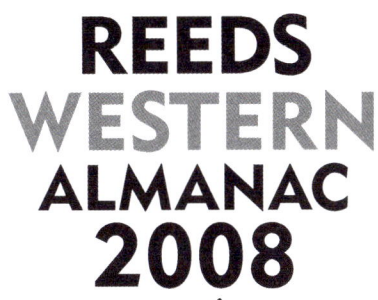

# REEDS
## WESTERN
## ALMANAC
## 2008

**ADLARD COLES NAUTICAL**

EDITORS Neville Featherstone and Andy Du Port

*Free updates are available at www.reedsalmanac.co.uk*

Published by Adlard Coles Nautical 2007

Copyright © Nautical Data Ltd 1999–2003

Copyright © Adlard Coles Nautical 2004–2007

## IMPORTANT SAFETY NOTE AND LEGAL DISCLAIMER

This Almanac is intended as an aid to navigation only and to assist with basic planning for your passage. The information, charts, maps and diagrams in this Almanac should not be relied on for navigational purposes and should always be used in conjunction with current official hydrographic data. Whilst every care has been taken in its compilation, this Almanac may contain inaccuracies and is no substitute for the relevant official hydrographic charts and data, which should always be consulted in advance of, and whilst, navigating in the relevant area. Before setting out you should also check local conditions with the harbourmaster or other appropriate office responsible for your intended area of navigation.

Before using any waypoint or coordinate listed in this Almanac it must first be plotted on an appropriate official hydrographic chart to check its usefulness, accuracy and appropriateness for the prevailing weather and tidal conditions.

To the extent that the editors or publishers become aware that corrections are required, these will be published on the website www.reedsalmanac.co.uk. Readers should therefore regularly check the website for any such corrections. Data in this Almanac is corrected up to Weekly Edition 25/2007 of Admiralty Notices to Mariners.

The publishers, editors and their agents accept no responsibility for any errors or omissions, or for any accident, loss or damage (including without limitation any indirect, consequential, special or exemplary damages) arising from the use or misuse of, or reliance upon, the information contained in this Almanac.

The decision to use and rely on any of the data in this Almanac is entirely at the discretion of, and is the sole responsibility of, the Skipper or other individual in control of the vessel in connection with which it is being used or relied upon.

**Adlard Coles Nautical**
38 Soho Square
London, W1D 3HB
Tel: +44 (0)207 758 0200
Fax: +44 (0)207 758 0222/0333
Email: info@reedsalmanac.co.uk
www.reedsalmanac.co.uk

**Almanac manager**
Chris Stevens

**Cartography**
Chris Stevens, Garold West

**Cover photograph**
Jersey Tourism  www.jersey.com

**ISBN 978 0 7136 8502 2 - Reeds Western Almanac 2008**

A CIP catalogue record for this book is available from the British Library.

Printed in the UK.

**ADVERTISEMENT SALES**
Enquiries about advertising should be addressed to:
MS Publications,
2nd Floor, Ewer House,
44-46 Crouch Street,
Colchester, Essex CO3 3HH.
*Tel: +44 (0)1206 506223*
*Fax: +44 (0)1206 500228*

# Reference Contents

# Wireless is more.

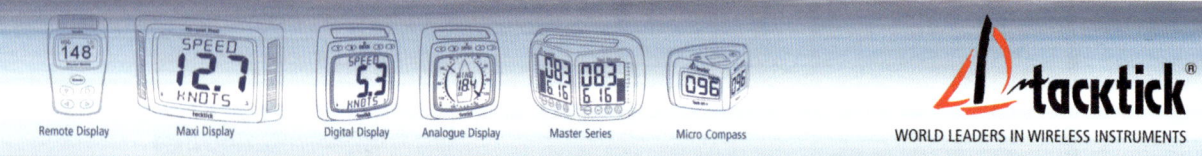

# Navigational Contents

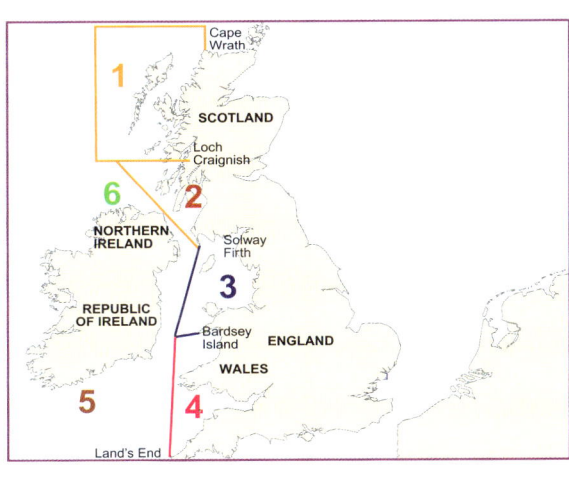

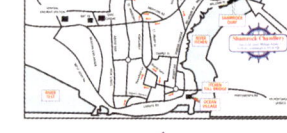

# QUAY
## M·A·R·I·N·A·S

Bangor Marina is situated on the south shore of Belfast Lough, close to the Irish Sea cruising routes and is Northern Ireland's largest marina.

Besides offering all the usual facilities, maintained to a high standard and operated 24 hours a day by friendly staff, the marina is perfectly situated for visitors to explore the town and the North Down area.

Quay Marinas operate four other large marinas within the UK at Conwy, Penarth, Portishead and Newcastle upon Tyne.

## bangor marina

2008/NC7/s

# Yacht Insurance

Nothing is ever certain at sea and, however careful a skipper may be, a boat is always at risk of being seriously damaged, even becoming a total loss or causing damage to third parties.

Owners should insure their boat for her full value, not necessarily the same as the purchase price. Any appreciable discrepancy between price paid and proposed insured value should however be explained to the insurer and agreed with them as, in the event of a claim, they may repudiate on the grounds of mis-disclosure of material facts. A reasonable basis for the insured value is that in normal market conditions how much would you have to pay for a boat that is the same and of similar age and condition? In any case you should read the proposal form carefully, and answer the various questions accurately and truthfully. Remember that answers to questions such as where is the boat normally kept? What fuel is used? etc, if altered, become a material fact. Otherwise insurers may subsequently be entitled to avoid liability in the event of a claim.

A policy normally covers the boat for a certain period in commission each year. If you need to extend the period, be sure to tell the company beforehand. Similarly cover is arranged for a certain cruising area. Make certain that the agreed limits are kept to, or make special arrangements when necessary.

The policy contains a number of warranties and conditions, either implied or expressed. These can be identified by reading the various sections carefully, and usually include the following important points:

1. If any loss or damage occurs the owner must take all steps necessary to minimise further loss, and the underwriters will contribute to charges properly incurred in taking such steps.

2. Charter or hire of the boat is not covered, except by special arrangement.

3. If an incident may give rise to a claim, prompt notice must be given to the underwriters.

4. The amount payable for a claim may be reduced for fair wear and tear of sails, rigging etc.

5. Theft of equipment is only covered where forcible entry or removal can be shown. Outboards must be locked to the boat. Check that there is no exclusion for outboard falling overboard.

6. Sails which are split by the wind are not generally insured, unless caused by the yacht being stranded or in collision. Also excluded is damage to sails while racing, unless caused by the boat being stranded, sunk, on fire or in collision.

7. Damage to or loss of an engine or other mechanical or electrical items is only covered if caused by the yacht being flooded, sunk, stranded, burned or in collision; or by theft of the entire boat; or by theft following forcible entry; or by malicious acts.

8. Personal effects can be included, if specially arranged.

9. Boats with a maximum designed speed of 17 knots or more are subject to 'Speedboat Clauses' which specify certain conditions and generally attract higher premiums.

10. Cover for at least £1,000,000 Third Party Liability is recommended. Normally somebody using the boat with the consent of the owner is covered, but this should be confirmed.

11. When in transit or trailing by road, a boat may be covered for accidental loss or damage, but the policy excludes all third party liabilities or offences against the road traffic legislation.

12. If no claim is made under the policy, most insurers will grant a no-claim bonus.

13. In the case of yachts over 15 years old, most under-writers require a recent survey on first insurance and after a change of ownership, followed by periodic surveys thereafter.

14. A Marine policy is not assignable. The moment the ownership changes the old policy is dead and should be cancelled.

Marine Insurance policies contain 'conditions' which usually includes that the owner must keep the boat and its equip-ment in seaworthy condition and in a proper state of repair.

Some insurers argue that single handed sailing infers under manning and therefore the boat is not seaworthy. Failure to disclose on the proposal that the yacht is habitually sailed single or short-handed may be held as failure to disclose material facts, so tell your insurer and get it agreed.

Marine insurance is a specialised business. Either deal with a broker or intermediary who is experienced in yacht insurance or get proposal forms from several established firms who advertise in the yachting press; it will be apparent that some insurers give wider cover than others. Return those forms which best seem to meet your needs, and then compare the quotations. However, firms with the lowest premiums are not necessarily the best at settling claims. Useful information is given in RYA booklet G9 *The Yachtsman's Lawyer* and *Marine Law for Boat Owners* by Edmund Whelan.

Extract from the *Reeds Yachtsman's Handbook*
Copyright © Nautical Data Ltd 2002

# Yacht Brokers

Yacht brokers and agents provide an important service and if you are buying a boat of any size, it is highly advisable to deal through one. They can advise on the suitability of a boat for your particular purpose, and can then track down those most likely to meet your needs. They can help to arrange both the slipping and the survey of the selected boat (very useful if you happen to live elsewhere), and information on providers of a marine mortgage if required, and insurance. They will also show prospective purchasers over the boat for you. They can check details such as the inventory of the boat, and ensure that the documentation is properly completed so that title is fully transferred. ABYA members work to the ABYA Code of Practice which has recently been up-dated.

A standard form of agreement is used, setting out various terms including: the agreed purchase price; 10% deposit which is paid when the agreement is signed, allowing the purchaser to have the yacht lifted out and surveyed at his own expense; the fact that the survey should normally be completed within 14 days, although this can be longer, by agreement. Within a stated period from completion of survey, if any material defects (generally this is taken to mean *significant* cost) have been found, the purchaser may either reject the yacht (giving notice of the defects discovered), or ask the seller either to make good such shortcomings or reduce the price. The form also details the obligations of the two parties, default by the purchaser, the transfer of risk, and arbitration procedure in the event of a dispute.

If the sale proceeds, the agreement states that the yacht is considered to have been accepted by the buyer and the balance of the agreed price is due if:

a) a period of 14 days elapses, and no survey has been made; or
b) after an agreed time after the survey the purchaser has not acted; or
c) the seller remedies any specified defects to the satisfaction of the surveyor; or
d) an agreed reduction in price is made.

The buyer should also be aware that if the seller is a private individual, ie he or she is not selling the boat in the course of trade or business (and that business does not have to be selling boats), and if that fact is known to the buyer, there is no question of any guarantee on the sale of a second-hand boat because the buyer is quite at liberty to inspect the craft and to satisfy himself as to her condition – either personally or by employing a surveyor. Unquestionably a survey should always be made, except perhaps in the case of a very small and cheap boat where the buyer has enough knowledge and experience to detect any serious faults. A boat sold in the course of business has implied warranties under the Sale of Goods Acts.

Buying yachts can be a complex business, particularly when the boat, the seller and the buyer are all miles apart. Two brokers are often involved, and access must be provided by the yard or marina where the boat is lying. Consequently the ABYA Guidance Notes provides for a fair split of the total commission between those involved. The seller of the boat pays an agreed commission based on the selling price. For guidance the normal rates (plus VAT) are: 6–8% of the price for vessels in the UK; 10% for vessels on inland waters. 10% also applies if the vessel, owner or buyer are abroad.

## SELLING THROUGH A YACHT BROKER

Selling a yacht through a yacht broker may be a useful and appropriate course of action for a number of people. It eliminates most of the work and problems involved with a private sale, and because a broker has access to a wide market it may enable a higher price to be obtained or a quicker sale to be achieved.

When instructing a broker to sell a boat, the owner will be asked to complete a form which requires full particulars of the boat and of her material condition. It is important that these are accurately stated. The vendor must also agree with the broker at the outset whether or not he is to be the sole agent. It is important that the vendor provides the broker with documentation proving he has legal title, of the VAT paid status of the vessel, and of RCD compliance if she was built after June 1998 or is coming into the EU market for the first time.

A broker acts as a go-between for buyers and sellers of yachts all over the world. If a broker is appointed as sole agent he may pass full details of the boat to other selected brokers, who will usually receive half of the eventual commission if they produce a sale. These central listing facilities allow the interchange of information about all the boats for sale between all the various participating brokerage firms, so that the net is spread as wide as possible.

Very importantly, a broker is able to advise on the correct price at which a boat should be offered – a price that is likely to attract response, but which will be fair to the seller. It is in the broker's interest to obtain the best price, as his commission is based on it.

Any advertising copy or materials produced by the broker must be accurate because he is liable under the Trade Descriptions Act, although he is often dependent upon the vendor for his information. He will advertise the boat and handle all enquiries and inspections. When a potential buyer appears the broker will prepare a Sale Agreement on a standard form of contract. If the sale proceeds after survey, he can advise the owner regarding any defects that may have been found in order to negotiate a fair price. Finally the broker prepares the Bill of Sale, and ensures that title is not transferred until the purchase money has been received. He also arranges for VAT paid status and RCD compliance documentation to be passed to the new owner, as applicable.

Extract from the *Reeds Yachtsman's Handbook* updated by Association of Brokers and Yacht Agents 2007. Copyright © Nautical Data Ltd 2002.

# Yacht Surveyors

The idea of getting a boat surveyed usually arises when you are thinking about buying a boat or you've had a collision or a serious grounding. Alternatively your insurers might have asked for one or you are trying to get Part I British Registry. Perhaps you have become involved in a dispute and need an expert witness. Whatever your reason, it is essential to select a surveyor with the proper qualifications who has been personally recommended by someone experienced that you trust.

There are several different types of survey available, and which one you select will depend on what you need. The best known is the Full Condition Survey which will tell you the condition of the boat you are considering buying. Certainly it would be very foolish to buy a second-hand boat without having a proper survey done, with the boat out of the water. It is also often appropriate to have your boat surveyed before selling her, so that you can discover and rectify any problems before the buyer discovers them and demands an overgenerous discount to cover them.

The purpose of a Full Survey is to determine the condition of the entire yacht: hull, machinery, gear and all the equipment relating to her operation. A competent surveyor should report on every aspect of the boat's structure, depending on the materials concerned. He should comment on whether the condition of the various items is attributable to fair wear and tear, or whether other factors such as poor design, inferior materials, bad workmanship or lack of maintenance are involved. His examination should include all items such as fastenings, chain plates, shafting, steering gear and rudder fittings.

The surveyor will not usually provide an Engine Survey, and the engine itself may need to be surveyed separately as this is the province of the marine engineer. However the surveyor should certainly be able to assess its general condition. If you have any concerns about the engines, ask the surveyor or broker to help you find a local marine engineer. Similarly surveyors are not usually insured to go up the mast and tell you about the masthead fittings. There are modern rigging testing techniques and equipment which will give you information about this. Again, you should ask for a specialist report if you are concerned, or if this is of particular importance to you.

A Hull Condition Survey is just that, and is clearly more limited in scope. As well as Full and Hull Condition Surveys, surveyors assess accident damage for insurance purposes, and oversee repairs or modifications.

Insurers need surveys for accident reports and for when you insure your boat. These are two different types of survey - the accident report may need to be very detailed, giving insurers the information they need to assess the level of damage and whether it is repairable, etc. If, for instance, the accident was due to fire, they will want to know how the fire started. A Full Condition Survey will often be requested before an insurance policy is provided.

For Part 1 Registration a tonnage measurement is a much quicker survey and does not relate to the condition of the boat. It is simply a measurement and verification of the boat.

In cases where a dispute arises, some of the more senior members of the YDSA are experienced in providing expert witness reports for the Court, and others can act as arbitrators to settle technical disputes. Some surveyors specialise in particular types of boat, such as steel inland waterways boats, or old wooden boats.

The surveyor will ask you for information on the boat before he agrees to do the survey for you. Be clear what it is that you are asking for so that you get what you intended. Instruct the surveyor in writing; the details are important as they will form the basis of a contract with him.

To get a proper survey you need a professional surveyor, and sadly a small minority of surveyors lack the knowledge and experience required. Members of the Yacht Designers and Surveyors Association (YDSA) submit documentation for assessment before being accepted as members (there is an up-grading exam from Affiliate to Associate grade) and hold Professional Indemnity insurance.

The names of all members are listed on the YDSA website at www.ydsa.co.uk or telephone 01730 710425; email info@ydsa.co.uk; or fax 01730 710423 for a list.

Other organisations, dealing partly with yachts and commercial vessels, are:

The International Institute of Marine Surveying, Stone Lane, Gosport, Hants PO12 1SS: tel 023 9258 8000; fax 023 9258 8002; email iims@compuserve.com; www.iims.org.uk

The Society of Consulting Marine Engineers and Ships Surveyors, c/o 202 Lambeth Rd, London SE1 7LQ: tel 0207 261 0869; fax 0207 261 0871; email sec@scmshq.org

The Institute of Marine Engineering, Science & Technology, 80 Coleman Street, London EC2R 5BJ: tel 0207 382 2600; fax 0207 382 2670; email ssg@imarest.org; www.imarest.org

Royal Institution of Naval Architects, 10 Upper Belgrave Street, London SW1X 8BQ: tel 0207 235 4622; fax 02070259 5912; email hq@rina.org.uk; www.rina.org.uk

Extract from the *Reeds Yachtsman's Handbook* updated by Yacht Designers and Surveyors Association (YDSA) 2007. Copyright © Nautical Data Ltd 2002.

# Yacht Charter

Chartering has become very big business in recent years. On one side of the coin a yachtsman can help to pay some of his running costs or the instalments on his marine mortgage by chartering his boat. On the other side, chartering allows a person who does not own a boat, for whatever reason, to get afloat and enjoy a holiday not necessarily in home waters but perhaps in more reliably sunny climes. In either case it is important to have a proper written agreement, which covers every conceivable eventuality.

Many people prefer to charter a yacht for two or three weeks a year, rather than face the continuing responsibility and costs of looking after a boat throughout the year. There are plenty of charter boats on offer around the UK, with some of them in delightful areas such as the west coasts of Scotland and Ireland. Chartering in home waters is usually cheaper, because travel costs are much reduced. Also, if required, it is feasible to change crews during the charter. Since air fares are now cheaper in real terms, it may make good economic sense to sail in established areas like the Mediterranean or Caribbean (including the British Virgin Islands, the Bahamas and Florida), where the weather is likely to be reliable. One of the attractions of chartering is to explore different places and these now extend as far afield as the Indian and Pacific Oceans, including the Great Barrier Reef in Australia.

All charter yachts are fitted with radio, allowing them to keep in touch with base, and invaluable should any problem arise with the boat. The charter company should be able to provide a service whereby in a few hours they can reach any yacht which has trouble with gear or engine, for example. With the larger companies the spares backup is usually very impressive, with makes and types of equipment rationalised amongst their fleet, which may number 50 boats or more. Apply early, so as to take up any cheap fares on offer, although a number of companies are now specialising in late bookings. Also remember that a three-week holiday is more economical per week than a fortnight's holiday, both in terms of travel costs and particularly since a few charter companies offer reductions for the third week of a charter.

Most companies will arrange for provisioning the boat in advance, to a scale agreed by the charterers. It is often wise to take advantage of such a scheme, since there may be no convenient shops on arrival. 'Split provisioning' provides enough food if three or four main meals are taken ashore each week. The equipment inventory is normally very comprehensive and the company should provide a detailed list. Although items such as snorkel gear are included, binoculars are sometimes not. Pilot Guides are usually provided although you may wish to take your own for the area concerned. The company will almost certainly give a 'chart briefing' ashore, which will describe the better anchorages and shore facilities, where to get items such as ice, and provisions etc.

Flotilla sailing is a good opportunity for less experienced sailors to start cruising, with advice from the flotilla 'leader' always readily available. The boats will be fitted with VHF radios, so that help is always on call. Most flotilla operations are in relatively small yachts, sleeping four or six people, and often ideal for a family holiday. The leader knows the area, the best anchorages, the more attractive harbours, and the places ashore where food and drink are good and cheap. He can also help, where necessary, with language problems, Customs formalities and the like.

Whatever company or private owner you charter from, find out as much as possible about the firm or individual concerned, preferably from people who have had first-hand experience of the boats or boat. All boats offered for charter must by law comply with the Maritime and Coastguard Agencies Code of Practice; check that yours does. Ensure that you carefully check the equipment provided against a comprehensive list, which the charter company is required to supply. Pay particular regard to navigational items and to safety equipment. What is the age of the boat, and is she the best type for your purpose? Does the accommodation really match your requirements? Look closely at insurance to see what excess is included, and check the third party cover, which should be for at least £1,000,000. What sort of service is provided in the event of some problem developing with the boat during the charter period (probably none, if you are chartering from a private individual). If the boat becomes unusable, what refund will be offered?

A proper form of written agreement is essential, covering such items as: the date, time and place to take over and hand back the boat; booking deposit; balance of the charter money (payable before the charter starts); arrangements for cancellation; a security deposit for loss or damage (returnable within 14 days of the completion of the charter); any insurance excess which the charterer may have to bear; cruising limits, where applicable; payment for items such as fuel, harbour dues, food, laundry etc; what penalty may be imposed for late return of the boat; and, if crew are carried, who pays for their food.

The Yacht Charter Association (YCA) was the organisation overseeing the yacht charter business but has now been merged with other BMF associations to form the Marine Leisure Association (MLA). This new Association is part of the BMF and one of its primary aims is to raise standards and protect customers. UK charter companies that are members abide by these standards and the BMF and MLA Codes of Conduct in respect of operations and service.

Further information is available from the General Secretary, Marine Leisure Association, 24 Peterscroft Avenue, Ashurst, Southampton SO40 7AB.

Telephone and fax: 023 8029 3822

E-mail: info@marineleisure.co.uk

Website: www.marineleisure.co.uk

# CHARTERS GUIDE

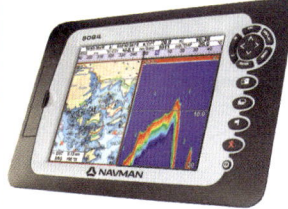

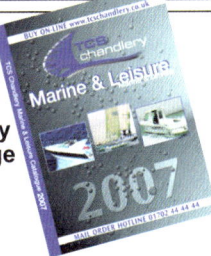

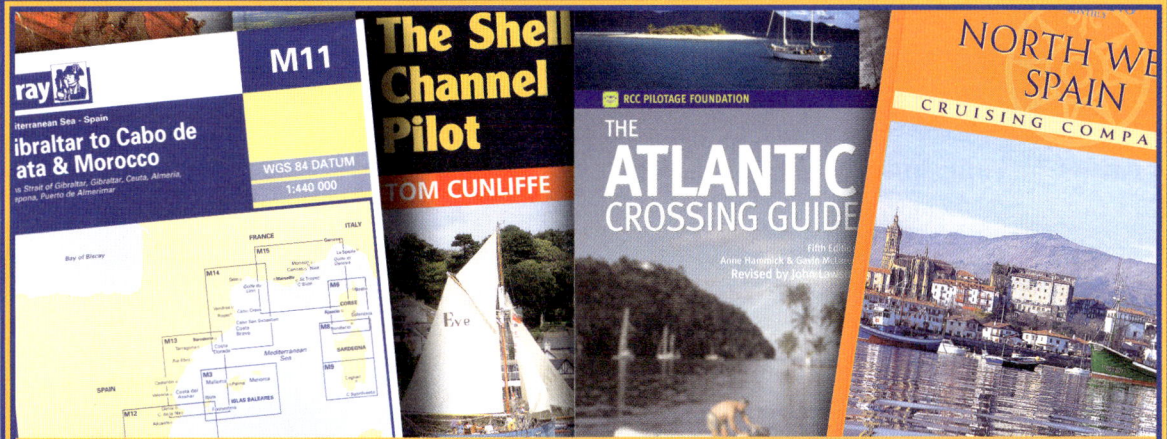

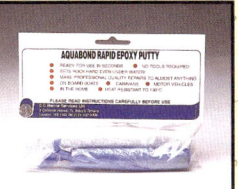
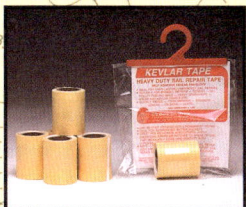

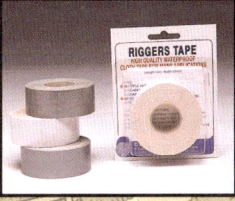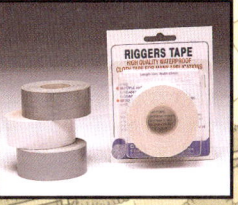
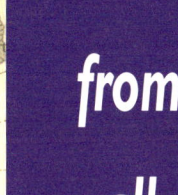

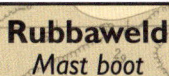
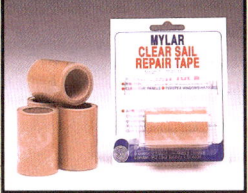
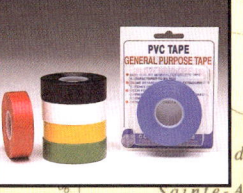
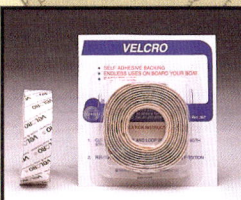

# Sail right into the heart of it.

## DUBLIN CITY MOORINGS

One of the benefits of berthing at Dublin City Moorings is that you are right in the heart of one of Europe's most exciting capitals – a cosmopolitan young city with a world-renowned cultural scene.

- Berthing available for yachts up to 1000 tonnes
- Draught 4.2 m. LAT
- 3 phase electricity, water, pump-out, wheelchair access

Contact: info@dublindocklands.ie

**DUBLIN DOCKLANDS**
DEVELOPMENT AUTHORITY

2008/NC81/e

52-55 Sir John Rogerson's Quay, Docklands, Dublin 2.
t: +353 1 818 3300   f:+353 1 818 3399   www.dublindocklands.ie

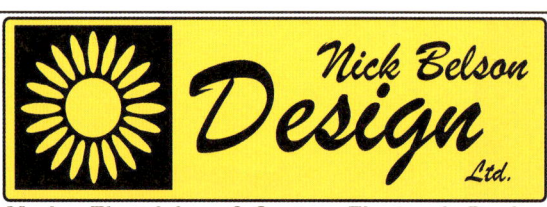

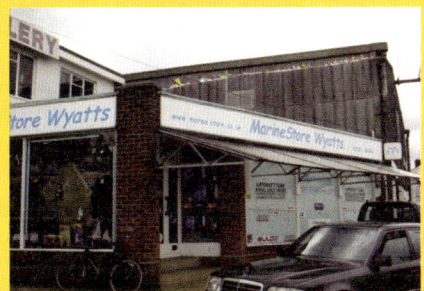

# Milford Haven Port Authority

### Milford Marina & Docks

## Ideally placed for land and sea operations

Situated in a non-tidal basin on the North Shore of one of Europe's best known Ports, Milford Haven provides superb shelter and access to some of the finest leisure boating in the UK.

With first class berthing and unloading facilities, this is also an ideal choice for West-of-UK commercial operations.

**Milford Marina:** Cleddau House, The Docks, MILFORD HAVEN, Pembrokeshire  SA73 3AF
**Milford Docks:** Unit 4, Victory House, The Docks, MILFORD HAVEN, Pembrokeshire  SA73 3AF
**Marina:** Tel: +44 (0)1646 696312   **Docks:** Tel: +44 (0)1646 696300
website: www.mhpa.co.uk

# S. ROBERTS MARINE LIMITED

at

## Liverpool Marina

*YOUR ONE STOP SHOP FOR ALL YOUR MARINE NEEDS !!*

- ✔ **Boatbuilding**
- ✔ **Repairs**
- ✔ **Surveying**
- ✔ **Consultancy**
- ✔ **Chandlery**
- ✔ **Rigging** up to 12mm

Barge Turbot, Coburg Wharf,
South Ferry Quay, Liverpool L3 4BP
Tel/Fax 0151 707 8300

email: stephen@robmar.freeserve.co.uk
website: www.srobertsmarine.com

2008/NC68/z

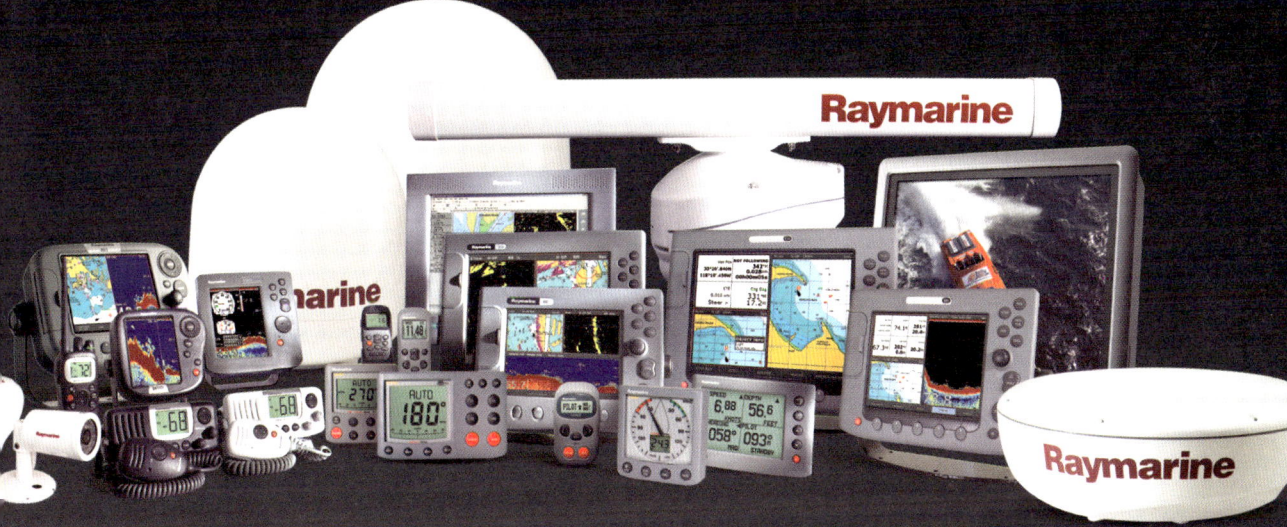

# MEET THE FAMILY.

## IF YOU'RE RESTORING YOUR VESSEL OR UPGRADING INSTRUMENTS, RAYMARINE HAS THE EQUIPMENT TO ENHANCE YOUR PERFORMANCE.

Your choice of marine electronics is one of the most important decisions you will have to make as a boat owner, next to choosing the boat itself of course. Thousands of boaters head to the water everyday, confident in the performance and accuracy of their chosen Raymarine equipment.

When you buy Raymarine equipment, you are buying into world-class performance, top-notch integration, and the latest proven design technologies. Years of research and development, and customer feedback have resulted in the 'simple-on-the-outside, sophisticated-on-the-inside' design philosophy that is behind all our intuitive easy-to-use equipment.

To see what Raymarine can do for you telephone: +44 (0) 8080 729627 for your FREE copy of our product brochure or visit our website **raymarine.com**

**Raymarine**®

2008/NC45/e

Lifestyle Photo: Oyster and Cranchi

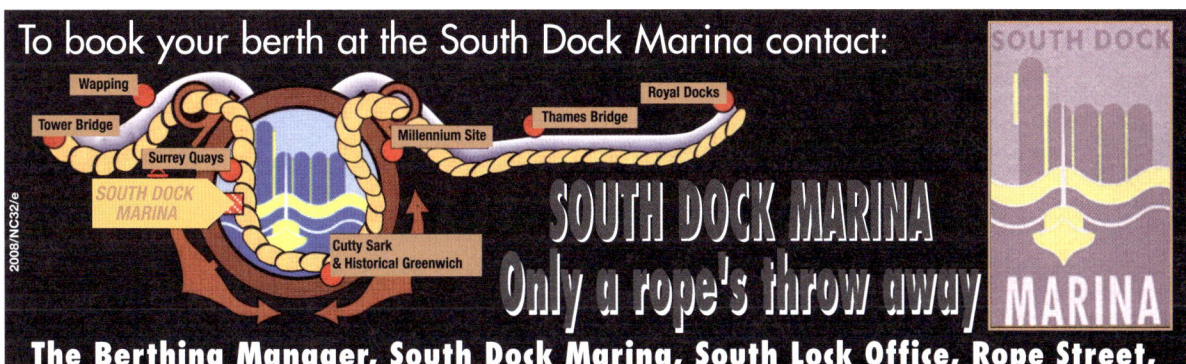

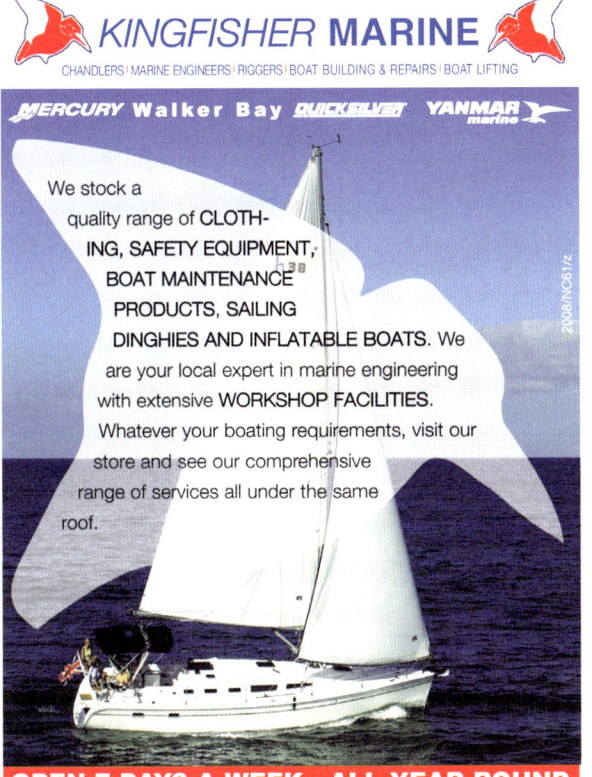

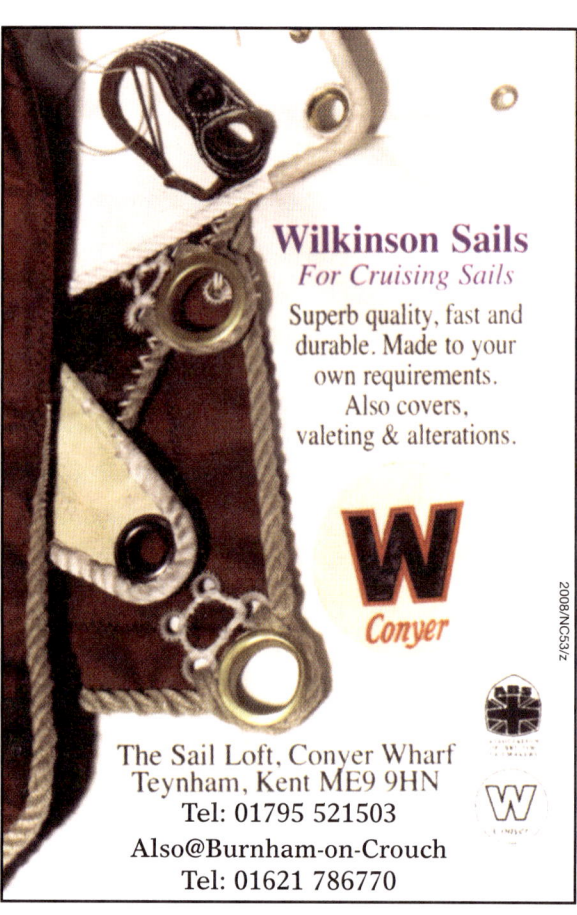

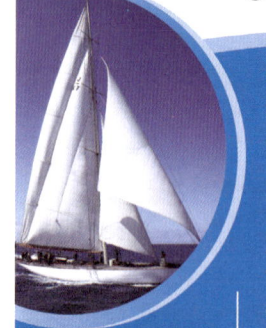

# Reference data

## 0.1 THE ALMANAC

### • Acknowledgements

The Editors thank the many official bodies and individuals for information and advice given in the compilation of this Almanac. These include: UKHO, Trinity House, HM Nautical Almanac Office, SHOM, HMSO, HM Revenue & Customs, Meteorological Office, BBC, IBA, MCA, RNLI, ABP, countless Harbourmasters and our many individual harbour agents.

### • Permissions

Chartlets, tidal stream diagrams and curves are reproduced from Admiralty charts and publications (ie ALL, ASD, ATT and ALRS) by permission of the UKHO (Licence No GB DQ – 001 – Adlard Coles) and the Controller of HMSO.

UK and foreign tidal predictions are supplied by and with the permission of UKHO.

Extracts from the *International Code of Signals, 1987* and *Meteorological Office Weather Services for Shipping* are published by permission of the Controller of HMSO.

Ephemerides are derived from HM Nautical Almanac by permission of HM Nautical Almanac Office and the Council for the Central Laboratory of the Research Councils.

### • Disclaimer

No National HO has verified the information in this product and none accepts liability for the accuracy of reproduction or any modifications made thereafter. No National HO warrants that this product satisfies national or inter-national regulations regarding the use of the appropriate products for navigation.

Chartlets in this Almanac are not intended for navigational use; only for reference. Always consult fully updated navigational charts for the latest information.

### • Improvements

This edition contains 4 major and many minor improvements:

- Information on AIS, overhead clearances and a clearer diagram of IALA buoyage.
- A simpler system of times of Sun and Moon rise/set.

Readers' suggestions, even minor ideas, for improving the content or layout are welcome, especially those based on experience and practical use at sea. Not every suggestion can be implemented, but all are carefully considered.

Please send your comments on the Update card or by letter, fax or email direct to: The Editors, RNA, Adlard Coles Nautical, 38 Soho Square, London W1D 3HB. ☎ 020 7758 0200. 🖷 020 7758 0222. info@reedsalmanac.co.uk.

### • Notifying errors

Although the Almanac has been very carefully compiled from countless sources, a few errors may still occur. Please tell the Editors of any such errors.

### • Harbour agents

Our harbour agents provide the local information which may not appear in official sources. Vacancies are advertised on our website www.reedsalmanac.co.uk. If you would like to earn a free copy of Reeds Nautical Almanac every year, please apply to the address under improvements with a brief summary of your nautical qualifications.

### • Sources of corrections

This Almanac is corrected to Weekly edition No. 25/2007 of Admiralty Notices to Mariners, downloaded 13 June 2007. Corrections to Admiralty charts and publications can be downloaded from www.ukho.gov.uk or obtained from Admiralty chart agents (ACA) and certain Port authorities.

### • Updates

Free updates, monthly from January to June, can be downloaded at www.reedsalmanac.co.uk. Please register online if you would like to receive an email reminder when the updates are available for download.

A printed Update of corrections up to the end of March, can be obtained from April by returning the enclosed reply card with a cheque for £2 to cover admin costs and an A4 sized, self-addressed envelope stamped for £0.70 (1st class) or £0.52 (2nd class) to the address under Improvements.

## 0.2 ABBREVIATIONS AND SYMBOLS

The following more common abbreviations and symbols feature in Reeds Almanacs. Other Admiralty chart symbols are on the flap of the inside back cover. Chart 5011 (a booklet) is the complete reference for Symbols and Abbreviations on charts.

| | |
|---|---|
| @ | Internet café/access |
| AB | Alongside berth |
| ABP | Associated British Ports |
| AC, ⌁ | Shore power (electrical) |
| AC, ACA | Admiralty Chart, AC Agent |
| ACN | Adlard Coles Nautical (Publisher) |
| Aff Mar | Affaires Maritimes |
| AIS | Automatic Identification System |
| aka | Also known as |
| ALL | Admiralty List of Lights |
| ALRS | Admiralty List of Radio Signals |
| Al | Alternating light |
| AM | Amplitude Modulation |
| ANWB | Association of road & waterway users (Dutch) |
| Appr | Approach(es) |
| ASD | Admiralty Sailing Directions (Pilot) |
| ATM | Automatic telling machine, cashpoint |
| ATT | Admiralty Tide Tables |
| ATT | Atterisage (landfall/SWM) buoy |
| Auto | Météo Répondeur Automatique |
| B. | Bay, Black |
| Bar, ⌾ | Licensed bar, Public house, Inn |
| BH | Boat Hoist (+ tons) |
| Bkwtr | Breakwater |
| BMF | British Marine Federation |
| BMS | Bulletin Météorologique Spécial |
| Bn, bcn(s) | Beacon, beacon(s) |
| BSH | German Hydrographic Office/chart(s) |
| BST | British Summer Time (= DST) |
| Bu | Blue |
| BWB | British Waterways Board |
| By(s) | Buoy, buoys |
| BY, ⌘ | Boatyard |
| C. | Cape, Cabo, Cap |
| C | Crane (+ tons) |
| © | National Coastwatch Institution station |
| ca | Cable (approx 185m long) |
| Cas | Castle |
| CD | Chart datum (vertical) |
| CEVNI | Code Européen de Voies de la Navigation Intérieure (inland waterways signs etc) |
| cf | Compare, cross-refer to |
| CG | Coastguard |

| | |
|---|---|
| CH, ⚓ | Chandlery |
| chan | Channel (navigational) |
| Ch | Channel (VHF) |
| Ch, ⊕ | Church |
| Chy | Chimney |
| Col | Column, pillar, obelisk |
| CROSS | Centre Régional Opérationnel de Surveillance et Sauvetage (= MRCC) |
| CRS | Coast Radio Station |
| D | Diesel (supply by hose) |
| Dec | Declination (of the Sun) |
| dest | Destroyed |
| DG | De-gaussing (range) |
| DGPS | Differential GPS |
| Dia | Diaphone (fog signal) |
| discont | Discontinued |
| Dn(s) | Dolphin(s) |
| DR | Dead Reckoning |
| DSC | Digital Selective Calling |
| DST | Daylight Saving Time |
| DW | Deep Water (route) |
| DYC | Dutch Yacht Chart(s) |
| DZ | Danger Zone (buoy) |
| E | East |
| ECM | East cardinal mark (buoy/beacon) |
| ED | Existence doubtful, European Datum |
| EEA | European Economic Area |
| EI | Electrical repairs |
| Ⓔ | Electronic repairs |
| Elev | Elevation |
| Ent | Entrance, entry, enter |
| EP, △ | Estimated position |
| ETA | Estimated Time of Arrival |
| ETD | Estimated Time of Departure |
| F | Fixed light |
| f | Fine (eg sand) |
| F&A | Fore and aft (berth/mooring) |
| Fcst | Forecast |
| FFL | Fixed and Flashing light |
| Fl | Flashing light |
| FM | Frequency Modulation |
| Foc | Free of charge |
| Fog Det lt | Fog Detector light |
| Freq, Fx | Frequency |
| FS | Flagstaff, Flagpole |
| ft | Foot, feet |
| Ft | Fort |
| FV | Fishing vessel |
| FW, 🚰 | Fresh water supply |
| G | Gravel, Green |
| Gas | Calor Gas |
| Gaz | Camping Gaz |
| GC | Great Circle |
| GDOP | Geometrical Dilution of Precision (GPS) |
| GHA | Greenwich Hour Angle |
| GLA | General Lighthouse Authority |
| GMDSS | Global Maritime Distress & Safety System |
| grt | Gross Registered Tonnage |
| Gy | Grey |
| H, h, Hrs | Hour(s) |
| H–, H+ | Minutes before, after the whole hour |
| H24 | Continuous |

| | |
|---|---|
| HAT | Highest Astronomical Tide |
| HF | High Frequency |
| HFP | High Focal Plane (buoy) |
| HIE | Highlands & Islands Enterprise |
| HJ | Day service only, sunrise to sunset |
| HM | Harbour Master |
| HMRC | HM Revenue & Customs |
| HMSO | Her Majesty's Stationery Office |
| HN | Night service only, sunset to sunrise |
| HO | Office hours, Hydrographic Office |
| (hor) | Horizontally disposed (lights) |
| hPa | Hectopascal (= 1millibar) |
| HT | High Tension (overhead electricity line) |
| HW | High Water |
| HX | No fixed hours |
| IALA | International Association of Lighthouse Authorities |
| iaw | In accordance with |
| ICAO | International Civil Aviation Organisation |
| IDM | Isolated Danger Mark (buoy/beacon) |
| IHO | International Hydrographic Organisation |
| IMO | International Maritime Organisation |
| INMARSAT | International Maritime Satellite Organisation |
| intens | Intensified (light sector) |
| IPTS | International Port Traffic Signals |
| IQ | Interrupted quick flashing light |
| IRPCS | International Regulations for the Prevention of Collisions at Sea |
| Is, I | Island, Islet |
| ISAF | International Sailing Federation |
| Iso | Isophase light |
| ITU | International Telecommunications Union |
| ITZ | Inshore Traffic Zone (TSS) |
| IUQ | Interrupted ultra quick flashing light |
| IVQ | Interrupted very quick flashing light |
| kn | knot(s) |
| Kos | Kosangas |
| kW | Kilowatts |
| L | Lake, Loch, Lough, Landing place |
| Lat | Latitude |
| LAT | Lowest Astronomical Tide |
| Lanby, ⬭ | Large automatic navigational buoy |
| LB, ♦ | Lifeboat, inshore lifeboat |
| Ldg | Leading (light) |
| LF | Low frequency |
| L Fl | Long flash |
| LH | Left hand |
| L/L | Latitude/Longitude |
| LNG | Liquefied Natural Gas |
| LNTM | Local Notice To Mariners |
| LOA | Length overall |
| Long | Longitude |
| LPG | Liquefied Petroleum Gas |
| LT | Local time |
| Lt(s), ☆ ✫ | Light(s) |
| ⬭ | Light float, minor |
| Lt V, ⬭ | Light vessel; Lt float, major; Lanby |
| M | Moorings, nautical (sea) mile(s), Mud |
| m | Metre(s) |
| Mag | Magnetic, magnitude (of Star) |
| mb | Millibar (= 1 hectopascal, hPa) |
| MCA | Maritime and Coastguard Agency |
| ME | Marine engineering repairs |

| | |
|---|---|
| Météo | Météorologie (weather) |
| MHWN | Mean High Water Neaps |
| MHWS | Mean High Water Springs |
| MHz | Megahertz |
| ML | Mean Level (tidal) |
| MLWN | Mean Low Water Neaps |
| MLWS | Mean Low Water Springs |
| MMSI | Maritime Mobile Service Identity |
| Mo | Morse |
| Mon | Monument, Monday |
| MRCC | Maritime Rescue Co-ordination Centre |
| MSI | Maritime Safety Information |
| | |
| N | North |
| Navi | Navicarte (French charts) |
| NB | Nota Bene, Notice Board |
| NCI, © | National Coastwatch Institution |
| NCM | North Cardinal Mark (buoy/beacon) |
| NGS | Naval Gunfire Support (buoy) |
| NM | Notice(s) to Mariners |
| nps | Neap tides |
| NP | Naval Publication (plus number) |
| NT | National Trust (land/property) |
| | |
| Obscd | Obscured |
| Obstn | Obstruction |
| Oc | Occulting light |
| ODAS | Ocean Data Acquisition System (buoy) |
| Or | Orange |
| OT | Other times |
| OWF | Offshore wind farm |
| | |
| P | Petrol (supply by hose), Pebbles |
| (P) | Preliminary (NM) |
| PA | Position approximate |
| Pax | Passenger(s) |
| PC | Portuguese chart |
| PD | Position doubtful |
| PHM | Port-hand Mark (buoy/beacon) |
| PLA | Port of London Authority |
| PO, ✉ | Post Office |
| prom | Prominent |
| PSSA | Particularly Sensitive Sea Area |
| Pt(e). | Point(e) |
| ⚓ | Pump-out facility |
| Pta | Punta (point) |
| | |
| Q | Quick flashing light |
| QHM | Queen's Harbour Master |
| | |
| R | Red, Restaurant ✗, River, Rock |
| Racon | Radar transponder beacon |
| Ramark | Radar beacon |
| RCD | Recreational Craft Directive |
| RG | Emergency RDF station |
| RH | Right hand |
| Rk, Rky | Rock, Rocky |
| RMWG | Reeds Marina & Waypoint Guide |
| RNLI | Royal National Lifeboat Institution |
| ROI | Republic of Ireland |
| R/T | Radiotelephony |
| Ru | Ruins |
| RYA | Royal Yachting Association |
| | |
| S | South, Sand |
| S, St, Ste | Saint(s) |
| SAMU | Service d'Aide Médicale Urgente (ambulance) |

| | |
|---|---|
| SAR | Search and Rescue |
| SC | Sailing Club, Spanish chart |
| SCM | South Cardinal Mark (buoy/beacon) |
| SD | Sailing Directions, Semi-diameter (of sun) |
| SD | Sounding of doubtful depth |
| sf | Stiff |
| Sh | Shells, Shoal |
| SHM | Simplified Harmonic Method (tides), |
| SHM | Starboard-hand Mark (buoy/beacon) |
| SHOM | French Hydrographic Office/Chart |
| Si | Silt |
| SIGNI | Signalisation de la Navigation Intérieure |
| SM | Sailmaker |
| ✗ | Shipwright (esp wooden hulls) |
| SMS | Short Message Service (mobile texting) |
| SNSM | Société Nationale de Sauvetage en Mer |
| so | Soft (eg mud) |
| SOLAS | Safety of Life at Sea (IMO Convention) |
| sp | Spring tides |
| SPM | Special Mark (buoy/beacon) |
| SR | Sunrise |
| SRR | Search and Rescue Region |
| SS | Sunset, Signal Station |
| SSB | Single Sideband (Radio) |
| Stbd | Starboard |
| subm | Submerged |
| SWM | Safe Water Mark (buoy/beacon) |
| | |
| (T), (Temp) | Tem#porary |
| tbc | To be confirmed |
| tbn | To be notified |
| TD | Temporarily Discontinued (fog signal) |
| TE | Temporarily Extinguished (light) |
| tfn | Till further notice |
| Tr, twr | Tower |
| T/R | Traffic Report (tells the CG your route etc) |
| TSS | Traffic Separation Scheme |
| ≠ | In transit with, ie ldg marks/lts |
| | |
| u/mkd | Unmarked (feature/hazard) |
| UQ | Ultra Quick flashing light |
| UT | Universal Time (= approx GMT) |
| | |
| Var | Variation (magnetic) |
| Vel | Velocity |
| (vert) | Vertically disposed (lights) |
| Vi | Violet |
| VLCC | Very large crude carrier (Oil tanker) |
| VNF | Voie Navigable de France (canals) |
| VQ | Very Quick flashing light |
| VTS | Vessel Traffic Service |
| | |
| W | West, White |
| WCM | West Cardinal Mark (buoy/beacon) |
| � | Wind turbine |
| wef | With effect from |
| WGS | World Geodetic System (GPS datum) |
| WIP | Work in progress |
| Wk, ⌇ ⊕ | Wreck |
| WPT, ⊕ | Waypoint |
| Wx | Weather |
| WZ | Code for UK coastal navigation warning |
| | |
| Y | Yellow, Amber, Orange |
| YC, ⌐ | Yacht Club |

## 0.3    PASSAGE PLANNING CHECKLIST

DATE ............... FROM ............................ETD ................ VIA ............................ TO ................................. ETA ........................

TIMES OF SUNRISE ................. SUNSET ................... MOON RISE ................... MOONSET ............... WATCH SYSTEM ☐

CHARTS ☐      DOCUMENTS ☐      CUSTOMS ☐      PAY DUES ☐      CG (T/R) ☐      FUEL ☐      WATER ☐      FOOD ☐

WEATHER FORECAST ...........................................................................................................................................

---

**DEPARTURE PORT**  VHF ............... HM ☎ ...............................

BRIDGE TIMES ..........................................................

LOCK/GATE TIMES .....................................................

BAR CROSSING TIMES ...............................................

DEPARTURE WINDOW ................................................

DEPARTURE PROCEDURE ...........................................

...........................................................................................

...........................................................................................

VTS DETAILS ..............................................................

...........................................................................................

...........................................................................................

STANDARD PORT, TIDES (SP/NP, HW/LW TIMES & HEIGHTS)

...........................................................................................

...........................................................................................

...........................................................................................

DEPARTURE PORT TIDES (HW/LW TIMES & HEIGHTS) ............

...........................................................................................

...........................................................................................

...........................................................................................

TIDAL STREAMS ON DEPARTURE ....................................

...........................................................................................

---

**EN ROUTE**

TIDAL STREAM ANALYSIS ............................................

...........................................................................................

...........................................................................................

...........................................................................................

...........................................................................................

TIDAL GATES (TIMES) ................................................

...........................................................................................

TIDE RACES ...............................................................

...........................................................................................

TRAFFIC SEPARATION SCHEMES .....................................

...........................................................................................

PROHIBITED AREAS/DANGERS .........................................

PRINCIPAL LIGHTS/MARKS ............................................

...........................................................................................

...........................................................................................

---

**LEG DETAILS**

| FROM | TO | WPT | TRK°M | DIST | TIME | REMARKS |
|---|---|---|---|---|---|---|
|  |  |  |  |  |  |  |
|  |  |  |  |  |  |  |
|  |  |  |  |  |  |  |
|  |  |  |  |  |  |  |
|  |  |  |  |  |  |  |
|  |  |  |  |  |  |  |
|  |  |  |  |  |  |  |

---

**DESTINATION PORT**  VHF ............... HM ☎ ........................

ARRIVAL  PROCEDURE ....................................................

...........................................................................................

BAR CROSSING TIMES ...................................................

LOCK/GATE/SILL TIMES .................................................

BRIDGE TIMES .............................................................

ACCESS WINDOW .........................................................

**ALTERNATE PORT**  VHF ............... HM ☎ .........................

ARRIVAL  PROCEDURE ....................................................

...........................................................................................

BAR CROSSING TIMES ...................................................

LOCK/GATE/SILL TIMES .................................................

BRIDGE TIMES .............................................................

ACCESS WINDOW .........................................................

## 0.4 PASSAGE PLANNING

Before you start to navigate you need to plan: where you are going, how to get there and what factors may influence the plan. To most people this is commonsense, but now it is also the law. Visit www.mcga.gov.uk for guidance.

**SOLAS V, Regulation 34** requires that all passage plans, however short, should consider the following:
- **Limitations of the vessel.** Seaworthy, well equipped.
- **Limitations of the crew.** Experience and ability.
- **Navigational dangers**, awareness and avoidance of.
- **Tides.** Tide times & heights. Best use of tidal streams.
- **Weather.** Suitable 'window' and bolt-holes.
- **Contingency plan.** Able to cope with all emergencies.
- **GPS**, over-reliance on. DR navigation.
- **CG 66:** Complete this voluntary identification form so as to help the CG find you if in difficulty.

Legally all voyages/passages by any vessel that goes to sea must be pre-planned. 'Going to sea' is defined as proceeding beyond sheltered waters. Even in very familiar waters every passage, however short, must be pre-planned, but for small craft the degree of planning may be less than for big ships.

The passage plan need not be in writing. However a written plan, in the event of legal action, is clear proof that planning has been done. A checklist, which when completed forms the passage plan, is therefore included overleaf; it may be photocopied or modified to suit individual needs.

Before reaching the checklist stage, much thought and study must go into drafting the plan. Any plan for any project goes through some or all of the following phases:

- Deciding the aim. It is not always obvious.
- Gathering the facts; time consuming but essential.
- Assessing the information now available.
- Formulating the plan. Think laterally of all the options.

## 0.5 GPS HORIZONTAL DATUM

GPS fixes are referenced to the World Geodetic System 84 (WGS84) datum. Satellite fixes cannot be plotted directly onto those charts which are still referenced to older datums. Corrections must first be applied to obtain the full accuracy of GPS.

Admiralty charts of UK waters have been converted to WGS84, or ETRS 89, a compatible datum. All chartlets and Lat/Long coordinates in the Reeds Almanacs are now to WGS84. Charts of N Europe are mostly to WGS84. Further south the changeover from ED50 to WGS84 continues steadily.

The datum used on a chart is always printed below the title under 'Satellite-derived positions', with the correction, or shift, needed to adjust the chart's datum to WGS84. If the changeover to WGS84 is still incomplete, the navigator has two options when using a non-WGS84 chart:

- Set the receiver to WGS84 and manually apply the datum shifts before plotting positions on the chart.

- Or, set the receiver to the datum of the chart in use. The software in the receiver will convert the satellite signal from WGS84 to the datum of the chart in use, usually less accurately but quicker than the manual method above.

The differences between WGS84 and other horizontal datums vary with location but errors can be substantial.

## 0.6 COMMUNICATIONS

### Radio Telephony (R/T)

VHF gives a range about 30–40M depending on the aerial heights of both the shore station and the yacht.

Give your position in Lat/Long or as the yacht's bearing and distance **from** a charted object, eg 'My position 225° Lundy Island 4M' means you are 4M SW of Lundy Island. Use the 360° True bearing notation and the 24 hour clock (0000 to 2359), specifying UT, LT, etc.

VHF sets may be Simplex, ie transmit and receive on the same frequency, so that only one person can talk at a time; Semi-Duplex, ie transmit and receive on different frequencies; or Duplex, ie simultaneous semi-duplex, so that conversation is normal.

Marine VHF frequencies are in the band 156·00–174·00 MHz. Frequencies are known by their international channel number (Ch), as shown below.

Channels are grouped according to three main purposes, but some can be used for more than one purpose. They are shown in their preferred order of usage:

- *Public correspondence:* (via Coast Radio Stations). Ch 26, 27, 25, 24, 23, 28, 04, 01, 03, 02, 07, 05, 84, 87, 86, 83, 85, 88, 61, 64, 65, 62, 66, 63, 60, 82, 78, 81. All channels can be used for duplex.

- *Inter-ship:* Ch 06, 08, 10, 13, 09, 72, 73, 69, 77, 15, 17. These are all simplex channels. It is as well to know at least 3 or 4 of these channels so that, if called on Ch 16 , you can nominate an inter-ship working channel without delay.

- *Port operations:*
Simplex: Ch 12, 14, 11, 13, 09, 68, 71, 74, 69, 73, 17, 15.
Duplex: Ch 20, 22, 18, 19, 21, 05, 07, 02, 03, 01, 04, 78, 82, 79, 81, 80, 60, 63, 66, 62, 65, 64, 61, 84.

The following channels have one specific purpose:

**Ch 0** (156·00 MHz): SAR ops, not available to yachts.

**Ch 10** (156·50 MHz), **23** (161·750 MHz), **73** (156·675 MHz), **84** (161·825 MHz) and **86** (161·925 MHz): MSI broadcasts. The optimum channel is broadcast in the prior announcement on Ch 16.

**Ch 13** (156·650 MHz): Inter-ship communications relating to safety of navigation; a possible channel for calling a merchant ship if no contact on Ch 16.

**Ch 16** (156·80 MHz): Distress, Safety and calling. Ch 16, in parallel with DSC Ch 70, will be monitored by ships, CG rescue centres (and, in some areas, any remaining Coast radio stations) for Distress and Safety until further notice. Yachts should monitor Ch 16. After an initial call, stations concerned **must** switch to a working channel, except for Safety matters.

**Ch 67** (156·375 MHz): Small craft safety channel used by all UK CG centres, accessed via Ch 16.

**Ch 70** (156·525 MHz): Digital Selective Calling for Distress and Safety purposes under GMDSS.

**Ch 80** (157·025 MHz): Primary working channel between yachts and UK marinas.

**Ch M** (157·85 MHz): Secondary working channel, formerly known as Ch 37, but no longer.

**Ch M2** (161·425 MHz): for race control, with Ch M as stand-by. YCs may apply to use Ch M2.

## 0.7 DISTRESS CALLS

### MAYDAY – Distress signal

A MAYDAY call should usually be sent on VHF Ch 16 or MF 2182 kHz, but any frequency may be used if help may thus be obtained more quickly.

Distress, Urgency and Safety messages from vessels at sea are free of charge. A Distress call has priority over all other transmissions. If heard, cease all transmissions that may interfere with the Distress call or messages, and listen on the frequency concerned.

Train your crew, as necessary, so they can all send a Distress message. It helps greatly to display the MAYDAY message format near the radio. Before making the call:

- Check main battery switch ON
- Switch radio ON
- Select HIGH power (25 watts)
- Select VHF Ch 16 (or 2182 kHz for MF)
- Press and hold down the transmit button, and say slowly and distinctly:

- **MAYDAY MAYDAY MAYDAY**
- **THIS IS** ...........................................................
  (name of boat, spoken three times)
- **MAYDAY** ..........................................................
  (name of boat spoken once)
- **MY POSITION IS** ..............................................
  (latitude and longitude, or true bearing and distance from a known point)
- **Nature of distress** .........................................
  (sinking, on fire, etc)
- **Help required** .................................................
  (immediate assistance)
- **Number of persons on board** ........................
- **Any other important, helpful information** ...........
  (eg if the yacht is drifting, whether distress rockets are being fired)
- **OVER**

On completion of the Distress message, release the transmit button and listen. The boat's position is of vital importance, and should be repeated if time allows.

Vessels with GMDSS equipment should make a MAYDAY call on Ch 16 *after* sending a DSC Distress alert on VHF Ch 70 or MF 2187·5 kHz.

### 0.7.1 MAYDAY acknowledgement

In coastal waters an immediate acknowledgement should be expected, as follows:

> **MAYDAY** ...........................................................
> (name of station sending the Distress message, spoken three times)
> **THIS IS** ...........................................................
> (name of station acknowledging, spoken three times)
> **RECEIVED MAYDAY**

If an acknowledgement is not received, check the set and repeat the Distress call.

If you hear a Distress message, write down the details, and if you can help you should acknowledge accordingly, but only after giving an opportunity for the nearest Coastguard station or some larger vessel to do so.

### 0.7.2 MAYDAY relay

If you hear a Distress message from a vessel, and it is not acknowledged, you should pass on the message as follows:

> **MAYDAY RELAY** ..............................................
> (spoken three times)
> **THIS IS** ...........................................................
> (name of vessel re-transmitting the Distress message, spoken three times), followed by the intercepted message.

### 0.7.3 Control of MAYDAY traffic

A MAYDAY call imposes general radio silence until the vessel concerned or some other authority (eg the nearest Coastguard) cancels the Distress. If necessary the station controlling Distress traffic may impose radio silence as follows:

> **SEELONCE MAYDAY**, followed by its name or other identification, on the Distress frequency.
>
> If some other station nearby believes it necessary to do likewise, it may transmit:
>
> **SEELONCE DISTRESS**, followed by its name or other identification.

### 0.7.4 Relaxing radio silence

When complete radio silence is no longer necessary on a frequency being used for Distress traffic, the controlling station may relax radio silence as follows, indicating that restricted working may be resumed:

> **MAYDAY**
> **ALL STATIONS, ALL STATIONS, ALL STATIONS**
> **THIS IS** ...........................................................
> (name or callsign)
> The time ...........................................................
> The name of the vessel in distress ...............................
> **PRUDONCE**

Normal working on the Distress frequency may then be resumed, having listened carefully before transmitting. Subsequent calls from the casualty should be prefixed by the Urgency signal (0.8).

If Distress working continues on other frequencies these will be identified. For example, PRUDONCE on 2182 kHz, but SEELONCE on VHF Ch 16.

### 0.7.5 Cancelling radio silence

When the problem is resolved, the Distress call must be cancelled by the co-ordinating station using the prowords SEELONCE FEENEE as follows:

> **MAYDAY**
> **ALL STATIONS, ALL STATIONS, ALL STATIONS**
> **THIS IS** ...........................................................
> (name or callsign)
> The time ...........................................................
> The name of the vessel in distress ...............................
> **SEELONCE FEENEE**

## 0.8 URGENCY AND SAFETY CALLS

### PAN PAN – Urgency signal

The R/T Urgency signal, consisting of the words PAN PAN spoken three times, indicates that a vessel, or station, has a very urgent message concerning the safety of a ship or person. It is appropriate for a man overboard situation or when urgent medical advice or attention is needed.

Here is an example of an Urgency call and message from the yacht *Seabird*, disabled off the Needles.

> **PAN PAN, PAN PAN, PAN PAN**
>
> **ALL STATIONS, ALL STATIONS, ALL STATIONS**
>
> **THIS IS YACHT SEABIRD, SEABIRD, SEABIRD**
>
> Two nine zero degrees Needles lighthouse two miles
>
> Dismasted and propeller fouled
>
> Anchor dragging and drifting east north east towards Shingles Bank
>
> Require urgent tow
>
> **OVER**

PAN PAN messages take priority over all traffic except Distress, and are sent on Ch 16 or 2182 kHz. They should be cancelled when the urgency is over.

If the message itself is long or is a medical call, or communications traffic is heavy, it should be passed on a working frequency after an initial call on Ch 16 or 2182 kHz. At the end of the initial call it should be indicated that you are switching to a working frequency.

If you hear an Urgency call respond in the same way as for a Distress call.

### 0.8.1 SÉCURITÉ – Safety signal

This consists of the word SÉCURITÉ (pronounced SAY-CURE-E-TAY) spoken three times, and indicates that the station is about to transmit an important navigational or meteorological warning. Such messages usually originate from a CG Centre or a Coast radio station, and are transmitted on a working channel after an announcement on the Distress channel.

Safety messages are usually addressed to 'All stations', and are often transmitted at the end of the first available silence period. An example of a Sécurité message might be:

> **SÉCURITÉ, SÉCURITÉ, SÉCURITÉ** .....................................
>
> **THIS IS** ................................................................................
> (CG Centre or Coast Radio Station callsign, spoken three times)
>
> **ALL STATIONS** ...................................................................
> (spoken three times) followed by instructions to change channel, then the message.

## 0.9 GMDSS

The Global Maritime Distress and Safety System (GMDSS) is a sophisticated, but complex, semi-automatic, third-generation communications system. Although not compulsory for yachts, its potential for saving life, particularly when far offshore and out of VHF range, is so great that every yachtsman should consider it most seriously. Training courses, leading to the award of the Short Range Certificate (SRC) of Competence, are widely available. Equipment costs continue to fall.

### 0.9.1 Purpose

GMDSS enables a coordinated SAR operation to be mounted rapidly and reliably anywhere at sea. To this end, terrestrial and satellite communications and navigation equipment is used to alert SAR authorities ashore and ships in the vicinity to a Distress incident or Urgency situation. GMDSS also promulgates MSI (Maritime Safety Information).

### 0.9.2 Sea areas

For the purposes of GMDSS, the world's sea areas are divided into 4 categories (A1-4), defined mainly by the range of radio communications. These are:

> **A1** An area within R/T coverage of at least one VHF Coastguard or Coast radio station in which continuous VHF alerting is available via DSC. Range: 20–50M from the CG/CRS.
>
> **A2** An area, excluding sea area A1, within R/T coverage of at least one MF CG/CRS in which continuous DSC alerting is available. Range: approx 50–250M from the CG/CRS.
>
> **A3** An area between 70°N and 70°S, excluding sea areas A1 and A2, within coverage of HF or an Inmarsat satellite in which continuous alerting is available.
>
> **A4** An area outside sea areas A1, A2 and A3, ie the polar regions, within coverage of HF.

In each category of sea area certain types of radio equipment must be carried. In A1 areas VHF DSC; A2 areas MF or HF DSC; A3 areas SatCom; A4 MF/HF.

### 0.9.3 Digital Selective Calling

DSC is a vital component of GMDSS. It is so called because information is sent by a burst of digital code; selective because it can be addressed to a specific DSC-equipped vessel or to a selected group of vessels.

In GMDSS every vessel and shore station has a 9-digit number, or MMSI (Maritime Mobile Service Identity), in effect an automatic, electronic callsign.

DSC is used to transmit Distress alerts from ships; to receive Distress acknowledgements; to send Urgency and Safety alerts; to relay Distress alerts; and for routine calling and answering.

A VHF/DSC Distress alert might be sent as follows:

> • Momentarily press the (red, guarded) Distress button. The set automatically switches to Ch 70 (DSC Distress chan) and transmits a basic Distress alert with position and time. It then reverts to Ch I6.
>
> • If time permits, select from the DSC menu the nature of the distress, eg Collision. Then press the Distress button for 5 seconds to send a full Distress alert.

A CG centre or CRS automatically sends a Distress acknowledgement on Ch 70, before replying on Ch 16. Ships in range should reply directly on Ch 16.

> • When a DSC Distress acknowledgement has been received, or after about 15 seconds, the vessel in distress should transmit a MAYDAY message by voice on Ch 16 adding its MMSI.

*Fig 0(4)   Distress and life saving signals*

## (1) Signals to be used by Ships, Aircraft or Persons in Distress

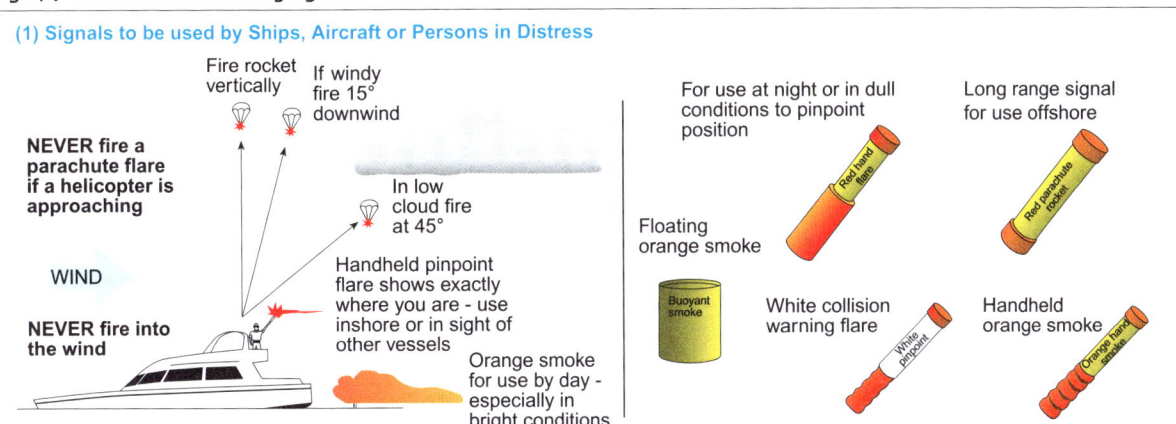

Fire rocket vertically

If windy fire 15° downwind

**NEVER fire a parachute flare if a helicopter is approaching**

WIND

**NEVER fire into the wind**

In low cloud fire at 45°

Handheld pinpoint flare shows exactly where you are - use inshore or in sight of other vessels

Orange smoke for use by day - especially in bright conditions

For use at night or in dull conditions to pinpoint position

Long range signal for use offshore

Red hand flares

Red parachute rocket

Floating orange smoke

Buoyant smoke

White collision warning flare

White pinpoint

Handheld orange smoke

Orange hand smoke

## (2) Replies from life-saving stations etc. to distress signals made by ships or persons

Orange smoke signal

White star rocket - three single signals fired at intervals of about one minute

**Meaning**
**'You are seen - assistance will be given as soon as possible'**

## (3) Surface to Air Signals

| Message | International Code of Signals | | ICAO Visual Signals |
|---|---|---|---|
| 'I require assistance' | 'V' (red X) | (· · · —) | V |
| 'I require medical assistance' | 'W' (red square) | (· — —) | X |
| 'No' or 'negative' | 'N' (blue/white check) | (— ·) | N |
| 'Yes' or 'affirmative' | 'C' (blue/white/red) | (— · — ·) | Y |
| 'Proceed in this direction' | ↑ | | |

## (4) Air to Surface replies

**'Message understood'**

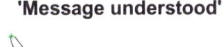

Drop a message   Rocking wings   Flash landing or navigation lights twice

or 'T' ( — )
or 'R' (· — ·)

Morse code signal by light

**'Message not understood - repeat'**

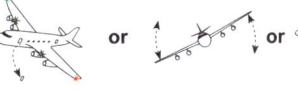

Straight and level flight

Circling

or 'RPT'
(· — · · — · — · — )

Morse code signal by light

## (5) Air to Surface Direction Signals

**Sequence of 3 manœuvres meaning proceed in this direction**

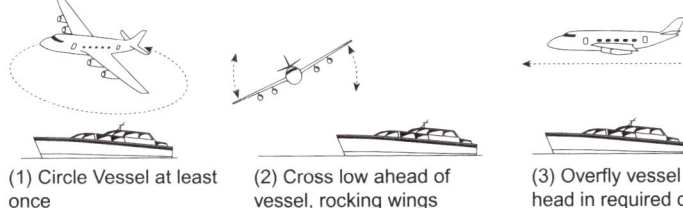

(1) Circle Vessel at least once

(2) Cross low ahead of vessel, rocking wings

(3) Overfly vessel and head in required direction

**Your assistance is no longer required**

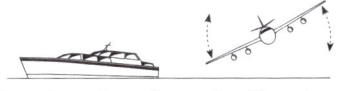

Cross low astern of vessel rocking wings

**Note:** as an alternative to rocking wings, the aircraft engine pitch or volume may be varied

## (6) Surface to Air replies

**'Message understood - I will comply'**

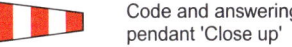

Change course or direction

**or**

'T' ( — )   Morse Code signal by light

**or**

Code and answering pendant 'Close up'

**'I am unable to comply'**

'N' ( — ·)   Morse Code signal by light

**or**

(blue/white check flag)   International flag 'N'

## 0.10 WEATHER BROADCASTS IN THE UK

### BBC Radio 4 Shipping forecast

BBC Radio 4 broadcasts shipping forecasts at:

| | |
|---|---|
| 0048 LT[1] | LW, MW, FM |
| 0520 LT[1] | LW, MW, FM |
| 1201 LT | LW only |
| 1754 LT | LW, FM (Sat/Sun) |

[1] Includes weather reports from coastal stations

### Frequencies

| | | |
|---|---|---|
| LW | | 198 kHz |
| MW | London and N Ireland: | 720 kHz |
| | Redruth: | 756 kHz |
| | Plymouth & Enniskillen: | 774 kHz |
| | Carlisle: | 1485 kHz |
| FM | England: | 92·4–94·6 MHz |
| | Scotland: | 91·3–96·1 MHz |
| | | 103·5–104·9 MHz |
| | Wales: | 92·8–96·1 MHz & |
| | | 103·5–104·9 MHz |
| | N Ireland | 93·2–96·0 MHz |
| | | 103·5–104·6 MHz |

### Contents of the Shipping forecast

The forecast contains:

A summary of gale warnings in force at time of issue; a general synopsis of weather systems and their expected development over the next 24 hours; and a forecast of wind direction/force, weather and visibility in each sea area for the next 24 hours.

Gale warnings are also broadcast at the earliest juncture in Radio 4 programmes after receipt, as well as after the next news bulletin. Sea area Trafalgar is only included in the 0048 forecast.

**Strong Wind Warnings** are issued by the Met Office whenever winds of Force 6 or more are expected over coastal waters up to 5M offshore.

Shipping forecasts cover large sea areas, and rarely include the detailed variations that may occur near land. The Inshore waters forecast (see 0.10.1) can be more helpful to mariners on coastal passages.

**Weather reports from coastal stations** follow the 0048 and 0520 forecasts. They include wind direction and force, present weather, visibility, and sea-level pressure and tendency, if available. The stations are shown below in 0.10.1 and in Fig 0(2).

### 0.10.1 BBC Radio 4 Inshore waters forecast

A forecast for inshore waters (up to 12M offshore) around the UK and N Ireland, valid until 1800, is broadcast after the 0048 and 0520 coastal station reports.

It includes a general synopsis, forecasts of wind direction and force, visibility and weather for stretches of inshore waters, extending from Land's End to Cape Wrath. Areas are defined by well-known places such as St David's Hd, Great Ormes Hd, Mull of Galloway and Ardnamurchan.

**Reports of actual weather** at the stations below are only broadcast after the 0048 inshore waters forecast: *Scilly\**, Milford Haven, Aberporth, Valley, Liverpool (Crosby), *Ronaldsway*, Larne, Machrihanish\*, Greenock and *Stornoway*. These stations are shown in Fig 0(2). Asterisk\* denotes an automatic station. Stations in italics also feature in the 0048 and 0520 shipping forecasts.

## 0.10.2 Terms used in weather bulletins

### Speed of movement of pressure systems

| | |
|---|---|
| *Slowly* | < 15 knots |
| *Steadily* | 15–25 knots |
| *Rather quickly* | 25–35 knots |
| *Rapidly* | 35–45 knots |
| *Very rapidly* | > 45 knots |

### Visibility

| | |
|---|---|
| *Good* | > 5 miles |
| *Moderate* | 2–5 miles |
| *Poor* | 1000 metres–2 miles |
| *Fog* | Less than 1000 metres |

### Timing of gale warnings

| | |
|---|---|
| *Imminent:* | Within 6 hrs from time of issue |
| *Soon:* | 6–12 hrs from time of issue |
| *Later:* | >12 hrs from time of issue |

### Barometric pressure changes (tendency)

*Rising or falling slowly:* Pressure change of 0·1 to 1·5 hPa/mb in the preceding 3 hours.

*Rising or falling:* Pressure change of 1·6 to 3·5 hPa/mb in the preceding 3 hours.

*Rising or falling quickly:* Pressure change of 3·6 to 6 hPa/mb in the preceding 3 hours.

*Rising or falling very rapidly:* Pressure change of more than 6 hPa/mb in the preceding 3 hours.

*Now rising (or falling):* Pressure has been falling (rising) or steady in the preceding 3 hours, but at the observation time was definitely rising (falling).

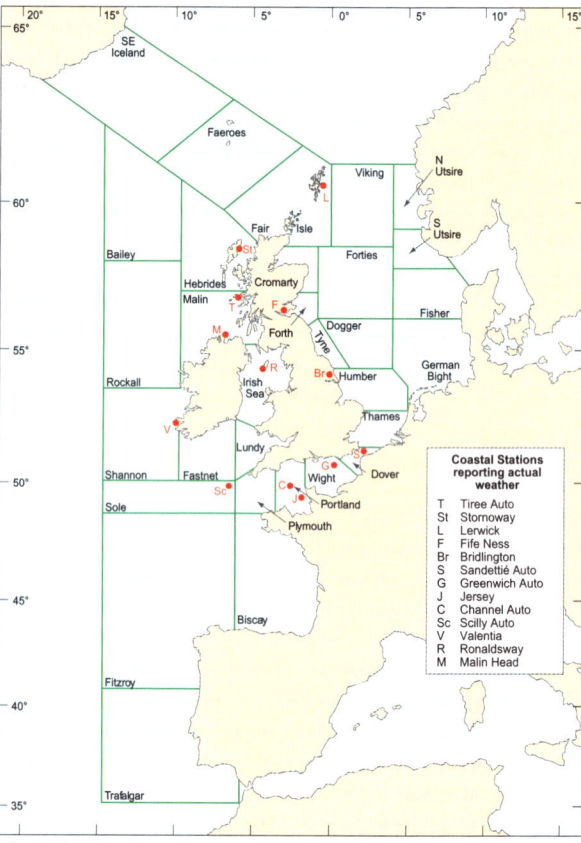

**Coastal Stations reporting actual weather**

| | |
|---|---|
| T | Tiree Auto |
| St | Stornoway |
| L | Lerwick |
| F | Fife Ness |
| Br | Bridlington |
| S | Sandettié Auto |
| G | Greenwich Auto |
| J | Jersey |
| C | Channel Auto |
| Sc | Scilly Auto |
| V | Valentia |
| R | Ronaldsway |
| M | Malin Head |

*Fig 0(2) UK – Forecast areas*

## 0.11  NAVTEX

Navtex uses a dedicated aerial, receiver and integral printer or LCD screen. The user programmes the receiver for the required station(s) and message categories. MSI is automatically printed or displayed. Interference between stations is avoided by time sharing and by limiting the range of transmitters to about 300M. Coverage of Europe is excellent. Navtex information applies only to the geographic area for which each station is responsible. Navtex is especially valuable if there is a language problem, when out of range of other sources, or otherwise occupied.

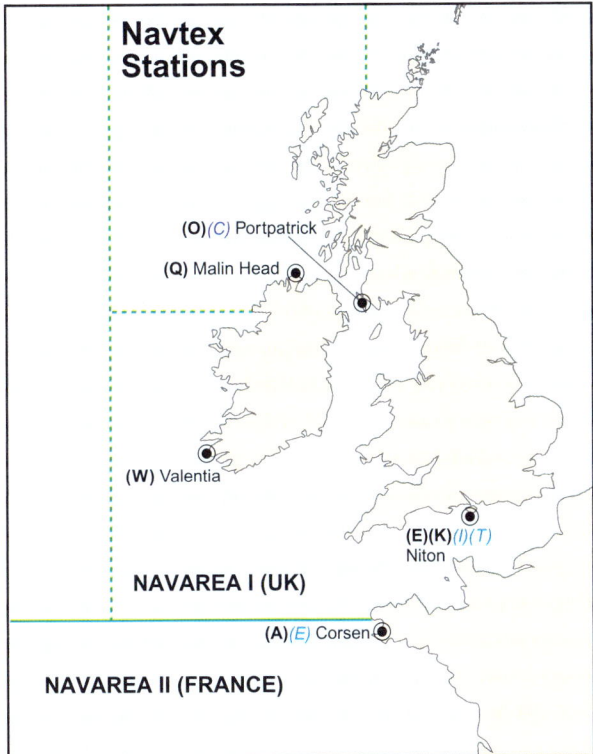

*Fig 0(3) Navtex stations/areas – UK & Ireland*

Two frequencies are used, 518 kHz and 490 kHz:

518 kHz messages are always in English (occasionally in the national language as well).

490 kHz (for clarity shown in red throughout this section) is used abroad for transmissions in the national language. In the UK it is used for inshore waters forecasts. 490 kHz and 518 kHz stations have different identification letters.

### 0.11.1  Message numbering

Each message is prefixed by a four-character group:

The first character is the code letter of the transmitting station (eg **E** for Niton).

The second character is the message category, see 0.11.2.

The third and fourth are message serial numbers, running from 01 to 99 and then re-starting at 01.

The serial number 00 denotes urgent messages which are always printed.

Messages which are corrupt or have already been printed are rejected. Weather messages, and certain other message types, are dated and timed. All Navtex messages end with NNNN.

### 0.11.2  Message categories

| | |
|---|---|
| A* | Navigational warnings |
| B* | Meteorological warnings |
| C | Ice reports |
| D* | SAR info and Piracy attack warnings |
| E | Weather forecasts |
| F | Pilot service |
| H | Loran-C |
| J | Satellite navigation |
| K | Other electronic Navaids |
| L | Subfacts and Gunfacts (UK) |
| V | Amplifying navwarnings initially sent under A; also weekly oil and gas rig moves |
| W-Y | Special service – trial allocation |
| Z | No messages on hand at scheduled time |
| G, I & M-U | Not allocated at present |

\* These categories cannot be rejected by the receiver.

### 0.11.3  UK 518 kHz stations

The times (UT) of weather messages are in bold; the times of an extended outlook (a further 2 or 3 days beyond the shipping forecast period) are in italics.

| O – | **Portpatrick** Lundy clockwise to SE Iceland. | *0220* | **0620** | 1020 | 1420 | **1820** | 2220 |
|---|---|---|---|---|---|---|---|
| E – | **Niton** Thames clockwise to Fastnet, excluding Trafalgar. | *0040* | 0440 | **0840** | 1240 | 1640 | **2040** |

### 0.11.4  UK 490 kHz stations

These provide forecasts for the Inshore waters (12M offshore) of the UK, including Shetland, plus a national 3 day outlook for inshore waters. Times are UT.

| C – | **Portpatrick** St David's Head to Cape Wrath | | 0820 | | 2020 |
|---|---|---|---|---|---|
| I – | **Niton** The Wash to Colwyn Bay | 0520 | | 1720 | |

### 0.11.5  Navtex coverage in Ireland  and Brittany

Times of weather messages are shown in **bold**. Gale warnings are usually transmitted 4 hourly.

| METAREA I (Co-ordinator – UK) | Transmission times (UT) | | | | | |
|---|---|---|---|---|---|---|
| Q  –  **Malin Head**, Ireland | 0240 | **0640** | **1040** | 1440 | **1840** | 2240 |
| W  –  **Valentia**, Ireland | 0340 | **0740** | **1140** | 1540 | **1940** | 2340 |
| METAREA II (Co-ordinator – France) | | | | | | |
| A  –  **Corsen**, France | 0000 | 0400 | 0800 | **1200** | 1600 | 2000 |

## 0.12   WEATHER BY TELEPHONE

Marinecall offer 3 types of recorded weather bulletins. Call from any landline or mobile network within the UK (inc Channel Islands). In case of difficulty contact Customer Services on 0871 200 3985.

### 0.12.1   Actual weather

Current weather, updated hourly, gives hourly summaries for next 6 hours at over 160 locations around the UK. Dial **09068 969** + the required area number, in green on Fig 0(4).

### 0.12.2   5-day forecasts for Inshore waters

For any of 15 UK inshore areas, call **09068 9696 + the Area number** shown in green on Fig 0(4). For an inshore waters forecast covering the whole UK for 3 to 5 days ahead, dial **09068 9696** 40.

Forecasts cover the waters out to 12M offshore for up to 5 days and include: General situation, strong wind or gale warnings in force, wind, weather, visibility, sea state, max air temp and mean sea temp.

The initial 2-day forecast is followed by a forecast for days 3 and 4 and outlook for day 5. Forecasts are updated at 0700 daily. The Channel Islands area (656) is additionally updated at 1300.

The local inshore forecast for Shetland is only available from Shetland CG on ☎ 01595 692976.

09068 calls cost 60p/min from a landline. Calls from mobiles may be subject to network charges.

Discounts are available via Marinecall Club, ie

10 forecasts £20; 20 for £40; 30 for £55; and 40 for £70. Pay in advance and dial a Marinecall freefone number using a unique PIN.

### 0.12.3   Offshore planning forecasts

For 2- to 5-day planning forecasts for offshore areas, updated by 0700 daily, call **09068 9696** + the number for the offshore area, shown in red on Fig 0(4), ie:

| | |
|---|---|
| 57 | English Channel |
| 59 | Irish Sea |
| 60 | Biscay |
| 61 | NW Scotland |
| 62 | Northern North Sea |

These forecasts contain elements similar to those in 0.12.2.

### 0.12.4   Contacting Marinecall

For further information contact:
Marinecall Customer Services, iTouch (UK) Ltd, Avalon House, 57-63 Scrutton Street, London EC2A 4PF. ☎ 0871 200 3985; 🖷 0870 600 4229. www.marinecall.co.uk marinecall@itouch.co.uk

## 0.13   WEATHER BY FAX

Fax forecasts contain the same data as those listed under 0.12, but are updated thrice daily. The Advance forecast (🖷 09065 @ £1.50/min) contains slightly more detail than the Standard forecast (🖷 09060 @ £1/min). The Fax numbers in Fig 0(9) are for the Advance service.

To obtain a forecast dial 🖷 09065 22 23 plus the 2 digit area number in Fig 0(4), either green for inshore waters or red for offshore. After dialling press the Start or Receive button to start the transmission; be prepared for a slight delay as the data is downloaded to your fax machine.

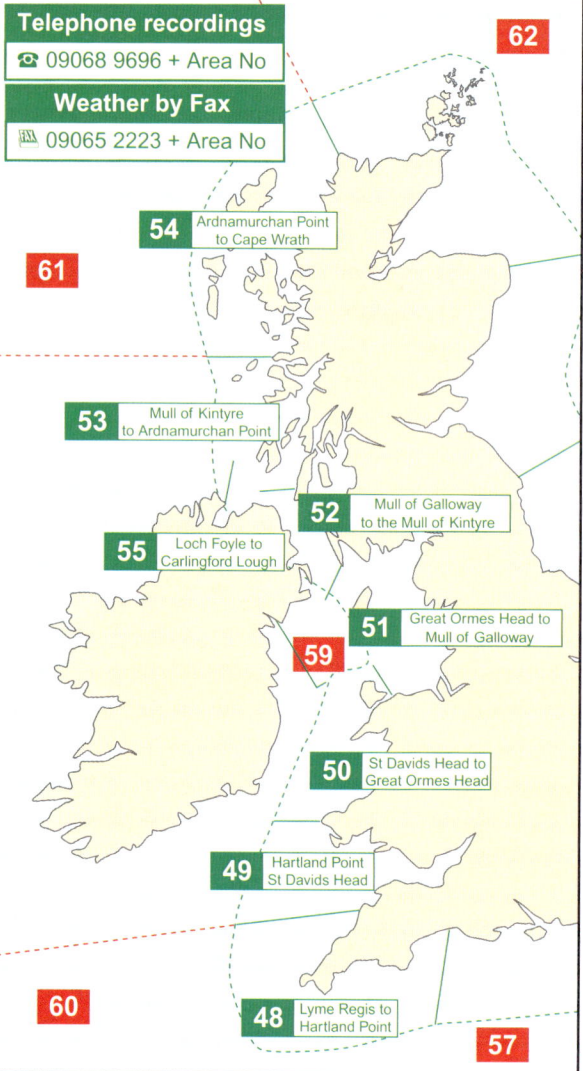

Fig 0(4) Inshore/Offshore forecast areas by Telephone and Fax

### 0.13.1   Marinecall FaxDirect

Discounts to regular users of the Advance services include, for example over 3 months: 1 fax per week costs £38.76 inc VAT; 3 faxes per week £102.23; and 7 faxes per week £211.50. Monthly and annual subscriptions are available.

## EUROPEAN WEATHER BY TELEPHONE & FAX
### 0.13.2   4-digit codes

Over 200 such codes give quicker, cheaper access to a required area or port by reducing the preamble. They apply to Tel and Fax messages for UK and Europe. Dial ☎ 09068 96 96 or 🖷 09065 22 23, and the 2 digit area code, ie the offshore areas 57-62 shown in red in Fig. 0(4). Add the 4-digit code, eg 6360 for Oban, as soon as the call connects or you are prompted to do so. A full listing of 4-digit codes is in the Marinecall Handbook or visit www.marinecall.co.uk

For European coastal locations dial ☎ 09068 96 96 or 🖷 09065 22 23, and the 2 digit area code; add the 4-digit code as stated above. For example for Dublin 59 2928.

Other 2-digit Area codes include:

**Northern Ireland** Area code 59, + 4 digits, ie: Lough Foyle

6560; Portrush 6562; Ballycastle 6563; Larne 6564; Bangor 6565; Portavogie 6566; Strangford Lough 6567.

**Irish Republic** Area code 59: Carlingford Lough 2924; Dublin 2928; Wicklow Head 2925; Mine Head 2926; Baltimore 2927, Malin Head 6561. W coast locations are not covered.

## 0.14 WEATHER BY MOBILE PHONE

Marinecall offers 3 ways to get forecasts via your mobile. Note: Calls from mobiles may be subject to network charges. Not all mobiles can receive MMS or WAP messages.

• **SMS** (Short Message Service, ie texting). A message includes: current weather; a forecast for 5 hrs later, at one of the coastal locations below; updated hrly. Format: Location, date, time; max temp °C; mean wind direction/ speed; visibility; % risk of precipitation. For example:

> Iona: 1/10/08
> 10am: 11c, WD 250d, WS 12kt, VIS 17.59km, RAIN 10%.
> 3pm: 12c, WD 290d, WS 14kt, VIS 13.50km, RAIN 12%.

To obtain this message, by return @ 25p per message, type **AC** and the location's name; then send it to 83141.

Or type **AC Sub** and location's name; send it to 83141, to receive data by 0900 daily @ £1.50 for 6 messages.

• **MMS** (Multi Media Messaging) receives the same data as SMS. Type **AC MMS**, location's name and send to 83141; £1 a message. **AC MMS Sub** is as per **AC Sub** above.

• **WAP** (Wireless Application Protocol) connects your mobile to the internet. Forecasts contain the same data as MMS, but there are fewer locations. Type **AC WAP**, location's name and send to 83141; 75p a message. **AC WAP Sub** is as per **AC Sub** above.

### Area 1, NW Scotland

| | |
|---|---|
| Craobh marina | Oban |
| Iona | Tobermory |

### Area 2, SW Scotland

| | |
|---|---|
| Ardrossan | Lamlash |
| Burrow Head | Largs |
| Campbeltown | Mull of Kintyre |
| East Loch Tarbert | Portpatrick |
| Kip marina | Rhu marina |
| Kirkcudbright | Troon |

### Area 3, NW England, IoM, N Wales

| | |
|---|---|
| Beaumaris | Liverpool |
| Caernarfon | Maryport |
| Conwy | Preston |
| Glasson Dock | Whitehaven |
| Holyhead | Wyre Dock (Fleetwood) |

### Area 4, Wales – Land's End

| | |
|---|---|
| Aberystwyth | Padstow |
| Bardsey Island | Penarth (Cardiff) |
| Bristol | Portishead |
| Milford Dock | Pwllheli |
| Newquay (Cornwall) | Swansea |

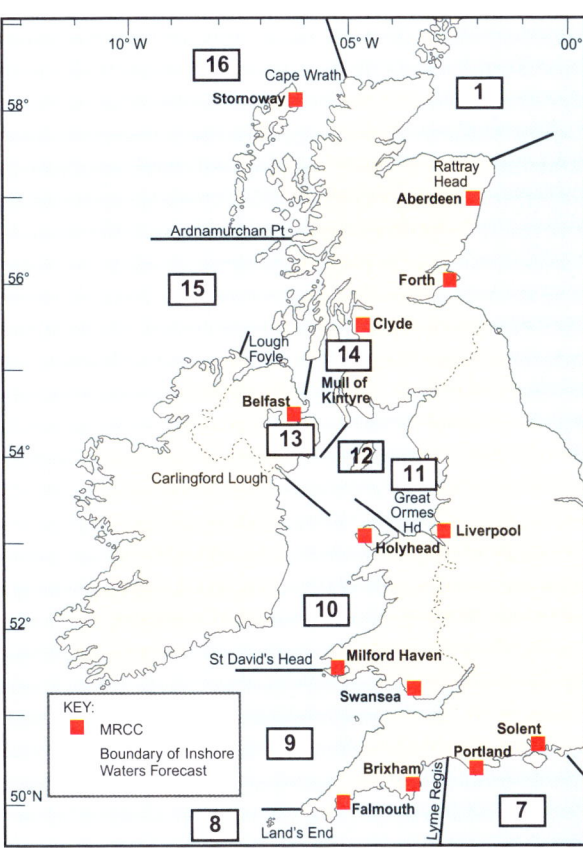

*Fig 0(5) Stations reporting actual weather via BBC Radio 4, SMS or telephone recordings*

*Fig 0(6) Boundaries of the areas used by the CG for forecasts covering inshore waters*

## 0.15   BROADCASTS BY HM COASTGUARD

HM CG Centres routinely broadcast MSI every 3 hours at the times below. VHF channels are pre-stated on Ch 16.

Each broadcast contains one of 3 different Groups of MSI: **Group A**, the full broadcast, contains the Shipping forecast, a new Inshore waters forecast and 24 hrs outlook, Gale warnings, a Fisherman's 3 day forecast* (1 Oct-31 Mar), Navigational (WZ) warnings and Subfacts & Gunfacts

where appropriate ‡. Times of 'A' broadcasts are in bold. **Group B** contains a new Inshore waters forecast, plus the previous outlook, and Gale warnings. 'B' broadcast times are in plain type.

**Group C** is a repeat of the Inshore forecast and Gale warnings (as per the previous Group A or B) plus new Strong wind warnings. 'C' broadcast times are italicised.

| Coastguard | Shipping forecast areas | Inshore areas | Broadcast times LT | | | | | | | |
|---|---|---|---|---|---|---|---|---|---|---|
| | | | B | C | A | C | B | C | A | C |
| **West Coast** | | | | | | | | | | |
| **Stornoway**‡* | Rockall, Malin, Hebrides, Bailey, Fair Is, Faeroes, SE Iceland | 16 | 0110 | *0410* | **0710** | *1010* | 1310 | *1610* | **1910** | *2210* |
| **Clyde**‡ | Rockall, Malin, Hebrides, Bailey | 14, 15 | 0210 | *0510* | **0810** | *1110* | 1410 | *1710* | **2010** | *2310* |
| **Belfast**‡ | Irish Sea, Malin | 12–14 | 0110 | *0410* | **0710** | *1010* | 1310 | *1610* | **1910** | *2210* |
| **Liverpool** | Irish Sea | 11, 12 | 0130 | *0430* | **0730** | *1030* | 1330 | *1630* | **1930** | *2230* |
| **Holyhead** | Irish Sea | 10, 11 | 0150 | *0450* | **0750** | *1050* | 1350 | *1650* | **1950** | *2250* |
| **Milford Haven** | Lundy, Fastnet, Irish Sea | 9, 10 | 0150 | *0450* | **0750** | *1050* | 1350 | *1650* | **1950** | *2250* |
| **Swansea** | Lundy, Fastnet, Irish Sea | 9, 10 | 0150 | *0450* | **0750** | *1050* | 1350 | *1650* | **1950** | *2250* |

## 0.16   REPUBLIC OF IRELAND

Met Éireann (the Irish Met Office) is at Glasnevin Hill, Dublin 9, Ireland. ☎ 1 806 4250, 🖷 1 806 4250, www.met.ie. General forecasting division (H24, charges may apply) ☎ 1 806 4255, 🖷 1 806 4275.

### 0.16.1   Irish Coast Radio Stations

CRS and their VHF channels are listed below (anti-clockwise from Malin Head) and shown on Fig 0(7). Weather bulletins for 30M offshore and the Irish Sea are broadcast on VHF at 0103, 0403, 0703, 1003, 1303, 1603, 1903 and 2203UT after an announcement on Ch 16. Broadcasts are made 1 hour earlier when DST is in force. Bulletins include gale warnings, synopsis and a 24-hour forecast.

| | | | |
|---|---|---|---|
| Malin Head | 23 | Bantry | 23 |
| Glen Head | 24 | Mizen Head | 04 |
| Donegal Bay | 02 | Cork | 26 |
| Belmullet | 83 | Mine Head | 83 |
| Clifden | 26 | Rosslare | 23 |
| Galway | 04 | Wicklow Head | 02 |
| Shannon | 28 | Dublin | 83 |
| Valentia | 24 | Carlingford | 04 |

Gale warnings are broadcast on these VHF channels on receipt and at 0033, 0633, 1233 and 1833 UT, after an announcement on Ch 16.

**MF** Valentia Radio broadcasts forecasts for sea areas Shannon and Fastnet on 1752 kHz at 0833 & 2033 UT, and on request.

Gale warnings are broadcast on 1752 kHz on receipt and at 0303, 0903, 1503 and 2103 (UT) after an announcement on 2182 kHz.

Malin Head does not broadcast weather information on 1677 kHz. At Dublin there is no MF transmitter.

### 0.16.2   Radio Telefís Éireann  (RTE) Radio 1

Met Éireann (the Irish Met Office) is at Glasnevin Hill, Dublin 9, Ireland. ☎ 1 806 4250, 🖷 1 806 4250, www.met.ie. General forecasting division: ☎ 1 806 4255, 🖷 1 806 4275, forecasts@met.ie (Charges may apply for individual forecasts)

CRS and their VHF channels are listed below (anti-clockwise from Malin Head) and shown on Fig 0(7). Weather bulletins for 30M offshore and the Irish Sea are broadcast on VHF at

0103, 0403, 0703, 1003, 1303, 1603, 1903 and 2203LT after an announcement on Ch 16. Bulletins include gale warnings, synopsis and a 24-hour forecast.

| | | | |
|---|---|---|---|
| *MALIN HEAD* | *23* | *Bantry* | *23* |
| *Glen Head* | *24* | *Mizen Head* | *04* |
| *Donegal Bay* | *02* | *Cork* | *26* |
| *Belmullet* | *83* | *Mine Head* | *83* |
| *Clifden* | *26* | *Rosslare* | *23* |
| *Galway* | *04* | *Wicklow Head* | *02* |
| *Shannon* | *28* | *DUBLIN* | *83* |
| *VALENTIA* | *24* | *Carlingford* | *04* |

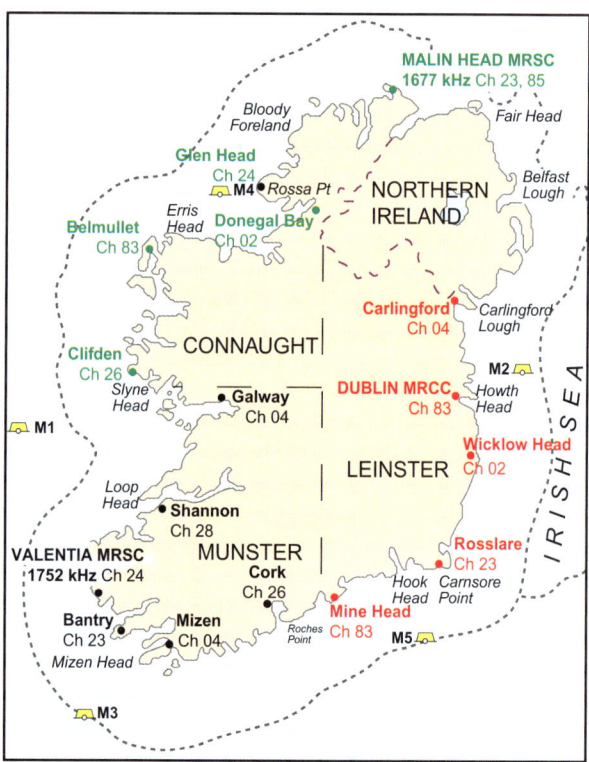

*Fig 0(7) shows CRS, Met buoys M1–M5, PROVINCES and headlands named in forecasts*

Gale warnings are broadcast on receipt and at 0033, 0633, 1233 and 1833 UT, after an announcement on Ch 16.

**MF** Valentia Radio broadcasts forecasts for Shannon and Fastnet on 1752 kHz at 0833 & 2033 UT, and on request.

Gale warnings are broadcast on receipt and at 0303, 0903, 1503 and 2103 (UT) after an announcement on 2182 kHz.

Weather is not broadcast on MF by Malin Head or Dublin.

### 0.16.3   Weather by telephone

The latest sea area forecasts and gale warnings are available H24 from Weatherdial as recorded messages. Dial ☎ 1550 123 plus the following suffixes:

850 Munster; 851 Leinster; 852 Connaught; 853 Ulster; 854 Dublin (plus winds in Dublin Bay and HW times); 855 Coastal waters and Irish Sea.

### 0.16.4   Weather by fax

Similar information, plus isobaric, swell and wave charts and any Small craft warnings (>F6 up to 10M offshore; Apr–Sep inc) is available H24 by Weatherdial Fax.

Dial ✉ 1570 131 838 (from within ROI only). From the menu below select the required 4-digit product code (see code 0400 for full listing):

- 0015: Latest analysis chart
- 0016: Forecast valid for next 24 hrs
- 0017: Forecast valid for next 36 hrs
- 0018: Forecast valid for next 48 hrs
- 0021: Forecasts for coastal waters and Irish Sea
- 0031, 0032, 0033, 0034: Forecast (days 1–4) for sea and swell wave heights and periods
- 5-day forecasts (plain language, farming/national) 0001: Munster. 0002: Leinster. 0003: Connaught. 0004: Ulster. 0005: Dublin.

*Sea Planners* provide graphic forecasts for up to 5 days (updated at 0430 daily) of expected winds and waves at the following seven offshore positions:

| | |
|---|---|
| 0041: 53°N 05° 30'W. | 0045: 54°N 11°W. |
| 0042: 51°N 06°W. | 0046: 55°N 10°W. |
| 0043: 51°N 10°30'W. | 0047: 56°N 08°W. |
| 0044: 53°N 11°W. | |

### 0.16.5   Radio Telefís Éireann  (RTE) Radio 1

RTE Radio 1 broadcasts weather bulletins daily at 0602, 1255, 1657 & 2355LT (1hr earlier when DST is in force) on 567kHz (Tullamore), 729kHz (Cork) and FM (88·2–95·2MHz).

Bulletins contain a situation, forecast and coastal reports for Irish Sea and coastal waters. The forecast includes: wind, weather, vis, swell (if higher than 4m) and a 24 hrs outlook.

Gale warnings are included in hourly news bulletins on FM & MF.

Coastal reports include wind, weather, visibility, pressure, with pressure change over the last 3 hrs described as:

| | | |
|---|---|---|
| Steady | = | 0–0·4 hPa change |
| Rising/falling slowly | = | 0·5–1·9 |
| Rising/falling | = | 2·0–3·4 |
| Rising/falling rapidly | = | 3·5–5·9 |
| Rising/falling very rapidly | = | > 6·0 |

## 0.17   HM COASTGUARD - CONTACT DETAILS OF CG CENTRES

### SCOTLAND AND NORTHERN IRELAND REGION

**†ABERDEEN  COASTGUARD**
57°08'N 02°05'W. MMSI 002320004
Marine House, Blaikies Quay, Aberdeen AB11 5PB.
☎ 01224 592334. ✉ 01224 575920.
Area: Doonies Pt to Cape Wrath, incl Pentland Firth.

**†SHETLAND  COASTGUARD**
60°09'N 01°08'W. MMSI 002320001
Knab Road, Lerwick ZE1 0AX.
☎ 01595 692976. ✉ 01595 693634.
Area: Orkney, Fair Isle and Shetland.

**†*STORNOWAY  COASTGUARD**
58°12'N 06°22'W. MMSI 002320024
Battery Point, Stornoway, Isle of Lewis H51 2RT.
☎ 01851 702013. ✉ 01851 706796.
Area: Cape Wrath to Ardnamurchan Pt, Western Isles and St Kilda.

**†*CLYDE  COASTGUARD**
55°58'N 04°48'W. MMSI 002320022
Navy Buildings, Eldon St, Greenock PA16 7QY.
☎ 01475 729988. ✉ 01475 888095.
Area: Ardnamurchan Pt to Mull of Galloway inc islands.

***BELFAST  COASTGUARD**
54°40'N 05°40'W. MMSI 002320021
Bregenz House, Quay St, Bangor, Co Down BT20 5ED.
☎ 02891 463933. ✉ 02891 469854.
Area: Carlingford Lough to Lough Foyle.

### WESTERN REGION

**LIVERPOOL  COASTGUARD**
53°30'N 03°03'W. MMSI 002320019
Hall Road West, Crosby, Liverpool L23 8SY.
☎ 0151 9313341. ✉ 0151 9320978
Area: Mull of Galloway to Queensferry (near Chester).

**†HOLYHEAD  COASTGUARD**
53°19'N 04°38'W. MMSI 002320018
Prince of Wales Rd, Holyhead, Anglesey LL65 1ET.
☎ 01407 762051. ✉ 01407 761613
Area: Queensferry to Friog (1·6M S of Barmouth).

**†MILFORD HAVEN COASTGUARD**
51°42'N 05°03'W. MMSI 002320017
Gorsewood Drive, Hakin, Milford Haven, SA73 2HD.
☎ 01646 690909. ✉ 01646 697287.
Area: Friog to River Towy (11M N of Worms Head).

**SWANSEA  COASTGUARD**
51°34'N 03°58'W. MMSI 002320016
Tutt Head, Mumbles, Swansea SA3 4EX.
☎ 01792 366534. ✉ 01792 368371.
Area: River Towy to Marsland Mouth (near Bude).

NOTES: †Monitors DSC MF 2187.5 kHz.
*Broadcasts Gunfacts/Subfacts.

## 0.18   IRISH REPUBLIC

The Irish CG co-ordinates SAR operations around the coast of Eire via Dublin MRCC, Malin Head and Valentia MRSCs and remote sites. It may liaise with the UK and France during any rescue operation within 100M of the Irish coast. It is part of the Dept of Marine, Leeson Lane, Dublin 2. ☎ (01) 6620922; ✉ (01) 6620795. The Irish EPIRB Registry is at the same address;  ☎ (01) 6199280; ✉ (01) 6621571.

The MRCC/MRSCs are co-located with the Coast radio stations of the same name and manned by the same staff. All stations keep watch H24 on VHF Ch 16 and DSC Ch 70. If ashore dial 999 or 112 in an emergency and ask for Marine Rescue.

Details of the MRCC/MRSCs are as follows:

**DUBLIN (MRCC)**
53°20'N 06°15W. DSC MMSI 002500300 (+2187·5 kHz).
☎ +353 1 662 0922/3; ▨ +353 1 662 0795.
Area: Carlingford Lough to Youghal.

**VALENTIA (MRSC)**
51°56'N 10°21'W.DSC MMSI 002500200 (+2187·5 kHz).
☎ +353 669 476 109; ▨ +353 669 476 289.
Area: Youghal to Slyne Head.

**MALIN HEAD (MRSC)**
55°22'N 07°20W. DSC MMSI 002500100 (+2187·5 kHz).
☎ +353 74 9370103; ▨ +353 74 9370221.
Area: Slyne Head to Lough Foyle.

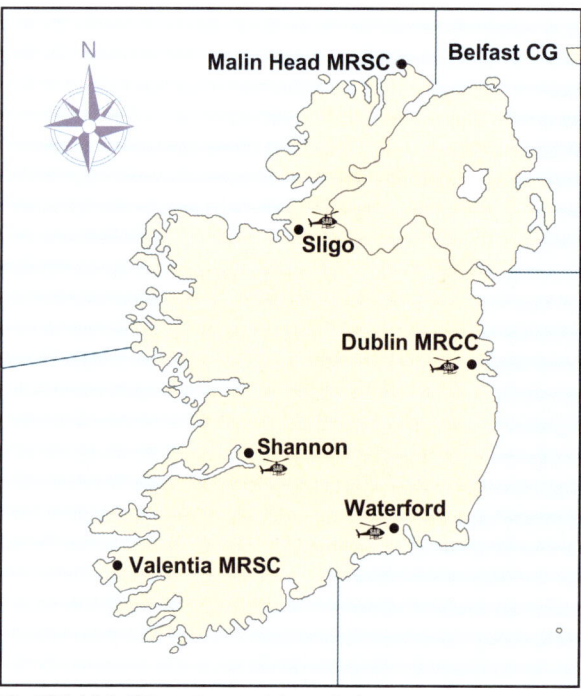

*Fig 0(9) Irish CG centres and boundaries*

## 0.18.1   SAR resources
The Irish coastguard provides some 50 units around the coast and is on call H24. The RNLI maintains four stations around the coast and operates 42 lifeboats. Additionally, six community-run inshore rescue boats are available.

Sikorsky S-61 helicopters, based at Dublin, Waterford, Shannon and Sligo, can respond within 15 to 45 minutes and operate to a radius of 200M.  They are equipped with infrared search equipment and can uplift 30 survivors.

Military and civilian aircraft and vessels, together with the Garda and lighthouse service, can also be called upon.

Some stations provide specialist cliff climbing services. They are manned by volunteers, who are trained in first aid and equipped with inflatables, breeches buoys, cliff ladders etc. Their ☎ numbers (the Leader's residence) are given, where appropriate, under each port.

## 0.19   AUTOMATIC IDENTIFICATION SYSTEM (AIS)

AIS was originated to monitor shipping patterns in key areas so as to safeguard the marine environment; see last para below. It is also widely used to assist in collision avoidance by automatically and continuously identifying, tracking and displaying other vessels' movements.

Each ship's course & speed vector is shown by a tadpole-like symbol on an AIS screen or overlaid on radar, chart plotter or PC. This data may also appear in a text box as hdg, COG & SOG, range, CPA (in some sets); plus Lat/Long, ship's name (derived from its MMSI); and her status, ie under power or sail, anchored, constrained by draught, restricted in her manoeuvrability, not under command, fishing etc. Range scales are usually 1, 2, 4, 8, 16 and 32M.

AIS must be fitted in commercial vessels >300 GRT, in particular oil tankers and vessels carrying hazardous cargos. **Caveats**: Some ships do not switch on their AIS; some only display 3 lines of text, not a plot; in busy areas only the strongest signals may be shown; AIS may distract a bridge watchkeeper from his radar watch (yachts will therefore not be detected); unlike eyes and radar AIS does not yet feature in IRPCS; GPS/electronic failures invalidate AIS.

AIS is not mandatory for leisure craft, but it is well worth having. Accurate and continuous display of the target's COG and SOG removes doubts engendered when these parameters are manually calculated from radar. Receive-only equipment at about £250 is available for small craft – basically a VHF dual frequency (161.975 & 162.025 MHz) transceiver, aerial, GPS input and a mini-computer. Note: *AIS is not a radar* despite what some advertisements imply.

Most of the AIS shore stations around the UK monitor traffic routeing in choke points, eg the Dover Strait, or environmentally sensitive areas, eg The Minches.

## 0.20 CALCULATING CLEARANCES BELOW OVERHEAD OBJECTS

A diagram often helps when calculating vertical clearance below bridges, power cables etc. The height of such objects, as given on the chart, is now* measured above HAT, so the actual clearance will usually be more than the charted value. Fig 0(11) shows the relationship to CD. The height of HAT above CD is given at the foot of each page of tide tables. *Admiralty charts are only adjusted to HAT when a new edition is published; check the **Heights** block below the chart Title.

Insert the dimensions into the following formula, carefully observing the conventions for brackets:

Masthead clearance = (Height of object above HAT + height of HAT above CD) minus (height of tide at the time + height of the masthead above waterline)

Overhead object
Masthead clearance
Height of object
Height of mast above water
HAT
Sea level
Height of HAT
Height of tide
Chart datum


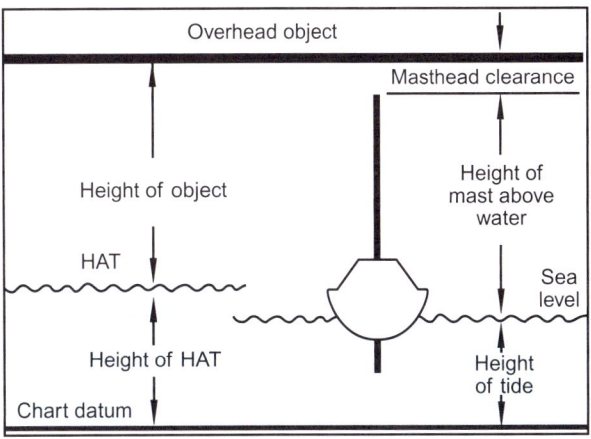

*Fig 0(11) Calculating masthead clearance*

## 0.21 IALA BUOYAGE

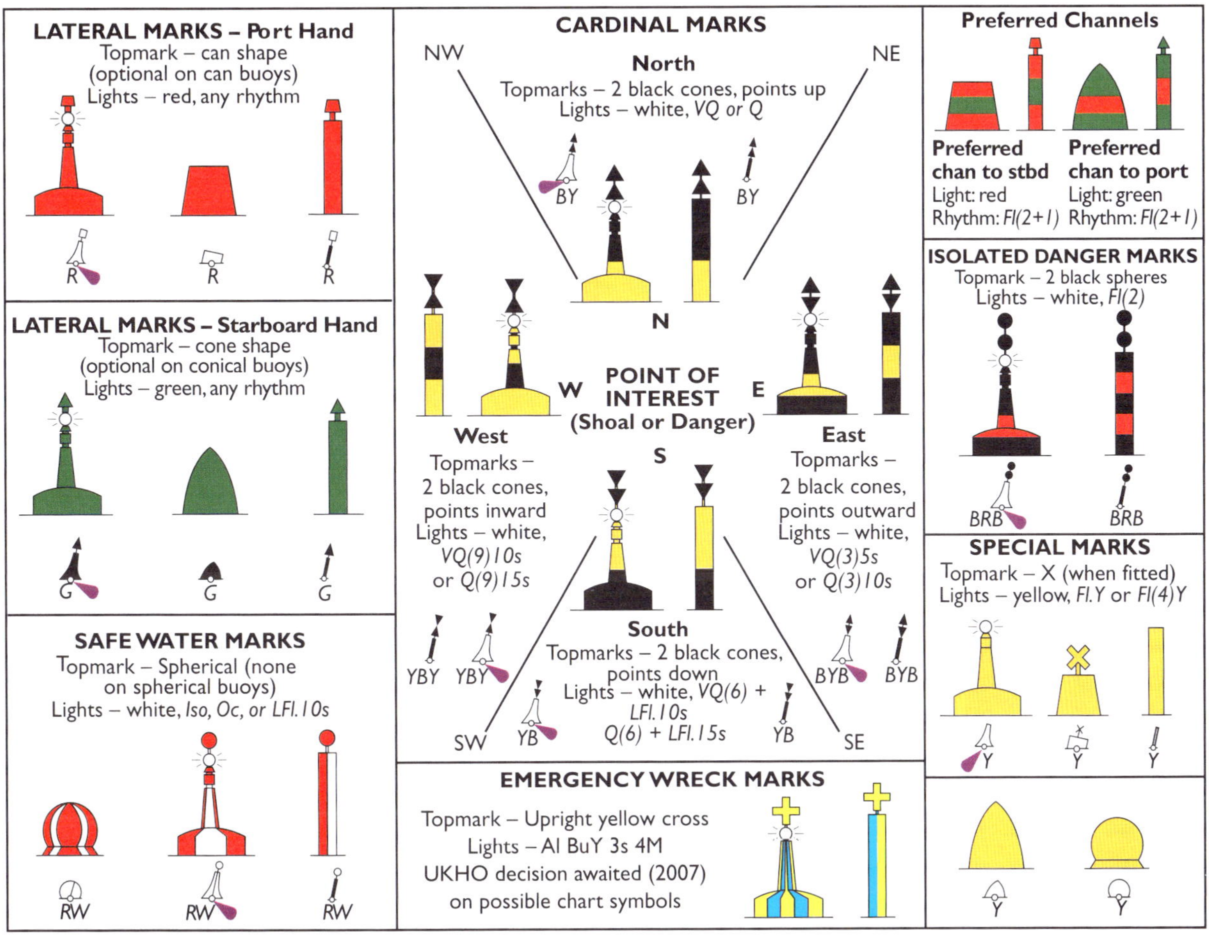

LATERAL MARKS – Port Hand
Topmark – can shape
(optional on can buoys)
Lights – red, any rhythm
R
R
R
LATERAL MARKS – Starboard Hand
Topmark – cone shape
(optional on conical buoys)
Lights – green, any rhythm
G
G
G
SAFE WATER MARKS
Topmark – Spherical (none on spherical buoys)
Lights – white, Iso, Oc, or LFl.10s
RW
RW
RW
CARDINAL MARKS
NW
NE
North
Topmarks – 2 black cones, points up
Lights – white, VQ or Q
BY
BY
N
W
POINT OF INTEREST
(Shoal or Danger)
E
S
West
Topmarks – 2 black cones, points inward
Lights – white, VQ(9)10s or Q(9)15s
East
Topmarks – 2 black cones, points outward
Lights – white, VQ(3)5s or Q(3)10s
YBY
YBY
BYB
BYB
South
Topmarks – 2 black cones, points down
Lights – white, VQ(6) + LFl.10s
Q(6) + LFl.15s
YB
YB
SW
SE
EMERGENCY WRECK MARKS
Topmark – Upright yellow cross
Lights – Al BuY 3s 4M
UKHO decision awaited (2007) on possible chart symbols
Preferred Channels
Preferred chan to stbd
Light: red
Rhythm: Fl(2+1)
Preferred chan to port
Light: green
Rhythm: Fl(2+1)
ISOLATED DANGER MARKS
Topmark – 2 black spheres
Lights – white, Fl(2)
BRB
BRB
SPECIAL MARKS
Topmark – X (when fitted)
Lights – yellow, Fl.Y or Fl(4)Y
Y
Y
Y
Y
Y

## 0.22   FLAGS AND ENSIGNS

UK WHITE ENSIGN

UK BLUE ENSIGN

UK RED ENSIGN

AUSTRALIA

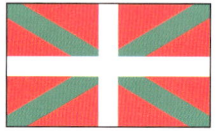
BASQUE FLAG

BELGIUM

BERMUDA

CANADA

CYPRUS

DENMARK

EU

FINLAND

FRANCE

GERMANY

GREECE

GUERNSEY

IRELAND

ISRAEL

ITALY

LIBERIA

MALTA

MONACO

MOROCCO

NETHERLANDS

NEW ZEALAND

NORWAY

PANAMA

POLAND

PORTUGAL

SOUTH AFRICA

SPAIN

SWEDEN

SWITZERLAND

TUNISIA

TURKEY

USA

## 0.23 LIGHTS AND SHAPES

**Vessels being towed and towing**

Vessel towed shows sidelights (forward) and sternlight

Tug shows two masthead lights, sidelights, sternlight, yellow towing light

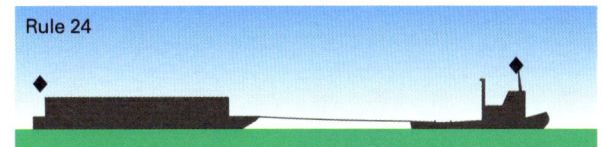

**Towing by day — Length of tow more than 200m**

Towing vessel and tow display diamond shapes. By night, the towing vessel shows three masthead lights instead of two as for shorter tows

**Motor sailing**

Cone point down, forward. At night the lights of a power-driven vessel underway

**Vessel fishing**

All-round red light over all-round white, plus sidelights and sternlight when making way

**Fishing/Trawling**

A shape consisting of two cones point to point in a vertical line one above the other

**Vessel trawling**

All-round green light over all-round white, plus sidelights and sternlight when making way

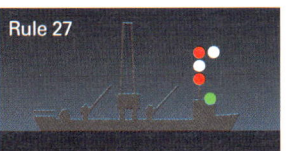

**Vessel restricted in her ability to manoeuvre**

All-round red, white, red lights vertically, plus normal steaming lights when making way

Three shapes in a vertical line: ball, diamond, ball

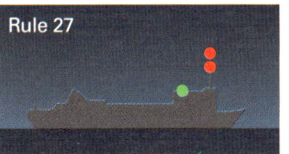

**Not under command**

Two all-round red lights, plus sidelights and sternlight when making way

Two balls vertically

**Dredger**

All round red, white, red lights vertically, plus two all-round red lights (or two balls) on foul side, and two all-round green (or two diamonds) on clear side

**Divers down**

Letter 'A' International Code

**Constrained by draught**

Three all-round red lights in a vertical line, plus normal steaming lights. By day — a cylinder

**Pilot boat**

All-round white light over all-round red, plus sidelights and sternlight when underway, or anchor light

**Vessel at anchor**

All-round white light; if over 50m, a second light aft and lower

Ball forward

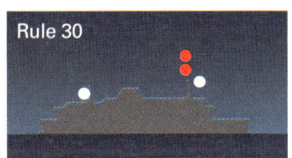

**Vessel aground**

Anchor light(s), plus two all-round red lights in a vertical line

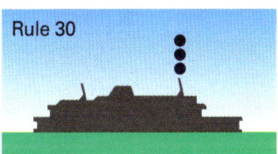

Three balls in a vertical line

## 0.24   NAVIGATION LIGHTS

Port sidelight (red) shows from ahead to 22½° abaft the beam

112½°

Abeam

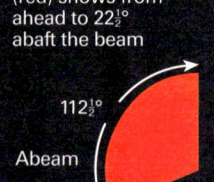

For yachts 12-50m overall, visibility – 2 miles. For yachts under 12m – 1 mile

(May be combined with starboard sidelight in one centreline lantern in boats under 20m overall)

White masthead light shows over arc of 225° – from ahead to 22½° abaft the beam each side. Shown by vessels under power only

**Ahead**

225°

(Masthead light and sternlight may be combined in one all-round white light in boats under 12m overall)

**Astern**

White sternlight shows over arc of 135°, 67½° on each side of vessel

135°

For yachts 20-50m overall, visibility – 5 miles. For yachts 12-20m – 3 miles. For yachts under 12m – 2 miles

For yachts under 50m overall, visibility – 2 miles

Starboard sidelight (green) shows from ahead to 22½° abaft the beam

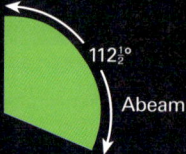

112½°

Abeam

For yachts 12-50m overall, visibility – 2 miles. For yachts under 12m – 1 mile

(May be combined with port sidelight in one centreline lantern in boats under 20m overall)

### Lights for power-driven vessels underway (plan views)

*Note:* Also apply to sailing yachts or other sailing craft when under power

Motor boat under 7m, less than 7 knots

Motor boat under 12m (combined masthead & sternlight)

Motor yacht under 20m (combined lantern for sidelights)

Motor yacht over 20m

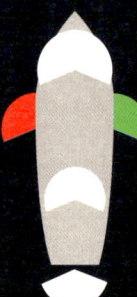

Larger vessel, over 50m, with two masthead lights – the aft one higher

### Lights for sailing vessels underway (plan views)

*Note:* These lights apply to sailing craft when under sail ONLY. If motor-sailing, the appropriate lights for a power-driven vessel must be shown, as above

Sailing boat under 7m shows white light to prevent collision. If practicable, she should show sidelights and sternlight

Combined sidelights plus sternlight

or

Tricolour lantern at masthead

Sailing yacht under 20m

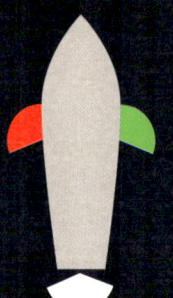

Separate sidelights and sternlight for sailing vessel over 20m

### Bow view

If *not* using tricolour masthead lantern, a sailing yacht may show (in addition to other lights) two all-round lights near masthead, the upper red and the lower green

**Times are in UT - add 1 hour in non-shaded areas to convert to BST**

## 0.25 SUNRISE/SET TIMES

Showing times of Sunrise (SR) and Sunset (SS) for every 4th day, the table below is much simpler than in earlier editions.

This does not imply any lack of accuracy since the times of Sunrise and Sunset never change by more than 8 minutes (and often by only 1–3 minutes) between the given dates.

The table is based on Longitude 0°, so longitude corrections are required, ie add 4 minutes of time for every degree West of Greenwich; subtract if East.

### LATITUDE 56°N

|  | Rise | Set | Rise | Set | Rise | Set | Rise | Set | Rise | Set | Rise | Set |
|---|---|---|---|---|---|---|---|---|---|---|---|---|
|  | JANUARY | | FEBRUARY | | MARCH | | APRIL | | MAY | | JUNE | |
| 1 | 08 31 | 15 35 | 07 56 | 16 32 | 06 51 | 17 35 | 05 30 | 18 39 | 04 15 | 19 40 | 03 22 | 20 35 |
| 4 | 08 30 | 15 39 | 07 50 | 16 38 | 06 43 | 17 41 | 05 22 | 18 45 | 04 09 | 19 46 | 03 19 | 20 39 |
| 7 | 08 29 | 15 44 | 07 44 | 16 45 | 06 35 | 17 48 | 05 14 | 18 51 | 04 02 | 19 52 | 03 16 | 20 42 |
| 10 | 08 27 | 15 48 | 07 38 | 16 51 | 06 28 | 17 54 | 05 06 | 18 57 | 03 56 | 19 58 | 03 15 | 20 45 |
| 13 | 08 24 | 15 53 | 07 31 | 16 58 | 06 20 | 18 00 | 04 59 | 19 03 | 03 50 | 20 04 | 03 13 | 20 47 |
| 16 | 08 21 | 15 59 | 07 25 | 17 05 | 06 12 | 18 06 | 04 51 | 19 10 | 03 45 | 20 09 | 03 13 | 20 49 |
| 19 | 08 17 | 16 05 | 07 18 | 17 11 | 06 04 | 18 12 | 04 44 | 19 16 | 03 40 | 20 15 | 03 13 | 20 50 |
| 22 | 08 13 | 16 11 | 07 10 | 17 18 | 05 56 | 18 19 | 04 36 | 19 22 | 03 35 | 20 20 | 03 13 | 20 51 |
| 25 | 08 08 | 16 17 | 07 03 | 17 24 | 05 48 | 18 25 | 04 29 | 19 28 | 03 30 | 20 25 | 03 15 | 20 51 |
| 28 | 08 03 | 16 23 | 06 56 | 17 31 | 05 40 | 18 31 | 04 22 | 19 34 | 03 26 | 20 29 | 03 16 | 20 50 |
| 31 | 07 58 | 16 29 | | | 05 32 | 18 37 | | | 03 23 | 20 34 | | |

|  | Rise | Set | Rise | Set | Rise | Set | Rise | Set | Rise | Set | Rise | Set |
|---|---|---|---|---|---|---|---|---|---|---|---|---|
|  | JULY | | AUGUST | | SEPTEMBER | | OCTOBER | | NOVEMBER | | DECEMBER | |
| 1 | 03 19 | 20 49 | 04 04 | 20 07 | 05 05 | 18 54 | 06 04 | 17 34 | 07 08 | 16 19 | 08 07 | 15 31 |
| 4 | 03 21 | 20 47 | 04 10 | 20 01 | 05 11 | 18 46 | 06 10 | 17 27 | 07 14 | 16 12 | 08 12 | 15 28 |
| 7 | 03 25 | 20 45 | 04 16 | 19 54 | 05 17 | 18 38 | 06 16 | 17 19 | 07 20 | 16 06 | 08 16 | 15 27 |
| 10 | 03 28 | 20 42 | 04 22 | 19 48 | 05 22 | 18 30 | 06 22 | 17 11 | 07 27 | 16 00 | 08 20 | 15 25 |
| 13 | 03 32 | 20 38 | 04 28 | 19 41 | 05 28 | 18 22 | 06 28 | 17 04 | 07 33 | 15 55 | 08 24 | 15 25 |
| 16 | 03 37 | 20 34 | 04 33 | 19 34 | 05 34 | 18 14 | 06 34 | 16 56 | 07 39 | 15 50 | 08 26 | 15 25 |
| 19 | 03 42 | 20 30 | 04 39 | 19 26 | 05 40 | 18 06 | 06 40 | 16 49 | 07 45 | 15 45 | 08 29 | 15 26 |
| 22 | 03 46 | 20 25 | 04 45 | 19 19 | 05 46 | 17 58 | 06 46 | 16 41 | 07 51 | 15 41 | 08 30 | 15 27 |
| 25 | 03 52 | 20 20 | 04 51 | 19 12 | 05 52 | 17 50 | 06 53 | 16 34 | 07 57 | 15 37 | 08 31 | 15 29 |
| 28 | 03 57 | 20 15 | 04 57 | 19 04 | 05 58 | 17 42 | 06 59 | 16 28 | 08 02 | 15 33 | 08 32 | 15 32 |
| 31 | 04 03 | 20 09 | 05 03 | 18 56 | | | 07 05 | 16 21 | | | 08 31 | 15 35 |

## 0.26 MOONRISE/SET TIMES

The table below is much simpler than that in earlier editions. It gives the times of Moonrise (MR) and Moonset (MS) for every 4th day; interpolation is necessary for other days. The aim is simply to indicate whether the night in question will be brightly moonlit, partially moonlit or pitch black – depending, of course, on cloud cover.

The table is based on Longitude 0°. To correct for longitude, add 4 minutes of time for every degree West; subtract if East.
** Indicates that the phenomenon does not occur.

### LATITUDE 56°N

|  | Rise | Set | Rise | Set | Rise | Set | Rise | Set | Rise | Set | Rise | Set |
|---|---|---|---|---|---|---|---|---|---|---|---|---|
|  | JANUARY | | FEBRUARY | | MARCH | | APRIL | | MAY | | JUNE | |
| 1 | 01 26 | 11 17 | 04 22 | 10 17 | 04 20 | 09 32 | 04 14 | 12 19 | 02 48 | 14 15 | 01 29 | 18 01 |
| 4 | 05 22 | 11 53 | 07 09 | 12 56 | 05 56 | 13 20 | 04 41 | 16 47 | 03 12 | 18 59 | 02 58 | 22 26 |
| 7 | 08 35 | 14 01 | 08 01 | 17 18 | 06 26 | 17 50 | 05 07 | 21 41 | 04 20 | 23 45 | 07 18 | 23 49 |
| 10 | 09 43 | 18 11 | 08 23 | 21 46 | 06 48 | 22 32 | 06 28 | 00 54 | 08 11 | 01 12 | 11 43 | 00 07 |
| 13 | 10 06 | 22 32 | 08 51 | 00 53 | 07 46 | 01 48 | 10 29 | 03 10 | 12 37 | 01 52 | 15 39 | 00 27 |
| 16 | 10 30 | 01 33 | 10 38 | 05 18 | 11 11 | 04 43 | 14 48 | 03 43 | 16 32 | 02 11 | 19 33 | 01 03 |
| 19 | 11 49 | 06 17 | 15 02 | 06 57 | 15 39 | 05 26 | 18 44 | 04 01 | 20 29 | 02 40 | 22 06 | 03 02 |
| 22 | 15 57 | 08 35 | 19 22 | 07 23 | 19 41 | 05 45 | 22 43 | 04 32 | 23 32 | 04 09 | 22 56 | 06 53 |
| 25 | 20 26 | 09 08 | 23 22 | 07 41 | 23 42 | 06 09 | 00 52 | 06 13 | 00 24 | 07 43 | 23 18 | 11 01 |
| 28 | ** ** | 09 26 | 02 02 | 08 19 | 02 07 | 07 25 | 02 19 | 09 57 | 00 55 | 11 52 | 23 48 | 15 30 |
| 31 | 03 04 | 09 56 | | | 03 59 | 10 53 | | | 01 18 | 16 21 | | |

|  | Rise | Set | Rise | Set | Rise | Set | Rise | Set | Rise | Set | Rise | Set |
|---|---|---|---|---|---|---|---|---|---|---|---|---|
|  | JULY | | AUGUST | | SEPTEMBER | | OCTOBER | | NOVEMBER | | DECEMBER | |
| 1 | 00 43 | 20 06 | 03 44 | 20 12 | 07 16 | 18 53 | 09 00 | 17 28 | 11 41 | 17 16 | 11 30 | 18 25 |
| 4 | 04 42 | 21 53 | 08 19 | 20 37 | 11 23 | 19 20 | 12 53 | 18 34 | 13 27 | 20 38 | 12 09 | 22 22 |
| 7 | 09 21 | 22 22 | 12 25 | 21 00 | 15 09 | 20 37 | 15 04 | 21 37 | 14 02 | ** ** | 12 32 | 01 03 |
| 10 | 13 24 | 22 43 | 16 19 | 22 00 | 17 03 | 23 57 | 15 47 | 00 20 | 14 26 | 03 31 | 13 12 | 05 38 |
| 13 | 17 21 | 23 29 | 18 39 | ** ** | 17 40 | 02 46 | 16 11 | 04 35 | 15 16 | 08 20 | 15 50 | 09 49 |
| 16 | 20 08 | 00 53 | 19 23 | 03 45 | 18 02 | 07 04 | 16 50 | 09 18 | 18 22 | 12 02 | 20 39 | 11 09 |
| 19 | 21 05 | 04 39 | 19 45 | 07 58 | 18 45 | 11 46 | 19 15 | 13 25 | 23 01 | 13 03 | ** ** | 11 36 |
| 22 | 21 28 | 08 49 | 20 17 | 12 29 | 21 25 | 15 30 | 23 46 | 14 45 | 01 48 | 13 28 | 03 36 | 12 03 |
| 25 | 21 54 | 13 10 | 22 17 | 16 43 | 00 28 | 16 38 | 02 37 | 15 12 | 05 48 | 13 56 | 07 24 | 13 12 |
| 28 | 23 23 | 17 47 | 01 13 | 18 18 | 04 53 | 17 02 | 06 41 | 15 36 | 09 32 | 15 14 | 09 34 | 16 14 |
| 31 | 02 05 | 19 56 | 05 50 | 18 46 | | | 10 37 | 16 35 | | | 10 17 | 20 09 |

## 0.27 INTERNATIONAL CODE OF SIGNALS

Code flags, phonetic alphabet, Morse code, single-letter signals. IALA BUOYAGE SYSTEM 'A'. INTERNATIONAL PORT TRAFFIC SIGNALS.

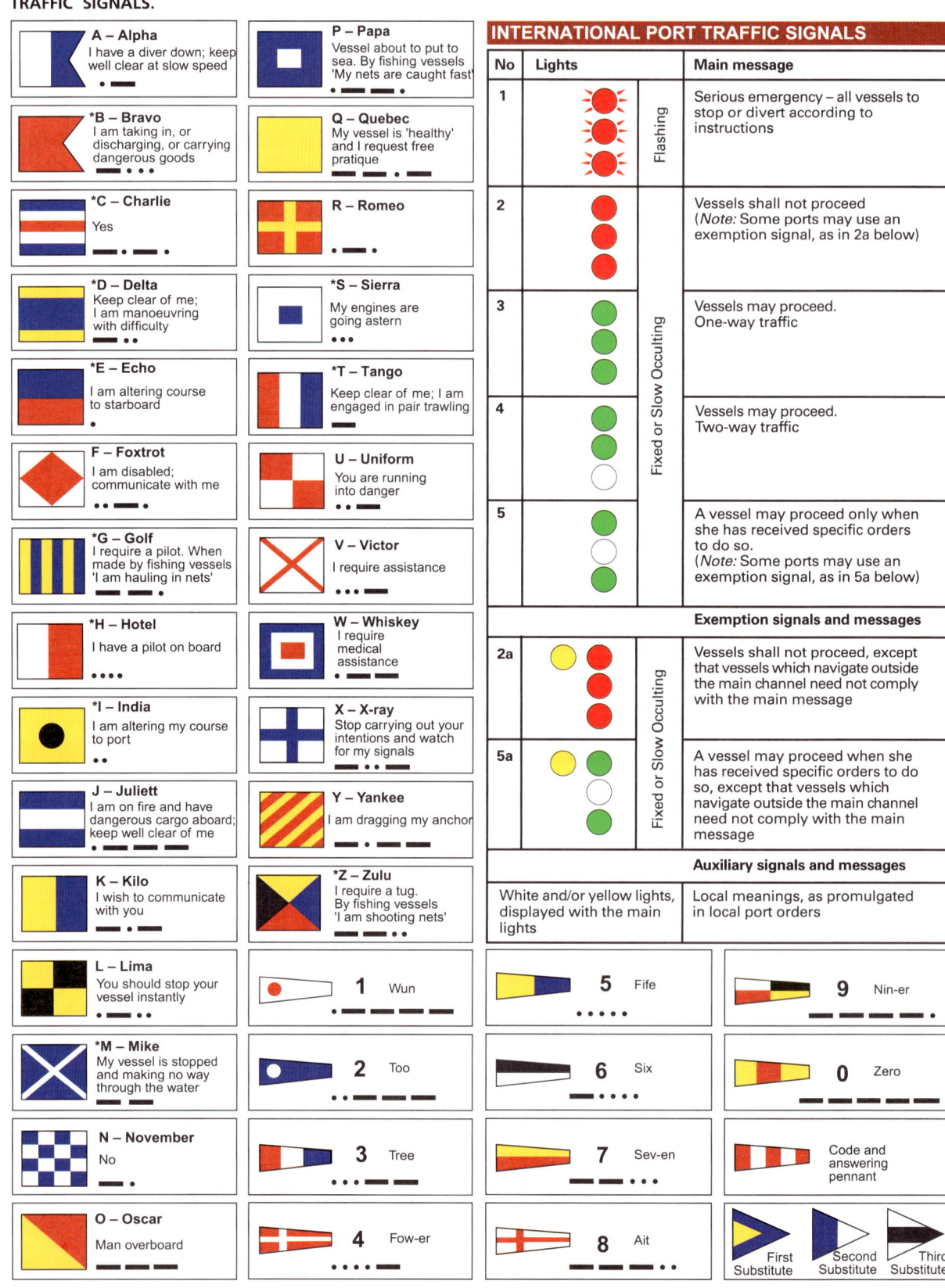

**A – Alpha**
I have a diver down; keep well clear at slow speed

**\*B – Bravo**
I am taking in, or discharging, or carrying dangerous goods

**\*C – Charlie**
Yes

**\*D – Delta**
Keep clear of me; I am manoeuvring with difficulty

**\*E – Echo**
I am altering course to starboard

**F – Foxtrot**
I am disabled; communicate with me

**\*G – Golf**
I require a pilot. When made by fishing vessels 'I am hauling in nets'

**\*H – Hotel**
I have a pilot on board

**\*I – India**
I am altering my course to port

**J – Juliett**
I am on fire and have dangerous cargo aboard; keep well clear of me

**K – Kilo**
I wish to communicate with you

**L – Lima**
You should stop your vessel instantly

**\*M – Mike**
My vessel is stopped and making no way through the water

**N – November**
No

**O – Oscar**
Man overboard

**P – Papa**
Vessel about to put to sea. By fishing vessels 'My nets are caught fast'

**Q – Quebec**
My vessel is 'healthy' and I request free pratique

**R – Romeo**

**\*S – Sierra**
My engines are going astern

**\*T – Tango**
Keep clear of me; I am engaged in pair trawling

**U – Uniform**
You are running into danger

**V – Victor**
I require assistance

**W – Whiskey**
I require medical assistance

**X – X-ray**
Stop carrying out your intentions and watch for my signals

**Y – Yankee**
I am dragging my anchor

**\*Z – Zulu**
I require a tug. By fishing vessels 'I am shooting nets'

**1** Wun
**2** Too
**3** Tree
**4** Fow-er
**5** Fife
**6** Six
**7** Sev-en
**8** Ait
**9** Nin-er
**0** Zero

Code and answering pennant

First Substitute
Second Substitute
Third Substitute

### INTERNATIONAL PORT TRAFFIC SIGNALS

| No | Lights | | Main message |
|---|---|---|---|
| 1 | (3 red flashing) | Flashing | Serious emergency – all vessels to stop or divert according to instructions |
| 2 | (3 red) | Fixed or Slow Occulting | Vessels shall not proceed (Note: Some ports may use an exemption signal, as in 2a below) |
| 3 | (3 green) | Fixed or Slow Occulting | Vessels may proceed. One-way traffic |
| 4 | (green, green, green, white) | Fixed or Slow Occulting | Vessels may proceed. Two-way traffic |
| 5 | (green, white, green) | Fixed or Slow Occulting | A vessel may proceed only when she has received specific orders to do so. (Note: Some ports may use an exemption signal, as in 5a below) |

**Exemption signals and messages**

| No | Lights | | Main message |
|---|---|---|---|
| 2a | (yellow, 3 red) | Fixed or Slow Occulting | Vessels shall not proceed, except that vessels which navigate outside the main channel need not comply with the main message |
| 5a | (yellow, green, white, green) | Fixed or Slow Occulting | A vessel may proceed when she has received specific orders to do so, except that vessels which navigate outside the main channel need not comply with the main message |

**Auxiliary signals and messages**

| White and/or yellow lights, displayed with the main lights | Local meanings, as promulgated in local port orders |
|---|---|

## 0.28  AREA INFORMATION

Harbour, coastal and tidal information is given for each of the geographic areas which are arranged as follows:

**A map of the area** showing the positions of harbours, principal lights, emergency RDF stations, CG Centres with their boundaries, magnetic variation and a distance table.

**Tidal stream chartlets** showing hourly rates and set.

**Lights, buoys and waypoints** list characteristics of selected lights, their daytime appearance, fog signals, Racons and lat/long. Arcs of visibility and alignment of leading lights are true bearings as seen from seaward. Lights are white unless otherwise stated. Any colours are shown between the bearings of the relevant arcs.

**Passage information** briefly describes the coast, offlying dangers, tidal gates, tide races, the better anchorages, recommended routes and local weather patterns.

**Special notes** give data specific to that country or area.

## 0.29  HARBOUR INFORMATION

Below the **harbour name**, the County or Unitary Council (or foreign equivalent) is given, followed by the lat/long of the harbour entrance for use as the final waypoint.

The **harbour ratings**, inevitably subjective, grade a port for ease of access, facilities and attractiveness as a place to visit, based on the following criteria:

**Ease of access**:
- ❀❀❀  *Can be entered in gales from most directions and at all states of tide, by day or night.*
- ❀❀  *Accessible in strong winds from most directions; possible tidal or pilotage constraints.*
- ❀  *Only accessible in calm, settled conditions by day with little or no swell; possible bar and difficult pilotage.*

**Facilities available**:
- ⚓⚓⚓  *Good facilities for vessel and crew.*
- ⚓⚓  *Most domestic needs catered for, but limited boatyard facilities.*
- ⚓  *Possibly some domestic facilities, but little else.*

**Attractiveness**:
- ✿✿✿  *An attractive place; well worth visiting.*
- ✿✿  *Average for this part of the coast.*
- ✿  *Holds no particular attraction.*

**Chart numbers** for Admiralty (AC), Imray, Stanford (Stan) and foreign charts are given, smallest scale first. Admiralty Leisure Editions and Leisure Folios (56XX) are in *italics*. Ordnance Survey (1:50,000) map numbers are also given.

**Tide tables and tidal curves** are given for Standard Ports and the differences for Secondary Ports.

**Harbour chartlets** are based on AC or relevant foreign charts.

> **They are not intended to be used for navigation, although great care has been taken to ensure that they accurately portray the harbour. The publisher and editors disclaim any responsibility for resultant accidents or damage if they are so used. The largest scale official chart, properly corrected, should always be used.**

Drying areas and the 5m depth contour are coloured as follows: Dries          <5m          >5m

Due to limitations of scale, chartlets do not always cover the whole area referred to in the text nor do they show every depth, mark, feature or the approach waypoint, ⊕.

**Shelter** assesses how protected a harbour is from wind, sea, surge and swell. It warns of access difficulties and advises on safe berths and anchorages.

**Navigation** gives the lat/long of an approach waypoint, ⊕, with its bearing and distance to the harbour entrance or next significant feature; some waypoints may be off the harbour chartlet. Approach channels, buoyage, speed limits and hazards are also described.

Access times, if quoted, are based on a nominal 1·5m draft, plus a safety margin, for an average tide. Any significant swell may affect these times. Lock and bridge opening times are in local time.

**Wrecks** around the UK which are of archaeological or historic interest are protected by law. About 20 sites are listed under the nearest harbour or in Passage Information. Unauthorised interference, including anchoring and diving on such sites, may lead to a substantial fine.

**Lights and Marks** describe, in more detail than is shown on the chartlets, any unusual characteristics of marks, their appearance by day and features not listed elsewhere.

**IPTS** (International Port Traffic Signals) are in Chapter 4.

**R/T** lists VHF channels related to the port, marina or VTS. Callsigns, if not obvious, are in *italics*.

**Telephone** gives any area code in brackets (which is not repeated for individual telephone numbers unless different or additional codes apply). International calls from/to the UK are described in Special Notes, as are national numbers for marine emergencies abroad including Ambulance, Fire, Police. In the EU 112 is the main emergency number; in the UK it is 999.

**Facilities** describe man-made features: pontoons, ⚓s, quays, pile moorings, etc at harbours, marinas and YCs, followed by commercial technical services. YC facilities are usually available to bona fide crews who belong to a recognised club and arrive by sea. See also the free *Reeds Marina Guide*. Town facilities are listed, with rail, ferry and air links.

**The overnight cost of a visitor's alongside berth** (AB), at the previous year's rates, is per metre LOA (unless otherwise stated) during high season, usually June to Sept. It includes harbour dues, if applicable, and VAT. The cost of pile moorings, ⚓s or ⚓ where these are the norm, may also be given. Shore electricity is usually free abroad, but extra in the UK.

The number of ⓥ berths is a marina's estimate of how many visitors may be accommodated at any one time. It is always advisable to call the marina beforehand.

**Slipways**. Access and launch/recovery fees per day, eg Slip HW±2 (£6.00), are given where possible for craft < 6.5m LOA.

## 0.30  FACILITIES FOR DISABLED PEOPLE

*RYA Sailability* operates under the RYA's auspices to open up sailing and its related benefits to disabled sailors. Facilities include car parking, wheelchair ramps to buildings and pontoons and purpose-built toilets and showers. Facilities for those with sight or hearing disabilities are becoming more widely available. Standard symbols (♿ ♿ ♿ ♿) are self-explanatory.

## 0.31 ENVIRONMENTAL GUIDANCE

- Comply with regulations for navigation and conduct within Marine Nature Reserves, Particularly Sensitive Sea Areas (PSSA) and National Water Parks.
- In principle never ditch rubbish at sea, keep it on board and dispose of it in harbour refuse bins.
- Readily degradable foodstuffs may be ditched at sea when >3M offshore (>12M in the English Channel).
- Foodstuffs and other materials which are not readily degradable should never be ditched at sea.
- Do not discharge foul water into a marina, anchorage or moorings area and minimise on washing-up water.
- Sewage. If you do not have a holding tank, only use the onboard heads when well offshore. A holding tank should be fitted as many countries require them. Pump-out facilities (⚓) are shown in the text. Do not pump out holding tanks until >3M offshore.
- Deposit used engine oil and oily waste ashore at a recognised facility. Do not allow an automatic bilge pump to discharge oily bilge water overboard.
- Dispose of toxic waste (eg some antifoulings, cleaning chemicals, old batteries) at an approved disposal facility.
- Row ashore whenever possible – to minimise noise, wash and disturbance. Land at recognised places.
- Respect wild birds, plants, fish and marine animals. Avoid protected nesting sites and breeding colonies.
- Do not anchor or dry out on vulnerable seabed species, eg soft corals, eel grass.

## 0.32 DISTANCES (M) ACROSS THE IRISH SEA

Approximate distances in nautical miles are by the most direct route, avoiding dangers and allowing for TSS.

| Scotland England Wales / Ireland | Port Ellen (Islay) | Campbeltown | Troon | Portpatrick | Mull of Galloway | Kirkcudbright | Maryport | Fleetwood | Pt of Ayre (IOM) | Port St Mary (IOM) | Liverpool | Holyhead | Pwllheli | Fishguard | Milford Haven | Swansea | Avonmouth | Ilfracombe | Padstow | Longships |
|---|---|---|---|---|---|---|---|---|---|---|---|---|---|---|---|---|---|---|---|---|
| Tory Island | 75 | 107 | 132 | 119 | 134 | 170 | 185 | 215 | 156 | 171 | 238 | 207 | 260 | 279 | 307 | 360 | 406 | 355 | 372 | 399 |
| Malin Head | 45 | 76 | 101 | 88 | 103 | 139 | 154 | 184 | 125 | 140 | 207 | 176 | 229 | 248 | 276 | 329 | 375 | 324 | 341 | 368 |
| Lough Foyle | 38 | 61 | 86 | 73 | 88 | 124 | 139 | 169 | 110 | 125 | 192 | 161 | 214 | 233 | 261 | 314 | 360 | 309 | 326 | 353 |
| Portrush | 31 | 50 | 76 | 64 | 80 | 116 | 131 | 161 | 102 | 117 | 184 | 153 | 206 | 225 | 253 | 306 | 352 | 301 | 318 | 345 |
| Carnlough | 42 | 35 | 57 | 32 | 45 | 81 | 96 | 126 | 67 | 78 | 149 | 115 | 168 | 187 | 215 | 268 | 314 | 263 | 280 | 307 |
| Larne | 51 | 39 | 58 | 24 | 37 | 72 | 88 | 118 | 58 | 70 | 141 | 106 | 159 | 178 | 206 | 259 | 305 | 254 | 271 | 298 |
| Carrickfergus | 64 | 48 | 65 | 26 | 34 | 69 | 85 | 115 | 55 | 66 | 138 | 101 | 154 | 173 | 201 | 254 | 300 | 249 | 266 | 293 |
| Bangor | 63 | 48 | 64 | 22 | 30 | 65 | 81 | 111 | 51 | 62 | 134 | 97 | 150 | 169 | 197 | 250 | 296 | 245 | 262 | 289 |
| Strangford L. | 89 | 72 | 84 | 36 | 30 | 63 | 76 | 97 | 41 | 37 | 107 | 69 | 121 | 141 | 167 | 219 | 265 | 214 | 231 | 258 |
| Carlingford L. | 117 | 100 | 112 | 64 | 60 | 90 | 103 | 112 | 70 | 51 | 118 | 67 | 111 | 124 | 149 | 202 | 248 | 197 | 214 | 241 |
| Dun Laoghaire | 153 | 136 | 148 | 100 | 93 | 119 | 126 | 120 | 93 | 69 | 119 | 56 | 82 | 94 | 109 | 162 | 208 | 157 | 174 | 201 |
| Wicklow | 170 | 153 | 165 | 117 | 108 | 133 | 140 | 127 | 108 | 83 | 123 | 56 | 67 | 71 | 90 | 143 | 189 | 138 | 155 | 182 |
| Arklow | 182 | 165 | 177 | 129 | 120 | 144 | 149 | 133 | 117 | 93 | 131 | 64 | 71 | 65 | 79 | 132 | 179 | 128 | 144 | 167 |
| Rosslare | 215 | 202 | 208 | 161 | 154 | 179 | 180 | 164 | 152 | 125 | 156 | 90 | 83 | 55 | 58 | 109 | 157 | 110 | 119 | 137 |
| Tuskar Rock | 216 | 203 | 209 | 162 | 155 | 179 | 182 | 165 | 152 | 126 | 152 | 91 | 82 | 48 | 51 | 105 | 150 | 103 | 112 | 130 |
| Dunmore East | 250 | 237 | 243 | 196 | 189 | 213 | 216 | 199 | 186 | 160 | 189 | 127 | 116 | 79 | 76 | 130 | 177 | 124 | 127 | 136 |
| Youghal | 281 | 268 | 274 | 227 | 220 | 244 | 247 | 230 | 217 | 191 | 220 | 158 | 147 | 110 | 103 | 156 | 200 | 148 | 139 | 138 |
| Crosshaven | 300 | 287 | 293 | 246 | 239 | 263 | 266 | 249 | 236 | 210 | 239 | 177 | 166 | 131 | 118 | 170 | 216 | 163 | 151 | 144 |
| Baltimore | 346 | 333 | 339 | 292 | 285 | 309 | 312 | 295 | 282 | 256 | 285 | 223 | 212 | 172 | 160 | 209 | 254 | 198 | 178 | 161 |
| Fastnet Rock | 354 | 341 | 347 | 300 | 293 | 317 | 320 | 303 | 290 | 264 | 293 | 231 | 220 | 181 | 169 | 216 | 260 | 207 | 185 | 170 |

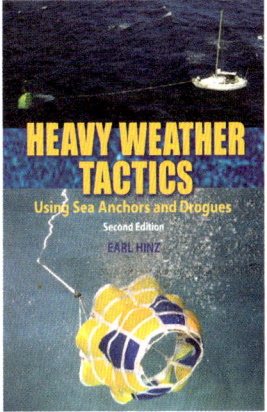

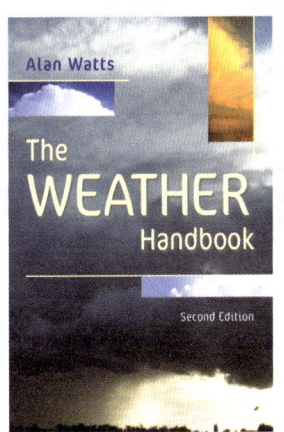

**British Waterways**

Scotland

# Welcome

## To Scotland's Canals

## Marina and Yachting Facilities

- Superb value Marina Berthing

- Winter Lay-up at keen prices

- Skipper's Guides and Passage Information

- A network of Waterways linking Scotland's cruising waters

- A comprehensive range of licence options to suit your needs

## Shoreside

- Experience the unique Falkirk Wheel

- Cycle or walk the canal banks

- Magnificent scenery rich in wildlife

- There is so much to see and do – the ideal family experience

## Website

- Everything you need to know Online!

## www.scottishcanals.co.uk

2008/NM18/v

# West Scotland

## Cape Wrath to Solway Firth

**W Scotland**

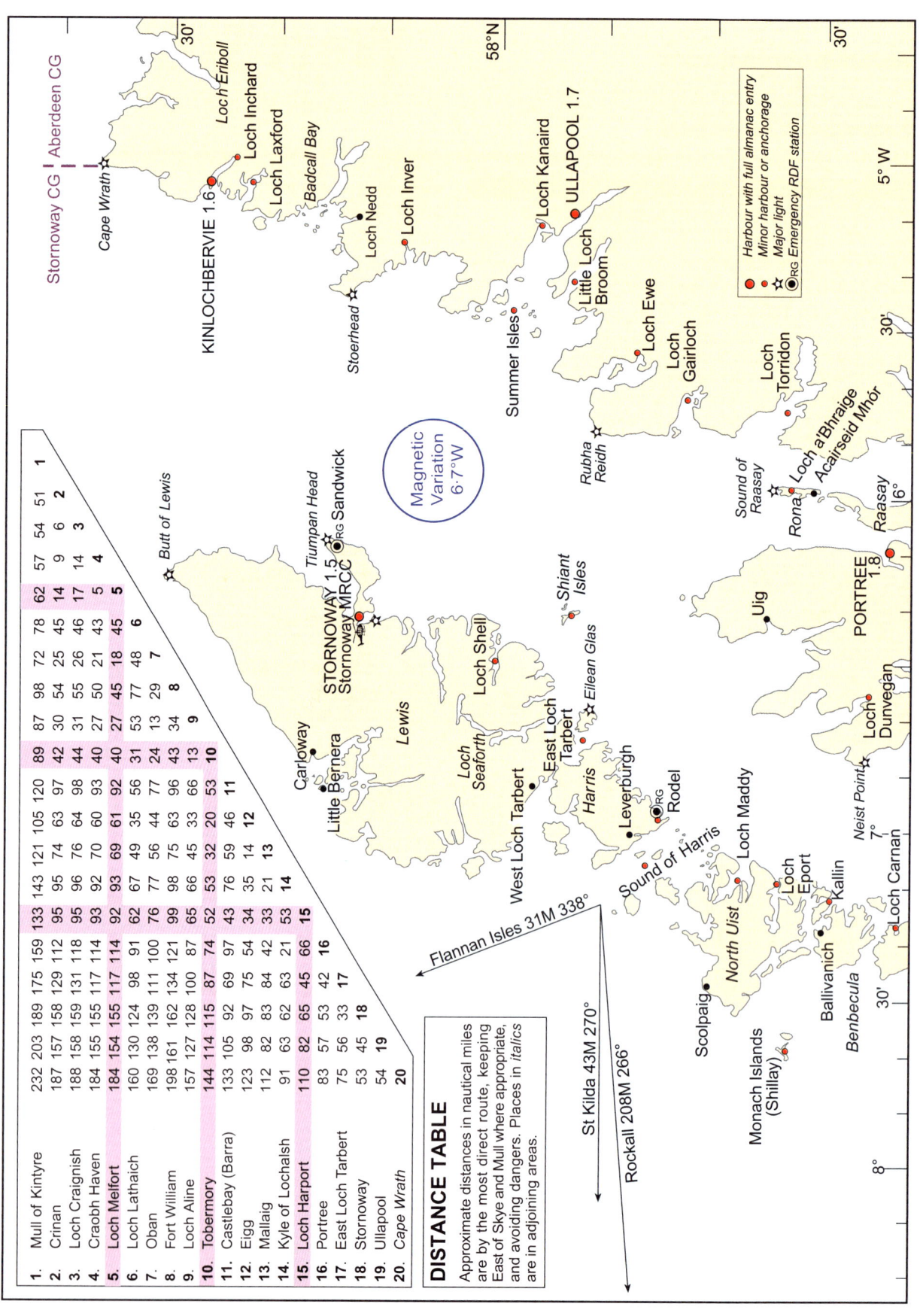

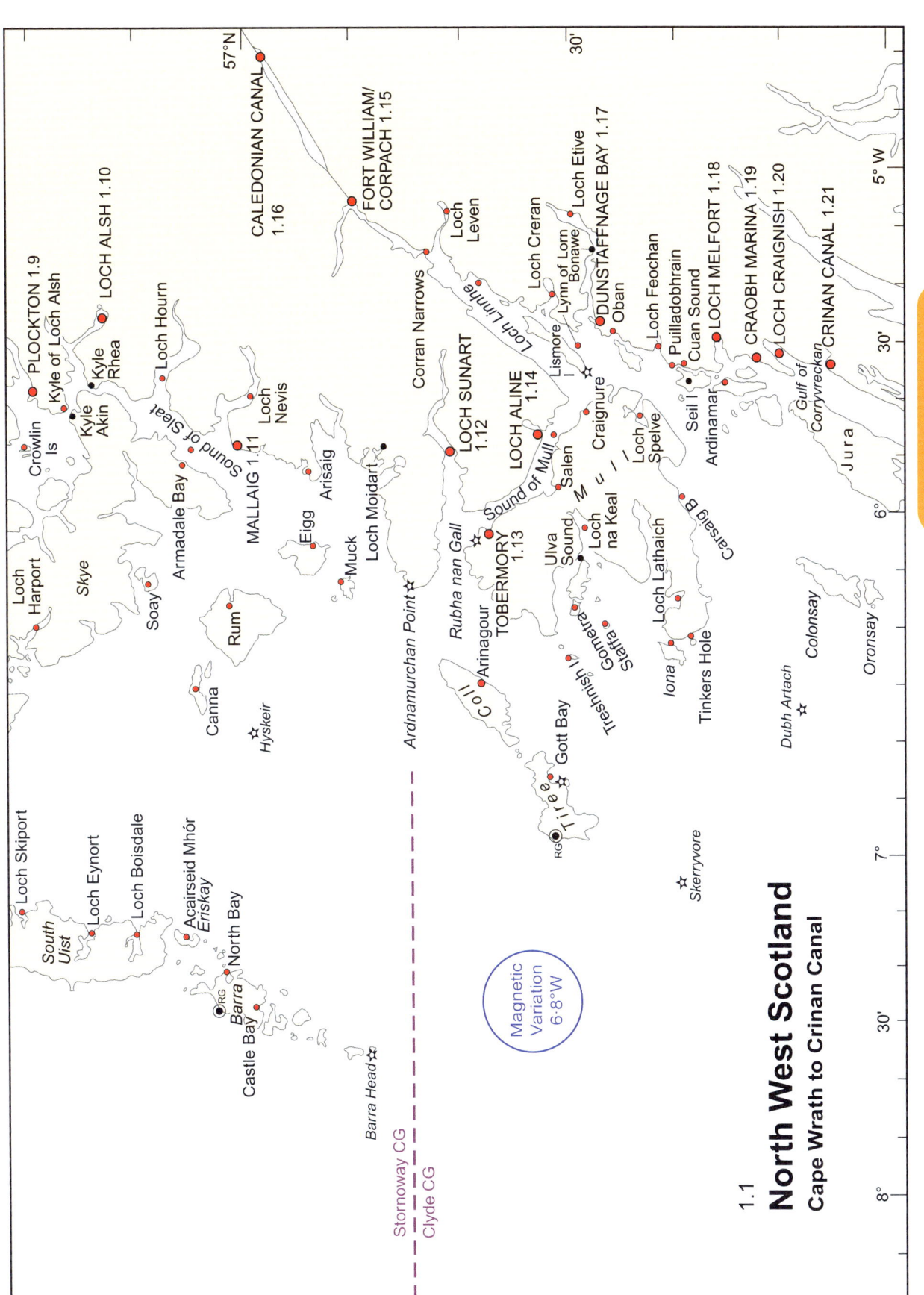

1.1
# North West Scotland
**Cape Wrath to Crinan Canal**

CALEDONIAN CANAL 1.16

FORT WILLIAM/ CORPACH 1.15

Loch Leven

PLOCKTON 1.9

LOCH ALSH 1.10

Kyle of Loch Alsh

Loch Hourn

Loch Creran

Loch Etive

DUNSTAFFNAGE BAY 1.17

LOCH MELFORT 1.18

CRAOBH MARINA 1.19

LOCH CRAIGNISH 1.20

CRINAN CANAL 1.21

Corran Narrows

Lynn of Lorn

Bonawe

Oban

Loch Feochan

Puilladobhrain

Cuan Sound

Crowlin Is

Kyle Akin

Kyle Rhea

Loch Nevis

Loch Linnhe

Lismore

Ardinamar

Gulf of Corryvreckan

Armadale Bay

Sound of Sleat

LOCH SUNART 1.12

LOCH ALINE 1.14

Seil I

Jura

Loch Harport

Skye

MALLAIG 1.11

Eigg

Arisaig

Loch Moidart

Sound of Mull

Craignure

Salen

Loch Spelve

Soay

Muck

Rubha nan Gall

Mull

Loch na Keal

Carsaig B

Rum

Arinagour

TOBERMORY 1.13

Ulva Sound

Loch Lathaich

Canna

☆ Hyskeir

Ardnamurchan Point ☆

Coll

Gometra

Staffa

Iona

Tinkers Hole

Colonsay

Oronsay

Treshnish I

Tiree

Gott Bay

Dubh Artach ☆

Loch Skiport

Loch Eynort

Loch Boisdale

Acairseid Mhór

Eriskay

North Bay

South Uist

RG

Castle Bay

Barra

RG

Barra Head ☆

☆ Skerryvore

Magnetic Variation 6·8'W

Stornoway CG

Clyde CG

57°N

30'

5° W

30'

6°

7°

30'

8°

## 1.2 NW SCOTLAND TIDAL STREAMS

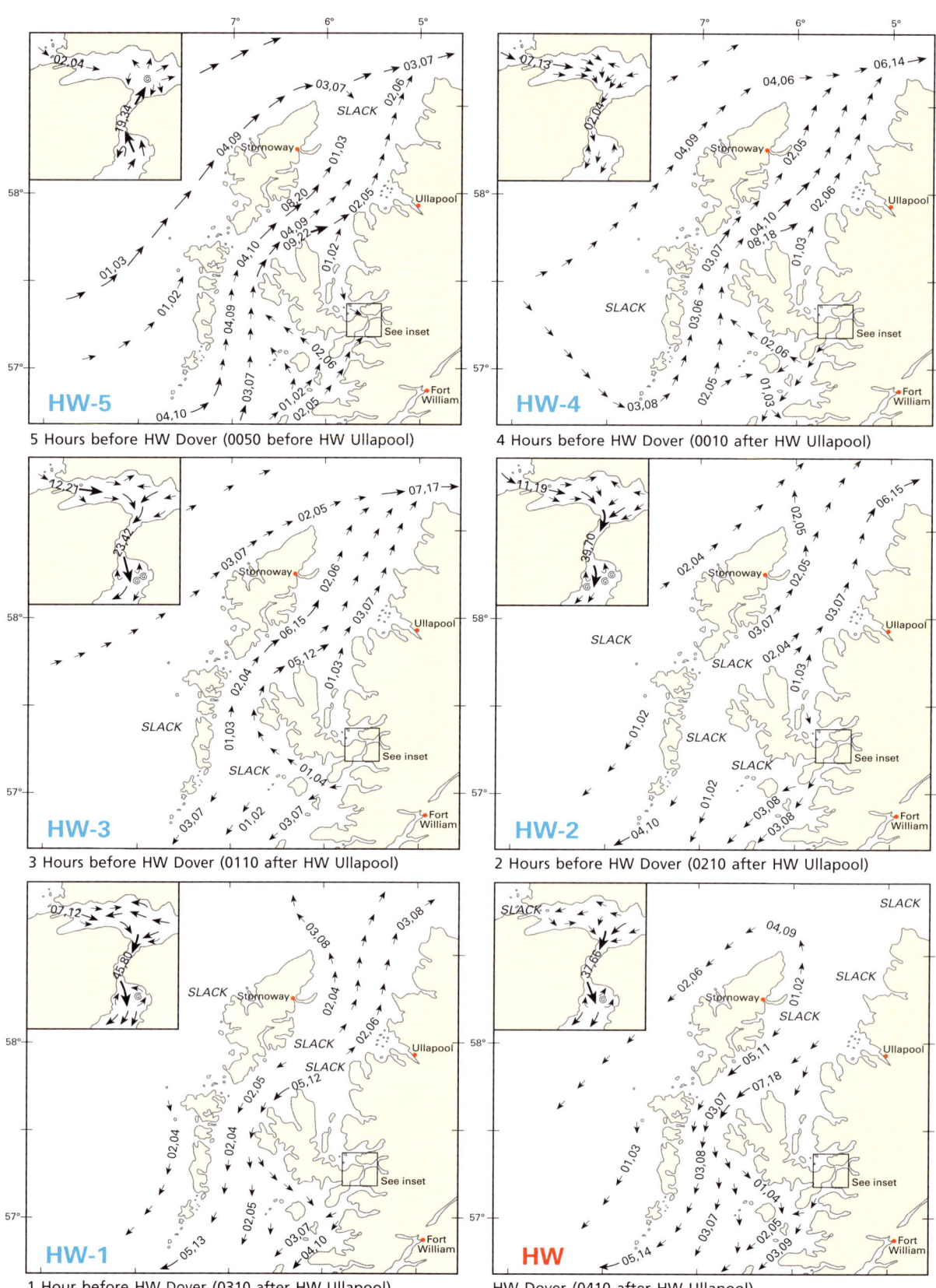

**HW-5**

5 Hours before HW Dover (0050 before HW Ullapool)

**HW-4**

4 Hours before HW Dover (0010 after HW Ullapool)

**HW-3**

3 Hours before HW Dover (0110 after HW Ullapool)

**HW-2**

2 Hours before HW Dover (0210 after HW Ullapool)

**HW-1**

1 Hour before HW Dover (0310 after HW Ullapool)

**HW**

HW Dover (0410 after HW Ullapool)

Southward 2.2    Mull of Kintyre 2.10

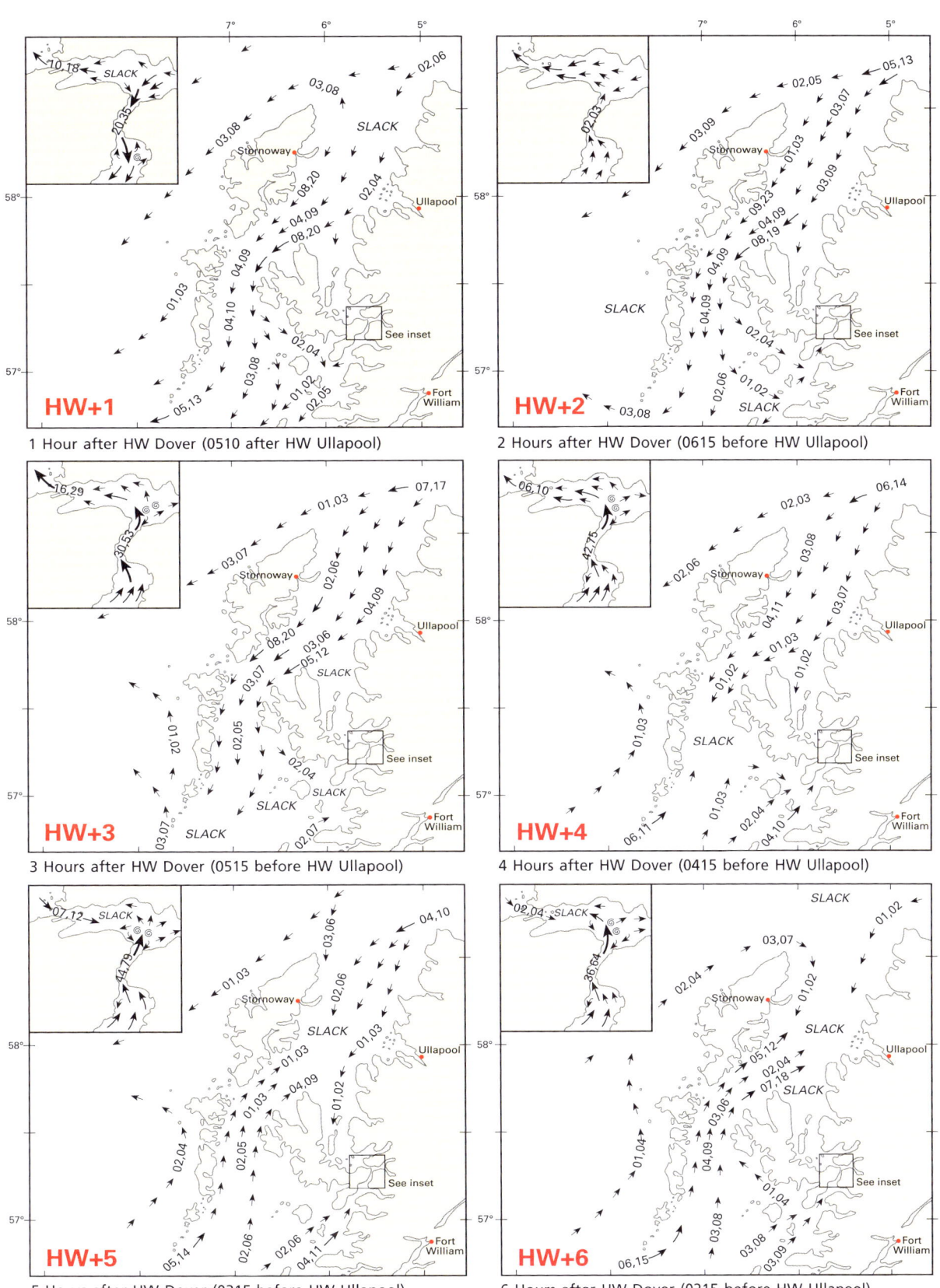

HW+1
1 Hour after HW Dover (0510 after HW Ullapool)

HW+2
2 Hours after HW Dover (0615 before HW Ullapool)

HW+3
3 Hours after HW Dover (0515 before HW Ullapool)

HW+4
4 Hours after HW Dover (0415 before HW Ullapool)

HW+5
5 Hours after HW Dover (0315 before HW Ullapool)

HW+6
6 Hours after HW Dover (0215 before HW Ullapool)

NW Scotland

## 1.3 LIGHTS, BUOYS AND WAYPOINTS

**Bold** print = light with a nominal range of 15M or more. CAPITALS = place or feature. *CAPITAL ITALICS* = light-vessel, light float or Lanby. *Italics* = Fog signal. ***Bold italics*** = Racon. See 0.2 for Abbreviations.

### CAPE WRATH TO LOCH TORRIDON

**Cape Wrath** ☆ 58°37'·54N 04°59'·99W Fl (4) 30s 122m **22M**; W twr.

### LOCH INCHARD and LOCH LAXFORD

Rubha na Lecaig ⚲ Fl (2) 10s 30m 8M; 58°27'·41N 05°04'·58W.
Bodha Ceann na Saile ⚲ Q; 58°27'·24N 05°04'·01W.
**Kinlochbervie Dir lt** 327° ☆. 58°27'·49N 05°03'·08W WRG 15m **16M**; vis: 326°-FG-326·5°-Al GW-326·75°-FW-327·25°-Al RW-327·5°-FR-328°.
Creag Mhòr Dir lt 147°; Iso WRG 2s 16m 4M; vis: 136·5°-R -146·5°-W-147·5°-G-157·5°; 58°26'·99N 05°02'·45W.
**Stoer Head** ☆ 58°14'·43N 05°24'·07W Fl 15s 59m **24M**; W twr.

### LOCH INVER, SUMMER ISLES and ULLAPOOL

Soyea I ⚲ Fl (2) 10s 34m 6M; 58°08'·56N 05°19'·67W.
Glas Leac ⚲ Fl WRG 3s 7m 5M; vis: 071°- W-078°-R-090°-G-103°-W-111°, 243°-W-247°-G-071°; 58°08'·68N 05°16'·36W.
L. InverHbr Bkwtr Hd ⚲ QG 3m 1M 58°08'·93N 05°15'·08W.
L. Inver Culag Pier Hd ⚲ 2 FG (vert) 6m; 58°08'·90N 05°14'·89W.
Old Dornie Pier Head ⚲ Fl G 3s 5m; 58°02'·56N 05°25'·39W.
Rubha Cadail ⚲ Fl WRG 6s 11m W9M, R6M, G6M; W twr; vis: 311°-G-320°-W-325°-R-103°-W-111°-G-118°-W-127°-R-157°-W-199°; 57°55'·51N 05°13'·40W.
Ullapool Pt ⚲ QR; 57°53'·70N 05°10'·68W.
Ullapool Pt ⚲ Iso R 4s 8m 6M; W twr; vis:258°-108°; 57°53'·59N 05°09'·93W.
Ferry Pier SE corner ⚲ Fl R 3s 6m 1M; 57°53'·70N 05°09'·43W.
Cailleach Head ⚲ Fl (2) 12s 60m 9M; W twr; vis: 015°-236°; 57°55'·81N 05°24'·23W.

### LOCH EWE and LOCH GAIRLOCH

Fairway ⚲ L Fl 10s; 57°51'·98N 05°40'·09W.
No. 1 ⚲ Fl (3) G 10s; 57°50'·97N 05°40'·09W.
⚲ Fl (4) R 10s; 57°49'·84N 05°35'·49W.
NATO POL Jetty, NW corner ⚲ Fl G 4s 5m 3M; 57°49'·66N 05°35'·12W.
E ⚲ Fl R 2s; 57°49'·42N 05°35'·51W.
D ⚲ Fl (2) R 10s; 57°49'·11N 05°36'·11W.
**Rubha Reidh** ☆ 57°51'·52N 05°48'·72W Fl (4) 15s 37m **24M**.
Glas Eilean ⚲Fl WRG 6s 9m W6M, R4M; vis: 080°-W-102°-R-296°-W-333°-G-080°; 57°42'·79N 05°42'·42W.
Gairloch Pier ⚲ QR 6m 2M; 57°42'·59N 05°41'·03W .

### OUTER HEBRIDES – EAST SIDE

#### LEWIS

**Butt of Lewis** ☆ 58°30'·89N 06°15'·84W Fl 5s 52m **25M**; R twr; vis: 056°-320°.
**Tiumpan Head** ☆ 58°15'·66N 06°08'·29W Fl (2) 15s 55m **25M**; W twr.
Broad Bay Tong Anch. Ldg Lts 320°, Oc R 8s 8m 4M; 58°14'·48N 06°19'·98W. Rear, 70m from front, Oc R 8s 9m 4M.

#### STORNOWAY

Reef Rock ⚲ QR; 58°11'·58N 06°21'·97W.
**Arnish Point** ☆ Fl WR 10s 17m W9M, R7M; W ○ twr; vis: 088°-W-198°-R-302°-W-013°; 58°11'·50N 06°22'·16W.
Sandwick Bay, NW side ⚲ Oc WRG 6s 10m 9M; vis: 334°-G-341°-W-347°-R-354°; 58°12'·20N 06°22'·11W.
Eilean na Gobhail ⚲ Fl G 6s 8m; 58°12'·14N 06°22'·99W.
No. 1 Pier SW corner ⚲ Q WRG 5m 11M; vis: shore-G-335°-W-352°-R-shore; 58°12'·36N 06°23'·43W.
No. 3 Pier ⚲ Q (2) G 10s 7m 2M 58°12'·31N 06°23'·28W.
Glumaig Hbr ⚲ Iso WRG 3s 8m 3M; 58°11'·27N 06°22'·9W; grey framework twr; vis: 150°-G-174°-W-180°-R-205°.

### LOCH ERISORT, LOCH SHELL and EAST LOCH TARBERT

Tabhaidh Bheag ⚲ Fl 3s 13m 3M; 58°07'·19N 06°23'·06W.
Eilean Chalabrigh ⚲ QG 5m 3M; 58°06'·82N 06°26'·67W.
Gob na Milaid Pt ⚲ Fl 15s 17m 10M; 58°01'·08N 06°22'·04W.
Rubh' Uisenis ⚲ Fl 5s 24m 11M; W twr; 57°56'·25N 06°28'·36W.
Shiants ⚲ QG; 57°54'·57N 06°25'·70W.
Sgeir Inoe ⚲ Fl G 6s; 57°50'·93N 06°33'·93W.
Scalpay, **Eilean Glas** ☆ 57°51'·41N 06°38'·55W Fl (3) 20s 43m **23M**; W twr, R bands; ***Racon (T) 16-18M***.
Scalpay N Hbr ⚲ Fl G 2s; 57°52'·57N 06°42'·22W.
Sgeir Bràigh Mor ⚲ Fl G 6s; 57°51'·51N 06°43'·84W.
Dun Cor Mòr ⚲ Fl R 5s 10m 5M; 57°51'·03N 06°44'·01W.
Sgeir Graidach ⚲ Q (6) + L Fl 15s; 57°50'·36N 06°41'·37W.
Sgeir Ghlas ⚲ Iso WRG 4s 9m W9M, R6M, G6M; W ○ twr; vis: 282°-G-319°-W-329°-R-153°-W-164°-G-171°; 57°52'·36N 06°45'·24W.
Tarbert ⚲ Fl WRG 6s 10m 5M 57°53'·82N 06°47'·93W Oc WRG 6s 10m 5M

### SOUND OF HARRIS, LEVERBURGH and BERNERAY

Fairway ⚲ L Fl 10s; 57°40'·35N 07°02'·15W.
No.1 ⚲ QG; 57°41'·20N 07°02'·67W.
No. 3 ⚲ Fl G 5s; 57°41'·86N 07°03'·44W.
No. 4 ⚲ Fl R 5s; 57°41'·76N 07°03'·63W.
Suilven ⚲ Fl (3)R 10s; 57°41'·68N 07°04'·36W.
Cabbage ⚲ Fl (2) R 6s; ***Racon (T) 5M (3cm);*** 57°42'·13N 07°03'·96W.
L1 ⚲ Fl (2) G 5s; 57°42'·59N 07°03'·21W.
L 4 ⚲ Fl R 2s; 57°43'·68N 07°01'·60W.
Grocis N ⚲ Fl R 8s; 57°44'·29N 07°01'·44W.
Mile Sgeir ⚲ Fl G 5s; 57°43'·97N 07°01'·53SW.
Stumbles Rk ⚲ Fl (2) R 10s; 57°45'·13N 07°01'·79W.
Dubh Sgeir ⚲ Q (2) 5s 9m 6M; R twr, B bands; 57°45'·52N 07°02'·62W
Bo Stainan ⚲ 57°45'·76N 07°02'·40W VQ(6) + LF 10s.
Leverburgh Ldg Lts 014·7°. Front, Q 10m 4M 57°46'·23N 07°02'·04W. Rear, Oc 3s 12m 4M.
Jane's Tower ⚲ Q (2) G 5s 6m 4M; vis: obscured 273°-318°; 57°45'·76N 07°02'·12W.
Leverburgh Reef ⚲ Fl R 2s 4m 57°45'·97N 07°01'·86W.
Leverburgh Pier Hd ⚲ Oc WRG 8s 5m 2M; Gy col; vis: 305°-G-059°-W-066°-R-125°; 57°46'·01N 07°01'·62W.
Berneray Bkwtr Hd ⚲ Iso R 4s 6m 4M; 57°42'·87N 07°10'·07W.
Drowning Rock ⚲ Q (2) G 8s 2m 2M; 57°42'·47N 07°09'·34W.
Portain ⚲ Fl G 3s; 57°41'·71N 07°08'·31W.
Ceann Na Dige ⚲ QR; 57°41'·77N 07°08'·48W.
Trench ⚲ Q (3) G 10s; 57°41'·89N 07°09'·00W.
Reef Chan No. 1 ; 57°42'·95N 07°09'·08W.
Reef Chan No. 2 ; 57°42'·96N 07°09'·06W.

### NORTH UIST

Fairway ⚲ L Fl 10s; 57°40'·23N 07°01'·39W.
No.1 ⚲ QG; 57°41'·20N 07°02'·67W.
No. 3 ⚲ Fl G 5s; 57°41'·86N 07°03'·44W.
No. 4 ⚲ Fl R 5s; 57°41'·76N 07°03'·63W.
NF 3 ⚲ Fl G 10s; 57°41'·47N 07°06'·68W.
NF 6 ⚲ Fl R 5s; 57°41'·56N 07°07'·93W.
Eilean Fuam ⚲ Q 6m 2M; W col; 57°41'·93N 07°10'·69W.
Vallay Island ⚲ Fl WRG 3s 4m 8M; vis: 206°-W-085°-G-140°-W-145°-R-206°; 57°39'·69N 07°26'·42W.
Griminish Hbr Ldg Lts 183°. Front, QG 6m 4M; 57°39'·38N 07°26'·75W. Rear, 110m from front, QG 7m 4M.
Pier Hd ⚲ 2 FG (vert) 6m 4M; Gy col; 57°39'·26N 07°26'·36W.

### LOCH MADDY

Weaver's Pt ⚲ Fl 3s 24m 7M; W hut. 57°36'·49N 07°06'·00W
Glas Eilean Mòr ⚲ Fl (2) G 4s 8m 5M. 57°35'·95N 07°06'·70W
Rubna Nam Pleàc ⚲ Fl R 4s 7m 5M. 57°35'·76N 07°06'·76W
Ruigh Liath E Islet ⚲ QG 6m 5M. 57°35'·72N 07°08'·42W
Vallaquie I ⚲ Fl (3) WRG 8s 11m W7M, R5M, G5M; W pillar; vis: shore-G-205°-W-210°-R-240°-G-254°-W-257°-R-shore; 57°35'·50N 07°09'·40W.
Lochmaddy Ldg Lts 298°. Front, Ro-Ro Pier 2 FG (vert) 8m 4M.

## WGS84 DATUM
### *Plot waypoints on chart before use*

Rear, 110m from front, Oc G 8s 10m 4M; vis: 284°-304°; 57°35'·76N 07°09'·36W.
⟨ Fl R 3s 4M; 57°35'·92N 07°08'·68W.

### GRIMSAY
No. 1 ⚲ Fl (2) R 8s; 57°28'·26N 07°11'·82W.
No. 2 ⚲ Fl R 5s; 57°28'·62N 07°11'·80W.
No. 3 ▲ Fl G 2s; 57°28'·71N 07°11'·84W.

Kallin Harbour Bkwtr NE corner ⚡ 2 FR (vert)6m5M;Gycol; 57°28'·88N 07°12'·31W.

### SOUTH UIST and LOCH CARNAN
Landfall ⟨ L Fl 10s; 57°22'·27N 07°11'·52W.
No. 1 ▲ Fl G 2·5s 57°22'·42N 07°14'·93W.
No. 2 ⚲ Fl R 2s; 57°22'·39N 07°14'·93W.
No. 3 ⚲ Fl R 5s; 57°22'·32N 07°15'·61W.
No. 4 ⚲ QR; 57°22'·25N 07°15'·88W.
No. 2 ▲ QG; 57°22'·11N 07°16'·20W.

Ldg Lts 222°. Front Fl R 2s 7m 5M; W ◇ on post; 57°22'·00N 07°16'·34W. Rear, 58m from front, Iso R 10s 11m 5M; W ◇ on post.
**Ushenish** ☆ (S Uist) 57°17'·89N 07°11'·58W Fl WR 20s 54m **W19M, R15M**; W twr; vis: 193°-W-356°-R-018°.

### LOCH BOISDALE
MacKenzie Rk ⚲ Fl (3) R 15s 3m 4M; 57°08'·24N 07°13'·71W.
Calvay E End ⚡ Fl (2) WRG 10s 16m W7M, R4M, G4M; W twr; vis: 111°-W-190°-G-202°-W-286°-R-111°; 57°08'·53N 07°15'·38W.
N side ⚡ Fl G 6s 3m 3M; 57°08'·99N 07°17'·05W.
Eilean Dubh ⚡ Fl (2) R 5s 2m 3M; 57°09'·07N 07°18'·18W.
Gasay I ⚡ Fl WR 5s 10m W7M, R4M; W twr; vis: 120°-W-284°-R-120°; 57°08'·93N 07°17'·39W.
Gasay Spar ⟨ QG 4m 5M; 57°09'·02N 07°17'·45W.
Sgeir Rock ▲ Fl G 3s 2m 4M; 57°09'·09N 07°17'·76W.
Eilean Dubh ⚡ Fl (2) R 5s 2m 3M; 57°09'·07N 07°18'·18W.
Ro-Ro Jetty Head ⚡ Iso RG 4s 8m 2M; vis: shore-G-283°-R-shore; 2 FG (vert) 8m 3M on dn; 57°09'·12N 07°18'·22W.

### LUDAIG and ERISKAY
The Witches ⚲ Fl R 5s; 57°05'·72N 07°20'·84W.
Off Ludaig ◢ 57°05'·94N 07°19'·56W.
Ludaig Bwtr ⚡ 2 FR (vert) 6m 3M; 57°06'·17N 07°19'·49W.
Bank Rk ⚡ Q (2) 4s 5m 4M; 57°05'·56N 07°17'·60W.
Pier ⚡2 FR (vert) 5m 5M; 57°05'·25N 07°18'·17W .
Acairseid Mhor Ldg Lts 285°. Front, Oc R 6s 9m 4M; 57°03'·89N 07°17'·25W. Rear, 24m from front, Oc R 6s 10m 4M.

▲ Fl G 5s; 57°03'·89N 07°17'·10W.
Acairseid Pier ⚡ 2 FG (vert) 5m 4M; 57°04'·03N 07°17'·61W.

### BARRA, CASTLEBAY and VATERSAY SOUND
Drover Rocks ⟨ Q (6) + L Fl 15s; 57°04'·08N 07°23'·54W.
Binch Rock ⟨ Q (6) + L Fl 15s; 57°01'·71N 07°17'·16W.
Curachan ⟨ Q (3) 10s; 56°58'·56N 07°20'·51W.

Ardveenish ⚡ Oc WRG 6m 9/6M; vis: 300°-G-304°-W-306°-R-310°; 57°00'·21N 07°24'·43W.
Aird Mhor RoRo terminal ⚡ Fl G 2·5s 3M; 57°00'·54N 07°24'·09W.
Bo Vich Chuan ⟨ Q(6) + L Fl 15s; *Racon (M) 5M*; 56°56'·15N 07°23'·31W.
Channel Rk ⚡ Fl WR 6s 4m W6M, R4M; vis: 121·5°-W-277°-R-121·5°; 56°56'·24N 07°28'·94W.
Sgeir a Scape ▲ Fl (2) G 8s; 56°56'·25N 07°27'·21W.
Castle Bay S ⚲ Fl (2) R 8s; *Racon (T) 7M*; 56°56'·09N 07°27'·21W.
Sgeir Dubh ⚡ Q (3) G 6s 6m 5M; 56°56'·40N 07°28'·92W.
Castlebay ⚡Fl R 5s 2m 3M; 56°57'·16N 07°29'·63W .

Rubha Glas. Ldg Lts 295°. Front ⟨ FBu 9m 6M; Or △ on W twr; 56°56'·77N 07°30'·64W. Rear ⟨, 457m from front, FBu 15m 6M; Or ▽ on W twr; vis: 15° and 8° respectively either side of ldg line.

**Barra Hd** ☆ 56°47'·11N 07°39'·26W Fl 15s 208m **18M**; W twr; obsc by islands to NE.

### OUTER HEBRIDES – WEST SIDE
**Flannan I** ☆, Eilean Mór Fl (2) 30s 101m **20M**; W twr; 58°17'·32N 07°35'·23W, obsc in places by Is to W of Eilean Mór.
Rockall ⚡ Fl 15s 19m 8M (unreliable); 57°35'·76N 13°41'·27W.
Gasker Lt ⚡ Fl (3) 10s 38m 10M; 57°59'·05N 07°17'·20W.
Whale Rock ⟨ Q (3) 10s 5m 5M; 57°54'·40N 07°59·91W.
**Haskeir I** ☆ 57°41'·98N 07°41·36W Fl 20s 44m **23M**; W twr; *Racon (M) 17–15M.*

### EAST LOCH ROAG
Aird Laimishader Carloway ⚡ Fl 6s 63m 8M; W hut; obsc on some brgs; 58°17'·06N 06°49'·50W.
Ardvanich Pt ⚡ Fl G 3s 4m 2M; 58°13'·48N 06°47'·68W.
Tidal Rk ⚡ Fl R 3s 2m 2M (synch with Ardvanich Pt above); 58°13'·45N 06°47'·57W.
Gt Bernera Kirkibost Jetty ⚡ 2 FG (vert) 7m 2M.
Grèinam ⚡ Fl WR 6s 8m W8M, R7M; W Bn; vis: R143°-169°, W169°-143°; 58°13'·30N 06°46'·16W.
Rubha Arspaig Jetty Hd ⚡ 2 FR (vert) 10m 4M.

### NORTH UIST and SOUTH UIST
Vallay I ⚡ Fl WRG 3s 8M; vis: 206°-W-085°-G-140°-W-145°-R-206°; 57°39'·70N 07°26'·34W.
Falconet twr ⚡ FR 25m 8M (3M by day); shown 1hr before firing, changes to Iso R 2s 15 min before firing until completion; 57°22'·04N 07°23'·58W.

### ST KILDA
Ldg Lts 270°. Front, Oc 5s 26m 3M; 57°48'·32N 08°34'·31W. Rear, 100m from front, Oc 5s 38m 3M; synch.

### LOCH TORRIDON TO MALLAIG
### LITTLE MINCH and W SKYE
Eugenie Rock t Q 6 + LF 15s; 57°46'·47N 06°27'·28W.
Eilean Troddday ⚡ Fl (2) WRG 10s 52m W12M, R9M, G9M; W Bn; vis: W062°-R088°-130°-W-322°-G-062°; 57°43'·64N 06°17'·89W.
Comet Rock ⚲ Fl R 6s; 57°44'·60N 06°20'·50W.
Uig, Edward Pier Hd ⚡ 57°35'·09N 06°22'·29W Iso WRG 4s 9m W7M, R4M, G4M; vis: 180°-W-006°-G-050°-W-073°-R-180°.
Bo Na Farmachd ▲ Fl G 5s; 57°26'·79N 06°35'·86W.
Waternish Pt ⚡ Fl 20s 21m 8M; W twr; 57°36'·48N 06°37'·99W.
Loch Dunvegan, Uiginish Pt ⚡ Fl WRG 3s 16m W7M,R5M,G5M; W metal-framed Twr; vis: 041°-G-132°-W-145°-R-148°-W-253°-R-263°-W-273°-G-306°, obsc by Fiadhairt Pt when brg > 148°; 57°26'·84N 06°36'·53W.
**Neist Point** ☆ 57°25'·41N 06°47'·30W Fl 5s 43m **16M**; W twr.
Loch Harport, Ardtreck Pt ⚡ 57°20'·38N 06°25'·80W Fl 6s 18m 9M; small W twr.

### RONA, LOCH A'BHRAIGE and INNER SOUND
Na Gamhnachain ⟨ Q; 57°35'·89N 05°57'·71W.
**Rona NE Point** ☆ 57°34'·68N 05°57'·56W Fl 12s 69m **19M**; W twr; vis: 050°-358°.
Loch A'Bhraige, Sgeir Shuas ⚡ Fl R 2s 6m 3M; vis: 070°-199°; 57°35'·02N 05°58'·61W.
Jetty, SW corner ⚡ 2 FR (vert); 57°34'·66N 05°57'·93W.
Rock ⟨ QR 4m 3M; 57°34'·59N 05°58'·01W.
Ldg Lts 136·5°. Front, No. 9 ⟨ Q WRG 3m W4M, R3M; vis: 135°-W- 138°-R- 318°-G-135°; 57°34'·41N 05°58'·09W. Rear, No. 10 ⟨ Iso 6s 28m 5M.
No. 1 ⟨ Fl G 3s 91m 3M; Or bn; 57°34'·27N 05°58'·34W.
Rubha Chùiltairbh ⟨ Fl 3s 6m 5M; 57°34'·12N 05°57'·17W.
No. 11 ⟨ QY 6m 4M; 57°33'·12N 05°57'·60W.
No. 3 ⟨ Fl (2) 10s 9m 4M; 57°32'·59N 05°57'·86W.
No. 12 ⟨ QR 5m 3M; 57°32'·04N 05°58'·15W.
Garbh Eilean SE Pt No. 8 ⟨ Fl 3s 8m 5M; W Bn; 57°30'·67N 05°58'·60W.
Ru Na Lachan ⚡ Oc WR 8s 21m 10M; twr; vis: 337°-W-022°- R-117°-W-162°; 57°29'·02N 05°52'·15W.

### SOUND OF RAASAY, PORTREE and CROWLIN ISLANDS
Sgeir Mhór ₄Fl G 5s; 57°24'·57N 06°10'·53W.
Portree Pier Hd ⚓ 2 FR (vert) 6m 4M; (occas); 57°24'·64N 06°11'·42W.
Eilean Beag ⚓ Fl 6s 32m 6M; W Bn; 57°21'·21N 05°51'·42W.

### RAASAY and LOCH SLIGACHAN
Suisnish ⚓ 2 FG (vert) 8m 2M; 57°19'·87N 06°03'·91W.
Eyre Point ⚓ Fl WR 3s 6m W9M, R6M; W twr; vis: 215°-W-266°-R-288°-W-063°; 57°20'·01N 06°01'·29W.
Sconser Ferry Terminal ⚓ QR 8m 3M; 57°18'·88N 06°06'·67W.
McMillan's Rock ₄ Fl (2) G 12s; 57°21'·11N 06°06'·32W.
Penfold Rock ₌ Fl R 5s; 57°20'·62N 06°05'·54W.
Jackal Rock ₄ Fl G 5s; 57°20'·34N 06°04'·76W.

### PLOCKTON and LOCH CARRON
Plockton Rocks ₤ Fl R 3s 2m 1M; 57°20'·54N 05°38'·29W.
Sgeir Golach ₤ 57°21'·20N 05°39'·01W.
Bogha Dubh Sgeir ₤ 57°20'·92N 05°37'·85W.
Old Lt Ho (13) 57°20'·95N 05°38'·88W (unlit).

### KYLEAKIN and KYLE OF LOCH ALSH
Carragh Rk ₄ Fl (2) G 12s; *Racon (T) 5M*; 57°17'·18N 05°45'·36W.
Bow Rk ₌ Fl (2) R 12s; 57°16'·71N 05°45'·85W.
Fork Rks ₄ Fl G 6s; 57°16'·85N 05°44'·93W.
Black Eye Rk ₌ Fl R 6s; 57°16'·72N 05°45'·31W.
Skye Bridge Centre ⚓ Oc 6s; 57°16'·57N 05°44'·58W.
Eileanan Dubha East ⚓ Fl (2) 10s 9m 8M; vis: obscured 104°-146°; 57°16'·56N 05°42'·32W.
8 Metre Rock ⚓ Fl G 6s 5m 4M; 57°16'·60N 05°42'·69W.
String Rock ₌ Fl R 6s; 57°16'·50N 05°42'·89W.
Allt-an-Avaig Jetty ⚓ 2 FR (vert) 10m; vis: 075°-270°.
S shore, Ferry slipway ⚓ QR 6m; 57°16'·42N 05°43'·40W.
Ferry Pier, W and E sides ⚓ 2 FG (vert) 6/5m 5/4M.
Butec Jetty W end, N corner ⚓ Oc G 6s 5m 3M each end, synch; 57°16'·74N 05°42'·53W.
Sgeir-na-Caillich ⚓ Fl (2) R 6s 3m 4M; 57°15'·59N 05°38'·90W.

### SOUND OF SLEAT
Kyle Rhea ⚓ Fl WRG 3s 7m W8M, R5M, G5M; W Bn; vis: shore-R-217°-W-226°-G-336°-W-345°-R-shore; 57°14'·22N 05°39'·93W.
Sandaig I, NW point ⚓ Fl 6s 13m 8M; W twr; 57°10'·05N 05°42'·29W.
Ornsay, N end ⚓ Fl R 6s 8m 4M; W twr; 57°09'·08N 05°46'·95W.
**Ornsay, SE end** ☆ 57°08'·59N 05°46'·88W Oc 8s 18m **15M**; W twr; vis: 157°-030°.
Eilean Iarmain, off Pier Hd ⚓ 2 FR (vert) 3m 2M; 57°08'·78N 05°47'·89W.
Armadale Bay Pier Centre ⚓Oc R 6s 6m 6M; 57°03'·86N 05°53'·58W.
Pt. of Sleat ⚓ Fl 3s 20m9M; W twr; 57°01'·08N06°01'·08W.
Elgol ⚓ Fl G 3s 4m 4M; 57°08'·78N 06°06'·53W.

### MALLAIG and LOCH NEVIS ENTRANCE
Sgeir Dhearg ₄QG; 57°00'·74N 05°49'·50W.
Northern Pier E end ⚓ Iso WRG 4s 6m W9M, R6M, G6M; Gy twr; vis: 181°-G-185°-W-197°-R-201°. Fl G 3s 14m 6M; same structure; 57°00'·47N 05°49'·50W.
Sgeir Dhearg ⚓ 57°00'·63N 05°49'·61W Fl (2) WG 8s 6m 5M; Gy Bn; vis: 190°-G-055°-W-190°.

### SMALL ISLES AND WEST OF MULL

### CANNA and RUM
Canna, E end Sanday Is ⚓ Fl 10s 32m 9M; W twr; vis: 152°-061°; 57°02'·82N 06°28'·02W.
Loch Scresort ☆ 2F.R(vert) 7m 2M; 57°00'·71N 06°15'·72W.
Loch Scresort ₤ Q; 57°00'·79N 06°14'·61W.

### HYSKEIR, EIGG, MUCK and ARISAIG
Humla ₄ Fl G 6s 3m 4M 57°00'·46N 06°37'·39W.
**Hyskeir** ☆ 56°58'·14N 06°40'·87W Fl (3) 30s 41m **24M**; W twr. *Racon (T) 14-17M*.

SE point Eigg (Eilean Chathastail) ⚓ Fl 6s 24m 8M; W twr; vis: 181°-shore; 56°52'·25N 06°07'·28W.
Eigg, Sgeir nam Bagh (Ferry Terminal) ⚓ Dir 245°; Fl WRG 3s 9m W14, R11, G11; H24; steel pole; vis: 242·5°-G-244°-W-246°-R-247·5°. 2FR(vert) on same structure; 56°52'·80N 06°07'·60W.
Isle of Muck (Port Mor) ⚓ Dir Fl WRG 3s 7m W14, R11, G11, by day W1, R1, G1; steel twr; vis: 319·5°-G-321°-W-323°-R-324·5°; 56°49'·96N 06°13'·64W.
Bogha Ruadh⚓ Fl G 5s 4m 3M; 56°49'·56N 06°13'·05W.
Bo Faskadale ₄ Fl (3) G 18s; 56°48'·18N 06°06'·37W.
**Ardnamurchan** ☆ 56°43'·63N 06°13'·58W Fl (2) 20s 55m **24M**; Gy twr; vis: 002°-217°.
Cairns of Coll, Suil Ghorm ⚓ Fl 12s 23m 10M; W twr; 56°42'·26N 06°26'·75W.

### TIREE, COLL and ARINAGOUR
Loch Eatharna, Bogha Mór ₄ Fl G 6s; 56°36'·63N 06°30'·95W.
Arinagour Pier ⚓ 2 FR (vert) 12m; 56°36'·85N 06°31'·31W.
Roan Bogha ₤ Q (6) + L Fl 15s 3m 5M; 56°32'·23N 06°40'·18W.
Placaid Bogha ₄ Fl G 4s; 56°33'·22N 06°44'·06W.
**Scarinish** ☆, S side of ent 56°30'·01N 06°48'·27W Fl 3s 11m **16M**; W □ twr; vis: 210°-030°.
Cairn na Burgh More (Treshnish Is), Fl (3) 15s 36m 8M; solar panels on framework tr; 56°31'·05N 06°22'·95W.
Gott Bay Ldg Lts 286·5°. Front FR 8m; 56°30'·61N 06°47'·82W. Rear 30m from front FR 11m.
Cairn na Burgh More (Treshnish Is), Fl (3) 15s 36m 8M; solar panels on framework tr; 56°31'·05N 06°22'·95W.
**Skerryvore** ☆ Fl 10s 46m **23M**; Gy twr; *Racon (M) 18M*. 56°19'·36N 07°06'·88W

### LOCH NA LÀTHAICH (LOCH LATHAICH)
Eileanan na Liathanaich, SE end ⚓ Fl WR 6s 12m W8M, R6M; vis: R088°- W108°-088°; 56°20'·56N 06°16'·38W.
**Dubh Artach** ☆ 56°07'·94N 06°38'·08W Fl (2) 30s 44m **20M**; Gy twr, R band.

### SOUND OF MULL

### LOCH SUNART, TOBERMORY and LOCH ALINE
Ardmore Pt ⚓ Fl (2) 10s 18m 13M; 56°39'·37N 06°07'·70W.
New Rks ₄ Fl G 6s 56°39'·05N 06°03'·30W.
**Rubha nan Gall** ☆ 56°38'·33N 06°04'·00W Fl 3s 17m **15M**; W twr.
Bogha Bhuilg ₄ 56°36'·13N 05°59'·13W Fl G 5s.
Hispania Wreck ₌ 56°34'·95N 05°59'·12W Fl (2) R 10s.
Bo Rocks ₄ 56°31'·53N 05°55'·53W Fl (2) G 6s.
Eileanan Glasa (Dearg Sgeir) ⚓ 56°32'·25N 05°54'·80W Fl 6s 7m 8M; W ○ twr.
Fiunary Spit ₄ 56°32'·66N 05°53'·17W Fl G 6s.
Avon Rock ₌ Fl (4) R 12s; 56°30'·78N 05°46'·80W.
Lochaline ₌ QR; 56°32'·09N 05°46'·48W.
Lochaline Ldg Lts 356°. Front, F 2m; 56°32'·39N 05°46'·49W. Rear, 88m from front, F 4m; both H24.
Ardtornish Pt ⚓ Fl (2) WRG 10s 8m W8M, R6M, G6M; W twr; vis: G shore- 302°-W-308°-R-342°-W-057°-R-095°-W-108°-G-shore; 56°31'·10N 05°45'·23W.
Yule Rocks ₌ Fl R 15s; 56°30'·01N 05°43'·96W.
Glas Eileanan Gy Rks ⚓ Fl 3s 11m 6M; W ○ twr on W base; 56°29'·77N 05°42'·83W.
Craignure Ldg Lts 240·9°. Front, FR 10m; 56°28'·26N 05°42'·28W. Rear, 150m from front, FR 12m; vis: 225·8°-255·8°.

### MULL TO CALEDONIAN CANAL AND OBAN
**Lismore** ☆, SW end 56°27'·34N 05°36'·45W Fl 10s 31m **17M**; W twr; vis: 237°-208°.
Lady's Rk ₄ Fl 6s 12m 5M; 56°26'·92N 05°37'·05W.
Duart Pt ⚓ Fl (3) WR 18s 14m W5M, R3M; vis: 162°-W-261°-R-275°-W-353°-R-shore; 56°26'·84N 05°38'·77W.

## LOCH LINNHE

Corran Shoal ⌇ QR 56°43'·69N 05°14'·39W.

Ent W side, Corran Pt ∡ Iso WRG 4s 12m W10M, R7M, G7M; W twr; vis: shore-R-195°-W-215°-G-020-W-030°-R-shore;56°43'·25N 05°14'·54W.

Corran Narrows NE ∡Fl 5s 4m 4M; W twr; vis: S shore-214°; 56°43'·62N 05°13'·90W .

Jetty ∡ Fl R 5s 7m 3M; Gy mast; 56°43'·40N 05°14'·64W.

⌇ Fl (2) R 10s; 56°42'·85N 05°14'·93W.

Clovullin Spit ⌇ Fl (2) R 15s; 56°42'·29N 05°15'·56W.

Cuil-cheanna Spit ▲ Fl G 6s; 56°41'·17N 05°15'·72W.

## FORT WILLIAM and CALEDONIAN CANAL

Corpach, Caledonian Canal Lock ent ∡ Iso WRG 4s 6m 5M; W twr; vis: G287°- W310°- R335°-030°; 56°50'·52N 05°07'·44W.

Eilean na Creiche ⌇ Fl R 3s 3m 4M; 56°50'·40N 05°07'·38W.

Eilean na Creiche (E of) ⌇ Fl R 6s; 56°50'·29N 05°07'·01W.

Lochy Flat S ▲ QG; 56°49'·53N 05°07'·02W.

McLean Rock ⌇ Fl (2) R 12s 3m 4M; 56°49'·81N 05°07'·04W.

## LYNN OF LORN

Sgeir Bhuidhe Appin ⌇ Fl (2) WR 7s 8m W9M R6M; W Bn; vis: W013·5°- R184°-220°; 56°33'·63N 05°24'·65W.

Appin Point ▲ Fl G 6s; 56°32'·69N 05°25'·97W.

Dearg Sgeir, off Aird's Point ⌇ Fl WRG 2s 2m W3M, R1M, G1M; vis: 196°-R-246°-W-258°-G-311°-W-058°-R-093°-W-139°; 56°32'·20N 05°25'·22W.

Rubha nam Faoileann (Eriska) ⌇ QG 2m 2M; G col; vis 128°-329°; 56°32'·20N 05°24'·11W.

## DUNSTAFFNAGE BAY/OBAN

Pier Hd ∡ NE end, 2 FG (vert) 4m 2M; 56°27'·21N 05°26'·18W.

N spit of Kerrera ∡ Fl R 3s 9m 5M; W col, R bands; 56°25'·49N 05°29'·56W.

Dunollie ∡ Fl (2) WRG 6s 6m W8M, R6M, G6M; vis: 351°-G- 020°-W-047°-R-120°-W-138°-G-143°; 56°25'·37N 05°29'·05W.

Rubbh'a' Chruidh ∡ QR 4m 2M; 56° 25'·32N 05°29'·29W.

Corran Ledge ⌇ VQ (9) 10s; 56°25'·19N 05°29'·11W.

Oban N Pier Mid ∡ 2 FG (vert) 8m 5M; 56°24'·87N 05°28'·49W.

## OBAN TO LOCH CRAIGNISH

Sgeir Rathaid North ⌇ Q; 56°24'·92N 05°29'·24W.

Sgeir Rathaid South ⌇ Q (6) + L Fl 15s; 56°24'·74N 05°29'·37W.

Ardbhan ▲ Fl G 5s; 56°24'·18N 05°30'·39W.

Ferry Rocks NW ▲ QG; 56°24'·11N 05°30'·70W.

Ferry Rocks SE ⌇ Fl R 5s; 56°23'·99N 05°30'·53W.

Little Horse Shoe ⌇ Fl (4) R 12s; 56°23'·22N 05°31'·83W.

Kerrera Sound, Dubha Sgeirean ∡ Fl (2) 12s 7m 5M; W ○ twr; 56°22'·81N 05°32'·27W.

Bogha Nuadh ⌇ Q (6) + LFl 15s; 56°21'·69N 05°37'·88W.

Bono Rock ⌇ Fl (4) R 12s; 56°16'·23N 05°40'·98W.

Fladda ∡ Fl (2) WRG 9s 13m W11M, R9M, G9M; W twr; vis: 169°-R-186°-W-337°-G-344°-W-356°-R-026°; 56°14'·89N 05°40'·83W.

Dubh Sgeir (Luing) ∡ Fl WRG 6s 9m W6M, R4M. G4M; W twr; vis: W000°- R010°- W025°- G199°-000°; *Racon (M) 5M*; 56°14'·76N 05°40'·20W.

The Garvellachs, Eileach an Naoimh, SW end ∡ Fl 6s 21m 9M; W Bn; vis: 240°-215°; 56°13'·04N 05°49'·06W.

## LOCH MELFORT and CRAOBH HAVEN

Melfort Pier ∡ Dir FR 6m 3M; (Private shown 1/4 to 31/10); 56°16'·14N 05°30'·19W.

▲ 56°12'·88N 05°33'·59W.

Craobh Marina Bkwtr Hd ∡ Iso WRG 5s 10m, W5M, R3M, G3M ; vis:114°-G-162°-W-183°-R-200°; 56°12'·78N 05°33'·52W.

---

# 1.4 PASSAGE INFORMATION

It is essential to carry large scale charts and current Pilot Books: Admiralty *W Coast of Scotland Pilot*; Clyde Cruising Club's *Sailing Directions, Pt 2 Kintyre to Ardnamurchan* and *Pt 3 Ardnamurchan to Cape Wrath*; and the *Yachtsman's Pilot to W Coast of Scotland;Vol 2 Crinan to Canna, Vol 3 The Western Isles, Vol 4 Skye & NW Scotland* (Lawrence/Imray).

The West coast of Scotland provides splendid, if sometimes boisterous, sailing and matchless scenery. In summer the long daylight hours and warmth of the Gulf Stream compensate for the lower air temperatures and higher wind speeds experienced when depressions run typically north of Scotland. Inshore winds are often unpredictable, due to geographical effects of lochs, mountains and islands offshore; calms and squalls can alternate rapidly.

Good anchors, especially on kelp/weed, are essential. ⚓s are listed but it should not be assumed that these will always be available. Particularly in N of area, facilities are very dispersed. A '*Rover Ticket*' from Highland Council allows berthing for 15 days; the scheme includes: Kinlochbervie, Lochinver, Gairloch, Kyle of Lochalsh, Kyleakin, Portree and Uig. VHF communications with shore stations may be limited by high ground. Beware ever more fish farms in many inlets. Local magnetic anomalies occur in Kilbrannan Sound, Passage of Tiree, Sound of Mull, Canna, and East Loch Roag. Submarines exercise throughout these waters.

## CAPE WRATH TO ULLAPOOL

(AC 1785, 1794) C Wrath (lt, fog sig) is a steep headland (110m). ▶ *To N of it the E-going stream begins at HW Ullapool – 0350, and W- going at HW Ullapool + 0235, sp rates 3kn. Eddies close inshore cause almost continuous W-going stream E of Cape, and N-going stream SW of it. Where they meet is turbulence, with dangerous seas in bad weather.* ◀ Duslic Rk, 7ca NE of lt ho, dries 3·4m. 6M SW of

C Wrath, islet of Am Balg (45m)is foul for 2ca around.

There are anchs in Loch Inchard (AC 2503), the best shelter being in Kinlochbervie on N shore; also good anchs among Is along S shore of Loch Laxford, entered between Ardmore Pt and Rubha Ruadh. Handa Is to WSW is a bird sanctuary. Handa Sound is navigable with care, but beware Bogha Morair in mid-chan and associated overfalls. ▶ *Tide turns 2hrs earlier in the Sound than offshore. Strong winds against tide raise a bad sea off Pt of Stoer.* ◀ The best shelter is 8M S at Loch Inver (AC 2504), with good anch off hotel near head of loch. S lies Enard Bay.

## ULLAPOOL TO LOCH TORRIDON

(AC 1794, 2210) The Summer Isles (AC 2501), 12M NW of the major fishing port of Ullapool, offer some sheltered anchs and tight approaches. The best include the Bay on E side of Tanera Mor; off NE of Tanera Beg (W of Eilean Fada Mor); and in Caolas Eilean Ristol, between the Is and mainland.

Loch Ewe (AC 3146) provides good shelter and easy access. Best anchs are in Poolewe Bay (beware Boor Rks off W shore) and in SW corner of Loch Thuirnaig (entering, keep close to S shore to avoid rks extending from N side). Off Rubha Reidh (lt) seas can be dangerous. ▶ *The NE-going stream begins at HW Ullapool – 0335; the SW-going at HW Ullapool + 0305. Sp rates 3kn, but slacker to SW of point.* ◀ Longa Is lies N of ent to Loch Gairloch (AC 2528). The chan N of it is navigable but narrow at E end. Outer loch is free of dangers, but exposed to swell. Best anch is on S side of loch in Caolas Bad a' Chrotha, W of Eilean Horrisdale.

Entering L Torridon (AC 2210) from S or W beware Murchadh Breac (dries 1·5m) 3ca NNW of Rubha na Fearna. Best anchs are SW of Eilean Mor (to W of Ardheslaig); in Loch a 'Chracaich, 7ca further SE; E of Shieldaig Is; and near head of Upper L Torridon. ▶ *Streams are weak except where they run 2-3 kn in narrows between L Shieldaig and Upper L Torridon.* ◀

## OUTER HEBRIDES

(AC 1785, 1794, 1795) The E sides of these Is have many good, sheltered anchs, but W coasts give little shelter. The CCC's *Outer Hebrides SDs* or *The Western Isles* (Imray) are advised.

▶ *The Minches and Sea of the Hebrides can be very rough, particularly in the Little Minch between Skye and Harris, and around Shiant Is where tide runs locally 4kn at sp, and heavy overfalls can occur. The NE going stream on both shores begins at HW Dover +0430 (HW Ullapool -0340), with the strongest flow from mid channel to the Skye coast. There is a W going counter tide E of Vaternish Pt.* ◀

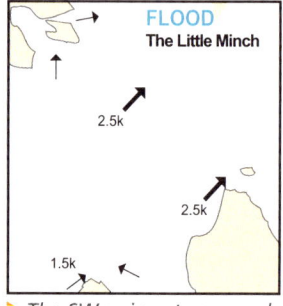
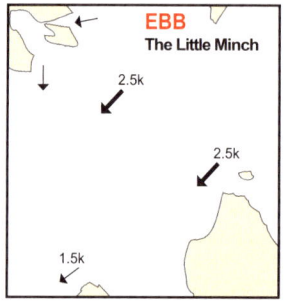

▶ *The SW going stream on both shores begins at HW Dover – 0130 (HW Ullapool +0240), with the strongest flow from mid channel to the Skye coast, sp rates 2·5kn. The E going stream in Sound of Scalpay runs at up to 2k. The E going flood and W going ebb in Sound of Scalpay run at up to 2k.* ◀

▶ ***Sound of Harris:*** *the behaviour of tidal streams varies from day to night, sp to np, and winter to summer. The following data applies to daylight, in summer at sp tides in the Cope Chan. For further information refer to the Admiralty West of Scotland Pilot.*

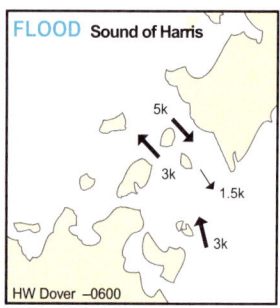
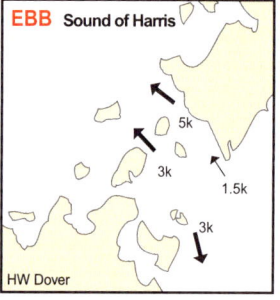

HW Dover - HW D +0200: SE stream.
HW D +0300 - HW D +0600: Incoming stream from both ends.
HW D –0600 - HW D –0500: NW stream.
HW D –0500 - HW Dover: Outgoing stream from both ends.
*At neaps in summer the stream will run SE for most of the day. Tide rates shown are the maxima likely to be encountered at any time.* ◀

From N to S, the better hbrs in Outer Hebrides include:

*Lewis.* Stornoway; Loch Grimshader (beware Sgeir a'Chaolais, dries in entrance); Loch Erisort; Loch Odhairn; Loch Shell. Proceeding S from here, or to E Loch Tarbert beware Sgeir Inoe (dries 2·3m) 3M ESE of Eilean Glas lt ho at SE end of Scalpay.

*Harris.* E Loch Tarbert; Loch Scadaby; Loch Stockinish; Loch Finsby; W Loch Tarbert; Loch Rodel (⚓). A well marked ferry chan connects Leverburgh (South Harris) to Berneray.

*N Uist.* Loch Maddy (⚓); Loch Eport, Kallin Hbr (⚓).

*S Uist.* Loch Carnan (⚓); Loch Skiport; Loch Eynort; Loch Boisdale (⚓).

*Barra.* Castlebay (⚓), and Berneray, on N side, E of Shelter Rk.

Activity at the Hebrides Range, S. Uist ☎ (01870) 604441, is broadcast daily at 0950LT and Mon-Fri 1100-1700LT on VHF Ch **12** (Ch 73 in emergency) and on MF 2660 kHz.

## SKYE TO ARDNAMURCHAN

(AC 1795, 2210, 2209, 2208, 2207) Skye and the islands around it provide many good and attractive anchs, of which the most secure are: Acairseid Mhor on the W side of Rona; Portree (1.8); Isleornsay; Portnalong, near the ent to Loch Harport, and Carbost at the head; Loch Dunvegan; and Uig Bay in Loch Snizort. ⚓s at Stein (Loch Dunvegan), Portree, Acairseid Mhor (Rona), Churchton Bay (Raasay) and Armadale Bay (S tip).

▶ *Tides are strong off Rubha Hunish at N end of Skye, and heavy overfalls occur with tide against fresh or strong winds.* ◀ Anch behind Fladday Is near the N end of Raasay can be squally and uncomfortable; and Loch Scavaig (S. Skye, beneath the Cuillins) more so, though the latter is so spectacular as to warrant a visit in fair weather. Soay Is has a small, safe hbr on its N side, but the bar at ent almost dries at LW sp.

Between N Skye and the mainland there is the choice of Sound of Raasay or Inner Sound. **The direction of buoyage in both Sounds is Northward.** In the former, coming S from Portree, beware Sgeir Chnapach (3m) and Ebbing Rk (dries 2·9m), both NNW of Oskaig Pt. Beware McMillan's Rk (0·4m depth) in mid-chan, marked by SHM lt buoy. ▶ *At the Narrows (chart 2534) the SE- going stream begins at HW Ullapool – 0605, and the NW-going at HW Ullapool + 0040; sp rate 1·4kn in mid-chan, but more near shoals each side.* ◀

The chan between Scalpay and Skye narrows to 2.5ca with drying reefs each side and least depth 0·1m. ▶ *Here the E-going stream begins at HW Ullapool + 0550, and W-going at HW Ullapool – 0010, sp rate 1kn.* ◀

Inner Sound, which is a Submarine exercise area, is wider and easier than Sound of Raasay; the two are connected by Caol Rona and Caol Mor, respectively N and S of Raasay. Dangers extend about 1M N of Rona, and Cow Is lies off the mainland 8M to S; otherwise approach from N is clear to Crowlin Is, which should be passed to W. There is a good anch between Eilean Mor and Eilean Meadhonach.

A torpedo range in the Inner Sound does not normally restrict passage, but vessels may be requested to keep to the E side of the Sound if the range is active. Range activity is broadcast at 0800 and 1800LT first on VHF Ch 16 and then on Ch 8, and is indicated by Red Flags flown at the range building at Applecross, by all range vessels and at the naval pier at Kyle of Lochalsh, ☎ (01599) 534262.

Approaching Kyle Akin (AC 2540) from W, beware dangerous rks to N, off Bleat Is (at S side of entrance to Loch Carron); on S side of chan, Bogha Beag (dries 1·2m) and Black Eye Rk (depth 3·2m), respectively 6ca and 4ca W of bridge. Pass at least 100m N or S of Eileanan Dubha in Kyle Akin. On S side of chan String Rk (dries) is marked by PHM lt buoy.

Kyle Rhea connects Loch Alsh with NE end of Sound of Sleat. ▶ *The tidal streams are very strong: N-going stream begins HW Ullapool + 0600, sp rate 6-7kn; S-going stream begins at HW Ullapool, sp rate 8kn. N going stream in Kyle Rhea begins HW Dover +0140 (HW Ullapool +0555) and runs for 6 hours. The E going stream in Kyle Akin begins (Sp) HW Dover +0350 (HW Ullapool –0415). (Nps) HW Dover –0415 (HW Ullapool ).*

*S going stream in Kyle Rhea begins HW Dover -0415 (HW Ullapool) and runs for 6 hours. The W going stream in Kyle Akin begins (Sp) HW Dover –0015 (HW Ullapool +0400). (Nps) HW Dover +0140 (HW Ullapool +0555). Eddies form both sides of the Kyle and there are dangerous overfalls off S end in fresh S'ly winds on S-going stream.* ◀ Temp anch in Sandaig Bay, 3M to SW.

The Sound of Sleat widens to 4M off Point of Sleat and is exposed to SW winds unless Eigg and Muck give a lee. Mallaig is a busy fishing and ferry hbr, convenient for supplies. Further S the lochs require intricate pilotage. 6M NE of Ardnamurchan Pt (lt, fog sig)

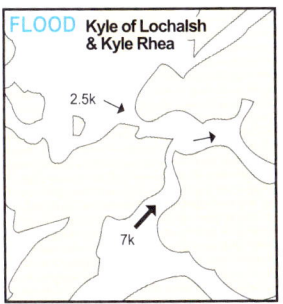

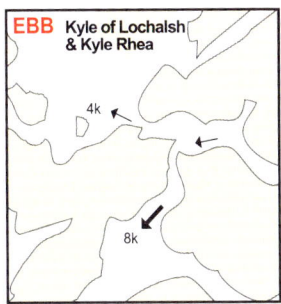

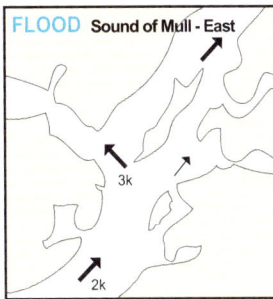

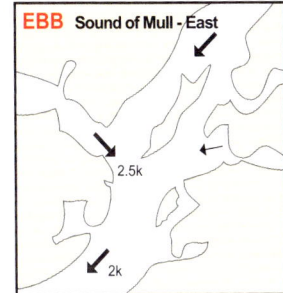

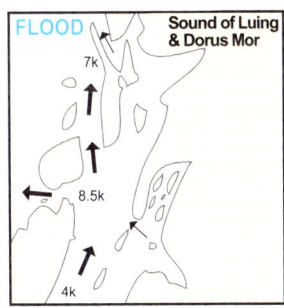

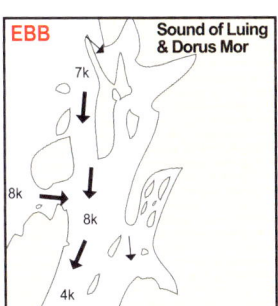

begins at HW Dover +0105 (HW Oban –0550). The ingoing tides at Lochs Feochan, Etive and Creran begin at HW Dover +0300, –0100 & +0030.

*The S going stream in the Firth of Lorne begins at HW Dover +0500 (HW Oban –0155). The E going stream in the Sound of Mull begins at HW Dover +0555 (HW Oban –0025). The outgoing tides at Lochs Feochan, Etive and Creran begin at HW Dover – 0500, –0520 & –0505.* ◄

On the mainland shore Puilladobhrain is a sheltered anch. Cuan Sound is a useful short cut to Loch Melfort, and Craobh Marina. Good shelter, draft permitting, in Ardinamar B, SW of Torsa.

Sound of Luing (AC 2326) between Fladda (lt), Lunga and Scarba on the W side, and Luing and Dubh Sgeir (lt) on the E side, is the normal chan to or from Sound of Jura, despite dangers at the N end and strong tidal streams. ► *The N and W-going flood begins at HW Oban + 0430; the S and E-going ebb at HW Oban –0155. Sp rates are 2·5kn at S end of Sound, increasing to 6kn or more in Islands off N entrance, where there are eddies, races and overfalls.* ◄

► *The N or W going stream begins in the following sequence:*
*Dorus Mor:*       *HW Dover –0200 (HW Oban +0330). Sp: 8 kn.*
*Corryvreckan:*   *HW D –0120 (HW O +0410). Sp: 8.5 kn.*
*Cuan Sound:*     *HW D –0110 (HW O +0420). Sp: 6 kn.*
*Sound of Jura:*  *HW D –0130 (HW O +0400). Sp: 4 kn.*
*Sound of Luing:* *HW D –0100 (HW O +0430). Sp: 7 kn.*

*The S or E going stream begins as follows:*
*Dorus Mor:*       *HW Dover +0440 (HW Oban –0215). Sp: 8 kn.*
*Corryvreckan:*   *HW D +0445 (HW O –0210). Sp: 8.5 kn.*
*Cuan Sound:*     *HW D +0455 (HW O –0200). Sp: 6 kn.*
*Sound of Jura:*  *HW D +0450 (HW O –0205). Sp: 4 kn.*
*Sound of Luing:* *HW D +0500 (HW O –0155). Sp: 7 kn.*
*From the N, beware very strong streams, eddies and whirlpools in Dorus Mór, off Craignish Pt. Streams begin to set W and N away from Dorus Mór at HW Oban + 0345, and E and S towards Dorus Mór at HW Oban – 0215, sp rates 7kn.* ◄

At N end of Sound of Jura (AC 2326) is Loch Craignish For Gulf of Corryvreckan, Colonsay, Islay, Loch Crinan and passage south through the Sound of Jura, see 2.4.

are Bo Faskadale rks, drying 0·5m and marked by SHM lt buoy, and Elizabeth Rk with depth of 0·7m. ► *Ardnamurchan Pt is an exposed headland onto which the ebb sets. With onshore winds, very heavy seas extend 2M offshore and it should be given a wide berth. Here the N-going stream begins at HW Oban – 0525, and the S-going at HW Oban + 0100, sp rates 1·5kn.* ◄

## THE SMALL ISLES

(AC 2207, 2208) These consist of Canna, Rum, Eigg and Muck. The hbrs at Eigg (SE end), Rhum (Loch Scresort) and Canna (between Canna and Sanday) are all exposed to E'lies; Canna has best shelter and is useful for the Outer Hebrides. Dangers extend SSW from Canna: at 1M Jemina Rk (depth 1·5m) and Belle Rk (depth 3·6m); at 2M Humla Rk (5m high), marked by buoy and with offlying shoals close W of it; at 5M Hyskeir (lt, fog sig), the largest of a group of small islands; and at 7M Mill Rks (with depths of 1·8m).
► *The tide runs hard here, and in bad weather the sea breaks heavily up to 15M SW of Canna. Between Skerryvore and Neist Pt the stream runs generally N and S, starting N-going at HW Ullapool + 0550, and S-going at HW Ullapool – 0010. It rarely exceeds 1kn, except near Skerryvore, around headlands of The Small Isles, and over rks and shoals.* ◄

1M off the N side of Muck are Godag Rks, some above water but with submerged dangers extending 2ca further N. Most other dangers around the Small Isles are closer inshore, but there are banks on which the sea breaks heavily in bad weather. A local magnetic anomaly exists about 2M E of Muck.

## ARDNAMURCHAN TO CRINAN

(AC 2171, 2169) S of Ardnamurchan the route lies either W of Mull via Passage of Tiree (where headlands need to be treated with respect in bad weather); or via the more sheltered Sound of Mull and Firth of Lorne. The former permits a visit to Coll and Tiree, where best anchs are at Arinagour (⚓s) and Gott Bay respectively. Beware Cairns of Coll, off the N tip.

The W coast of Mull is rewarding in settled weather, but careful pilotage is needed. Beware tide rip off Caliach Pt (NW corner) and Torran Rks off SW end of Mull (large scale AC 2617 required). Apart from the attractions of Iona and of Staffa (Fingal's Cave), the remote Treshnish Is are worth visiting. The best anchs in this area are at Ulva, Gometra, Bull Hole and Tinker's Hole in Iona Sound. The usual passage through Iona Sound avoids overfalls W of Iona, but heed shoal patches. Loch Lathaich on the N side of Ross of Mull is 5M to the E; a good base with anch at Bunessan.

The Sound of Mull gives access to Tobermory, Dunstaffnage Bay, Oban, and up Loch Linnhe through Corran Narrows (where tide runs strongly) to Fort William and to Corpach for the Caledonian Canal. Apart from these places, there are dozens of lovely anchs in the sheltered lochs inside Mull, as for example in Loch Sunart with ⚓s at Kilchoan; also at Craignure and Salen Bays on Sound of Mull.
► *Firth of Lorne: the N going stream begins at HW Dover –0100 (HW Oban +0430). The W going stream in the Sound of Mull*

## 1.5 STORNOWAY

Lewis (Western Isles) **58°11'·58N 06°21'·82W** ❁❁❁▲▲✿✿

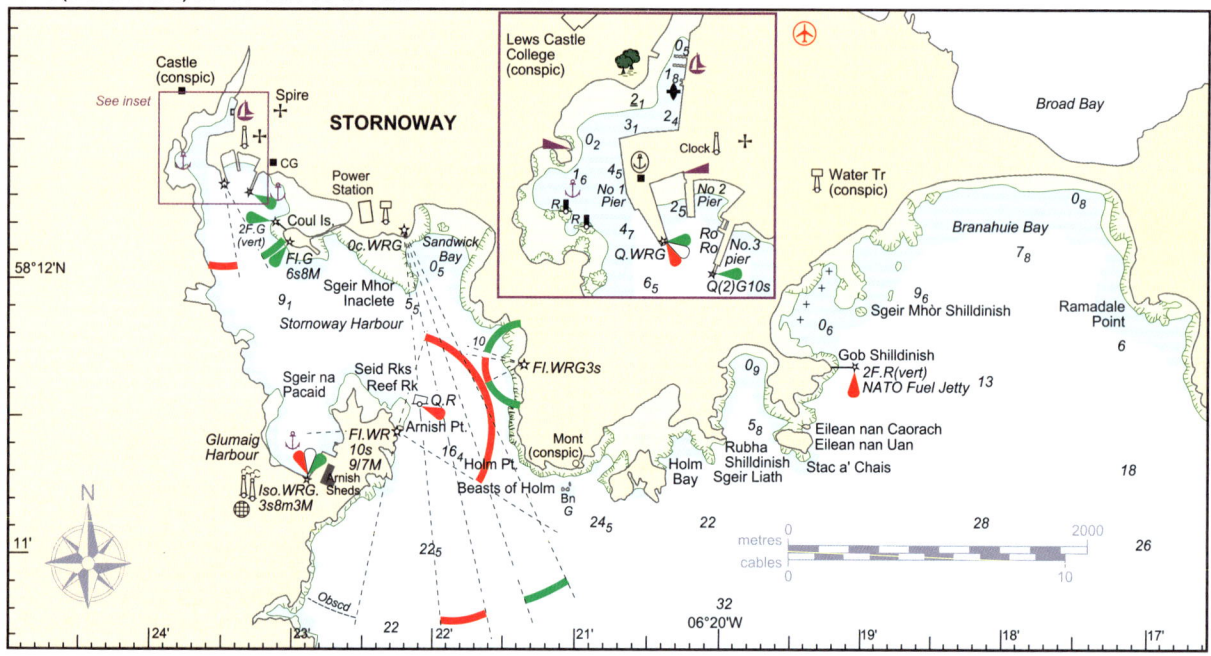

**CHARTS** AC 1785, 1794, 2529; Imray C67; OS 8

**TIDES** –0428 Dover; ML 2·8; Duration 0610

**Standard Port STORNOWAY (→)**

| Times | | | | Height (metres) | | | |
|---|---|---|---|---|---|---|---|
| High Water | | Low Water | | MHWS | MHWN | MLWN | MLWS |
| 0100 | 0700 | 0300 | 0900 | 4·8 | 3·7 | 2·0 | 0·7 |
| 1300 | 1900 | 1500 | 2100 | | | | |

***East side of Outer Hebrides, N to S***
**Differences LOCH SHELL** (Harris)

| | | | | | | | |
|---|---|---|---|---|---|---|---|
| –0013 | 0000 | 0000 | –0017 | 0·0 | –0·1 | –0·1 | 0·0 |
| **EAST LOCH TARBERT** (Harris) | | | | | | | |
| –0025 | –0010 | –0010 | –0020 | +0·2 | 0·0 | +0·1 | +0·1 |
| **LOCH MADDY** (N Uist) | | | | | | | |
| –0044 | –0014 | –0016 | –0030 | 0·0 | –0·1 | –0·1 | 0·0 |
| **LOCH CARNAN** (S Uist) | | | | | | | |
| –0050 | –0010 | –0020 | –0040 | –0·3 | –0·5 | –0·1 | –0·1 |
| **LOCH SKIPORT** (S Uist) | | | | | | | |
| –0100 | –0025 | –0024 | –0024 | –0·2 | –0·4 | –0·3 | –0·2 |
| **LOCH BOISDALE** (S Uist) | | | | | | | |
| –0055 | –0030 | –0020 | –0040 | –0·7 | –0·7 | –0·3 | –0·2 |
| **BARRA** (North Bay) | | | | | | | |
| –0103 | –0031 | –0034 | –0048 | –0·6 | –0·5 | –0·2 | –0·1 |
| **CASTLE BAY** (Barra) | | | | | | | |
| –0115 | –0040 | –0045 | –0100 | –0·5 | –0·6 | –0·3 | –0·1 |
| **BARRA HEAD** (Berneray) | | | | | | | |
| –0115 | –0040 | –0045 | –0055 | –0·8 | –0·7 | –0·2 | +0·1 |
| ***West side of Outer Hebrides, N to S*** | | | | | | | |
| **CARLOWAY** (W Lewis) | | | | | | | |
| –0040 | +0020 | –0035 | –0015 | –0·6 | –0·5 | –0·4 | –0·1 |
| **LITTLE BERNERA** (W Lewis) | | | | | | | |
| –0021 | –0011 | –0017 | –0027 | –0·5 | –0·6 | –0·4 | –0·2 |
| **WEST LOCH TARBERT** (W Harris) | | | | | | | |
| –0015 | –0015 | –0046 | –0046 | –1·1 | –0·9 | –0·5 | 0·0 |
| **SCOLPAIG** (W North Uist) | | | | | | | |
| –0033 | –0033 | –0040 | –0040 | –1·0 | –0·9 | –0·5 | 0·0 |
| **SHILLAY** (Monach Islands) | | | | | | | |
| –0103 | –0043 | –0047 | –0107 | –0·6 | –0·7 | –0·7 | –0·3 |
| **BALIVANICH** (W Benbecula) | | | | | | | |
| –0103 | –0017 | –0031 | –0045 | –0·7 | –0·6 | –0·5 | –0·2 |

**SHELTER** Good. A small marina, max LOA 12m, at the N end of the Inner Hbr, beyond the LB berth, has depths 1·4–3·3m. Or AB for larger boats on adjacent Cromwell St Quay, close S; or lie

alongside FVs in the inner hbr. Visitors should report to HM. Ullapool ferries use the new No 3 pier and commercial vessels on Nos 1 and 2 Piers. S'ly swells can make anchoring uncomfortable. Much of the hbr is foul with old wire hawsers. ‡s as on chartlet at: Poll nam Portan on the W side of inner chan, opposite No 1 Pier; Glumaig Hbr is best ‡, but oil works may preclude this; in bay NW of Coul Island (Eilean na Gobhail).

**NAVIGATION** WPT 58°09'·98N 06°20'·87W, 343°/2·3M to Oc WRG lt. Reef Rk, N of Arnish Pt on W side of ent, is marked by PHM buoy, QR. At the E side of ent an unlit G bn marks the Beasts of Holm, a rky patch off Holm Pt, on which is a conspic memorial. A local magnetic anomaly exists over a small area in mid-hbr, 1·75ca N of Seid Rks PHM bn.

**LIGHTS AND MARKS** Arnish sheds are conspic 3ca SW of Arnish Pt lt, W sector 302°-013° covers ent. Then in turn follow W sectors of: Sandwick Bay lt, (close E of water tr, 3 power stn chys and fuel tanks; all conspic); then Stoney Field astern, Fl WRG 3s, across hbr; and finally No 1 Pier, Q WRG.

**R/T** VHF Ch 12 16 (H24).

**TELEPHONE** (Code 01851) HM 702688, ✆ 705714; MRCC 702013; ☎ 703626; Marinecall 09068 969654; Police 702222; Dr 703145.

**FACILITIES Marina** 27 berths, inc 8 ❷, £9.40 via HM Ch 12; FW. **Nos 1 & 2 Piers** FW, C (10 ton), CH, AB, Slip, P. **No3 Pier** AB(E side), FW, C (Mobile10+ ton), D(road tanker) **Services:** ACA, ME, EI, ✕. **Town** P (cans), D, EI, ▨, ▣, R, Bar, Gas, ✉, ⓑ, ⇌ (ferry to Ullapool, bus to Garve), ✈.

**HARBOURS AND ANCHORAGES ON THE EAST SIDE OF THE OUTER HEBRIDES, from N to S:**

*Visitor moorings mentioned in this section are inspected annually, have pick up buoys, can take yachts <15tons, and there is no charge <7days. Refer to www.w-isles.gov.uk/harbour master.*

**LOCH SHELL**, Lewis, **57°59'·98N 06°25'·07W**. AC 1794. HW –0437 on Dover; ML 2·7m. See 1.5. Pass S of Eilean Iuvard; beware rks to W of Is. ‡ in Tob Eishken, 2½M up loch on N shore (beware rk awash on E side of ent), or at head of loch (exposed to E winds; dries some distance). **Facilities:** ⊠/Stores at Lemreway.

**SHIANT ISLANDS**, Lewis, **57°53'·68N 06°21'·37W**. AC 1794, 1795. Tides as Loch Shell 1.5. Beware strong tidal streams and overfalls in Sound of Shiant. Strictly a fair weather ‡ ; in W winds ‡ E of Mol Mor, isthmus between Garbh Eileen (160m) and Eileen an Tighe. In E winds ‡ W of Mol Mor. No lights or facilities.

**EAST LOCH TARBERT**, Harris, **57°49'·98N 06°41'·07W**. AC 2905. HW –0446 on Dover; ML 3·0m; Duration 0605. See 1.5. Appr via Sound of Scalpay; beware Elliot Rk (2m) 2½ca SSW of Rubha Crago. A bridge (20m clearance) at 57°52'·80N 06°41'·73W joins Scalpay to Harris. Bridge lts: Centre Oc 6s; N side Iso G 4s 35m; S side Iso R 4s 35m. Eilean Glas lt ho at E end of Scalpay, Fl (3) 20s 43m 23M; W tr, R bands. In Sound of Scalpay, stream sets W from HW +3, and E from HW –3. ‡ off Tarbert WSW of steamer pier in about 2·5m. ☎ (01589) 502444. Facilities: Bar, D, Dr, FW, P, ⊠, R, 🛒, ferry to Uig. Alternatively Scalpay N Hbr gives good shelter. Beware rk 5ca off Aird an Aiseig, E side of ent. SHM buoy marks wk off Coddem; 5ca E of the buoy is a rk, depth 1·1m. Ldg Lt Oc WRG 6s 10m 5M. Both piers have 2FG (vert) lts; ‡ 7ca N, in about 3m. **Facilities:** FW at pier, ⊠, 🛒, ferry to Harris.

**Sound of Harris, 57°43'N 06°58'W**. Passages through this difficult Sound are detailed in the *W Coast of Scotland Pilot*. The Stanton and Outer Stromay Chans off the Harris shore are the most feasible for yachts. AC 2642 shows the newly marked ferry routes from Leverburgh to Berneray. Be aware of the following;

• Unusual orientation of this chart – not North-up.
• The charted notes regarding navigation in the Cope Passage, Stanton and Leverburgh Channels and the direction of buoyage – Sound of Harris Ferry Route.

**Loch Rodel**, Harris. AC 2642. 3 🛥s at 57°44'·2N 06°57'·4W in Poll an Tigh-mhàil; enter from SW past jetties. No lts.

**LOCH MADDY**, North Uist, **57°35'·98N 07°06'·07W**. AC 2825. HW –0500 on Dover. See 1.5. With strong wind against tide there can be bad seas off ent. Appr clear, but from S beware submerged rk ½ca N of Leacnam Madadh. Lts: Weaver's Pt Fl 3s 21m 7M; Glas Eilean Mor Fl (2) G 4s 8m 5M; Rubna Nam Pleac Fl R 4s 7m 5M. Inside loch: Ruigh Liath QG 6m 5M; Vallaquie Is Dir Fl (3) WRG 8s. Ferry pier ldg lts 298°: front 2FG(vert) 4M; rear Oc G 8s 10m 4M, vis 284°-304°. 2 🛥s Bagh Aird nam Madadh; 2 🛥s W of and 4 🛥s SW of ferry pier ☎ (01870) 602425; 2 🛥s E of Oronsay. ‡s: clear S of ferry pier; NE of Vallaquie Is; Charles Hbr; Oronsay (‡ not advised due to moorings), tidal berth on private pier; Sponish Hbr; Loch Portain. VHF Ch 12 16. Port Manager ☎ (01876) 5003337 (day), 5003226 (night). **Facilities:** Lochmaddy, Shop, ⒷⒷ, Gas, ⊠, P, D, FW; Loch Portain ⊠, Shop.

**LOCH EPORT**, North Uist, **57°33'·45N 07°08'·12W**. AC 2825, but not the head of loch. Tides, approx as L Maddy; 3kn sp stream. On the S side of ent are rks, some drying. The ent proper is clean but very narrow (about 100m) for 5ca, then widens. Follow the charted clearing line 082°. Best ‡s are: Bàgh a' Bhiorain (S of chan; line up cairn and Bu boulder on 129°); and Acairseid Lee (N bank) E or W of Deer Is. 🛒, R, Bar, ⊠ at Clachan, hd of loch.

**KALLIN**, Grimsay. 57°28'·9N 07°12'·2W. AC 2904. 1 🛥 in NE of hbr. 3 chan lt buoys and 2 FR (vert) on hbr bkwtr. ☎ (01870) 602425.

**LOCH CARNAN**, South Uist, **57°22'·03N 07°16'·39W**. AC 2825. Tides, see 1.5. SWM buoy, L Fl 10s, at 57°22'·30N 07°11'·57W is almost 2M E of app chan proper, marked by Nos 1 and 2 buoys, Fl G 2·5s and Fl R 2s, at 57°22'·45N 07°14'·90W. Round No 3 PHM buoy, Fl R 5s, between Gasay and Taigh Iamain, then pick up ldg lts 222° to Sandwick Quay; front Fl R 2s, rear Iso R 10s, both 5M, W ◊s on posts. Power stn and 2 chys are conspic close to SE of quay. ☎ (01870) 602425 for permission to berth on the quay (MoD property). There is ‡ or 2 🛥s about 2ca WNW of the quay in deep water. ☎ (01870) 610238. The passage S of Gasay is unmarked and needs careful pilotage. FW, D available.

**LOCH SKIPPORT**, South Uist, **57°19'·98N 07°13'·67W**. AC 2904, 2825. HW –0602 on Dover; see 1.5. Easy ent 3M NNE of Hecla (604m). No lights, but 2¼M SSE is Usinish lt ho Fl WR 20s 54m 19/15M. ‡s at: Wizard Pool in 7m; beware Float Rk, dries 2·3m; on N side of Caolas Mor in 7m; Bagh Charmaig in 5m. Linne Arm has narrow ent, many fish farms and poor holding. No facilities.

**LOCH EYNORT**, South Uist, **57°13'·13N 07°16'·87W**. AC 2825. Tides: interpolate between Lochs Skipport and Boisdale, see 1.5. ‡s in the outer loch at Cearcdal Bay and on the N side just before the narrows are exposed to the E. The passage to Upper L Eynort is very narrow and streams reach 5-7kn; best not attempted unless local fishermen offer guidance. Good ‡ inside at Bàgh Lathach.

**LOCH BOISDALE**, South Uist, **57°08'·78N 07°16'·07W**. AC 2770. HW –0455 on Dover; ML 2·4m; Duration 0600. See 1.5. Good shelter except in SE gales when swell runs right up the 2M loch. From N, appr between Rubha na Cruibe and Calvay Is; ldg line 245°: Hollisgeir (0·3m) on with pier (ru). From S beware Clan Ewan Rk, dries 1·2m, and McKenzie Rk (2·4m), marked by PHM lt buoy Fl (3) R 15s. Chan to Boisdale Hbr lies N of Gasay Is; beware rks off E end. ‡ off pier in approx 4m, or SW of Gasay Is in approx 9m. 4 🛥s NE of pier ☎ (01870) 602425. There are fish cages W of Rubha Bhuailt. Lts: E end of Calvay Is Fl (2) WRG 10s 16m 7/4M. Gasay Is Fl WR 5s 10m 7/4M. N side of loch, opp Gasay Is, Fl G 6s. Ro-Ro terminal Iso RG 4s 8m 2M; and close SE, Fl (2) R 5s. See 1.3. ☎ (0187) 700288. **Facilities:** Bar, FW (on pier), P, ⊠, R, ferry to mainland.

**ACAIRSEID MHÓR**, Eriskay, ⊕ **57°03'·78N 07°16'·35W**. AC 2770. Tides approx as for North Bay (Barra), see 1.5. Ben Scrien (183m) is conspic, pointed peak N of hbr. Ldg lts 285°, both Oc R 6s 9/10m 4M, W △ ▽ on orange posts, lead for 0·5M from the above lat/long between two drying rks into the outer loch. A SHM buoy, Fl G 6s, marks a rk drying 3m. 3 🛥s are at 57°03'·95N 07°17'·40W on S side of inner loch, opp pier, 2 FG (vert). ☎ (01870) 602425. 🛒, R, Bar, ⊠ at Haun, 1·5M at N end of island.

**NORTH BAY**, Barra, **57°00'·11N 07°24'·67W**. AC 2770. Tides see 1.5. Well marked approach to inlet sheltered from S and W winds. WPT 56°58'·68N 07°20'·31W is about 200m NE of Curachan ECM buoy, Q (3) 10s, and in the white sector (304°-306°) of Ardveenish dir ☆ 305°, Oc WRG 3s, 2·5M to the WNW. ‡ 1ca WNW of Black Island or in N part of Bay Hirivagh where there are 🛥s; or tempy AB on the quay in 4·5m. FW, Bar, 🛒, bus to Castlebay.

**CASTLEBAY**, Barra, **56°56'·78N 07°29'·67W**. AC 2769. HW –0525 on Dover; ML 2·3m; Duration 0600. See 1.5. Very good shelter & holding. Best ‡ in approx 8m NW of Kiessimul Castle (on an island); NE of castle are rks. 8 🛥s lie to W of pier ☎ (01870) 602425. Or ‡ in Vatersay Bay in approx 9m. W end of Vatersay Sound is closed by a causeway. Beware rks NNW of Sgeir Dubh a conspic W/G tr, Q(3)G 6s 6m 5M, which leads 283° in transit with Sgeir Liath bn. Chan Rk, 2ca to the S, is marked by Fl WR 6s 4m 6/4M. Close-in ldg lts 295°, both FBu 6M on W framework trs: front 9m Or △ on Rubha Glas; rear, 457m from front, 15m Or ▽, vis: 15° and 8° respectively either side of ldg line. ☎ (01871) 810306. **Facilities:** Bar, D, FW, P, ⊠, R, 🛒, Ferry to mainland.

## STORNOWAY  LAT 58°12'N  LONG 6°23'W
### TIMES AND HEIGHTS OF HIGH AND LOW WATERS

TIME ZONE (UT)
For Summer Time add ONE hour in non-shaded areas

Dates in red are SPRINGS
Dates in blue are NEAPS

YEAR 2008

### JANUARY

| Time | m | | Time | m |
|---|---|---|---|---|
| **1** 0105 | 3.5 | | **16** 0011 | 3.7 |
| 0643 | 2.1 | | 0613 | 1.6 |
| TU 1326 | 3.8 | | W 1238 | 4.0 |
| 1941 | 1.9 | | 1854 | 1.4 |
| **2** 0218 | 3.5 | | **17** 0127 | 3.7 |
| 0754 | 2.2 | | 0722 | 1.8 |
| W 1440 | 3.7 | | TH 1352 | 3.9 |
| 2050 | 2.0 | | 2003 | 1.6 |
| **3** 0323 | 3.6 | | **18** 0243 | 3.7 |
| 0911 | 2.2 | | 0847 | 1.8 |
| TH 1547 | 3.6 | | F 1508 | 3.9 |
| 2155 | 1.9 | | 2123 | 1.6 |
| **4** 0416 | 3.8 | | **19** 0354 | 3.9 |
| 1018 | 2.1 | | 1013 | 1.6 |
| F 1641 | 3.7 | | SA 1620 | 4.0 |
| 2248 | 1.8 | | 2238 | 1.5 |
| **5** 0500 | 4.0 | | **20** 0455 | 4.2 |
| 1111 | 1.9 | | 1122 | 1.4 |
| SA 1726 | 3.8 | | SU 1721 | 4.2 |
| 2332 | 1.7 | | 2338 | 1.3 |
| **6** 0538 | 4.1 | | **21** 0547 | 4.5 |
| 1156 | 1.7 | | 1218 | 1.0 |
| SU 1804 | 3.9 | | M 1813 | 4.4 |
| **7** 0012 | 1.5 | | **22** 0028 | 1.1 |
| 0613 | 4.3 | | 0633 | 4.7 |
| M 1236 | 1.5 | | TU 1307 | 0.8 |
| 1839 | 4.0 | | ○ 1858 | 4.5 |
| **8** 0050 | 1.3 | | **23** 0112 | 0.9 |
| 0646 | 4.5 | | 0714 | 4.9 |
| TU 1314 | 1.2 | | W 1351 | 0.6 |
| ● 1912 | 4.1 | | 1939 | 4.6 |
| **9** 0125 | 1.2 | | **24** 0153 | 0.8 |
| 0719 | 4.6 | | 0752 | 5.0 |
| W 1350 | 1.0 | | TH 1430 | 0.5 |
| 1945 | 4.2 | | 2016 | 4.5 |
| **10** 0200 | 1.0 | | **25** 0230 | 0.8 |
| 0752 | 4.7 | | 0829 | 5.0 |
| TH 1426 | 0.9 | | F 1508 | 0.6 |
| 2018 | 4.3 | | 2052 | 4.4 |
| **11** 0234 | 1.0 | | **26** 0307 | 0.9 |
| 0827 | 4.7 | | 0904 | 4.8 |
| F 1502 | 0.8 | | SA 1544 | 0.7 |
| 2052 | 4.2 | | 2127 | 4.2 |
| **12** 0310 | 1.0 | | **27** 0343 | 1.0 |
| 0903 | 4.6 | | 0939 | 4.6 |
| SA 1540 | 0.8 | | SU 1621 | 1.0 |
| 2129 | 4.1 | | 2204 | 4.0 |
| **13** 0347 | 1.1 | | **28** 0420 | 1.3 |
| 0943 | 4.5 | | 1017 | 4.3 |
| SU 1621 | 0.9 | | M 1658 | 1.3 |
| 2211 | 4.0 | | 2245 | 3.8 |
| **14** 0428 | 1.3 | | **29** 0459 | 1.6 |
| 1030 | 4.3 | | 1101 | 3.9 |
| M 1705 | 1.1 | | TU 1739 | 1.6 |
| 2304 | 3.8 | | 2337 | 3.6 |
| **15** 0516 | 1.4 | | **30** 0544 | 1.9 |
| 1129 | 4.2 | | 1157 | 3.6 |
| TU 1756 | 1.2 | | W 1827 | 1.9 |
| ◑ | | | |
| | | | **31** 0049 | 3.4 |
| | | | 0639 | 2.2 |
| | | | TH 1320 | 3.4 |
| | | | 1930 | 2.1 |

### FEBRUARY

| Time | m | | Time | m |
|---|---|---|---|---|
| **1** 0229 | 3.4 | | **16** 0229 | 3.6 |
| 0758 | 2.3 | | 0842 | 1.9 |
| F 1512 | 3.3 | | SA 1508 | 3.6 |
| 2108 | 2.2 | | 2119 | 1.9 |
| **2** 0344 | 3.5 | | **17** 0350 | 3.8 |
| 0948 | 2.2 | | 1022 | 1.6 |
| SA 1622 | 3.4 | | SU 1624 | 3.8 |
| 2225 | 2.0 | | 2241 | 1.6 |
| **3** 0438 | 3.7 | | **18** 0453 | 4.1 |
| 1056 | 2.0 | | 1125 | 1.3 |
| SU 1712 | 3.6 | | M 1721 | 4.0 |
| 2316 | 1.8 | | 2336 | 1.3 |
| **4** 0521 | 4.0 | | **19** 0542 | 4.4 |
| 1143 | 1.7 | | 1214 | 0.9 |
| M 1751 | 3.8 | | TU 1806 | 4.2 |
| 2358 | 1.5 | | |
| **5** 0557 | 4.2 | | **20** 0020 | 1.1 |
| 1222 | 1.4 | | 0622 | 4.7 |
| TU 1825 | 4.0 | | W 1256 | 0.6 |
| | | | 1843 | 4.4 |
| **6** 0034 | 1.3 | | **21** 0059 | 0.8 |
| 0629 | 4.5 | | 0657 | 4.9 |
| W 1258 | 1.0 | | TH 1333 | 0.5 |
| 1855 | 4.2 | | ○ 1917 | 4.5 |
| **7** 0109 | 1.0 | | **22** 0135 | 0.7 |
| 0700 | 4.7 | | 0729 | 5.0 |
| TH 1332 | 0.7 | | F 1407 | 0.4 |
| ● 1925 | 4.4 | | 1948 | 4.5 |
| **8** 0142 | 0.8 | | **23** 0208 | 0.6 |
| 0732 | 4.9 | | 0800 | 4.9 |
| F 1406 | 0.5 | | SA 1439 | 0.5 |
| 1955 | 4.5 | | 2018 | 4.5 |
| **9** 0216 | 0.6 | | **24** 0241 | 0.7 |
| 0804 | 4.9 | | 0829 | 4.8 |
| SA 1440 | 0.4 | | SU 1511 | 0.6 |
| 2026 | 4.5 | | 2047 | 4.4 |
| **10** 0249 | 0.6 | | **25** 0313 | 0.8 |
| 0837 | 4.9 | | 0858 | 4.5 |
| SU 1516 | 0.4 | | M 1542 | 0.9 |
| 2059 | 4.4 | | 2118 | 4.2 |
| **11** 0325 | 0.7 | | **26** 0346 | 1.1 |
| 0914 | 4.8 | | 0930 | 4.2 |
| M 1553 | 0.5 | | TU 1614 | 1.2 |
| 2136 | 4.2 | | 2152 | 3.9 |
| **12** 0403 | 0.9 | | **27** 0421 | 1.4 |
| 0958 | 4.5 | | 1006 | 3.9 |
| TU 1634 | 0.8 | | W 1650 | 1.6 |
| 2221 | 4.0 | | 2235 | 3.7 |
| **13** 0447 | 1.1 | | **28** 0500 | 1.8 |
| 1053 | 4.2 | | 1053 | 3.6 |
| W 1720 | 1.2 | | TH 1731 | 1.9 |
| 2323 | 3.7 | | 2338 | 3.5 |
| **14** 0539 | 1.5 | | **29** 0548 | 2.1 |
| 1209 | 3.9 | | 1210 | 3.3 |
| TH 1816 | 1.5 | | F 1826 | 2.2 |
| ◑ | | | ◑ | |
| **15** 0056 | 3.6 | | | |
| 0650 | 1.8 | | | |
| F 1340 | 3.7 | | | |
| 1931 | 1.8 | | | |

### MARCH

| Time | m | | Time | m |
|---|---|---|---|---|
| **1** 0110 | 3.3 | | **16** 0222 | 3.6 |
| 0655 | 2.3 | | 0854 | 1.8 |
| SA 1431 | 3.2 | | SU 1511 | 3.5 |
| 1959 | 2.4 | | 2122 | 2.0 |
| **2** 0300 | 3.4 | | **17** 0343 | 3.8 |
| 0910 | 2.3 | | 1021 | 1.5 |
| SU 1557 | 3.3 | | M 1623 | 3.7 |
| 2159 | 2.2 | | 2234 | 1.7 |
| **3** 0406 | 3.6 | | **18** 0444 | 4.1 |
| 1035 | 2.0 | | 1115 | 1.2 |
| M 1649 | 3.5 | | TU 1714 | 4.0 |
| 2253 | 1.9 | | 2322 | 1.4 |
| **4** 0452 | 3.9 | | **19** 0528 | 4.4 |
| 1120 | 1.7 | | 1157 | 0.9 |
| TU 1727 | 3.8 | | W 1751 | 4.2 |
| 2334 | 1.6 | | |
| **5** 0530 | 4.2 | | **20** 0001 | 1.1 |
| 1157 | 1.3 | | 0604 | 4.6 |
| W 1759 | 4.1 | | TH 1234 | 0.7 |
| | | | 1822 | 4.4 |
| **6** 0009 | 1.2 | | **21** 0037 | 0.9 |
| 0602 | 4.6 | | 0635 | 4.7 |
| TH 1231 | 0.9 | | F 1307 | 0.5 |
| 1828 | 4.4 | | ○ 1851 | 4.5 |
| **7** 0044 | 0.9 | | **22** 0111 | 0.7 |
| 0634 | 4.9 | | 0703 | 4.8 |
| F 1305 | 0.5 | | SA 1338 | 0.5 |
| ● 1858 | 4.7 | | 1918 | 4.5 |
| **8** 0117 | 0.6 | | **23** 0143 | 0.7 |
| 0706 | 5.1 | | 0730 | 4.7 |
| SA 1339 | 0.3 | | SU 1408 | 0.6 |
| 1929 | 4.8 | | 1945 | 4.5 |
| **9** 0151 | 0.4 | | **24** 0214 | 0.7 |
| 0739 | 5.2 | | 0757 | 4.6 |
| SU 1414 | 0.2 | | M 1437 | 0.7 |
| 2000 | 4.8 | | 2013 | 4.5 |
| **10** 0226 | 0.4 | | **25** 0245 | 0.9 |
| 0814 | 5.1 | | 0825 | 4.4 |
| M 1449 | 0.2 | | TU 1506 | 1.0 |
| 2033 | 4.7 | | 2043 | 4.3 |
| **11** 0303 | 0.5 | | **26** 0317 | 1.1 |
| 0852 | 4.9 | | 0856 | 4.1 |
| TU 1527 | 0.5 | | W 1537 | 1.2 |
| 2110 | 4.5 | | 2116 | 4.1 |
| **12** 0342 | 0.7 | | **27** 0350 | 1.4 |
| 0938 | 4.6 | | 0931 | 3.8 |
| W 1607 | 0.8 | | TH 1611 | 1.6 |
| 2155 | 4.2 | | 2157 | 3.8 |
| **13** 0427 | 1.1 | | **28** 0428 | 1.7 |
| 1037 | 4.1 | | 1015 | 3.5 |
| TH 1652 | 1.3 | | F 1650 | 1.9 |
| 2301 | 3.8 | | 2258 | 3.6 |
| **14** 0521 | 1.5 | | **29** 0514 | 2.0 |
| 1205 | 3.7 | | 1137 | 3.3 |
| F 1748 | 1.7 | | SA 1741 | 2.2 |
| | | | ◑ | |
| **15** 0047 | 3.6 | | **30** 0024 | 3.4 |
| 0644 | 1.8 | | 0618 | 2.2 |
| SA 1342 | 3.5 | | SU 1335 | 3.2 |
| 1915 | 2.1 | | 1904 | 2.4 |
| | | | **31** 0157 | 3.4 |
| | | | 0806 | 2.2 |
| | | | M 1515 | 3.3 |
| | | | 2111 | 2.3 |

### APRIL

| Time | m | | Time | m |
|---|---|---|---|---|
| **1** 0316 | 3.6 | | **16** 0421 | 4.1 |
| 0951 | 2.0 | | 1048 | 1.2 |
| TU 1611 | 3.6 | | W 1654 | 3.9 |
| 2214 | 2.0 | | 2254 | 1.5 |
| **2** 0410 | 3.9 | | **17** 0505 | 4.3 |
| 1040 | 1.6 | | 1129 | 1.0 |
| W 1651 | 3.9 | | TH 1728 | 4.1 |
| 2257 | 1.7 | | 2334 | 1.3 |
| **3** 0452 | 4.3 | | **18** 0540 | 4.4 |
| 1119 | 1.2 | | 1204 | 0.9 |
| TH 1725 | 4.2 | | F 1757 | 4.3 |
| 2334 | 1.3 | | |
| **4** 0529 | 4.6 | | **19** 0010 | 1.1 |
| 1156 | 0.8 | | 0609 | 4.5 |
| F 1757 | 4.6 | | SA 1237 | 0.8 |
| | | | 1824 | 4.4 |
| **5** 0011 | 0.9 | | **20** 0044 | 0.9 |
| 0604 | 5.0 | | 0637 | 4.5 |
| SA 1233 | 0.5 | | SU 1308 | 0.8 |
| 1829 | 4.8 | | ○ 1851 | 4.5 |
| **6** 0048 | 0.6 | | **21** 0117 | 0.9 |
| 0639 | 5.2 | | 0704 | 4.5 |
| SU 1309 | 0.3 | | M 1338 | 0.8 |
| ● 1902 | 5.0 | | 1918 | 4.5 |
| **7** 0126 | 0.4 | | **22** 0149 | 0.9 |
| 0716 | 5.2 | | 0732 | 4.4 |
| M 1347 | 0.2 | | TU 1407 | 0.9 |
| 1937 | 5.0 | | 1947 | 4.5 |
| **8** 0204 | 0.4 | | **23** 0221 | 1.0 |
| 0755 | 5.1 | | 0802 | 4.2 |
| TU 1425 | 0.3 | | W 1437 | 1.1 |
| 2014 | 4.9 | | 2019 | 4.3 |
| **9** 0245 | 0.5 | | **24** 0254 | 1.2 |
| 0839 | 4.9 | | 0837 | 4.0 |
| W 1504 | 0.6 | | TH 1509 | 1.3 |
| 2056 | 4.6 | | 2056 | 4.1 |
| **10** 0329 | 0.8 | | **25** 0329 | 1.4 |
| 0931 | 4.5 | | 0916 | 3.8 |
| TH 1546 | 1.0 | | F 1543 | 1.6 |
| 2148 | 4.3 | | 2140 | 3.9 |
| **11** 0418 | 1.1 | | **26** 0408 | 1.6 |
| 1040 | 4.0 | | 1008 | 3.5 |
| F 1634 | 1.5 | | SA 1623 | 1.9 |
| 2307 | 4.0 | | 2239 | 3.7 |
| **12** 0522 | 1.5 | | **27** 0456 | 1.8 |
| 1208 | 3.7 | | 1123 | 3.3 |
| SA 1734 | 1.9 | | SU 1713 | 2.1 |
| ◑ | | | 2352 | 3.6 |
| **13** 0041 | 3.8 | | **28** 0559 | 2.0 |
| 0654 | 1.7 | | 1249 | 3.3 |
| SU 1335 | 3.5 | | M 1828 | 2.3 |
| 1910 | 2.1 | | ◑ | |
| **14** 0206 | 3.8 | | **29** 0106 | 3.6 |
| 0840 | 1.7 | | 0719 | 2.0 |
| M 1459 | 3.6 | | TU 1411 | 3.4 |
| 2058 | 2.1 | | 1959 | 2.3 |
| **15** 0322 | 3.9 | | **30** 0216 | 3.7 |
| 0957 | 1.4 | | 0842 | 1.8 |
| TU 1607 | 3.7 | | W 1517 | 3.6 |
| 2206 | 1.8 | | 2114 | 2.0 |

Chart Datum: 2·71 metres below Ordnance Datum (Newlyn). HAT is 5·5 metres above Chart Datum.

FREE monthly updates from
www.reedsalmanac.co.uk

**TIME ZONE (UT)**
For Summer Time add ONE hour in **non-shaded areas**

## STORNOWAY  LAT 58°12'N  LONG 6°23'W
### TIMES AND HEIGHTS OF HIGH AND LOW WATERS

Dates in red are SPRINGS
Dates in blue are NEAPS

YEAR **2008**

NW Scotland

### MAY

| Day | Time m | | Day | Time m | |
|---|---|---|---|---|---|
| **1** TH | 0317 4.0 / 0945 1.5 / 1606 3.9 / 2207 1.7 | | **16** F | 0433 4.1 / 1052 1.3 / 1659 3.9 / 2301 1.5 | |
| **2** F | 0408 4.3 / 1034 1.2 / 1646 4.2 / 2253 1.4 | | **17** SA | 0512 4.1 / 1131 1.2 / 1730 4.1 / 2341 1.4 | |
| **3** SA | 0452 4.6 / 1117 0.9 / 1724 4.5 / 2336 1.1 | | **18** SU | 0546 4.2 / 1207 1.1 / 1800 4.2 | |
| **4** SU | 0534 4.9 / 1159 0.6 / 1801 4.8 | | **19** M | 0018 1.3 / 0617 4.2 / 1241 1.1 / 1829 4.4 | |
| **5** M | 0019 0.8 / 0615 5.0 / 1242 0.5 / ● 1839 4.9 | | **20** TU | 0055 1.2 / 0647 4.2 / 1313 1.1 / ○ 1859 4.4 | |
| **6** TU | 0104 0.6 / 0659 5.1 / 1323 0.5 / 1919 5.0 | | **21** W | 0129 1.2 / 0719 4.1 / 1345 1.1 / 1931 4.4 | |
| **7** W | 0148 0.6 / 0745 5.0 / 1405 0.6 / 2003 4.9 | | **22** TH | 0204 1.2 / 0753 4.0 / 1417 1.2 / 2007 4.3 | |
| **8** TH | 0235 0.6 / 0835 4.7 / 1448 0.8 / 2052 4.7 | | **23** F | 0239 1.2 / 0831 3.9 / 1451 1.3 / 2045 4.2 | |
| **9** F | 0325 0.8 / 0933 4.4 / 1534 1.1 / 2151 4.5 | | **24** SA | 0317 1.3 / 0913 3.8 / 1527 1.5 / 2129 4.1 | |
| **10** SA | 0420 1.1 / 1040 4.1 / 1625 1.5 / 2303 4.2 | | **25** SU | 0358 1.5 / 1002 3.6 / 1607 1.7 / 2220 3.9 | |
| **11** SU | 0525 1.3 / 1154 3.8 / 1727 1.8 | | **26** M | 0444 1.6 / 1101 3.5 / 1655 1.9 / 2319 3.8 | |
| **12** M | 0019 4.1 / 0640 1.5 / 1309 3.6 / ◐ 1846 2.1 | | **27** TU | 0538 1.6 / 1207 3.4 / 1755 2.0 | |
| **13** TU | 0133 4.0 / 0759 1.6 / 1425 3.6 / 2011 2.1 | | **28** W | 0021 3.8 / 0640 1.6 / 1313 3.5 / ◐ 1904 2.0 | |
| **14** W | 0244 4.0 / 0911 1.5 / 1532 3.6 / 2122 1.9 | | **29** TH | 0124 3.9 / 0744 1.6 / 1417 3.6 / 2012 1.9 | |
| **15** TH | 0345 4.0 / 1008 1.4 / 1621 3.8 / 2216 1.7 | | **30** F | 0224 4.0 / 0848 1.4 / 1515 3.8 / 2115 1.7 | |
| | | | **31** SA | 0322 4.2 / 0947 1.2 / 1606 4.1 / 2212 1.5 | |

### JUNE

| Day | Time m | | Day | Time m | |
|---|---|---|---|---|---|
| **1** SU | 0417 4.4 / 1040 1.0 / 1653 4.4 / 2305 1.2 | | **16** M | 0528 3.8 / 1141 1.5 / 1741 4.1 / 2359 1.5 | |
| **2** M | 0508 4.6 / 1131 0.9 / 1738 4.6 / 2358 1.0 | | **17** TU | 0606 3.9 / 1220 1.4 / 1815 4.2 | |
| **3** TU | 0559 4.7 / 1220 0.8 / 1823 4.8 / ● | | **18** W | 0039 1.4 / 0640 3.9 / 1256 1.3 / ○ 1848 4.3 | |
| **4** W | 0050 0.8 / 0649 4.8 / 1308 0.7 / 1909 4.9 | | **19** TH | 0117 1.3 / 0715 4.0 / 1331 1.2 / 1921 4.4 | |
| **5** TH | 0142 0.7 / 0741 4.7 / 1354 0.8 / 1957 4.9 | | **20** F | 0153 1.2 / 0749 4.0 / 1405 1.2 / 1956 4.4 | |
| **6** F | 0233 0.7 / 0833 4.6 / 1440 0.9 / 2047 4.8 | | **21** SA | 0229 1.1 / 0825 3.9 / 1439 1.2 / 2032 4.3 | |
| **7** SA | 0324 0.7 / 0927 4.4 / 1526 1.1 / 2141 4.7 | | **22** SU | 0306 1.1 / 0902 3.9 / 1514 1.3 / 2110 4.2 | |
| **8** SU | 0416 0.9 / 1023 4.2 / 1615 1.4 / 2240 4.5 | | **23** M | 0344 1.1 / 0942 3.8 / 1551 1.4 / 2151 4.1 | |
| **9** M | 0510 1.1 / 1122 3.9 / 1708 1.6 / 2342 4.2 | | **24** TU | 0425 1.2 / 1027 3.7 / 1632 1.5 / 2239 4.0 | |
| **10** TU | 0607 1.3 / 1225 3.7 / 1808 1.8 / ◐ | | **25** W | 0510 1.2 / 1120 3.6 / 1721 1.7 / 2335 4.0 | |
| **11** W | 0048 4.0 / 0708 1.5 / 1334 3.6 / 1914 2.0 | | **26** TH | 0601 1.3 / 1220 3.6 / 1817 1.7 / ◑ | |
| **12** TH | 0156 3.9 / 0813 1.6 / 1442 3.5 / 2026 2.0 | | **27** F | 0036 3.9 / 0657 1.4 / 1324 3.6 / 1920 1.8 | |
| **13** F | 0301 3.8 / 0916 1.6 / 1541 3.6 / 2132 1.9 | | **28** SA | 0140 4.0 / 0759 1.4 / 1429 3.7 / 2030 1.7 | |
| **14** SA | 0359 3.8 / 1011 1.6 / 1627 3.8 / 2227 1.8 | | **29** SU | 0246 4.0 / 0905 1.4 / 1532 3.9 / 2141 1.6 | |
| **15** SU | 0447 3.8 / 1059 1.5 / 1706 3.9 / 2316 1.7 | | **30** M | 0352 4.1 / 1012 1.3 / 1630 4.2 / 2248 1.4 | |

### JULY

| Day | Time m | | Day | Time m | |
|---|---|---|---|---|---|
| **1** TU | 0454 4.3 / 1113 1.2 / 1724 4.4 / 2350 1.1 | | **16** W | 0557 3.7 / 1204 1.5 / 1802 4.2 | |
| **2** W | 0552 4.4 / 1209 1.0 / 1814 4.7 | | **17** TH | 0028 1.5 / 0632 3.9 / 1243 1.3 / 1835 4.3 | |
| **3** TH | 0046 0.9 / 0645 4.6 / 1300 0.9 / ● 1902 4.9 | | **18** F | 0105 1.2 / 0705 4.0 / 1317 1.2 / ○ 1907 4.5 | |
| **4** F | 0139 0.6 / 0735 4.6 / 1347 0.8 / 1948 5.0 | | **19** SA | 0139 1.0 / 0736 4.1 / 1350 1.1 / 1938 4.5 | |
| **5** SA | 0226 0.5 / 0822 4.6 / 1431 0.8 / 2033 5.0 | | **20** SU | 0212 0.9 / 0807 4.2 / 1422 1.0 / 2010 4.6 | |
| **6** SU | 0312 0.5 / 0907 4.5 / 1513 0.9 / 2117 4.8 | | **21** M | 0246 0.8 / 0838 4.2 / 1455 1.0 / 2043 4.5 | |
| **7** M | 0356 0.6 / 0952 4.3 / 1555 1.1 / 2203 4.6 | | **22** TU | 0321 0.7 / 0912 4.1 / 1529 1.0 / 2118 4.4 | |
| **8** TU | 0440 0.9 / 1039 4.0 / 1638 1.4 / 2253 4.3 | | **23** W | 0358 0.8 / 0948 4.0 / 1606 1.2 / 2159 4.3 | |
| **9** W | 0525 1.2 / 1131 3.8 / 1725 1.6 / 2351 4.0 | | **24** TH | 0438 0.9 / 1033 3.9 / 1648 1.3 / 2250 4.1 | |
| **10** TH | 0614 1.5 / 1233 3.6 / 1817 1.9 / ◐ | | **25** F | 0524 1.1 / 1130 3.7 / 1737 1.5 / ◑ 2356 4.0 | |
| **11** F | 0059 3.8 / 0709 1.7 / 1345 3.5 / 1921 2.1 | | **26** SA | 0616 1.3 / 1241 3.6 / 1839 1.7 | |
| **12** SA | 0215 3.6 / 0816 1.9 / 1456 3.5 / 2042 2.1 | | **27** SU | 0110 3.8 / 0718 1.5 / 1358 3.7 / 1958 1.8 | |
| **13** SU | 0327 3.5 / 0930 1.9 / 1556 3.6 / 2200 2.0 | | **28** M | 0229 3.8 / 0836 1.6 / 1514 3.8 / 2133 1.7 | |
| **14** M | 0427 3.5 / 1031 1.9 / 1645 3.8 / 2259 1.9 | | **29** TU | 0346 3.9 / 1002 1.6 / 1622 4.1 / 2251 1.4 | |
| **15** TU | 0516 3.6 / 1121 1.7 / 1726 4.0 / 2347 1.7 | | **30** W | 0454 4.1 / 1111 1.4 / 1719 4.4 / 2351 1.1 | |
| | | | **31** TH | 0550 4.3 / 1205 1.1 / 1808 4.7 | |

### AUGUST

| Day | Time m | | Day | Time m | |
|---|---|---|---|---|---|
| **1** F | 0042 0.8 / 0638 4.5 / 1252 0.9 / ● 1851 4.9 | | **16** SA | 0044 1.1 / 0642 4.2 / 1256 1.1 / ○ 1844 4.7 | |
| **2** SA | 0128 0.5 / 0721 4.6 / 1334 0.8 / 1931 5.1 | | **17** SU | 0115 0.9 / 0711 4.4 / 1327 0.9 / 1913 4.8 | |
| **3** SU | 0210 0.4 / 0800 4.6 / 1414 0.7 / 2009 5.1 | | **18** M | 0146 0.6 / 0740 4.5 / 1358 0.8 / 1943 4.9 | |
| **4** M | 0248 0.4 / 0837 4.6 / 1451 0.8 / 2045 4.9 | | **19** TU | 0219 0.5 / 0809 4.5 / 1430 0.7 / 2014 4.9 | |
| **5** TU | 0326 0.5 / 0914 4.4 / 1527 0.9 / 2122 4.7 | | **20** W | 0252 0.5 / 0839 4.5 / 1503 0.8 / 2048 4.8 | |
| **6** W | 0403 0.6 / 0952 4.2 / 1604 1.2 / 2201 4.4 | | **21** TH | 0328 0.6 / 0913 4.3 / 1539 0.9 / 2127 4.5 | |
| **7** TH | 0441 1.2 / 1034 3.9 / 1643 1.5 / 2245 4.0 | | **22** F | 0407 0.8 / 0954 4.1 / 1620 1.2 / 2218 4.2 | |
| **8** F | 0521 1.5 / 1125 3.7 / 1727 1.8 / ◐ 2345 3.7 | | **23** SA | 0450 1.1 / 1051 3.9 / 1708 1.5 / ◑ 2331 3.9 | |
| **9** SA | 0607 1.9 / 1238 3.5 / 1821 2.1 | | **24** SU | 0541 1.5 / 1216 3.7 / 1812 1.8 | |
| **10** SU | 0124 3.4 / 0706 2.1 / 1410 3.5 / 1941 2.3 | | **25** M | 0103 3.7 / 0648 1.8 / 1347 3.7 / 1954 1.9 | |
| **11** M | 0259 3.3 / 0847 2.3 / 1525 3.6 / 2141 2.3 | | **26** TU | 0232 3.7 / 0829 2.0 / 1510 3.8 / 2147 1.7 | |
| **12** TU | 0409 3.4 / 1010 2.1 / 1622 3.7 / 2247 2.0 | | **27** W | 0351 3.8 / 1008 1.8 / 1620 4.1 / 2255 1.4 | |
| **13** W | 0501 3.6 / 1103 1.9 / 1706 4.0 / 2333 1.8 | | **28** TH | 0454 4.1 / 1108 1.5 / 1713 4.5 / 2346 1.0 | |
| **14** TH | 0541 3.8 / 1146 1.7 / 1742 4.2 | | **29** F | 0543 4.3 / 1155 1.2 / 1757 4.8 | |
| **15** F | 0010 1.4 / 0613 4.0 / 1223 1.4 / 1814 4.4 | | **30** SA | 0029 0.7 / 0623 4.5 / 1237 0.9 / ● 1834 5.0 | |
| | | | **31** SU | 0109 0.5 / 0659 4.7 / 1314 0.8 / 1908 5.1 | |

Chart Datum: 2·71 metres below Ordnance Datum (Newlyn). HAT is 5·5 metres above Chart Datum.

**TIME ZONE (UT)**
For Summer Time add ONE hour in **non-shaded areas**

## STORNOWAY  LAT 58°12'N  LONG 6°23'W
TIMES AND HEIGHTS OF HIGH AND LOW WATERS

Dates in red are SPRINGS
Dates in blue are NEAPS

YEAR **2008**

### SEPTEMBER

| Time m | Time m |
|---|---|
| **1** 0145 0.4 / 0732 4.7 / M 1350 0.7 / 1941 5.1 | **16** 0115 0.5 / 0710 4.8 / TU 1330 0.7 / 1916 5.2 |
| **2** 0218 0.5 / 0804 4.7 / TU 1424 0.8 / 2012 4.9 | **17** 0149 0.4 / 0740 4.9 / W 1404 0.7 / 1949 5.2 |
| **3** 0251 0.6 / 0835 4.5 / W 1457 0.9 / 2042 4.7 | **18** 0223 0.4 / 0812 4.8 / TH 1439 0.7 / 2025 5.0 |
| **4** 0324 0.9 / 0908 4.3 / TH 1531 1.2 / 2114 4.3 | **19** 0300 0.6 / 0847 4.6 / F 1517 0.9 / 2108 4.7 |
| **5** 0358 1.3 / 0944 4.1 / F 1606 1.5 / 2151 4.0 | **20** 0339 0.9 / 0931 4.3 / SA 1600 1.2 / 2204 4.3 |
| **6** 0433 1.6 / 1029 3.8 / SA 1646 1.9 / 2242 3.6 | **21** 0423 1.3 / 1034 4.0 / SU 1652 1.6 / 2331 3.9 |
| **7** 0515 2.0 / 1136 3.6 / SU 1735 2.2 ◑ | **22** 0517 1.8 / 1034 3.8 / M 1807 1.9 ◑ |
| **8** 0019 3.4 / 0608 2.3 / M 1315 3.5 / 1845 2.5 | **23** 0107 3.7 / 0633 2.1 / TU 1343 3.8 / 2012 2.0 |
| **9** 0227 3.3 / 0746 2.5 / TU 1445 3.6 / 2119 2.4 | **24** 0235 3.7 / 0838 2.2 / W 1505 4.0 / 2148 1.7 |
| **10** 0343 3.4 / 0945 2.4 / W 1549 3.8 / 2227 2.1 | **25** 0350 3.9 / 1001 1.9 / TH 1611 4.3 / 2245 1.3 |
| **11** 0435 3.6 / 1039 2.1 / TH 1636 4.0 / 2307 1.8 | **26** 0446 4.1 / 1054 1.6 / F 1700 4.6 / 2329 1.0 |
| **12** 0513 3.9 / 1119 1.8 / F 1713 4.3 / 2340 1.4 | **27** 0528 4.4 / 1136 1.3 / SA 1740 4.8 |
| **13** 0544 4.2 / 1153 1.5 / SA 1745 4.6 | **28** 0007 0.8 / 0602 4.6 / SU 1214 1.1 / 1813 4.9 |
| **14** 0011 1.1 / 0612 4.4 / SU 1226 1.2 / 1815 4.9 | **29** 0043 0.7 / 0633 4.7 / M 1249 0.9 / ● 1844 5.0 |
| **15** 0043 0.8 / 0641 4.7 / M 1258 0.9 / ○ 1845 5.1 | **30** 0115 0.6 / 0703 4.7 / TU 1323 0.9 / 1913 4.9 |

### OCTOBER

| Time m | Time m |
|---|---|
| **1** 0146 0.7 / 0732 4.7 / W 1356 0.9 / 1941 4.8 | **16** 0120 0.5 / 0715 5.1 / TH 1341 0.7 / 1930 5.2 |
| **2** 0217 0.9 / 0801 4.6 / TH 1428 1.1 / 2009 4.6 | **17** 0158 0.6 / 0751 5.0 / F 1421 0.8 / 2012 5.0 |
| **3** 0248 1.1 / 0832 4.5 / F 1501 1.3 / 2041 4.3 | **18** 0238 0.8 / 0833 4.8 / SA 1504 1.0 / 2102 4.7 |
| **4** 0320 1.4 / 0907 4.3 / SA 1537 1.6 / 2117 4.0 | **19** 0320 1.1 / 0924 4.5 / SU 1552 1.3 / 2208 4.3 |
| **5** 0355 1.7 / 0952 4.0 / SU 1616 1.9 / 2207 3.7 | **20** 0406 1.5 / 1039 4.2 / M 1652 1.6 / 2336 4.0 |
| **6** 0435 2.1 / 1058 3.8 / M 1704 2.2 / ● 2339 3.4 | **21** 0504 1.9 / 1207 4.1 / TU 1817 1.9 ◑ |
| **7** 0528 2.4 / 1223 3.7 / TU 1810 2.4 ◑ | **22** 0100 3.8 / 0629 2.2 / W 1328 4.0 / 2000 1.8 |
| **8** 0136 3.3 / 0650 2.6 / W 1348 3.7 / 2004 2.4 | **23** 0221 3.8 / 0817 2.2 / TH 1445 4.1 / 2123 1.6 |
| **9** 0259 3.5 / 0858 2.5 / TH 1500 3.8 / 2141 2.2 | **24** 0332 3.9 / 0935 2.0 / F 1550 4.3 / 2219 1.4 |
| **10** 0356 3.7 / 0959 2.2 / F 1553 4.1 / 2224 1.8 | **25** 0426 4.1 / 1027 1.7 / SA 1639 4.5 / 2302 1.2 |
| **11** 0435 4.0 / 1040 1.9 / SA 1634 4.4 / 2259 1.5 | **26** 0506 4.3 / 1109 1.5 / SU 1718 4.6 / 2339 1.0 |
| **12** 0508 4.3 / 1115 1.6 / SU 1710 4.7 / 2333 1.1 | **27** 0538 4.5 / 1148 1.3 / M 1751 4.7 |
| **13** 0539 4.6 / 1150 1.3 / M 1744 5.0 | **28** 0013 1.0 / 0608 4.6 / TU 1224 1.2 / ● 1821 4.7 |
| **14** 0008 0.8 / 0609 4.9 / TU 1226 1.0 / ○ 1817 5.2 | **29** 0046 1.0 / 0637 4.7 / W 1258 1.1 / 1849 4.7 |
| **15** 0044 0.6 / 0641 5.0 / W 1302 0.8 / 1852 5.3 | **30** 0117 1.0 / 0705 4.7 / TH 1332 1.1 / 1918 4.6 |
| | **31** 0148 1.1 / 0735 4.7 / F 1406 1.2 / 1948 4.4 |

### NOVEMBER

| Time m | Time m |
|---|---|
| **1** 0220 1.3 / 0808 4.5 / SA 1440 1.4 / 2023 4.2 | **16** 0223 0.9 / 0829 4.9 / SU 1500 0.9 / 2104 4.6 |
| **2** 0253 1.5 / 0846 4.4 / SU 1516 1.6 / 2103 4.0 | **17** 0309 1.2 / 0925 4.7 / M 1553 1.1 / 2208 4.3 |
| **3** 0328 1.7 / 0932 4.2 / M 1556 1.8 / 2156 3.7 | **18** 0358 1.5 / 1032 4.5 / TU 1654 1.4 / 2320 4.1 |
| **4** 0409 2.0 / 1031 4.0 / TU 1644 2.0 / 2311 3.5 | **19** 0456 1.8 / 1145 4.3 / W 1804 1.6 ◑ |
| **5** 0500 2.3 / 1141 3.8 / W 1743 2.2 | **20** 0033 3.9 / 0608 2.1 / TH 1257 4.2 / 1920 1.7 |
| **6** 0033 3.5 / 0609 2.4 / TH 1250 3.8 / ● 1858 2.2 | **21** 0146 3.8 / 0731 2.1 / F 1408 4.2 / 2035 1.6 |
| **7** 0151 3.5 / 0735 2.4 / F 1355 3.9 / 2017 2.1 | **22** 0256 3.8 / 0848 2.1 / SA 1514 4.2 / 2138 1.6 |
| **8** 0256 3.7 / 0852 2.3 / SA 1455 4.1 / 2121 1.8 | **23** 0354 4.0 / 0949 1.9 / SU 1609 4.2 / 2227 1.5 |
| **9** 0345 4.0 / 0946 2.0 / SU 1545 4.3 / 2209 1.5 | **24** 0438 4.1 / 1039 1.7 / M 1654 4.3 / 2309 1.4 |
| **10** 0426 4.3 / 1031 1.7 / M 1630 4.6 / 2252 1.2 | **25** 0514 4.3 / 1122 1.6 / TU 1731 4.3 / 2346 1.3 |
| **11** 0503 4.6 / 1113 1.4 / TU 1711 4.9 / 2333 1.0 | **26** 0546 4.4 / 1202 1.4 / W 1805 4.3 |
| **12** 0540 4.8 / 1156 1.1 / W 1753 5.0 | **27** 0021 1.3 / 0618 4.5 / TH 1240 1.4 / ● 1836 4.3 |
| **13** 0015 0.8 / 0617 5.0 / TH 1240 0.9 / ○ 1835 5.1 | **28** 0056 1.3 / 0649 4.6 / F 1316 1.3 / 1908 4.3 |
| **14** 0057 0.7 / 0657 5.1 / F 1325 0.8 / 1920 5.1 | **29** 0129 1.3 / 0722 4.6 / SA 1352 1.3 / 1941 4.2 |
| **15** 0140 0.8 / 0740 5.1 / SA 1411 0.8 / 2009 4.9 | **30** 0203 1.3 / 0757 4.5 / SU 1428 1.4 / 2017 4.1 |

### DECEMBER

| Time m | Time m |
|---|---|
| **1** 0237 1.4 / 0834 4.4 / M 1504 1.4 / 2057 4.0 | **16** 0302 1.0 / 0914 5.0 / TU 1548 0.8 / 2151 4.4 |
| **2** 0313 1.6 / 0916 4.3 / TU 1544 1.5 / 2142 3.8 | **17** 0349 1.2 / 1008 4.8 / W 1639 1.0 / 2247 4.2 |
| **3** 0352 1.8 / 1003 4.1 / W 1627 1.7 / 2235 3.7 | **18** 0438 1.5 / 1108 4.5 / TH 1733 1.2 / 2349 3.9 |
| **4** 0436 1.9 / 1057 4.0 / TH 1716 1.8 / 2338 3.6 | **19** 0533 1.7 / 1212 4.3 / F 1831 1.5 ◑ |
| **5** 0531 2.1 / 1156 3.9 / F 1812 1.8 ◑ | **20** 0056 3.7 / 0636 2.0 / SA 1321 4.1 / 1934 1.7 |
| **6** 0043 3.6 / 0633 2.2 / SA 1255 3.9 / 1913 1.8 | **21** 0207 3.7 / 0747 2.1 / SU 1431 3.9 / 2043 1.8 |
| **7** 0147 3.7 / 0740 2.1 / SU 1355 4.0 / 2016 1.7 | **22** 0313 3.7 / 0902 2.1 / M 1536 3.9 / 2147 1.8 |
| **8** 0247 3.9 / 0846 2.0 / M 1454 4.2 / 2117 1.6 | **23** 0408 3.8 / 1008 1.9 / TU 1631 3.9 / 2240 1.7 |
| **9** 0340 4.1 / 0946 1.8 / TU 1551 4.4 / 2213 1.4 | **24** 0452 4.0 / 1102 1.8 / W 1717 3.9 / 2324 1.6 |
| **10** 0429 4.4 / 1041 1.5 / W 1644 4.6 / 2305 1.2 | **25** 0531 4.2 / 1148 1.6 / TH 1756 4.0 |
| **11** 0515 4.6 / 1135 1.3 / TH 1736 4.7 / 2354 1.0 | **26** 0005 1.5 / 0606 4.3 / F 1230 1.5 / 1831 4.0 |
| **12** 0601 4.8 / 1227 1.0 / F 1827 4.8 ○ | **27** 0043 1.3 / 0640 4.5 / SA 1308 1.3 / ● 1904 4.1 |
| **13** 0042 0.9 / 0648 5.0 / SA 1319 0.8 / 1917 4.9 | **28** 0118 1.2 / 0714 4.5 / SU 1344 1.2 / 1936 4.1 |
| **14** 0130 0.9 / 0735 5.1 / SU 1409 0.7 / 2007 4.8 | **29** 0152 1.2 / 0746 4.6 / M 1418 1.1 / 2008 4.1 |
| **15** 0216 0.9 / 0824 5.1 / M 1458 0.7 / 2058 4.7 | **30** 0225 1.2 / 0820 4.5 / TU 1452 1.1 / 2041 4.1 |
| | **31** 0259 1.2 / 0854 4.4 / W 1527 1.1 / 2116 4.0 |

Chart Datum: 2·71 metres below Ordnance Datum (Newlyn). HAT is 5·5 metres above Chart Datum.

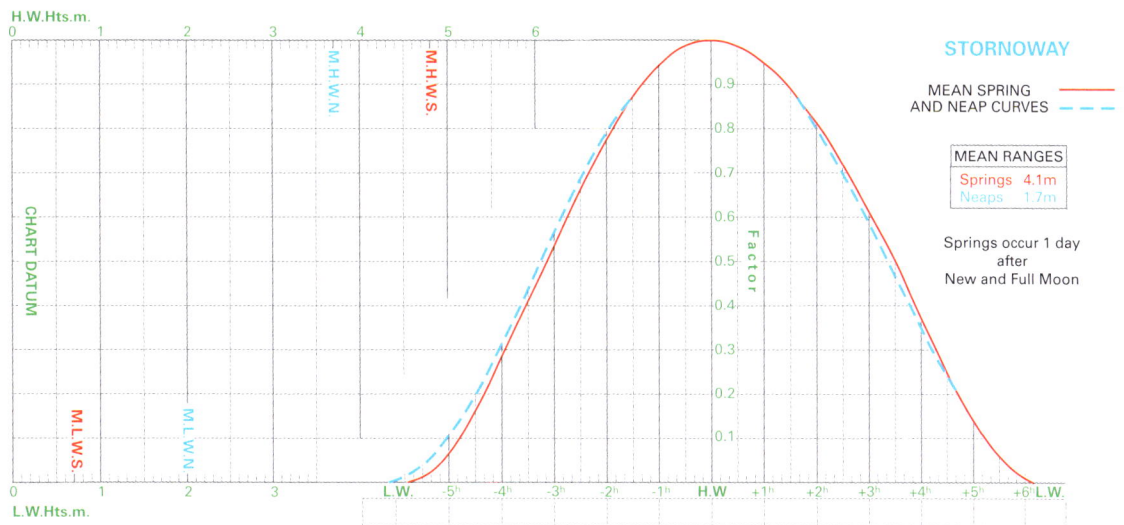

## ISLANDS WEST OF THE OUTER HEBRIDES (N to S)

### TIDES

Standard Port STORNOWAY (←—)

| Times | | | | Height (metres) | | | |
|---|---|---|---|---|---|---|---|
| High Water | | Low Water | | MHWS | MHWN | MLWN | MLWS |
| 0100 | 0700 | 0300 | 0900 | 4·8 | 3·7 | 2·0 | 0·7 |
| 1300 | 1900 | 1500 | 2100 | | | | |
| Differences FLANNAN ISLES | | | | | | | |
| −0026 | −0016 | −0016 | −0026 | −0·9 | −0·7 | −0·6 | −0·2 |
| VILLAGE BAY (St Kilda) | | | | | | | |
| −0040 | −0040 | −0045 | −0045 | −1·4 | −1·2 | −0·8 | −0·3 |
| ROCKALL | | | | | | | |
| −0055 | −0055 | −0105 | −0105 | −1·8 | −1·5 | −0·9 | −0·2 |

**FLANNAN ISLES,** Western Isles, centred on **58°17´·28N 07°35´·27W** (Eilean Mór). AC 2524, 2721. Tides, as above. Uninhabited group of several rky islets, 18M WNW of Gallan Head (Lewis). The main islet is Eilean Mór where landing can be made on SW side in suitable conditions. Lt ho, Fl (2) 30s 101m 20M, is a 23m high W tr on NE tip of Eilean Mór; the lt is obscured by islets to the W which are up to 57m high. No recommended ⚓s and the few charted depths are by lead-line surveys.

**ST KILDA,** Western Isles, 57°48´·28N 08°33´·07W. AC 2721, 2524. Tides at Village Bay, Hirta: HW −0510 on Dover; ML 1·9m; Duration 0615; see above. A group of four isles and three stacks, the main island is Hirta from which the Army withdrew in April 1998 after 30 years. The facility is now manned by a civilian company, Qinetiq ☎ (01870) 604443, based at South Uist. Hirta is owned by National Trust for Scotland and leased to Scottish National Heritage who employ a Seasonal Warden, ☎ 01870 604628. ⚓ in Village Bay, SE-facing, in approx 5m about 1·5ca off the pier. Ldg lts 270°, both Oc 5s 26/38m 3M. If wind is between NE and SSW big swells enter the bay; good holding, but untenable if winds strong. Levenish Is (55m) is 1·5M E of Hirta with offlying rks. Call *Kilda Radio* VHF Ch 16 **12** 73 (HJ) for permission to land; ☎ (01870) 604406 (HO), 604612 (OT); 🖂 604601. Alternative ⚓ at Glen Bay on N side is only safe in S & E winds. Facilities: FW from wells near landings.

**ROCKALL,** 57°35´·7N 13°41´·2W. AC 1128, 2524. Tides, as above. A 19m high granite rock, 200M W of N Uist. Best access by helicopter. Lt, Fl 15s 13M, is often extinguished for long periods due to weather damage. Helen's Reef, 1·4m, on which the sea breaks is 2M ENE.

**MONACH ISLANDS** (Heisker Is) centred on 57°31´·28N 07°38´·07W. AC 2721, 2722. Tides, see 1.5 Shillay. The group lies 5M SW of N Uist and 8M WNW of Benbecula. The 5 main islands (W-E) are Shillay, Ceann Iar, Shivinish, Ceann Ear and Stockay; all uninhabited. Many rky offliers from NW through N to SE of the group. On Shillay there is a conspic, disused, red brick lt ho. ⚓s at: E of disused lt ho; Croic Hbr, bay N of Shivinish; and S Hbr on W side of Shivinish.

## 1.6 KINLOCHBERVIE

Highland **58°27´·26N 05°02´·78W** ✿✿✿⚓⚓☆☆

CHARTS AC 1954, 1785, 2503; Imray C67; OS 9

TIDES −0400 Dover; ML 2·7; Duration 0610

Standard Port ULLAPOOL (—→)

| Times | | | | Height (metres) | | | |
|---|---|---|---|---|---|---|---|
| High Water | | Low Water | | MHWS | MHWN | MLWN | MLWS |
| 0000 | 0600 | 0300 | 0900 | 5·2 | 3·9 | 2·1 | 0·7 |
| 1200 | 1800 | 1500 | 2100 | | | | |
| Differences LOCH BERVIE | | | | | | | |
| +0020 | +0010 | +0010 | +0020 | −0·4 | −0·3 | −0·2 | 0·1 |
| LOCH LAXFORD | | | | | | | |
| +0015 | +0015 | +0005 | +0005 | −0·3 | −0·4 | −0·2 | 0·0 |
| BADCALL BAY | | | | | | | |
| +0005 | +0005 | +0005 | +0005 | −0·7 | −0·5 | −0·5 | +0·2 |
| LOCH NEDD | | | | | | | |
| 0000 | 0000 | 0000 | 0000 | −0·3 | −0·2 | −0·2 | 0·0 |
| LOCH INVER | | | | | | | |
| −0005 | −0005 | −0005 | −0005 | −0·2 | 0·0 | 0·0 | +0·1 |

SHELTER Very good in Kinlochbervie Hbr off the N shore of Loch Inchard. A useful passage port, only 14.5 track miles S of Cape Wrath. It is an active FV port, but yachts AB in NNE corner on 18m long pontoon in 4m on SW side only; NE side is shoal/foul. If full, ⚓ at Loch Clash, open to W; landing jetty in 2·7m. Other ⚓s at: Camus Blair on S shore, 5ca SW of hbr ent, and up the loch at L Sheigra, Achriesgill Bay and 5ca short of the head of the loch.

NAVIGATION WPT 58°27´·34N 05°05´·08W (at mouth of Loch Inchard), 100°/1·3M to hbr ent. The sides of the loch are clean, but keep to N side of Loch Inchard to clear Bodha Ceann na Saile NCM and rk (3m depth) almost in mid-chan.

LIGHTS AND MARKS From offshore in good vis Ceann Garbh, a conspic mountain 899m (6M inland), leads 110° toward ent of Loch Inchard. Rubha na Leacaig, Fl (2) 10s 30m 8M, marks N side of loch ent. Dir ✫ WRG (H24) 15m 16M, Y framework tr (floodlit) leads 327° into hbr; see 1.3 for its sectors. The 25m wide ent chan (and hbr) is dredged 4m and marked by 2 PHM poles, Fl R 4s and QR, and by a SHM pole, Fl G 4s. On S shore of loch Creag Mhòr, Dir Oc lt WRG 2.8s 16m 9M, is aligned 147°/327° with hbr ent chan; see 1.3.

R/T VHF Ch **14** 16 HX. Ch 06 is used by FVs in the Minches.

TELEPHONE (Code 01971) HM ☎ 521235, 🖂 521718, mob 07787 151446; MRCC (01851) 702013; ⊖ (0141) 887 9369 (H24); Marinecall 09068 969654; Police 521222; Dr 502002.

FACILITIES AB(pontoon) £1.50<10m for 48hrs, FW, D at FV quay, P (cans), Gas, CH, ME, 🖂, Bar, 🍽, R, Showers (Mission & Hbr Office), ♿. In summer, bus to Inverness.

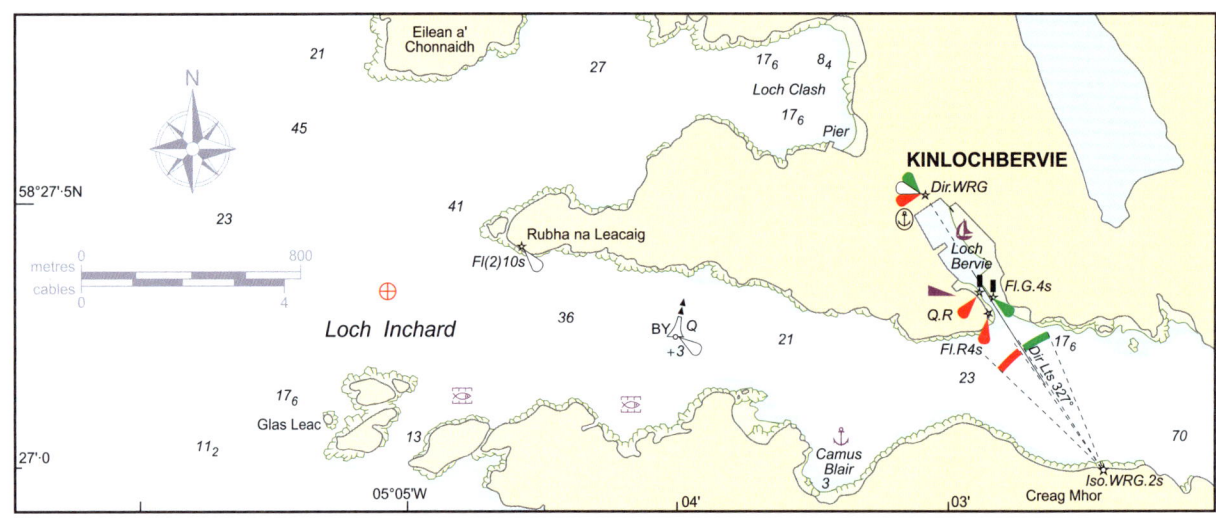

## ⚓ & HBR BETWEEN KINLOCHBERVIE AND ULLAPOOL

**LOCH LAXFORD** Highland, **58°24′·78N 05°07′·18W.** AC 2503. HW –0410 on Dover. ML 2·7m. See 1.6. Ent between Rubha Ruadh and Ardmore Pt, 1M ENE, clearly identified by 3 isolated mountains (N-S) Ceann Garbh, Ben Arkle and Ben Stack. The many ⚓s in the loch include: Loch a'Chadh-fi, on N/NE sides of islet (John Ridgeway's Adventure School on Pt on W side of narrows has moorings); Bagh nah-Airde Beag, next bay to E, (beware rk 5ca off SE shore which covers at MHWS); Weaver's Bay on SW shore, 3M from ent (beware drying rk off NW Pt of ent); Bagh na Fionndalach Mor on SW shore (4-6m); Fanagmore Bay on SW shore (beware head of bay foul with old moorings). Beware many fish farming cages. Facilities: none, nearest stores at Scourie (5M).

**LOCH INVER** Highland, **58°08′·98N 05°15′·08W.** AC 2504. HW –0433 on Dover; ML 3·0m. See 1.6. Good shelter in all weathers at head of loch in busy fishing hbr on S side. Appr N or S of Soyea Is, Fl (2) 10s 34m 6M; beware rock drying 1·7m about 50m off Kirkaig Point (S side of ent). Glas Leac, a small islet 7ca WSW of hbr, may be passed on either side. Its ☆, Fl WRG 3s, has 3 WRG sectors (see 1.3) covering the chans N and S of Soyea Is and into the hbr. The church, hotel (S side) and white ho (N side) are all conspic. A pontoon for yachts, <12m LOA, is in 5m between the bkwtr (QG) and the first FV pier. Or, in W'ly gales, ⚓ in the lee of bkwtr in about 8m; or where HM directs. Other ⚓s on S shore of Loch Inver. VHF Ch 09 16. HM ☎ (01571) 844265. **Facilities:** FW, P, D, ▣, ▦, ✉, Gas.

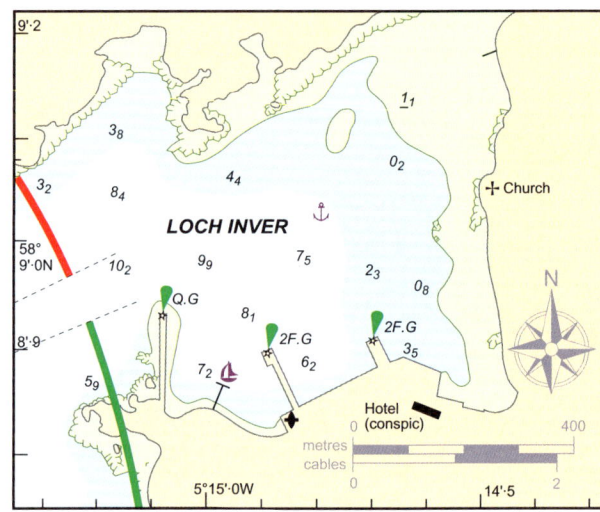

## 1.7 ULLAPOOL

Highland **57°53′·70N 05°09′·38W** ✿✿✿⚓⚓✿✿

**CHARTS** AC 1794, 2500, 2501, 2509; Imray C67; OS 19

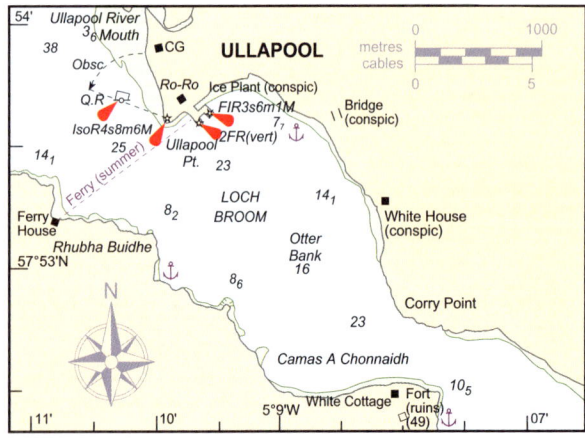

**TIDES** –0415 Dover; ML 3·0; Duration 0610

**Standard Port ULLAPOOL (→)**

| Times | | | | Height (metres) | | | |
|---|---|---|---|---|---|---|---|
| High Water | | Low Water | | MHWS | MHWN | MLWN | MLWS |
| 0000 | 0600 | 0300 | 0900 | 5·2 | 3·9 | 2·1 | 0·7 |
| 1200 | 1800 | 1500 | 2100 | | | | |
| Differences SUMMER ISLES (Tanera Mor) | | | | | | | |
| –0005 | –0005 | –0010 | –0010 | –0·1 | +0·1 | 0·0 | +0·1 |
| LOCH EWE (Mellon Charles, 57°51′N 05°38′W) | | | | | | | |
| –0010 | –0010 | –0010 | –0010 | –0·1 | –0·1 | –0·1 | 0·0 |
| LOCH GAIRLOCH | | | | | | | |
| –0020 | –0020 | –0010 | –0010 | 0·0 | +0·1 | –0·3 | –0·1 |

**SHELTER** Good in ⚓ E of pier. A commercial port and may be congested. Visiting yachts are welcome but consult HM for berth. Loch Kanaird (N of ent to Loch Broom) has good ⚓ E of Isle Martin. Possible ⚓s 6ca S of Ullapool Pt, and beyond the narrows 3ca ESE of W cottage. The upper loch is squally in strong winds.

**NAVIGATION** WPT L Broom ent 57°55′·78N 05°15′·08W, 129°/3.5M to Ullapool Pt lt. N of Ullapool Pt extensive drying flats off the mouth of Ullapool R are marked by QR buoy. Beware fish pens and unlit buoys SE of narrows off W shore.

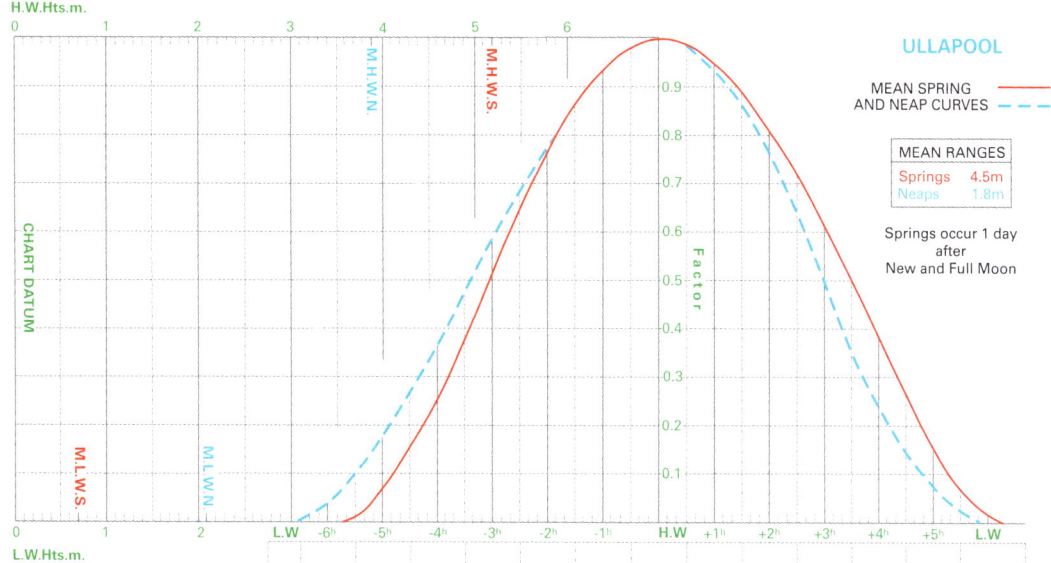

ULLAPOOL

MEAN SPRING AND NEAP CURVES

| MEAN RANGES | |
|---|---|
| Springs | 4.5m |
| Neaps | 1.8m |

Springs occur 1 day after New and Full Moon

**LIGHTS AND MARKS** Rhubha Cadail, N of L. Broom ent, Fl WRG 6s 11m 9/6M. Cailleach Hd, W of ent, Fl (2) 12s 60m 9M. Ullapool Pt Iso R 4s 8m 6M; grey mast, vis 258°-108°.

**R/T** VHF Ch 14 16 12 H24 (at Pier).

**TELEPHONE** (Code 01854) HM 612091/612724, ✆ 612678; CG (non-emergency) 613076; ⊖ (0141) 887 9369; Marinecall 09068 969654; Police 612017; Dr 612015; Dentist 613289 or 612660.

**FACILITIES Pier** AB or M - consult HM, D, FW, CH; **Loch Broom SC Services:** Gas, ME & GRP repairs Mobile Marine Services ✆ 633719, mob 07866 516067, El, Ⓔ, El, Ⓔ, ✕A.Morgan ✆ 666383; **Town** D & P (cans 0700-2100), @ at Captains Cabin, Library and Ceilidh Place Hotel, all domestic facilities, showers at swimming pool, 🛒, R, Bar, 🚍 (bus to Garve). Daily buses to Inverness (✈), ferries three times a day (summer) to Stornoway. No Sunday bus services.

**ADJACENT ANCHORAGES**

**LOCH KANAIRD, 57°56′60′N 05°12′20′W.** AC 2500. HW –0425 Dover; See 1.7; streams are weak and irreg. Situated E of the entrance to Loch Broom, S of the Summer Is and protected by Isle Martin. Good ⚓'s (strong tripping line recommended) ENE of Sgeir Mhor (rock 1m high) or E of Isle Martin in the bight N of Rubha Beag, as suitable for wind direction. Beware cables and marine farms. Ent from S (1ca wide) between two rocky spits, leading line E extremity of Isle Martin in transit with dark streak on cliff behind brg 000°. Ent from N, deep and clear of dangers. Facilities: Ardmair Boat Centre ✆ P.Fraser (01854) 612054, M, FW, showers, some repairs. Isle Martin, Landing permitted (voluntary donation to Trust, ✆ (01854) 612531).

**SUMMER ISLES, 58°01′N 05°25′W.** AC 2509, 2501. HW –0425 Dover; See 1.7; streams are weak and irregular. In the N apps to Loch Broom some 30 islands and rks, the main ones being Eilean Mullagrach, Isle Ristol, Glas-leac Mor, Tanera Beg, Eilean a' Char, Eilean Fada Mor. Beware rocks at S end of Horse Sound. ⚓s:

**Isle Ristol,** ⚓ to S of drying causeway and clear of moorings; beware landings frequented by local FVs. Close to slip is lt Fl G 3s. Facilities: 🛒 (at Polbain 2M).

**Tanera Beg,** ⚓ in the chan to the E inside Eilean Fada Mor.

**Tanera Mor,** on E side, ⚓ in bay to N off pier or in W corner off stone jetty ; beware many moorings and fish pens. Also poss ⚓ close NW of Is and close E of Eilean na Saille, but N of drying rock. Facilities: ✆ (01854) 622272 B Wilder for M, showers, FW, Tea Room.

**Badentarbat Bay,** Temp'y ⚓ NW part of bay ESE of pier which is busy with marina farm activity. Beware N part of bay is shoal. Suitable for Achiltibuie or Polbain on mainland. Facilities: 🛒, R, Gas, FW, D (emerg) ✆ (01854) 622261.

**LITTLE LOCH BROOM, 57°54′·98N 05°24′·68W.** AC 2500. HW –0415 Dover as per Ullapool, see 1.7; streams are weak (approx 1kn).

Between Loch Broom and Gruinard Bay, entered S of Cailleach Hd it is deep (115m in centre) and shoreline steep to. In approaches beware of Ardross Rk (depth 0.6m). 0.38M ENE of Stattic Pt.

**Camusnagaul,** on S side of loch 1.6M from head and Dundonnel Hotel, ⚓ to E of hamlet.

**Scoraig,** inside narrows on N shore in N'ly conditions, ⚓ off jetty clear of submarine cables and marine farm. ✕C.Dawson ✆ 01845 613380.

**⚓s BETWEEN LITTLE LOCH BROOM AND LOCH GAIRLOCH**

**LOCH EWE, 57°52′·0N 05°40′·0W** (SWM buoy, L Fl 10s). AC 2509, 3146. Tides: See 1.7; HW –0415 on Dover; ML 2·9m; Duration 0610. Shelter in all winds. Easy ent with no dangers in loch. Rhubha Reidh lt, Fl (4) 15s 37m 24M, W tr, is 4·5M W of ent. No 1 buoy Fl (3) G 10s. Loch approx 7M long with Isle Ewe and 2 small islets about 2M from ent in centre; can be passed on either side. Temp ⚓ in bay of Isle Ewe. Beware unlit buoy A2 between E side Isle Ewe & Aultbea Pier, 2 FG (vert). NATO fuelling jetty and dolphins, all Fl G 4s.

**Loch Thurnaig,** 1.7M SSE of Isle of Ewe, sheltered ⚓ off Ob na Bà Rùaidhe, SE of pier to W of drying reef. Beware of numerous marine farms in approaches.

**Aultbea:** ⚓ off Aultbea Hotel on E shore or in NW'lies close of pier. N part of bay is shoal. Facilities: Dr, P, ✉, R, 🛒, Bar.

**Poolewe Bay** ⚓ in SW part of bay in 3·5m, at head of loch: Boor Rks(3m) with drying rocks extending 1ca NW lie off W shore about 9ca NW of Poolewe. Facilities: FW, D, L on pier, P (at garage), ✉, R, Bar, 🛒, Gas.

**Inverewe Gdns** on NE side of bay, ⚓ to SW of Jetty at Port na Cloiche Gile.

**LOCH GAIRLOCH, 57°43′N 05°45′W.** AC 228, 2528. HW –0440 on Dover. See 1.7. A wide loch facing W. Ent clear of dangers but Submarine Exercise Area (see 1.21) to S of Longa Is. Quite heavy seas enter in bad weather. Lts: Glas Eilean Fl WRG 6s 9m 6/4M, Gairloch Pier Hd, QR 9m.

**Badachro,** good shelter SW of Eilean Horrisdale on SW side of loch but busy with FVs and local craft. Also ⚓'ge to NNW of Sgeir Dhubh Bheag SSE of Eilean Horrisdale, passage to S of this island is possible with caution. R, Bar, (Bad Inn HM ✆ (01445) 741255 for M availability.

**Loch Shieldaig,** at SE end of the loch with many moorings for local craft, if congested ⚓ to SSW of Eilean an t-Sabhail. Beware marine farms.

**Flowerdale Bay,** ⚓ in approx 6m near Gairloch pier or berth on pontoons (2m depth N side, 3m S side) at pier. HM ✆ (01445) 712140. VHF Ch 16 (occas). Gairloch Pier: AB fees charged. P (cans), D, FW, SC, Hotel, Bar, Showers, Gas, 🛒, CH, ✉.

**TIME ZONE (UT)**
For Summer Time add ONE hour in **non-shaded areas**

**ULLAPOOL**   LAT 57°54'N   LONG 5°10'W
TIMES AND HEIGHTS OF HIGH AND LOW WATERS

Dates in red are SPRINGS
Dates in blue are NEAPS

YEAR **2008**

## JANUARY

| Time | m | | Time | m |
|---|---|---|---|---|
| **1** 0110 | 4.0 | | **16** 0016 | 4.3 |
| 0653 | 2.3 | | 0620 | 1.9 |
| TU 1329 | 4.1 | | W 1240 | 4.5 |
| 1944 | 2.2 | | 1856 | 1.8 |
| **2** 0219 | 3.9 | | **17** 0131 | 4.2 |
| 0802 | 2.5 | | 0732 | 2.1 |
| W 1443 | 4.0 | | TH 1357 | 4.4 |
| 2054 | 2.2 | | 2010 | 1.9 |
| **3** 0326 | 4.0 | | **18** 0249 | 4.2 |
| 0919 | 2.5 | | 0858 | 2.1 |
| TH 1550 | 4.0 | | F 1517 | 4.4 |
| 2202 | 2.2 | | 2133 | 2.0 |
| **4** 0422 | 4.2 | | **19** 0404 | 4.4 |
| 1027 | 2.3 | | 1021 | 1.9 |
| F 1646 | 4.1 | | SA 1633 | 4.5 |
| 2257 | 2.1 | | 2247 | 1.8 |
| **5** 0508 | 4.4 | | **20** 0506 | 4.7 |
| 1119 | 2.1 | | 1128 | 1.6 |
| SA 1731 | 4.3 | | SU 1735 | 4.7 |
| 2341 | 1.9 | | 2347 | 1.6 |
| **6** 0546 | 4.6 | | **21** 0557 | 5.0 |
| 1203 | 1.9 | | 1224 | 1.3 |
| SU 1810 | 4.4 | | M 1826 | 5.0 |
| **7** 0021 | 1.8 | | **22** 0036 | 1.3 |
| 0621 | 4.8 | | 0640 | 5.3 |
| M 1243 | 1.7 | | TU 1313 | 1.0 |
| 1845 | 4.6 | | ○ 1909 | 5.1 |
| **8** 0057 | 1.6 | | **23** 0121 | 1.1 |
| 0654 | 5.0 | | 0720 | 5.4 |
| TU 1320 | 1.5 | | W 1357 | 0.8 |
| ● 1918 | 4.7 | | 1950 | 5.2 |
| **9** 0133 | 1.5 | | **24** 0202 | 1.0 |
| 0726 | 5.1 | | 0758 | 5.5 |
| W 1356 | 1.3 | | TH 1437 | 0.7 |
| 1950 | 4.8 | | 2027 | 5.1 |
| **10** 0207 | 1.4 | | **25** 0241 | 1.0 |
| 0759 | 5.2 | | 0835 | 5.4 |
| TH 1431 | 1.2 | | F 1515 | 0.8 |
| 2024 | 4.8 | | 2103 | 5.0 |
| **11** 0242 | 1.3 | | **26** 0318 | 1.1 |
| 0834 | 5.2 | | 0910 | 5.2 |
| F 1507 | 1.1 | | SA 1552 | 0.9 |
| 2059 | 4.8 | | 2139 | 4.8 |
| **12** 0318 | 1.3 | | **27** 0354 | 1.3 |
| 0911 | 5.2 | | 0944 | 5.0 |
| SA 1545 | 1.1 | | SU 1627 | 1.2 |
| 2138 | 4.7 | | 2215 | 4.5 |
| **13** 0356 | 1.4 | | **28** 0430 | 1.5 |
| 0951 | 5.1 | | 1019 | 4.6 |
| SU 1625 | 1.2 | | M 1703 | 1.5 |
| 2221 | 4.6 | | 2256 | 4.3 |
| **14** 0437 | 1.5 | | **29** 0508 | 1.8 |
| 1037 | 4.9 | | 1059 | 4.3 |
| M 1708 | 1.3 | | TU 1742 | 1.8 |
| 2313 | 4.4 | | 2348 | 4.0 |
| **15** 0524 | 1.7 | | **30** 0551 | 2.1 |
| 1132 | 4.7 | | 1154 | 4.0 |
| TU 1758 | 1.5 | | W 1829 | 2.2 |
| ◑ | | | ◗ | |
| | | | **31** 0101 | 3.8 |
| | | | 0645 | 2.4 |
| | | | TH 1326 | 3.8 |
| | | | 1933 | 2.4 |

## FEBRUARY

| Time | m | | Time | m |
|---|---|---|---|---|
| **1** 0227 | 3.8 | | **16** 0232 | 4.0 |
| 0808 | 2.6 | | 0847 | 2.2 |
| F 1505 | 3.7 | | SA 1518 | 4.1 |
| 2111 | 2.5 | | 2127 | 2.2 |
| **2** 0346 | 3.9 | | **17** 0401 | 4.2 |
| 0954 | 2.5 | | 1027 | 1.9 |
| SA 1624 | 3.8 | | SU 1638 | 4.3 |
| 2233 | 2.4 | | 2249 | 2.0 |
| **3** 0445 | 4.1 | | **18** 0504 | 4.5 |
| 1103 | 2.3 | | 1131 | 1.5 |
| SU 1718 | 4.1 | | M 1735 | 4.6 |
| 2325 | 2.1 | | 2344 | 1.6 |
| **4** 0528 | 4.4 | | **19** 0551 | 4.9 |
| 1149 | 2.0 | | 1220 | 1.2 |
| M 1758 | 4.3 | | TU 1818 | 4.8 |
| **5** 0006 | 1.8 | | **20** 0029 | 1.3 |
| 0604 | 4.7 | | 0629 | 5.2 |
| TU 1229 | 1.6 | | W 1302 | 0.8 |
| 1830 | 4.5 | | 1854 | 5.0 |
| **6** 0043 | 1.5 | | **21** 0108 | 1.0 |
| 0636 | 5.0 | | 0704 | 5.3 |
| W 1304 | 1.3 | | TH 1340 | 0.6 |
| 1900 | 4.8 | | ○ 1928 | 5.1 |
| **7** 0117 | 1.3 | | **22** 0144 | 0.8 |
| 0707 | 5.2 | | 0736 | 5.4 |
| TH 1339 | 1.0 | | F 1415 | 0.6 |
| ● 1931 | 5.0 | | 1959 | 5.1 |
| **8** 0151 | 1.1 | | **23** 0218 | 0.8 |
| 0739 | 5.4 | | 0807 | 5.3 |
| F 1413 | 0.8 | | SA 1447 | 0.6 |
| 2002 | 5.1 | | 2029 | 5.0 |
| **9** 0225 | 0.9 | | **24** 0251 | 0.9 |
| 0812 | 5.5 | | 0836 | 5.2 |
| SA 1447 | 0.7 | | SU 1518 | 0.8 |
| 2035 | 5.1 | | 2059 | 4.9 |
| **10** 0259 | 0.9 | | **25** 0323 | 1.0 |
| 0847 | 5.4 | | 0905 | 4.9 |
| SU 1523 | 0.7 | | M 1549 | 1.0 |
| 2111 | 5.0 | | 2129 | 4.6 |
| **11** 0335 | 0.9 | | **26** 0355 | 1.3 |
| 0925 | 5.3 | | 0935 | 4.6 |
| M 1559 | 0.8 | | TU 1620 | 1.4 |
| 2150 | 4.8 | | 2202 | 4.4 |
| **12** 0414 | 1.1 | | **27** 0428 | 1.6 |
| 1009 | 5.1 | | 1008 | 4.3 |
| TU 1639 | 1.0 | | W 1653 | 1.7 |
| 2236 | 4.6 | | 2241 | 4.1 |
| **13** 0457 | 1.4 | | **28** 0505 | 1.9 |
| 1101 | 4.7 | | 1049 | 4.0 |
| W 1724 | 1.4 | | TH 1730 | 2.1 |
| 2335 | 4.3 | | 2340 | 3.8 |
| **14** 0549 | 1.8 | | **29** 0551 | 2.3 |
| 1212 | 4.4 | | 1203 | 3.7 |
| TH 1820 | 1.8 | | F 1821 | 2.4 |
| ◑ | | | ◐ | |
| **15** 0058 | 4.1 | | | |
| 0701 | 2.1 | | | |
| F 1343 | 4.1 | | | |
| 1938 | 2.2 | | | |

## MARCH

| Time | m | | Time | m |
|---|---|---|---|---|
| **1** 0122 | 3.7 | | **16** 0225 | 4.0 |
| 0700 | 2.5 | | 0854 | 2.1 |
| SA 1414 | 3.5 | | SU 1520 | 3.9 |
| 2003 | 2.6 | | 2128 | 2.3 |
| **2** 0258 | 3.7 | | **17** 0352 | 4.1 |
| 0914 | 2.6 | | 1024 | 1.8 |
| SU 1554 | 3.6 | | M 1633 | 4.2 |
| 2208 | 2.5 | | 2241 | 1.9 |
| **3** 0411 | 3.9 | | **18** 0452 | 4.4 |
| 1040 | 2.2 | | 1119 | 1.4 |
| M 1653 | 3.9 | | TU 1722 | 4.5 |
| 2303 | 2.2 | | 2330 | 1.6 |
| **4** 0459 | 4.2 | | **19** 0535 | 4.7 |
| 1126 | 1.9 | | 1202 | 1.0 |
| TU 1732 | 4.2 | | W 1800 | 4.7 |
| 2343 | 1.8 | | | |
| **5** 0536 | 4.6 | | **20** 0010 | 1.2 |
| 1203 | 1.4 | | 0609 | 5.0 |
| W 1803 | 4.5 | | TH 1240 | 0.8 |
| | | | 1831 | 4.9 |
| **6** 0018 | 1.4 | | **21** 0047 | 1.0 |
| 0608 | 4.9 | | 0641 | 5.1 |
| TH 1238 | 1.0 | | F 1314 | 0.6 |
| 1833 | 4.8 | | ○ 1901 | 5.0 |
| **7** 0052 | 1.0 | | **22** 0120 | 0.8 |
| 0639 | 5.2 | | 0710 | 5.2 |
| F 1312 | 0.7 | | SA 1346 | 0.6 |
| ● 1903 | 5.1 | | 1929 | 5.0 |
| **8** 0126 | 0.7 | | **23** 0152 | 0.8 |
| 0711 | 5.5 | | 0738 | 5.1 |
| SA 1347 | 0.4 | | SU 1416 | 0.7 |
| 1935 | 5.2 | | 1956 | 5.0 |
| **9** 0201 | 0.6 | | **24** 0223 | 0.8 |
| 0746 | 5.6 | | 0805 | 5.0 |
| SU 1421 | 0.3 | | M 1445 | 0.8 |
| 2008 | 5.3 | | 2024 | 4.9 |
| **10** 0236 | 0.5 | | **25** 0253 | 1.0 |
| 0822 | 5.5 | | 0834 | 4.8 |
| M 1457 | 0.4 | | TU 1513 | 1.0 |
| 2044 | 5.2 | | 2053 | 4.7 |
| **11** 0313 | 0.6 | | **26** 0324 | 1.2 |
| 0903 | 5.3 | | 0904 | 4.5 |
| TU 1534 | 0.6 | | W 1543 | 1.3 |
| 2124 | 4.9 | | 2124 | 4.4 |
| **12** 0353 | 0.9 | | **27** 0357 | 1.5 |
| 0949 | 5.0 | | 0937 | 4.2 |
| W 1614 | 1.0 | | TH 1614 | 1.7 |
| 2210 | 4.6 | | 2201 | 4.2 |
| **13** 0437 | 1.3 | | **28** 0433 | 1.8 |
| 1047 | 4.6 | | 1020 | 3.9 |
| TH 1659 | 1.4 | | F 1650 | 2.0 |
| 2311 | 4.3 | | 2253 | 3.9 |
| **14** 0532 | 1.7 | | **29** 0517 | 2.1 |
| 1209 | 4.1 | | 1113 | 3.6 |
| F 1756 | 1.9 | | SA 1736 | 2.3 |
| ◑ | | | ◐ | |
| **15** 0044 | 4.0 | | **30** 0026 | 3.7 |
| 0652 | 2.1 | | 0620 | 2.4 |
| SA 1345 | 3.9 | | SU 1328 | 3.5 |
| 1925 | 2.3 | | 1900 | 2.6 |
| | | | **31** 0203 | 3.7 |
| | | | 0816 | 2.4 |
| | | | M 1503 | 3.5 |
| | | | 2121 | 2.5 |

## APRIL

| Time | m | | Time | m |
|---|---|---|---|---|
| **1** 0320 | 3.8 | | **16** 0427 | 4.3 |
| 0954 | 2.1 | | 1051 | 1.3 |
| TU 1610 | 3.8 | | W 1657 | 4.3 |
| 2224 | 2.1 | | 2302 | 1.6 |
| **2** 0415 | 4.1 | | **17** 0509 | 4.5 |
| 1045 | 1.7 | | 1133 | 1.1 |
| W 1653 | 4.1 | | TH 1733 | 4.5 |
| 2307 | 1.7 | | 2343 | 1.3 |
| **3** 0456 | 4.5 | | **18** 0544 | 4.7 |
| 1126 | 1.3 | | 1210 | 0.9 |
| TH 1728 | 4.5 | | F 1804 | 4.7 |
| 2344 | 1.3 | | | |
| **4** 0532 | 4.9 | | **19** 0019 | 1.1 |
| 1203 | 0.9 | | 0615 | 4.8 |
| F 1800 | 4.8 | | SA 1244 | 0.8 |
| | | | 1833 | 4.8 |
| **5** 0020 | 0.9 | | **20** 0054 | 1.0 |
| 0607 | 5.2 | | 0644 | 4.8 |
| SA 1240 | 0.5 | | SU 1316 | 0.8 |
| 1832 | 5.1 | | ○ 1901 | 4.9 |
| **6** 0057 | 0.6 | | **21** 0126 | 0.9 |
| 0643 | 5.4 | | 0712 | 4.8 |
| SU 1317 | 0.3 | | M 1345 | 0.9 |
| ● 1907 | 5.3 | | 1929 | 4.9 |
| **7** 0135 | 0.4 | | **22** 0157 | 1.0 |
| 0721 | 5.5 | | 0741 | 4.7 |
| M 1354 | 0.2 | | TU 1415 | 1.0 |
| 1943 | 5.3 | | 1957 | 4.8 |
| **8** 0213 | 0.4 | | **23** 0228 | 1.1 |
| 0802 | 5.4 | | 0812 | 4.6 |
| TU 1433 | 0.3 | | W 1444 | 1.2 |
| 2022 | 5.2 | | 2028 | 4.6 |
| **9** 0254 | 0.5 | | **24** 0300 | 1.2 |
| 0848 | 5.2 | | 0845 | 4.4 |
| W 1513 | 0.6 | | TH 1515 | 1.4 |
| 2105 | 5.0 | | 2101 | 4.5 |
| **10** 0338 | 0.8 | | **25** 0335 | 1.4 |
| 0942 | 4.8 | | 0924 | 4.1 |
| TH 1555 | 1.1 | | F 1548 | 1.7 |
| 2157 | 4.6 | | 2141 | 4.3 |
| **11** 0428 | 1.2 | | **26** 0413 | 1.7 |
| 1051 | 4.4 | | 1013 | 3.9 |
| F 1644 | 1.5 | | SA 1625 | 1.9 |
| 2308 | 4.3 | | 2234 | 4.0 |
| **12** 0530 | 1.6 | | **27** 0458 | 1.9 |
| 1214 | 4.0 | | 1121 | 3.7 |
| SA 1747 | 2.0 | | SU 1713 | 2.2 |
| ◑ | | | 2349 | 3.8 |
| **13** 0039 | 4.1 | | **28** 0558 | 2.1 |
| 0657 | 1.9 | | 1246 | 3.6 |
| SU 1340 | 3.9 | | M 1826 | 2.4 |
| 1921 | 2.3 | | ◑ | |
| **14** 0210 | 4.0 | | **29** 0112 | 3.8 |
| 0842 | 1.8 | | 0723 | 2.1 |
| M 1504 | 3.9 | | TU 1405 | 3.6 |
| 2105 | 2.2 | | 2011 | 2.3 |
| **15** 0329 | 4.1 | | **30** 0223 | 3.9 |
| 0959 | 1.6 | | 0850 | 1.9 |
| TU 1610 | 4.1 | | W 1513 | 3.8 |
| 2213 | 1.9 | | 2128 | 2.0 |

Chart Datum: 2·75 metres below Ordnance Datum (Newlyn). HAT is 5·9 metres above Chart Datum.

»» FREE monthly updates from ««
www.reedsalmanac.co.uk

**TIME ZONE (UT)**
For Summer Time add ONE hour in **non-shaded areas**

## ULLAPOOL  LAT 57°54'N  LONG 5°10'W
TIMES AND HEIGHTS OF HIGH AND LOW WATERS

Dates in red are SPRINGS
Dates in blue are NEAPS

YEAR **2008**

**NW Scotland**

### MAY

| Day | Time m | Day | Time m |
|---|---|---|---|
| **1** TH | 0322 4.1 / 0952 1.6 / 1605 4.1 / 2220 1.7 | **16** F | 0438 4.3 / 1057 1.3 / 1702 4.3 / 2310 1.5 |
| **2** F | 0411 4.4 / 1041 1.2 / 1648 4.4 / 2304 1.3 | **17** SA | 0517 4.4 / 1137 1.2 / 1737 4.5 / 2351 1.4 |
| **3** SA | 0454 4.8 / 1124 0.9 / 1726 4.8 / 2347 1.0 | **18** SU | 0551 4.4 / 1213 1.2 / 1809 4.6 |
| **4** SU | 0536 5.1 / 1206 0.6 / 1804 5.1 | **19** M | 0028 1.3 / 0623 4.5 / 1248 1.1 / 1839 4.7 |
| **5** M | 0029 0.7 / 0618 5.3 / 1249 0.4 / ● 1843 5.2 | **20** TU | 0103 1.2 / 0655 4.5 / 1320 1.2 / ○ 1909 4.7 |
| **6** TU | 0112 0.5 / 0702 5.3 / 1331 0.4 / 1924 5.3 | **21** W | 0137 1.2 / 0728 4.5 / 1352 1.2 / 1940 4.7 |
| **7** W | 0156 0.5 / 0751 5.2 / 1413 0.5 / 2008 5.2 | **22** TH | 0210 1.2 / 0802 4.4 / 1424 1.3 / 2013 4.6 |
| **8** TH | 0242 0.6 / 0844 5.0 / 1458 0.8 / 2057 5.0 | **23** F | 0245 1.3 / 0839 4.3 / 1457 1.5 / 2049 4.5 |
| **9** F | 0332 0.8 / 0945 4.7 / 1545 1.2 / 2155 4.7 | **24** SA | 0321 1.4 / 0919 4.2 / 1532 1.6 / 2131 4.4 |
| **10** SA | 0426 1.1 / 1053 4.4 / 1638 1.5 / 2305 4.4 | **25** SU | 0401 1.5 / 1006 4.0 / 1611 1.8 / 2219 4.2 |
| **11** SU | 0530 1.4 / 1204 4.1 / 1741 1.9 | **26** M | 0445 1.6 / 1100 3.9 / 1658 1.9 / 2318 4.1 |
| **12** M | 0021 4.2 / 0644 1.6 / 1316 4.0 / ◑ 1858 2.1 | **27** TU | 0538 1.7 / 1205 3.8 / 1758 2.1 |
| **13** TU | 0139 4.1 / 0804 1.7 / 1429 3.9 / 2020 2.0 | **28** W | 0023 4.0 / 0640 1.8 / 1313 3.8 / ◑ 1911 2.1 |
| **14** W | 0252 4.1 / 0914 1.6 / 1532 4.0 / 2129 1.9 | **29** TH | 0130 4.1 / 0749 1.7 / 1418 3.9 / 2025 2.0 |
| **15** TH | 0351 4.2 / 1010 1.5 / 1622 4.2 / 2224 1.7 | **30** F | 0231 4.2 / 0855 1.5 / 1517 4.1 / 2129 1.7 |
| | | **31** SA | 0327 4.4 / 0955 1.3 / 1609 4.4 / 2225 1.5 |

### JUNE

| Day | Time m | Day | Time m |
|---|---|---|---|
| **1** SU | 0421 4.6 / 1048 1.1 / 1657 4.7 / 2317 1.2 | **16** M | 0533 4.2 / 1147 1.5 / 1749 4.4 |
| **2** M | 0512 4.8 / 1138 0.9 / 1742 4.9 | **17** TU | 0008 1.6 / 0611 4.3 / 1226 1.5 / 1823 4.6 |
| **3** TU | 0007 0.9 / 0603 5.0 / 1227 0.7 / ● 1827 5.1 | **18** W | 0047 1.4 / 0647 4.3 / 1302 1.4 / ○ 1857 4.7 |
| **4** W | 0057 0.7 / 0655 5.1 / 1315 0.7 / 1913 5.2 | **19** TH | 0124 1.3 / 0722 4.4 / 1337 1.4 / 1930 4.7 |
| **5** TH | 0147 0.6 / 0748 5.1 / 1402 0.8 / 2002 5.2 | **20** F | 0159 1.3 / 0756 4.4 / 1411 1.4 / 2003 4.7 |
| **6** F | 0237 0.6 / 0842 4.9 / 1449 0.9 / 2052 5.1 | **21** SA | 0235 1.2 / 0831 4.4 / 1445 1.4 / 2038 4.7 |
| **7** SA | 0328 0.7 / 0938 4.7 / 1537 1.1 / 2147 4.9 | **22** SU | 0311 1.2 / 0907 4.3 / 1521 1.4 / 2116 4.6 |
| **8** SU | 0421 0.9 / 1036 4.5 / 1628 1.4 / 2245 4.6 | **23** M | 0348 1.2 / 0946 4.3 / 1558 1.5 / 2157 4.5 |
| **9** M | 0515 1.1 / 1135 4.2 / 1722 1.6 / 2348 4.4 | **24** TU | 0428 1.3 / 1030 4.2 / 1640 1.6 / 2244 4.4 |
| **10** TU | 0613 1.4 / 1236 4.0 / 1820 1.8 ◑ | **25** W | 0512 1.4 / 1122 4.1 / 1728 1.7 / 2339 4.3 |
| **11** W | 0054 4.2 / 0713 1.6 / 1340 3.9 / 1925 2.0 | **26** TH | 0602 1.5 / 1223 4.0 / 1825 1.8 ◑ |
| **12** TH | 0202 4.0 / 0816 1.7 / 1444 3.9 / 2033 2.0 | **27** F | 0041 4.2 / 0659 1.5 / 1330 4.0 / 1931 1.9 |
| **13** F | 0307 4.0 / 0919 1.7 / 1542 4.0 / 2139 2.0 | **28** SA | 0147 4.2 / 0805 1.6 / 1436 4.1 / 2043 1.8 |
| **14** SA | 0403 4.0 / 1016 1.7 / 1630 4.1 / 2236 1.9 | **29** SU | 0254 4.3 / 0914 1.5 / 1539 4.3 / 2154 1.7 |
| **15** SU | 0451 4.1 / 1104 1.6 / 1712 4.3 / 2325 1.7 | **30** M | 0400 4.4 / 1021 1.4 / 1638 4.5 / 2259 1.4 |

### JULY

| Day | Time m | Day | Time m |
|---|---|---|---|
| **1** TU | 0503 4.6 / 1121 1.3 / 1731 4.8 / 2358 1.1 | **16** W | 0602 4.1 / 1210 1.7 / 1810 4.5 |
| **2** W | 0601 4.8 / 1216 1.1 / 1821 5.0 | **17** TH | 0034 1.6 / 0637 4.3 / 1248 1.5 / 1843 4.7 |
| **3** TH | 0052 0.8 / 0653 5.0 / 1307 0.9 / ● 1908 5.2 | **18** F | 0111 1.3 / 0710 4.5 / 1323 1.4 / ○ 1915 4.8 |
| **4** F | 0143 0.6 / 0743 5.0 / 1354 0.9 / 1954 5.3 | **19** SA | 0146 1.2 / 0740 4.6 / 1357 1.3 / 1946 4.9 |
| **5** SA | 0231 0.5 / 0830 5.0 / 1440 0.9 / 2039 5.2 | **20** SU | 0220 1.0 / 0811 4.6 / 1430 1.2 / 2018 5.0 |
| **6** SU | 0318 0.5 / 0917 4.9 / 1524 1.0 / 2124 5.1 | **21** M | 0254 0.9 / 0843 4.6 / 1504 1.1 / 2052 5.0 |
| **7** M | 0403 0.7 / 1003 4.6 / 1607 1.1 / 2211 4.8 | **22** TU | 0328 0.9 / 0918 4.6 / 1539 1.2 / 2129 4.9 |
| **8** TU | 0447 0.9 / 1051 4.4 / 1651 1.4 / 2301 4.5 | **23** W | 0404 1.0 / 0956 4.5 / 1616 1.3 / 2211 4.7 |
| **9** W | 0531 1.2 / 1143 4.1 / 1737 1.6 / 2357 4.2 | **24** TH | 0443 1.1 / 1041 4.3 / 1658 1.5 / 2259 4.6 |
| **10** TH | 0619 1.6 / 1242 3.9 / 1829 1.9 ◑ | **25** F | 0527 1.3 / 1137 4.2 / 1748 1.7 ◑ |
| **11** F | 0102 4.0 / 0712 1.8 / 1348 3.8 / 1930 2.1 | **26** SA | 0000 4.4 / 0618 1.5 / 1248 4.1 / 1850 1.9 |
| **12** SA | 0214 3.8 / 0817 2.0 / 1457 3.8 / 2047 2.2 | **27** SU | 0116 4.2 / 0724 1.8 / 1406 4.2 / 2011 2.0 |
| **13** SU | 0327 3.8 / 0932 2.1 / 1559 3.9 / 2205 2.2 | **28** M | 0237 4.1 / 0846 1.9 / 1523 4.2 / 2142 1.9 |
| **14** M | 0430 3.8 / 1037 2.0 / 1650 4.1 / 2306 2.0 | **29** TU | 0357 4.2 / 1011 1.8 / 1633 4.4 / 2258 1.6 |
| **15** TU | 0521 4.0 / 1127 1.9 / 1733 4.3 / 2353 1.8 | **30** W | 0506 4.5 / 1118 1.6 / 1729 4.7 / 2358 1.2 |
| | | **31** TH | 0601 4.7 / 1212 1.3 / 1816 5.0 |

### AUGUST

| Day | Time m | Day | Time m |
|---|---|---|---|
| **1** F | 0048 0.8 / 0647 5.0 / 1259 1.0 / ● 1858 5.3 | **16** SA | 0051 1.2 / 0646 4.6 / 1303 1.3 / ○ 1851 5.0 |
| **2** SA | 0135 0.6 / 0729 5.1 / 1342 0.8 / 1937 5.4 | **17** SU | 0124 1.0 / 0715 4.8 / 1335 1.1 / 1921 5.2 |
| **3** SU | 0217 0.4 / 0808 5.1 / 1422 0.7 / 2015 5.4 | **18** M | 0156 0.8 / 0743 4.9 / 1407 0.9 / 1951 5.3 |
| **4** M | 0256 0.4 / 0845 5.0 / 1501 0.8 / 2053 5.2 | **19** TU | 0228 0.6 / 0814 5.0 / 1440 0.9 / 2024 5.3 |
| **5** TU | 0334 0.6 / 0923 4.8 / 1538 1.0 / 2130 4.9 | **20** W | 0301 0.6 / 0847 4.9 / 1514 0.9 / 2100 5.2 |
| **6** W | 0410 0.9 / 1001 4.5 / 1616 1.2 / 2208 4.6 | **21** TH | 0336 0.7 / 0924 4.8 / 1551 1.1 / 2141 5.0 |
| **7** TH | 0447 1.2 / 1043 4.3 / 1654 1.6 / 2250 4.3 | **22** F | 0414 0.9 / 1006 4.6 / 1632 1.3 / 2230 4.7 |
| **8** F | 0526 1.6 / 1135 4.0 / 1737 1.9 / ◑ 2348 3.9 | **23** SA | 0456 1.3 / 1100 4.3 / 1720 1.6 / ◑ 2336 4.3 |
| **9** SA | 0610 2.0 / 1246 3.8 / 1830 2.2 | **24** SU | 0546 1.7 / 1218 4.1 / 1825 2.0 |
| **10** SU | 0117 3.7 / 0709 2.3 / 1408 3.7 / 1949 2.4 | **25** M | 0106 4.1 / 0655 2.1 / 1353 4.0 / 2001 2.1 |
| **11** M | 0252 3.6 / 0845 2.4 / 1526 3.8 / 2137 2.4 | **26** TU | 0240 4.0 / 0840 2.2 / 1521 4.1 / 2149 1.9 |
| **12** TU | 0410 3.7 / 1015 2.3 / 1627 4.0 / 2251 2.2 | **27** W | 0404 4.2 / 1014 2.0 / 1631 4.4 / 2301 1.5 |
| **13** W | 0505 3.9 / 1111 2.1 / 1713 4.3 / 2338 1.9 | **28** TH | 0506 4.5 / 1115 1.6 / 1722 4.8 / 2353 1.1 |
| **14** TH | 0545 4.1 / 1153 1.8 / 1749 4.5 | **29** F | 0553 4.8 / 1202 1.3 / 1804 5.1 |
| **15** F | 0016 1.5 / 0617 4.4 / 1229 1.5 / 1821 4.8 | **30** SA | 0036 0.8 / 0631 5.0 / 1244 1.0 / ● 1840 5.3 |
| | | **31** SU | 0117 0.5 / 0706 5.2 / 1323 0.8 / 1914 5.4 |

Chart Datum: 2·75 metres below Ordnance Datum (Newlyn). HAT is 5·9 metres above Chart Datum.

**TIME ZONE (UT)**
For Summer Time add ONE hour in **non-shaded areas**

## ULLAPOOL   LAT 57°54'N   LONG 5°10'W
### TIMES AND HEIGHTS OF HIGH AND LOW WATERS

Dates in red are SPRINGS
Dates in blue are NEAPS

YEAR **2008**

### SEPTEMBER

| Time | m | | Time | m |
|---|---|---|---|---|
| **1** 0153 | 0.4 | | **16** 0126 | 0.6 |
| 0739 | 5.2 | | 0713 | 5.2 |
| M 1359 | 0.7 | | TU 1340 | 0.7 |
| 1947 | 5.4 | | 1923 | 5.5 |
| **2** 0228 | 0.5 | | **17** 0159 | 0.5 |
| 0811 | 5.1 | | 0744 | 5.2 |
| TU 1433 | 0.8 | | W 1414 | 0.7 |
| 2019 | 5.2 | | 1957 | 5.5 |
| **3** 0300 | 0.7 | | **18** 0233 | 0.5 |
| 0842 | 4.9 | | 0819 | 5.2 |
| W 1507 | 0.9 | | TH 1450 | 0.8 |
| 2050 | 5.0 | | 2036 | 5.3 |
| **4** 0332 | 0.9 | | **19** 0309 | 0.7 |
| 0914 | 4.7 | | 0856 | 5.0 |
| TH 1541 | 1.2 | | F 1528 | 1.0 |
| 2122 | 4.6 | | 2120 | 5.0 |
| **5** 0405 | 1.3 | | **20** 0348 | 1.0 |
| 0948 | 4.4 | | 0940 | 4.7 |
| F 1616 | 1.6 | | SA 1612 | 1.3 |
| 2157 | 4.3 | | 2215 | 4.6 |
| **6** 0439 | 1.7 | | **21** 0432 | 1.4 |
| 1030 | 4.2 | | 1037 | 4.4 |
| SA 1655 | 1.9 | | SU 1704 | 1.7 |
| 2242 | 3.9 | | 2335 | 4.2 |
| **7** 0517 | 2.1 | | **22** 0525 | 1.9 |
| 1135 | 3.9 | | 1209 | 4.1 |
| SU 1742 | 2.3 | | M 1818 | 2.0 |
| ◗ | | | ◗ | |
| **8** 0019 | 3.6 | | **23** 0111 | 4.0 |
| 0609 | 2.4 | | 0645 | 2.3 |
| M 1316 | 3.7 | | TU 1348 | 4.1 |
| 1854 | 2.5 | | 2011 | 2.1 |
| **9** 0213 | 3.5 | | **24** 0243 | 4.0 |
| 0750 | 2.6 | | 0844 | 2.3 |
| TU 1445 | 3.8 | | W 1516 | 4.2 |
| 2106 | 2.5 | | 2149 | 1.8 |
| **10** 0342 | 3.7 | | **25** 0400 | 4.3 |
| 0951 | 2.5 | | 1007 | 2.0 |
| W 1555 | 4.0 | | TH 1620 | 4.5 |
| 2227 | 2.2 | | 2249 | 1.4 |
| **11** 0439 | 3.9 | | **26** 0454 | 4.5 |
| 1047 | 2.2 | | 1100 | 1.7 |
| TH 1643 | 4.3 | | F 1707 | 4.8 |
| 2311 | 1.9 | | 2335 | 1.1 |
| **12** 0518 | 4.2 | | **27** 0535 | 4.8 |
| 1126 | 1.8 | | 1143 | 1.3 |
| F 1719 | 4.6 | | SA 1745 | 5.1 |
| 2347 | 1.5 | | | |
| **13** 0548 | 4.5 | | **28** 0014 | 0.8 |
| 1201 | 1.5 | | 0609 | 5.0 |
| SA 1751 | 4.9 | | SU 1222 | 1.1 |
| | | | 1818 | 5.3 |
| **14** 0020 | 1.1 | | **29** 0051 | 0.7 |
| 0615 | 4.8 | | 0640 | 5.2 |
| SU 1234 | 1.2 | | M 1258 | 0.9 |
| 1820 | 5.2 | | ● 1849 | 5.3 |
| **15** 0053 | 0.8 | | **30** 0125 | 0.6 |
| 0644 | 5.0 | | 0710 | 5.2 |
| M 1307 | 0.9 | | TU 1332 | 0.8 |
| ○ 1850 | 5.4 | | 1919 | 5.3 |

### OCTOBER

| Time | m | | Time | m |
|---|---|---|---|---|
| **1** 0156 | 0.7 | | **16** 0130 | 0.5 |
| 0739 | 5.1 | | 0719 | 5.4 |
| W 1405 | 0.9 | | TH 1350 | 0.7 |
| 1948 | 5.1 | | 1936 | 5.5 |
| **2** 0227 | 0.9 | | **17** 0208 | 0.6 |
| 0808 | 5.0 | | 0756 | 5.4 |
| TH 1437 | 1.1 | | F 1430 | 0.8 |
| 2018 | 4.9 | | 2020 | 5.3 |
| **3** 0257 | 1.1 | | **18** 0247 | 0.8 |
| 0838 | 4.8 | | 0838 | 5.2 |
| F 1510 | 1.3 | | SA 1513 | 1.0 |
| 2050 | 4.6 | | 2112 | 5.0 |
| **4** 0328 | 1.4 | | **19** 0330 | 1.2 |
| 0910 | 4.6 | | 0927 | 4.9 |
| SA 1544 | 1.6 | | SU 1602 | 1.3 |
| 2125 | 4.3 | | 2217 | 4.6 |
| **5** 0401 | 1.8 | | **20** 0418 | 1.6 |
| 0948 | 4.3 | | 1033 | 4.6 |
| SU 1622 | 1.9 | | M 1701 | 1.7 |
| 2210 | 4.0 | | 2340 | 4.3 |
| **6** 0438 | 2.1 | | **21** 0517 | 2.1 |
| 1043 | 4.1 | | 1203 | 4.3 |
| M 1708 | 2.2 | | TU 1822 | 2.0 |
| 2334 | 3.7 | | ◗ | |
| **7** 0526 | 2.5 | | **22** 0105 | 4.1 |
| 1220 | 3.9 | | 0641 | 2.3 |
| TU 1814 | 2.5 | | W 1334 | 4.3 |
| ◗ | | | 2002 | 2.0 |
| **8** 0124 | 3.6 | | **23** 0228 | 4.1 |
| 0651 | 2.7 | | 0824 | 2.3 |
| W 1353 | 3.8 | | TH 1455 | 4.4 |
| 2008 | 2.5 | | 2125 | 1.8 |
| **9** 0253 | 3.7 | | **24** 0339 | 4.3 |
| 0902 | 2.6 | | 0940 | 2.1 |
| TH 1506 | 4.0 | | F 1557 | 4.6 |
| 2139 | 2.2 | | 2222 | 1.5 |
| **10** 0356 | 3.9 | | **25** 0431 | 4.5 |
| 1006 | 2.3 | | 1033 | 1.8 |
| F 1600 | 4.3 | | SA 1644 | 4.8 |
| 2229 | 1.9 | | 2307 | 1.3 |
| **11** 0438 | 4.2 | | **26** 0511 | 4.7 |
| 1048 | 1.9 | | 1117 | 1.5 |
| SA 1640 | 4.6 | | SU 1722 | 4.9 |
| 2307 | 1.5 | | 2347 | 1.1 |
| **12** 0511 | 4.5 | | **27** 0545 | 4.9 |
| 1125 | 1.6 | | 1157 | 1.3 |
| SU 1714 | 4.9 | | M 1756 | 5.0 |
| 2343 | 1.1 | | | |
| **13** 0541 | 4.9 | | **28** 0022 | 1.0 |
| 1200 | 1.2 | | 0615 | 5.1 |
| M 1747 | 5.2 | | TU 1234 | 1.2 |
| | | | ● 1826 | 5.1 |
| **14** 0018 | 0.8 | | **29** 0056 | 1.0 |
| 0612 | 5.1 | | 0644 | 5.1 |
| TU 1235 | 0.9 | | W 1308 | 1.1 |
| ○ 1821 | 5.5 | | 1857 | 5.0 |
| **15** 0054 | 0.6 | | **30** 0128 | 1.1 |
| 0644 | 5.3 | | 0713 | 5.1 |
| W 1312 | 0.7 | | TH 1341 | 1.2 |
| 1857 | 5.6 | | 1927 | 4.9 |
| | | | **31** 0159 | 1.2 |
| | | | 0743 | 5.0 |
| | | | F 1414 | 1.3 |
| | | | 1959 | 4.8 |

### NOVEMBER

| Time | m | | Time | m |
|---|---|---|---|---|
| **1** 0229 | 1.4 | | **16** 0233 | 1.0 |
| 0814 | 4.9 | | 0831 | 5.3 |
| SA 1447 | 1.5 | | SU 1507 | 1.0 |
| 2033 | 4.6 | | 2113 | 5.0 |
| **2** 0301 | 1.6 | | **17** 0320 | 1.3 |
| 0847 | 4.7 | | 0925 | 5.1 |
| SU 1522 | 1.7 | | M 1600 | 1.2 |
| 2111 | 4.3 | | 2217 | 4.7 |
| **3** 0335 | 1.9 | | **18** 0411 | 1.6 |
| 0927 | 4.5 | | 1029 | 4.8 |
| M 1601 | 1.9 | | TU 1700 | 1.5 |
| 2158 | 4.1 | | 2327 | 4.5 |
| **4** 0413 | 2.1 | | **19** 0510 | 1.9 |
| 1017 | 4.3 | | 1144 | 4.6 |
| TU 1646 | 2.1 | | W 1810 | 1.7 |
| 2303 | 3.9 | | ◗ | |
| **5** 0459 | 2.4 | | **20** 0040 | 4.3 |
| 1128 | 4.1 | | 0621 | 2.2 |
| W 1744 | 2.3 | | TH 1302 | 4.5 |
| | | | 1926 | 1.8 |
| **6** 0027 | 3.8 | | **21** 0153 | 4.2 |
| 0606 | 2.6 | | 0740 | 2.2 |
| TH 1252 | 4.0 | | F 1417 | 4.4 |
| ◗ 1902 | 2.4 | | 2039 | 1.8 |
| **7** 0146 | 3.8 | | **22** 0302 | 4.3 |
| 0743 | 2.6 | | 0855 | 2.1 |
| F 1404 | 4.1 | | SA 1524 | 4.5 |
| 2027 | 2.2 | | 2142 | 1.7 |
| **8** 0255 | 3.9 | | **23** 0359 | 4.4 |
| 0903 | 2.4 | | 0957 | 2.0 |
| SA 1503 | 4.3 | | SU 1616 | 4.5 |
| 2131 | 1.9 | | 2233 | 1.6 |
| **9** 0347 | 4.2 | | **24** 0444 | 4.6 |
| 0958 | 2.1 | | 1048 | 1.8 |
| SU 1552 | 4.5 | | M 1700 | 4.6 |
| 2219 | 1.6 | | 2317 | 1.5 |
| **10** 0429 | 4.5 | | **25** 0522 | 4.7 |
| 1043 | 1.7 | | 1132 | 1.7 |
| M 1635 | 4.8 | | TU 1738 | 4.7 |
| 2302 | 1.3 | | 2356 | 1.4 |
| **11** 0507 | 4.9 | | **26** 0556 | 4.9 |
| 1125 | 1.4 | | 1212 | 1.5 |
| TU 1715 | 5.1 | | W 1812 | 4.8 |
| 2343 | 1.0 | | | |
| **12** 0544 | 5.1 | | **27** 0032 | 1.4 |
| 1206 | 1.1 | | 0627 | 5.0 |
| W 1756 | 5.4 | | TH 1249 | 1.5 |
| | | | ● 1845 | 4.8 |
| **13** 0024 | 0.8 | | **28** 0106 | 1.4 |
| 0621 | 5.4 | | 0658 | 5.0 |
| TH 1249 | 0.9 | | F 1325 | 1.4 |
| ○ 1839 | 5.5 | | 1918 | 4.8 |
| **14** 0107 | 0.7 | | **29** 0139 | 1.5 |
| 0701 | 5.5 | | 0729 | 5.0 |
| F 1332 | 0.8 | | SA 1359 | 1.5 |
| 1925 | 5.5 | | 1952 | 4.7 |
| **15** 0149 | 0.8 | | **30** 0212 | 1.5 |
| 0744 | 5.5 | | 0802 | 5.0 |
| SA 1418 | 0.8 | | SU 1434 | 1.5 |
| 2016 | 5.3 | | 2026 | 4.6 |

### DECEMBER

| Time | m | | Time | m |
|---|---|---|---|---|
| **1** 0245 | 1.7 | | **16** 0313 | 1.2 |
| 0836 | 4.9 | | 0917 | 5.4 |
| M 1509 | 1.6 | | TU 1554 | 0.9 |
| 2103 | 4.5 | | 2201 | 4.9 |
| **2** 0319 | 1.8 | | **17** 0401 | 1.4 |
| 0913 | 4.7 | | 1010 | 5.1 |
| TU 1547 | 1.7 | | W 1646 | 1.2 |
| 2144 | 4.3 | | 2257 | 4.7 |
| **3** 0356 | 2.0 | | **18** 0452 | 1.6 |
| 0957 | 4.6 | | 1109 | 4.9 |
| W 1629 | 1.9 | | TH 1740 | 1.4 |
| 2231 | 4.2 | | 2358 | 4.4 |
| **4** 0439 | 2.1 | | **19** 0547 | 1.9 |
| 1048 | 4.4 | | 1215 | 4.6 |
| TH 1716 | 2.0 | | F 1838 | 1.7 |
| 2329 | 4.0 | | ◗ | |
| **5** 0530 | 2.3 | | **20** 0103 | 4.2 |
| 1149 | 4.3 | | 0648 | 2.1 |
| F 1811 | 2.1 | | SA 1326 | 4.4 |
| ◗ | | | 1941 | 1.9 |
| **6** 0038 | 4.0 | | **21** 0213 | 4.1 |
| 0634 | 2.4 | | 0757 | 2.2 |
| SA 1258 | 4.3 | | SU 1439 | 4.2 |
| 1915 | 2.1 | | 2049 | 2.0 |
| **7** 0148 | 4.0 | | **22** 0319 | 4.2 |
| 0748 | 2.3 | | 0911 | 2.3 |
| SU 1403 | 4.3 | | M 1545 | 4.2 |
| 2023 | 2.0 | | 2154 | 2.0 |
| **8** 0251 | 4.2 | | **23** 0416 | 4.3 |
| 0859 | 2.2 | | 1018 | 2.2 |
| M 1502 | 4.5 | | TU 1640 | 4.3 |
| 2127 | 1.8 | | 2249 | 1.9 |
| **9** 0347 | 4.4 | | **24** 0502 | 4.5 |
| 1000 | 1.9 | | 1112 | 2.0 |
| TU 1558 | 4.7 | | W 1725 | 4.4 |
| 2223 | 1.5 | | 2335 | 1.8 |
| **10** 0436 | 4.7 | | **25** 0541 | 4.7 |
| 1054 | 1.7 | | 1158 | 1.9 |
| W 1651 | 4.9 | | TH 1805 | 4.7 |
| 2315 | 1.3 | | | |
| **11** 0522 | 5.0 | | **26** 0016 | 1.7 |
| 1144 | 1.4 | | 0616 | 4.8 |
| TH 1742 | 5.1 | | F 1238 | 1.7 |
| | | | 1840 | 4.6 |
| **12** 0004 | 1.1 | | **27** 0053 | 1.6 |
| 0606 | 5.3 | | 0649 | 4.9 |
| F 1235 | 1.1 | | SA 1315 | 1.6 |
| ○ 1832 | 5.3 | | ● 1913 | 4.7 |
| **13** 0052 | 1.0 | | **28** 0127 | 1.6 |
| 0652 | 5.5 | | 0721 | 5.0 |
| SA 1324 | 0.9 | | SU 1350 | 1.5 |
| 1923 | 5.4 | | 1945 | 4.7 |
| **14** 0139 | 1.0 | | **29** 0201 | 1.5 |
| 0738 | 5.5 | | 0752 | 5.1 |
| SU 1413 | 0.8 | | M 1424 | 1.4 |
| 2015 | 5.3 | | 2016 | 4.7 |
| **15** 0226 | 1.0 | | **30** 0233 | 1.5 |
| 0826 | 5.5 | | 0824 | 5.0 |
| M 1503 | 0.8 | | TU 1457 | 1.4 |
| 2107 | 5.2 | | 2048 | 4.7 |
| | | | **31** 0306 | 1.6 |
| | | | 0857 | 5.0 |
| | | | W 1532 | 1.4 |
| | | | 2121 | 4.6 |

Chart Datum: 2·75 metres below Ordnance Datum (Newlyn). HAT is 5·9 metres above Chart Datum.

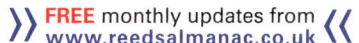

**WGS84 DATUM**

**NW Scotland**

## 1.8  PORTREE

Skye (Highland) **57°24'·73N 06°11'·07W** ✿✿✿🏵🏵✿✿✿

**CHARTS**  AC 2209, 2534; Imray C66; OS 23

**TIDES**  –0445 Dover; ML no data; Duration 0610

**Standard Port ULLAPOOL** (⟵)

| Times | | | | Height (metres) | | | |
|---|---|---|---|---|---|---|---|
| High Water | | Low Water | | MHWS | MHWN | MLWN | MLWS |
| 0000 | 0600 | 0300 | 0900 | 5·2 | 3·9 | 2·1 | 0·7 |
| 1200 | 1800 | 1500 | 2100 | | | | |
| **Differences PORTREE (Skye)** | | | | | | | |
| –0025 | –0025 | –0025 | –0025 | +0·1 | –0·2 | –0·2 | 0·0 |
| **SHIELDAIG (Loch Torridon)** | | | | | | | |
| –0020 | –0020 | –0015 | –0015 | +0·4 | +0·3 | +0·1 | 0·0 |
| **LOCH A'BHRAIGE (Rona)** | | | | | | | |
| –0020 | 0000 | –0010 | 0000 | –0·1 | –0·1 | –0·1 | –0·2 |
| **PLOCKTON** | | | | | | | |
| +0005 | –0025 | –0005 | –0010 | +0·5 | +0·5 | +0·5 | +0·2 |
| **LOCH SNIZORT (Uig Bay, Skye)** | | | | | | | |
| –0045 | –0020 | –0005 | –0025 | +0·1 | –0·4 | –0·2 | 0·0 |
| **LOCH DUNVEGAN (Skye)** | | | | | | | |
| –0105 | –0030 | –0020 | –0040 | 0·0 | –0·1 | 0·0 | 0·0 |
| **LOCH HARPORT (Skye)** | | | | | | | |
| –0115 | –0035 | –0020 | –0100 | –0·1 | –0·1 | 0·0 | +0·1 |
| **SOAY (Camus nan Gall)** | | | | | | | |
| –0055 | –0025 | –0025 | –0045 | –0·4 | –0·2 | No data | |
| **KYLE OF LOCHALSH** | | | | | | | |
| –0040 | –0020 | –0005 | –0025 | +0·1 | 0·0 | 0·0 | –0·1 |
| **DORNIE BRIDGE (Loch Alsh)** | | | | | | | |
| –0040 | –0010 | –0005 | –0020 | +0·1 | 0·0 | 0·0 | 0·0 |
| **GLENELG BAY (Kyle Rhea)** | | | | | | | |
| –0105 | –0035 | –0035 | –0055 | –0·4 | –0·4 | –0·9 | –0·1 |
| **LOCH HOURN** | | | | | | | |
| –0125 | –0050 | –0040 | –0110 | –0·2 | –0·1 | –0·1 | +0·1 |

**SHELTER**  Secure in all but strong S to SW'lies, when Camas Bàn is more sheltered. In the NW of the bay there are 8 🛟s for <15 tons. Short stay pontoon on pier.

**NAVIGATION**  WPT 57°24'·58N 06°10'·07W, 275°/0·72M to pier. From the S, avoid rks off An Tom Pt (1·5M to E, off chartlet).

**LIGHTS AND MARKS**  Only lts are a SHM buoy Fl G 5s marking Sgeir Mhór, 2 FR (vert) 6m 4M (occas) on the pier and a SPM buoy Fl Y 5s.

**R/T**  VHF Ch 16 12 (occas).

**TELEPHONE**  (Code 01478)  HM ☎ 612926; Moorings 612341; MRCC (01851) 702013; ⊖ (0141) 887 9369; Marinecall 09068 969654; Police 612888; Dr 612013; Ⓗ 612704.

**FACILITIES**  Pier AB £13, D (cans), L, FW. **Town** P, 🍴, Gas, Gaz, 🛢, R, Bar, ✉, Ⓑ, bus to Kyle of Lochalsh, ⇌.

### ANCHORAGES AROUND OR NEAR SKYE

**LOCH TORRIDON**, Highland, **57°36'N 05°49'W**. AC 228. Tides, see 1.8. Three large lochs: ent to outer loch (Torridon) is 3M wide, with isolated Sgeir na Trian (2m) almost in mid-chan; ↓s on SW side behind Eilean Mór and in L Beag. L Sheildaig is middle loch with good ↓ between the Is and village. 1M to the N, a 2ca wide chan leads into Upper L Torridon; many fish cages and prone to squalls. Few facilities, except Shieldaig: FW, 🍴, R, Bar, ✉, Garage.

**LOCH A'BHRAIGE**, Rona (Highland), **57°34'·6N 05°57'·9W**. AC 2479, 2534. HW –0438 on Dover; ML 2·8m; Duration 0605. See 1.8. A good ↓ in NW of the island, safe except in NNW winds. Beware rks on NE side up to 1ca off shore. Hbr in NE corner of loch head. Ldg lts 137°, see 1.3. Facilities: jetty, FW and a helipad, all owned by MOD (DRA). Before ent, call *Rona Range Control* VHF Ch 13.

**Acarseid Mhór** is ↓ on W of Rona. One 🛟 £12. App S of Eilean Garbh marked by W arrow. SD sketch of rks at ent is necessary. FW (cans), showers. At **Churchton Bay**, SW tip of Raasay, there are 4 HIE 🛟s; ☎ (01478) 612341; Slip, showers, R, 🛢.

**LOCH DUNVEGAN**, 4 🛟s off Stein, **57°30'·9N 06°34'·5W**. 3 🛟s off Dunvegan, 57°26'·3N 06°35'·2W. Fuel, FW, R. ☎ (01478) 612341.

**LOCH HARPORT**, Skye (Highland), **57°20'·6N 06°25'·8W**. AC 1795. HW –0447 (sp), –0527 (np) on Dover. See 1.8. On E side of Loch Bracadale, entered between Oronsay Is and Ardtreck Pt (W lt ho, Fl 6s 18m 9M). SW end of Oronsay has conspic rk pillar, called The Castle; keep ¼M off-shore here and off E coast of Oronsay which is joined to Ullinish Pt by drying reef. ↓ Oronsay Is, N side of drying reef (4m), or on E side, but beware rk (dries) 0·5ca off N shore of Oronsay. Fiskavaig Bay 1M S of Ardtreck (7m); Loch Beag on N side of loch, exposed to W winds; Port na Long E of Ardtreck, sheltered except from E winds (beware fish farm); 1 🛟 off the distillery and 2 🛟 off *The Old Inn* at Carbost on SW shore. Facilities: (Carbost) 🛒, Bar, R, P (garage), ✉, FW. (Port na Long) Bar, FW, 🍴.

**SOAY HARBOUR**, Skye (Highland), **57°09'·5N 06°13'·4W**. AC 2208. Tides see 1.8. Narrow inlet on NW side of Soay; enter from Soay Sound above half flood to clear bar, dries 0·6m. Appr on 135° from 5ca out to avoid reefs close each side of ent. Cross bar slightly E of mid-chan, altering 20° stbd for best water; ent is 15m wide between boulder spits marked by W poles with Or tops. ↓ in 3m mid-pool or shoal draft boats can enter inner pool. Good shelter and holding. Camas nan Gall (poor holding); no other facilities.

**ARMADALE BAY**, Skye (Highland), 4M NW of Mallaig. AC 2208. 6 🛟s £12 at **57°04'·0N 05°53'·6W**, ☎ (01471) 844216. Bay is sheltered from SE to N winds but subject to swell in winds from N to SE. From S, beware the Eilean Maol & Sgorach rocks. Ferry pier, Oc R 6s 6m 6M, with conspic W shed. Facilities, Skye Yachts ☎ 01471 844216, 🖪 844387: M (£12), FW at pontoon or by hose to charter M's, D, 🍴, showers, Gas, free pontoon for tenders, ferry to Mallaig for ⇌. Ardvasar ¾ mile: Slip HW±3 at BY (launching/parking £5), P (cans)(not Sat/Sun), showers, 🚾, Gaz at ¼ mile; R, Bar.

**CROWLIN ISLANDS**, Highland, **57°21'·1N 05°50'·6W**. AC 2209, 2498. HW –0435 on Dover, –0020 on Ullapool; HW +0·3m on Ullapool. See 1.7. ↓ between Eilean Meadhonach and Eilean Mor, appr from N, keep E of Eilean Beg. Excellent shelter except in strong N winds. There is an inner ↓ with 3½m but ent chan dries. Eilean Beg lt ho Fl 6s 32m 6M, W tr. No facilities.

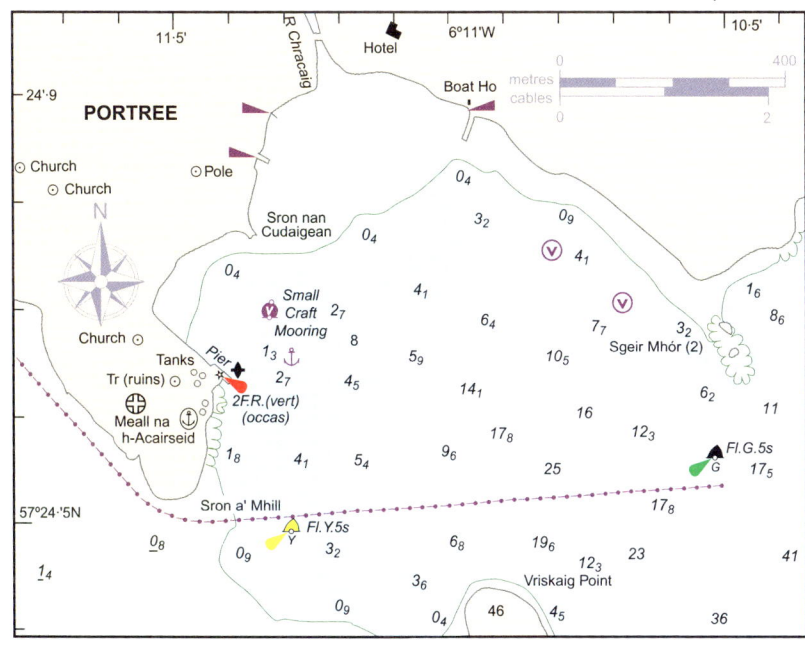

## 1.9  PLOCKTON

Highland **57°20´·52N 05°38´·47W** ✿✿✿⚓✿✿✿

**CHARTS**  AC 2209, 2528; Imray C66; OS 24, 33

**TIDES**  −0435 Dover; ML 3·5m; Duration 0600; See 1.8

**SHELTER**  Good, exposed only to N/NE'lies. 5 Y ⚓s or ⚓ in centre of bay in approx 3·5m. Inner part of bay shoals and dries to the SW.

**NAVIGATION**  WPT 57°21´·16N 05°39´·44W; thence towards Bogha Dubh Sgeir PHM bn, between Cat Is disused Lt ho and Sgeir Golach PHM Bcn and High Stone (1m) to the N. Hawk (0.1m) will be cleared when Duncraig Castle bears 158°. Alter S to the ⚓. Beware Plockton Rks (<u>3</u>·1m) on E side of bay.

**LIGHTS AND MARKS**  See 1.3 and chartlet. Old lt ho (13m) on Cat Is is conspic, as is Duncraig Castle. Plockton Rks marked by lit PHM Bcn.

**R/T**  None.

**TELEPHONE**  HM (01599) 534589, 🖷 534167, Mobile 07802 367253 (at Kyle of Lochalsh); MRCC (01851) 702013; ⊝ (0141) 887 9369; Marinecall 09068 969654; Police/Dr via HM.

**FACILITIES**  **Village** FW, M £5, L at 50m dinghy pontoon (H24 except MLWS), D (cans), CH, 🛒, R, Bar, ✉, ⇌, airstrip, (bus to Kyle of Lochalsh).

**LOCH CARRON**. Strome Narrows are not buoyed or lit. At head of loch are 3 Y ⚓s (max LOA 14m) in 3m off drying jetty at 57°23´·95N 05°29´·0W; call ☎ 01520 722321. Appr on 328° between Sgeir Chreagach and Sgeir Fhada.

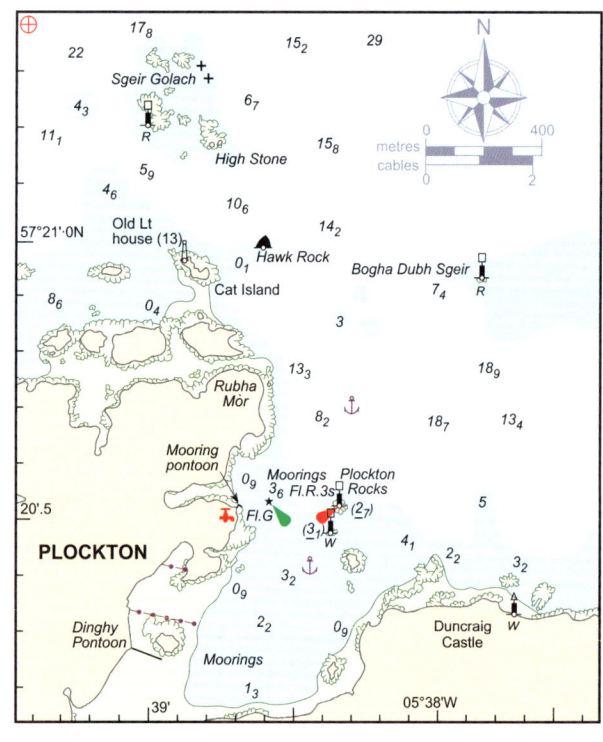

## 1.10  LOCH ALSH

Highland **57°16´·68N 05°42´·87W** ✿✿✿⚓⚓✿✿✿

**CHARTS**  AC 2540; Imray C66; OS 33

**TIDES**  −0450 Dover; ML 3·0m; Duration 0555; See 1.8

**SHELTER**  **Kyle of Lochalsh:** AB on Railway Pier, with FVs, or on 40m L-shaped pontoon (seasonal), close W of Railway Pier; or ⚓ off the hotel there in 11m. **Kyle Akin:** 3 free ⚓s are subject to tidal stream. Lit pontoon on NW side of hbr, shoal on N side.

⚓s, safe depending on winds, are (clockwise from Kyle): Avernish B, (2ca N of Racoon Rk) in 3m clear of power cables, open to SW; NW of Eilean Donnan Cas (conspic); in Ratagan B at head of L Duich in 7m; in Totaig B facing Loch Long ent in 3·5m; on S shore in Ardintoul B in 5·5m; at head of Loch na Béiste in 7m close inshore and W of fish cages.

**NAVIGATION**  WPT (from Inner Sound) 57°16´·98N 05°45´·77W, 123°/0·75M to bridge. Chan to bridge is marked by 2 PHM and 2 SHM lt buoys. Bridge to Skye, 30m clearance, is lit Oc 6s in centre of main span, Iso R 4s on S pier and Iso G4s on N pier. The secondary NE span is lit, but has only 4.5m clearance.

**LIGHTS AND MARKS**  See chartlet. Direction of buoyage is N in Kyle Rhea, thence E up Loch Alsh; but W through Kyle Akin and the bridge, ie SHMs are on N side of chan.

**R/T**  VHF Ch 11 16. Skye bridge VHF Ch 12.

**TELEPHONE**  (Code 01599)  HM 534589, 🖷 534167, Mobile 07802 367253; MRCC (01851) 702013; ⊝ (0141) 887 9369; Marinecall 09068 969654; Police, Dr, Ⓗ : via HM. Skye br ☎ 534844, 🖷 534969.

**FACILITIES**  **Kyle of Lochalsh:** AB pontoon, £1.40 (second day free), FW, D (Fish pier via HM), P (cans), ME, Ⓔ, CH, ✉, Ⓑ, R, Bar, 🛒, Gas, ⇌ (useful railhead), Bus to Glasgow & Inverness; buses every ½hr to/from Kyleakin. **Kyleakin:** ☎ 534167 or VHF Ch 11, 120m AB (£12/craft) depth varies from 3m to drying, M, FW, 🛒, R, Bar.

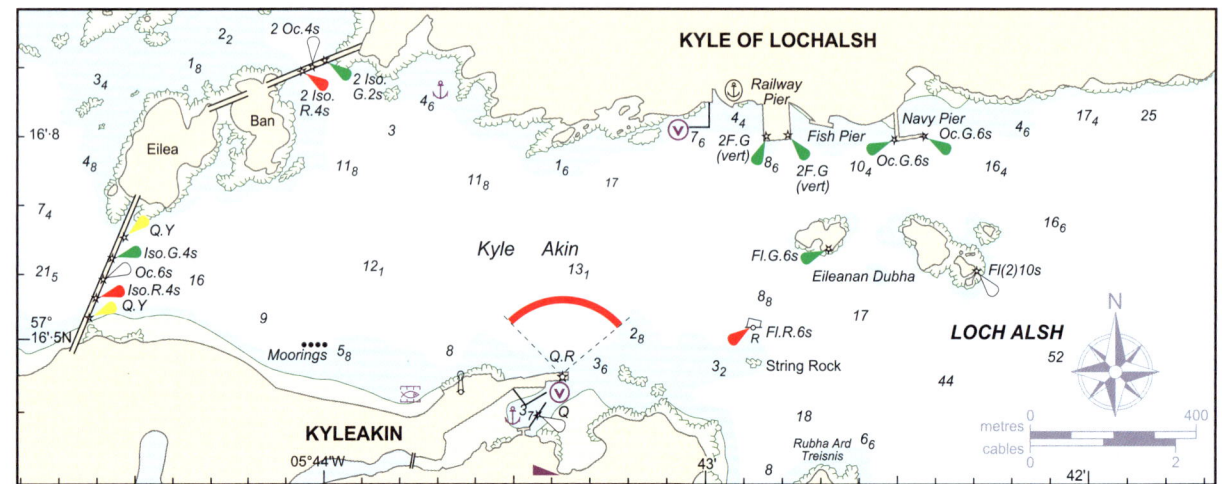

### ANCHORAGES IN THE SOUND OF SLEAT (see also 1.8)

**SOUND OF SLEAT**: There are ⚓s at: **Glenelg Bay (57°12´·57N 05°37´·95W)** SW of pier out of the tide, but only moderate holding. Usual facilities in village. At **Sandaig Bay (57°10´·0N 05°41´·4W)**, exposed to SW. Sandaig Is are to NW of the bay; beware rks off Sgeir nan Eun. Eilean Mór has lt Fl 6s. At **Isleornsay Hbr** (57°09´N 05°48´W) 2ca N of pier, 2FR (vert) and floodlit. Give drying N end of Ornsay Is a wide berth. Lts: SE tip of Ornsay, Oc 8s 18m 15M, W tr; N end, Fl R 6s 8m 4M. Facilities: FW, ⊠, Hotel.

**LOCH HOURN**, Highland, **57°08´N 05°42´W**. AC 2208, 2541. Tides see 1.8. Ent is S of Sandaig Is and opposite Isle Ornsay, Skye. Loch extends 11M inland via 4 narrows to Loch Beag; it is scenically magnificent, but violent squalls occur in strong winds. Sgeir Ulibhe, drying 2·1m, bn, lies almost in mid-ent; best to pass S of it to clear Clansman Rk, 2·1m, to the N. ⚓s on N shore at Eilean Ràrsaidh and Camas Bàn, within first 4M. For pilotage further E, consult SDs. Facilities at Arnisdale (Camas Bàn): FW, 🍴, R, Bar, ⊠. Doune Marine (01687 462667) FW, D.

**LOCH NEVIS**, Highland, **57°02´·2N 05°43´·3W**. AC 2208, 2541. HW –0515 on Dover. See 1.8. Beware rks Bogha cas Sruth (dries 1·8m), Bogha Don and Sgeirean Glasa both marked by bns. ⚓ NE of Eilean na Glaschoille, good except in S winds; or 9 Or 🛟s off Inverie, £5 (free if dining), 10m max LOA. Call *Old Forge* VHF Ch 16, 12; FW, Bar, R, showers, 🗓. In strong winds expect violent unpredictable squalls. Enter the inner loch with caution, and ⚓ N or SE of Eilean Maol.

### ANCHORAGES IN THE SMALL ISLANDS

**CANNA**, The Small Islands, **57°03´·3N 06°29´·4W**. AC 1796, 2208. HW –0457 (Sp), –0550 (Np) on Dover; HW –0035 and –0·4m on Ullapool; Duration 0605. Good shelter, except in strong E'lies, in hbr between Canna and Sanday Is but holding is poor due to kelp. Appr along Sanday shore, keeping N of Sgeir a' Phuirt, dries 4·6m. Ldg marks as in SDs. ⚓ in 3–4m W of Canna pier, off

which beware drying rky patch. ⚓ Lt is advised due to FVs. Conspic W lt bn, Fl 10s 32m 9M, vis 152°-061°, at E end of Sanday Is. Magnetic anomaly off NE Canna. Facilities: FW, shower at farm, R(☎01687 462937) with limited 🍴, ⊠, Note: NT manage island.

**RUM**, The Small Islands, **57°00´·1N 06°15´·7W**. AC 2207, 2208. HW –0500 on Dover; –0035 and –0·3m on Ullapool; ML 2·4m; Duration 0600. SNH owns Is. The mountains (809m) are unmistakeable. Landing is only allowed at L Scresort on E side; no dogs beyond village limit. Beware drying rks 1ca off N point of ent and almost 3ca off S point. The head of the loch dries 2ca out; ⚓ off slip on S side or further in, to NE of jetty. Hbr is open to E winds/swell. Facilities: ⊠, FW, 🍴 (limited), R, Bar, ferry to Mallaig.

**EIGG HARBOUR**, The Small Islands, **56°52´·6N 06°07´·6W**. AC 2207. HW –0523 on Dover. See 1.11. Entering from N or E use Sgeir nam Bagh(Ferry Terminal) Dir lt 245° Fl WRG 3s, leads between Garbh Sgeir Bn Fl (2) G 10s & Flod Sgeir Bn Fl R 5s. An Sgùrr is a conspic 391m high peak/ridge brg 281°/1·3M from Sgeir nam Bagh. Most of hbr dries, but good ⚓ 1ca NE of Galmisdale Pt pier, except in NE winds when yachts should go through the narrows and ⚓ in South Bay in 6-8m; tide runs hard in the narrows. Also ⚓ in 2·5m at Poll nam Partan, about 2ca N of Flod Sgeir. SE point of Eilean Chathastail Fl 6s 24m 8M, vis 181°-shore, W tr. VHF Ch 08 *Eigg Hbr*. HM ☎ via (01687) 482428. FW, repairs. **Pierhead** Showers, ⊠, R, 🍴, Gas. **Cleadale village** (2M to N) Bar.

**MUCK**, The Small Islands, **56°49´·8N 06°13´·3W**. AC 2207. Tides approx as Eigg, 1.11. Port Mór at SE end is the main hbr, with a deep pool inside offlying rks, but open to S'lies. Approach: Dir lt Fl WRG 3s 7m vis 1M by day leads between Dubh Sgeir (Fl(2) R 10s) and Bogha Ruadh (Fl G 5s) rks; see 1.3. ⚓ towards the NW side of inlet; NE side has drying rks. To N of Is, Bagh a' Ghallanaich is ⚓ protected from S; ent needs SDs and careful identification of marks. Few facilities.

## 1.11 MALLAIG

Highland 57°00´·47N 05°49´·47W ✿✿✿❄️🌿🌿🌸🌸

**CHARTS** AC 2208, 2541; Imray C65, C66; OS 40

**TIDES** –0515 Dover; ML 2·9; Duration 0605

**Standard Port OBAN (➡)**

| Times | | | | Height (metres) | | | |
|---|---|---|---|---|---|---|---|
| High Water | | Low Water | | MHWS | MHWN | MLWN | MLWS |
| 0000 | 0600 | 0100 | 0700 | 4·0 | 2·9 | 1·8 | 0·7 |
| 1200 | 1800 | 1300 | 1900 | | | | |
| **Differences MALLAIG** | | | | | | | |
| +0017 | +0017 | +0017 | +0017 | +1·0 | +0·7 | +0·3 | +0·1 |
| **INVERIE BAY** (Loch Nevis) | | | | | | | |
| +0030 | +0020 | +0035 | +0020 | +1·0 | +0·9 | +0·2 | 0·0 |
| **BAY OF LAIG** (Eigg) | | | | | | | |
| +0015 | +0030 | +0040 | +0005 | +0·7 | +0·6 | –0·2 | –0·2 |
| **LOCH MOIDART** | | | | | | | |
| +0015 | +0015 | +0040 | +0020 | +0·8 | +0·6 | –0·2 | –0·2 |
| **LOCH EATHARNA** (Coll) | | | | | | | |
| +0025 | +0010 | +0015 | +0025 | +0·4 | +0·3 | No data | |
| **GOTT BAY** (Tiree) | | | | | | | |
| 0000 | +0010 | +0005 | +0010 | 0·0 | +0·1 | 0·0 | 0·0 |

**SHELTER** Good in SW'lies but open to N. Access H24. ⚓ in SE part of hbr or find a berth on Fish Pier. No 🛟s. Hbr is often full of FVs; also Skye ferry.

**NAVIGATION** WPT 57°00´·75N 05°49´·40W, 191°/0·3m to Steamer Pier lt, passing E of Sgeir Dhearg lt bn. The former W chan is now permanently closed to navigation.

**LIGHTS AND MARKS** As chartlet & 1.3. Town lts may obscure Sgeir Dhearg lt. Outer Hbr Pier Hds floodlit. IPTS (3 FR vert at pier hd) when ferries manoeuvring, no other traffic allowed except by HM's permission.

**R/T** Call: *Mallaig Hbr Radio* VHF Ch 09 16 (HO).

**TELEPHONE** (Code 01687) HM 462154, outside office hrs 462411; MRCC (01851) 702013; ⊖ (0141) 887 9369; Marinecall 09068 969654; Police 462177.

**FACILITIES** **Hbr** AB £6 whenever alongside for FW/fuel/stores (⚓ is free), M, P (cans), D, FW, ME, El, 🔧, C (mobile 10 ton), CH, Ⓔ,

ACA, Slip; a busy FV hbr, yacht berths may be provided at a later date near root of the Fish Pier. **Town** Dr 462202. 🛒, R, Gas, Gaz, Bar, ⊠, Ⓑ, 🚉.

### ADJACENT ANCHORAGE

**ARISAIG**, (Loch nan Ceall), Highland, **56°53´·64N 05°55´·77W** (ent). AC 2207. HW –0515 on Dover; +0030 and +0·9m on Oban. S side of ent is identifiable by W mark on Rubh' Arisaig. SDs essential. S Chan is winding, but marked by 8 perches; each must be identified. Appr HW±4 to avoid strongest streams LW±1½. Caution: many unmarked rks; no lts. Sheltered ⚓ at head of loch, clear of moorings. Call **Arisaig Marine** ☎ (01687) 450224, 🖷 450678, VHF Ch 16, M; few 🛟s, C (10 ton), CH, D & FW at ferry pier (HW), P (cans), El, ME, 🔧, Slip. **Village** FW at hotel, Bar, ⊠, R, Gas, 🛒, 🚉.

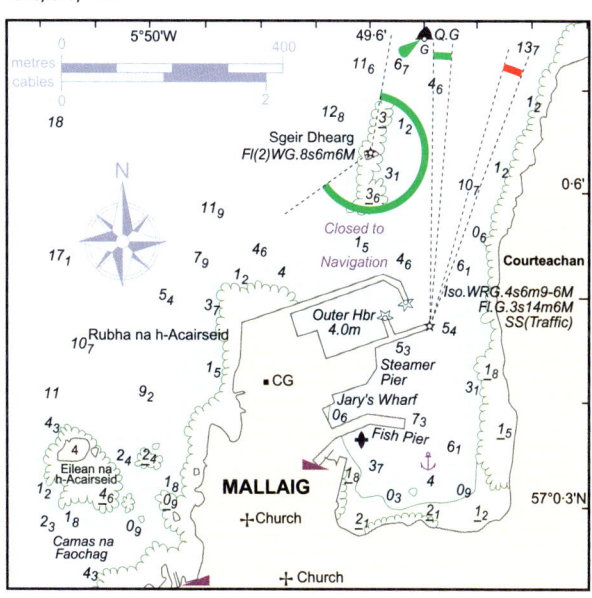

# 1.12  LOCH SUNART

Highland 56°39'·49N 06°00'·07W ✿❀⚓⛰⚘⚘

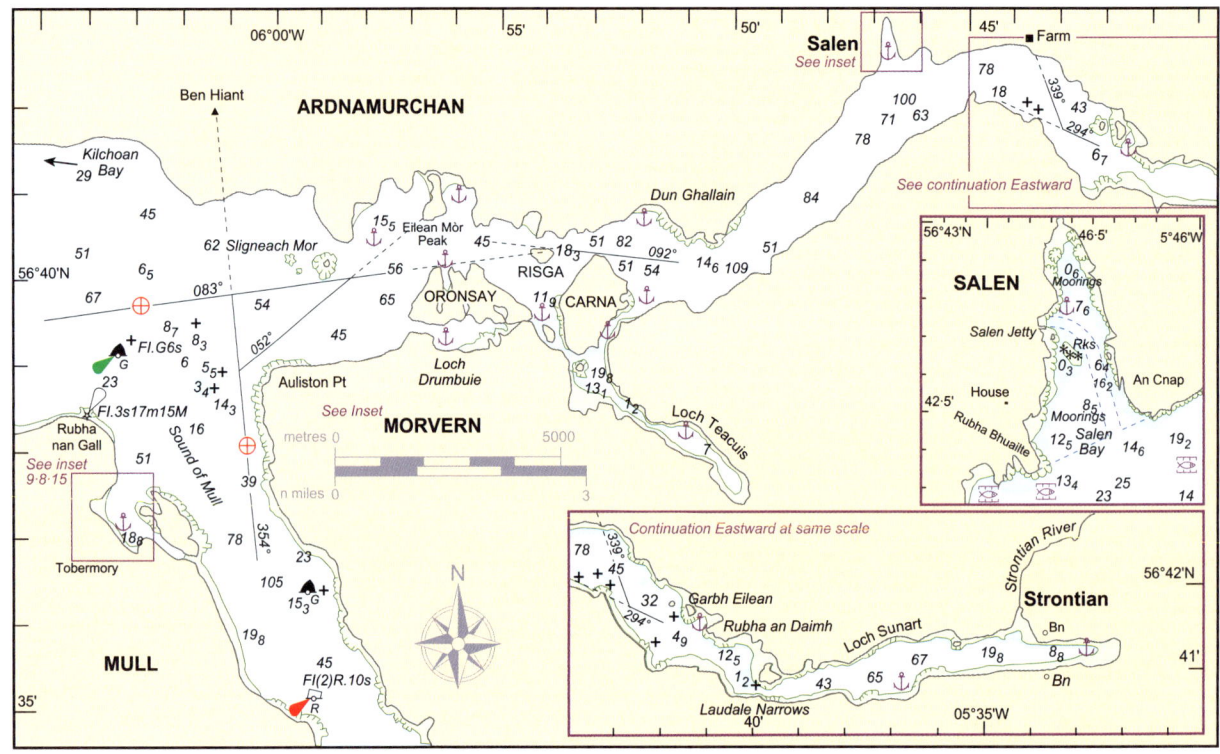

**CHARTS**  AC *5611, 2171,* 2392, 2394; Imray C65; OS 45, 47, 49

**TIDES**  Salen –0500 Dover; ML 2·0

**Standard Port OBAN (→)**

| Times | | | | Height (metres) | | | |
|---|---|---|---|---|---|---|---|
| High Water | | Low Water | | MHWS | MHWN | MLWN | MLWS |
| 0100 | 0700 | 0100 | 0800 | 4·0 | 2·9 | 1·8 | 0·7 |
| 1300 | 1900 | 1300 | 2000 | | | | |
| Differences SALEN (Loch Sunart) | | | | | | | |
| –0015 | +0015 | +0010 | +0005 | +0·6 | +0·5 | –0·1 | –0·1 |

**SHELTER**  8 ⚓s at Kilchoan Bay (56°41'·5N 06°07'·3W); ☎ (01972) 510209. ⚓s in Loch Drumbuie (S of Oronsay) sheltered in all winds; in Sailean Mór (N of Oronsay) convenient and easy ent; between Oronsay and Carna; in Loch Teacuis (very tricky ent); E of Carna; Salen Bay, with ⚓s and jetty, open only to SSE (see facilities); Garbh Eilean (NW of Rubha an Daimh), and E of sand spit by Strontian R.

**NAVIGATION  West WPT**, 56°39'·69N 06°03'·07W, 083°/3·7M to Creag nan Sgarbh (NW tip of Orinsay). **South WPT**, 56°38'·00N 06°00'·65W, 1M S of Auliston Pt; there are extensive rky reefs, The Stirks W of this pt. AC 2394 and detailed directions are needed to navigate the 17M long loch, particularly in its upper reaches. Beware Ross Rk, S of Risga; Broad Rk, E of Risga; Dun Ghallain Rk; shoals extending 3ca NNW from Eilean mo Shlinneag off S shore; drying rock 1ca W of Garbh Eilean and strong streams at sp in Laudale Narrows. Fish farms on both sides of the loch.

**LIGHTS AND MARKS**  Unlit. Transits as on the chart: from W WPT, Risga on with N tip of Oronsay at 083°; N pt of Carna on with top of Risga 092°. From S WPT, Ben Hiant bearing 354°, thence Eilean Mor Peak at 052°. Further up the loch, 339° and 294°, as on chartlet, are useful. Many other transits are shown on AC 2394.

**R/T**  None, except under Salen Bay opposite.

**TELEPHONE** (Code 01967)  MRCC (01475) 729014; ⊜ (0141) 887 9369; Marinecall 09068 969653; Dr 431231.

**FACILITIES  Salen Bay** jetty (56°42'·39N 05°46'·17W). ☎ 01967 431333. VHF Ch 16 (occas). Access HW±2 to jetty, keeping on E side of ent to avoid a drying reef on W side; two R ⚓s (15 ton) £10 (other moorings are private); ⚓ buoy advised as bottom is generally foul. L (£2 unless on ⚓), FW, D by hose, ⛽, Slip, SM, ME, El, CH, Gas, Gaz, Diver, ⬛, 🛒, R, Bar. **Acharacle** (2½M), P, 🛒, ✉, Ⓑ (Tues/Wed, mobile), ≥ (bus to Loch Ailort/Fort William), ✈ (Oban). **Strontian** FW, P, 🛒, hotel, ✉, Gas, Gaz, Bar. Bus to Fort William.

**ANCHORAGES IN COLL AND TIREE (Argyll and Bute)**

**ARINAGOUR**, Loch Eatharna, Coll, **56°37'·0N 06°31'·2W**. AC *5611*, 2171, 2474. HW –0530 on Dover; ML 1·4m; Duration 0600; see 1.11. Good shelter with SE swell or strong winds from ENE to SSW. Enter at SHM buoy, Fl G 6s, marking Bogha Mòr. Thence NW to Arinagour ferry pier, 2 FR(vert) 10m. Beware McQuarrie's Rk (dries 2·9m) 1ca E of pier hd and unmarked drying rks further N on E side of fairway. Ch and hotel are conspic ahead. Continue N towards old stone pier; ⚓ S of it or pick up a buoy. Six ⚓s on W side of hbr, between the two piers. Also ⚓ E of Eilean Eatharna. Piermaster ☎ (01879) 230347; VHF Ch 31. **Facilities:** HIE Trading Post ☎ 230349, M, D, FW, Gas, 🛒, CH, R. **Village** ⬛, FW, P, ✉, ferry to Oban (≥).

**GOTT BAY**, Tiree, **56°30'·74N 06°48'·07W**. AC *5611*, 2474. Tides as 1.11; HW –0540 on Dover. HM ☎ (01879) 230337, VHF Ch 31. Adequate shelter in calm weather, but exposed in winds ENE to S. (in which case use Wilson hbr in Balephetrish Bay IM W, Ldg lts F.G/ Oc.G). The bay, at NE end of island, can be identified by conspic latticed tr at Scarinish about 8ca SW of ent, with lt Fl 3s 11m 16M close by (obscd over hbr). Appr on NW track, keeping to SW side of bay which is obstructed on NE side by Soa Is and drying rks. The ferry pier at S side of ent has FR ldg lts 286½°. ⚓ 1ca NW of pier head in 3m on sand; L at pier. Facilities: P & D (cans), Gas, 🛒, R, Bar, ✉ at Scarinish (½M), ferry to Oban (≥).

## 1.13 TOBERMORY

Mull (Argyll and Bute) **56°37'·19N 06°03'·87W** ✿✿✿⚓⚓✿✿✿

**CHARTS** AC *5611, 2171, 2390*, 2474; Imray C65; OS 47

**TIDES** –0519 Dover; ML 2·4; Duration 0610

**Standard Port OBAN (➡)**

| Times | | | | Height (metres) | | | |
|---|---|---|---|---|---|---|---|
| High Water | | Low Water | | MHWS | MHWN | MLWN | MLWS |
| 0100 | 0700 | 0100 | 0800 | 4·0 | 2·9 | 1·8 | 0·7 |
| 1300 | 1900 | 1300 | 2000 | | | | |
| **Differences TOBERMORY** (Mull) | | | | | | | |
| +0025 | +0010 | +0015 | +0025 | +0·4 | +0·4 | 0·0 | 0·0 |
| **CARSAIG BAY** (S Mull) | | | | | | | |
| –0015 | –0005 | –0030 | +0020 | +0·1 | +0·2 | 0·0 | –0·1 |
| **IONA** (SW Mull) | | | | | | | |
| –0010 | –0005 | –0020 | +0015 | 0·0 | +0·1 | –0·3 | –0·2 |
| **BUNESSAN** (Loch Lathaich, SW Mull) | | | | | | | |
| –0015 | –0015 | –0010 | –0015 | +0·3 | +0·1 | 0·0 | –0·1 |
| **ULVA SOUND** (W Mull) | | | | | | | |
| –0010 | –0015 | 0000 | –0005 | +0·4 | +0·3 | 0·0 | –0·1 |

**SHELTER** Good, but some swell in strong N/NE winds. 22 ⚓s are marked by a blue ⚓ with a Y pick-up. ⚓ clear of fairway, where marked; at SE end of The Doirlinn.

**NAVIGATION** WPT 56°37'·59N 06°03'·17W, 224°/0·5M to moorings. N ent is wide and clear of dangers. S ent via The Doirlinn is only 80m wide at HW, and dries at LW; at HW±2 least depth is 2m. Enter between 2 bns on 300°.

**LIGHTS AND MARKS** Rhubha nan Gall, Fl 3s 17m 15M, W tr is 1M N of ent. Ch spire and hotel turret are both conspic.

**R/T** VHF Ch 16 12 (HO), M.

**TELEPHONE** (Code 01688) Piermaster 302017, 🖷 302660; MRCC (01475) 729014; Local CG 302200; Marinecall 09068 969653; Police 302016; Dr 302013.

**FACILITIES** **Cal-Mac Pier**, only short stay AB for P, D; landing stage FW £2; **Western Isles YC** ☎ 302371; **Services:** ⚓ £9 <8m £12 >8m or, 10 nights/£70-£90, ME, CH, ACA, Gaz, Gas, Divers. **Town** FW, P, Dr, 🖳, R, Bar, ⊠, ⓑ, ⇌ (ferry to Oban), ✈ (grass strip; helipad on golf course).

**SOUND OF MULL** (Mull, **56°31'·44N 05°56'·82W**). Beware drying rocks 6ca E of the bay; ent on SE side. **Salen Jetty**, ⚓ £10. Landing from yacht at ⚓ £1 per person/H24. FW, D. **Village**, 🖳, ME, ⓔ, CH, R, Dr, ⊠. Land at jetty in SW corner.

**CRAIGNURE**, (Mull, **56°28'·37N 05°42'·25W**) ldg lts 241°, both FR 10/12m. Facilities: 🖳, Bar, ⊠, Gas, ferry to Oban. Tides, see 1.14.

## 1.14 LOCH ALINE

Highland **56°32'·09N 05°46'·47W** ✿✿✿⚓ ✿✿✿

**CHARTS** AC *5611, 2390*; Imray C65; OS 49

**TIDES** –0523 Dover; Duration 0610

**Standard Port OBAN (➡)**

| Times | | | | Height (metres) | | | |
|---|---|---|---|---|---|---|---|
| High Water | | Low Water | | MHWS | MHWN | MLWN | MLWS |
| 0100 | 0700 | 0100 | 0800 | 4·0 | 2·9 | 1·8 | 0·7 |
| 1300 | 1900 | 1300 | 2000 | | | | |
| **Differences LOCH ALINE** | | | | | | | |
| +0012 | +0012 | No data | | +0·5 | +0·3 | No data | |
| **SALEN** (Sound of Mull) | | | | | | | |
| +0045 | +0015 | +0020 | +0030 | +0·2 | +0·2 | –0·1 | 0·0 |
| **CRAIGNURE** (Sound of Mull) | | | | | | | |
| +0030 | +0005 | +0010 | +0015 | 0·0 | +0·1 | –0·1 | –0·1 |

**SHELTER** Very good. ⚓s in SE end of loch and in N and E part of loch. Temp berth on the old stone slip in the ent on W side, depth and ferries permitting.

**NAVIGATION** WPT 56°31'·49N 05°46'·37W, 176°/0·9M to front ldg bn. Bns (not easily seen) lead 356°, 100m W of Bogha Lurcain, drying rk off Bolorkle Pt on E side of ent. The buoyed ent is easy, but narrow with a bar (min depth 2·1m); stream runs 2½kn at sp. Beware coasters (which completely fill the ent) from the sand mine going to/from the jetty and ferries to/from Mull. Last 5ca of loch dries.

**LIGHTS AND MARKS** Ardtornish Pt lt ho, 1M SSE of ent, Fl (2) WRG 10s 7m 8/5M. Lts and buoys as chartlet. War memorial (conspic, 9m high) stands on W side of ent. Ldg lts are FW 2/4m (H24). 1M up the loch on E side a Y bn with Y ○ topmark marks a reef, and ¾M further up similar bn marks a larger reef on W side. Both top marks need new coat of paint. Clock tr is very conspic at head of loch.

**R/T** None.

**TELEPHONE** (Code 01967) MRCC (01475) 729014; ⊖ (0141) 887 9369; Marinecall 09068 969653; Ⓗ (01631) 563727; Dr 421252.

**FACILITIES** **Village** FW at pier, Gas, 🖳, R, Bar, P, ⊠, (ⓑ, ⇌, ✈ at Oban), Ferry to Fishnish Bay (Mull).

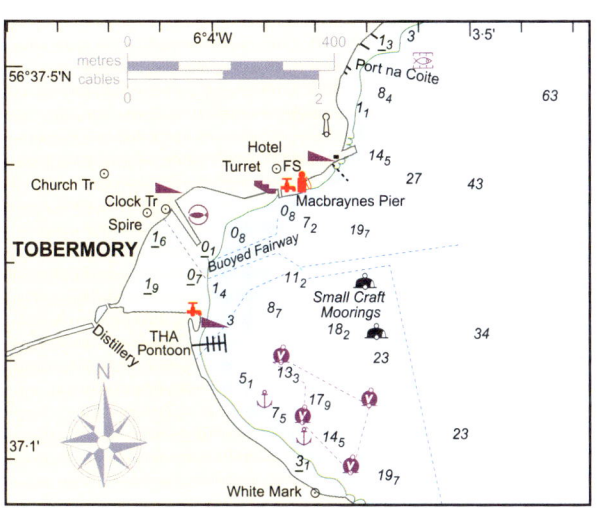

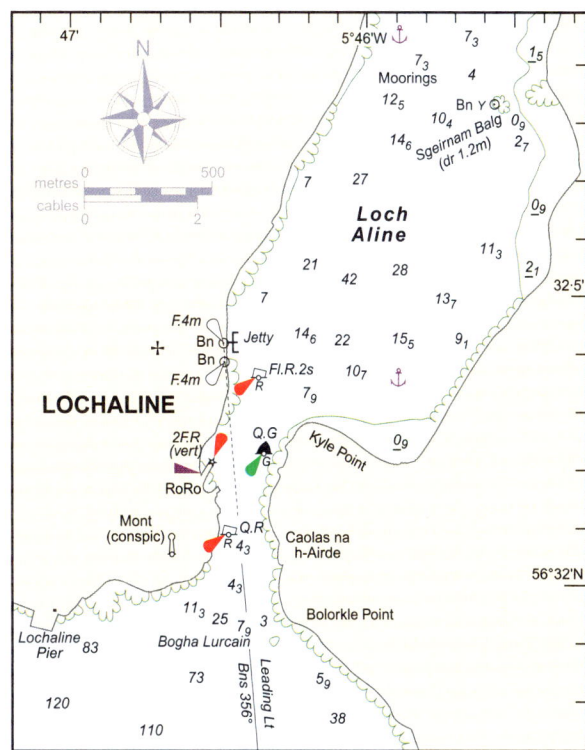

**ANCHORAGES on WEST and SOUTH COASTS OF MULL (Anti-clockwise from the north. SDs essential)** (See AC *5611*)

**TRESHNISH ISLES, 56°29'N 06°31'W.** AC 2652. The main Is (N to S) are: Cairn na Burgh, Fladda, Lunga, Bac Mòr and Bac Beag. Tides run hard and isles are exposed to swell, but merit a visit in calm weather. Appr with caution on ldg lines as in CCC SDs; temp ⚓ off Lunga's N tip in 4m.

**STAFFA, 56°25'·96N 06°20'·34W.** AC 2652. Spectacular isle with Fingal's Cave, but same caveats as above. Very temp ⚓ off SE tip where there is landing; beware unmarked rks.

**GOMETRA, 56°28'·85N 06°23'W.** AC 2652. Tides as 1.13. The narrow inlet between Gometra and Ulva Is offers sheltered ⚓, except in S'lies. Appr on 020° between Staffa and Little Colonsay, or N of the former. Beware rks drying 3·2m, to stbd and 5ca S of ent. Inside, E side is cleaner.

**LOCH NA KEAL, 56°26'N 06°18'W** (ent). AC 2652. Tides in 1.13. Appr S of Geasgill Is and N of drying rks off **Inch Kenneth**; E of this Is and in **Sound of Ulva** are sheltered ⚓s, except in S'lies. Beware MacQuarrie's Rk, dries 0·8m.

**LOCH LATHAICH,** Mull, **56°19'·29N 06°15'·47W.** AC 2617. HW –0545 on Dover; ML 2·4. See 1.13. Excellent shelter with easy access; good base for cruising W Mull. Eilean na Liathanaich (a group of islets) lie off the ent, marked by a W bn at the E end, Fl WR 6s 12m 8/6M, R088°-108°, W108°-088°. Keep to W side of loch and ⚓ off Bendoran BY in SW, or SE of Eilean Ban off the pier in approx 5m. **Facilities:** (Bunessan) Shop, ✉, Bar, R, FW.

**SOUND OF IONA, 56°19'·45N 06°23'·12W.** AC 2617. Tides see 1.13. From N, enter in mid-chan; from S keep clear of Torran Rks. Cathedral brg 012° closes the Iona shore past 2 SHM buoys and SCM buoy. Beware a bank 0·1m in mid-sound, between cathedral and Fionnphort; also tel cables and ferries. ⚓ S of ferry close in to Iona, or in Bull Hole. Consult SDs. Crowded in season; limited facilities.

**TINKER'S HOLE,** Ross of Mull, **56°17'·49N 06°23'·07W.** AC 2617. Beware Torran Rks, reefs extending 5M S and SW of Erraid. Usual app from S, avoiding Rankin's Rks, drying 0·8m, and rk, dries 2·3m, between Eilean nam Muc and Erraid. Popular ⚓ in mid-pool between Eilean Dubh and Erraid.

**CARSAIG BAY,** Ross of Mull, **56°19'·19N 05°59'·07W.** Tides see 1.13. AC 2386. Temp, fair weather ⚓s to N of Gamhnach Mhòr, reef 2m high, or close into NW corner of bay. Landing at stone quay on NE side. No facilities.

**LOCH SPELVE,** Mull, **56°23'N 05°41'W.** AC 2387. Tides as Oban. Landlocked water, prone to squalls off surrounding hills. Ent narrows to ½ca due to shoal S side and drying rk N side, 56°23'·24N 05°41'·95W, ☆ FlG 5s 3m 2M, G pole. CCC SDs give local ldg lines. ⚓s in SW and NW arms, clear of fish farms. Pier at Croggan; no facilities.

**ANCHORAGES ALONG LOCH LINNHE** (AC *5611*, 2378, 2379, 2380)

**LYNN OF LORN, 56°33'N 05°25'·2W:** At NE end are ⚓s off **Port Appin,** clear of ferry and cables (beware Appin Rks); and in **Airds Bay,** open to SW. At NW tip of Lismore, **Port Ramsey** offers good ⚓s between the 3 main islets. **Linnhe Marina** ☎ 01631 730401 offers pontoon and mooring berths.

**LOCH CRERAN, 56°32'·14N 05°25'·22W.** Tides 1.15. Ent at Airds Pt, Dir lt 050°, Fl WRG 2s, W vis 041-058°. Chan turns 90° stbd with streams of 4kn. Sgeir Callich, rky ridge extends NE to SHM By, Fl G 3s; ⚓ W of it. ⚓s (max LOA 7m) off Barcaldine; also 3 ⚓s max LOA 9m off Creagan Inn, ☎ (01631) 573250. Bridge has 12m clearance. Beware of extensive marine farms in loch.

**LOCH LEVEN, 56°42'N 05°12'W.** (see inset 1.15 Tides 1.15. Fair weather ⚓s in Ballachulish Bay, at Kentallen B (deep), Onich and off St Brides on N shore. App bridge (17m clnce) on 114°; 4ca ENE of br are moorings and ⚓ at Poll an Dùnan, entered W of perch. Facilities at Ballachulish: Hotels, 🛒, R, ✉, Ⓑ. Loch is navigable 7M to Kinlochleven.

**CORRAN NARROWS, 56°43'·27N 05°14'·34W.** AC 2372. Sp rate 6kn. Well buoyed; Corran Pt lt ho, Iso WRG 4s, and lt bn 5ca NE. ⚓ 5ca NW of Pt, off Camas Aiseig pier/slip.

## 1.15  FORT WILLIAM/CORPACH

Highland 56°48'·99N 05°07'·07W (off Fort William)

**CHARTS**  AC *5611*, 2372, 2380; Imray C65, C23; OS 41

**TIDES**  –0535 Dover; ML 2·3; Duration 0610

**Standard Port OBAN** (→)

| Times | | | | Height (metres) | | | |
|---|---|---|---|---|---|---|---|
| High Water | | Low Water | | MHWS | MHWN | MLWN | MLWS |
| 0100 | 0700 | 0100 | 0800 | 4·0 | 2·9 | 1·8 | 0·7 |
| 1300 | 1900 | 1300 | 2000 | | | | |
| **Differences CORPACH** | | | | | | | |
| 0000 | +0020 | +0040 | 0000 | 0·0 | 0·0 | –0·2 | –0·2 |
| **LOCH EIL** (Head) | | | | | | | |
| +0025 | +0045 | +0105 | +0025 | | No data | | No data |
| **CORRAN NARROWS** | | | | | | | |
| +0007 | +0007 | +0004 | +0004 | +0·4 | +0·4 | –0·1 | 0·0 |
| **LOCH LEVEN** (Head) | | | | | | | |
| +0045 | +0045 | +0045 | +0045 | | No data | | No data |
| **LOCH LINNHE** (Port Appin) | | | | | | | |
| –0005 | –0005 | –0030 | 0000 | +0·2 | +0·2 | +0·1 | +0·1 |
| **LOCH CRERAN** (Barcaldine Pier) | | | | | | | |
| +0010 | +0020 | +0040 | +0015 | +0·1 | +0·1 | 0·0 | +0·1 |
| **LOCH CRERAN** (Head) | | | | | | | |
| +0015 | +0025 | +0120 | +0020 | –0·3 | –0·3 | –0·4 | –0·3 |

**SHELTER**  Exposed to winds SW thro' N to NE. ⚓s off Fort William pier; in Camus na Gall; SSW of Eilean A Bhealaidh; and off Corpach Basin, where there is also a waiting pontoon; or inside the canal where it is more sheltered. The sea lock is normally available HW±4 during canal hrs. For Caledonian Canal see 1.16.

**NAVIGATION**  Corpach WPT 56°50'·29N 05°07'·07W, 315°/0·3M to lock ent.

> Beware McLean Rk, dries 0·3m, buoyed, 8ca N of Fort William. Lochy Flats dry 3ca off the E bank. In Annat Narrows at ent to Loch Eil streams reach 5kn.

**LIGHTS AND MARKS**  Iso WRG 4s lt is at N jetty of sea-lock ent, W310°-335°. A long pier/viaduct off Ft William is unlit.

**R/T**  Call: *Corpach Lock* VHF Ch **74** 16 (during canal hours).

**TELEPHONE**  (Code 01397) HM 772249, 🖷 772484 (Corpach); MRCC (01475) 729014; ⊖ 702948; Marinecall 09068 969653; Police 702361; Dr 703136.

**FACILITIES**  **Fort William: Pier** ☎ 703881, AB; **Services:** Slip, L, CH, ACA. **Town:** P, ME, El, 🔧, YC, 🛒, R, Bar, Ⓗ, ✉, Ⓑ, 🚂. **Corpach: Corpach Basin** ☎ 772249, AB, L, FW, D; **Lochaber YC** ☎ 703576, M, FW, L, Slip; **Services:** ME, El, 🔧, D (cans), M, CH, Slip, Divers. **Village:** P, 🛒, R, Bar, ✉, Ⓑ, 🚂.

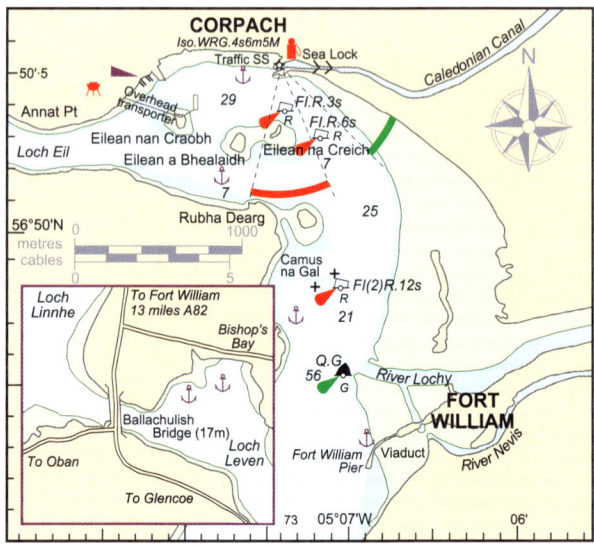

## 1.16 CALEDONIAN CANAL

Highland ❀❀⛵⛵✿✿✿

**CHARTS** AC 1791; Imray C23; OS 41, 34, 26; *BWB Skippers Guide*

**TIDES** Tidal differences: Corpach –0455 on Dover; See 1.15. Clachnaharry: +0116 on Dover.

**SHELTER** Corpach is at the SW ent of the Caledonian Canal, see 1.15; the sea locks at both ends do not open LW±2 at springs. For best shelter transit the sea lock and lie above the double lock. Numerous pontoons along the canal; cost is included in the canal dues.

**NAVIGATION** The 60M canal consists of 38M through 3 lochs, (Lochs Lochy, Oich and Ness), connected by 22M of canal.

Loch Oich is part of a hydro-electric scheme which may vary the water level. The passage normally takes two full days, possibly longer in the summer; absolute minimum is 14 hrs. Speed limit is 5kn in the canal sections. There are 10 swing bridges; road traffic has priority at peak hrs. Do not pass bridges without the keeper's instructions.

**LOCKS** There are 29 locks: 14 between Loch Linnhe (Corpach), via Lochs Lochy and Oich up to the summit (106ft above sea level); and 15 locks from the summit down via Loch Ness to Inverness.

**2005 information**

**Hours:** Winter Mon-Fri 0900-1600
Spring Mon-Sun 0830-1730
Summer Mon-Sun 0800-1730
Autumn Mon-Sun 0830-1730

**Dues** payable at Corpach: transit/lock fee Outward £16 per metre for 8 day passage or less; Return £12 per metre. £20 per metre is charged for a 2 week sojourn. For regulations and useful booklet *BWS Skipper's Guide* apply: Canal Manager, Canal Office, Seaport Marina, Muirtown Wharf, Inverness IV3 5LE, ☎ (01463) 233140, 🖷 710942 or download from: www.waterscape.com

**LIGHTS AND MARKS**
See 1.15 for ent lts. Channel is marked by posts, cairns and unlit buoys, PHM on the NW side of the chan and SHM on the SE side.

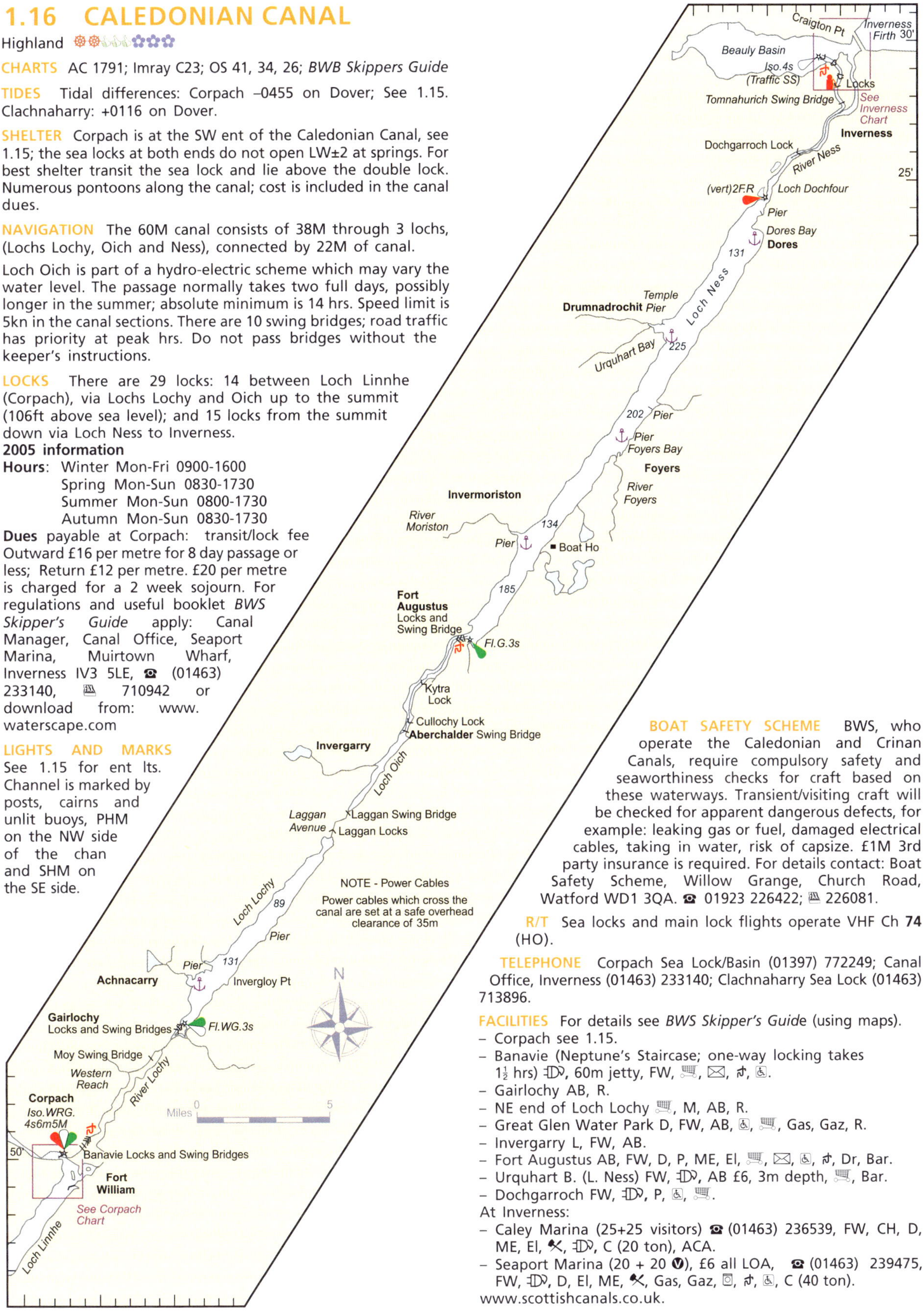

**BOAT SAFETY SCHEME** BWS, who operate the Caledonian and Crinan Canals, require compulsory safety and seaworthiness checks for craft based on these waterways. Transient/visiting craft will be checked for apparent dangerous defects, for example: leaking gas or fuel, damaged electrical cables, taking in water, risk of capsize. £1M 3rd party insurance is required. For details contact: Boat Safety Scheme, Willow Grange, Church Road, Watford WD1 3QA. ☎ 01923 226422; 🖷 226081.

**R/T** Sea locks and main lock flights operate VHF Ch **74** (HO).

**TELEPHONE** Corpach Sea Lock/Basin (01397) 772249; Canal Office, Inverness (01463) 233140; Clachnaharry Sea Lock (01463) 713896.

**FACILITIES** For details see *BWS Skipper's Guide* (using maps).
– Corpach see 1.15.
– Banavie (Neptune's Staircase; one-way locking takes 1½ hrs) ⟲, 60m jetty, FW, 🛒, ✉, ⛽, ♿.
– Gairlochy AB, R.
– NE end of Loch Lochy 🛒, M, AB, R.
– Great Glen Water Park D, FW, AB, ♿, 🛒, Gas, Gaz, R.
– Invergarry L, FW, AB.
– Fort Augustus AB, FW, D, P, ME, El, 🛒, ✉, ♿, ⛽, Dr, Bar.
– Urquhart B. (L. Ness) FW, ⟲, AB £6, 3m depth, 🛒, Bar.
– Dochgarroch FW, ⟲, P, ♿, 🛒.
At Inverness:
– Caley Marina (25+25 visitors) ☎ (01463) 236539, FW, CH, D, ME, El, 🔧, ⟲, C (20 ton), ACA.
– Seaport Marina (20 + 20 ❶), £6 all LOA, ☎ (01463) 239475, FW, ⟲, D, El, ME, 🔧, Gas, Gaz, ▣, ⛽, ♿, C (40 ton).
www.scottishcanals.co.uk

### Map labels

Craigton Pt
Inverness Firth 30'
Beauly Basin
Iso.4s
(Traffic SS)
Tomnahurich Swing Bridge
Inverness
See Inverness Chart
Dochgarroch Lock
River Ness
25'
(vert)2F.R
Loch Dochfour
Pier
Dores Bay
Dores
131
Loch Ness
Temple Pier
Drumnadrochit
Urquhart Bay
225
202 Pier
Pier
Foyers Bay
Foyers
River Foyers
Invermoriston
River Moriston
134
Pier
Boat Ho
185
Fort Augustus
Locks and Swing Bridge
Fl.G.3s
Kytra Lock
Cullochy Lock
Aberchalder Swing Bridge
Invergarry
Loch Oich
Laggan Avenue
Laggan Swing Bridge
Laggan Locks

**NOTE - Power Cables**
Power cables which cross the canal are set at a safe overhead clearance of 35m

Loch Lochy
89
Pier
Achnacarry
Pier
131
Invergloy Pt
N
Gairlochy
Locks and Swing Bridges
Fl.WG.3s
Moy Swing Bridge
Western Reach
River Lochy
Corpach
Iso.WRG. 4s6m5M
Miles 0 5
50'
Banavie Locks and Swing Bridges
Fort William
Loch Linnhe
See Corpach Chart

# Oban Tides

**TIME ZONE (UT)**
For Summer Time add ONE hour in **non-shaded areas**

**OBAN**  LAT 56°25'N   LONG 5°29'W
TIMES AND HEIGHTS OF HIGH AND LOW WATERS

Dates in red are SPRINGS
Dates in blue are NEAPS

**YEAR 2008**

## JANUARY

| Day | Time m | Time m | Time m | Time m |
|---|---|---|---|---|
| 1 TU | 0523 1.6 | 1122 3.1 | 1828 2.0 | |
| 2 W | 0017 2.9 | 0619 1.8 | 1238 3.0 | 1934 2.0 |
| 3 TH | 0142 3.0 | 0721 1.9 | 1404 3.0 | 2043 2.0 |
| 4 F | 0246 3.1 | 0830 1.9 | 1508 3.1 | 2139 1.8 |
| 5 SA | 0338 3.3 | 0938 1.8 | 1557 3.3 | 2224 1.7 |
| 6 SU | 0423 3.4 | 1032 1.7 | 1640 3.5 | 2302 1.5 |
| 7 M | 0504 3.6 | 1116 1.5 | 1720 3.6 | 2339 1.3 |
| 8 TU | 0543 3.8 | 1157 1.4 | 1758 3.7 ● | |
| 9 W | 0013 1.2 | 0620 3.9 | 1236 1.3 | 1833 3.7 |
| 10 TH | 0047 1.1 | 0655 3.9 | 1313 1.2 | 1904 3.7 |
| 11 F | 0120 1.0 | 0728 3.9 | 1349 1.2 | 1934 3.7 |
| 12 SA | 0153 1.0 | 0802 3.9 | 1423 1.2 | 2007 3.6 |
| 13 SU | 0228 1.0 | 0838 3.8 | 1500 1.3 | 2044 3.5 |
| 14 M | 0308 1.1 | 0919 3.7 | 1543 1.4 | 2126 3.4 |
| 15 TU | 0354 1.3 | 1007 3.5 | 1635 1.5 | ☽ 2215 3.2 |
| 16 W | 0451 1.4 | 1108 3.4 | 1740 1.6 | 2319 3.1 |
| 17 TH | 0605 1.6 | 1236 3.2 | 1854 1.7 | |
| 18 F | 0052 3.0 | 0730 1.6 | 1423 3.2 | 2010 1.6 |
| 19 SA | 0237 3.2 | 0859 1.5 | 1540 3.4 | 2120 1.5 |
| 20 SU | 0351 3.4 | 1017 1.3 | 1638 3.6 | 2220 1.2 |
| 21 M | 0444 3.7 | 1115 1.1 | 1723 3.7 | 2311 1.0 |
| 22 TU | 0527 3.9 | 1203 1.0 | 1802 3.8 | ○ 2358 0.8 |
| 23 W | 0607 4.1 | 1247 0.9 | 1838 3.9 | |
| 24 TH | 0041 0.7 | 0644 4.1 | 1327 0.9 | 1912 3.9 |
| 25 F | 0122 0.6 | 0721 4.1 | 1405 1.0 | 1945 3.8 |
| 26 SA | 0200 0.7 | 0755 4.0 | 1441 1.1 | 2016 3.7 |
| 27 SU | 0237 0.8 | 0828 3.8 | 1514 1.3 | 2046 3.5 |
| 28 M | 0313 1.1 | 0900 3.6 | 1548 1.5 | 2117 3.4 |
| 29 TU | 0351 1.3 | 0933 3.4 | 1627 1.8 | 2154 3.2 |
| 30 W | 0433 1.6 | 1010 3.2 | 1716 1.9 | ☽ 2240 3.0 |
| 31 TH | 0523 1.8 | 1057 2.9 | 1819 2.1 | 2358 2.8 |

## FEBRUARY

| Day | Time m | Time m | Time m | Time m |
|---|---|---|---|---|
| 1 F | 0625 2.0 | 1246 2.8 | 1938 2.1 | |
| 2 SA | 0214 2.9 | 0740 2.1 | 1507 2.9 | 2113 2.0 |
| 3 SU | 0328 3.0 | 0923 2.0 | 1600 3.1 | 2213 1.7 |
| 4 M | 0415 3.3 | 1033 1.7 | 1637 3.3 | 2252 1.5 |
| 5 TU | 0455 3.5 | 1113 1.5 | 1713 3.5 | 2326 1.2 |
| 6 W | 0532 3.7 | 1148 1.2 | 1748 3.7 | 2358 1.0 |
| 7 TH | 0607 3.9 | 1222 1.0 | 1819 3.8 ● | |
| 8 F | 0028 0.8 | 0639 4.0 | 1256 0.8 | 1847 3.8 |
| 9 SA | 0100 0.7 | 0710 4.1 | 1328 0.8 | 1914 3.8 |
| 10 SU | 0133 0.6 | 0741 4.1 | 1400 0.8 | 1944 3.8 |
| 11 M | 0209 0.7 | 0815 4.0 | 1435 0.9 | 2019 3.7 |
| 12 TU | 0248 0.8 | 0852 3.8 | 1515 1.1 | 2058 3.5 |
| 13 W | 0332 1.0 | 0936 3.5 | 1604 1.3 | 2142 3.3 |
| 14 TH | 0428 1.3 | 1012 3.0 | 1706 1.5 | ☽ 2241 3.0 |
| 15 F | 0546 1.6 | 1210 2.9 | 1825 1.7 | |
| 16 SA | 0028 2.9 | 0721 1.7 | 1433 2.9 | 1951 1.7 |
| 17 SU | 0251 3.0 | 0917 1.6 | 1551 3.1 | 2112 1.5 |
| 18 M | 0403 3.3 | 1030 1.3 | 1642 3.4 | 2215 1.2 |
| 19 TU | 0445 3.6 | 1117 1.1 | 1719 3.6 | 2303 0.9 |
| 20 W | 0520 3.9 | 1155 0.9 | 1751 3.8 | 2345 0.7 |
| 21 TH | 0553 4.0 | 1231 0.8 | 1821 3.9 ○ | |
| 22 F | 0024 0.5 | 0625 4.1 | 1305 0.8 | 1849 3.9 |
| 23 SA | 0101 0.5 | 0657 4.1 | 1337 0.8 | 1917 3.9 |
| 24 SU | 0136 0.6 | 0726 4.0 | 1407 1.0 | 1944 3.9 |
| 25 M | 0207 0.8 | 0754 3.9 | 1435 1.2 | 2011 3.7 |
| 26 TU | 0239 1.0 | 0822 3.7 | 1505 1.4 | 2039 3.5 |
| 27 W | 0312 1.3 | 0849 3.4 | 1538 1.6 | 2112 3.3 |
| 28 TH | 0349 1.6 | 0918 3.2 | 1622 1.9 | 2151 3.1 |
| 29 F | 0437 1.9 | 0951 2.9 | 1728 2.0 | ☾ 2245 2.9 |

## MARCH

| Day | Time m | Time m | Time m | Time m |
|---|---|---|---|---|
| 1 SA | 0546 2.1 | 1046 2.7 | 1851 2.1 | |
| 2 SU | 0150 2.7 | 0711 2.1 | 1507 2.7 | 2035 2.0 |
| 3 M | 0314 2.9 | 0921 2.0 | 1549 2.9 | 2148 1.7 |
| 4 TU | 0358 3.2 | 1016 1.6 | 1621 3.2 | 2227 1.4 |
| 5 W | 0434 3.5 | 1051 1.3 | 1653 3.4 | 2300 1.1 |
| 6 TH | 0508 3.8 | 1124 1.0 | 1724 3.6 | 2331 0.8 |
| 7 F | 0542 4.0 | 1157 0.7 | 1753 3.8 ● | |
| 8 SA | 0002 0.5 | 0614 4.1 | 1229 0.5 | 1819 3.9 |
| 9 SU | 0036 0.4 | 0645 4.2 | 1302 0.5 | 1848 3.9 |
| 10 M | 0112 0.3 | 0717 4.1 | 1335 0.5 | 1920 3.9 |
| 11 TU | 0151 0.4 | 0751 4.0 | 1413 0.6 | 1956 3.8 |
| 12 W | 0233 0.6 | 0830 3.7 | 1455 0.9 | 2036 3.6 |
| 13 TH | 0321 0.9 | 0914 3.3 | 1544 1.1 | 2122 3.3 |
| 14 F | 0422 1.3 | 1012 3.0 | 1648 1.4 | ☾ 2224 3.0 |
| 15 SA | 0543 1.6 | 1225 2.7 | 1808 1.6 | |
| 16 SU | 0037 2.8 | 0731 1.7 | 1435 2.8 | 1937 1.6 |
| 17 M | 0253 3.0 | 0926 1.5 | 1544 3.0 | 2100 1.4 |
| 18 TU | 0353 3.3 | 1021 1.2 | 1627 3.3 | 2159 1.1 |
| 19 W | 0427 3.5 | 1057 1.0 | 1657 3.5 | 2244 0.8 |
| 20 TH | 0457 3.8 | 1134 0.9 | 1724 3.7 | 2324 0.7 |
| 21 F | 0528 3.9 | 1205 0.8 | 1752 3.8 ○ | |
| 22 SA | 0001 0.6 | 0558 4.0 | 1235 0.8 | 1820 3.9 |
| 23 SU | 0035 0.6 | 0627 4.0 | 1304 0.8 | 1847 3.9 |
| 24 M | 0107 0.7 | 0655 3.9 | 1332 0.9 | 1913 3.9 |
| 25 TU | 0137 0.8 | 0723 3.8 | 1400 1.1 | 1940 3.8 |
| 26 W | 0207 1.1 | 0749 3.6 | 1428 1.3 | 2010 3.6 |
| 27 TH | 0238 1.4 | 0815 3.4 | 1458 1.5 | 2042 3.4 |
| 28 F | 0312 1.6 | 0842 3.1 | 1536 1.8 | 2120 3.1 |
| 29 SA | 0357 1.9 | 0915 2.9 | 1641 2.0 | ☽ 2213 2.9 |
| 30 SU | 0516 2.1 | 1010 2.6 | 1806 2.1 | |
| 31 M | 0047 2.7 | 0648 2.1 | 1421 2.6 | 1935 2.0 |

## APRIL

| Day | Time m | Time m | Time m | Time m |
|---|---|---|---|---|
| 1 TU | 0237 2.9 | 0831 1.9 | 1511 2.8 | 2054 1.7 |
| 2 W | 0323 3.2 | 0932 1.5 | 1547 3.1 | 2142 1.4 |
| 3 TH | 0400 3.5 | 1013 1.2 | 1620 3.4 | 2220 1.0 |
| 4 F | 0435 3.8 | 1049 0.9 | 1650 3.6 | 2256 0.7 |
| 5 SA | 0510 4.0 | 1123 0.6 | 1719 3.8 | 2333 0.4 |
| 6 SU | 0544 4.2 | 1158 0.4 | 1750 3.9 ● | |
| 7 M | 0011 0.3 | 0618 4.2 | 1234 0.4 | 1823 4.0 |
| 8 TU | 0053 0.3 | 0654 4.1 | 1312 0.4 | 1900 3.9 |
| 9 W | 0136 0.4 | 0733 3.9 | 1354 0.5 | 1940 3.8 |
| 10 TH | 0224 0.6 | 0815 3.6 | 1440 0.8 | 2024 3.6 |
| 11 F | 0317 1.0 | 0904 3.2 | 1533 1.1 | 2115 3.3 |
| 12 SA | 0422 1.3 | 1010 2.8 | 1636 1.3 | ☾ 2225 3.0 |
| 13 SU | 0542 1.5 | 1232 2.6 | 1751 1.5 | |
| 14 M | 0037 2.9 | 0736 1.6 | 1413 2.7 | 1915 1.5 |
| 15 TU | 0226 3.0 | 0903 1.4 | 1517 2.9 | 2033 1.3 |
| 16 W | 0322 3.2 | 0954 1.2 | 1556 3.1 | 2131 1.1 |
| 17 TH | 0355 3.4 | 1031 1.1 | 1623 3.4 | 2217 0.9 |
| 18 F | 0426 3.6 | 1103 1.0 | 1650 3.6 | 2256 0.8 |
| 19 SA | 0457 3.7 | 1133 0.9 | 1719 3.7 | 2332 0.7 |
| 20 SU | 0527 3.8 | 1201 0.9 | 1749 3.8 ○ | |
| 21 M | 0006 0.8 | 0557 3.8 | 1231 0.9 | 1817 3.9 |
| 22 TU | 0038 0.8 | 0627 3.8 | 1301 1.0 | 1846 3.8 |
| 23 W | 0110 1.0 | 0656 3.7 | 1331 1.1 | 1917 3.7 |
| 24 TH | 0142 1.2 | 0726 3.5 | 1402 1.3 | 1950 3.6 |
| 25 F | 0215 1.5 | 0754 3.3 | 1433 1.5 | 2025 3.4 |
| 26 SA | 0250 1.7 | 0825 3.1 | 1510 1.7 | 2105 3.2 |
| 27 SU | 0338 1.9 | 0906 2.9 | 1602 1.8 | 2159 3.0 |
| 28 M | 0451 2.0 | 1009 2.7 | 1715 1.9 | ☾ 2323 2.9 |
| 29 TU | 0616 1.9 | 1243 2.6 | 1831 1.9 | |
| 30 W | 0127 3.0 | 0736 1.8 | 1415 2.8 | 1942 1.7 |

Chart Datum: 2·10 metres below Ordnance Datum (Newlyn). HAT is 4·5 metres above Chart Datum.

》》 **FREE** monthly updates from 《《
www.reedsalmanac.co.uk

**TIME ZONE (UT)**
For Summer Time add ONE hour in **non-shaded areas**

## OBAN   LAT 56°25′N   LONG 5°29′W
### TIMES AND HEIGHTS OF HIGH AND LOW WATERS

Dates in red are SPRINGS
Dates in blue are NEAPS

**YEAR 2008**

**NW Scotland**

### MAY

| Day | Time | m | Time | m |
|---|---|---|---|---|
| 1 TH | 0230 | 3.2 | 0839 | 1.5 |
| | 1500 | 3.0 | 2043 | 1.4 |
| 2 F | 0316 | 3.5 | 0927 | 1.2 |
| | 1536 | 3.3 | 2134 | 1.1 |
| 3 SA | 0357 | 3.8 | 1009 | 0.9 |
| | 1610 | 3.5 | 2220 | 0.8 |
| 4 SU | 0437 | 4.0 | 1049 | 0.7 |
| | 1646 | 3.8 | 2305 | 0.5 |
| 5 M ● | 0516 | 4.1 | 1129 | 0.5 |
| | 1724 | 3.9 | 2351 | 0.4 |
| 6 TU | 0557 | 4.1 | 1210 | 0.4 |
| | 1805 | 4.0 | | |
| 7 W | 0038 | 0.4 | 0638 | 4.0 |
| | 1254 | 0.4 | 1846 | 3.9 |
| 8 TH | 0127 | 0.5 | 0722 | 3.8 |
| | 1340 | 0.6 | 1931 | 3.8 |
| 9 F | 0219 | 0.7 | 0809 | 3.5 |
| | 1429 | 0.7 | 2020 | 3.6 |
| 10 SA | 0315 | 1.0 | 0903 | 3.2 |
| | 1522 | 1.0 | 2114 | 3.4 |
| 11 SU | 0418 | 1.3 | 1012 | 2.9 |
| | 1621 | 1.2 | 2221 | 3.1 |
| 12 M ☽ | 0533 | 1.5 | 1201 | 2.7 |
| | 1726 | 1.3 | 2357 | 3.0 |
| 13 TU | 0703 | 1.5 | 1326 | 2.8 |
| | 1839 | 1.4 | | |
| 14 W | 0132 | 3.0 | 0820 | 1.5 |
| | 1428 | 2.9 | 1950 | 1.4 |
| 15 TH | 0234 | 3.1 | 0914 | 1.4 |
| | 1510 | 3.0 | 2052 | 1.3 |
| 16 F | 0315 | 3.2 | 0955 | 1.3 |
| | 1543 | 3.2 | 2142 | 1.2 |
| 17 SA | 0350 | 3.3 | 1029 | 1.2 |
| | 1615 | 3.4 | 2224 | 1.1 |
| 18 SU | 0424 | 3.5 | 1059 | 1.2 |
| | 1648 | 3.6 | 2302 | 1.1 |
| 19 M | 0457 | 3.5 | 1130 | 1.1 |
| | 1721 | 3.7 | 2337 | 1.1 |
| 20 TU ○ | 0532 | 3.6 | 1202 | 1.1 |
| | 1755 | 3.8 | | |
| 21 W | 0013 | 1.2 | 0606 | 3.6 |
| | 1236 | 1.1 | 1828 | 3.8 |
| 22 TH | 0049 | 1.2 | 0641 | 3.6 |
| | 1310 | 1.2 | 1903 | 3.7 |
| 23 F | 0126 | 1.3 | 0715 | 3.5 |
| | 1344 | 1.3 | 1939 | 3.6 |
| 24 SA | 0203 | 1.5 | 0748 | 3.3 |
| | 1417 | 1.4 | 2016 | 3.5 |
| 25 SU | 0242 | 1.6 | 0824 | 3.2 |
| | 1453 | 1.5 | 2057 | 3.3 |
| 26 M | 0327 | 1.7 | 0906 | 3.0 |
| | 1536 | 1.6 | 2145 | 3.2 |
| 27 TU | 0423 | 1.8 | 0959 | 2.9 |
| | 1629 | 1.7 | 2243 | 3.2 |
| 28 W ☽ | 0529 | 1.7 | 1105 | 2.8 |
| | 1732 | 1.7 | 2357 | 3.2 |
| 29 TH | 0638 | 1.7 | 1227 | 2.9 |
| | 1839 | 1.6 | | |
| 30 F | 0119 | 3.3 | 0742 | 1.5 |
| | 1347 | 3.0 | 1947 | 1.4 |
| 31 SA | 0226 | 3.4 | 0840 | 1.3 |
| | 1446 | 3.2 | 2051 | 1.2 |

### JUNE

| Day | Time | m | Time | m |
|---|---|---|---|---|
| 1 SU | 0321 | 3.6 | 0931 | 1.1 |
| | 1536 | 3.5 | 2151 | 1.0 |
| 2 M | 0411 | 3.8 | 1020 | 0.9 |
| | 1623 | 3.7 | 2246 | 0.8 |
| 3 TU ● | 0458 | 3.9 | 1107 | 0.7 |
| | 1709 | 3.8 | 2339 | 0.7 |
| 4 W | 0545 | 3.9 | 1154 | 0.6 |
| | 1755 | 3.9 | | |
| 5 TH | 0031 | 0.6 | 0632 | 3.8 |
| | 1241 | 0.5 | 1842 | 4.0 |
| 6 F | 0124 | 0.7 | 0719 | 3.7 |
| | 1329 | 0.6 | 1929 | 3.9 |
| 7 SA | 0216 | 0.8 | 0807 | 3.5 |
| | 1418 | 0.7 | 2017 | 3.7 |
| 8 SU | 0309 | 1.0 | 0858 | 3.3 |
| | 1507 | 0.8 | 2106 | 3.5 |
| 9 M | 0404 | 1.2 | 0954 | 3.1 |
| | 1559 | 1.0 | 2159 | 3.3 |
| 10 TU ☽ | 0503 | 1.4 | 1100 | 2.9 |
| | 1653 | 1.2 | 2259 | 3.1 |
| 11 W | 0607 | 1.6 | 1215 | 2.8 |
| | 1750 | 1.4 | | |
| 12 TH | 0010 | 3.0 | 0716 | 1.6 |
| | 1321 | 2.8 | 1851 | 1.5 |
| 13 F | 0124 | 3.0 | 0819 | 1.6 |
| | 1415 | 2.9 | 1954 | 1.5 |
| 14 SA | 0225 | 3.0 | 0911 | 1.6 |
| | 1501 | 3.1 | 2055 | 1.5 |
| 15 SU | 0313 | 3.1 | 0954 | 1.5 |
| | 1543 | 3.2 | 2149 | 1.5 |
| 16 M | 0356 | 3.2 | 1031 | 1.4 |
| | 1623 | 3.4 | 2234 | 1.4 |
| 17 TU | 0436 | 3.3 | 1107 | 1.3 |
| | 1702 | 3.5 | 2316 | 1.4 |
| 18 W ○ | 0517 | 3.4 | 1143 | 1.2 |
| | 1741 | 3.6 | 2356 | 1.3 |
| 19 TH | 0557 | 3.5 | 1219 | 1.2 |
| | 1819 | 3.7 | | |
| 20 F | 0036 | 1.3 | 0634 | 3.5 |
| | 1255 | 1.2 | 1856 | 3.7 |
| 21 SA | 0116 | 1.3 | 0710 | 3.5 |
| | 1329 | 1.2 | 1932 | 3.7 |
| 22 SU | 0154 | 1.3 | 0743 | 3.4 |
| | 1401 | 1.2 | 2007 | 3.6 |
| 23 M | 0231 | 1.4 | 0816 | 3.3 |
| | 1434 | 1.3 | 2043 | 3.6 |
| 24 TU | 0308 | 1.4 | 0852 | 3.2 |
| | 1510 | 1.3 | 2123 | 3.5 |
| 25 W | 0350 | 1.5 | 0934 | 3.1 |
| | 1554 | 1.4 | 2209 | 3.4 |
| 26 TH ☽ | 0441 | 1.5 | 1024 | 3.1 |
| | 1648 | 1.4 | 2306 | 3.3 |
| 27 F | 0543 | 1.6 | 1125 | 3.0 |
| | 1752 | 1.5 | | |
| 28 SA | 0018 | 3.3 | 0650 | 1.5 |
| | 1243 | 3.0 | 1906 | 1.5 |
| 29 SU | 0144 | 3.3 | 0759 | 1.4 |
| | 1408 | 3.1 | 2022 | 1.4 |
| 30 M | 0300 | 3.4 | 0903 | 1.3 |
| | 1518 | 3.3 | 2136 | 1.2 |

### JULY

| Day | Time | m | Time | m |
|---|---|---|---|---|
| 1 TU | 0403 | 3.5 | 1002 | 1.1 |
| | 1616 | 3.6 | 2241 | 1.0 |
| 2 W | 0457 | 3.7 | 1055 | 0.8 |
| | 1707 | 3.8 | 2339 | 0.8 |
| 3 TH ● | 0547 | 3.8 | 1145 | 0.7 |
| | 1755 | 4.0 | | |
| 4 F | 0031 | 0.7 | 0632 | 3.8 |
| | 1233 | 0.5 | 1839 | 4.0 |
| 5 SA | 0121 | 0.7 | 0716 | 3.7 |
| | 1319 | 0.5 | 1923 | 4.0 |
| 6 SU | 0207 | 0.8 | 0758 | 3.5 |
| | 1404 | 0.6 | 2005 | 3.9 |
| 7 M | 0252 | 0.9 | 0838 | 3.5 |
| | 1447 | 0.7 | 2045 | 3.7 |
| 8 TU | 0336 | 1.1 | 0918 | 3.3 |
| | 1530 | 0.9 | 2125 | 3.5 |
| 9 W | 0420 | 1.3 | 0959 | 3.1 |
| | 1614 | 1.1 | 2206 | 3.3 |
| 10 TH ☽ | 0506 | 1.6 | 1046 | 3.0 |
| | 1700 | 1.4 | 2252 | 3.1 |
| 11 F | 0558 | 1.7 | 1149 | 2.9 |
| | 1751 | 1.6 | 2351 | 2.9 |
| 12 SA | 0659 | 1.8 | 1312 | 2.8 |
| | 1849 | 1.8 | | |
| 13 SU | 0116 | 2.8 | 0813 | 1.8 |
| | 1424 | 2.9 | 1956 | 1.8 |
| 14 M | 0243 | 2.9 | 0923 | 1.7 |
| | 1522 | 3.1 | 2115 | 1.8 |
| 15 TU | 0343 | 3.0 | 1015 | 1.6 |
| | 1610 | 3.2 | 2222 | 1.7 |
| 16 W | 0429 | 3.2 | 1056 | 1.4 |
| | 1653 | 3.4 | 2308 | 1.5 |
| 17 TH | 0511 | 3.4 | 1133 | 1.2 |
| | 1733 | 3.6 | 2348 | 1.4 |
| 18 F ○ | 0550 | 3.5 | 1207 | 1.1 |
| | 1810 | 3.8 | | |
| 19 SA | 0026 | 1.2 | 0626 | 3.6 |
| | 1240 | 1.0 | 1845 | 3.8 |
| 20 SU | 0103 | 1.1 | 0659 | 3.6 |
| | 1311 | 0.9 | 1918 | 3.9 |
| 21 M | 0138 | 1.1 | 0727 | 3.6 |
| | 1341 | 0.9 | 1949 | 3.8 |
| 22 TU | 0210 | 1.1 | 0755 | 3.6 |
| | 1411 | 1.0 | 2021 | 3.8 |
| 23 W | 0242 | 1.1 | 0826 | 3.5 |
| | 1445 | 1.0 | 2056 | 3.7 |
| 24 TH | 0318 | 1.2 | 0904 | 3.4 |
| | 1526 | 1.1 | 2137 | 3.5 |
| 25 F | 0403 | 1.3 | 0947 | 3.2 |
| | 1616 | 1.3 | 2228 | 3.3 |
| 26 SA | 0501 | 1.5 | 1043 | 3.1 |
| | 1721 | 1.5 | 2338 | 3.1 |
| 27 SU | 0614 | 1.6 | 1203 | 3.0 |
| | 1843 | 1.6 | | |
| 28 M | 0127 | 3.1 | 0733 | 1.6 |
| | 1400 | 3.0 | 2014 | 1.6 |
| 29 TU | 0308 | 3.2 | 0849 | 1.4 |
| | 1529 | 3.3 | 2142 | 1.4 |
| 30 W | 0415 | 3.4 | 0955 | 1.2 |
| | 1627 | 3.6 | 2249 | 1.1 |
| 31 TH | 0506 | 3.6 | 1050 | 0.9 |
| | 1712 | 3.8 | 2341 | 0.9 |

### AUGUST

| Day | Time | m | Time | m |
|---|---|---|---|---|
| 1 F ● | 0548 | 3.7 | 1138 | 0.7 |
| | 1752 | 4.0 | | |
| 2 SA | 0026 | 0.7 | 0625 | 3.8 |
| | 1223 | 0.5 | 1829 | 4.2 |
| 3 SU | 0107 | 0.7 | 0701 | 3.9 |
| | 1304 | 0.4 | 1906 | 4.1 |
| 4 M | 0147 | 0.7 | 0734 | 3.8 |
| | 1344 | 0.5 | 1941 | 4.0 |
| 5 TU | 0224 | 0.9 | 0807 | 3.7 |
| | 1422 | 0.6 | 2014 | 3.9 |
| 6 W | 0259 | 1.1 | 0837 | 3.5 |
| | 1458 | 0.9 | 2045 | 3.6 |
| 7 TH | 0334 | 1.3 | 0907 | 3.4 |
| | 1535 | 1.1 | 2117 | 3.4 |
| 8 F ☽ | 0412 | 1.5 | 0942 | 3.2 |
| | 1616 | 1.4 | 2152 | 3.1 |
| 9 SA | 0459 | 1.8 | 1027 | 3.0 |
| | 1705 | 1.7 | 2233 | 2.9 |
| 10 SU | 0600 | 1.9 | 1148 | 2.8 |
| | 1804 | 2.0 | 2357 | 2.7 |
| 11 M | 0719 | 2.0 | 1403 | 2.8 |
| | 1918 | 2.1 | | |
| 12 TU | 0253 | 2.7 | 0902 | 1.9 |
| | 1517 | 3.0 | 2114 | 2.0 |
| 13 W | 0352 | 2.9 | 1003 | 1.6 |
| | 1604 | 3.2 | 2224 | 1.7 |
| 14 TH | 0425 | 3.2 | 1044 | 1.3 |
| | 1641 | 3.5 | 2301 | 1.5 |
| 15 F | 0459 | 3.4 | 1118 | 1.2 |
| | 1717 | 3.7 | 2334 | 1.2 |
| 16 SA ○ | 0534 | 3.6 | 1148 | 1.0 |
| | 1752 | 3.9 | | |
| 17 SU | 0007 | 1.0 | 0606 | 3.7 |
| | 1218 | 0.8 | 1824 | 4.0 |
| 18 M | 0040 | 0.9 | 0635 | 3.8 |
| | 1246 | 0.7 | 1855 | 4.1 |
| 19 TU | 0112 | 0.8 | 0700 | 3.8 |
| | 1316 | 0.7 | 1923 | 4.0 |
| 20 W | 0142 | 0.8 | 0726 | 3.8 |
| | 1347 | 0.7 | 1954 | 4.0 |
| 21 TH | 0214 | 0.9 | 0758 | 3.7 |
| | 1423 | 0.8 | 2028 | 3.8 |
| 22 F | 0251 | 1.0 | 0835 | 3.5 |
| | 1504 | 1.0 | 2108 | 3.6 |
| 23 SA | 0335 | 1.2 | 0917 | 3.3 |
| | 1555 | 1.3 | 2157 | 3.2 |
| 24 SU | 0434 | 1.4 | 1012 | 3.1 |
| | 1707 | 1.6 | 2314 | 3.0 |
| 25 M | 0553 | 1.6 | 1147 | 2.9 |
| | 1841 | 1.7 | | |
| 26 TU | 0150 | 2.9 | 0719 | 1.7 |
| | 1426 | 3.0 | 2031 | 1.7 |
| 27 W | 0318 | 3.1 | 0842 | 1.5 |
| | 1538 | 3.3 | 2159 | 1.4 |
| 28 TH | 0415 | 3.3 | 0948 | 1.2 |
| | 1624 | 3.6 | 2250 | 1.1 |
| 29 F | 0457 | 3.6 | 1040 | 0.9 |
| | 1701 | 3.9 | 2331 | 0.9 |
| 30 SA ● | 0532 | 3.8 | 1123 | 0.6 |
| | 1735 | 4.1 | | |
| 31 SU | 0008 | 0.7 | 0603 | 3.9 |
| | 1204 | 0.5 | 1807 | 4.2 |

Chart Datum: 2·10 metres below Ordnance Datum (Newlyn). HAT is 4·5 metres above Chart Datum.

# Oban Tides – Dunstaffnage

**TIME ZONE (UT)**
For Summer Time add ONE hour in **non-shaded areas**

**OBAN**  LAT 56°25′N   LONG 5°29′W
TIMES AND HEIGHTS OF HIGH AND LOW WATERS

Dates in **red** are **SPRINGS**
Dates in **blue** are **NEAPS**

YEAR **2008**

## SEPTEMBER

| Time m | Time m |
|---|---|
| **1** 0043 0.7 / 0633 4.0 / M 1243 0.4 / 1839 4.2 | **16** 0009 0.7 / 0602 3.9 / TU 1218 0.6 / 1825 4.2 |
| **2** 0116 0.7 / 0703 4.0 / TU 1318 0.5 / 1909 4.1 | **17** 0041 0.6 / 0628 3.9 / W 1250 0.5 / 1854 4.2 |
| **3** 0148 0.9 / 0731 3.9 / W 1352 0.7 / 1938 3.9 | **18** 0113 0.6 / 0658 3.9 / TH 1326 0.6 / 1927 4.0 |
| **4** 0219 1.1 / 0758 3.7 / TH 1424 1.0 / 2006 3.7 | **19** 0149 0.7 / 0733 3.8 / F 1406 0.8 / 2004 3.8 |
| **5** 0251 1.3 / 0826 3.6 / F 1458 1.3 / 2034 3.5 | **20** 0229 0.9 / 0812 3.6 / SA 1452 1.0 / 2046 3.5 |
| **6** 0328 1.5 / 0859 3.3 / SA 1538 1.6 / 2103 3.2 | **21** 0317 1.2 / 0857 3.4 / SU 1551 1.4 / 2139 3.1 |
| **7** 0415 1.8 / 0941 3.1 / SU 1627 1.9 / ☽ 2135 2.9 | **22** 0419 1.4 / 0958 3.1 / M 1710 1.7 / ☽ 2315 2.8 |
| **8** 0518 2.0 / 1045 2.9 / M 1733 2.1 / 2226 2.7 | **23** 0538 1.6 / 1210 2.9 / TU 1849 1.8 |
| **9** 0640 2.1 / 1356 2.8 / TU 1857 2.2 | **24** 0155 2.8 / 0706 1.6 / W 1424 3.1 / 2049 1.6 |
| **10** 0253 2.7 / 0831 1.9 / W 1504 3.0 / 2120 2.0 | **25** 0310 3.0 / 0829 1.4 / TH 1525 3.4 / 2151 1.3 |
| **11** 0335 2.9 / 0937 1.7 / TH 1545 3.3 / 2203 1.7 | **26** 0359 3.3 / 0932 1.1 / F 1605 3.7 / 2233 1.1 |
| **12** 0404 3.2 / 1016 1.4 / F 1618 3.6 / 2235 1.4 | **27** 0435 3.5 / 1020 0.9 / SA 1637 3.9 / 2308 0.9 |
| **13** 0435 3.4 / 1049 1.1 / SA 1651 3.8 / 2306 1.1 | **28** 0504 3.7 / 1101 0.7 / SU 1707 4.1 / 2340 0.8 |
| **14** 0507 3.6 / 1118 0.9 / SU 1724 4.0 / 2338 0.9 | **29** 0532 3.9 / 1140 0.6 / M 1738 4.2 / ● |
| **15** 0537 3.8 / 1147 0.7 / M 1755 4.2 / ○ | **30** 0012 0.8 / 0601 4.0 / TU 1216 0.6 / 1807 4.1 |

## OCTOBER

| Time m | Time m |
|---|---|
| **1** 0043 0.9 / 0629 4.0 / W 1250 0.7 / 1836 4.1 | **16** 0010 0.6 / 0600 4.0 / TH 1228 0.6 / 1829 4.2 |
| **2** 0113 1.0 / 0657 4.0 / TH 1322 0.9 / 1904 3.9 | **17** 0048 0.6 / 0636 4.0 / F 1310 0.6 / 1906 4.0 |
| **3** 0144 1.1 / 0725 3.9 / F 1354 1.2 / 1932 3.7 | **18** 0129 0.7 / 0715 3.9 / SA 1356 0.8 / 1947 3.8 |
| **4** 0216 1.3 / 0756 3.7 / SA 1428 1.5 / 2000 3.5 | **19** 0214 0.9 / 0759 3.7 / SU 1449 1.1 / 2034 3.4 |
| **5** 0253 1.6 / 0831 3.5 / SU 1507 1.8 / 2029 3.2 | **20** 0306 1.1 / 0851 3.5 / M 1552 1.4 / 2134 3.1 |
| **6** 0338 1.8 / 0903 3.2 / M 1558 2.0 / 2102 3.0 | **21** 0408 1.3 / 0958 3.2 / TU 1709 1.7 / ☽ 2330 2.8 |
| **7** 0440 2.0 / 1014 3.0 / TU 1709 2.2 / ☽ 2155 2.7 | **22** 0521 1.5 / 1215 3.1 / W 1851 1.7 |
| **8** 0558 2.1 / 1325 2.9 / W 1837 2.2 | **23** 0135 2.9 / 0642 1.5 / TH 1359 3.2 / 2027 1.6 |
| **9** 0208 2.7 / 0731 2.0 / TH 1430 3.1 / 2020 2.1 | **24** 0245 3.0 / 0802 1.4 / F 1458 3.4 / 2124 1.4 |
| **10** 0256 2.9 / 0847 1.8 / F 1511 3.4 / 2117 1.7 | **25** 0331 3.3 / 0904 1.2 / SA 1536 3.6 / 2205 1.3 |
| **11** 0330 3.2 / 0932 1.5 / SA 1545 3.6 / 2155 1.4 | **26** 0403 3.5 / 0942 1.1 / SU 1607 3.8 / 2239 1.1 |
| **12** 0402 3.4 / 1007 1.2 / SU 1617 3.9 / 2229 1.1 | **27** 0431 3.7 / 1035 0.9 / M 1637 3.9 / 2310 1.1 |
| **13** 0432 3.6 / 1040 1.0 / M 1650 4.1 / 2302 0.9 | **28** 0500 3.8 / 1113 0.9 / TU 1707 4.0 / ● 2340 1.0 |
| **14** 0501 3.8 / 1113 0.7 / TU 1723 4.2 / ○ 2335 0.7 | **29** 0530 4.0 / 1149 0.9 / W 1737 4.0 |
| **15** 0529 4.0 / 1149 0.6 / W 1755 4.3 | **30** 0010 1.0 / 0600 4.0 / TH 1223 1.0 / 1807 4.0 |
|  | **31** 0042 1.1 / 0631 4.0 / F 1256 1.2 / 1838 3.9 |

## NOVEMBER

| Time m | Time m |
|---|---|
| **1** 0116 1.2 / 0703 3.9 / SA 1330 1.4 / 1910 3.7 | **16** 0114 0.7 / 0707 4.0 / SU 1352 0.9 / 1940 3.7 |
| **2** 0151 1.4 / 0737 3.8 / SU 1406 1.6 / 1941 3.5 | **17** 0202 0.8 / 0756 3.8 / M 1446 1.1 / 2030 3.5 |
| **3** 0227 1.6 / 0815 3.6 / M 1447 1.9 / 2013 3.3 | **18** 0255 1.0 / 0849 3.6 / TU 1547 1.4 / 2129 3.2 |
| **4** 0309 1.8 / 0858 3.4 / TU 1537 2.1 / 2052 3.1 | **19** 0352 1.2 / 0952 3.4 / W 1657 1.6 / ☽ 2254 2.9 |
| **5** 0400 2.0 / 0953 3.2 / W 1642 2.2 / 2148 2.9 | **20** 0455 1.4 / 1121 3.3 / TH 1819 1.7 |
| **6** 0504 2.1 / 1119 3.1 / TH 1759 2.2 / ☽ 2343 2.8 | **21** 0044 2.9 / 0605 1.5 / F 1307 3.3 / 1941 1.7 |
| **7** 0616 2.0 / 1327 3.2 / F 1916 2.1 | **22** 0157 3.0 / 0718 1.5 / SA 1415 3.3 / 2044 1.6 |
| **8** 0155 2.9 / 0727 1.9 / SA 1421 3.4 / 2018 1.8 | **23** 0248 3.1 / 0825 1.4 / SU 1501 3.4 / 2131 1.5 |
| **9** 0242 3.1 / 0827 1.7 / SU 1502 3.6 / 2106 1.5 | **24** 0325 3.3 / 0920 1.4 / M 1536 3.5 / 2208 1.5 |
| **10** 0318 3.3 / 0916 1.4 / M 1539 3.8 / 2147 1.2 | **25** 0358 3.5 / 1007 1.3 / TU 1609 3.6 / 2240 1.4 |
| **11** 0352 3.6 / 0959 1.1 / TU 1616 4.0 / 2226 1.0 | **26** 0431 3.7 / 1048 1.3 / W 1641 3.7 / 2312 1.3 |
| **12** 0426 3.8 / 1043 0.9 / W 1654 4.2 / 2305 0.8 | **27** 0506 3.8 / 1126 1.3 / TH 1715 3.8 / ● 2345 1.3 |
| **13** 0502 4.0 / 1127 0.8 / TH 1732 4.2 / ○ 2345 0.7 | **28** 0540 3.9 / 1202 1.3 / F 1749 3.8 |
| **14** 0541 4.1 / 1213 0.7 / F 1813 4.2 | **29** 0020 1.3 / 0615 4.0 / SA 1238 1.4 / 1824 3.8 |
| **15** 0028 0.6 / 0623 4.1 / SA 1301 0.8 / 1855 4.0 | **30** 0057 1.3 / 0651 3.9 / SU 1316 1.5 / 1900 3.7 |

## DECEMBER

| Time m | Time m |
|---|---|
| **1** 0133 1.4 / 0727 3.8 / M 1354 1.6 / 1935 3.6 | **16** 0152 0.7 / 0752 4.0 / TU 1440 1.0 / 2024 3.6 |
| **2** 0209 1.5 / 0805 3.7 / TU 1433 1.8 / 2009 3.4 | **17** 0241 0.8 / 0841 3.8 / W 1532 1.2 / 2113 3.4 |
| **3** 0244 1.6 / 0844 3.6 / W 1515 1.9 / 2046 3.3 | **18** 0331 1.0 / 0931 3.6 / TH 1627 1.4 / 2207 3.2 |
| **4** 0321 1.8 / 0928 3.4 / TH 1604 2.0 / 2130 3.1 | **19** 0424 1.2 / 1027 3.4 / F 1726 1.6 / ☽ 2314 3.0 |
| **5** 0406 1.8 / 1020 3.3 / F 1702 2.0 / ☽ 2225 3.0 | **20** 0521 1.4 / 1135 3.2 / SA 1832 1.8 |
| **6** 0502 1.9 / 1126 3.3 / SA 1807 2.0 / 2334 3.0 | **21** 0035 3.0 / 0622 1.5 / SU 1301 3.1 / 1942 1.8 |
| **7** 0607 1.9 / 1251 3.3 / SU 1912 1.9 | **22** 0145 3.0 / 0729 1.7 / M 1415 3.1 / 2046 1.8 |
| **8** 0102 3.0 / 0715 1.8 / M 1405 3.5 / 2010 1.7 | **23** 0242 3.1 / 0839 1.7 / TU 1509 3.2 / 2137 1.7 |
| **9** 0217 3.2 / 0822 1.6 / TU 1501 3.7 / 2104 1.4 | **24** 0328 3.3 / 0941 1.7 / W 1550 3.3 / 2218 1.6 |
| **10** 0312 3.4 / 0925 1.4 / W 1550 3.8 / 2154 1.2 | **25** 0411 3.5 / 1031 1.6 / TH 1628 3.4 / 2255 1.5 |
| **11** 0401 3.7 / 1022 1.1 / TH 1636 4.0 / 2242 1.0 | **26** 0451 3.6 / 1114 1.5 / F 1705 3.6 / 2331 1.4 |
| **12** 0447 3.9 / 1116 0.9 / F 1722 4.0 / ○ 2329 0.8 | **27** 0530 3.8 / 1152 1.5 / SA 1743 3.7 / ● |
| **13** 0533 4.1 / 1207 0.8 / SA 1807 4.0 | **28** 0008 1.3 / 0607 3.9 / SU 1229 1.4 / 1820 3.7 |
| **14** 0016 0.7 / 0619 4.1 / SU 1259 0.8 / 1851 4.0 | **29** 0044 1.2 / 0644 3.9 / M 1306 1.4 / 1855 3.7 |
| **15** 0104 0.6 / 0706 4.1 / M 1349 0.9 / 1937 3.8 | **30** 0119 1.2 / 0719 3.9 / TU 1343 1.5 / 1927 3.7 |
|  | **31** 0151 1.3 / 0753 3.8 / W 1417 1.5 / 1957 3.6 |

Chart Datum: 2·10 metres below Ordnance Datum (Newlyn). HAT is 4·5 metres above Chart Datum.

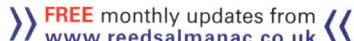
**FREE** monthly updates from
www.reedsalmanac.co.uk

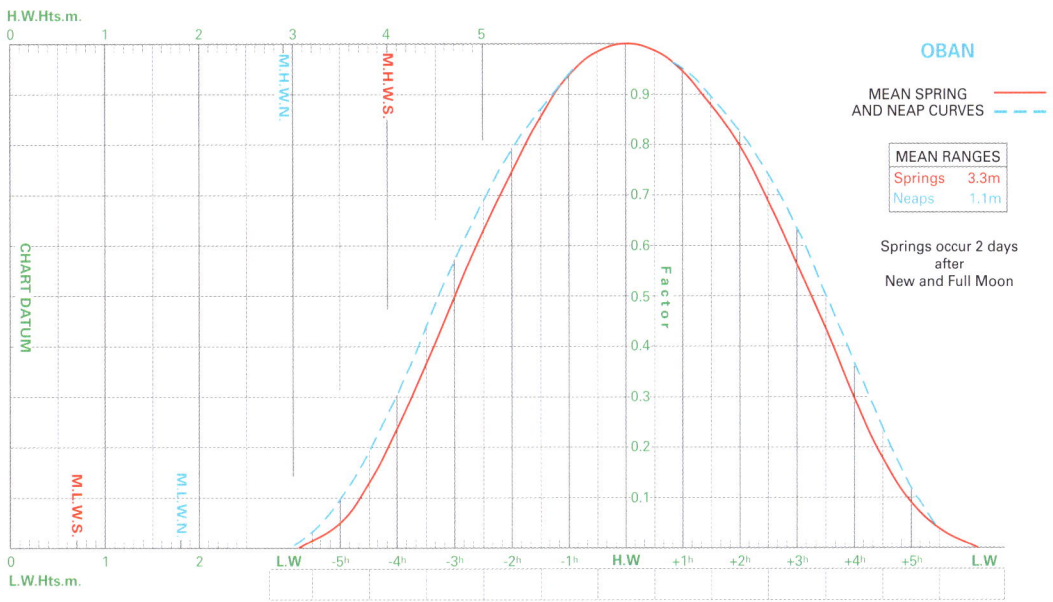

OBAN

MEAN SPRING ——————
AND NEAP CURVES  - - - - - - -

| MEAN RANGES | |
|---|---|
| Springs | 3.3m |
| Neaps | 1.1m |

Springs occur 2 days
after
New and Full Moon

## 1.17   DUNSTAFFNAGE

**DUNSTAFFNAGE BAY**, Argyll and Bute, **56°27′·04N 05°25′·97W**.
✺✺✹✺⚓⚓⚓✿✿✿

**CHARTS**  AC *5611, 2171*, 2387, *1790*; Imray C65; OS 49

**TIDES**  –0530 Dover; ML 2·4; Duration 0610

**Standard Port OBAN** (⟵)

| Times | | | | Height (metres) | | | |
|---|---|---|---|---|---|---|---|
| High Water | | Low Water | | MHWS | MHWN | MLWN | MLWS |
| 0100 | 0700 | 0100 | 0800 | 4·0 | 2·9 | 1·8 | 0·7 |
| 1300 | 1900 | 1300 | 2000 | | | | |
| **Differences DUNSTAFFNAGE BAY** | | | | | | | |
| +0005 | 0000 | 0000 | +0005 | +0·1 | +0·1 | +0·1 | +0·1 |
| **CONNEL** | | | | | | | |
| +0020 | +0005 | +0010 | +0015 | –0·3 | –0·2 | –0·1 | +0·1 |
| **BONAWE** | | | | | | | |
| +0150 | +0205 | +0240 | +0210 | –2·0 | –1·7 | –1·3 | –0·5 |

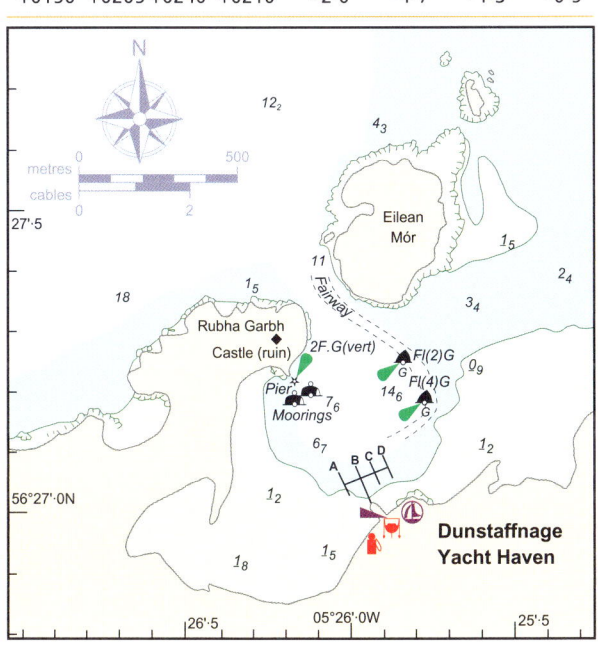

**SHELTER** Good at marina in SE side of bay, little room to ⚓, within the bay the tidal stream is rotary but sets mainly E through the marina.

**NAVIGATION** Entered between Rubha Garbh and Eilean Mór. No navigational hazards, spd limit 4kn in bay/⚓. Do not approach marina through moorings, use buoyed fairway. W and SW sides of bay dry.

**LIGHTS AND MARKS**  See 1.3. and chartlet.

**R/T**  Call: *Dunstaffnage Marina* VHF Ch M.

**TELEPHONE**  Marinecall 09068 969653; ⊖ 08457231110; MRCC (01475) 729988; Police 510500; Dr 563175.

**FACILITIES** **Dunstaffnage Marina,** (Code 01631) 566555, ▨ 567422, 150 inc 10❤ AB £2.00, Wi-fi, D (0830-2000 summer), Gas, Slip (launching H24 except LWS ±2hrs, £9.00 each way) BH (18 ton), CH, C (masting), ME, BY, ▢, SM, R, Bar; Facilities: P (cans, ¾M), 🛒 (½M), Bus, ≠ Oban (2M), Glasgow (✈) 2-3hrs and Connel (airstrip).

**ADJACENT ANCHORAGES AND MARINA** (See AC *5611*)
**LOCH ETIVE**, AC 2378 to Bonawe, thence AC 5076. Connel Bridge, 15m clrnce, and Falls of Lora can be physical and tidal barriers. HT cables at Bonawe have 13m clearance. See *Clyde Cruising Club SDs.*

**OBAN** Argyll and Bute **56°24′·99N 05°29′·07W** ✺✺✺⚓⚓⚓✿✿
Standard port HW –0530 on Dover; see 1.18. Good shelter except in strong SW/NW winds, but sheltered from these is **Oban Marina** in Ardantrive Bay (Kerrera) with water taxi to Oban (0800-2200). The only ⚓s convenient for town are in deep water off the Esplanade. and NW of Sailing Club, beware of moorings. Alternatively ⚓ at N end of Kerrera to S of Rubh'a Chruidh Is or Horseshoe Bay and Little Horseshoe Bay, Kerera Sound.

**NAVIGATION** WPT (N) 56°25′·84N 05°30′·07W, 129° to Dunollie lt, 0·73M and WPT (S) 56°21′·99N 05°32′·95W, 030° to 140m ESE of Sgeirean Dubha 9 ca. Beware Sgeir Rathaid, buoyed, in middle of the bay; also CalMac ferries running to/from Railway Quay.

• Ferry Rks in mid-chan at 56°24′·0N can be passed on either side Note the direction of the buoyage is **NE**, thus pass to the E'ward of  PHM unlit buoy or to W'ward of the SHM QG buoy. The N'ly SHM buoy must be passed to the W'ward.

**LIGHTS AND MARKS**  See 1.3. and Oban chartlet.

**R/T**  Call: *North Pier*  Ch 12 16 (0900-1700). For Railway Quay, call *CalMac* Ch  06 12 16. **Oban Marina**, call *Oban Yachts* Ch 80.

*Continued on page 61*

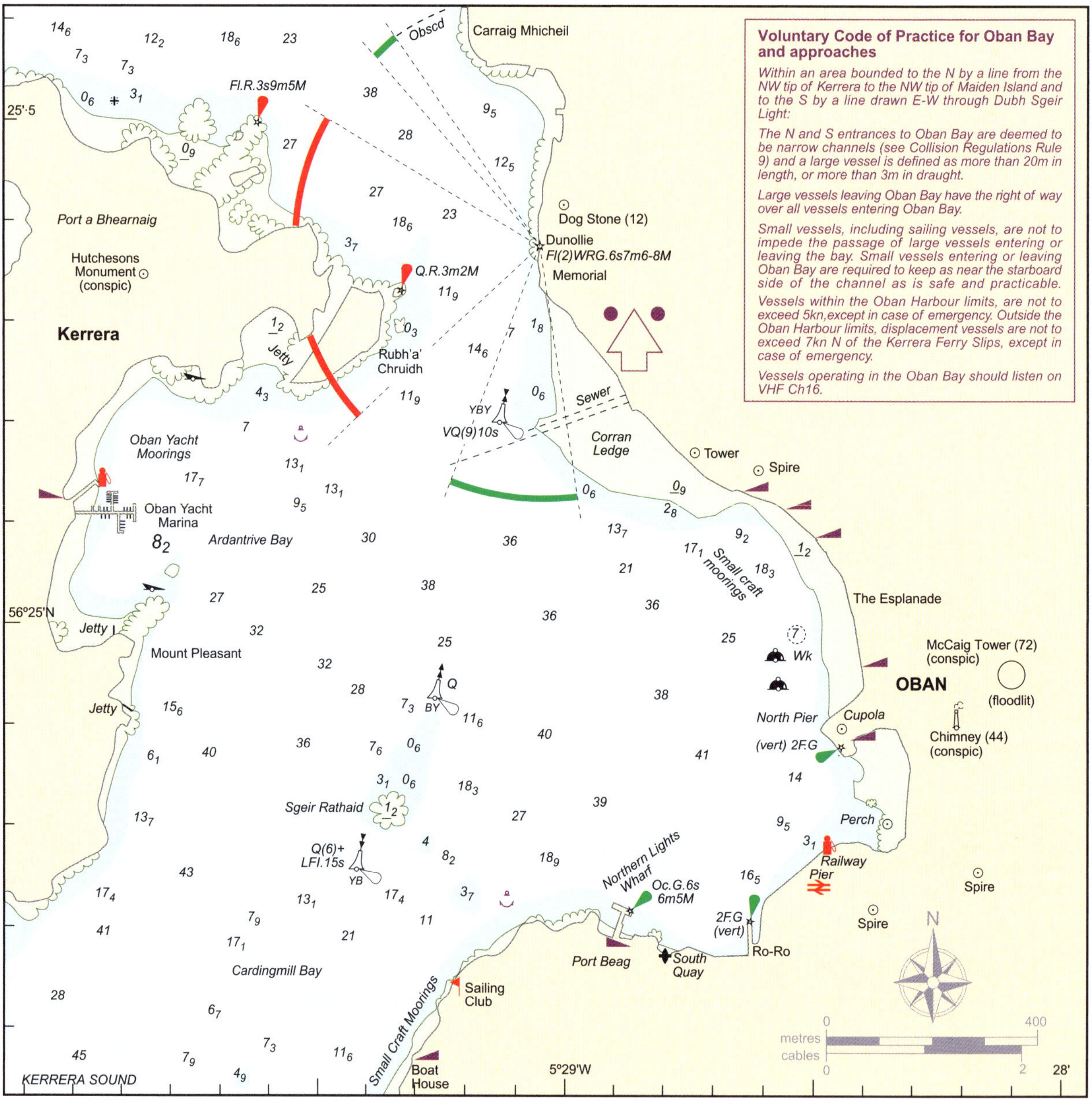

Carraig Mhicheil

Obscd

Fl.R.3s9m5M

Port a Bhearnaig

Hutchesons
Monument ⊙
(conspic)

**Kerrera**

Jetty

Q.R.3m2M

Rubh'a'
Chruidh

Dog Stone (12)

Dunollie
Fl(2)WRG.6s7m6-8M
Memorial

Sewer

YBY
VQ(9)10s

Corran
Ledge

Oban Yacht
Moorings

Oban Yacht
Marina

Ardantrive Bay

⊙ Tower        ⊙ Spire

Small craft
moorings

The Esplanade

McCaig Tower (72)
(conspic)

**OBAN**

(floodlit)

Wk

Chimney (44)
(conspic)

Cupola

North Pier
(vert) 2F.G

Railway
Pier

Perch

Northern Lights
Wharf
Oc.G.6s
6m5M

2F.G
(vert)

Ro-Ro

South
Quay

Port Beag

Spire

⊙
Spire

N

Mount Pleasant

Jetty

Jetty

Sgeir Rathaid

Q(6)+
LFl.15s
YB

BY

Q

Cardingmill Bay

Small Craft Moorings

Sailing
Club

Boat
House

KERRERA SOUND

5°29'W

56°25'N

25'·5

metres
cables

0     400

0    2    28'

2008/VVM14/z

**OBAN** *continued*

☎ (Code 01631) Pier 562892; Marinecall 09068 969653; ⊖ 08457231110; MRCC (01475) 729988; Police 510500; Dr 563175.

**FACILITIES   N Pier** ☎ 562892, L, FW, C (15 ton mobile) via Piermaster; **Rly Quay,** L, Slip, D (H24, ☎ 562849), FW, CH; **Services:** Slip, ACA, Gas, ME, El, divers. **Town** P (cans, ½M), all facilities, ℍ, ⇌, Glasgow (✈) 2-3hrs & Connel (airstrip) 3M, ferries to Inner & Outer Hebrides.

**ARDANTRIVE BAY, KERRERA** Argyll and Bute **56°25'·15N 05°29'·80W** ❀❀❀❀♨♨♨✿✿✿ AC 1790. HW -0530 on Dover. **Oban Yachts Marina,** www.obanyachts.com, VHF Ch80/16, ☎ 565333, 🖷 565888. 56 AB (pontoons,inc 30Ⓥ) £2.20, 30🛥s £1.95; D, FW, Gas, ⟐, ▣, Showers, 🆆🅲, ME, BY, ⚒, C (masting), CH, Slip, BH (16 ton), marina water taxi 0800-2200 in season, (call *Oban Yachts* Ch 80 for timetable); 10min crossing to Oban.

**ANCHORAGES ON MAINLAND SHORE OF FIRTH OF LORN**

**LOCH FEOCHAN,** Argyll and Bute, **56°21'·39N 05°29'·77W.** AC *5611,* 2387. HW = HW Oban; flood runs 4 hrs, ebb for 8 hrs. Caution: strong streams off Ardentallan Pt. Good shelter, 5M S of Oban and 1·5M SE of Kerrera. Best appr at local slack LW = LW Oban +0200. Narrow buoyed channel, ⚓ off pier, or moor off **Ardoran Marine** ☎ (01631) 566123, 🖷 566611; 4 🛥s £10 <11m, D, FW, ME, CH, Slip, Showers.

**PUILLADOBHRAIN,** Argyll and Bute, **56°19'·47N 05°35'·22W.** AC *5611,* 2386/2387. Tides as Oban. Popular ⚓ on the SE shore of the Firth of Lorne, approx 7M S of Oban, sheltered by the islets to the W of it. At N end of Ardencaple Bay identify Eilean Dùin (18m) and steer SE keeping 1½ca off to clear a rk awash at its NE tip. Continue for 4ca between Eilean nam Beathach, with Orange drum on N tip, and Dun Horses rks drying 2·7m. Two W cairns on E side of Eilean nam Freumha lead approx 215° into the inner ⚓ in about 4m. Landing at head of inlet. Nearest facilities: Bar, ☎, at Clachan Br (½M); ☎, ✉ at Clachan Seil.

**CUAN SOUND,** Argyll and Bute, **56°15'·84N 05°37'·47W.** AC 2386, 2326. Tides see 1.18 SEIL SOUND. Streams reach 6kn at sp; N-going makes at HW Oban +0420, S-going at HW Oban −2. The Sound is a useful doglegged short cut from Firth of Lorne to Lochs Melfort and Shuna, but needs care due to rks and tides. There are ⚓s at either end to await the tide. At the 90° dogleg, pass close N of Cleit Rk onto which the tide sets; it is marked by a Y △ perch. The chan is only ¾ca wide here due to rks off Seil. Overhead cables (35m) cross from Seil to Luing. There are ⚓s out of the tide to the S of Cleit Rk. No lts/facilities. See CCC SDs.

**ARDINAMAR,** Luing/Torsa, **56°14'·92N 05°37'·04W.** AC 2326. HW −0555 on Dover; ML 1·7m; see 1.18 SEIL SOUND. A small cove and popular ⚓ between Luing and Torsa, close W of ent to L. Melfort. Appr on brg 290°. Narrow, shallow (about 1m CD) ent has drying rks either side, those to N marked by 2 SHM perches. Keep about 15m S of perches to ⚓ in 2m in centre of cove; S part dries. Few facilities: 🛒, ✉, ☎, at Cullipool 1·5M WNW. Gas at Cuan Sound ferry 2M NNW.

# 1.18   LOCH MELFORT

Argyll and Bute **56°14'·59N 05°34'·07W** ❀❀❀❀♨♨♨✿✿✿

**CHARTS**   AC *5611,* 2169, 2326; Imray C65; OS 55

**TIDES**   Loch Shuna −0615 Dover; ML Loch Melfort 1·7; Duration Seil Sound 0615

**Standard Port OBAN (⟵)**

| Times | | | | Height (metres) | | | |
|---|---|---|---|---|---|---|---|
| High Water | | Low Water | | MHWS | MHWN | MLWN | MLWS |
| 0100 | 0700 | 0100 | 0800 | 4·0 | 2·9 | 1·8 | 0·7 |
| 1300 | 1900 | 1300 | 2000 | | | | |
| **Differences LOCH MELFORT** | | | | | | | |
| −0055 | −0025 | −0040 | −0035 | −1·2 | −0·8 | −0·5 | −0·1 |
| **SEIL SOUND** | | | | | | | |
| −0035 | −0015 | −0040 | −0015 | −1·3 | −0·9 | −0·7 | −0·3 |

**SHELTER**   Good at Kilmelford Yacht Haven in Loch na Cille; access at all tides for 3m draft, W lts at end of pier and along its length. Or lt at Melfort Pier (Fearnach Bay at N end of loch): pier/pontoon in 2m, but chan to inner hbr dries; good ⚓ in N winds. ⚓'ge sheltered from S to W at Kames Bay clear of moorings, rks and marine farms. ⚓'ge N of Arduaine denied to small craft due extensive marine farm activity (2005).

**NAVIGATION**   WPT 56°13'·90N 05°34'·80W, 000°/3·5ca to Eilean Gamhna. Pass either side of Eilean Gamhna. 8ca NE lies Campbell Rk (1·8m). A rk drying 1m lies 1½ca ESE of the FS on Eilean Coltair. The S side of L Melfort is mostly steep-to, except in Kames Bay. At Loch na Cille, beware drying reef ¾ca off NE shore (PHM perch), and rk near S shore (SHM perch); boats may obscure perches.

**LIGHTS AND MARKS**   A Dir FR ☆ 6m 3M on Melfort pier (also depth gauge) and a Dir FG ☆ close NE on the shore are not ldg lts, nor do they form a safe transit. Approach on a N'ly track keeping them an equal angle off each bow.

**R/T**   Kilmelford VHF Ch **80** M (HO).

**TELEPHONE**   (Code 01852)   MRCC (01475) 729014; ⊖ (0141) 887 9369;   Police (01631) 562213;   Marinecall 09068 969653; ℍ (01546) 602323.

**FACILITIES**   **Kilmelford Yacht Haven** ☎ 200248, 🖷 200343, £14·50/ craft, D (Mon-Sat 0800-2000), FW, ▣,BH (20 ton), Slip HW±4, ME, El, ⚒, Gas, 🛒 village (¾M); **Melfort Pier** ☎ 200333, 🖷 200329, AB £1.30, 🛥 £1.30, Slip, @. Village (1¼M) 🛒, Bar, ✉.

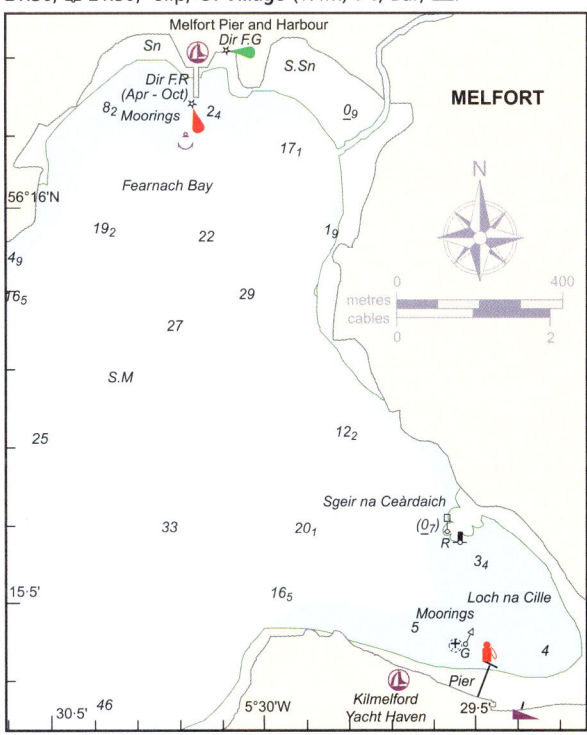

MELFORT

## 1.19   CRAOBH MARINA (L SHUNA)

Argyll & Bute **56°12´·80N 05°33´·54W** ❀❀❀⚓⚓⚓♖♖♖

**CHARTS**   AC *5611, 2169, 2326*; Imray C65; OS 55

**TIDES**   HW Loch Shuna  –0100 Oban;  –0615 Dover; Seil Sound Duration 0615, ML 1·4. For tidal figures see 1.18.

**SHELTER**   Very good. Craobh (pronounced Croove) Marina (access H24) on SE shore of Loch Shuna is enclosed by N and S causeways between islets. The ent is between 2 bkwtrs on the N side. In the marina, a shoal area S of the E bkwtr is marked by 9 PHM and 2 SHM buoys. A Y perch in W corner of hbr marks a spit; elsewhere ample depth. There are ⚓s in Asknish Bay 1M to the N, and in the bays E of Eilean Arsa and at Bàgh an Tigh-Stòir, S of Craobh.

**NAVIGATION**   WPT 56°13´·01N 05°33´·57W, 173°/2ca to ent. Tidal streams in Loch Shuna are weak. Beware fish farm 2ca N of Shuna, lobster pots in appr's and unmarked rks (dr 1·5m) 4ca NNE of ent. An unlit SHM buoy marks a rk (1m) 150m NNW of the W bkwtr. 1M N of marina, Eich Donna, an unmarked reef (dr 1·5m), lies between Eilean Creagach and Arduaine Pt.

**LIGHTS AND MARKS**   The W sector, 162°-183°, of Dir Lt, Iso WRG 5s 10m 5/3M, on E bkwtr hd leads 172° between the close-in rks above. Multi coloured marina buildings are conspic.

**R/T**   VHF Ch M, 80 (summer 0830-2000; winter 0830-1800).

**TELEPHONE**   (Code 01852)  HM 500222, 🖷 500252; MRCC (01475) 729014; ⊖ (0141) 887 9369; Marinecall 09068 969653; Police (01546) 602222; Ⓗ (01546) 602323.

**FACILITIES**   **Craobh Marina** (200+50 Ⓥ) ☎ 500222, 🖷 500252, £2.00, D, SM, BY, CH, Slip (launch/recovery £3.70/m), BH (15 ton), C (12 ton), Gas, Gaz, ME, El, ✕, R, SC, Ⓔ, ▣, Divers. **Village** 🍴, Bar, Ⓑ (Fri), ✉ (Kilmelford), ≈ (Oban by bus), ✈ (Glasgow).

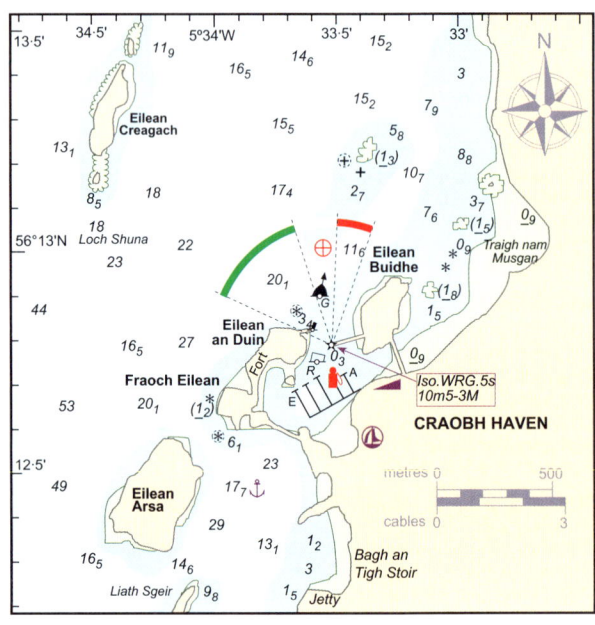

## 1.20   LOCH CRAIGNISH

Argyll and Bute **56°07´·99N 05°35´·07W** (Ardfern)  ❀❀❀⚓⚓⚓♖♖♖

**CHARTS**   AC *5611, 2169, 2326*; Imray C65, C63; OS 55

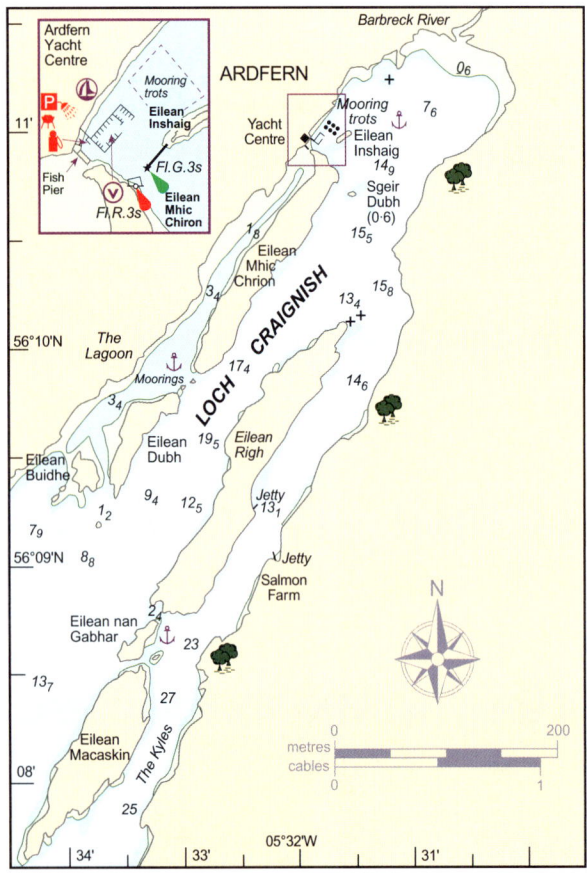

**TIDES**   +0600 Dover; ML (Loch Beag)1·2; Duration (Seil Sound) 0615

**Standard Port OBAN (←→)**

| Times | | | | Height (metres) | | | |
|---|---|---|---|---|---|---|---|
| High Water | | Low Water | | MHWS | MHWN | MLWN | MLWS |
| 0100 | 0700 | 0100 | 0800 | 4·0 | 2·9 | 1·8 | 0·7 |
| 1300 | 1900 | 1300 | 2000 | | | | |

**Differences LOCH BEAG** (Sound of Jura)

| | | | | | | | |
|---|---|---|---|---|---|---|---|
| –0110 | –0045 | –0035 | –0045 | –1·6 | –1·2 | –0·8 | –0·4 |

NOTE: HW Ardfern is approx HW Oban –0045; times/heights much affected by local winds and barometric pressure

**SHELTER**   Good at Ardfern, 56°11´·0N 05°31´·8W, access H24; ⚓s at
• Eilean nan Gabhar; appr from E chan and ⚓ E of island.
• Eilean Righ; midway up the E side of the island.
• Eilean Dubh in the 'lagoon' between the ls and mainland.
• Beware squalls in E'lies, especially on E side of loch.

**NAVIGATION**   See 1.4.WPT 56°07´·59N 05°35´·37W (off chartlet) between Dorus Mór and Liath-sgier Mhòr.

Beware: strong tidal streams (up to 8kn) in Dorus Mór see 1.4; a reef extending 1ca SSW of the SE chain of islands; rk 1½ca SSW of Eilean Dubh; fish cages especially on E side of loch; a drying rock at N end of Ardfern ⚓ with a rock awash ¼ca E of it. (These 2 rocks are ½ca S of the more S'ly of little islets close to mainland). The main fairway is free from hazards, except for Sgeir Dhubh, an unmarked rock 3½ca SSE of Ardfern, with a reef extending about ¼ca all round. Ardfern is 1ca W of Eilean Inshaig.

**LIGHTS AND MARKS**   Ent to Ardfern Yacht Centre marked by PHM buoy, Fl R 3s, and end of floating breakwater, Fl G 3s, which extends 90m SW from Eilean Inshaig.

**R/T**   Ardfern Yacht Centre VHF Ch 80 M (office hrs).

**TELEPHONE**   (Code 01852) HM (Yacht Centre) 500247, 🖷 500624, www.ardfernyacht.co.uk,  MRCC (01475) 729014;  Marinecall 09068 969653; ⊖ (0141) 887 9369; Dr (01546) 602921; Ⓗ (01546) 602449.

**FACILITIES**   **Ardfern Yacht Centre** (87+20Ⓥ, 12⚓) AB £1.53, M £1.10, Wi-fi, D (HO), BH (20 ton), Slip (HW±3, £1.50/m inc parking), ME, El, ✕, SM, ACA, C (12 ton), CH, ▥, Gas, Gaz. **Village** R, 🍴, Ⓑ (Fri), ✉ , ≈ (Oban), Bar, ✈ (Glasgow).

## 1.21 SUBMARINE EXERCISE AREAS (SUBFACTS)

Areas North of Mull in which submarine activity is planned for the next 16 hrs are broadcast by MRCCs on a specified VHF Ch after an initial announcement on Ch 16 at the times below. The areas are referred to by the names given below, rather than by the numbers indicated. For Areas 22 – 81 (South of Mull), see 2.18.

| | |
|---|---|
| **Stornoway** | 0110 0510 0910 1310 1710 and 2110 UT |
| **Clyde** | 0020 0420 0820 1220 1620 and 2020 UT |

During notified NATO exercises, Subfacts are also broadcast on MF by **Stornoway** (1743 kHz) and **Clyde** (1883 kHz), at the same times as above.

General information on Subfacts is also broadcast twice daily at 0620 & 1820 UT by **Portpatrick** Navtex **(O)**. **Stornoway** and **Clyde** MRCCs will also supply Subfacts on request. Call Ch 16.

A Fisherman's hotline (☎ (01436) 674321) deals with queries. FOSNNI Ops (☎ (01436) 674321 ext 3206/6778) may also help. Submarines on the surface and at periscope depth always listen on Ch 16. See also 2.18.

| | | | |
|---|---|---|---|
| 1 | Tiumpan | 14 | Raasay |
| 2 | Minch North | 15 | Neist |
| 3 | Stoer | 16 | Bracadale |
| 4 | Shiant | 17 | Ushenish |
| 5 | Minch South | 18 | Hebrides North |
| 6 | Ewe | 19 | Canna |
| 7 | Troddday | 20 | Rhum |
| 8 | Rona West | 21 | Sleat |
| 9 | Rona North | 22 | Barra |
| 10 | Lochmaddy | 23 | Hebrides Central |
| 11 | Dunvegan | 24 | Hawes |
| 12 | Portree | 25 | Eigg |
| 13 | Rona South | 26 | Hebrides South |

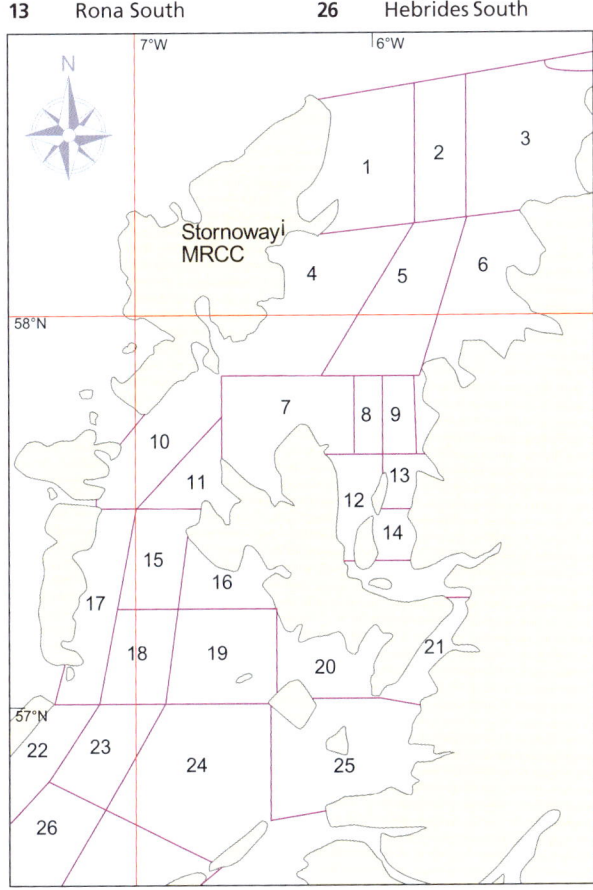

## 1.22 FERRIES ON THE WEST COAST OF SCOTLAND

The following is a brief summary of the many ferries plying between mainland and island harbours and may prove useful when plans or crews change in remote places. It covers Area 1 (Stornoway to Oban) and Area 2 (Jura to the Clyde).

The major operator is Caledonian MacBrayne: Head Office, The Ferry Terminal, Gourock PA19 1QP; ☎ 08705-650000 for reservations, 🖷 (08705) 650000. www.calmac.co.uk

Many routes are very short and may not be pre-bookable; seasonal routes are marked *.

| From | To | Time | Remarks |
|---|---|---|---|
| **Area 8** | | | |
| Berneray | Leverburgh | 1¼ | |
| Ullapool | Stornoway | 2¾ hrs | |
| Uig (Skye) | Tarbert (Harris) | 1¾ hrs | Not Sun |
| Uig | Lochmaddy (N Uist) | 1¾ hrs | |
| Oban | Castlebay/Lochboisdale | 5-7 hrs | |
| Sconser (Skye) | Raasay | 15 mins | Not Sun |
| Mallaig* | Armadale (Skye) | 20 mins | |
| Mallaig | Eigg-Muck-Rhum-Canna | Varies | Not Sun |
| Oban | Coll-Tiree | Varies | Not Thurs |
| Tobermory | Kilchoan | 35 mins | |
| Fionnphort | Iona | 5 mins | |
| Lochaline | Fishnish (Mull) | 15 mins | |
| Oban | Craignure (Mull) | 45 mins | |
| Oban | Lismore | 50 mins | Not Sun |
| **Areas 8/9** | | | |
| Oban | Colonsay | 2¼ hrs | Sun/W/Fri |
| **Area 9** | | | |
| Kennacraig | Port Askaig/Colonsay | Varies | Wed |
| Kennacraig | Port Ellen | 2h 10m | |
| Kennacraig | Port Askaig | 2 hrs | |
| Tayinloan | Gigha | 20 mins | |
| Ardrossan | Brodick | 55 mins | |
| Claonaig | Lochranza (Arran) | 30 mins | |
| Largs | Cumbrae Slip | 10 mins | |
| Tarbert (L Fyne) | Portavadie* | 25 mins | |
| Colintraive | Rhubodach (Bute) | 5 mins | |
| Wemyss Bay | Rothesay (Bute) | 35 mins | |
| Gourock | Dunoon | 20 mins | |

**Other Island Ferry Operators**

| Area | From | Operator | Telephone |
|---|---|---|---|
| Corran - V | Ardgour | Highland Council | 01855 841243 |
| Easdale - P | Seil | Area Manager | 01631 562125 |
| Firth of Lorn - P | Colonsay | K & C Byrne | 01951 200320 |
| | Uisken (Ross of Mull) | | |
| | Scalasaig (Colonsay) | | |
| | Tarbert (Jura) | | |
| | Port Askaig (Islay) | | |
| Jura - V | Port Askaig (Islay) | Serco Denholm | 01496 840681 |
| Kerrara - P | Oban | Oban Yachts | 01631 565333 |
| Kilgregan - P | Gourock | Clyde Marine Motoring | 01475 721281 |
| Lismore - P | Port Appin | Area Manager | 01631 562125 |
| Loch Nevis - P | Mallaig | Bruce Watt | 01687 462233 |
| Luing - P/V | Seil | Area Manager | 01631 562125 |
| Morvern | Sunart | Pre-book via | 01688 302851 |
| Mull | Drimnin | Sound of Mull | or mobile |
| Ardnamurchan | Tobermory Kilchoan | Transport | 07799 608199 |
| Skye - V | Gleneig | R Macleod | 01599 511302 |
| Staffa - P | Iona | D Kirkpatrick | 01681 700373 |
| Staffa - P | Mull | Gordon Grant | 01681 700338 |
| Staffa - P | Mull | Turus Mara | 01688 400242 |

P = Passenger only          V = Cars and Passengers

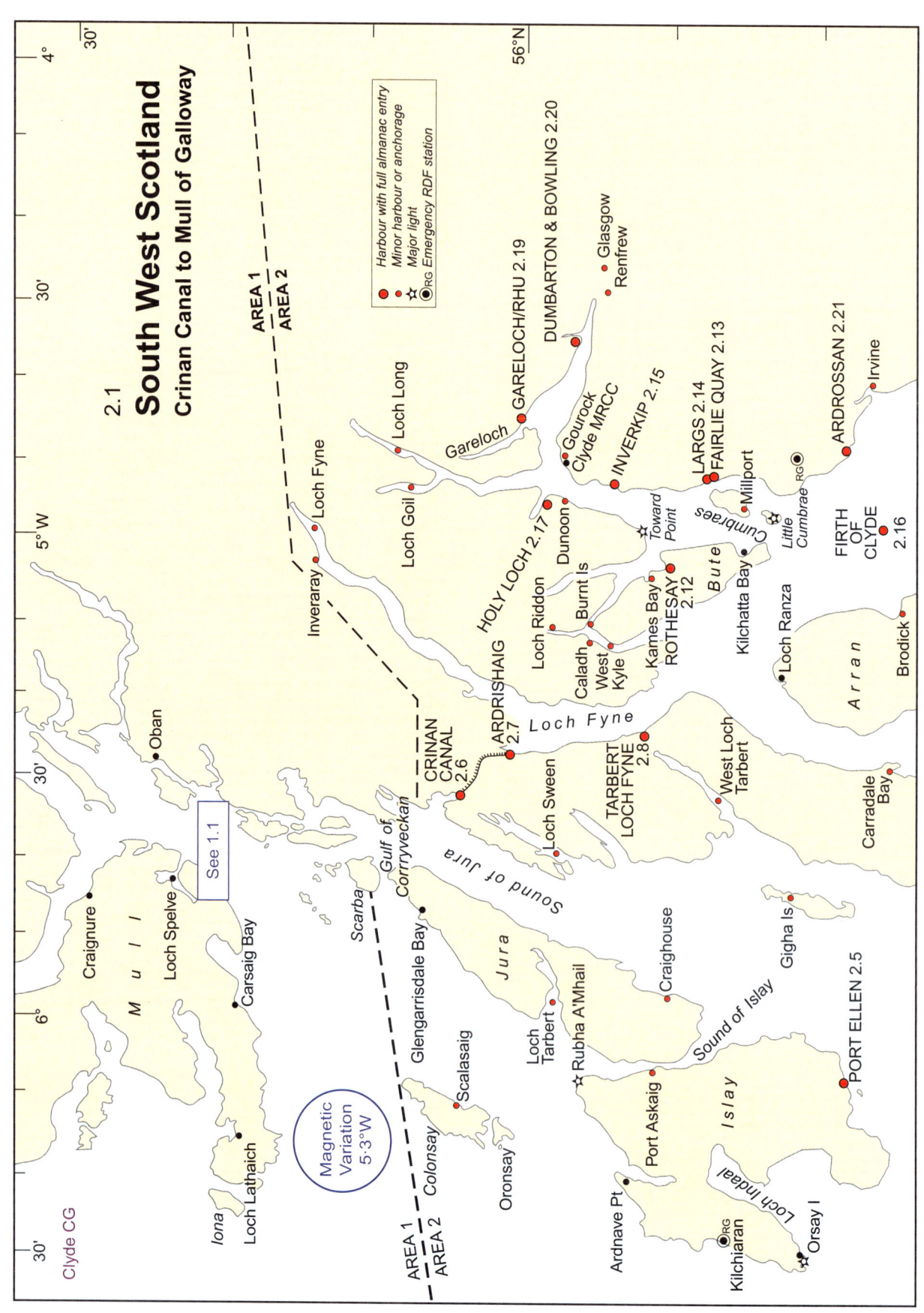

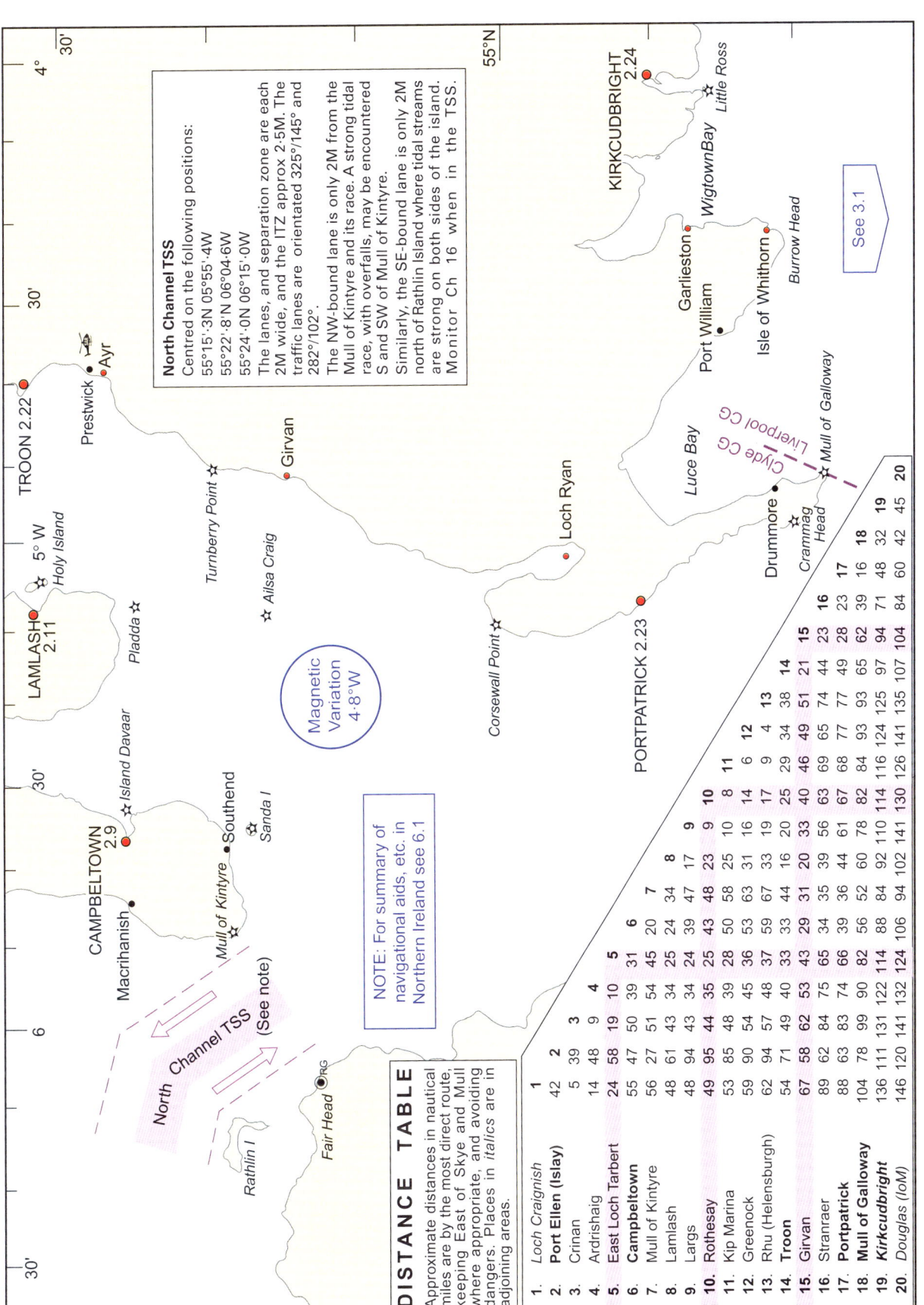

**North Channel TSS**

Centred on the following positions:
55°15'·3N 05°55'·4W
55°22'·8N 06°04·6W
55°24'·0N 06°15'·0W
The lanes, and separation zone are each 2M wide, and the ITZ approx 2·5M. The traffic lanes are orientated 325°/145° and 282°/102°.
The NW-bound lane is only 2M from the Mull of Kintyre and its race. A strong tidal race, with overfalls, may be encountered S and SW of Mull of Kintyre.
Similarly, the SE-bound lane is only 2M north of Rathlin Island where tidal streams are strong on both sides of the island. Monitor Ch 16 when in the TSS.

NOTE: For summary of navigational aids, etc. in Northern Ireland see 6.1

Magnetic Variation 4·8°W

North Channel TSS (See note)

See 3.1

Clyde CG
Liverpool CG

# DISTANCE TABLE

Approximate distances in nautical miles are by the most direct route, keeping East of Skye and Mull where appropriate, and avoiding dangers. Places in *italics* are in adjoining areas.

| | 1 | 2 | 3 | 4 | 5 | 6 | 7 | 8 | 9 | 10 | 11 | 12 | 13 | 14 | 15 | 16 | 17 | 18 | 19 | 20 |
|---|---|---|---|---|---|---|---|---|---|---|---|---|---|---|---|---|---|---|---|---|
| 1. *Loch Craignish* | 1 | | | | | | | | | | | | | | | | | | | |
| 2. **Port Ellen (Islay)** | 42 | 2 | | | | | | | | | | | | | | | | | | |
| 3. Crinan | 5 | 39 | 3 | | | | | | | | | | | | | | | | | |
| 4. Ardrishaig | 14 | 48 | 9 | 4 | | | | | | | | | | | | | | | | |
| 5. East Loch Tarbert | 24 | 58 | 19 | 10 | 5 | | | | | | | | | | | | | | | |
| 6. **Campbeltown** | 55 | 47 | 50 | 39 | 31 | 6 | | | | | | | | | | | | | | |
| 7. Mull of Kintyre | 56 | 27 | 51 | 54 | 45 | 20 | 7 | | | | | | | | | | | | | |
| 8. Lamlash | 48 | 61 | 43 | 34 | 25 | 24 | 34 | 8 | | | | | | | | | | | | |
| 9. Largs | 48 | 94 | 43 | 34 | 24 | 39 | 47 | 17 | 9 | | | | | | | | | | | |
| 10. **Rothesay** | 49 | 95 | 44 | 35 | 25 | 43 | 48 | 23 | 9 | 10 | | | | | | | | | | |
| 11. Kip Marina | 53 | 85 | 48 | 39 | 28 | 50 | 58 | 25 | 10 | 8 | 11 | | | | | | | | | |
| 12. Greenock | 59 | 90 | 54 | 45 | 36 | 53 | 63 | 31 | 16 | 14 | 6 | 12 | | | | | | | | |
| 13. Rhu (Helensburgh) | 62 | 94 | 57 | 48 | 37 | 55 | 67 | 33 | 19 | 17 | 9 | 4 | 13 | | | | | | | |
| 14. **Troon** | 54 | 71 | 49 | 40 | 33 | 33 | 44 | 16 | 20 | 25 | 29 | 34 | 38 | 14 | | | | | | |
| 15. **Girvan** | 67 | 58 | 62 | 53 | 43 | 29 | 31 | 20 | 33 | 40 | 46 | 49 | 51 | 21 | 15 | | | | | |
| 16. Stranraer | 89 | 62 | 84 | 75 | 65 | 34 | 35 | 39 | 56 | 63 | 69 | 65 | 74 | 44 | 23 | 16 | | | | |
| 17. **Portpatrick** | 88 | 63 | 83 | 74 | 66 | 39 | 36 | 44 | 61 | 67 | 68 | 77 | 77 | 49 | 28 | 23 | 17 | | | |
| 18. **Mull of Galloway** | 104 | 78 | 99 | 90 | 82 | 56 | 52 | 60 | 78 | 82 | 84 | 93 | 93 | 65 | 62 | 39 | 16 | 18 | | |
| 19. **Kirkcudbright** | 136 | 111 | 131 | 122 | 114 | 88 | 84 | 92 | 110 | 114 | 116 | 124 | 125 | 97 | 94 | 71 | 48 | 32 | 19 | |
| 20. *Douglas (IoM)* | 146 | 120 | 141 | 132 | 124 | 106 | 94 | 102 | 141 | 130 | 126 | 141 | 135 | 107 | 104 | 84 | 60 | 42 | 45 | 20 |

55°N

KIRKCUDBRIGHT 2.24
Little Ross
Wigtown Bay
Burrow Head
Garlieston
Port William
Isle of Whithorn
Crammag Head
Mull of Galloway
Drummore
Luce Bay
PORTPATRICK 2.23
Corsewall Point
Loch Ryan
Girvan
Alisa Craig
Turnberry Point
TROON 2.22
Ayr
Prestwick
5° W
Holy Island
LAMLASH 2.11
Pladda
Island Davaar
CAMPBELTOWN 2.9
Macrihanish
Mull of Kintyre
Southend
Sanda I
Fair Head
Rathlin I

## 2.2 SW SCOTLAND TIDAL STREAMS

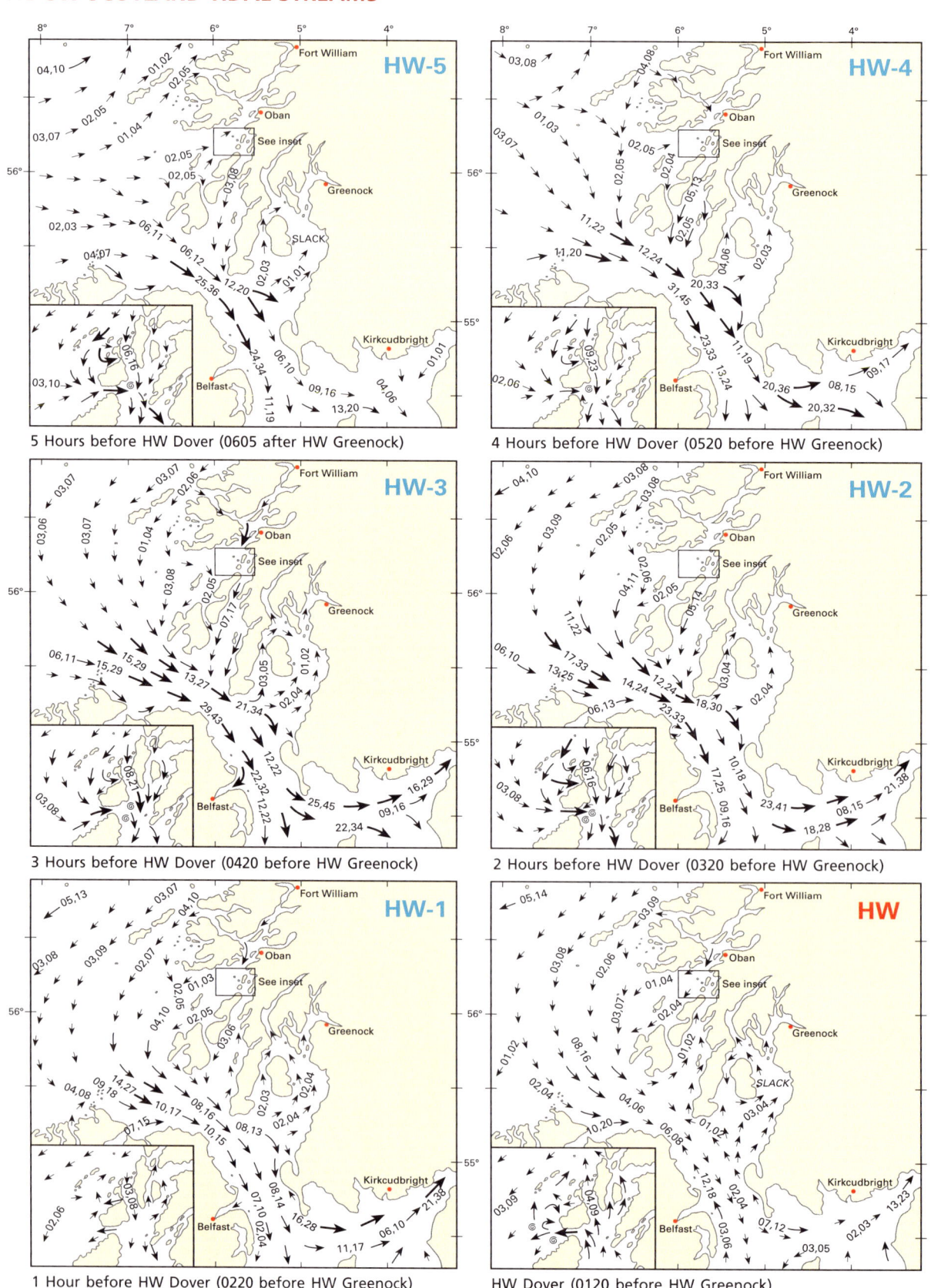

5 Hours before HW Dover (0605 after HW Greenock)

4 Hours before HW Dover (0520 before HW Greenock)

3 Hours before HW Dover (0420 before HW Greenock)

2 Hours before HW Dover (0320 before HW Greenock)

1 Hour before HW Dover (0220 before HW Greenock)

HW Dover (0120 before HW Greenock)

Northward 1.2    Mull of Kintyre 2.10    Irish Sea 4.2    Northern Ireland 6.2

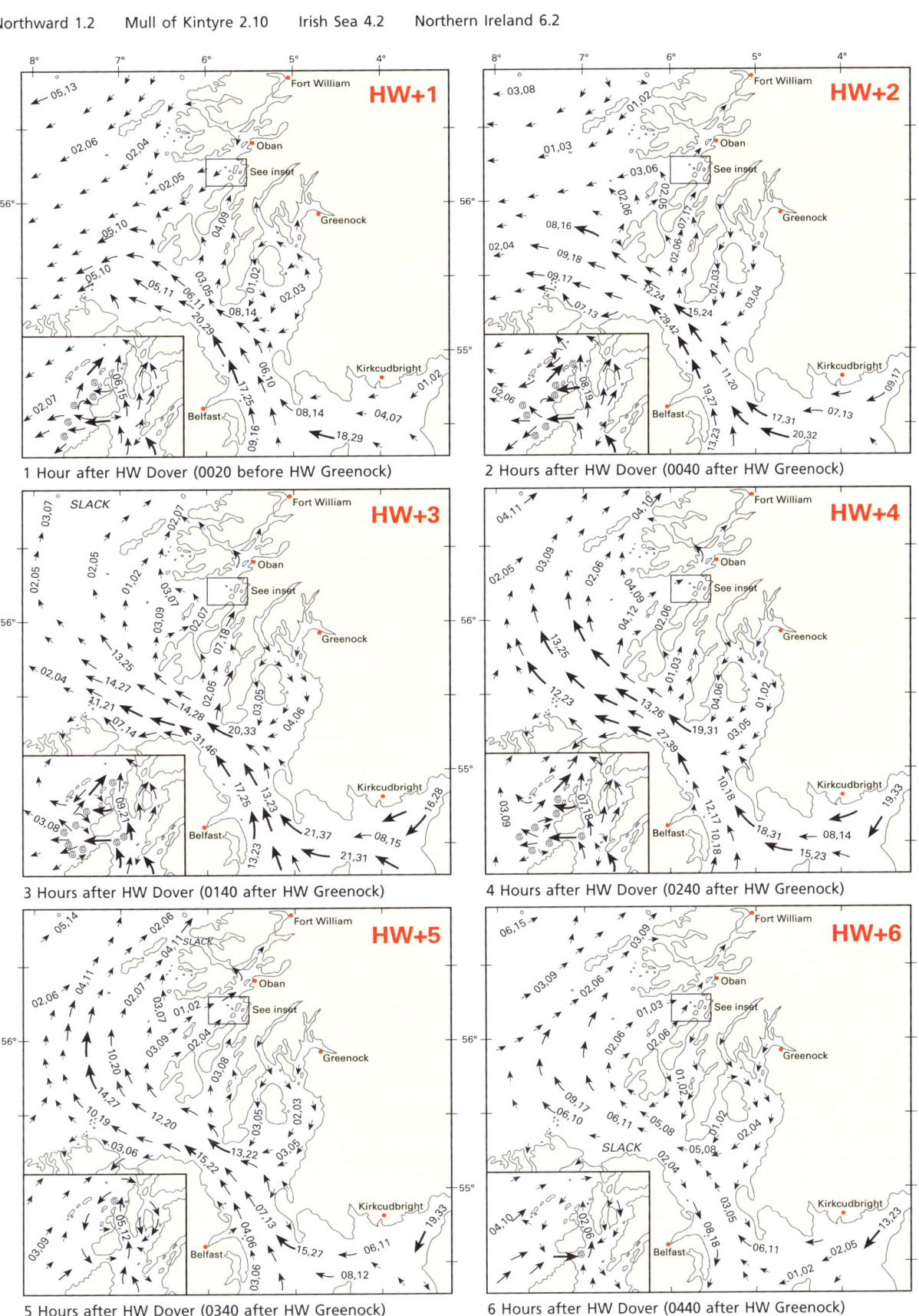

1 Hour after HW Dover (0020 before HW Greenock)

2 Hours after HW Dover (0040 after HW Greenock)

3 Hours after HW Dover (0140 after HW Greenock)

4 Hours after HW Dover (0240 after HW Greenock)

5 Hours after HW Dover (0340 after HW Greenock)

6 Hours after HW Dover (0440 after HW Greenock)

SW Scotland

## 2.3 LIGHTS, BUOYS AND WAYPOINTS

**Bold** print = light with a nominal range of 15M or more. CAPITALS = place or feature. *CAPITAL ITALICS* = light-vessel, light float or Lanby. *Italics* = Fog signal. ***Bold italics*** = Racon. See 0.2 for Abbreviations.

### COLONSAY TO ISLAY

#### COLONSAY
Scalasaig, Rubha Dubh ⚓ Fl (2) WR 10s 8m W8M, R6M; W bldg; vis: shore-R- 230°-W-337°-R-354°; 56°04'·01N 06°10'·90W.
Pier Hd Ldg Lts ⚓ 262°, FR 8/10m (occas); 56°04'·12N 06°11'·02W.

#### SOUND OF ISLAY
**Rhubh' a Mháil (Ruvaal)** ☆ 55°56'·18N 06°07'·46W Fl (3) WR 15s 45m **W24M, R21M**; W twr; vis: 075°-R-180°-W-075°.
Carragh an t'Struith ⚓ Fl  3s 8m 9M; W twr; vis: 354°-180°; 55°52'·30N 06°05'·78W.
Carraig Mòr ⚓ Fl (2) WR 6s 7m W8M, R6M; W twr; vis: shore-R-175°-W-347°-R-shore; 55°50'·42N 06°06'·13W.
Black Rocks ▲ Fl G 6s; 55°47'·50N 06°04'·09W.
McArthur's Hd ⚓ Fl (2) WR 10s 39m W14M, R11M; W twr; W in Sound of Islay from NE coast,159°-R-244°-W-E coast of Islay; 55°45'·84N 06°02'·90W.
Eilean a Chùirn ⚓ Fl (3) 18s 26m 8M;   W Bn; obsc when brg more than 040°; 55°40'·12N 06°01'·22W.
Gigha Rocks ⚓ Q (9) 15s; 55°39'·20N 05°43'·65W.
Otter Rock ⚓ Q (6) + L Fl 15s; 55°33'·86N 06°07'·92W.

#### PORT ELLEN and LOCH INDAAL
Port Ellen ⚓ QG; 55°37'·00N 06°12'·27W.
Carraig Fhada ⚓ Fl WRG 3s 20m W8M, R6M, G6M; W⬜ twr; vis: W shore- 248°-G-311°-W-340°-R-shore; 55°37'·22N 06°12'·71W.
Sgeir nan Ròn ⚓ Fl R 5s 3M; 55°37'·62N 06°11'·54W.
Ro-Ro terminal ⚓ 2 FG (vert) 7m 3M; 55°37'·61N 06°11'·44W.
Bruichladdich Pier Hd ⚓ 55°45'·83N 06°21'·67 W 2 FR (vert) 6m 5M.
Rubh'an Dùin ⚓ Fl (2) WR 7s 15m W13M, R12M; W twr; vis: 218°-W-249°-R-350°-W-036°; 55°44'·70N 06°22'·28 W.
Orsay Is, **Rhinns of Islay** ☆ 55°40'·40N 06°30'·84W Fl 5s 46m **24M**; W twr; vis: 256°-184°.

### JURA TO MULL OF KINTYRE

#### SOUND OF JURA, CRAIGHOUSE, L SWEEN and GIGHA
Reisa an t-Struith, S end of Is ⚓ Fl (2) 12s 12m 7M; W col; 56°07'·77N 05°38'·91W.
Ruadh Sgeir ⚓ Fl 6s 15m 9M; W○ twr; 56°04'·32N 05°39'·77W.
Skervuile ⚓ Fl 15s 22m 9M; W twr; 55°52'·46N 05°49'·85W.
Ninefoot Rk ⚓ Q (3) 10s; 55°52'·46N 05°52'·95W.
Eilean nan Gabhar ⚓ Fl 5s 7m 8M; framework twr; vis: 225°-010°; 55°50'·04N 05°56'·25W.
Na Cùiltean ⚓ Fl 10s 9m 9M; 55°48'·64N 05°54'·90W.
Gamhna Gigha ⚓ Fl (2) 6s 7m 5M; 55°43'·78N 05°41'·08W.
Badh Rk ▲ Fl (2) G 12s; 55°42'·30N 05°41'·24W.
Sgeir Nuadh ⚓ Fl R 6s; 55°41'·78N 05°42'·06W.
Sgeir Gigalum ▲ Fl G 6s 3m 4M; 55°39'·96N 05°42'·67W.
Cath Sgeir ⚓ Q (9) 15s; 55°39'·66N 05°47'·50W.
Gigalum Rks ⚓ Q (9) 15s; 55°39'·20N 05°43'·70W.
Caolas Gigalum ⚓ 55°39'·15N 05°44'·57W.

#### WEST LOCH TARBERT
Dunskeig Bay ⚓ Q (2) 10s 11m 8M; 55°45'·22N 05°35'·00W.
Eileen Tráighe (off S side) ⚓ Fl (2) R 5s 5m 3M; R post; 55°45'·37N 05°35'·75W.
Corran Pt ⚓ QG 3m 3M; G post; 55°46'·12N 05°34'·35W.
Sgeir Mhein ⚓ QR 3m 3M; R post; 55°47'·06N 05°32'·42W.
Black Rocks ⚓ QG 3M; G post; 55°47'·89N 05°30'·20W.
Kennacraig Ferry Terminal ⚓ 2 FG (vert) 7m 3M; silver post; 55°48'·40N 05°29'·01W.
Kennacraig ⚓ QR; unreliable; 55°48'·66N 05°29'·18W.

**Mull of Kintyre** ☆ 55°18'·64N 05°48'·25W Fl (2) 20s 91m **24M**; W twr on W bldg; vis: 347°-178°.

### CRINAN CANAL and ARDRISHAIG
Crinan, E of lock ent ⚓ Fl WG 3s 8m 4M; W twr, R band; vis: shore-W-146°-G-shore; 56°05'·48N 05°33'·37W.
Ardrishaig Bkwtr Hd ⚓ L Fl WRG 6s 9m 4M; vis: 287°-G-339°-W-350°-R-035°; 56°00'·76N 05°26'·59W.
Sgeir Sgalag No. 49 ▲ Fl G 5s; 56°00'·36N 05°26'·30W.
Gulnare Rk No. 48 ⚓ Fl R 4s; 56°00'·18N 05°26'·31W.

### LOCH FYNE TO SANDA ISLAND

#### UPPER LOCH FYNE and INVERARY
'P' Lt By ⚓ Fl R 3s; 56°00'·23N 05°22'·07W.
Otter Spit ⚓ Fl G 3s 7m 8M; 56°00'·63N 05°21'·10W.
Glas Eilean ⚓ Fl R 5s 12m 7M; 56°01'·10N 05°21'·16W.
'Q' ⚓ Fl R 3s; 56°00'·95N 05°20'·67W.
Brideagan Rks 'X' ⚓ Fl R 3s; 56°06'·32N 05°14'·06W.
Sgeir an Eirionnaich ⚓ Fl WR 3s 7m 8M; vis: 044°-R-087°-W- 192°-R-210°-W-044°; 56°06'·47N 05°13'·55W.
Furnace Wharf ⚓ 2 FR (vert) 9m 5M; 56°09'·05N 05°10'·45W.

#### EAST LOCH TARBERT
Madadh Maol ⚓ Fl R 2·5s 4m 3M; 55°52'·02N 05°24'·25W.
Eilean a'Choic, SE side ⚓ QG 3m 2M; 55°51'·99N 05°24'·37W.
Eilean na Beithe ⚓ Fl WRG 3s 7m 5M; vis: G036°- W065°- R078°-106°; 55°52'·68N 05°19'·62W.
Portavadie Bkwtr ⚓ 2 FG (vert) 6/4m 4M; 55°52'·52N 05°19'·24W.
Sgat Mór ⚓ Fl 3s 9m 12M; W○ twr; 55°50'·85N 05°18'·50W.
No. 51 ⚓ Fl R 4s; 55°45'·56N 05°19'·68W.
Skipness range ⚓ Iso R 8s 7m 10M; Y ◇ on bldg; vis 292·2°-312·2°. Oc (2) Y 10s **24M** when range in use (occas); 55°46'·72N 05°19'·06W.

#### KILBRANNAN SOUND, CRANNAICH and CARRADALE BAY
Port Crannaich Bkwtr Hd ⚓ Fl R 10s 5m 6M; vis: 099°-279°; 55°35'·60N 05°27'·84W.
Crubon Rock ⚓ Fl (2) R 12s; 55°34'·48N 05°27'·07W.
Otterard Rock ⚓ Q (3) 10s; 55°27'·07N 05°31'·11W.

#### CAMPBELTOWN LOCH
**Davaar N Pt** ☆ 55°25'·69N 05°32'·42W Fl (2) 10s 37m **23M**; W twr; vis: 073°-330°.
Methe Bank 'C' ⚓ Fl (2) 6s; 55°25'·30N 05°34'·42W.
Arranman's Barrels ⚓ Fl (2) R 12s; 55°19'·40N 05°32'·87W.
Macosh Rock ⚓ Fl R 6s; 55°17'·95N 05°37'·00W.
**Sanda Island** ☆ 55°16'·50N 05°35'·01W Fl 10s 50m **15M**; W twr.
Patersons Rock ⚓ Fl (3) R 18s; 55°16'·90N 05°32'·48W.

### KYLES OF BUTE TO RIVER CLYDE

#### KYLES OF BUTE and CALADH
Ardlamont Point No. 47 ⚓ W Fl R 4s; 55°49'·59N 05°11'·76.
Carry Point No. 46 ⚓ Fl R 4s; 55°51'·39N 05°12'·24W.
Rubha Ban ⚓ Fl R 4s; 55°54'·95N 05°12'·40W.
Burnt Is ▲ (NE of Eilean Fraoich) Fl G 3s; 55°55'·78N 05°10'·49W.
Burnt I No. 42 ⚓ (S of Eilean Buidhe) Fl R 2s; 55°55'·76N 05°10'·39W.
Creyke Rock No. 45 ⚓ 55°55'·67N 05°10'·89W.
Beere Rock No. 44 ▲ 55°55'·55N 05°10'·63W.
Wood Farm Rock No. 43 ▲ 55°55'·41N 05°10'·34W.
Rubha á Bhodaich ▲ Fl G; 55°55'·38N 05°09'·59W.
Ardmaleish Point No. 41 ⚓ Q; 55°53'·02N 05°04'·70W.
Bogany Point No.36 ⚓ Fl R 4s; 55°50'·78N 05°01'·41W.

#### ROTHESAY
Front Pier, E end ⚓ 2 FG (vert) 7m 5M; 55°50'·32N 05°03'·10W.
Pier W end ⚓ 2 FR (vert) 7m 5M; 55°50'·35N 05°03'·32W.
Albert Pier near N end ⚓ 2 FR (vert) 8m 5M.

#### FIRTH OF CLYDE
Ascog Patches No. 13 ⚓ Fl (2) 10s 5m 5M; 55°49'·71N 05°00'·25W.

**WGS84 DATUM**

*Plot waypoints on chart before use*

**Toward Pt** ☆ 55°51'·73N 04°58'·79W Fl 10s 21m **22M**; W twr.
No. 34 ⨎ 55°51'·44N 04°59'·11W.
Toward Bank No. 35 ▲ Fl G 3s; 55°51'·04N 05°00'·01W.
Skelmorlie ⨼ Iso 5s; 55°51'·65N 04°56'·34W.

### WEMYSS and INVERKIP
Wemyss Bay Pier ⨎ 2 FG (vert) 7m 5M; 55°52'·56N 04°53'·47W.
'M' ▲ Fl G 5s; 55°53'·52N 04°54'·41W.
'O' ▲ Fl G 2·5s; 55°54'·55N 04°54'·55W.
Kip ▲ QG; 55°54'·49N 04°52'·98W.
Warden Bank ▲ Fl G 2s; 55°54'·77N 04°54'·54W.
Cowal ⨾ L Fl 10s; 55°56'·00N 04°54'·83W.
The Gantocks ⨼ Fl R 6s 12m 6M; ○ twr; 55°56'·45N 04°55'·08W.

### DUNOON
Dunoon Pier, S end 55°56'·76N 04°55'·31W; & N end ⨎ both 2 FR (vert) 5m 6M.
Cloch Point ⨎ Fl 3s 24m 8M; W ○ twr, B band, W dwellings; 55°56'·55N 04°52'·74W.
McInroy's Point, Ro-Ro Ferry terminal Hd ⨎ 2 FG (vert) 5/3m 6M; 55°57'·08N 04°51'·26W.

### HOLY LOCH
Hunter's Quay(Ro-Ro) ⨎ 2 FR (vert) 6/4m 6M; 55°58'·26N 04°54'·50W.
Holy Loch Marina 2 FR (vert) 4m 1M; 55°59'·00N 04°56'·80W.

### LOCH LONG and LOCH GOIL
Loch Long ⨾ Oc 6s; 55°59'·15N 04°52'·42W.
Baron's Pt No. 3 ⨎ Oc (2) Y 10s 5m 3M; 55°59'·18N 04°51'·12W.
Blairmore ⨎ Fl R 5s 5m 2M; 55°59'·66N 04°53'·61W.
Ravenrock Pt ⨎ Fl 4s 12m 10M; W twr on W col. Dir lt 204°, WRG 9m (same twr); vis: 201·5°-F R-203°-Al WR(W phase incr with brg)-203·5°-FW-204·5°-Al WG(G phase incr with brg)-205°-FG-206·5°; 56°02'·14N 04°54'·39W.
Port Dornaige ⨎ Fl 6s 8m 11M; W col; vis: 026°-206°; 56°03·75N 04°53'·65W.
Carraig nan Ron (Dog Rock) ⨎ Fl 2s 7m 11M; W col; 56°06'·00N 04°51'·71W.
Rubha Ardnahein ⨎ Fl R 5s 3m 3M; vis: 132°-312°; 56°06'·15N 04°53'·60W.
The Perch, Ldg Lts 318° Front, F WRG 3m 5M; vis: 311°-G-317°-W-320°-R-322°. Same structure, Fl R 3s 3m 3M; vis: 187°-322°; 56°06'·90N 04°54'·31W. Rear, 700m from front, F 7m 5M; vis: 312°-322·5°.
Cnap Pt ⨎ Ldg Lts 031°. Front, Q 8m 10M; W col; 56°07'·40N 04°49'·97W. Rear, 87m from front F 13m; R line on W twr.
Ashton ⨾ Iso 5s; 55°58'·10N 04°50'·65W.

### GOUROCK
Railway Pier Hd ⨎ 2 FG (vert) 10m 3M; 55°57'·77N 04°49'·06W.
Kempock Pt No. 4 ⨎ Oc (2) Y 10s 6m 3M; 55°57'·71N 04°49'·37W.
Whiteforeland ⨾ L Fl 10s; 55°58'·11N 04°47'·28W.
Rosneath Patch ⨼ Fl (2) 10s 5m 10M; 55°58'·52N 04°47'·45W.

### ROSNEATH, RHU NARROWS and GARELOCH
Ldg Lts 356°. **Front, No. 7N** ⨼ 56°00'·05N 04°45'·36W Dir lt 356°. WRG 5m **W16M**, R13M, G13M; vis: 353°-Al WG- 355°-FW-357°-Al WR-000°-FR-002°.
**Dir lt 115°** WRG 5m **W16M**, R13M, G13M; vis: 111°-Al WG-114°-FW- 116°-Al WR-119°-FR-121°. Passing lt Oc G 6s 6m 3M; G △ on G pile. Rear, Ardencaple Castle Centre ⨎ 56°00'·54N 04°45'·43W 2 FG (vert) 26m 12M; twr on Castle NW corner; vis: 335°-020°.
**No. 8N Lt Bn** ⨼ 55°59'·09N 04°44'·21W Dir lt 080° WRG 4m; **W16M**, R13M,G13M;vis: 075°-FG-077·5°-Al WG-079·5°-FW-080·5°-AltWR-082·5°-FR-085°. **Dir lt 138°** WRG 4m **W16M**, R13M, G13M; vis: 132°-FG-134°-Al WG- FW137°-139°-Al WR-142°. Passing lt Fl Y 3s 6m 3M.
Garelock No. 1 Lt Bn ⨎ VQ (4) Y 5s 9m; Y 'X' on Y structure; 55°59'·12N 04°43'·89W.
Row ▲ Fl G 5s; 55°59'·84N 04°45'·13W.
Cairndhu ▲ Fl G 2·5s; 56°00'·35N 04°46'·00W.
Castle Pt ⨎ Fl (2) R 10s 8m 6M; R mast; 56°00'·19N 04°46'·50W.

⨎ Fl G 4s; 56°00'·61N 04°46'·53W.
**No. 3 N Lt Bn** ⨼ 56°00'·07N 04°46'·72W Dir lt 149° WRG 9m **W16M**, R13M, G13M F & Al; vis: 144°-FG-145°-Al WG-148°-FW-150°-Al WR-153°-FR-154°. Passing lt Oc R 8s 9m 3M.
Rosneath DG Jetty ⨎ 2 FR (vert) 5M; W col; vis: 150°-330°; 56°00'·39N 04°47'·51W.
Rhu SE ▲ Fl G 3s; 56°00'·64N 04°47'·17W.
Rhu Pt ⨼ Q (3) WRG 6s 9m W10M, R7M, G7M; vis: 270°-G-000°-W-114°-R-188°; 56°00'·95N 04°47'·19W.
Dir lt 318° WRG **W16M**, R13M,G13M; vis: 315°-Al WG-317°-F-319°-Al WR-321°-FR-325°.
**Limekiln No. 2N Lt Bn** ⨼ 56°00'·67N 04°47'·64W Dir lt 295° WRG 5m **W16M**, R13M, G13M F & Al; R □ on R Bn; vis: 291°-Al WG-294°-FW- 296°-Al WR-299°-FR-301°.
Rhu NE ▲ QG; 56°01'·02N 04°47'·58W.
Rhu Spit ⨼ Fl 3s 6m 6M; 56°00'·84N 04°47'·34W.
Mambeg Dir lt 331°, Q (4) WRG 8s 10m 14M; vis: 328·5°-G-330°-W-332°-R-333°; H24; 56°03'·74N 04°50'·47W.
Helensburgh Pier Hd ⨎ 2 FG (vert) 5M; 56°00'·06N 04°44'·27W.

### GREENOCK and PORT GLASGOW
Anchorage Lts in line 196°. Front, FG 7m 12M; Y col; 55°57'·62N 04°46'·58W. Rear, 32m from front, FG 9m 12M. Y col.
Lts in line 194·5°. Front, FG 18m; 55°57'·45N 04°45'·91W. Rear, 360m from front, FG 33m.
Clydeport Container Terminal NW corner ⨎ QG 8m 8M.
Victoria Hbr W side ⨎ 2 FG 5m (vert); 55°56'·77N 04°44'·70W.
Garvel W end ⨎ Oc G 10s 9m 4M; 55°56'·81N 04°43'·55W.
E end, Maurice Clark Pt ⨎ QG 7m 2M; 55°56'·60N 04°42'·85W.
Port Glasgow Bn off ent Õ FG 7m 9M; 55°56'·25N 04°41'·26W.
Steamboat Quay, W end ⨎ FG 12m 12M; B&W chequered col; vis 210°-290°; 55°56'·25N 04°41'·44W. From here to Glasgow Lts on S bank are Fl G and Lts on N bank are Fl R.

## CLYDE TO MULL OF GALLOWAY
### LARGS
Approach ⨀ L Fl 10s; 55°46'·40N 04°51'·85W.
Marina S Bkwtr Hd ⨎ Oc G 10s 4m 4M; 55°46'·36N 04°51'·73W.
W Bkwtr Hd ⨎ Oc R 10s 4m 4M; 55°46'·37N 04°51'·67W.

### FAIRLIE
Fairlie Patch ▲ Fl G 1·5s; 55°45'·38N 04°52'·34W.
Hunterston Jetty S ⨎ 2 FG (vert) 11m 5M; 55°45'·10N 04°52'·88W.
Pier N ⨎ 2 FG (vert) 11m 5M; 55°45'·30N 04°52'·65W.
Fairlie Quay Pier Hd N ⨎ 2 FG (vert); 55°46'·06N 04°51'·78W.

### MILLPORT and GREAT CUMBRAE
The Eileans, W end ⨎ QG 5m 2M; 55°44'·89N 04°55'·59W.
Ldg Lts 333°. Pier Head front, 55°45'·04N 04°55'·85W FR 7m 5M. Rear, 137m from front, FR 9m 5M.
Mountstuart ⨾ L Fl 10s; 55°48'·00N 04°57'·57W.
Portachur ▲ Fl G 3s; 55°44'·35N 04°58'·52W.
Runnaneun Pt (Rubha'n Eun) ⨎ Fl R 6s 8m 12M; W twr; 55°43'·79N 05°00'·23W.
Sheanawally Point ⨎ Fl 10s 6m 5M; vis: 061°300°; 55°44'·12N 04°56'·37W.
Little Cumbrae Is, Cumbrae Elbow ⨎ Fl 6s 28m 14M; W twr; vis: 334°-193°; 55°43'·22N 04°58'·06W.

### ARDROSSAN
Approach Dir lt 055°, WRG 15m W14M, R11M, G11M; vis: 050°-F G-051·2°-Alt WG(W phase inc with Brg)- 053·8°-FW-056·2°-Alt WR(R phase inc with brg)-058·8°-FR-060°; 55°38'·66N 04°49'·22W. Same structure FR 13m 6M; vis: 325°-145°.
N Bkwtr Hd ⨎ Fl R 5s 7m 5M; R gantry; 55°38'·53N 04°49'·64W.
W Crinan Rk ⨾ Fl R 4s; 55°38'·47N 04°49'·89W.
Lt ho Pier Hd ⨎ Iso WG 4s 11m 9M; W twr; vis: 035°-W-317°-G-035°; 55°38'·47N 04°49'·57W.
Eagle Rock ▲ 55°38'·21N 04°49'·69W Fl G 5s.

### IRVINE

Ent N side ⚓ Fl R 3s 6m 5M; R col; 55°36'·21N 04°42'·09W.
S side ⚓ Fl G 3s 6m 5M; G col; 55°36'·17N 04°42'·04W.
Ldg Lts 051°. Front, FG 10m 5M; 55°36'·40N 04°41'·57W. Rear, 101m from front, FR 15m 5M; G masts, both vis: 019°-120°.

### TROON

Troon ⚓ Fl G 4s; 55°33'·06N 04°41'·35W.
Troon Approach ⚓ Fl R 2s 4m 3M; 55°33'·06N 04°41'·35W.
W Pier Hd ⚓ Fl (2) WG 5s 11m 9M; W twr; vis: 036°-G-090°-W-036°; 55°33'·07N 04°41'·02W.
E Pier Hd ⚓ Fl R 10s 6m 3M; 55°33'·03N 04°40'·96W.
Lady I ⚓ Fl 2s 19m 11M; W Tr R vert stripes; *Racon (T) 13-11M*; 55°31'·63N 04°44'·05W.

### ARRAN, RANZA, LAMLASH and BRODICK

Brodick Pier Hd ⚓ 2 FR (vert) 9m 4M; 55°32'·64N 05°08'·28W.
Hamilton Rk ⚓ Fl R 6s; 55°32'·63N 05°04'·90W.
**Pillar Rk Pt** ☆ (Holy Island), 55°31'·04N 05°03'·67W Fl (2) 20s 38m **25M**; W☐twr.
Fullarton Rk ⚓ Fl (2) R 12s; 55°30'·64N 05°04'·57W.
Holy I SW end ⚓ Fl G 3s 14m 10M; W twr; vis: 282°-147°; 55°30'·73N 05°04'·21W.
**Pladda** ☆ 55°25'·50N 05°07'·12W Fl (3) 30s 40m **17M**; W twr.

### AYR

S. Nicholas ⚓ 55°28'·12N 04°39'·44W Fl G 2s.
N Bkwtr Hd ⚓ QR 9m 5M; 55°28'·21N 04°38'·78W.
S Pier Hd ⚓ Q 7m 7M; R twr; vis: 012°-161°. Also FG 5m 5M; vis: 012°-082°; 55°28'·17N 04°38'·74W.
Ldg Lts 098°. Front, FR 10m 5M; Tfc sigs; 55°28'·15N 04°38'·38W. Rear, 130m from front Oc R 10s 18m 9M.
**Turnberry Point** ☆, near castle ruins 55°19'·56N 04°50'·71W Fl 15s 29m **24M**; W twr.
**Ailsa Craig** ☆ 55°15'·12N 05°06'·52W Fl 4s 18m **17M**; W twr; vis: 145°-028°.

### GIRVAN

S Pier Hd ⚓2 FG (vert) 8m 4M; W twr; 55°14'·72N 04°51'·90W.
N Bkwtr Hd ⚓ Fl (2) R 6s 7m 4M; 55°14'·74N 04°51'·85W.
N Groyne Hd ⚓ Iso 4s 3m 4M; 55°14'·71N 04°51'·71W.

### LOCH RYAN and STRANRAER

Milleur Point ⚓ Q; 55°01'·28N 05°05'·66W.

Forbes Shoal ⚓ QR; 54°59'·47N 05°02'·96W.
Loch Ryan W ⚓QG;54°59'·23N 05°03'·24W .
Cairn Pt ⚓ Fl (2) R 10s 14m 12M; W twr; 54°58'·46N 05°01'·85W.
Cairnryan ⚓ Fl R 5s 5m 5M; 54°57'·77N 05°00'·99W.
Stranraer No.1 ⚓ Oc G 6s; 54°56'·67N 05°01'·32W.
No. 3 ⚓ QG; 54°55'·87N 05°01'·60W.
No. 5 ⚓ Fl G 3s; 54°55'·08N 05°01'·86W.
Ross Pier Hd ⚓ 2 F Bu (vert); 54°54'·54N 05°01'·64W.
E Pier Hd ⚓ 2 FR (vert) 9m; 54°54'·61N 05°01'·60W.
W Pier Hd ⚓ 2 FG (vert) 8m 4M; Gy col; 54°54'·51N 05°01'·75W.
**Corsewall Point** ☆ 55°00'·41N 05°09'·58W Fl (5) 30s 34m **22M**; W twr; vis: 027°-257°.

### PORTPATRICK

Ldg Lts 050·5°. Front, FG (occas); 54°50'·50N 05°07'·02W. Rear, 68m from front, FG 8m (occas).
**Crammag Hd** ☆ 54°39'·90N 04°57'·92W Fl 10s 35m **18M**; W twr.
**Mull of Galloway** ☆, SE end 54°38'·08N 04°51'·45W Fl 20s 99m **28M**; W twr; vis: 182°-105°.

### DRUMMORE, ISLE OF WHITHORN and GARLIESTON

Port William Ldg Lts 105°. Front, Pier Hd Fl G 3s 7m 3M; 54°45'·66N 04°35'·28W. Rear, 130m from front, FG 10m 2M.
Whithorn Hbr E Pier Hd ⚓ QG 4m 5M; 54°41'·88N 04°21'·86W.
Ldg Lts 335°. Front, Oc R 8s 7m 7M; Or ♦; 54°42'·01N 04°22'·05W. Rear, 35m from front, Oc R 8s 9m 7M; Or ♦, synch.
Garlieston Pier Hd ⚓ 2 FR (vert) 8m 3M; 54°47'·32N 04°21'·81W.
Little Ross ⚓ Fl 5s 50m 12M; W twr; obsc in Wigtown B when brg more than 103°; 54°45'·93N 04°05'·10W.

### KIRKCUDBRIGHT BAY and KIPPFORD

Little Ross NNE end of Is ⚓ Fl (2) 5s 21m 5M; Stone bcn; 54°46'·06N 04°05'·02W.
No. 1 Lifeboat Ho ⚓ Fl 3s 7m 3M; 54°47'·68N 04°03'·74W.
No.12 ⚓ Fl R 3s; 54°49'·15N 04°04'·83W.
Perch No.14 ⚓ Fl 3s 5m; 54°49'·24N 04°04'·83W.
No. 22 ⚓ Fl R 3s 2m; 54°50'·08N 04°04'·02W.
Outfall ⚓ Fl Y 5s 3m 2M; Y twr; 54°50'·18N 04°03'·84W.
Hestan I, E end ⚓ Fl (2) 10s 42m 9M; 54°49'·95N 03°48'·53W.
Barnkirk Pt ⚓ Fl 2s 18m 2M; 54°58'·00N 03°16'·02W.

---

## 2.4 PASSAGE INFORMATION

Conditions in the SW of Scotland are generally less rugged south of Mull. Some of the remarks at the start of 1.4 are equally applicable to this area. The area is well covered by Admiralty Leisure Folios. Refer to the Clyde Cruising Club's SDs, Admiralty *West Coast of Scotland Pilot*; and to *Yachtsman's Pilot to the W Coast of Scotland, Clyde to Colonsay* (Imray/Lawrence). Submarines exercise throughout these waters; see Subfacts for information on active areas.

Some of the following more common *Gaelic* terms may help with navigation: *Acairseid*: anchorage. *Ailean*: meadow. *Aird, ard*: promontory. *Aisir, aisridh*: passage between rocks. *Beag*: little. *Beinn*: mountain. *Bo, boghar, bodha*: rock. *Cala*: harbour. *Camas*: channel, bay. *Caol*: strait. *Cladach*: shore, beach. *Creag*: cliff. *Cumhamn*: narrows. *Dubh, dhubh*: black. *Dun*: castle. *Eilean, eileanan*: island. *Garbh*: rough. *Geal, gheal*: white. *Glas, ghlas*: grey, green. *Inis*: island. *Kyle*: narrow strait. *Linn, Linne*: pool. *Mor, mhor*: large. *Mull*: promontory. *Rinn, roinn*: point. *Ruadh*: red, brown. *Rubha, rhu*: cape. *Sgeir*: rock. *Sruth*: current. *Strath*: river valley. *Tarbert*: isthmus. *Traigh*: beach. *Uig*: bay.

### CORRYVRECKAN TO CRINAN

(AC 2326, 2343) ▶ *Between Scarba and Jura is the Gulf of Corryvreckan (AC 2343) which is best avoided, and should*

*never be attempted by small craft except at slack water and in calm conditions. (In any event the Sound of Luing is always a safer and not much longer alternative.) The Gulf has a least width of 6ca and is free of dangers apart from its very strong tides which, in conjunction with a very uneven bottom, cause extreme turbulence. This is particularly dangerous with strong W winds over a W-going (flood) tide which spews out several miles to seaward of the gulf, with overfalls extending 5M from the W of ent (The Great Race). Keep to the S side of the gulf to avoid the worst turbulence and the whirlpool known as The Hag, caused by depths of only 29m, as opposed to more than 100m in the fairway. The W-going stream in the gulf begins at HW Oban + 0410, and the E-going at HW Oban – 0210. Sp rate W-going is 8·5kn, and E-going about 6kn. The range of tide at sp can vary nearly 2m between the E end of the gulf (1·5m) and the W end (3·4m), with HW 30mins earlier at the E end. Slack water occurs at HW Oban +0400 and –0230 and lasts almost 1 hr at nps, but only 15 mins at sps. On the W-going (flood) stream eddies form both sides of the gulf, but the one on the N (Scarba) shore is more important. Where this eddy meets the main stream off Camas nam Bairneach there is violent turbulence, with heavy overfalls extending W at the division of the eddy and the main stream.* ◀ There are temp anchs with the wind in the right quarter in Bàgh Gleann a' Mhaoil in the SE corner of Scarba, and in Bàgh Gleann nam Muc at N end of Jura but the latter has rks in approaches E and SW of Eilean Beag.

SE of Corryvreckan is Loch Crinan, which leads to the Crinan Canal. Beware Black Rk, 2m high and 2ca N of the canal sea lock, and dangers extending 100m from the rock.

## WEST OF JURA TO ISLAY

(AC 2481, 2168) The W coasts of Colonsay and Oronsay (AC 2169) are fringed with dangers up to 2M offshore. The two islands are separated by a narrow chan which dries and has an overhead cable (10m). There are HIE ⚓s at Scalasaig.

The Sound of Islay presents no difficulty; hold to the Islay shore, where all dangers are close in. ▶ *The N-going stream begins at HW Oban + 0440, and the S-going at HW Oban – 0140. Main flood begins +0015 HW Dover (HW Oban +0545). Streams turn approx 1 hr earlier in Gigha Sd and at Kintyre and Jura shores. S going stream for 9hrs close inshore between Gigha and Machrihanish starting HW Dover (HW Oban –0530).*

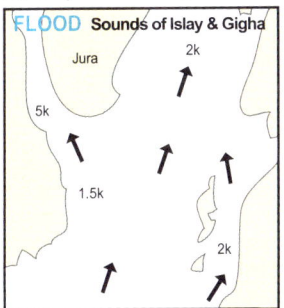
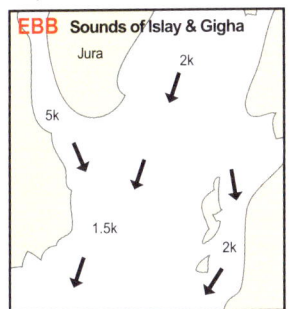

*Main ebb begins HW Dover –0545 (HW Oban –0015). Streams turn 1 hr earlier in Gigha Sd, Kintyre and Jura shores. Overfalls off McArthur's Hd. The sp rates are 2·5kn at N entrance and 1·5kn at S* **entrance, but reaching 5kn in the narrows off Port Askaig.** ◀ There are anchs in the Sound, but holding ground is mostly poor. The best places are alongside at Port Askaig, or at anch off the distillery in Bunnahabhain B, 2·5M to N. ▶ *There are overfalls off McArthur's Hd (Islay side of S entrance) during the S-going stream.* ◀

The N coast of Islay and Rhinns of Islay are very exposed. In the N there is anch SE of Nave Island at entrance to Loch Gruinart; beware Balach Rks which dry, just to N. ▶ *To the SW off Orsay (lt), Frenchman's Rks and W Bank there is a race and overfalls which should be cleared by 3M. Here the NW-going stream begins at HW Oban + 0530, and the SE-going at HW Oban – 0040;* **sp rates are 6-8kn inshore**, *but decrease to 3kn 5M offshore.* ◀ Loch Indaal gives some shelter; beware rks extending from Laggan Pt on E side of ent. Off the Mull of Oa there are further overfalls. Port Ellen, the main hbr on Islay, has HIE ⚓s; there are some dangers in approach, and it is exposed to S; see AC 2474.

## SOUND OF JURA TO GIGHA

(AC 2397, 2396, 2168) From Crinan to Gigha the Sound of Jura is safe if a mid-chan course is held. Ruadh Sgeir (lt) are rocky ledges in mid-fairway, about 3M W of Crinan. Loch Sween (AC 2397) can be approached N or SE of MacCormaig Islands, where there is an attractive anch on NE side of Eilean Mor, but exposed to NE. Coming from N beware Keills Rk and Danna Rk. Sgeirean a Mhain is a rk in fairway 1·5M NE of Castle Sween (conspic on SE shore). Anch at Tayvallich, near head of loch on W side.

W Loch Tarbert (AC 2477) is long and narrow, with good anchs and lts near ent, but unmarked shoals. On entry give a berth of at least 2½ca to Eilean Traighe off N shore, E of Ardpatrick Pt. Dun Skeig, an isolated hill, is conspic on S shore. Good anch near head of loch, 1M by road from E Loch Tarbert, Loch Fyne.

On W side of Sound, near S end of Jura, are The Small Is (AC 2396) across the mouth of Loch na Mile. Beware Goat Rk (dries 0·3m) 1.5ca off s'most Is, Eilean nan Gabhar, behind which is good anch.

Also possible to go alongside Craighouse Pier (HIE ⚓). Another anch is in Lowlandman's B, about 3M to N, but exposed to S winds; Ninefoot Rks with depth of 2·4m and ECM lt buoy lie off ent. Skervuile (lt) is a reef to the E, in middle of the Sound.

S of W Loch Tarbert, and about 2M off the Kintyre shore, is Gigha Is (AC 2475). Good anchs on E side in Druimyeon B and Ardminish B (HIE ⚓s), respectively N and S of Ardminish Pt. Outer and Inner Red Rks (least depth 2m) lie 2M SW of N end of Gigha Is. Dangers extend 1M W off S end of Gigha Is. Gigalum Is and Cara Is are off the S end. Gigha Sound needs very careful pilotage, since there are several dangerous rks, some buoyed/lit, others not. ▶ *The N-going stream begins at HW Oban + 0430, and S-going at HW Oban – 0155, sp rates 1·3kn.* ◀

## MULL OF KINTYRE

(AC 2126, 2199, 2798) From Crinan to Mull of Kintyre is about 50M. ▶ *This long peninsula much affects the tidal streams in North Chan. Off Mull of Kintyre (lt, fog sig) the N-going stream begins at HW Oban + 0400, and the S-going at HW Oban – 0225, sp rate 5kn. A strong race and overfalls exist S and SW of Mull of Kintyre, dangerous in strong S winds against S-going tide. Careful timing is needed, especially W-bound. Main flood begins HW Dover –0600 (HW Greenock +0505). Races off Mull of Kintyre, Altacarry Hd and Fair Hd. Counter tides in bays of Antrim coast. W-going streams in Rathlin Sd, counter tide from Sanda Sd to Machrihanish last 1h30 - 2 hrs.*

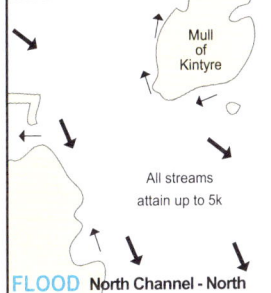
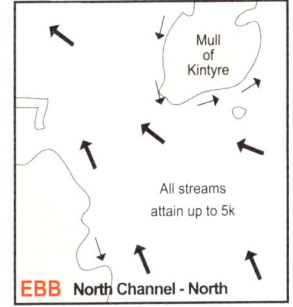

*Main ebb begins HW Dover (HW Greenock –0120). Races off Mull of Kintyre & Altacarry Hd. Counter tides in bays of Antrim coast, counter tide from Macrihanish to Sanda Sd last 1h30 - 2 hrs.* ◀ The Traffic Separation Scheme in the North Channel, is only 2M W of the Mull and may limit sea-room in the ITZ.

Sanda Sound separates Sanda Is (lt) and its rks and islets, from Kintyre. On the mainland shore beware Macosh Rks (dry, PHM lt buoy) forming part of Barley Ridges, 2ca offshore; Arranman Barrels, drying and submerged, marked by PHM lt buoy; and Blindman Rk (depth 2m) 1·3M N of Ru Stafnish, where 3 radio masts are 5ca inland. Sanda Is has Sheep Is 3ca to the N; Paterson's Rk (dries) is 1M E. There is anch in Sanda hbr on N side. ▶ *In Sanda Sound the E-going stream begins at HW Greenock + 0340, and the W-going at HW Greenock – 0230, sp rates 5kn. Tide races extend W, N and NE from Sanda, and in strong S or SW winds the Sound is dangerous.* ◀ In these conditions pass 2M S of Mull of Kintyre and Sanda and E of Paterson's Rk.

## MULL OF KINTYRE TO UPPER LOCH FYNE

(AC 2126, 2383, 2381, 2382). ▶ *Once E of Mull of Kintyre, tidal conditions and pilotage much improve.* ◀ Campbeltown is entered N of Island Davaar (lt). 1·5M N off lt ho is Otterard Rk (depth 3·8m), with Long Rk (dries 1·1m) 5ca W of it; only Otterard Rock is buoyed. ▶ *E of Island Davaar tide runs 3kn at sp, and there are overfalls.* ◀

Kilbrannan Sound runs 21M from Island Davaar to Skipness Pt, where it joins Inchmarnock Water, Lower Loch Fyne and Bute Sound. ▶ *There are few dangers apart from overfalls on Erins*

*Bank, 10M S of Skipness, on S-going stream.◄* Good anch in Carradale Bay, off Torrisdale Castle. *►There are overfalls off Carradale Pt on S-going stream.◄*

Lower L Fyne (AC 2381) is mainly clear of dangers to East L Tarbert. On E shore beware rks off Ardlamont Pt; 4M to NW is Skate Is which is best passed to W. 3M S of Ardrishaig beware Big Rk (depth 2·1m). Further N, at entrance to Loch Gilp (mostly dries) note shoals (least depth 1·5m) round Gulnare Rk, PHM lt buoy; also Duncuan Is with dangers extending SW to Sgeir Sgalag (depth 0·6m), buoyed.

Where Upper L Fyne turns NE (The Narrows) it is partly obstructed by Otter Spit (dries 0·9m), extending 8ca WNW from E shore and marked by lt bn. The stream runs up to 2kn here. A buoyed/lit rk, depth less than 2m, lies about 7ca SW of Otter Spit bn. In Upper L Fyne (AC 2382) off Minard Pt, the chan between rks and islands in the fairway is buoyed/lit.

## ARRAN, BUTE AND FIRTH OF CLYDE

(AC1906, 1907) Bute Sound leads into Firth of Clyde, and is clear in fairway. Arran's mountains tend to cause squalls or calms, but it has good anchs at Lamlash, Brodick and Loch Ranza. Sannox Rock (depth 1·5m) is 2½ca off Arran coast 8M N of Lamlash. 1ca off W side of Inchmarnock is Tra na-h-uil, a rk drying 1·5m. In Inchmarnock Sound, Shearwater Rk (depth 0·9m) lies in centre of S entrance.

Kyles of Bute are attractive chan N of Bute from Inchmarnock Water to Firth of Clyde, and straightforward apart from Burnt Islands. Here it is best to take the north channel, narrow but well buoyed, passing S of Eilean Buidhe, and N of Eilean Fraoich and Eilean Mor. *► Care is needed, since sp stream may reach 5kn.◄* Caladh Hbr is a beautiful anch 7ca NW of Burnt Is.

The N lochs in Firth of Clyde are less attractive. Loch Goil is worth a visit; Loch Long is squally and has few anchs but has no hidden dangers, while Gareloch (has Rhu marina, the submarine base and hotel with mooring near the northern end (west shore)). *► Navigation in Firth of Clyde is easy since tidal streams are weak, seldom exceeding 1kn. ◄* Channels are well marked; but beware unlit moorings commercial and naval shipping. There are marinas on the mainland at Largs, Fairlie and Inverkip. Rothesay Hbr on E Bute, and Kilchattan B (anch 6M to S) are both sheltered from SSE to WNW.

## FIRTH OF CLYDE TO MULL OF GALLOWAY

(AC 2131, 2126, 2199, 2198) Further S the coast is less inviting, with mostly commercial hbrs until reaching Ardrossan and Troon, NW of which there are various dangers: beware Troon Rk (depth 5·6m, but sea can break), Lappock Rk (dries 0·6m, marked by bn), and Mill Rk (dries 0·4m, buoyed). Lady Isle (lt, racon), shoal to NE, is 2M WSW of Troon.

*► There is a severe race off Bennane Hd (8M SSE of Ailsa Craig, conspic) when tide is running strongly.◄* Loch Ryan offers little for yachtsmen but there is anch S of Kirkcolm Pt, inside the drying spit which runs in SE direction 1·5M from the point. There is also a useful anch in Lady Bay, sheltered except from NE. Portpatrick is a useful passage hbr, but not in onshore winds.

*▶ North Channel South (6.4 for N.Chan N): Irish coast – the S-going flood begins HW Dover +0610 (HW Belfast –0600). Counter tide off Donaghadee and Island Magee for last 3 hrs of flood. Scottish coast between Corsewall Pt and Mull of Galloway – HW Dover +0430 (HW Greenock +0310). Sp rate off Corsewall Pt is 2–3 kn, increasing* **to 5kn off and S of Black Hd.** *Races occur off Copeland Is. Morroch B, Money Hd Mull of Logan and Mull of Galloway.*

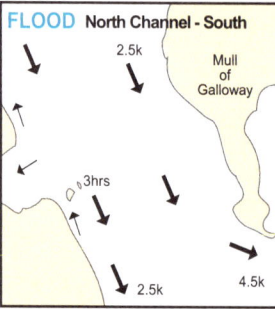
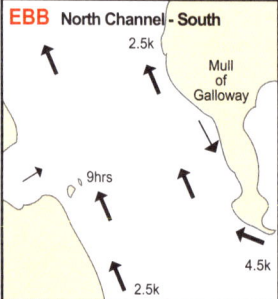

*Irish coast – N going ebb begins HW Dover –0015 (HW Belfast). Scottish coast - HW Dover –0130 (HW Greenock –0250). Races off Copeland Is. & Mull of Galloway. Flood begins 2 hrs early close inshore N of Mull of Galloway. A race SSE of Crammag Hd is bad if wind against tide. Mull of Galloway (lt) is a high (82m), steep-to headland with* **a dangerous race extending nearly 3M to S.** *On E-going stream it extends NNE into Luce B; on W-going stream it extends SW and W. Give the race a wide berth, or pass close inshore at slack water nps and calm weather. SW wind >F4 against W-going stream, do not attempt inshore route.◄*

## SCOTLAND – SW COAST

The Scares, two groups of rocks, lie at the mouth of Luce Bay which elsewhere is clear more than 3ca offshore; but the whole bay is occupied by a practice bombing range, marked by 12 DZ SPM lt buoys. Good anch at E Tarbert B to await the tide around the Mull of Galloway, or good shelter in drying hbr of Drummore . Off Burrow Hd there is a bad race in strong W winds with W-going tide. Luce Bay Firing Range (D402/403) lies at the NW end. For info on activity ☎ (01776) 888792. In Wigtown B the best anch is in Isle of Whithorn B, but exposed to S. It is also possible to dry out in Garlieston.

A tank firing range, between the E side of ent to Kirkcudbright Bay and Abbey Hd, 4M to E, extends 14M offshore. If unable to avoid the area, cross it at N end close inshore. For information contact the Range safety boat 'Gallovidian' on VHF Ch 16, 73. The range operates 0900-1600LT Mon-Fri, but weekend and night firing may also occur.

See 3.4 for continuation E into Solway Firth and S into the Irish Sea. For notes on crossing the Irish Sea, see 6.4.

## HARBOURS AND ANCHORAGES IN COLONSAY, JURA, ISLAY AND THE SOUND OF JURA

**SCALASAIG**, Colonsay, **56°04´·14N 06°10´·86W**. AC *2169*, 2474. HW +0542 on Dover; ML 2·2m. See 2.5. Conspic monument ½M SW of hbr. Beware group of rks N of pier hd marked by bn. 2 HIE Ⓥ berths on N side of pier, inner end approx 2·5m. Inner hbr to SW of pier is safe, but dries. Ldg lts 262°, both FR 8/10m on pier. Also ⚓ clear of cable in **Loch Staosnaig**; SW of Rubha Dubh lt, Fl (2) WR 10s 8m 8/6M; shore-R-230°-W-337°-R-354°. Facilities: D, P, 🛒 (all at ✉), FW, Hotel ☎ (01951) 200316, Dr (0951) 200328.

**LOCH TARBERT**, W Jura, **55°57´·69N 06°00´·06W**. AC *2169*, 2481. Tides as Rubha A'Mhàil (N tip of Islay). See 2.5. HW −0540 on Dover; ML 2·1m; Duration 0600. Excellent shelter inside the loch, but subject to squalls in strong winds; ⚓ outside in Glenbatrick Bay in approx 6m in S winds, or at Bagh Gleann Righ Mor in approx 2m in N winds. To enter inner loch via Cumhann Beag, there are four pairs of ldg marks (W stones) at approx 120°, 150°, 077°, and 188°, the latter astern, to be used in sequence; pilot book required. There are no facilities.

**PORT ASKAIG**, Islay, **55°50´·87N 06°06´·26W**. AC 2168, 2481. HW +0610 on Dover; ML 1·2m. See 2.5. Hbr on W side of Sound of Islay. ⚓ close inshore in 4m or secure to ferry pier. Beware strong tide/eddies. ☆ FR at LB. Facilities: FW (hose on pier), Gas, P, R, Hotel, 🛒, ✉, ferries to Jura and Kintyre. Other ⚓s in the Sound at: Bunnahabhain (2M N); Whitefarland Bay, Jura, opp Caol Ila distillery; NW of Am Fraoch Eilean (S tip of Jura); Aros Bay, N of Ardmore Pt.

**CRAIGHOUSE**, SE Jura, **55°49´·99N 05°56´·31W**. AC 2168, 2481, 2396. HW +0600 on Dover; ML 0·5m; Duration 0640 np, 0530 sp. See 2.5. Good shelter, but squalls occur in W winds. Enter between lt bn on SW end of Eilean nan Gabhar, Fl 5s 7m 8M vis 225°-010°, and unlit bn close SW. There are 8 HIE Ⓥs N of pier (☎ (01496) 810332), where yachts may berth alongside; or ⚓ in 5m in poor holding at the N end of Loch na Mile. Facilities: very limited, Bar, FW, ✉, R, 🛒, Gas, P & D (cans). **Lowlandman's Bay** is 1M further N, with ECM buoy, Q (3) 10s, marking Nine Foot Rk (2·4m) off the ent. ⚓ to SW of conspic houses, off stone jetty.

**LOCH SWEEN**, Argyll and Bute, **55°55´·69N 05°41´·26W**. AC 2397. HW +0550 on Dover; ML 1·5m; Duration = 0610. See 2.6 Carsaig Bay. Off the ent to loch, **Eilean Mòr** (most SW'ly of MacCormaig Isles) has tiny ⚓ on N side in 3m; local transit marks keep clear of two rks, 0·6m and 0·9m. Inside the loch, beware Sgeirean a'Mhain, a rk in mid-chan to S of Taynish Is, 3M from ent. Good shelter in Loch a Bhealaich (⚓ outside **Tayvallich** in approx 7m on boulders) or enter inner hbr to ⚓ W of central reef. There are no lts. Facilities: Gas, Bar, ✉, FW (🛥 by ✉), R, 🛒. Close to NE are ⚓s at **Caol Scotnish** and **Fairy Is**, the former obstructed by rks 3ca from ent.

**WEST LOCH TARBERT**, Argyll and Bute, (Kintyre), **55°45'N 05°36'W**. AC 2477. Tides as Gigha Sound, 2.5. Good shelter. Ent is S of Eilean Traighe, Fl (2) R 5s, and NW of Dun Skeig, Q (2) 10s, where there is also conspic conical hill (142m). Loch is lit for 5M by 3 bns, QG, QR and QG in sequence, up to Kennacraig ferry pier, 2FG (vert). PHM buoy, QR, is 2½ca NW of pier. Caution: many drying rks and fish farms outside the fairway and near head of loch. ⚓s are NE of Eilean Traighe (beware weed and ferry wash); near Rhu Pt, possible Ⓥs; NE of Eilean dà Gallagain, and at loch hd by pier (ru). Tarbert (2.8) is 1·5M walk/bus.

**GIGHA ISLAND**, Argyll and Bute, **55°40´·6N 05°44´·0W**. AC 2168, 2475. HW +0600 on Dover; ML 0·9m; Duration 0530. See 2.5. Main ⚓ is **Ardminish Bay**: 12 HIE Ⓥs in the centre. Reefs extend off both points, the S'ly reef marked by an unlit PHM buoy. Kiln Rk (dries 1·5m) is close NE of the old ferry jetty. **Druimyeon Bay** is more sheltered in E'lies, but care needed entering from S. ⚓s sheltered from winds in ( ): Port Mór (S-W), Bàgh na Dòirlinne (SE-S), W Tarbert Bay (NE). Caolas Gigalum (⚓ 50m SE of pier) is safe in all but NE-E winds. Beware many rks in Gigha Sound. Lts: Fl (2) 6s, on Gamhna Gigha (off NE tip); WCM buoy Fl (9) 15s marks Gigalum Rks, at S end of Gigha. **Ardminish** ☎/🏥 (01583) 505254: FW, Gas, P & D (cans), 📮, ✉, Bar, R, 🛒.

# 2.5 PORT ELLEN

Islay (Argyll and Bute) **55°37´·29N 06°12´·26W** ✿✿⌂⌂✿✿

**CHARTS** AC 2168, 2474; Imray C64

**TIDES** HW +0620 np, +0130 sp on Dover; ML 0·6. Sea level is much affected by the weather, rising by 1m in S/E gales; at nps the tide is sometimes diurnal and range negligible.

**Standard Port OBAN (←——)**

| Times | | | | Height (metres) | | | |
|---|---|---|---|---|---|---|---|
| High Water | | Low Water | | MHWS | MHWN | MLWN | MLWS |
| 0100 | 0700 | 0100 | 0800 | 4·0 | 2·9 | 1·8 | 0·7 |
| 1300 | 1900 | 1300 | 2000 | | | | |
| **Differences PORT ELLEN (S Islay)** | | | | | | | |
| −0530 | −0050 | −0045 | −0530 | −3·1 | −2·1 | −1·3 | −0·4 |
| **SCALASAIG (E Colonsay)** | | | | | | | |
| −0020 | −0005 | −0015 | +0005 | −0·1 | −0·2 | −0·2 | −0·2 |
| **GLENGARRISDALE BAY (N Jura)** | | | | | | | |
| −0020 | 0000 | −0010 | 0000 | −0·4 | −0·2 | 0·0 | −0·2 |
| **CRAIGHOUSE (SE Jura)** | | | | | | | |
| −0230 | −0250 | −0150 | −0230 | −3·0 | −2·4 | −1·3 | −0·6 |
| **RUBHA A'MHÀIL (N Islay)** | | | | | | | |
| −0020 | 0000 | +0005 | −0015 | −0·3 | −0·1 | −0·3 | −0·1 |
| **ARDNAVE POINT (NW Islay)** | | | | | | | |
| −0035 | +0010 | 0000 | −0025 | −0·4 | −0·2 | −0·35 | −0·1 |
| **ORSAY ISLAND (SW Islay)** | | | | | | | |
| −0110 | −0110 | −0040 | −0040 | −1·4 | −0·6 | −0·5 | −0·2 |
| **BRUICHLADDICH (Islay, Loch Indaal)** | | | | | | | |
| −0105 | −0035 | −0110 | −0110 | −1·8 | −1·3 | −0·4 | +0·1 |
| **PORT ASKAIG (Sound of Islay)** | | | | | | | |
| −0110 | −0030 | −0020 | −0020 | −1·9 | −1·4 | −0·8 | −0·3 |
| **GIGHA SOUND (Sound of Jura)** | | | | | | | |
| −0450 | −0210 | −0130 | −0410 | −2·5 | −1·6 | −1·0 | −0·1 |
| **MACHRIHANISH** | | | | | | | |
| −0520 | −0350 | −0340 | −0540 | Mean range 0·5 metres. | | | |

**SHELTER** Good shelter on pontoons (3m at MLWS), but in S winds swell sets into the bay. 10 HIE Ⓥs to W of Rubha Glas; adjacent rks marked by 3 Bcns with reflective topmarks. In W'lies ⚓ in Kilnaughton Bay, N of Carraig Fhada lt ho; or 4M ENE at Loch-an-t-Sàilein.

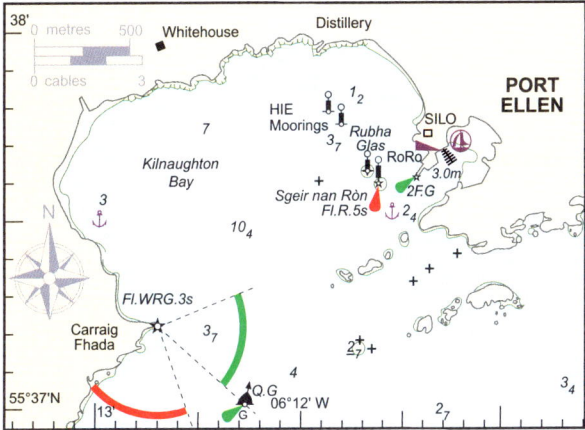

**NAVIGATION** WPT 55°36´·69N 06°12´·06W, 326°/0·63M to Carraig Fhada lt ho. Beware Otter Rk 4M SE of hbr, rks on both sides of ent and in NE corner of bay. Keep close to pier.

**LIGHTS AND MARKS** On W side 10 Radio masts (103m) and Carraig Fhada lt ho (conspic), Fl WRG 3s 20m 8/6M; keep in W sector until past the SHM lt buoy. Sgeir nan Ròn Bn Fl R 5s, Ro-Ro Pier 2 FG (vert) and Marina pontoon Fl G 4s. Limits of dredged area around Ro-Ro Pier and pontoon area marked by buoys.

**R/T** None.

**TELEPHONE** Moorings (01496)300301/mob 0773219133; MRCC (01475) 729988.

**FACILITIES** **Marina** (30 inc Ⓥ - welcome, 🚿 in bay), ☎ 300301 for fuel and assistance, dredged to 3m, £12<10m, £14 >10m, D, Slip; **Village** Bar, FW, ✉, R, 🛒, Gas.

## 2.6 CRINAN CANAL

Argyll and Bute **56°05'·50N 05°33'·38W** Crinan ✿✿♒♒✿✿✿

**CHARTS** AC *2326*, 2320; Imray C65; OS 55

**TIDES** −0608 Dover; ML 2·1; Duration 0605; HW Crinan is at HW Oban −0045

**Standard Port OBAN (←—)**

| Times | | | | Height (metres) | | | |
|---|---|---|---|---|---|---|---|
| High Water | | Low Water | | MHWS | MHWN | MLWN | MLWS |
| 0100 | 0700 | 0100 | 0800 | 4·0 | 2·9 | 1·8 | 0·7 |
| 1300 | 1900 | 1300 | 2000 | | | | |

**Differences CARSAIG BAY (56°02'N 05°38'W)**

| | | | | | | | |
|---|---|---|---|---|---|---|---|
| −0105 | −0040 | −0050 | −0050 | −2·1 | −1·6 | −1·0 | −0·4 |

NOTE: In the Sound of Jura, S of Loch Crinan, the rise of tide occurs mainly during the 3½ hrs after LW; the fall during the 3½ hrs after HW. At other times the changes in level are usually small and irregular.

**SHELTER** Complete shelter in canal basin; yachts are welcome. Good shelter in Crinan Hbr (E of Eilean da Mheinn) but full of moorings. Except in strong W/N winds, ⚓ E of the canal ent, clear of fairway. Gallanach Bay on N side of L Crinan has good holding in about 3m. Berths may be reserved at Bellanoch Bay on a medium to long term basis but compliance with Boat Safety Scheme required.

**NAVIGATION** WPT 56°05'·70N 05°33'·64W, 146°/0·27M to Fl WG 3s lt. Beware Black Rock (2m high) in appr NE of ldg line 146° to dir Fl WG 3s lt. Off NW corner of chartlet, no ⚓ in a nearly rectangular shellfish bed, 6ca by 6ca. SPM lt buoys mark each corner: Fl (4) Y 12s at the NE and NW corners, Fl Y 6s at the SW and SE corners; the latter being about 100m NE of Black Rock.

**CANAL** Canal is 9M long with 15 locks and 7 opening bridges. Least transit time is 5 to 6 hrs, observing 4kn speed limit. If short-handed, helpers may be available via canal staff or 01546 602458. Entry at all tides. Max LOA: 26·82m, 6·09m beam, 2·89m draft (add 0.10m to your salt water draft), mast 28.95m. Vessels NW-bound have right of way. **Lock hrs**: The canal operates 7 days a week during the summer but during the winter periods of closure or partial closure can be expected. Contact the Canal Office for current operating schedule. The canal is normally closed from Christmas to the New Year. Do not pump out bilge water or toilets in the canal. Contact canal staff if reqd.

**BOAT SAFETY SCHEME** Transit craft liable to safety checks on gas, fuel, electrics; £1M 3rd party insurance required. Resident craft subject to full safety checks. See 1.16.

**LIGHTS AND MARKS** Crinan Hotel is conspic W bldg. A conspic chy, 3ca SW of hotel, leads 187° into Crinan Hbr. E of sea-lock:

Dir Fl WG 3s 8m 4M, vis 114°-W-146°-G-280°. Ent: 2 FG (vert) and 2FR (vert).

**R/T** VHF Ch **74** 16 only at sea locks.

**TELEPHONE** (Code 01546) Sea lock 830285; Canal HQ 603210; MRCC (01475) 729988; Marinecall 09068 500463; Police 702200; Dr 462001.

**FACILITIES** Canal HQ ☎ 603210, www.waterscape.com. All fees are under review; contact office for details. M, L, FW, *Skippers Guide* is essential reading; **Sea Basin** AB (overnight rate available). **Services:** BY, D, Slip, ME, El, ✕, Gas, ACA, C (5 ton), ▣, CH, P (cans), ⚒, R, Bar. Use shore toilets, not yacht heads, whilst in canal. **Village** ✉, Ⓑ (Ardrishaig), ⇌ (Oban), ✈ (Glasgow or Macrihanish). There is a wintering park, plus BY and CH, at Cairnbaan for yachts <10m LOA.

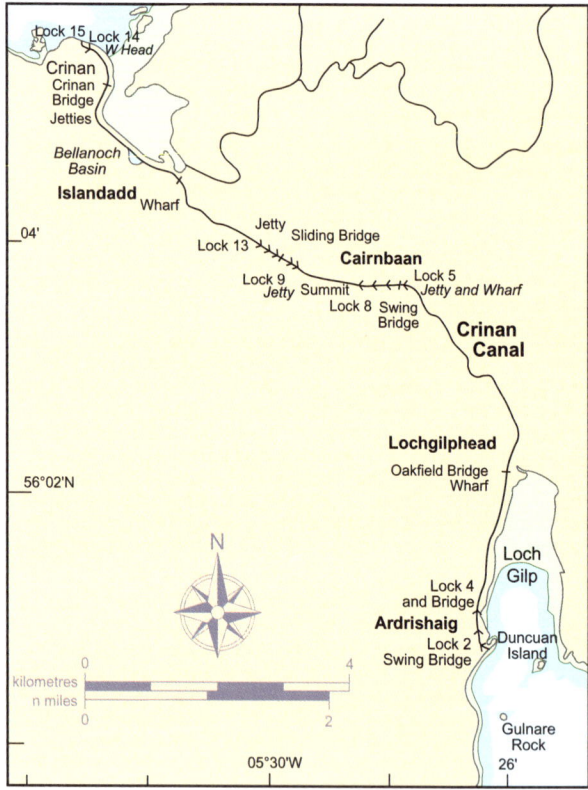

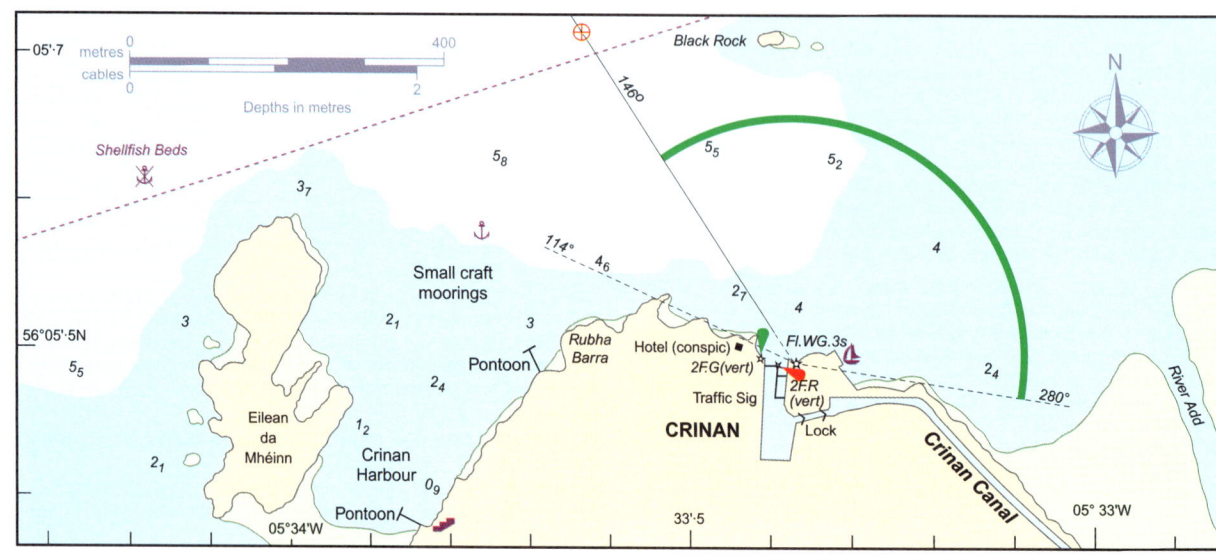

# 2.7  ARDRISHAIG

Argyll and Bute **56°00′·78N 05°26′·62W** ❀❀🚢⚓ ✿✿

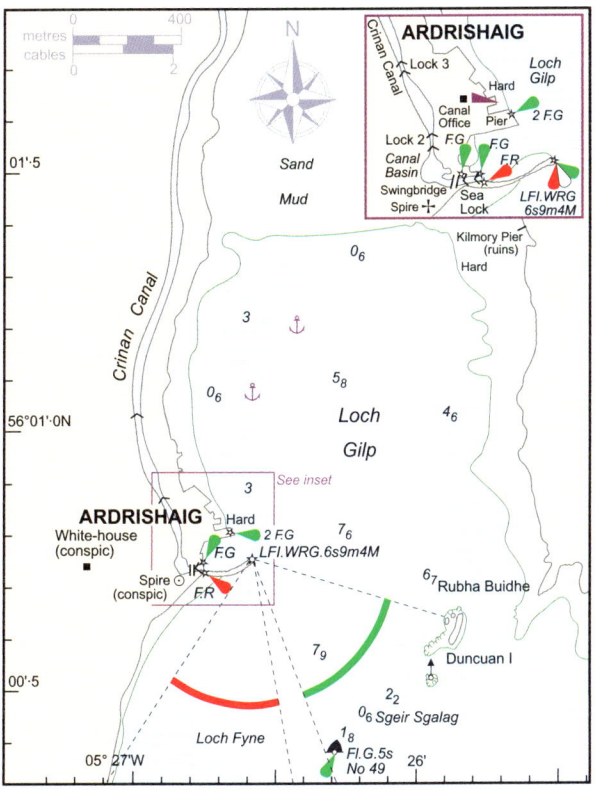

**CHARTS**  AC *5610, 2131*, 2381; Imray C63; OS 55

**TIDES**  +0120 Dover; ML 1·9; Duration 0640

**Standard Port GREENOCK (→)**

| Times | | | | Height (metres) | | | |
|---|---|---|---|---|---|---|---|
| High Water | | Low Water | | MHWS | MHWN | MLWN | MLWS |
| 0000 | 0600 | 0000 | 0600 | 3·4 | 2·8 | 1·0 | 0·3 |
| 1200 | 1800 | 1200 | 1800 | | | | |
| **Differences ARDRISHAIG** | | | | | | | |
| +0006 | +0006 | -0015 | +0020 | 0·0 | 0·0 | +0·1 | -0·1 |
| **INVERARAY** | | | | | | | |
| +0011 | +0011 | +0034 | +0034 | -0·1 | +0·1 | -0·5 | -0·2 |

**SHELTER** Hbr is sheltered except from strong E'lies; do not berth on pier or ⚓ due to commercial vessels H24. Sea lock into the Crinan Canal is usually left open, however, a waiting pontoon has been installed outside the lock, with restricted depth, for use in fair weather only. Access at all tides. Complete shelter in the canal basin, or beyond lock No 2; see 2.6. Also ⚓ 2ca N of hbr, off the W shore of L Gilp.

**NAVIGATION** WPT No 48 PHM lt buoy, 56°00′·18N 05°26′·31W, 345°/0·6M to bkwtr lt. Dangerous drying rocks to E of appr chan are marked by No 49 Fl.G.5s SHM buoy.

**LIGHTS AND MARKS** Conspic W Ho on with block of flats leads 315°between Nos 48 and 49 buoys. Bkwtr lt, L Fl WRG 6s, W339°-350°. Pier is floodlit.  Other lights as plan.

**R/T**  VHF Ch **74** 16.

**TELEPHONE** (Code 01546) HM 603210, 🖷 603941; Sea lock 602458; MRCC (01475) 729988; Marinecall 09068 969652; Police 702200; Dr 462001.

**FACILITIES**  **Pier/Hbr** ☎ 603210, AB (fees under review), Slip, FW; **Sea Lock** ☎ 602458; **Crinan Canal** www.waterscape.com, AB, M, L, FW, R, Bar; dues, see 2.6. **Services:** BY, ME, El, ✕, CH, D (cans), Gas. **Village** P & D (cans), 🛢, R, Bar, ✉, Ⓑ, ≈ (bus to Oban), ✈ (Glasgow or Campbeltown).

# 2.8  TARBERT, LOCH FYNE

Also known as East Loch Tarbert

Argyll and Bute **55°52′·05N 05°24′·22W** ❀❀🚢⚓ ✿✿

**CHARTS**  AC *5610, 2131*, 2381; Imray C63; OS 62

**TIDES**  +0120 Dover; ML 1·9; Duration 0640

**Standard Port GREENOCK (→)**

| Times | | | | Height (metres) | | | |
|---|---|---|---|---|---|---|---|
| High Water | | Low Water | | MHWS | MHWN | MLWN | MLWS |
| 0000 | 0600 | 0000 | 0600 | 3·4 | 2·8 | 1·0 | 0·3 |
| 1200 | 1800 | 1200 | 1800 | | | | |
| **Differences EAST LOCH TARBERT** | | | | | | | |
| -0005 | -0005 | 0000 | -0005 | +0·2 | +0·1 | 0·0 | 0·0 |

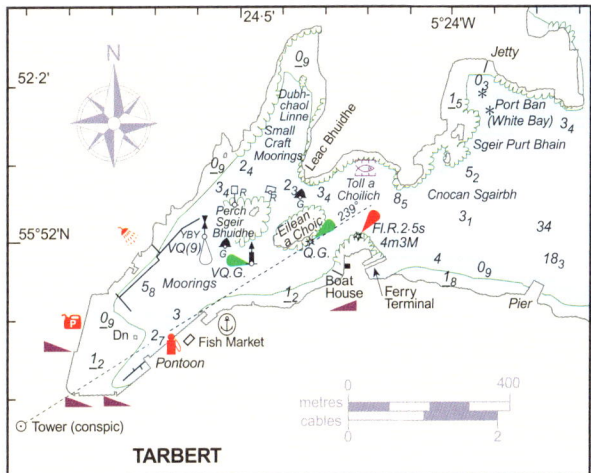

**SHELTER** Very good in all weathers but gets crowded. Access H24. Visitors berth only on SE side of yacht pontoons in 2·4m to 5m and alongside FV's on Fish Quay.

**NAVIGATION** WPT 55°52′·02N 05°23′·03W, 270°/0·7M to Fl R 2·5s lt. Ent is very narrow. Cock Isle divides the ent in half: Main hbr to the S, Buteman's Hole to the N, where ⚓s are fouled by heavy moorings and lost chains. Speed limit 3kn.

**LIGHTS AND MARKS** Outer ldg lts 252° to S ent: Fl R 2·5s on with Cock Is lt QG. Inner ldg line 239°:  same QG, G column, on with conspic ✠ tr. Note: The W sector, 065°-078°, of Eilean na Beithe ☆, Fl WRG 3s 7m 5M (on E shore of Lower Loch Fyne), could be used to position for the initial appr to Tarbert.

**R/T**  Call VHF Ch 16; work Ch **14** (0900-1700LT).

**TELEPHONE** (Code 01880) HM 820344, 🖷 820719, email tarbertharbour@btconnect.com; MRCC (01475) 729988; Marinecall 09068 969652; Police 820200; Ⓗ (01546) 602323.

**FACILITIES** Yacht Berthing Facility 100 visitors, AB £1.70, FW, AC; **Fish Quay** D (Mon-Fri 0800-1800), FW; **Tarbert YC** Slip, L; **Services:** SM, 🖷, ACA, ✕, CH. **Town** P & D (0800-1800 cans), Gas, Gaz, L, 🛢, R, Bar, ✉, Ⓑ, Wi-fi, ≈ (bus to Glasgow), ✈ (Glasgow/ Campbeltown).

### ANCHORAGES IN LOCH FYNE
• *Beware discarded wires on sea bed throughout the area.*

**INVERARAY**, Argyll and Bute, **56°13′·95N 05°04′·07W**. AC *2131*, 2382. HW +0126 on Dover. See 2.7. In Upper Loch Fyne (see 2.4) 4 ⚓ laid at the head of the loch are for patrons of the oyster Bar. Beware An Oitir drying spit 2ca offshore, ⅓M S of pier. ⚓ SSW of pier in 4m or dry out NW of the pier. FW (on pier), ✉, 🛢, R, Bar, Gas, bus to Glasgow.  Beyond Otter Spit, are ⚓s on NW bank at Port Ann, Loch Gair and Minard Bay; and on SE bank at Otter Ferry, Strachur Bay (5 ⚓s off Creggans Inn, ☎ (01369) 860279) and St Catherine's. In Lower L Fyne, 6M NNE of East Loch Tarbert there is a ⚓ at Kilfinan Bay, ☎ (01700) 821201.

## 2.9 CAMPBELTOWN

Argyll & Bute **55°25'·90N 05°32'·56W** Hbr ent ✿✿✿♨♨♨❀❀❀

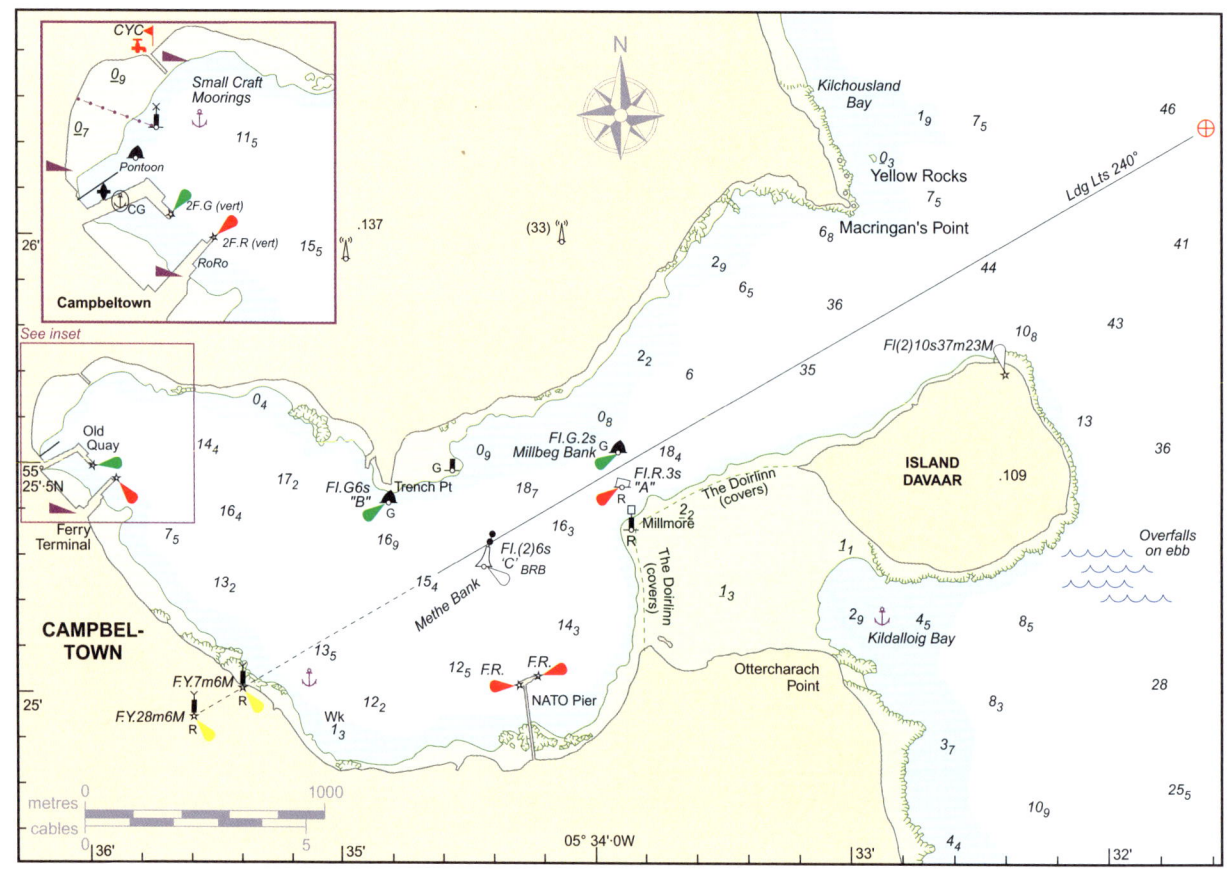

**CHARTS** AC *5610, 2126,* 1864; Imray C63; OS 68

**TIDES** +0125 Dover; ML 1·8; Duration 0630

**Standard Port GREENOCK (→)**

| Times | | | | Height (metres) | | | |
|---|---|---|---|---|---|---|---|
| High Water | | Low Water | | MHWS | MHWN | MLWN | MLWS |
| 0000 | 0600 | 0000 | 0600 | 3·4 | 2·8 | 1·0 | 0·3 |
| 1200 | 1800 | 1200 | 1800 | | | | |
| Differences CAMPBELTOWN | | | | | | | |
| –0025 | –0005 | –0015 | +0005 | –0·5 | –0·3 | +0·1 | +0·2 |
| CARRADALE BAY | | | | | | | |
| –0015 | –0005 | 0000 | +0005 | –0·3 | –0·2 | +0·1 | +0·1 |
| SOUTHEND, (Mull of Kintyre) | | | | | | | |
| –0030 | –0010 | +0005 | +0035 | –1·3 | –1·2 | –0·5 | –0·2 |

**SHELTER** Good, but gusts off the hills in strong SW'lies. Yacht pontoon (10+20❤) dredged 3·0m is close NW of Old Quay and gives excellent sheltered berthing. Yachts >12m LOA should notify ETA to Berthing Master by ☎ (below). Excellent ⚓ close E of front ldg lt (240°); ⚓ near moorings NNE of the hbr is cluttered and exposed to SE winds: use only in settled conditions and do not pick up private mooring buoys. S of Island Davaar there is a temp ⚓ in Kildalloig Bay, but no access to the loch.

**NAVIGATION** WPT 55°26'·24N 05°31'·61W, 240°/1·4M to first chan buoys. The ent is easily identified by radio masts N and NE of Trench Pt (conspic W bldg) and conspic lt ho on N tip of Island Davaar off which streams are strong (4kn sp). Caution: The Dhorlin, a bank drying 2·5m which covers at HW, is close S of the ldg line.

**LIGHTS AND MARKS** See 2.4 and chartlet. Otterard Rk (3·8m depth, off chartlet, 1·5M NNE of Island Davaar), is marked by ECM lt buoy.

**R/T** VHF Ch 12 13 16 (Mon-Fri 0900-1700).

**TELEPHONE** (Code 01586) HM ☎/⊠ 552552; Yacht pontoon Berthing Master ☎/⊠ 552199, mobile 07798 524821; MRCC (01475) 729988; Marinecall 09068 969652; Police 862000; Dr 552105.

**FACILITIES Yacht pontoon** £1.30, FW, ⬓; **Aquilibrium** – dedicated facilities for yacht crews: @, showers, toilets, ▨, R. Also swimming pool, gym and sauna. **Old Quay** D (HO ☎ No on tank), FW, AB, LB; **Ferry Terminal** (used by RoRo vessels); no charge, but yachts not encouraged to berth; drying berths at nearby slipway, FW, ⬓; **Campbeltown SC** Slip (dinghies), Bar, regular racing. **Town** ME, ACA, C (10 ton), P & D(HO Mon-Sat, cans or bowser to craft berthed on Old Quay), El, CH, Ⓔ, Gas, Gaz, ▨ (2 supermarkets), R, Bar, ⊠, Ⓑ, ▨, Ⓗ, ⬓ toilet about 100m from yacht pontoon, key at Tourist office or police station (H24). Bus 3/ day to Glasgow, ✈ twice daily to Glasgow, ⇌ (nearest is Arrochar, 90 miles N by road). Car hire/taxi.

**ADJACENT ANCHORAGE IN KILBRANNAN SOUND**

**CARRADALE BAY**, Argyll and Bute, **55°34'·40N 05°28'·66W**. AC *5610, 2131,* HW+0115 on Dover. ML 1·8m. See 2.9. Good ⚓ in 7m off Torrisdale Castle in SW corner of Carradale Bay. In N & E winds ⚓ in NE corner of bay, W of Carradale Pt 3ca E of this Pt, a PHM buoy Fl (2) R 12s marks Cruban Rk. With S & SE winds a swell sets into bay, when good shelter can be found 1M N in **Carradale Harbour** (Port Crannaich); if full of FVs, ⚓ 100m N of Hbr. Bkwtr lt, Fl R 10s 5m 6M. Piermaster ☎ (01586) 431228. Facilities: FW on pier, D (cans), Gas, ▨, R, Bar, ⊠.

# 2.10 TIDAL STREAMS AROUND THE MULL OF KINTYRE

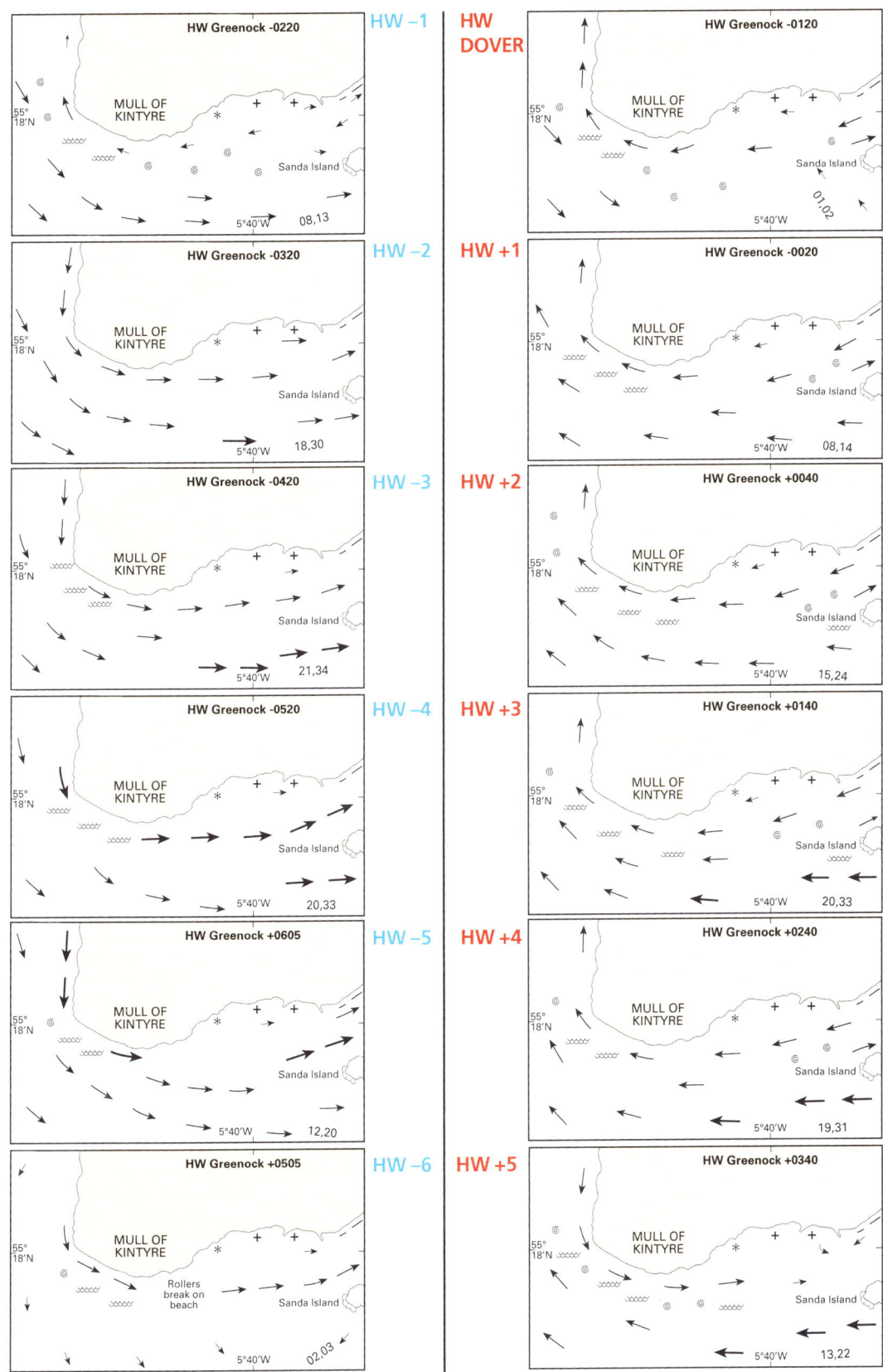

HW –1 | HW DOVER

HW –2 | HW +1

HW –3 | HW +2

HW –4 | HW +3

HW –5 | HW +4

HW –6 | HW +5

## 2.11 LAMLASH

Isle of Arran, N Ayrshire    55°32´·00N    05°07´·06W
❀❀❀⚓⚓⚓❀❀❀

**CHARTS** AC 5610, 2131, 2220, 1864; Imray C63; OS 69

**TIDES** +0115 Dover; ML no data; Duration 0635

**Standard Port GREENOCK (→)**

| Times | | | | Height (metres) | | | |
|---|---|---|---|---|---|---|---|
| High Water | | Low Water | | MHWS | MHWN | MLWN | MLWS |
| 0000 | 0600 | 0000 | 0600 | 3·4 | 2·8 | 1·0 | 0·3 |
| 1200 | 1800 | 1200 | 1800 | | | | |
| **Differences LAMLASH** | | | | | | | |
| –0016 | –0036 | –0024 | –0004 | –0·2 | –0·2 | No data | |
| **BRODICK BAY** | | | | | | | |
| –0013 | –0013 | –0008 | –0008 | –0·2 | –0·1 | 0·0 | +0·1 |
| **LOCH RANZA** | | | | | | | |
| –0015 | –0005 | –0010 | –0005 | –0·4 | –0·3 | –0·1 | 0·0 |

**SHELTER** Very good in all weathers. Lamlash is a natural hbr with sheltered anchorages as follows: ⚓ off Lamlash except in E'lies - note depth may be 20m; off Kingscross Point, good except in strong N/NW winds; off the Farm at NW of Holy Island in E'lies. Or pick up ⚓ off Lamlash Pier. Or dry out against pier if in need of repairs. See also Brodick 5M N, and Loch Ranza 14M N (RH col).

**NAVIGATION** WPT 55°32´·63N 05°03´·06W, 270°/1M to N Chan buoy (Fl R 6s).

> Beware: submarines exercise frequently in this area (see 2.18), and also wreck of landing craft (charted) off farmhouse on Holy Is.

**LIGHTS AND MARKS** See 2.4 and chartlet.

**R/T** None.

**TELEPHONE** (Code 01770) MRCC (01475) 729988; Marinecall 09068 969652; Police 302573; Ⓗ 600777.

**FACILITIES** **Lamlash Old Pier** Slip (£3 - £5), L, FW, CH, ⚒ (hull repairs); **Arran YC** 25 ⚓ £10 via: ☎ 01770 600333. **Village** (Lamlash/Brodick); ME, P & D (cans), Bar, R, 🍴, ✉, ⇌ (bus to Brodick, ferry to Ardrossan), ✈ (Glasgow or Prestwick).

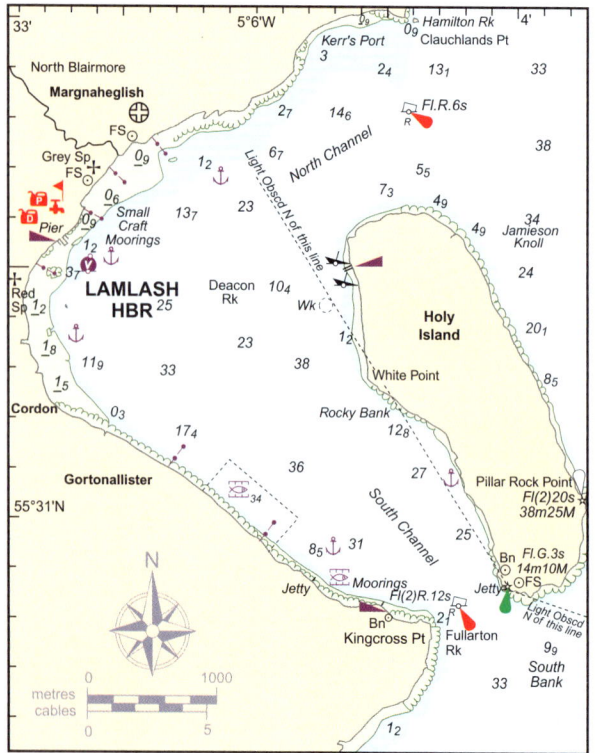

**OTHER HARBOURS ON ARRAN** (See AC 5610)

**BRODICK**, Arran, **55°35´·50N 05°08´·66W**. AC 2131, 2220, 1864. HW +0115 on Dover; ML 1·8m; Duration 0635. See 2.11. Shelter is good except in E winds. ⚓ W of ferry pier in 3m; on NW side just below the Castle in 4·5m, or further N off Merkland Pt in 3-4m. Also 5 ⚓s. There are no navigational dangers but the bay is in a submarine exercise area; see 2.18. Only lts are 2FR (vert) 9/7m 4M on pier hd and Admiralty buoy, Fl Y 2s, 5ca N of pier. Facilities: Ⓑ, Bar, P & D (cans), FW (at pier hd), ME, ✉, R, 🍴. Ferry to Ardrossan.

**LOCH RANZA**, Arran, **55°42´·60N 05°17´·96W**. AC 2131, 2383, 2221. HW +0120 on Dover; ML 1·7m; Duration 0635. See 2.11. Good shelter, but swell enters loch with N'lies. The 850m mountain 4M to S causes fierce squalls in the loch with S winds. Beware Screda Reef extending SW off Newton Pt. 5 ⚓s. ⚓ in 5m off castle (conspic); holding is suspect in soft mud. 2F.G lts on RoRo pier at Coillemore. S shore dries. Facilities: Bar, FW at ferry slip, ✉, R, 🍴. Ferry to Claonaig.

**HARBOURS AND ANCHORAGES AROUND BUTE
(Clockwise from Garroch Head, S tip of Bute)** (See AC 5610)

**ST NINIAN'S BAY**, Bute, **55°48´·15N 05°07´·86W**. AC 2221, 2383. Inchmarnock Is gives some shelter from the W, but Sound is exposed to S'lies. At S end, beware Shearwater Rk, 0·9m, almost in mid-sound. ⚓ in about 7m, 2ca E of St Ninian's Pt; beware drying spit to S of this Pt. Or ⚓ off E side of Inchmarnock, close abeam Midpark Farm.

**WEST KYLE**, Bute, **55°54´N 05°12´·7W**. AC1906. Tides, see 2.12 (Tighnabruaich). On W bank PHM buoys, each Fl R 4s, mark Ardlamont Pt, Carry Pt and Rubha Ban; N of which are two Fl Y buoys (fish farms). ⚓ close off Kames or Tighnabruaich, where space allows; or in Black Farland Bay (N of Rubha Dubh). Some ⚓s off Kames and Royal Hotels, maintained by them on a 'use at own risk basis': Kames Hotel ☎ (01700) 811489; Kyles of Bute Hotel 811350; Royal Hotel 811239; and Tighnabruaich Hotel 811615. Facilities: FW, D (cans), BY, 🍴.

**CALADH HARBOUR**, Argyll and Bute, **55°56´·00N, 05°11´·73W**. AC 1906. HW (Tighnabruaich) +0015 on Dover; ML 2·1m. See 2.12. Perfectly sheltered natural hbr on W side of ent to Loch Riddon. Enter Caladh Hbr to N or S of Eilean Dubh; keep to the middle of the S passage. When using the N ent, keep between R and G bns to clear a drying rk marked by perch. ⚓ in the middle of hbr clear of moorings. No facilities/stores; see West Kyle above.

**LOCH RIDDON**, Argyll and Bute, **55°57´N 05°11´·6W**. AC 1906. Tides, see 2.12. Water is deep for 1·3M N of Caladh and shore is steep-to; upper 1·5M of loch dries. ⚓ on W side close N of Ormidale pier; on E side at Salthouse; off Eilean Dearg (One Tree Is); and at NW corner of Fearnoch Bay.

**BURNT ISLANDS**, Bute, **55°55´·76N 05°10´·39W**. AC 1906. Tides, see 2.12. The three islands (Eilean Mor, Fraoich and Buidhe) straddle the East Kyle. There are 2 channels: North, between Buidhe and the other 2 islets, is narrow, short and marked by 2 SHM buoys (the NW'ly one is Fl G 3s), and one PHM buoy, Fl R 2s. South chan lies between Bute and Fraoich/Mor; it is unlit, but marked by one PHM and two SHM buoys. A SHM buoy, Fl G 3s, is off Rubha a' Bhodaich, 4ca ESE. Direction of buoyage is to SE. Sp streams reach 5kn in N Chan and 3kn in S Chan. ⚓ in Wreck Bay, Balnakailly Bay or in the lee of Buidhe and Mor in W'lies; also W of Colintraive Pt, clear of ferry and cables. There are 4 ⚓s off the hotel, ☎ (01700) 841207.

**KAMES BAY**, Bute, **55°51´·7N 05°04´·81W**. AC 1906, 1867. Tides as Rothesay. Deep water bay, but dries 2ca off head of loch and 1ca off NW shore. AB (55 inc Ⓥ) in marina at Port Bannatyne in 2·5m; P & D in cans, CH, Gas, BY, BH (25 ton). ⚓ off (clear of moorings) Port Bannatyne (S shore) W of unmarked ruined jetty. Beware drying rks 1ca off Ardbeg Pt. No lts. Facilities: BY, FW, Gas, 🍴, Bar, ✉.

**KILCHATTAN BAY**, Bute, **55°45´N 05°01´·1W**. AC 1907. Bay is deep, but dries 3ca off the W shore. Temp ⚓s only in offshore winds: off the village on SW side, or on N side near Kerrytonlia Pt. ⚓s for hotel guests. Rubh' an Eun Lt, Fl R 6s, is 1·1M to SSE. Facilities: FW, 🍴, ✉, bus Rothesay.

# 2.12 ROTHESAY

Isle of Bute, Argyll and Bute 55°50´·32N 05°03´·08W
❀❀❀✿✿ ✿✿✿

**CHARTS** AC *5610, 2131, 1907, 1906, 1867*; Imray C63, 2900 Series; OS 63

**TIDES** +0100 Dover; ML 1·9; Duration 0640

**Standard Port GREENOCK (→)**

| Times | | | | Height (metres) | | | |
|---|---|---|---|---|---|---|---|
| High Water | | Low Water | | MHWS | MHWN | MLWN | MLWS |
| 0000 | 0600 | 0000 | 0600 | 3·4 | 2·8 | 1·0 | 0·3 |
| 1200 | 1800 | 1200 | 1800 | | | | |
| Differences ROTHESAY BAY | | | | | | | |
| –0020 | –0015 | –0010 | –0002 | +0·2 | +0·2 | +0·2 | +0·2 |
| RUBHA BHODACH (Burnt Is) | | | | | | | |
| –0020 | –0010 | –0007 | –0007 | –0·2 | –0·1 | +0·2 | +0·2 |
| TIGHNABRUAICH | | | | | | | |
| +0007 | –0010 | –0002 | –0015 | 0·0 | +0·2 | +0·4 | +0·5 |

**SHELTER** Good on yacht pontoons in Outer Hbr (2m) and at W end inside Front Pier (2m on N side only), but subject to ferry wash. Proposed development of Inner Hbr to include 20 berths. No berthing on north and east faces of Front Pier (works in progress). 40 ⚓ WNW of pier or good ⚓ in bay ¾M W of Isle of Bute SC but exposed to N/NE when Kyles of Bute or Kames Bay offer better shelter.

**NAVIGATION** WPT 55°51´·00N 05°02´·76W, 194°/0·69M to Outer hbr ent. From E keep 1ca off Bogany Pt PHM buoy, Fl R 4s.

**LIGHTS AND MARKS** Lts as chartlet, hard to see against shore lts. Conspicuous church spire leads 190° to outer hbr; at night beware large, unlit Admiralty buoy 'MK' on this bearing 5½ca from harbour. 3½ca N of hbr is Rothesay 'A' mooring buoy, Fl Y 2s.

**R/T** Ch **12** 16 (1 May-30 Sep: 0600-2100; 1 Oct-30 Apr: 0600-1900).

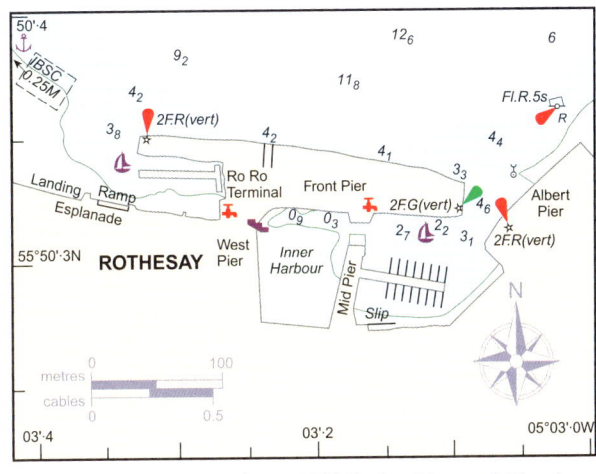

**TELEPHONE** (Code 01700) HM 503842; Berthing and Moorings 500630, mob 07799 724225; MRCC (01475) 729988; Marinecall 09068 969652; Police 894000; Dr 503985;  Ⓗ 503938.

**FACILITIES** **Outer Hbr** AB £14/yacht, 🔌, FW, Slip, L, FW, ME, ♿; **Inner Hbr** L, AB; **Front Pier (W)** only suitable for larger craft, £12/yacht, D by arrangement week days only (min 200 galls). **Town** P & D (closes 1800), @ (0900-1700) 🛒, R, Bar, ✉, Ⓑ, ≈ (ferry to Wemyss Bay), ✈ (Glasgow).

## GREAT CUMBRAE ISLAND

**MILLPORT**, Great Cumbrae, N Ayrshire, 55°45´·00N 04°55´·82W. AC *5610*, 1867, 1907. HW +0100 on Dover; ML 1·9m; Duration 0640. See 2.13. Good shelter, except in S'lies. ⚓ in approx 3m S of pier or E of the Eileans. 12 ⚓s 1½ca SSE of pier. Ldg marks: pier hd on with ✠ twr 333°; or ldg lts 333°, both FR 7/9m 5M, between the Spoig and the Eileans, QG. Unmarked, drying rk is close E of ldg line. HM ☎ (01475) 530826. **Town** CH, Bar, Gas, D, P, FW, ✉, R, Slip, 🛒.

# 2.13 FAIRLIE QUAY

N Ayrshire 55°46´·07N 04°51´·78W ❀✿✿✿✿ ✿

**CHARTS** AC *5610, 2131, 1907, 1867*; Imray C63, 2900 Series; OS 63

**TIDES** +0105 Dover; ML 1·9; Duration 0640

**Standard Port GREENOCK (→)**

| Times | | | | Height (metres) | | | |
|---|---|---|---|---|---|---|---|
| High Water | | Low Water | | MHWS | MHWN | MLWN | MLWS |
| 0000 | 0600 | 0000 | 0600 | 3·4 | 2·8 | 1·0 | 0·3 |
| 1200 | 1800 | 1200 | 1800 | | | | |
| Differences MILLPORT | | | | | | | |
| –0005 | –0025 | –0025 | –0005 | 0·0 | –0·1 | 0·0 | 0·1 |

**SHELTER** Access H24 with 2.6m deep berths. Pontoon subject to swell in fresh conditions and wash from passing vessels. No shelter from prevailing SW'lies and craft should not be left unsupervised unless calm settled weather is forecast. Cumbrae Is gives shelter from W'lies; Largs Chan is open to S or N winds.

**NAVIGATION** WPT 55°46´·08N 04°51´·84W. From S beware Hunterston Sands, Southannan Sands and outfalls from Hunterston Power Stn (conspic).

**LIGHTS AND MARKS** Lts as on chartlet. Fairlie Quay, 2 FG (vert) N & S ends of Pier.

**R/T** *Fairlie Quay Marina* Ch **80** M (H24).

**TELEPHONE** (Code 01475) Fairlie Quay 568267; MRCC 729988; Dr 673380; Ⓗ 733777; Marinecall 09068 969652; Police 674651.

**FACILITIES** **Fairlie Quay** Some Ⓥ £11/yacht, Fuel H24: D, SM, BY, ME, El, 🔧, BH (80 ton), CH, Gas. **Fairlie YC**; **Town** 🛒, R, Bar, ✉, Ⓑ, ≈ (dep Largs every H –10; 50 mins to Glasgow), ✈.

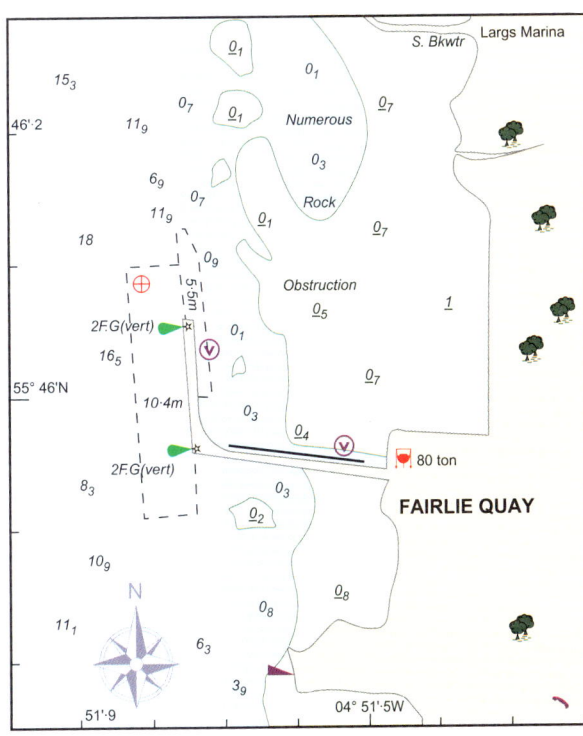

## 2.14 LARGS

N Ayrshire 55°46'·40N 04°51'·84W ✿✿✿⚓⚓⚓✿✿

**CHARTS** AC *5610, 2131,* 1907, 1867; Imray C63, 2900 Series; OS 63

**TIDES** +0105 Dover; ML 1·9; Duration 0640

**Standard Port GREENOCK (→)**

| Times | | | | Heights (metres) | | | |
|---|---|---|---|---|---|---|---|
| High Water | | Low Water | | MHWS | MHWN | MLWN | MLWS |
| 0000 | 0600 | 0000 | 0600 | 3·4 | 2·8 | 1·0 | 0·3 |
| 1200 | 1800 | 1200 | 1800 | | | | |
| Differences MILLPORT | | | | | | | |
| −0005 | −0025 | −0025 | −0005 | 0·0 | −0·1 | 0·0 | +0·1 |

**SHELTER** Excellent in Largs Yacht Haven, access all tides (2·5m in ent; 3m deep berths). 7 pontoons; ❶ on 'C/D'. Cumbrae Is gives shelter from W'lies; Largs Chan is open to S or N winds.

**NAVIGATION** WPT 55°46'·40N 04°51'·84W, SWM lt buoy, off ent. From S beware Hunterston Sands, Southannan Sands and outfalls from Hunterston Power Stn (conspic). From the S bkwtr to Fairlie Quay is a restricted, no ⚓ area.

**LIGHTS AND MARKS** 'Pencil' monument (12m) conspic 4ca N of ent. Lts as on chartlet. Largs Pier, 2 FG (vert) when vessel expected.

**R/T** *Largs Yacht Haven* Ch **80** M (H24).

**TELEPHONE** (Code 01475) Largs Yacht Haven 675333, *www.yachthavens.com;* 📠 672245; Largs SC 670000; MRCC 729988; Dr 673380; Ⓗ 733777; Marinecall 09068 969652; Police 674651.

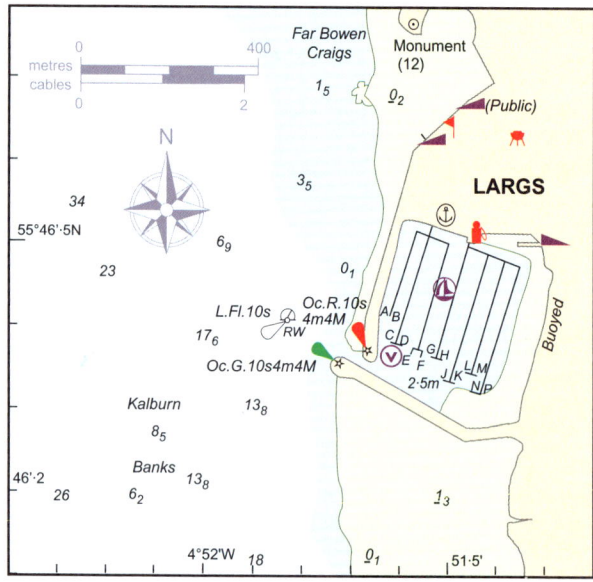

**FACILITIES** **Largs Yacht Haven** (750, some ❶), £2·43, Wi-fi, Fuel H24: D, P, ♿, SM, BY, C (17 ton), ME, El, ✕, ⚓, BH (70 ton), Divers, Ⓔ,CH, ⬚, Ice, Gas, Gaz, Slip (access H24), Bar, R.**Town** 🛒, R, Bar, ✉, Ⓑ, ⇌ (dep Largs every H −10; 50 mins to Glasgow), ✈.

## 2.15 INVERKIP (KIP MARINA)

Inverclyde 55°54'·50N 04°53'·00W ✿✿✿⚓⚓⚓✿✿

**CHARTS** AC *5610, 2131, 1907;* Imray C63, 2900 Series; OS 63

**TIDES** +0110 Dover; ML 1·8; Duration 0640

**Standard Port GREENOCK (→)**

| Times | | | | Height (metres) | | | |
|---|---|---|---|---|---|---|---|
| High Water | | Low Water | | MHWS | MHWN | MLWN | MLWS |
| 0000 | 0600 | 0000 | 0600 | 3·4 | 2·8 | 1·0 | 0·3 |
| 1200 | 1800 | 1200 | 1800 | | | | |
| Differences WEMYSS BAY | | | | | | | |
| −0005 | −0005 | −0005 | −0005 | 0·0 | 0·0 | +0·1 | +0·1 |

**SHELTER** Excellent inside marina. Chan and marina are dredged 3·5m; accessible H24. Inverkip Bay is exposed to SW/NW winds.

**NAVIGATION** WPT 55°54'·49N 04°52'·95W, Kip SHM buoy, QG, at ent to buoyed chan; beware shifting bank to the N.

**LIGHTS AND MARKS** SHM 55°54'·55N 04°54'·47W Fl G 1·06M 093° to entr which is ½M N of conspic chmy (238m). SPM buoy marks sewer outfall off Ardgowan Pt. From Kip SHM buoy, 3 SHM and 3 PHM buoys mark 365m long appr chan.

**R/T** *Kip Marina* Ch **80** M (H24). *Clydeport Estuary Radio* VHF Ch **12** 16 (H24). Info on weather and traffic available on request.

**TELEPHONE** (Code 01475) MRCC 729988; Marinecall 09068 969652; Police 521222; Dr 520248; Ⓗ 33777.

**FACILITIES** **Kip Marina** ☎ 521485, 📠 521298, www.scottishmarinas.co.uk; (700 + ❶) £2·05, £11 <5hrs), Wi-fi, D, P (cans), ✕, C, ME, El, Ⓔ, SM, CH, Diver, BH (50 ton), 🛒, R, Bar, ⬚, Gas, Gaz, YC. **Town** ✉, Ⓑ (Gourock), ⇌, ✈ (Glasgow).

### ADJACENT ANCHORAGE

**DUNOON**, Argyll and Bute, **55°56'·70N 04°55'·20W.** AC *5610, 2131,* 1907, 1994. Use Greenock tides. Temp ⚓ in West or East Bays (S and N of Dunoon Pt). The former is open to the S; the latter more shoal. Six HIE ⚓s (free, but condition uncertain) in each bay; call ☎ (01369) 703785. The Gantocks, drying rks 3ca SE of Dunoon Pt, have W ◯ bn tr, Fl R 6s 12m 6M. 2FR (vert) on ferry pier. Facilities: P & D (cans), 🛒, R, Bar, ✉, Gas, ferry to Gourock. 3 ⚓s off Inellan, 3·7M S of Dunoon, ☎ (01369) 830445.

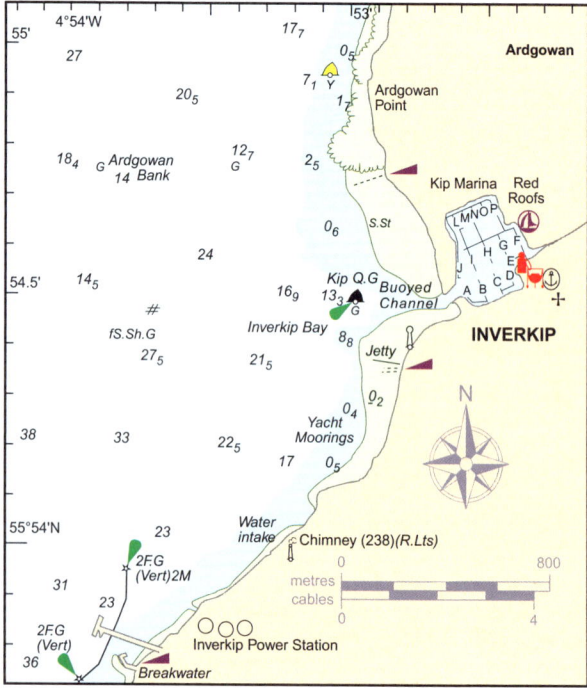

### ANCHORAGE IN THE UPPER FIRTH OF CLYDE

**GOUROCK**, Inverclyde, **55°58'·00N 04°49'·00W.** AC *5610, 2131, 1994,* Imray C63, 2900 Series; OS 63. Use Greenock tides. Good ⚓ in West Bay, beware of moorings. It is exposed in NW/NE'lies. Beware foul ground in Gourock Bay. No navigational dangers, but much shipping and ferries in the Clyde. The S edge of the Firth of Clyde recommended channel lies 2ca N of Kempock Pt. The pier at the S end of Gourock Bay is disused and unsafe. Facilities: Royal Gourock YC ☎ 632983 M, L, FW, ME, Slip, 🛒, R, Bar. Services: SM. Town: P, D (cans), 🛒, R, Bar, ✉, Ⓑ, ⇌, Ferry(to Dunoon) ✈ (Glasgow).

## 2.16   FIRTH OF CLYDE AREA

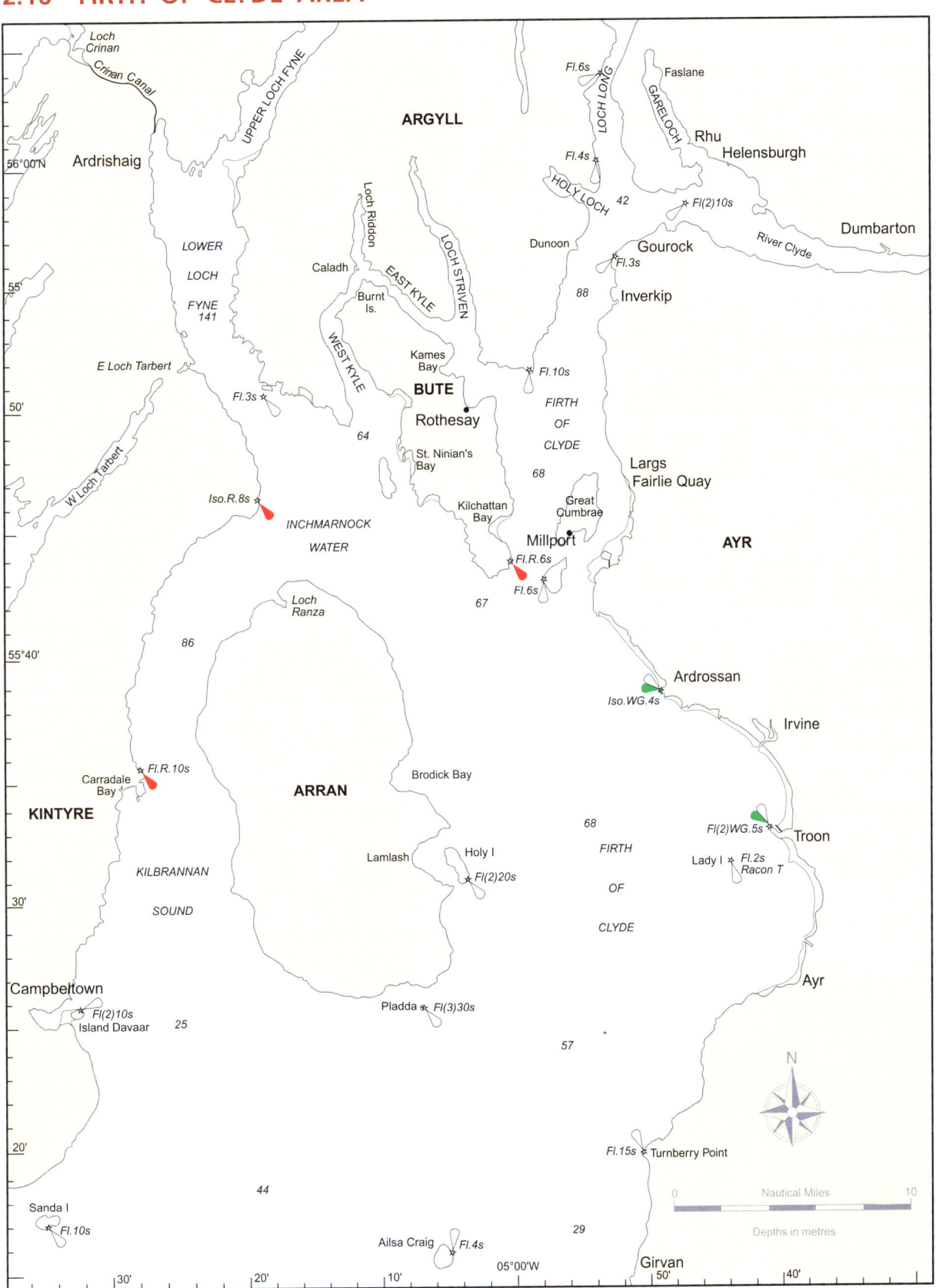

Loch Crinan

Crinan Canal

UPPER LOCH FYNE

LOCH LONG

Fl.6s

Faslane

GARELOCH

Rhu

Helensburgh

**ARGYLL**

56°00'N   Ardrishaig

Fl.4s

HOLY LOCH

42

Fl(2)10s

River Clyde

Dumbarton

55'

*LOWER
LOCH
FYNE
141*

Loch Riddon

EAST KYLE

LOCH STRIVEN

Dunoon

Gourock

Fl.3s

Inverkip

88

Caladh

Burnt
Is.

WEST KYLE

Kames
Bay

Fl.10s

*FIRTH
OF
CLYDE*

50'   E Loch Tarbert

Fl.3s

**BUTE**

Rothesay

W Loch Tarbert

64

St. Ninian's
Bay

68

Largs
Fairlie Quay

Iso.R.8s

*INCHMARNOCK
WATER*

Kilchattan
Bay

Great
Cumbrae

Fl.R.6s

Millport

**AYR**

67

Fl.6s

Loch
Ranza

55°40'   86

Fl(2)20s

Ardrossan

Iso.WG.4s

Irvine

Fl.R.10s

Carradale
Bay

**ARRAN**

Brodick Bay

68

Fl(2)WG.5s

Troon

**KINTYRE**

*KILBRANNAN*

Lamlash

Holy I

Lady I   Fl.2s
Racon T

30'   *SOUND*

Fl(2)20s

*FIRTH
OF
CLYDE*

Ayr

Campbeltown

Fl(2)10s
Island Davaar

25

Pladda   Fl(3)30s

57

20'

Fl.15s   Turnberry Point

N

Sanda I

Fl.10s

44

29

Ailsa Craig   Fl.4s

05°00'W

Girvan

0   Nautical Miles   10

Depths in metres

30'   20'   10'   50'   40'

## 2.17  HOLY LOCH

Argyll **55°59'·03N 04°56'·82W** ✿✿✿✿✿▴▴▴✿✿✿

**CHARTS**  AC *5610, 2131, 1994*; Imray C63, 2900 Series; OS 63

**TIDES**  +0122 Dover; ML 2·0; Duration 0640

**Standard Port GREENOCK** (→)

**SHELTER** Good, but exposed to to E/NE.

**NAVIGATION** WPT 55°59'·03N 04°55'·75W 270° to marina ent 0.60M. No offshore dangers. Holy Loch is controlled by QHM Clyde but navigation is not restricted.

**LIGHTS AND MARKS** No 30 SCM 55°58'·75N 04°53'·82W off Strone Pt. 2FR at SE end of pier. Marina floodlit.

**R/T** Call *Holy Loch Marina* Ch 80 M.

**TELEPHONE** (Code 01369) MRCC (01475) 729988; Marinecall 09068 969652; Police 702222; Dr 703279; Ⓗ 704341.

**FACILITIES Marina** (260 + Ⓥ in 3m) £1.90, £5 < 4hrs. Berth as directed by HM. ☎ 701800, 🖷 704749, info@holylochmarina. co.uk, D, P, C, BH (23 ton), BY, Gas, Wi-fi. **Holy Loch SC** ☎ 702707. **Sandbank** (town) PO, ⬛. Ferries from Sandbank to Gourock connecting with trains and coaches to Glasgow Airport.

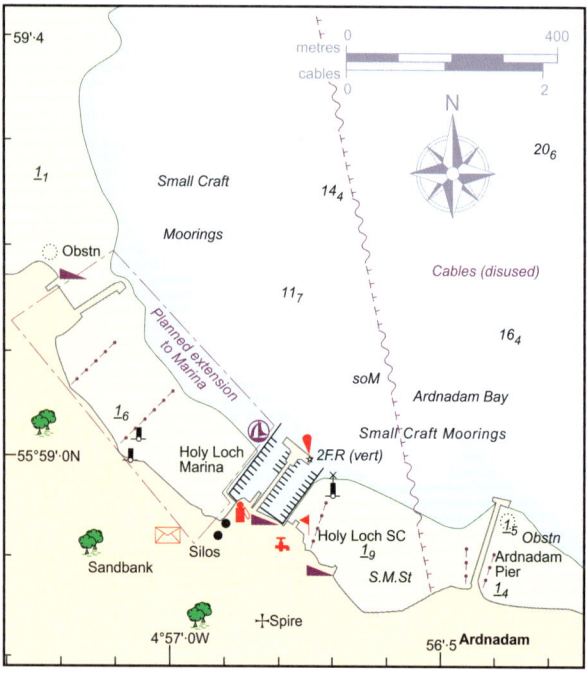

## 2.18  SUBMARINE EXERCISE AREAS

Submarines on the surface and at periscope depth always listen on Ch 16. Submarines on the surface will comply strictly with IRPCS; submarines at periscope depth will not close to within 1500 yds of a FV without its express permission. See 3.13.1 for more guidance.

Subfacts for areas between Barra and the Isle of Man are broadcast, after an initial announcement on Ch 16, by the MRCCs below on a specified VHF Ch at the following times:

| | |
|---|---|
| Stornoway | 0110 0510 0910 1310 1710 and 2110 UT |
| Clyde | 0020 0420 0820 1220 1620 and 2020 UT |
| Belfast | 0305 0705 1105 1505 1905 and 2305 UT |

During notified NATO exercises, Subfacts are also broadcast on MF SSB by Stornoway 1743 kHz, and Clyde 1883 kHz, at the same times as above.

The areas are referred to not by numbers, but by the names as listed below. See 1.21 for areas to the North of Mull.

General information on Subfacts is also broadcast twice daily at 0620 and 1820 UT by Portpatrick (O) Navtex. Clyde, Oban and Belfast Coastguards will also supply Subfacts on request Ch 16.

A Fisherman's Hotline, ☎ (01436) 674321, answers queries. FOSNNI Ops, ☎ (01436) 674321 ext 3206/6778 may help.

| | | | |
|---|---|---|---|
| 22 | Barra | 52 | Boyle |
| 23 | Hebrides Central | 53 | Orsay |
| 24 | Hawes | 54 | Islay |
| 25 | Eigg | 55 | Otter |
| 26 | Hebrides South | 56 | Gigha |
| 27 | Ford | 57 | Earadale |
| 28 | Tiree | 58 | Lochranza |
| 29 | Staffa | 59 | Davaar |
| 30 | Mackenzie | 60 | Brodick |
| 31 | Mull | 61 | Irvine |
| 32 | Linnhe | 62 | Lamlash |
| 33 | Jura Sound | 63 | Ayr |
| 34 | Fyne | 64 | Skerries |
| 35 | Minard | 65 | Rathlin |
| 36 | Tarbert | 66 | Kintyre |
| 37 | Skipness | 67 | Sanda |
| 38 | West Kyle | 68 | Stafnish |
| 39 | Striven | 69 | Pladda |
| 40 | East Kyle | 70 | Turnberry |
| 41 | Goil | 71 | Torr |
| 42 | Long | 72 | Mermaid |
| 43 | Cove | 73 | Ailsa |
| 44 | Gareloch | 74 | Maiden |
| 45 | Rosneath | 75 | Corsewall |
| 46 | Cumbrae | 76 | Ballantrae |
| 47 | Garroch | 77 | Magee |
| 48 | Laggan | 78 | Londonderry |
| 49 | Blackstone | 79 | Beaufort |
| 50 | Place | 80 | Ardglass |
| 51 | Colonsay | 81 | Peel |

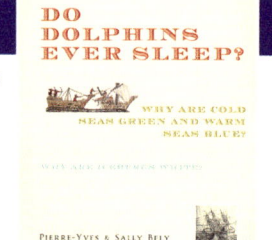

# SUBMARINE EXERCISE AREA MAP

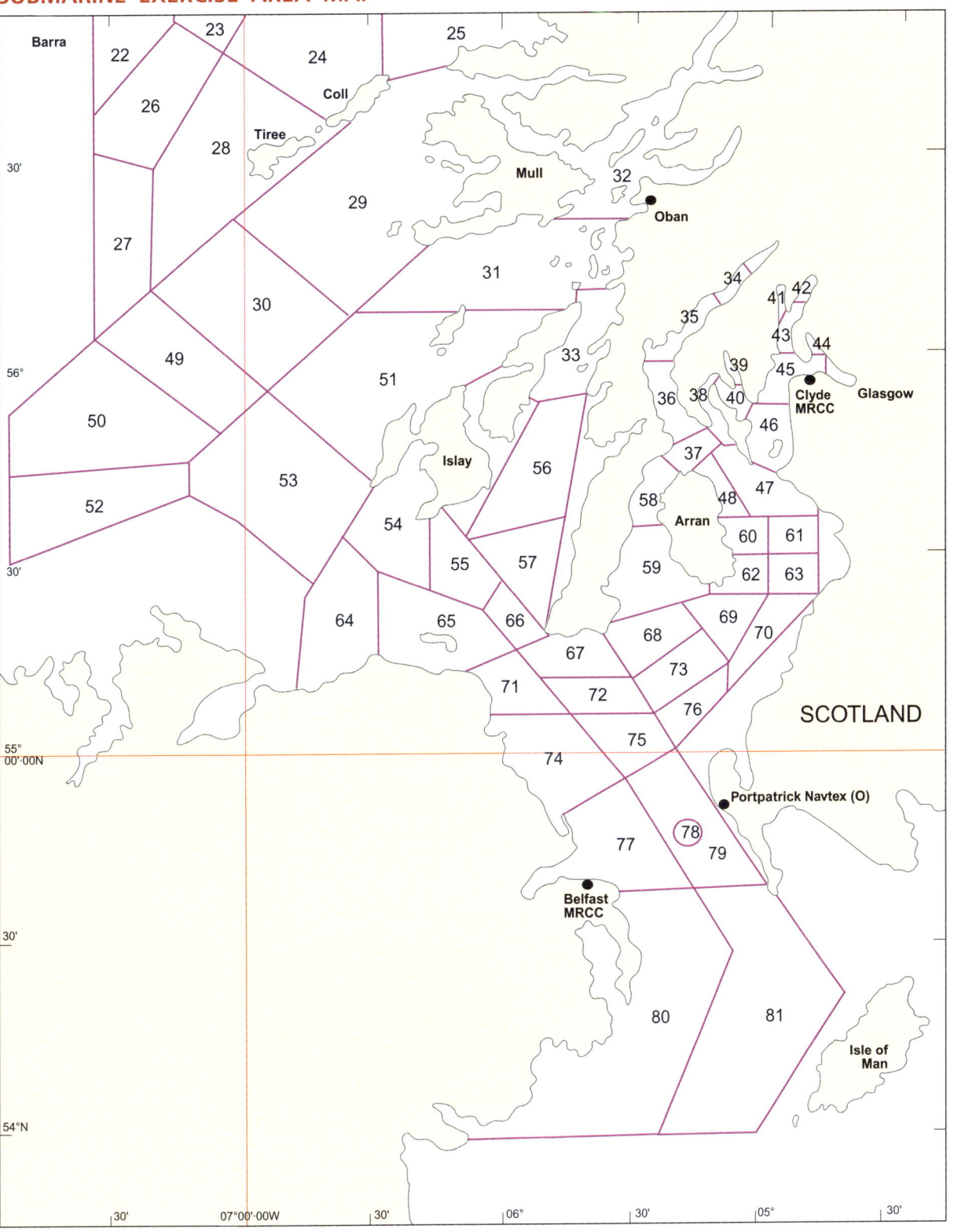

## 2.19 GARELOCH/RHU

Argyll and Bute 56°00'·70N 04°46'·57W (Rhu marina)
Rhu ✸✸✸⟡⟡❀❀✿; Sandpoint (W Dunbartonshire) ✸✸✸⟡❀✿

**CHARTS** AC *5610, 2131, 1994, 2000;* Imray C63, 2900 Series; OS 56, 63

**TIDES** +0110 Dover; ML 1·9; Duration 0640. Tides at Helensburgh are the same as at Greenock

**Standard Port GREENOCK (⟶)**

| Times | | | | Height (metres) | | | |
|---|---|---|---|---|---|---|---|
| High Water | | Low Water | | MHWS | MHWN | MLWN | MLWS |
| 0000 | 0600 | 0000 | 0600 | 3·4 | 2·8 | 1·0 | 0·3 |
| 1200 | 1800 | 1200 | 1800 | | | | |
| **Differences RHU MARINA** | | | | | | | |
| −0007 | −0007 | −0007 | −0007 | −0·1 | −0·1 | −0·1 | −0·2 |
| **FASLANE** | | | | | | | |
| −0010 | −0010 | −0010 | −0010 | 0·0 | 0·0 | −0·1 | −0·2 |
| **GARELOCHHEAD** | | | | | | | |
| 0000 | 0000 | 0000 | 0000 | 0·0 | 0·0 | 0·0 | −0·1 |
| **COULPORT** | | | | | | | |
| −0011 | −0011 | −0008 | −0008 | 0·0 | 0·0 | 0·0 | 0·0 |
| **LOCHGOILHEAD** | | | | | | | |
| +0015 | 0000 | −0005 | −0005 | −0·2 | −0·3 | −0·3 | −0·3 |
| **ARROCHAR** | | | | | | | |
| −0005 | −0005 | −0005 | −0005 | 0·0 | 0·0 | −0·1 | −0·1 |

**BYELAWS** Loch Long and Gareloch are classified as Dockyard Ports under the jurisdiction of the Queen's Harbour Master. All submarines and other warships at anchor or underway have an Exclusion Zone around them. Do not enter it or impede their passage.

**SHELTER** Rhu Marina is entered between low, floating wavebreaks on its S and W sides, not easy to find at night; caution cross-tides. On E/SE sides a rock bkwtr 1m above MHWS protects from strong SE'lies. Helensburgh Pier is a temp'y drying berth, rather exposed, used by occas steamers. ⚓ E of marina or in Rosneath Bay. Moorings N of the narrows at Stroul B & Clynder; and at the head of the loch. Clyde Naval Base at Faslane must be avoided by yachts.

**NAVIGATION** WPT 55°59'·29N 04°45'·26W, 356°/1·3M to bn No 7. Beaches between Cairndhu Pt and Helensburgh Pier (dries almost to the head) are strewn with large boulders above/below MLWS. Gareloch ent is about 225m wide due to drying spit off Rhu Pt. Beware a seaplane service operates (May-Oct) from Rhu Marina; large unlit MoD buoys and barges off W shore of Gareloch; for Garelochhead keep to W shore until well clear of Faslane Base area.

**LIGHTS AND MARKS** Ldg/dir lts into Gareloch 356°, 318°, 295°, 329° and 331°. Conspic ✠ tr at Rhu. Gareloch Fuel Depot lt, Iso WRG 4s 10m 14M, 351°-G-356°-W-006°-R-011°, is clearly visible from the S. Many shore lts and an unlit floating boom make night sailing near the Base area inadvisable.

**R/T** VHF Ch 16. Rhu Marina Ch **80** M (H24 in season).

**TELEPHONE** (Code 01436) Marina 820238; Queen's HM 674321; MRCC (01475) 729014; Marinecall 09068 969652; Police 672141; Ⓗ (01389) 754121; Dr 672277.

**FACILITIES** **Rhu Marina** (200) ☎ 820238, 🖷 821039, AB £2·10, @, D, M, BH (35 ton), CH, ME, El, Slip, M, C hire, Gas, Gaz; **Royal Northern and Clyde YC** ☎ 820322. Possible ⚓s, L, R, Bar; **Helensburgh SC** ☎ 672778 Slip (dinghies) L, FW; **Town** (1M) all services, ⇌, ✈ (Glasgow). **DRB Marine** ☎ 831231, some AB and ⚓s, Slip (launching £10), Wi-fi.

**Naval activity**: Beware submarines from Faslane Base. See 2.21 for submarine activity (Subfacts) in the Clyde and offshore or call FOSNNI Ops ☎ (01436) 674321 Ext 3206.

**Protected Areas**: Vessels are never allowed within 150m of naval shore installations at Faslane and Coulport.

**Restricted Areas** (Faslane, Rhu Chan and Coulport): These are closed to all vessels during submarine movements (see opposite and *W Coast of Scotland Pilot*, App 2). MoD Police patrols enforce areas which are shown on charts. The S limit of Faslane Restricted area is marked by two Or posts with X topmarks on Shandon foreshore. The W limit is marked by Iso WRG 4s, vis W356°-006°, at Gareloch Oil fuel depot N jetty. The following signals are shown when restrictions are in force:

**Entrance to Gareloch**
Day & Night: 🔴 🟢 🟢 (vert), supplemented by R flag with W diagonal bar.

**Faslane and Coulport**
Day & Night: 🟢🟢🟢 (vert), supplemented by International Code pendant over pendant Nine.

**LOCH LONG/LOCH GOIL**, Argyll and Bute, approx 56°00′N 04°52′·5W to 56°12′·00N 04°45′·00W. AC *5610*, 3746. Tides: See 2.19 for differences. ML 1·7m; Duration 0645.

**SHELTER** Loch Long is about 15M long. Temp ‡s (south to north)at: Cove, Blairmore (not in S'lies), Ardentinny, Portincaple, Coilessan (about 1M S of Ardgartan Pt), and near head of loch (Arrochar) on either shore. In Loch Goil ‡ at Swines Hole and off Carrick Castle (S of the pier, in N'lies a swell builds). Avoid ‡ near Douglas Pier. The head of the loch is crowded with private/dinghy moorings, and is either too steep-to or too shallow to ‡. The loch is frequently closed to navigation due to the trial range half way down.

**LIGHTS** Coulport Jetty, 2FG (vert) each end and two Fl G 12s on N jetty; Port Dornaige Fl 6s 8m 11M, vis 026°-206°; Dog Rock (Carraig nan Ron) Fl 2s 11M; Finnart Oil Terminal has FG lts and ldg lts 031° QW/FW on Cnap Pt. Upper Loch Long is unlit. Loch Goil ent is marked by 2 PHM buoys (Fl R 3s and QR), a SHM buoy (QG) and ldg lts 318°: front (The Perch) Dir FWRG and Fl R 3s; rear FW. Rubha Ardnahein Fl R5s.

**FACILITIES** Loch Long (Cove), Cove SC, FW, Bar; ⚓, FW (pier); (Portincaple) shops, hotel, ✉, FW; (Ardentinny) shop, ⚓, R, hotel, M; (Blairmore) shops, ✉, Slip, FW; (Arrochar) shops, hotel, FW, Gas, ✉. Loch Goil (Carrick Castle) has ✉, shop, hotel; (Lochgoilhead) has a store, ✉, hotel, FW, Gas.

---

## 2.20   DUMBARTON (SANDPOINT) AND BOWLING HARBOUR

Dunbartonshire 55°56′·50N 04°34′·27W ✿✿✿✿❀

**CHARTS** AC *5610*, 2131, 1994, 2007: BW Skipper's Guide for Forth and Clyde Canal, BW Skipper's Brief for Lowland Canals; Imray 63, 2900 Series.

**TIDES** +0122 Dover; ML 2·0; Duration 0640

**Standard Port GREENOCK (→)**

| Times | | | | Height (metres) | | | |
|---|---|---|---|---|---|---|---|
| High Water | | Low Water | | MHWS | MHWN | MLWN | MLWS |
| 0000 | 0600 | 0000 | 0600 | 3·4 | 2·8 | 1·0 | 0·3 |
| 1200 | 1800 | 1200 | 1800 | | | | |
| Differences PORT GLASGOW (55°56′·10N 04°40′·50W) | | | | | | | |
| +0010 | +0005 | +0010 | +0020 | +0·2 | +0·1 | 0·0 | 0·0 |
| DUMBARTON | | | | | | | |
| +0015 | +0010 | +0020 | +0040 | +0·4 | +0·3 | +0·1 | 0·0 |
| BOWLING | | | | | | | |
| +0020 | +0010 | +0030 | +0055 | +0·6 | +0·5 | +0·3 | +0·1 |
| RENFREW | | | | | | | |
| +0025 | +0015 | +0035 | +0100 | +0·9 | +0·8 | +0·5 | +0·2 |
| GLASGOW | | | | | | | |
| +0025 | +0015 | +0035 | +0105 | +1·3 | +1·2 | +0·6 | +0·4 |

**SHELTER** Good at Dumbarton (Sandpoint Marina) and Bowling Hbr 3M further east. Hbrs are controlled by Clyde Port Authority.

**NAVIGATION** WPT 55°57′·61N 04°45′·96W, No 1 SHM buoy, 2ca NNW of Clydeport container terminal (conspic blue cranes). No navigational dangers, but much shipping and ferries in the Clyde. Keep just inboard of chan lateral marks as depths shoal rapidly outboard. For Dumbarton cross the river at 90° abeam No 39 SHM buoy. Depths in R Leven may be less than charted. For Bowling Hbr cross abeam No 45 SHM buoy. Follow ldg marks as charted.

**LIGHTS AND MARKS** The R Clyde is well buoyed/lit.

**R/T** Call *Clydeport Estuary Radio* Ch **12** 16 (H24) when abm No 1 buoy E-bound. Weather and traffic info on request. Marina Ch M. Bowling lockkeeper Ch 74, HW±2.

**TELEPHONE** (Codes: Greenock 01475; Glasgow 0141, followed by 7 digit Tel No). HM 725775; Estuary Control 726221; British Waterways Board 332 6936; MRCC 729988; Police 01389 822000; Dr 634617; Marinecall 09068 969652; ⊞ 01389 754121.

**FACILITIES** Sandpoint Marina 55°56′·48N 04°34′·07W. ☎ 01389 762396/731500, 🖷 732605. Limited visitors berths, £10 per night. VHF Ch M. BH (40 ton), Slip, BY, D (can), CH ☎ 01389 742438. **Town** ⚓, R, Bar, Ⓑ, ✉, ⇌ 30 mins to Glasgow.

**Bowling Basin** 55°55′·8N 04°29′·0W, W end of Forth & Clyde Canal. ☎ 01389 877969. Lock access HW±2 to Basin and Canal. For lock hrs call VHF Ch 74 asap for latest schedule. *Skipper's Brief* essential obtain from www.scottishcanals.co.uk. **Facilities** AB £2·25, FW, Showers, 🚾, D by prior notice, C (mast), Wi-fi. **Town** P&D (cans), ⚓, R, Bar, ✉, Ⓑ, ⇌ .

There are no yachting facilities on R Clyde E of Bowling Basin.

**GLASGOW** 55°55′·94N 04°34′·25W; Clyde Yacht Clubs Association is at 8 St James St, Paisley. ☎ 8878296. Clyde Cruising Club is at Suite 408, Pentagon Centre, 36 Washington Street, Glasgow G3 8AZ, ☎ 221 2774, 🖷 221 2775. **Services:** ACA, CH.

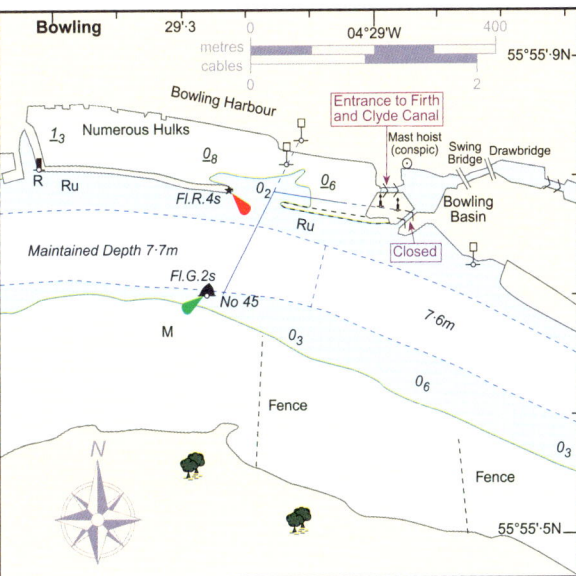

**TIME ZONE (UT)**
For Summer Time add ONE hour in **non-shaded areas**

## GREENOCK  LAT 55°57'N  LONG 4°46'W
TIMES AND HEIGHTS OF HIGH AND LOW WATERS

Dates in red are SPRINGS
Dates in blue are NEAPS

YEAR **2008**

### JANUARY

| Time | m | | Time | m |
|---|---|---|---|---|
| **1** TU | 0620 2.9 / 1153 1.1 / 1807 3.2 | **16** W | 0522 3.1 / 1106 0.8 / 1744 3.3 / 2352 0.6 |
| **2** W | 0027 0.9 / 0712 2.9 / 1303 1.2 / 1901 3.0 | **17** TH | 0611 3.0 / 1210 0.9 / 1847 3.1 |
| **3** TH | 0133 1.0 / 0815 2.9 / 1416 1.2 / 2006 2.9 | **18** F | 0102 0.7 / 0714 2.9 / 1329 1.0 / 2015 3.0 |
| **4** F | 0235 1.0 / 0923 3.0 / 1516 1.0 / 2119 2.9 | **19** SA | 0218 0.8 / 0852 2.9 / 1450 0.9 / 2149 3.0 |
| **5** SA | 0327 1.0 / 1022 3.1 / 1605 0.9 / 2224 3.0 | **20** SU | 0325 0.7 / 1014 3.1 / 1556 0.7 / 2301 3.1 |
| **6** SU | 0413 0.9 / 1111 3.3 / 1647 0.8 / 2315 3.1 | **21** M | 0422 0.6 / 1112 3.3 / 1650 0.5 / 2359 3.2 |
| **7** M | 0453 0.9 / 1152 3.4 / 1725 0.7 / 2359 3.1 | **22** TU | 0513 0.5 / 1202 3.5 / 1737 0.3 ○ |
| **8** TU | 0530 0.8 / 1228 3.5 / 1801 0.6 ● | **23** W | 0052 3.3 / 0600 0.5 / 1248 3.6 / 1821 0.2 |
| **9** W | 0040 3.2 / 0604 0.8 / 1302 3.6 / 1834 0.6 | **24** TH | 0141 3.3 / 0644 0.4 / 1331 3.7 / 1902 0.2 |
| **10** TH | 0120 3.2 / 0639 0.7 / 1335 3.6 / 1908 0.5 | **25** F | 0225 3.3 / 0726 0.4 / 1411 3.7 / 1943 0.3 |
| **11** F | 0159 3.2 / 0717 0.7 / 1410 3.6 / 1945 0.5 | **26** SA | 0304 3.2 / 0807 0.5 / 1449 3.7 / 2022 0.3 |
| **12** SA | 0238 3.3 / 0758 0.6 / 1447 3.6 / 2025 0.4 | **27** SU | 0339 3.2 / 0846 0.5 / 1526 3.6 / 2101 0.4 |
| **13** SU | 0317 3.3 / 0840 0.6 / 1526 3.6 / 2109 0.4 | **28** M | 0412 3.2 / 0924 0.6 / 1602 3.5 / 2142 0.5 |
| **14** M | 0357 3.3 / 0925 0.6 / 1608 3.5 / 2157 0.4 | **29** TU | 0446 3.1 / 1005 0.7 / 1640 3.4 / 2226 0.7 |
| **15** TU | 0438 3.2 / 1013 0.7 / 1653 3.4 / 2251 0.5 ◗ | **30** W | 0524 3.0 / 1050 0.9 / 1722 3.2 / 2316 0.9 ◗ |
| | | **31** TH | 0607 2.9 / 1149 1.1 / 1809 2.9 |

### FEBRUARY

| Time | m | | Time | m |
|---|---|---|---|---|
| **1** F | 0019 1.1 / 0701 2.8 / 1315 1.2 / 1906 2.8 | **16** SA | 0037 0.9 / 0628 2.9 / 1309 1.0 / 1956 2.7 |
| **2** SA | 0144 1.2 / 0820 2.7 / 1446 1.1 / 2019 2.7 | **17** SU | 0208 0.9 / 0821 2.8 / 1448 0.9 / 2200 2.8 |
| **3** SU | 0300 1.2 / 0952 2.9 / 1544 0.9 / 2201 2.7 | **18** M | 0322 0.8 / 1008 2.9 / 1555 0.6 / 2304 3.0 |
| **4** M | 0354 1.0 / 1050 3.1 / 1628 0.7 / 2303 2.9 | **19** TU | 0418 0.6 / 1106 3.2 / 1645 0.4 / 2356 3.2 |
| **5** TU | 0437 0.9 / 1133 3.3 / 1706 0.6 / 2348 3.0 | **20** W | 0506 0.4 / 1152 3.4 / 1728 0.2 |
| **6** W | 0513 0.8 / 1209 3.4 / 1741 0.4 | **21** TH | 0042 3.2 / 0548 0.3 / 1236 3.5 / 1806 0.1 ○ |
| **7** TH | 0028 3.1 / 0546 0.7 / 1244 3.4 / 1813 0.4 ● | **22** F | 0124 3.3 / 0627 0.3 / 1315 3.6 / 1842 0.2 |
| **8** F | 0107 3.1 / 0619 0.6 / 1317 3.5 / 1845 0.3 | **23** SA | 0201 3.2 / 0704 0.3 / 1352 3.6 / 1915 0.2 |
| **9** SA | 0143 3.2 / 0655 0.5 / 1353 3.6 / 1920 0.2 | **24** SU | 0233 3.2 / 0738 0.3 / 1426 3.6 / 1948 0.3 |
| **10** SU | 0219 3.3 / 0734 0.4 / 1431 3.6 / 2000 0.2 | **25** M | 0302 3.2 / 0810 0.4 / 1458 3.5 / 2022 0.4 |
| **11** M | 0255 3.3 / 0816 0.3 / 1510 3.6 / 2042 0.3 | **26** TU | 0332 3.2 / 0844 0.4 / 1532 3.5 / 2057 0.5 |
| **12** TU | 0332 3.4 / 0859 0.3 / 1550 3.6 / 2129 0.3 | **27** W | 0404 3.2 / 0920 0.5 / 1607 3.3 / 2134 0.7 |
| **13** W | 0409 3.3 / 0945 0.4 / 1632 3.5 / 2220 0.4 | **28** TH | 0439 3.1 / 1001 0.7 / 1646 3.1 / 2215 0.9 |
| **14** TH | 0449 3.2 / 1037 0.6 / 1718 3.2 / 2321 0.7 ◗ | **29** F | 0518 2.9 / 1052 1.0 / 1732 2.8 / 2307 1.2 ◗ |
| **15** F | 0534 3.1 / 1140 0.8 / 1815 2.9 | | |

### MARCH

| Time | m | | Time | m |
|---|---|---|---|---|
| **1** SA | 0607 2.7 / 1208 1.2 / 1828 2.6 | **16** SU | 0030 1.0 / 0604 2.8 / 1314 0.9 / 2029 2.6 |
| **2** SU | 0032 1.4 / 0715 2.6 / 1411 1.1 / 1938 2.5 | **17** M | 0202 1.0 / 0820 2.7 / 1443 0.7 / 2159 2.8 |
| **3** M | 0229 1.3 / 0914 2.7 / 1516 0.9 / 2141 2.6 | **18** TU | 0311 0.8 / 0955 2.9 / 1543 0.5 / 2254 3.0 |
| **4** TU | 0330 1.1 / 1022 2.9 / 1601 0.6 / 2244 2.8 | **19** W | 0405 0.6 / 1049 3.2 / 1630 0.3 / 2339 3.2 |
| **5** W | 0413 0.9 / 1105 3.1 / 1638 0.4 / 2327 3.0 | **20** TH | 0450 0.4 / 1133 3.4 / 1710 0.1 |
| **6** TH | 0448 0.7 / 1141 3.3 / 1712 0.2 | **21** F | 0019 3.2 / 0529 0.3 / 1214 3.4 / 1744 0.1 ○ |
| **7** F | 0006 3.1 / 0520 0.5 / 1217 3.4 / 1743 0.1 ● | **22** SA | 0057 3.2 / 0606 0.2 / 1252 3.5 / 1816 0.2 |
| **8** SA | 0043 3.1 / 0553 0.4 / 1253 3.4 / 1816 0.1 | **23** SU | 0129 3.2 / 0638 0.3 / 1326 3.4 / 1844 0.3 |
| **9** SU | 0119 3.2 / 0630 0.3 / 1332 3.5 / 1853 0.0 | **24** M | 0157 3.3 / 0707 0.3 / 1357 3.4 / 1913 0.4 |
| **10** M | 0155 3.3 / 0709 0.2 / 1412 3.6 / 1935 0.1 | **25** TU | 0226 3.3 / 0736 0.3 / 1429 3.4 / 1945 0.4 |
| **11** TU | 0231 3.4 / 0752 0.1 / 1453 3.6 / 2019 0.1 | **26** W | 0256 3.3 / 0808 0.4 / 1502 3.3 / 2019 0.5 |
| **12** W | 0307 3.5 / 0837 0.2 / 1533 3.6 / 2108 0.3 | **27** TH | 0327 3.3 / 0844 0.5 / 1537 3.2 / 2056 0.7 |
| **13** TH | 0344 3.4 / 0924 0.3 / 1616 3.4 / 2201 0.5 | **28** F | 0400 3.2 / 0925 0.6 / 1617 3.0 / 2138 0.9 |
| **14** F | 0424 3.4 / 1018 0.5 / 1703 3.1 / 2304 0.8 ◗ | **29** SA | 0437 3.0 / 1016 0.8 / 1703 2.8 / 2230 1.1 ◗ |
| **15** SA | 0509 3.1 / 1127 0.8 / 1803 2.8 | **30** SU | 0523 2.8 / 1125 1.0 / 1759 2.6 / 2339 1.3 |
| | | **31** M | 0627 2.6 / 1315 1.0 / 1907 2.5 |

### APRIL

| Time | m | | Time | m |
|---|---|---|---|---|
| **1** TU | 0127 1.3 / 0801 2.6 / 1432 0.8 / 2053 2.6 | **16** W | 0245 0.8 / 0926 3.0 / 1517 0.4 / 2227 3.0 |
| **2** W | 0247 1.1 / 0936 2.8 / 1521 0.5 / 2209 2.8 | **17** TH | 0340 0.6 / 1020 3.2 / 1603 0.3 / 2310 3.1 |
| **3** TH | 0335 0.8 / 1025 3.0 / 1601 0.3 / 2253 3.0 | **18** F | 0426 0.4 / 1105 3.3 / 1642 0.2 / 2348 3.2 |
| **4** F | 0414 0.6 / 1104 3.2 / 1636 0.1 / 2332 3.1 | **19** SA | 0506 0.3 / 1145 3.3 / 1716 0.3 |
| **5** SA | 0450 0.4 / 1144 3.3 / 1711 0.0 | **20** SU | 0023 3.2 / 0541 0.3 / 1222 3.3 / 1746 0.3 ○ |
| **6** SU | 0010 3.2 / 0526 0.2 / 1226 3.4 / 1748 0.0 ● | **21** M | 0054 3.3 / 0611 0.3 / 1256 3.3 / 1814 0.4 |
| **7** M | 0049 3.3 / 0606 0.1 / 1309 3.5 / 1829 0.0 | **22** TU | 0124 3.3 / 0639 0.3 / 1328 3.3 / 1843 0.5 |
| **8** TU | 0128 3.4 / 0648 0.1 / 1354 3.6 / 1914 0.1 | **23** W | 0153 3.4 / 0708 0.4 / 1400 3.3 / 1916 0.5 |
| **9** W | 0207 3.5 / 0732 0.1 / 1438 3.6 / 2002 0.2 | **24** TH | 0224 3.4 / 0742 0.4 / 1435 3.2 / 1953 0.6 |
| **10** TH | 0246 3.5 / 0820 0.1 / 1522 3.4 / 2054 0.4 | **25** F | 0256 3.4 / 0820 0.5 / 1512 3.1 / 2034 0.7 |
| **11** F | 0325 3.5 / 0912 0.3 / 1608 3.2 / 2152 0.6 | **26** SA | 0329 3.3 / 0903 0.6 / 1553 3.0 / 2119 0.8 |
| **12** SA | 0407 3.3 / 1013 0.5 / 1702 2.9 / 2300 0.8 ◑ | **27** SU | 0405 3.1 / 0954 0.7 / 1639 2.8 / 2211 1.0 |
| **13** SU | 0454 3.1 / 1132 0.6 / 1822 2.7 | **28** M | 0449 2.9 / 1058 0.8 / 1735 2.7 / 2313 1.2 ◑ |
| **14** M | 0019 1.0 / 0557 2.9 / 1305 0.7 / 2024 2.6 | **29** TU | 0549 2.7 / 1217 0.8 / 1838 2.6 |
| **15** TU | 0138 1.0 / 0803 2.8 / 1420 0.6 / 2136 2.8 | **30** W | 0027 1.2 / 0704 2.7 / 1333 0.7 / 1953 2.7 |

Chart Datum: 1·62 metres below Ordnance Datum (Newlyn). HAT is 4·0 metres above Chart Datum.

**SW Scotland**

## GREENOCK  LAT 55°57'N  LONG 4°46'W
### TIMES AND HEIGHTS OF HIGH AND LOW WATERS

**TIME ZONE (UT)**
For Summer Time add ONE hour in **non-shaded areas**

Dates in red are SPRINGS
Dates in blue are NEAPS

YEAR 200?

Chart Datum: 1·62 metres below Ordnance Datum (Newlyn). HAT is 4·0 metres above Chart Datum.

### MAY

| Day | Time m | Time m | Time m | Time m |
|---|---|---|---|---|
| 1 TH | 0145 1.1 | 0829 2.8 | 1431 0.4 | 2112 2.8 |
| 2 F | 0247 0.8 | 0934 3.0 | 1517 0.2 | 2208 3.0 |
| 3 SA | 0336 0.6 | 1024 3.2 | 1559 0.1 | 2253 3.1 |
| 4 SU | 0420 0.4 | 1111 3.3 | 1640 0.0 | 2337 3.2 |
| 5 M ● | 0502 0.2 | 1159 3.4 | 1723 0.0 | |
| 6 TU | 0020 3.4 | 0545 0.1 | 1248 3.5 | 1808 0.1 |
| 7 W | 0104 3.5 | 0630 0.0 | 1338 3.5 | 1858 0.2 |
| 8 TH | 0147 3.5 | 0718 0.1 | 1427 3.4 | 1950 0.3 |
| 9 F | 0229 3.6 | 0810 0.1 | 1517 3.3 | 2046 0.4 |
| 10 SA | 0312 3.5 | 0906 0.2 | 1611 3.1 | 2144 0.6 |
| 11 SU | 0357 3.4 | 1009 0.4 | 1713 2.9 | 2246 0.7 |
| 12 M ◐ | 0448 3.2 | 1121 0.5 | 1828 2.8 | 2353 0.9 |
| 13 TU | 0555 3.0 | 1235 0.5 | 1947 2.7 | |
| 14 W | 0102 0.9 | 0723 2.9 | 1343 0.5 | 2052 2.8 |
| 15 TH | 0208 0.8 | 0842 3.0 | 1439 0.5 | 2146 2.9 |
| 16 F | 0306 0.7 | 0941 3.1 | 1527 0.4 | 2231 3.0 |
| 17 SA | 0355 0.5 | 1029 3.1 | 1609 0.4 | 2311 3.1 |
| 18 SU | 0438 0.4 | 1112 3.2 | 1645 0.4 | 2348 3.2 |
| 19 M | 0516 0.4 | 1150 3.2 | 1718 0.5 | |
| 20 TU ○ | 0022 3.3 | 0548 0.4 | 1225 3.1 | 1748 0.6 |
| 21 W | 0055 3.4 | 0619 0.4 | 1259 3.1 | 1821 0.6 |
| 22 TH | 0127 3.4 | 0650 0.5 | 1334 3.1 | 1856 0.6 |
| 23 F | 0159 3.4 | 0725 0.5 | 1411 3.1 | 1936 0.7 |
| 24 SA | 0232 3.4 | 0804 0.5 | 1451 3.1 | 2019 0.7 |
| 25 SU | 0306 3.3 | 0847 0.5 | 1533 3.0 | 2104 0.8 |
| 26 M | 0343 3.2 | 0935 0.6 | 1619 2.9 | 2154 0.8 |
| 27 TU | 0425 3.1 | 1030 0.6 | 1710 2.9 | 2247 0.9 |
| 28 W ◐ | 0517 2.9 | 1133 0.6 | 1806 2.8 | 2347 1.0 |
| 29 TH | 0622 2.9 | 1238 0.5 | 1906 2.8 | |
| 30 F | 0052 0.9 | 0734 2.9 | 1340 0.4 | 2012 2.9 |
| 31 SA | 0159 0.8 | 0846 3.0 | 1435 0.3 | 2118 3.0 |

### JUNE

| Day | Time m | Time m | Time m | Time m |
|---|---|---|---|---|
| 1 SU | 0259 0.6 | 0948 3.2 | 1526 0.2 | 2216 3.1 |
| 2 M | 0352 0.4 | 1044 3.3 | 1615 0.1 | 2308 3.2 |
| 3 TU ● | 0441 0.2 | 1138 3.3 | 1703 0.1 | 2357 3.4 |
| 4 W | 0529 0.1 | 1233 3.4 | 1753 0.2 | |
| 5 TH | 0045 3.5 | 0618 0.1 | 1329 3.3 | 1845 0.3 |
| 6 F | 0132 3.6 | 0708 0.1 | 1423 3.3 | 1939 0.4 |
| 7 SA | 0217 3.6 | 0800 0.1 | 1517 3.2 | 2033 0.4 |
| 8 SU | 0302 3.6 | 0854 0.2 | 1611 3.1 | 2127 0.5 |
| 9 M | 0348 3.5 | 0951 0.3 | 1706 3.0 | 2221 0.6 |
| 10 TU ◐ | 0438 3.3 | 1050 0.4 | 1801 2.9 | 2317 0.7 |
| 11 W | 0532 3.2 | 1153 0.5 | 1855 2.8 | |
| 12 TH | 0018 0.8 | 0633 3.0 | 1257 0.6 | 1951 2.8 |
| 13 F | 0122 0.8 | 0740 2.9 | 1355 0.6 | 2048 2.8 |
| 14 SA | 0225 0.8 | 0847 2.9 | 1447 0.6 | 2143 2.9 |
| 15 SU | 0322 0.7 | 0947 2.9 | 1534 0.6 | 2232 3.0 |
| 16 M | 0411 0.6 | 1037 3.0 | 1616 0.7 | 2316 3.1 |
| 17 TU | 0453 0.5 | 1120 3.0 | 1655 0.7 | 2356 3.3 |
| 18 W ○ | 0531 0.5 | 1159 3.0 | 1731 0.7 | |
| 19 TH | 0032 3.4 | 0606 0.5 | 1237 3.0 | 1805 0.7 |
| 20 F | 0106 3.4 | 0639 0.5 | 1314 3.0 | 1842 0.7 |
| 21 SA | 0139 3.4 | 0713 0.5 | 1353 3.1 | 1920 0.7 |
| 22 SU | 0212 3.4 | 0749 0.4 | 1433 3.1 | 2001 0.6 |
| 23 M | 0247 3.4 | 0828 0.4 | 1514 3.1 | 2044 0.6 |
| 24 TU | 0324 3.4 | 0911 0.4 | 1557 3.1 | 2130 0.6 |
| 25 W | 0404 3.3 | 0959 0.4 | 1642 3.0 | 2218 0.7 |
| 26 TH ◐ | 0449 3.2 | 1053 0.6 | 1730 3.0 | 2310 0.7 |
| 27 F | 0543 3.1 | 1153 0.4 | 1822 2.9 | |
| 28 SA | 0010 0.8 | 0648 3.0 | 1257 0.4 | 1920 2.9 |
| 29 SU | 0118 0.8 | 0804 3.0 | 1401 0.4 | 2031 2.9 |
| 30 M | 0228 0.7 | 0920 3.0 | 1501 0.4 | 2145 3.0 |

### JULY

| Day | Time m | Time m | Time m | Time m |
|---|---|---|---|---|
| 1 TU | 0332 0.5 | 1028 3.1 | 1558 0.3 | 2248 3.2 |
| 2 W | 0428 0.3 | 1130 3.2 | 1651 0.3 | 2343 3.3 |
| 3 TH ● | 0520 0.2 | 1228 3.2 | 1743 0.3 | |
| 4 F | 0033 3.5 | 0609 0.1 | 1325 3.2 | 1834 0.3 |
| 5 SA | 0121 3.5 | 0657 0.0 | 1419 3.2 | 1924 0.3 |
| 6 SU | 0207 3.6 | 0745 0.1 | 1509 3.2 | 2013 0.4 |
| 7 M | 0250 3.6 | 0832 0.1 | 1555 3.1 | 2101 0.4 |
| 8 TU | 0333 3.6 | 0920 0.2 | 1638 3.1 | 2147 0.5 |
| 9 W | 0415 3.5 | 1008 0.3 | 1718 3.0 | 2235 0.6 |
| 10 TH ◐ | 0458 3.3 | 1100 0.5 | 1758 2.9 | 2326 0.7 |
| 11 F | 0543 3.1 | 1158 0.7 | 1842 2.8 | |
| 12 SA | 0027 0.9 | 0633 2.9 | 1302 0.8 | 1934 2.8 |
| 13 SU | 0140 1.0 | 0733 2.8 | 1406 0.9 | 2041 2.8 |
| 14 M | 0250 0.9 | 0848 2.7 | 1504 0.9 | 2154 2.9 |
| 15 TU | 0347 0.8 | 1005 2.7 | 1554 0.8 | 2251 3.1 |
| 16 W | 0435 0.6 | 1101 2.8 | 1638 0.8 | 2336 3.2 |
| 17 TH | 0515 0.5 | 1145 2.9 | 1716 0.7 | |
| 18 F ○ | 0014 3.3 | 0551 0.4 | 1223 3.0 | 1751 0.7 |
| 19 SA | 0048 3.4 | 0624 0.4 | 1300 3.0 | 1824 0.6 |
| 20 SU | 0120 3.4 | 0655 0.4 | 1336 3.0 | 1859 0.6 |
| 21 M | 0153 3.5 | 0727 0.3 | 1414 3.1 | 1937 0.5 |
| 22 TU | 0228 3.5 | 0802 0.3 | 1452 3.1 | 2018 0.5 |
| 23 W | 0305 3.5 | 0842 0.2 | 1531 3.2 | 2101 0.5 |
| 24 TH | 0344 3.4 | 0926 0.3 | 1611 3.2 | 2147 0.5 |
| 25 F ◐ | 0425 3.3 | 1017 0.5 | 1654 3.1 | 2237 0.6 |
| 26 SA | 0511 3.2 | 1114 0.5 | 1740 3.0 | 2334 0.7 |
| 27 SU | 0609 3.0 | 1221 0.6 | 1835 2.9 | |
| 28 M | 0043 0.8 | 0727 2.8 | 1336 0.7 | 1948 2.9 |
| 29 TU | 0207 0.7 | 0908 2.8 | 1449 0.6 | 2127 2.9 |
| 30 W | 0324 0.6 | 1030 3.0 | 1552 0.5 | 2240 3.1 |
| 31 TH | 0424 0.4 | 1131 3.1 | 1646 0.4 | 2335 3.3 |

### AUGUST

| Day | Time m | Time m | Time m | Time m |
|---|---|---|---|---|
| 1 F ● | 0514 0.2 | 1226 3.2 | 1735 0.3 | |
| 2 SA | 0024 3.5 | 0559 0.1 | 1317 3.2 | 1820 0.3 |
| 3 SU | 0110 3.6 | 0642 0.0 | 1404 3.2 | 1904 0.3 |
| 4 M | 0152 3.6 | 0723 0.1 | 1446 3.2 | 1947 0.3 |
| 5 TU | 0232 3.6 | 0802 0.1 | 1523 3.1 | 2028 0.4 |
| 6 W | 0309 3.6 | 0841 0.2 | 1556 3.1 | 2108 0.4 |
| 7 TH | 0345 3.5 | 0922 0.4 | 1628 3.1 | 2148 0.5 |
| 8 F ◐ | 0422 3.4 | 1004 0.6 | 1704 3.0 | 2233 0.7 |
| 9 SA | 0502 3.1 | 1053 0.8 | 1745 2.9 | 2328 0.9 |
| 10 SU | 0547 2.9 | 1156 1.0 | 1834 2.8 | |
| 11 M | 0047 1.1 | 0641 2.7 | 1323 1.2 | 1938 2.7 |
| 12 TU | 0223 1.1 | 0752 2.6 | 1441 1.1 | 2118 2.8 |
| 13 W | 0326 0.9 | 0945 2.6 | 1537 1.0 | 2230 3.0 |
| 14 TH | 0414 0.7 | 1050 2.8 | 1621 0.8 | 2315 3.2 |
| 15 F | 0454 0.5 | 1132 2.9 | 1658 0.7 | 2352 3.3 |
| 16 SA ○ | 0529 0.4 | 1208 3.0 | 1730 0.6 | |
| 17 SU | 0026 3.4 | 0559 0.3 | 1242 3.0 | 1800 0.6 |
| 18 M | 0058 3.4 | 0628 0.3 | 1315 3.1 | 1832 0.5 |
| 19 TU | 0132 3.5 | 0658 0.2 | 1350 3.2 | 1909 0.4 |
| 20 W | 0208 3.5 | 0734 0.2 | 1427 3.2 | 1950 0.4 |
| 21 TH | 0246 3.6 | 0814 0.2 | 1504 3.3 | 2033 0.4 |
| 22 F | 0324 3.6 | 0858 0.2 | 1542 3.3 | 2119 0.4 |
| 23 SA ◐ | 0404 3.4 | 0947 0.4 | 1623 3.3 | 2209 0.5 |
| 24 SU | 0448 3.2 | 1045 0.6 | 1708 3.1 | 2308 0.8 |
| 25 M | 0542 3.0 | 1158 0.8 | 1801 3.0 | |
| 26 TU | 0024 0.9 | 0705 2.7 | 1329 0.9 | 1917 2.8 |
| 27 W | 0207 0.9 | 0923 2.7 | 1449 0.8 | 2125 2.9 |
| 28 TH | 0325 0.6 | 1035 3.0 | 1549 0.5 | 2234 3.2 |
| 29 F | 0420 0.4 | 1128 3.1 | 1638 0.4 | 2324 3.4 |
| 30 SA ● | 0504 0.2 | 1215 3.2 | 1722 0.3 | |
| 31 SU | 0009 3.5 | 0544 0.1 | 1258 3.3 | 1803 0.3 |

》》 **FREE** monthly updates from 《《
www.reedsalmanac.co.uk

## GREENOCK  LAT 55°57'N  LONG 4°46'W
### TIMES AND HEIGHTS OF HIGH AND LOW WATERS

TIME ZONE (UT)
For Summer Time add ONE hour in non-shaded areas

Dates in red are SPRINGS
Dates in blue are NEAPS

YEAR 2008

### SEPTEMBER

| Time | m | Time | m |
|---|---|---|---|
| **1** 0051 | 3.6 | **16** 0030 | 3.5 |
| 0621 | 0.1 | 0557 | 0.2 |
| M 1338 | 3.2 | TU 1248 | 3.2 |
| 1841 | 0.3 | 1805 | 0.4 |
| **2** 0130 | 3.6 | **17** 0108 | 3.6 |
| 0655 | 0.2 | 0630 | 0.2 |
| TU 1412 | 3.2 | W 1324 | 3.3 |
| 1917 | 0.3 | 1843 | 0.3 |
| **3** 0206 | 3.6 | **18** 0147 | 3.6 |
| 0728 | 0.3 | 0708 | 0.2 |
| W 1442 | 3.2 | TH 1401 | 3.4 |
| 1951 | 0.4 | 1925 | 0.3 |
| **4** 0240 | 3.6 | **19** 0227 | 3.6 |
| 0802 | 0.4 | 0750 | 0.2 |
| TH 1512 | 3.2 | F 1439 | 3.5 |
| 2027 | 0.4 | 2009 | 0.3 |
| **5** 0314 | 3.5 | **20** 0308 | 3.6 |
| 0838 | 0.5 | 0837 | 0.4 |
| F 1544 | 3.2 | SA 1518 | 3.5 |
| 2104 | 0.6 | 2057 | 0.4 |
| **6** 0349 | 3.4 | **21** 0349 | 3.6 |
| 0915 | 0.7 | 0929 | 0.6 |
| SA 1619 | 3.1 | SU 1559 | 3.4 |
| 2146 | 0.7 | 2151 | 0.6 |
| **7** 0427 | 3.1 | **22** 0435 | 3.2 |
| 0957 | 0.9 | 1030 | 0.8 |
| SU 1700 | 3.0 | M 1644 | 3.2 |
| ◑ 2238 | 1.0 | ◑ 2255 | 0.8 |
| **8** 0511 | 2.9 | **23** 0533 | 2.9 |
| 1050 | 1.2 | 1152 | 1.1 |
| M 1748 | 2.8 | TU 1741 | 3.0 |
| 2356 | 1.2 | | |
| **9** 0607 | 2.6 | **24** 0029 | 1.0 |
| 1224 | 1.4 | 0729 | 2.7 |
| TU 1852 | 2.7 | W 1328 | 1.1 |
| | | 1913 | 2.9 |
| **10** 0153 | 1.2 | **25** 0208 | 0.9 |
| 0718 | 2.5 | 0928 | 2.8 |
| W 1416 | 1.3 | TH 1441 | 0.9 |
| 2034 | 2.8 | 2116 | 3.0 |
| **11** 0258 | 0.9 | **26** 0315 | 0.6 |
| 0927 | 2.6 | 1026 | 3.1 |
| TH 1514 | 1.1 | F 1537 | 0.7 |
| 2159 | 3.0 | 2217 | 3.3 |
| **12** 0345 | 0.7 | **27** 0404 | 0.3 |
| 1027 | 2.8 | 1111 | 3.2 |
| F 1556 | 0.9 | SA 1623 | 0.5 |
| 2245 | 3.2 | 2304 | 3.5 |
| **13** 0424 | 0.4 | **28** 0446 | 0.2 |
| 1107 | 3.0 | 1152 | 3.3 |
| SA 1631 | 0.7 | SU 1704 | 0.3 |
| 2322 | 3.3 | 2347 | 3.6 |
| **14** 0458 | 0.3 | **29** 0523 | 0.2 |
| 1143 | 3.1 | 1230 | 3.3 |
| SU 1702 | 0.6 | M 1742 | 0.3 |
| 2355 | 3.4 | ● | |
| **15** 0529 | 0.2 | **30** 0026 | 3.6 |
| 1215 | 3.2 | 0556 | 0.2 |
| M 1732 | 0.5 | TU 1305 | 3.3 |
| ○ | | 1816 | 0.3 |

### OCTOBER

| Time | m | Time | m |
|---|---|---|---|
| **1** 0103 | 3.6 | **16** 0044 | 3.6 |
| 0626 | 0.3 | 0605 | 0.2 |
| W 1335 | 3.3 | TH 1258 | 3.5 |
| 1847 | 0.4 | 1821 | 0.3 |
| **2** 0138 | 3.6 | **17** 0128 | 3.7 |
| 0656 | 0.4 | 0647 | 0.3 |
| TH 1404 | 3.4 | F 1338 | 3.6 |
| 1918 | 0.4 | 1906 | 0.4 |
| **3** 0211 | 3.5 | **18** 0212 | 3.7 |
| 0728 | 0.5 | 0734 | 0.4 |
| F 1435 | 3.4 | SA 1419 | 3.6 |
| 1952 | 0.5 | 1953 | 0.4 |
| **4** 0245 | 3.5 | **19** 0257 | 3.6 |
| 0802 | 0.6 | 0824 | 0.5 |
| SA 1508 | 3.4 | SU 1500 | 3.6 |
| 2029 | 0.6 | 2045 | 0.5 |
| **5** 0320 | 3.3 | **20** 0343 | 3.4 |
| 0839 | 0.8 | 0920 | 0.8 |
| SU 1543 | 3.3 | M 1543 | 3.5 |
| 2112 | 0.8 | 2143 | 0.6 |
| **6** 0359 | 3.2 | **21** 0435 | 3.1 |
| 0920 | 1.0 | 1024 | 1.0 |
| M 1622 | 3.2 | TU 1631 | 3.3 |
| 2203 | 1.0 | ◑ 2255 | 0.8 |
| **7** 0444 | 2.9 | **22** 0547 | 2.9 |
| 1010 | 1.3 | 1144 | 1.1 |
| TU 1709 | 3.0 | W 1733 | 3.1 |
| ◑ 2315 | 1.2 | | |
| **8** 0540 | 2.7 | **23** 0027 | 0.9 |
| 1124 | 1.5 | 0739 | 2.8 |
| W 1812 | 2.8 | TH 1307 | 1.1 |
| | | 1911 | 3.0 |
| **9** 0105 | 1.2 | **24** 0147 | 0.8 |
| 0650 | 2.6 | 0904 | 2.9 |
| TH 1321 | 1.5 | F 1416 | 1.0 |
| 1936 | 2.8 | 2047 | 3.1 |
| **10** 0217 | 1.0 | **25** 0249 | 0.6 |
| 0838 | 2.7 | 0959 | 3.1 |
| F 1433 | 1.3 | SA 1513 | 0.8 |
| 2110 | 3.0 | 2148 | 3.3 |
| **11** 0306 | 0.7 | **26** 0338 | 0.4 |
| 0949 | 2.9 | 1043 | 3.3 |
| SA 1519 | 1.0 | SU 1600 | 0.6 |
| 2202 | 3.2 | 2236 | 3.5 |
| **12** 0347 | 0.5 | **27** 0420 | 0.4 |
| 1033 | 3.1 | 1122 | 3.4 |
| SU 1556 | 0.8 | M 1642 | 0.5 |
| 2242 | 3.3 | 2319 | 3.5 |
| **13** 0422 | 0.3 | **28** 0457 | 0.4 |
| 1109 | 3.2 | 1158 | 3.4 |
| M 1630 | 0.6 | TU 1719 | 0.4 |
| 2321 | 3.5 | ● 2359 | 3.6 |
| **14** 0454 | 0.2 | **29** 0530 | 0.4 |
| 1143 | 3.3 | 1231 | 3.5 |
| TU 1704 | 0.5 | W 1753 | 0.5 |
| ○ | | | |
| **15** 0001 | 3.6 | **30** 0035 | 3.5 |
| 0528 | 0.2 | 0600 | 0.5 |
| W 1220 | 3.4 | TH 1302 | 3.5 |
| 1741 | 0.4 | 1823 | 0.5 |
| | | **31** 0110 | 3.5 |
| | | 0630 | 0.6 |
| | | F 1333 | 3.6 |
| | | 1854 | 0.6 |

### NOVEMBER

| Time | m | Time | m |
|---|---|---|---|
| **1** 0144 | 3.5 | **16** 0203 | 3.6 |
| 0702 | 0.7 | 0723 | 0.5 |
| SA 1405 | 3.6 | SU 1404 | 3.8 |
| 1928 | 0.6 | 1943 | 0.4 |
| **2** 0220 | 3.4 | **17** 0253 | 3.5 |
| 0738 | 0.8 | 0816 | 0.6 |
| SU 1439 | 3.6 | M 1448 | 3.7 |
| 2007 | 0.7 | 2038 | 0.5 |
| **3** 0257 | 3.3 | **18** 0345 | 3.4 |
| 0817 | 0.9 | 0912 | 0.8 |
| M 1514 | 3.5 | TU 1534 | 3.7 |
| 2050 | 0.8 | 2137 | 0.6 |
| **4** 0337 | 3.2 | **19** 0442 | 3.2 |
| 0900 | 1.0 | 1013 | 0.9 |
| TU 1552 | 3.3 | W 1625 | 3.5 |
| 2140 | 0.9 | ◐ 2245 | 0.7 |
| **5** 0422 | 3.0 | **20** 0551 | 3.0 |
| 0949 | 1.2 | 1119 | 1.0 |
| W 1637 | 3.1 | TH 1727 | 3.3 |
| 2241 | 1.1 | | |
| **6** 0515 | 2.9 | **21** 0000 | 0.7 |
| 1048 | 1.4 | 0707 | 2.9 |
| TH 1734 | 3.0 | F 1231 | 1.1 |
| ◐ | | 1842 | 3.2 |
| **7** 0000 | 1.1 | **22** 0111 | 0.7 |
| 0618 | 2.8 | 0818 | 3.0 |
| F 1205 | 1.4 | SA 1339 | 1.0 |
| 1842 | 2.9 | 2001 | 3.2 |
| **8** 0116 | 1.0 | **23** 0213 | 0.7 |
| 0734 | 2.8 | 0917 | 3.1 |
| SA 1325 | 1.4 | SU 1440 | 0.9 |
| 1959 | 3.0 | 2108 | 3.3 |
| **9** 0215 | 0.8 | **24** 0305 | 0.6 |
| 0852 | 3.0 | 1006 | 3.2 |
| SU 1427 | 1.2 | M 1532 | 0.8 |
| 2107 | 3.2 | 2203 | 3.3 |
| **10** 0302 | 0.6 | **25** 0350 | 0.6 |
| 0948 | 3.1 | 1049 | 3.3 |
| M 1515 | 0.9 | TU 1617 | 0.6 |
| 2200 | 3.3 | 2250 | 3.4 |
| **11** 0343 | 0.4 | **26** 0431 | 0.6 |
| 1032 | 3.3 | 1128 | 3.4 |
| TU 1558 | 0.7 | W 1658 | 0.6 |
| 2247 | 3.5 | 2332 | 3.4 |
| **12** 0422 | 0.3 | **27** 0507 | 0.7 |
| 1113 | 3.4 | 1204 | 3.5 |
| W 1639 | 0.5 | TH 1734 | 0.7 |
| 2335 | 3.6 | ● | |
| **13** 0503 | 0.2 | **28** 0011 | 3.4 |
| 1154 | 3.5 | 0540 | 0.7 |
| TH 1721 | 0.4 | F 1238 | 3.6 |
| ○ | | 1807 | 0.6 |
| **14** 0023 | 3.6 | **29** 0048 | 3.3 |
| 0546 | 0.3 | 0612 | 0.8 |
| F 1237 | 3.6 | SA 1311 | 3.6 |
| 1805 | 0.3 | 1840 | 0.6 |
| **15** 0113 | 3.6 | **30** 0124 | 3.3 |
| 0632 | 0.4 | 0646 | 0.8 |
| SA 1321 | 3.7 | SU 1344 | 3.7 |
| 1852 | 0.3 | 1915 | 0.7 |

### DECEMBER

| Time | m | Time | m |
|---|---|---|---|
| **1** 0201 | 3.3 | **16** 0252 | 3.4 |
| 0723 | 0.8 | 0805 | 0.5 |
| M 1418 | 3.6 | TU 1441 | 3.8 |
| 1952 | 0.7 | 2027 | 0.3 |
| **2** 0239 | 3.3 | **17** 0343 | 3.4 |
| 0802 | 0.9 | 0857 | 0.6 |
| TU 1453 | 3.6 | W 1527 | 3.8 |
| 2033 | 0.7 | 2120 | 0.4 |
| **3** 0319 | 3.2 | **18** 0435 | 3.3 |
| 0843 | 0.9 | 0949 | 0.7 |
| W 1530 | 3.5 | TH 1615 | 3.7 |
| 2117 | 0.8 | 2217 | 0.5 |
| **4** 0402 | 3.1 | **19** 0527 | 3.1 |
| 0928 | 1.0 | 1045 | 0.8 |
| TH 1611 | 3.3 | F 1707 | 3.5 |
| 2207 | 0.9 | ◐ 2318 | 0.6 |
| **5** 0449 | 3.0 | **20** 0620 | 3.0 |
| 1017 | 1.1 | 1146 | 0.9 |
| F 1659 | 3.2 | SA 1802 | 3.3 |
| ◐ 2304 | 0.9 | | |
| **6** 0541 | 2.9 | **21** 0024 | 0.7 |
| 1114 | 1.2 | 0716 | 3.0 |
| SA 1756 | 3.1 | SU 1254 | 1.0 |
| | | 1903 | 3.2 |
| **7** 0008 | 0.9 | **22** 0129 | 0.8 |
| 0639 | 2.9 | 0818 | 2.9 |
| SU 1220 | 1.3 | M 1402 | 1.0 |
| 1901 | 3.1 | 2011 | 3.1 |
| **8** 0113 | 0.8 | **23** 0228 | 0.9 |
| 0744 | 3.0 | 0920 | 3.0 |
| M 1329 | 1.2 | TU 1502 | 0.9 |
| 2012 | 3.1 | 2122 | 3.1 |
| **9** 0213 | 0.7 | **24** 0321 | 0.9 |
| 0854 | 3.1 | 1016 | 3.2 |
| TU 1433 | 1.0 | W 1555 | 0.8 |
| 2119 | 3.2 | 2223 | 3.1 |
| **10** 0306 | 0.5 | **25** 0407 | 0.8 |
| 0954 | 3.2 | 1104 | 3.3 |
| W 1528 | 0.8 | TH 1640 | 0.7 |
| 2220 | 3.4 | 2313 | 3.1 |
| **11** 0356 | 0.4 | **26** 0449 | 0.8 |
| 1046 | 3.4 | 1145 | 3.5 |
| TH 1618 | 0.6 | F 1720 | 0.6 |
| 2316 | 3.4 | 2357 | 3.2 |
| **12** 0444 | 0.4 | **27** 0527 | 0.8 |
| 1135 | 3.5 | 1222 | 3.5 |
| F 1706 | 0.5 | SA 1757 | 0.6 |
| ○ | | ● | |
| **13** 0010 | 3.5 | **28** 0035 | 3.2 |
| 0531 | 0.4 | 0602 | 0.8 |
| SA 1222 | 3.6 | SU 1257 | 3.6 |
| 1754 | 0.3 | 1831 | 0.6 |
| **14** 0105 | 3.5 | **29** 0112 | 3.2 |
| 0621 | 0.4 | 0635 | 0.8 |
| SU 1308 | 3.7 | M 1329 | 3.6 |
| 1843 | 0.3 | 1904 | 0.6 |
| **15** 0159 | 3.5 | **30** 0148 | 3.2 |
| 0713 | 0.5 | 0708 | 0.8 |
| M 1355 | 3.8 | TU 1401 | 3.6 |
| 1934 | 0.3 | 1937 | 0.6 |
| | | **31** 0225 | 3.2 |
| | | 0744 | 0.8 |
| | | W 1435 | 3.6 |
| | | 2012 | 0.6 |

SW Scotland

Chart Datum: 1·62 metres below Ordnance Datum (Newlyn). HAT is 4·0 metres above Chart Datum.

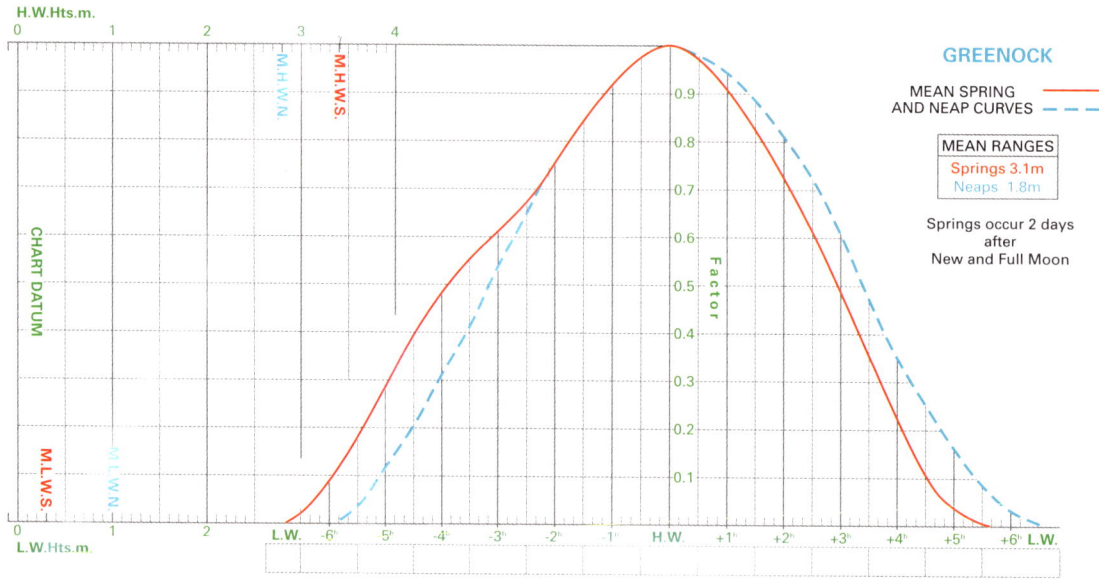

GREENOCK

MEAN SPRING
AND NEAP CURVES -----

MEAN RANGES
Springs 3.1m
Neaps 1.8m

Springs occur 2 days after
New and Full Moon

## 2.21 ARDROSSAN

N Ayrshire **55°38'·50N 04°49'·61W** ✿✿✿🛥🛥🛥⚓✿

**CHARTS** AC *5610, 2126,* 2221, *2491, 1866;* Imray C63; OS 63/70

**TIDES** +0055 Dover; ML 1·9; Duration 0630

**Standard Port GREENOCK (←—)**

| Times | | | | Height (metres) | | | |
|---|---|---|---|---|---|---|---|
| High Water | | Low Water | | MHWS | MHWN | MLWN | MLWS |
| 0000 | 0600 | 0000 | 0600 | 3·4 | 2·8 | 1·0 | 0·3 |
| 1200 | 1800 | 1200 | 1800 | | | | |
| **Differences ARDROSSAN** | | | | | | | |
| −0020 | −0010 | −0010 | −0010 | −0·2 | −0·2 | +0·1 | +0·1 |
| **IRVINE** | | | | | | | |
| −0020 | −0020 | −0030 | −0010 | −0·3 | −0·3 | −0·1 | 0·0 |

**SHELTER** Good in marina (formerly Eglinton Dock), access at all tides over sill, 5·2m least depth. A storm gate is fitted; max acceptable beam is 8·6m (28ft). Strong SW/NW winds cause heavy seas in the apprs and the hbr may be closed in SW gales. Ferries berth on both sides of Winton Pier.

**NAVIGATION** WPT 55°38'·13N 04°50'·55W, 055°/0·65M to hbr ent. From the W/NW keep clear of low-lying Horse Isle (conspic W tower on its S end) ringed by drying ledges. The passage between Horse Isle and the mainland is obstructed by unmarked drying rks and should not be attempted. Be aware of following dangers: From the S/SE, Eagle Rk 3ca S of hbr ent, marked by SHM buoy, Fl G 5s. 3ca SE of Eagle Rk lies unmarked Campbell Rk (0·2m). W Crinan Rk (1·1m) is 300m W of hbr ent, marked by PHM buoy, Fl R 4s.

**LIGHTS AND MARKS** Dir lt WRG 15m W14M, R/G11M (see 2.3); W sector leads 055° to hbr ent between lt ho and detached bkwtr. Lt ho Iso WG 4s 11m 9M, 317°-G-035°, W elsewhere. On S end of detached bkwtr, Fl R 5s 7m 5M.

**Traffic Signals,** shown H24 from control twr at ent to marina:

3 F 🔴 lts (vert) = hbr and marina closed; no entry/exit for commercial and pleasure vessels.

3 F 🟢 lts (vert) = marina open, hbr closed; pleasure craft may enter/exit the marina, no commercial movements.

2 F 🔴 lts over 1 F 🟢 = hbr open, marina closed; in severe weather marina storm gate is closed. Commercial vessels may enter/exit hbr, subject to approval by Hbr Control on VHF. Pleasure craft must clear the approach channel, ferry turning area (between the detached bkwtr and Winton Pier) and the outer basin. Yachts may not manoeuvre under sail alone until seaward of the outer breakwater.

**R/T** *Clyde Marina* VHF Ch **80** M. *Hbr Control* Ch 12 14 16 (H24).

**TELEPHONE** (Code 01294) Marina 607077, 🖷 607076, www.clydemarina.com; Ardrossan Hbr 469468, 🖷 601289; MRCC (01475) 729988; Marinecall 09068 969652; Police 404500; Dr 463011.

**FACILITIES** Clyde Marina (250 inc 50 Ⓥ) £2·15, short stay £10<4hrs, access H24, Marina Office hrs 0900-1800, Wi-fi, D, ME, El, Ⓔ, CH, BH (50 ton). **Town** 🍴, R, Bar, 🗔, Gas, ✉, Ⓑ, Wi-fi. 🚆, ✈ (Prestwick/Glasgow). Ferry to Brodick (Arran).

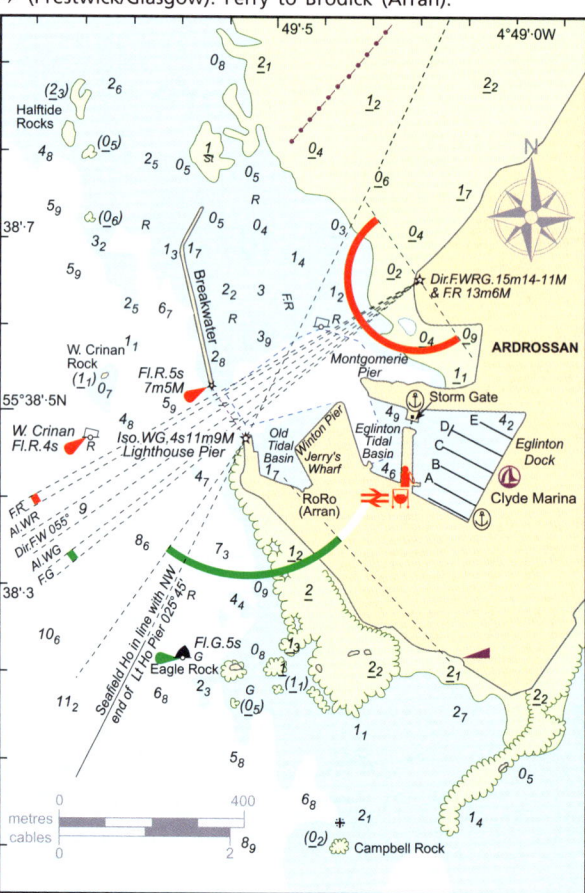

## HARBOUR BETWEEN ARDROSSAN AND TROON

**IRVINE**, N Ayrshire, 55°36′·17N 04°42′·07W. AC *2126*, 2220, 1866. HW +0055 on Dover. Tides: see 2.21.

- Do not attempt ent in heavy onshore weather.
- Good shelter once across the bar (0·5m CD); access approx HW ±3½ for 1·4m draft.

The IB-B SPM buoy, Fl Y 3s, is 1·15M from hbr ent, close NW of ldg line. 5 blocks of flats and chys are conspic ENE of ent. Ldg lts 051°: front, FG 10m 5M; rear, FR 15m 5M. The ent groynes have bns, Fl R 3s and Fl G 3s; groynes inside the ent have unlit perches. White Pilot tr with mast is conspic 3ca inside ent. Visitors' pontoons on N side or on S side at visitors' quay (2·2m). ⚓ prohib. VHF Ch 12 (0800-1600 Tues and Thurs; 0800-1300 Wed). HM ☎ (01294) 487286, 🖷 487111. Berths available above opening footbridge which opens at 5 mins notice ☎ 08708 403123 or VHF Ch 12 (call *Irvine Bridge*). Facilities: **Quay** AB < 5m £4, >5m <10m £6, >10m <15m £9, FW, Slip, C (3 ton), Showers, SM. **Town** P & D (cans, 1·5km), Gas, 🛒, R, ⇌, ✈ (Prestwick).

## 2.22 TROON

S Ayrshire 55°33′·10N 04°40′·97W ✳✳✳🌿🌿🌿❀❀

**CHARTS** AC *5610, 2126, 2220, 1866*; Imray C63; OS 70

**TIDES** +0050 Dover; ML 1·9; Duration 0630

**Standard Port GREENOCK (←—)**

| Times | | | | Height (metres) | | | |
|---|---|---|---|---|---|---|---|
| High Water | | Low Water | | MHWS | MHWN | MLWN | MLWS |
| 0000 | 0600 | 0000 | 0600 | 3·4 | 2·8 | 1·0 | 0·3 |
| 1200 | 1800 | 1200 | 1800 | | | | |
| **Differences TROON** | | | | | | | |
| −0025 | −0025 | −0020 | −0020 | −0·2 | −0·2 | 0·0 | 0·0 |
| **AYR** | | | | | | | |
| −0025 | −0025 | −0030 | −0015 | −0·4 | −0·3 | +0·1 | +0·1 |
| **GIRVAN** | | | | | | | |
| −0025 | −0040 | −0035 | −0010 | −0·3 | −0·3 | −0·1 | 0·0 |
| **LOCH RYAN (Stranraer)** | | | | | | | |
| −0030 | −0025 | −0010 | −0010 | −0·2 | −0·1 | 0·0 | +0·1 |

**SHELTER** Complete in marina (2·4m at ent, 1·6m at SE end); speed limit 5kn. *Strong SW/NW winds cause heavy seas in the apprs to hbr.*

**NAVIGATION** WPT 55°33′·20N 04°42′·00W, 103°/0·6M to W pier lt. Appr in sector SW to NW. Beware Lady Isle, Fl (4) 30s 19m 8M, W bn, 2·2M SW; Troon Rock (5·6m, occas breaks) 1·1M W; Lappock Rock (0·6m, bn with G barrel topmark) 1·6M NNW; Mill Rock (0·4m) ½M NNE of hbr ent, marked by unlit PHM buoy.

**LIGHTS AND MARKS** No ldg lts. Sheds (35m) at Ailsa Shipyard are conspic and floodlit at night. Traffic signals VQ.Y. occas when Fast Ferries arriving/departing. 14m SE of W pier hd lt, Fl (2) WG 5s, there is a floodlit dolphin, W with dayglow patches. A SHM lt buoy, FG, marks the chan in the ent to marina.

**R/T** HM Ch 14. Marina Ch 80 M (H24).

**TELEPHONE** (Code 01292) HM 281687, 🖷 287787; Troon CC 311865; Troon YC 316770. MRCC (01475) 729988; Marinecall 09068 969652; Police 313100; Dr 313593; Ⓗ 610555 (Ayr).

**FACILITIES Troon Yacht Haven** (300+50 Ⓥ), £1.93, access all tides. ☎ 315553, 🖷 312836, www.yachthavens.com Ⓥ berths on pontoon A, first to stbd. AB for LOA 36m x 3m draft at hammerheads. Wi-fi, D (H24), ME, El, Ⓔ, CH, ✗, SM (daily pick-up), BH (50 ton), C (20 ton), Slip, 🛒, R ☎ 311523, Bar, ▣, Gas, Gaz. **Town** ✉, Ⓑ, ⇌, ✈ (Prestwick/Glasgow). Fast RoRo ferry to Belfast.

## HARBOURS ON THE FIRTH OF CLYDE SOUTH OF TROON

**AYR**, S Ayrshire, 55°28′·22N 04°38′·78W. AC *5610, 2126, 2220, 1866*. HW +0050 on Dover; ML 1·8m. Duration 0630. See 2.22. After heavy rains large amounts of debris may be washed down the R Ayr. From the W, hbr ent lies between conspic gasholder to the N and townhall spire to the S. Outer St Nicholas SHM buoy, Fl G 2s, warns of shoals and Rk (0·8m) 150m S of ent. Ldg lts 098°: front, by Pilot Stn, FR 10m 5M R tr, also tfc sigs; rear (130m from front), Oc R 10s 18m 9M. N bkwtr hd, QR 9m 5M. S pier hd, Q 7M 7M, vis 012°-161°, and FG 5m 5M, same structure, vis 012°-082°, over St Nicholas Rk. Tfc sigs (near front ldg lt): 2 ● (vert) = hbr closed to incoming traffic. HM ☎ (01292) 281687; VHF Ch 14 16.

**Ayr Y & CC** at S dock, limited AB on pontoon on N side of hbr (access key, £10 deposit) from Ship Inn), M. **Services:** ✗, ME, El, CH. **Town** Ⓑ, Bar, Gas, P & D, FW, ✉, R, ⇌, 🛒.

**GIRVAN**, S Ayrshire, 55°14′·77N 04°51′·87W. AC 2199, 1866. HW +0043 on Dover; ML 1·8m; Duration 0630. See 2.22. Good shelter at inner hbr for 16 yachts on 60m pontoon (1·7m) beyond LB. Coasters and FVs berth on adjacent quay. No access LW±2 over bar 1·5m. Beware Girvan Patch, 1·7m, 4ca SW of ent, and Brest Rks, 3·5M N of hbr extending 6ca offshore. Ch spire (conspic) brg 104° leads between N bkwtr, Fl (2) R 6s 7m 4M, and S pier, 2 FG (vert) 8m 4M. Inner N groyne, Iso 4s 3m 4M. Tfc sigs at root of S pier: 2 B discs (hor), at night 2 ● (hor) = hbr shut. VHF Ch 12 16 (HO). HM ☎ (01465) 713648; FW, Slip. **Town** Ⓑ, ✉, 🛒, R, ⇌, P & D (cans).

## ANCHORAGES WITHIN LOCH RYAN

**LOCH RYAN**, Dumfries and Galloway, 55°01′N 05°05′W. AC 2198, 1403. HW (Stranraer) +0055 on Dover; ML 1·6m; Duration 0640. See tides 2.22. See adjacent chartlet. Very good shelter except in strong NW winds. Ent between Milleur Pt and Finnarts Pt. ⚓s in Lady Bay, 1·3M SSE of Milleur Pt, but exposed to heavy wash from HSS; in The Wig in 3m (avoid weed patches); or off Stranraer 3ca NW of W pier hd. Larger yachts berth on NE side of E pier, by arrangement with

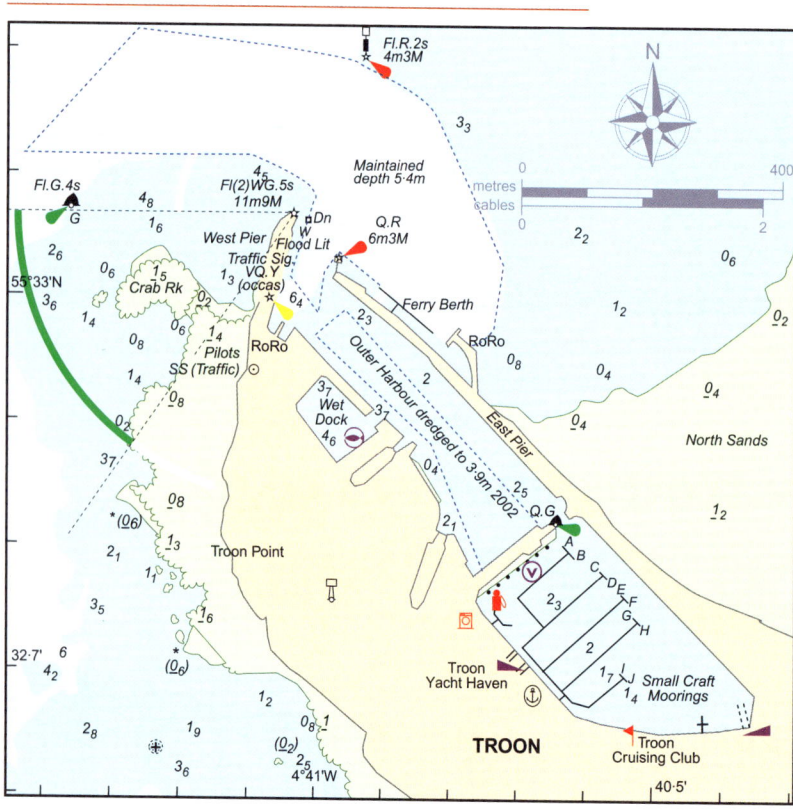

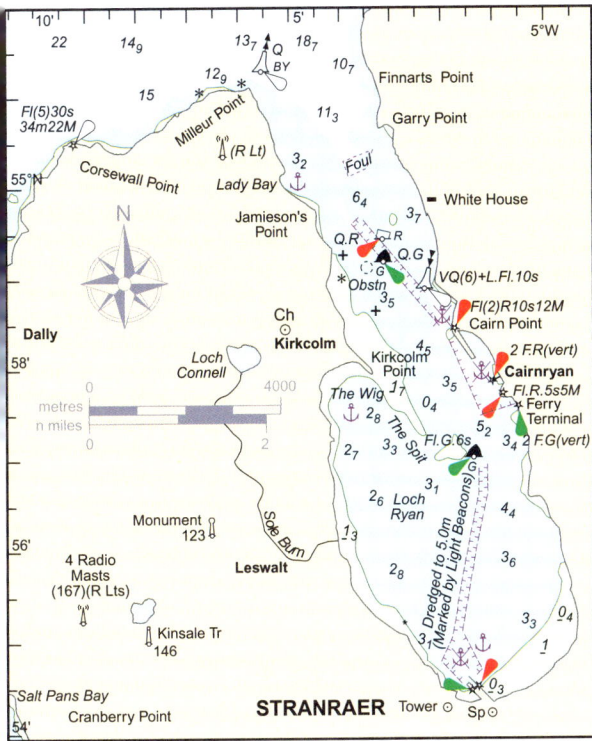

HM, VHF Ch **14** (H24) or ☎ (01776) 702460. Beware The Beef Barrel, rk 1m high 6ca SSE of Milleur Pt; the sand spit running 1·5M to SE from W shore opposite Cairn Pt lt ho Fl (2) R10s 14m 12M. Lt at Cairnryan ferry terminal Fl R 5s 5m 5M. Lts at Stranraer: centre pier hd 2FBu (vert), E pier hd 2FR (vert), W pier hd 2 FG (vert) 8m 4M. Facilities (Stranraer): Ⓑ, Bar, D, FW, P, ✉, R, ⇌, 🛒.

## HARBOURS FROM MULL OF GALLOWAY TO WIGTOWN BAY

**DRUMMORE,** Dumfries and Galloway, **54°41'·57N 04°53'·49W.** AC 2094. HW +0040m on Dover; ML 3.3m; Duration 0610. Recently acquired from MOD by Drummore Hbr Trust ☎ 01557 330337. Good shelter from all conditions in small drying harbour convenient for awaiting weather/tidal conditions for rounding Mull of Galloway westbound. Temp'y ⚓ 5.5ca NNE of hbr ent in 4m. Access HW ±0245; approach entrance heading 140° from 1ca off. Depth in hbr varies due to silting but suitable for craft of <1.3m draft. Berth on pier (fender board required with fenders). Facilities FW, Slip, P (cans), Gas, 🛒, R, Bar, ✉, ⇌ (bus to Stranraer), ✈ (Carlisle).

**ISLE OF WHITHORN,** Dumfries and Galloway, **54°41'·91N 04°21'·88W.** AC 1826, 2094. HW +0035 on Dover; ML 3.7m; Duration 0545. See 2.24. Shelter good but hbr dries, having approx 2·5m at HW±3. On W side of ent beware the Skerries ledge. St Ninian's Tr (Fl WR 3s 20m 6/4M viz: 310°-W-005°-R-040°; W ☐ tr) is conspic at E side of ent. E pier hd has QG 4m 5M; ldg lts 335°, both Oc R 8s 7/9m 7M, synch, Or masts and ◇. HM ☎ (01988) 500468, www.isleofwhithorn.com; Facilities: AB on quay £4.83/yacht, 2 Slips (launching £1.00), P, D (by arrangement with HM), FW, ME, ⚒, CH, 🛒, Bar, ✉, VHF Ch08 (occas).

**GARLIESTON,** Dumfries and Galloway, **54°47'·36N 04°21'·83W.** AC 1826, 2094. HW +0035 on Dover; ML no data; Duration 0545. See 2.24. Hbr affords complete shelter but dries. Access (2m) HW±3. Pier hd lt 2FR (vert) 5m 3M. Beware rky outcrops in W side of bay marked by a perch. HM ☎ (01988) 600295, Mobile 07734 073422. Facilities: M £3, FW, AC on quay, Slip. **Town:** 🛒, ME, P, D. ⚓s NE or W of Hestan Is to await tide. VHF: Ch M call Kippford Startline (YC) HW±2 in season. Ch 16 Kippford Slipway (Pilotage). Facilities: **Solway YC** (01556) 600221, www.thesyc.com; AB, ⟲, FW, M; **Services:** AB £6, M, Slip, D (cans), CH, Gaz, BY Kippford Slipway Ltd(01556) 620249, ME. **Town** P, SM, 🛒, ✉, Bar, Slip.

## 2.23 PORTPATRICK

Dumfries and Galloway 54°50'·42N 05°07'·18W ✿✿✿⚓⚓⚓❀❀

**CHARTS** AC 2724, 2198; Imray C62; OS 82

**TIDES** +0032 Dover; ML 2·1; Duration 0615

**Standard Port LIVERPOOL (→)**

| Times | | | | Heights (metres) | | | |
|---|---|---|---|---|---|---|---|
| High Water | | Low Water | | MHWS | MHWN | MLWN | MLWS |
| 0000 | 0600 | 0200 | 0800 | 9·3 | 7·4 | 2·9 | 0·9 |
| 1200 | 1800 | 1400 | 2000 | | | | |
| Differences PORTPATRICK | | | | | | | |
| +0018 | +0026 | 0000 | –0035 | –5·5 | –4·4 | –2·0 | –0·6 |

**SHELTER** Good in tiny Inner hbr, but ent is difficult in strong SW/NW winds.

**NAVIGATION** WPT 54°50'·00N 05°08'·07W, 055°/0·7M to ent. Ent to outer hbr by short narrow chan with hazards either side, including rky shelf covered at HW. Beware cross tides off ent, up to 3kn springs. Barrel buoy (a mooring buoy) marks end of Half Tide Rk; do not cut inside.

**LIGHTS AND MARKS** Ldg lts 050°, FG (H24) 6/8m: Front on sea wall; rear on bldg; 2 vert orange stripes by day. Conspic features include: TV mast 1M NE, almost on ldg line; large hotel on cliffs about 1½ca NNW of hbr ent; Dunskey Castle (ru) 4ca SE of hbr.

**R/T** None.

**TELEPHONE** (Code 01776) HM 810355; MRCC (01475) 729988; Marinecall 09068 969652; Police 702112; Ⓗ 702323.

**FACILITIES** **Hbr** Slip (small craft), AB £9, M, FW, L. **Village** P (cans), D (bulk tanker), Gas, 🛒, R, Bar, ✉, Ⓑ (Stranraer), ⇌ (bus to Stranraer), ✈ (Prestwick).

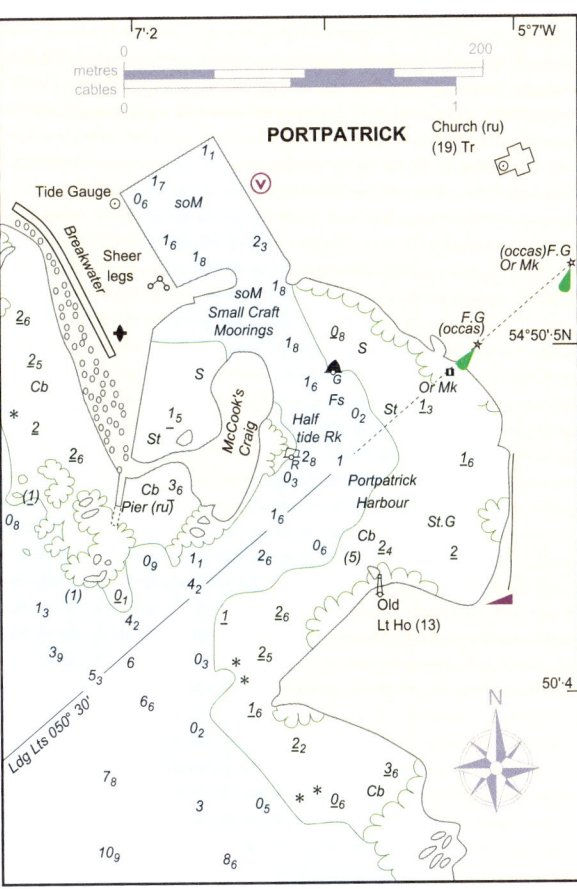

## 2.24  KIRKCUDBRIGHT

Dumfries and Galloway **54°50'·33N 04°03'·47W** ✿✿⚓⚓⚓

**CHARTS**  AC *1826,* 2094, 1346, 1344; Imray C62; OS 84

**TIDES**  +0030 Dover; ML 4·1; Duration 0545

**Standard Port LIVERPOOL** (3.16) (→)

| Times | | | | Height (metres) | | | |
|---|---|---|---|---|---|---|---|
| High Water | | Low Water | | MHWS | MHWN | MLWN | MLWS |
| 0000 | 0600 | 0200 | 0800 | 9·3 | 7·4 | 2·9 | 0·9 |
| 1200 | 1800 | 1400 | 2000 | | | | |
| **Differences KIRKCUDBRIGHT BAY** | | | | | | | |
| +0015 | +0015 | +0010 | 0000 | −1·8 | −1·5 | −0·5 | −0·1 |
| **DRUMMORE** | | | | | | | |
| +0030 | +0040 | +0015 | +0020 | −3·4 | −2·5 | −0·9 | −0·3 |
| **PORT WILLIAM** | | | | | | | |
| +0030 | +0030 | +0025 | 0000 | −2·9 | −2·2 | −0·8 | No data |
| **GARLIESTON** | | | | | | | |
| +0025 | +0035 | +0030 | +0005 | −2·3 | −1·7 | −0·5 | No data |
| **ISLE OF WHITHORN** | | | | | | | |
| +0020 | +0025 | +0025 | +0005 | −2·4 | −2·0 | −0·8 | −0·2 |
| **HESTAN ISLET** (Kippford) | | | | | | | |
| +0025 | +0025 | +0020 | +0025 | −1·0 | −1·1 | −0·5 | 0·0 |
| **SOUTHERNESS POINT** | | | | | | | |
| +0030 | +0030 | +0030 | +0010 | −0·7 | −0·7 | No data | |
| **ANNAN WATERFOOT** | | | | | | | |
| +0050 | +0105 | +0220 | +0310 | −2·2 | −2·6 | −2·7 | * |
| **TORDUFF POINT** | | | | | | | |
| +0105 | +0140 | +0520 | +0410 | −4·1 | −4·9 | *Not below CD | |
| **REDKIRK** | | | | | | | |
| +0110 | +0215 | +0715 | +0445 | −5·5 | −6·2 | *Not below CD | |

NOTES: At Annan Waterfoot, Torduff Pt and Redkirk the LW time differences are for the start of the rise, which at sp is very sudden. *At LW the tide does not usually fall below CD.

**SHELTER**  Very good. Depths at LW: 1·0–2·0m at the floating pontoon, visitors should always berth/raft on N side of it. Craft drawing 2·0–3·0m, drying moorings, and drying out against Town Quay (not advised as used H24 by many FVs) by advance arrangement with HM. Down-river there are good ⚓s close W, N, and NE of Little Ross and ½ca N of Torrs Pt, except in S'lies which raise heavy swell.

**NAVIGATION**  WPT 54°45'·51N 04°04'·08W, 005°/1·4M to Torrs Pt. The Bar is 1ca N of Torrs Pt; access HW±2½. R Dee has depths of 0·1m to 4·3m. Spring tides run up to 3–4kn. A firing range straddles the ent but no restrictions on transit of firing area; call Range Safety Officer ☎ (01557) 500271 (out of hours), 830236 office hours) or VHF 73 Range Safety Craf Gallavidian on Ch 16.

**LIGHTS AND MARKS**  Little Ross Lt ho, W of ent, Fl 5s 50m 12M, NNE end of Is, Stone bcn Fl (2) 5s 21m 5M. No 1 lt bn, Fl 3s 7m 3M, on LB shed (54°47'·70N). River is well lit/buoyed, Fl G lts at the marina.

**R/T**  Ch 12 (0730-1700). *Range Control* Ch 16 73.

**TELEPHONE** (Code 01557) HM ☎/📠 331135 Mobile 07709 479663; MRCC 0151-931 3341; Marinecall 09068 969652; Police 330600; Dr 330755; GM Marine Services (Fuel) 07970 109814.

**FACILITIES**  **Pontoon/jetty** £1.40 inc showers & 🚿, FW; **Town Quay** P (hose), D (stictly by arrangement with HM), FW, El, C (15 ton) CH, ME. **KYC** ☎ 330963; **SC** ☎ 330032, Slip, M, FW; **Town** 🛒, R, Bar, ✉, Ⓑ, ⊨ (Dumfries 30M), ✈ (Glasgow 100M).

### HARBOUR IN THE SOLWAY FIRTH APPROACHES

**KIPPFORD**, Dumfries and Galloway, **54°52'·36N 03°48'·93W**. AC *1826*, 1346. HW +0040 on Dover; ML 4·2m (Hestan Is). See 2.24. Good shelter on drying moorings/pontoons off Kippford, 2·75M up drying Urr Estuary from Hestan Is lt ho Fl (2) 10s 42m 9M. Access HW±2 via marked, unlit chan. *Clyde Cruising Club* or *Solway Sailing Directions* (from Solway YC) are strongly advised. Beware Craig Roan on E side of ent. Temp ⚓s NE or W of Hestan Is to await tide. VHF: Ch M call *Kippford Startline* (YC) HW±2 in season. Ch 16 *Kippford Slipway* (Pilotage). Facilities: **Solway YC** (01556) 600221, www.thesyc.com; AB, 🚿, FW, M; **Services:** AB £6, M, Slip, D (cans), CH, Gaz, BY *Kippford Slipway Ltd*(01556) 620249, ME. **Town** P, SM, 🛒, ✉, Bar, Slip.

# Adlard Coles Nautical
## THE BEST SAILING BOOKS

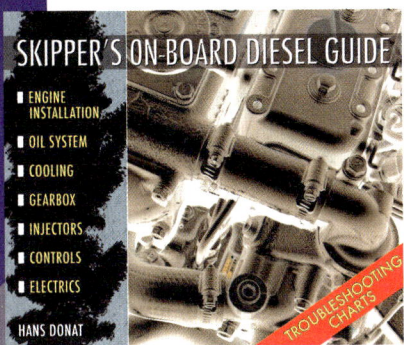

**Skipper's Onboard Diesel Guide**
*Hans Donat*
9 780713 676181
**£9.99**

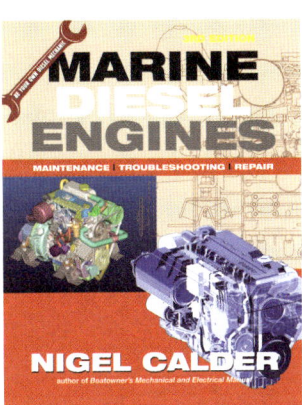

**Marine Diesel Engines**
*Nigel Calder*
9 780713 682663
**£24.99**

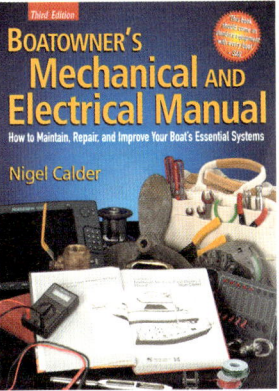

**Boatowner's Mechanical and Electrical Manual**
*Nigel Calder*
9 780713 672268
**£45.00**

# Practical Books from
# Adlard Coles Nautical

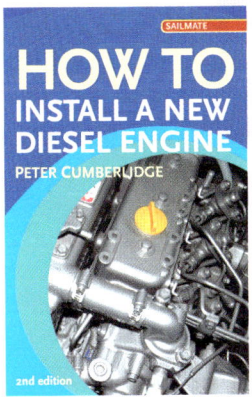

**How to install a new Diesel Engine**
*Peter Cumberlidge*
9 780713 675801
**£10.99**

**The Adlard Coles Book of Diesel Engines**
*Tim Bartlett*
9 780713 674022
**£12.99**

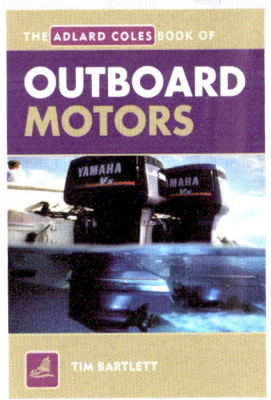

**The Adlard Coles Book of Outboard Motors**
*Tim Bartlett*
9 780713 675757
**£12.99**

**TO ORDER**

Available from chandlers & bookshops or order direct from:
MDL, Brunel Road, Houndmills, Basingstoke RG21 6XS
Tel: **01256 302699** email: **direct@macmillan.co.uk** or **www.adlardcoles.com**

# Predict the unpredictable

**Our localised, six-hour Met Office forecasts are updated hourly. So you never have to resort to plan B. Stick to plan A. Marinecall 0871 200 3985**

| COASTAL/INSHORE AREA | 5-DAY BY PHONE 09068 969 + area no | 2-DAY BY FAX 09065 222 + area no |
|---|---|---|
| National Inshore Waters (3-5 day forecast) | 640 | 340 |
| Scotland North | 641 | 341 |
| Scotland East | 642 | 342 |
| North East | 643 | 343 |
| East | 644 | 344 |
| Anglia | 645 | 345 |
| Channel East | 646 | 346 |
| Mid Channel | 647 | 347 |
| South West | 648 | 348 |
| Bristol | 649 | 349 |
| Wales | 650 | 350 |
| North West | 651 | 351 |
| Clyde | 652 | 352 |
| Caledonia | 653 | 353 |
| Minch | 654 | 354 |
| Northern Ireland | 655 | 355 |
| Channel Islands | 656 | - |

| OFFSHORE AREA | 2-5 DAY BY PHONE 09068 969 + area no | 2-5 DAY BY FAX 09065 222 + area no |
|---|---|---|
| English Channel | 657 | 357 |
| Southern North Sea | 658 | 358 |
| Irish Sea | 659 | 359 |
| Biscay | 660 | 360 |
| North West Scotland | 661 | 361 |
| Northern North Sea | 662 | 362 |
| Index page to all fax products | – | 09068 24 66 80 |

**Marinecall by SMS**

Have today's weather delivered direct to your mobile. Text at any time for the latest forecast. Your choice of forecast received daily by 9am. Each text contains a forecast for now, and 6-hours ahead. Create a TEXT MESSAGE. Type AC plus the NAME of the INSHORE/COASTAL LOCATION you require. By Subscription follow the above, but type AC SUB, plus the location. Send all messages to 83141.

**Buy the latest Marinecall forecasts online at www.marinecall.co.uk**

### don't guess
### ⊙ marinecall

2008/NC27/d

# West England, IoM & Wales

## Solway Firth to Land's End

W England, IoM, Wales

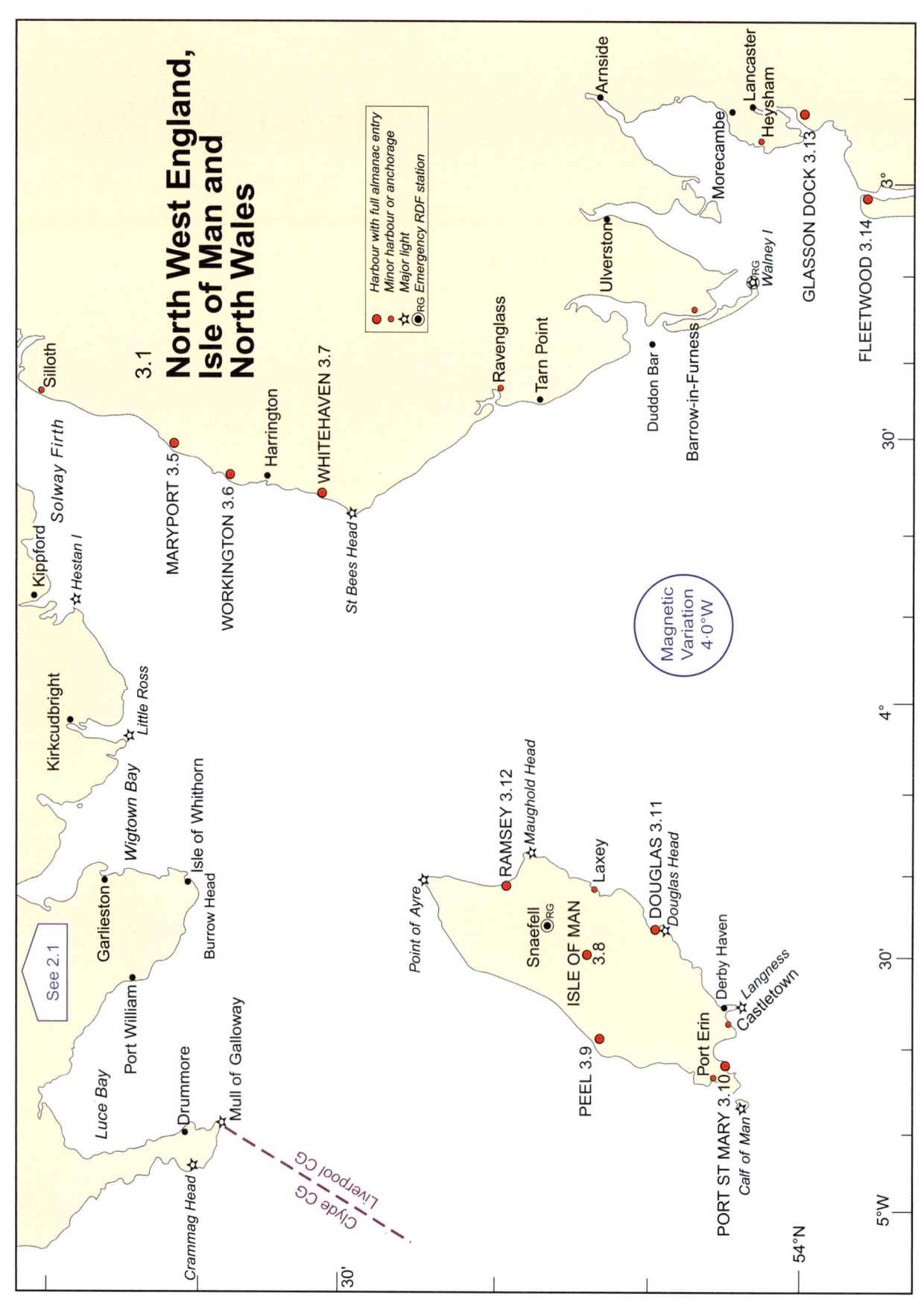

3.1

# North West England, Isle of Man and North Wales

Harbour with full almanac entry
Minor harbour or anchorage
Major light
RG Emergency RDF station

Silloth

Solway Firth

Kippford

Hestan I

MARYPORT 3.5

Harrington

WORKINGTON 3.6

WHITEHAVEN 3.7

St Bees Head

Kirkcudbright

Little Ross

Wigtown Bay

Isle of Whithorn

Garlieston

Burrow Head

See 2.1

Port William

Luce Bay

Drummore

Mull of Galloway

Crammag Head

Clyde CG
Liverpool CG

Ravenglass

Tarn Point

Duddon Bar

Barrow-in-Furness

Ulverston

RG
Walney I

Arnside

Morecambe

Lancaster

Heysham

GLASSON DOCK 3.13

FLEETWOOD 3.14

3°

Magnetic Variation 4·0°W

4°

RAMSEY 3.12

Maughold Head

Point of Ayre

Snaefell
RG

Laxey

ISLE OF MAN
3.8

DOUGLAS 3.11

Douglas Head

Derby Haven

Langness

Castletown

Port Erin

PEEL 3.9

PORT ST MARY 3.10

Calf of Man

54°N

5°W

30'

30'

30'

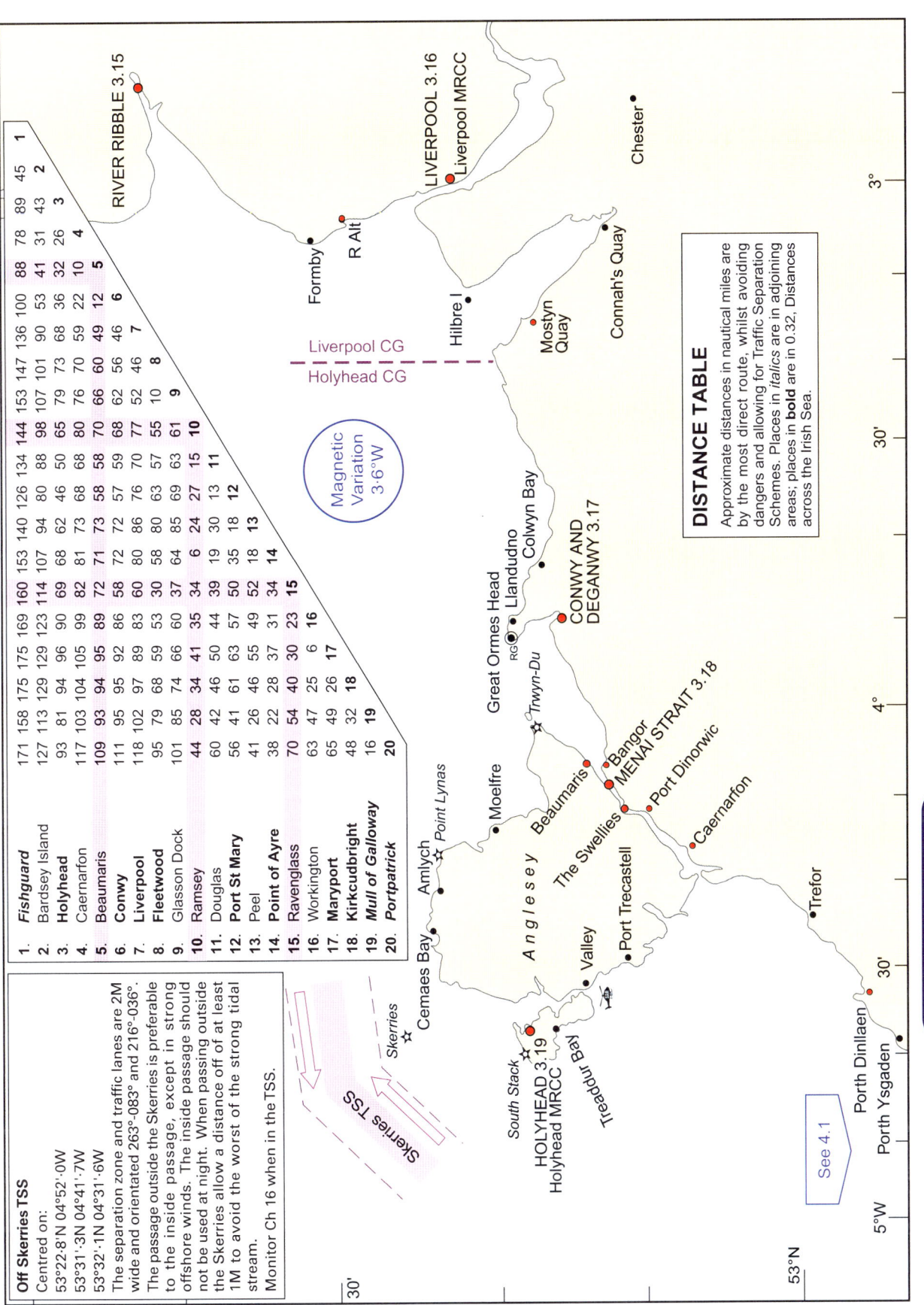

**Off Skerries TSS**

Centred on:
53°22'·8N 04°52'·0W
53°31'·3N 04°41'·7W
53°32'·1N 04°31'·6W

The separation zone and traffic lanes are 2M wide and orientated 263°-083° and 216°-036°. The passage outside the Skerries is preferable to the inside passage, except in strong offshore winds. The inside passage should not be used at night. When passing outside the Skerries allow a distance off of at least 1M to avoid the worst of the strong tidal stream.

Monitor Ch 16 when in the TSS.

**DISTANCE TABLE**

Approximate distances in nautical miles are by the most direct route, whilst avoiding dangers and allowing for Traffic Separation Schemes. Places in *italics* are in adjoining areas; places in **bold** are in 0.32. Distances across the Irish Sea.

Distance table:

|  | | |
|---|---|---|
| 1. *Fishguard* | 171 158 175 175 169 160 153 140 126 134 144 153 147 136 100 88 78 89 45 | **1** |
| 2. *Bardsey Island* | 127 113 129 123 114 107 94 88 80 98 107 101 90 53 41 31 43 | **2** |
| 3. **Holyhead** | 93 81 96 103 105 92 89 83 60 80 86 76 70 59 36 26 | **3** |
| 4. Caernarfon | 117 103 104 105 99 95 97 89 74 85 80 73 68 58 10 | **4** |
| 5. Beaumaris | 109 93 95 89 72 58 60 53 37 64 69 63 22 12 | **5** |
| 6. **Conwy** | 111 95 92 86 72 57 59 76 80 85 58 49 46 | **6** |
| 7. Liverpool | 118 102 97 89 83 60 80 86 76 70 52 46 | **7** |
| 8. Fleetwood | 95 79 68 59 53 30 58 63 69 55 10 | **8** |
| 9. Glasson Dock | 101 85 74 66 60 37 64 69 63 61 | **9** |
| 10. **Ramsey** | 44 28 34 41 35 34 6 24 27 15 | **10** |
| 11. Douglas | 60 42 46 50 44 39 19 30 13 | **11** |
| 12. **Port St Mary** | 56 41 61 63 57 30 35 18 | **12** |
| 13. Peel | 41 26 46 55 49 52 18 | **13** |
| 14. **Point of Ayre** | 38 22 28 37 31 34 | **14** |
| 15. Ravenglass | 70 54 40 30 23 | **15** |
| 16. Workington | 63 47 25 6 | **16** |
| 17. **Maryport** | 65 49 26 | **17** |
| 18. Kirkcudbright | 48 32 | **18** |
| 19. *Mull of Galloway* | 16 | **19** |
| 20. *Portpatrick* | | **20** |

Magnetic Variation 3·6°W

Liverpool CG
Holyhead CG

RIVER RIBBLE 3.15

LIVERPOOL 3.16
Liverpool MRCC

Formby
R Alt
Hilbre I
Mostyn Quay
Connah's Quay
Chester

Great Ormes Head
RG
Llandudno
Colwyn Bay
CONWY AND DEGANWY 3.17
Twyn-Du
Bangor
MENAI STRAIT 3.18
Beaumaris
Port Dinorwic
The Swellies
Caernarfon

Moelfre
*Point Lynas*
Amlych
Anglesey
Port Trecastell
Valley
Trefor
Cemaes Bay
Skerries
Skerries TSS
South Stack
HOLYHEAD 3.19
Holyhead MRCC
Treaddur Bay

See 4.1
Porth Dinllaen
Porth Ysgaden

5°W
53°N
30'
4°
30'
3°
30'

## 3.2 NW ENGLAND, IOM & N WALES TIDAL STREAMS

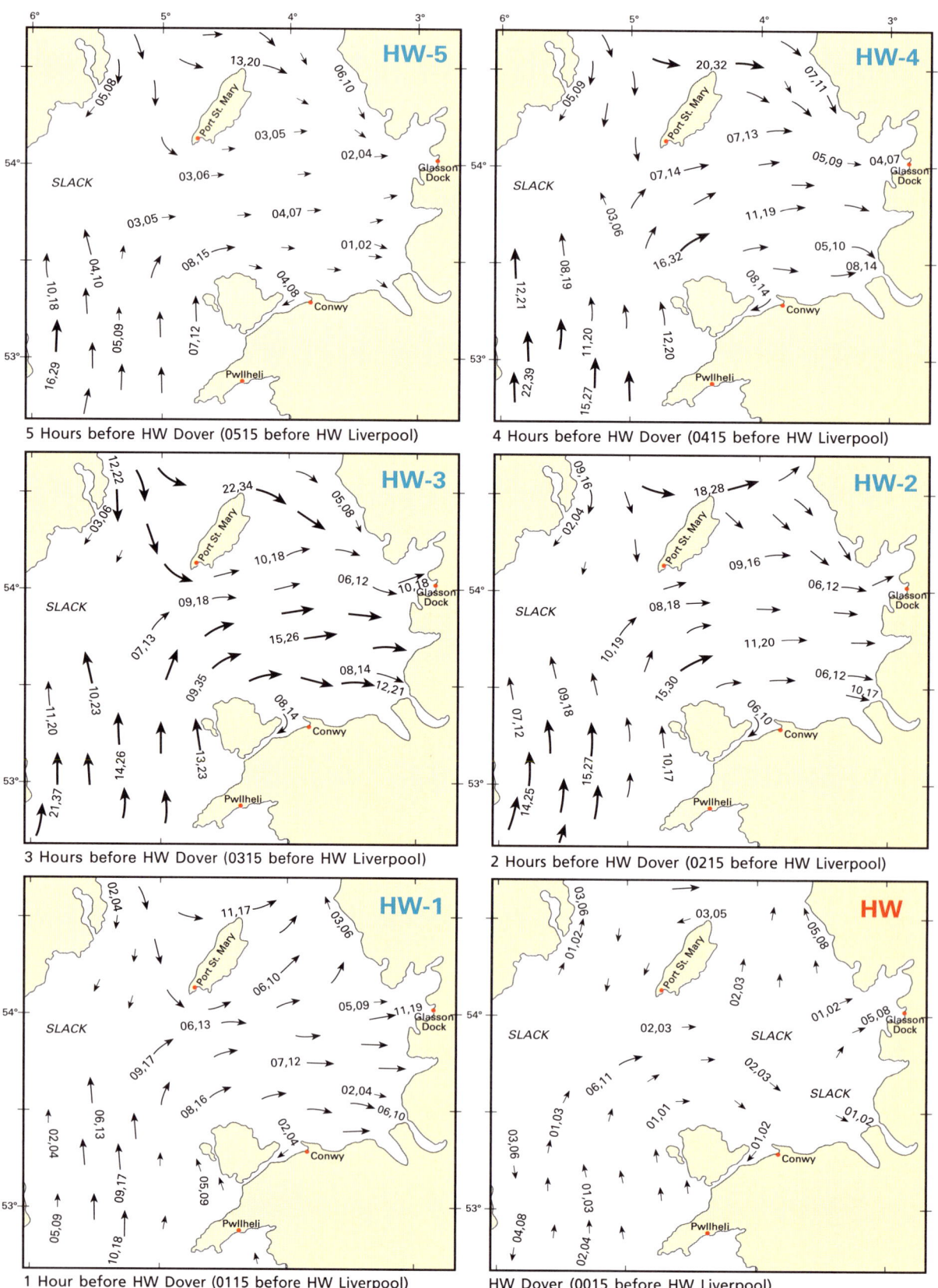

5 Hours before HW Dover (0515 before HW Liverpool)

4 Hours before HW Dover (0415 before HW Liverpool)

3 Hours before HW Dover (0315 before HW Liverpool)

2 Hours before HW Dover (0215 before HW Liverpool)

1 Hour before HW Dover (0115 before HW Liverpool)

HW Dover (0015 before HW Liverpool)

Northward 2.2    Southward 4.2    North Ireland 6.2    Mull of Kintyre 2.10    South Ireland 5.2

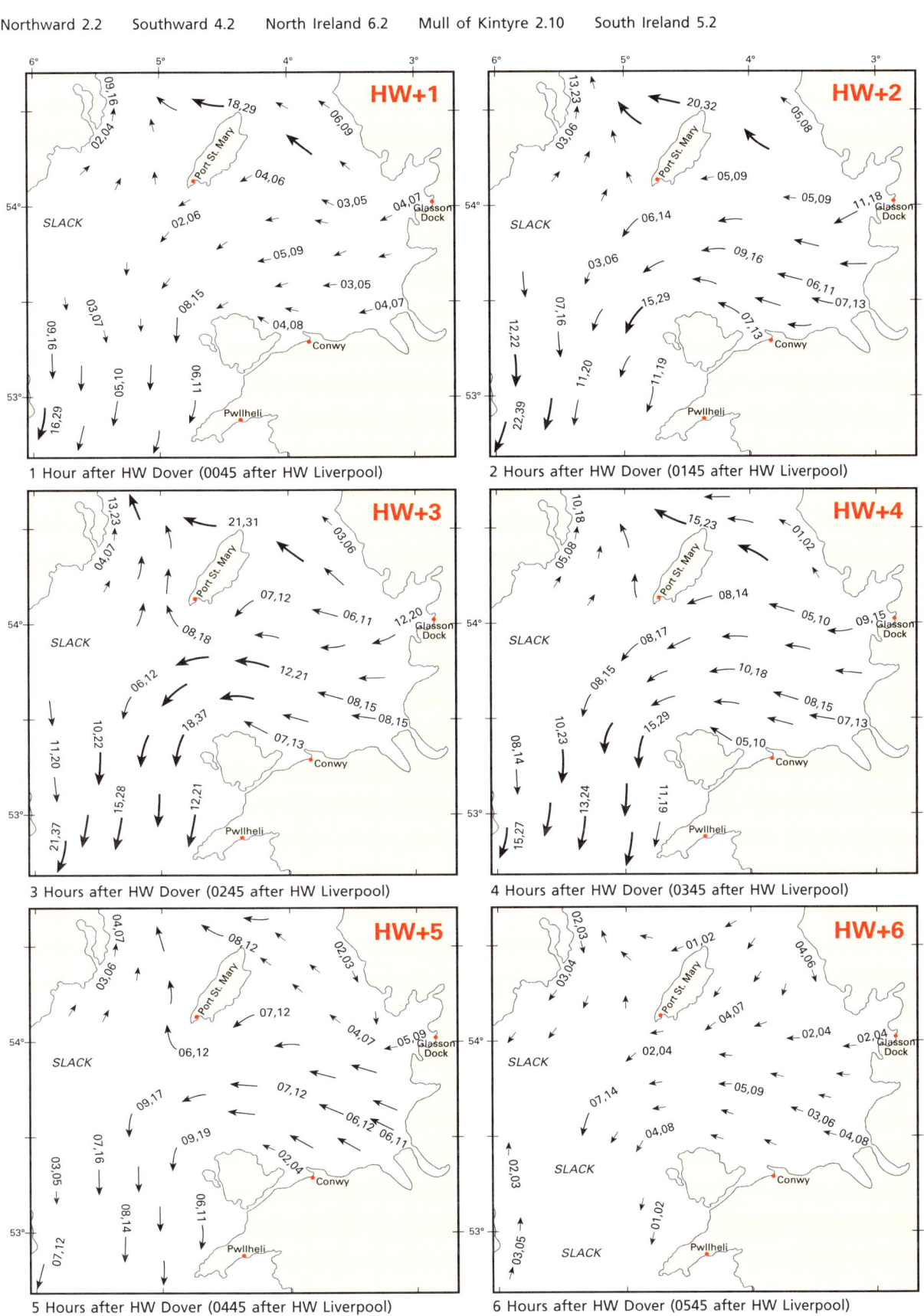

1 Hour after HW Dover (0045 after HW Liverpool)

2 Hours after HW Dover (0145 after HW Liverpool)

3 Hours after HW Dover (0245 after HW Liverpool)

4 Hours after HW Dover (0345 after HW Liverpool)

5 Hours after HW Dover (0445 after HW Liverpool)

6 Hours after HW Dover (0545 after HW Liverpool)

**W England, IoM, Wales**

*Plot waypoints on chart before use*

## 3.3 LIGHTS, BUOYS AND WAYPOINTS

**Blue** print = light with a nominal range of 15M or more. CAPITALS = place or feature. *CAPITAL ITALICS* = light-vessel, light float or Lanby. *Italics* = Fog signal. ***Bold italics*** = Racon. See 0.2 for Abbreviations.

### SOLWAY FIRTH TO BARROW-IN-FURNESS

**SILLOTH, MARYPORT and WORKINGTON**
Two Feet Bank Q (9) 15s; 54°42'·90N 03°47'·10W.
Solway Fl G 4s; 54°46'·80N 03°30'·14W.
Maryport S Pier Hd .Fl 1·5s 10m 6M; 54°43'·07N 03°30'·64W.
N Workington Q; 54°40'·10N 03°38'·18W.
S Workington VQ (6) + L Fl 10s; 54°37'·01N 03°38'·58W.
Workington Pier Hd QG 5m; 54°39'·14N 03°34'·80W.

**WHITEHAVEN and RAVENGLASS**
W Pier Hd Fl G 5s 16m 13M; W○ twr; 54°33'·17N 03°35'·92W.
**Saint Bees Hd** ☆ 54°30'·81N 03°38'·23W Fl (2) 20s 102m **18M**; W○ twr; obsc shore-340°.
Selker Fl (3) G 10s; *Bell;* 54°16'·14N 03°29'·58W.

**BARROW-IN-FURNESS**
Barrow Wind Farm VQ (6) + L Fl 10s; 53°58'·20N 03°17'·40W.
Lightning Knoll L Fl 10s; *Bell;* 53°59'·83N 03°14'·28W.
Halfway Shoal QR 19m 10s; R&W chequer Bn; ***Racon (B) 10M***; 54°01'·46N 03°11'·88W.
Bar Fl (2) R 5s; 54°02'·54N 03°10'·31W.
**Isle of Walney** ☆ 54°02'·92N 03°10'·64W Fl 15s 21m **23M**; stone twr; obsc 122°-127° within 3M of shore.

### ISLE OF MAN

Whitestone Bank Q (9) 15s; 54°24'·58N 04°20'·41W.
**Point of Ayre** ☆ 54°24'·94N 04°22'·13W Fl (4) 20s 32m **19M**; W twr, two R bands, *Horn (3) 60s*, ***Racon (M) 13-15M***.
Low Lt 54°25'·03N 04°21'·86W Fl 3s 10m 8M; R twr, lower part W, on B Base; part obsc 335°-341°.

**PEEL, P ERIN, P ST MARY, CASTLETOWN and DERBY HAVEN**
Peel Bkwtr Hd Oc 7s 11m 6M; W twr; 54°13'·67N 04°41'·69W.
Peel Groyne Hd Oc R 2s 4m; 54°13'·56N 04°41'·67W.
Port Erin Raglan Pier Hd Oc G 5s 8m 5M; 54°05'·12N 04°45'·86W.
**Calf of Man** ☆ W Pt 54°03'·19N 04°49'·78W Fl 15s 93m **26M**; W 8-sided twr; vis 274°-190°; *Horn 45s*.
Chicken Rk Fl 5s 38m 18M; twr; *Horn 60s;* 54°02'·26N 04°50'·32W.
Alfred Pier Hd Oc R 10s 8m 6M; W twr, R band; 54°04'·33N 04°43'·82W.
Dreswick Pt Fl (2) 30s 23m 12M; W twr; 54°03'·29N 04°37'·45W.
Castletown Bay Fl R 3s: *Bell;* 54°03'·73N 04°38'·62W.
Derby Haven, Bkwtr SW end Iso G 2s 5m 5M; W twr, G band; 54°04'·58N 04°37'·06W.

**DOUGLAS**
**Douglas Head** ☆ 54°08'·60N 04°27'·95W Fl 10s 32m **24M**; W twr; obsc brg more than 037°. FR Lts on radio masts 1 and 3M West.
No. 1 Q (3) G 5s; 54°09'·04N 04°27'·68W.
Princess Alexandra Pier Hd Fl R 5s 16m 8M; R mast; *Whis (2) 40s;* 54°08'·84N 04°27'·85W.

**LAXEY and RAMSEY**
**Maughold Head** ☆ 54°17'·72N 04°18'·58W Fl (3) 30s 65m **21M**.
Bahama VQ (6) + L Fl 10s; 54°20'·01N 04°08'·57W.
Ramsey N Pier Hd QG 9m 10M; W twr, B base; 54°19'·46N 04°22'·50W.
King William Bank Q (3) 10s; 54°26'·01N 04°00'·08W.

### BARROW TO RIVERS MERSEY AND DEE

**MORECAMBE**
Lightning Knoll L Fl 10s; 53°59'·84N 03°14'·28W.
Morecambe Q (9) 15s; *Whis;* 53°51'·99N 03°24'·10W.
Lune Deep Q (6) + L Fl 15s; *Whis;* ***Racon (T);*** 53°55'·81N 03°11'·08W.

Shell Wharf Fl G 2·5s; 53°55'·46N 03°08'·96W.
King Scar Fl (2) G 5s; 53°56'·96N 03°04'·38W.

### R LUNE, GLASSON DOCK, FLEETWOOD and BLACKPOOL
R Lune Q (9) 15s; 53°58'·63N 03°00'·03W.
S Bank Fl (2) G 4s; 53°58'·12N 02°56'·12W.
Plover Scar Fl 2s 6m 6M; W twr, B lantern; 53°58'·89N 02°52'·96W.
Crook Perch, No. 7 Fl G 5s 3M; G △ on mast; 53°59'·46N 02°52'·36W.
Bazil Perch, No.16 Fl (3) R 10s 3M; 54°00'·20N 02°51'·65W.
Glasson Quay FG 1M; 54°00'·03N 02°51·03W.
Fleetwood Fairway 53°57'·67N 03°02'·03W Q; *Bell.*
Fleetwood Esplanade Ldg Lts 156°. Front, Iso G 2s 14m 9M; 53°55'·71N 03°00'·56W. Rear, 320m from front, Iso G 4s 28m 9M. Both vis on Ldg line only. (H24) (chan liable to change).
Black Scar Perch No. 11 QG 4m 2M *Horn (1) 15s;* 53°56'·24N 03°01'·06W.
Blackpool N Pier Hd 2 FG (vert) 3M; 53°49'·16N 03°03'·77W.

### RIVER RIBBLE, RIVER MERSEY and LIVERPOOL
Gut L Fl 10s; 53°41'·74N 03°08'·98W.
Perches show Fl R on N side, and Fl G on S side of chan.
S side, 14¼M Perch Fl G 5s 6m 3M; 53°42'·75N 03°04'·90W.
Southport Pier Hd 2 FG (vert) 6m 5M; vis: 033°-213°; 53°39'·33N 03°01'·31W.
Jordan's Spit Q (9) 15s; 53°35'·76N 03°19'·28W.
FT Q; 53°34'·56N 03°13'·20W.

Bar L Fl 10s; ***Racon (T) 10M***; 53°32'·01N 03°20'·98W.
Q1 VQ; 53°31'·00N 03°16'·72W.
Q2 VQ R; 53°31'·47N 03°14'·95W.
Formby Iso 4s 11m 6M; R hull, W stripes; 53°31'·13N 03°13'·50W.
C4 Fl R 3s R hull; 53°31'·82N 03°08'·51W.
Crosby Oc 5s 11m 8M; R hull, W stripes; 53°30'·72N 03°06'·29W.
C14 Fl R 3s; R hull; 53°29'·91N 03°05'·34W.
Brazil QG; G hull; 53°26'·84N 03°02'·24W.
Pluckington Bank VQ (9)10s; 53°23'·00N 02°59'·56W.

### RIVER DEE, MOSTYN, WELSH and MID HOYLE CHANNEL
HE1 Q (9) 15s; 53°26'·33N 03°18'·08W.
HE2 Q (3) 10s; 53°25'·13N 03°13'·07W.
HE3 QG; 53°24'·62N 03°12'·82W.
Hilbre I Fl R 3s 14m 5M; W twr; 53°22'·99N 03°13'·72W.
HE4 53°22'·32N 03°14'·29W.
M1 QG; 53°20'·98N 03°16'·39W.
Mostyn S Bkwtr Hd Fl G 5s; 53°19'·22N 03°15'·67W.
Dee Q (6) + L Fl 15s; 53°21'·99N 03°18'·68W.
Air Fl G 5s; 53°21'·85N 03°19'·29W.
SH7 Fl (4) G 15s; 53°21'·82N 03°22'·23W.
SH3 W Fl (2) G 5s; 53°21'·23N 03°24'·43W.
South Hoyle Outer Fl R 2·5s; 53°21'·47N 03°27'·48W.
E Hoyle Spit Fl G 5s; 53°22'·52N 03°18'·95W.
Mid Hoyle Fl R 2·5s; 53°22'·92N 03°19'·50W.
NW Hoyle Fl R 2·5s; 53°23'·32N 03°23'·89W.
N Hoyle VQ; 53°26'·68N 03°30'·58W.

### WALES – NORTH COAST AND INNER PASSAGE
West Hoyle Spit Bn 53°21'·20N 03°24'·08W QG 5M. OuterDirLt 096·5° Iso WRG 2s 7M; vis 094°-G-096°-W-097°-R-099°;Occas when vessels expected; By day 3M.
Prestatyn QG; 53°21'·51N 03°28'·51W.
Inner Passage Fl R 5s; 53°21'·91N 03°31'·95W.
Mid Patch Spit QR; 53°22'·25N 03°32'·67W.
N Rhyl Q; 53°22'·76N 03°34'·58W.
North Hoyle Wind Farm (30 turbines, see 9.10.5) centred on 53°25'·00N 03°27'·00W. NW, NE, SW, SE extremities (F.R Lts) Fl Y 2·5s 5M Horn Mo (U) 30s.
Mast Mo (U) 15s 12m 10M & 2FR(vert); Horn Mo (U) 30s; Mast (80); 53°28'·84N 03°30'·50W.
W Constable Q (9) 15s; ***Racon (M) 10M;*** 53°23'·14N 03°49'·26W.

### RHYL, LLANDUDNO and CONWY

Llandudno Pier Hd ⚓ 2 FG (vert) 8m 4M; 53°19'·90N 03°49'·51W.
Great Ormes Hd Lt Ho, (unlit); 53°20'·56N 03°52'·17W.
Conwy Fairway ⚓ L Fl 10s; 53°17'·95N 03°55'·58W.
C2 ⚓ Fl (2) R 10s; 53°17'·64N 03°54'·69W.
C6 ⚓ Fl (6) R 30s; 53°17'·78N 03°52'·27W.
C8 ⚓ Fl (8) R 10s; 53°18'·00N 03°52'·05W.
C7 ⚓ QG; 53°18'·06N 03°50'·75W.
Conway R ent S side ⚓ Fl WR 5s 5m 2M; vis: 076°-W-088°-R- 171°-W-319°-R-076°; 53°18'·07N 03°50'·86W.

### ANGLESEY

**Point Lynas** ☆ 53°24'·98N 04°17'·35W Oc 10s 39m **18M**;
W castellated twr; vis: 109°-315°; *Horn 45s;* H24.
Archdeacon Rock ⚓ Q; 53°26'·71N 04°30'·87W.
Victoria Bank ⚓ VQ; 53°25'·61N 04°31'·37W.
Coal Rk ⚓ Q (6) + L Fl 15s; 53°25'·91N 04°32'·79W.
Ethel Rk ⚓ VQ; 53°26'·64N 04°33'·67W.
W Mouse ⚓ 53°25'·05N 04°33'·27W.

**The Skerries** ☆ 53°25'·27N 04°36'·55W Fl (2) 15s 36m **20M**; W ○ twr, R band; *Racon (T) 25M.* Iso R 4s 26m 10M; same twr; vis: 233°-253°; *Horn (2) 60s.* H24 in periods of reduced visibility.
Langdon ⚓ Q (9) 15s; 53°22'·74N 04°38'·74W.
Wk ⚓ Fl (2) R 10s; 53°20'·43N 04°36'·60W.

### HOLYHEAD

Bkwtr Head ⚓ Fl (3) G 10s 21m 14M; W □ twr, B band; Fl Y vis: 174°-226°; *Siren 20s;* 53°19'·86N 04°37'·16W.
Marina Bkwtr Hd ⚓ 2 FR (vert); 53°19'·31N 04°38'·63W.

**South Stack** ☆ 53°19'·31N 04°41'·98W Fl 10s 60m **24M**; (H24); W ○ twr; obsc to N by N Stack and part obsc in Penrhos bay; *Horn 30s.* Fog Det lt vis: 145°-325°.

## MENAI STRAIT TO BARDSEY ISLAND

Trwyn-Du ⚓ Fl 5s 19m 12M; W ○ castellated twr, B bands; vis: 101°-023°; *Bell (1) 30s,* sounded continuously; 53°18'·77N 04°02'·44W. FR on radio mast 2M SW.

Ten Feet Bank ⚓ QR; 53°19'·47N 04°02'·82W.
Dinmor ⚓ QG; 53°19'·34N 04°03'·32W.

### BEAUMARIS and BANGOR
**(Direction of buoyage ⟳ NE to SW)**
Perch Rock ⚓ Fl R 5s; 53°18'·73N 04°02'·09W.
B1 ⚓ Fl (2) G 10s; 53°18'·12N 04°02'·37W.
B3 ⚓ QG; 53°17'·72N 04°02'·77W.
B8 ⚓ Fl (3) R 10s; 53°16'·47N 04°04'·47W.
B5 ⚓ Fl G 5s; 53°15'·77N 04°04'·91W.
Beaumaris Pier ⚓ F WG 5m 6M;vis: 212°-G-286°-W-041°-G-071°; 53°15'·67N 04°05'·41W.
B12 ⚓ QR; 53°15'·47N 04°05'·58W.
B7 ⚓ Fl (2) G 5s; 53°15'·10N 04°06'·13W.
Bangor ⚓ 53°14'·47N 04°07'·59W.

### PORT DINORWIC and CAERNARFON
Port Dinorwic Pier Hd ⚓ 53°11'·18N 04°12'·64W F WR 5m 2M; vis: 225°-R- 357°-W-225°.

C9 ⚓ 53°08'·52N 04°16'·87W.
Channel ⚓ 53°10'·34N 04°15'·19W.
C14 ⚓ 53°10'·19N 04°15'·37W.
C11 ⚓ 53°09'·92N 04°15'·67W.
**(Direction of buoyage ⟳ SW to NE)**
Change ⚓ 53°08'·82N 04°16'·72W.
C10 ⚓ QR; 53°07'·96N 04°18'·27W.
Abermenai Point ⚓ Fl WR 3·5s 6m 3M; W mast; vis: 065°-R-245°-W-065°; 53°07'·62N 04°19'·72W
C1 ⚓ Fl G 5s; 53°06'·95N 04°24'·52W.
C2 ⚓ Fl R 10s; 53°07'·07N 04°24'·52W.

### PORTH DINLLÄEN
Careg y Chwislen ⚓ 52°56'·99N 04°33'·51W.

**Bardsey I** ☆ 52°44'·97N 04°48'·02W Fl (5) 15s 39m **26M**; W □ twr, R bands; obsc by Bardsey Is 198°-250° and in Tremadoc B when brg less than 260°; *Horn Mo (N) 45s;* H24.

---

## 3.4 PASSAGE INFORMATION

For detailed directions covering these waters and harbours refer to the Admiralty Pilot *W Coast of England and Wales; Lundy and Irish Sea Pilot* (Taylor/Imray). Admiralty Leisure Folio 5609 covers NW Wales from Aberystwyth to Colwyn Bay including Menai Strait.

### SOLWAY FIRTH

(AC 1346) Between Abbey Hd and St Bees Hd lies the Solway Firth, most of which is encumbered by shifting sandbanks.The *Solway SDs* are essential. Off the entrances to the Firth, and in the approaches to Workington beware shoals over which strong W winds raise a heavy sea. There are navigable, buoyed chans as far as Annan on the N shore, but buoys are laid primarily for the aid of Pilots. ▶ *Local knowledge is required, particularly in the upper Firth, where streams run very strongly in the chans when the banks are dry, and less strongly over the banks when covered. In Powfoot chan for example the in-going stream begins at HW Liverpool – 0300, and the outgoing at HW Liverpool + 0100, sp rates up to 6kn.* ◀

Between Silloth and Walney Is are Maryport, Workington, Harrington, Whitehaven, and Ravenglass. South along the Cumbrian coast past St Bees Hd to Walney Is there are no dangers more than 2M offshore, but no shelter either.

### ISLE OF MAN (IOM)

(charts 2094, 2696) For general pilotage information, tidal streams and hbr details of IOM, see *IOM Sailing Directions, Tidal Streams and Anchorages,* published by Hunter Publications. For notes on crossing the Irish Sea, see 6.4.

There are four choices when rounding S of IoM:
In bad weather, or at night, keep S of Chicken Rk. In good conditions, pass between Chicken Rk and Calf of Man (lt). With winds of < Force 3 and a reliable engine giving < 5kn, and only by day use Calf Sd between Calf of Man and IoM, passing W of Kitterland Is but E of Thousla Rk, which is marked by lt bn and is close to Calf of Man shore. Little Sd, a minor chan, runs E of Kitterland Is.

▶ *The stream runs strongly through Calf Sound, starting N-going at HW Liverpool – 0145, and S-going at HW Liverpool + 0345, sp rates 3·5kn. W of Calf of Man the stream runs N and S, but changes direction off Chicken Rk and runs W and E between Calf of Man and Langness Pt 6M to E. Overfalls extend E from Chicken Rk on E-going stream, which begins at HW Liverpool + 0610, and N from the rk on W-going stream, which begins at HW Liverpool.* ◀
▶ *Off Langness Pt (lt) the Skerranes (dry) extend 1ca SW, and*

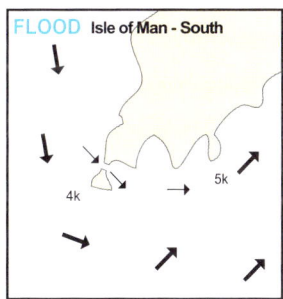

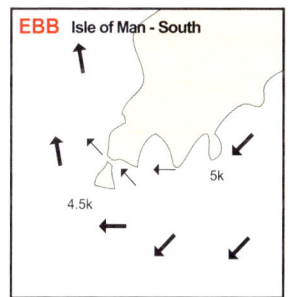

*tidal stream runs strongly, with eddies and a race. E side of Langness peninsula is foul ground, over which a dangerous sea can build in strong winds. Here the NE-going stream begins at HW Liverpool +0545, and the SW-going at HW Liverpool –0415, sp rates 2·25kn.* ◄

Anch in Derby Haven, N of St Michael's Is, but exposed to E. From here to Douglas and on to Maughold Hd (lt), there are no dangers more than 4ca offshore. ▶ *Near the coast the SW-going stream runs for 9 hours and the NE-going for 3 hours, since an eddy forms during the second half of the main NE-going stream. Off Maughold Hd the NE-going stream begins at HW Liverpool +0500, and the SW-going at HW Liverpool –0415.* ◄

SE, E and NW of Pt of Ayre are dangerous banks, on which seas break in bad weather. These are Whitestone Bk (least depth 2·0m), Bahama Bk (1·5m), Ballacash Bk (2·7 m), King William Bks (3·3m), and Strunakill Bk (6·7m).

▶ *E going stream at Point of Ayre begins HW Dover –0545 (HW Liverpool –0600). Counter tide inside banks E of Point. In Ramsey Bay the S going tide runs for 3h from +0530 Dover (+0515 Liverpool).*

*W going stream at Point of Ayre begins HW Dover +0015 (HW Liverpool). Counter tide inside banks W of Point. In Ramsey Bay the N going tide runs for 9h from –0330 Dover (–0345 Liverpool).* ◄

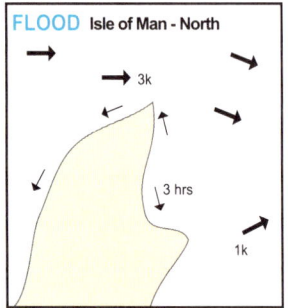 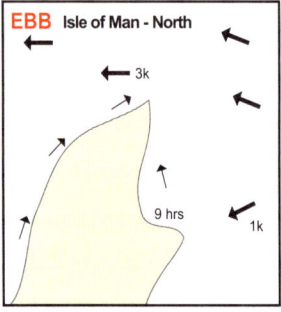

The W coast of IOM has few pilotage hazards. A spit with depth of 1·4m runs 2ca offshore from Rue Pt. Jurby Rk (depth 2·7m) lies 3ca off Jurby Hd. Craig Rk (depth 4 m) & shoals lie 2·5M NNE of Peel.

## BARROW TO CONWY

(AC 2010, 1981, 1978) Ent to Barrow-in-Furness (AC 3164) is about 1M S of Hilpsford Pt at S end of Walney Island where the lt ho is prominent. ▶ *The stream sets across the narrow chan, which is well marked but shallow in patches.* ◄ W winds cause rough sea in the ent. Moorings and anch off Piel and Roa Islands, but space is limited. ▶ *Stream runs hard on ebb. Coming from the S it is possible with sufficient rise of tide to cross the sands between Fleetwood and Barrow.* ◄

Barrow Wind Farm (construction in progress 2007) is marked by SCM lt buoy, and all structures are marked FlY 2·5s 2M lts. The site is centred approx 7M SSW of Barrow-in-Furness.

Lune Deep, 2M NW of Rossall Pt, is ent to Morecambe B (chart 2010), and gives access to the ferry/commercial port of Heysham, Glasson Dock, & Fleetwood; it is well buoyed. ▶ *Streams run 3·5kn at sp.* ◄ Most of Bay is encumbered withdrying sands, intersected by chans which are subject to change. S of Morecambe B, beware shoals and drying outfall (2·0m) extending 3M W of Rossall Pt. Further S, R. Ribble gives access via a long drying chan to the marina at Preston.

Queen's Chan and Crosby Chan (AC 1951 &1978) are entered E of the Bar Lat Buoy SWM. They are well buoyed, dredged and preserved by training banks, & give main access to R. Mersey & Liverpool. Keep clear of commercial shipping. From the N the old Formby chan is abandoned, but possible near HW. Towards HW and in moderate winds a yacht can cross the training bank (level of which varies between 2m and 3m above CD) E of Great Burbo Bk,

if coming from the W. Rock Ch, which is unmarked & parts of which dry, may also be used but beware wrecks.

In good weather at nps, the Dee Estuary (AC 1953, 1978) is accessible for boats able to take the ground. But most of estuary dries and banks extend 6M seaward. Chans shift, and buoys are moved as required. ▶ *Stream runs hard in chans when banks are dry.* ◄ Main ent is Welsh Chan, but if coming from N, Hilbre Swash runs W of Hilbre Is.

Sailing W from the Dee on the ebb, it is feasible to take the Inner Passage (buoyed) S of West Hoyle Spit, which gives some protection from onshore winds at half tide or below. Rhyl is a tidal hbr, not accessible in strong onshore winds, but gives shelter for yachts able to take the ground. Abergele Rd, Colwyn B and Llandudno B are possible anchs in settled weather & S winds. Conwy & Deganwy offer good shelter in both marinas and harbour. ▶ *Between Point of Ayr and Great Ormes Head the E-going stream begins at HW Liverpool +0600, and the W-going at HW Liverpool –0015, sp rates 3kn.* ◄

North Hoyle Wind Farm consists of 30 turbines and is centred on 53°25'·00N 03°27'·00W. Each turbine is 58m high, with 80m diameter blades and clearance of 18m. Many of them are lit. Vessels to keep well clear and not enter the area.

## MENAI STRAIT

(AC 1464) The main features of this narrow chan include: Puffin Is, seaward of NE end; Beaumaris; Garth Pt at Bangor, where NE end of Strait begins; Menai Suspension Bridge (30·5m); The Swellies, a narrow 1M stretch with strong tide and dangers mid-stream; Britannia Rail Bridge (27·4m), with cables close W at elevation of 22m; Port Dinorwic and Caernarfon ; Abermenai Pt and Fort Belan, where narrows mark SW end of Strait; and Caernarfon Bar.

The following brief notes only cover very basic pilotage. For detailed directions see *W Coasts of England and Wales Pilot*, or *Cruising Anglesey and N Wales* (NW Venturers Yacht Club). ▶ *For tidal streams 'Arrowsmiths' is recommended, from Arrowsmiths, Winterstoke Rd., Bristol, BS3 2NT. The Swellies should be taken near local HW slack, and an understanding of tidal streams is essential. The tide is about 1 hour later, and sp range about 2·7m more, at NE end of Strait than at SW end. Levels differ most at about HW +1 (when level at NE end is more than 1·8m above level at SW end); and at about HW – 0445 (when level at NE end is more than 1·8m below level at SW end). Normally the stream runs as follows (times referred to HW Holyhead). HW –0040 to HW +0420: SW between Garth Pt and Abermenai Pt. HW +0420 to HW +0545: outwards from about The Swellies, ie NE towards Garth Pt and SW towards Abermenai Pt. HW +0545 to HW – 0040: NE between Abermenai Pt and Garth Pt. Sp rates are generally about 3kn, **but more in narrows, eg 5kn off Abermenai Pt, 6kn between the bridges, and 8kn at The Swellies.** The timings and rates of streams may be affected by strong winds in either direction.* ◄

▶ *From NE, enter chan W of Puffin Island, taking first of ebb to reach the Swellies at slack HW (HW Holyhead –0100). Slack HW only lasts about 20 mins at sps, a little more at nps.* ◄

Pass under centre of suspension bridge span, and steer to leave Platters (dry) on mainland shore to port and Swellies lt bn close to stbd. From Swellies lt bn to Britannia Bridge hold mainland shore, leaving bn on Price Pt to port, and Gored Goch and Gribbin Rk to stbd. Leave Britannia Rk (centre pier of bridge) to stbd. Thence to SW hold to buoyed chan near mainland shore. (A Historic Wreck is 4ca SW of Britannia Bridge at 53°12'·77N 04°11'·72W.) Port Dinorwic is useful to await right tidal conditions for onward passage in either direction. **Note: Direction of buoyage becomes NE off Caernarfon.**

▶ *Caernarfon Bar is impassable even in moderately strong winds against ebb, and narrows at Abermenai Pt demand a fair tide, or slackish water, since tide runs strongly here. Going seaward on first* of ebb, when there is water over the banks, it may not be practicable to return to the Strait if conditions on the bar are bad. ◄

Then it is best to anchor near Mussel Bank buoy and await slack water, before returning to Caernarfon, for example. Leaving Abermenai Pt on last of ebb means banks to seaward are exposed and there is little water in chan or over bar.

Going NE'ward it is safe to reach the Swellies with last of flood, leaving Caernarfon about HW Holyhead – 0230. Do not leave too late, or full force of ebb will be met before reaching Bangor.

### ANGLESEY TO BARDSEY ISLAND

(AC 1977, 1970, 1971) On N coast of Anglesey, a race extends 5ca off Pt Lynas (lt, fog sig, RC) on E-going stream. Amlwch is a small hbr (partly dries) 1·5M W of Pt Lynas. A drying rk lies 100m offshore on W side of appr, which should not be attempted in strong onshore winds. From here to Carmel Hd beware E Mouse (and shoals to SE), Middle Mouse, Harry Furlong's Rks (dry), Victoria Bank (least depth 1·8m), Coal Rk (awash), and W Mouse (with dangers to W & SW). The outermost of these dangers is 2M offshore. There are overfalls and races at headlands and over the many rks and shoals along this coast.

Simplest passage, or at night or in bad weather, is to pass 1M off Skerries, in the TSS ITZ. In good conditions by day and at slack water, Carmel Hd can be rounded close inshore; but beware short, steep, breaking seas here in even moderate winds against tide. Holyhead (port of refuge), access H24 in all weathers, within New Hbr; beware fast ferries.

► Between Carmel Hd and The Skerries the NE-going stream begins at HW Holyhead + 0550, and the SW-going at HW Holyhead – 0010, **sp rates 5kn.** 1M NW of Skerries the stream turns 0130 later, and runs less strongly. **Flood tide close to the coast runs at over 5k springs,** and at about 2.5k 7 miles offshore. The brief period of slack water offshore is HW Dover - 0100 ( HW L'pool - 0115). Slack water lasts longer in Holyhead Bay.

Ebb tide close to the coast runs at over 5k springs, and at about 2.5k 7 miles offshore. Slack water is 5h after HW Dover (4h45 after HW L'pool). There is no significant counter tide in Holyhead Bay, but the ebb starts first there, giving about 9h W-going tide N of the harbour. ◄

► Races occur off N Stack and (more severe) off S Stack , up to 1·5M offshore on NNE-going stream which begins at HW Holyhead – 0605, **sp rate 5kn.** Races do not extend so far on SSW-going stream which begins at HW Holyhead + 0020, **sp rate 5kn.** ◄

The W coast of Anglesey is rugged with rks, some drying, up to 1·5M offshore. There are races off Penrhyn Mawr and Rhoscolyn Hd. Pilot's Cove, E of Llanddwyn Is, is good anch to await the right conditions for Menai Strait.

On the Lleyn Peninsula Porth Dinllaen is good anch, but exposed to N and NE. Braich y Pwll is the steep, rky point at end of Lleyn Peninsula (AC 1971). About 1M N of it and up to 1M offshore lie The Tripods, a bank on which there are o'falls and a bad sea with wind against tide.

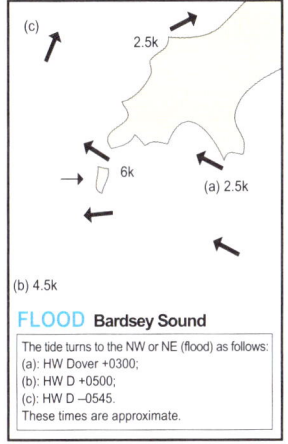

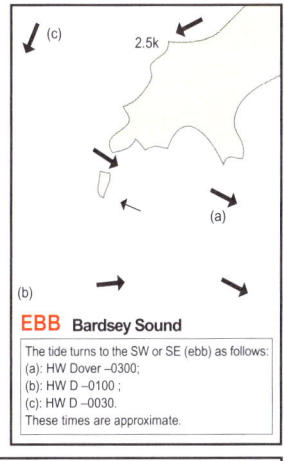

NOTE: There is a strong eddy down tide off Bardsey Island and overfalls throughout the area.

► Bardsey Sound, 1·5M wide, can be used by day in moderate winds. **Stream reaches 6kn at sp, and passage should be made at slack water,** Holyhead – 0015 HW or + 0035 LW. ◄

Avoid Carreg Ddu on N side and Maen Bugail Rk (dries 4·1m) on S side of Sound, where there are dangerous races. If passing outside Bardsey Is make a good offing to avoid o'falls which extend 1·5M W and 2·5M S of Island. Turbulence occurs over Bastram Shoal, Devil's Tail & Devil's Ridge, which lie SSE and E of Bardsey Is.

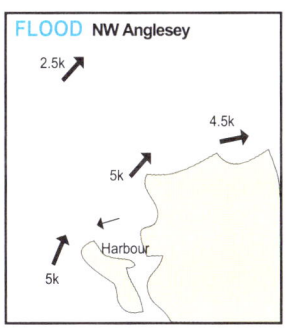

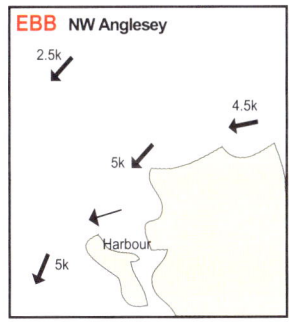

W England, IoM, Wales

## 3.5 MARYPORT

Cumbria **54°43'·03N 03°30'·38W** ✿✿🌿🌿🌿✿✿✿

**CHARTS** AC*1826*, 1346, 2013; Imray C62; OS 89

**TIDES** +0038 Dover; ML no data; Duration 0550

**Standard Port LIVERPOOL** (→)

| Times | | | | Height (metres) | | | |
|---|---|---|---|---|---|---|---|
| High Water | | Low Water | | MHWS | MHWN | MLWN | MLWS |
| 0000 | 0600 | 0200 | 0800 | 9·3 | 7·4 | 2·9 | 0·9 |
| 1200 | 1800 | 1400 | 2000 | | | | |
| **Differences MARYPORT** | | | | | | | |
| +0017 | +0032 | +0020 | +0005 | −0·7 | −0·8 | −0·4 | 0·0 |
| **SILLOTH** | | | | | | | |
| +0030 | +0040 | +0045 | +0055 | −0·1 | −0·3 | −0·6 | −0·1 |

**SHELTER** Good in marina, access HW ±2½ nps over sill 1·75m; at other times Workington is a refuge. Elizabeth Basin dries 2m, access HW±1½; commercial, not used by yachts.

**NAVIGATION** WPT 54°43'·09N 03°32'·47W, 090°/1M to S pier. Overfalls at ent with W/SW winds over ebb. At HW−3 1·8m over bar at ent and in river chan; mud banks cover HW −2.

**LIGHTS AND MARKS** See 3.3 and chartlet. SHM bn Fl G 5s marks outfall 6ca SW of S pier.

**R/T** Port VHF Ch 12 16. Marina (H24) Ch 12 16.

**TELEPHONE** (Code 01900) HM 817440; Hbr Authority 604351; CG 812782; MRCC (0151) 931 3341; Marinecall 09068 969651; Police 602422; Dr 815544; Ⓗ 812634.

**FACILITIES Maryport Marina** (200 inc ♥ £14.69/craft inc ⏦), ☎ 814431, 🖷 810212, www.maryportmarina.com, BY, BH, El, CH, 🗑, ME, Slip (±3HW), D, P, (fresh fish from Fisherman's Co-op); **Maryport Yachting Ass'n** ☎ 64964. **Town** P, D, ME, 🛒, R, Bar, ✉, Ⓑ, ⇌, ✈ (Newcastle).

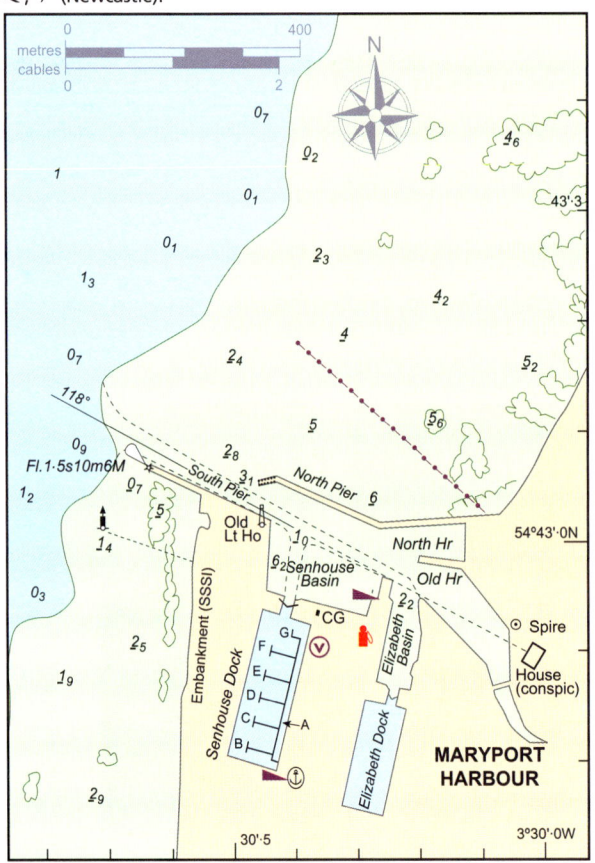

## 3.6 WORKINGTON

Cumbria **54°39'·03N 03°34'·38W** ✿🌿✿

**CHARTS** AC *1826*, 1346, 2013; Imray C62; OS 89

**TIDES** +0025 Dover; ML 4·5; Duration 0545

**Standard Port LIVERPOOL** (→)

| Times | | | | Height (metres) | | | |
|---|---|---|---|---|---|---|---|
| High Water | | Low Water | | MHWS | MHWN | MLWN | MLWS |
| 0000 | 0600 | 0200 | 0800 | 9·3 | 7·4 | 2·9 | 0·9 |
| 1200 | 1800 | 1400 | 2000 | | | | |
| **Differences WORKINGTON** | | | | | | | |
| +0020 | +0020 | +0020 | +0010 | −1·2 | −1·1 | −0·3 | 0·0 |

**SHELTER** Good; ent and chan to Prince of Wales Dock are dredged 1·8m. Berth where you can (free) or ⚓ in Turning Basin. Lock (HW±1½) into PoW Dock 1·8m (for coasters). Low (1·8m) fixed railway bridge across ent to inner tidal hbr.

**NAVIGATION** WPT 54°39'·59N 03°35'·38W, 131°/1M to front ldg lt.

• Tide sets strongly across ent. In periods of heavy rain a strong freshet from R Derwent may be encountered in the hbr ent.

**LIGHTS AND MARKS** Workington Bank, least depth 5·5m, is 2M W of hbr ent; and is marked by NCM and SCM lt buoys (see 3.3). A SHM buoy, Fl G 5s, 1·3M NW of hbr ent is a mark for English Chan. Ldg lts 132°, both FR 10/12m 3M, on W pyramidal trs with Y bands. Two sets of F Bu lts in line mark NE and SW edges of chan.

• There are 16 wind-turbines between ¾M and 2M NE of hbr ent.

**R/T** VHF Ch 14 16 (HW−2½ to HW+2 approx).

**TELEPHONE** (Code 01900) HM 602301 🖷 604696 ; CG 2238; MRCC (0151) 931 3341; Marinecall 09068 969651; Police 602422; Dr 64866; Ⓗ 602244.

**FACILITIES Dock** D, FW, ME, El; **Vanguard SC** ☎ 826886, M, FW. **Town** P, 🛒, R, Bar, ✉, Ⓑ, ⇌, ✈ (Carlisle).

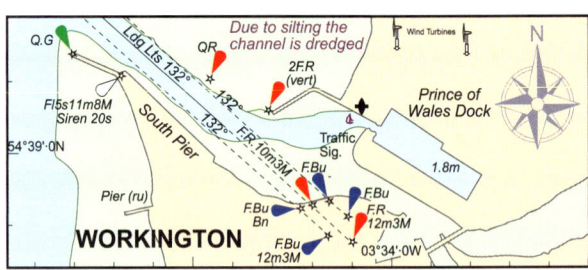

**MINOR HARBOUR 10M NNE OF MARYPORT**

**SILLOTH**, Cumbria, **54°52'·16N 03°23'·86W**. AC*1826*, 1346, 2013. HW −0050 on Dover; ML no data; Duration 0520. See 3.5. Appr via English or Middle Chans, approx 8M long, requires local knowledge. Beware constantly shifting chans and banks. Yachts are not encouraged. ⚓ SW of ent in about 4m off Lees Scar, Fl G 10s 11m 2M; exposed to SW winds. Outer hbr dries; lock into New Dock (note sill 1.2 above CD), which is mainly commercial. East Cote Dir lt 052° FG 15m 12M; vis 046°-058°, intens 052°. Ldg lts, both F, 115°. Groyne 2 FG (vert). Tfc sigs on mast at New Dock: no entry unless Y signal arm raised by day or Q Bu lt by night. VHF Ch 16 12 (HW−2½ to HW+1½). HM ☎ (016973) 31358. Facilities: FW, Ⓑ, Bar, ✉, R, 🛒.

**MINOR HARBOUR 2M S OF WORKINGTON**

**HARRINGTON**, Cumbria, **54°36'·77N 03°34'·29W**. AC *1826*, 1346, 2013. HW +0025 on Dover; Duration 0540; Use Diff's Workington 3.6. Good shelter in small hbr only used by local FVs and yachts; dries 3ca offshore. Ent difficult in strong W winds. Berth on N wall of inner hbr (free). Call ☎ (01946) 823741 Ext 148 for moorings. Limited facilities. SC.

## 3.7 WHITEHAVEN

Cumbria **54°33´·18N 03°35´·82W** ✿✿✿⛵⛵🌸🌸

**CHARTS** AC *1826*, 1346, 2013; Imray C62; OS 89

**TIDES** +0015 Dover; ML 4·5; Duration 0550

**Standard Port LIVERPOOL** (→)

| Times | | | | Height (metres) | | | |
|---|---|---|---|---|---|---|---|
| High Water | | Low Water | | MHWS | MHWN | MLWN | MLWS |
| 0000 | 0600 | 0200 | 0800 | 9·3 | 7·4 | 2·9 | 0·9 |
| 1200 | 1800 | 1400 | 2000 | | | | |
| **Differences WHITEHAVEN** | | | | | | | |
| +0005 | +0015 | +0010 | +0005 | −1·3 | −1·1 | −0·5 | +0·1 |
| **TARN POINT** (54°17´N 03°25´W) | | | | | | | |
| +0005 | +0005 | +0010 | 0000 | −1·0 | −1·0 | −0·4 | 0·0 |
| **DUDDON BAR** (54°09´N 03°20´W) | | | | | | | |
| +0003 | +0003 | +0008 | +0002 | −0·8 | −0·8 | −0·3 | 0·0 |

**SHELTER** Very good, entry safe in most weathers. One of the more accessible ports of refuge in NW England, with a new marina in the inner hbr. Appr chan across the outer hbr is dredged to 1·0m above CD giving access approx HW±4. Sea lock (30m x 13.7m), with sill at CD, maintains 7m within inner hbr. Yacht pontoons are in Inner Hbr. Queen's Dock (from which the lock gates have been decommissioned) and N Hbr remain for commercial and FV use.

**NAVIGATION** WPT 54°33´·34N 03°36´·21W, 133°/4½ca to W pier hd. There are no hazards in the offing. Hold closer to the North Pier, and beware stone bar at end of W Pier.

**LIGHTS AND MARKS** Several tall chimneys are charted within 1·5M S of hbr. St Bees Head Lt ho is 2·7M SSW of hbr ent. SHM bn, Fl G 2·5s, 4½ca S of W pierhead marks sewer outfall. IPTS sigs 1-3 shown from N side of lock ent to seaward only at present: priority to inward bound vessels.

**R/T** HM VHF Ch 12 16 (as for access times).

**TELEPHONE** (Code 01946)HM 692435, 🖷 691135; Sealock 694672; MRCC (0151) 931 3341; Police 692616; Marinecall 09068 969651.

**FACILITIES Marina** (200 inc Ⓥ) ☎ 692435, office@whitehaven-harbour.co.uk, <12m £15, <12m £8 on quay wall, contact HM, D, Gas, BY, CH, ME, Ⓔ, El, ⚓, BH, Slip, 🛢. **SC. Town** Market days Thurs, Sat; P (cans), Bar, Ⓑ, ✉, R, 🛒, 🚂.

**MINOR HARBOUR BETWEEN ST BEES HD AND MORECAMBE BAY**
**RAVENGLASS**, Cumbria, **54°20´·00N 03°26´·80W** (drying line). AC 1346, *1826*. HW +0020 on Dover; ML no data; Duration 0545. See 3.7 (Tarn Pt). Large drying hbr, into which R's Mite, Irt and Esk flow; approx 2·5m in ent at HW−2. Sellafield power stn with WCM lt buoy and outfall buoys are 5M NNW. FG ☆ (occas) on blockhouse at S side of ent. *Solway Sailing Directions* with pilotage notes by Ravenglass Boating Ass'n, local knowledge advisable. From N beware Drigg Rk and from S Selker Rks, SHM lt buoy, 5M SSW of ent. Firing range D406 close S at Eskmeals; Mon-Thur 0800-1600LT (1500 Fri). When in use R flags flown, R lts at night; *Eskmeals Gun Range* VHF Ch 16 13, ☎ (01229) 717631 Ext 245/6. **Village:** FW, Slip, Bar, 🛒, ✉.

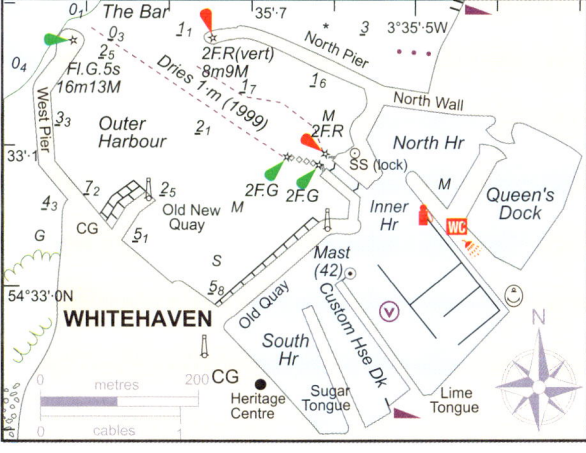

WHITEHAVEN

## 3.8 ISLE OF MAN

**Charts** AC Irish Sea *1826*, *1411*; 2094 (small scale); 2696 (ports). *Imray, C26, Y70. OS 95.*

**The Isle of Man** is one of the British Islands, set in the Irish Sea roughly equidistant from England, Scotland, Wales and Ireland but it is not part of the UK. It has a large degree of self-government. Lights are maintained by the Commissioners of Northern Lighthouses in Scotland. Manx hbrs are administered by the IOM Government.

**Directions** *Isle of Man – Tides, Directions and Anchorages* is recommended; from Hunter Publications, Wild Boar Cottage, Rawcliffe Rd, St Michaels, Preston PR3 0UH, ☎ 01995-679240, 🖷 679740.

**Passage information** See 3.4.

**Distances** See 3.1 for distances between ports in Area 10 and 0.31 for distances across the Irish Sea, North Channel and St George's Channel.

**Harbours and anchorages** Most of the hbrs are on the E and S sides, but a visit to the W coast with its characteristic cliffs is worth while. The four main hbrs are treated below in an anti-clockwise direction from Peel on the W coast to Ramsey in the NE. There are good ⚓s at: Port Erin in the SW, Castletown and Derby Haven in the SE, and Laxey Bay in the E. All IOM hbrs charge the same overnight berthing fee, £8·73, regardless of LOA. In addition, a charge of £12.75 is levied on all visiting craft using the pontoons in Douglas Harbour.

**R/T** If contact with local Harbour Offices cannot be established on VHF, vessels should call *Douglas Hbr Control* Ch 12 16 for urgent messages or other info.

**Coastguard** Call Liverpool MRCC Ch 16 67 86; the Snaefell (IoM) aerial is linked to Liverpool by land line.

**Customs** The IOM is under the same customs umbrella as the rest of the UK, and there are no formalities on landing from or returning to UK.

**Weather** Forecasts can be obtained direct from the forecaster at Ronaldsway Met Office ☎ 0900 6243 3200, H24. **Douglas Hbr Control** (3.15) can supply visibility and wind info on request.

**MINOR HARBOURS IN THE ISLE OF MAN**

**PORT ERIN**, Isle of Man, **54°05´·31N 04°46´·34W**. AC 2094, 2696. HW −0020 on Dover; ML 2·9m; Duration 0555. See 3.14. From S and W, Milner's Twr on Bradda Hd is conspic. Ldg lts, both FR 10/19m 5M, lead 099° into the bay. Beware the ruined bkwtr (dries 2·9m) extending N from the SW corner, marked by an unlit SHM buoy. A small hbr on the S side dries 0·8m. Raglan Pier (E arm of hbr), Oc G 5s 8m 5M. Two ⚓s W of Raglan Pier. Good ⚓ in 3-8m N of Raglan Pier, but exposed to W'lies. Call Port St. Mary Harbour (VHF Ch 12) ☎ 833205

**CASTLETOWN BAY**, Isle of Man, **54°03´·51N 04°38´·57W**. AC 2094, 2696. HW +0025 on Dover; ML 3·4m; Duration 0555. The bay gives good shelter except in SE to SW winds. From the E, keep inside the race off Dreswick Pt, or give it a wide berth. Beware Lheeah-rio Rks in W of bay, marked by PHM buoy, Fl R 3s, Bell. Hbr dries 3·1m to level sand. Access HW±2½. Berth in outer hbr or go via swing footbridge (manually opened) into inner hbr below fixed bridge. ⚓ between Lheeah-rio Rks and pier in 3m; or W of Langness Pt. Lts: Langness lt, on Dreswick Pt, Fl (2) 30s 23m 12M. Hbr S (New) Pier, Oc R 15s 8m 5M; Inner S pier (Irish Quay), Oc R 4s 5m 5M, vis 142°-322°. 150m NW is swing bridge marked by 2 FR (hor). N pier, Oc G 4s 3m (W metal post on concrete column). VHF Ch 12 16 (when vessel due). HM ☎ 823549; Dr 823597. Facilities: **Outer hbr** Slip, L, C (mobile), AB; **Irish Quay** AB, C, FW; **Inner hbr** AB, C, FW; **Town** P, D, Gas, ME.

**LAXEY**, Isle of Man, **54°13´·46N 04°23´·32W**. AC 2094. HW +0025 on Dover; +0010 and −2·0m on Liverpool; ML 4m; Duration 0550. The bay gives good shelter in SW to N winds. 2 yellow ⚓s (seasonal) are close E of hbr ent; 2 more are 1M S in Garwick Bay. ⚓ about 2ca S of pier hds or in Garwick Bay. The hbr dries 3·0m to rk and is only suitable for small yachts; access HW±3 for 1·5m draft. Beware rks on N side of the narrow ent. Keep close to pier after entering to avoid training wall on NE side. AB on inside of pier; inner basin is full of local boats. Pier hd lt Oc R 3s 7m 5M, obsc when brg <318°. Bkwtr hd lt Oc G 3s 7m. Harbour Office ☎ 861663. Facilities: FW, R, ✉, Ⓑ, Bar.

# 3.9  PEEL

Isle of Man 54°13'·61N 04°41'·68W ✿❋◐⚓⚓✿✿✿

**CHARTS**  AC 2094, 2696; Imray C62; Y70; OS 95

**TIDES**  +0005 Dover; ML 2·9; Duration 0545

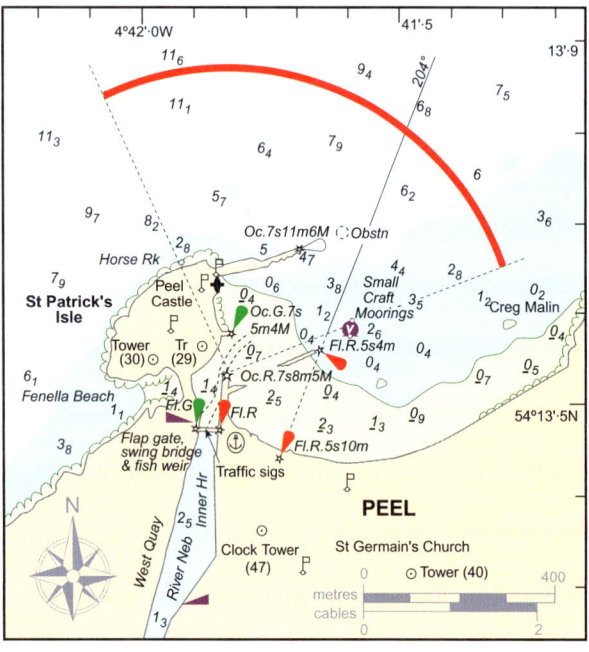

**Standard Port LIVERPOOL (→)**

| Times | | | | Height (metres) | | | |
|---|---|---|---|---|---|---|---|
| High Water | | Low Water | | MHWS | MHWN | MLWN | MLWS |
| 0000 | 0600 | 0200 | 0700 | 9·3 | 7·4 | 2·9 | 0·9 |
| 1200 | 1800 | 1400 | 1900 | | | | |
| **Differences PEEL** | | | | | | | |
| +0005 | +0005 | -0015 | -0025 | −4·1 | −3·1 | −1·4 | −0·5 |

**SHELTER**  Good, except in strong NW to NE winds when ent should not be attempted. 4 Y ⚓s (seasonal) off S groyne in about 2m. Fin keelers may be able to berth on N bkwtr in 5m. Inner hbr approaches dry approx 1·4m, flat sand; access HW±2 when flapgate lowered and through swing bridge. AB on W quay. A water retention scheme is now operational and Inner Hbr maintained depth 2·5m reducing to 1.3m at the inner end.

**NAVIGATION**  WPT 54°13'·97N 04°41'·43W, 200°/0·42M to groyne lt. When close in, beware groyne on S side of hbr ent, submerged at half tide.

**LIGHTS AND MARKS**  Power stn chy (80m, grey with B top) at S end of inner hbr is conspic from W and N; chy brg 203° leads to hbr ent. Groyne lt and Clock Tr (conspic) in transit 200° are almost on same line. Peel Castle and 2 twrs are conspic on St Patrick's Isle to NW of hbr. Ldg lts in transit 204° on Groyne Fl R 5s 3m. Traffic sigs for Inner Hbr.

**R/T**  Peel Hbr VHF Ch **12** 16 (HW±2, HO for Swing Bridge – other times call Douglas Hbr Control Ch 12 for remote bridge opening).

**TELEPHONE** (Code 01624) Harbour Office ☎/🖷 842338, Mobile 07624 495036; MRCC 0151-931 3341; Weather 0900 6243 322; Marinecall 09068 969651; Police 697327; Dr 843636.

**FACILITIES**  Outer and Inner Hbrs, AB see 3.8, M, Slip, FW, ME, El, ⚒, C (mobile); **Peel Sailing and Cruising Club** ☎ 842390, Showers (key from Harbour Office), R, 🗑, Bar; **Services:** Gas, BY, CH, ACA. **Town** P (cans), 🖷, R, Bar, ✉, Ⓑ, ⇌ (bus to Douglas, qv for ferries), ✈ Ronaldsway. Facilities: Bar, D, P, FW, R, Slip, 🛒.

# 3.10  PORT ST MARY

Isle of Man **54°04'·43N 04°43'·73W** ✿❋◐⚓⚓✿✿

**CHARTS**  AC 2094, 2696; Imray C62; Y70; OS 95

**TIDES**  +0020 Dover; ML 3·2; Duration 0605

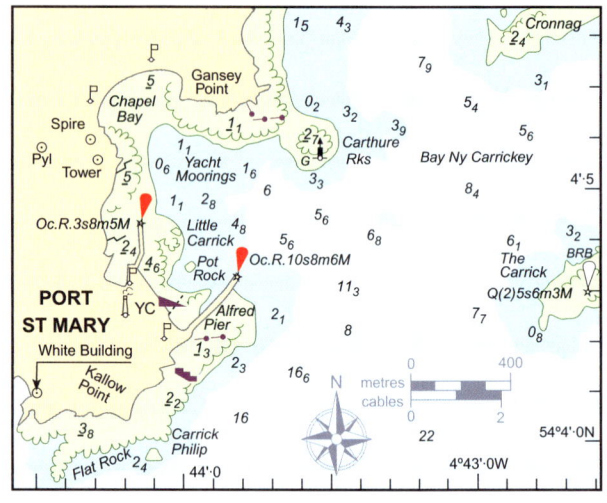

**Standard Port LIVERPOOL (→)**

| Times | | | | Height (metres) | | | |
|---|---|---|---|---|---|---|---|
| High Water | | Low Water | | MHWS | MHWN | MLWN | MLWS |
| 0000 | 0600 | 0200 | 0700 | 9·3 | 7·4 | 2·9 | 0·9 |
| 1200 | 1800 | 1400 | 1900 | | | | |
| **Differences PORT ST MARY** | | | | | | | |
| +0005 | +0015 | −0010 | −0030 | −3·4 | −2·6 | −1·3 | −0·4 |
| **CALF SOUND** | | | | | | | |
| +0005 | +0005 | −0015 | −0025 | −3·2 | −2·6 | −0·9 | −0·3 |
| **PORT ERIN** | | | | | | | |
| −0005 | +0015 | −0010 | −0050 | −4·1 | −3·2 | −1·3 | −0·5 |

**SHELTER**  Very good except in E or SE winds. ⚓ S of Gansey Pt, but poor holding. 5 yellow ⚓s (seasonal) between Alfred Pier and Little Carrick.

**NAVIGATION**  WPT 54°04'·21N 04°43'·37W, 295°/0·3M to Alfred Pier lt. Rocky outcrops to SE of pier to 2ca offshore. Beware lobster/crab pots, especially between Calf Island and Langness Pt.

**LIGHTS AND MARKS**  Alfred Pier, Oc R 10s 8m 6M. Inner pier, Oc R 3s 8m 5M; both lts on W trs + R band, in transit 295° lead clear S of The Carrick Rk, in centre of bay, which is marked by IDM bn, Q (2) 5s 6m 3M. A conspic TV mast (133m), 5ca WNW of hbr, in transit with Alfred Pier lt leads 290° towards the hbr and also clears The Carrick rock.

**R/T**  Call Port St Mary Hbr VHF Ch 12 16 (when vessel due or through Douglas Hbr Control Ch 12).

**TELEPHONE** (Code 01624)  HM 833205; MRCC 0151 931 3341; Weather 0900 6243 322, Marinecall 09068 969651; Police 697327; Dr 832281.

**FACILITIES**  **Alfred Pier** AB see 3.8, Slip, D, L, FW, C (mobile); **Inner Hbr** dries 2·4m on sand; AB, Slip, D, L, FW; **Isle of Man YC** ☎ 832088, FW, Showers, Bar; **Services:** ME, CH, D, El, SM. **Town** CH, 🖷, R, Bar, ✉, Ⓑ, ⇌ (bus to Douglas, qv for ferries), ✈ Ronaldsway.

## MINOR HARBOUR EAST OF CASTLETOWN

**DERBY HAVEN**, Isle of Man, **54°04'·65N 04°36'·45W**. Tides & charts as above. Rather remote bay exposed only to NE/E winds. ⚓ in centre of bay, NW of St Michael's Island, in 3-5m. A detached bkwtr on NW side of the bay gives shelter to craft able to dry out behind it. Lts: Iso G 2s on S end of bkwtr. Aero FR (occas) at Ronaldsway airport, NW of bay. Facilities: at Castletown (1½M) and Port St Mary.

# 3.11  DOUGLAS

Isle of Man **54°08'·87N 04°27'·96W** ✿✿✿⚙🌊⚓✿✿✿

**CHARTS**  AC 2094, 2696; Imray C62; Y70; OS 95

**TIDES**  +0009 Dover; ML 3·8; Duration 0600

**Standard Port LIVERPOOL (→)**

| Times | | | | Height (metres) | | | |
|---|---|---|---|---|---|---|---|
| High Water | | Low Water | | MHWS | MHWN | MLWN | MLWS |
| 0000 | 0600 | 0200 | 0700 | 9·3 | 7·4 | 2·9 | 0·9 |
| 1200 | 1800 | 1400 | 1900 | | | | |
| Differences DOUGLAS | | | | | | | |
| +0005 | +0015 | –0015 | –0025 | –2·4 | –2·0 | –0·5 | –0·1 |

**SHELTER**  Good except in NE winds. Very heavy seas run in during NE gales. Outer hbr: Victoria and King Edward VIII piers are for commercial vessels/ferries.  At inner end of Battery Pier in summer about 18 boats can raft up on pontoon; untenable in NE/E winds. Complete shelter in inner hbr, with possible pontoon berths, flapgate lowers on the flood and rises on the ebb at 4·4m above CD, lifting bridge opens every ½H subject to tide/road traffic conditions (request opening on VHF Ch12).

**NAVIGATION**  WPT 54°09'·01N 04°27'·67W (abeam No 1 SHM buoy, Q (3) G 5s), 229°/0·47M to front ldg lt.  Appr from NE of No 1 buoy (to avoid overfalls E of Princess Alexandra Pier) and await port entry sig, or call on VHF Ch 12. There is no bar. Keep clear of large vessels and ferries. Beware concrete step at end of dredged area (◇ mark on King Edward VIII Pier) and cill at ent to inner hbr.

**LIGHTS AND MARKS**  Douglas Head Fl 10s 32m 24M. Ldg lts 229°, both Oc 10s 9/12m 5M, synch; front W △; rear W ▽, both on R border. IPTS Nos 2, 3 and 5 shown from mast on Victoria Pier. Dolphin at N end of Alexandra Pier 2FR (vert).

**R/T**  *Douglas Hbr Control* VHF Ch **12** 16 (H24); also broadcasts nav warnings for IoM ports and coastal waters on Ch 12 including weather and tidal info on request.

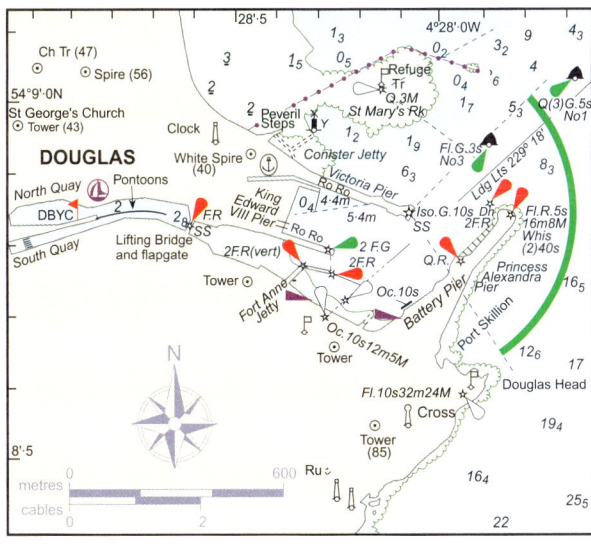

**TELEPHONE**  (Code 01624) Hr Control 686628 🖷 626403 (H24); MRCC 0151-931 3341; Weather 0900 6243 322, Marinecall 09068 969651; Police 697327; Ⓗ 650000.

**FACILITIES  Outer Hbr** AB see 3.8, M, FW at pontoon, ME, El, ⚒, C (mobile), Slip; **Inner Hbr (Pontoons and N and S Quays)** (110); Ⓥ according to space (no reservations), AB (£10.87/craft), M, ⏻, FW, ME, C, El, ⚒, CH, Slip; **Douglas Bay YC** ☎ 673965, Bar, Slip, L, showers 0930-2300. **Services:** P (cans), D, CH, ACA, El, Divers, Gas, Gaz, Kos. **Town** www.gov.im, 🖷, R, Bar, ⊠, Ⓑ, 🖸, Ferry to Heysham and Liverpool; also in summer to Dublin and Belfast; ✈ Ronaldsway.

# 3.12  RAMSEY

Isle of Man **54°19'·44N 04°22'·49W** ✿✿⚙🌊✿✿

**CHARTS**  AC 2094, 2696; Imray C62; Y70; OS 95

**TIDES**  +0020 Dover; ML 4·2; Duration 0545

**Standard Port LIVERPOOL (→)**

| Times | | | | Height (metres) | | | |
|---|---|---|---|---|---|---|---|
| High Water | | Low Water | | MHWS | MHWN | MLWN | MLWS |
| 0000 | 0600 | 0200 | 0700 | 9·3 | 7·4 | 2·9 | 0·9 |
| 1200 | 1800 | 1400 | 1900 | | | | |
| Differences RAMSEY | | | | | | | |
| +0005 | +0015 | –0005 | –0015 | –1·9 | –1·5 | –0·6 | 0·0 |

**SHELTER**  Very good except in strong NE winds. Hbr dries 1·8m–6m. Access and ent only permitted HW –2½ to HW +2. Berth on Town quay (S side) or as directed by HM on entry. 4 yellow ⚓s are close NW of Queen's Pier hd (seasonal). Note: Landing on Queen's Pier is prohibited.

**NAVIGATION**  WPT 54°19'·44N 04°21'·89W, 270°/0.37M to ent. The foreshore dries out 1ca to seaward of the pier hds.

**LIGHTS AND MARKS**  No ldg lts/marks. Relative to hbr ent, Pt of Ayre, Fl (4) 20s 32m 19M, is 5·5M N; Maughold Hd, Fl (3) 30s 65m 21M, is 3M SE; Albert Tr (☐ stone tr 14m, on hill 130m) is conspic 7ca S; and Snaefell (617m) bears 220°/5M. Inside the hbr an Iso G 4s, G SHM post, marks the S tip of Mooragh Bank; it is not visible from seaward. 2FR (hor) on each side mark the centre of swing bridge.

**R/T**  *Ramsey Hbr* VHF Ch **12** 16 (0800-1600LT and when a vessel is due); Other times call *Douglas Hbr Control* Ch **12**.

**TELEPHONE**  (Code 01624) Harbour Office 812245, mob 07624 460304; MRCC 0151 931 3341; Weather 0900 6243 322, Marinecall 09068 969651; Police 812234; Dr 813881; Ⓗ 811811.

**FACILITIES  Outer Hbr: E Quay** ☎ 812245, strictly for commercial vessels (frequent movements H24), no AB for yachts, FW; **Town Quay** (S side) AB see 3.8, ⏻, FW. **Inner Hbr, W Quay** AB, ⏻, FW, Slip (Grid); **N Quay** AB, FW; **Shipyard Quay** Slip; **Old Hbr** AB, Slip, M; **Manx S&CC:** ☎ 813494 AB £7.26; **Services:** P (cans) from garages, D, ME, El, Ⓔ, ⚒, ⛽. **Town** 🖷, R, Gas, Gaz, Kos, Bar, @ in Library, 🖸, ⊠, Ⓑ, ⇌ (bus to Douglas, which see for ferries), ✈ Ronaldsway.

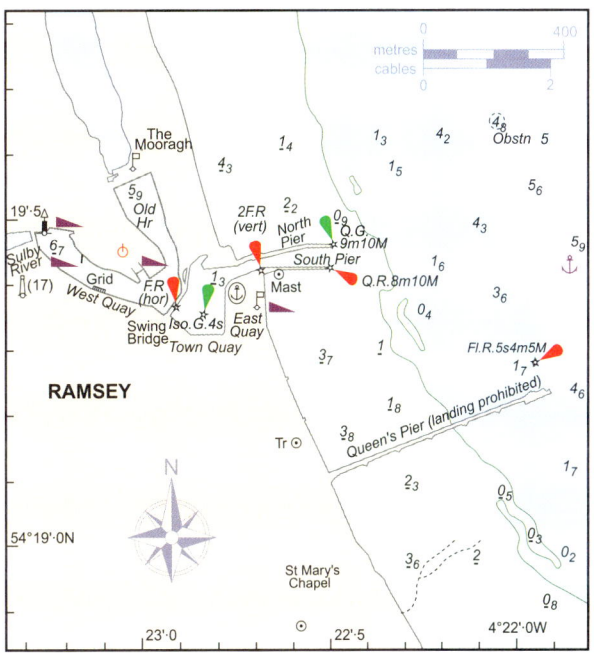

## 3.13 GLASSON DOCK

Lancashire 53°59'·98N 02°50'·93W ✹✹◊◊◊✿✿

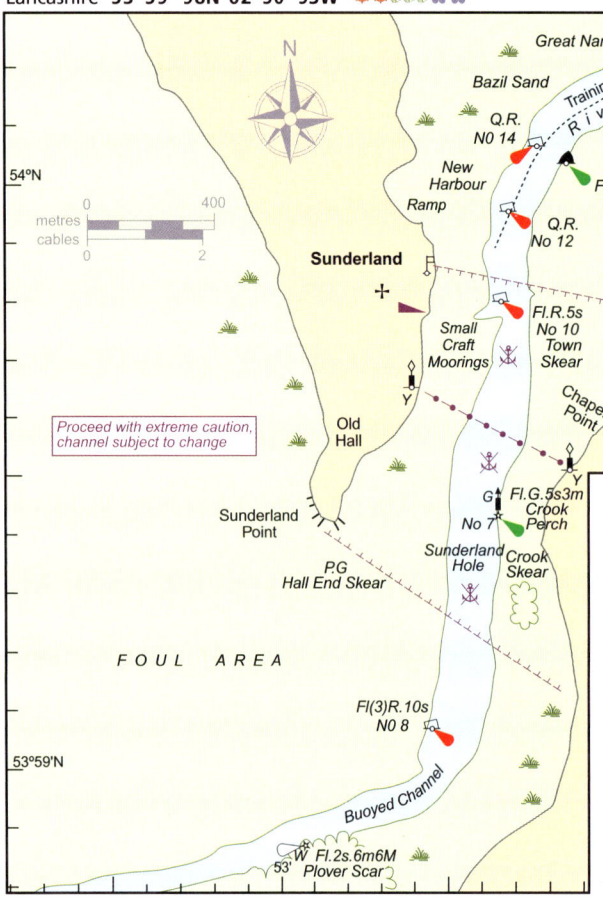

Proceed with extreme caution, channel subject to change

a tide gauge showing depth over the lock sill at Glasson Dock. ⚓ is prohib between Sutherland Pt and No 10 PHM lt buoy. Beyond this a training wall, marked by PHM lt buoys/bn, extends to lock ent. R Lune is navigable to Lancaster.

• **It is dangerous to proceed downriver later than HW +1.**

**LIGHTS AND MARKS** Plover Scar, Fl 2s, on with Cockersand, FW, leads 084° up to Nos 2/3 buoys; then follow buoyed chan which shifts.

**Tfc Sigs** at E side of lock from estuary
- 🔴 = lock manned, but shut
- 🟢 = lock open, clear to enter

**Tfc Sigs** inside dock
- 🔴 = Gate closed or vessel(s) entering dock
- 🟢 = Gate open. Vessels may leave

**R/T** VHF Ch 16 69 (HW–1½ to HW Liverpool).

**TELEPHONE** (Code 01524) HM 751724, 📠 753601; MRCC 0151 931 3341; Marinecall 09068 969651; Police 63333; 🏥 765944.

**FACILITIES** Glasson Basin Marina (240 + 20 ⓥ) £12.00/craft) ☎ 751491, www.BWML.co.uk. Slip, D (0830-1630), ME, El, Ⓔ, ✂, C, (50 ton), BH (50 ton), CH, ⚒; **Glasson SC** ☎ 751089 Slip, M, C; **Lune CC** Access HW±2. **Town** P (cans), ⚫, R, Bar, ✉, Ⓑ (Lancaster), ⇌ (bus to Lancaster 4M), ✈ (Blackpool).

**CHARTS** AC*1826*, 1552, 2010; Imray C62; OS 102, 97

**TIDES** +0020 Dover; ML No data; Duration 0535

Standard Port LIVERPOOL (→)

| Times | | | | Height (metres) | | | |
|---|---|---|---|---|---|---|---|
| High Water | | Low Water | | MHWS | MHWN | MLWN | MLWS |
| 0000 | 0600 | 0200 | 0700 | 9·3 | 7·4 | 2·9 | 0·9 |
| 1200 | 1800 | 1400 | 1900 | | | | |
| **Differences BARROW-IN-FURNESS** (Ramsden Dock) | | | | | | | |
| +0015 | +0015 | +0015 | +0015 | 0·0 | –0·3 | +0·1 | +0·2 |
| **ULVERSTON** | | | | | | | |
| +0020 | +0040 | No data | | 0·0 | –0·1 | No data | |
| **ARNSIDE** | | | | | | | |
| +0100 | +0135 | No data | | +0·5 | +0·2 | No data | |
| **MORECAMBE** | | | | | | | |
| +0005 | +0010 | +0030 | +0015 | +0·2 | 0·0 | 0·0 | +0·2 |
| **HEYSHAM** | | | | | | | |
| +0005 | +0005 | +0015 | 0000 | +0·1 | 0·0 | 0·0 | +0·2 |
| **GLASSON DOCK** | | | | | | | |
| +0020 | +0030 | +0220 | +0240 | –2·7 | –3·0 | No data | |
| **LANCASTER** | | | | | | | |
| +0110 | +0030 | Dries out | | –5·0 | –4·9 | Dries out | |

NOTE: At Glasson Dock LW time differences give the end of a LW stand which lasts up to 2 hrs at sp.

**SHELTER** Very good in marina; also sheltered ⚓ in R Lune to await sea lock, opens HW–1 (Liverpool) to HW, into Glasson Dock. Inner lock/swing bridge lead into BWB basin.

**NAVIGATION** WPT 53°58'·41N 03°00'·09W (close R Lune WCM lt buoy), 084°/4·2M to front ldg lt. Leave WPT at HW–1½ via buoyed/lit chan which is subject to frequent change. For latest info call Port Commission (☎ 01524 751724). Plover Scar lt bn has

**ADJACENT HARBOURS IN MORECAMBE BAY**

**BARROW-IN-FURNESS**, Cumbria, **54°05'·64N 03°13'·44W**. AC *1826*, 2010, 3164. HW +0030 on Dover; See 3.8. ML 5·0m; Duration 0530. Good shelter but open to SE winds. Drying moorings off Piel and Roa Islands or ⚓ clear of fairway. Marks/lts: Walney Island Lt ho (conspic stone tr), Fl 15s 21m 23M (obsc 122°-127° within 3M of shore). Directions: From Lightning Knoll SWM lt buoy, ldg lts, front Q 7m 10M; rear (6ca from front), Iso 2s 13m 10M (lattice structures) lead 041°/3·7M past Halfway Shoal bn, QR 16m 10M with RY chequers, Racon, to Bar lt buoy (abeam Walney Island lt ho). Inner Channel ldg lts, front Q 9m 10M, rear Iso 2s 14m 6M, lead 005° past Piel Is with least charted depth 1·7m. Piel Is, conspic ruined castle, slip and moorings on E side. Roa Is, 5ca N, has jetty at S end and moorings on E & W sides. Slip (Roa Is Boat Club ☎ (01229) 825291). Causeway joins to mainland. Commercial docks, 3M NW at Barrow, reached via buoyed/lit Walney Chan, dredged to 2·5m, which must be kept clear. HM (Barrow) ☎ (01229) 822911, 📠 835822; VHF *Barrow Port Control* Ch 12 16 (H24). Facilities: Hotel at Rampside, ⚫.

**HEYSHAM**, Lancashire, **54°02'·01N 02°55'·96W**. AC *1826*, 2010, 1552. HW +0015 on Dover; ML 5·1m; Duration 0545. See 3.8. Good shelter, but yachts not normally accepted without special reason. Beware high speed ferries and oil rig supply ships. Ldg lts 102°, both F Bu 11/14m 2M, Y+B ◊ on masts. S jetty lt 2 FG (vert), Siren 30s. S pier hd ,Oc G 7·5s 9m 6M. N pier hd, 2FR (vert) 11m, obsc from seaward. Ent sigs: R flag or 🔴 = no entry; no sig = no dep; 2 R flags or 2 🔴 = no ent or dep. VHF Ch 14 74 16 (H24). HM ☎ (01524) 852373. Facilities: Bar, FW, R, ⚫ at Morecambe (2M).

# 3.14 FLEETWOOD

Lancashire 53°55'·49N 03°00'·15W ✿✿✿☆☆☆❀❀

**CHARTS** AC *1826,* 2010, 1552; Imray C62; OS 102

**TIDES** +0015 Dover; ML 5.2; Duration 0530

**Standard Port LIVERPOOL (→)**

| Times | | | | Height (metres) | | | |
|---|---|---|---|---|---|---|---|
| High Water | | Low Water | | MHWS | MHWN | MLWN | MLWS |
| 0000 | 0600 | 0200 | 0700 | 9·3 | 7·4 | 2·9 | 0·9 |
| 1200 | 1800 | 1400 | 1900 | | | | |
| **Differences WYRE LIGHTHOUSE** | | | | | | | |
| −0010 | −0010 | +0005 | 0000 | −0·1 | −0·1 | No data | |
| **FLEETWOOD** | | | | | | | |
| −0008 | −0008 | −0003 | −0003 | −0·1 | −0·1 | +0·1 | +0·3 |
| **BLACKPOOL** | | | | | | | |
| −0015 | −0005 | −0005 | −0015 | −0·4 | −0·4 | −0·1 | +0·1 |

**SHELTER** Very good in Fleetwood Village Marina 5·5m. Sheltered ⚓ off Knott End pier on E bank to await tide. Passage up-river to

Skippool (5M) needs local knowledge and shoal draft; access HW±1·5 hrs (if ht of tide is >8·5m).

**NAVIGATION** WPT 53°57'·57N 03°02'·33W, Fairway NCM buoy, VQ, 143°/3ca to No 3 SHM lt buoy; here the appr chan turns S.

• Avoid ferries and dredgers turning in lower hbr, dredged 4·5m.

• Further up the hbr, Nos 23 SHM and 24 PHM buoys mark start of marina ent chan dredged to drying height of 3m.

• Freeflow access through lock HW±1½ except some np tides. In addition, on many dates specified by the HM between Mar 29 and October 13 access is extended to HW±2½ by locking in and out.

• For best water keep 15m NW of the 300m long training wall (3 perches with R □ topmarks).

**LIGHTS AND MARKS** Chan is well buoyed/lit, but AC 1552 does not depict individual buoys which are subject to frequent change due to silting. Ldg lts, front Iso G 2s; rear Iso G 4s, 156° (only to be used between Nos 8 buoy and 11 perch bn). Lock sigs (only enter on instructions): 1 ● (1 ●) = Gates open for entry; 2 ● (2 ●) = open for departures.

**R/T** Call *RoRo Ships* directly on Ch 11 for info on movements. Call *Fleetwood Dock* Ch **12**, HW±1·5 for marina/Fish Dock.

**TELEPHONE** (Code 01253) HM (ABP) ☎ 879060, 🖷 777549; MRCC (0151) 931 3341; Marinecall 09068 969651; Police (01524) 63333; Dr 873312.

**FACILITIES Marina** (300) ☎ 879062, 🖷 777549, £1·96, D (0800-1700), 🅿, C (25 ton), CH, SM, ACA, ✕, Ⓔ (☎ 8253535), C (mobile 50 ton by arrangement). **River Wyre YC** 811948, 1 Ⓥ. **Blackpool & Fleetwood YC** (Skippool) ☎ 884205, AB, Slip, FW, Bar; **Town** P & D (cans), ME, El, ✕, CH, 🛒, R, Bar, ✉, Ⓑ, ⇌ (Poulton-le-Fylde or Blackpool), ✈ (Blackpool).

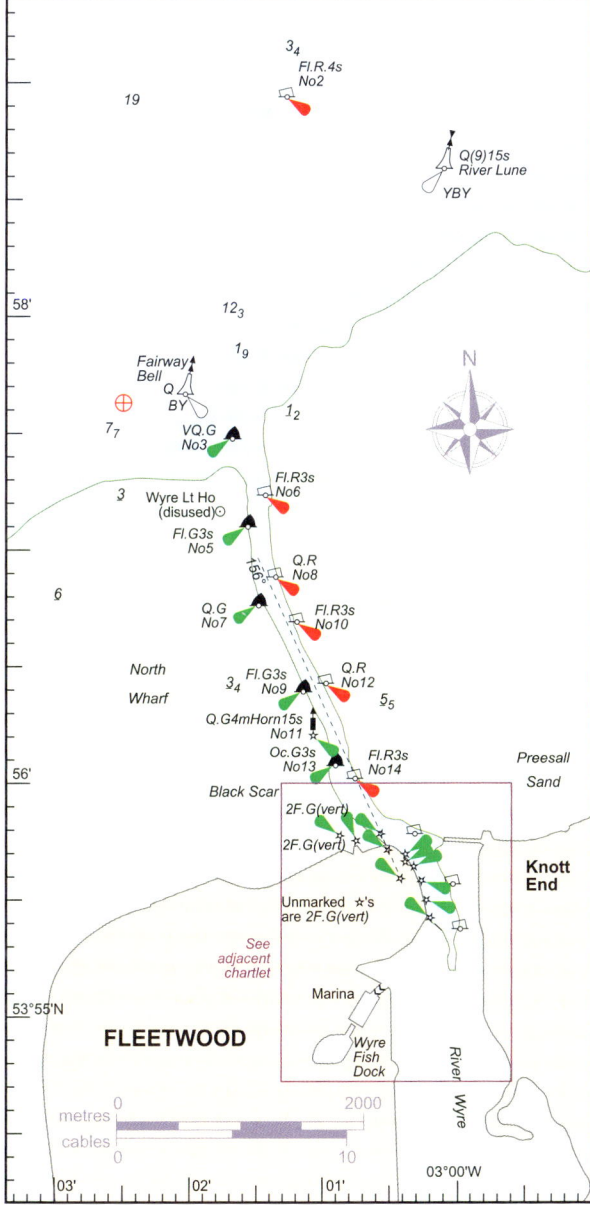

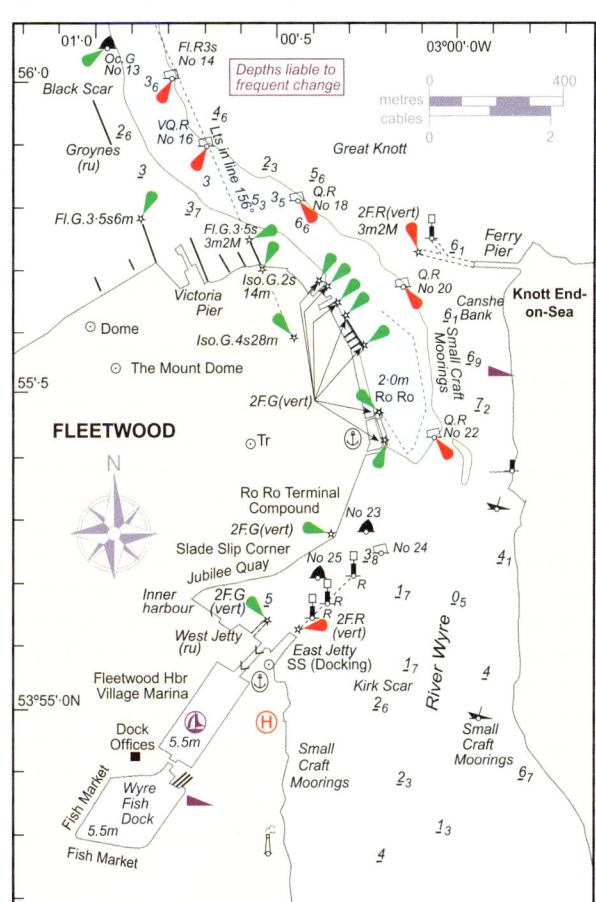

## 3.15 RIVER RIBBLE/PRESTON

Lancashire 53°43'·51N 03°00'·08W ✿✿✿▵▵▵✿✿

**CHARTS** AC *1826*, 1981; Imray C62; OS 102

**TIDES** +0013 Dover; ML No data; Duration 0520

**Standard Port LIVERPOOL (→)**

| Times | | | | Height (metres) | | | |
|---|---|---|---|---|---|---|---|
| High Water | | Low Water | | MHWS | MHWN | MLWN | MLWS |
| 0000 | 0600 | 0200 | 0700 | 9·3 | 7·4 | 2·9 | 0·9 |
| 1200 | 1800 | 1400 | 1900 | | | | |

**Differences PRESTON**

| | | | | | | | |
|---|---|---|---|---|---|---|---|
| +0010 | +0010 | +0335 | +0310 | −4·0 | −4·1 | −2·8 | −0·8 |

LW time differences give the end of a LW stand lasting 3½ hrs.

**SOUTHPORT**

| | | | | | | | |
|---|---|---|---|---|---|---|---|
| −0020 | −0010 | No data | | −0·3 | −0·3 | No data | |

**FORMBY**

| | | | | | | | |
|---|---|---|---|---|---|---|---|
| −0015 | −0010 | −0020 | −0020 | −0·3 | −0·1 | 0·0 | +0·1 |

**SHELTER** Good in Preston marina (5m depth) 15M upriver. Possible drying berths on the N bank at Lytham or Freckleton, or 2M up R Douglas access HW±1.

**NAVIGATION** WPT **A** 53°41'·75N 03°08'·90W, Gut SWM lt buoy. The chartlet shows only the outer 6M of the estuary. The seaward 2·5M of the Gut chan is silted up. Best water is now via South Gut chan (liable to shift), navigable HW±2. Leave WPT **A** at HW

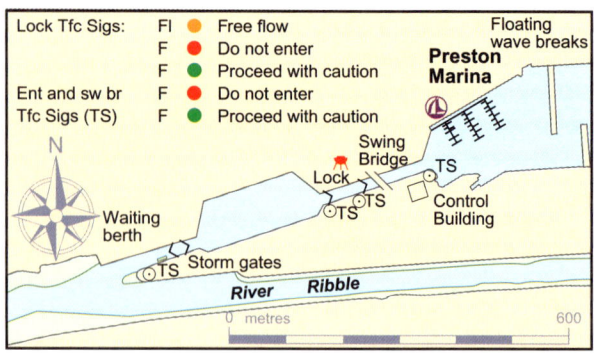

**TELEPHONE** (Code 01772) Preston locks 726871; MRCC (0151) 9313341; Marinecall 09068 969651; Police 203203; Ⓗ 710408.

**FACILITIES** Waiting berth for 2m draft outside storm gates which are usually open. Tfc lts at lock into marina; see plan below. Lock in HW−1 to +2, 0700-2100 Apr-Oct (no commercial tfc). Swing bridge opens in unison with locks. **Preston Marina** ☎ 733595, 🖷 731881, www.prestonmarina. co.uk, £1·25, D, CH, ME, ✖, Gas, C (25 ton, 45 ton by arrangement), R, ▨, ACA, ⬤. **Douglas BY**, ☎/ 🖷 812462, mob 07740 780899, AB, £0·70, C (20 ton), CH, D, FW, ✖, Slip, ME. **Freckleton BY** ☎ 632439, mob 07957 820881, AB, £5/ yacht, slip, FW, CH, ME. **Ribble Cruising Club** ☎ (01253) 739983.

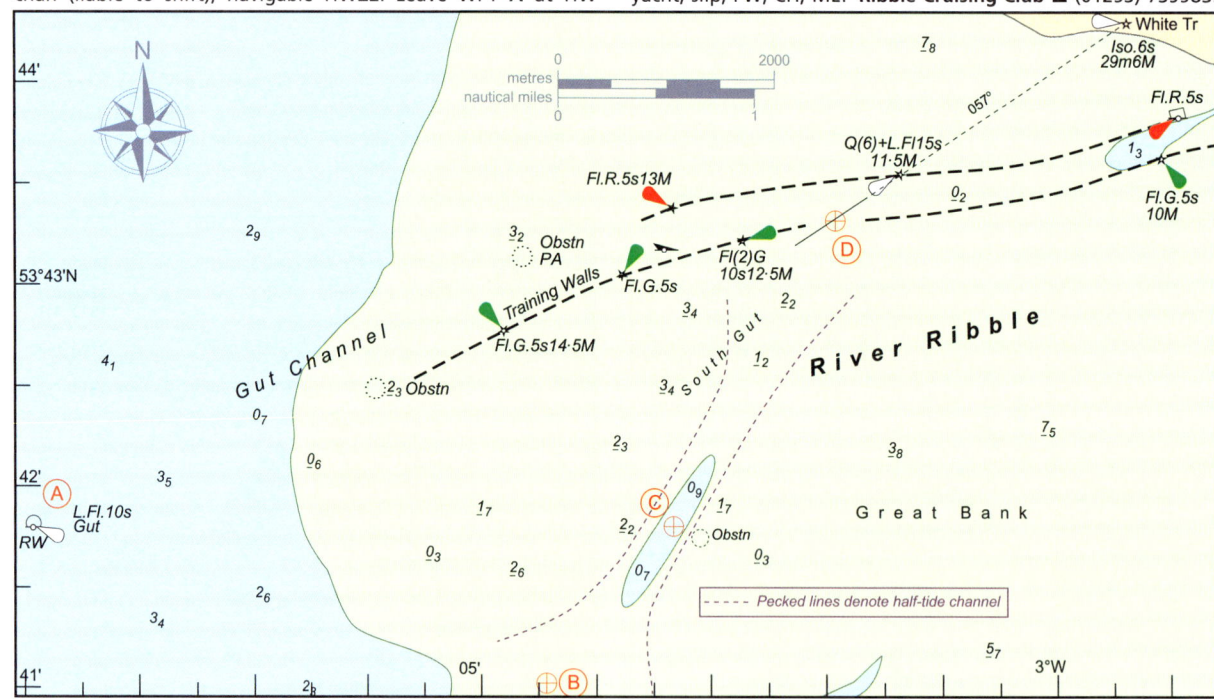

Liverpool −2. Track 105°/2·9M to WPT **B** 53°40'·96N 03°04'·22W; thence 032°/0·9M to WPT **C** 53°41'·70N 03°03'·43W; thence 026°/ 1·8M to WPT **D** 53°43'·29N 03°02'·10W. Enter Gut Chan via the gap, leaving *11¾M* perch 100m to port. The river trends 080° between training walls 3m, marked by lit perches. The remaining 15M is straightforward but night appr not advised. Shortcut if draught < 2m: from WPT **A** track 090°/3·2M to WPT **C**. Then 026°/ 1·8M to WPT **D** and the transit of the 11½M SCM lt perch with conspic W twr.

**LIGHTS AND MARKS** 14½M perch is the most seaward chan mark. Up-river of 11½M perch there is a PHM buoy and perch (off chartlet), both Fl R 5s. 4 SHM perches, Fl G 5s, lead to 5M perch, Fl (2) G 10s, marking mouth of unlit R Douglas. 3M and 2M perches are Fl G 5s; 1M perch is Fl G 10s. Warton airfield beacon, Mo (WQ) G 9s occas, is N abeam 6M perch, Fl G 5s.

**R/T** At Preston, for locks call *Riversway* Ch **14**; Marina Ch **80**, both (HW±2). Douglas BY Ch 16 when vessel due.

**TIME ZONE (UT)**
For Summer Time add ONE hour in **non-shaded areas**

# LIVERPOOL (ALFRED DOCK)   LAT 53°24'N   LONG 3°01'W
TIMES AND HEIGHTS OF HIGH AND LOW WATERS

Dates in red are **SPRINGS**
Dates in blue are **NEAPS**

YEAR **2008**

## JANUARY

| Day | Time | m | Day | Time | m |
|---|---|---|---|---|---|
| **1** TU | 0457 / 1124 / 1720 | 7.5 / 3.1 / 7.6 | **16** W | 0422 / 1048 / 1650 / 2324 | 8.1 / 2.5 / 8.4 / 2.5 |
| **2** W | 0009 / 0600 / 1223 / 1825 | 3.0 / 7.3 / 3.3 / 7.4 | **17** TH | 0525 / 1156 / 1757 | 7.8 / 2.8 / 8.1 |
| **3** TH | 0108 / 0709 / 1328 / 1935 | 3.1 / 7.3 / 3.3 / 7.4 | **18** F | 0038 / 0639 / 1320 / 1912 | 2.7 / 7.7 / 2.9 / 8.0 |
| **4** F | 0210 / 0812 / 1434 / 2037 | 3.0 / 7.6 / 3.1 / 7.6 | **19** SA | 0202 / 0758 / 1446 / 2032 | 2.7 / 7.9 / 2.6 / 8.2 |
| **5** SA | 0307 / 0905 / 1531 / 2129 | 2.8 / 7.9 / 2.8 / 7.9 | **20** SU | 0319 / 0908 / 1559 / 2139 | 2.4 / 8.4 / 2.0 / 8.6 |
| **6** SU | 0356 / 0950 / 1620 / 2213 | 2.5 / 8.3 / 2.4 / 8.2 | **21** M | 0422 / 1005 / 1659 / 2235 | 1.9 / 8.9 / 1.5 / 9.0 |
| **7** M | 0439 / 1031 / 1704 / 2252 | 2.2 / 8.6 / 2.1 / 8.4 | **22** TU | 0515 / 1055 / 1751 / ○2324 | 1.5 / 9.3 / 1.0 / 9.2 |
| **8** TU | 0519 / 1109 / 1746 / ●2329 | 2.0 / 8.8 / 1.9 / 8.6 | **23** W | 0603 / 1141 / 1838 | 1.3 / 9.6 / 0.8 |
| **9** W | 0559 / 1146 / 1827 | 1.8 / 9.0 / 1.7 | **24** TH | 0008 / 0646 / 1224 / 1921 | 9.3 / 1.2 / 9.7 / 0.7 |
| **10** TH | 0006 / 0637 / 1218 / 1906 | 8.7 / 1.7 / 9.1 / 1.5 | **25** F | 0050 / 0726 / 1304 / 2001 | 9.3 / 1.2 / 9.6 / 0.8 |
| **11** F | 0044 / 0715 / 1301 / 1945 | 8.8 / 1.7 / 9.2 / 1.5 | **26** SA | 0128 / 0804 / 1342 / 2038 | 9.1 / 1.4 / 9.4 / 1.1 |
| **12** SA | 0123 / 0753 / 1341 / 2023 | 8.8 / 1.7 / 9.2 / 1.5 | **27** SU | 0204 / 0838 / 1419 / 2112 | 8.9 / 1.7 / 9.1 / 1.5 |
| **13** SU | 0202 / 0831 / 1422 / 2100 | 8.8 / 1.8 / 9.2 / 1.6 | **28** M | 0239 / 0910 / 1456 / 2144 | 8.6 / 2.0 / 8.7 / 2.0 |
| **14** M | 0244 / 0911 / 1505 / 2140 | 8.7 / 1.9 / 9.0 / 1.8 | **29** TU | 0316 / 0942 / 1534 / 2217 | 8.2 / 2.5 / 8.2 / 2.5 |
| **15** TU | 0329 / 0955 / 1554 / ◑2226 | 8.4 / 2.2 / 8.8 / 2.1 | **30** W | 0357 / 1021 / 1618 / ◑2301 | 7.7 / 2.9 / 7.7 / 3.0 |
| | | | **31** TH | 0448 / 1117 / 1715 | 7.3 / 3.3 / 7.2 |

## FEBRUARY

| Day | Time | m | Day | Time | m |
|---|---|---|---|---|---|
| **1** F | 0003 / 0558 / 1231 / 1831 | 3.4 / 7.0 / 3.6 / 6.9 | **16** SA | 0005 / 0615 / 1305 / 1903 | 3.1 / 7.3 / 3.1 / 7.4 |
| **2** SA | 0116 / 0725 / 1347 / 2001 | 3.5 / 7.1 / 3.5 / 7.0 | **17** SU | 0148 / 0751 / 1446 / 2034 | 3.1 / 7.5 / 2.7 / 7.8 |
| **3** SU | 0228 / 0838 / 1500 / 2108 | 3.3 / 7.5 / 3.1 / 7.5 | **18** M | 0318 / 0905 / 1600 / 2138 | 2.7 / 8.1 / 2.0 / 8.3 |
| **4** M | 0331 / 0930 / 1600 / 2156 | 2.8 / 8.0 / 2.6 / 7.9 | **19** TU | 0421 / 1000 / 1655 / 2228 | 2.1 / 8.8 / 1.3 / 8.9 |
| **5** TU | 0421 / 1013 / 1649 / 2237 | 2.4 / 8.5 / 2.1 / 8.4 | **20** W | 0510 / 1045 / 1741 / 2311 | 1.5 / 9.3 / 0.8 / 9.2 |
| **6** W | 0505 / 1052 / 1733 / 2314 | 1.9 / 8.9 / 1.6 / 8.7 | **21** TH | 0552 / 1126 / 1822 / ○2350 | 1.2 / 9.6 / 0.6 / 9.3 |
| **7** TH | 0546 / 1129 / 1814 / ●2351 | 1.6 / 9.2 / 1.3 / 9.0 | **22** F | 0630 / 1204 / 1900 | 1.0 / 9.7 / 0.6 |
| **8** F | 0625 / 1206 / 1852 | 1.3 / 9.4 / 1.0 | **23** SA | 0026 / 0706 / 1240 / 1934 | 9.3 / 1.0 / 9.6 / 0.7 |
| **9** SA | 0027 / 0702 / 1243 / 1929 | 9.1 / 1.2 / 9.6 / 0.9 | **24** SU | 0059 / 0738 / 1314 / 2005 | 9.2 / 1.1 / 9.4 / 1.0 |
| **10** SU | 0104 / 0738 / 1322 / 2003 | 9.3 / 1.1 / 9.7 / 0.9 | **25** M | 0131 / 0807 / 1346 / 2032 | 9.0 / 1.4 / 9.1 / 1.5 |
| **11** M | 0142 / 0813 / 1401 / 2037 | 9.2 / 1.2 / 9.6 / 1.1 | **26** TU | 0202 / 0831 / 1418 / 2054 | 8.8 / 1.7 / 8.8 / 1.9 |
| **12** TU | 0221 / 0849 / 1442 / 2112 | 9.1 / 1.4 / 9.3 / 1.5 | **27** W | 0235 / 0856 / 1452 / 2119 | 8.4 / 2.2 / 8.3 / 2.4 |
| **13** W | 0302 / 0929 / 1528 / 2154 | 8.7 / 1.8 / 8.9 / 2.0 | **28** TH | 0310 / 0931 / 1532 / 2157 | 8.0 / 2.7 / 7.7 / 3.0 |
| **14** TH | 0350 / 1018 / 1622 / ◑2248 | 8.2 / 2.3 / 8.3 / 2.6 | **29** F | 0353 / 1022 / 1622 / ◑2259 | 7.4 / 3.2 / 7.1 / 3.5 |
| **15** F | 0453 / 1127 / 1733 | 7.7 / 2.9 / 7.7 | | | |

## MARCH

| Day | Time | m | Day | Time | m |
|---|---|---|---|---|---|
| **1** SA | 0454 / 1140 / 1735 | 6.9 / 3.6 / 6.6 | **16** SU | 0608 / 1307 / 1906 | 7.2 / 3.0 / 7.2 |
| **2** SU | 0026 / 0630 / 1307 / 1924 | 3.8 / 6.8 / 3.6 / 6.7 | **17** M | 0146 / 0744 / 1443 / 2027 | 3.3 / 7.5 / 2.5 / 7.7 |
| **3** M | 0150 / 0806 / 1427 / 2043 | 3.6 / 7.1 / 3.2 / 7.2 | **18** TU | 0311 / 0852 / 1549 / 2124 | 2.7 / 8.1 / 1.8 / 8.3 |
| **4** TU | 0302 / 0903 / 1534 / 2132 | 3.0 / 7.8 / 2.5 / 7.8 | **19** W | 0408 / 0943 / 1638 / 2210 | 2.0 / 8.7 / 1.2 / 8.8 |
| **5** W | 0358 / 0947 / 1625 / 2212 | 2.4 / 8.4 / 1.9 / 8.4 | **20** TH | 0452 / 1026 / 1720 / 2249 | 1.5 / 9.2 / 0.8 / 9.1 |
| **6** TH | 0443 / 1026 / 1709 / 2249 | 1.8 / 8.9 / 1.3 / 8.9 | **21** F | 0531 / 1104 / 1757 / ○2325 | 1.2 / 9.4 / 0.7 / 9.2 |
| **7** F | 0525 / 1103 / 1750 / ●2326 | 1.3 / 9.4 / 0.9 / 9.2 | **22** SA | 0606 / 1139 / 1831 / 2357 | 1.0 / 9.4 / 0.7 / 9.2 |
| **8** SA | 0604 / 1141 / 1828 | 1.0 / 9.7 / 0.6 | **23** SU | 0639 / 1212 / 1902 | 1.0 / 9.3 / 0.9 |
| **9** SU | 0002 / 0641 / 1220 / 1904 | 9.5 / 0.7 / 9.9 / 0.5 | **24** M | 0028 / 0708 / 1244 / 1928 | 9.1 / 1.1 / 9.2 / 1.2 |
| **10** M | 0041 / 0718 / 1259 / 1939 | 9.6 / 0.6 / 9.9 / 0.6 | **25** TU | 0058 / 0733 / 1314 / 1950 | 9.0 / 1.4 / 8.9 / 1.6 |
| **11** TU | 0119 / 0753 / 1340 / 2012 | 9.5 / 0.8 / 9.7 / 0.9 | **26** W | 0128 / 0756 / 1346 / 2011 | 8.8 / 1.6 / 8.6 / 1.9 |
| **12** W | 0158 / 0830 / 1422 / 2049 | 9.3 / 1.1 / 9.3 / 1.4 | **27** TH | 0200 / 0823 / 1419 / 2039 | 8.5 / 2.0 / 8.2 / 2.4 |
| **13** TH | 0240 / 0912 / 1509 / 2131 | 8.8 / 1.6 / 8.7 / 2.0 | **28** F | 0234 / 0858 / 1458 / 2116 | 8.1 / 2.5 / 7.7 / 2.9 |
| **14** F | 0329 / 1004 / 1606 / ◑2228 | 8.2 / 2.3 / 8.0 / 2.8 | **29** SA | 0315 / 0947 / 1546 / ◑2213 | 7.6 / 3.0 / 7.1 / 3.5 |
| **15** SA | 0434 / 1119 / 1725 / 2350 | 7.6 / 2.8 / 7.3 / 3.3 | **30** SU | 0411 / 1101 / 1653 / 2341 | 7.1 / 3.4 / 6.7 / 3.8 |
| | | | **31** M | 0533 / 1228 / 1834 | 6.8 / 3.4 / 6.6 |

## APRIL

| Day | Time | m | Day | Time | m |
|---|---|---|---|---|---|
| **1** TU | 0107 / 0716 / 1346 / 2001 | 3.6 / 7.1 / 3.0 / 7.1 | **16** W | 0245 / 0822 / 1521 / 2056 | 2.6 / 8.1 / 1.7 / 8.2 |
| **2** W | 0221 / 0821 / 1454 / 2054 | 3.1 / 7.7 / 2.4 / 7.8 | **17** TH | 0340 / 0914 / 1609 / 2141 | 2.1 / 8.6 / 1.3 / 8.6 |
| **3** TH | 0321 / 0909 / 1549 / 2137 | 2.4 / 8.3 / 1.7 / 8.4 | **18** F | 0424 / 0958 / 1650 / 2220 | 1.7 / 8.9 / 1.1 / 8.9 |
| **4** F | 0410 / 0951 / 1636 / 2216 | 1.7 / 9.0 / 1.1 / 9.0 | **19** SA | 0502 / 1037 / 1725 / 2255 | 1.4 / 9.0 / 1.1 / 9.0 |
| **5** SA | 0454 / 1032 / 1718 / 2255 | 1.2 / 9.4 / 0.7 / 9.4 | **20** SU | 0537 / 1112 / 1757 / ○2327 | 1.3 / 9.0 / 1.1 / 9.0 |
| **6** SU | 0536 / 1113 / 1759 / ●2335 | 0.8 / 9.8 / 0.4 / 9.6 | **21** M | 0608 / 1144 / 1825 / 2357 | 1.3 / 9.0 / 1.3 / 9.0 |
| **7** M | 0617 / 1155 / 1837 | 0.5 / 9.9 / 0.4 | **22** TU | 0637 / 1215 / 1850 | 1.4 / 8.8 / 1.5 |
| **8** TU | 0015 / 0657 / 1238 / 1914 | 9.7 / 0.5 / 9.9 / 0.5 | **23** W | 0028 / 0703 / 1246 / 1913 | 8.9 / 1.5 / 8.7 / 1.7 |
| **9** W | 0057 / 0737 / 1322 / 1951 | 9.6 / 0.6 / 9.6 / 0.9 | **24** TH | 0100 / 0729 / 1319 / 1940 | 8.7 / 1.7 / 8.4 / 2.0 |
| **10** TH | 0140 / 0818 / 1409 / 2032 | 9.3 / 1.0 / 9.1 / 1.5 | **25** F | 0133 / 0801 / 1355 / 2012 | 8.5 / 2.0 / 8.1 / 2.3 |
| **11** F | 0226 / 0905 / 1500 / 2119 | 8.8 / 1.5 / 8.5 / 2.1 | **26** SA | 0209 / 0838 / 1434 / 2052 | 8.2 / 2.3 / 7.8 / 2.8 |
| **12** SA | 0320 / 1004 / 1602 / ◑2220 | 8.2 / 2.1 / 7.8 / 2.8 | **27** SU | 0252 / 0927 / 1522 / 2146 | 7.8 / 2.7 / 7.3 / 3.2 |
| **13** SU | 0430 / 1124 / 1724 / 2345 | 7.7 / 2.6 / 7.3 / 3.2 | **28** M | 0345 / 1032 / 1623 / ◑2302 | 7.4 / 3.0 / 7.0 / 3.5 |
| **14** M | 0558 / 1259 / 1850 | 7.4 / 2.6 / 7.3 | **29** TU | 0454 / 1148 / 1741 | 7.2 / 3.1 / 6.9 |
| **15** TU | 0129 / 0719 / 1420 / 2000 | 3.1 / 7.7 / 2.2 / 7.7 | **30** W | 0020 / 0614 / 1300 / 1903 | 3.4 / 7.3 / 2.8 / 7.2 |

Chart Datum: 4·93 metres below Ordnance Datum (Newlyn). HAT is 10·5 metres above Chart Datum.

**NW England**

**TIME ZONE (UT)**
For Summer Time add ONE hour in **non-shaded areas**

## LIVERPOOL (ALFRED DOCK)  LAT 53°24'N  LONG 3°01'W
TIMES AND HEIGHTS OF HIGH AND LOW WATERS

Dates in red are **SPRINGS**
Dates in blue are **NEAPS**

YEAR **2008**

### MAY

| Time | m | | Time | m |
|---|---|---|---|---|
| **1** 0131 | 3.0 | | **16** 0259 | 2.4 |
| 0726 | 7.8 | | 0838 | 8.2 |
| TH 1406 | 2.3 | | F 1531 | 1.9 |
| 2005 | 7.8 | | 2105 | 8.2 |
| **2** 0234 | 2.4 | | **17** 0347 | 2.1 |
| 0823 | 8.3 | | 0925 | 8.4 |
| F 1506 | 1.7 | | SA 1612 | 1.7 |
| 2055 | 8.4 | | 2147 | 8.5 |
| **3** 0330 | 1.8 | | **18** 0427 | 1.9 |
| 0913 | 8.9 | | 1007 | 8.5 |
| SA 1558 | 1.2 | | SU 1648 | 1.6 |
| 2141 | 9.0 | | 2224 | 8.6 |
| **4** 0420 | 1.2 | | **19** 0503 | 1.7 |
| 1000 | 9.4 | | 1044 | 8.6 |
| SU 1645 | 0.8 | | M 1720 | 1.6 |
| 2225 | 9.4 | | 2258 | 8.7 |
| **5** 0508 | 0.8 | | **20** 0536 | 1.7 |
| 1046 | 9.7 | | 1119 | 8.6 |
| M 1730 | 0.6 | | TU 1750 | 1.7 |
| ● 2308 | 9.6 | | ○ 2331 | 8.8 |
| **6** 0554 | 0.6 | | **21** 0608 | 1.7 |
| 1133 | 9.8 | | 1151 | 8.5 |
| TU 1812 | 0.6 | | W 1818 | 1.7 |
| 2353 | 9.6 | | | |
| **7** 0640 | 0.5 | | **22** 0004 | 8.7 |
| 1220 | 9.7 | | 0639 | 1.7 |
| W 1854 | 0.7 | | TH 1225 | 8.4 |
| | | | 1848 | 1.9 |
| **8** 0039 | 9.5 | | **23** 0038 | 8.6 |
| 0726 | 0.6 | | 0712 | 1.8 |
| TH 1310 | 9.4 | | F 1300 | 8.3 |
| 1937 | 1.1 | | 1921 | 2.0 |
| **9** 0128 | 9.3 | | **24** 0114 | 8.5 |
| 0814 | 0.9 | | 0748 | 2.0 |
| F 1401 | 9.0 | | SA 1338 | 8.2 |
| 2023 | 1.6 | | 1957 | 2.3 |
| **10** 0219 | 8.9 | | **25** 0153 | 8.3 |
| 0907 | 1.4 | | 0828 | 2.2 |
| SA 1455 | 8.5 | | SU 1418 | 8.0 |
| 2114 | 2.1 | | 2039 | 2.5 |
| **11** 0315 | 8.4 | | **26** 0236 | 8.1 |
| 1007 | 1.8 | | 0914 | 2.4 |
| SU 1556 | 8.0 | | M 1504 | 7.7 |
| 2215 | 2.6 | | 2128 | 2.8 |
| **12** 0421 | 8.0 | | **27** 0325 | 7.9 |
| 1116 | 2.1 | | 1008 | 2.5 |
| M 1705 | 7.6 | | TU 1557 | 7.5 |
| ◑ 2327 | 2.9 | | 2228 | 3.0 |
| **13** 0532 | 7.8 | | **28** 0422 | 7.8 |
| 1228 | 2.3 | | 1109 | 2.6 |
| TU 1817 | 7.5 | | W 1659 | 7.4 |
| | | | ◐ 2334 | 3.0 |
| **14** 0047 | 3.0 | | **29** 0527 | 7.8 |
| 0641 | 7.8 | | 1213 | 2.5 |
| W 1339 | 2.2 | | TH 1807 | 7.5 |
| 1921 | 7.6 | | | |
| **15** 0200 | 2.7 | | **30** 0041 | 2.8 |
| 0744 | 8.0 | | 0632 | 8.0 |
| TH 1440 | 2.0 | | F 1319 | 2.2 |
| 2017 | 7.9 | | 1914 | 7.9 |
| | | | **31** 0148 | 2.4 |
| | | | 0736 | 8.4 |
| | | | SA 1423 | 1.9 |
| | | | 2014 | 8.3 |

### JUNE

| Time | m | | Time | m |
|---|---|---|---|---|
| **1** 0251 | 2.0 | | **16** 0348 | 2.4 |
| 0835 | 8.8 | | 0938 | 8.0 |
| SU 1522 | 1.5 | | M 1610 | 2.2 |
| 2108 | 8.8 | | 2157 | 8.3 |
| **2** 0350 | 1.5 | | **17** 0430 | 2.2 |
| 0931 | 9.1 | | 1021 | 8.2 |
| M 1616 | 1.2 | | TU 1647 | 2.1 |
| 2158 | 9.2 | | 2235 | 8.5 |
| **3** 0445 | 1.1 | | **18** 0509 | 2.0 |
| 1025 | 9.4 | | 1059 | 8.3 |
| TU 1706 | 1.0 | | W 1722 | 2.0 |
| ● 2248 | 9.4 | | ○ 2312 | 8.6 |
| **4** 0538 | 0.8 | | **19** 0547 | 1.9 |
| 1117 | 9.5 | | 1135 | 8.3 |
| W 1755 | 0.9 | | TH 1757 | 1.9 |
| 2337 | 9.5 | | 2347 | 8.7 |
| **5** 0630 | 0.7 | | **20** 0624 | 1.8 |
| 1209 | 9.4 | | 1211 | 8.3 |
| TH 1842 | 1.0 | | F 1832 | 1.9 |
| **6** 0027 | 9.5 | | **21** 0023 | 8.7 |
| 0721 | 0.7 | | 0701 | 1.8 |
| F 1301 | 9.3 | | SA 1247 | 8.4 |
| 1929 | 1.2 | | 1908 | 1.9 |
| **7** 0118 | 9.3 | | **22** 0101 | 8.7 |
| 0813 | 0.8 | | 0740 | 1.8 |
| SA 1352 | 9.0 | | SU 1324 | 8.3 |
| 2017 | 1.5 | | 1946 | 2.0 |
| **8** 0209 | 9.1 | | **23** 0139 | 8.6 |
| 0904 | 1.1 | | 0819 | 1.8 |
| SU 1443 | 8.7 | | M 1403 | 8.3 |
| 2106 | 1.9 | | 2026 | 2.1 |
| **9** 0301 | 8.8 | | **24** 0220 | 8.6 |
| 0956 | 1.4 | | 0900 | 1.9 |
| M 1536 | 8.3 | | TU 1444 | 8.2 |
| 2158 | 2.3 | | 2108 | 2.3 |
| **10** 0356 | 8.4 | | **25** 0304 | 8.5 |
| 1048 | 1.8 | | 0943 | 2.0 |
| TU 1631 | 7.9 | | W 1530 | 8.1 |
| ◑ 2253 | 2.6 | | 2156 | 2.5 |
| **11** 0453 | 8.1 | | **26** 0353 | 8.4 |
| 1143 | 2.1 | | 1031 | 2.2 |
| W 1731 | 7.6 | | TH 1622 | 7.9 |
| 2352 | 2.8 | | ◐ 2251 | 2.6 |
| **12** 0555 | 7.8 | | **27** 0449 | 8.2 |
| 1240 | 2.4 | | 1127 | 2.3 |
| TH 1833 | 7.5 | | F 1722 | 7.8 |
| | | | 2355 | 2.7 |
| **13** 0055 | 2.9 | | **28** 0551 | 8.2 |
| 0657 | 7.7 | | 1233 | 2.4 |
| F 1341 | 2.5 | | SA 1829 | 7.8 |
| 1932 | 7.6 | | | |
| **14** 0200 | 2.8 | | **29** 0107 | 2.6 |
| 0756 | 7.7 | | 0657 | 8.2 |
| SA 1438 | 2.5 | | SU 1344 | 2.3 |
| 2027 | 7.8 | | 1937 | 8.1 |
| **15** 0259 | 2.6 | | **30** 0221 | 2.3 |
| 0850 | 7.9 | | 0806 | 8.4 |
| SU 1528 | 2.4 | | M 1454 | 2.0 |
| 2114 | 8.1 | | 2042 | 8.4 |

### JULY

| Time | m | | Time | m |
|---|---|---|---|---|
| **1** 0330 | 1.9 | | **16** 0405 | 2.5 |
| 0912 | 8.7 | | 1002 | 7.9 |
| TU 1557 | 1.7 | | W 1623 | 2.4 |
| 2142 | 8.9 | | 2217 | 8.4 |
| **2** 0432 | 1.4 | | **17** 0451 | 2.2 |
| 1013 | 9.0 | | 1048 | 8.1 |
| W 1653 | 1.4 | | TH 1704 | 2.1 |
| 2236 | 9.2 | | 2256 | 8.6 |
| **3** 0530 | 1.0 | | **18** 0532 | 1.9 |
| 1108 | 9.2 | | 1121 | 8.3 |
| TH 1745 | 1.2 | | F 1743 | 1.9 |
| ● 2327 | 9.5 | | ○ 2333 | 8.8 |
| **4** 0624 | 0.7 | | **19** 0612 | 1.7 |
| 1200 | 9.3 | | 1157 | 8.5 |
| F 1835 | 1.1 | | SA 1820 | 1.8 |
| **5** 0016 | 9.6 | | **20** 0008 | 8.9 |
| 0715 | 0.5 | | 0650 | 1.5 |
| SA 1250 | 9.3 | | SU 1232 | 8.6 |
| 1921 | 1.1 | | 1856 | 1.7 |
| **6** 0105 | 9.5 | | **21** 0044 | 9.0 |
| 0803 | 0.6 | | 0727 | 1.4 |
| SU 1336 | 9.2 | | M 1307 | 8.7 |
| 2006 | 1.3 | | 1933 | 1.6 |
| **7** 0151 | 9.4 | | **22** 0121 | 9.0 |
| 0848 | 0.8 | | 0803 | 1.4 |
| M 1421 | 8.9 | | TU 1343 | 8.7 |
| 2048 | 1.6 | | 2009 | 1.7 |
| **8** 0236 | 9.1 | | **23** 0159 | 9.0 |
| 0930 | 1.1 | | 0839 | 1.5 |
| TU 1504 | 8.6 | | W 1421 | 8.7 |
| 2130 | 1.9 | | 2046 | 1.8 |
| **9** 0320 | 8.7 | | **24** 0239 | 9.0 |
| 1011 | 1.6 | | 0915 | 1.6 |
| W 1547 | 8.1 | | TH 1502 | 8.5 |
| 2213 | 2.3 | | 2126 | 2.0 |
| **10** 0406 | 8.3 | | **25** 0324 | 8.8 |
| 1054 | 2.1 | | 0955 | 1.9 |
| TH 1634 | 7.7 | | F 1548 | 8.2 |
| ◑ 2301 | 2.8 | | ◐ 2213 | 2.4 |
| **11** 0456 | 7.8 | | **26** 0416 | 8.4 |
| 1142 | 2.6 | | 1045 | 2.3 |
| F 1730 | 7.4 | | SA 1645 | 7.9 |
| 2356 | 3.1 | | 2315 | 2.7 |
| **12** 0557 | 7.4 | | **27** 0518 | 8.1 |
| 1237 | 3.0 | | 1152 | 2.6 |
| SA 1836 | 7.2 | | SU 1754 | 7.7 |
| **13** 0100 | 3.2 | | **28** 0037 | 2.9 |
| 0707 | 7.2 | | 0630 | 7.8 |
| SU 1339 | 3.1 | | M 1315 | 2.8 |
| 1945 | 7.4 | | 1913 | 7.7 |
| **14** 0208 | 3.1 | | **29** 0205 | 2.7 |
| 0816 | 7.3 | | 0752 | 7.9 |
| M 1442 | 2.9 | | TU 1439 | 2.5 |
| 2044 | 7.7 | | 2031 | 8.1 |
| **15** 0311 | 2.8 | | **30** 0324 | 2.2 |
| 0914 | 7.6 | | 0908 | 8.3 |
| TU 1537 | 2.7 | | W 1550 | 2.1 |
| 2134 | 8.1 | | 2135 | 8.7 |
| | | | **31** 0430 | 1.5 |
| | | | 1009 | 8.8 |
| | | | TH 1648 | 1.6 |
| | | | 2229 | 9.2 |

### AUGUST

| Time | m | | Time | m |
|---|---|---|---|---|
| **1** 0525 | 1.0 | | **16** 0515 | 1.7 |
| 1101 | 9.1 | | 1101 | 8.5 |
| F 1739 | 1.2 | | SA 1727 | 1.7 |
| ● 2317 | 9.5 | | ○ 2312 | 9.0 |
| **2** 0615 | 0.6 | | **17** 0554 | 1.4 |
| 1148 | 9.3 | | 1136 | 8.7 |
| SA 1825 | 1.0 | | SU 1803 | 1.5 |
| | | | 2346 | 9.2 |
| **3** 0002 | 9.7 | | **18** 0631 | 1.2 |
| 0701 | 0.4 | | 1209 | 8.9 |
| SU 1232 | 9.4 | | M 1839 | 1.3 |
| 1907 | 1.0 | | | |
| **4** 0045 | 9.7 | | **19** 0021 | 9.3 |
| 0742 | 0.5 | | 0706 | 1.0 |
| M 1313 | 9.3 | | TU 1244 | 9.0 |
| 1946 | 1.1 | | 1914 | 1.2 |
| **5** 0125 | 9.5 | | **20** 0057 | 9.4 |
| 0821 | 0.7 | | 0740 | 1.0 |
| TU 1350 | 9.0 | | W 1319 | 9.0 |
| 2022 | 1.4 | | 1948 | 1.3 |
| **6** 0203 | 9.2 | | **21** 0134 | 9.4 |
| 0857 | 1.1 | | 0813 | 1.2 |
| W 1426 | 8.7 | | TH 1355 | 9.0 |
| 2056 | 1.8 | | 2023 | 1.6 |
| **7** 0240 | 8.8 | | **22** 0214 | 9.2 |
| 0930 | 1.7 | | 0847 | 1.5 |
| TH 1502 | 8.3 | | F 1435 | 8.8 |
| 2129 | 2.2 | | 2100 | 1.8 |
| **8** 0318 | 8.3 | | **23** 0258 | 8.8 |
| 1004 | 2.3 | | 0925 | 1.9 |
| F 1540 | 7.9 | | SA 1520 | 8.4 |
| ◑ 2207 | 2.7 | | ◐ 2146 | 2.3 |
| **9** 0401 | 7.7 | | **24** 0350 | 8.3 |
| 1045 | 2.8 | | 1014 | 2.5 |
| SA 1627 | 7.4 | | SU 1617 | 7.8 |
| 2300 | 3.2 | | 2250 | 2.8 |
| **10** 0454 | 7.2 | | **25** 0456 | 7.7 |
| 1141 | 3.3 | | 1125 | 3.0 |
| SU 1731 | 7.1 | | M 1733 | 7.4 |
| **11** 0011 | 3.5 | | **26** 0025 | 3.1 |
| 0610 | 6.8 | | 0621 | 7.4 |
| M 1252 | 3.5 | | TU 1303 | 3.2 |
| 1901 | 7.0 | | 1907 | 7.5 |
| **12** 0128 | 3.5 | | **27** 0207 | 2.8 |
| 0745 | 6.9 | | 0756 | 7.6 |
| TU 1405 | 3.4 | | W 1439 | 2.8 |
| 2019 | 7.4 | | 2030 | 8.0 |
| **13** 0243 | 3.1 | | **28** 0326 | 2.1 |
| 0853 | 7.3 | | 0907 | 8.2 |
| W 1511 | 3.0 | | TH 1548 | 2.2 |
| 2114 | 7.9 | | 2130 | 8.7 |
| **14** 0345 | 2.6 | | **29** 0425 | 1.4 |
| 0943 | 7.8 | | 1001 | 8.8 |
| TH 1604 | 2.5 | | F 1641 | 1.6 |
| 2158 | 8.4 | | 2218 | 9.3 |
| **15** 0433 | 2.1 | | **30** 0514 | 0.8 |
| 1024 | 8.2 | | 1047 | 9.2 |
| F 1648 | 2.1 | | SA 1726 | 1.2 |
| 2237 | 8.8 | | ● 2302 | 9.6 |
| | | | **31** 0558 | 0.5 |
| | | | 1129 | 9.4 |
| | | | SU 1807 | 0.9 |
| | | | 2341 | 9.8 |

Chart Datum: 4·93 metres below Ordnance Datum (Newlyn). HAT is 10·5 metres above Chart Datum.

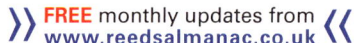
**FREE** monthly updates from
www.reedsalmanac.co.uk

**TIME ZONE (UT)**
For Summer Time add ONE hour in **non-shaded areas**

## LIVERPOOL (ALFRED DOCK)   LAT 53°24'N   LONG 3°01'W
TIMES AND HEIGHTS OF HIGH AND LOW WATERS

Dates in red are **SPRINGS**
Dates in blue are **NEAPS**

YEAR **2008**

### SEPTEMBER

| Time | m | Time | m |
|---|---|---|---|
| **1** 0638 | 0.4 | **16** 0603 | 0.9 |
| 1207 | 9.4 | 1140 | 9.2 |
| M 1845 | 0.9 | TU 1816 | 1.0 |
| | | 2353 | 9.6 |
| **2** 0019 | 9.7 | **17** 0639 | 0.8 |
| 0714 | 0.6 | 1215 | 9.3 |
| TU 1242 | 9.3 | W 1852 | 0.9 |
| 1919 | 1.1 | | |
| **3** 0055 | 9.5 | **18** 0031 | 9.7 |
| 0748 | 0.9 | 0714 | 0.8 |
| W 1315 | 9.1 | TH 1253 | 9.3 |
| 1950 | 1.3 | 1927 | 1.0 |
| **4** 0128 | 9.2 | **19** 0111 | 9.6 |
| 0818 | 1.1 | 0748 | 1.1 |
| TH 1347 | 8.8 | F 1331 | 9.2 |
| 2018 | 1.7 | 2004 | 1.3 |
| **5** 0201 | 8.8 | **20** 0153 | 9.2 |
| 0844 | 1.9 | 0823 | 1.5 |
| F 1420 | 8.5 | SA 1413 | 8.9 |
| 2045 | 2.2 | 2044 | 1.7 |
| **6** 0236 | 8.3 | **21** 0239 | 8.7 |
| 0910 | 2.4 | 0904 | 2.0 |
| SA 1455 | 8.0 | SU 1501 | 8.4 |
| 2117 | 2.7 | 2133 | 2.3 |
| **7** 0315 | 7.7 | **22** 0335 | 8.1 |
| 0944 | 3.0 | 0957 | 2.7 |
| SU 1537 | 7.5 | M 1601 | 7.8 |
| ◗ 2206 | 3.2 | ◗ 2245 | 2.9 |
| **8** 0405 | 7.1 | **23** 0449 | 7.4 |
| 1042 | 3.5 | 1114 | 3.3 |
| M 1634 | 7.1 | TU 1726 | 7.4 |
| 2325 | 3.6 | | |
| **9** 0517 | 6.6 | **24** 0030 | 3.0 |
| 1207 | 3.8 | 0626 | 7.3 |
| TU 1812 | 6.8 | W 1303 | 3.3 |
| | | 1905 | 7.6 |
| **10** 0052 | 3.6 | **25** 0207 | 2.6 |
| 0715 | 6.7 | 0753 | 7.7 |
| W 1330 | 3.6 | TH 1434 | 2.8 |
| 1949 | 7.2 | 2019 | 8.2 |
| **11** 0212 | 3.2 | **26** 0316 | 1.9 |
| 0828 | 7.2 | 0854 | 8.3 |
| TH 1443 | 3.2 | F 1535 | 2.1 |
| 2046 | 7.8 | 2113 | 8.8 |
| **12** 0318 | 2.6 | **27** 0409 | 1.2 |
| 0916 | 7.8 | 0943 | 8.8 |
| F 1539 | 2.6 | SA 1624 | 1.6 |
| 2130 | 8.4 | 2159 | 9.3 |
| **13** 0406 | 2.0 | **28** 0453 | 0.8 |
| 0956 | 8.3 | 1025 | 9.2 |
| SA 1622 | 2.0 | SU 1705 | 1.2 |
| 2208 | 8.9 | 2240 | 9.6 |
| **14** 0447 | 1.5 | **29** 0532 | 0.6 |
| 1032 | 8.7 | 1103 | 9.3 |
| SU 1702 | 1.6 | M 1743 | 1.0 |
| 2243 | 9.2 | ● 2317 | 9.6 |
| **15** 0526 | 1.1 | **30** 0608 | 0.7 |
| 1106 | 9.0 | 1138 | 9.3 |
| M 1739 | 1.2 | TU 1817 | 1.0 |
| ○ 2318 | 9.5 | 2351 | 9.5 |

### OCTOBER

| Time | m | Time | m |
|---|---|---|---|
| **1** 0641 | 0.9 | **16** 0611 | 0.7 |
| 1210 | 9.2 | 1149 | 9.6 |
| W 1849 | 1.2 | TH 1831 | 0.8 |
| **2** 0023 | 9.3 | **17** 0008 | 9.8 |
| 0711 | 1.2 | 0649 | 0.8 |
| TH 1241 | 9.1 | F 1230 | 9.5 |
| 1918 | 1.4 | 1910 | 0.9 |
| **3** 0055 | 9.0 | **18** 0053 | 9.6 |
| 0737 | 1.6 | 0727 | 1.1 |
| F 1312 | 8.8 | SA 1313 | 9.3 |
| 1943 | 1.8 | 1952 | 1.2 |
| **4** 0127 | 8.6 | **19** 0139 | 9.2 |
| 0800 | 2.0 | 0807 | 1.6 |
| SA 1344 | 8.6 | SU 1359 | 8.9 |
| 2010 | 2.2 | 2039 | 1.7 |
| **5** 0202 | 8.2 | **20** 0230 | 8.6 |
| 0826 | 2.5 | 0854 | 2.2 |
| SU 1420 | 8.2 | M 1452 | 8.5 |
| 2043 | 2.6 | 2136 | 2.2 |
| **6** 0241 | 7.7 | **21** 0331 | 8.0 |
| 0902 | 3.0 | 0952 | 2.8 |
| M 1501 | 7.7 | TU 1557 | 8.0 |
| 2129 | 3.1 | ◗ 2252 | 2.6 |
| **7** 0329 | 7.2 | **22** 0448 | 7.5 |
| 0956 | 3.5 | 1110 | 3.2 |
| TU 1555 | 7.2 | W 1720 | 7.7 |
| ◗ 2244 | 3.5 | | |
| **8** 0435 | 6.7 | **23** 0024 | 2.7 |
| 1121 | 3.9 | 0615 | 7.5 |
| W 1713 | 6.9 | TH 1249 | 3.2 |
| | | 1843 | 7.8 |
| **9** 0012 | 3.6 | **24** 0146 | 2.4 |
| 0622 | 6.6 | 0729 | 7.8 |
| TH 1247 | 3.7 | F 1409 | 2.8 |
| 1859 | 7.1 | 1951 | 8.2 |
| **10** 0129 | 3.2 | **25** 0250 | 1.9 |
| 0746 | 7.1 | 0827 | 8.3 |
| F 1400 | 3.3 | SA 1509 | 2.3 |
| 2004 | 7.7 | 2046 | 8.7 |
| **11** 0234 | 2.6 | **26** 0342 | 1.4 |
| 0837 | 7.7 | 0916 | 8.7 |
| SA 1458 | 2.7 | SU 1557 | 1.8 |
| 2050 | 8.3 | 2133 | 9.0 |
| **12** 0326 | 2.0 | **27** 0425 | 1.2 |
| 0918 | 8.3 | 0958 | 9.0 |
| SU 1546 | 2.0 | M 1638 | 1.5 |
| 2130 | 8.9 | 2214 | 9.2 |
| **13** 0411 | 1.4 | **28** 0503 | 1.1 |
| 0956 | 8.8 | 1035 | 9.1 |
| M 1629 | 1.5 | TU 1715 | 1.4 |
| 2209 | 9.3 | ● 2251 | 9.2 |
| **14** 0453 | 1.0 | **29** 0536 | 1.2 |
| 1032 | 9.2 | 1109 | 9.2 |
| TU 1710 | 1.1 | W 1749 | 1.4 |
| ○ 2247 | 9.6 | 2324 | 9.1 |
| **15** 0533 | 0.8 | **30** 0607 | 1.3 |
| 1110 | 9.5 | 1140 | 9.1 |
| W 1751 | 0.9 | TH 1820 | 1.5 |
| 2327 | 9.8 | 2356 | 9.0 |
| | | **31** 0636 | 1.6 |
| | | 1211 | 9.0 |
| | | F 1850 | 1.7 |

### NOVEMBER

| Time | m | Time | m |
|---|---|---|---|
| **1** 0027 | 8.8 | **16** 0041 | 9.5 |
| 0702 | 1.8 | 0714 | 1.2 |
| SA 1244 | 8.9 | SU 1302 | 9.5 |
| 1918 | 1.9 | 1950 | 1.1 |
| **2** 0101 | 8.5 | **17** 0132 | 9.2 |
| 0728 | 2.1 | 0800 | 1.6 |
| SU 1318 | 8.6 | M 1353 | 9.2 |
| 1948 | 2.2 | 2042 | 1.4 |
| **3** 0137 | 8.2 | **18** 0226 | 8.7 |
| 0759 | 2.5 | 0850 | 2.0 |
| M 1355 | 8.3 | TU 1447 | 8.8 |
| 2023 | 2.5 | 2139 | 1.8 |
| **4** 0217 | 7.8 | **19** 0325 | 8.3 |
| 0837 | 2.9 | 0948 | 2.5 |
| TU 1437 | 8.0 | W 1548 | 8.4 |
| 2109 | 2.9 | ◖ 2244 | 2.1 |
| **5** 0304 | 7.4 | **20** 0431 | 7.9 |
| 0928 | 3.3 | 1054 | 2.8 |
| W 1527 | 7.6 | TH 1656 | 8.1 |
| 2212 | 3.2 | 2354 | 2.3 |
| **6** 0401 | 7.1 | **21** 0543 | 7.7 |
| 1038 | 3.6 | 1208 | 3.0 |
| TH 1630 | 7.3 | F 1807 | 8.0 |
| ◖ 2326 | 3.3 | | |
| **7** 0516 | 6.9 | **22** 0105 | 2.3 |
| 1155 | 3.6 | 0651 | 7.8 |
| F 1746 | 7.4 | SA 1324 | 2.9 |
| | | 1914 | 8.1 |
| **8** 0038 | 3.1 | **23** 0211 | 2.2 |
| 0639 | 7.2 | 0752 | 8.0 |
| SA 1306 | 3.3 | SU 1430 | 2.6 |
| 1900 | 7.7 | 2012 | 8.3 |
| **9** 0143 | 2.6 | **24** 0306 | 2.0 |
| 0743 | 7.7 | 0843 | 8.3 |
| SU 1409 | 2.8 | M 1523 | 2.3 |
| 1958 | 8.2 | 2103 | 8.5 |
| **10** 0241 | 2.1 | **25** 0352 | 1.8 |
| 0833 | 8.3 | 0928 | 8.6 |
| M 1505 | 2.2 | TU 1608 | 2.1 |
| 2048 | 8.8 | 2148 | 8.7 |
| **11** 0333 | 1.6 | **26** 0430 | 1.7 |
| 0917 | 8.8 | 1008 | 8.8 |
| TU 1555 | 1.7 | W 1647 | 1.9 |
| 2134 | 9.2 | 2227 | 8.8 |
| **12** 0420 | 1.2 | **27** 0505 | 1.7 |
| 1000 | 9.2 | 1044 | 8.9 |
| W 1643 | 1.3 | TH 1723 | 1.8 |
| 2219 | 9.6 | ● 2303 | 8.8 |
| **13** 0505 | 0.9 | **28** 0537 | 1.8 |
| 1043 | 9.5 | 1118 | 9.0 |
| TH 1729 | 1.0 | F 1757 | 1.8 |
| ○ 2305 | 9.7 | 2336 | 8.7 |
| **14** 0548 | 0.9 | **29** 0608 | 1.8 |
| 1127 | 9.6 | 1151 | 8.9 |
| F 1815 | 0.9 | SA 1830 | 1.8 |
| 2352 | 9.7 | | |
| **15** 0631 | 1.0 | **30** 0009 | 8.6 |
| 1213 | 9.6 | 0638 | 2.0 |
| SA 1902 | 0.9 | SU 1225 | 8.9 |
| | | 1902 | 2.0 |

### DECEMBER

| Time | m | Time | m |
|---|---|---|---|
| **1** 0044 | 8.5 | **16** 0124 | 9.4 |
| 0710 | 2.1 | 0756 | 1.4 |
| M 1301 | 8.7 | TU 1344 | 9.6 |
| 1936 | 2.1 | 2039 | 0.9 |
| **2** 0121 | 8.3 | **17** 0215 | 9.1 |
| 0744 | 2.3 | 0844 | 1.6 |
| TU 1339 | 8.6 | W 1434 | 9.3 |
| 2013 | 2.3 | 2129 | 1.2 |
| **3** 0200 | 8.1 | **18** 0306 | 8.7 |
| 0823 | 2.6 | 0933 | 2.0 |
| W 1419 | 8.4 | TH 1526 | 8.9 |
| 2055 | 2.5 | 2219 | 1.6 |
| **4** 0243 | 7.9 | **19** 0359 | 8.3 |
| 0907 | 2.9 | 1024 | 2.4 |
| TH 1504 | 8.1 | F 1620 | 8.5 |
| 2144 | 2.7 | ◖ 2312 | 2.1 |
| **5** 0331 | 7.6 | **20** 0456 | 7.9 |
| 1001 | 3.1 | 1120 | 2.7 |
| F 1555 | 7.9 | SA 1719 | 8.1 |
| ◖ 2240 | 2.8 | | |
| **6** 0428 | 7.4 | **21** 0009 | 2.4 |
| 1102 | 3.2 | 0600 | 7.6 |
| SA 1655 | 7.8 | SU 1221 | 3.0 |
| 2343 | 2.9 | 1824 | 7.8 |
| **7** 0533 | 7.4 | **22** 0112 | 2.7 |
| 1209 | 3.2 | 0706 | 7.6 |
| SU 1759 | 7.9 | M 1329 | 3.0 |
| | | 1931 | 7.8 |
| **8** 0049 | 2.7 | **23** 0216 | 2.7 |
| 0641 | 7.6 | 0807 | 7.8 |
| M 1317 | 2.9 | TU 1438 | 2.9 |
| 1904 | 8.2 | 2032 | 7.9 |
| **9** 0155 | 2.4 | **24** 0312 | 2.6 |
| 0745 | 8.0 | 0900 | 8.1 |
| TU 1423 | 2.5 | W 1536 | 2.6 |
| 2006 | 8.5 | 2124 | 8.1 |
| **10** 0256 | 2.0 | **25** 0359 | 2.4 |
| 0841 | 8.5 | 0946 | 8.4 |
| W 1524 | 2.0 | TH 1623 | 2.4 |
| 2103 | 8.9 | 2209 | 8.3 |
| **11** 0352 | 1.6 | **26** 0439 | 2.2 |
| 0934 | 9.0 | 1026 | 8.5 |
| TH 1621 | 1.5 | F 1704 | 2.1 |
| 2158 | 9.3 | 2249 | 8.4 |
| **12** 0443 | 1.3 | **27** 0516 | 2.0 |
| 1024 | 9.4 | 1103 | 8.8 |
| F 1714 | 1.2 | SA 1742 | 2.0 |
| ○ 2250 | 9.5 | ● 2324 | 8.5 |
| **13** 0532 | 1.1 | **28** 0552 | 2.0 |
| 1113 | 9.6 | 1139 | 8.9 |
| SA 1806 | 0.9 | SU 1818 | 1.9 |
| 2342 | 9.6 | 2358 | 8.6 |
| **14** 0621 | 1.1 | **29** 0626 | 1.9 |
| 1203 | 9.7 | 1213 | 8.9 |
| SU 1858 | 0.8 | M 1854 | 1.9 |
| **15** 0033 | 9.5 | **30** 0032 | 8.6 |
| 0708 | 1.2 | 0659 | 2.0 |
| M 1253 | 9.7 | TU 1249 | 8.9 |
| 1949 | 0.8 | 1928 | 1.9 |
| | | **31** 0108 | 8.6 |
| | | 0733 | 2.2 |
| | | W 1325 | 8.9 |
| | | 2003 | 1.9 |

Chart Datum: 4·93 metres below Ordnance Datum (Newlyn). HAT is 10·5 metres above Chart Datum.

NW England

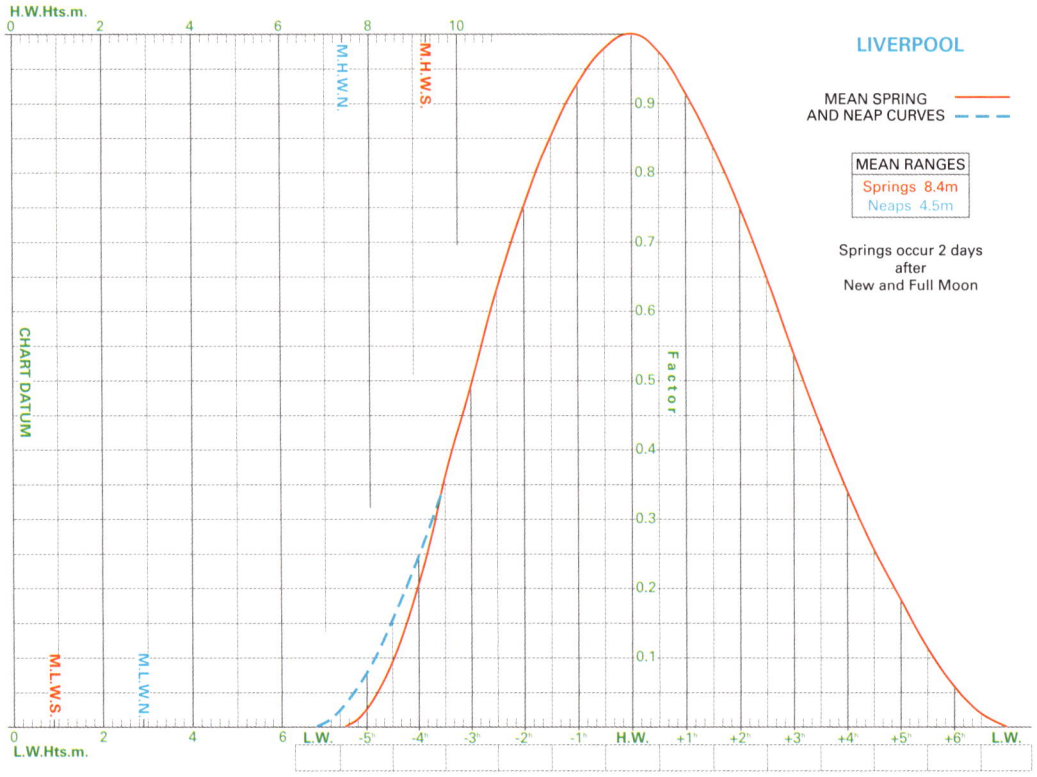

## 3.16 LIVERPOOL

Merseyside **53°24'·22N 03°00'·28W** (Liver Bldg) 🌼🌼🌼🌊🌊🌼🌼

**CHARTS** AC *1826, 1978*, 1951, 3490; Imray C62; OS 108

**TIDES** +0015 Dover; ML 5·2; Duration 0535

**Standard Port LIVERPOOL (ALFRED DOCK)** (⟷)

| Times | | | | Height (metres) | | | |
|---|---|---|---|---|---|---|---|
| High Water | | Low Water | | MHWS | MHWN | MLWN | MLWS |
| 0000 | 0600 | 0200 | 0700 | 9·3 | 7·4 | 2·9 | 0·9 |
| 1200 | 1800 | 1400 | 1900 | | | | |
| **Differences GLADSTONE DOCK** | | | | | | | |
| −0003 | −0003 | −0003 | −0003 | −0·1 | −0·1 | 0·0 | −0·1 |
| **EASTHAM** (River Mersey) | | | | | | | |
| +0010 | +0010 | +0009 | +0009 | +0·3 | +0·1 | −0·1 | −0·3 |
| **HALE HEAD** (River Mersey) | | | | | | | |
| +0030 | +0025 | No data | | −2·4 | −2·5 | No data | |
| **WIDNES** (River Mersey) | | | | | | | |
| +0040 | +0045 | +0400 | +0345 | −4·2 | −4·4 | −2·5 | −0·3 |
| **FIDDLER'S FERRY** (River Mersey) | | | | | | | |
| +0100 | +0115 | +0540 | +0450 | −5·9 | −6·3 | −2·4 | −0·4 |
| **HILBRE ISLAND** (River Dee) | | | | | | | |
| −0015 | −0012 | −0010 | −0015 | −0·3 | −0·2 | +0·2 | +0·4 |
| **MOSTYN DOCKS** (River Dee) | | | | | | | |
| −0020 | −0015 | −0020 | −0020 | −0·8 | −0·7 | No data | |
| **CONNAH'S QUAY** (River Dee) | | | | | | | |
| 0000 | +0015 | +0355 | +0340 | −4·6 | −4·4 | Dries | |
| **CHESTER** (River Dee) | | | | | | | |
| +0105 | +0105 | +0500 | +0500 | −5·3 | −5·4 | Dries | |
| **COLWYN BAY** | | | | | | | |
| −0020 | −0020 | No data | | −1·5 | −1·3 | No data | |
| **LLANDUDNO** | | | | | | | |
| −0020 | −0020 | −0035 | −0040 | −1·7 | −1·4 | −0·7 | −0·3 |

NOTE: LW time differences at Connah's Quay give the end of a LW stand lasting about 3¾hrs at sp and 5hrs at nps. A bore occurs in the R Dee at Chester.

**SHELTER** Good at marinas in Brunswick/Coburg docks and in Canning/Albert Docks. Fair weather ⚓ on the SW side of river. In strong NW'lies there is swell on the bar. Wind against tide causes steep, breaking seas in outer reaches of River Mersey. Inside, the buoyed chan is safe; elsewhere local knowledge and great caution needed as the whole area (R Dee, R Mersey to R Alt and N to Morecambe Bay) is littered with sandbanks.

**NAVIGATION** WPT 53°32'·02N 03°20'·98W, Bar SWM lt buoy, 111°/2·8M to Q1 NCM lt F. From Q1 to marina is 15·5M via Queen's and Crosby Chans. Both chans have training banks which cover and it is unwise to navigate between the floats/buoys and the trng banks. Sp tidal streams exceed 5kn within the river.

**Leeds and Liverpool Canal** (BWB) gives access to E Coast, ent at Stanley Dock. Max draft 1·0m, air draft 2·2m, beam 4·3m, LOA 18·3m. Liverpool to Goole 161M, 103 locks.

**Manchester Ship Canal**, ent at Eastham Locks, leads 31M to Salford Quays or R Weaver for boatyards at Northwich. Obtain licence from MSC Co ☎ 0151 327 1461.

**R Dee:** WPT 53°25'·13N 03°13'·17W, Hilbre Swash HE2 ECM buoy, Q (3) 10s, (chan shifts). From the W use Welsh Chan. The Dee estuary mostly dries.

**LIGHTS AND MARKS** Bar SWM lt buoy, L Fl 10s Racon. Keep 5ca clear of SPM, 5ca W of Bar lt buoy. Formby SWM lt F, Iso 4s, is at the ent to Queen's Chan which is marked by PHM lt Flts and SHM buoys, and 3 NCM buoys, numbered Q1-Q12. Crosby Chan is similarly marked, C1-C23. From Crosby SWM lt F, Oc 5s, the track up-river is approx 145°. The Liver Bldg (twin spires) and Port of Liverpool Bldg (dome) are conspic on the E bank opposite Birkenhead Docks.

**R/T** Monitor *Mersey Radio* VHF Ch **12** 16 (H24). Local nav and gale warnings are broadcast on receipt on Ch 12. Traffic movements, nav warnings and weather reports are broadcast on Ch 09 at HW−3 and −2. Radar Ch 18 covers a radius of 20M and in poor vis can offer continuous fixing. *Liverpool Marina* Ch **M**. Eastham Locks Ch 07 (H24). Manchester Ship Canal Ch 14.

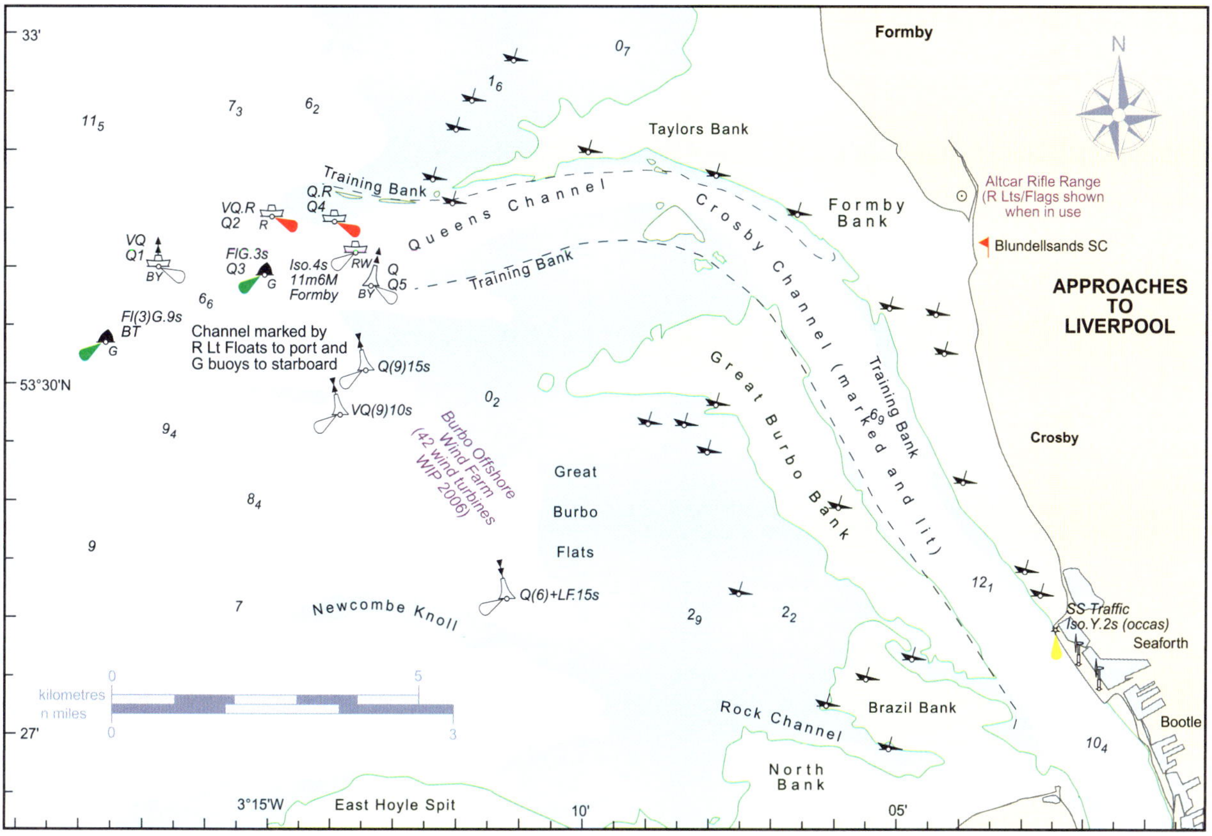

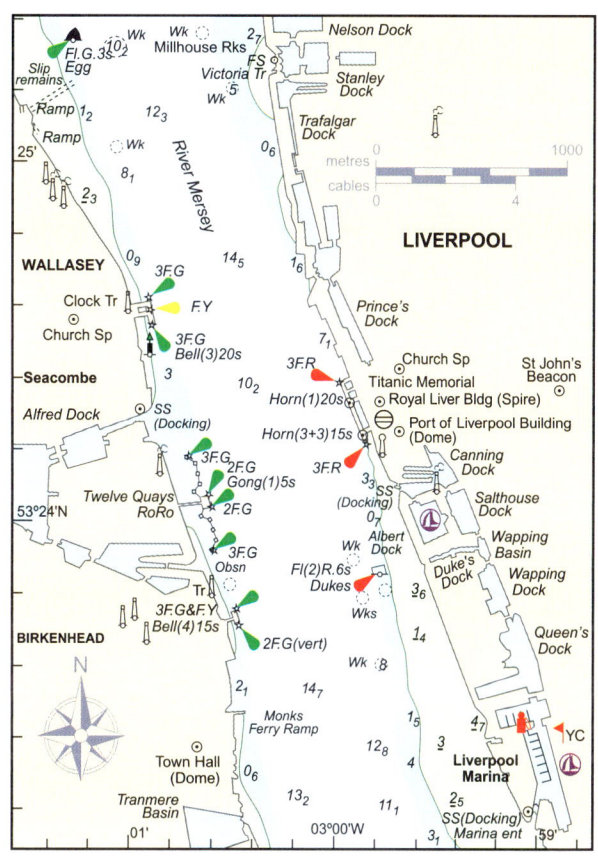

## Chart – Approaches to Liverpool

33'

Formby

0₇

1₆

11₅

7₃

6₂

Taylors Bank

Training Bank

Q.R
Q4

Queens Channel

Crosby Bank

Formby Bank

Altcar Rifle Range
(R Lts/Flags shown
when in use)

Blundellsands SC

**APPROACHES
TO
LIVERPOOL**

VQ.R
Q2

VQ
Q1
BY

FI.G.3s
Q3
G

6₆

RW
BY

Iso.4s
11m6M
Formby

Q
Q5

Crosby Channel (marked and lit)

FI(3)G.9s
BT
G

Channel marked by
R Lt Floats to port and
G buoys to starboard

Q(9)15s

Training Bank

6₉

Crosby

53°30'N

VQ(9)10s

0₂

9₄

Burbo Offshore
Wind Farm
(42 wind turbines
WIP 2006)

Great Burbo Bank

Great

Burbo

Flats

12₁

SS Traffic
Iso.Y.2s (occas)
Seaforth

8₄

9

Newcombe Knoll

Q(6)+LF.15s

2₉

2₂

7

Rock Channel

Brazil Bank

North
Bank

10₄

Bootle

kilometres
n miles

27'

3°15'W    East Hoyle Spit    10'    05'

kilometres / n miles scale 0–5 / 0–3

---

**TELEPHONE** (Code 0151) Port Ops 949 6134/5, ☒ 949 56090; MRCC 931 3341; Marinecall 09068 969651; Police 709 6010; Ⓗ 709 0141.

**FACILITIES Liverpool Marina** entrance is 1M S of the Liver Bldg, abeam Pluckington Bank WCM buoy. **IPTS** (sigs 2, 3 & 5) from conspic black control bldg at lock ent. Access approx HW ±2¼ sp, ±1½ nps, 0600-2200 Mar-Oct, via Brunswick Dock lock, pontoons inside, min depth 3·5m; night locking as pre-arranged. www.liverpoolmarina.co.uk ☎ 7076777, (0600-2200 Mar–Oct), ☒ 7076770. 350 AB + 50 Ⓥ, £2.36. D, P (½M), BH (60 ton), Slip, CH, SM, ☐, &, Bar, R (☎ 7076888).

**Albert Dock** ☎ 7096558; access HW–2 to HW via Canning Dock, but not on every tide. VHF Ch M when ent manned, AB, FW, AC.

**Royal Mersey YC** ☎ 6453204, Slip, M, P, D, L, FW, R, Bar.

**W Kirby SC** ☎ 6255579, AB (at HW), Slip, M (in Dee Est) L, FW, C (30ton), Bar.

**Hoylake SC** ☎ 6322616, Slip, M, FW, Bar; **Services:** CH, SM, ME, El, ✂, ACA, Ⓔ.

**City** all facilities, ⇌, ✈.

## ADJACENT ANCHORAGE

**RIVER ALT**, Merseyside, **53°31'·42N 03°03'·80W**. AC *1978, 1951*. HW –0008 on Dover; see 3.11. Good shelter but only for LOA <8·5m x 1·2m draft on a HW of at least 8m. Mersey E training wall can be crossed HW±2. Ent to chan (shifts frequently) is E of C14 PHM lt float, thence marked by locally-laid Y Fairway buoy and perches on the training wall. Unsafe to ⚓ in R Alt; pick up a free mooring off the SC and contact club. Local knowledge advised. Facilities very limited. **Blundellsands SC** ☎ (0151) 929 2101 (occas), Slip, L (at HW), FW, Bar.

## Chart – Liverpool

Nelson Dock

FI.G.3s
Egg

Wk

Wk

2₇

Millhouse Rks

FS

Victoria Tr

Stanley
Dock

Slip
remains

Ramp

1₂

12₃

Wk

5

Trafalgar
Dock

Ramp

Wk

25'

8₁

River Mersey

0₆

metres
cables
0–1000 / 0–4

**LIVERPOOL**

2₃

WALLASEY

0₉

3F.G

14₅

Prince's
Dock

Clock Tr

Church Sp

F.Y

3F.G
Bell(3)20s

7₁

3F.R

Church Sp

St John's
Beacon

Seacombe

SS
(Docking)

10₂

Horn(1)20s

Titanic Memorial
Royal Liver Bldg (Spire)

Alfred Dock

Horn(3+3)15s

Port of Liverpool Building
(Dome)

3F.G
2F.G
Gong(1)5s

3F.R

Canning
Dock

Twelve Quays
RoRo

2F.G

3₃

SS
(Docking)

0₇

Salthouse
Dock

53°24'N

3F.G
Obsn

Albert
Dock

Wapping
Basin

Tr

FI(2)R.6s
Dukes

Duke's
Dock

3₆

Wapping
Dock

**BIRKENHEAD**

N

3F.G&F.Y
Bell(4)15s

Wks

1₄

Queen's
Dock

2F.G(vert)

Wk

8

2₁

14₇

1₅

4₇

YC

Monks
Ferry Ramp

12₈

Liverpool
Marina

Town Hall
(Dome)

0₆

13₂

11₁

2₅

SS(Docking)
Marina ent

Tranmere
Basin

01'    03°00'W

3₁

59'

## 3.17  CONWY AND DEGANWY

Conwy   **53°17'·48N 03°50'·23W** (marina) ✿✿✿✿✿✿✿✿✿
Deganwy **53°17'·41N 03°49'·66W** (marina) ✿✿✿✿✿✿✿✿✿

**CHARTS** AC *5609, 1826, 1977, 1978, 1463*; Imray C52; OS 115; Stan 27

**TIDES** –0015 Dover; ML 4·3; Duration 0545

**Standard Port HOLYHEAD** (→)

| Times | | | | Height (metres) | | | |
|---|---|---|---|---|---|---|---|
| High Water | | Low Water | | MHWS | MHWN | MLWN | MLWS |
| 0000 | 0600 | 0500 | 1100 | 5·6 | 4·4 | 2·0 | 0·7 |
| 1200 | 1800 | 1700 | 2300 | | | | |
| **Differences CONWY** | | | | | | | |
| +0025 | +0035 | +0120 | +0105 | +2·3 | +1·8 | +0·6 | +0·4 |

NOTE: HW Conwy is approx HW Liverpool –0040 sp and –0020 nps.

**SHELTER** Good, except in strong NW'lies.

**NAVIGATION** WPT Fairway buoy, 53°17'·95N 03°55'·58W, 120°/6·5ca to No 2 PHM. Access HW±2; if Conwy Sands (to the N) are covered, there is enough water in chan for a 2m draught boat. A bar 1·0m forms at The Scabs between Nos 4 and 8 buoys.

After No 2 buoy the channel up to Deganwy Point is marked by lt buoys in sequence: Nos 1 SHM, 4 PHM, 6 PHM, 8 PHM, 3 SHM, 5 SHM; Perch lt bcn (53°18'·06N 03°50'·84W; leave approx 30m to stbd), 7 SHM; unlit PHM at Narrows into R Conwy. See 3.3 for buoy lights. 10kn spd limit above Perch lt bcn. Sp ebb up to 5kn.

North Deep, a buoyed inshore passage (close SW of Gt Orme's Hd to Deganwy Point), is only advised with local knowledge.

Beware: unlit Beacons Jetty (close N of Conwy marina); unlit moorings off Deganwy; and two unlit pontoons upriver of Bodlondeb Pt.

**LIGHTS AND MARKS** Penmaenmawr SPM outfall buoy (SW of No 2 buoy) is not a channel mark. The 4 towers of Conwy castle and the 2 adjacent bridge towers are conspic.

**R/T** HM Ch **14**. Summer 0900-1700LT daily; winter, same times Mon-Fri). Conwy Marina, pre-call Ch 80 (H24) for a berth. Deganwy Quay Ch 80. N Wales CC launch Ch M, water taxi.

**TELEPHONE** (Code 01492) HM 596253, 🖷 585222. MRCC (01407) 762051. Marinecall 09068 969650. Police 517171. Dr 592424.

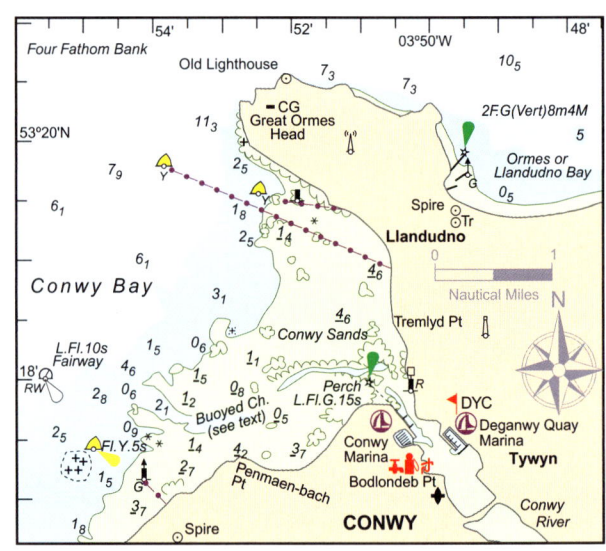

**FACILITIES Conwy Marina** Access when height of tide above CD exceeds 3·5m, ie approx HW ±3¼. Gate times are on an electronic noticeboard. Waiting pontoon outside. Obey R/G entry lts. ☎ 593000, 🖷 572111. www.quaymarinas.com, 500 AB inc Ⓥ, £3.09m; < 5hrs, £10. D & P (0700-2200), BH (30 ton), BY, 🔧, ⚓, CH, Gas, SM, Wi-fi, ⊡, R, Bar.

**Harbour** Between Bodlondeb Pt and Conwy bridge contact HM for: Pontoon AB £11.00; Town Quay AB dries (12·3m max LOA, short stay for loading); and ⚓'s. D (Town Quay/pontoon HW±2, call Ch 14 to confirm), FW, ♿. Slip HW±3 at Beacons Jetty £16/day.

**Deganwy Quay Marina** Keep close to 3 PHM lt buoys marking the appr channel (see lower chartlet). Min depth in chan is 2·5m when marina gate open. Access when height of tide above CD exceeds 4m, ie approx HW ±3¼. www.deganwyquay.com/marina ☎ 576888. deganwymarina@tiscali.co.uk 200 AB inc Ⓥ, £3.30. ♿, 🔧, ME, El, Ⓔ, Slip, BH (20 ton).

**Conwy YC** (Deganwy) ☎ 583690, Slip, M, L, FW, R, Bar.

**N Wales Cruising Club** (in Conwy) ☎ 593481, AB, M, FW, Bar.
**Services:** ME, Gas, Gaz, 🔧, El, Ⓔ.

**Town** P & D (cans), 🛒, R, Bar, ✉, Ⓑ, ⇌, ✈ (Liverpool).

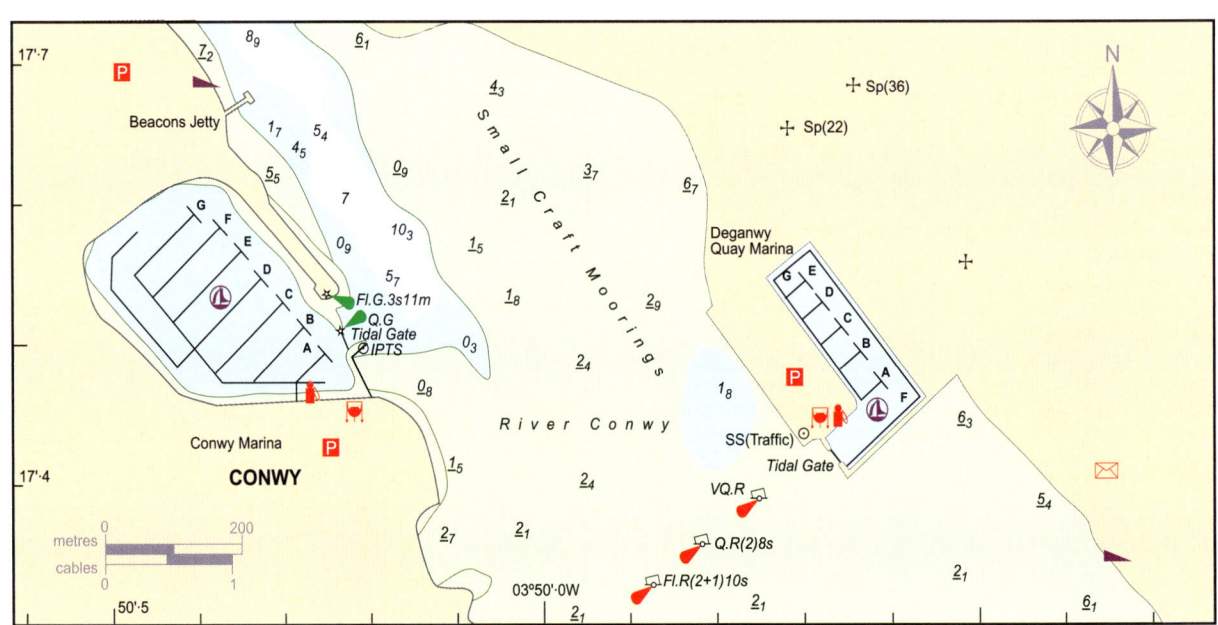

# 3.18 MENAI STRAIT

Gwynedd/Isle of Anglesey

**CHARTS** AC *5609, 1464*, Imray C52; Stanfords 27; OS 114, 115.
NOTE: The definitive Pilot book is *Cruising Anglesey and the North Wales Coast* by R Morris, 5th edition 1995: North West Venturers YC

**TIDES** Beaumaris –0025 Dover; ML Beaumaris 4·2; Duration 0540
**Standard Port HOLYHEAD (⟶)**

| Times | | | | Height (metres) | | | |
|---|---|---|---|---|---|---|---|
| High Water | | Low Water | | MHWS | MHWN | MLWN | MLWS |
| 0000 | 0600 | 0500 | 1100 | 5·6 | 4·4 | 2·0 | 0·7 |
| 1200 | 1800 | 1700 | 2300 | | | | |
| **Differences BEAUMARIS** | | | | | | | |
| +0025 | +0010 | +0055 | +0035 | +2·0 | +1·6 | +0·5 | +0·1 |
| **MENAI BRIDGE** | | | | | | | |
| +0030 | +0010 | +0100 | +0035 | +1·7 | +1·4 | +0·3 | 0·0 |
| **PORT DINORWIC** | | | | | | | |
| –0015 | –0025 | +0030 | 0000 | 0·0 | 0·0 | 0·0 | +0·1 |
| **CAERNARFON** | | | | | | | |
| –0030 | –0030 | +0015 | –0005 | –0·4 | –0·4 | –0·1 | –0·1 |
| **FORT BELAN** | | | | | | | |
| –0040 | –0015 | –0025 | –0005 | –1·0 | –0·9 | –0·2 | –0·1 |
| **LLANDDWYN ISLAND** | | | | | | | |
| –0115 | –0055 | –0030 | –0020 | –0·7 | –0·5 | –0·1 | 0·0 |

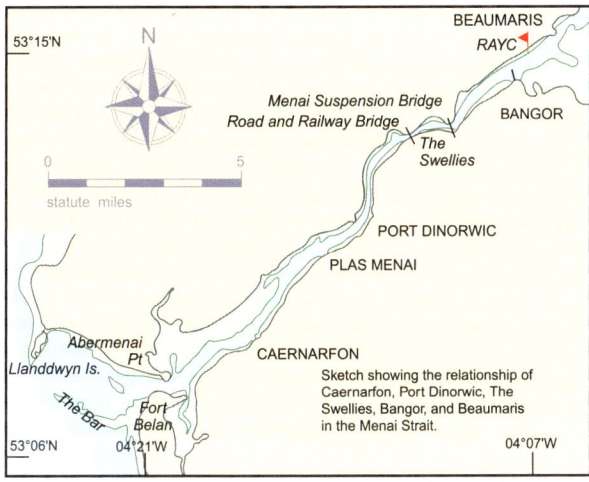

Sketch showing the relationship of Caernarfon, Port Dinorwic, The Swellies, Bangor, and Beaumaris in the Menai Strait.

## SOUTH WEST ENTRANCE – CAERNARFON BAR

**NAVIGATION** WPT 53°06'·70N 04°25'·40W, 6ca WSW of C1 SHM. A dangerous sea can build in even a moderate breeze against tide, especially if a swell is running. Bar Chan should not be used at any time other than HW-3 to HW+3. Caernarfon Bar shifts often and unpredictably. See 3.4.

**LIGHTS AND MARKS** See 3.3. and chartlet. **Direction of buoyage changes at Caernarfon.**

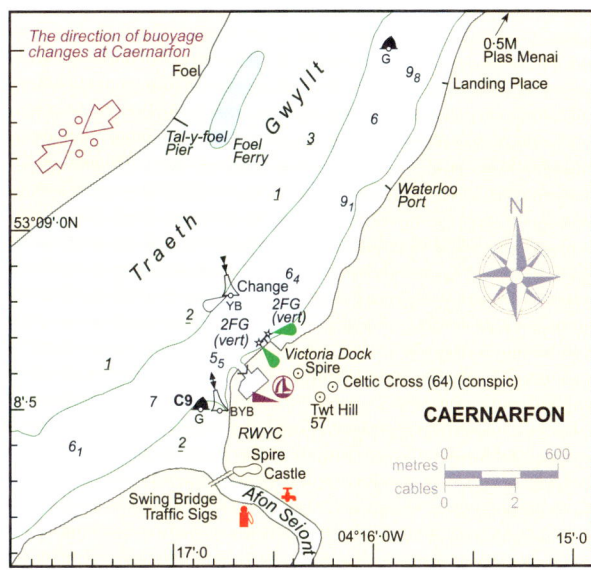

*The direction of buoyage changes at Caernarfon*

## CAERNARFON 53°08'·51N 04°16'·83W

**SHELTER** Good in Victoria Dock marina, access HW±2 via gates, trfc lts; pontoons at SW end in 2m. Or in river hbr (S of conspic castle), dries to mud/gravel, access HW±3 via swing bridge; for opening sound B (─····). ⚓ off Foel Ferry, with local knowledge; or temp ⚓ in fair holding off Abermenai Pt, sheltered from W'lies, but strong streams. ⚓ waiting 1½ca SW of C9.

**R/T** Victoria Dock marina VHF Ch 80. Port Ch 14 16 (HJ).

**TELEPHONE** (Code 01286) HM 672118, 📠 678729, Mobile 07786 730865; Police 673333; Ⓗ 01248 384384; Dr (emergency) 01248 384001.

**FACILITIES** **Dock** £1·80 **River** £13·50/craft, 0700-2300 (Summer), FW, Slip, C (2 ton), 🛒, ME, El, Ⓔ, ➶; **Caernarfon SC** ☎ (01248) 672861, L, Bar; **Royal Welsh YC** ☎ (01248) 672599, Bar; **Town** P (cans), ✉, Ⓑ.

## PORT DINORWIC 53°11'·23N 04°13'·70W

**TELEPHONE** (Code 01248) Marina 671500; MRCC (01407) 762051; Dr 670423.

**FACILITIES** Port Dinorwic Marina (230 berths in fresh water) Ⓥ £21/craft. Call *Dinorwic Marina* VHF Ch 80 M (HO)3 ⚓ 1ca NE of lock. **Tidal basin** dries at sp; lock opens HW±2. ☎ 671500 📠 671252, D, P (cans), 🔌, CH, SM; Pier hd F WR 5m 2M, vis R225°-W357°-225°. **Services:** SM, ME, El, ✕, Slip, C, CH. Dinas Boatyard ☎ 671642 all BY facilities. **Town** Ⓔ, ✉ (Bangor or Caernarfon), Ⓑ, ⚄ (Bangor), ✈ (Liverpool). **Plas Menai** (between Port Dinorwic and Caernarfon), the Sport Council for Wales Sailing and Sports Centre: ☎ 670964. *Menai Base* Ch 80 M; day moorings only; ♿.

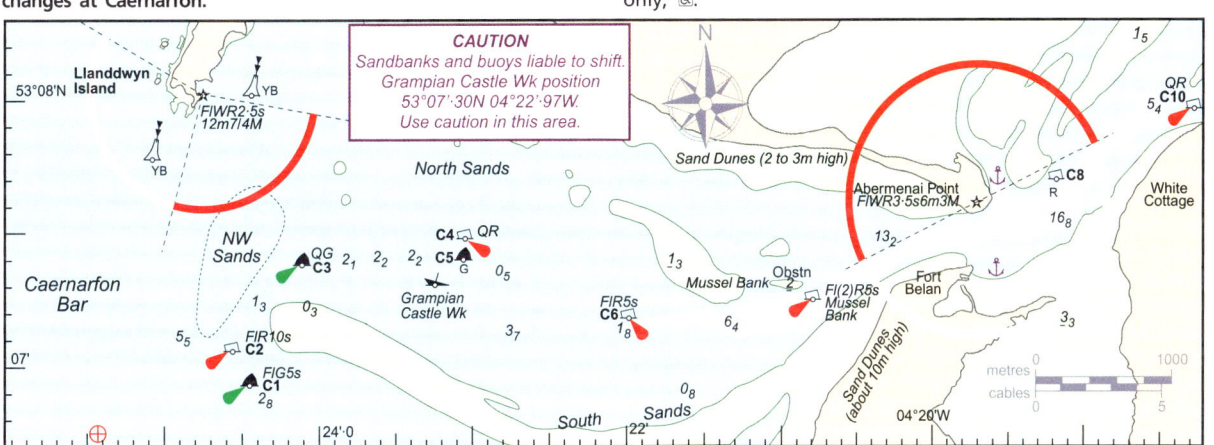

CAUTION
Sandbanks and buoys liable to shift. Grampian Castle Wk position 53°07'·30N 04°22'·97W. Use caution in this area.

## NORTH EAST ENTRANCE

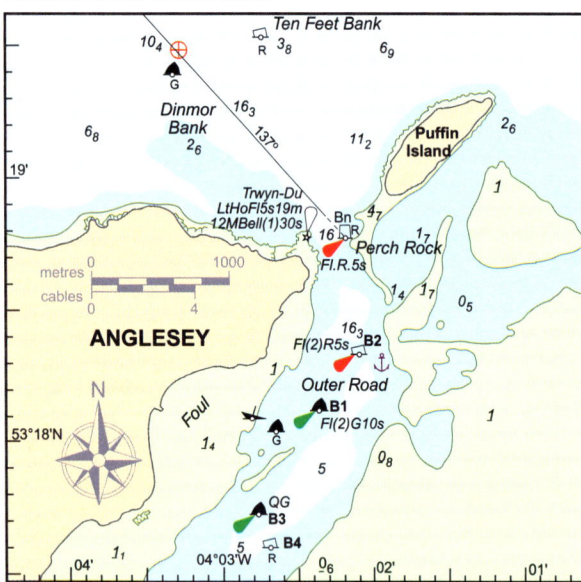

**NAVIGATION** WPT 53°19′·48N 04°03′·28W, 137°/1M to Perch Rk PHM Bn.

- In N'ly gales seas break on Ten Feet Bank.
- In N Strait keep to buoyed chan, nearer Anglesey.
- Night pilotage not advised due to many unlit buoys/moorings.

**LIGHTS AND MARKS** See 3.3. and chartlet. At NE end of Strait, Trwyn-Du Lt ho and Conspic tr on Puffin Is. Chan is laterally buoyed, some lit. Beaumaris pier has FWG sectored lt (see 3.3).

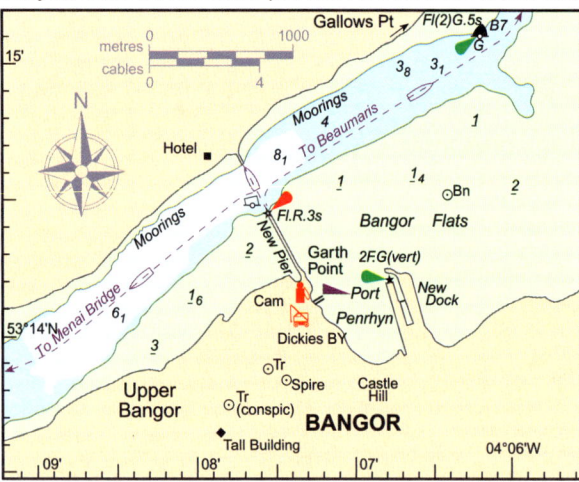

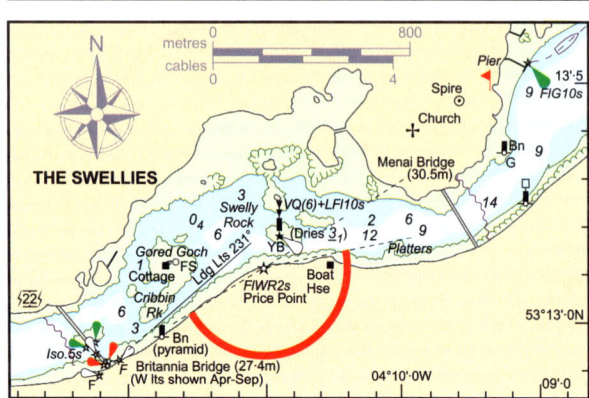

## MENAI BRIDGE/BEAUMARIS 53°15′·66N 04°05′·38W

**SHELTER** Reasonable off Beaumaris except from NE winds. ⚓ S of B10 PHM buoy or call YCs for mooring. At Menai Bridge, call HM VHF Ch 69 16 for mooring or temp'y berth on St George's Pier (S of which a marina is planned).

**TELEPHONE** (Code 01248) HM Menai 712312, mobile 07990 531595; MRCC (01407) 762051; Marinecall 09068 969650; Police (01286) 673333; Dr (emergency) 01248 384001.

**FACILITIES St George's Pier** (Fl G 10s) L at all tides; **Royal Anglesey YC** ☎ 810295, Slip, M, L, R, Bar, P; **North West Venturers YC** ☎ 810023, M, L, FW, water taxi at w/ends only; **Menai Bridge SC**. Services: Slip, P & D (cans), FW, ME, BH (20 ton), ⚒, C (2 ton), CH, El, Ⓔ, Gas. **Both towns** ✉, Ⓑ, ⇌ (bus to Bangor), ✈ (Liverpool).

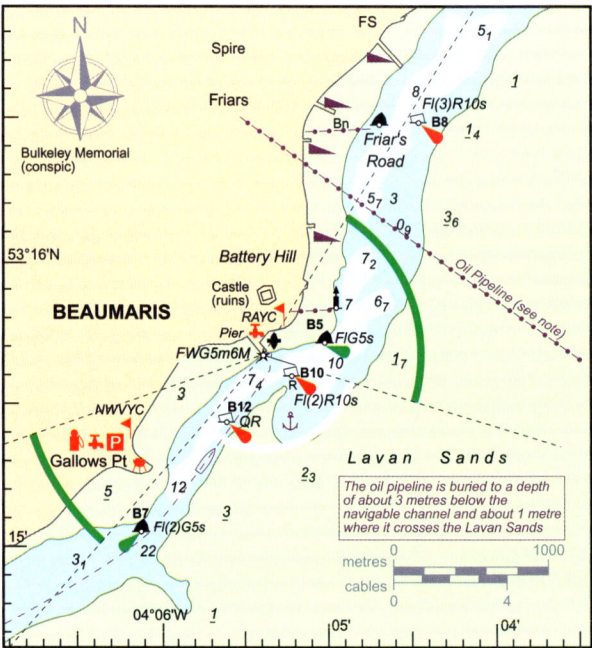

## BANGOR 53°14′·46N 04°07′·58W

**SHELTER** Good, except in E'lies, at Dickies BY or Port Penrhyn dock (both dry; access HW±2).

**R/T** *Dickies* VHF Ch 09 M 16 (0930-1730), all year.

**TELEPHONE** (Code 01248) Penrhyn HM 352525, 🖷 352525; MRCC (01407) 762051; Police (01286) 673333; Dr (emergency) 384001.

**FACILITIES Services:** Slip, D, P (cans), FW, ME, El, ⚒, C, CH, Ⓔ, SM, BH (30 ton), Gas, Gaz, ACA; **Port Penrhyn**, Slip, AB, D. **Town** ✉, Ⓑ, ⇌, ✈ (Chester).

## THE SWELLIES 53°13′·14N 04°10′·46W

### NAVIGATION
- For pilotage notes, see 3.4. The passage should only be attempted at slack HW, which is about –0100 HW Holyhead.
- The shallow rky narrows between the bridges are dangerous for yachts at other times, when the stream can reach 8kn.
- At slack HW there is 3m over The Platters and the outcrop off Price Pt, which can be ignored.
- For shoal-draft boats passage is also possible at slack LW nps, but there are depths of 0·5m close E of Britannia Bridge.
- The bridges and power cables have a least clearance of 22m at MHWS. Night passage is not recommended.

**LIGHTS AND MARKS** See 3.3. and chartlet. Britannia Bridge, E side, ldg lts 231°, both FW (shown Apr-Sep). Bridge lts, both sides: Centre span Iso 5s 27m 3M; S end, FR 21m 3M; N end, FG 21m 3M.

# 3.19 HOLYHEAD

Isle of Anglesey 53°19'·72N 04°37'·07W

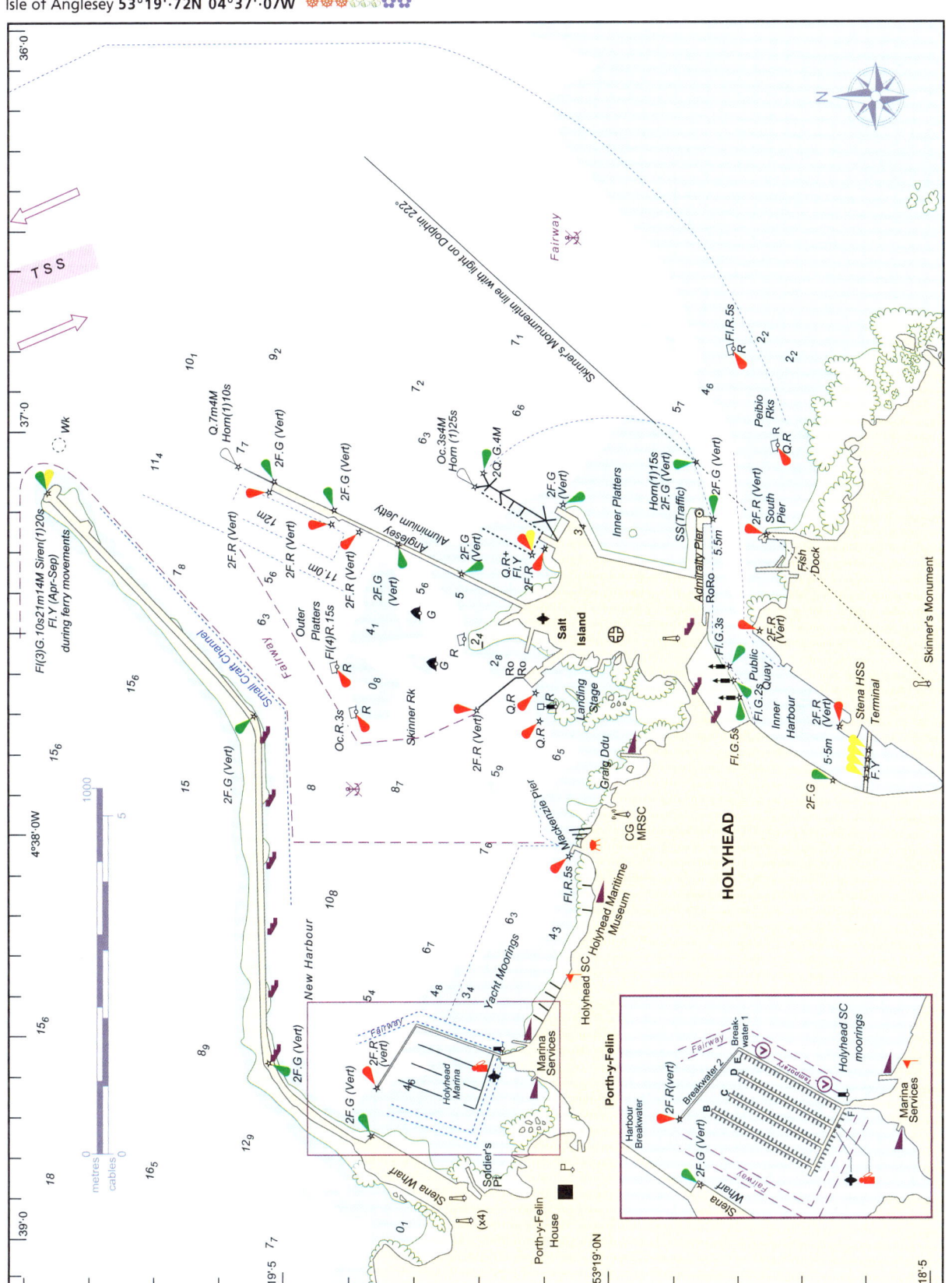

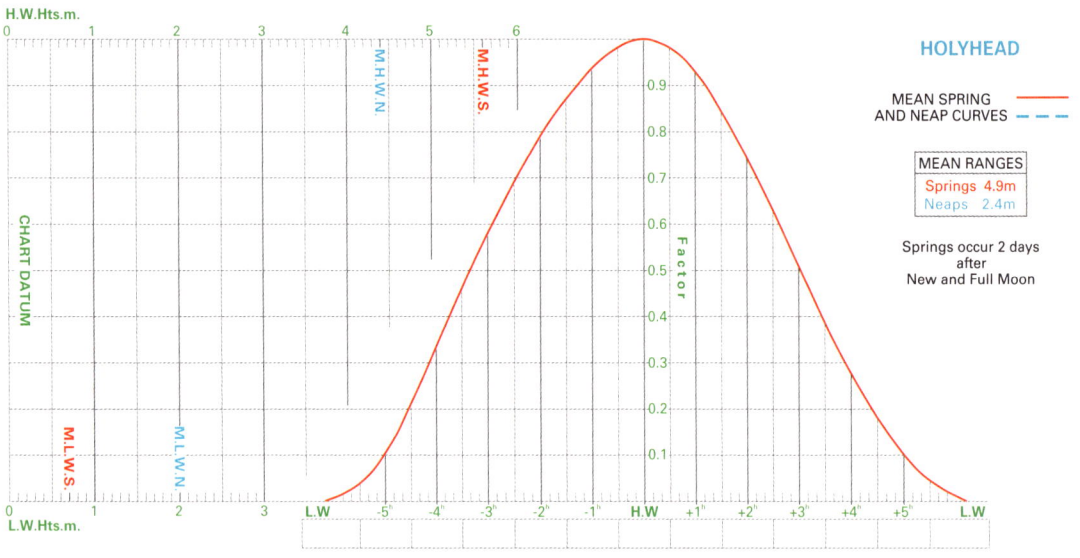

HOLYHEAD

MEAN SPRING ——— AND NEAP CURVES – – –

MEAN RANGES
Springs 4.9m
Neaps 2.4m

Springs occur 2 days after New and Full Moon

**CHARTS** AC *5609, 1826*, 1970, *1977*, 1413, 2011; Imray C61, C52; Stanfords 27; OS 114

**TIDES** –0035 Dover; ML 3·2; Duration 0615

**Standard Port HOLYHEAD (→)**

| Times | | | | Height (metres) | | | |
|---|---|---|---|---|---|---|---|
| High Water | | Low Water | | MHWS | MHWN | MLWN | MLWS |
| 0000 | 0600 | 0500 | 1100 | 5·6 | 4·4 | 2·0 | 0·7 |
| 1200 | 1800 | 1700 | 2300 | | | | |
| **Differences TRWYN DINMOR** (W of Puffin Is) | | | | | | | |
| +0025 | +0015 | +0050 | +0035 | +1·9 | +1·5 | +0·5 | +0·2 |
| **MOELFRE** (NE Anglesey) | | | | | | | |
| +0025 | +0020 | +0050 | +0035 | +1·9 | +1·4 | +0·5 | +0·2 |
| **AMLWCH** (N Anglesey) | | | | | | | |
| +0020 | +0010 | +0035 | +0025 | +1·6 | +1·3 | +0·5 | +0·2 |
| **CEMAES BAY** (N Anglesey) | | | | | | | |
| +0020 | +0025 | +0040 | +0035 | +1·0 | +0·7 | +0·3 | +0·1 |
| **TREARDDUR BAY** (W Anglesey) | | | | | | | |
| –0045 | –0025 | –0015 | –0015 | –0·4 | –0·4 | 0·0 | +0·1 |
| **PORTH TRECASTELL** (SW Anglesey) | | | | | | | |
| –0045 | –0025 | –0005 | –0015 | –0·6 | –0·6 | 0·0 | 0·0 |
| **TREFOR** (Lleyn peninsula) | | | | | | | |
| –0115 | –0100 | –0030 | –0020 | –0·8 | –0·9 | –0·2 | –0·1 |
| **PORTH DINLLAEN** (Lleyn peninsula) | | | | | | | |
| –0120 | –0105 | –0035 | –0025 | –1·0 | –1·0 | –0·2 | –0·2 |
| **PORTH YSGADEN** (Lleyn peninsula) | | | | | | | |
| –0125 | –0110 | –0040 | –0035 | –1·1 | –1·0 | –0·1 | –0·1 |
| **BARDSEY ISLAND** | | | | | | | |
| –0220 | –0240 | –0145 | –0140 | –1·2 | –1·2 | –0·5 | –0·1 |

**SHELTER** Good in marina, least depth 2m, but temp'y visitors berths on E side of floating bwtr are exposed to fresh E'lies. Alternatively ⚓ or use Y ⚓ off HSC; drying AB on bkwtr in emergency only; or in Fish Dock. Strong NE winds raise an uncomfortable sea.

**NAVIGATION** WPT 53°20'·12N 04°37'·27W, 165°/0·28M to Bkwtr Lt ho. Yachts should approach New Harbour via the Small Craft Channel, parallel to and within 70m of the bkwtr; but beware shoal, drying 0·5m, which extends 35m SE of bkwtr head. Keep close SE of the breakwater until clear of the Fairway area in the New Harbour. No anchoring in fairways.

Frequent HSS and Ro-Ro ferries to and from Dun Laoghaire comply with a mini-TSS at the hbr ent by entering within 100-500m of bkwtr hd for Ro-Ro terminals in New Hbr or the Inner Hbr; outbound ferries pass within 2½ca WSW of Clipera PHM buoy, Fl(4) R 15s. Yachts should keep well clear.

**LIGHTS AND MARKS** Ldg marks 165°: bkwtr lt ho on with chy (127m, grey + B top; R lts); chy and Holyhead Mountain (218m) are conspic from afar. Cranes on aluminium jetty conspic closer to. Inner hbr tfc sigs from old lt ho at E end of Admiralty pier:
● = Ent is impracticable. ○ = Ent is clear.

**R/T** *Holyhead Marina* and *Holyhead SC*: Ch **M**. Monitor *Holyhead* Ch 14 16 (H24) for ferry traffic. Broadcast of local nav info/ warnings 1200UT daily on Ch 14.

**TELEPHONE** (Code 01407) Marina 764242; Port Control 763071 🖷 606622; MRCC 762051; Marinecall 09068 969650; Police (01286) 673333; Dr via MRCC.

**FACILITIES** Holyhead Marina ☎ 764242, mob 07714 292990, 🖷 769152, www.holyheadmarina.co.uk, £2.00, Ⓥ 20 approx, D (0800-1800), Gas, Gaz, BY, CH, ME, Ⓔ, El, ✕, BH (14 tons), Slip, R.
**Holyhead SC (HSC)** ☎ 762526, M £8.00, L, FW, launch (call Ch M: 0900-2100, Fri/Sat to 2330), Slip, R (Wed, Fri, Sat, Sun only), Bar ☎ 762496.
**Fish Dock** ☎ 760139 AB on pontoons, but little room, FW, D by hose.
**Inner Hbr** ☎ 762304, used by Stena HSS; not advised for yachts.
**Services:** BY, ACA, CH, ME, El, ✕, C (100 ton), BH, Slip, Ⓔ.
**Town** P, 🛒, R, Bar, ◎, ✉, Ⓑ, ⇌, ✈ (Liverpool/Manchester). Ferry/ HSS to Dun Laoghaire and Dublin.
**Trearddur Bay** (3M south) M (small craft only), L; BY ☎ 860501, D, FW, ✕, CH. **Village** P, 🛒, R, Bar.

### MINOR HARBOUR ON THE LLEYN PENINSULA

**PORTH DINLLAEN**, Gwynedd, **52°56'·68N 04°33'·66W**. AC 1971, 1512. HW –0240 on Dover; ML 2·5m; Duration 0535. See 3.19. Shelter good in S to W winds but strong NNW to NNE winds cause heavy seas in the bay. Beware Carreg-y-Chad (1·8m) 0·75M SW of the point, and Carreg-y-Chwislen (dries, with unlit IDM Bn) 2ca ENE of the point. From N, Garn Fadryn (369m) brg 182° leads into the bay. Best ⚓ 1ca S of LB ho in approx 2m. HM ☎ (01758) 720276; CG ☎ 01407 762051. Facilities: EC Wed; Bar, 🛒 by landing stage. At Morfa Nefyn (1M), Bar, P, R, 🛒.

*See 4.5 for Bardsey Island and Aberdaron Bay anchorages.*

## HOLYHEAD  LAT 53°19'N  LONG 4°37'W
### TIMES AND HEIGHTS OF HIGH AND LOW WATERS

**TIME ZONE (UT)**
For Summer Time add ONE hour in **non-shaded areas**

Dates in red are SPRINGS
Dates in blue are NEAPS

YEAR **2008**

### JANUARY

| Time m | Time m |
|---|---|
| **1** 0420 4.4 / 1020 2.2 / TU 1637 4.6 / 2308 2.0 | **16** 0330 4.7 / 0937 1.7 / W 1552 5.1 / 2217 1.6 |
| **2** 0526 4.4 / 1128 2.3 / W 1745 4.5 | **17** 0438 4.6 / 1048 1.9 / TH 1705 4.9 / 2330 1.7 |
| **3** 0011 2.1 / 0632 4.4 / TH 1237 2.3 / 1854 4.5 | **18** 0558 4.6 / 1208 1.8 / F 1827 4.9 |
| **4** 0111 2.1 / 0732 4.6 / F 1338 2.2 / 1954 4.6 | **19** 0045 1.7 / 0713 4.8 / SA 1324 1.7 / 1943 5.0 |
| **5** 0204 1.9 / 0821 4.8 / SA 1430 1.9 / 2044 4.7 | **20** 0154 1.6 / 0818 5.1 / SU 1431 1.3 / 2048 5.2 |
| **6** 0249 1.8 / 0903 5.0 / SU 1513 1.7 / 2126 4.9 | **21** 0253 1.3 / 0912 5.4 / M 1527 1.0 / 2142 5.4 |
| **7** 0327 1.6 / 0939 5.2 / M 1551 1.5 / 2202 5.0 | **22** 0344 1.1 / 1000 5.6 / TU 1617 0.8 / ○ 2229 5.5 |
| **8** 0403 1.5 / 1014 5.4 / TU 1627 1.3 / ● 2237 5.1 | **23** 0429 1.0 / 1044 5.8 / W 1701 0.6 / 2313 5.5 |
| **9** 0438 1.3 / 1048 5.5 / W 1702 1.1 / 2312 5.2 | **24** 0510 0.9 / 1125 5.9 / TH 1743 0.6 / 2353 5.5 |
| **10** 0513 1.2 / 1124 5.6 / TH 1739 1.0 / 2348 5.2 | **25** 0550 0.9 / 1206 5.8 / F 1823 0.7 |
| **11** 0549 1.2 / 1201 5.6 / F 1816 1.0 | **26** 0032 5.3 / 0628 1.0 / SA 1245 5.7 / 1901 0.9 |
| **12** 0026 5.2 / 0626 1.2 / SA 1240 5.6 / 1854 1.0 | **27** 0110 5.2 / 0705 1.2 / SU 1322 5.4 / 1939 1.1 |
| **13** 0106 5.1 / 0706 1.2 / SU 1321 5.5 / 1936 1.1 | **28** 0146 5.0 / 0743 1.4 / M 1359 5.2 / 2018 1.4 |
| **14** 0148 5.0 / 0749 1.4 / M 1404 5.4 / 2022 1.2 | **29** 0224 4.7 / 0824 1.7 / TU 1439 4.9 / 2101 1.8 |
| **15** 0235 4.9 / 0838 1.5 / TU 1454 5.2 / ◑ 2114 1.4 | **30** 0309 4.5 / 0912 2.1 / W 1527 4.5 / ◑ 2153 2.1 |
| | **31** 0406 4.3 / 1015 2.3 / TH 1634 4.3 / 2303 2.3 |

### FEBRUARY

| Time m | Time m |
|---|---|
| **1** 0523 4.2 / 1139 2.5 / F 1802 4.2 | **16** 0536 4.5 / 1158 1.9 / SA 1826 4.6 |
| **2** 0024 2.4 / 0647 4.3 / SA 1304 2.3 / 1929 4.3 | **17** 0037 2.0 / 0707 4.7 / SU 1325 1.7 / 1950 4.7 |
| **3** 0136 2.2 / 0754 4.5 / SU 1409 2.1 / 2029 4.5 | **18** 0154 1.8 / 0815 5.0 / M 1432 1.3 / 2051 5.0 |
| **4** 0230 2.0 / 0843 4.8 / M 1456 1.7 / 2113 4.7 | **19** 0251 1.4 / 0907 5.3 / TU 1523 1.0 / 2138 5.2 |
| **5** 0311 1.7 / 0922 5.1 / TU 1534 1.4 / 2148 5.0 | **20** 0337 1.1 / 0950 5.6 / W 1606 0.7 / 2218 5.4 |
| **6** 0346 1.4 / 0956 5.3 / W 1609 1.1 / 2221 5.2 | **21** 0415 0.9 / 1029 5.7 / TH 1644 0.6 / ○ 2253 5.5 |
| **7** 0420 1.1 / 1030 5.6 / TH 1643 0.8 / ● 2254 5.3 | **22** 0451 0.8 / 1105 5.8 / F 1720 0.5 / 2327 5.5 |
| **8** 0454 0.9 / 1104 5.7 / F 1717 0.6 / 2328 5.4 | **23** 0525 0.7 / 1140 5.8 / SA 1753 0.6 |
| **9** 0528 0.8 / 1140 5.8 / SA 1753 0.6 | **24** 0000 5.4 / 0558 0.8 / SU 1215 5.6 / 1826 0.8 |
| **10** 0003 5.5 / 0604 0.7 / SU 1218 5.8 / 1829 0.6 | **25** 0033 5.3 / 0631 1.0 / M 1247 5.4 / 1858 1.1 |
| **11** 0041 5.4 / 0642 0.8 / M 1257 5.8 / 1908 0.7 | **26** 0105 5.1 / 0705 1.2 / TU 1319 5.2 / 1931 1.4 |
| **12** 0120 5.3 / 0723 1.0 / TU 1338 5.6 / 1951 1.0 | **27** 0138 4.9 / 0741 1.5 / W 1354 4.8 / 2008 1.7 |
| **13** 0203 5.1 / 0810 1.2 / W 1426 5.3 / 2041 1.3 | **28** 0215 4.6 / 0823 1.9 / TH 1434 4.5 / 2052 2.1 |
| **14** 0255 4.8 / 0907 1.6 / TH 1524 4.9 / ◑ 2144 1.7 | **29** 0303 4.4 / 0918 2.2 / F 1532 4.2 / ◑ 2154 2.4 |
| **15** 0403 4.6 / 1024 1.9 / F 1645 4.6 / 2307 2.0 | |

### MARCH

| Time m | Time m |
|---|---|
| **1** 0414 4.2 / 1038 2.4 / SA 1708 4.0 / 2329 2.6 | **16** 0528 4.4 / 1157 1.8 / SU 1832 4.4 |
| **2** 0553 4.1 / 1221 2.4 / SU 1859 4.1 | **17** 0033 2.1 / 0700 4.6 / M 1321 1.5 / 1949 4.7 |
| **3** 0102 2.4 / 0718 4.4 / M 1338 2.1 / 2006 4.4 | **18** 0147 1.8 / 0805 5.0 / TU 1422 1.2 / 2043 4.9 |
| **4** 0202 2.0 / 0813 4.7 / TU 1428 1.6 / 2049 4.7 | **19** 0239 1.4 / 0853 5.2 / W 1508 0.9 / 2123 5.1 |
| **5** 0245 1.6 / 0854 5.0 / W 1506 1.2 / 2123 5.0 | **20** 0320 1.1 / 0932 5.5 / TH 1546 0.7 / 2156 5.3 |
| **6** 0320 1.2 / 0929 5.3 / TH 1541 0.9 / 2155 5.2 | **21** 0355 0.9 / 1007 5.6 / F 1620 0.6 / ○ 2228 5.4 |
| **7** 0354 0.9 / 1003 5.6 / F 1615 0.6 / ● 2227 5.4 | **22** 0427 0.8 / 1040 5.6 / SA 1651 0.6 / 2258 5.4 |
| **8** 0428 0.6 / 1038 5.8 / SA 1649 0.4 / 2301 5.6 | **23** 0459 0.7 / 1112 5.6 / SU 1722 0.7 / 2329 5.4 |
| **9** 0503 0.5 / 1115 6.0 / SU 1725 0.3 / 2337 5.6 | **24** 0530 0.8 / 1144 5.5 / M 1752 0.9 / 2359 5.3 |
| **10** 0540 0.4 / 1153 6.0 / M 1803 0.4 | **25** 0602 1.0 / 1215 5.3 / TU 1822 1.1 |
| **11** 0015 5.6 / 0619 0.5 / TU 1234 5.8 / 1843 0.6 | **26** 0030 5.2 / 0634 1.2 / W 1247 5.1 / 1854 1.4 |
| **12** 0056 5.4 / 0702 0.7 / W 1318 5.6 / 1927 0.9 | **27** 0103 5.0 / 0710 1.4 / TH 1321 4.8 / 1929 1.7 |
| **13** 0140 5.2 / 0751 1.1 / TH 1408 5.2 / 2019 1.4 | **28** 0139 4.8 / 0750 1.7 / F 1401 4.5 / 2010 2.0 |
| **14** 0233 4.9 / 0854 1.5 / F 1513 4.7 / ◑ 2126 1.9 | **29** 0223 4.5 / 0842 2.0 / SA 1454 4.2 / ◑ 2108 2.4 |
| **15** 0346 4.5 / 1019 1.8 / SA 1647 4.4 / 2259 2.1 | **30** 0326 4.3 / 0955 2.3 / SU 1622 3.9 / 2235 2.5 |
| | **31** 0459 4.1 / 1131 2.2 / M 1813 4.0 |

### APRIL

| Time m | Time m |
|---|---|
| **1** 0013 2.4 / 0627 4.3 / TU 1251 1.9 / 1924 4.3 | **16** 0123 1.8 / 0740 4.9 / W 1357 1.2 / 2018 4.9 |
| **2** 0119 2.0 / 0729 4.6 / W 1345 1.5 / 2010 4.7 | **17** 0213 1.5 / 0827 5.1 / TH 1441 1.0 / 2056 5.0 |
| **3** 0206 1.6 / 0814 5.0 / TH 1428 1.1 / 2048 5.0 | **18** 0254 1.2 / 0906 5.3 / F 1518 0.9 / 2129 5.2 |
| **4** 0245 1.2 / 0853 5.3 / F 1505 0.7 / 2122 5.3 | **19** 0329 1.1 / 0940 5.3 / SA 1551 0.9 / 2159 5.3 |
| **5** 0321 0.8 / 0931 5.5 / SA 1542 0.5 / 2157 5.5 | **20** 0401 0.9 / 1013 5.4 / SU 1622 0.9 / ○ 2230 5.3 |
| **6** 0358 0.5 / 1009 5.9 / SU 1619 0.3 / ● 2233 5.7 | **21** 0433 0.9 / 1046 5.3 / M 1652 0.9 / 2301 5.3 |
| **7** 0436 0.4 / 1049 6.0 / M 1658 0.2 / 2312 5.7 | **22** 0505 1.0 / 1118 5.2 / TU 1722 1.0 / 2332 5.3 |
| **8** 0517 0.3 / 1132 5.9 / TU 1740 0.6 / 2353 5.7 | **23** 0538 1.1 / 1150 5.1 / W 1754 1.2 |
| **9** 0601 0.4 / 1217 5.8 / W 1823 0.7 | **24** 0004 5.2 / 0611 1.2 / TH 1224 4.9 / 1826 1.4 |
| **10** 0037 5.5 / 0649 0.7 / TH 1307 5.4 / 1911 1.1 | **25** 0038 5.0 / 0648 1.4 / F 1300 4.7 / 1903 1.7 |
| **11** 0126 5.2 / 0745 1.0 / F 1403 5.0 / 2008 1.5 | **26** 0116 4.9 / 0730 1.6 / SA 1342 4.5 / 1946 1.9 |
| **12** 0225 4.9 / 0853 1.4 / SA 1515 4.6 / ◑ 2120 1.9 | **27** 0200 4.5 / 0821 1.8 / SU 1434 4.3 / 2041 2.2 |
| **13** 0341 4.7 / 1018 1.6 / SU 1650 4.4 / 2249 2.1 | **28** 0257 4.5 / 0925 2.0 / M 1547 4.1 / ◑ 2154 2.3 |
| **14** 0515 4.6 / 1145 1.6 / M 1821 4.4 | **29** 0412 4.4 / 1042 2.0 / TU 1718 4.1 / 2316 2.2 |
| **15** 0014 2.0 / 0637 4.7 / TU 1300 1.4 / 1929 4.6 | **30** 0532 4.4 / 1156 1.8 / W 1830 4.3 |

Chart Datum: 3·05 metres below Ordnance Datum (Newlyn). HAT is 6·3 metres above Chart Datum.

**N Wales**

## HOLYHEAD LAT 53°19'N LONG 4°37'W
### TIMES AND HEIGHTS OF HIGH AND LOW WATERS

**TIME ZONE (UT)**
For Summer Time add ONE
hour in **non-shaded areas**

Dates in red are **SPRINGS**
Dates in blue are **NEAPS**

YEAR 2008

Chart Datum: 3·05 metres below Ordnance Datum (Newlyn). HAT is 6·3 metres above Chart Datum.

### MAY

| Time | m | | Time | m |
|---|---|---|---|---|
| **1** 0025 | 2.0 | **16** 0138 | 1.7 |
| 0636 | 4.7 | | 0752 | 4.9 |
| TH 1255 | 1.4 | | F 1407 | 1.3 |
| 1923 | 4.6 | | 2023 | 4.8 |
| **2** 0119 | 1.6 | **17** 0223 | 1.5 |
| 0729 | 5.0 | | 0835 | 5.0 |
| F 1344 | 1.1 | | SA 1446 | 1.2 |
| 2007 | 5.0 | | 2059 | 5.0 |
| **3** 0205 | 1.2 | **18** 0302 | 1.3 |
| 0815 | 5.3 | | 0913 | 5.0 |
| SA 1428 | 0.8 | | SU 1522 | 1.2 |
| 2047 | 5.5 | | 2132 | 5.1 |
| **4** 0248 | 0.9 | **19** 0337 | 1.2 |
| 0858 | 5.6 | | 0948 | 5.1 |
| SU 1510 | 0.5 | | M 1555 | 1.2 |
| 2127 | 5.5 | | 2205 | 5.2 |
| **5** 0330 | 0.6 | **20** 0412 | 1.2 |
| 0943 | 5.8 | | 1023 | 5.1 |
| M 1552 | 0.4 | | TU 1627 | 1.2 |
| ● 2209 | 5.6 | | ○ 2237 | 5.2 |
| **6** 0415 | 0.4 | **21** 0446 | 1.2 |
| 1029 | 5.8 | | 1057 | 5.0 |
| TU 1636 | 0.4 | | W 1659 | 1.2 |
| 2252 | 5.7 | | 2310 | 5.2 |
| **7** 0501 | 0.4 | **22** 0520 | 1.2 |
| 1117 | 5.8 | | 1132 | 5.0 |
| W 1722 | 0.6 | | TH 1733 | 1.3 |
| 2338 | 5.7 | | 2344 | 5.2 |
| **8** 0551 | 0.5 | **23** 0556 | 1.3 |
| 1207 | 5.6 | | 1207 | 4.9 |
| TH 1811 | 0.8 | | F 1808 | 1.5 |
| **9** 0026 | 5.6 | **24** 0020 | 5.1 |
| 0644 | 0.7 | | 0634 | 1.4 |
| F 1302 | 5.3 | | SA 1246 | 4.7 |
| 1903 | 1.2 | | 1846 | 1.6 |
| **10** 0120 | 5.3 | **25** 0100 | 5.0 |
| 0744 | 0.9 | | 0716 | 1.5 |
| SA 1402 | 5.0 | | SU 1328 | 4.6 |
| 2001 | 1.5 | | 1929 | 1.8 |
| **11** 0220 | 5.1 | **26** 0144 | 4.9 |
| 0850 | 1.2 | | 0803 | 1.6 |
| SU 1512 | 4.7 | | M 1417 | 4.5 |
| 2108 | 1.8 | | 2019 | 1.9 |
| **12** 0329 | 4.9 | **27** 0234 | 4.7 |
| 1002 | 1.4 | | 0857 | 1.6 |
| M 1630 | 4.5 | | TU 1515 | 4.3 |
| ◑ 2224 | 2.0 | | 2118 | 2.0 |
| **13** 0446 | 4.8 | **28** 0333 | 4.7 |
| 1116 | 1.5 | | 0959 | 1.6 |
| TU 1746 | 4.6 | | W 1623 | 4.3 |
| 2338 | 2.0 | | ◐ 2224 | 2.0 |
| **14** 0559 | 4.7 | **29** 0439 | 4.7 |
| 1222 | 1.4 | | 1103 | 1.6 |
| W 1851 | 4.6 | | TH 1732 | 4.4 |
| | | | 2331 | 1.9 |
| **15** 0043 | 1.8 | **30** 0544 | 4.8 |
| 0701 | 4.8 | | 1205 | 1.4 |
| TH 1320 | 1.4 | | F 1833 | 4.6 |
| 1942 | 4.7 | | |
| | | **31** 0032 | 1.6 |
| | | | 0644 | 5.0 |
| | | | SA 1302 | 1.2 |
| | | | 1926 | 4.9 |

### JUNE

| Time | m | | Time | m |
|---|---|---|---|---|
| **1** 0127 | 1.3 | **16** 0237 | 1.6 |
| 0739 | 5.2 | | 0849 | 4.7 |
| SU 1354 | 1.0 | | M 1456 | 1.5 |
| 2016 | 5.1 | | 2109 | 4.9 |
| **2** 0219 | 1.0 | **17** 0318 | 1.5 |
| 0832 | 5.4 | | 0930 | 4.8 |
| M 1444 | 0.8 | | TU 1534 | 1.4 |
| 2103 | 5.4 | | 2145 | 5.1 |
| **3** 0310 | 0.8 | **18** 0356 | 1.4 |
| 0924 | 5.6 | | 1007 | 4.9 |
| TU 1533 | 0.7 | | W 1609 | 1.4 |
| ● 2150 | 5.6 | | ○ 2219 | 5.2 |
| **4** 0401 | 0.6 | **19** 0432 | 1.3 |
| 1016 | 5.6 | | 1043 | 4.9 |
| W 1622 | 0.7 | | TH 1643 | 1.3 |
| 2239 | 5.7 | | 2254 | 5.2 |
| **5** 0453 | 0.5 | **20** 0507 | 1.2 |
| 1108 | 5.6 | | 1118 | 4.9 |
| TH 1712 | 0.7 | | F 1718 | 1.3 |
| 2328 | 5.7 | | 2329 | 5.3 |
| **6** 0546 | 0.5 | **21** 0543 | 1.2 |
| 1201 | 5.5 | | 1154 | 4.9 |
| F 1802 | 0.9 | | SA 1754 | 1.3 |
| **7** 0018 | 5.6 | **22** 0005 | 5.2 |
| 0639 | 0.6 | | 0620 | 1.2 |
| SA 1256 | 5.3 | | SU 1232 | 4.9 |
| 1853 | 1.1 | | 1831 | 1.4 |
| **8** 0111 | 5.5 | **23** 0044 | 5.2 |
| 0734 | 0.8 | | 0659 | 1.2 |
| SU 1351 | 5.0 | | M 1311 | 4.8 |
| 1947 | 1.3 | | 1910 | 1.5 |
| **9** 0205 | 5.3 | **24** 0125 | 5.1 |
| 0831 | 1.0 | | 0741 | 1.2 |
| M 1449 | 4.8 | | TU 1353 | 4.7 |
| 2043 | 1.6 | | 1954 | 1.5 |
| **10** 0303 | 5.1 | **25** 0208 | 5.0 |
| 0931 | 1.2 | | 0826 | 1.3 |
| TU 1550 | 4.6 | | W 1440 | 4.6 |
| ◑ 2144 | 1.8 | | 2043 | 1.6 |
| **11** 0404 | 4.9 | **26** 0257 | 5.0 |
| 1033 | 1.4 | | 0918 | 1.4 |
| W 1654 | 4.5 | | TH 1534 | 4.6 |
| 2249 | 1.9 | | ◐ 2139 | 1.7 |
| **12** 0509 | 4.7 | **27** 0353 | 4.9 |
| 1135 | 1.6 | | 1016 | 1.4 |
| TH 1758 | 4.4 | | F 1638 | 4.5 |
| 2354 | 1.9 | | 2243 | 1.7 |
| **13** 0613 | 4.6 | **28** 0457 | 4.9 |
| 1233 | 1.6 | | 1120 | 1.4 |
| F 1856 | 4.5 | | SA 1746 | 4.6 |
| | | | 2352 | 1.7 |
| **14** 0055 | 1.9 | **29** 0606 | 4.9 |
| 0712 | 4.6 | | 1226 | 1.4 |
| SA 1327 | 1.6 | | SU 1853 | 4.8 |
| 1946 | 4.6 | | |
| **15** 0150 | 1.8 | **30** 0059 | 1.5 |
| 0804 | 4.7 | | 0714 | 5.0 |
| SU 1415 | 1.6 | | M 1329 | 1.3 |
| 2030 | 4.8 | | 1953 | 5.0 |

### JULY

| Time | m | | Time | m |
|---|---|---|---|---|
| **1** 0202 | 1.3 | **16** 0303 | 1.7 |
| 0818 | 5.2 | | 0917 | 4.7 |
| TU 1428 | 1.1 | | W 1517 | 1.6 |
| 2049 | 5.2 | | 2128 | 5.0 |
| **2** 0301 | 1.0 | **17** 0342 | 1.5 |
| 0916 | 5.3 | | 0955 | 4.8 |
| W 1522 | 1.0 | | TH 1553 | 1.5 |
| 2140 | 5.5 | | 2203 | 5.2 |
| **3** 0356 | 0.7 | **18** 0418 | 1.3 |
| 1011 | 5.5 | | 1028 | 4.9 |
| TH 1614 | 0.9 | | F 1627 | 1.3 |
| ● 2230 | 5.7 | | ○ 2237 | 5.3 |
| **4** 0448 | 0.5 | **19** 0451 | 1.1 |
| 1102 | 5.5 | | 1101 | 5.0 |
| F 1702 | 0.8 | | SA 1700 | 1.2 |
| 2318 | 5.8 | | 2311 | 5.4 |
| **5** 0538 | 0.4 | **20** 0525 | 1.0 |
| 1151 | 5.5 | | 1135 | 5.1 |
| SA 1749 | 0.8 | | SU 1735 | 1.1 |
| | | | 2346 | 5.5 |
| **6** 0006 | 5.8 | **21** 0600 | 0.9 |
| 0625 | 0.5 | | 1210 | 5.1 |
| SU 1240 | 5.3 | | M 1810 | 1.1 |
| 1835 | 0.9 | | |
| **7** 0053 | 5.7 | **22** 0022 | 5.5 |
| 0713 | 0.6 | | 0635 | 0.9 |
| M 1326 | 5.2 | | TU 1247 | 5.1 |
| 1921 | 1.1 | | 1846 | 1.1 |
| **8** 0139 | 5.5 | **23** 0100 | 5.4 |
| 0800 | 0.9 | | 0713 | 0.9 |
| TU 1413 | 4.9 | | W 1325 | 5.0 |
| 2008 | 1.4 | | 1925 | 1.2 |
| **9** 0226 | 5.2 | **24** 0140 | 5.3 |
| 0849 | 1.2 | | 0753 | 1.1 |
| W 1501 | 4.7 | | TH 1407 | 4.9 |
| 2058 | 1.6 | | 2009 | 1.4 |
| **10** 0316 | 4.9 | **25** 0224 | 5.2 |
| 0941 | 1.5 | | 0840 | 1.2 |
| TH 1553 | 4.5 | | F 1455 | 4.8 |
| ◑ 2154 | 1.9 | | ◐ 2101 | 1.6 |
| **11** 0411 | 4.6 | **26** 0316 | 5.0 |
| 1038 | 1.8 | | 0936 | 1.4 |
| F 1653 | 4.4 | | SA 1554 | 4.6 |
| 2259 | 2.1 | | 2206 | 1.7 |
| **12** 0516 | 4.4 | **27** 0422 | 4.8 |
| 1142 | 2.0 | | 1045 | 1.6 |
| SA 1801 | 4.3 | | SU 1711 | 4.6 |
| | | | 2325 | 1.8 |
| **13** 0009 | 2.2 | **28** 0544 | 4.7 |
| 0628 | 4.3 | | 1203 | 1.7 |
| SU 1246 | 2.0 | | M 1833 | 4.7 |
| 1907 | 4.4 | | |
| **14** 0118 | 2.1 | **29** 0046 | 1.7 |
| 0737 | 4.4 | | 0707 | 4.8 |
| M 1346 | 1.9 | | TU 1318 | 1.6 |
| 2003 | 4.6 | | 1944 | 4.9 |
| **15** 0216 | 1.9 | **30** 0158 | 1.4 |
| 0832 | 4.5 | | 0818 | 5.0 |
| TU 1436 | 1.8 | | W 1423 | 1.4 |
| 2049 | 4.8 | | 2043 | 5.2 |
| | | **31** 0259 | 1.0 |
| | | | 0916 | 5.2 |
| | | | TH 1517 | 1.1 |
| | | | 2134 | 5.5 |

### AUGUST

| Time | m | | Time | m |
|---|---|---|---|---|
| **1** 0351 | 0.7 | **16** 0355 | 1.1 |
| 1005 | 5.4 | | 1007 | 5.1 |
| F 1605 | 0.9 | | SA 1604 | 1.2 |
| ● 2220 | 5.7 | | ○ 2213 | 5.5 |
| **2** 0438 | 0.5 | **17** 0427 | 1.0 |
| 1050 | 5.5 | | 1037 | 5.2 |
| SA 1648 | 0.8 | | SU 1636 | 1.0 |
| 2303 | 5.9 | | 2246 | 5.6 |
| **3** 0521 | 0.4 | **18** 0459 | 0.7 |
| 1132 | 5.5 | | 1109 | 5.3 |
| SU 1730 | 0.7 | | M 1709 | 0.8 |
| 2345 | 5.9 | | 2320 | 5.7 |
| **4** 0603 | 0.5 | **19** 0532 | 0.7 |
| 1213 | 5.4 | | 1142 | 5.4 |
| M 1810 | 0.8 | | TU 1743 | 0.7 |
| | | | 2355 | 5.7 |
| **5** 0026 | 5.7 | **20** 0606 | 0.7 |
| 0643 | 0.6 | | 1218 | 5.3 |
| TU 1253 | 5.3 | | W 1819 | 0.9 |
| 1849 | 1.0 | | |
| **6** 0106 | 5.5 | **21** 0032 | 5.7 |
| 0722 | 0.9 | | 0643 | 0.8 |
| W 1331 | 5.0 | | TH 1256 | 5.3 |
| 1929 | 1.2 | | 1857 | 1.0 |
| **7** 0146 | 5.2 | **22** 0112 | 5.6 |
| 0802 | 1.2 | | 0723 | 1.0 |
| TH 1410 | 4.8 | | F 1336 | 5.1 |
| 2010 | 1.6 | | 1941 | 1.2 |
| **8** 0226 | 4.9 | **23** 0157 | 5.3 |
| 0845 | 1.6 | | 0809 | 1.3 |
| F 1454 | 4.6 | | SA 1424 | 4.9 |
| ◐ 2058 | 1.9 | | ◑ 2035 | 1.5 |
| **9** 0314 | 4.6 | **24** 0251 | 5.0 |
| 0935 | 2.0 | | 0907 | 1.6 |
| SA 1548 | 4.4 | | SU 1526 | 4.7 |
| 2159 | 2.2 | | 2146 | 1.8 |
| **10** 0417 | 4.3 | **25** 0404 | 4.7 |
| 1041 | 2.3 | | 1024 | 1.9 |
| SU 1700 | 4.2 | | M 1652 | 4.5 |
| 2320 | 2.4 | | 2318 | 1.9 |
| **11** 0543 | 4.1 | **26** 0544 | 4.5 |
| 1203 | 2.4 | | 1156 | 2.0 |
| M 1825 | 4.3 | | TU 1827 | 4.6 |
| **12** 0047 | 2.3 | **27** 0047 | 1.7 |
| 0714 | 4.2 | | 0714 | 4.7 |
| TU 1319 | 2.3 | | W 1318 | 1.8 |
| 1937 | 4.5 | | 1941 | 5.0 |
| **13** 0156 | 2.1 | **28** 0159 | 1.4 |
| 0818 | 4.4 | | 0821 | 5.0 |
| W 1416 | 2.0 | | TH 1420 | 1.5 |
| 2028 | 4.8 | | 2037 | 5.3 |
| **14** 0244 | 1.7 | **29** 0255 | 1.0 |
| 0901 | 4.7 | | 0911 | 5.2 |
| TH 1458 | 1.7 | | F 1509 | 1.1 |
| 2107 | 5.0 | | 2123 | 5.6 |
| **15** 0322 | 1.4 | **30** 0340 | 0.7 |
| 0936 | 4.9 | | 0953 | 5.4 |
| F 1532 | 1.4 | | SA 1550 | 0.9 |
| 2141 | 5.3 | | ● 2203 | 5.8 |
| | | **31** 0420 | 0.5 |
| | | | 1030 | 5.5 |
| | | | SU 1628 | 0.8 |
| | | | 2242 | 5.8 |

>> **FREE** monthly updates from <<
www.reedsalmanac.co.uk

**TIME ZONE (UT)**
For Summer Time add ONE hour in **non-shaded areas**

## HOLYHEAD   LAT 53°19'N   LONG 4°37'W
### TIMES AND HEIGHTS OF HIGH AND LOW WATERS

Dates in red are SPRINGS
Dates in blue are NEAPS

YEAR **2008**

### SEPTEMBER

| Time | m | | Time | m |
|---|---|---|---|---|
| **1** 0457 | 0.5 | **16** 0427 | 0.6 | |
| 1106 | 5.5 | 1039 | 5.5 | |
| M 1704 | 0.7 | TU 1640 | 0.7 | |
| 2319 | 5.9 | 2251 | 5.9 | |
| **2** 0533 | 0.6 | **17** 0501 | 0.5 | |
| 1142 | 5.5 | 1113 | 5.6 | |
| TU 1740 | 0.8 | W 1715 | 0.7 | |
| 2356 | 5.7 | 2328 | 5.9 | |
| **3** 0608 | 0.8 | **18** 0537 | 0.6 | |
| 1216 | 5.3 | 1150 | 5.6 | |
| W 1815 | 1.0 | TH 1753 | 0.7 | |
| **4** 0031 | 5.5 | **19** 0007 | 5.8 | |
| 0642 | 1.0 | 0616 | 0.7 | |
| TH 1251 | 5.2 | F 1230 | 5.5 | |
| 1851 | 1.2 | 1835 | 0.9 | |
| **5** 0106 | 5.2 | **20** 0051 | 5.6 | |
| 0717 | 1.4 | 0658 | 1.0 | |
| F 1325 | 5.0 | SA 1313 | 5.3 | |
| 1929 | 1.6 | 1923 | 1.2 | |
| **6** 0142 | 4.9 | **21** 0139 | 5.3 | |
| 0754 | 1.7 | 0748 | 1.4 | |
| SA 1403 | 4.7 | SU 1405 | 5.0 | |
| 2012 | 1.9 | 2023 | 1.6 | |
| **7** 0224 | 4.5 | **22** 0240 | 4.9 | |
| 0839 | 2.1 | 0851 | 1.9 | |
| SU 1451 | 4.5 | M 1513 | 4.7 | |
| ☽ 2108 | 2.3 | ☽ 2143 | 1.9 | |
| **8** 0322 | 4.2 | **23** 0408 | 4.5 | |
| 0940 | 2.4 | 1018 | 2.2 | |
| M 1601 | 4.3 | TU 1649 | 4.6 | |
| 2229 | 2.5 | 2320 | 1.9 | |
| **9** 0457 | 4.0 | **24** 0553 | 4.5 | |
| 1113 | 2.6 | 1154 | 2.2 | |
| TU 1736 | 4.2 | W 1822 | 4.8 | |
| **10** 0010 | 2.4 | **25** 0045 | 1.7 | |
| 0646 | 4.1 | 0714 | 4.7 | |
| W 1245 | 2.5 | TH 1311 | 1.9 | |
| 1900 | 4.5 | 1931 | 5.1 | |
| **11** 0124 | 2.1 | **26** 0150 | 1.3 | |
| 0752 | 4.4 | 0812 | 5.0 | |
| TH 1346 | 2.1 | F 1407 | 1.6 | |
| 1956 | 4.8 | 2023 | 5.4 | |
| **12** 0213 | 1.7 | **27** 0240 | 1.0 | |
| 0834 | 4.7 | 0856 | 5.3 | |
| F 1428 | 1.8 | SA 1452 | 1.2 | |
| 2036 | 5.1 | 2105 | 5.6 | |
| **13** 0250 | 1.4 | **28** 0320 | 0.8 | |
| 0907 | 5.0 | 0932 | 5.4 | |
| SA 1502 | 1.4 | SU 1529 | 1.0 | |
| 2110 | 5.3 | 2142 | 5.8 | |
| **14** 0323 | 1.0 | **29** 0356 | 0.7 | |
| 0937 | 5.2 | 1005 | 5.5 | |
| SU 1534 | 1.1 | M 1604 | 0.9 | |
| 2143 | 5.6 | ● 2217 | 5.8 | |
| **15** 0355 | 0.8 | **30** 0430 | 0.7 | |
| 1007 | 5.4 | 1038 | 5.5 | |
| M 1606 | 0.9 | TU 1638 | 0.8 | |
| ○ 2216 | 5.8 | 2252 | 5.7 | |

### OCTOBER

| Time | m | | Time | m |
|---|---|---|---|---|
| **1** 0502 | 0.8 | **16** 0433 | 0.5 | |
| 1111 | 5.5 | 1047 | 5.8 | |
| W 1712 | 0.9 | TH 1652 | 0.6 | |
| 2326 | 5.6 | 2305 | 6.0 | |
| **2** 0534 | 1.0 | **17** 0513 | 0.6 | |
| 1143 | 5.4 | 1127 | 5.8 | |
| TH 1745 | 1.1 | F 1735 | 0.7 | |
| 2359 | 5.4 | 2350 | 5.8 | |
| **3** 0606 | 1.2 | **18** 0556 | 0.8 | |
| 1215 | 5.3 | 1211 | 5.6 | |
| F 1820 | 1.3 | SA 1822 | 0.9 | |
| **4** 0032 | 5.1 | **19** 0038 | 5.6 | |
| 0639 | 1.5 | 0643 | 1.2 | |
| SA 1249 | 5.1 | SU 1300 | 5.4 | |
| 1857 | 1.6 | 1917 | 1.2 | |
| **5** 0108 | 4.9 | **20** 0134 | 5.2 | |
| 0715 | 1.8 | 0738 | 1.6 | |
| SU 1326 | 4.9 | M 1356 | 5.2 | |
| 1939 | 1.9 | 2023 | 1.5 | |
| **6** 0148 | 4.6 | **21** 0242 | 4.8 | |
| 0758 | 2.2 | 0846 | 2.0 | |
| M 1411 | 4.7 | TU 1509 | 4.9 | |
| 2032 | 2.2 | ☽ 2144 | 1.7 | |
| **7** 0243 | 4.3 | **22** 0412 | 4.6 | |
| 0855 | 2.5 | 1027 | 2.2 | |
| TU 1514 | 4.4 | W 1638 | 4.8 | |
| ☽ 2145 | 2.4 | 2310 | 1.7 | |
| **8** 0411 | 4.1 | **23** 0543 | 4.6 | |
| 1019 | 2.7 | 1136 | 2.2 | |
| W 1643 | 4.3 | TH 1802 | 4.9 | |
| 2319 | 2.4 | | | |
| **9** 0557 | 4.1 | **24** 0025 | 1.6 | |
| 1154 | 2.6 | 0655 | 4.8 | |
| TH 1809 | 4.5 | F 1248 | 1.9 | |
| | | 1907 | 5.1 | |
| **10** 0035 | 2.1 | **25** 0127 | 1.3 | |
| 0707 | 4.4 | 0749 | 5.0 | |
| F 1300 | 2.2 | SA 1343 | 1.7 | |
| 1910 | 4.8 | 1959 | 5.3 | |
| **11** 0128 | 1.7 | **26** 0215 | 1.2 | |
| 0753 | 4.7 | 0831 | 5.2 | |
| SA 1346 | 1.9 | SU 1428 | 1.4 | |
| 1955 | 5.1 | 2041 | 5.5 | |
| **12** 0209 | 1.4 | **27** 0255 | 1.0 | |
| 0829 | 5.0 | 0907 | 5.3 | |
| SU 1425 | 1.5 | M 1506 | 1.2 | |
| 2033 | 5.4 | 2118 | 5.6 | |
| **13** 0245 | 1.0 | **28** 0330 | 1.0 | |
| 0902 | 5.3 | 0939 | 5.4 | |
| M 1500 | 1.1 | TU 1541 | 1.1 | |
| 2109 | 5.7 | ● 2153 | 5.6 | |
| **14** 0320 | 0.8 | **29** 0403 | 1.1 | |
| 0935 | 5.5 | 1012 | 5.5 | |
| TU 1535 | 0.9 | W 1615 | 1.1 | |
| ○ 2146 | 5.9 | 2227 | 5.5 | |
| **15** 0356 | 0.6 | **30** 0435 | 1.1 | |
| 1010 | 5.7 | 1044 | 5.5 | |
| W 1612 | 0.7 | TH 1649 | 1.2 | |
| 2224 | 6.0 | 2301 | 5.4 | |
| | | **31** 0506 | 1.2 | |
| | | 1116 | 5.5 | |
| | | F 1723 | 1.3 | |
| | | 2335 | 5.3 | |

### NOVEMBER

| Time | m | | Time | m |
|---|---|---|---|---|
| **1** 0538 | 1.4 | **16** 0544 | 0.9 | |
| 1149 | 5.4 | 1200 | 5.8 | |
| SA 1758 | 1.4 | SU 1818 | 0.8 | |
| **2** 0009 | 5.1 | **17** 0033 | 5.5 | |
| 0612 | 1.6 | 0635 | 1.2 | |
| SU 1223 | 5.2 | M 1253 | 5.6 | |
| 1835 | 1.6 | 1915 | 1.0 | |
| **3** 0045 | 4.9 | **18** 0132 | 5.2 | |
| 0648 | 1.8 | 0732 | 1.5 | |
| M 1301 | 5.1 | TU 1351 | 5.4 | |
| 1917 | 1.8 | 2018 | 1.3 | |
| **4** 0127 | 4.6 | **19** 0238 | 4.9 | |
| 0731 | 2.1 | 0835 | 1.8 | |
| TU 1345 | 4.9 | W 1457 | 5.2 | |
| 2007 | 2.0 | ☽ 2128 | 1.5 | |
| **5** 0218 | 4.4 | **20** 0353 | 4.7 | |
| 0823 | 2.3 | 0947 | 2.0 | |
| W 1440 | 4.7 | TH 1611 | 5.0 | |
| 2108 | 2.2 | 2241 | 1.6 | |
| **6** 0327 | 4.2 | **21** 0509 | 4.7 | |
| 0931 | 2.5 | 1101 | 2.1 | |
| TH 1551 | 4.5 | F 1725 | 5.0 | |
| ☽ 2222 | 2.2 | 2350 | 1.6 | |
| **7** 0454 | 4.2 | **22** 0618 | 4.7 | |
| 1051 | 2.5 | 1210 | 2.0 | |
| F 1708 | 4.6 | SA 1832 | 5.0 | |
| 2334 | 2.0 | | | |
| **8** 0607 | 4.4 | **23** 0051 | 1.5 | |
| 1201 | 2.3 | 0715 | 4.9 | |
| SA 1814 | 4.8 | SU 1310 | 1.8 | |
| | | 1927 | 5.1 | |
| **9** 0033 | 1.8 | **24** 0143 | 1.5 | |
| 0702 | 4.7 | 0802 | 5.0 | |
| SU 1257 | 1.9 | M 1400 | 1.7 | |
| 1907 | 5.1 | 2014 | 5.2 | |
| **10** 0123 | 1.4 | **25** 0227 | 1.4 | |
| 0747 | 5.0 | 0841 | 5.2 | |
| M 1343 | 1.6 | TU 1443 | 1.5 | |
| 1953 | 5.3 | 2055 | 5.2 | |
| **11** 0206 | 1.1 | **26** 0305 | 1.4 | |
| 0827 | 5.3 | 0916 | 5.3 | |
| TU 1426 | 1.3 | W 1522 | 1.4 | |
| 2036 | 5.4 | 2133 | 5.3 | |
| **12** 0247 | 0.9 | **27** 0340 | 1.3 | |
| 0906 | 5.5 | 0951 | 5.4 | |
| W 1508 | 1.0 | TH 1559 | 1.4 | |
| 2119 | 5.8 | ● 2209 | 5.3 | |
| **13** 0329 | 0.7 | **28** 0414 | 1.4 | |
| 0946 | 5.7 | 1024 | 5.4 | |
| TH 1551 | 0.8 | F 1634 | 1.4 | |
| ○ 2204 | 5.9 | 2244 | 5.2 | |
| **14** 0412 | 0.7 | **29** 0446 | 1.4 | |
| 1028 | 5.8 | 1057 | 5.5 | |
| F 1637 | 0.7 | SA 1708 | 1.4 | |
| 2251 | 5.9 | 2318 | 5.1 | |
| **15** 0456 | 0.8 | **30** 0520 | 1.5 | |
| 1112 | 5.9 | 1131 | 5.4 | |
| SA 1725 | 0.7 | SU 1744 | 1.4 | |
| 2340 | 5.8 | 2353 | 5.1 | |

### DECEMBER

| Time | m | | Time | m |
|---|---|---|---|---|
| **1** 0554 | 1.6 | **16** 0027 | 5.6 | |
| 1206 | 5.3 | 0626 | 1.0 | |
| M 1821 | 1.5 | TU 1244 | 5.8 | |
| | | 1906 | 0.8 | |
| **2** 0030 | 4.9 | **17** 0121 | 5.4 | |
| 0631 | 1.7 | 0718 | 1.3 | |
| TU 1244 | 5.2 | W 1336 | 5.7 | |
| 1900 | 1.6 | 2001 | 1.0 | |
| **3** 0110 | 4.8 | **18** 0216 | 5.1 | |
| 0711 | 1.9 | 0812 | 1.5 | |
| W 1325 | 5.1 | TH 1431 | 5.4 | |
| 1944 | 1.7 | 2058 | 1.2 | |
| **4** 0155 | 4.6 | **19** 0315 | 4.9 | |
| 0756 | 2.0 | 0910 | 1.8 | |
| TH 1411 | 4.9 | F 1531 | 5.2 | |
| 2033 | 1.8 | ☽ 2159 | 1.5 | |
| **5** 0247 | 4.5 | **20** 0418 | 4.7 | |
| 0849 | 2.2 | 1014 | 2.0 | |
| F 1505 | 4.8 | SA 1636 | 5.0 | |
| ☽ 2130 | 1.9 | 2303 | 1.7 | |
| **6** 0349 | 4.4 | **21** 0525 | 4.6 | |
| 0951 | 2.2 | 1122 | 2.1 | |
| SA 1607 | 4.8 | SU 1744 | 4.8 | |
| 2232 | 1.9 | | | |
| **7** 0459 | 4.5 | **22** 0006 | 1.8 | |
| 1058 | 2.2 | 0630 | 4.6 | |
| SU 1713 | 4.8 | M 1230 | 2.1 | |
| 2335 | 1.7 | 1850 | 4.8 | |
| **8** 0605 | 4.6 | **23** 0106 | 1.8 | |
| 1203 | 2.0 | 0728 | 4.7 | |
| M 1817 | 5.0 | TU 1331 | 2.0 | |
| | | 1949 | 4.8 | |
| **9** 0035 | 1.6 | **24** 0200 | 1.8 | |
| 0702 | 4.9 | 0817 | 4.9 | |
| TU 1303 | 1.7 | W 1425 | 1.8 | |
| 1915 | 5.2 | 2039 | 4.9 | |
| **10** 0130 | 1.3 | **25** 0245 | 1.7 | |
| 0754 | 5.1 | 0859 | 5.1 | |
| W 1357 | 1.4 | TH 1510 | 1.7 | |
| 2009 | 5.4 | 2121 | 5.0 | |
| **11** 0221 | 1.1 | **26** 0325 | 1.6 | |
| 0842 | 5.4 | 0936 | 5.2 | |
| TH 1448 | 1.1 | F 1549 | 1.5 | |
| 2101 | 5.6 | 2159 | 5.0 | |
| **12** 0310 | 1.0 | **27** 0400 | 1.5 | |
| 0929 | 5.6 | 1010 | 5.4 | |
| F 1539 | 0.9 | SA 1624 | 1.4 | |
| ○ 2152 | 5.7 | ● 2234 | 5.1 | |
| **13** 0358 | 0.9 | **28** 0433 | 1.4 | |
| 1016 | 5.8 | 1044 | 5.4 | |
| SA 1629 | 0.7 | SU 1658 | 1.3 | |
| 2244 | 5.8 | 2307 | 5.1 | |
| **14** 0447 | 0.8 | **29** 0506 | 1.4 | |
| 1103 | 5.9 | 1117 | 5.5 | |
| SU 1721 | 0.6 | M 1731 | 1.2 | |
| 2335 | 5.7 | 2340 | 5.1 | |
| **15** 0536 | 0.9 | **30** 0540 | 1.4 | |
| 1153 | 5.9 | 1151 | 5.5 | |
| M 1813 | 0.6 | TU 1806 | 1.2 | |
| | | **31** 0014 | 5.1 | |
| | | 0614 | 1.4 | |
| | | W 1227 | 5.4 | |
| | | 1841 | 1.3 | |

**N Wales**

Chart Datum: 3·05 metres below Ordnance Datum (Newlyn). HAT is 6·3 metres above Chart Datum.

# Milford Haven Port Authority

**Milford Marina & Docks**

## Ideally placed for land and sea operations

Situated in a non-tidal basin on the North Shore of one of Europe's best known Ports, Milford Haven provides superb shelter and access to some of the finest leisure boating in the UK.

With first class berthing and unloading facilities, this is also an ideal choice for West-of-UK commercial operations.

**Milford Marina:** Cleddau House, The Docks, MILFORD HAVEN, Pembrokeshire SA73 3AF

**Milford Docks:** Unit 4, Victory House, The Docks, MILFORD HAVEN, Pembrokeshire SA73 3AF

**Marina:** Tel: +44 (0)1646 696312    **Docks:** Tel: +44 (0)1646 696300

website: www.mhpa.co.uk

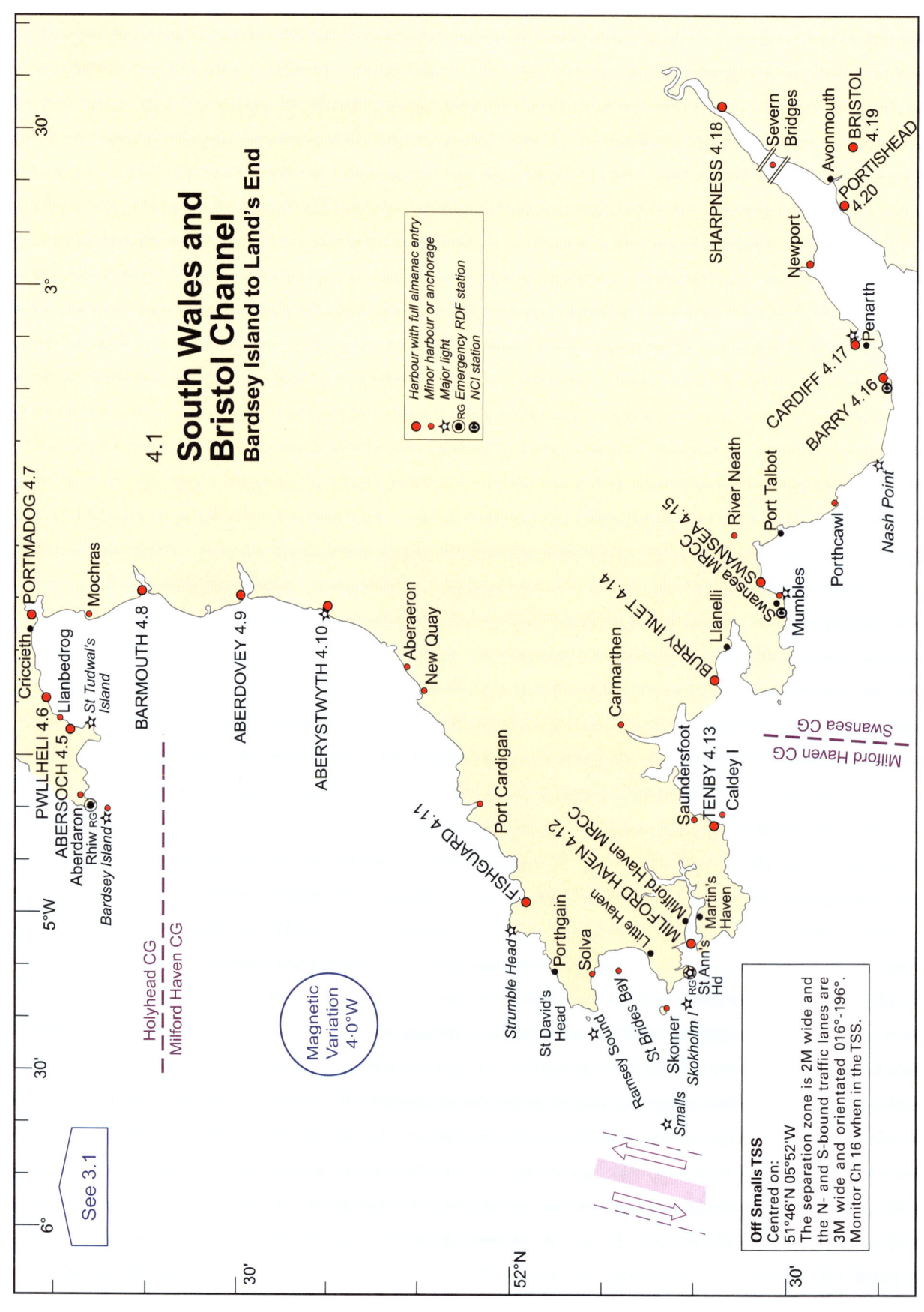

4.1

# South Wales and Bristol Channel
**Bardsey Island to Land's End**

Harbour with full almanac entry
Minor harbour or anchorage
Major light
RG Emergency RDF station
NCI station

See 3.1

Magnetic Variation 4·0°W

Holyhead CG
Milford Haven CG

PORTMADOG 4.7
Criccieth
Mochras
PWLLHELI 4.6
Llanbedrog
St Tudwal's Island
BARMOUTH 4.8
ABERSOCH 4.5
Aberdaron
Rhiw RG
Bardsey Island
ABERDOVEY 4.9
New Quay
Aberaeron
ABERYSTWYTH 4.10
Port Cardigan
FISHGUARD 4.11
Strumble Head
St David's Head
Porthgain
Solva
Ramsey Sound
St Brides Bay
Smalls
Skomer
Skokholm I
St Ann's Hd
RG
Little Haven
MILFORD HAVEN 4.12
Milford Haven MRCC
St Martin's Haven
Caldey I
TENBY 4.13
Saundersfoot
Carmarthen
BURRY INLET 4.14
Llanelli
River Neath
Port Talbot
Porthcawl
Nash Point
Swansea MRCC
SWANSEA 4.15
Mumbles
BARRY 4.16
CARDIFF 4.17
Penarth
Newport
SHARPNESS 4.18
Severn Bridges
Avonmouth
BRISTOL 4.19
PORTISHEAD 4.20

Milford Haven CG
Swansea CG

**Off Smalls TSS**
Centred on:
51°46'N 05°52'W
The separation zone is 2M wide and the N- and S-bound traffic lanes are 3M wide and orientated 016°–196°. Monitor Ch 16 when in the TSS.

30'
3°
5°W
6°
52°N
30'
30'

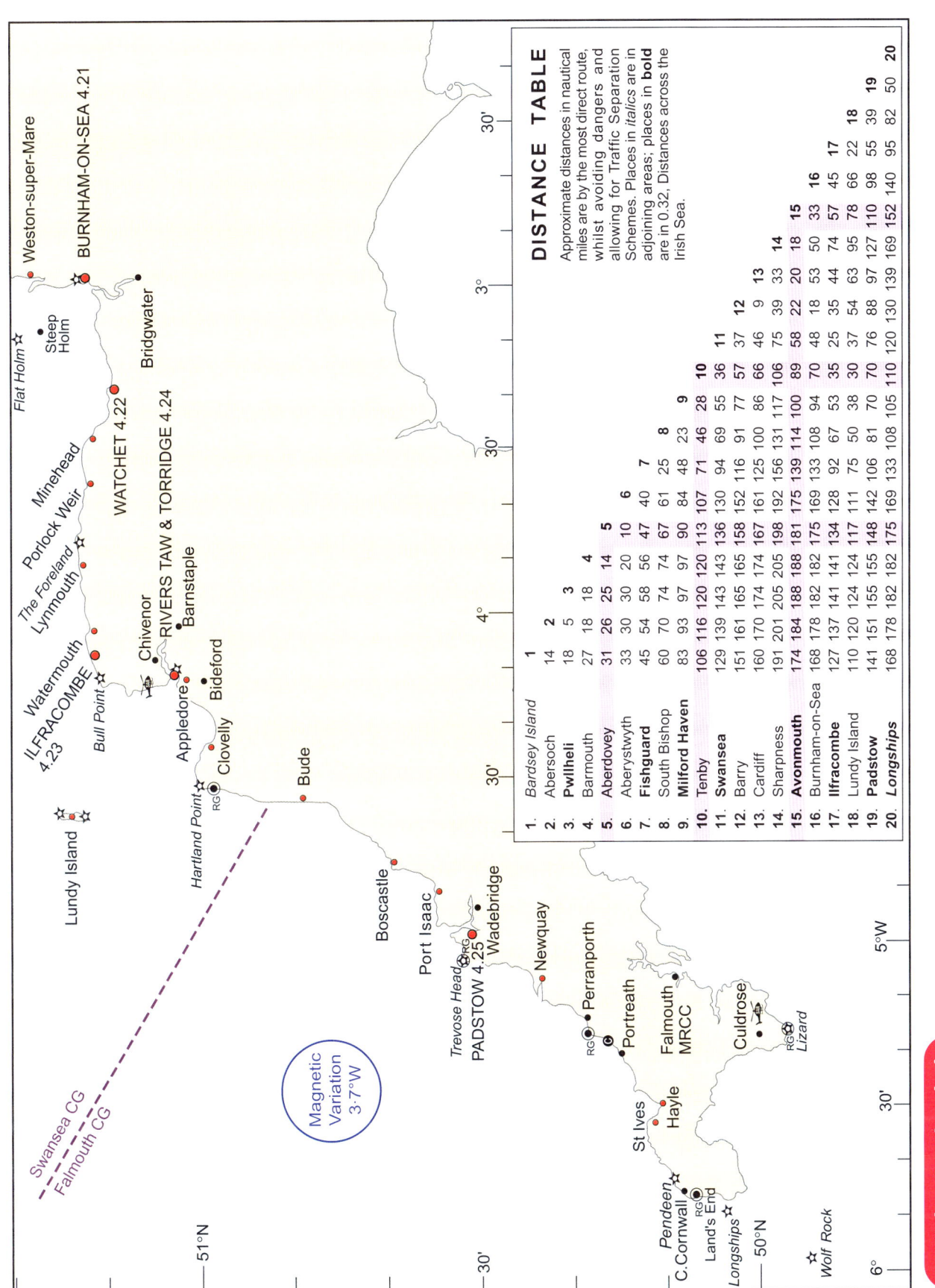

**DISTANCE TABLE**

Approximate distances in nautical miles are by the most direct route, whilst avoiding dangers and allowing for Traffic Separation Schemes. Places in *italics* are in adjoining areas; places in **bold** are in 0.32, Distances across the Irish Sea.

| | | | | | | | | | | | | | | | | | | | | |
|---|---|---|---|---|---|---|---|---|---|---|---|---|---|---|---|---|---|---|---|---|
| 1. *Bardsey Island* | **1** | | | | | | | | | | | | | | | | | | | |
| 2. Abersoch | 14 | **2** | | | | | | | | | | | | | | | | | | |
| 3. **Pwllheli** | 18 | 5 | **3** | | | | | | | | | | | | | | | | | |
| 4. Barmouth | 27 | 18 | 18 | **4** | | | | | | | | | | | | | | | | |
| 5. Aberdovey | 31 | 26 | 25 | 14 | **5** | | | | | | | | | | | | | | | |
| 6. Aberystwyth | 33 | 30 | 30 | 20 | 10 | **6** | | | | | | | | | | | | | | |
| 7. **Fishguard** | 45 | 54 | 58 | 56 | 47 | 40 | **7** | | | | | | | | | | | | | |
| 8. South Bishop | 60 | 70 | 74 | 74 | 67 | 61 | 25 | **8** | | | | | | | | | | | | |
| 9. **Milford Haven** | 83 | 93 | 97 | 97 | 90 | 84 | 48 | 23 | **9** | | | | | | | | | | | |
| 10. Tenby | 106 | 116 | 120 | 120 | 113 | 107 | 71 | 46 | 28 | **10** | | | | | | | | | | |
| 11. Swansea | 129 | 139 | 143 | 143 | 136 | 130 | 94 | 69 | 55 | 36 | **11** | | | | | | | | | |
| 12. Barry | 151 | 161 | 165 | 165 | 158 | 152 | 116 | 91 | 77 | 57 | 37 | **12** | | | | | | | | |
| 13. Cardiff | 160 | 170 | 174 | 174 | 167 | 161 | 125 | 100 | 86 | 66 | 46 | 9 | **13** | | | | | | | |
| 14. Sharpness | 191 | 201 | 205 | 205 | 198 | 192 | 156 | 131 | 117 | 106 | 75 | 39 | 33 | **14** | | | | | | |
| 15. **Avonmouth** | 174 | 184 | 188 | 188 | 181 | 175 | 139 | 114 | 100 | 89 | 58 | 22 | 20 | 18 | **15** | | | | | |
| 16. Burnham-on-Sea | 168 | 178 | 182 | 182 | 175 | 169 | 133 | 108 | 94 | 70 | 48 | 18 | 53 | 50 | 33 | **16** | | | | |
| 17. Ilfracombe | 127 | 137 | 141 | 141 | 134 | 128 | 92 | 67 | 53 | 35 | 25 | 35 | 44 | 74 | 57 | 45 | **17** | | | |
| 18. Lundy Island | 110 | 120 | 124 | 124 | 117 | 111 | 75 | 50 | 38 | 30 | 37 | 54 | 63 | 95 | 78 | 66 | 22 | **18** | | |
| 19. **Padstow** | 141 | 151 | 155 | 155 | 148 | 142 | 106 | 81 | 70 | 70 | 76 | 88 | 97 | 127 | 110 | 98 | 55 | 39 | **19** | |
| 20. *Longships* | 168 | 178 | 182 | 182 | 175 | 169 | 133 | 108 | 105 | 110 | 120 | 130 | 139 | 169 | 152 | 140 | 95 | 82 | 50 | **20** |

Weston-super-Mare

BURNHAM-ON-SEA 4.21

Flat Holm ☆

Steep Holm ☆

Bridgwater

Minehead

Porlock Weir

WATCHET 4.22

The Foreland

Lynmouth

RIVERS TAW & TORRIDGE 4.24

Watermouth

Chivenor

Barnstaple

ILFRACOMBE 4.23

Bull Point

Appledore

Bideford

Clovelly

Hartland Point

Bude

Lundy Island ☆

Boscastle

Port Isaac

Wadebridge

Newquay

Trevose Head

PADSTOW 4.25

Perranporth

Portreath

Falmouth MRCC

Culdrose

Lizard

St Ives

Hayle

Pendeen

C. Cornwall

Land's End ☆

*Longships*

☆ Wolf Rock

*Magnetic Variation 3·7°W*

Swansea CG

Falmouth CG

51°N

30'

50°N

30'

6°

30'

4°

3°

5°W

## 4.2  S WALES & BRISTOL CHANNEL TIDAL STREAMS

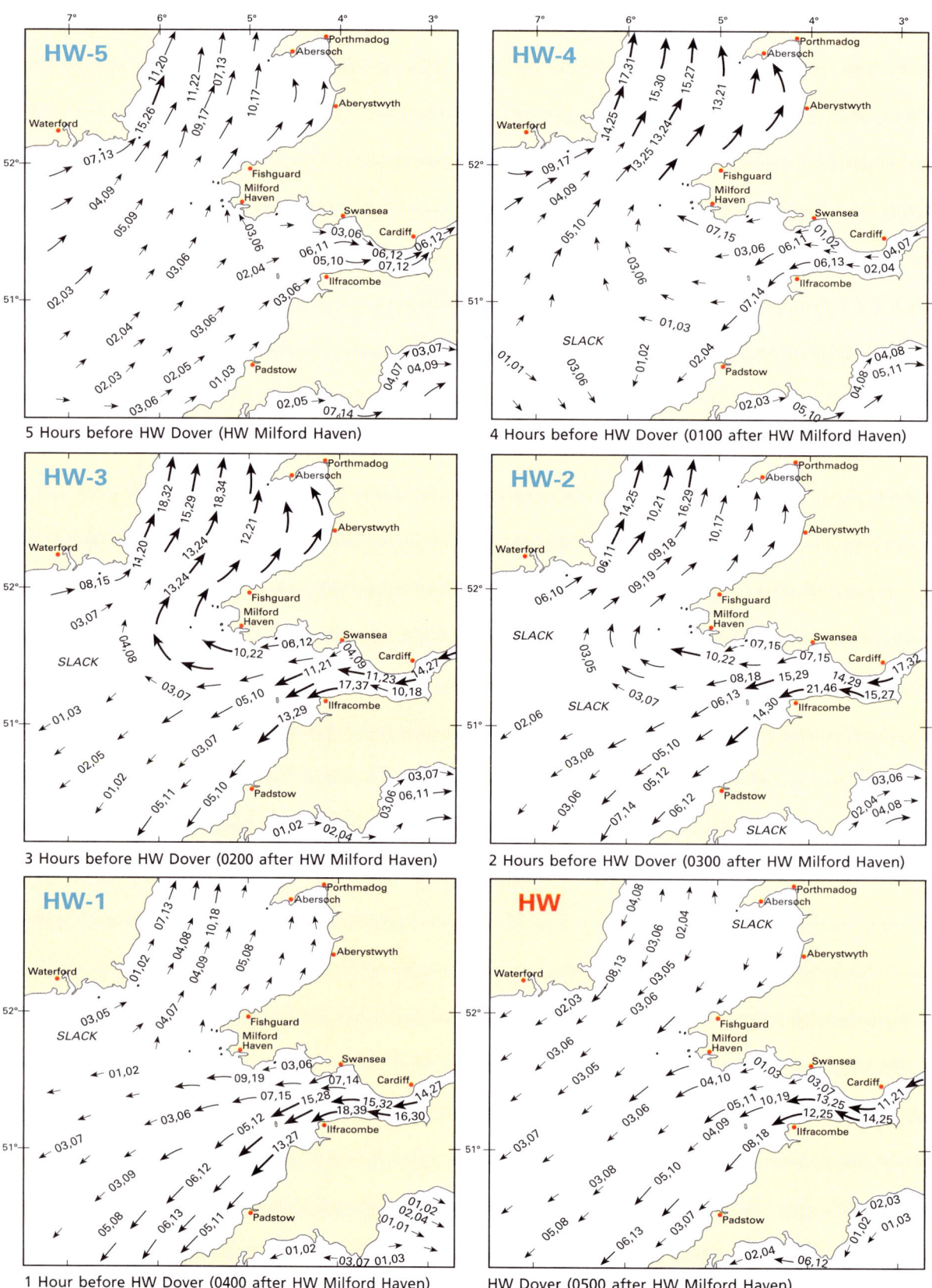

5 Hours before HW Dover (HW Milford Haven)

4 Hours before HW Dover (0100 after HW Milford Haven)

3 Hours before HW Dover (0200 after HW Milford Haven)

2 Hours before HW Dover (0300 after HW Milford Haven)

1 Hour before HW Dover (0400 after HW Milford Haven)

HW Dover (0500 after HW Milford Haven)

Northward 3.2    South Ireland 4.2

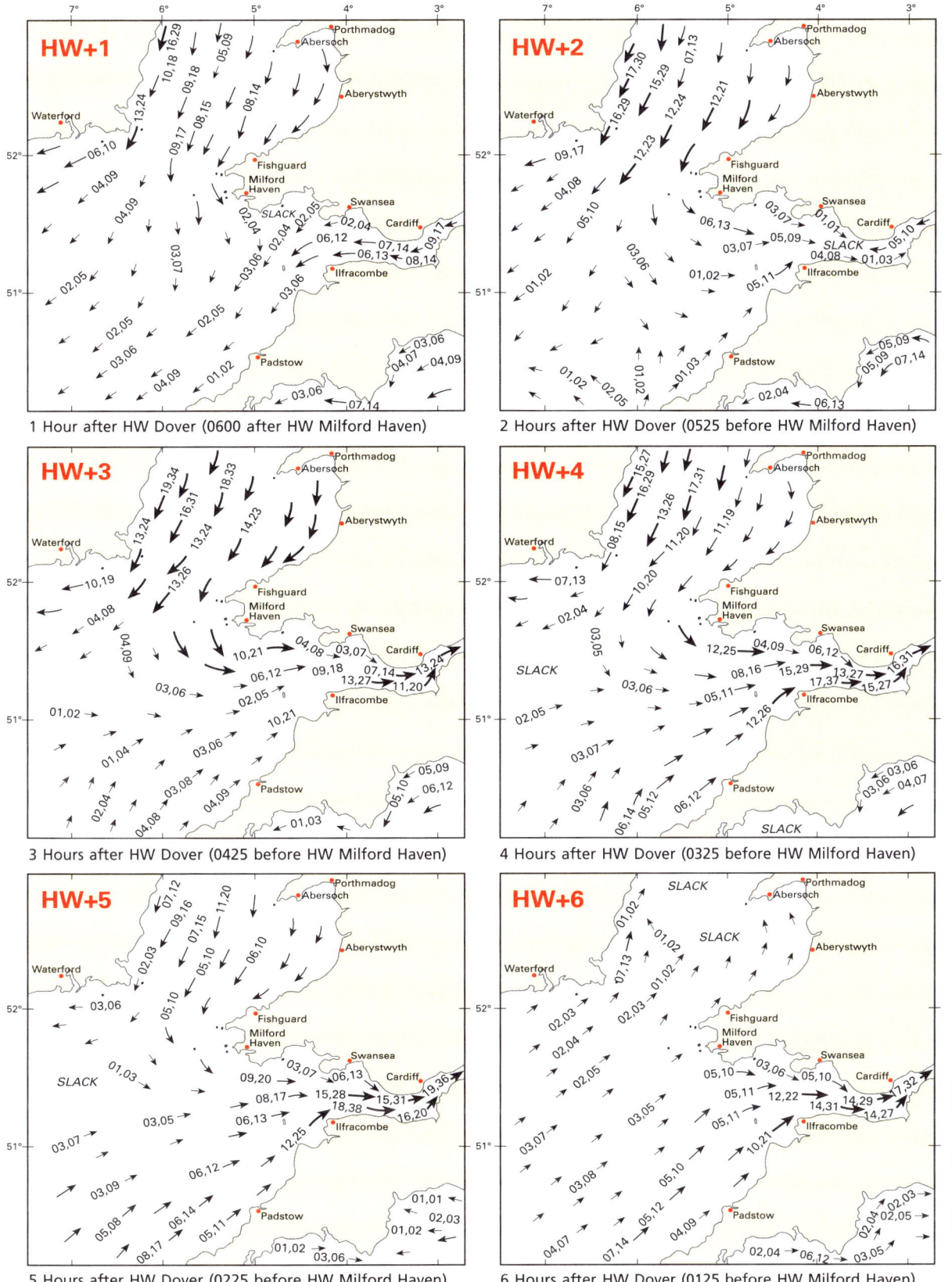

1 Hour after HW Dover (0600 after HW Milford Haven)

2 Hours after HW Dover (0525 before HW Milford Haven)

3 Hours after HW Dover (0425 before HW Milford Haven)

4 Hours after HW Dover (0325 before HW Milford Haven)

5 Hours after HW Dover (0225 before HW Milford Haven)

6 Hours after HW Dover (0125 before HW Milford Haven)

## 4.3 LIGHTS, BUOYS AND WAYPOINTS

**Bold** print = light with a nominal range of 15M or more. CAPITALS = place or feature. *CAPITAL ITALICS* = light-vessel, light float or Lanby. *Italics* = Fog signal. ***Bold italics*** = Racon. See 0.2 for Abbreviations.

### CARDIGAN BAY (see also 3.3)

**Bardsey I** ☆ 52°45'·00N 04°47'·98W Fl (5) 15s 39m **26M**; W☐twr, R bands; obsc by Bardsey I 198°-250° and in Tremadoc B when brg less than 260°; *Horn Mo(N) 45s.*

St Tudwal's ⚓ Fl WR 15s 46m W14, R10M; vis: 349°-W-169°-R-221°-W-243°-R-259°-W-293°-R-349°; obsc by East I 211°-231°; 52°47'·92N 04°28'·30W.

### PWLLHELI, PORTHMADOG and MOCHRAS LAGOON

Pwllheli App ⚓ Iso 2s; 52°53'·02N 04°23'·07W.
Training Arm Hd ⚓ QG 3m 3M; 52°53'·25N 04°23'·74W.
Abererch ⚓ (Apr-Oct); 52°53'·52N 04°23'·07W.
Gimblet Shoals ⚓(Apr-Oct); 52°50'·20N 04°22'·70W Fl Y 5s.
West End ⚓ (Apr-Oct); 52°52'·42N 04°25'·57W.
Porthmadog Fairway ⚓ L Fl 10s; 52°52'·97N 04°11'·18W.
Shell Is, NE Corner ⚓ Fl WRG 4s; vis: 079°-G-124°-W-134°-R-179°; (Mar-Nov); 52°49'·56N 04°07'·71W.

### BARMOUTH and ABERDOVEY

Diffuser ⚓ Fl Y 5s; 52°43'·19N 04°05'·38W.
Barmouth Outer ⚓ L Fl 10s; 52°42'·62N 04°04'·83W.
N Bank Y Perch ⚓ QR 4m 5M; 52°42'·83N 04°03'·74W.
Ynys y Brawd, SE end ⚓ Fl R 5s 5M; 52°42'·99N 04°03'·12W.
Sarn Badrig Causeway ⚓Q (9) 15s; *Bell;* 52°41'·19N 04°25'·36W.
Sarn-y-Bwch ⚓ VQ (9) 10s; 52°34'·81N 04°13'·58W.

Aberdovey Outer ⚓ Iso 4s; 52°32'·00N 04°05'·56W.
Cynfelyn Patches, Patches ⚓ Q (9) 15s; 52°25'·83N 04°16'·41W.

### ABERYSTWYTH, ABERAERON and NEW QUAY

Aberystwyth S Bkwtr Hd ⚓ Fl (2) WG 10s 12m 10M; vis: 030°-G-053°-W-210°; 52°24'·40N 04°05'·52W.
Ldg Lts 133°. Front, FR 4m 5M; 52°24'·37N 04°05'·39W. Rear, 52m from front, FR 7m 6M.
Aberaeron S Pier ⚓ Fl (3) G 10s 11m 6M; vis: 050°-243°; 52°14'·61N 04°15'·94W.
N Pier ⚓ Fl (4) WRG 15s 10m 6M; vis: 050°-G-104°-W-178°-R-232°; 52°14'·61N 04°15'·87W.
Carreg Ina ⚓ Q; 52°13'·25N 04°20'·75W.
⚓ Q (3) 10s; 52°12'·94N 04°21'·29W.
New Quay Pier Hd ⚓ Fl WG 3s 12m W8M, G5M; G △; vis: 135°-W-252°-G-295; 52°12'·95N 04°21'·35W.

### CARDIGAN and FISHGUARD

Cardigan CG Bldg ⚓ 2 FR (vert); 52°06'·98N 04°41'·21W.
Cardigan Channel ⚓ Fl (2) 5s; 52°06'·44N 04°41'·43W.
Fishguard N Bkwtr Hd ⚓ Fl G 4·5s 18m 13M; *Bell (1) 8s;* 52°00'·76N 04°58'·23W.
E Bkwtr Hd ⚓ Fl R 3s 10m 5M; 52°00'·31N 04°58'·86W.
Lts in line 282°. Front FG 77m 5M W ◇ on mast; 52°00'·68N 04°59'·27W. Rear, 46m from front, FG 89m 5M.
Penanglas, 152m S of Pt, *Dia (2) 60s*; W obelisk.
**Strumble Head** ☆ 52°01'·79N 05°04'·43W Fl (4) 15s 45m **26M**; vis: 038°-257°; (H24).

### BISHOPS and SMALLS

**South Bishop** ☆ 51°51'·14N 05°24'·74W Fl 5s 44m **16M**; W ◯ twr; *Horn (3) 45s;* ***Racon (O)10M***; (H24).

**The Smalls** ☆ 51°43'·27N 05°40'·19W Fl (3) 15s 36m **18M**; ***Racon (T)***. *Horn (2) 60s.* Same twr, Iso R 4s 33m 13M; vis: 253°-285° over Hats & Barrels Rk; both Lts shown H24 in periods of reduced visibility.

**Skokholm I** ☆, 51°41'·64N 05°17'·22W Fl WR 10s 54m **W18M, R15M**; vis: 301°-W-154°-R-301°; partially obsc 226°-258°.

### WALES – SOUTH COAST – BRISTOL CHANNEL

### MILFORD HAVEN

**St Ann's Head** ☆ 51°40'·87N 05°10'·42W Fl WR 5s 48m **W18M, R17M**, R14M; W 8-sided twr; vis: 233°-W-247°-R-285°-R(intens)- 314°-R-332°-W131°, partially obscured between 124°-129°; *Horn (2) 60s.*

W Blockhouse Point ⚓ Ldg Lts 022·5°. Front, F 54m 13M; B stripe on W twr; vis: 004·5°-040·5°; intens on lead. By day 10M; vis: 004·5°-040·5°; ***Racon (Q)***; 51°41'·31N 05°09'·56W.
**Watwick Point Common Rear** ☆, 0·5M from front, F 80m **15M**; vis: 013·5°-031·5°. By day 10M; vis: 013·5°-031·5°; ***Racon (Y)***..
W Blockhouse Point ⚓ Q WR 21m W9M, R7M; R lantern on W base: vis: 220°-W-250°-R-020°-W-036°-R-049°; 51°41'·31N 05°09'·56W.
Dale Fort ⚓ Fl (2) WR 5s 20m W5M, R3M; vis: 222°-R-276°-W-019°; 51°42'·16N 05°09'·01W.
Gt Castle Hd ⚓ F WRG 27m W5M, R3M, G3M; vis: 243°-R-281°-G-299°-W-029°; also Dir WRG (040°) 038·25°-G-039°-Al WG-039·5°-W-040·5°-AlWR-041°-R-041·75°; 51°42'·67N 05°07'·07W (not used in conjunction with the following front light) also Ldg Lts 039·7°.
**Front,** Oc 4s 27m **15M**; vis: 031·2°-048·2°. **Rear**, 890m from front, **Little Castle Head** ⚓ 51°43'·03N 05°06'·60W Oc 8s 53m **15M** (by day 10M) vis: 031·2°-048·2°.
St Ann's ⚓ Fl R 2·5s; 51°40'·25N 05°10'·51W.
Mid Channel Rks ⚓ Q (9) 15s; 51°40'·18N 05°10'·14W.
Middle Chan Rks ⚓ Fl (3) G 7s 18m 8M; 51°40'·32N 05°09'·83W.
Sheep ⚓ QG; 51°40'·06N 05°08'·31W.
Millbay ⚓ Fl (2) R 5s; 51°41'·05N 05°09'·45W.
W Chapel ⚓ Fl G 10s; 51°40'·98N 05°08'·67W.
E Chapel ⚓ Fl R 5s; 51°40'·87N 05°08'·15W.
Rat ⚓ Fl G 5s; 51°40'·80N 05°07'·86W.
Angle ⚓ VQ; 51°41'·63N 05°08'·27W.
Thorn Rock ⚓ Q (9) 15s; 51°41'·53N 05°07'·76W.
Dakotian ⚓ Q (3) 10s; 51°42'·15N 05°08'·29W.
Chapel ⚓ 51°41'·66N 05°06'·86W Fl G 5s.
Stack ⚓ Fl R 2·5s; 51°42'·03N 05°06'·52W.
S Hook ⚓ Q (6) +L Fl 15s; 51°41'·83N 05°06'·10W.
Esso ⚓ Q; 51°41'·74N 05°05'·24W.
E Angle ⚓ Fl (3) G 10s; 51°41'·72N 05°04'·26W.
Turbot Bank ⚓ VQ (9) 10s; 51°37'·41N 05°10'·08W.
ODAS ⚓ Fl (5) 20s; 51°36'·80N 05°08'·80W.
St Gowan ⚓ Q (6) + L Fl 15s, ***Racon (T) 10M***; 51°31'·93N 04°59'·77W.

### TENBY/SAUNDERSFOOT/CARMARTHEN BAY/BURRY INLET

Caldey I ⚓ Fl (3) WR 20s 65m W13M, R9M; vis: R173°- W212°-R088°-102°; 51°37'·90N 04°41'·08W.
Eel Point ⚓ Fl G 2·5s; 51°38'·86N 04°42'·24W.
Giltar Spit ⚓ Fl R 2·5s; 51°39'·03N 04°42'·12W.
Spaniel ⚓ Q (3) 10s; 51°38'·06N 04°39'·74W.
Woolhouse ⚓ Q (6) + L Fl 15s; 51°39'·35N 04°39'·69W.
North Highcliff ⚓ Q; 51°39'·38N 04°40'·77W.
Tenby Pier Hd ⚓ FR 7m 7M; 51°40'·40N 04°41'·89W.
Saundersfoot Pier Hd ⚓ Fl R 5s 6m 7M; 51°42'·59N 04°41'·73W.
DZ1 ⚓ 51°42'·05N 04°36'·00W.
DZ2 ⚓ Fl Y 2·5s; 51°39'·98N 04°37'·73W.
DZ3 ⚓ 51°37'·37N 04°37'·84W.
DZ7 ⚓ Fl Y 10s; 51°38'·09N 04°30'·12W.
DZ4 ⚓ Fl Y 5s; 51°35'·73N 04°30'·05W.
DZ8 ⚓ 51°41'·51N 04°24'·42W.
DZ6 ⚓ 51°38'·02N 04°24'·37W.
DZ5 ⚓ Fl Y 2·5s; 51°36'·37N 04°24'·39W.
Burry Port Barrel Post ⚓ Fl R 3s 5M; 51°40'·49N 04°15'·01W.
**Burry Port Inlet** ⚓ 51°40'·62N 04°15'·06W Fl 5s 7m **15M**.
Llanelli Ent N side ⚓ Fl R 5s 2M.
W. Helwick (W HWK) ⚓ (9) 15s; ***Racon (T) 10M***; *Whis;* 51°31'·40N 04°23'·65W Q.
E. Helwick ⚓ VQ (3) 5s; *Bell;* 51°31'·80N 04°12'·68W.

### SWANSEA BAY and SWANSEA

Ledge ⚓ VQ (6) + L Fl 10s; 51°29'·93N 03°58'·77W.

*Plot waypoints on chart before use*

Mixon ⌐ Fl (2) R 5s; *Bell;* 51°33'·12N 03°58'·78W.
Outer Spoil Gnd ⌐ Fl Y 2·5s; 51°32'·11N 03°55'·73W.
Grounds ⚲ VQ (3) 5s; 51°32'·81N 03°53'·47W.
**Mumbles** ☆ 51°34'·01N 03°58'·27W Fl (4) 20s 35m **15M**; W twr; *Horn (3) 60s.*
Railway Pier Hd ⚡ 2 FR (vert) 11m 9M; 51°34'·21N 03°58'·44W.
SW Inner Green Grounds ⚲ Q (6) + L Fl 15s; *Bell;* 51°34'·06N 03°57'·03W.
Outer Fairway ⚑ QG; *Bell;* 51°35'·52N 03°56'·09W.
Swansea West Fairway ⌐ QR; 51°35'·56N 03°56'·24W.
Swansea Inner Fairway ⚑ Fl G 2·5s; *Bell;* 51°36'·23N 03°55'·67W.
E Bkwtr Hd ⚡ 2 FG (vert) 10m 6M; *Siren30s;* 51°36'·38N 03°55'·62W.
W Pier Hd ⚡ Fl (2) R 10s 11m 9M; 51°36'·50N 03°55'·73W.
Lts in line 020°. Jetty Head Front, Oc G 4s 5m 2M; 51°36'·55N 03°55'·52W. Rear, 260m from front, FG 6M.

## SWANSEA BAY, RIVER NEATH and PORT TALBOT
Neath App Chan ⚑ Fl G 5s; 51°35'·71N 03°52'·83W.
Monkstone ⚡ Fl (2) G 6s 6m 5M; 51°36'·32N 03°51'·97W.
Neath SE Trg Wall N End ⚡ Fl (3) G 10s 6m 5M; 51°37'·09N 03°50'·85W.
Neath SE Trg Wall Mid. ⚡ Fl G 1·5s 6m 5M; 51°36'·70N 03°51'·41W.
Neath SE Trg Wall N end inner ⚡ Fl(3)G 10s 6m 5M; 51°37'·09N 03°50'·85W.
Cabenda ⚲ VQ (6) + L Fl 10s; *Racon (Q);* 51°33'·36N 03°52'·23W.
P Talbot S Outer ⚑ Fl G 5s; 51°33'·71N 03°51'·30W.
P Talbot N Outer ⌐ Fl R 5s; 51°33'·78N 03°51'·38W.
N. Inner ⌐ 51°34'·22N 03°50'·25W Fl R 3s.
Ldg Lts 059·8° (occas). Front, Oc R 3s 12m 6M; 51°34'·92N 03°48'·10W. Rear, 400m from front, Oc R 6s 32m 6M.
N Bkwtr Hd ⚡ Fl (4) R 10s 11m 3M; 51°34'·77N 03°49'·00W.
S Bkwtr Hd ⚡ Fl G 3s 11m 3M; 51°34'·46N 03°49'·04W.

Kenfig ⚲ VQ (3) 5s; 51°29'·44N 03°46'·06W.
W Scar ⚲ Q (9) 15s, *Bell,* **Racon (T) 10M**; 51°28'·31N 03°55'·57W.
South Scar (S SCAR) ⚲ Q (6) + L Fl 15s; 51°27'·61N 03°51'·58W.
Hugo ⌐ QR; 51°28'·63N 03°48'·07W.
E. Scarweather ⚲ Q (3) 10s; *Bell;* 51°27'·98N 03°46'·76W.

### PORTHCAWL
Fairy ⚲ Q (9) 15s; *Bell;* 51°27'·86N 03°42'·07W.
Tusker ⌐ Fl (2) R 5s *Bell;* 51°26'·85N 03°40'·74W.
Porthcawl Bkwtr Hd ⚡ Fl WRG 10m W6M, R4M, G4M; vis: 302°-G-036°-W-082°-R-122°.
W Nash ⚲ VQ (9) 10s; *Bell;* 51°25'·99N 03°45'·95W.
Middle Nash ⚲ Q (6) + L Fl 15s; 51°24'·83N 03°39'·41W.
East Nash ⚲ Q (3) 10s; 51°24'·06N 03°34'·10W.
**Nash** ☆ 51°24'·03N 03°33'·06W Fl (2) WR 15s 56m **W21M, R16M**; vis: 280°-R-290°-W-100°-R-120°-W-128°.
Saint Hilary ⚡ Aero QR 346m 11M; radio mast; 4 FR (vert) on same mast 6M; 51° 27'·43N 03°24'·18W.
Breaksea Point intake ⚡ Fl R 11m; 51°22'·51N 03°24'·53W.
Breaksea ⚲ L Fl 10s; *Racon (T) 10M;* 51°19'·88N 03°19'·08W.
Wenvoe ⚡ Aero Q 365m 12M; radio mast (H24); 51°27'·55N 03°16'·93W.
Merkur ⌐ QR; 51°21'·88N 03°15'·95W.
Welsh Water Barry W ⌐ Fl R 5s; 51°22'·27N 03°16'·94W.

### BARRY
W Bkwtr Hd ⚡ Fl 2·5s 12m 10M; 51°23'·46N 03°15'·52W.
E Bkwtr Hd ⚡ QG 7m 8M; 51°23'·50N 03°15'·43W.
Lavernock Spit ⚲ VQ (6) + L Fl 10s; 51°23'·02N 03°10'·82W.
N. One Fathom ⚲ Q; 51°20'·94N 03°12'·17W.
Mackenzie ⌐ QR; 51°21'·75N 03°08'·24W.
Holm Middle ⚑ Fl G 2·5s; 51°21'·71N 03°06'·72W.
Wolves ⚲ Q; 51°23'·13N 03°08'·88W.
**Flat Holm** ☆, SE Pt 51°22'·54N 03°07'·14W Fl (3) WR 10s 50m **W15M, R12M**; W ⚪ twr; vis: 106°-R-140°-W-151°-R-203°-W-106°; (H24).

Weston ⌐ Fl (2) R 5s; 51°22'·60N 03°05'·75W.
Monkstone Rock ⚡ Fl 5s 13m 12M; 51°24'·89N 03°06'·02W.

Lavernock Outfall ⌐ Fl Y 5s; 51°23'·95N 03°09'·50W.
Ranie ⌐ Fl (2) R 5s; 51°24'·23N 03°09'·39W.
S Cardiff ⚲ Q (6) + L Fl 15s; *Bell;* 51°24'·18N 03°08'·57W.
Mid Cardiff ⚑ Fl (3) G 10s; 51°25'·60N 03°08'·09W.
Cardiff Spit ⌐ QR; 51°24'·57N 03°07'·12W.
N Cardiff ⚑ QG; 51°26'·52N 03°07'·19W.

### PENARTH and CARDIFF
Penarth Pier near Hd ⚡ 2 FR (vert) 8/6m 3M; *Reed Mo (BA) 60s.* when vessel expected; 51°26'·08N 03°09'·90W.
Wrach Chan Dir lt 348·5°. Oc WRG 10s 5m; W3M, R3M, G3M; vis: 344·5°-G-347°-W-350°-R-352°; H24; 51°27'·16N 03°09'·75W.
Outer Wrach ⚲ Q (9) 15s; 51°26'·20N 03°09'·46W.
Inner Wrach ⚑ Fl G 2·5s; 51°26'·74N 03°09'·65W.
Barrage ⌐ Fl (2+1) R 10s; 51°26'·63N 03°09'·76W.
Queen Alexandra Dock ent S Jetty Hd ⚡ 2 FG (vert); Tfc sigs; *Dia 60s;* 51°27'·09N 03°09'·58W.
Tail Patch ⚑ QG; 51°23'·53N 03°03'·65W.
Hope ⚲ Q (3) 10s; 51°24'·84N 03°02'·68W.
NW Elbow ⚲ VQ (9) 10s; *Bell;* 51°26'·28N 02°59'·93W.
EW Grounds ⚲ L Fl 10s 7M; *Bell; Racon (T) 7M;* 51°27'·12N 02°59'·95W.

Newport Deep ⚑ Fl (3) G 10s; *Bell;* 51°29'·36N 02°59'·12W.
**East Usk** ☆ 51°32'·40N 02°58'·01W; Fl(2) WRG 10s 11m W11M,R10M, G10M; vis: 284°-W-290° -obscured shore-324°-R- 017°-W-037°-G-115°-W-120°. Also Oc WRG 10s 10m W11M, R9M, G9M; vis: 018°-G-022°-W- 024°-R-028°.
Alexandra Dock, S Lock W Pier Hd ⚡ 2 FR (vert) 9m 6M; *Horn 60s;* 51°32'·87N 02°59'·26W.
E Pier Head ⚡ 2 FG (vert) 9m 6M; 51°32'·96N 02°59'·11W.
Julians Pill Ldg Lts 062°. Front, FG 5m 4M; 51°33'·30N 02°57'·94W. Rear, 61m from front, FG 8m 4M.
Birdport Jetty ⚡ 2 FG (vert) 6m; 51°33'·66N 02°58'·10W.
Dallimores Wharf ⚡ 2 FG (vert); 51°33'·88N 02°58'·60W.
Transporter Bridge, W side ⚡2 FR (vert); 2 FY (vert) shown on transporter car; 51°34'·25N 02°59'·23W .
E side ⚡ 2 FG (vert). Centres of George Street and Newport Bridges marked by FY Lts.

### BRISTOL DEEP
N Elbow ⚑ QG; *Bell;* 51°26'·97N 02°58'·65W.
S Mid Grounds ⚲ VQ (6) + L Fl 10s; 51°27'·62N 02°58'·68W.
E Mid Grounds ⌐ Fl R 5s; 51°27'·83N 02°54'·68W.
Clevedon ⚲ VQ; 51°27'·39N 02°54'·93W.
Welsh Hook ⚲ Q (6) + L Fl 15s; *Bell;* 51°28'·53N 02°51'·86W.
Avon ⚑ Fl G 2·5s; 51°27'·92N 02°51'·73W.
**Black Nore Point** ☆ 51°29'·09N 02°48'·05W Fl (2) 10s 11m **17M**; obsc by Sand Pt when brg less than 049°; vis: 044°-243°.
Newcome ⌐ 51°30'·01N 02°46'·71W Fl (3) R 10s.
Denny Shoal ⚲ VQ (6) + L Fl 10s; 51°30'·15N 02°45'·45W.
Firefly ⚑ Fl (2) G 5s; 51°29'·96N 02°45'·35W.
Outer ⚑ Fl G 5s; 51°29'·99N 02°44'·79W.
Middle ⚑ QG; 51°29'·93N 02°44'·22W.
Inner ⚑ Fl (3) G 15s; 51°29'·86N 02°43'·87W.
Cockburn ⌐ Fl R 2·5s; 51°30'·46N 02°44'·07W.
**Portishead Point** ☆ 51°29'·68N 02°46'·42W Q (3) 10s 9m **16M**; B twr, W base; vis: 060°-262°; *Horn 20s.*

### PORTISHEAD
Pier Hd ⚡ Iso G 2s 5m 3M; 51°29'·69N 02°45'·27W.
Seabank. Lts in line 086·8°. Front, IQ 13m 5M; vis: 070·3°-103·3°; by day 1M vis: 076·8°-096·8°; 51°30'·07N 02°43'·81W. Rear, 500m from front, IQ 16m 5M; vis: 070·3°-103·3°; by day 1M, vis: 076·8°-096·8°.

Royal Portbury Dock ☆ L Fl G 15s 5m 6M; 51°30'·15N 02°43'·75W.
Pier corner ☆ Fl G 2s 7m 7M; Gy pillar; 51°30'·12N 02°43'·84W.
Knuckle Lts in line 099·6°, Oc G 5s 6m 6M; 51°29'·94N 02°43'·67W.
Rear, 165m from front, FG 13m 6M; vis: 044°-134°.

## AVONMOUTH
Royal Edward Dock N Pier Hd ☆ Fl 4s 15m 10M; vis: 060°-228·5°;
51°30'·49N 02°43'·09W.
King Road Ldg Lts 072·4°. N Pier Hd ☆ Front, Oc R 5s 5m 9M; W
obelisk, R bands; vis: 062°-082°; 51°30'·49N 02°43'·09W. Rear ☆,
546m from front, QR 15m 10M; vis: 066°- 078°.

## RIVER AVON, CUMBERLAND BASIN and AVON BRIDGE
S Pier Hd ☆ Oc RG 30s 9m 10M; vis: 294°-R-036°-G-194°;
51°30'·37N 02°43'·10W.
Ldg Lts 127·2°. Front ⸛, Iso R 2s 6m 3M, vis: 010°-160°; 51°30'·10N
02°42'·59W. Rear ⸛, Iso R 2s10m 3M, vis: 048°-138°.
Monoliths ⸛ 51°30'·25N 02°42'·76W Fl R 5s 5m 3M; vis: 317°-137°.
Saint George Ldg Lts 173·3°, both Oc G 5s 7/13m 1M, vis: 158°-
305°; synchronised; 51°29'·76N 02°42'·67W.
Nelson Point ☆ Fl R 3s 9m 3M; 51°29'·86N 02°42'·50W.
Broad Pill ☆ QR 4m 1M; 51°29'·68N 02°41'·97W.
Avonmouth Bridge, NE end ☆L Fl R 10s 5m 3M, SW end L Fl G 10s
5m 3M, show up and downstream; 51°29'·39N 02°41'·55W. From
here to City Docks, G Lts are shown on S bank, and R Lts on N bank.
Cumberland Basin Ent N side ☆ 2FR(vert)6m 1M; S side W end
2 FG (vert) 7m 1M; 51°26'·98N 02°37'·44W.
Avon Bridge; N side ☆ FR 6m 1M on Bridge pier; 51°26'·83N
02°37'·43W. Centre of span ☆ Iso 5s 6m 1M; 51°26'·82N 02°37'·44W.
S side ☆ FG 6m 1M on Bridge pier; 51°26'·81N 02°37'·44W.

## SEVERN ESTUARY
### THE SHOOTS AND RIVER WYE
Redcliffe Ldg Lts 012·9° Front, F Bu 16m; vis: 358°-028°; 51°36'·20N
02°41'·37W. Rear, 320m from front, F Bu 33m 10M.
Lower Shoots ⸛ Q (9) 15s 6m 7M; 51°33'·85N 02°42'·05W.
North Mixoms ⸛ Fl (3) R 10s 6m 6M; 51°34'·04N 02°42'·61W.
Second Severn Crossing, Centre span ☆ Q Bu 5M; *Racon (O) (3cm)
range unknown*; 51°34'·45N 02°42'·03W.
Old Man's Hd ⸛ VQ (9) W 10s 6m 7M; 51°34'·74N 02°41'·69W.
Lady Bench (Lts in line 234°) ⸛ QR 6m 6M; 51°34'·85N 02°42'·20W.
Rear, Oc R 5s 38m 3M.
Charston Rock ☆ Fl 3s 5m 8M; 51°35'·35N 02°41'·68W.
Chapel Rock ☆ Fl WRG 2·6s 6m 8M, vis: W213°- G284°- W049°-
R051·5°-160°; 51°35'·44N 02°39'·21W.
Wye Bridge ☆ 51°37'·05N 02°39'·65W 2 F Bu (hor); centre span.

### SEVERN BRIDGE
Aust ☆ 2 QG (vert) 11m 6M; 51°36'·16N 02°38'·00W.
West Tower ☆ 3 QR (hor) on upstream/downstream sides; *Siren
(3) 30s*; obscured 040°-065°; 51°36'·73N 02°38'·80W.
Centre of span ☆ Q Bu, each side; 51°36'·59N 02°38'·43W.
East Tower ☆ 3 QG (hor) on up/downstream sides; 51°36'·46N
02°38'·07W.
Lyde Rock ☆ Q WR 5m 5M; vis: 148°-R-237°-W-336°-R-067°;
51°36'·89N 02°38'·67W.
Sedbury ☆ 2 FR (vert) 10m 3M; 51°37'·81N 02°39'·04W.
Slime Road Ldg Lts 210·4°. Front, F Bu 9m 5M; 51°37'·24N
02°39'·08W. Rear, 91 m from front, F Bu 16m 5M; B twr,
Inward Rocks Ldg Lts 252·5°. Front, F 6m 6M; B twr; 51°39'·26N
02°37'·47W. Rear, 183m from front, F 23m 2M.
COUNTS ⸗ Q; 51°39'·48N 02°35'·84W .
Sheperdine Ldg Lts 070·4°. Front, F 8m 5M 51°40'·06N 02°33'·31W.
Rear, 168m from front, F 13m 5M.
LEDGES ⸗ 51°39'·77N 02°34'·15W Fl (3) G 10s.
Narlwood Rocks Ldg Lts 224·9°. Front, Fl 2s 5m 8M; 51°39'·57N
02°34'·77W. Rear, 198m from front Fl 2s 9m 8M.
Hills Flats ▲ Fl G 4s; 51°40'·68N 02°32'·67W.

---

Hayward Rock ⸛ Q 6m 4M; 51°41'·24N 02°31'·18W.
Conigre Ldg Lts 077·5°. Front, F Bu 21m 8M; 51°41'·46N 02°30'·03W.
Rear, 213m from front, F Bu 29m 8M.
Fishing House Ldg Lts 217·7°. Front, F 5m 2M; 51°40'·98N
02°31'·00W. Rear, F 11m 2M.

## BERKELEY
Bull Rock ☆ Fl 3s 6m 8M; 51°41'·80N 02°29'·89W.
Berkeley Pill Ldg Lts 187·8°. Front, FG 5m 2M; 51°41'·99N
02°29'·41W. Rear, 152m from front, FG 11m 2M.
Panthurst Pill ☆ F Bu 6m 1M; Y pillar; 51°42'·59N 02°29'·02W.
Lydney Pier Hd ☆ 2 FR (vert) 6m; 51°42'·63N 02°30'·35W.

## SHARPNESS DOCKS
S Pier Hd ☆ 2 FG (vert) 6m 3M; *Siren 20s;* 51°42'·97N 02°29'·12W.
N Pier ☆ 2 FR (vert) 6m 3M; 51°43'·07N 02°29'·10W.
Old ent, S side; *Siren 5s* (tidal); 51°43'·52N 02°28'·93W.

## BRISTOL CHANNEL (SOUTH SHORE)
### WESTON-SUPER-MARE
Pier Hd ☆ 2 FG (vert) 6m; 51°20'·88N 02°59'·26W.
E Culver ⸛ Q (3) 10s; 51°18'·00N 03°15'·44W.
W Culver ⸛ VQ (9) 10s; 51°17'·37N 03°18'·68W.
Gore ⸑ Iso 5s; *Bell;* 51°13'·94N 03°09'·79W.

### BURNHAM-ON-SEA and RIVER PARRETT
Ent ☆ Fl 7·5s 7m 12M; vis: 074°-164°; 51°14'·89N 03°00'·36W.
Dir lt076°. FWRG 4m W12M, R10M, G10M; vis: 071°-G-075°-W-077°-R-081°.
Bridgewater Bar No. 1 ⸑ QR; 51°14'·53N 03°03'·75W.
Seafront Lts in line 112°, moved for changing chan, Front, FR 6m
3M W□, Or stripe on sea wall; 51°14'·39N 02°59'·95W. Rear, FR
12m 3M; on church twr.
Stert Reach ☆ Fl 3s 4m 7M; vis: 187°-217°; 51°13'·53N 03°00'·29W.
Brue Bn ☆ Fl R 3s 4m 3M; 51°13'·53N 03°00'·29W.
DZ No. 1 ⸑ Fl Y 2·5s; 51°15'·28N 03°09'·49W.
Hinkley Point ☆ 2 FG (vert) 7m 3M; 51°12'·93N 03°08'·05W.
DZ No. 2 ⸑ Fl Y 10s; 51°13'·77N 03°17'·19W.
DZ No. 3 ⸑ Fl Y 5s; 51°15'·52N 03°14'·98W.

### WATCHET, MINEHEAD and PORLOCK WEIR
Watchet W Bkwtr Hd ☆ Oc G 3s 9m 9M; 51°11'·03N 03°19'·74W.
Watchet E Pier ☆ 2 FR (vert) 3M; 51°11'·01N 03°19'·72W.
Minehead Bkwtr Hd ☆Fl(2) G 5s 4M; vis: 127°-262°; 51°12'·81N 03°28'·36W.
Sewer Outfall ⸛ 51°12'·97N 03°28'·31W QG 6m 7M.
**Lynmouth Foreland** ☆ 51°14'·73N 03°47'·21W Fl (4) 15s 67m **18M**;
W ○ twr; vis: 083°-275°; (H24).

### LYNMOUTH and WATERMOUTH
River Training Arm ☆ 2 FR (vert) 6m 5M; 51°13'·90N 03°49'·83W.
Harbour Arm ☆ 2 FG (vert) 6m 5M; 51°13'·92N 03°49'·84W.
Sand Ridge ⸑ Q G; 51°15'·01N 03°49'·77W.
Copperas Rock ▲ 51°13'·78N 04°00'·60W.
Watermouth ☆ Oc WRG 5s 1m 3M; W△; vis: 149·5°-G-151·5°-W-
154·5°-R-156·5°; 51°12'·93N 04°04'·60W.

### ILFRACOMBE
Lantern Hill ☆ Fl G 2·5s 39m 6M; 51°12'·66N 04°06'·78W.
Promenade Pier N end ☆ 2 FG (vert); 51°12'·69N 04°06'·68W.
Ldg Lts 188°. Front, Oc 10s 8m 3M; 51°12'·53N 04°06'·65W. Rear,
Oc 10s 6m 3M.

Horseshoe ⸛ Q; 51°15'·02N 04°12'·96W.
**Bull Point** ☆ 51°11'·94N 04°12'·09W Fl (3) 10s 54m **20M**; W ○ twr,
obscd shore-056°. Same twr; FR 48m 12M; vis: 058°-096°.
Morte Stone ▲ 51°11'·30N 04°14'·95W.
Baggy Leap ▲ 51°08'·92N 04°16'·97W.

### BIDEFORD, RIVERS TAW and TORRIDGE
Bideford Fairway ⸛ L Fl 10s; *Bell;* 51°05'·25N 04°16'·25W.
Bideford Bar ⸛ Q G; 51°04'·89N 04°14'·62W.
Middle Ridge ⸛ Fl G 5s; 51°04'·65N 04°13'·80W (subject to
change).

Outer Pulley ⚓ Fl G 2.5s; 51°04'·34N 04°12'·90W.
Pulley ⚓ Fl G 10s; 51°04'·08N 04°12'·70W.

**Instow** ☆ Ldg Lts 118°. **Front**, 51°03'·62N 04°10'·66W Oc 6s 22m **15M**; vis: 103·5°-132°. **Rear**, 427m from front, Oc 10s 38m **15M**; vis: 103°-132·5°; (H24).

Crow Pt ⚓ Fl WR 2. 5s 8m W6M R5M; vis: 225°-R-232°-W-237°-R-358°-W-015°-R-045°; 51°03'·96N 04°11'·39W.

Clovelly Hbr Quay Hd ⚓ 50°59'·92N 04°23'·83W Fl G 5s 5m 5M.

## LUNDY

**Near North Point** ☆ 51°12'·10N 04°40'·65W Fl 15s 48m **17M**; vis: 009°-285°.

**South East Point** ☆ 51°09'·72N 04°39'·37W Fl 5s 53m **15M**; vis: 170°-073°; *Horn 25s.*

Jetty Head ⚓ Fl R 3s 8m 3M; 51°09'·80N 04°39'·20W.

**Hartland Point** ☆ 51°01'·29N 04°31'·59W Fl (6) 15s 37m **25M**; (H24); *Horn 60s.*

## NORTH CORNWALL

### BUDE

Compass Point twr 50°49'·71N 04°33'·42W.

### PADSTOW

Stepper Point ⚓ L Fl 10s 12m 4M; 50°34'·12N 04°56'·72W.
Greenaway ⚓ Fl (2) R 10s; 50°33'·78N 04°56'·06W.

Bar ⚓ Fl G 5s; 50°33'·46N 04°56'·12W.
St Saviour's Pt ⚓ L Fl G 10s 1m; 50°32'·76N 04°56'·06W.
N Quay Hd ⚓ 2 FG (vert) 6m 2M; 50°32'·50N 04°56'·16W.

**Trevose Head** ☆ 50°32'·94N 05°02'·13W Fl 7·5s 62m **21M**; *Horn (2) 30s.*

## NEWQUAY

North Pier Hd ⚓ 2 FG (vert) 5m 2M; 50°25'·07N 05°05'·19W.
South Pier Hd ⚓ 2 FR (vert) 4m 2M; 50°25'·05N 05°05'·20W.

## HAYLE and ST IVES

The Stones ⚓ Q; 50°15'·64N 05°25'·51W.
Godrevy I ⚓ Fl WR 10s 37m W12M, R9M; vis: 022°-W-101°-R-145°-W-272°; 50°14'·54N 05°24'·04W.

Hayle App ⚓ QR; 50°12'·26N 05°26'·30W.
Lts in line 180°. Front, F 17m 4M; 50°11'·50N 05°26'·18W. Rear, 110m from front, F 23m 4M.

St Ives App ⚓ 50°12'·85N 05°28'·42W
East Pier Hd ⚓ 2 FG (vert) 8m 5M; 50°12'·80N 05°28'·61W.
West Pier Hd ⚓ 2 FR (vert) 5m 3M; 50°12'·77N 05°28'·73W.

**Pendeen** ☆ 50°09'·90N 05°40'·32W Fl (4) 15s 59m **16M**; vis: 042°-240°; in bay between Gurnard Hd and Pendeen it shows to coast; *Horn 20s.*

## 3.4 PASSAGE INFORMATION

For directions on this coast refer to the Admiralty *W Coasts of England and Wales Pilot*; *Lundy and Irish Sea Pilot* (Imray/Taylor). The area is well covered by Admiralty Leisure Folios. For additional tidal information for east of Ilfracombe/Swansea, *Arrowsmith's Bristol Channel Tide Tables,* from J.W. Arrowsmith Ltd ☎ (0117) 9667545.

It is useful to know some Welsh words with navigational significance. *Aber:* estuary. *Afon:* river. *Bach, bychan, fach:* little. *Borth:* cove. *Bryn:* hill. *Careg, craig:* rock. *Coch, goch:* red. *Dinas:* fort. *Ddu:* black. *Fawr, Mawr:* big. *Ffrydiau:* tiderip. *Llwyd:* grey. *Moel:* bare conical hill. *Mor:* sea. *Morfa:* sandy shore. *Mynydd:* mountain. *Penrhyn:* headland. *Porth:* cove. *Ynys, Ynysoedd:* island(s).

## CARDIGAN BAY

(AC 1971, 1972, 1973) Hbrs are mostly on a lee shore, and/or have bars which make them dangerous to approach in bad weather. Abersoch and Pwllheli offer best shelter from prevailing W'lies. There may be overfalls off Trwyn Cilan, SW of St Tudwal's Is (lit). In N part of bay there are three major dangers to coasting yachts, as described briefly below: St Patrick's Causeway (Sarn Badrig) runs 12M SW from Mochras Pt. It is mostly large loose stones, and dries (up to 1·5m) for much of its length. In strong winds the sea breaks heavily at all states of tide. The outer end is marked by a WCM lt buoy. At the inner end there is a chan about 5ca offshore, which can be taken with care at half tide.

Sarn-y-Bwch runs 4M WSW from Pen Bwch Pt. It is consists of rky boulders, drying in places close inshore and with least depth 0·3m over 1M offshore. There is a WCM buoy off W end. NW of Aberystwyth, Sarn Cynfelyn and Cynfelyn Patches extend a total of 6·5M offshore, with depths of 1·5m in places. A WCM buoy is at the outer end. Almost halfway along the bank is Main Chan, 3ca wide, running roughly N/S, but not marked.

Aberporth Range occupies much of Cardigan B. Beware targets and buoys, some unlit. Range activity is broadcast on VHF Ch 16, 0800-1600LT Mon-Fri or ☎ (01239) 813462.

If on passage N/S through St George's Chan (ie not bound for Cardigan B or Milford Haven) the easiest route, and always by night, is W of the Bishops and the Smalls, noting the TSS. If bound to/from Milford Haven or Cardigan Bay, passage inside both the Smalls and Grassholm is possible.

## RAMSEY SOUND, THE BISHOPS, THE SMALLS TO MILFORD HAVEN

(AC 1478, 1482) The Bishops and the Clerks are islets and rks 2·5M W and NW of Ramsey Is, a bird sanctuary SSW of St David's Hd. N Bishop is the N'ly of the group, 3ca ENE of which is Bell Rk (depth 1·9m). S Bishop (Lt, fog sig) is 3M to the SSW.

Between S Bishop and Ramsey Is the dangers include Daufraich with offliers to the E and heavy o'falls; Llech Isaf and Llech Uchaf drying rks are further ENE. Carreg Rhoson and offliers are between Daufraich and N Bishop. The navigable routes between most of these islets and rks trend NE/SW, use only by day, in good visibility and with local knowledge. The N/S route close W of Ramsey I is considered easier than Ramsey Snd.

▶ 2M W of The Bishops the S-going stream begins at HW Milford Haven +4, and the N-going at HW –2½, sp rates 2kn. Between The Bishops and Ramsey Is the SW-going stream begins at HW Milford Haven +3½, and the NE-going at HW –3, **sp rates 5kn**. Ramsey Sound should be taken at slack water. The S-going stream begins at HW Milford Haven +3, and the N-going at HW –3½,

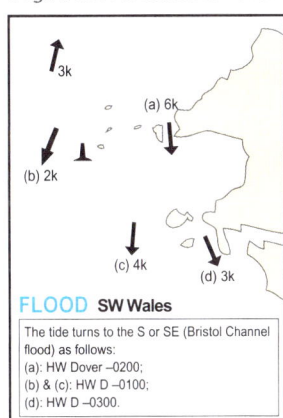

**FLOOD** SW Wales

The tide turns to the S or SE (Bristol Channel flood) as follows:
(a): HW Dover –0200;
(b) & (c): HW D –0100;
(d): HW D –0300.

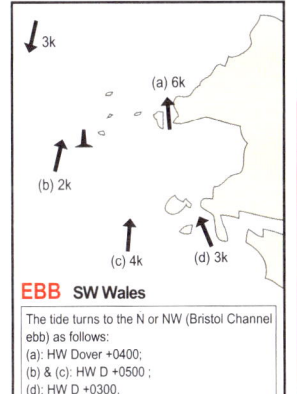

**EBB** SW Wales

The tide turns to the N or NW (Bristol Channel ebb) as follows:
(a): HW Dover +0400;
(b) & (c): HW D +0500 ;
(d): HW D +0300.

*sp rates 6kn at The Bitches, where chan is narrowest (2ca), decreasing N and S.* ◄

The Bitches are rks up to 4m high and extending 2ca from E side of Ramsey Is. Other dangers are: Gwahan and Carreg-gafeiliog, both 3m high at N end of Sound, to W and E; Horse Rk (dries 0·9m) almost in mid-chan about 5ca NNE of The Bitches, with associated overfalls; Shoe Rk (dries 3m) at SE end of chan; and rks extending 5ca SSE from S end of Ramsey Is.

St Brides Bay provides anch in settled weather/offshore winds. It is also a regular anchorage for tankers, but is a trap in westerlies. Solva is a little hbr with shelter for boats able to take the ground, or anch behind Black Rk (dries 3·6m) in the middle of the entrance.

The Smalls Lt, where there is a Historic Wreck (see 0.29) is 13M W of the Welsh mainland (Wooltack Pt). 2M and 4M E of The Smalls are the Hats and Barrels, rky patches on which the sea breaks. ► *7M E of The Smalls is Grassholm Island with a race either end and strong tidal eddies so that it is advisable to pass about 1M off. The chan between Barrels and Grassholm is 2·5M wide, and here the S-going stream begins at HW Milford Haven + 0440, and the N-going at HW Milford Haven – 0135, sp rates 5kn.* ◄ *5M of clear water lie between Grassholm and Skomer Is/Skokholm Is to the E. But Wildgoose Race, which forms W of Skomer and Skokholm is very dangerous, so keep 2M W of these two Islands.*

To E of Skomer is Midland Is, and between here and Wooltack Pt is Jack Sound, least width about 1ca. Do not attempt it without AC 1482, detailed pilotage directions, and only at slack water nps. ► *Correct timing is important. The S-going stream begins at HW Milford Haven +2, and the N-going at HW –4½, sp rates 6-7kn.* ◄ Rocks which must be identified include, from N to S: On E side of chan off Wooltack Pt, Tusker Rk (2m), steep-to on its W side; and off Anvil Pt, The Cable (2·4m), The Anvil and Limpet Rks (3·7m). On the W side lie the Crabstones (3·7m) and the Blackstones (1·5m).

## MILFORD HAVEN TO MUMBLES HEAD

(AC 1179, 1076) Milford Haven is a long natural, all-weather hbr with marinas beyond the oil terminals. Beware Turbot Bank (WCM lt buoy) 3M S of the ent. Crow Rk (dries 5·5m) is 5ca SSE of Linney Hd, and The Toes are dangerous submerged rks close W and SE of Crow Rk. There is a passage inshore of these dangers. There are overfalls on St Gowan Shoals which extend 4M SW of St Govan's Hd, and the sea breaks on the shallow patches in bad weather. There are firing areas from Linney Hd to Carmarthen Bay.

Caldey Is (Lt) lies S of Tenby. Off its NW pt is St Margaret's Is connected by a rky reef. Caldey Sound, between St Margaret's Is and Giltar Pt (AC 1482), is buoyed, but beware Eel Spit near W end of Caldey Is where there can be a nasty sea with wind against tide, and Woolhouse Rks (dry 3·6m) 1ca NE of Caldey Is. Saundersfoot hbr (dries) is 2M N of Tenby, with anch well sheltered from N and W but subject to swell. Streams are weak here. Carmarthen Bay has no offshore dangers for yachts, other than the extensive drying sands at head of B and on its E side off Burry Inlet.

S of Worms Hd, Helwick Sands (buoyed at each end) extend 7M W from Port Eynon Pt; least depth of 1·3m is near their W end. Stream sets NE/SW across the sands. There is a narrow chan inshore, close to Port Eynon Pt.

► *Between here and Mumbles Hd the stream runs roughly along coast, sp rates 3kn off Pts, but there are eddies in Port Eynon B and Oxwich B (both yacht anchs), & overfalls SSE of Oxwich Pt.* ◄

## MUMBLES HEAD TO CARDIFF

(AC 1165, 1182) Off Mumbles Hd (Lt, fog sig) beware Mixon Shoal (dries 0·3m), marked by PHM buoy. In good conditions pass N of shoal, 1ca off Mumbles Hd. Anch N of Mumbles Hd, good holding but exposed to swell. At W side of Swansea Bay, Green Grounds, rky shoals, lie in appr's to Swansea.

Scarweather Sands, much of which dry (up to 3·3m) with seas breaking heavily, extend 7M W from Porthcawl (4.15) and are well buoyed (AC 1161). There is a chan between the sands and coast to E, but beware Hugo Bank (dries 2·6m) and Kenfig Patches (0·5m) with o'falls up to 7ca offshore between Sker Pt and Porthcawl.

Nash Sands extend 7·5M WNW from Nash Pt. Depths vary and are least at inshore end (dries 3m), but Nash Passage, 1ca wide, runs close inshore between E Nash ECM buoy and ledge off Nash Pt. ► *On E-going stream there are heavy overfalls off Nash Pt and at W end of Nash Sands. Between Nash Pt and Breaksea Pt the E-going stream begins at HW Avonmouth + 0535, and the W-going at HW Avonmouth –0035, sp rates 3kn. Off Breaksea Pt there may be overfalls.* ◄

From Rhoose Pt to Lavernock Pt the coast is fringed with foul ground. Lavernock Spit extends 1·75M S of Lavernock Pt, and E of the spit is main chan to Cardiff; the other side of the chan being Cardiff Grounds, a bank drying 5·4m which lies parallel with the shore and about 1·5M from it.

## SEVERN ESTUARY

(AC 1176, 1166) Near the centre of Bristol Chan, either side of the buoyed fairway, are the islands of Flat Holm (Lt, fog sig) and Steep Holm. 7M SW of Flat Holm lies Culver Sand (0·9m), 3M in length, with W and ECM bys. Monkstone Rk (Lt, dries) is 2M NW of the buoyed chan to Avonmouth and Bristol. Extensive drying banks cover the N shore of the estuary, beyond Newport and the Severn bridges (AC 1176).

► *The range of tide in the Bristol Chan is exceptionally large, 12·2m sp and 6·0m np, and tidal streams are very powerful, particularly above Avonmouth. Between Flat Holm and Steep Holm the E-going stream begins at HW Avonmouth – 0610, sp 3kn, and the W-going at HW Avonmouth + 0015, sp 4kn.* ◄

The ent to the R. Avon is just to the S of Avonmouth S Pier Hd. Bristol City Docks lie some 6M up river. Approach the ent via King Road and the Newcombe and Cockburn lt buoys and thence via the Swash chan into the Avon. The ent dries at LW but the river is navigable at about half tide. ► *Tidal streams are strong in the approaches to Avonmouth, up to 5kn at sp. The tide is also strong in the R. Avon which is best entered no earlier than HW Avonmouth – 0200.* ◄

From Avonmouth it is 16M to Sharpness which yachts should aim to reach at about HW Avonmouth. ► *Spring streams can run 8kn at the Shoots, and 6kn at the Severn bridges.* At the Shoots the flood begins at HW Avonmouth –0430 and the ebb at HW Avonmouth + 0045. The Severn Bore can usually be seen if Avonmouth range is 13·5m or more. ◄

## AVONMOUTH TO HARTLAND POINT

(AC 1152, 1165) From Avonmouth to Sand Pt, the part-drying English Grounds extend 3M off the S shore. Portishead Quays Marina offers good shelter. Extensive mud flats fill the bays S to Burnham-on-Sea. Westward, the S shore of Bristol Chan is cleaner than N shore. But there is less shelter since the approaches to hbrs such as Watchet, Minehead, Porlock Weir and Watermouth dry out.

► *In bad weather dangerous overfalls occur NW and NE of Foreland Pt. 5M to W there is a race off Highveer Pt. Between Ilfracombe and Bull Pt the E-going stream begins at HW Milford Haven + 0540, and the W-going at HW Milford Haven – 0025, sp rates 3kn. Overfalls occur up to 1·5M N of Bull Pt and over Horseshoe Rks, which lie 3M N. There is a dangerous race off Morte Pt, 1·5M to W of Bull Pt.* ◄

Shelter is available under the lee of Lundy Is; but avoid bad races to NE (White Horses), NW (Hen and Chickens), and SE; also overfalls over NW Bank. ► *W of Lundy streams are moderate, but strong around the Is and much stronger towards Bristol Chan proper.* ◄

Proceeding WSW from Rivers Taw/Torridge, keep 3M off to avoid the race N of Hartland Pt (Lt, fog sig, conspic radome). There is shelter off Clovelly in S/SW winds.

## HARTLAND POINT TO LAND'S END

(AC 1156, 1149) The N coast of Cornwall and SW approaches to Bristol Chan are very exposed. Yachts need to be sturdy and well equipped since, if bad weather develops, no shelter may be at hand. Bude dries, and is not approachable in W winds; only accessible in calm weather or offshore winds. Boscastle is a tiny hbr (dries) 3M NE of Tintagel Hd. Only approach in good weather or offshore winds; anch off or dry out alongside.

Padstow can be a refuge, but in strong NW winds the sea breaks on bar and prevents entry. Off Trevose Hd beware Quies Rks which extend 1M to W. From here S the coast is relatively clear to Godrevy Is, apart from Bawden Rks 1M N of St Agnes Hd.

Newquay B is good anch in offshore winds, and the hbr (dries) is sheltered but uncomfortable in N winds. Off Godrevy Is are The Stones, drying rky shoals extending 1·5M offshore, marked by NCM lt buoy.

In St Ives Bay (AC 1168), Hayle is a commercial port (dries); seas break heavily on bar at times, especially with a ground swell. ▶ *Stream is strong, so enter just before HW.* ◄ The bottom is mostly sand. St Ives (dries) gives shelter from winds E to SW, but is very exposed to N; there is sometimes a heavy breaking sea if there is ground swell.

From St Ives to Land's End coast is rugged and exposed. There are o'falls SW of Pendeen Pt . Vyneck Rks lie awash about 3ca NW of C Cornwall. The Brisons are two high rky islets 5ca SW of C Cornwall, with rky ledges inshore and to the S. The Longships group of rks is about 1M W of Land's End. The inshore passage (001° on Brisons) is about 4ca wide with unmarked drying rks on the W side; only to be considered in calm weather and beware of fishing gear marker buoys.

## 4.5 ABERSOCH

Gwynedd **52°49'·29N 04°29'·20W** (⚓) ✻✻🏠🏠🌸🌸

**CHARTS** AC *5609, 1410, 1411, 1971, 1512*; Imray C61, C52; Stanfords 27; OS 123

**TIDES** –0315 Dover; ML 2·5; Duration 0520; Zone 0 (UT)

**Standard Port MILFORD HAVEN** (→)

| Times | | | | Height (metres) | | | |
|---|---|---|---|---|---|---|---|
| High Water | | Low Water | | MHWS | MHWN | MLWN | MLWS |
| 0100 | 0800 | 0100 | 0700 | 7·0 | 5·2 | 2·5 | 0·7 |
| 1300 | 2000 | 1300 | 1900 | | | | |
| **Differences ST TUDWAL'S ROADS** | | | | | | | |
| +0155 | +0145 | +0240 | +0310 | –2·2 | –1·9 | –0·7 | –0·2 |
| **ABERDARON** | | | | | | | |
| +0210 | +0200 | +0240 | +0310 | –2·4 | –1·9 | –0·6 | –0·2 |

**SHELTER** There are few moorings for visitors. Apply to HM or SC. ⚓ in St Tudwal's Roads clear of moored yachts; sheltered from SSE through S to NE.

**NAVIGATION** WPT 52°48'·52N 04°26'·13W, 293°/2·4M to YC jetty. There are no navigational dangers, but steer well clear of the drying rks to the E of East Island; Carred y Trai buoy FlR 2·5s is 2ca E of these rks (just off chartlet). St Tudwal's islands themselves are fairly steep-to, except at N ends. St Tudwal's Sound is clear of dangers.

**LIGHTS AND MARKS** The only lt is on St Tudwal's West Island, Fl WR 15s 46m 14/10M (see chartlet and 4.3).

**R/T** S Caernarfon YC Ch **80** M.

**TELEPHONE** (Code 01758) HM 712203; MRCC (01407) 762051; Marinecall 09068 969650; Police (01286) 673333; Dr 612535.

**FACILITIES** **South Caernarvonshire YC** ☎ 712338, Slip, M, L, FW, R, Bar (May-Sept), D, **Abersoch Power Boat Club** ☎ 812027. **Services** BY, Slip, ME, El, ✕, ACA, CH, P, C (12 ton), LPG. **Town** CH, 🛒, R, Bar, ✉, Ⓑ, ➥ (Pwllheli), ✈ (Chester).

## ADJACENT ANCHORAGES

**BARDSEY ISLAND – YNYS ENNLI**, Gwynedd, **52°45'·00N 04°47'·40W**. AC *5609, 1410, 1411, 1971*. HW –0240 on Dover, see 3.19. Lights and Marks see 4.3. ⚓ in settled conditions only, is useful on passage N when awaiting tide through Bardsey Sound, see 3.4. ⚓ to W of Pen Cristin in approach to Henllwyn Cove in 4m. Sheltered in winds from WSW through N to NE but may be subject to swell at times. Possible with caution for smaller craft to anchor in the cove but beware of isolated rocks and shoals. Landing at jetty in rocks at cove marked by small boathouse at top of slip. Island is of historical interest with ruined abbey and religious settlement since 6th century. Now run as managed farm and nature reserve, see 0.31 Environmental Guidance.

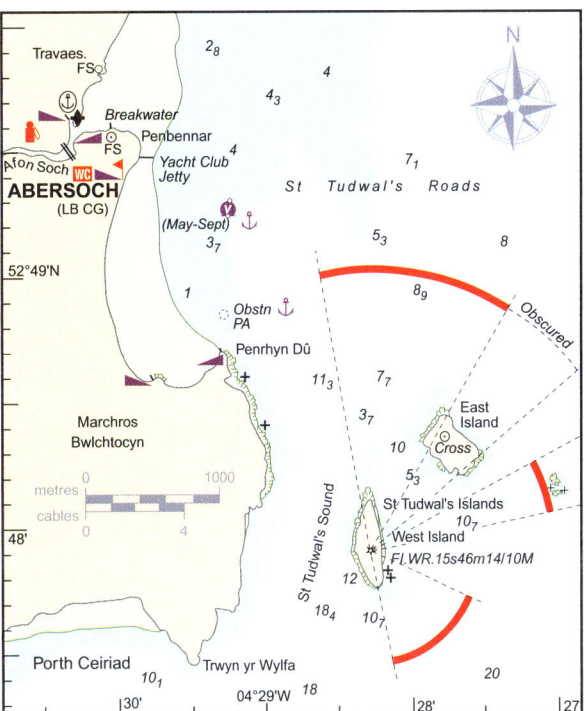

**ABERDARON BAY**, Gwynedd, **52°47'·75N 04°42'·82W**. AC *5609, 1410, 1411, 1971, 5609*. HW –0240 on Dover, see 3.19 Bardsey Is. In settled conditions only, is useful on passage N when awaiting tide through Bardsey Sound, see 3.4. In SE appr to bay are 2 islets Ynys Gwylan-fawr and Ynys Gwylan-bâch with a deep water passage between them, also passage between Ynys Gwylan-fawr and Trwyn Gwningaer(shore). ⚓ 4ca SSW of church in 5-10m, limited protection and subject to swell at times but sheltered in winds from W through N to NE. Do not leave craft unattended due to poor holding ground. Dinghy landing with care on shingle beach at Porth Meudwy, W side of bay. **Village** limited facilities: FW, R, Bar, ✉, ➥ (Pwllheli).

**LLANBEDROG**, Gwynedd, **52°51'·14N 04°28'·09W**. AC *5609, 1410, 1411, 1971, 1512*. HW –0245 on Dover, see 4.5 (St Tudwal's Roads). Good ⚓ N of Trwyn Llanbedrog (steep sided headland 131m) 1.0ca ENE of Bcn PHM in 2-3m. Beach has numerous conspicuous bathing huts. Sheltered in winds from N through W to SW. ⚓ well clear of local craft moorings as they have a long scope. Dinghy landing near boathouse. **Village** limited facilities: P & D (cans ½M), FW , R, Bar, ➥ (Pwllheli).

## 4.6 PWLLHELI

Gwynedd **52°53′·23N 04°23′·75W** ✿✿✿✿✿✿✿✿

**CHARTS** AC *1410*, 1971, 1512; Imray C61, C52; OS 123; Stanfords 27

**TIDES** –0315 Dover; ML 2·6; Duration 0510

**Standard Port MILFORD HAVEN (→)**

| Times | | | | Height (metres) | | | |
|---|---|---|---|---|---|---|---|
| High Water | | Low Water | | MHWS | MHWN | MLWN | MLWS |
| 0100 | 0800 | 0100 | 0700 | 7·0 | 5·2 | 2·5 | 0·7 |
| 1300 | 2000 | 1300 | 1900 | | | | |
| Differences PWLLHELI | | | | | | | |
| +0210 | +0150 | +0245 | +0320 | –2·0 | –1·8 | –0·6 | –0·2 |
| CRICCIETH | | | | | | | |
| +0210 | +0155 | +0255 | +0320 | –2·0 | –1·8 | –0·7 | –0·3 |

**SHELTER** Good in hbr and marina. Drying moorings in inner hbr (SW and NW bights).

**NAVIGATION** WPT 52°53′·02N 04°23′·07W, SWM lt buoy 299°/0·47M to QG lt at head of Training Arm.

- Ent is safe in most winds, but in strong E to SW winds sea breaks on offshore shoals.
- Ent subject to silting and bar and hbr chan are dredged but only to 0·6m below CD; 3 tide gauges. Max tidal stream 2kn.
- No ⚓ in hbr; 4kn speed limit.

**LIGHTS AND MARKS** See 4.3 and chartlet. Gimblet Rock (30m) is conspic conical rock 3ca SW of ent.

**R/T** Marina: Ch **80** M H24. HM: VHF Ch **12** 16 (0900-1715).

**TELEPHONE** (Code 01758) HM 704081, mob 07879 433145; MRCC (01407) 762051; Ⓗ Bangor (A&E) 01248 384384; Marinecall 09068 969650; Police (01286) 673333; Dr 701457.

**FACILITIES** **Marina** ☎ 701219, 🖷 701443, www.yachthavens.com 400 AB, £2.12, £9.40 <4hrs. Pontoon numbers are 4–12 from S–N. Pile berths on S side of appr chan. Wi-fi, P&D, LPG, BH (40 ton), C, Slip, 🗑, ♿, ⚓; **Boat Club** ☎ 612271, Slip, FW. **Pwllheli SC** pwllhelisailingclub@btinternet.com ☎ 614442, 🖷 612134.
**Services:** BY, ME, Gas, Gaz, ✗, CH, ACA, C (14 ton), El, Ⓔ, SM. **Town** 🛒, R, Bar, ✉, Ⓑ, ⇌, ✈ (Chester).

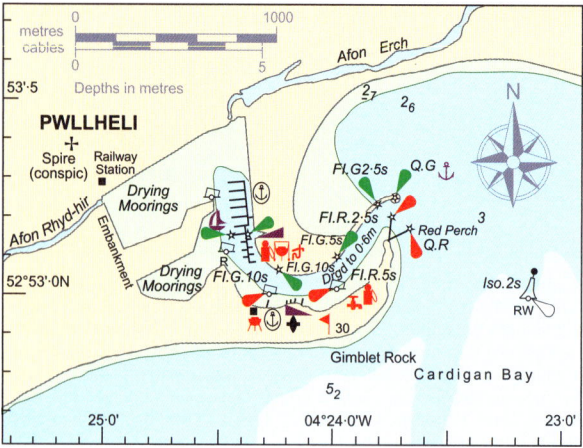

### ADJACENT HARBOUR

**MOCHRAS,** Gwynedd, **52°49′·57N 04°07′·77W.** AC 1971, 1512. HW –0245 on Dover. Small yacht hbr in drying Mochras lagoon on SE side of Shell Is. Bar, about 2ca seaward. Appr advised HW±2. 3 grey posts, R topmarks, mark NE side of chan. Ebb tide runs strongly in the narrow ent between the sea wall and Shell Is (lt Fl WRG 4s, 079°-G-124°-W-134°-R-179°; Mar-Nov); at sp beware severe eddies inside. Inside ent, buoyed chan runs WSW to Shell Island Yacht Hbr ☎ 01341 241453. Facilities: M, FW, Slip, R, Bar, shwrs. Shifting chan, marked by posts and buoys, runs NE to Pensarn, where permanent moorings limit space. Drying AB, ⇌.

## 4.7 PORTHMADOG

Gwynedd **52°55′·32N 04°07′·77W** ✿✿✿✿✿✿

**CHARTS** AC *1410*, 1971, 1512,; Imray C61, C51; Stanfords 27; OS 124

**TIDES** –0247 Dover; ML no data; Duration 0455

**Standard Port MILFORD HAVEN (→)**

| Times | | | | Height (metres) | | | |
|---|---|---|---|---|---|---|---|
| High Water | | Low Water | | MHWS | MHWN | MLWN | MLWS |
| 0100 | 0800 | 0100 | 0700 | 7·0 | 5·2 | 2·5 | 0·7 |
| 1300 | 2000 | 1300 | 1900 | | | | |
| Differences PORTHMADOG | | | | | | | |
| +0235 | +0210 | No data | | –1·9 | –1·8 | No data | |

**SHELTER** Inner hbr (N of Cei Ballast): Good all year round; visitors' drying AB adjacent Madoc YC or afloat rafted on moored yachts off YC. Outer hbr: Summer only, exposed to S winds. Speed limit 6kn in hbr upstream of No 8 buoy.

**NAVIGATION** WPT Fairway SWM buoy, 52°52′·97N 04°11′·09W, 041°/1·9M to conspic white Ho at W side of ent.

- Chan shifts and may divide. Bar changes frequently, but is near to No 3 and 4 buoys; dries approx 0·3m.
- In SW'lies, waves are steep-sided and close, especially on the ebb.
- Latest info from HM on request. Advise entering HW±1½.

**LIGHTS AND MARKS** Fairway buoy RW, L Fl 10s. Chan marker buoys (14) Nos 1–9 lit (May-Oct), have R/G reflective top marks and W reflective numbers. Moel-y-Gest is conspic hill (259m) approx 1M WNW of hbr. Harlech Castle (ru) is about 3M SE of appr chan.

**R/T** HM Ch 12 16 (HO and when vessel due). Madoc YC Ch M.

**TELEPHONE** (Code 01766) HM 512927, mobile (07879) 433147; MRCC (01407) 762051; Pilot 530684; Hbr Authority Gwynedd Council (01758) 704066; Marinecall 09068 969650; Police (01286) 673333; Dr 512284.

**FACILITIES** **Hbr** (265 berths) ☎ 512927, £7.00 all craft; D, FW, C, Slip access HW±4 (launching £10); **Madoc YC** ☎ 512976, AB, M, FW, Bar; **Porthmadog SC** ☎ 513546, AB, M, FW, Slip; **Services:** CH, ACA, ✗, D(quay), D & P (cans), C (8 ton), M, BY, El, Pilot. **Town** ✉, Ⓑ, ⇌, ✈ (Chester).

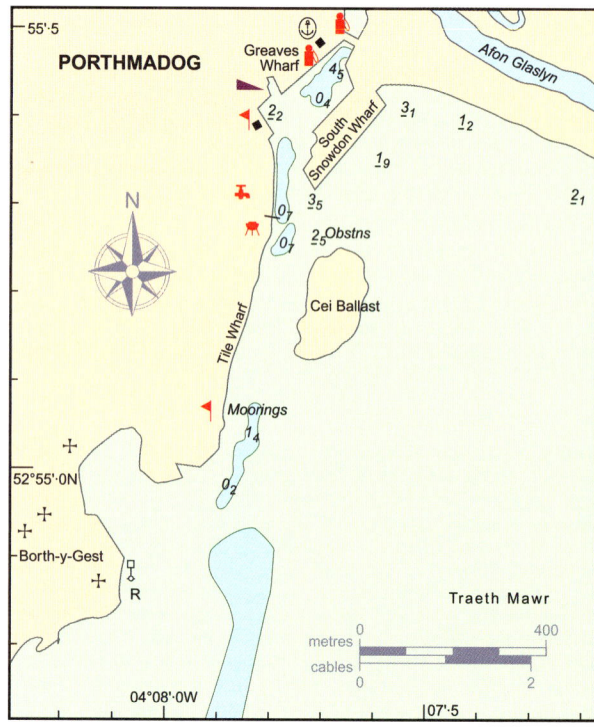

## 4.8 BARMOUTH

Gwynedd **52°42'·97N 04°03'·07W** ✿✿◌◌✿✿✿

**CHARTS** AC *5609, 1410,* 1971, 1484; Imray C61, C51; Stanfords 27; OS 124

**TIDES** –0305 Dover; ML 2·6; Duration 0515

**Standard Port MILFORD HAVEN (⟶)**

| Times | | | | Height (metres) | | | |
|---|---|---|---|---|---|---|---|
| High Water | | Low Water | | MHWS | MHWN | MLWN | MLWS |
| 0100 | 0800 | 0100 | 0700 | 7·0 | 5·2 | 2·5 | 0·7 |
| 1300 | 2000 | 1300 | 1900 | | | | |
| **Differences BARMOUTH** | | | | | | | |
| +0215 | +0205 | +0310 | +0320 | –2·0 | –1·7 | –0·7 | 0·0 |

**SHELTER** Good. Entry HW±2½ safe, but impossible with strong SW'lies. Exposed ⚓ W of Barmouth Outer buoy in 6 to 10m. Serious silting reported. In hbr there are 5 Ⓜs; secure as directed by HM, because of submarine cables and strong tidal streams. A Ⓥ berth is marked at W end of quay, dries at half-tide. Drying ⚓ inside Penrhyn Pt.

**NAVIGATION** WPT, Barmouth Outer SWM buoy, 52°42´·72N 04°05´·02W, 082°/0·8M to Y perch lt, QR. Appr from SW between St Patrick's Causeway (Sarn Badrig) and Sarn-y-Bwch (see 4.4). Barmouth can be identified by Cader Idris, a mountain 890m high, 5M ESE. Fegla Fawr, a rounded hill, lies on S side of hbr.

- The Bar, 0·75M W of Penrhyn Pt, with min depth 0·3m is subject to constant change. Chan is marked by buoys, all unlit, fitted with radar reflectors and reflective tape and moved as required.
- Spring ebb runs 3 – 5kn.
- The estuary and river (Afon Mawddach) are tidal and can be navigated for about 7M above rly br (clearance approx 5·5m); but chan is not buoyed, and sandbanks move constantly – local knowledge essential.

**LIGHTS AND MARKS** Outer SWM L Fl 10s. SHM Q Fl G. Bar No2 PHM Fl R. Inner buoy. Y perch QR 4m 5M on R framework tr, marks S end of stony ledge extending 3ca SW from Ynys y Brawd across N Bank. Ynys y Brawd groyne, SE end, marked by lit bn, Fl R 5s 5M. NW end of rly bridge 2 FR (hor).

**R/T** Call *Barmouth Hbr* VHF Ch **12** 16 (Apr-Sep 0900-1700 later for HW; Oct-Mar 0900-1600); wind and sea state are available.

**TELEPHONE** (Code 01341) HM 280671 mob 07795 012747; MRCC (01407) 762051; Marinecall 09068 969650; Police (01286) 673333; Dr 280521. Local information www.barmouthwebcam.co.uk

**FACILITIES** Quay £10.50/9m yacht, M (incl 3 drying Ⓜ) contact HM in advance if deep water Ⓜ required, D, FW, El, ⓓ, 2 Slips(HW±3, launching £8.50); Merioneth YC ☎ 280000; Services: CH, ACA. **Town** P, D, 🛒, R, Bar, ✉, @, Ⓑ, ⇌, ✈ (Chester), ferry to Penrhyn Pt. **Fairbourne** ✉, 🛒, ⇌, ferry to Barmouth.

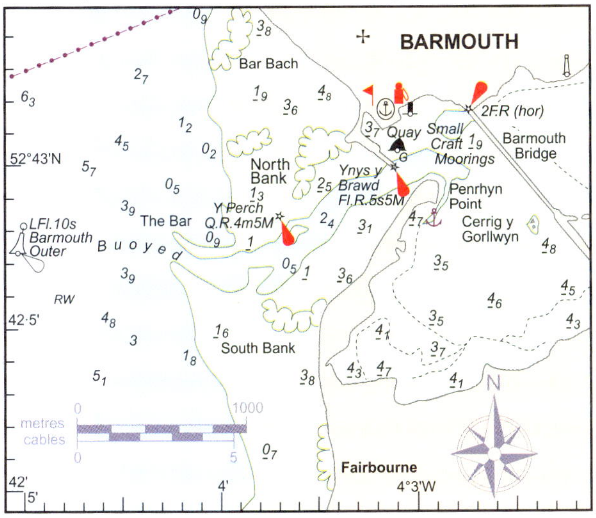


## 4.9 ABERDOVEY

Gwynedd **52°32'·57N 04°02'·72W** (Jetty) ✿✿◌◌✿✿✿

**CHARTS** AC *5609, 1410,* 1972, 1484; Imray C61, C51; Stanfords 27; OS 135

**TIDES** –0320 Dover; ML 2·6; Duration 0535. For differences see 4.10.

**SHELTER** Good except in strong W/SW winds. Berth on jetty in 3m; to the E there is heavy silting.

**NAVIGATION** WPT Aberdovey Outer SWM buoy, 52°32´·00N 04°05´·56W, 093°/0.43M to Bar buoy.

- Bar and channel constantly shift and are hazardous below half-tide; buoys moved accordingly.
- Enter the channel at gateway between Bar SHM and PHM Fl R 5s. Visitors should call HM on VHF before entering.

**LIGHTS AND MARKS** See 4.3 and chartlet. No daymarks. Lts may be unreliable. Submarine cables (prohib ⚓s) marked by bns with R ◊ topmarks.

**R/T** Call *Aberdovey Hbr* VHF Ch 12 16.

**TELEPHONE** (Code 01654) HM 767626, mobile 07879 433148; MRCC (01646) 690909; Marinecall 09068 969650; Police (01286) 673333; Dr 710414; Ⓗ 710411.

**FACILITIES** **Jetty** AB £7.00 <9m, £10.50 >9m; M, FW; **Wharf** Slip, AB, L, FW, C; **Dovey YC** ☎ 767607, Bar, Slip(launching £4.50 if engine <10hp), L, FW; **Services:** BY, ME, El, ⚒, CH, ACA, Ⓔ. **Town** P & D (cans), ME, El, CH, 🛒, R, Bar, ✉, Ⓑ, ⇌, ✈ (Chester).

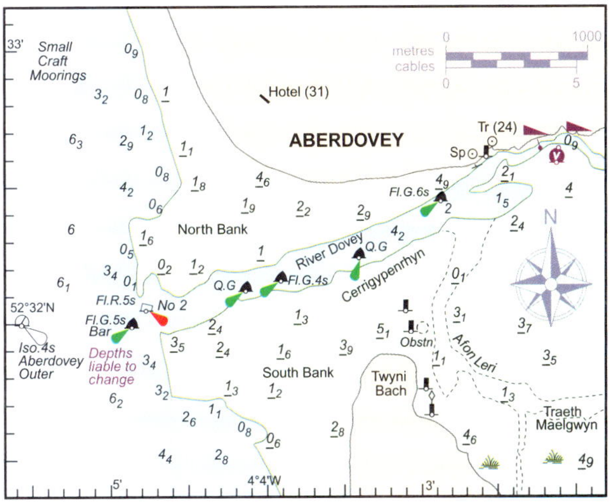


### OTHER HARBOURS IN SOUTH PART OF CARDIGAN BAY

**ABERAERON**, Ceredigion, **52°14´·62N 04°15´·94W**. AC *1410,* 1972, 1484. HW –0325 on Dover; +0140 and –1·9m on Milford Haven; ML 2·7m; Duration 0540. A small, popular drying hbr at the mouth of the R Aeron; access HW±1½. Short drying piers extend each side of river ent. In strong NW'lies there is little shelter. AB £4.60 on NW wall. Foul ground with depths of 1·5m extend 3ca offshore to SW of Aberaeron. Beware Carreg Gloyn (0·3m) 4ca WSW of hbr, and Sarn Cadwgan (1·8m) shoals 5ca N of the hbr ent. Lts (see 4.3 for sectors): N pier Fl (4) WRG 15s 10m 6M. S pier Fl (3) G 10s 11m 6M. VHF **14** 16. HM ☎ (01545) 571645; FW, D (hose) via aquarium. **YC** ☎ 570077.

**NEW QUAY**, Ceredigion, **52°12´·92N 04°21´·22W**. AC *1410,* 1972, 1484. HW –0335 on Dover; Duration 0540; see 4.10. Good shelter in offshore winds, but untenable in NW'lies. On E side of bay Carreg Ina, rks drying 1·3m, are marked by NCM buoy, Q. Two Y bns mark a sewer outfall running 7ca NNW from Ina Pt. The hbr (dries 1·6m) is protected by a pier with lt, Fl WG 3s 12m 8/5M; 135°-W-252°-G-295°. Groyne extends 80m SSE of pierhd to a SHM bn; close ENE of which is a ECM bn, Q (3) 10s. VHF Ch **14** 16. HM ☎ (01545) 560368. MRCC (01646) 690909; Dr ☎ 560203; YC ☎ 560516. Facilities: FW, D (from fishermen), slip (£6). **Town** P (3M), ✉, R, Bar.

## 4.10 ABERYSTWYTH

Ceredigion 52°24'·42N 04°05'·47W ✿✿◉▲▲▲✿✿✿

**CHARTS** AC *5609, 5620, 1410,* 1972, 1484; Imray C61, C51; Stanfords 27; OS 135

**TIDES** –0330 Dover; ML 2·7; Duration 0540

**Standard Port MILFORD HAVEN (➡)**

| Times | | | | Height (metres) | | | |
|---|---|---|---|---|---|---|---|
| High Water | | Low Water | | MHWS | MHWN | MLWN | MLWS |
| 0100 | 0800 | 0100 | 0700 | 7·0 | 5·2 | 2·5 | 0·7 |
| 1300 | 2000 | 1300 | 1900 | | | | |
| **Differences ABERDOVEY** | | | | | | | |
| +0215 | +0200 | +0230 | +0305 | –2·0 | –1·7 | –0·5 | 0·0 |
| **ABERYSTWYTH** | | | | | | | |
| +0145 | +0130 | +0210 | +0245 | –2·0 | –1·7 | –0·7 | 0·0 |
| **NEW QUAY** | | | | | | | |
| +0150 | +0125 | +0155 | +0230 | –2·1 | –1·8 | –0·6 | –0·1 |
| **ABERPORTH** | | | | | | | |
| +0135 | +0120 | +0150 | +0220 | –2·1 | –1·8 | –0·6 | –0·1 |

**SHELTER** Good, in marina (1·7m) on E side of chan; or dry against Town Quay. Access approx HW±3 (HW±2 for strangers).

**NAVIGATION** WPT 52°24'·83N 04°06'·22W,133/0·6M* to ent. Appr dangerous in strong on-shore winds. The Bar, close off S pier hd, has 0·7m least depth. From N, beware Castle Rks, in R sector of N bkwtr lt; also rks drying 0·5m W of N bkwtr and boulders below S pier hd. Turn 90° port inside narrow ent. E edge of inner hbr chan 0·3m is defined by WCM bn which in line with Y daymark gives a daytime lead into the Hbr.

**LIGHTS AND MARKS** N Bkwtr Hd ≠ 140° Wellington Mon't (on top Pendinas, conspic hill 120m high) clears to S of Castle Rks. Ldg lts 133°, both FR on Ystwyth Bridge, white daymarks. WCM bn on with Y daymark leads 100° across bar into hbr ent.

**R/T** HM Ch **14** 16. Marina Ch 80.

**TELEPHONE** (Code 01970) HM ☎/📠 611433 Mobile 07974 023965; Marina 611422; MRCC (01646) 690909; Marinecall 09068 969650; Police 612791; Dr 624855.

**FACILITIES** Marina (Y Lanfa), ☎ 611422, 📠 624122. 88 + 15 ♥, £2.60. D, Slip (launch £8.00), BH (10 ton), C (max 15 ton by arrangement), ⛽, ♿. **Town Quay** AB £5.50, FW, El, CH, Ⓔ, ME, ⚒, M, 2 Slips (launch £6), C (25 ton), Gas. **Y C** ☎ 612907, Slip, M, Bar.
**Town** P (cans), CH, 🛒, R, Bar, SM, ♿, 🗑, ✉, Ⓑ, ➤, ✈ (Swansea).

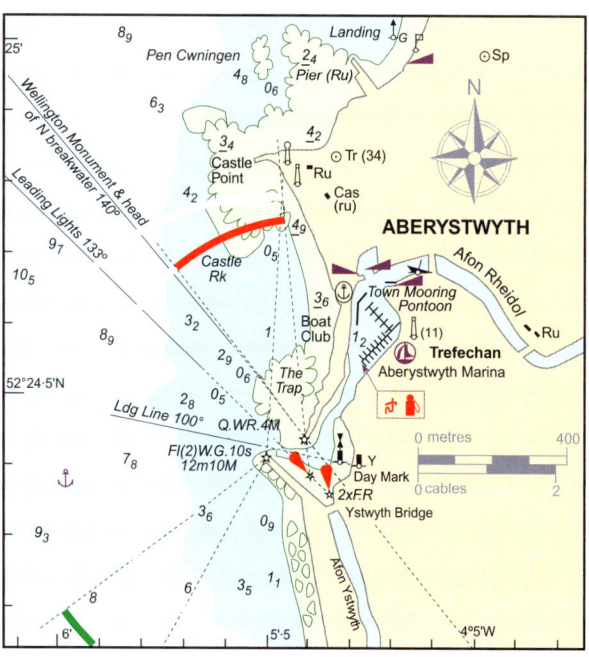

### MINOR HARBOUR, 12M NE of Fishguard

**PORT CARDIGAN**, Ceredigion, **52°07'·02N 04°42'·07W**. AC 1973, 1484. HW –0405 on Dover; ML 2·4m; Duration 0550. Shelter is good, but ent dangerous in strong N/NW winds. Large scale chart (1484) and local advice essential. Bar has 0·3m or less; breakers form esp on sp ebb. ⚓ near Hotel (conspic) on E side of ent. Chan is usually close to E side; IDM bn, Fl (2) 5s, should be left to stbd when clear of the bar. From Pen-yr-Ergyd to Bryn-Du chan is marked with lit mid channel markers but shifts constantly. St Dogmaels has ⚓ or a ♉ via Mooring Master ☎ (01329) 621437 mob 07774 126342. Or ⚓ in pools off Pen-yr-Ergyd. Short stay pontoons in the Teifi; possible ♉s off Teifi Boating Club. **Moorings:** administered by Afon Teifi Fairway Committee, Mooring Master ☎ (01239) 613966, mob 07799 284206.
**Teifi Boating Club** ☎ 613846, FW, Bar; **Services:** ME, ⚒.
**Town** Ⓑ, 🛒, CH, P&D (cans), FW, ME, Bar, R.

## 4.11 FISHGUARD

Pembrokeshire 52°00'·12N 04°58'·40W
Commercial Hbr ✿✿✿▲▲✿; Lower Hbr ✿◉▲✿✿✿

**CHARTS** AC *5620, 1178, 1410,* 1973, 1484; Imray C61, C51, C60; Stanfords 27; OS 157

**TIDES** –0400 Dover; ML 2·6; Duration 0550

**Standard Port MILFORD HAVEN (➡)**

| Times | | | | Height (metres) | | | |
|---|---|---|---|---|---|---|---|
| High Water | | Low Water | | MHWS | MHWN | MLWN | MLWS |
| 0100 | 0800 | 0100 | 0700 | 7·0 | 5·2 | 2·5 | 0·7 |
| 1300 | 2000 | 1300 | 1900 | | | | |
| **Differences FISHGUARD** | | | | | | | |
| +0115 | +0100 | +0110 | +0135 | –2·2 | –1·8 | –0·5 | +0·1 |
| **PORT CARDIGAN** | | | | | | | |
| +0140 | +0120 | +0220 | +0130 | –2·3 | –1·8 | –0·5 | 0·0 |
| **CARDIGAN** (Town) | | | | | | | |
| +0220 | +0150 | No data | | –2·2 | –1·6 | No data | |
| **PORTHGAIN** | | | | | | | |
| +0055 | +0045 | +0045 | +0100 | –2·5 | –1·8 | –0·6 | 0·0 |
| **RAMSEY SOUND** | | | | | | | |
| +0030 | +0030 | +0030 | +0030 | –1·9 | –1·3 | –0·3 | 0·0 |
| **SOLVA** | | | | | | | |
| +0015 | +0010 | +0035 | +0015 | –1·5 | –1·0 | –0·2 | 0·0 |
| **LITTLE HAVEN** | | | | | | | |
| +0010 | +0010 | +0025 | +0015 | –1·1 | –0·8 | –0·2 | 0·0 |
| **MARTIN'S HAVEN** | | | | | | | |
| +0010 | +0010 | +0015 | +0015 | –0·8 | –0·5 | +0·1 | +0·1 |
| **SKOMER IS** | | | | | | | |
| –0005 | –0005 | +0005 | +0005 | –0·4 | –0·1 | 0·0 | 0·0 |

**SHELTER** Good, except in strong NW/NE winds. Beware large swell, especially in N winds. No ⚓, except SW of ferry quay. Good holding in most of the bay. At Lower town ⚓ off Saddle or Castle Points in 2m. Strong S'lies funnel down the hbr.

**NAVIGATION** WPT 52°01'·02N 04°57'·57W, 237°/0·48M to N bkwtr lt. *Keep at least 1ca clear of N bkwtr head; beware of ferries and High-Speed SeaCats manoeuvring.*

**LIGHTS AND MARKS** See 4.3 and chartlet. Strumble Hd Lt ho, Fl (4) 15s 45m 26M, is approx 4M WNW of hbr. The SHM (bn) at Aber Gwaun is very small.

**R/T** HM Ch **14** 16. Goodwick Marine Ch M (occas).

**TELEPHONE** (Code 01348) Commercial Hbr Supervisor 404425; MRCC (01646) 690909; Marinecall 09068 969650; Police 873073; Dr 872802.

**FACILITIES** Fishguard (Lower town) dries 3·2m; access HW±1, limited AB. 10 Or ♉ (drying), 5 Y ♉, FW, ⛽. HM (Lower hbr) ☎ 873369; mob 07775 523846. Slip, BY, ⚒, FW, D (cans) from Goodwick Marine, ME, ACA, Slip, CH, El.

**Fishguard Bay YC**, FW, Bar, ♿.

**Town** P & D (cans), 🛒, R, Gas, Bar, ✉, 🗑, @, Ⓑ, ➤, ✈ (Cardiff), Ferry–Rosslare.

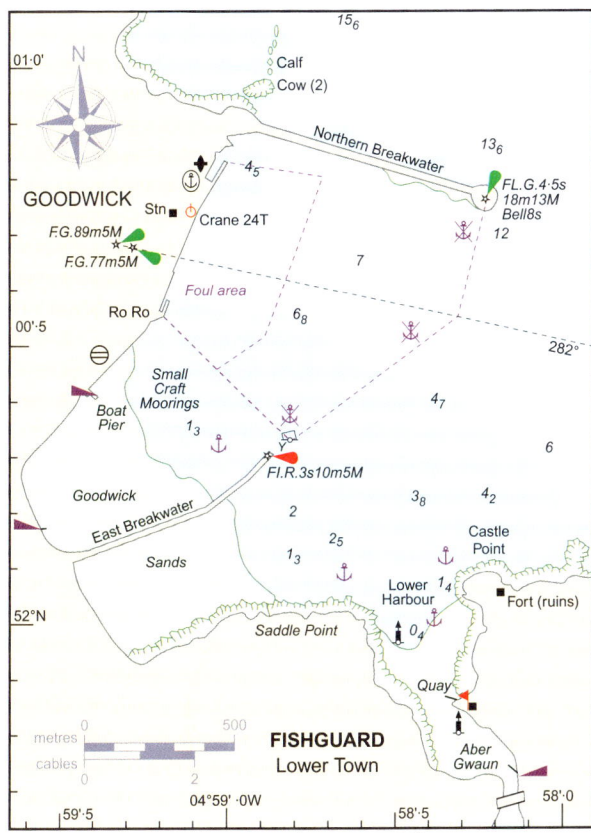

**FISHGUARD**
Lower Town

## HARBOURS IN ST BRIDES BAY (See AC 5620)

**SOLVA**, Pembrokeshire, **51°52'02N 05°11'·67W**. AC 1478. HW – 0450 on Dover; ML 3·2m; Duration 0555. See 4.11. Good shelter for small boats that can take the ground; access HW±3. Avoid in strong S winds. Black Scar, Green Scar and The Mare are rks 5ca S. Ent via SSE side; best water near Black Rk in centre of ent. Beware stone spit at Trwyn Caws on W just inside ent. There are 9 Or Øs drying on hard sand (£5.00), drying/rafting ABs for <9·5m LOA; or ⚓ behind the rk in approx 3m. Yachts can go up to the quay (£6.50) Facilities: showers, 🚾, Bar, R in village. FW on quay, Slip (launching £5). HM (01437) 721703 mob 07974 020139, VHF Ch 16 8, M, CH. **Solva Boat Owners Assn** ☎ 721489 mob 07974 020139.

**ST BRIDES BAY**, Pembrokeshire, **51°49'02N 05°10'·07W**. AC 1478. HW (Little Haven) –0450 on Dover; ML 3·2m; Duration 0555. See 4.11. A SPM buoy, Fl (5) Y 20s, is midway between Ramsey and Skomer islands at 51°48'·2N 05°20'·0W. Keep at least 100m offshore 1/9-28/2 to avoid disturbing seals, and nesting sea birds 1/3-31/7. Many good ⚓s, especially between Little Haven and Borough Head in S or E winds or between Solva and Dinas Fawr in N or E winds. In W'lies boats should shelter in Solva (above), Skomer (below) or Pendinas Bach. Tankers anchor in mouth of B. For apprs from the N or S see 4.4. Facilities: (Little Haven) CH, 🚾, R, Bar, FW (cans).

## 4.12  MILFORD HAVEN

Pembrokeshire **51°40'·13N 05°08'·16W** ✦✦✦⚓⚓🚩🚩

**CHARTS** AC 5620, 1410, 1178, 1478, 2878, 3273/4/5; Imray C60, C13; Stanfords 27; OS 157

**TIDES** –0500 Dover; ML 3·8; Duration 0605

**Standard Port MILFORD HAVEN (→)**

| Times | | | | Height (metres) | | | |
|---|---|---|---|---|---|---|---|
| High Water | | Low Water | | MHWS | MHWN | MLWN | MLWS |
| 0100 | 0800 | 0100 | 0700 | 7·0 | 5·2 | 2·5 | 0·7 |
| 1300 | 2000 | 1300 | 1900 | | | | |
| **Differences DALE ROADS** | | | | | | | |
| –0005 | –0005 | –0008 | –0008 | 0·0 | 0·0 | 0·0 | –0·1 |
| **NEYLAND** | | | | | | | |
| +0002 | +0010 | 0000 | 0000 | 0·0 | 0·0 | 0·0 | 0·0 |
| **HAVERFORDWEST** | | | | | | | |
| +0010 | +0025 | Dries out | | –4·8 | –4·9 | Dries out | |
| **LLANGWM** (Black Tar) | | | | | | | |
| +0010 | +0020 | +0005 | 0000 | +0·1 | +0·1 | 0·0 | –0·1 |

**SHELTER** Very good in various places round the hbr, especially in Milford Marina and Neyland Yacht Haven. ⚓s in Dale Bay; off Chapel Bay and Angle Pt on S shore; off Scotch Bay, E of Milford marina; and others beyond Pembroke Dock. Free pontoons (May-Oct) include: Dale Bay, Gelliswick Bay; waiting pontoons off Milford Dock and Hobbs Pt (for Pembroke Dock); and drying pontoons at Dale Beach, Hazelbeach, Neyland and Burton; mainly intended for tenders. It is possible to dry out safely at inshore areas of Dale, Sandy Haven and Angle Bay, depending on weather.

**NAVIGATION** West Channel WPT 51°40'·21N 05°10'·28W. **East Channel** WPT 51°40'·12N 05°08'·67W.

The tide sets strongly across the ent to the Haven particularly at sp. In bad weather avoid passing over Mid Chan Rks and St Ann's Hd shoal, where a confused sea and swell will be found (see AC 3273). Give St Ann's Head a wide berth especially on the ebb, when East Chan by Sheep Island is better.

Beware large tankers entering/departing the Haven and ferries moving at high speed in the lower Haven. Caution: Only 15m clearance below cables between Thorn Is and Thorn Pt.

Milford Haven Port Authority has a jetty, Port Control and offices near Hubberston Pt. Their launches have G hulls and W upperworks with 'PILOT' in black letters and fly a Pilot flag while on patrol; Fl Bu lt at night. Their instructions must be obeyed. No vessel may pass within 100m of any terminal or any tanker, whether at ⚓ or under way.

River Cleddau is navigable 6M to Picton Pt, at junction of West and East arms, at all tides for boats of moderate draught. Clearance under Cleddau Bridge above Neyland is 37m; and 25m under power cable 1M upstream. Chan to Haverfordwest has 2m at HW and clearances of only 6m below cables and bridge; only feasible for shoal draft/lifting keel and unmasted craft.

**LIGHTS AND MARKS** See 4.3 and chartlets. The ldg lts are specifically for VLCCs entering/leaving hbr and proceeding to/from the oil refineries. The Haven is very well buoyed and lit as far as Cleddau bridge. Milford Dock ldg lts 348°, both F.Bu, with W ○ daymarks. Dock entry sigs on E side of lock: 2 FG (vert) = gates open, vessels may enter. VHF Ch 18 is normally used for ent/exit by day and night.

**R/T** Monitor *Milford Haven Port Control* Ch 12 (H24) while underway in the Haven. *Milford Haven Patrol* launches Ch11/12 (H24). To lock in to Milford Dock marina call *Pierhead*, Ch 18, for clearance, then call *Milford Marina*, Ch M, for a berth. Neyland Yacht Haven Ch 80/M.

**Broadcasts**: Local forecasts on Ch 12 14 at 0300, 0900, 1500 and 2100 (all UT). Nav warnings follow on Ch14. Gale warnings issued on receipt Ch 12 14. Expected shipping movements for next 24 hours on Ch 12, 0800–0830, 2000–2030LT and on request. Tide hts and winds on request. Bcsts on Ch 16 67 at 0335 then every 4 hrs to 2335.

**TELEPHONE** (Code 01646) Lock 696310; Port Ctrl 696136/7, 🖷 696125; MRCC 690909; Marinecall 09068 969649; Police (01437) 763355; Ⓗ Haverfordwest (01437) 764545; Dr 690674.

**FACILITIES** Marinas/Berthing (from seaward): **Dale Bay** 🚾, FW, R, Slip, Pontoon, YC.

## Milford Marina
### MILFORD DOCKS • MILFORD HAVEN
### PEMBROKESHIRE • SA73 3AF

Milford Marina is set in a non-tidal basin on the magnificent Milford Haven waterway, where the 22 miles of sheltered estuary offer all-year-round sailing. The amenity building provides comprehensive range of facilities to a very high standard. There are boat repair facilities and storage available within the docks. Secure hard standing area and easy access slipway. Boat hoist and cranage facilities are also available.

- Easy access via M4
- London 4 hours
- British Rail station next to dock
- Close to town centre
- Retail Park on site
- Water and electricity to every berth
- Staff on duty 24 hours
- Member of the Yacht Harbour Association

### Tel: 01646 696312
### E-mail: enquiries@mhpa.co.uk
### www.mhpa.co.uk
### VHF: Ch 37

2008/WM10/e

**Milford Haven Port Authority jetty** ☎ 696133 (occas use by visitors with approval from HM), AB, FW.

**Milford Marina** (280) ☎ 696312, Pierhead ☎ 696310; £2·05. VHF Ch 14 M. Lock hrs: ent HW–4, exit –3½, free flow HW –2¼ to HW– ¼, ent +1½, exit +1¾, ent +2¾, exit +3¼; waiting pontoon or shelter in lock, 3·5m water at MLWS. D (H24), C, BH (16 ton), CH, El, ME, ✕, ⒠, D, Gas, Gaz, ⬚, R, Bar, Ice, ⬚, ⬚, ✉, ⒝, Wi-fi.

**Lawrenny Yacht Station** (100) ☎ 651212/651065, ⚓ £5, L, FW, BY, CH, D, P, ✕, C (15 ton), ME, Slip (launching £5), ⬚, Bar, R, ⬚, ⬚, ✉, Gas.

**Neyland Yacht Haven** (420 inc Ⓥ, £2) ☎ 601601, 🖷 600713; Wi-fi, D, CH, ⒠, Gas, Gaz, ⬚, C (20 ton), SM, SC, ME, El, ✕, R, ⬚, Wi-fi; Access lower basin H24, upper basin HW±3½ (sill+depth gauges and R/G lit perches); marina and approaches dredged annually Oct/Mar – proceed with extreme caution.

**Services**: All marine services available; check with HM, marinas or YC/SC. **Dale Sailing Co** (@ Neyland), BY, CH, ME, ✕, D, LPG, BH (35T). **East Llannion Marine**: access HW±3, Slip, scrubbing piles, BH (30 ton), fuel. **Rudder's BY**, small but useful, is just upstream of Burton Pt.

**Yacht Clubs**: Dale YC ☎ 636362; Pembrokeshire YC ☎ 692799; Neyland YC ☎ 600267; Pembroke Haven YC ☎ 684403; Lawrenny YC ☎ 651212.

**Towns**: Milford Haven, ✉, ⒝, ≉. Pembroke Dock; ✉, ⒝, ≉, Ⓗ. Neyland, ✉, ⒝. Haverfordwest, ✉, Ⓗ, ⒝, ≉, ✈ (Swansea or Cardiff). Ferry: Pembroke Dock–Rosslare.

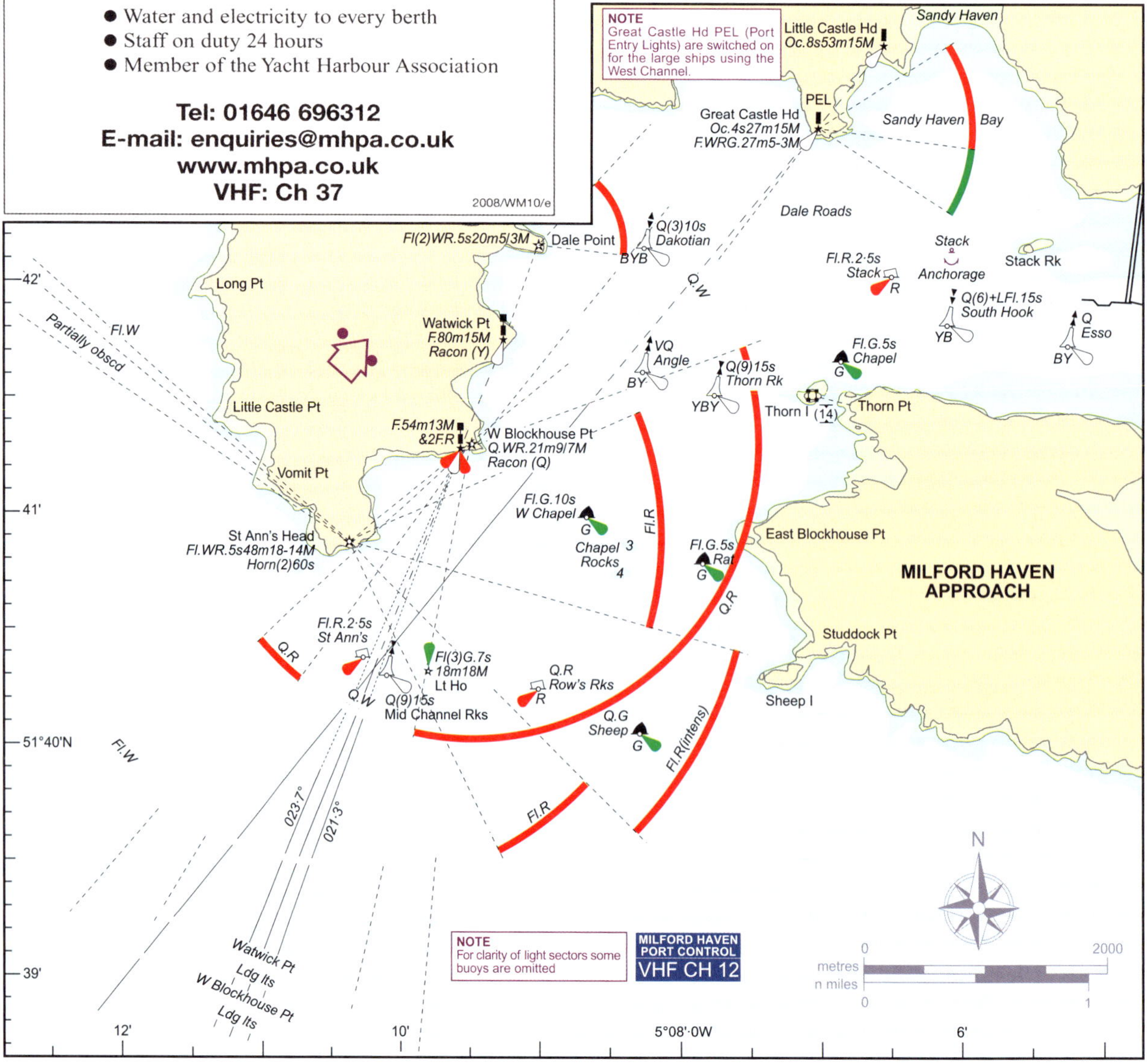

NOTE
Great Castle Hd PEL (Port Entry Lights) are switched on for the large ships using the West Channel.

Little Castle Hd
Oc.8s53m15M

Sandy Haven

PEL

Great Castle Hd
Oc.4s27m15M
F.WRG.27m5-3M

Sandy Haven Bay

Dale Roads

Stack
Stack Rk

Fl.R.2·5s
Stack
Anchorage
R

Q(6)+LFl.15s
South Hook
YB

Q
Esso
BY

Fl(2)WR.5s20m5/3M
Dale Point
BYB

Q(3)10s
Dakotian

Q.W

VQ
Angle
BY

Q(9)15s
Thorn Rk
YBY

Fl.G.5s
Chapel
G

Thorn I (14)
Thorn Pt

Long Pt

Fl.W

Partially obscd

Watwick Pt
F.80m15M
Racon (Y)

Little Castle Pt

F.54m13M
&2F.R

W Blockhouse Pt
Q.WR.21m9/7M
Racon (Q)

Vomit Pt

42'

Fl.G.10s
W Chapel
G

Chapel
Rocks
3
4

Fl.G.5s
Rat
G

East Blockhouse Pt

Fl.R

**MILFORD HAVEN
APPROACH**

41'

St Ann's Head
Fl.WR.5s48m18-14M
Horn(2)60s

Studdock Pt

Fl.R.2·5s
St Ann's
Q.R

Sheep I

Q.R
Row's Rks
R

Fl(3)G.7s
18m18M
Lt Ho

Q.W
Q(9)15s
Mid Channel Rks

Q.G
Sheep
G

Fl.R(intens)

51°40'N

Fl.W

023.7°
021.3°

Fl.R

39'

Watwick Pt
Ldg lts

W Blockhouse Pt
Ldg lts

NOTE
For clarity of light sectors some buoys are omitted

**MILFORD HAVEN
PORT CONTROL
VHF CH 12**

N

0          2000
metres
n miles
0          1

12'          10'          5°08'·0W          6'

MILFORD HAVEN *continued*

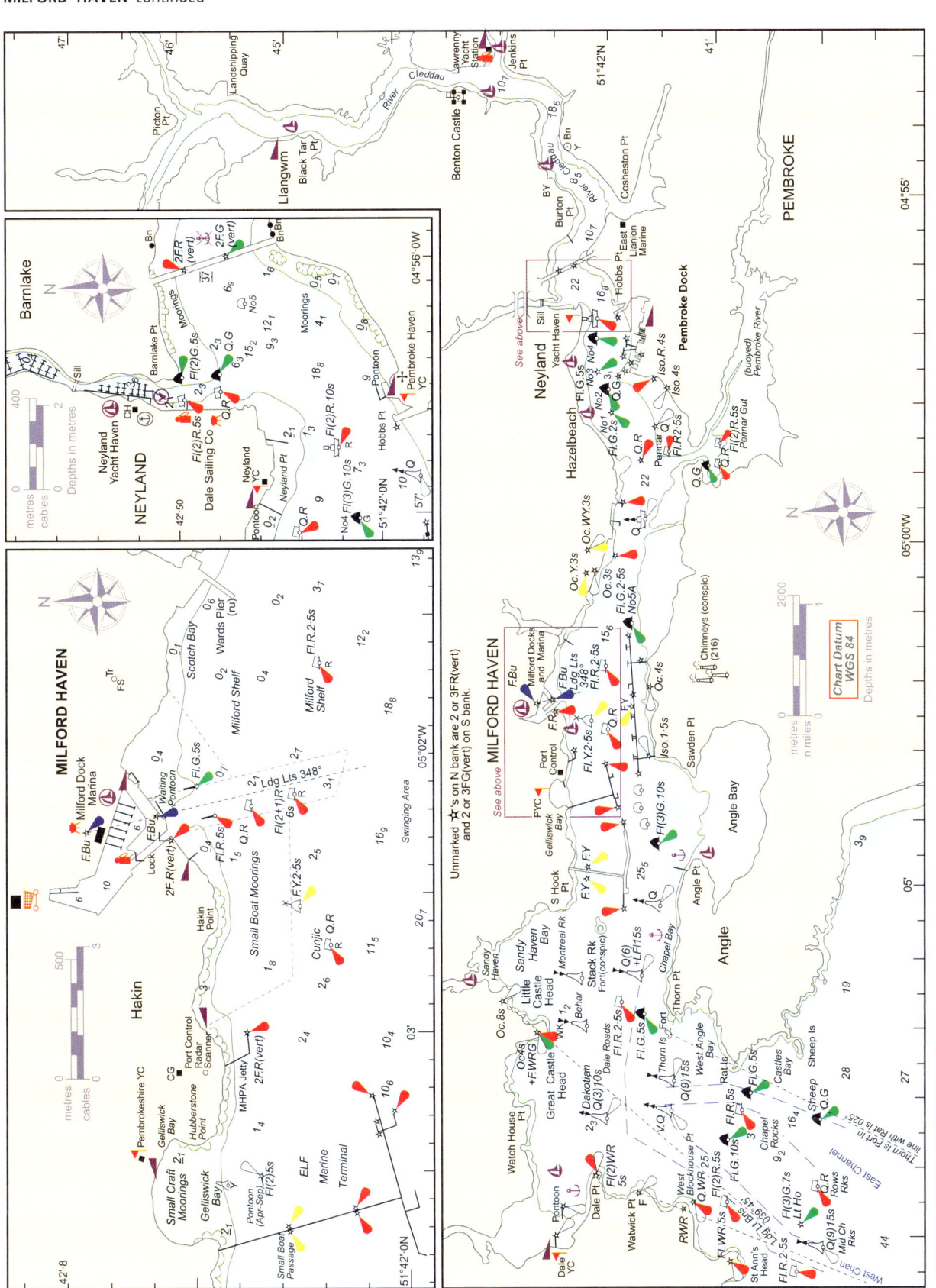

## MILFORD HAVEN  LAT 51°42'N  LONG 5°03'W
### TIMES AND HEIGHTS OF HIGH AND LOW WATERS

**TIME ZONE (UT)**
For Summer Time add ONE hour in **non-shaded areas**

Dates in **red** are **SPRINGS**
Dates in **blue** are **NEAPS**

YEAR **2008**

### JANUARY

| Time | m | | Time | m |
|---|---|---|---|---|
| **1** TU | 0558 2.4 / 1209 5.5 / 1838 2.5 | | **16** W | 0520 1.9 / 1137 6.0 / 1758 2.0 |
| **2** W | 0045 5.2 / 0701 2.6 / 1315 5.3 / 1943 2.6 | | **17** TH | 0006 5.6 / 0626 2.2 / 1245 5.7 / 1910 2.2 |
| **3** TH | 0156 5.2 / 0813 2.6 / 1425 5.1 / 2053 2.5 | | **18** F | 0121 5.5 / 0750 2.2 / 1404 5.6 / 2034 2.2 |
| **4** F | 0302 5.3 / 0921 2.5 / 1528 5.4 / 2153 2.3 | | **19** SA | 0243 5.6 / 0916 2.1 / 1523 5.8 / 2151 1.9 |
| **5** SA | 0359 5.6 / 1018 2.2 / 1623 5.6 / 2242 2.1 | | **20** SU | 0358 6.0 / 1029 1.7 / 1633 6.1 / 2254 1.6 |
| **6** SU | 0447 5.9 / 1105 1.9 / 1708 5.9 / 2324 1.8 | | **21** M | 0501 6.4 / 1129 1.3 / 1731 6.5 / 2348 1.2 |
| **7** M | 0529 6.2 / 1146 1.7 / 1749 6.1 | | **22** TU | 0554 6.8 / 1220 0.9 / 1821 6.7 ○ |
| **8** TU | 0002 1.6 / 0606 6.4 / 1225 1.5 / 1826 6.3 ● | | **23** W | 0036 0.9 / 0640 7.1 / 1307 0.7 / 1905 6.9 |
| **9** W | 0039 1.4 / 0643 6.6 / 1301 1.3 / 1902 6.4 | | **24** TH | 0119 0.8 / 0723 7.2 / 1348 0.7 / 1946 6.9 |
| **10** TH | 0115 1.3 / 0719 6.6 / 1338 1.1 / 1938 6.5 | | **25** F | 0159 0.8 / 0802 7.1 / 1426 0.7 / 2023 6.8 |
| **11** F | 0151 1.2 / 0756 6.8 / 1415 1.1 / 2015 6.4 | | **26** SA | 0236 0.9 / 0840 7.0 / 1501 1.0 / 2059 6.6 |
| **12** SA | 0228 1.2 / 0834 6.8 / 1453 1.1 / 2053 6.5 | | **27** SU | 0310 1.1 / 0915 6.7 / 1534 1.3 / 2133 6.3 |
| **13** SU | 0306 1.2 / 0914 6.7 / 1532 1.2 / 2133 6.3 | | **28** M | 0342 1.5 / 0949 6.3 / 1605 1.7 / 2207 5.9 |
| **14** M | 0345 1.4 / 0956 6.5 / 1614 1.4 / 2216 6.1 | | **29** TU | 0415 1.8 / 1024 5.9 / 1638 2.0 / 2244 5.6 |
| **15** TU | 0429 1.6 / 1043 6.3 / 1701 1.7 / 2306 5.9 ◑ | | **30** W | 0452 2.2 / 1103 5.5 / 1719 2.4 / 2329 5.2 ◑ |
| | | | **31** TH | 0542 2.6 / 1154 5.1 / 1818 2.7 |

### FEBRUARY

| Time | m | | Time | m |
|---|---|---|---|---|
| **1** F | 0034 4.9 / 0658 2.8 / 1312 4.9 / 1947 2.8 | | **16** SA | 0054 5.3 / 0733 2.4 / 1348 5.2 / 2022 2.4 |
| **2** SA | 0210 4.9 / 0834 2.8 / 1450 4.9 / 2118 2.7 | | **17** SU | 0234 5.3 / 0916 2.2 / 1523 5.4 / 2148 2.1 |
| **3** SU | 0330 5.2 / 0952 2.5 / 1601 5.0 / 2220 2.3 | | **18** M | 0358 5.8 / 1030 1.7 / 1634 5.9 / 2251 1.6 |
| **4** M | 0427 5.6 / 1046 2.1 / 1651 5.6 / 2306 1.9 | | **19** TU | 0457 6.3 / 1126 1.2 / 1726 6.4 / 2341 1.2 |
| **5** TU | 0511 6.0 / 1130 1.6 / 1732 6.0 / 2346 1.5 | | **20** W | 0545 6.8 / 1211 0.9 / 1809 6.7 |
| **6** W | 0549 6.4 / 1208 1.3 / 1809 6.4 | | **21** TH | 0023 0.8 / 0626 7.0 / 1251 0.6 / 1847 6.9 ○ |
| **7** TH | 0023 1.2 / 0625 6.7 / 1245 0.9 / 1845 6.7 ● | | **22** F | 0101 0.7 / 0703 7.2 / 1326 0.6 / 1922 7.0 |
| **8** F | 0059 0.9 / 0702 7.0 / 1321 0.7 / 1921 6.8 | | **23** SA | 0135 0.6 / 0738 7.1 / 1358 0.6 / 1955 6.9 |
| **9** SA | 0135 0.7 / 0738 7.1 / 1357 0.6 / 1956 6.9 | | **24** SU | 0207 0.7 / 0810 7.0 / 1428 0.8 / 2026 6.7 |
| **10** SU | 0211 0.7 / 0815 7.2 / 1434 0.6 / 2033 6.9 | | **25** M | 0237 0.9 / 0840 6.7 / 1456 1.1 / 2055 6.5 |
| **11** M | 0247 0.7 / 0853 7.1 / 1510 0.8 / 2110 6.7 | | **26** TU | 0305 1.2 / 0910 6.4 / 1522 1.4 / 2124 6.1 |
| **12** TU | 0324 1.0 / 0932 6.8 / 1548 1.1 / 2149 6.4 | | **27** W | 0333 1.6 / 0939 6.0 / 1549 1.8 / 2156 5.8 |
| **13** W | 0403 1.3 / 1015 6.3 / 1630 1.5 / 2234 6.0 | | **28** TH | 0404 2.0 / 1012 5.6 / 1621 2.2 / 2233 5.3 |
| **14** TH | 0450 1.7 / 1106 5.9 / 1722 2.0 / 2332 5.6 ◑ | | **29** F | 0444 2.4 / 1054 5.1 / 1706 2.7 / 2326 4.9 ◐ |
| **15** F | 0554 2.2 / 1201 5.5 / 1838 2.4 | | | |

### MARCH

| Time | m | | Time | m |
|---|---|---|---|---|
| **1** SA | 0549 2.8 / 1159 4.7 / 1832 3.0 | | **16** SU | 0044 5.2 / 0735 2.4 / 1345 5.1 / 2018 2.5 |
| **2** SU | 0059 4.7 / 0743 2.9 / 1402 4.6 / 2036 2.9 | | **17** M | 0231 5.3 / 0915 2.1 / 1520 5.4 / 2141 2.1 |
| **3** M | 0255 4.9 / 0920 2.6 / 1533 5.0 / 2151 2.4 | | **18** TU | 0348 5.8 / 1022 1.6 / 1622 5.9 / 2239 1.6 |
| **4** TU | 0358 5.4 / 1019 2.1 / 1625 5.5 / 2240 1.9 | | **19** W | 0442 6.3 / 1110 1.2 / 1708 6.4 / 2323 1.1 |
| **5** W | 0443 6.0 / 1103 1.5 / 1706 6.0 / 2320 1.4 | | **20** TH | 0525 6.7 / 1150 0.9 / 1747 6.7 |
| **6** TH | 0522 6.5 / 1142 1.1 / 1743 6.5 / 2358 1.1 | | **21** F | 0001 0.9 / 0603 6.9 / 1225 0.7 / 1821 6.8 ○ |
| **7** F | 0600 6.9 / 1219 0.7 / 1820 6.9 ● | | **22** SA | 0035 0.7 / 0637 7.0 / 1256 0.7 / 1854 6.9 |
| **8** SA | 0035 0.6 / 0637 7.2 / 1257 0.4 / 1856 7.1 | | **23** SU | 0107 0.7 / 0708 7.0 / 1326 0.7 / 1924 6.9 |
| **9** SU | 0112 0.4 / 0714 7.4 / 1334 0.3 / 1932 7.2 | | **24** M | 0137 0.8 / 0738 6.9 / 1354 0.9 / 1953 6.7 |
| **10** M | 0149 0.3 / 0752 7.4 / 1410 0.3 / 2009 7.1 | | **25** TU | 0205 0.9 / 0807 6.6 / 1421 1.1 / 2021 6.5 |
| **11** TU | 0226 0.5 / 0831 7.2 / 1447 0.6 / 2047 6.9 | | **26** W | 0233 1.2 / 0835 6.4 / 1447 1.4 / 2049 6.2 |
| **12** W | 0304 0.8 / 0911 6.9 / 1525 1.0 / 2127 6.5 | | **27** TH | 0301 1.5 / 0904 6.0 / 1513 1.8 / 2119 5.9 |
| **13** TH | 0344 1.2 / 0954 6.3 / 1607 1.5 / 2213 6.0 | | **28** F | 0332 1.9 / 0936 5.6 / 1544 2.2 / 2155 5.5 |
| **14** F | 0433 1.7 / 1047 5.8 / 1701 2.1 / 2314 5.5 ◐ | | **29** SA | 0411 2.3 / 1015 5.2 / 1625 2.6 / 2244 5.1 ◐ |
| **15** SA | 0543 2.2 / 1201 5.2 / 1825 2.5 | | **30** SU | 0508 2.7 / 1116 4.7 / 1735 2.9 |
| | | | **31** M | 0004 4.8 / 0653 2.8 / 1259 4.6 / 1943 2.9 |

### APRIL

| Time | m | | Time | m |
|---|---|---|---|---|
| **1** TU | 0200 4.9 / 0832 2.6 / 1447 4.9 / 2106 2.5 | | **16** W | 0321 5.9 / 0954 1.6 / 1553 5.9 / 2210 1.6 |
| **2** W | 0314 5.4 / 0937 2.0 / 1545 5.5 / 2201 1.9 | | **17** TH | 0413 6.6 / 1040 1.3 / 1639 6.2 / 2254 1.3 |
| **3** TH | 0404 6.0 / 1025 1.5 / 1629 6.0 / 2245 1.4 | | **18** F | 0456 6.5 / 1119 1.1 / 1717 6.5 / 2331 1.1 |
| **4** F | 0447 6.5 / 1108 1.0 / 1709 6.6 / 2326 0.9 | | **19** SA | 0533 6.6 / 1152 1.0 / 1752 6.6 |
| **5** SA | 0527 7.0 / 1148 0.6 / 1749 7.0 | | **20** SU | 0004 1.0 / 0606 6.7 / 1224 0.9 / 1823 6.7 ○ |
| **6** SU | 0006 0.5 / 0607 7.3 / 1229 0.3 / 1827 7.2 ● | | **21** M | 0037 0.9 / 0638 6.7 / 1254 1.0 / 1853 6.7 |
| **7** M | 0047 0.3 / 0648 7.4 / 1308 0.2 / 1907 7.3 | | **22** TU | 0108 1.0 / 0708 6.6 / 1323 1.1 / 1923 6.6 |
| **8** TU | 0127 0.3 / 0729 7.4 / 1348 0.3 / 1947 7.2 | | **23** W | 0138 1.1 / 0738 6.4 / 1351 1.2 / 1953 6.4 |
| **9** W | 0207 0.4 / 0811 7.2 / 1428 0.6 / 2028 7.0 | | **24** TH | 0208 1.3 / 0808 6.2 / 1420 1.5 / 2023 6.2 |
| **10** TH | 0249 0.8 / 0855 6.7 / 1509 1.1 / 2113 6.5 | | **25** F | 0239 1.6 / 0839 5.9 / 1449 1.8 / 2056 5.9 |
| **11** F | 0335 1.2 / 0943 6.2 / 1556 1.6 / 2204 6.1 | | **26** SA | 0313 1.9 / 0913 5.6 / 1523 2.1 / 2134 5.6 |
| **12** SA | 0431 1.8 / 1041 5.6 / 1655 2.1 / 2310 5.6 | | **27** SU | 0354 2.2 / 0956 5.3 / 1607 2.4 / 2223 5.3 |
| **13** SU | 0548 2.2 / 1157 5.2 / 1822 2.5 | | **28** M | 0449 2.4 / 1054 5.0 / 1710 2.7 / 2333 5.1 ◐ |
| **14** M | 0037 5.4 / 0727 2.3 / 1333 5.1 / 2000 2.4 | | **29** TU | 0610 2.5 / 1214 4.9 / 1846 2.7 |
| **15** TU | 0210 5.5 / 0853 2.0 / 1455 5.4 / 2116 2.0 | | **30** W | 0059 5.1 / 0737 2.4 / 1344 5.0 / 2010 2.4 |

Chart Datum: 3·71 metres below Ordnance Datum (Newlyn). HAT is 7·8 metres above Chart Datum.

**FREE** monthly updates from
www.reedsalmanac.co.uk

**TIME ZONE (UT)**
For Summer Time add ONE hour in **non-shaded areas**

# MILFORD HAVEN  LAT 51°42'N  LONG 5°03'W
### TIMES AND HEIGHTS OF HIGH AND LOW WATERS

Dates in red are **SPRINGS**
Dates in blue are **NEAPS**

YEAR **2008**

## MAY

| Time | m | | Time | m |
|---|---|---|---|---|
| **1** 0217 | 5.5 | **16** 0333 | | 6.0 |
| 0845 | 2.0 | 1000 | | 1.6 |
| TH 1452 | 5.5 | F 1600 | | 5.9 |
| 2112 | 1.9 | 2216 | | 1.6 |
| **2** 0316 | 6.0 | **17** 0419 | | 6.1 |
| 0940 | 1.5 | 1041 | | 1.5 |
| F 1545 | 6.0 | SA 1642 | | 6.1 |
| 2203 | 1.4 | 2257 | | 1.5 |
| **3** 0406 | 6.4 | **18** 0500 | | 6.2 |
| 1029 | 1.1 | 1118 | | 1.4 |
| SA 1632 | 6.5 | SU 1720 | | 6.3 |
| 2251 | 1.0 | 2334 | | 1.4 |
| **4** 0453 | 6.9 | **19** 0537 | | 6.3 |
| 1115 | 0.7 | 1153 | | 1.3 |
| SU 1716 | 6.9 | M 1755 | | 6.4 |
| 2337 | 0.7 | | | |
| **5** 0539 | 7.1 | **20** 0009 | | 1.3 |
| 1200 | 0.5 | 0611 | | 6.3 |
| M 1801 | 7.1 | TU 1226 | | 1.3 |
| ● | | ○ 1828 | | 6.4 |
| **6** 0022 | 0.5 | **21** 0043 | | 1.3 |
| 0624 | 7.3 | 0644 | | 6.3 |
| TU 1245 | 0.4 | W 1258 | | 1.3 |
| 1845 | 7.2 | 1900 | | 6.4 |
| **7** 0108 | 0.4 | **22** 0117 | | 1.3 |
| 0711 | 7.2 | 0717 | | 6.2 |
| W 1330 | 0.5 | TH 1330 | | 1.4 |
| 1930 | 7.1 | 1933 | | 6.4 |
| **8** 0155 | 0.6 | **23** 0150 | | 1.4 |
| 0758 | 7.0 | 0750 | | 6.1 |
| TH 1414 | 0.8 | F 1402 | | 1.5 |
| 2017 | 6.9 | 2006 | | 6.2 |
| **9** 0242 | 0.8 | **24** 0225 | | 1.6 |
| 0847 | 6.6 | 0824 | | 5.9 |
| F 1501 | 1.2 | SA 1435 | | 1.7 |
| 2106 | 6.6 | 2042 | | 6.0 |
| **10** 0334 | 1.2 | **25** 0302 | | 1.7 |
| 0939 | 6.2 | 0902 | | 5.7 |
| SA 1552 | 1.6 | SU 1513 | | 1.9 |
| 2201 | 6.2 | 2123 | | 5.9 |
| **11** 0432 | 1.6 | **26** 0344 | | 1.9 |
| 1036 | 5.7 | 0945 | | 5.5 |
| SU 1652 | 2.0 | M 1557 | | 2.1 |
| 2303 | 5.8 | 2210 | | 5.7 |
| **12** 0542 | 1.9 | **27** 0434 | | 2.0 |
| 1143 | 5.4 | 1037 | | 5.3 |
| M 1805 | 2.2 | TU 1651 | | 2.2 |
| ◑ | | 2308 | | 5.5 |
| **13** 0015 | 5.6 | **28** 0534 | | 2.1 |
| 0658 | 2.0 | 1139 | | 5.3 |
| TU 1259 | 5.3 | W 1758 | | 2.3 |
| 1923 | 2.2 | ◐ | | |
| **14** 0131 | 5.6 | **29** 0013 | | 5.5 |
| 0810 | 2.0 | 0643 | | 2.1 |
| W 1411 | 5.4 | TH 1248 | | 5.3 |
| 2033 | 2.1 | 1912 | | 2.2 |
| **15** 0238 | 5.8 | **30** 0122 | | 5.7 |
| 0911 | 1.8 | 0751 | | 1.9 |
| TH 1511 | 5.7 | F 1358 | | 5.6 |
| 2129 | 1.8 | 2020 | | 1.9 |
| | | **31** 0228 | | 5.9 |
| | | 0854 | | 1.6 |
| | | SA 1500 | | 5.9 |
| | | 2121 | | 1.6 |

## JUNE

| Time | m | | Time | m |
|---|---|---|---|---|
| **1** 0327 | 6.3 | **16** 0428 | | 5.8 |
| 0952 | 1.3 | 1047 | | 1.8 |
| SU 1556 | 6.3 | M 1651 | | 6.0 |
| 2218 | 1.3 | 2307 | | 1.7 |
| **2** 0422 | 6.6 | **17** 0512 | | 5.9 |
| 1046 | 1.0 | 1127 | | 1.6 |
| M 1648 | 6.6 | TU 1732 | | 6.1 |
| 2312 | 1.0 | 2348 | | 1.6 |
| **3** 0516 | 6.8 | **18** 0551 | | 6.0 |
| 1138 | 0.8 | 1205 | | 1.5 |
| TU 1740 | 6.9 | W 1809 | | 6.3 |
| ● | | ○ | | |
| **4** 0005 | 0.7 | **19** 0025 | | 1.5 |
| 0608 | 6.9 | 0628 | | 6.1 |
| W 1228 | 0.7 | TH 1240 | | 1.5 |
| 1830 | 7.0 | 1845 | | 6.3 |
| **5** 0057 | 0.6 | **20** 0102 | | 1.4 |
| 0659 | 6.9 | 0703 | | 6.1 |
| TH 1317 | 0.7 | F 1315 | | 1.4 |
| 1920 | 7.1 | 1920 | | 6.4 |
| **6** 0148 | 0.6 | **21** 0137 | | 1.4 |
| 0750 | 6.8 | 0738 | | 6.1 |
| F 1406 | 0.9 | SA 1349 | | 1.4 |
| 2010 | 7.0 | 1955 | | 6.4 |
| **7** 0238 | 0.8 | **22** 0213 | | 1.4 |
| 0840 | 6.6 | 0813 | | 6.1 |
| SA 1454 | 1.1 | SU 1425 | | 1.5 |
| 2100 | 6.7 | 2032 | | 6.3 |
| **8** 0329 | 1.1 | **23** 0251 | | 1.4 |
| 0930 | 6.3 | 0851 | | 6.0 |
| SU 1543 | 1.4 | M 1502 | | 1.5 |
| 2151 | 6.5 | 2111 | | 6.2 |
| **9** 0421 | 1.4 | **24** 0330 | | 1.5 |
| 1020 | 6.0 | 0930 | | 5.9 |
| M 1635 | 1.7 | TU 1543 | | 1.7 |
| 2243 | 6.1 | 2153 | | 6.1 |
| **10** 0515 | 1.7 | **25** 0413 | | 1.6 |
| 1114 | 5.7 | 1014 | | 5.8 |
| TU 1731 | 1.9 | W 1627 | | 1.8 |
| ◑ 2339 | 5.9 | 2240 | | 6.0 |
| **11** 0613 | 1.9 | **26** 0501 | | 1.7 |
| 1212 | 5.5 | 1105 | | 5.7 |
| W 1832 | 2.1 | TH 1719 | | 1.9 |
| | | ◑ 2334 | | 5.8 |
| **12** 0040 | 5.7 | **27** 0556 | | 1.9 |
| 0713 | 2.1 | 1203 | | 5.6 |
| TH 1316 | 5.4 | F 1821 | | 2.0 |
| 1935 | 2.2 | | | |
| **13** 0144 | 5.6 | **28** 0036 | | 5.8 |
| 0815 | 2.1 | 0701 | | 1.9 |
| F 1419 | 5.4 | SA 1310 | | 5.6 |
| 2038 | 2.2 | 1932 | | 2.0 |
| **14** 0245 | 5.6 | **29** 0146 | | 5.8 |
| 0912 | 2.0 | 0812 | | 1.8 |
| SA 1516 | 5.6 | SU 1422 | | 5.7 |
| 2134 | 2.0 | 2047 | | 1.9 |
| **15** 0339 | 5.7 | **30** 0256 | | 6.0 |
| 1003 | 1.9 | 0922 | | 1.7 |
| SU 1607 | 5.8 | M 1529 | | 6.0 |
| 2223 | 1.9 | 2156 | | 1.6 |

## JULY

| Time | m | | Time | m |
|---|---|---|---|---|
| **1** 0402 | 6.2 | **16** 0453 | | 5.7 |
| 1026 | 1.4 | 1108 | | 1.9 |
| TU 1631 | 6.4 | W 1714 | | 6.0 |
| 2259 | 1.2 | 2332 | | 1.7 |
| **2** 0503 | 6.5 | **17** 0536 | | 5.9 |
| 1124 | 1.1 | 1148 | | 1.6 |
| W 1729 | 6.7 | TH 1754 | | 6.2 |
| 2356 | 0.9 | | | |
| **3** 0600 | 6.7 | **18** 0011 | | 1.5 |
| 1217 | 0.9 | 0613 | | 6.1 |
| TH 1823 | 6.9 | F 1225 | | 1.4 |
| ● | | ○ 1829 | | 6.4 |
| **4** 0050 | 0.7 | **19** 0047 | | 1.3 |
| 0652 | 6.8 | 0648 | | 6.2 |
| F 1308 | 0.8 | SA 1300 | | 1.3 |
| 1912 | 7.1 | 1904 | | 6.6 |
| **5** 0140 | 0.6 | **20** 0122 | | 1.1 |
| 0741 | 6.9 | 0723 | | 6.4 |
| SA 1355 | 0.8 | SU 1334 | | 1.2 |
| 2000 | 7.1 | 1939 | | 6.6 |
| **6** 0228 | 0.6 | **21** 0157 | | 1.0 |
| 0826 | 6.7 | 0757 | | 6.4 |
| SU 1440 | 0.9 | M 1409 | | 1.1 |
| 2045 | 7.0 | 2015 | | 6.7 |
| **7** 0312 | 0.8 | **22** 0233 | | 1.0 |
| 0910 | 6.5 | 0832 | | 6.4 |
| M 1523 | 1.1 | TU 1445 | | 1.1 |
| 2128 | 6.7 | 2051 | | 6.6 |
| **8** 0354 | 1.1 | **23** 0309 | | 1.1 |
| 0952 | 6.2 | 0909 | | 6.3 |
| TU 1605 | 1.4 | W 1521 | | 1.3 |
| 2211 | 6.4 | 2130 | | 6.5 |
| **9** 0435 | 1.5 | **24** 0347 | | 1.3 |
| 1034 | 5.9 | 0948 | | 6.2 |
| W 1647 | 1.7 | TH 1600 | | 1.5 |
| 2255 | 6.0 | 2211 | | 6.3 |
| **10** 0518 | 1.8 | **25** 0428 | | 1.5 |
| 1120 | 5.6 | 1031 | | 5.9 |
| TH 1734 | 2.1 | F 1645 | | 1.7 |
| ◑ 2343 | 5.6 | ◑ 2300 | | 6.0 |
| **11** 0607 | 2.2 | **26** 0517 | | 1.8 |
| 1213 | 5.3 | 1124 | | 5.7 |
| F 1829 | 2.3 | SA 1741 | | 2.0 |
| | | 2359 | | 5.7 |
| **12** 0040 | 5.3 | **27** 0620 | | 2.1 |
| 0706 | 2.4 | 1232 | | 5.5 |
| SA 1319 | 5.1 | SU 1858 | | 2.2 |
| 1936 | 2.5 | | | |
| **13** 0150 | 5.2 | **28** 0115 | | 5.5 |
| 0817 | 2.5 | 0743 | | 2.2 |
| SU 1431 | 5.2 | M 1356 | | 5.5 |
| 2051 | 2.5 | 2030 | | 2.1 |
| **14** 0301 | 5.2 | **29** 0240 | | 5.6 |
| 0926 | 2.3 | 0909 | | 2.0 |
| M 1536 | 5.4 | TU 1518 | | 5.8 |
| 2155 | 2.3 | 2151 | | 1.8 |
| **15** 0403 | 5.4 | **30** 0357 | | 5.9 |
| 1022 | 2.1 | 1020 | | 1.6 |
| TU 1630 | 5.7 | W 1627 | | 6.2 |
| 2248 | 2.0 | 2257 | | 1.4 |
| | | **31** 0501 | | 6.3 |
| | | 1119 | | 1.2 |
| | | TH 1725 | | 6.7 |
| | | 2352 | | 0.9 |

## AUGUST

| Time | m | | Time | m |
|---|---|---|---|---|
| **1** 0555 | 6.7 | **16** 0553 | | 6.2 |
| 1210 | 0.9 | 1204 | | 1.3 |
| F 1815 | 7.0 | SA 1808 | | 6.6 |
| ● | | ○ | | |
| **2** 0041 | 0.6 | **17** 0026 | | 1.1 |
| 0641 | 6.9 | 0626 | | 6.5 |
| SA 1256 | 0.7 | SU 1239 | | 1.0 |
| 1900 | 7.2 | 1842 | | 6.9 |
| **3** 0126 | 0.5 | **18** 0100 | | 0.8 |
| 0724 | 7.0 | 0700 | | 6.7 |
| SU 1338 | 0.6 | M 1313 | | 0.9 |
| 1942 | 7.2 | 1917 | | 7.0 |
| **4** 0207 | 0.5 | **19** 0135 | | 0.7 |
| 0804 | 6.9 | 0734 | | 6.8 |
| M 1417 | 0.7 | TU 1348 | | 0.8 |
| 2021 | 7.1 | 1952 | | 7.0 |
| **5** 0244 | 0.7 | **20** 0210 | | 0.7 |
| 0841 | 6.7 | 0808 | | 6.8 |
| TU 1454 | 0.9 | W 1422 | | 0.8 |
| 2058 | 6.8 | 2027 | | 7.0 |
| **6** 0318 | 1.0 | **21** 0245 | | 0.8 |
| 0916 | 6.4 | 0843 | | 6.7 |
| W 1528 | 1.2 | TH 1458 | | 1.0 |
| 2133 | 6.5 | 2104 | | 6.8 |
| **7** 0351 | 1.4 | **22** 0321 | | 1.1 |
| 0951 | 6.1 | 0921 | | 6.4 |
| TH 1601 | 1.6 | F 1535 | | 1.3 |
| 2208 | 6.1 | 2145 | | 6.4 |
| **8** 0424 | 1.8 | **23** 0400 | | 1.5 |
| 1028 | 5.7 | 1003 | | 6.1 |
| F 1637 | 2.0 | SA 1619 | | 1.7 |
| ◑ 2246 | 5.6 | ◑ 2232 | | 6.0 |
| **9** 0501 | 2.2 | **24** 0447 | | 1.9 |
| 1111 | 5.3 | 1055 | | 5.7 |
| SA 1723 | 2.4 | SU 1716 | | 2.1 |
| 2334 | 5.2 | 2334 | | 5.5 |
| **10** 0554 | 2.6 | **25** 0554 | | 2.3 |
| 1210 | 5.0 | 1209 | | 5.3 |
| SU 1833 | 2.8 | M 1845 | | 2.4 |
| **11** 0045 | 4.9 | **26** 0102 | | 5.2 |
| 0717 | 2.8 | 0735 | | 2.5 |
| M 1343 | 4.9 | TU 1350 | | 5.3 |
| 2009 | 2.8 | 2034 | | 2.3 |
| **12** 0227 | 4.8 | **27** 0242 | | 5.4 |
| 0854 | 2.7 | 0910 | | 2.2 |
| TU 1510 | 5.1 | W 1520 | | 5.7 |
| 2133 | 2.5 | 2155 | | 1.8 |
| **13** 0344 | 5.1 | **28** 0400 | | 5.8 |
| 1001 | 2.4 | 1018 | | 1.7 |
| W 1610 | 5.5 | TH 1626 | | 6.3 |
| 2229 | 2.1 | 2255 | | 1.3 |
| **14** 0436 | 5.5 | **29** 0456 | | 6.3 |
| 1049 | 2.0 | 1112 | | 1.2 |
| TH 1655 | 6.0 | F 1717 | | 6.8 |
| 2313 | 1.7 | 2343 | | 0.9 |
| **15** 0517 | 5.9 | **30** 0542 | | 6.7 |
| 1129 | 1.6 | 1157 | | 0.8 |
| F 1733 | 6.3 | SA 1800 | | 7.1 |
| 2351 | 1.4 | ● | | |
| | | **31** 0025 | | 0.6 |
| | | 0623 | | 7.0 |
| | | SU 1237 | | 0.6 |
| | | 1840 | | 7.3 |

Chart Datum: 3·71 metres below Ordnance Datum (Newlyn). HAT is 7·8 metres above Chart Datum.

**S Wales**

**TIME ZONE (UT)**
For Summer Time add ONE hour in **non-shaded areas**

# MILFORD HAVEN   LAT 51°42'N   LONG 5°03'W
### TIMES AND HEIGHTS OF HIGH AND LOW WATERS

Dates in red are SPRINGS
Dates in blue are NEAPS

YEAR **2008**

## SEPTEMBER

| Time | m | Time | m |
|---|---|---|---|
| **1** 0103 | 0.5 | **16** 0033 | 0.7 |
| 0700 | 7.1 | 0632 | 7.0 |
| M 1314 | 0.6 | TU 1248 | 0.7 |
| 1917 | 7.3 | 1850 | 7.3 |
| **2** 0138 | 0.6 | **17** 0109 | 0.5 |
| 0735 | 7.0 | 0707 | 7.1 |
| TU 1348 | 0.7 | W 1323 | 0.6 |
| 1951 | 7.1 | 1926 | 7.3 |
| **3** 0210 | 0.8 | **18** 0144 | 0.6 |
| 0808 | 6.8 | 0743 | 7.1 |
| W 1420 | 0.9 | TH 1400 | 0.7 |
| 2023 | 6.8 | 2003 | 7.2 |
| **4** 0240 | 1.1 | **19** 0221 | 0.8 |
| 0839 | 6.6 | 0820 | 6.9 |
| TH 1450 | 1.2 | F 1437 | 0.9 |
| 2054 | 6.5 | 2043 | 6.9 |
| **5** 0308 | 1.4 | **20** 0258 | 1.1 |
| 0910 | 6.2 | 0859 | 6.6 |
| F 1520 | 1.6 | SA 1517 | 1.3 |
| 2125 | 6.1 | 2125 | 6.4 |
| **6** 0336 | 1.9 | **21** 0339 | 1.6 |
| 0942 | 5.8 | 0944 | 6.2 |
| SA 1551 | 2.1 | SU 1605 | 1.8 |
| 2158 | 5.6 | 2216 | 5.9 |
| **7** 0407 | 2.3 | **22** 0431 | 2.1 |
| 1020 | 5.4 | 1042 | 5.7 |
| SU 1631 | 2.5 | M 1710 | 2.3 |
| ☽ 2240 | 5.1 | ☾ 2326 | 5.4 |
| **8** 0451 | 2.7 | **23** 0547 | 2.5 |
| 1113 | 5.0 | 1205 | 5.3 |
| M 1735 | 2.9 | TU 1855 | 2.5 |
| 2344 | 4.7 | | |
| **9** 0616 | 3.0 | **24** 0104 | 5.1 |
| 1245 | 4.8 | 0738 | 2.6 |
| TU 1929 | 3.0 | W 1351 | 5.4 |
| | | 2038 | 2.3 |
| **10** 0148 | 4.6 | **25** 0243 | 5.4 |
| 0819 | 3.0 | 0850 | 2.2 |
| W 1440 | 5.0 | TH 1515 | 5.9 |
| 2105 | 2.7 | 2149 | 1.7 |
| **11** 0318 | 5.0 | **26** 0351 | 5.9 |
| 0934 | 2.5 | 1008 | 1.7 |
| TH 1542 | 5.5 | F 1612 | 6.4 |
| 2203 | 2.2 | 2241 | 1.3 |
| **12** 0409 | 5.5 | **27** 0440 | 6.4 |
| 1022 | 2.0 | 1055 | 1.2 |
| F 1626 | 6.0 | SA 1658 | 6.8 |
| 2245 | 1.7 | 2324 | 0.9 |
| **13** 0449 | 6.0 | **28** 0522 | 6.8 |
| 1101 | 1.6 | 1136 | 0.9 |
| SA 1704 | 6.5 | SU 1739 | 7.1 |
| 2322 | 1.2 | | |
| **14** 0524 | 6.4 | **29** 0001 | 0.8 |
| 1137 | 1.2 | 0558 | 7.0 |
| SU 1739 | 6.8 | M 1212 | 0.8 |
| 2358 | 0.9 | ● 1814 | 7.2 |
| **15** 0558 | 6.8 | **30** 0035 | 0.7 |
| 1212 | 0.9 | 0632 | 7.0 |
| M 1815 | 7.1 | TU 1246 | 0.8 |
| ○ | | 1848 | 7.1 |

## OCTOBER

| Time | m | Time | m |
|---|---|---|---|
| **1** 0106 | 0.8 | **16** 0043 | 0.5 |
| 0704 | 7.0 | 0641 | 7.3 |
| W 1318 | 0.8 | TH 1301 | 0.6 |
| 1920 | 7.0 | 1903 | 7.4 |
| **2** 0136 | 1.0 | **17** 0122 | 0.6 |
| 0735 | 6.8 | 0721 | 7.2 |
| TH 1348 | 1.0 | F 1341 | 0.7 |
| 1950 | 6.7 | 1945 | 7.2 |
| **3** 0205 | 1.2 | **18** 0202 | 0.8 |
| 0805 | 6.6 | 0802 | 7.0 |
| F 1418 | 1.3 | SA 1424 | 1.0 |
| 2020 | 6.4 | 2028 | 6.8 |
| **4** 0232 | 1.5 | **19** 0244 | 1.2 |
| 0835 | 6.3 | 0846 | 6.7 |
| SA 1447 | 1.7 | SU 1510 | 1.4 |
| 2050 | 6.1 | 2117 | 6.4 |
| **5** 0259 | 1.9 | **20** 0330 | 1.7 |
| 0906 | 5.9 | 0938 | 6.3 |
| SU 1518 | 2.1 | M 1604 | 1.8 |
| 2122 | 5.6 | 2214 | 5.8 |
| **6** 0330 | 2.3 | **21** 0428 | 2.2 |
| 0943 | 5.6 | 1041 | 5.8 |
| M 1558 | 2.5 | TU 1717 | 2.2 |
| 2203 | 5.2 | ☾ 2326 | 5.4 |
| **7** 0411 | 2.7 | **22** 0549 | 2.5 |
| 1033 | 5.2 | 1203 | 5.6 |
| TU 1656 | 2.9 | W 1854 | 2.3 |
| ☽ 2303 | 4.8 | | |
| **8** 0522 | 3.1 | **23** 0055 | 5.3 |
| 1152 | 4.9 | 0726 | 2.5 |
| W 1842 | 3.0 | TH 1335 | 5.6 |
| | | 2020 | 2.1 |
| **9** 0045 | 4.6 | **24** 0221 | 5.5 |
| 0727 | 3.0 | 0844 | 2.1 |
| TH 1347 | 5.0 | F 1450 | 6.0 |
| 2018 | 2.7 | 2125 | 1.8 |
| **10** 0232 | 5.0 | **25** 0324 | 5.9 |
| 0850 | 2.7 | 0942 | 1.7 |
| F 1458 | 5.4 | SA 1546 | 6.4 |
| 2120 | 2.2 | 2215 | 1.4 |
| **11** 0328 | 5.5 | **26** 0413 | 6.3 |
| 0943 | 2.1 | 1029 | 1.4 |
| SA 1546 | 6.0 | SU 1632 | 6.6 |
| 2207 | 1.7 | 2256 | 1.2 |
| **12** 0410 | 6.0 | **27** 0454 | 6.6 |
| 1025 | 1.6 | 1109 | 1.2 |
| SU 1627 | 6.5 | M 1712 | 6.8 |
| 2247 | 1.3 | 2332 | 1.1 |
| **13** 0448 | 6.5 | **28** 0531 | 6.8 |
| 1104 | 1.2 | 1145 | 1.1 |
| M 1705 | 6.9 | TU 1747 | 6.9 |
| 2325 | 0.9 | ● | |
| **14** 0526 | 6.9 | **29** 0005 | 1.1 |
| 1142 | 0.9 | 0604 | 6.8 |
| TU 1744 | 7.2 | W 1219 | 1.1 |
| ○ | | 1820 | 6.8 |
| **15** 0004 | 0.7 | **30** 0037 | 1.1 |
| 0603 | 7.2 | 0636 | 6.8 |
| W 1221 | 0.7 | TH 1251 | 1.2 |
| 1823 | 7.4 | 1852 | 6.7 |
| | | **31** 0107 | 1.2 |
| | | 0708 | 6.7 |
| | | F 1322 | 1.3 |
| | | 1923 | 6.6 |

## NOVEMBER

| Time | m | Time | m |
|---|---|---|---|
| **1** 0137 | 1.4 | **16** 0150 | 0.9 |
| 0739 | 6.6 | 0753 | 7.1 |
| SA 1353 | 1.5 | SU 1418 | 0.9 |
| 1954 | 6.3 | 2022 | 6.8 |
| **2** 0206 | 1.6 | **17** 0237 | 1.2 |
| 0810 | 6.3 | 0842 | 6.8 |
| SU 1425 | 1.7 | M 1509 | 1.3 |
| 2026 | 6.0 | 2114 | 6.4 |
| **3** 0236 | 1.9 | **18** 0328 | 1.6 |
| 0843 | 6.1 | 0936 | 6.5 |
| M 1459 | 2.0 | TU 1606 | 1.6 |
| 2101 | 5.7 | 2210 | 6.0 |
| **4** 0309 | 2.2 | **19** 0425 | 1.9 |
| 0921 | 5.8 | 1036 | 6.2 |
| TU 1540 | 2.3 | W 1712 | 1.9 |
| 2142 | 5.4 | ☽ 2313 | 5.7 |
| **5** 0352 | 2.6 | **20** 0535 | 2.2 |
| 1009 | 5.4 | 1144 | 5.9 |
| W 1633 | 2.6 | TH 1826 | 2.1 |
| 2237 | 5.1 | | |
| **6** 0451 | 2.8 | **21** 0025 | 5.5 |
| 1114 | 5.2 | 0650 | 2.3 |
| TH 1750 | 2.8 | F 1258 | 5.8 |
| ☾ 2351 | 4.9 | 1939 | 2.1 |
| **7** 0623 | 2.9 | **22** 0139 | 5.6 |
| 1236 | 5.2 | 0803 | 2.2 |
| F 1916 | 2.6 | SA 1408 | 5.9 |
| | | 2044 | 2.0 |
| **8** 0119 | 5.0 | **23** 0243 | 5.8 |
| 0748 | 2.7 | 0904 | 2.0 |
| SA 1355 | 5.5 | SU 1508 | 6.1 |
| 2024 | 2.3 | 2138 | 1.8 |
| **9** 0231 | 5.4 | **24** 0338 | 6.0 |
| 0850 | 2.3 | 0956 | 1.8 |
| SU 1455 | 5.9 | M 1559 | 6.2 |
| 2119 | 1.9 | 2223 | 1.7 |
| **10** 0323 | 5.9 | **25** 0424 | 6.2 |
| 0942 | 1.8 | 1040 | 1.6 |
| M 1544 | 6.3 | TU 1643 | 6.4 |
| 2207 | 1.4 | 2303 | 1.5 |
| **11** 0409 | 6.4 | **26** 0504 | 6.4 |
| 1028 | 1.4 | 1119 | 1.5 |
| TU 1630 | 6.8 | W 1722 | 6.4 |
| 2252 | 1.1 | 2339 | 1.5 |
| **12** 0453 | 6.8 | **27** 0541 | 6.5 |
| 1113 | 1.1 | 1156 | 1.5 |
| W 1715 | 7.1 | TH 1759 | 6.5 |
| 2336 | 0.8 | ● | |
| **13** 0537 | 7.1 | **28** 0013 | 1.4 |
| 1158 | 0.8 | 0616 | 6.6 |
| TH 1800 | 7.3 | F 1232 | 1.4 |
| ○ | | 1833 | 6.4 |
| **14** 0020 | 0.7 | **29** 0047 | 1.5 |
| 0620 | 7.3 | 0649 | 6.6 |
| F 1244 | 0.7 | SA 1306 | 1.5 |
| 1846 | 7.3 | 1907 | 6.4 |
| **15** 0105 | 0.7 | **30** 0119 | 1.5 |
| 0706 | 7.3 | 0723 | 6.5 |
| SA 1330 | 0.8 | SU 1339 | 1.5 |
| 1933 | 7.1 | 1940 | 6.3 |

## DECEMBER

| Time | m | Time | m |
|---|---|---|---|
| **1** 0150 | 1.6 | **16** 0232 | 1.0 |
| 0756 | 6.4 | 0837 | 7.1 |
| M 1413 | 1.7 | TU 1505 | 0.9 |
| 2013 | 6.1 | 2106 | 6.7 |
| **2** 0223 | 1.8 | **17** 0320 | 1.2 |
| 0831 | 6.2 | 0927 | 6.9 |
| TU 1448 | 1.8 | W 1556 | 1.2 |
| 2049 | 5.9 | 2155 | 6.4 |
| **3** 0258 | 2.0 | **18** 0410 | 1.5 |
| 0909 | 6.0 | 1017 | 6.5 |
| W 1528 | 2.0 | TH 1648 | 1.5 |
| 2128 | 5.7 | 2246 | 6.0 |
| **4** 0338 | 2.2 | **19** 0503 | 1.8 |
| 0952 | 5.8 | 1111 | 6.2 |
| TH 1613 | 2.2 | F 1743 | 1.9 |
| 2214 | 5.5 | ☽ 2341 | 5.7 |
| **5** 0426 | 2.4 | **20** 0601 | 2.1 |
| 1042 | 5.7 | 1209 | 5.9 |
| F 1706 | 2.3 | SA 1843 | 2.1 |
| ☽ 2309 | 5.3 | | |
| **6** 0525 | 2.5 | **21** 0044 | 5.5 |
| 1142 | 5.6 | 0705 | 2.3 |
| SA 1811 | 2.4 | SU 1314 | 5.7 |
| | | 1948 | 2.3 |
| **7** 0013 | 5.3 | **22** 0151 | 5.5 |
| 0638 | 2.5 | 0814 | 2.3 |
| SU 1249 | 5.6 | M 1420 | 5.6 |
| 1921 | 2.3 | 2053 | 2.3 |
| **8** 0125 | 5.4 | **23** 0256 | 5.6 |
| 0750 | 2.4 | 0918 | 2.3 |
| M 1358 | 5.6 | TU 1522 | 5.7 |
| 2027 | 2.0 | 2149 | 2.1 |
| **9** 0232 | 5.7 | **24** 0353 | 5.8 |
| 0856 | 2.1 | 1013 | 2.1 |
| TU 1501 | 5.9 | W 1617 | 5.8 |
| 2127 | 1.7 | 2238 | 2.0 |
| **10** 0331 | 6.1 | **25** 0442 | 6.0 |
| 0955 | 1.7 | 1059 | 1.9 |
| W 1558 | 6.4 | TH 1704 | 6.0 |
| 2223 | 1.4 | 2320 | 1.8 |
| **11** 0425 | 6.5 | **26** 0524 | 6.2 |
| 1050 | 1.3 | 1141 | 1.7 |
| TH 1653 | 6.8 | F 1745 | 6.1 |
| 2315 | 1.1 | 2358 | 1.6 |
| **12** 0517 | 6.9 | **27** 0603 | 6.4 |
| 1143 | 1.0 | 1219 | 1.6 |
| F 1745 | 7.0 | SA 1822 | 6.2 |
| ○ | | ● | |
| **13** 0006 | 0.9 | **28** 0033 | 1.5 |
| 0607 | 7.1 | 0638 | 6.5 |
| SA 1235 | 0.8 | SU 1255 | 1.5 |
| 1837 | 7.1 | 1856 | 6.3 |
| **14** 0055 | 0.8 | **29** 0107 | 1.5 |
| 0658 | 7.3 | 0712 | 6.6 |
| SU 1325 | 0.7 | M 1328 | 1.4 |
| 1927 | 7.1 | 1929 | 6.3 |
| **15** 0143 | 0.8 | **30** 0139 | 1.4 |
| 0748 | 7.2 | 0745 | 6.6 |
| M 1415 | 0.7 | TU 1402 | 1.4 |
| 2017 | 6.9 | 2002 | 6.3 |
| | | **31** 0212 | 1.5 |
| | | 0819 | 6.5 |
| | | W 1435 | 1.4 |
| | | 2035 | 6.3 |

Chart Datum: 3·71 metres below Ordnance Datum (Newlyn). HAT is 7·8 metres above Chart Datum.

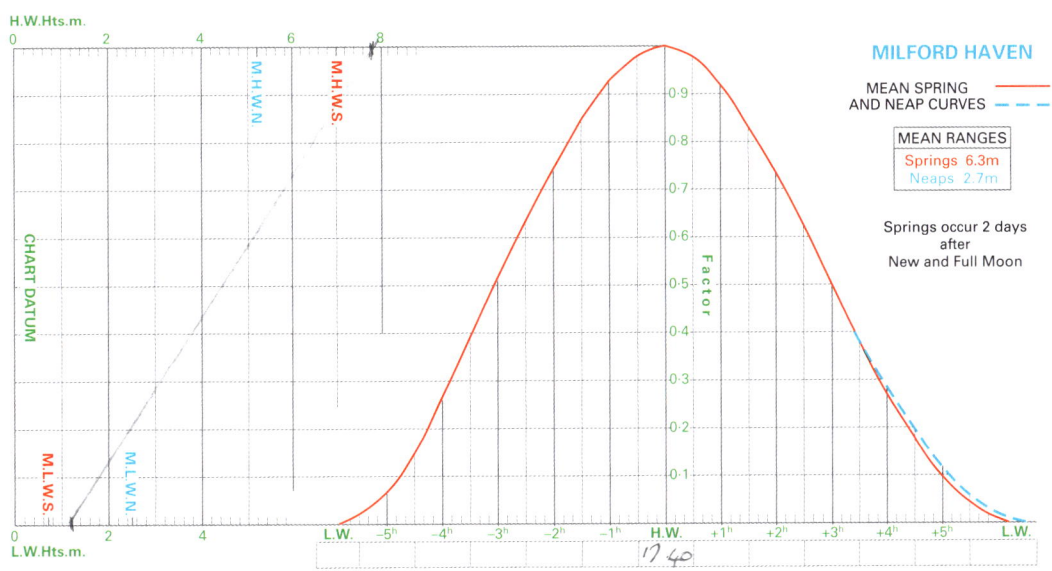

**MILFORD HAVEN**

MEAN SPRING
AND NEAP CURVES

MEAN RANGES
Springs 6.3m
Neaps 2.7m

Springs occur 2 days after
New and Full Moon

## 4.13   TENBY

Pembrokeshire  51·40'·42N 04°41'·93W

**CHARTS**  AC *5620*, *1179*, *1076*, *1482*; Imray C60; Stanfords 14; OS 158

**TIDES**  –0510 Dover; ML 4·5; Duration 0610

### Standard Port MILFORD HAVEN (◄─►)

| Times | | | | Height (metres) | | | |
|---|---|---|---|---|---|---|---|
| High Water | | Low Water | | MHWS | MHWN | MLWN | MLWS |
| 0100 | 0800 | 0100 | 0700 | 7·0 | 5·2 | 2·5 | 0·7 |
| 1300 | 2000 | 1300 | 1900 | | | | |
| **Differences TENBY** | | | | | | | |
| –0015 | –0010 | –0015 | –0020 | +1·4 | +1·1 | +0·5 | +0·2 |
| **STACKPOLE QUAY** (7M W of Caldey Island) | | | | | | | |
| –0005 | +0025 | –0010 | –0010 | +0·9 | +0·7 | +0·2 | +0·3 |

**SHELTER**  Good, but hbr dries up to 5m; access HW±2½. Sheltered ⚓s, depending on wind direction, to NE in Tenby Roads, in Lydstep Haven (2·5M SW), and around Caldey Is as follows: Priory

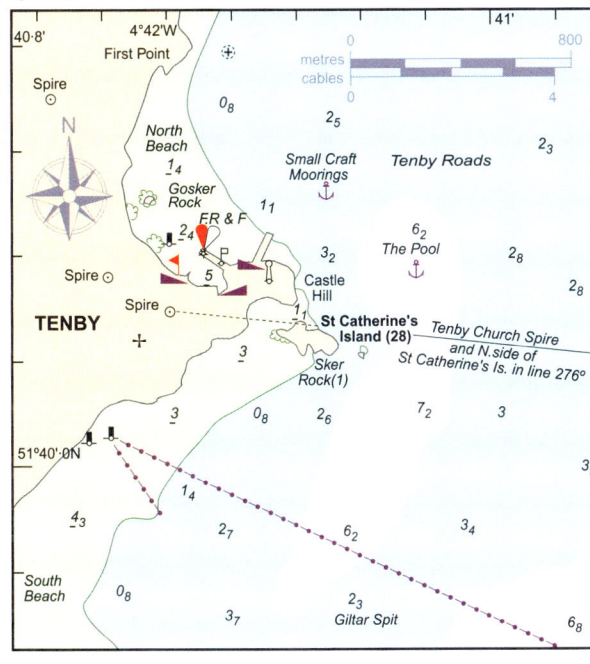

Bay to the N but shallow, Jone's Bay (NE), Drinkim Bay (E) or Sandtop Bay (W).

**NAVIGATION**  WPT 51°40'·02N 04°38'·08W, 279°/2·2M to monument on Castle Hill. The ⊕ WPT (off chartlet) is 2ca W of DZ2 SPM lit buoy. Beware Woolhouse Rks (3·6m) 1·5M SExE of the Hbr, marked by lit SCM buoy; and Sker Rk (1m high) closer in off St Catherine's Island (28m). From the W, Caldey Sound is navigable with care between Eel Pt SHM and Giltar Spit PHM lit buoys. Approaching Tenby Roads, keep outside the line of mooring buoys. For adjacent Firing ranges, see overleaf. Caldey Island is private and no landing without permission from the Abbot.

**LIGHTS AND MARKS**  See 4.3 and chartlet. Church spire transit N side of St Catherine's Is 276°.  FR 7m 7M on pier hd. Inside hbr, FW 6m 1M marks landing steps PHM beacon (unlit) marks outcrop from Gosker Rk on beach close N of hbr ent. Hbr is floodlit.

**R/T**  Ch 16, 80 (listening during HO).

**TELEPHONE** (Code 01834)  HM ☎/🖷 842717 (end May-end Sept), Mobile 07977 609947; MRCC (01646) 690909; Marinecall 09068 969649; Police (01437) 763355 ; Dr 844161; Ⓗ 842040.

**FACILITIES**  **Hbr** AB, Slip (up to 4·2m). **Town** P & D (cans), Ⓞ, CH, 🖳, R, Bar, Gas, ✉, Ⓑ, ⇌, ✈ (Swansea; and a small airfield at Haverfordwest).

**OTHER ADJACENT HARBOURS** (See AC *5620*)

**SAUNDERSFOOT**, Pembrokeshire, 51°42'·60N 04°41'·76W. AC *1179, 1076, 1482*. HW –0510 on Dover; ML 4·4m; Duration 0605. See 4.13. A half-tide hbr with good shelter, but there may be a surge in prolonged E winds. On appr, beware buoys marking restricted area (power boats, etc) between Coppett Hall Pt and Perry's Pt. AB may be available (see HM), or moorings in the middle. Pier hd lt Fl R 5s 6m 7M on stone cupola. VHF: HM 11 16. HM ☎/🖷 (01834) 812094/(Home 831389). Facilities: 6 AB, CH, FW (on SW wall), Slip, P & D (cans), ME, BH. **Town** 🖳, R, Bar, ✉, Ⓑ, ⇌ (Tenby/Saundersfoot).

**CARMARTHEN**, Carmarthenshire, 51°46'·27N 04°22'·53W. AC *1179, 1076*. HW –0455 on Dover. See 4.14. R Towy & Taf dry; access HW±2. Beware Carmarthen Bar in S winds F4 and over with strong sp streams. Nav info is available from Carmarthen Bar Navigation Committee ☎ (01267) 231250 or YC's. Appr on N'ly hdg toward Wharley Pt, leaving DZ8 & 9 buoys 5ca to stbd.  Chan shifts frequently and is unmarked so local knowledge reqd unless conditions ideal. ⚓ in mid-stream or 🖴s at R Towy YC off Ferryside (7M below Carmarthen) or R Towey Boat Club 1M N on W bank. Access for both HW±2. 4 power lines cross in last 2·5M before Carmarthen, clearance 7·4m. **R Towy YC** ☎ (01267) 238356, M, FW, Bar. **R Towy BC** ☎ (01267) 238316. **Town** Ⓑ, Bar, Gas, ✉, 🖳, ⇌, ✈ (Cardiff).

## FIRING RANGES between LINNEY HEAD and BURRY INLET

For daily info on all range firing times call *Milford Haven CG* Ch 16/67 or ☎ 01646 690909.

**Castlemartin Range** Danger Area extends 12M WNW from Linney Hd, thence in an anti-clockwise arc to a point 12M S of St Govan's Hd. The exact Danger Area operative on any one day depends on the ranges/ammunition used; it is primarily a tank range. When firing is in progress R flags are flown (Fl R lts at night) along the coast from Freshwater West to Linney Hd to St Govan's Hd. Yachts are requested to keep clear of ranges when active.

Firing takes place on weekdays 0900 –1630, exceptionally to 1700. Night firing takes place on Mon to Thurs, up to 2359, depending on the hours of darkness. In Jan only small arms are usually fired and the danger area is reduced.

Days/times of firing are published locally and can be obtained by VHF from *Castlemartin Range* Ch 16 or ☎ 01646 662367 (H24 answering service); Range safety launches Ch 16 or 12; and Milford Haven CG Ch 16. Also from the Range Office ☎ (01646) 662287 or Warren Tower 01646 662336.

**Manorbier Range** (further E) covers a sector arc radius 12M centred on Old Castle Hd; E/W extent is approx between St Govan's Hd and Caldey Is (see AC Q6402). It is usually active Mon-Fri 0900-1700LT, occas Sat/Sun, and is primarily a surface to air missile range, but active parts depend on the weapons in use on any given day. On firing days warnings are broadcast on Ch 16, 73 at 0830, 1430 and on completion; R flags are flown either side of Old Castle Hd. Yachts on passage should either stay 12M offshore or close inshore via Stackpole Hd, Trewent Pt, Priest's Nose and Old Castle Hd. Firing days/times are available from local HMs and YCs. For further info call: *Manorbier Range Control* Ch 16, 73 (also manned by Range safety launches); *Milford Haven CG* Ch 16; or Range Control ☎ (01834) 871282 ext 209, ☎ 871283.

**Penally Range** (further E at Giltar Pt) is for small arms only and seldom interferes with passage through Caldey Sound. Info ☎ (01834) 843522.

**Pendine Range** (between Tenby and Burry Inlet) is a MOD range for testing explosive devices. It is usually possible to steer the rhumb line course from Tenby to Worms Hd without interference. Info ☎ (01994) 453243. Broadcasts on VHF Ch 16, 73 at 0900 and 1400LT. Range active 0800-1615.

**Pembrey Range** (approx 5M NW of Burry Inlet) is used for bombing practice by the RAF. Info ☎ (01554) 891224.

## 4.14 BURRY INLET

Carmarthenshire **51°40'·52N 04°14'·93W** (Burry Port) ✿✿🛶🛶✿

**CHARTS** AC *5620, 5608 1179*, 1076, 1167; Imray C59, C60; Stanfords 14; OS 159

**TIDES** –0500 Dover; ML 4·7; Duration 0555

**Standard Port MILFORD HAVEN** (←)

| Times | | | | Height (metres) | | | |
|---|---|---|---|---|---|---|---|
| High Water | | Low Water | | MHWS | MHWN | MLWN | MLWS |
| 0100 | 0800 | 0100 | 0700 | 7·0 | 5·2 | 2·5 | 0·7 |
| 1300 | 2000 | 1300 | 1900 | | | | |
| **Differences BURRY PORT** | | | | | | | |
| +0003 | +0003 | +0007 | +0007 | +1·6 | +1·4 | +0·5 | +0·4 |
| **LLANELLI** | | | | | | | |
| –0003 | –0003 | +0150 | +0020 | +0·8 | +0·6 | No data | |
| **FERRYSIDE** | | | | | | | |
| 0000 | –0010 | +0220 | 0000 | –0·3 | –0·7 | –1·7 | –0·6 |
| **CARMARTHEN** | | | | | | | |
| +0010 | 0000 | Dries | | –4·4 | –4·8 | Dries | |

**SHELTER** Good in Burry Port via new lock with flapgate controlled by R/G lts. Access HW±2 over sill depth 2m. Pontoons for visitors on W side of Hbr. Sp tides run hard. Note: If bad weather precludes access, see 4.13 for ⚓s around Caldey Island, especially in W'lies. Call Hbr Office (01554 935691 mob 07817 395710). Visitors welcome but few facilities.

**NAVIGATION** WPT 51°36'·37N 04°24'·38W, 087°/3·3M to Burry Holms, thence 4·5M to Burry Port.

- Carmarthen Bar, extending from the R Towy ent SE to Burry Holms, should not be attempted in W winds >F5 nor at night.
- Best entry is close NW of Burry Holms at HW–2; thence track 018° with Worms Hd on a stern transit (198°) between Burry Holms and Limekiln Pt. When Whiteford lt ho (disused) bears about 082°, alter to approx 050° into deeper water and steer to leave the Barrel Post at least 1½ ca to port as a large sand bank has formed to E of it.
- Near apprs to hbr marked by buoyed chan (3.2m) access HW±2. Barrel Post now marks W end of new sandbank, only to be used as reference point – do not round close to. E end of this bank marked by unlit buoy PHM. Appr from here on NW'ly heading, chan marked by 5 pairs unlit buoys PHMs & SHMs beyond which 2 unlit PHMs in near appr to lock/flapgate
- Chan is liable to shift.
- Before appr, check Firing Range activity (contact HM or Pendine Range Control, see above).

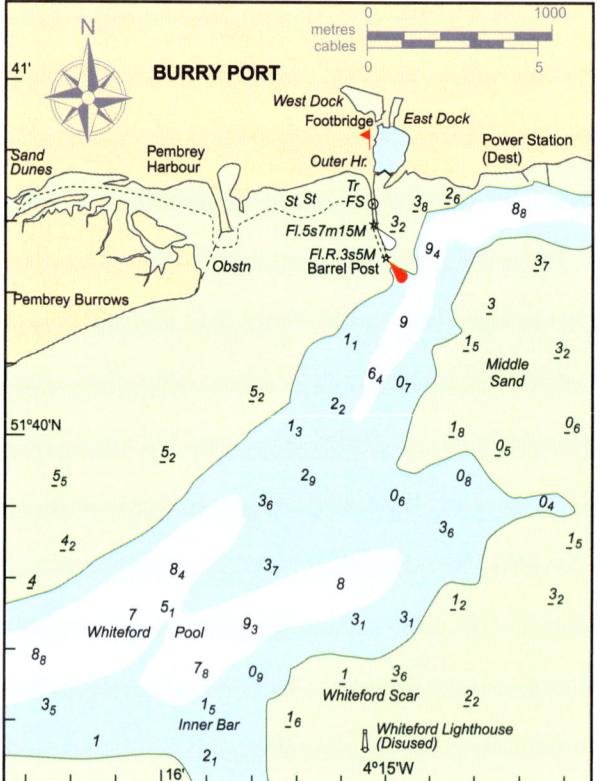

**LIGHTS AND MARKS** Whiteford lt ho is conspic, but no longer lit. On head of W bkwtr is Barrel post, Fl R 3s 5M; 1½ca N is conspic old lt ho (W tr, R top) Fl 5s 7m 15M, and flagstaff.

**R/T** Ch M (Hbr Office),16.

**TELEPHONE** (Code 01554); HM 835691, mob 07817 395710; MRCC (01792) 366534; Pendine Range (01994) 453243 Ext 240; Marinecall 09068 969649; Police 0845 3302000; Dr 832240.

**FACILITIES** Slip, M, L, CH; **E Pier** (small craft only): Slip; **Burry Port YC** Bar; **Services:** D, ME, El, ⚒, C, Gas. **Town** P, D, CH, 🛒, R, Bar, ✉, Ⓑ, ⇌, ✈ (Cardiff).

# 4.15  SWANSEA

**Swansea 51°36'·43N 03°55'·67W** ✿✿✿☆♠♠✿✿✿

**CHARTS**  AC *5608, 1179, 1165,* 1161; Imray C59; Stanfords 14; OS 159

**TIDES**  –0500 Dover; ML 5·2; Duration 0620

**Standard Port MILFORD HAVEN** (⟵)

| Times | | | | Height (metres) | | | |
|---|---|---|---|---|---|---|---|
| High Water | | Low Water | | MHWS | MHWN | MLWN | MLWS |
| 0100 | 0800 | 0100 | 0700 | 7·0 | 5·2 | 2·5 | 0·7 |
| 1300 | 2000 | 1300 | 1900 | | | | |
| **Differences SWANSEA** | | | | | | | |
| +0004 | +0006 | –0006 | –0003 | +2·6 | +2·1 | +0·7 | +0·3 |
| **MUMBLES** | | | | | | | |
| +0005 | +0010 | –0020 | –0015 | +2·3 | +1·7 | +0·6 | +0·2 |
| **PORT TALBOT** | | | | | | | |
| 0000 | +0005 | –0010 | –0005 | +2·8 | +2·2 | +1·0 | +0·4 |
| **PORTHCAWL** | | | | | | | |
| +0005 | +0010 | –0010 | –0005 | +2·9 | +2·3 | +0·8 | +0·3 |

**SHELTER**  Very good in marina.

**NAVIGATION**  WPT 51°35'·53N 03°56'·08W (SHM buoy) 020°/ 0·92M to E bkwtr lt. Keep seaward of Mixon Shoal. When N of SW Inner Green Grounds (SWIGG) SCM lt buoy keep to W of dredged chan and clear of commercial ships. *Yachts must motor in approaches and in harbour,* max speed 4kn. In Swansea Bay tidal streams flow anti-clockwise for 9½ hrs (Swansea HW –3½ to +6), with at times a race off Mumbles Hd. From HW–6 to –3 the stream reverses, setting N past Mumbles Hd towards Swansea.

**LOCKS**  Enter via R Tawe barrage lock, which operates on request HW±4½ (co-ordinated with the marina lock), 0700-2200BST; out of season, 0700-1900UT, but to 2200 at w/ends. Lock fee £2.40 per week. There are pontoons in both locks.

Yachts usually exit Tawe barrage lock at H+00, and enter at H+30. Locks are closed when ht of tide falls to 1·5m above CD, usually at MLWS. At sp, do not enter river until LW+1½. Two large Or holding buoys below barrage in mid-stream; also, at W side of barrage lock, a landing pontoon (dries, foul ground).

**LIGHTS AND MARKS**  See 4.3 and chartlet. Mumbles Hd, Fl (4) 20s35m16M, is 3M SSW of hbr ent. A conspic TV mast (R lts) NNE of hbr is almost aligned with the fairway. Ldg lts 020° mark E side of chan dredged 3m. When N of Swansea Middle West (QR) and Swansea Middle East (QG) chan buoys stay inside dredged chan. Barrage lock lit by 2FR/FG (vert) to seaward.

**Port Traffic sigs** are conspic at W side of ent to King's Dock; there are 9 lts, 🔴 or 🟢, arranged in a 3 x 3 frame. Yachts arriving must obey the middle lt in left column:

🔴  = Do not enter the river; hold SW of W Pier.

🟢  = Yachts may enter the river, keeping to mid-chan, then to W of holding buoys.

Lock Master will advise on tfc movements Ch 18.
**Lock sigs** for barrage and marina locks alike are:

🔴🔴 ] = Lock closed. Do not proceed

🔴  = Wait

🟢  = Enter with caution

🔴🟢 ] = Free flow operating; proceed with caution

**R/T**  Barrage, *Tawe Lock* Ch 18. *Swansea Marina* Ch **80**. For commercial docks call *Swansea Docks Radio* VHF Ch14 (H24).

**TELEPHONE** (Code 01792) HM 653787 🖷 650729; Barrage 456014; MRCC 366534; Police 456999; Marinecall 09068 969649; 🏥 205666; Dr 653452; DVLA (for SSR) 783355.

**FACILITIES**  Swansea Marina (350+50 Ⓥ) ☎ 470310, 🖷 463948, £1·85, D (no P), C (1 ton), BH (25 ton), ⚓, Gas, Gaz, Ice, CH, ME, ACA, SM, El, Ⓔ, ✕, ▣, ♿, Bar, R.
**Swansea Yacht & Sub Aqua Club (SY & SAC)** ☎ 654863, No visitors, M, L, FW, C (5 ton static), R, Bar. **City** 🛒, R, Bar, ✉, Ⓑ, ⇌, ✈.

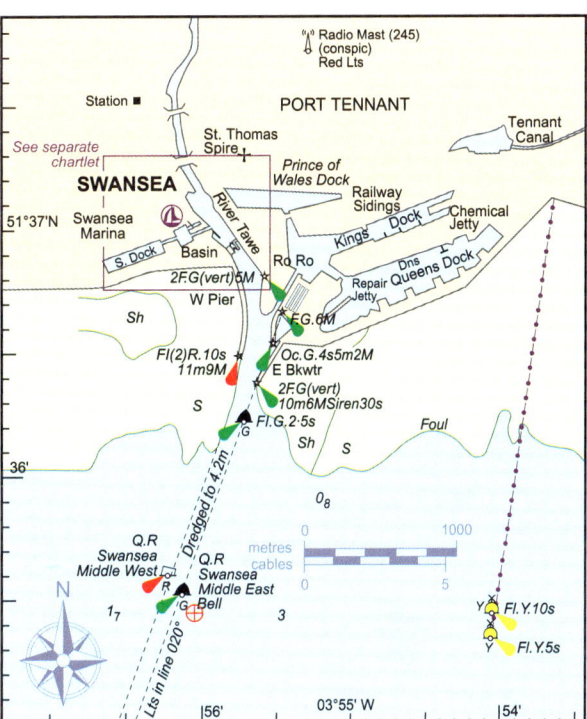

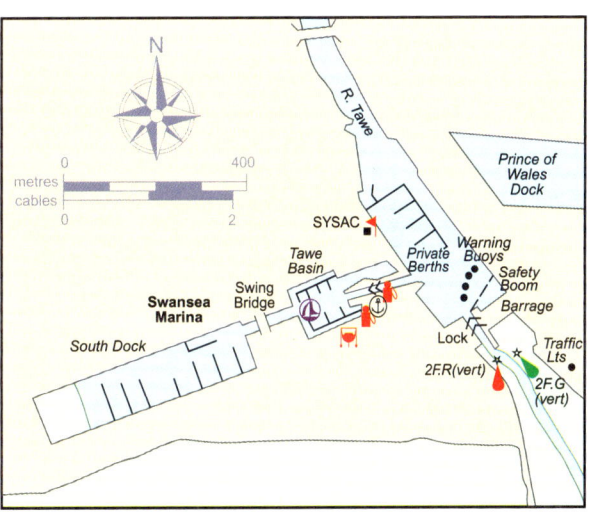

## ADJACENT HARBOURS AND ANCHORAGES

**Mumbles, 51°34'·2N 03°58'·2W.** Good ⚓ in W'lies 5ca N of Mumbles Hd lt ho. **Bristol Chan YC** ☎ (01792) 366000, Slip, M; **Mumbles YC** ☎ 369321, Slip, M, L, FW, C (hire).

**R Neath, 51°37'·88N 03°49'·97W.** Ent over bar HW±2½ via 1·5M chan, marked/lit training wall to stbd. Tfc info from *Neath Pilot* VHF Ch 77, if on stn. **Monkstone Marina,** W bank just S of bridge, dries 4m: AB, 2 Y ⚓s, D, FW, Slip, BH (15 ton), R, Bar, Visitors welcome. **Monkstone C & SC,** ☎ (01792) 812229; VHF Ch M (occas).

**PORTHCAWL, Bridgend, 51°28'·48N 03°42'·02W.** AC *1165,* 1169. HW –0500 on Dover; ML 5·3m. See 4.15. A tiny drying hbr (access HW±2) protected by bkwtr running SE from Porthcawl Pt. Beware rk ledge (dries) W of bkwtr. Porthcawl lt ho, F WRG (see 4.3) in line 094° with St Hilary radio mast (QR & FR) leads through Shord chan. Tidal streams can reach 6kn at sp off end of bkwtr. 3 ⚓s or ⚓ approx 3ca SSE of lt ho. HM ☎ (01656) 782756. Facilities: **Porthcawl Hbr B C** ☎ 782342. **Town** P & D (cans), CH, 🛒, R, Bar, ✉, Ⓑ, ⇌ (Bridgend), ✈ (Cardiff).

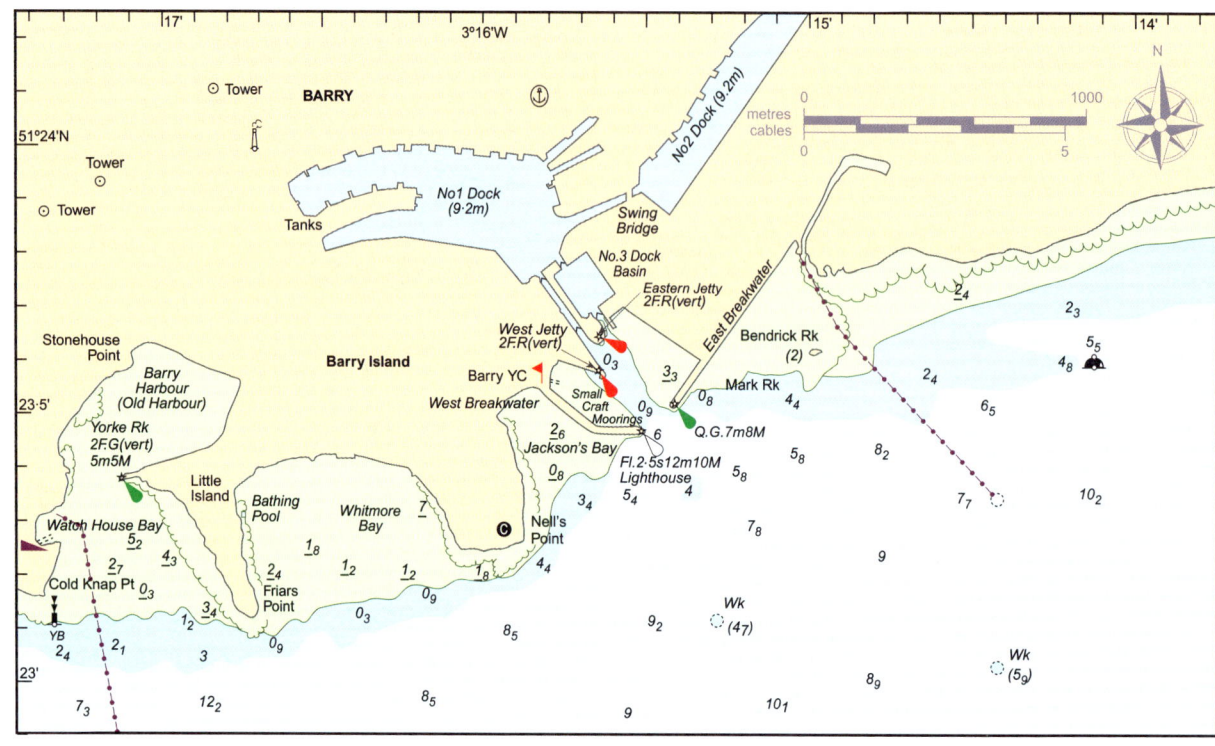

## 4.16 BARRY

Vale of Glamorgan **51°23'·48N 03°15'·45W** ❀❀❀✿✿✿

**CHARTS** AC *5608, 1179, 1152, 1182;* Imray C59; Stanfords 14; OS 171

**TIDES** –0423 Dover; ML 6·1; Duration 0630

**Standard Port BRISTOL (AVONMOUTH) (→)**

| Times | | | | Height (metres) | | | |
|---|---|---|---|---|---|---|---|
| High Water | | Low Water | | MHWS | MHWN | MLWN | MLWS |
| 0600 | 1100 | 0300 | 0800 | 13·2 | 9·8 | 3·8 | 1·0 |
| 1800 | 2300 | 1500 | 2000 | | | | |
| **Differences BARRY** | | | | | | | |
| –0025 | –0025 | –0130 | –0045 | –1·6 | –1·0 | –0·2 | 0·0 |
| **FLAT HOLM** | | | | | | | |
| –0015 | –0015 | –0035 | –0035 | –1·4 | –1·0 | –0·5 | 0·0 |
| **STEEP HOLM** | | | | | | | |
| –0020 | –0020 | –0040 | –0040 | –1·7 | –1·1 | –0·5 | –0·4 |

**SHELTER** Good, but in strong E/SE winds avoid Barry; No 1 Dock is not available for pleasure craft. Access H24 to the Outer hbr. No AB; pick up a mooring (free) and see YC.

**NAVIGATION** WPT 51°23'·03N 03°15'·08W, 332°/0·53M to ent. Beware heavy commercial traffic. Approaching from E keep well out from the shore. Strong tidal stream across ent.

**LIGHTS AND MARKS** Welsh Water Barry West PHM buoy, Fl R 5s, and Merkur PHM buoy, Fl R 2·5s, lie respectively 217°/1·5M and 191°/1·65M from hbr ent. W bkwtr Fl 2·5s 10M. E bkwtr QG 8M.

**R/T** *Barry Radio* VHF Ch **11** 10 16 (HW–4 to HW+3); tidal info on request. *Bristol Pilot* via Ch 16 may advise on vacant moorings.

**TELEPHONE** HM 0870 609 6699 ▥ 029 2083 5001; MRCC (01792) 366534; Marinecall 09068 969649; Police 01446 734451; Dr 01446 739543.

**FACILITIES Barry YC** (130) ☎ 735511, access HW±3½, Slip, M, Bar, FW, D, Gas, ME, El, ✕, SM.
**Town** P (cans, 1M away), CH, 🛒, R, Bar, ✉, Ⓑ, ⇄, ✈ (Cardiff).

## 4.17 CARDIFF (PENARTH)

Vale of Glamorgan **51°26'·74N 03°09'·92W** (marina) ❀❀✿✿✿✿

**CHARTS** AC *5608, 1179, 1176, 1182;* Imray C59; Stanfords 14; OS 171

**TIDES** –0425 Dover; ML 6·4; Duration 0610

**Standard Port BRISTOL (AVONMOUTH) (→)**

| Times | | | | Height (metres) | | | |
|---|---|---|---|---|---|---|---|
| High Water | | Low Water | | MHWS | MHWN | MLWN | MLWS |
| 0600 | 1100 | 0300 | 0800 | 13·2 | 9·8 | 3·8 | 1·0 |
| 1800 | 2300 | 1500 | 2000 | | | | |
| **Differences CARDIFF** | | | | | | | |
| –0015 | –0015 | –0100 | –0030 | –1·0 | –0·5 | 0·0 | 0·0 |
| **NEWPORT** | | | | | | | |
| –0020 | –0010 | 0000 | –0020 | –1·1 | –0·9 | –0·6 | –0·6 |
| **CHEPSTOW (River Wye)** | | | | | | | |
| +0020 | +0020 | No data | | No data | | No data | |

NOTE: At Newport the ht of LW does not normally fall below MLWS. Tidal hts are based on a minimum river flow; max flow may raise ht of LW by as much as 0·3m.

**SHELTER** Very good in marina. See above for barrage locks. Waiting trot berths in outer hbr; or ⚓ off Penarth seafront in W'lies; in E'lies cramped ⚓ off Alexandra Dock ent in 2m.

**NAVIGATION** WPT 51°24'·03N 03°08'·81W (2½ca SW of S Cardiff SCM lt buoy), 349°/2·9M to barrage locks.

The outer approaches from W or SW are via Breaksea lt float and N of One Fathom Bk. Keep S of Lavernock Spit SCM lt buoy and NW of Flat Holm and Wolves NCM lt buoy drying rk. From NE, drying ledges and shoals extend >1M offshore. From E, appr via Monkstone Lt ho and S Cardiff SCM buoy. Ranny Spit (dries 0·4m) is 3½ca to the W, and Cardiff Grounds (dries 5·4m) 3½ca to the E.

The Wrach Chan is buoyed/lit and dredged 1·2m; it passes 1½ca E of Penarth Hd. The locks appr chan, buoyed, is dredged 0·7m below CD.

*Do not impede merchant ships, especially those entering/leaving Alexandra Dock.*

**WGS84 DATUM**

## Cardiff Bay Barrage and Marina lock

- Call *Barrage Control* VHF Ch 18 or ☎ 02920 700234 to request lock-in or lock-out. Waiting berth on a barge in outer hbr.
- If entering near LW ask Barrage Control for up-to-date depths.
- Subject to VHF instructions, enter the outer hbr (Wpt 51°26'·71N 03°09'·84W) and lock in.
- IPTS (sigs 1, 2, 3, 5) are shown at lock ent.
- Departures at H and H +30. Arrivals at H +15 and H +45.
- Lock into marina operates H24 on free-flow from the bay.

**LIGHTS AND MARKS** Directional light, Oc WRG 10s 5m3M, on a W metal post marks Wrach Channel.

**R/T** Port VHF Ch **14** 16 (HW−4 to HW+3). *Barrage Control* Ch 18 H24. Penarth Quays marina Ch 80 H24.

**TELEPHONE** (Code 02920) HM 400500; 🖷 471071 Barrage control 700234; MRCC (01792) 366534; Marinecall 09068 969649; Weather Centre 397020; Police (01446) 734451; Dr 415258; Cardiff Bay Authority 877900.

**FACILITIES** **Penarth Quay Marina** ☎ 705021 H24, 🖷 712170, www.quaymarinas.com 350+ Ⓥ welcome, £2, max draft 3m; Wi-fi, D&P (0930-1630, E pontoon), El, ME, ⚒, CH, BY, BH (20 ton), SM, C (20 ton), ACA, Ⓔ, Gas, LPG, Ⓞ, R.

**Penarth YC** ☎ 708196, Slip, FW, Bar.

**Cardiff YC** ☎ 463697, Slip, M, FW, L (floating pontoon), Bar.

**Cardiff Bay YC** ☎ 226575, M, L, C, FW, Slip, Bar.

**City** 🛒, R, Bar, ✉, Ⓑ, ⇌, ✈ (15 mins).

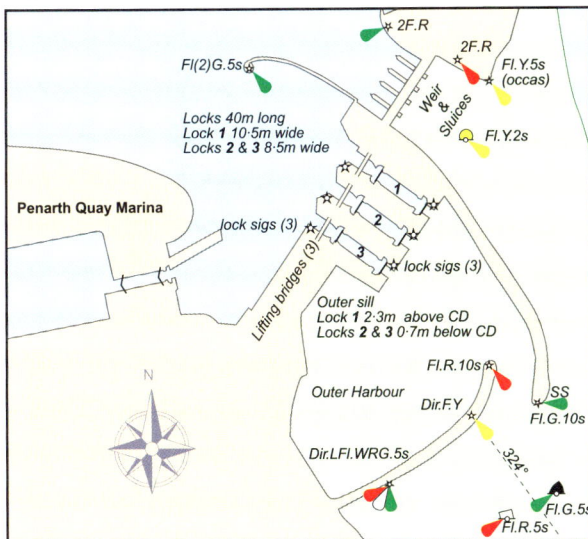

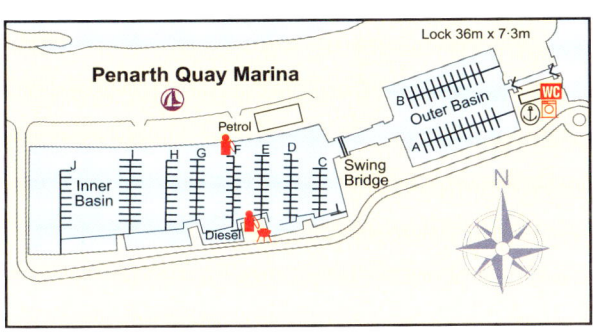

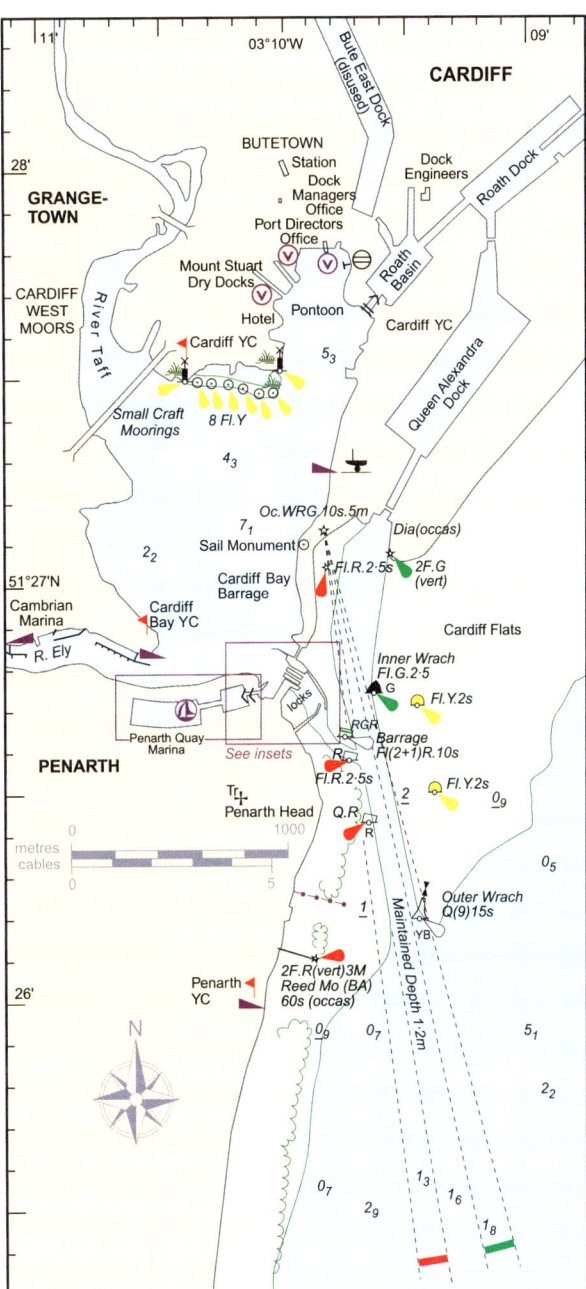

## ADJACENT HARBOUR

**NEWPORT**, Newport, **51°32'·95N 02°59'·13W**. AC *5608, 1179, 1152, 1176*. HW −0425 on Dover; ML 6·0m; Duration 0620. See 4.17. A commercial port controlled by ABP, but a safe shelter for yachts. Enter R Usk over bar (approx 0·5m) E of West Usk buoy, QR Bell) and follow buoyed and lit chan to S Lock ent; turn NE (ldg lts 062°) for yacht moorings on S side between power stn pier and YC. Beware overhead cables in Julian's Pill, clearance 3·8m.

Lights, see 4.3. East Usk lt ho Fl (2) WRG 10s. Ldg lts 062°, both FG. Alexandra Dock, S lock W pier head 2 FR (vert) 9/7m 6M. E pier head 2 FG (vert) 9/7m 6M.

Port VHF, *Newport Radio*, and VTS: Ch 09, **71**, 74 (HW ±4). HM (ABP) ☎ 0870 609 6699, 🖷 01633 221 285. Facilities: CH, El, ME, ⚒, Ⓔ. **Newport and Uskmouth SC** Bar, M. **Town** all facilities.

**THE SEVERN BRIDGES** The Second Severn Crossing (37m clearance), from 51°34'·88N 02°43'·80W to 51°34'·14N 02°39'·82W, is 4M upriver from Avonmouth and 3M below the Severn Bridge. The following brief directions, coupled with strong tidal streams and shifting banks, emphasise the need for local knowledge together with AC 1166.

Going upriver, pass both bridges at about HW Avonmouth −1¾ (see also 4.18); max sp stream is 8kn at The Shoots and 6kn at the Severn Bridge, setting across the channel when the banks are covered.

Redcliffe F Bu ldg lts in transit with Charston Rock lt lead 013° through The Shoots, a narrow passage between English Stones (6·2m) and the rocky ledges (5·1m) off the Welsh shore. 5ca S of the Second Crossing, the chan is marked by Lower Shoots WCM bcn and Mixoms PHM bcn.

No vessel may navigate between the shore and the nearer Tower of the 2nd Crossing, except in emergency.

4ca N of the 2nd Crossing, leave the 013° transit before passing Old Man's Hd WCM bcn and Lady Bench PHM bcn. From abeam Charston Rk, keep Chapel Rk, Fl WRG 2·6s, brg 050° until the E twr of Severn Bridge bears 068°; maintain this brg until Lyde Rk, QWR, bears about 355°, when alter 010° to transit the bridge (36·6m cl'nce) close to rks drying 1m.

**Radar Warning.** In certain conditions and tidal states, radar displays may show misleading echoes in the vicinity of the 2nd Severn Crossing. *Racon (O)* is at centre span of second crossing.

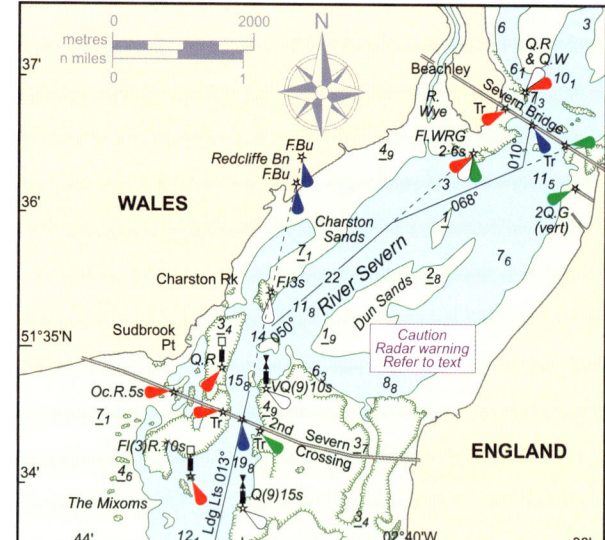

# 4.18  SHARPNESS

Gloucestershire 51°43'·03N 02°29'·08W ✿⊕◊◊✿✿

**CHARTS** AC *5608, 1166*, Imray C59; Stanfords 14; OS 162

**TIDES** −0315 Dover; Duration 0415. Note: The tidal regime is irregular and deviates from Avonmouth curve.

**Standard Port BRISTOL (AVONMOUTH) (⟶)**

| Times | | | | Height (metres) | | | |
|---|---|---|---|---|---|---|---|
| High Water | | Low Water | | MHWS | MHWN | MLWN | MLWS |
| 0000 | 0600 | 0000 | 0700 | 13·2 | 9·8 | 3·8 | 1·0 |
| 1200 | 1800 | 1200 | 1900 | | | | |
| Differences SUDBROOK (Second Severn Crossing) | | | | | | | |
| +0010 | +0010 | +0025 | +0015 | +0·2 | +0·1 | −0·1 | +0·1 |
| BEACHLEY/AUST (Severn Bridge) | | | | | | | |
| +0010 | | +0015 | +0040 | +0025 | −0·2 | −0·2 | −0·5 |
| −0·3 | | | | | | | |
| INWARD ROCKS (River Severn) | | | | | | | |
| +0020 | +0020 | +0105 | +0045 | −1·0 | −1·1 | −1·4 | −0·6 |
| NARLWOOD ROCKS | | | | | | | |
| +0025 | +0025 | +0120 | +0100 | −1·9 | −2·0 | −2·3 | −0·8 |
| WHITE HOUSE | | | | | | | |
| +0025 | +0025 | +0145 | +0120 | −3·0 | −3·1 | −3·6 | −1·0 |
| BERKELEY | | | | | | | |
| +0030 | +0045 | +0245 | +0220 | −3·8 | −3·9 | −3·4 | −0·5 |
| SHARPNESS DOCK | | | | | | | |
| +0035 | +0050 | +0305 | +0245 | −3·9 | −4·2 | −3·3 | −0·4 |
| WELLHOUSE ROCK | | | | | | | |
| +0040 | +0055 | +0320 | +0305 | −4·1 | −4·4 | −3·1 | −0·2 |

**SHELTER** Very good. The sea lock into the commercial dock is generally open HW-2 to HW but this depends on commercial shipping movements. The advice is plan your passage to arrive no sooner than HW-1 and no later than HW. For more detailed information on lock fees, canal licences and the passage from Avonmouth contact the HM at Sharpness on 01453 811862. The fog signal on Sharpness Point is available on request to Sharpness Radio on VHF channel 13 or 01453 511968.

**NAVIGATION** WPT 51°42'·83N 02°29'·28W, 028°/2ca to ent.
- Use transits shown on AC 1166. Request pilot notes from Sharpness HM in good time.
- Leave King Road, Avonmouth (17M downriver) not before HW Sharpness −3, to be off Hbr ent about HW −½. Stem strong flood S of F Bu lt; beware tidal eddy.
- Do not proceed above the Severn Bridge except HW±2. There is a 5H flood and a 7H ebb.

**LIGHTS AND MARKS** Lights as chartlet, but night passage not advised without local knowledge/pilot (07774 226143).

**R/T** Call *Sharpness Radio* VHF Ch 13 (HW −6 to +1) for lock. Gloucester and Sharpness Canal Ch 74 for bridges (no locks). Call *Bristol VTS* VHF Ch 12 when passing reporting points inwards/outwards: E/W Grounds PHM, Welsh Hook SCM and at Lower Shoots Bcn.

**TELEPHONE** (Code 01453) Pierhead 511968 (HW−5 to HW+1); HM 811862/64 (HO), 📠 811863; Police (01452) 521201; Ⓗ 810777.

**FACILITIES** Sharpness Marine ☎ 811476. 170 inc 2 🅥, £8 all LOA. El, D, ✕, CH, Gas, ME, C. **Town** D (above Fretherne Bridge), 🛒, R, Bar, ✉, Ⓑ (Berkeley), ⇌ (Stonehouse), ✈ (Bristol). Gloucester: D, ACA.

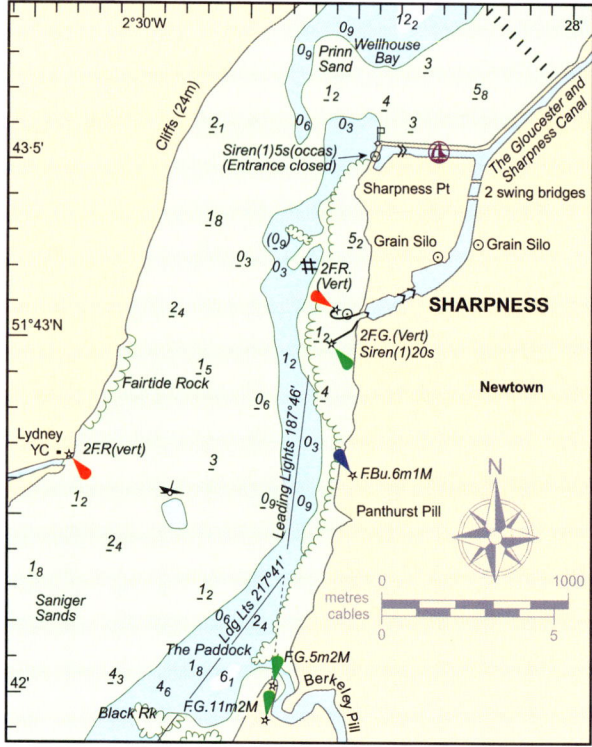

**TIME ZONE (UT)**
For Summer Time add ONE hour in **non-shaded areas**

# BRISTOL (AVONMOUTH)  LAT 51°30'N  LONG 2°44'W
## TIMES AND HEIGHTS OF HIGH AND LOW WATERS

Dates in red are SPRINGS
Dates in blue are NEAPS

YEAR **2008**

## JANUARY

| Day | Time m | Day | Time m |
|---|---|---|---|
| **1** TU | 0022 10.4 / 0634 3.3 / 1250 10.4 / 1902 3.4 | **16** W | 0615 2.7 / 1224 11.3 / 1847 2.8 |
| **2** W | 0116 10.0 / 0726 3.6 / 1352 10.1 / 1957 3.8 | **17** TH | 0050 10.9 / 0706 3.3 / 1330 10.7 / 1947 3.4 |
| **3** TH | 0226 9.8 / 0831 3.9 / 1501 10.0 / 2107 3.8 | **18** F | 0202 10.4 / 0823 3.8 / 1454 10.4 / 2127 3.7 |
| **4** F | 0337 10.0 / 0946 3.7 / 1605 10.3 / 2225 3.5 | **19** SA | 0334 10.4 / 1019 3.9 / 1619 10.7 / 2259 3.3 |
| **5** SA | 0437 10.6 / 1057 3.2 / 1701 10.8 / 2330 3.0 | **20** SU | 0452 11.0 / 1138 3.0 / 1729 11.4 |
| **6** SU | 0528 11.2 / 1155 2.6 / 1751 11.3 | **21** M | 0006 2.5 / 0554 11.9 / 1241 2.2 / 1826 12.2 |
| **7** M | 0023 2.5 / 0614 11.7 / 1246 2.2 / 1836 11.7 | **22** TU | 0106 1.9 / 0647 12.6 / 1338 1.6 / 1918 12.8 |
| **8** TU ● | 0112 2.2 / 0657 12.1 / 1335 2.1 / 1919 12.0 | **23** W | 0200 1.4 / 0736 13.2 / 1431 1.2 / 2005 13.1 |
| **9** W | 0158 2.1 / 0738 12.3 / 1422 2.0 / 2001 12.1 | **24** TH | 0249 1.1 / 0821 13.5 / 1518 1.0 / 2049 13.2 |
| **10** TH | 0242 2.1 / 0818 12.4 / 1506 2.0 / 2040 12.2 | **25** F | 0332 1.0 / 0903 13.4 / 1557 1.1 / 2128 13.1 |
| **11** F | 0320 2.2 / 0856 12.5 / 1544 2.0 / 2117 12.3 | **26** SA | 0407 1.2 / 0940 13.2 / 1628 1.5 / 2201 12.7 |
| **12** SA | 0353 2.2 / 0932 12.5 / 1617 2.0 / 2154 12.3 | **27** SU | 0433 1.6 / 1012 12.7 / 1649 1.9 / 2230 12.2 |
| **13** SU | 0423 2.1 / 1010 12.5 / 1648 2.0 / 2230 12.2 | **28** M | 0453 1.9 / 1041 12.2 / 1708 2.2 / 2257 11.6 |
| **14** M | 0455 2.1 / 1049 12.3 / 1722 2.1 / 2310 11.9 | **29** TU | 0516 2.3 / 1111 11.5 / 1733 2.5 / 2327 11.0 |
| **15** TU ◑ | 0532 2.3 / 1133 11.9 / 1801 2.4 / 2355 11.5 | **30** W ○ | 0546 2.7 / 1145 10.8 / 1806 3.0 |
| | | **31** TH | 0005 10.3 / 0626 3.3 / 1231 10.0 / 1850 3.6 |

## FEBRUARY

| Day | Time m | Day | Time m |
|---|---|---|---|
| **1** F | 0059 9.6 / 0725 3.9 / 1340 9.4 / 1958 4.2 | **16** SA | 0127 9.9 / 0738 4.1 / 1435 9.7 / 2059 4.3 |
| **2** SA | 0227 9.3 / 0847 4.2 / 1513 9.4 / 2128 4.2 | **17** SU | 0320 9.7 / 1013 4.1 / 1614 10.1 / 2250 3.7 |
| **3** SU | 0357 9.7 / 1013 3.8 / 1631 10.0 / 2253 3.6 | **18** M | 0446 10.6 / 1132 3.1 / 1724 11.1 / 2357 2.6 |
| **4** M | 0502 10.6 / 1126 3.1 / 1730 10.8 / 2358 2.8 | **19** TU | 0548 11.7 / 1231 2.1 / 1820 12.1 |
| **5** TU | 0554 11.4 / 1225 2.4 / 1819 11.6 | **20** W | 0053 1.7 / 0638 12.7 / 1325 1.3 / 1906 12.9 |
| **6** W | 0054 2.3 / 0639 12.1 / 1320 2.0 / 1903 12.1 | **21** TH ○ | 0145 1.0 / 0723 13.3 / 1414 0.8 / 1949 13.3 |
| **7** TH | 0146 2.0 / 0722 12.6 / 1412 1.7 / 1945 12.5 | **22** F | 0231 0.7 / 0804 13.6 / 1458 0.6 / 2028 13.4 |
| **8** F | 0234 1.8 / 0802 12.9 / 1458 1.6 / 2025 12.8 | **23** SA | 0312 0.6 / 0841 13.6 / 1535 0.8 / 2102 13.3 |
| **9** SA ● | 0316 1.7 / 0841 13.1 / 1538 1.5 / 2102 13.0 | **24** SU | 0346 0.9 / 0913 13.3 / 1603 1.3 / 2131 12.9 |
| **10** SU | 0350 1.6 / 0917 13.2 / 1610 1.6 / 2137 13.0 | **25** M | 0409 1.4 / 0941 12.8 / 1619 1.7 / 2155 12.4 |
| **11** M | 0416 1.6 / 0953 13.2 / 1635 1.5 / 2211 12.9 | **26** TU | 0423 1.7 / 1005 12.3 / 1631 2.0 / 2218 11.9 |
| **12** TU | 0441 1.7 / 1030 12.9 / 1701 1.7 / 2248 12.5 | **27** W | 0440 2.0 / 1030 11.7 / 1650 2.2 / 2243 11.3 |
| **13** W | 0510 1.9 / 1109 12.3 / 1732 2.1 / 2328 11.8 | **28** TH | 0504 2.3 / 1057 11.0 / 1717 2.7 / 2313 10.6 |
| **14** TH ◑ | 0545 2.4 / 1155 11.3 / 1811 2.8 | **29** F ◑ | 0537 3.0 / 1132 10.1 / 1753 3.4 / 2355 9.8 |
| **15** F ○ | 0016 10.8 / 0630 3.3 / 1256 10.3 / 1904 3.7 | | |

## MARCH

| Day | Time m | Day | Time m |
|---|---|---|---|
| **1** SA | 0624 3.8 / 1227 9.3 / 1851 4.2 | **16** SU | 0114 9.6 / 0726 4.4 / 1436 9.4 / 2106 4.5 |
| **2** SU | 0109 9.0 / 0752 4.4 / 1416 8.9 / 2037 4.6 | **17** M | 0316 9.6 / 1009 4.0 / 1605 10.0 / 2237 3.5 |
| **3** M | 0317 9.2 / 0935 4.2 / 1601 9.5 / 2221 4.0 | **18** TU | 0433 10.6 / 1116 2.8 / 1709 11.1 / 2337 2.4 |
| **4** TU | 0434 10.2 / 1101 3.3 / 1705 10.6 / 2337 3.1 | **19** W | 0531 11.7 / 1210 1.8 / 1800 12.2 |
| **5** W | 0529 11.3 / 1205 2.4 / 1756 11.6 | **20** TH | 0029 1.5 / 0618 12.7 / 1259 1.1 / 1843 12.9 |
| **6** TH | 0034 2.3 / 0616 12.2 / 1301 1.8 / 1840 12.4 | **21** F ○ | 0118 0.9 / 0700 13.3 / 1345 0.7 / 1923 13.3 |
| **7** F | 0127 1.8 / 0659 12.9 / 1352 1.4 / 1922 12.9 | **22** SA | 0202 0.6 / 0738 13.5 / 1427 0.7 / 1959 13.3 |
| **8** SA ● | 0215 1.5 / 0739 13.3 / 1438 1.2 / 2002 13.3 | **23** SU | 0243 0.7 / 0813 13.3 / 1504 0.9 / 2030 13.1 |
| **9** SU | 0257 1.2 / 0819 13.6 / 1518 1.0 / 2039 13.5 | **24** M | 0316 1.0 / 0843 13.0 / 1531 1.4 / 2057 12.7 |
| **10** M | 0332 1.2 / 0856 13.7 / 1550 1.1 / 2115 13.5 | **25** TU | 0339 1.4 / 0909 12.6 / 1547 1.8 / 2121 12.3 |
| **11** TU | 0400 1.2 / 0933 13.5 / 1615 1.3 / 2150 13.2 | **26** W | 0352 1.8 / 0932 12.1 / 1556 2.0 / 2143 11.9 |
| **12** W | 0424 1.4 / 1001 13.0 / 1639 1.6 / 2226 12.6 | **27** TH | 0407 1.9 / 0955 11.6 / 1614 2.1 / 2206 11.4 |
| **13** TH | 0450 1.8 / 1049 12.2 / 1707 2.1 / 2305 11.7 | **28** F | 0431 2.2 / 1021 11.0 / 1640 2.5 / 2236 10.8 |
| **14** F ◑ | 0523 2.5 / 1134 11.1 / 1745 3.0 / 2353 10.6 | **29** SA ◑ | 0502 2.7 / 1057 10.3 / 1714 3.1 / 2317 10.0 |
| **15** SA | 0607 3.5 / 1238 9.9 / 1840 4.0 | **30** SU | 0544 3.5 / 1149 9.5 / 1804 4.0 |
| | | **31** M | 0022 9.2 / 0658 4.3 / 1317 8.9 / 1939 4.6 |

## APRIL

| Day | Time m | Day | Time m |
|---|---|---|---|
| **1** TU | 0224 9.1 / 0854 4.2 / 1520 9.4 / 2139 4.1 | **16** W | 0404 10.8 / 1043 2.7 / 1638 11.1 / 2305 2.4 |
| **2** W | 0356 10.0 / 1024 3.4 / 1631 10.5 / 2302 3.2 | **17** TH | 0459 11.7 / 1135 1.9 / 1728 12.0 / 2355 1.6 |
| **3** TH | 0455 11.2 / 1133 2.5 / 1724 11.6 | **18** F | 0547 12.4 / 1223 1.3 / 1812 12.6 |
| **4** F | 0002 2.4 / 0544 12.2 / 1230 1.8 / 1810 12.5 | **19** SA | 0042 1.1 / 0628 12.8 / 1309 1.1 / 1850 12.9 |
| **5** SA | 0056 1.7 / 0629 13.0 / 1321 1.3 / 1853 13.2 | **20** SU ○ | 0127 1.0 / 0706 12.9 / 1351 1.1 / 1925 12.9 |
| **6** SU ● | 0144 1.3 / 0711 13.5 / 1408 1.0 / 1933 13.6 | **21** M | 0207 1.0 / 0740 12.8 / 1428 1.3 / 1957 12.7 |
| **7** M | 0228 1.0 / 0753 13.8 / 1449 0.8 / 2013 13.7 | **22** TU | 0242 1.3 / 0811 12.5 / 1457 1.7 / 2025 12.4 |
| **8** TU | 0307 0.9 / 0834 13.8 / 1524 0.9 / 2052 13.6 | **23** W | 0308 1.7 / 0839 12.1 / 1516 2.0 / 2051 12.1 |
| **9** W | 0340 1.0 / 0915 13.5 / 1554 1.2 / 2131 13.3 | **24** TH | 0326 1.9 / 0905 11.8 / 1530 2.1 / 2116 11.7 |
| **10** TH | 0409 1.3 / 0955 12.9 / 1622 1.6 / 2210 12.6 | **25** F | 0344 2.1 / 0931 11.4 / 1550 2.2 / 2142 11.3 |
| **11** F | 0439 1.9 / 1037 11.9 / 1653 2.3 / 2253 11.6 | **26** SA | 0410 2.3 / 1001 11.0 / 1618 2.5 / 2215 10.9 |
| **12** SA ◐ | 0514 2.6 / 1127 10.8 / 1734 3.2 / 2347 10.5 | **27** SU | 0443 2.6 / 1039 10.5 / 1655 2.9 / 2259 10.3 |
| **13** SU | 0606 3.6 / 1240 9.8 / 1838 4.1 | **28** M ◐ | 0527 3.2 / 1131 9.9 / 1744 3.6 |
| **14** M | 0122 9.7 / 0752 4.2 / 1424 9.6 / 2050 4.2 | **29** TU | 0000 9.8 / 0633 3.7 / 1245 9.5 / 1901 4.1 |
| **15** TU | 0257 10.0 / 0941 3.6 / 1538 10.2 / 2207 3.3 | **30** W | 0128 9.6 / 0807 3.8 / 1419 9.7 / 2045 3.9 |

Chart Datum: 6·50 metres below Ordnance Datum (Newlyn). HAT is 14·7 metres above Chart Datum.

**Bristol Channel**

》》 **FREE** monthly updates from 《《
www.reedsalmanac.co.uk

**TIME ZONE (UT)**
For Summer Time add ONE hour in **non-shaded areas**

# BRISTOL (AVONMOUTH)  LAT 51°30'N  LONG 2°44'W
TIMES AND HEIGHTS OF HIGH AND LOW WATERS

Dates in red are SPRINGS
Dates in blue are NEAPS

YEAR 200●

## MAY

| Time m | Time m |
|---|---|
| **1** 0302 10.2 / 0932 3.2 / TH 1542 10.5 / 2210 3.2 | **16** 0418 11.3 / 1050 2.4 / F 1647 11.4 / 2313 2.2 |
| **2** 0410 11.1 / 1047 2.6 / F 1643 11.5 / 2319 2.5 | **17** 0507 11.7 / 1141 2.0 / SA 1733 11.9 |
| **3** 0506 12.0 / 1149 1.9 / SA 1735 12.4 | **18** 0002 1.8 / 0551 12.0 / SU 1228 1.8 / 1814 12.2 |
| **4** 0016 1.8 / 0556 12.8 / SU 1245 1.4 / 1821 13.1 | **19** 0048 1.6 / 0631 12.1 / M 1311 1.7 / 1851 12.3 |
| **5** 0109 1.4 / 0643 13.3 / M 1334 1.1 / 1906 13.5 | **20** 0130 1.6 / 0708 12.1 / TU 1351 1.5 / 1926 12.2 |
| **6** 0157 1.0 / 0729 13.6 / TU 1420 0.9 / 1950 13.7 | **21** 0208 1.7 / 0743 12.0 / W 1425 1.9 / 1959 12.1 |
| **7** 0242 0.9 / 0815 13.5 / W 1502 1.0 / 2034 13.5 | **22** 0241 1.9 / 0817 11.8 / TH 1453 2.1 / 2031 11.9 |
| **8** 0323 1.0 / 0900 13.2 / TH 1539 1.2 / 2117 13.1 | **23** 0309 2.1 / 0849 11.5 / F 1515 2.3 / 2101 11.6 |
| **9** 0401 1.4 / 0946 12.7 / F 1615 1.7 / 2202 12.5 | **24** 0334 2.2 / 0920 11.3 / SA 1540 2.4 / 2132 11.4 |
| **10** 0439 1.9 / 1033 11.9 / SA 1652 2.3 / 2250 11.7 | **25** 0403 2.4 / 0954 11.1 / SU 1611 2.5 / 2208 11.1 |
| **11** 0521 2.5 / 1126 11.0 / SU 1737 3.0 / 2347 10.8 | **26** 0439 2.5 / 1034 10.9 / M 1650 2.7 / 2251 10.8 |
| **12** 0615 3.2 / 1233 10.3 / M 1839 3.6 ◑ | **27** 0524 2.8 / 1122 10.6 / TU 1738 3.1 / 2346 10.5 |
| **13** 0106 10.3 / 0729 3.5 / TU 1351 10.1 / 2003 3.7 | **28** 0620 3.0 / 1220 10.3 / W 1839 3.4 ◐ |
| **14** 0222 10.4 / 0849 3.3 / W 1458 10.3 / 2119 3.3 | **29** 0052 10.4 / 0945 3.2 / TH 1329 10.3 / 1954 3.5 |
| **15** 0324 10.8 / 0955 2.9 / TH 1556 10.8 / 2220 2.7 | **30** 0207 10.6 / 0840 3.0 / F 1445 10.6 / 2116 3.2 |
| | **31** 0321 11.1 / 0957 2.7 / SA 1558 11.2 / 2234 2.7 |

## JUNE

| Time m | Time m |
|---|---|
| **1** 0428 11.7 / 1109 2.2 / SU 1700 11.9 / 2340 2.1 | **16** 0513 11.1 / 1145 2.5 / M 1739 11.4 |
| **2** 0527 12.3 / 1211 1.8 / M 1754 12.6 | **17** 0008 2.2 / 0559 11.4 / TU 1234 2.2 / 1821 11.8 |
| **3** 0038 1.6 / 0620 12.8 / TU 1306 1.4 / 1844 13.1 ● | **18** 0056 2.0 / 0641 11.6 / W 1319 2.1 / 1902 11.9 ○ |
| **4** 0133 1.3 / 0711 13.1 / W 1358 1.2 / 1933 13.3 | **19** 0140 2.0 / 0722 11.6 / TH 1401 2.1 / 1940 12.0 |
| **5** 0225 1.1 / 0802 13.1 / TH 1447 1.1 / 2021 13.3 | **20** 0222 2.0 / 0801 11.6 / F 1439 2.2 / 2018 11.9 |
| **6** 0314 1.1 / 0851 13.0 / F 1532 1.3 / 2109 13.1 | **21** 0300 2.2 / 0839 11.6 / SA 1512 2.3 / 2053 11.8 |
| **7** 0359 1.3 / 0940 12.7 / SA 1614 1.6 / 2156 12.7 | **22** 0335 2.3 / 0915 11.6 / SU 1541 2.4 / 2128 11.7 |
| **8** 0442 1.6 / 1027 12.2 / SU 1654 2.0 / 2244 12.2 | **23** 0406 2.3 / 0950 11.5 / M 1612 2.4 / 2203 11.6 |
| **9** 0522 2.1 / 1115 11.6 / M 1733 2.4 / 2333 11.6 | **24** 0439 2.3 / 1027 11.3 / TU 1647 2.4 / 2243 11.5 |
| **10** 0604 2.5 / 1205 11.0 / TU 1817 2.8 ◑ | **25** 0517 2.3 / 1108 11.4 / W 1728 2.5 / 2321 11.3 |
| **11** 0029 11.0 / 0648 2.8 / W 1303 10.6 / 1907 3.1 | **26** 0601 2.4 / 1155 11.1 / TH 1816 2.8 ◐ |
| **12** 0132 10.7 / 0739 3.1 / TH 1404 10.4 / 2006 3.3 | **27** 0022 11.1 / 0652 2.6 / F 1251 10.9 / 1912 3.1 |
| **13** 0233 10.6 / 0838 3.2 / F 1504 10.4 / 2112 3.3 | **28** 0125 10.9 / 0753 2.9 / SA 1358 10.7 / 2025 3.3 |
| **14** 0330 10.6 / 0945 3.2 / SA 1600 10.6 / 2219 3.0 | **29** 0239 10.8 / 0911 3.0 / SU 1516 10.8 / 2156 3.2 |
| **15** 0424 10.8 / 1050 2.9 / SU 1652 11.0 / 2318 2.6 | **30** 0356 11.1 / 1036 2.8 / M 1631 11.3 / 2315 2.7 |

## JULY

| Time m | Time m |
|---|---|
| **1** 0505 11.6 / 1147 2.3 / TU 1734 12.0 | **16** 0533 10.9 / 1203 2.7 / W 1758 11.4 |
| **2** 0020 2.1 / 0605 12.2 / W 1249 1.8 / 1830 12.6 | **17** 0029 2.3 / 0620 11.3 / TH 1255 2.3 / 1843 11.9 |
| **3** 0120 1.6 / 0701 12.7 / TH 1346 1.4 / 1922 13.1 ● | **18** 0120 2.1 / 0705 11.7 / F 1345 2.1 / 1925 12.1 ○ |
| **4** 0217 1.2 / 0753 13.0 / F 1440 1.2 / 2012 13.3 | **19** 0209 2.0 / 0747 11.9 / SA 1431 2.1 / 2005 12.2 |
| **5** 0310 1.0 / 0843 13.1 / SA 1528 1.1 / 2100 13.3 | **20** 0255 2.0 / 0827 12.0 / SU 1512 2.2 / 2042 12.3 |
| **6** 0356 1.0 / 0930 13.0 / SU 1610 1.2 / 2145 13.2 | **21** 0335 2.0 / 0903 12.0 / M 1545 2.2 / 2117 12.3 |
| **7** 0436 1.2 / 1012 12.7 / M 1646 1.5 / 2226 12.7 | **22** 0407 2.0 / 0937 12.2 / TU 1612 2.2 / 2151 12.3 |
| **8** 0510 1.6 / 1051 12.2 / TU 1716 1.9 / 2305 12.2 | **23** 0434 2.0 / 1011 12.1 / W 1638 2.1 / 2226 12.2 |
| **9** 0537 2.0 / 1128 11.6 / W 1745 2.3 / 2344 11.5 | **24** 0503 2.0 / 1048 12.0 / TH 1710 2.2 / 2306 11.9 |
| **10** 0606 2.4 / 1206 11.0 / TH 1820 2.7 ◑ | **25** 0536 2.2 / 1129 11.6 / F 1748 2.5 / 2352 11.4 |
| **11** 0027 10.8 / 0643 2.9 / F 1252 10.4 / 1903 3.2 | **26** 0618 2.5 / 1217 11.1 / SA 1835 3.0 |
| **12** 0122 10.2 / 0730 3.4 / SA 1353 10.0 / 2001 3.6 | **27** 0050 10.8 / 0710 3.1 / SU 1320 10.5 / 1938 3.6 |
| **13** 0229 9.9 / 0832 3.7 / SU 1505 9.9 / 2113 3.7 | **28** 0207 10.3 / 0829 3.6 / M 1447 10.2 / 2132 3.8 |
| **14** 0337 10.0 / 0948 3.6 / M 1612 10.2 / 2231 3.4 | **29** 0338 10.4 / 1019 3.5 / TU 1616 10.7 / 2306 3.2 |
| **15** 0439 10.3 / 1103 3.2 / TU 1709 10.8 / 2335 2.8 | **30** 0457 11.0 / 1136 2.7 / W 1726 11.5 |
| | **31** 0014 2.3 / 0559 11.9 / TH 1240 2.0 / 1823 12.5 |

## AUGUST

| Time m | Time m |
|---|---|
| **1** 0114 1.5 / 0654 12.6 / F 1338 1.3 / 1914 13.2 ● | **16** 0104 2.0 / 0645 11.9 / SA 1330 2.0 / 1905 12.5 ○ |
| **2** 0210 1.0 / 0744 13.1 / SA 1430 0.9 / 2001 13.6 | **17** 0155 1.7 / 0727 12.3 / SU 1418 1.9 / 1945 12.7 |
| **3** 0259 0.6 / 0829 13.4 / SU 1516 0.7 / 2045 13.7 | **18** 0241 1.6 / 0806 12.5 / M 1501 1.8 / 2022 12.8 |
| **4** 0343 0.6 / 0911 13.3 / M 1556 0.8 / 2124 13.5 | **19** 0322 1.6 / 0842 12.6 / TU 1536 1.9 / 2057 12.9 |
| **5** 0419 0.9 / 0947 13.0 / TU 1627 1.2 / 2159 13.1 | **20** 0355 1.7 / 0916 12.6 / W 1602 1.9 / 2131 12.8 |
| **6** 0445 1.4 / 1019 12.5 / W 1649 1.7 / 2230 12.5 | **21** 0419 1.8 / 0949 12.6 / TH 1623 2.0 / 2206 12.6 |
| **7** 0503 1.9 / 1047 11.9 / TH 1708 2.1 / 2259 11.7 | **22** 0441 1.9 / 1024 12.3 / F 1649 2.1 / 2243 12.2 |
| **8** 0523 2.4 / 1116 11.2 / F 1734 2.6 / 2330 10.9 ◑ | **23** 0509 2.2 / 1103 11.8 / SA 1721 2.5 / 2326 11.6 ◐ |
| **9** 0552 2.8 / 1150 10.5 / SA 1810 3.2 | **24** 0545 2.7 / 1149 11.0 / SU 1802 3.2 |
| **10** 0012 10.0 / 0631 3.5 / SU 1241 9.7 / 1902 3.9 | **25** 0022 10.4 / 0633 3.6 / M 1253 10.1 / 1903 4.1 |
| **11** 0118 9.3 / 0732 4.1 / M 1407 9.3 / 2022 4.3 | **26** 0151 9.7 / 0802 4.3 / TU 1440 9.7 / 2140 4.3 |
| **12** 0255 9.2 / 0900 4.3 / TU 1539 9.6 / 2153 4.0 | **27** 0339 9.9 / 1019 3.8 / W 1613 10.4 / 2306 3.2 |
| **13** 0413 9.8 / 1032 3.7 / W 1645 10.4 / 2312 3.2 | **28** 0455 10.9 / 1130 2.7 / TH 1720 11.8 |
| **14** 0512 10.6 / 1142 2.9 / TH 1738 11.3 | **29** 0006 2.1 / 0555 12.0 / F 1228 1.7 / 1813 12.7 |
| **15** 0011 2.4 / 0601 11.4 / F 1238 2.3 / 1823 12.0 | **30** 0101 1.2 / 0641 12.9 / SA 1321 1.0 / 1900 13.5 ● |
| | **31** 0151 0.6 / 0725 13.4 / SU 1410 0.6 / 1942 13.9 |

Chart Datum: 6·50 metres below Ordnance Datum (Newlyn). HAT is 14·7 metres above Chart Datum.

# BRISTOL (AVONMOUTH)  LAT 51°30′N  LONG 2°44′W
## TIMES AND HEIGHTS OF HIGH AND LOW WATERS

**TIME ZONE (UT)**
or Summer Time add ONE hour in **non-shaded areas**

Dates in red are SPRINGS
Dates in blue are NEAPS

YEAR **2008**

## SEPTEMBER

| Time | m | | Time | m |
|------|---|---|------|---|
| **1** M | 0237 0.4 / 0806 13.6 / 1454 0.5 / 2021 13.9 | | **16** TU | 0217 1.4 / 0738 13.0 / 1436 1.6 / 1956 13.3 |
| **2** TU | 0318 0.5 / 0843 13.5 / 1531 0.7 / 2057 13.6 | | **17** W | 0257 1.4 / 0815 13.1 / 1513 1.6 / 2033 13.3 |
| **3** W | 0351 1.0 / 0916 13.1 / 1600 1.2 / 2127 13.1 | | **18** TH | 0331 1.5 / 0851 13.1 / 1542 1.7 / 2109 13.2 |
| **4** TH | 0413 1.6 / 0943 12.5 / 1617 1.8 / 2153 12.4 | | **19** F | 0357 1.7 / 0926 12.9 / 1605 1.8 / 2145 12.8 |
| **5** F | 0425 2.1 / 1007 11.9 / 1631 2.2 / 2217 11.7 | | **20** SA | 0419 1.9 / 1002 12.5 / 1630 2.1 / 2224 12.1 |
| **6** SA | 0439 2.4 / 1031 11.3 / 1652 2.6 / 2243 10.9 | | **21** SU | 0446 2.3 / 1042 11.7 / 1701 2.7 / 2308 11.1 |
| **7** SU | 0503 2.8 / 1100 10.5 / 1722 3.2 / ◑ 2314 10.0 | | **22** M | 0522 3.1 / 1129 10.7 / 1743 3.6 ◑ |
| **8** M | 0535 3.5 / 1139 9.7 / 1804 4.0 | | **23** TU | 0008 10.0 / 0612 4.0 / 1243 9.8 / 1854 4.5 |
| **9** TU | 0006 9.1 / 0627 4.3 / 1258 8.9 / 1930 4.7 | | **24** W | 0200 9.4 / 0831 4.6 / 1445 9.7 / 2142 4.1 |
| **10** W | 0212 8.7 / 0815 4.8 / 1510 9.2 / 2120 4.4 | | **25** TH | 0335 10.0 / 1010 3.7 / 1603 10.7 / 2251 2.9 |
| **11** TH | 0348 9.4 / 1007 4.2 / 1619 10.1 / 2251 3.4 | | **26** F | 0440 11.1 / 1112 2.5 / 1703 11.8 / 2345 1.8 |
| **12** F | 0447 10.4 / 1122 3.2 / 1712 11.2 / 2350 2.5 | | **27** SA | 0533 12.2 / 1204 1.5 / 1753 12.9 |
| **13** SA | 0536 11.4 / 1216 2.4 / 1757 12.1 | | **28** SU | 0034 1.0 / 0618 13.0 / 1254 0.9 / 1836 13.5 |
| **14** SU | 0041 1.9 / 0619 12.2 / 1306 1.9 / 1839 12.8 | | **29** M | 0122 0.6 / 0659 13.5 / 1340 0.6 / ● 1915 13.8 |
| **15** M | 0131 1.5 / 0700 12.7 / 1353 1.7 / ○ 1918 13.1 | | **30** TU | 0206 0.5 / 0737 13.5 / 1422 0.6 / 1952 13.7 |

## OCTOBER

| Time | m | | Time | m |
|------|---|---|------|---|
| **1** W | 0245 0.8 / 0811 13.3 / 1459 1.0 / 2026 13.3 | | **16** TH | 0225 1.2 / 0748 13.5 / 1444 1.4 / 2009 13.6 |
| **2** TH | 0317 1.3 / 0842 12.9 / 1527 1.5 / 2054 12.8 | | **17** F | 0302 1.3 / 0827 13.4 / 1519 1.5 / 2050 13.4 |
| **3** F | 0338 1.9 / 0908 12.4 / 1544 2.0 / 2119 12.2 | | **18** SA | 0334 1.5 / 0907 13.1 / 1550 1.7 / 2131 12.9 |
| **4** SA | 0348 2.3 / 0931 11.9 / 1558 2.3 / 2142 11.6 | | **19** SU | 0404 1.9 / 0947 12.6 / 1621 2.2 / 2214 12.1 |
| **5** SU | 0403 2.5 / 0954 11.3 / 1619 2.6 / 2206 10.9 | | **20** M | 0436 2.5 / 1031 11.8 / 1657 2.8 / 2302 11.1 |
| **6** M | 0426 2.8 / 1022 10.6 / 1647 3.1 / 2238 10.2 | | **21** TU | 0515 3.2 / 1124 10.8 / 1746 3.6 ◑ |
| **7** TU | 0457 3.4 / 1100 9.8 / 1726 3.9 / ◑ 2325 9.3 | | **22** W | 0008 10.1 / 0614 4.0 / 1249 10.0 / 1921 4.3 |
| **8** W | 0543 4.2 / 1202 9.1 / 1836 4.6 | | **23** TH | 0152 9.8 / 0818 4.3 / 1428 10.2 / 2114 3.8 |
| **9** TH | 0058 8.7 / 0713 4.9 / 1426 9.1 / 2036 4.6 | | **24** F | 0310 10.3 / 0940 3.5 / 1536 11.0 / 2218 2.9 |
| **10** F | 0308 9.2 / 0919 4.5 / 1542 10.0 / 2210 3.7 | | **25** SA | 0410 11.2 / 1039 2.6 / 1633 11.8 / 2312 2.0 |
| **11** SA | 0412 10.3 / 1044 3.5 / 1637 11.1 / 2315 2.7 | | **26** SU | 0502 12.0 / 1131 1.8 / 1722 12.6 |
| **12** SU | 0503 11.4 / 1141 2.6 / 1724 12.0 | | **27** M | 0000 1.4 / 0547 12.7 / 1219 1.2 / 1805 13.1 |
| **13** M | 0008 2.0 / 0547 12.3 / 1232 2.0 / 1807 12.8 | | **28** TU | 0046 1.1 / 0627 13.0 / 1305 1.0 / ● 1845 13.2 |
| **14** TU | 0057 1.5 / 0628 12.9 / 1319 1.7 / ○ 1848 13.3 | | **29** W | 0130 1.1 / 0704 13.1 / 1347 1.1 / 1922 13.1 |
| **15** W | 0143 1.3 / 0709 13.3 / 1404 1.5 / 1929 13.6 | | **30** TH | 0209 1.3 / 0739 12.9 / 1425 1.4 / 1956 12.8 |
| | | | **31** F | 0242 1.6 / 0810 12.6 / 1455 1.8 / 2026 12.4 |

## NOVEMBER

| Time | m | | Time | m |
|------|---|---|------|---|
| **1** SA | 0306 2.1 / 0839 12.2 / 1517 2.2 / 2054 11.9 | | **16** SU | 0319 1.4 / 0854 13.3 / 1542 1.6 / 2123 12.9 |
| **2** SU | 0322 2.4 / 0905 11.8 / 1535 2.4 / 2120 11.5 | | **17** M | 0358 1.8 / 0940 12.8 / 1623 2.0 / 2210 12.3 |
| **3** M | 0339 2.6 / 0931 11.3 / 1559 2.7 / 2147 11.0 | | **18** TU | 0437 2.3 / 1028 12.1 / 1705 2.5 / 2301 11.5 |
| **4** TU | 0405 2.8 / 1002 10.8 / 1630 3.0 / 2221 10.4 | | **19** W | 0521 2.9 / 1123 11.4 / 1756 3.1 ◐ |
| **5** W | 0439 3.2 / 1041 10.3 / 1710 3.5 / 2308 9.9 | | **20** TH | 0001 10.8 / 0616 3.4 / 1233 10.8 / 1901 3.5 |
| **6** TH | 0524 3.8 / 1137 9.7 / 1809 4.1 ● | | **21** F | 0118 10.4 / 0731 3.7 / 1351 10.7 / 2019 3.5 |
| **7** F | 0016 9.4 / 0631 4.3 / 1303 9.5 / 1938 4.2 | | **22** SA | 0229 10.5 / 0849 3.5 / 1457 11.0 / 2128 3.2 |
| **8** SA | 0152 9.4 / 0810 4.4 / 1441 10.0 / 2105 3.8 | | **23** SU | 0329 10.9 / 0953 3.0 / 1553 11.4 / 2227 2.8 |
| **9** SU | 0318 10.1 / 0939 3.8 / 1548 10.8 / 2221 3.1 | | **24** M | 0423 11.4 / 1050 2.5 / 1645 11.8 / 2320 2.3 |
| **10** M | 0419 11.1 / 1051 3.0 / 1643 11.7 / 2324 2.4 | | **25** TU | 0512 11.9 / 1141 2.1 / 1732 12.2 |
| **11** TU | 0510 12.0 / 1149 2.3 / 1733 12.5 | | **26** W | 0008 2.0 / 0555 12.3 / 1228 1.8 / 1814 12.3 |
| **12** W | 0018 1.8 / 0557 12.8 / 1242 1.8 / 1819 13.1 | | **27** TH | 0053 1.8 / 0634 12.5 / 1312 1.7 / ● 1854 12.4 |
| **13** TH | 0108 1.4 / 0641 13.3 / 1331 1.5 / ○ 1905 13.5 | | **28** F | 0135 1.8 / 0712 12.5 / 1353 1.8 / 1931 12.3 |
| **14** F | 0155 1.2 / 0725 13.6 / 1417 1.3 / 1950 13.5 | | **29** SA | 0212 1.9 / 0747 12.3 / 1429 2.0 / 2006 12.0 |
| **15** SA | 0238 1.2 / 0809 13.5 / 1501 1.3 / 2036 13.3 | | **30** SU | 0243 2.2 / 0820 12.1 / 1459 2.3 / 2039 11.8 |

## DECEMBER

| Time | m | | Time | m |
|------|---|---|------|---|
| **1** M | 0308 2.4 / 0852 11.8 / 1526 2.5 / 2110 11.5 | | **16** TU | 0357 1.4 / 0934 13.3 / 1625 1.5 / 2204 12.8 |
| **2** TU | 0330 2.6 / 0923 11.5 / 1553 2.7 / 2141 11.2 | | **17** W | 0438 1.7 / 1021 12.9 / 1706 1.8 / 2250 12.3 |
| **3** W | 0358 2.7 / 0955 11.2 / 1625 2.8 / 2216 11.0 | | **18** TH | 0517 2.1 / 1109 12.3 / 1745 2.2 / 2337 11.7 |
| **4** TH | 0432 2.9 / 1033 10.9 / 1704 3.0 / 2257 10.7 | | **19** F | 0556 2.6 / 1159 11.7 / 1825 2.7 ◐ |
| **5** F | 0515 3.2 / 1120 10.6 / 1751 3.3 / ◐ 2348 10.3 | | **20** SA | 0029 11.0 / 0640 3.0 / 1258 11.1 / 1910 3.1 |
| **6** SA | 0606 3.5 / 1218 10.4 / 1850 3.5 | | **21** SU | 0130 10.5 / 0733 3.4 / 1402 10.7 / 2006 3.5 |
| **7** SU | 0051 10.2 / 0711 3.8 / 1329 10.3 / 2001 3.6 | | **22** M | 0236 10.4 / 0837 3.6 / 1505 10.6 / 2117 3.6 |
| **8** M | 0205 10.2 / 0830 3.8 / 1446 10.6 / 2121 3.4 | | **23** TU | 0337 10.5 / 0952 3.5 / 1604 10.8 / 2230 3.4 |
| **9** TU | 0323 10.7 / 0956 3.4 / 1558 11.2 / 2238 2.9 | | **24** W | 0434 10.9 / 1058 3.1 / 1659 11.1 / 2329 2.9 |
| **10** W | 0431 11.5 / 1109 2.8 / 1701 11.9 / 2343 2.3 | | **25** TH | 0525 11.3 / 1152 2.6 / 1748 11.4 |
| **11** TH | 0528 12.3 / 1210 2.1 / 1756 12.6 | | **26** F | 0019 2.4 / 0609 11.8 / 1241 2.3 / 1832 11.7 |
| **12** F | 0040 1.7 / 0620 12.9 / 1307 1.7 / ○ 1848 13.1 | | **27** SA | 0106 2.2 / 0652 12.1 / 1327 2.1 / ● 1913 11.9 |
| **13** SA | 0133 1.4 / 0709 13.4 / 1401 1.4 / 1938 13.3 | | **28** SU | 0149 2.1 / 0730 12.2 / 1411 2.1 / 1952 11.9 |
| **14** SU | 0224 1.2 / 0758 13.6 / 1452 1.3 / 2028 13.3 | | **29** M | 0230 2.1 / 0808 12.2 / 1450 2.2 / 2028 11.9 |
| **15** M | 0312 1.2 / 0846 13.5 / 1540 1.3 / 2117 13.2 | | **30** TU | 0304 2.3 / 0843 12.1 / 1525 2.4 / 2102 11.8 |
| | | | **31** W | 0332 2.5 / 0916 11.9 / 1554 2.5 / 2134 11.7 |

Chart Datum: 6·50 metres below Ordnance Datum (Newlyn). HAT is 14·7 metres above Chart Datum.

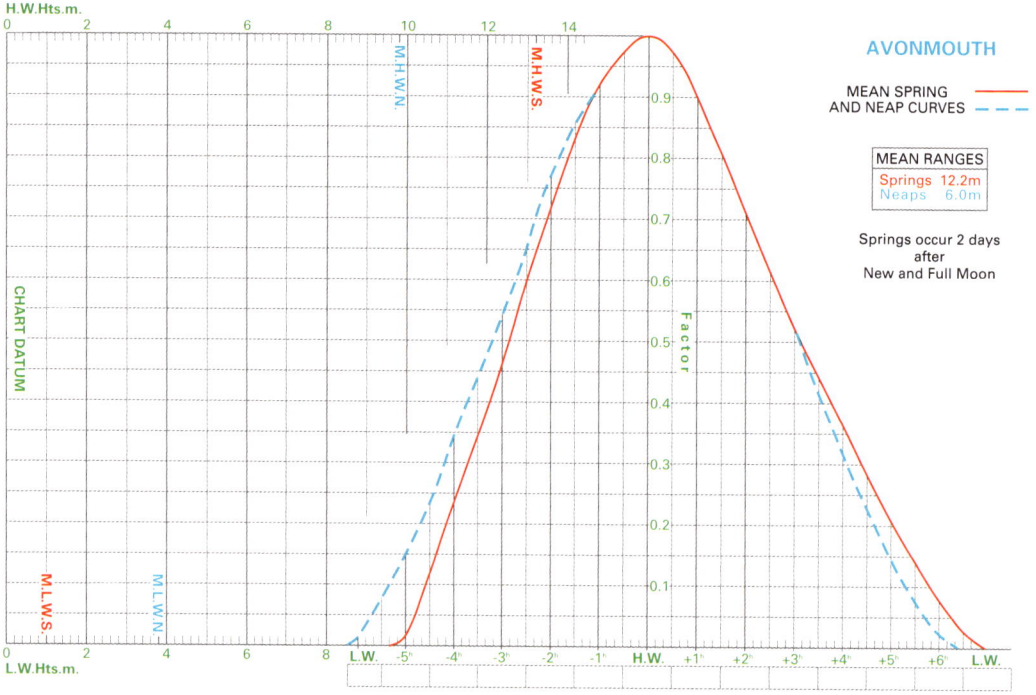

## 4.19 BRISTOL (CITY DOCKS)

Ent to R Avon **51°30'·44N 02°43'·31W** ✿⊛🌢🌢🌢✿✿✿

**CHARTS** AC *5608, 1179, 1176*, 1859; Imray C59; Stanfords 14; OS 172.

**TIDES** –0410 on Dover; ML 7·0; Duration 0620. NB very large range

**Standard Port BRISTOL (AVONMOUTH)** (◀—)

| Times | | | | Height (metres) | | | |
|---|---|---|---|---|---|---|---|
| High Water | | Low Water | | MHWS | MHWN | MLWN | MLWS |
| 0200 | 0800 | 0300 | 0800 | 13·2 | 9·8 | 3·8 | 1·0 |
| 1400 | 2000 | 1500 | 2000 | | | | |
| **Differences SHIREHAMPTON (R Avon, 51°29'N 02°41'W)** | | | | | | | |
| 0000 | 0000 | +0035 | +0010 | −0·7 | −0·7 | −0·8 | 0·0 |
| **SEA MILLS (R Avon, 51°29'N 02°39'W)** | | | | | | | |
| +0005 | +0005 | +0105 | +0030 | −1·4 | −1·5 | −1·7 | −0·1 |
| **CUMBERLAND BASIN (Ent)** | | | | | | | |
| +0010 | +0010 | Dries | | −2·9 | −3·0 | Dries | |

**SHELTER** Excellent in Bristol Floating Harbour. Avonmouth and Royal Portbury Docks are prohib to yachts, except in emergency. If early/late on the tide, ⚓ as close inshore as depth allows in Portishead Pool between Portishead Dock and Royal Portbury Dock, but avoid in onshore winds.

**NAVIGATION** **From the south and west:** from Avon SHM buoy (51°27'·92N 02°51'·73W) stay well clear to the S of the Bristol Deep shipping channel and use the *Inshore Route* (see chartlet), passing close to Portishead Pt. If using the *Offshore Route* to the north, cross the shipping channel immediately E of Denny Shoal SCM Buoy (51°30'·15N 02°45'·45W) and Firefly SHM Buoy.

**From the north:** use the *Inshore Route*, passing close to the entrance to Avonmouth Docks but keeping clear of disused fuel pier 2ca NE.

- Beware large ships transiting and turning in the main channel.
- Beware ships and tugs leaving the docks at any time.
- When on passage up/down the Severn estuary without stopping at Bristol or Portishead, use the *Offshore Route*.

Entering R Avon keep N of shallows (Swatch Bank) between Royal Portbury Dock and Avonmouth Docks. Speed limit 6kn in river.

**LIGHTS AND MARKS** Ldg lts 127°, both Iso R 2s, to R Avon ent abeam S pier lt, Oc RG 30s. St George ldg lts 173°, both Oc G 5s, front R/Or post, rear W/Or chequers on Or post, clear Swash Bank (dries). Upriver, G or R ✩s mark the outside of bends.

**Entry signals** to Bristol Hbr may be shown from E bank, 1½ and 2½ca S of Clifton Suspension Bridge: 🟢 = continue with caution; 🔴 = stop and await orders.

**LOCKS** Floating Harbour (approx 7M upriver) is accessed via Entrance Lock into Cumberland Basin and Junction Lock into Floating Hbr. Aim to reach the Ent lock no later than HW -0015; waiting pontoon (dries). Ent lock opens approx HW –2½, –1½ and –¼hr for arrivals; departures approx 15 mins after these times. Plimsoll swing bridge opens in unison with lock, except weekday rush hours 0800-0900 and 1700-1800.

Junction lock is always open, unless ht of HW is >9·6m ('stopgate' tide) when it closes; read special instructions. If you miss the last lock-in, call Ch 12 for advice. Options: dry out in soft mud at pontoons, or on N Wall (bow abreast ladder No 4 Survey Mark; no nearer the lock gate). Other areas are foul.

**BRIDGES** Prince St bridge usually opens H+15, 0915-2215 summer, by arrangement in winter; pre-notify Bridgemaster ☎ 9299338, Ch 73 or sound ●—●(R). Redcliffe bridge, pre-arrange same ☎. Clearances above HAT: St Augustine's Reach 1·8m & 0·7m; Prince St 0·7m; Redcliffe 2·1m; Bristol 2·6m. The R Avon leads to Netham lock ☎ 9776590, Keynsham, Bath and the Kennett & Avon canal.

**R/T VTS Areas:** *Severn VTS* Ch **69**, W of Brean Down/Flatholm/ Steepholm; *Bristol VTS* Ch **12**, East of *Severn VTS* area. *Bristol VTS* is friendly and helpful and will, on request, advise big ship movements and other MSI. If no radio, ☎ 0117 982 2257.

**R/T procedures for R Avon and Bristol City Docks**
- When inbound, call *Bristol VTS* with intentions at Welsh Hook PHM buoy and abeam Portishead Pt.
- This also applies to craft bound for Portishead marina.
- In R Avon at Nelson Point call *Bristol VTS* again, low power, confirming inbound to City Docks.
- At Black Rks (1M to run) call *City Docks Radio* Ch **14**, 11 low power, (HW–3 to HW+1) for locking instructions.
- For berth: *Bristol Hbr* Ch **73**, or Bristol Marina Ch **80** M.
- Departure procedure is the reverse.

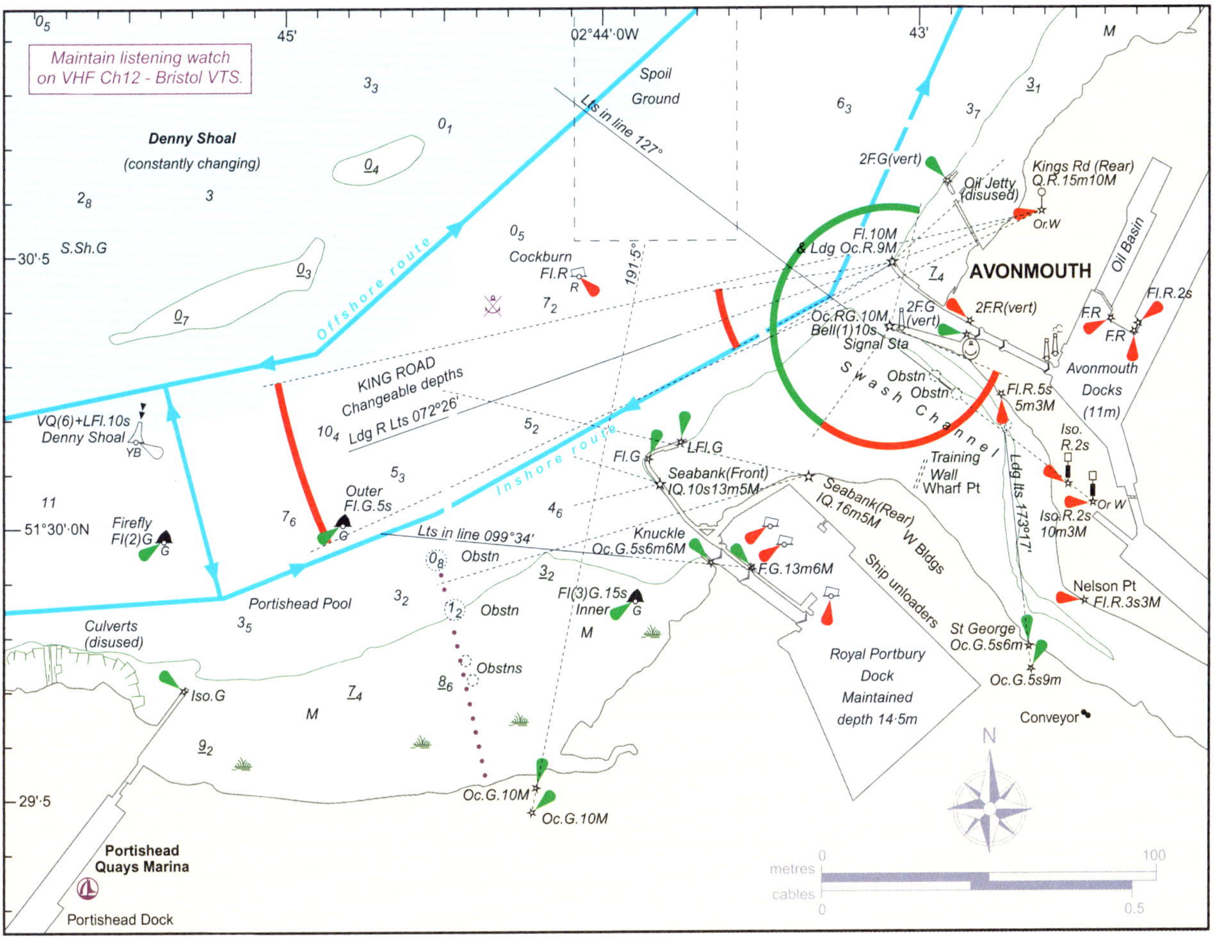

Maintain listening watch on VHF Ch12 - Bristol VTS.

Denny Shoal (constantly changing)

Spoil Ground

S.Sh.G

Cockburn Fl.R

AVONMOUTH

Oil Jetty (disused)

Kings Rd (Rear) Q.R.15m10M

Or.W

2F.G(vert)

Fl.10M & Ldg Oc.R.9M

Oc.RG.10M Bell(1)10s Signal Sta

2FG (vert)

2F.R(vert)

F.R

Fl.R.2s

Avonmouth Docks (11m)

Oil Basin

Swash Channel

Fl.R.5s 5m3M

Iso. R.2s

Or.W

Ldg lts 173°17'

Iso.R.2s 10m3M

Nelson Pt Fl.R.3s3M

Training Wall Wharf Pt

W Bldgs

KING ROAD Changeable depths

Ldg R Lts 072°26'

Offshore route

Inshore route

Lts in line 127°

VQ(6)+LFl.10s Denny Shoal YB

Outer Fl.G.5s G

Firefly Fl(2)G G

Portishead Pool

Lts in line 099°34'

Obstn

Fl.G

LFl.G

Seabank(Front) IQ.10s13m5M

Seabank(Rear) IQ.16m5M

Knuckle Oc.G.5s6m6M

Fl.G.13m6M

Ship unloaders

St George Oc.G.5s6m

Oc.G.5s9m

Fl(3)G.15s Inner G

Obstn M

Obstns

Royal Portbury Dock Maintained depth 14·5m

Conveyor

Culverts (disused)

Iso.G

Oc.G.10M

Oc.G.10M

Portishead Quays Marina

Portishead Dock

metres
cables

TELEPHONE (Bristol code 0117) Severn VTS 0845 6018870; Bristol VTS 982 2257; Dock Master (Cumberland Basin) 9273633; Bristol weather centre 927 9298; Swansea MRCC (01792) 366534; Marinecall 0891 500459; Police 9277777; H 923 0000.

FACILITIES from seaward. Portishead CC, at Crockerne Pill, SW bank, 5ca upstream of the M5 motorway bridge; ☎ 01275 373988, www.portisheadcruisingclub.org.uk  Drying (soft mud), Slip, grid (£5/day).

Bristol Hbr HM, Underfall Yard, Cumberland Rd, Bristol BS1 6XG. ☎ 9031484, 9031487, www.bristol-city.gov.uk/bristolharbour Approx 40 AB near ent to St Augustine's Reach, £1·50 inc licence

fee. FW, D, , , Slip (launching £5), CH, Gas, , R, Bar; ferries ply between various landing stages around the hbr.

Baltic Wharf Leisure Centre contact HM ☎ 9031484, Slip, L, Bar.

Bristol Marina ☎ 9213198, 9297672. www.bristolmarina.co.uk Access HW–3 to +1. 100 AB, inc (20m max LOA), £1·70. D, , BY, El, ME, , Gas, Gaz, SM, Wi-fi (some berths), Slip (£0.90/m), CH, C (9 & 12 ton), BH (50 ton), , .

Bathurst Basin Shower block.

Cabot CC ☎ 9268318, 9812458, AB, M, FW, Bar.

City All domestic facilities, ACA, , .

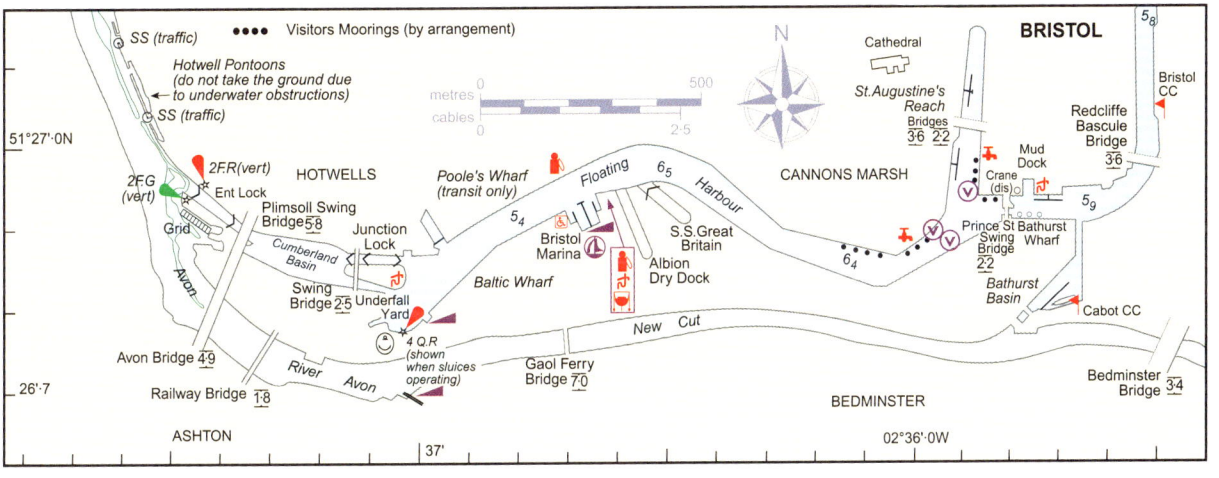

SS (traffic)

Hotwell Pontoons (do not take the ground due to underwater obstructions)

SS (traffic)

Visitors Moorings (by arrangement)

BRISTOL

Cathedral

St.Augustine's Reach Bridges 3·6 2·2

Bristol CC

Redcliffe Bascule Bridge 3·6

Mud Dock

Crane (dis)

2F.R(vert)

2FG (vert)

Ent Lock

Grid

HOTWELLS

Plimsoll Swing Bridge 5·8

Cumberland Basin

Junction Lock

Poole's Wharf (transit only)

Floating Harbour

Bristol Marina

Baltic Wharf

S.S.Great Britain

Albion Dry Dock

CANNONS MARSH

Prince St Bathurst Swing Wharf Bridge 2·2

Bathurst Basin

Cabot CC

Swing Bridge 2·5

Underfall Yard

4 Q.R (shown when sluices operating)

New Cut

Gaol Ferry Bridge 7·0

BEDMINSTER

Bedminster Bridge 3·4

Avon Bridge 4·9

Railway Bridge 1·8

River Avon

ASHTON

metres
cables

Bristol Channel

## 4.20  PORTISHEAD

Somerset **51°29'·56N 02°45'·41W**

**CHARTS**  AC *5608, 1176,* 1859; Imray C59; Stanfords 14; OS 171/2

**TIDES**  –0405 Dover; ML 6·8

Standard Port BRISTOL (AVONMOUTH) (←)

| Times | | | | Height (metres) | | | |
|---|---|---|---|---|---|---|---|
| High Water | | Low Water | | MHWS | MHWN | MLWN | MLWS |
| 0200 | 0800 | 0300 | 0800 | 13·2 | 9·8 | 3·8 | 1·0 |
| 1400 | 2000 | 1500 | 2000 | | | | |
| **Differences PORTISHEAD** | | | | | | | |
| –0002 | 0000 | No data | | –0·1 | –0·1 | No data | |
| **CLEVEDON** | | | | | | | |
| –0010 | –0020 | –0025 | –0015 | –0·4 | –0·2 | +0·2 | 0·0 |
| **ST THOMAS HEAD** | | | | | | | |
| 0000 | 0000 | –0030 | –0030 | –0·4 | –0·2 | +0·1 | +0·1 |
| **ENGLISH AND WELSH GROUNDS** | | | | | | | |
| –0008 | –0008 | –0030 | –0030 | –0·5 | –0·8 | –0·3 | 0·0 |
| **WESTON-SUPER-MARE** | | | | | | | |
| –0020 | –0030 | –0130 | –0030 | –1·2 | –1·0 | –0·8 | –0·2 |

**SHELTER**  Good in marina. Access by lock 9m x 40m x 3·5m draft (5·5m by prior arrangement) HW ±4½ (nps) ±3¾ (sp). Ⓥ's available in marina. ⚓ 1ca NE of pier hd (sheltered from SE to W) to await the tide for marina or Sharpness.

**NAVIGATION**  WPT 51°29'·96N 02°45'·35W, Firefly SHM lt buoy, 168°/500m to pier hd. Firefly Rks (0·9m) are close W of the 168° appr track. Appr's dry to mud and are exposed to N/NE winds. Close inshore a W-going eddy begins at HW –3 whilst the flood is still making E.

**LIGHTS AND MARKS**  Portishead Pt, Q (3) 10s9m 16M, is 7ca W of Portishead pierhd, Iso G 2s 5m 3M. Lock ent has FG and FR lts.

**R/T**  See 4.19. Monitor *Bristol VTS* Ch **12** for shipping movements. Portishead Quays Marina VHF Ch 80 24H.

**TELEPHONE**  (Code 01275) MRCC (01792) 366534; Marinecall 09068 969649; Police 818181; Health centre 847474; Ⓗ (Clevedon) 01179 872212.

**FACILITIES Marina** (200+Ⓥ), £1·60 (min charge £16), ☎ 841941, 📠 841942, www.quaymarinas.co.uk; Wi-fi, BH (35 ton), P & D, El, ME, CH, BY, Gas, Ⓒ. **Portishead Cruising Club; Town** ✉, Ⓑ, ⇌, ✈ (Bristol). 3M to Junction 19 of M5.

### ADJACENT HARBOUR

**WESTON-SUPER-MARE**, Somerset, **51°21'·03N 02°59'·28W**. AC *5608, 1179,* 1176,1152. HW –0435 on Dover; Duration 0655; ML 6·1m. See 4.20. Good shelter, except in S'lies, in Knightstone Hbr (dries) at N end of bay; access HW±1½. Causeway at ent marked by bn. Grand Pier hd 2 FG (vert) 6/5m. Or ⚓ in good weather in R Axe (dries), entry HW±2. Facilities: **Weston Bay YC** (located on beach) ☎ 01934 413366, M (lower R Axe), dry out on beach, FW, Bar, VHF Ch 80; **Services**: AB, CH, El, D, BH (10 ton), FW, Slip, ME, ✂; **Uphill Boat Centre** ☎ 01934 418617 AB, slip, Gas, Gaz; **Town** Bar, Ⓑ, FW, P, ✉, R, ⇌, 🛒.

## 4.21  BURNHAM-ON-SEA

Somerset **51°14'·23N 03°00'·33W**

**CHARTS**  AC *5608, 1179,* 1152; Imray C59; Stanfords 14; OS 182

**TIDES**  –0435 Dover; ML 5·4; Duration 0620

Standard Port BRISTOL (AVONMOUTH) (←)

| Times | | | | Height (metres) | | | |
|---|---|---|---|---|---|---|---|
| High Water | | Low Water | | MHWS | MHWN | MLWN | MLWS |
| 0200 | 0800 | 0300 | 0800 | 13·2 | 9·8 | 3·8 | 1·0 |
| 1400 | 2000 | 1500 | 2000 | | | | |
| **Differences BURNHAM-ON-SEA** | | | | | | | |
| –0020 | –0025 | –0030 | 0000 | –2·3 | –1·9 | –1·4 | –1·1 |
| **BRIDGWATER** | | | | | | | |
| –0015 | –0030 | +0305 | +0455 | –8·6 | –8·1 | Dries | |

**SHELTER**  Ent is very choppy in strong winds, especially from SW to W and from N to NE. ⚓ in 4m about 40m E of No 1 buoy or S of town jetty or, for best shelter, Ⓥ/⚓ in R Brue (dries).

**NAVIGATION**  WPT 51°15'·32N 03°08'·22W, 095°/5M to Low lt. Enter HW –3 to HW; not advised at night. Or from ½M S of Gore SWM buoy pick up brg 076° on Low lt ho. Approx 1½M past No 1 buoy, steer on ldg line/lts 112°; thence alter 180° into the river chan but banks and depths change frequently. Beware unmarked fishing stakes outside appr chan.

**LIGHTS AND MARKS**  Low lt ho Dir 076° as chartlet. Ldg lts/marks 112° (moved as chan shifts): front FR 6m 3M, Or stripe on ☐ W background on sea wall; rear FR 12m 3M, church tr.

**R/T**  HM and Pilot VHF Ch 08 16 (when vessel expected).

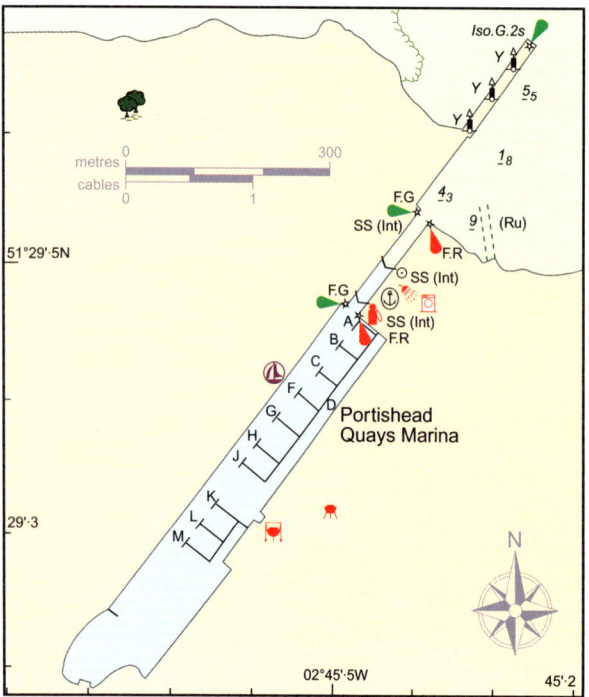

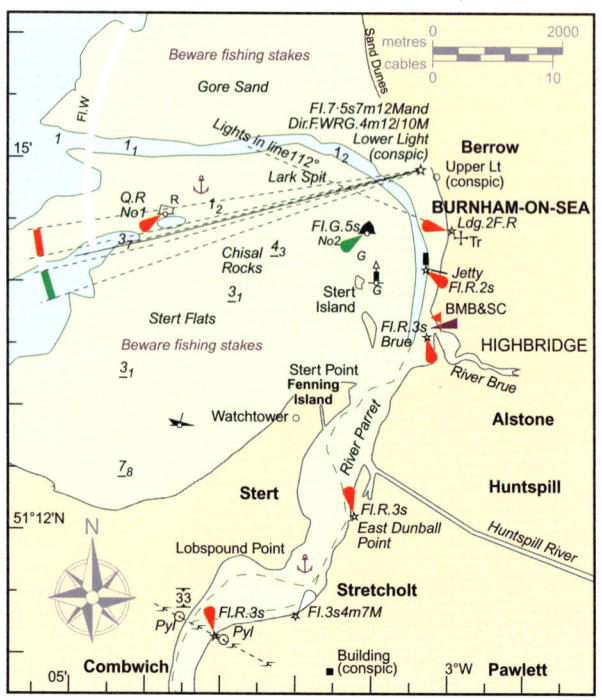

**TELEPHONE** (Code 01278) HM and Pilot 782180; MRCC (01792) 366534; Marinecall 09068 969649; Police (01823) 337911; Ⓗ 782262.

**FACILITIES** **Burnham-on-Sea MB&SC** ☎ 792911, M, few drying ⚓s in River Brue, L, Slip, Bar; **Brue Yachts** ☎ 783275 mob 07810 622209, drying pontoon £8, FW, D, ⚒. **Services:** ME, El, ✕, ACA (Bridgwater). **Town** Gas, ✉, Ⓑ, ⇌ (Highbridge), ✈ (Bristol). Note: No access to Bridgwater marina from sea/R Parrett.

## 4.22 WATCHET

Somerset 51°11′·03N 03°19′·72W ❀⚓⚓✿✿

**CHARTS** AC 5608, 1179, 1152, 1160; Imray C59; Stanfords 14; OS 181

**TIDES** –0450 Dover; ML 5·9; Duration 0655
**Standard Port BRISTOL (AVONMOUTH)** (←)

| Times | | | | Height (metres) | | | |
|---|---|---|---|---|---|---|---|
| High Water | | Low Water | | MHWS | MHWN | MLWN | MLWS |
| 0200 | 0800 | 0300 | 0800 | 13·2 | 9·8 | 3·8 | 1·0 |
| 1400 | 2000 | 1500 | 2000 | | | | |
| **Differences HINKLEY POINT** | | | | | | | |
| –0020 | –0025 | –0100 | –0040 | –1·7 | –1·4 | –0·2 | –0·2 |
| **WATCHET** | | | | | | | |
| –0035 | –0050 | –0145 | –0040 | –1·9 | –1·5 | +0·1 | +0·1 |
| **MINEHEAD** | | | | | | | |
| –0037 | –0052 | –0155 | –0045 | –2·6 | –1·9 | –0·2 | 0·0 |
| **PORLOCK BAY** | | | | | | | |
| –0045 | –0055 | –0205 | –0050 | –3·0 | –2·2 | –0·1 | –0·1 |
| **LYNMOUTH** | | | | | | | |
| –0055 | –0115 | No data | | –3·6 | –2·7 | No data | |

**SHELTER** Good, but open to N and E winds. The outer hbr ent dries 6·5m, but has about 6m depth at MHWS; access approx HW±2½. Marina entered through a dropping sill gate which is open when the tide level is at or above CD +6.92m (retained water level). Min clearance over the gate, when it has just opened or is about to close 2.5m. Approx gate opening times HW ±2½H sp, HW ±1½H np. Movement through the entrance is controlled by stop/go R/G lts. Entrance max width 8m. Min retained water depths vary 1.5–3.0m. Marina subject to constant silting and dredged berths may not be accessible at stated times. Obtain up to date information from Marina prior to arrival.

**NAVIGATION** WPT 51°12′·03N 03°18′·88W, 208°/1·1M to hbr ent. Rks/mud dry 5ca to seaward. Beware tidal streams 4-5kn at sp offshore and around W pier hd. Culver Sand (0·9m) is approx 6M NNE, marked by ECM and WCM lt buoys. 5M E of hbr are Lilstock range target buoys. DZ No 2 SPM buoy, Fl Y 10s, bears 030°/3·2M from Watchet. 3kn speed limit in marina.

**LIGHTS AND MARKS** Two unlit radio masts (206m) bearing 208° 1·6M from hbr ent are conspic approach marks. Hinkley Pt nuclear

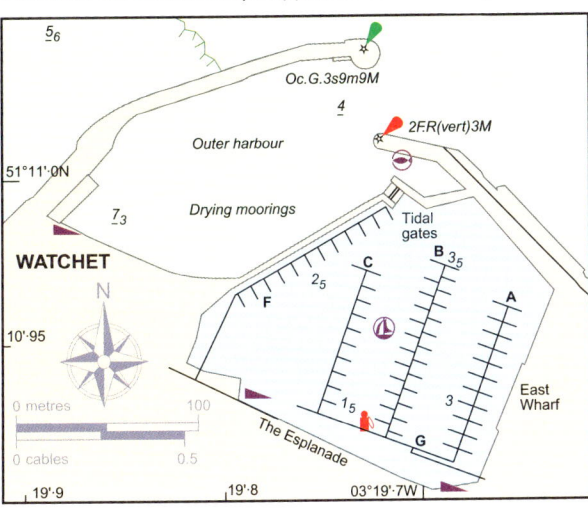

power stn is conspic 7·5M to the E. W pier hd Oc G 3s 9m 9M on Red (R) tr. E pier hd 2 FR (vert) 3M.

**R/T** VHF Ch 80 (from HW–2, but occas).

**TELEPHONE** (Code 01984) HM 631264 🖷 639238 mob 077477 785508; Watchet Boat Owners Association (01643) 702569; MRCC (01792) 366534; Marinecall 09068 969649; Police (01823) 337911.

**FACILITIES** **Watchet Harbour Marina** ☎ 631264 🖷 639238, AB (250 inc Ⓥ) £2·35 inc ⚡, D, ⛽, CH, Gaz, Slip(launching £5.00), ACA (Bridgwater). **Town** ✉, Ⓑ, ⚒, R, Bar. At Williton (2M): Gas, D & P (cans); Ⓗ (Minehead 8M), ⇌ (Taunton 18M), ✈ (Bristol).

### OTHER HARBOURS ON S SHORE OF BRISTOL CHANNEL

**MINEHEAD**, Somerset, 51°12′·79N 03°28′·37W. AC 1179, 1165, 1160. HW –0450 on Dover. ML 5·7m. See 4.22. Small hbr, dries 7·5m; access HW±2. Good shelter within pier curving E and then SE, over which seas may break in gales at MHWS; exposed to E'lies. Best appr from N or NW; beware The Gables, shingle bank (dries 3·7m) about 5ca ENE of pier. Keep E of a sewer outfall which passes ½ca E of pierhd and extends 1¾ca NNE of it; outfall is protected by rk covering, drying 2·8m and N end marked by SHM Bn QG 6m 7M. There are 6 pairs of fore and aft R ⚓s at hbr ent just seaward of 3 posts or drying alongside berth, £1.00 at inner end of pier. Hbr gets very crowded. Holiday camp is conspic 6ca SE. Pierhd lt Fl (2) G 5s 4M, vis 127°-262°. VHF Ch 16 12 14 (occas). HM ☎ (01643) 702566; Facilities: **Hbr** FW, Slip (launching £5.00). **Town** D, P, El, Gas, ME, ✕, R, Bar, ⚒, ✉, Ⓑ, ⇌ (Taunton).

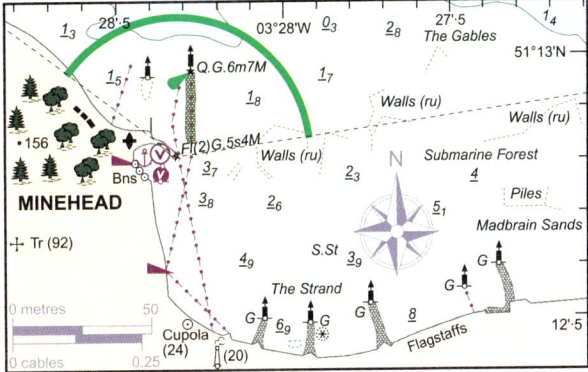

**PORLOCK WEIR**, Somerset, 51°13′·17N 03°37′·64W. AC 1179, 1165, 1160. HW –0500 on Dover; ML 5·6m. See 4.22. Access HW±1½. Ent chan (250°), about 15m wide marked by withies (3 PHM and 1 SHM), between shingle bank/wood pilings to stbd and sunken wooden wall to port is difficult in any seas. A small pool (1m) just inside ent is for shoal draft boats; others dry out on pebble banks. Or turn 90° stbd, via gates (but opening bridge usually closed), into inner drying dock with good shelter. No lts. HM ☎ 01643 863187 (not local). **Porlock Weir SC.** Facilities: FW and limited ⚒.

**LYNMOUTH**, Devon, 51°14′·16N 03°49′·79W. AC 1160,1165. HW–0515 on Dover. See 4.22. Tiny hbr, dries approx 5m; access HW±1, but not with particularly low Nps, but only in settled offshore weather. Appr from Sand Ridge SHM lt buoy, 1·6M W of Foreland Pt and 9ca N of hbr ent. The narrow appr chan through drying boulder ledges is marked by 7 unlit posts. After first 2 posts keep 10m away from next SH post then next 2PH posts keep to middle of ent. Hbr ent is between piers, 2FR/FG lts, on W side of river course. Berth on E pier, which covers (beware) at MHWS. Resort facilities. Admin by Council ☎ 01598 752384.

**WATERMOUTH**, Devon, 51°13′·03N 04°04′·6W. AC 1179, 1165. HW –0525 on Dover; ML 4·9m; Duration 0625. Use 4.23. Good shelter in drying hbr, but heavy surge runs in strong NW winds. Access HW±3 at sp; only as far as inner bkwtr at np. Dir lt 153° Oc WRG 5s 1m, W sector 151·5°-154·5°, W △ on structure, 1½ca inside ent on S shore. Bkwtr, covered at high tide, has Y poles along its length and a G pole with conical topmark at the end. 9 Y ⚓s with B handles £6.50. HM ☎ (01271) 865422. Facilities: **Hbr** D (cans), FW (cans), CH, C (12 ton), Slip; **YC**, Bar. **Combe Martin** 1½M all facilities.

## 4.23 ILFRACOMBE

Devon 51°12′·65N 04°06′·65W ✿✿✿✿✿

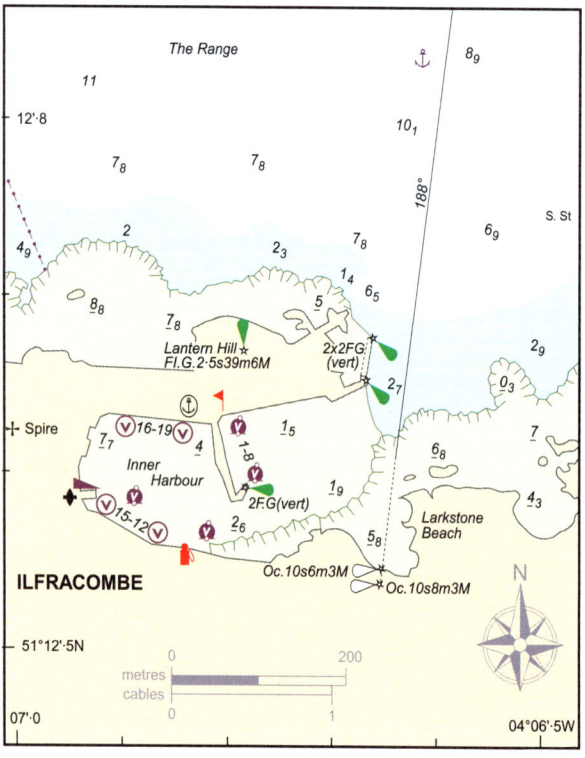

CHARTS  AC 5608, 1179, *1165*, 1160; Imray C59; Stanfords 14; OS 180

TIDES  –0525 Dover; ML 5·0; Duration 0625

Standard Port MILFORD HAVEN (←)

| Times | | | | Height (metres) | | | |
|---|---|---|---|---|---|---|---|
| High Water | | Low Water | | MHWS | MHWN | MLWN | MLWS |
| 0100 | 0700 | 0100 | 0700 | 7·0 | 5·2 | 2·5 | 0·7 |
| 1300 | 1900 | 1300 | 1900 | | | | |
| Differences ILFRACOMBE | | | | | | | |
| –0016 | –0016 | –0041 | –0031 | +2·3 | +1·8 | +0·6 | +0·3 |
| LUNDY ISLAND | | | | | | | |
| –0025 | –0025 | –0020 | –0035 | +0·9 | +0·7 | +0·3 | +0·1 |

SHELTER  Good except in NE/E winds. SW gales can cause surge in hbrs, which dry. 8 🛟s in outer hbr, access HW±3. Or ⚓ clear of pier. Visitors AB on N snd S walls of Inner Hbr, access HW±2 or dry out on chains off foot of N Pier.

NAVIGATION  WPT 51°13′·23N 04°06′·67W, 180°/0·55Mto pier hd. From E, beware Copperas Rks (4M to E), and tiderips on Buggy Pit, 7ca NE of ent. On entry keep toward Pier to clear drying ledges and lobster keep-pots obstructing Hbr ent on SE side.

LIGHTS AND MARKS  See 4.3. and chartlet

R/T  Call: *Ilfracombe Hbr* VHF Ch 12 16 (when manned).

TELEPHONE  (Code 01271) HM 862108 mob 07775 532606; MRCC (01792) 366534; Marinecall 09068 969649; Police 08705 777444; Dr 863119.

FACILITIES  **Hbr** AB and 🛟s £1·18 (inc use of showers), M, D, 🔌,(S Quay), FW, CH, Slip(launching £16·50/week), ME, EI, 🔧; **Ilfracombe YC** ☎ 863969, M, 🚽, Bar, C (35 ton, as arranged) **Town** 🛒, R, Bar, ✉, Ⓑ, bus to Barnstaple (🚆), ✈ (Exeter).

## 4.24 RIVERS TAW and TORRIDGE

Devon 51°04′·37N 04°12′·88W ✿✿✿✿✿✿

CHARTS  AC *5608, 1179, 1164*, 1160; Imray C58; Stanfords 14; OS 180

TIDES  –0525 (Appledore) Dover; ML 3·6; Duration 0600

Standard Port MILFORD HAVEN (←)

| Times | | | | Height (metres) | | | |
|---|---|---|---|---|---|---|---|
| High Water | | Low Water | | MHWS | MHWN | MLWN | MLWS |
| 0100 | 0700 | 0100 | 0700 | 7·0 | 5·2 | 2·5 | 0·7 |
| 1300 | 1900 | 1300 | 1900 | | | | |
| Differences APPLEDORE | | | | | | | |
| –0020 | –0025 | +0015 | –0045 | +0·5 | 0·0 | –0·9 | –0·5 |
| YELLAND MARSH (R Taw) | | | | | | | |
| –0010 | –0015 | +0100 | –0015 | +0·1 | –0·4 | –1·2 | –0·6 |
| FREMINGTON (R Taw) | | | | | | | |
| –0010 | –0015 | +0030 | –0030 | –1·1 | –1·8 | –2·2 | –0·5 |
| BARNSTAPLE (R Taw) | | | | | | | |
| 0000 | –0015 | –0155 | –0245 | –2·9 | –3·8 | –2·2 | –0·4 |
| BIDEFORD (R Torridge) | | | | | | | |
| –0020 | –0025 | 0000 | 0000 | –1·1 | –1·6 | –2·5 | –0·7 |
| CLOVELLY | | | | | | | |
| –0030 | –0030 | –0020 | –0040 | +1·3 | +1·1 | +0·2 | +0·2 |

SHELTER  Very well protected, but ent is dangerous in strong on-shore winds and/or swell. Yachts can ⚓ or pick up RNLI buoy (please donate to RNLI, Boathouse ☎ 473969) in Appledore Pool N of Skern Pt where spring stream can reach 5kn. Bideford quay dries to soft mud; used by coasters.

NAVIGATION  WPT 51°05′·43N 04°16′·11W, 118°/0·9M to Bar.

Bar and sands constantly shift; buoys are moved occasionally to comply. For advice on bar contact Bideford HM. Least depths over bar 0·1 and 0·4m. Estuary dries and access is only feasible from HW–2 to HW. Night entry not advised for strangers. Once tide is ebbing, breakers quickly form between Bideford Bar SHM lt buoy and Middle Ridge SHM lt buoy. Hold the ldg line 118° only up to Outer Pulley where chan deviates stbd toward Pulley buoy and Grey Sand Hill, thence to Appledore Pool. 2M passage to Bideford is not difficult. Barnstaple (7M): seek local advice or take pilot.

LIGHTS AND MARKS  See 4.3 and chartlet. Ldg marks are W trs, lit H24. R Torridge: Lt QY at E end of Bideford bridge, 2FR vert & 2FG vert indicate preferred chan; then SHM bn, QG, on W bank.

R/T  *2 Rivers Port/Pilots* VHF Ch 12 16 (From HW–2 occasional).

TELEPHONE  Appledore/Bideford: Code 01237. Appledore HM 474569; Pilot 477928; Bideford HM/Pilot 428700, mob 07967 333725, 🖷 478849; Dr 474994. Instow/Barnstaple: Code 01271. HM via Amenities Officer 388327; Dr 372672. Common Nos: MRCC (01792) 366534; Marinecall 09068 969649; Police 08705 777444.

FACILITIES

APPLEDORE: no AB; slips at town quay. **Services:** CH, D, EI, Ⓔ, BY, C (70 tons), Slip, ME, 🔧.

BIDEFORD: some AB (contact HM), FW, CH, 🚽, R, Gas, Bar. Ferry to Lundy Is.

INSTOW: **North Devon YC**, ☎ 860367, FW, Slip, R, Bar; **Services:** AB and a few moorings, £5 via Instow Marine ☎ 861081, CH, D, ME, M, Ⓔ, C (4 ton). **Town** R, FW, Bar.

BARNSTAPLE: AB (free for short stay, see HM), 🚽, Bar, Gas. FW: limited facilities; P & D: small quantities in cans. Bulk D (min 500 ltrs/110 galls) by bowser, see HM.

Towns ✉ (all four), Ⓑ (Barnstaple, Bideford), 🚆 (Barnstaple), ✈ (Exeter).

CLOVELLY, Devon, 51°00′·18N 04°23′·77W ✿✿✿✿✿. AC *1164*. Tides see above. HW –0524 on Dover. Tiny drying hbr, 5M E of Hartland Pt, is sheltered from S/SW winds; useful to await the tide into Bideford or around Hartland Pt. Some AB (max LOA 12m) £4 on pier, access only near HW; or ⚓ off in 5m. Lt Fl G 5s 5m 5M on hbr wall. HM ☎ (01237) 431761. Facilities: Slip, FW, ✉, limited 🚽, P, D.

## RIVERS TAW & TORRIDGE *continued*

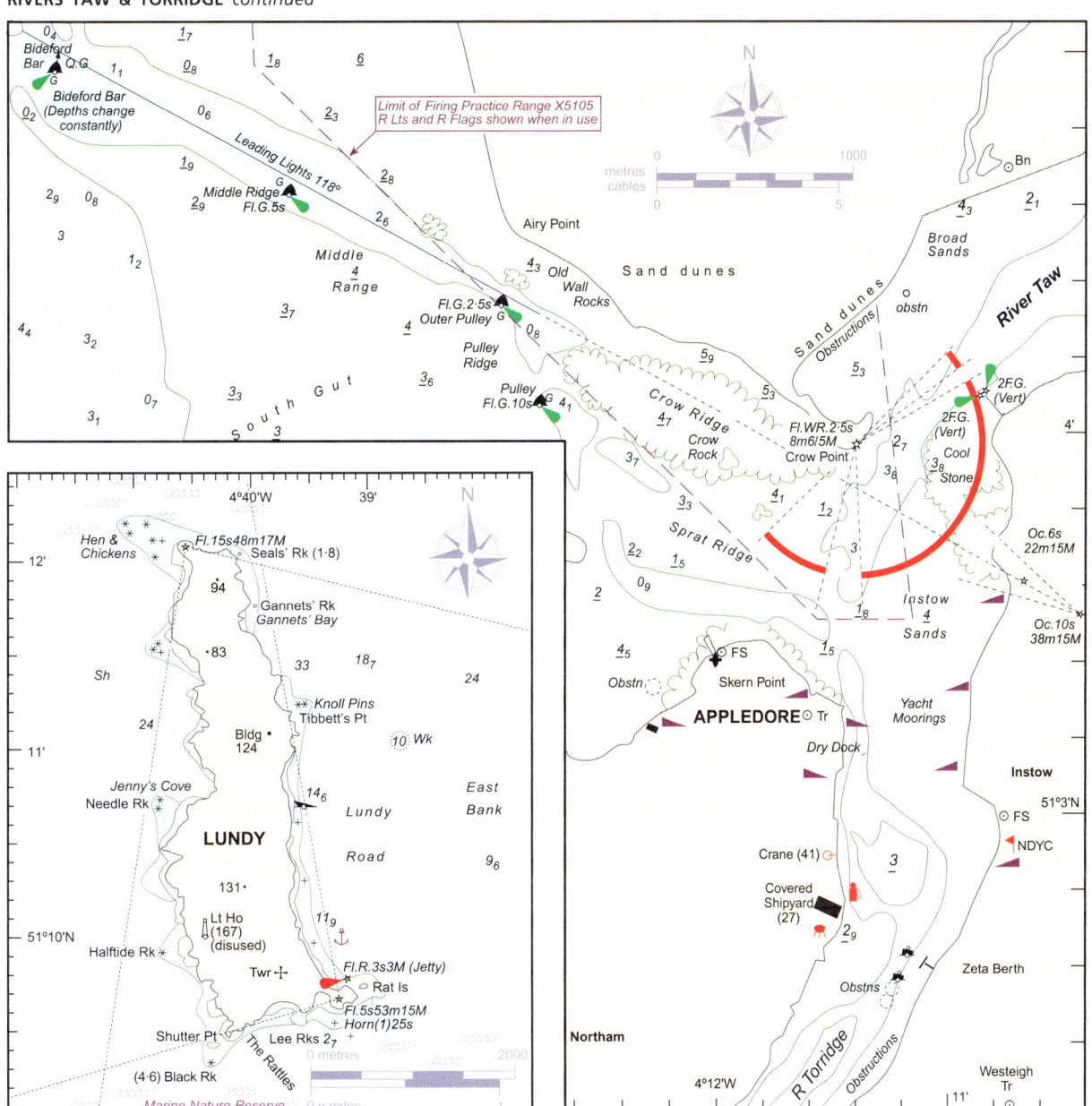

## ISLAND IN BRISTOL CHANNEL, 10M NNW of Hartland Pt

**LUNDY ISLAND**, Devon, **51°09'·83N 04°39'·27W**. AC *5608, 1179, 1164*. HW −0530 on Dover; ML 4·3m; Duration 0605. See 4.23. Shore Office ☎ 01237 470074, Island ☎ 01237 431831. Beware bad tide races, esp on E-going flood, off the N and SE tips of the island; and to the SW on the W-going ebb. A violent race forms over Stanley Bank 3M NE of the N tip. Shelter good in lee of island's high ground (145m). In SSW to NW winds, usual ⚓ is close inshore to NW of SE Pt and Rat Island, clear of ferry. In N'lies ⚓ in The Rattles, small bay on S side. In E'lies Jenny's Cove is safe if no W'ly swell. Lts: NW Pt, Fl 15s 48m 17M, vis 009°-285°, W ○ tr. On SE Pt, Fl 5s 53m 15M, vis 170°-073°, W ○ tr, horn 25s. Two Historic Wrecks (see 0.29) lie on the E side of island, at 51°11'N 04°39'·4W, and 4ca further E. Facilities: Landing by the ⚓ off SE end of island or using N side of jetty to disembark passengers only, boats may not remain alongside; £3.50/person landing fee. The waters around Lundy are a Marine Nature Reserve. **Lundy Co**: Gas, Bar, limited stores, ✉.

## MINOR HARBOURS ON THE NW COAST OF CORNWALL

**BUDE**, Cornwall, **50°49'·93N 04°33'·37W**. AC *5608*, 1156. HW − 0540 on Dover. Duration 0605. See 4.25. Limited shelter in drying hbr, access HW±2 in daylight, quiet weather, no swell conditions but sea-lock gives access to canal basin with 2m. Conspic W radar dish aerials 3·3M N of hbr. Outer ldg marks 075°, front W spar with Y ◇ topmark, rear W flagstaff; hold this line until inner ldg marks in line at 131°, front W pile, rear W spar, both with Y △ topmarks. There are no lts. VHF Ch 16 12 (when vessel expected). Advise HM of ETA with 24H notice ☎/🖷 (01288) 353111; FW on quay; **Town** (½M); Ⓑ, Bar, ✉, R, 🛒, Gas.

**BOSCASTLE**, Cornwall, **50°41'·48N 04°42·17W**. AC *5608*, 1156. HW −0543 on Dover; see 4.25. A tiny, picturesque hbr, almost a land-locked cleft in the cliffs. Access HW±2, but not in onshore winds when swell causes surge inside. An E'ly appr, S of Meachard Rk (37m high, 2ca NW of hbr), is best. 2 short bkwtrs at ent; moor bows-on to drying S quay. HM ☎ 01840 250453.

# 4.25 PADSTOW

Cornwall **50°32'·51N 04°56'·17W** ❀❀♨♨♨✿✿✿

**CHARTS** AC *5608*, 1156, 1168; Imray C58; Stanfords 13; OS 200

**TIDES** –0550 Dover; ML 4·0; Duration 0600

**Standard Port MILFORD HAVEN (←)**

| Times | | | | Height (metres) | | | |
|---|---|---|---|---|---|---|---|
| High Water | | Low Water | | MHWS | MHWN | MLWN | MLWS |
| 0100 | 0700 | 0100 | 0700 | 7·0 | 5·2 | 2·5 | 0·7 |
| 1300 | 1900 | 1300 | 1900 | | | | |
| **Differences BUDE** | | | | | | | |
| –0040 | –0040 | –0035 | –0045 | +0·7 | +0·6 | No data | |
| **BOSCASTLE** | | | | | | | |
| –0045 | –0010 | –0110 | –0100 | +0·3 | +0·4 | +0·2 | +0·2 |
| **PADSTOW** | | | | | | | |
| –0055 | –0050 | –0040 | –0050 | +0·3 | +0·4 | +0·1 | +0·1 |
| **WADEBRIDGE** (R Camel) | | | | | | | |
| –0052 | –0052 | +0235 | +0245 | –3·8 | –3·8 | –2·5 | –0·4 |
| **NEWQUAY** | | | | | | | |
| –0100 | –0110 | –0105 | –0050 | 0·0 | +0·1 | 0·0 | –0·1 |
| **PERRANPORTH** | | | | | | | |
| –0100 | –0110 | –0110 | –0050 | –0·1 | 0·0 | 0·0 | +0·1 |
| **ST IVES** | | | | | | | |
| –0050 | –0115 | –0105 | –0040 | –0·4 | –0·3 | –0·1 | +0·1 |
| **CAPE CORNWALL** | | | | | | | |
| –0130 | –0145 | –0120 | –0120 | –1·0 | –0·9 | –0·5 | –0·1 |

NOTE: At Wadebridge LW time differences give the start of the rise, following a LW stand of about 5 hours.

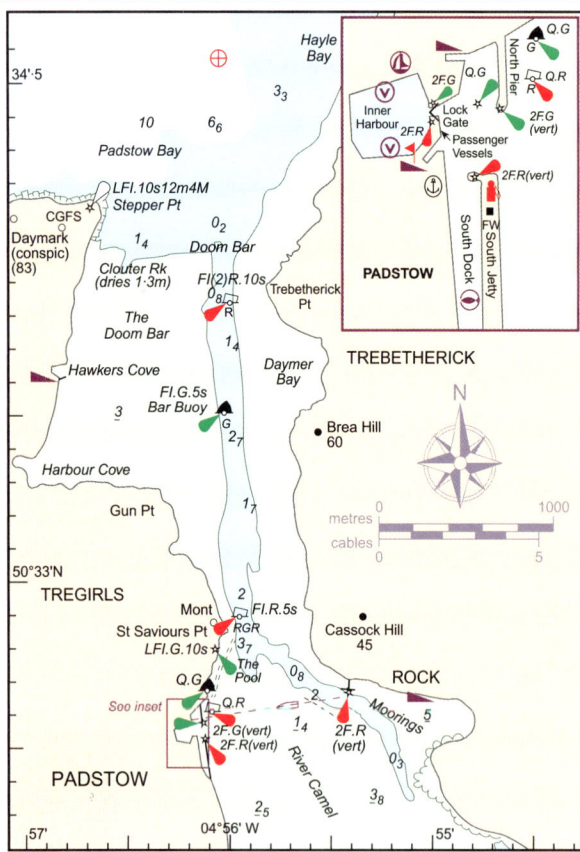

**SHELTER** Good in inner hbr 3m+, access via tidal gate HW±2 sp, ±1½ nps via tidal gate. If too late for gate, moor in the Pool or ⚓ close N in 1·5m LWS. Drying moorings available for smaller craft. Good AB at Wadebridge 4.5M up R Camel.

**NAVIGATION** WPT 50°34'·56N 04°56'·07W, 044°/ 0·6M to Stepper Pt. From SW, beware Quies Rks, Gulland Rk, The Hen, Gurley Rk,

Chimney Rks and a wreck 5ca W of Stepper Pt (all off the chartlet). From N, keep well off Newland Island and its offlying reef.

- Best appr HW–2½, do not try LW±1½; least depth on the bar is 0·5m at MLWS. Waiting ⚓s in Port Quin Bay in lee of Rumps Pt and Mother Ivey's Bay 3M WSW Stepper Pt.
- Shifting banks in estuary require care and a rising tide (ditto the drying R Camel to Wadebridge, 4M). In doubt, consult HM.
- Identify/align 180° the first 2 chan buoys before entry. In strong onshore winds or heavy ground swell, seas can break on Doom Bar and in the adjacent chan.
- S of St Saviour's Pt the chan lies very close to W shore.

**LIGHTS AND MARKS** See 4.3 and chartlet

**R/T** VHF Ch 12 16 (Mon-Fri 0800–1700 and HW±2). Water taxi.

**TELEPHONE** (Codes 01841; 01208 = Wadebridge) HM 532239 ✉ 533346; padstowharbour@btconnect.com; MRCC (01326) 317575; Marinecall 09068 500 458; Police 08705 777444; Dr 532346.

**FACILITIES** Hbr ☎ 532239, ✉ 533346, AB £1.40, ⛽, Slip( £3.50/£5.00 depends on engine hp), M, FW, El, C (60 ton), D, Gas, Gaz, ME, ▣, showers, ♨, R, Bar, Wi-fi; **Rock SC ☎** (01208) 862431, Slip; **Ferry 1** to Rock, also on request as water taxi, ☎ (01326) 317575 or VHF Ch 12 16. **Services:** BY, C, ME, CH, Slip, L, ⚒. **Town** ▣, P, ✉, ⑧, ⇌ (bus to Bodmin Parkway), ✈ (Newquay/Plymouth). **Wadebridge** HM as Padstow; AB only; **Town** ♨, R, Bar, ✉, ⑧, Wi-fi in Tourist Information Centre.

## MINOR HBRS BETWEEN BOSCASTLE AND LAND'S END

**PORT ISAAC**, Cornwall, **50°35'·75N 04°49'·57W**. AC 1156, 1168. HW –0548 on Dover; ML 4·1m. Small drying hbr, access HW±2. Conspic ⊕ tr bears 171°/1·3M. Rks close E of 50m wide ent between short bkwtrs. HM ☎ 01208 880607; ♨, R, Bar, ✉, LB.

**NEWQUAY**, Cornwall, **50°25'·06N 05°05'·19W**. AC 1149, 1168. HW –0604 on Dover; ML 3·7m; see 4.25. Ent to drying hbr ('The Gap') between two walls, is 23m wide. Beware Old Dane Rk and Listrey Rk outside hbr towards Towan Hd. Swell causes a surge in the hbr. Enter HW±2 but not in strong onshore winds. Berth as directed by HM. Lts: N pier 2 FG (vert) 2M; S pier 2 FR (vert) 2M. VHF Ch 08 16 14. HM ☎ (01637) 872809 mob 07813 064412. Facilities: Gas, Gaz, CH. **Town;** FW, Slip, D, ♨, R, Bar. Note: Shoal draft boats can dry out in Gannel Creek, close S of Newquay, but only in settled weather. Beware causeway bridge half way up creek.

**PORTREATH**, Cornwall, **50°15'·88N 05°17'·57W**. AC 1149. HW – 0600 on Dover. Conspic W daymark (38m) at E side of ent to small drying hbr, access HW±2. Gull Rk (23m) is 3ca W of ent and Horse Rk is close N. Keep close to pier on W side of chan. AB in either of 2 basins, both dry. ♨, R, Bar, ✉.

**HAYLE**, Cornwall, **50°11'·84N 05°26'·19W** (Chan ent) ❀♨✿. AC 1149, 1168. HW –0605 on Dover; ML 3·6m; Duration 0555. See 4.25. Drying hbr gives very good shelter, but is not advised for yachts. In ground swell dangerous seas break on the bar, drying 2·7m; approx 4m at ent @ MHWS. Cross the bar in good weather HW±1. Charted aids do not necessarily indicate best water. Ldg marks/lts 180°: both W □ R horiz band, ☆ FW 17/23m 4M. PHM buoy, QR is about 7ca N of the front ldg lt. Training wall on W side of ent chan is marked by 5 lit perches, all Oc G 4s. The hbr is divided by long central island (about 700m long, with lt bn QG at NW end) which should be left to stbd. Follow the SE arm of hbr to Hayle; the S arm leads to Lelant Quay. HM ☎ (01736) 754043, AB £5. Facilities: ⑧, Bar, FW (can), ⇌, R, ♨, Gas, P & D (cans).

**ST IVES**, Cornwall, **50°12'·79N 05°28'·67W** ❀❀♨♨✿✿✿. AC 1149, 1168. HW –0610 on Dover; ML 3·6m; Duration 0555. See 4.25. Drying hbr with about 4·5m @ MHWS. Good shelter except in on-shore winds when heavy swell works in. ⚓s and ⚓ in 3m between the hbr and Porthminster Pt to S and drying Or ⚓s in hbr. From the NW beware Hoe Rk off St Ives Hd, and from SE The Carracks. Keep E of SHM buoy about 1½ ca ENE of E pier. Lts: E pier hd 2 FG (vert) 8m 5M. W pier hd 2 FR (vert) 5m 3M. VHF Ch 12 16 (occas). HM ☎/✉ (01736) 795018. Facilities: ⚓s £12.13; **E Pier** FW. **Town** Gas, Gaz, ⑧, ▣, Bar, ✉, R, ♨, ⇌.

# Sailing HOLIDAYS IN IRELAND

## CALL US NOW FOR 2008

2008/NC4/z

NIT HARBOUR MARINA
+353-66-7136231

KILRUSH MARINA & BOATYARD
+353-65-9052072

BANGOR MARINA
028 9145 3297

CARLINGFORD MARINA
+353-4293-73073

DINGLE MARINA
+353-66-9151629

MALAHIDE MARINA
+353-1-8454129

LAWRENCE COVE MARINA
+353-27-75044

DUBLIN CITY MOORINGS
+353-1-818 3300

SALVE MARINE
+353-21-831145

DUN LAOGHAIRE MARINA
+353-1-2020040

ASTLEPARK MARINA
+353-21-4774959

CROSSHAVEN BOATYARD
+353-21-4831161

WATERFORD CITY MARINA
+353-51-309900

KILMORE QUAY MARINA
+353-53-29955

Map labels: LARNE, DONEGAL, BELFAST, SLIGO, GALWAY, R. Shannon, DUBLIN, Lough Derg, LIMERICK, ROSSLARE, KILLARNEY, CORK

## Sail in Ireland and enjoy the experience of a lifetime

Further information: Sailing Holidays in Ireland, Trident Hotel, Kinsale, Co. Cork, Ireland. Tel +353-21-477 2927.

www.sailingireland.com    www.irelandwatersports.net    Email:sailirl@indigo.ie

# Ireland

## All Ireland

Ireland

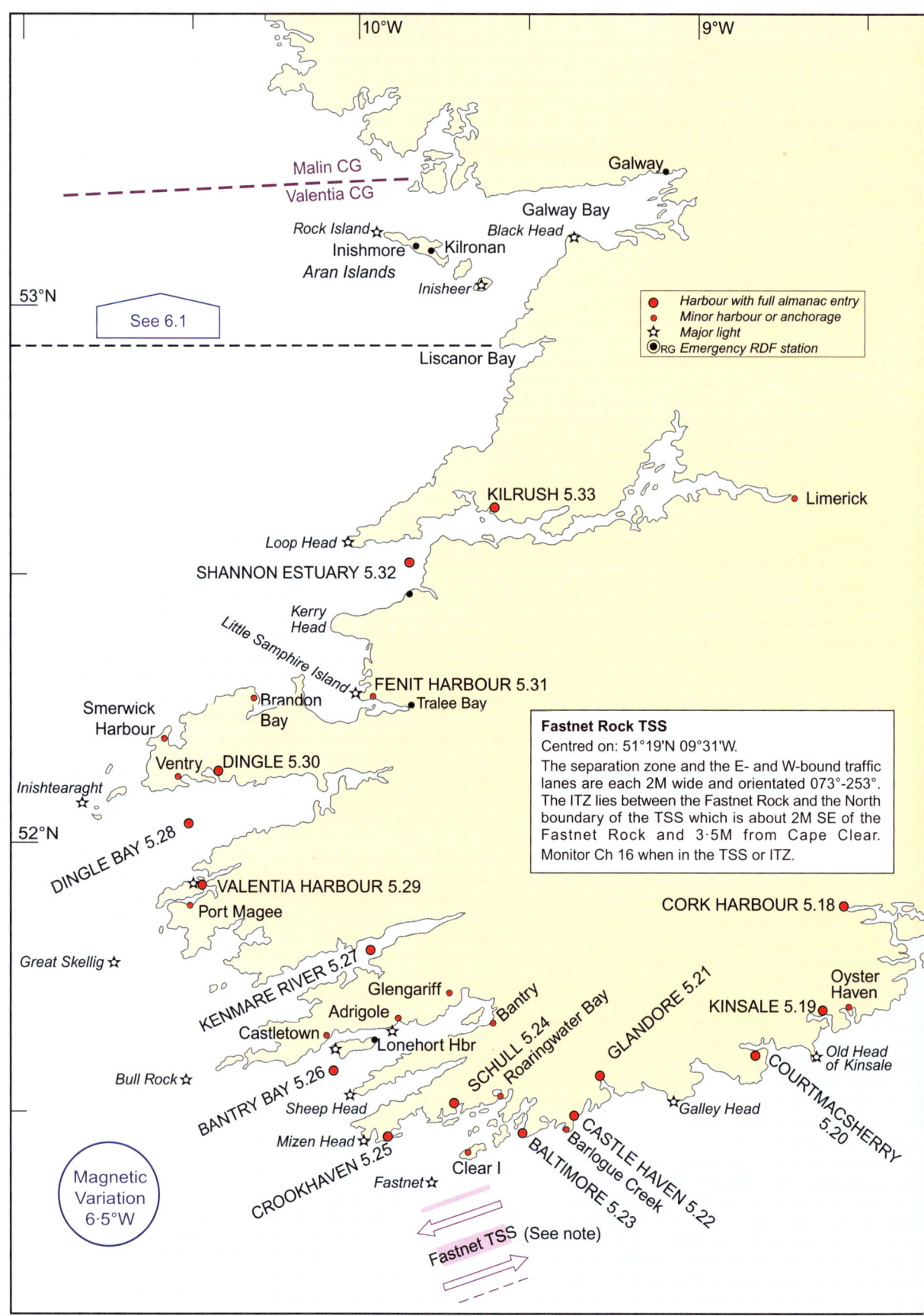

Malin CG
Valentia CG

Galway

Galway Bay

Rock Island ☆
Inishmore
Aran Islands
Kilronan
Black Head ☆

*Inisheer* ☆

53°N

See 6.1

| ● | Harbour with full almanac entry |
| ● | Minor harbour or anchorage |
| ☆ | Major light |
| ◉RG | Emergency RDF station |

Liscanor Bay

KILRUSH 5.33

Limerick

Loop Head ☆

SHANNON ESTUARY 5.32

Kerry
Head

Little Samphire Island

FENIT HARBOUR 5.31

Smerwick
Harbour

Brandon
Bay

Tralee Bay

Ventry

DINGLE 5.30

**Fastnet Rock TSS**
Centred on: 51°19'N 09°31'W.
The separation zone and the E- and W-bound traffic lanes are each 2M wide and orientated 073°-253°. The ITZ lies between the Fastnet Rock and the North boundary of the TSS which is about 2M SE of the Fastnet Rock and 3·5M from Cape Clear. Monitor Ch 16 when in the TSS or ITZ.

Inishtearaght ☆

52°N

DINGLE BAY 5.28

VALENTIA HARBOUR 5.29

Port Magee

CORK HARBOUR 5.18

Great Skellig ☆

KENMARE RIVER 5.27

Glengariff

Bantry

Oyster
Haven

KINSALE 5.19

Adrigole

Castletown

Lonehort Hbr

GLANDORE 5.21

Old Head
of Kinsale

Bull Rock ☆

BANTRY BAY 5.26

SCHULL 5.24

Roaringwater Bay

COURTMACSHERRY
5.20

Sheep Head

Galley Head ☆

Mizen Head ☆

CROOKHAVEN 5.25

Clear I

CASTLE HAVEN 5.22

Barlogue Creek

BALTIMORE 5.23

Magnetic
Variation
6·5°W

*Fastnet* ☆

Fastnet TSS (See note)

| | | | | | | | | | | | | | | | | | | | | |
|---|---|---|---|---|---|---|---|---|---|---|---|---|---|---|---|---|---|---|---|---|
| 1. | *Carlingford Lough* | **1** | | | | | | | | | | | | | | | | | | |
| 2. | Howth | 39 | **2** | | | | | | | | | | | | | | | | | |
| 3. | **Dun Laoghaire** | 48 | 8 | **3** | | | | | | | | | | | | | | | | |
| 4. | **Wicklow** | 63 | 25 | 21 | **4** | | | | | | | | | | | | | | | |
| 5. | **Arklow** | 75 | 37 | 36 | 15 | **5** | | | | | | | | | | | | | | |
| 6. | **Tuskar Rock** | 113 | 73 | 70 | 52 | 37 | **6** | | | | | | | | | | | | | |
| 7. | **Rosslare** | 108 | 70 | 66 | 47 | 34 | 8 | **7** | | | | | | | | | | | | |
| 8. | **Dunmore East** | 139 | 101 | 102 | 84 | 69 | 32 | 32 | **8** | | | | | | | | | | | |
| 9. | Youghal | 172 | 134 | 133 | 115 | 100 | 63 | 65 | 34 | **9** | | | | | | | | | | |
| 10. | **Crosshaven** | 192 | 154 | 155 | 137 | 122 | 85 | 85 | 59 | 25 | **10** | | | | | | | | | |
| 11. | Kinsale | 202 | 164 | 168 | 150 | 135 | 98 | 95 | 69 | 35 | 17 | **11** | | | | | | | | |
| 12. | **Baltimore** | 239 | 201 | 196 | 177 | 164 | 128 | 132 | 102 | 70 | 54 | 42 | **12** | | | | | | | |
| 13. | **Fastnet Rock** | 250 | 212 | 207 | 189 | 174 | 137 | 144 | 112 | 78 | 60 | 49 | 10 | **13** | | | | | | |
| 14. | Bantry | 281 | 243 | 241 | 223 | 208 | 171 | 174 | 146 | 112 | 94 | 83 | 42 | 34 | **14** | | | | | |
| 15. | **Darrynane** | 283 | 245 | 240 | 221 | 208 | 172 | 176 | 146 | 114 | 98 | 86 | 44 | 39 | 38 | **15** | | | | |
| 16. | Valentia | 295 | 257 | 252 | 242 | 227 | 184 | 188 | 165 | 131 | 113 | 102 | 56 | 48 | 55 | 16 | **16** | | | |
| 17. | Dingle | 308 | 270 | 265 | 246 | 233 | 197 | 201 | 171 | 139 | 123 | 111 | 69 | 61 | 63 | 29 | 13 | **17** | | |
| 18. | Kilrush | 361 | 323 | 318 | 299 | 286 | 250 | 254 | 224 | 192 | 176 | 164 | 122 | 114 | 116 | 82 | 66 | 64 | **18** | |
| 19. | *Galway* | 366 | 362 | 357 | 339 | 324 | 287 | 291 | 262 | 228 | 210 | 199 | 159 | 150 | 155 | 119 | 103 | 101 | 76 | **19** |
| 20. | *Slyne Head* | 317 | 351 | 346 | 328 | 313 | 276 | 283 | 251 | 217 | 199 | 188 | 153 | 139 | 144 | 113 | 97 | 95 | 75 | 49 | **20** |

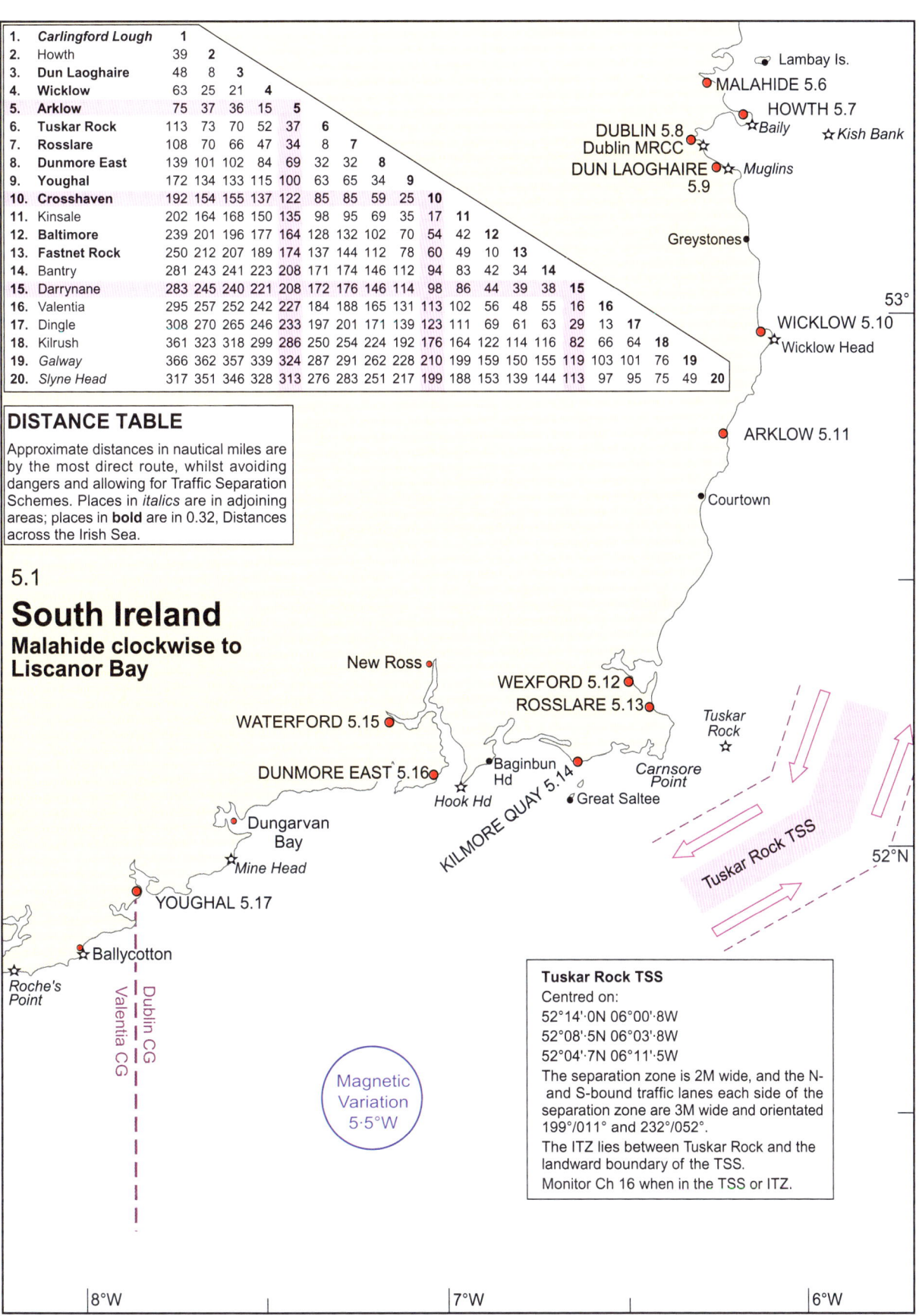

## DISTANCE TABLE

Approximate distances in nautical miles are by the most direct route, whilst avoiding dangers and allowing for Traffic Separation Schemes. Places in *italics* are in adjoining areas; places in **bold** are in 0.32, Distances across the Irish Sea.

5.1

# South Ireland

## Malahide clockwise to Liscanor Bay

Lambay Is.

MALAHIDE 5.6

HOWTH 5.7
☆*Baily*  ☆*Kish Bank*

DUBLIN 5.8
Dublin MRCC

DUN LAOGHAIRE ☆☆*Muglins*
5.9

Greystones

53°

WICKLOW 5.10
☆ Wicklow Head

ARKLOW 5.11

Courtown

New Ross

WEXFORD 5.12
ROSSLARE 5.13

*Tuskar Rock*
☆

WATERFORD 5.15

DUNMORE EAST 5.16
☆ *Hook Hd*

Baginbun Hd

KILMORE QUAY 5.14

*Carnsore Point*

Great Saltee

Tuskar Rock TSS

52°N

Dungarvan Bay

☆ *Mine Head*

YOUGHAL 5.17

☆ Ballycotton

*Roche's Point*

Dublin CG
Valentia CG

Magnetic Variation 5·5°W

### Tuskar Rock TSS

Centred on:
52°14'·0N 06°00'·8W
52°08'·5N 06°03'·8W
52°04'·7N 06°11'·5W

The separation zone is 2M wide, and the N- and S-bound traffic lanes each side of the separation zone are 3M wide and orientated 199°/011° and 232°/052°.

The ITZ lies between Tuskar Rock and the landward boundary of the TSS.

Monitor Ch 16 when in the TSS or ITZ.

8°W          7°W          6°W

## 5.2 SOUTH IRELAND TIDAL STREAMS

The tidal arrows (with no rates shown) off the S and W coasts of Ireland are printed by kind permission of the Irish Cruising Club, to whom the Editor is indebted. They have been found accurate, but should be used with caution.

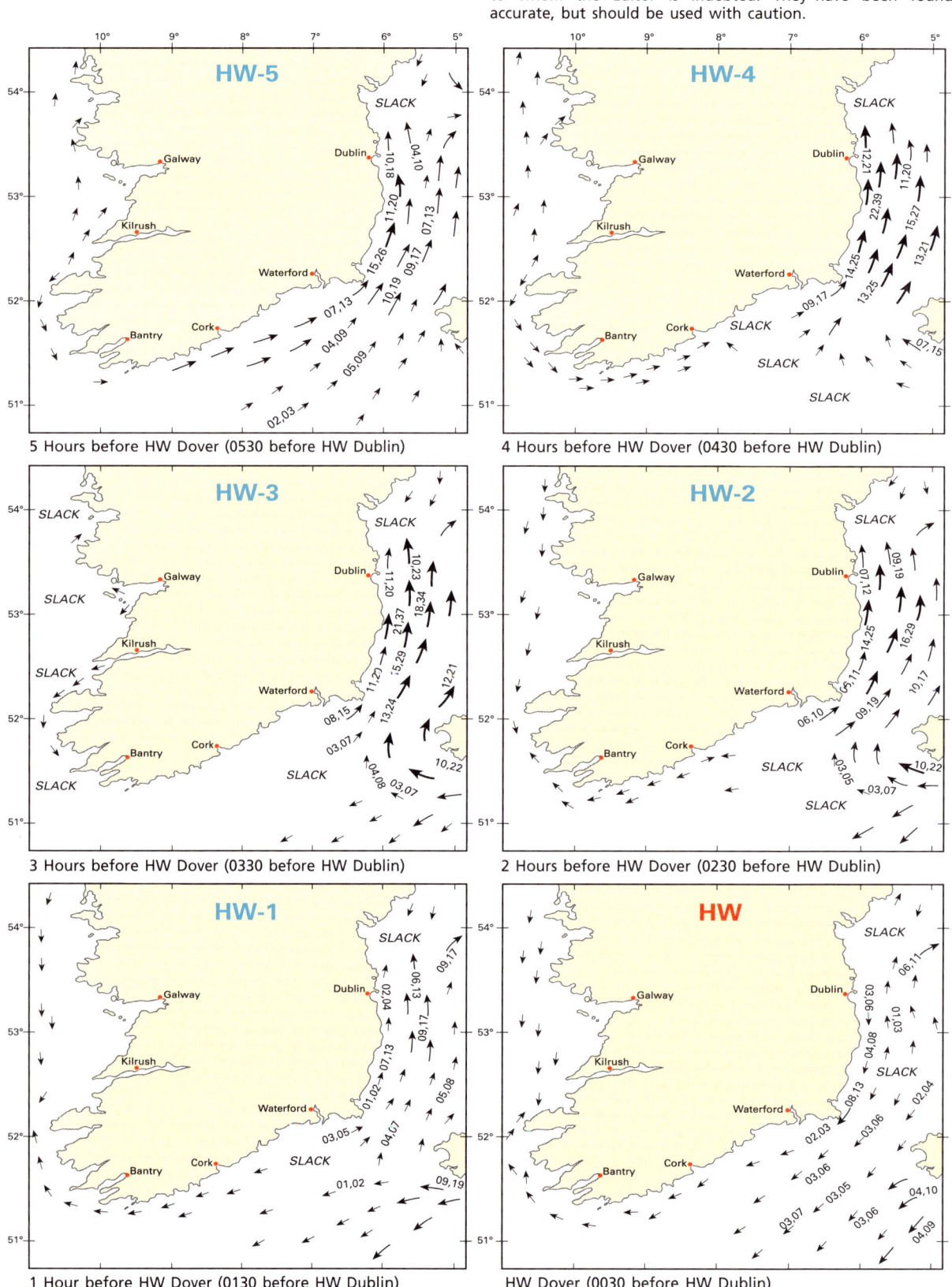

5 Hours before HW Dover (0530 before HW Dublin)

4 Hours before HW Dover (0430 before HW Dublin)

3 Hours before HW Dover (0330 before HW Dublin)

2 Hours before HW Dover (0230 before HW Dublin)

1 Hour before HW Dover (0130 before HW Dublin)

HW Dover (0030 before HW Dublin)

Northward 6.2     South Irish Sea 4.2

The tidal arrows (with no rates shown) off the S and W coasts of Ireland are printed by kind permission of the Irish Cruising Club, to whom the Editor is indebted. They have been found accurate, but should be used with caution.

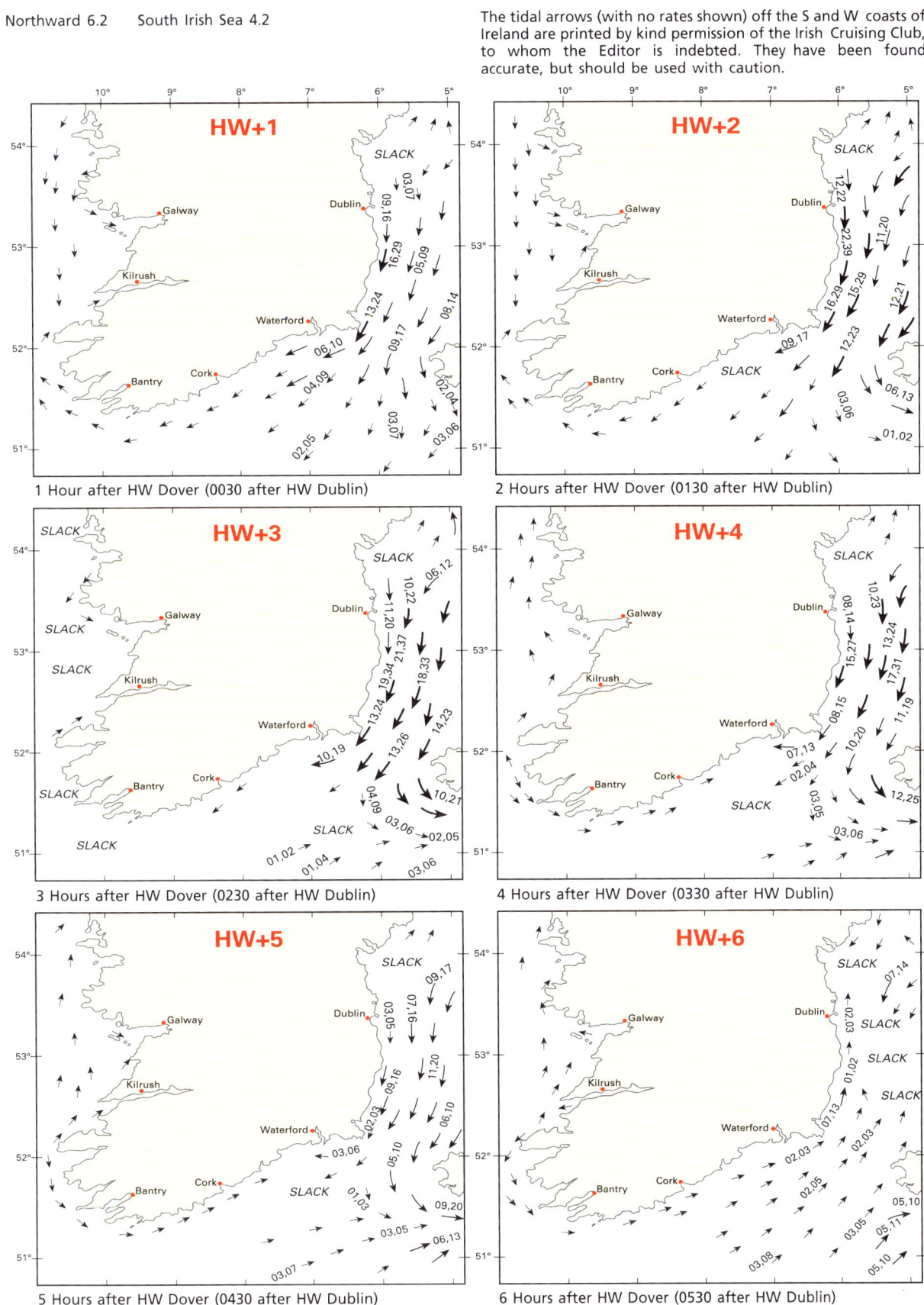

1 Hour after HW Dover (0030 after HW Dublin)

2 Hours after HW Dover (0130 after HW Dublin)

3 Hours after HW Dover (0230 after HW Dublin)

4 Hours after HW Dover (0330 after HW Dublin)

5 Hours after HW Dover (0430 after HW Dublin)

6 Hours after HW Dover (0530 after HW Dublin)

## 5.3 LIGHTS, BUOYS AND WAYPOINTS

**Bold** print = light with a nominal range of 15M or more. CAPITALS = place or feature. *CAPITAL ITALICS* = light-vessel, light float or Lanby. *Italics* = Fog signal. ***Bold italics*** = Racon. See 0.2 for Abbreviations.

### LAMBAY ISLAND TO TUSKAR ROCK

#### MALAHIDE, LAMBAY ISLAND and HOWTH

Tailor's Rks ↙ Q; 53°30'·21N 06°01'·87W.
Burren Rks ⅃ 53°29'·35N 06°02'·47W.
Howth ◣ Fl G 5s; 53°23'·74N 06°03'·59W.
Rowan Rocks ↙ Q (3) 10s; 53°23'·88N 06°03'·27W.
E Pier Hd ∳ Fl (2) WR 7·5s 13m W12M, R9M; W twr; vis: W256°-R295°-256°; 53°23'·66N 06°04'·03W.

**Baily** ☆ 53°21'·70N 06°03'·14W Fl 15s 41m **26M**; twr.
Rosbeg E ↙ Q (3) 10s; 53°21'·02N 06°03'·45W.
Rosbeg S ↙ Q (6) + L Fl 15s; 53°20'·22N 06°04'·17W.
N Burford ↙ Q; *Whis;* 53°20'·52N 06°01'·49W.
S Burford ↙ VQ (6) + L Fl 10s; *Whis;* 53°18'·07N 06°01'·27W.

#### PORT OF DUBLIN

Dublin Bay ↙ Mo (A) 10s; ***Racon (M);*** 53°19'·92N 06°04'·64W.
No. 3 ◣ IQ G; 53°20'·57N 06°06'·76W.
Great S Wall Hd Poolbeg ☆ Fl R 4s 20m 10M*(synchro with N.Bull);* R ○ twr; *Horn (2) 60s;* 53°20'·53N 06°09'·08W
N Bull ☆ Fl G 4s 15m 10M; G ○ twr; 53°20'·70N 06°08'·98W.
**N Bank** ☆ 53°20'·69N 06°10'·59W Oc G 8s 10m **16M**; G ☐ twr.

#### DUN LAOGHAIRE

**E Bkwtr Hd** ∳ 53°18'·15N 06°07'·62W Fl (2) R 10s 16m **17M**; twr, R lantern; *Horn 30s.*
Muglins ∳Fl 5s 14m 11M; 53°16'·55N 06°04'·58W.
Bennett Bank ↙ Q (6) + L Fl 15s; 53°20'·17N 05°55'·11W.
**Kish Bank** ☆ 53°18'·64N 05°55'·48W Fl (2) 20s 29m **22M**; W twr, R band; ***Racon (T) 15M***; *Horn (2) 30s.*
E Kish ⌐ Fl (2) R 10s; 53°14'·35N 05°53'·56W.
E Codling ⌐ Fl (4) R 10s; 53°08'·54N 05°47'·11W.
W Codling ◣ Fl G 10s; 53°06'·97N 05°54'·51W.
S Codling ↙ VQ (6) + L Fl 10s; 53°04'·74N 05°49'·76W.
Greystones ⌐ Fl Y 5s; 53°08'·42N 06°02'·54W.
Moulditch Bk ⌐ Fl R 10s; 53°08'·42N 06°01'·22W.
Breaches Shoal ⌐ Fl (2) R 6s; 53°05'·67N 05°59'·81W.
North India ↙ Q; 53°03'·12N 05°53'·46W.
South India ↙ Q (6) + L Fl 15s; 53°00'·36N 05°53'·31W.
*CODLING LANBY* ⌐ 53°03'·02N 05°40'·76W Fl 4s 12m **15M**; tubular structure on By; ***Racon (G)10M***; *Horn 20s.*

#### WICKLOW and ARKLOW

Wicklow E Pier Hd ∳ Fl WR 5s 11m 6M; W twr, R base and cupola; vis: 136°-R-293°-W-136°; 52°58'·99N 06°02'·07W.
**Wicklow Head** ☆ 52°57'·95N 05°59'·89W Fl (3) 15s 37m **23M**; W twr.
Horseshoe ⌐ Fl R 3s; 52°56'·62N 05°59'·31W.
N Arklow ↙ Q; 52°53'·86N 05°55'·21W.
No. 2 Arklow ⌐ Fl R 6s; 52°50'·22N 05°54'·56W.
Arklow Bank Wind Farm from 52°48'·47N 05°56'·57W to 52°46'·47N 05°57'·11W, N and S Turbines Fl Y 5s14m 10M + Fl W Aero lts. AIS transmitters. Other turbines Fl Y 5s. See 9.12.5.
Arklow S Pier Hd ∳ Fl WR 6s 11m 13M; twr; vis: R shore- W223°-R350°-shore; 52°47'·61N 06°08'·22W.
No. 1 Arklow ⌐ Fl (3) R 10s; 52°44'·32N 05°56'·05W.
S Arklow ↙ VQ (6) + L Fl 10s; 52°40'·82N 05°59'·21W.
*ARKLOW LANBY* ⌐ 52°39'·52N 05°58'·16W Fl (2) 12s 12m **15M**; ***Racon (O)10M***; *Horn Mo (A) 30s.*
No. 2 Glassgorman ⌐ Fl (4) R 10s; 52°44'·52N 06°05'·36W.
No. 1 Glassgorman ⌐ Fl (2) R 6s; 52°39'·08N 06°07'·42W.
N Blackwater ↙ Q; 52°32'·22N 06°09'·51W.
No. 1 Rusk ◣ Fl (2) G 5s; 52°28'·54N 06°11'·80W.
E Blackwater ↙ Q (3) 10s; 52°28'·02N 06°08'·06W.
W Blackwater ◣ Fl G 6s; 52°25'·87N 06°13'·56W.

SE Blackwater ⌐ Fl R 10s; 52°25'·64N 06°09'·66W.
S Blackwater ↙ Q (6) + L Fl 15s; 52°22'·76N 06°12'·86W.

#### WEXFORD and ROSSLARE

North Long ↙ Q; 52°21'·44N 06°17'·04W.
West Long ◣ QG; 52°18'·18N 06°17'·96W.
Lucifer ↙ VQ (3) 5s; 52°17'·02N 06°12'·67W.
S Long ↙ VQ (6) + L Fl 10s; 52°14'·84N 06°15'·64W.
Calmines ⌐ Fl R 2s; 52°15'·01N 06°17'·77W.
W Holdens ◣ Fl (3) G 10s; 52°15'·77N 06°18'·74W.
**Tuskar** ☆ 52°12'·17N 06°12'·42W Q (2) 7·5s 33m **24M**; W twr; *Horn (4) 45s, **Racon (T) 18M***.

### TUSKAR ROCK TO OLD HEAD OF KINSALE

S Rock ↙ Q (6) + L Fl 15s; 52°10'·80N 06°12'·84W.
Fundale ⌐ Fl (2) R 10s; 52°10'·64N 06°20'·26W.
Barrels ↙ Q (3) 10s; 52°08'·32N 06°22'·05W.

#### KILMORE

St Patrick's Bridge ⌐ Fl R 6s; (Apr-Sep); 52°09'·30N 06°34'·71W.
Kilmore Bkwtr Hd ∳ Q RG 7m 5M; vis: 269°-R-354°-G-003°-R-077°; 52°10'·20N 06°35'·15W.
Kilmore Quay SWM ↙ Iso 10s; (Apr-Sep); 52°09'·20N 06°35'·30W.
Coningbeg ↙ Q(6)+LFl 15s, Racon, AIS; 52°03'·20N 06°38'·57W.

#### WATERFORD and DUNMORE EAST

**Hook Hd** ☆ 52°07'·32N 06°55'·85W Fl 3s 46m **23M**; W twr, two B bands; ***Racon (K) 10M vis 237°-177°***; *Horn (2) 45s.*
Waterford ↙ Fl R 3s. Fl (3) 10s; 52°08'·95N 06°57'·00W.
Duncannon No. 1 ◣ Fl G 2s; 52°11'·02N 06°56'·28W.
Duncannon Dir lt 002°. F WRG 13m 10M, white tower on fort, 359·5°-FG-001·2°-Alt GW-001·7°-FW-002·4°-Alt WR-002·9°-FR-004·5°; Oc WR 4s 13m W 9M R 7M on same tower, 119°-R-149°-W-172°.
**Dunmore East Pier Head** ☆ 52°08'·93N 06°59'·37W Fl WR 8s 13m **W17M**, R13M; Gy twr, vis: W225°- R310°-004°.
E Bkwtr extn ∳ Fl R 2s 6m 4M; vis: 000°-310°; 52°08'·98N 06°59'·37W.

#### DUNGARVAN, YOUGHAL and BALLYCOTTON

Ballinacourty Point ∳ Fl (2) WRG 10s 16m W10M, R8M, G8M; W twr; vis: G245°- W274°- R302°- W325°-117°; 52°04'·69N 07°33'·18W.
Helvick ↙ Q (3) 10s; 52°03'·61N 07°32'·25W.
**Mine Head** ☆ 51°59'·52N 07°35'·25W Fl (4) 20s 87m **20M**; W twr, B band; vis: 228°-052°.
Bar Rocks ↙ Q (6) + L Fl 15s; 51°54'·85N 07°50'·05W.
Blackball Ledge ↙ 51°55'·34N 07°48'·53W Q (3) 10s.
**Youghal W side of ent** ☆ 51°56'·57N 07°50'·53W Fl WR 2·5s 24m **W17M**, R13M; W twr; vis: W183°- R273°- W295°- R307°- W351°-003°.
**Ballycotton** ☆ 51°49'·52N 07° 59'·09W Fl WR 10s 59m **W21M, R17M**; B twr, within W walls, B lantern; vis: W238°- R048°-238°; *Horn (4) 90s.*
The Smiths ⌐ Fl (3) R 10s; 51°48'·62N 08°00'·71W.
Power ↙ Q (6) + L Fl 15s; 51°45'·59N 08°06'·67W.

#### CORK

Cork ↙ L Fl 10s; ***Racon (T) 7M***; 51°42'·92N 08°15'·60W.
Daunt Rock ⌐ Fl (2) R 6s; 51°43'·52N 08°17'·65W.
**Fort Davis Ldg lts 354·1°. Front**, 51°48'·82N 08°15'·80W Dir WRG 29m **17M**; vis: FG351·5°- AlWG352·25°- FW353°- AlWR355°- FR355·75°-356·5°. Rear, Dognose Quay, 203m from front, Oc 5s 37m 10M; Or 3, synch with front.
**Roche's Point** ☆ 51°47'·59N 08°15'·29W Fl WR 3s 30m **W20M, R16M**; vis: Rshore- W292°- R016°- 033°, W(unintens) 033°- R159°- shore.
Outer Hbr Rk E2 ⌐ Fl R 2·5s; 51°47'·52N 08°15'·67W.
W1 ◣ Fl G 10s; 51°47'·69N 08°16'·05W.
The Sound E4 ↙ Q; 51°47'·92N 08°15'·77W.
C1 ◣ Fl G 10s; 51°48'·82N 08°16'·97W.
E Ferry Marina, E Pass ∳ 2 FR (vert) N & S ends; 51°51'·91N 08°12'·82W.

#### KINSALE and OYSTER HAVEN

Bulman ↙ Q (6) + L Fl 15s; 51°40'·14N 08°29'·74W.
Charle's Fort ∳ Fl WRG 5s 18m W9M, R6M, G7M; vis: G348°- W358°- R004°-168°; H24; 51°41'·74N 08°29'·97W.

## OLD HEAD OF KINSALE TO MIZEN HEAD

**Old Head of Kinsale** ☆, S point 51°36'·28N 08°32'·03W Fl (2) 10s 72m **20M**; B twr, two W bands; *Horn (3) 45s*.

### COURTMACSHERRY

Black Tom ▲ Fl G 5s; 51°36'·41N 08°37'·95W.
Wood Pt ⚓ Fl (2) WR 5s 15m 5M; vis: W315°- R332°-315°; 51°38'·16N 08°41'·00W.
**Galley Head** ☆ summit 51°31'·80N 08°57'·19W Fl (5) 20s 53m **23M**; W twr; vis: 256°-065°.

### GLANDORE and CASTLE HAVEN

⚓ Glandore SW Fl 2 G 10s; 51°33'·15N 09°06'·64W.
Sunk Rock ▲ Fl G 5s; 51°33'·46N 09°06'·93W.
Reen Point ⚓ Fl WRG 10s 9m W5M, R3M, G3M; W twr; vis: Gshore- W338°- R001°-shore; 51°30'·98N 09°10'·50W.
Kowloon Bridge ⚓ Q (6) + L Fl 15s; 51°27'·58N 09°13'·75W.

### BALTIMORE, SCHULL and CROOKHAVEN

Loo Rock ▲ Fl G 3s; 51°28'·43N 09°23'·45W.
Lousy Rocks ⚓ 51°28'·95N 09°23'·03W
**Fastnet** ☆, W end 51°23'·35N 09°36'·19W Fl 5s 49m **27M**; Gy twr, *Horn (4) 60s*, *Racon (G) 18M*.
Copper Pt Long Is, E end ⚓ Q (3)10s 16m 8M; W☐ twr; 51°30'·24N 09°32'·08W.
Amelia Rk ▲ Fl G 3s; 51°29'·97N 09°31'·45W.
Bull Rock ⚓ Fl (2) R 6s 4m 4M; 51°30'·75N 09°32'·20W.
Black Horse Rocks ⚓ 51°28'·44N 09°41'·66W.
Rock Is Pt ⚓ L Fl WR 8s 20m W13M, R11M; W twr; vis: W over Long Is B to 281°-R-340°; inside hbr 281°-R-348°- N shore; 51°28'·59N 09°42'·29W.
**Mizen Head** ☆ 51°27'·00N 09°49'·24W Iso 4s 55m **15M**; vis: 313°-133°.

## MIZEN HEAD TO DINGLE BAY

**Sheep's Hd** ☆ 51°32'·60N 09°50'·95W Fl (3) WR 15s 83m **W18M, R15M**; W bldg; vis: 007°-R-017°-W-212°.

### BANTRY BAY and CASTLETOWN BEARHAVEN

**Roancarrigmore** ☆ 51°39'·19N 09°44'·83W Fl WR 3s 18m **W18M, R14M**; W☐ twr, B band; vis: 312°-W-050°-R-122°-R(unintens)-242°-R-312°. Reserve lt W8M, R6M obsc 140°-220°.
**Ardnakinna Pt** ☆ 51°37'·11N 09°55'·08W Fl (2) WR 10s 62m **W17M, R14M**; W ○ twr; vis: 319°-R- 348°-W- 066°-R-shore.
Walter Scott Rock ⚓ Q (6) + L Fl 15s; 51°38'·54N 09°54'·24W.
**Bull Rock** ☆ 51°35'·51N 10°18'·08W Fl 15s 83m **21M**; W twr; vis: 220°-186°.

### KENMARE RIVER, DARRYNANE and BALLYCROVANE

Ballycrovane Hbr ⚓ Fl R 3s; 51°42'·63N 09° 57'·53W.
Darrynane Ldg lts 034°. Front, Oc 3s 10m 4M; 51°45'·90N 10°09'·20W. Rear, Oc 3s 16m 4M.
**Skelligs Rock** ☆ 51°46'·12N 10°32'·51W Fl (3) 15s 53m **19M**; W twr; vis: 262°-115°; part obsc within 6M 110°-115°.

### VALENTIA and PORTMAGEE

**Fort (Cromwell) Point** ☆ 51°56'·02N 10°19'·27W Fl WR 2s 16m **W17M, R15M**; W twr; vis: 304°-R-351°,102°-W-304°; obsc from seaward by Doulus Head when brg more than 180°.
Kay Rk ⚓ Fl (2) 6s; 51°56'·68N 10°17'·43W.

Harbour Rk ⚓ Q (3) 10s 4m 5M; vis: 080°-040°; 51°55'·82N 10°18'·92W.
The Foot ⚓ VQ (3) 5s; 51°55'·73N 10°17'·10W.

## DINGLE BAY TO LOOP HEAD

### DINGLE

Dingle, NE side of ent. ⚓ Fl G 3s 20m 6M; 52°07'·30N 10°15'·51W.
Black Point ▲ Fl (3) G 5s; 52°07'·40N 10°15'·84W.
Flaherty Point ⚓ QR; 52°07'·51N 10°16'·05W.
**Inishtearaght** ☆, W end Blasket Islands 52°04'·55N 10°39'·68W Fl (2) 20s 84m **19M**; W twr; vis: 318°-221°; *Racon (O)*.

### TRALEE BAY and FENIT HARBOUR

**Little Samphire Is** ☆ 52°16'·26N 09°52'·91W Fl WRG 5s 17m **W16M**, R13M; G13M; Bu ○ twr; vis: 262°-R- 275°, 280-R-090°-G-140°-W- 152°-R-172°.
Great Samphire I ⚓ QR 15m 3M; vis: 242°-097°; 52°16'·15N 09°51'·82W.
Fenit Marina Ent Hd ⚓ Iso G 6s 6m; 52°16'·25N 09°51'·66W.

### SHANNON ESTUARY

**Loop Head** ☆ 52°33'·68N 09°55'·96W Fl (4) 20s 84m **23M**.
Ballybunnion ⚓ VQ; *Racon (M) 6M*; 52°32'·52N 09°46'·93W.
Kilstiffin ⚓ Fl R 3s; 52°33'·80N 09°43'·83W.
**Kilcredaune Head** ☆ Fl 6s 41m **15M**; W twr; 52°34'·79N 09°42'·58W; obsc 224°-247° by hill within 1M.
Kilcredaune ⚓ Fl (2+1) R 10s; 52°34'·44N 09°41'·70W.
Tail of Beal ⚓ Q (9) 15s; 52°34'·39N 09°40'·75W.
Carrigaholt ⚓ Fl (2) R 6s; 52°34'·92N 09°40'·51W.
Beal Spit ⚓ VQ (9) 10s; 52°34'·82N 09°39'·98W.
Beal Bar ⚓ Q; 52°35'·18N 09°39'·23W.
Doonaha ⚓ Q (3) R 5s; 52°35'·46N 09°38'·50W.
Letter Point ⚓ Fl R 7s; 52°35'·44N 09°35'·89W.
Asdee ⚓ Fl R 5s; 52°35'·09N 09°34'·55W.
Rineanna ⚓ QR; 52°35'·59N 09°31'·24W.
North Carraig ⚓ Q; 52°35'·60N 09°29'·76W.

Scattery Is, Rineanna Pt ⚓ Fl (2) 8s 15m 10M; W twr; vis: 208°-092°; 52°36'·32N 09°31'·03W.
Tarbert Is N Point ⚓ Q WR 4s 18m W14M, R10M; W ○ twr; vis: W069°- R277°- W287°-339°; 52°35'·52N 09°21'·83W.
Tarbert (Ballyhoolahan Pt) Ldg lts 128·2° ⚓. Front, Iso 3s 13m 3M; △ on W twr; vis: 123·2°-133·2°; 52°34'·35N 09°18'·80W . Rear, 400m from front, Iso 5s 18m 3M; G stripe on W Bn.
Kilkerin ⚓ Fl (2) R 6s; 52°35'·53N 09°21'·02W.
Gorgon ▲ Fl (2) G 6s; 52°35'·18N 09°20'·84W.
Garraunbaun Pt ⚓ Fl (3) WR 10s 16m W8M, R5M; W☐ col, vis: R shore - W072°- R242°- shore; 52°35'·62N 09°13'·94W.
Loghill ▲ Fl G 3s; 52°36'·32N 09°12'·85W.
Rinealon Pt ⚓ Fl 2·5s 4m 7M; B col, W bands; vis: 234°-088°; 52°37'·12N 09°09'·82W.

### KILRUSH

Off Cappagh Pier ⚓ L Fl 10s; 52°37'·64N 09°30'·21W.
Marina Ent Chan Ldg lts 355°. Front, Oc 3s; 52°37'·99N 09°30'·27W. Rear, 75m from front, Oc 3s.

---

## 5.4 PASSAGE INFORMATION

The *Irish Cruising Club Sailing Directions* (ICC SD) are strongly recommended for all Irish waters. Particularly useful on the W coast where other information is scarce, they are published in two volumes: *E and N coasts of Ireland* covers anti-clockwise from Carnsore Pt to Bloody Foreland, and *S and W coasts of Ireland* covers clockwise. See also *Cruising Guide to the Coasts of Cork and Kerry* (Graham Swanson/Imray). For notes on crossing the Irish Sea, see 6.4; and for Distances across it see 0.32.

### MALAHIDE TO TUSKAR ROCK

(AC 1468, 1787) Malahide, 4M from both Lambay Is and Howth, can be entered in most weather via a channel which constantly shifts through drying sandbanks. Ireland's Eye, a rky island which rises steeply to a height of 99m, lies about 7½ca N of Howth with reefs running SE and SW from Thulla Rk at its SE end. Ben of Howth, on N side of Dublin Bay, is steep-to, with no dangers more than 1ca offshore.

Rosbeg Bank lies on the N side of Dublin Bay. Burford Bank, on which the sea breaks in E gales, and Kish Bank lie offshore in the approaches. ▶ *The N-going stream begins at HW Dublin – 0600, and the S-going at HW Dublin, sp rates 3kn.* ◀

From Dublin to Carnsore Pt as a cruising area, hbr facilities are being improved. The shallow offshore banks cause dangerous overfalls and dictate the route which is sheltered from the W winds. ▶ *Tidal streams run mainly N and S, but the N-going*

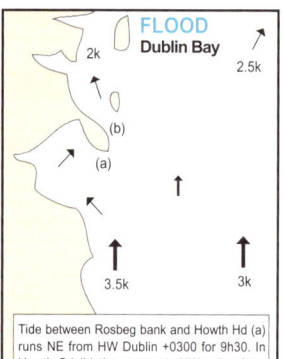

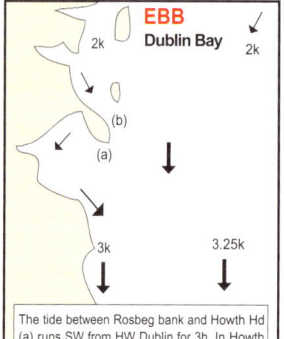

*flood sets across the banks on the inside, and the S-going ebb sets across them on the outside.* ◄

Leaving Dublin Bay, yachts normally use Dalkey Sound, but with a foul tide or light wind it is better to use Muglins Sound. Muglins (lt) is steep-to except for a rk about 1ca WSW of the lt. Beware Leac Buidhe (dries) 1ca E of Clare Rk. The inshore passage is best as far as Wicklow.

Thereafter yachts may either route offshore, passing east of Arklow Bank and its Lanby to fetch Tuskar Rock or Greenore Pt, or keep inshore of Arklow Bank, avoiding Glassgorman Banks; through the Rusk Channel, inside Blackwater and Lucifer Banks, to round Carnsore Pt NW of Tuskar Rock. Arklow is safe in offshore winds; Wexford has a difficult entrance. Rosslare lacks yacht facilities, but provides good shelter to wait out a SW'ly blow.

Arklow Bank Wind Farm is on the bank in the area W of No.2 and No1 Arklow buoys. It has 7 wind turbines, each 72.8m high with 104m diameter blades. They are lit, N'most and S'most are fitted with AIS (Automatic Identification System) transmitters.

### TUSKAR ROCK TO OLD HEAD OF KINSALE

(AC 2049) Dangerous rks lie up to 2ca NW and 6½ca SSW of Tuskar Rk and there can be a dangerous race off Carnsore Pt. In bad weather or poor visibility, use the Inshore Traffic Zone of the Tuskar Rock TSS, passing to seaward of Tuskar Rk (lt), the Barrels ECM lt buoy and Coningbeg buoy.

If taking the inshore passage from Greenore Pt, stay inside The Bailies to pass 2ca off Carnsore Pt. Beware of lobster pots in this area. Steer WSW to pass N of Black Rk and the Bohurs, S of which are

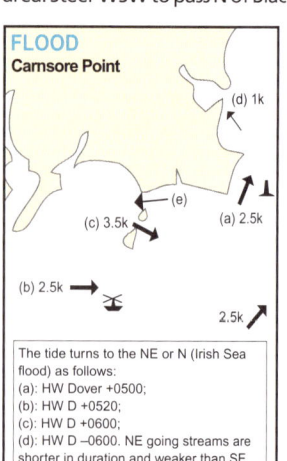

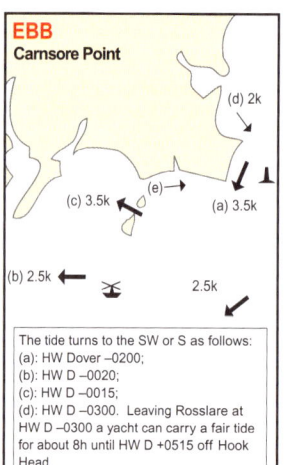

extensive overfalls. The small hbr of Kilmore Quay has been rebuilt with a new marina, but beware rks and shoals in the approaches.

Saltee Sound (AC 2740) is a safe passage, least width 3ca, between Great and Little Saltee, conspic islands to S and N. ▶ *Sebber Bridge extends 7½ca N from the NE point of Great Saltee and Jackeen Rk is 1M NW of the S end of Little Saltee, so care is needed through the sound, where the stream runs 3·5 kn at sp.* ◄ There are several rks S of the Saltees, but clear passage between many of them. There are no obstructions on a direct course for a point 1M S of Hook Head, to avoid the overfalls and Tower Race, which at times extend about 1M S of the Head.

Dunmore East (AC 2046) is a useful passage port at the mouth of Waterford Hbr. To the W, beware salmon nets and Falskirt, a dangerous rk off Swines Pt. There are few offlying rks from Tramore Bay to Ballinacourty Pt on the N side of Dungarvan Bay (AC 2017).Helvick is a small sheltered hbr approached along the S shore of the bay, keeping S of Helvick Rk (ECM lt buoy) and other dangers to the N.

Mine Hd (lt) has two dangerous rks, The Rogue about 2½ca E and The Longship 1M SW. To the W is a subm'gd rk 100m SE of Ram Hd. ▶ *Here the W-going stream starts at HW Cobh + 0230, and the E-going at HW Cobh –0215, sp rates 1·5kn.* ◄ Pass 2ca off Capel Island; the sound between it and Knockadoon Hd is not recommended.

The N side of Ballycotton B is foul up to 5ca offshore. Ballycotton Hbr is small and crowded, but usually there is sheltered anch outside. Sound Rk and Small Is lie between the mainland and Ballycotton Is (lt, fog sig). From Ballycotton to Cork keep at least 5ca off for dangers including The Smiths (PHM lt buoy) 1·5M WSW of Ballycotton Island. Pass between Hawk Rk, close off Power Hd, and Pollock Rk (PHM lt buoy) 1.25M SE.

Near the easy entrance and excellent shelter of Cork Harbour (AC 1777), Ringabella Bay offers temp anch in good weather. 7ca SE of Robert's Hd is Daunt Rk (3·5m) on which seas break in bad weather; marked by PHM lt buoy. Little Sovereign on with Reames Hd 241° leads inshore of it. The Sovereigns are large rks off Oyster Haven, a good hbr but prone to swell in S'lies. The ent is clear except for Harbour Rk which must be passed on its W side. Bulman Rk (SCM lt buoy) is 4ca S of Preghane Pt at the ent to Kinsale's fine harbour. ▶ *The tide on the Cork coast turns to the NE at HW Dover +0045. There is an eddy 5M ESE of Old Head of Kinsale at HW Dover +0400. The ingoing Cork Harbour tide begins at HW Dover +0055.*

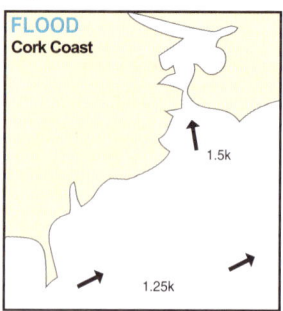

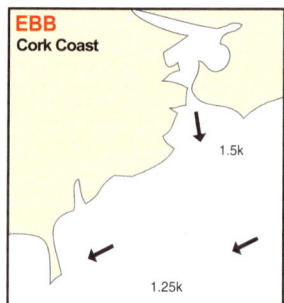

*The tide turns SW at HW Dover +0500. The outgoing Cork Harbour tide begins at HW Dover –0540. Old Head of Kinsale (lt, fog sig) is quite steep-to, but a race extends 1M to SW on W-going stream, and to SE on E-going stream.* ◄ There is an inshore passage in light weather, but in strong winds keep 2M off.

### OLD HEAD OF KINSALE TO MIZEN HEAD

(AC 2424) From Cork to Mizen Hd there are many natural hbrs. Only the best are mentioned here. ▶ *Offshore the stream seldom exceeds 1·5kn, but it is stronger off headlands causing races and overfalls with wind against tide. Prolonged W winds increase the*

---

**Image 1 (FLOOD Dublin Bay):** 2k, 2.5k, (b), (a), 3.5k, 3k

Tide between Rosbeg bank and Howth Hd (a) runs NE from HW Dublin +0300 for 9h30. In Howth Sd (b) the stream is NW going from +0430 to –0130.
New flood and ebb tides begin close to the S shore and N of Baily up to 1h before HW Dublin.

**Image 2 (EBB Dublin Bay):** 2k, 2k, (b), (a), 3k, 3.25k

The tide between Rosbeg bank and Howth Hd (a) runs SW from HW Dublin for 3h. In Howth Sd (b) the stream is SE going from –0130 to +0430.
Strengths of streams increase S of Dublin Bay, and decrease N of it.

**Image 3 (FLOOD Carnsore Point):** (d) 1k, (e), (c) 3.5k, (a) 2.5k, (b) 2.5k, 2.5k

The tide turns to the NE or N (Irish Sea flood) as follows:
(a): HW Dover +0500;
(b): HW D +0520;
(c): HW D +0600;
(d): HW D –0600. NE going streams are shorter in duration and weaker than SE going - careful passage planning is essential.

**Image 4 (EBB Carnsore Point):** (d) 2k, (e), (c) 3.5k, (a) 3.5k, (b) 2.5k, 2.5k

The tide turns to the SW or S as follows:
(a): HW Dover –0200;
(b): HW D –0020;
(c): HW D –0015;
(d): HW D –0300. Leaving Rosslare at HW D –0300 a yacht can carry a fair tide for about 8h until HW D +0515 off Hook Head.

NOTE: The tide turns on St Patrick's Bridge (e) up to 2 hours earlier than in Saltee Sound

**Image 5 (FLOOD Cork Coast):** 1.5k, 1.25k

**Image 6 (EBB Cork Coast):** 1.5k, 1.25k

rate/duration of the E-going stream, and strong E winds have a similar effect on the W-going stream. ◄

In the middle of Courtmacsherry Bay are several dangers, from E to W: Blueboy Rk, Barrel Rk (with Inner Barrels closer inshore), and Black Tom; Horse Rk is off Barry's Pt at the W side of the bay. These must be avoided going to or from Courtmacsherry, where the bar breaks in strong S/SE winds, but the river carries 2·3m.

Beware Cotton Rk and Shoonta Rk close E of Seven Heads, off which rks extend 50m. Clonakilty B has little to offer. Keep at least 5ca off Galley Hd to clear Dhulic Rk, and further off in fresh winds. ► Offshore the W-going stream makes at HW Cobh + 0200, and the E-going at HW Cobh – 0420, sp rates 1·5kn. ◄

Across Glandore Bay there are good anchs off Glandore, or Union Hall. Sailing W from Glandore, pass outside or inside High Is and Low Is; if inside beware Belly Rk (awash) about 3ca S of Rabbit Is. On passage Toe Head has foul ground 100m S, and 7½ca S is a group of rks called the Stags. Castle Haven, a sheltered and attractive hbr, is entered between Reen Pt (lt) and Battery Pt. Baltimore is 10M further W.

Fastnet Rk (lt, fog sig) is nearly 4M WSW of C Clear; 2½ca NE of it is an outlying rk. An E/W TSS lies between 2 and 8M SSE of the Fastnet. Long Island Bay can be entered from C Clear or through Gascanane Sound, between Clear Is and Sherkin Is. Carrigmore Rks lie in the middle of this chan, with Gascanane Rk 1ca W of them. The chan between Carrigmore Rks and Badger Island is best. If bound for Crookhaven, beware Bullig Reef, N of Clear Is.

Schull is N of Long Island, inside which passage can be made W'ward to Crookhaven. This is a well sheltered hbr, accessible at all states of tide, entered between Rock Is lt Ho and Alderman Rks, ENE of Streek Hd. Anch off the village. ► Off Mizen Hd (lt ho) the W-going stream starts at HW Cobh + 0120, and the E-going at HW Cobh – 0500. The sp rate is 4 kn, which with wind against tide forms a dangerous race, sometimes reaching to Brow Hd or Three Castle Hd, with broken water right to the shore. ◄

## THE WEST COAST

This coast offers wonderful cruising, although exposed to the Atlantic and any swell offshore; but this diminishes mid-summer. In bad weather however the sea breaks dangerously on shoals with quite substantial depths. There is usually a refuge close by, but if caught out in deteriorating weather and poor vis, a stranger may need to make an offing until conditions improve, so a sound yacht and good crew are required. Even in mid-summer at least one gale may be meet in a two-week cruise. Fog is less frequent than in the Irish Sea.

► Tidal streams are weak, except round headlands. ◄ There are few lights, so inshore navigation is unwise after dark, however coastal navigation is feasible at night in good visibility. Keep a good watch for drift nets off the coast, and for lobster pots in inshore waters. Stores, fuel and water are not readily available.

## MIZEN HEAD TO DINGLE BAY

(AC 2423) At S end of Dunmanus Bay Three Castle Hd has rks 1ca W, and sea can break on S Bullig 4ca off Hd. Dunmanus B (AC 2552) has three hbrs: Dunmanus, Kitchen Cove and Dunbeacon. Carbery, Cold and Furze Is lie in middle of B, and it is best to keep N of them. Sheep's Hd (lt) is at the S end of Bantry Bay (AC 1838, 1840) which has excellent hbrs, notably Glengariff and Castletown. There are few dangers offshore, except around Bear and Whiddy Islands. ► Off Blackball Hd at W entrance to Bantry B there can be a nasty race, particularly on W-going stream against the wind. Keep 3ca off Crow Is to clear dangers. ◄

Dursey Island is steep-to except for rk 7½ca NE of Dursey Hd and Lea Rk (1·4m)1½ca SW . The Bull (lt, fog sig, Racon) and two rks W of it lie 2·5M WNW of Dursey Hd. The Cow is midway between The Bull and Dursey Hd, with clear water each side. Calf and Heifer Rks are 7½ca SW of Dursey Hd, where there is often broken water. ► 2M W of The Bull the stream turns NW at HW Cobh + 0150, and SE at HW Cobh – 0420. Dursey Sound (chart 2495) is a good short cut, but the stream runs 4kn at sp; W-going starts at HW Cobh + 0135, and E-going at HW Cobh – 0450. ◄ Flag Rk lies almost awash in mid-chan at the narrows, which are crossed by cables 25m above MHWS. Hold very close to the Island shore. Beware wind changes in the sound, and broken water at N entrance.

Kenmare R. (AC 2495) has attractive hbrs and anchs, but its shores are rky, with no lights. The best places are Sneem, Kilmakilloge and Ardgroom. Off Lamb's Head, Two Headed Island is steep-to; further W is Moylaun Is with a rk 300m SW of it. Little Hog (or Deenish) Island is rky 1·5M to W, followed by Great Hog (or Scariff) Is which has a rk close N, and a reef extending 2ca W.

Darrynane is an attractive, sheltered hbr NNW of Lamb Hd. The entrance has ldg lts and marks, but is narrow and dangerous in bad weather. Ballinskelligs Bay has an anch N of Horse Is, which has two rks close off E end. Centre of bay is a prohib anch (cables reported).

Rough water is met between Bolus Hd and Bray Hd with fresh onshore winds or swell. The SW end of Puffin Island is steep-to, but the sound to the E is rky and not advised. Great Skellig (lit) is 6M, and Little Skellig 5M WSW of Puffin Is. Lemon Rk lies between Puffin Is and Little Skellig. ► Here the stream turns N at HW Cobh + 0500, and S at HW Cobh – 0110. ◄ There is a rk 3ca SW of Great Skellig. When very calm it is possible to go alongside at Blind Man's Cove on NE side of Great Skellig, where there are interesting ruins.

## DINGLE BAY TO LISCANNOR BAY

(AC 2254) Dingle Bay (AC 2789, 2790) is wide and deep, with few dangers around its shores. Cahersiveen & Dingle have small marinas. The best anchs are at Portmagee and Ventry. At the NW ent to the bay, 2·5M SSW of Slea Hd, is Wild Bank (or Three Fathom Pinnacle), a shallow patch with overfalls. 3M SW of Wild Bank is Barrack Rk, which breaks in strong winds.

The Blasket Islands are very exposed, ► with strong tides and overfalls ◄, but worth a visit in settled weather (AC 2790).

Great Blasket and Inishvickillane each have anch and landing on their NE side. Inishtearaght is the most W'ly Is (lt), but further W lie Tearaght Rks, and 3M S are Little Foze and Gt Foze Rks. Blasket Sound is the most convenient N-S route, 1M wide, and easy in daylight and reasonable weather with fair wind or tide; extensive rks and shoals form its W side. ► The N-going stream starts at HW Galway + 0430, and the S-going at HW Galway – 0155, with sp rate 3kn. ◄

Between Blasket Sound and Sybil Pt there is a race in W or NW winds with N-going tide, and often a nasty sea. Sybil Pt has steep cliffs, and offlying rks extend 3½ca.

Smerwick hbr, entered between Duncapple Is and the E Sister is sheltered, except from NW or N winds. From here the scenery is spectacular to Brandon Hd on the W side of which there is an anch, but exposed to N winds and to swell.

There is no lt from Inishtearaght to Loop Hd, apart from Little Samphire Is in Tralee B, where Fenit hbr provides the only secure refuge until entering the Shannon Estuary. The coast from Loop Hd to Liscanor Bay has no safe anchs, and no lts. Take care not to be set inshore, although there are few offlying dangers except near Mutton Is and in Liscanor Bay.

## THE SHANNON ESTUARY

(AC 1819, 1547, 1548, 1549) The estuary and lower reaches of the Shannon, are tidal for 50M, from its mouth between Loop Hd and Kerry Hd up to Limerick Dock, some 15M beyond the junction with R. Fergus. ▶ *The tides and streams are those of a deep-water inlet, with roughly equal durations of rise and fall, and equal rates of flood and ebb streams. In the entrance the flood stream begins at HW Galway – 0555, and the ebb at HW Galway + 0015.* ◀

There are several anchs available for yachts on passage up or down the coast. Kilbaha Bay (AC 1819) is about 3M E of Loop Hd, and is convenient in good weather or in N winds, but exposed to SE and any swell. Carrigaholt B (AC 1547), entered about 1M N of Kilcredaun Pt, is well sheltered from W winds and has little tidal stream. In N winds there is anch SE of Querrin Pt (AC 1547), 4·5M further up river on N shore. At Kilrush there is a marina and anchs E of Scattery Is and N of Hog Is. ▶ *Note that there are overfalls 0·75M S of Scattery Is with W winds and ebb tide.* ◀

▶ *Off Kilcredaun Pt the ebb reaches 4kn at sp, and in strong winds between S and NW a bad race forms. This can be mostly* avoided by keeping near the N shore, which is free from offlying dangers, thereby cheating the worst of the tide. When leaving the Shannon in strong W winds, aim to pass Kilcredaun Pt at slack water, and again keep near the N shore. Loop Hd (lt) marks the N side of Shannon Est, and should be passed 3ca off. Here the stream runs SW from HW Galway + 0300, and NE from HW Galway – 0300. ◀

▶ *Above the junction with R. Fergus (AC 1540) the tidal characteristics become more like those of most rivers, ie the flood stream is stronger than the ebb, but it runs for a shorter time. In the Shannon the stream is much affected by the wind. S and W winds increase the rate and duration of the flood stream, and reduce the ebb. Strong N or E winds have the opposite effect. Prolonged or heavy rain increases the rate and duration of the ebb.* ◀

The Shannon is the longest river in Ireland, rising at Lough Allen 100M above Limerick, thence 50M to the sea.

## 5.5 SPECIAL NOTES FOR IRELAND

*Céad Míle Fáilte! One hundred thousand Welcomes!*

**Lifejackets:** It is compulsory to wear lifejackets in Irish waters on all craft of <7m LOA. Children age under 16, must at all times wear a lifejacket or personal flotation device on deck when underway. Every vessel, irrespective of size, must carry a lifejacket or personal flotation device for each person on board. These regulations are mandatory.

**Ordnance Survey** map numbers refer to the Irish OS maps, scale 1:50,000 or 1¼ inch to 1 mile, which cover the whole island, including Ulster, in 89 sheets.

**Irish Customs:** First port of call should preferably be at Customs posts in one of the following hbrs: Dublin, Dun Laoghaire, Waterford, New Ross, Cork, Ringaskiddy, Bantry, Foynes, Limerick, Galway, Sligo and Killybegs. Yachts may, in fact, make their first call anywhere and if no Customs officer arrives within a reasonable time, the skipper should inform the nearest Garda (Police) station of the yacht's arrival. Only non-EC members should fly flag Q or show ● over ○ lts on arrival. Passports are not required by UK citizens. All current Northern Ireland 5 and 6 digit telephone numbers have become 8 digits 028 9012 3456.

**Telephone:** To call the Irish Republic from the UK, dial 00 - 353, then the area code (given in UK ☎ directories and below) minus the initial 0, followed by the ☎ number. To call UK from the Irish Republic: dial 00-44, followed by the area code minus the initial 0, then the number.

**Salmon drift nets** Use of these is decreasing but may be encountered along the S and W coasts, off headlands and islands during the summer and especially May–Jul. They may be 1½ to 3M long and are hard to see. FVs may give warnings on VHF Ch 16, 06, 08.

**Liquefied petroleum gas:** In Eire LPG is supplied by Kosan, a sister company of Calor Gas Ltd, but the bottles have different connections, and the smallest bottle is taller than the normal Calor one fitted in most yachts. Calor Gas bottles can be filled in most larger towns. Camping Gaz is widely available. The abbreviation Kos indicates where Kosan gas is available.

**Information:** The Irish Cruising Club publishes 2 highly recommended books of Sailing Directions, one for the S and W coasts of Ireland, the other for the N and E coasts. All three are distributed by Imray. See also *A cruising guide to the coasts of Cork and Kerry* by Graham Swanson. Further info is available from: Irish Sailing Association, 3 Park Road, Dun Laoghaire, Co Dublin, ☎ (01) 2800239, 🖷 2807558; or the Irish Tourist Board, 150 New Bond St, London W1Y 0AQ, ☎ (020 7) 518 0800.

**Email/Websites:**

| | |
|---|---|
| Commissioners of Irish Lights | www.cil.ie |
| Irish Sailing Association | www.sailing.ie |
| Irish Tourist Board (Eire) | www.ireland.travel.ie |
| Irish Forecasts from RTE | www.rte.ie/aertel/p160.htm |

**Currency** is the Euro (€), cash is most readily available from ATM's.

**ACCESS BY AIR:** There are airports in Eire at Dublin, Waterford, Cork, Kerry, Shannon, Galway, Connaught, Sligo and Donegal/Carrickfin.

**Northern Ireland:** Belfast CG (MRSC) is at Bangor, Co Down, ☎ (028 91) 463933, 🖷 465886. HM Customs (⊖) should be contacted H24 on ☎ (028 90) 358250 at the following ports, if a local Customs Officer is not available: Belfast, Warrenpoint, Kilkeel, Ardglass, Portavogie, Larne, Londonderry, Coleraine. Northern Ireland's main airport is Belfast (Aldergrove).

**Gaelic:** It helps to understand some of the commoner words for navigational features (courtesy of the Irish Cruising Club):

| | | | |
|---|---|---|---|
| *Ail, alt* | cliff, height | *Inish, illaun* | island |
| *Aird, ard* | height, high | *Inver* | river mouth |
| *Anna, annagh* | marsh | *Keal, keel* | narrow |
| *Ath* | ford | | place, sound |
| *Bal, Bally* | town | *Kill* | church, cell |
| *Barra* | sandbank | *Kin, ken* | promontory, |
| *Bel, beal* | mouth, strait | | head |
| *Beg* | little | *Knock* | hill |
| *Ben, binna* | hill | *Lag* | hollow |
| *Bo* | sunken rock | *Lahan* | broad |
| *Boy, bwee* | yellow | *Lea* | grey |
| *Bullig* | shoal, round | *Lenan* | weed- |
| | rock, breaker | | covered rock |
| *Bun* | end, river | *Lis* | ancient fort |
| | mouth | *Long, luing* | ship |
| *Caher* | fort | *Maan* | middle |
| *Camus* | bay, river | *Maol, mwee* | bare |
| | bend | *Mara* | of the sea |
| *Carrick* | rock | *More, mor* | big |
| *Cladach* | shore | *Rannagh* | point |
| *Cuan, coon* | harbour | *Ron, roan* | seal |
| *Derg, dearg* | red | *Roe, ruadh* | red |
| *Drum* | hill, ridge | *Scolt* | split, rky gut |
| *Duff, dubh* | black | *Scrow* | boggy, |
| *Dun, doon* | fort | | grassy sward |
| *Ennis* | island | *Slieve* | mountain |
| *Fad, fadda* | long | *Slig* | shells |
| *Fan* | slope | *Stag, stac* | high rock |
| *Fin* | white | *Tawney* | low hill |
| *Freagh, free* | heather | *Tigh, ti* | house |
| *Gall* | stranger | *Togher* | causeway |
| *Glas, glass* | green | *Tra, traw* | strand |
| *Glinsk* | clear water | *Turlin* | boulder |
| *Gorm* | blue | | beach |
| *Gub* | point of land | *Vad, bad* | boat |
| *Hassans* | swift current | | |

## 5.6 MALAHIDE

Dublin 53°27'·20N 06°08'·90W ❀❀🐚🐚🌸🌸

**CHARTS** AC 1468, 633, 5621; Imray C61, C62; Irish OS 50

**TIDES** +0030 Dover; ML 2·4; Duration 0615

**Standard Port DUBLIN (NORTH WALL)** (→)

| Times | | | | Height (metres) | | | |
|---|---|---|---|---|---|---|---|
| High Water | | Low Water | | MHWS | MHWN | MLWN | MLWS |
| 0000 | 0700 | 0000 | 0500 | 4·1 | 3·4 | 1·5 | 0·7 |
| 1200 | 1900 | 1200 | 1700 | | | | |
| Differences MALAHIDE | | | | | | | |
| +0002 | +0003 | +0009 | +0009 | +0·1 | −0·2 | −0·4 | −0·2 |

**SHELTER** Excellent in marina, dredged approx 2·3m. Access HW±4. Visitors berth on pontoon F. ⚓ between marina and Grand Hotel on S edge of fairway, clear of moorings.

**NAVIGATION** WPT: SWM LFl 10s 53°27'·10N 06°06'·81W. The approach channel lies between drying sandbanks.

- It is strongly recommended that visiting yachtsmen obtain up-to-date information by ☎ or VHF from the marina on the latest depths / buoyage and refer this to AC 633.

- Channel is marked by PHM and SHM perches which are lit.
- Entry not advised in strong onshore winds against the ebb. The flood reaches 3kn sp, and the ebb 3½kn.
- Speed limit 10kn in fairway and 4kn in marina.

**LIGHTS AND MARKS** The marina and apartment blocks close S of it are visible from the WPT. The Grand Hotel is no longer conspic from seaward, due to trees and bldgs.

**R/T** Marina, *Call sign Malahide Marina*, Ch **M** 80 (H24) . MYC, call *Yacht Base* Ch M (occas).

**TELEPHONE** (Code 01) Marina 8454129, 📠 8454255; MRCC 6620922/3; ⊖ 8746571; Police 666 4600; Dr 845 5994; Ⓗ 837 7755.

**FACILITIES** **Marina** (350) ☎ 8454129, 📠 8454255, Ⓥ (20) €3·90, ⬦⊳ (€6·50) D(hose H24), P(cans H24), Wi-fi, Gas, BH (30 ton), BY, R, Bar, Ice, ▣, 🚾, showers **Malahide YC** ☎ 8453372, Slip (for craft <5.5m, launching HW ±2), Scrubbing posts for <10m LOA; **Services:** Ⓔ, ✕, Kos. **Town** ▣, ✉, Ⓑ, ⇒, ✈ (Dublin).

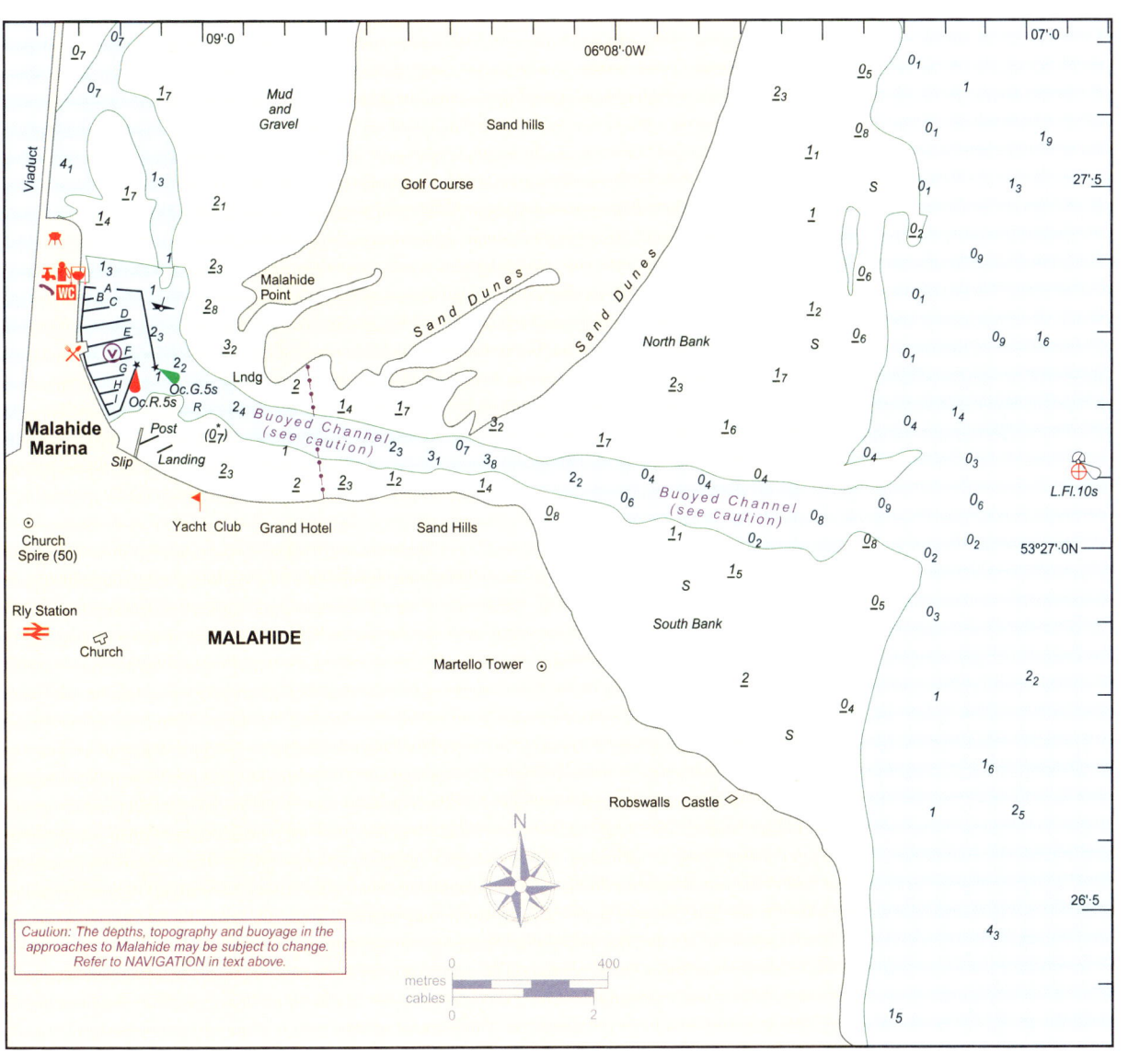

Caution: The depths, topography and buoyage in the approaches to Malahide may be subject to change. Refer to NAVIGATION in text above.

## 5.7  HOWTH

Dublin **53°23'·60N 06°04'·00W** ❀❀❀⚓⚓❁❁❁

**CHARTS** AC 1468, 1415, 5621; Imray C61, C62; Irish OS 50

**TIDES** +0025 Dover; ML 2·4; Duration 0625

**Standard Port DUBLIN (NORTH WALL) (→)**

| Times | | | | Height (metres) | | | |
|---|---|---|---|---|---|---|---|
| High Water | | Low Water | | MHWS | MHWN | MLWN | MLWS |
| 0000 | 0700 | 0000 | 0500 | 4·1 | 3·4 | 1·5 | 0·7 |
| 1200 | 1900 | 1200 | 1700 | | | | |
| **Differences HOWTH** | | | | | | | |
| –0007 | –0005 | +0001 | +0005 | 0·0 | –0·1 | –0·2 | –0·2 |

**SHELTER** Excellent in marina, available at all tides and in almost any conditions. After a severe ENE'ly storm, expect a dangerous scend in the app chan. Caution: many moorings in E part of outer hbr. No ent to FV basin for yachts. Inside the inner hbr keep strictly to chan to avoid drying shoals either side and a substantial wavebreak (gabion). Marina depth 2·2m. R PHM posts mark the outer limit of dredging around the marina. 4kn speed limit. There is a fair weather ⚓ in 2-3m at Carrigeen Bay, SW side of Ireland's Eye.

**NAVIGATION** WPT Howth SHM buoy, Fl G 5s, 53°23'·72N 06°03'·53W, 251°/0·27M to E pier lt. From the S beware Casana Rk 4ca S of the Nose of Howth and Puck's Rks extending about 50m off the Nose. Ireland's Eye is 0·6M N of hbr, with the Rowan Rks

SE and SW from Thulla, marked by Rowan Rks ECM, and S Rowan SHM lt buoys. The usual approach passes S of Ireland's Eye, but beware many lobster pots between the Nose of Howth and the hbr, and rocks off both pier hds. Howth Sound has 2·4m min depth; give way to FVs (constrained by draft) in the Sound and hbr entrance. 2·2m in marina approach channel but subject to silting (<1·6m reported in 2007).

**LIGHTS AND MARKS** Baily lt ho, Fl 15s 41m 26M, is 1·5M S of Nose of Howth. Disused lt ho on E pier is conspic. E pier lt, Fl (2) WR 7·5s 13m 12/9M; 256°-W-295°, R elsewhere. W sector leads safely to NE pierhead which should be rounded 50m off. Ent to FV Basin has QR and Fl G 3s. The chan to marina is marked by 8 R & G floating perches (some lit) with W reflective tape (2 bands = port, 1 = stbd).

**R/T** Marina Ch M 80 (H24). HM VHF Ch 16 11 (Mon-Fri 0700-2300LT; Sat/Sun occas).

**TELEPHONE** (Code 01) HM 832 2252; MRCC 6620922/3; ⊖ 8746571; Police 666 4900; Dr 832 3191; Ⓗ 837 7755.

**FACILITIES** **Howth Marina** (350 inc Ⓥ) ☎ 8392777, 📠 839 2430, www.hyc.ie; €2.75, Wi-fi, M, D (H24), P(cans), Slip(H24), C (15 ton), ⛽, ⬜, ♿. **Howth YC** ☎ 832 2141, Scrubbing posts <20m LOA, R (☎ 839 2100), Bar (☎ 8320606), ⬜, ♿. **Howth Boat Club** (no facilities). **Services:** LB, Gas, Kos, ME, SM, CH, El, Ⓔ. **Town** ✉, Ⓑ, ⬜, ⇌, ✈ (Dublin).

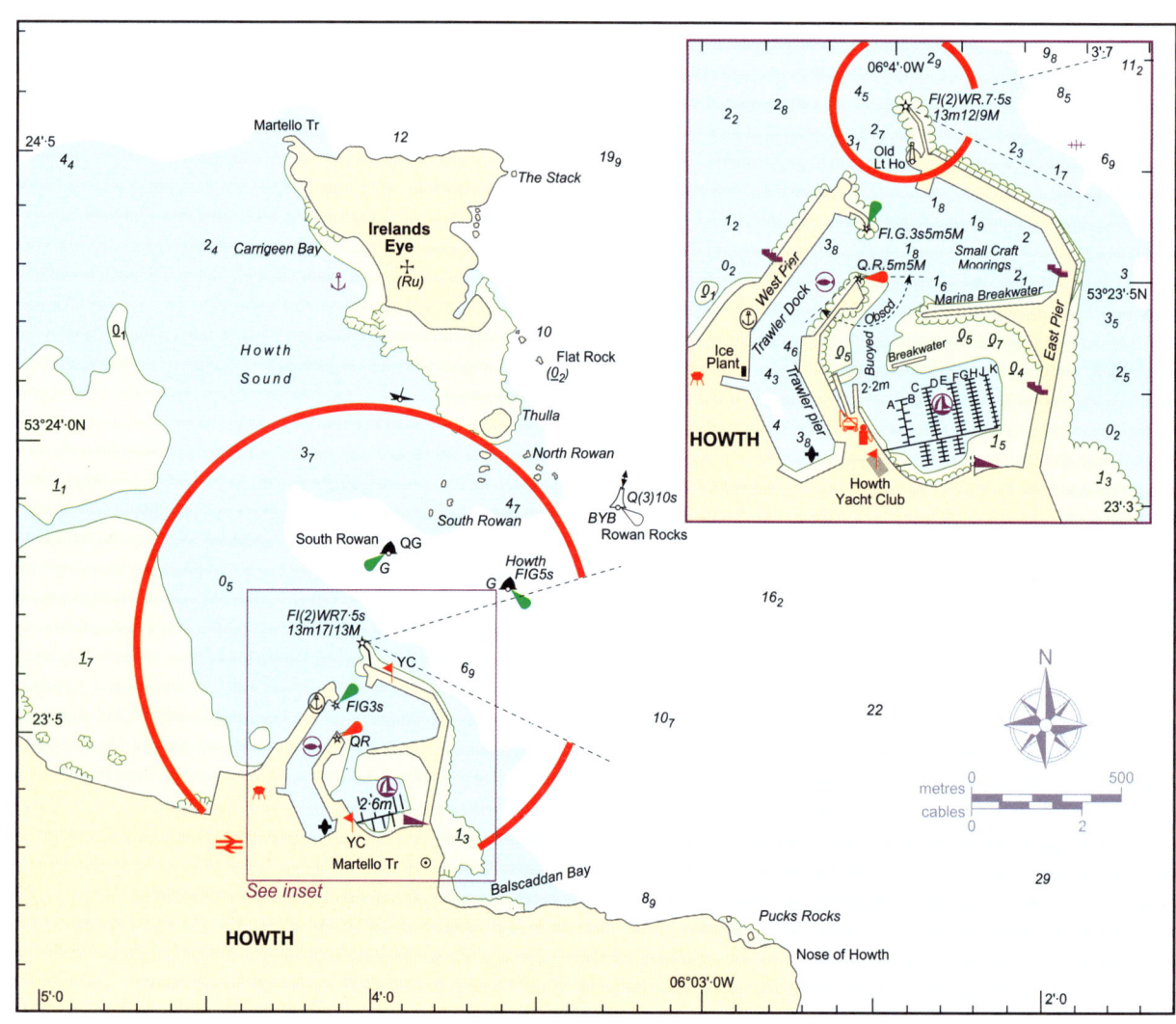

## 5.8 DUBLIN

Dublin 53°20'·85N 06°14'·80W ✿✿✿✿✿✿✿✿

**CHARTS** AC 1468, 1415, 1447, 5621; Imray C61, C62; Irish OS 50

**TIDES** +0042 Dover; ML 2·4; Duration 0640

**Standard Port DUBLIN (NORTH WALL) (→)**

| Times | | | | Height (metres) | | | |
|---|---|---|---|---|---|---|---|
| High Water | | Low Water | | MHWS | MHWN | MLWN | MLWS |
| 0000 | 0700 | 0000 | 0500 | 4·1 | 3·4 | 1·5 | 0·7 |
| 1200 | 1900 | 1200 | 1700 | | | | |
| **Differences DUBLIN BAR and DUN LAOGHAIRE** | | | | | | | |
| –0006 | –0001 | –0002 | –0003 | 0·0 | 0·0 | 0·0 | +0·1 |
| **GREYSTONES** (53°09'N 06°04'W) | | | | | | | |
| –0008 | –0008 | –0008 | –0008 | –0·5 | –0·4 | No data | |

**SHELTER Dublin Port,** excellent on N side 1ca below Matt Talbot Br on pontoons and Poolbeg YBC Marina, S of Alexandra Basin W.
**NAVIGATION Dublin Port** WPT 53°20'·50N 06°06'·71W, 275°/1·35M to hbr ent. Accessible H24, but the ent to R Liffey is rough in >E'ly F5 against ebb tide.

Note that Bull Wall covers 0.6 to 2.7m at HW. For clearance to enter call *Dublin Port Radio* Ch 12. Beware of shipping and ferries, esp astern. E Link Lifting Br (2·2m closed) opens 1100, 1500 and 2100, or on request HO and Bank Holidays. Call 00 353 1 855 5779.

**LIGHTS AND MARKS** Entance, N. Bull Lt Fl G 4s 15m 10M synchro with Gt. S. Wall Hd Poolbeg Lt Fl R 4s 20m 10M. Poolbeg power stn 2 R/W chimneys (VQ R) are conspic from afar.

**R/T** Call *Dublin Port Radio* Ch **12** 13 16 (H24). Lifting bridge (call *Eastlink*) Ch 12. *Poolbeg Marina* Ch **37** 12 16. Dublin Coast Radio Stn 16 67 83.

**TELEPHONE** (Code 00 353 1) HM Dublin 8748771; MRCC 6620922/3; Coast/Cliff Rescue Service 2803900; ⊖ 2803992; Weather 1550 123855; Police (Dublin) 6668000; Dr 2859244; Ⓗ 2806901.

**FACILITIES Dublin City Moorings** ☎ 818 3300, mobile 086856 8113, 20 ⓥ's AB in 3·3m, €2.60, FW, ⅅ, Showers. **Poolbeg YBC Marina** ☎ 6604681, ℻ 56 7790295, www.poolbegmarina.ie, 35 ⓥ's for 20m max LOA in 2.4m, €2.40, D, FW, ⅅ, Showers, ▣, Slip, Bar, R. Ferry to Holyhead. **Dublin City,** all needs, @ at Library, ⇌, ✈.

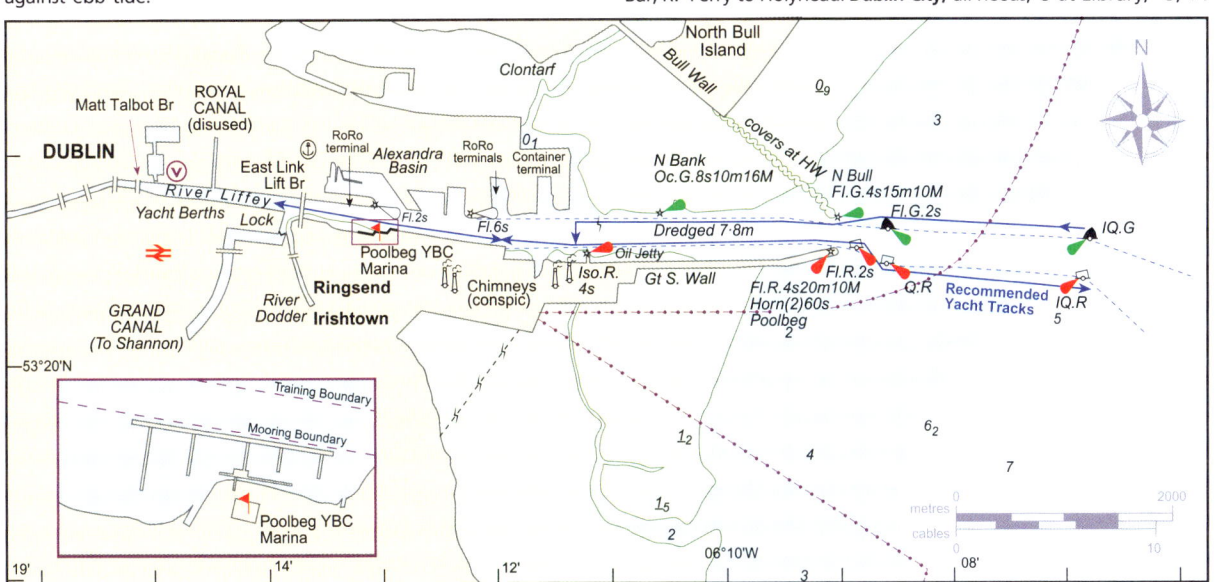

## 5.9 DUN LAOGHAIRE

Dublin (Port ent) 53°18'·16N 06°07'·68W ✿✿✿✿✿✿✿✿

**CHARTS** AC 1468, 1415, 1447, 5621; Imray C61, C62; Irish OS 50

**TIDES** +0042 Dover; ML 2·4; Duration 0640

**Standard Port DUBLIN (NORTH WALL) (→)**

| Times | | | | Height (metres) | | | |
|---|---|---|---|---|---|---|---|
| High Water | | Low Water | | MHWS | MHWN | MLWN | MLWS |
| 0000 | 0700 | 0000 | 0500 | 4·1 | 3·4 | 1·5 | 0·7 |
| 1200 | 1900 | 1200 | 1700 | | | | |
| **Differences DUBLIN BAR and DUN LAOGHAIRE** | | | | | | | |
| –0006 | –0001 | –0002 | –0003 | 0·0 | 0·0 | 0·0 | +0·1 |
| **GREYSTONES** (53°09'N 06°04'W) | | | | | | | |
| –0008 | –0008 | –0008 | –0008 | –0·5 | –0·4 | No data | |

**SHELTER** Excellent. Breakwaters within main hbr protect 800+ berth marina from ferry wash. ⓥ berths on end of pontoons or as directed. Additional berths inside Western Marina Breakwater. All YCs advertise ⚓s and/or pontoon berths.
**NAVIGATION** Dun Laoghaire is accessible H24, WPT 53°18'·40N 06°07'·00W, 240° 0·47M to ent. Keep clear of coasters, ferries/HSS, which turn off St Michael's Pier. Beware drying rocks approx 10m off E Pier Hd.

**TSS**: Two TSS ½M long, one at either end of the Burford Bank lead to/from an anti-clockwise circular TSS radius 2·3ca centred on Dublin Bay SWM lt buoy,(53°19'·90N 06°04'·58W, 2·5M NE of Dun Laoghaire/2·75M ESE of Dublin Port). Do not impede large vessels and keep clear of the TSS and fairway.

**LIGHTS AND MARKS** On Ro Ro Berth 2 x Fl.W = 'HSS under way; small craft keep clear of No 1 Fairway' (extends 600m seaward of ent).

**R/T** *Dun Laoghaire Hbr* VHF Ch **14** 16 (H24); Marina Ch **M**; YCs Ch M. Dublin Coast Radio Stn 16 67 83.

**TELEPHONE** (Code 00 353 1) HM Dun Laoghaire 2801130, ℻ 2809607; MRCC 6620922/3; Coast/Cliff Rescue Service 2803900; ⊖ 2803992; Weather 1550 123855; Police 6665000; Dr 2859244; Ⓗ 2806901.

**FACILITIES Dun Laoghaire Hbr Marina** ☎ 2020040, hal@dlmarina.com, www.dlmarina.com, (800 AB inc 20ⓥ) €5.00,BH, D&P, ▣, ♿, Wi-fi. **Yacht Clubs** (E to W): **National YC** ☎ 2805725, ℻ 2807837, Slip, M, L, C (12 ton), FW, D, R, Bar; **Royal St George YC** ☎ 2801811, ℻ 2843002, Boatman ☎ 2801208; AB by prior agreement, €3.00, Slip, M, D, L, FW, C (5 ton), R, Bar; **Royal Irish YC** ☎ 2809452, ℻ 2809723, Slip, M, D, L, FW, C (5 ton), R, Bar; **Dun Laoghaire Motor YC** ☎ 2801371, ℻ 2800870, Slip, FW, AB, Bar, R. **Services** SM, CH, ACA, ✗, Ⓔ, El, Gas. **Irish National SC** ☎ 28444195. HSS to Holyhead.

**DUN LAOGHAIRE** *chartlet overleaf*

**DUN LAOGHAIRE** *continued*

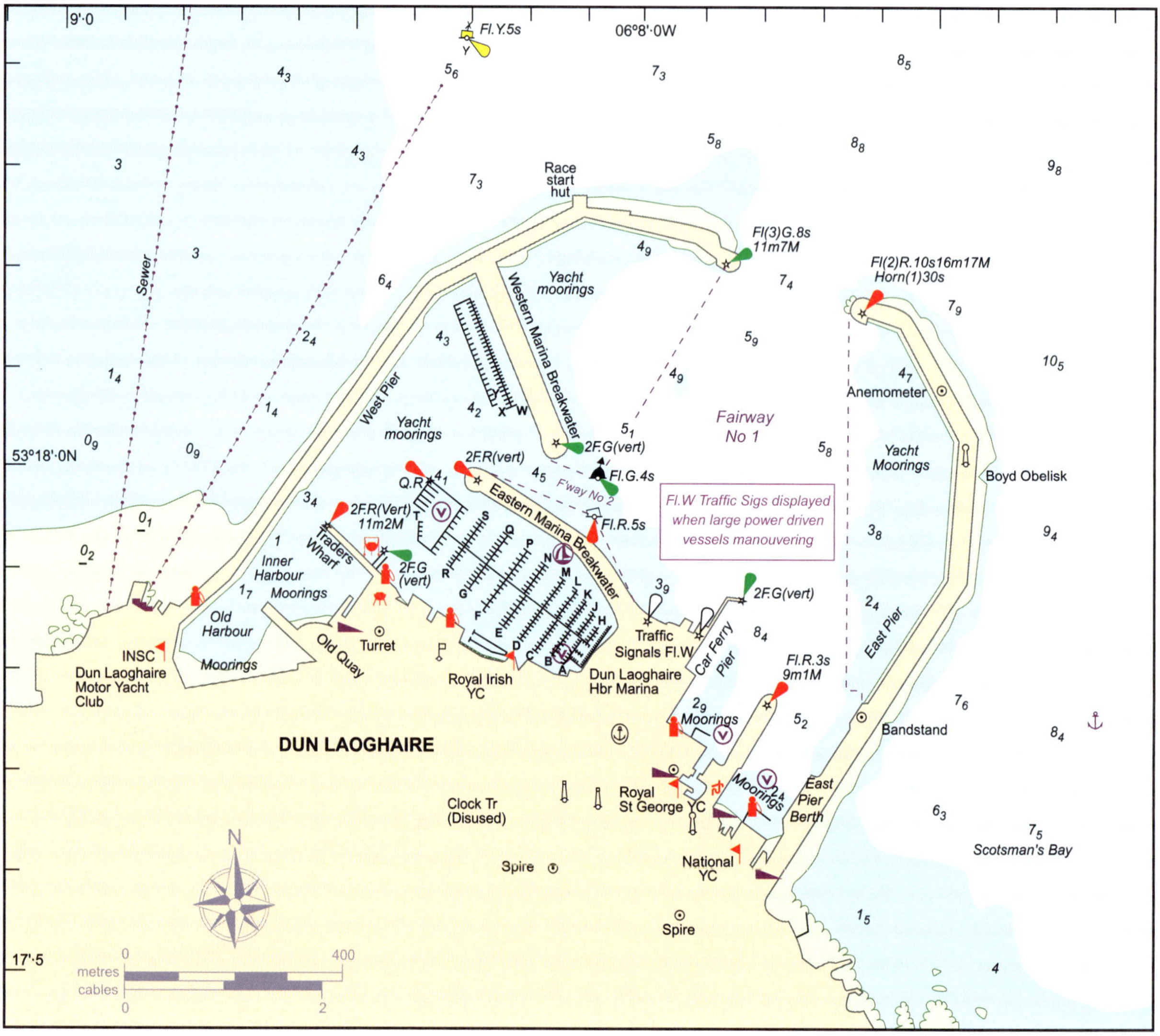

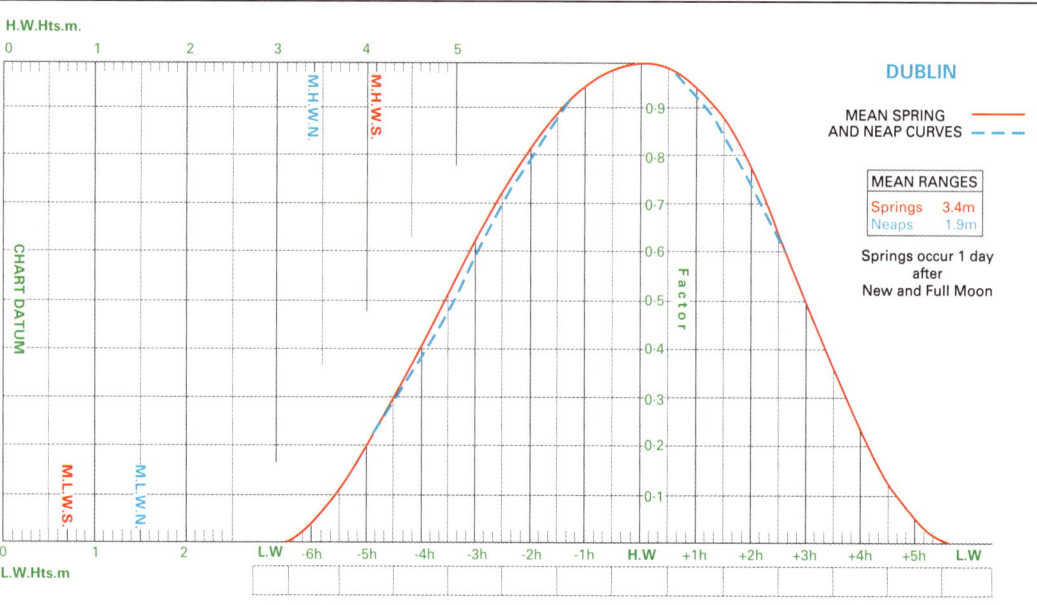

9'·0  
06°8'·0W

Fl.Y.5s

Race start hut

Yacht moorings

Western Marina Breakwater

Fl(3)G.8s 11m7M

Fl(2)R.10s16m17M Horn(1)30s

Anemometer

Fairway No 1

Yacht Moorings

Boyd Obelisk

West Pier

Yacht moorings

Q.R

2F.R(vert)

2F.R(Vert) 11m2M

2F.G (vert)

2F.G(vert)

Fl.G.4s

F'way No 2

Fl.R.5s

Fl.W Traffic Sigs displayed when large power driven vessels manouvering

2F.G(vert)

Eastern Marina Breakwater

Traders Wharf

Old Quay

Turret

Royal Irish YC

Traffic Signals Fl.W

Car Ferry Pier

Dun Laoghaire Hbr Marina

East Pier

53°18'·0N

Inner Harbour Moorings

Old Harbour

Moorings

INSC Dun Laoghaire Motor Yacht Club

Sewer

Fl.R.3s 9m1M

Moorings

Moorings

Moorings

East Pier Berth

Bandstand

Scotsman's Bay

**DUN LAOGHAIRE**

N

Clock Tr (Disused)

Royal St George YC

National YC

Spire

Spire

17'·5

metres  
cables

0 — 400  
0 — 2

**DUBLIN**

MEAN SPRING AND NEAP CURVES

| MEAN RANGES | |
|---|---|
| Springs | 3.4m |
| Neaps | 1.9m |

Springs occur 1 day after New and Full Moon

H.W.Hts.m.  
0  1  2  3  4  5

M.H.W.N.  M.H.W.S.

CHART DATUM

Factor

0·9 0·8 0·7 0·6 0·5 0·4 0·3 0·2 0·1

M.L.W.S.  M.L.W.N.

L.W  -6h -5h -4h -3h -2h -1h  H.W +1h +2h +3h +4h +5h  L.W

L.W.Hts.m

**TIME ZONE (UT)**
For Summer Time add ONE hour in **non-shaded areas**

## DUBLIN (NORTH WALL)  LAT 53°21'N  LONG 6°13'W
TIMES AND HEIGHTS OF HIGH AND LOW WATERS

Dates in red are SPRINGS
Dates in blue are NEAPS

YEAR 2008

S Ireland

### JANUARY

| Day | Time m | Day | Time m |
|---|---|---|---|
| 1 TU | 0554 3.3 / 1123 1.6 / 1813 3.5 / 2316 1.1 | 16 W | 0502 3.6 / 1039 1.3 / 1717 3.8 |
| 2 W | 0002 1.4 / 0654 3.3 / 1230 1.7 / 1915 3.4 | 17 TH | 0607 3.5 / 1148 1.4 / 1824 3.7 |
| 3 TH | 0107 1.5 / 0752 3.4 / 1340 1.7 / 2015 3.4 | 18 F | 0028 1.2 / 0719 3.5 / 1305 1.4 / 1941 3.6 |
| 4 F | 0212 1.5 / 0845 3.5 / 1445 1.6 / 2111 3.4 | 19 SA | 0146 1.3 / 0830 3.6 / 1420 1.3 / 2057 3.7 |
| 5 SA | 0306 1.5 / 0933 3.6 / 1536 1.4 / 2200 3.5 | 20 SU | 0257 1.2 / 0933 3.8 / 1526 1.0 / 2203 3.8 |
| 6 SU | 0348 1.4 / 1015 3.7 / 1616 1.3 / 2243 3.6 | 21 M | 0354 1.1 / 1028 4.0 / 1621 0.8 / 2259 3.9 |
| 7 M | 0424 1.3 / 1053 3.8 / 1650 1.2 / 2320 3.6 | 22 TU | 0441 0.9 / 1117 4.1 / 1709 0.6 / ○ 2347 3.9 |
| 8 TU | 0456 1.2 / 1127 3.9 / 1721 1.0 / ● 2354 3.7 | 23 W | 0522 0.8 / 1200 4.2 / 1752 0.5 |
| 9 W | 0526 1.1 / 1159 4.0 / 1752 0.9 | 24 TH | 0029 3.9 / 0600 0.8 / 1240 4.2 / 1832 0.4 |
| 10 TH | 0028 3.7 / 0558 1.0 / 1235 4.0 / 1825 0.8 | 25 F | 0108 3.8 / 0637 0.8 / 1319 4.2 / 1913 0.5 |
| 11 F | 0105 3.8 / 0633 1.0 / 1314 4.1 / 1903 0.7 | 26 SA | 0145 3.7 / 0715 0.9 / 1359 4.1 / 1954 0.6 |
| 12 SA | 0145 3.8 / 0713 0.9 / 1356 4.1 / 1945 0.7 | 27 SU | 0224 3.6 / 0757 1.0 / 1440 4.0 / 2036 0.8 |
| 13 SU | 0228 3.8 / 0757 1.0 / 1441 4.1 / 2031 0.7 | 28 M | 0306 3.5 / 0842 1.1 / 1524 3.8 / 2120 1.0 |
| 14 M | 0315 3.7 / 0846 1.0 / 1528 4.0 / 2121 0.8 | 29 TU | 0351 3.4 / 0931 1.3 / 1612 3.6 / 2208 1.2 |
| 15 TU | 0405 3.7 / 0939 1.1 / 1619 3.9 / ◑ 2215 0.9 | 30 W | 0443 3.3 / 1028 1.5 / 1710 3.4 / ◑ 2301 1.5 |
| | | 31 TH | 0548 3.2 / 1133 1.7 / 1822 3.2 |

### FEBRUARY

| Day | Time m | Day | Time m |
|---|---|---|---|
| 1 F | 0004 1.7 / 0700 3.2 / 1247 1.7 / 1935 3.1 | 16 SA | 0003 1.4 / 0659 3.4 / 1253 1.4 / 1938 3.4 |
| 2 SA | 0119 1.7 / 0805 3.3 / 1413 1.7 / 2041 3.2 | 17 SU | 0137 1.5 / 0820 3.5 / 1419 1.2 / 2100 3.5 |
| 3 SU | 0238 1.6 / 0902 3.4 / 1516 1.5 / 2138 3.3 | 18 M | 0256 1.3 / 0928 3.7 / 1526 1.0 / 2207 3.6 |
| 4 M | 0329 1.5 / 0951 3.6 / 1557 1.3 / 2223 3.5 | 19 TU | 0350 1.1 / 1025 3.9 / 1616 0.7 / 2259 3.7 |
| 5 TU | 0405 1.3 / 1031 3.8 / 1629 1.0 / 2301 3.6 | 20 W | 0433 0.9 / 1111 4.1 / 1658 0.5 / 2340 3.8 |
| 6 W | 0436 1.1 / 1105 3.9 / 1658 0.8 / 2333 3.7 | 21 TH | 0510 0.8 / 1150 4.1 / 1736 0.4 / ○ |
| 7 TH | 0505 0.9 / 1137 4.0 / 1728 0.6 / ● | 22 F | 0014 3.8 / 0543 0.7 / 1223 4.1 / 1811 0.4 |
| 8 F | 0004 3.8 / 0536 0.7 / 1211 4.1 / 1800 0.5 | 23 SA | 0042 3.8 / 0616 0.7 / 1254 4.1 / 1846 0.5 |
| 9 SA | 0038 3.9 / 0610 0.6 / 1248 4.2 / 1837 0.4 | 24 SU | 0110 3.7 / 0649 0.7 / 1328 4.0 / 1920 0.6 |
| 10 SU | 0115 3.9 / 0648 0.6 / 1328 4.2 / 1917 0.4 | 25 M | 0143 3.7 / 0724 0.8 / 1405 3.9 / 1956 0.8 |
| 11 M | 0156 3.9 / 0730 0.6 / 1412 4.2 / 2001 0.5 | 26 TU | 0219 3.6 / 0803 0.9 / 1444 3.7 / 2034 1.0 |
| 12 TU | 0240 3.8 / 0816 0.7 / 1500 4.1 / 2049 0.7 | 27 W | 0257 3.5 / 0844 1.1 / 1527 3.5 / 2114 1.2 |
| 13 W | 0329 3.7 / 0909 0.9 / 1551 3.9 / 2142 0.9 | 28 TH | 0341 3.4 / 0933 1.3 / 1616 3.3 / 2203 1.5 |
| 14 TH | 0425 3.6 / 1010 1.1 / 1651 3.7 / ◑ 2244 1.2 | 29 F | 0434 3.2 / 1039 1.5 / 1724 3.1 / ◑ 2310 1.7 |
| 15 F | 0534 3.4 / 1124 1.3 / 1806 3.5 | | |

### MARCH

| Day | Time m | Day | Time m |
|---|---|---|---|
| 1 SA | 0555 3.1 / 1200 1.7 / 1857 3.0 | 16 SU | 0647 3.4 / 1247 1.2 / 1940 3.3 |
| 2 SU | 0031 1.8 / 0725 3.1 / 1328 1.6 / 2013 3.1 | 17 M | 0128 1.6 / 0809 3.5 / 1412 1.1 / 2059 3.4 |
| 3 M | 0200 1.7 / 0831 3.3 / 1444 1.4 / 2113 3.2 | 18 TU | 0243 1.4 / 0918 3.7 / 1513 0.8 / 2159 3.6 |
| 4 TU | 0301 1.5 / 0922 3.5 / 1526 1.1 / 2159 3.4 | 19 W | 0334 1.1 / 1013 3.9 / 1559 0.6 / 2246 3.7 |
| 5 W | 0338 1.2 / 1003 3.7 / 1559 0.8 / 2235 3.6 | 20 TH | 0415 0.9 / 1057 4.0 / 1638 0.5 / 2324 3.7 |
| 6 TH | 0409 0.9 / 1037 3.9 / 1628 0.6 / 2306 3.8 | 21 F | 0450 0.8 / 1134 4.0 / 1714 0.5 / ○ 2352 3.7 |
| 7 F | 0439 0.7 / 1110 4.1 / 1659 0.5 / ● 2336 3.9 | 22 SA | 0523 0.7 / 1203 4.0 / 1747 0.5 |
| 8 SA | 0510 0.5 / 1144 4.2 / 1733 0.2 | 23 SU | 0013 3.7 / 0554 0.6 / 1231 3.9 / 1817 0.5 |
| 9 SU | 0008 4.0 / 0544 0.3 / 1221 4.3 / 1810 0.2 | 24 M | 0039 3.7 / 0625 0.6 / 1302 3.9 / 1848 0.7 |
| 10 M | 0045 4.0 / 0623 0.3 / 1303 4.3 / 1850 0.3 | 25 TU | 0109 3.7 / 0657 0.7 / 1337 3.8 / 1920 0.8 |
| 11 TU | 0126 4.0 / 0706 0.4 / 1348 4.2 / 1934 0.4 | 26 W | 0144 3.7 / 0732 0.8 / 1415 3.6 / 1955 1.0 |
| 12 W | 0211 3.9 / 0754 0.5 / 1438 4.0 / 2024 0.7 | 27 TH | 0222 3.6 / 0811 1.0 / 1457 3.4 / 2033 1.2 |
| 13 TH | 0301 3.8 / 0851 0.8 / 1533 3.8 / 2119 1.0 | 28 F | 0305 3.4 / 0857 1.2 / 1544 3.2 / 2120 1.4 |
| 14 F | 0359 3.6 / 0957 1.0 / 1639 3.5 / ◑ 2226 1.3 | 29 SA | 0354 3.3 / 0957 1.4 / 1645 3.0 / ◑ 2225 1.7 |
| 15 SA | 0513 3.4 / 1116 1.2 / 1808 3.3 / 2350 1.6 | 30 SU | 0459 3.1 / 1120 1.5 / 1816 2.9 / 2350 1.8 |
| | | 31 M | 0632 3.1 / 1241 1.5 / 1938 3.0 |

### APRIL

| Day | Time m | Day | Time m |
|---|---|---|---|
| 1 TU | 0110 1.7 / 0748 3.2 / 1352 1.3 / 2038 3.2 | 16 W | 0214 1.4 / 0855 3.7 / 1446 0.8 / 2136 3.5 |
| 2 W | 0214 1.4 / 0843 3.4 / 1442 1.0 / 2124 3.4 | 17 TH | 0306 1.2 / 0949 3.8 / 1533 0.7 / 2221 3.6 |
| 3 TH | 0258 1.1 / 0926 3.6 / 1520 0.7 / 2200 3.6 | 18 F | 0349 1.0 / 1034 3.9 / 1612 0.6 / 2258 3.7 |
| 4 F | 0334 0.8 / 1003 3.9 / 1555 0.4 / 2233 3.8 | 19 SA | 0426 0.8 / 1111 3.9 / 1648 0.6 / 2325 3.7 |
| 5 SA | 0408 0.5 / 1040 4.1 / 1630 0.2 / 2305 4.0 | 20 SU | 0501 0.8 / 1141 3.8 / 1720 0.7 / ○ 2347 3.7 |
| 6 SU | 0443 0.3 / 1117 4.2 / 1706 0.1 / ● 2340 4.1 | 21 M | 0533 0.7 / 1209 3.8 / 1751 0.7 |
| 7 M | 0521 0.2 / 1158 4.3 / 1746 0.1 | 22 TU | 0012 3.7 / 0605 0.8 / 1241 3.7 / 1821 0.8 |
| 8 TU | 0019 4.1 / 0602 0.2 / 1244 4.2 / 1827 0.3 | 23 W | 0043 3.7 / 0637 0.8 / 1315 3.6 / 1852 0.9 |
| 9 W | 0103 4.1 / 0649 0.3 / 1333 4.1 / 1914 0.5 | 24 TH | 0118 3.7 / 0712 0.9 / 1354 3.5 / 1926 1.1 |
| 10 TH | 0151 4.0 / 0742 0.5 / 1427 3.9 / 2007 0.8 | 25 F | 0157 3.7 / 0751 1.0 / 1436 3.4 / 2007 1.2 |
| 11 F | 0245 3.8 / 0844 0.7 / 1529 3.7 / 2107 1.1 | 26 SA | 0241 3.5 / 0837 1.1 / 1524 3.3 / 2055 1.4 |
| 12 SA | 0347 3.6 / 0953 0.9 / 1642 3.4 / ◑ 2216 1.4 | 27 SU | 0330 3.4 / 0934 1.3 / 1620 3.1 / 2155 1.5 |
| 13 SU | 0506 3.5 / 1110 1.0 / 1806 3.3 / 2335 1.5 | 28 M | 0428 3.3 / 1043 1.3 / 1730 3.1 / ◑ 2309 1.6 |
| 14 M | 0632 3.5 / 1232 1.1 / 1928 3.3 | 29 TU | 0538 3.2 / 1155 1.3 / 1846 3.1 |
| 15 TU | 0103 1.5 / 0749 3.6 / 1348 1.0 / 2039 3.4 | 30 W | 0020 1.6 / 0650 3.3 / 1259 1.1 / 1947 3.3 |

Chart Datum: 0·20 metres above Ordnance Datum (Dublin). HAT is 4·5 metres above Chart Datum.

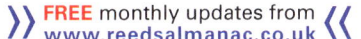

**TIME ZONE (UT)**
For Summer Time add ONE hour in **non-shaded areas**

## DUBLIN (NORTH WALL)  LAT 53°21'N  LONG 6°13'W
TIMES AND HEIGHTS OF HIGH AND LOW WATERS

Dates in red are SPRINGS
Dates in blue are NEAPS

YEAR **2008**

### MAY

| Time | m | Time | m |
|---|---|---|---|
| **1** 0121 | 1.4 | **16** 0230 | 1.3 |
| 0750 | 3.5 | 0916 | 3.7 |
| TH 1353 | 0.9 | F 1500 | 0.9 |
| 2037 | 3.5 | 2146 | 3.6 |
| **2** 0211 | 1.1 | **17** 0318 | 1.1 |
| 0841 | 3.7 | 1003 | 3.7 |
| F 1439 | 0.6 | SA 1543 | 0.9 |
| 2119 | 3.7 | 2223 | 3.6 |
| **3** 0255 | 0.8 | **18** 0401 | 1.0 |
| 0926 | 3.9 | 1043 | 3.7 |
| SA 1521 | 0.4 | SU 1621 | 0.9 |
| 2158 | 3.8 | 2254 | 3.7 |
| **4** 0337 | 0.6 | **19** 0439 | 1.0 |
| 1011 | 4.1 | 1117 | 3.7 |
| SU 1602 | 0.3 | M 1655 | 0.9 |
| 2237 | 4.0 | 2322 | 3.7 |
| **5** 0418 | 0.4 | **20** 0514 | 0.9 |
| 1056 | 4.2 | 1149 | 3.7 |
| M 1643 | 0.3 | TU 1727 | 1.0 |
| ● 2317 | 4.1 | ○ 2350 | 3.7 |
| **6** 0502 | 0.3 | **21** 0548 | 0.9 |
| 1143 | 4.2 | 1222 | 3.6 |
| TU 1726 | 0.3 | W 1758 | 1.0 |
| **7** 0001 | 4.1 | **22** 0022 | 3.8 |
| 0549 | 0.3 | 0621 | 1.0 |
| W 1233 | 4.1 | TH 1257 | 3.6 |
| 1811 | 0.5 | 1829 | 1.1 |
| **8** 0048 | 4.1 | **23** 0058 | 3.8 |
| 0640 | 0.3 | 0656 | 1.0 |
| TH 1326 | 4.0 | F 1336 | 3.5 |
| 1901 | 0.7 | 1905 | 1.1 |
| **9** 0140 | 4.0 | **24** 0138 | 3.7 |
| 0737 | 0.5 | 0734 | 1.0 |
| F 1424 | 3.8 | SA 1418 | 3.5 |
| 1955 | 0.9 | 1946 | 1.2 |
| **10** 0237 | 3.9 | **25** 0222 | 3.7 |
| 0839 | 0.6 | 0819 | 1.1 |
| SA 1527 | 3.4 | SU 1504 | 3.4 |
| 2055 | 1.2 | 2032 | 1.3 |
| **11** 0342 | 3.8 | **26** 0310 | 3.6 |
| 0945 | 0.8 | 0910 | 1.1 |
| SU 1636 | 3.5 | M 1554 | 3.3 |
| 2200 | 1.4 | 2126 | 1.4 |
| **12** 0454 | 3.7 | **27** 0402 | 3.5 |
| 1053 | 0.9 | 1007 | 1.1 |
| M 1748 | 3.4 | TU 1650 | 3.3 |
| ◑ 2309 | 1.5 | 2225 | 1.4 |
| **13** 0608 | 3.6 | **28** 0459 | 3.5 |
| 1204 | 1.0 | 1107 | 1.1 |
| TU 1859 | 3.4 | W 1751 | 3.3 |
| | | ◗ 2327 | 1.4 |
| **14** 0023 | 1.5 | **29** 0559 | 3.5 |
| 0717 | 3.6 | 1208 | 1.0 |
| W 1312 | 1.0 | TH 1851 | 3.4 |
| 2004 | 3.4 | | |
| **15** 0132 | 1.4 | **30** 0028 | 1.3 |
| 0820 | 3.7 | 0659 | 3.6 |
| TH 1410 | 0.9 | F 1306 | 0.9 |
| 2100 | 3.5 | 1947 | 3.5 |
| | | **31** 0125 | 1.1 |
| | | 0758 | 3.7 |
| | | SA 1400 | 0.8 |
| | | 2039 | 3.7 |

### JUNE

| Time | m | Time | m |
|---|---|---|---|
| **1** 0219 | 1.0 | **16** 0337 | 1.3 |
| 0854 | 3.9 | 1013 | 3.6 |
| SU 1451 | 0.6 | M 1555 | 1.2 |
| 2128 | 3.8 | 2223 | 3.7 |
| **2** 0310 | 0.8 | **17** 0420 | 1.2 |
| 0949 | 4.0 | 1053 | 3.6 |
| M 1539 | 0.6 | TU 1632 | 1.2 |
| 2216 | 4.0 | 2258 | 3.7 |
| **3** 0400 | 0.6 | **18** 0458 | 1.1 |
| 1042 | 4.1 | 1129 | 3.6 |
| TU 1627 | 0.5 | W 1706 | 1.1 |
| ● 2303 | 4.1 | ○ 2331 | 3.8 |
| **4** 0450 | 0.4 | **19** 0532 | 1.1 |
| 1134 | 4.1 | 1204 | 3.6 |
| W 1713 | 0.5 | TH 1738 | 1.1 |
| 2350 | 4.2 | | |
| **5** 0541 | 0.4 | **20** 0004 | 3.8 |
| 1226 | 4.1 | 0604 | 1.0 |
| TH 1801 | 0.6 | F 1239 | 3.6 |
| | | 1809 | 1.1 |
| **6** 0039 | 4.2 | **21** 0039 | 3.9 |
| 0634 | 0.4 | 0637 | 1.0 |
| F 1320 | 4.0 | SA 1315 | 3.6 |
| 1849 | 0.8 | 1843 | 1.1 |
| **7** 0131 | 4.1 | **22** 0118 | 3.9 |
| 0729 | 0.5 | 0713 | 1.0 |
| SA 1416 | 3.8 | SU 1355 | 3.6 |
| 1941 | 0.9 | 1922 | 1.1 |
| **8** 0226 | 4.0 | **23** 0200 | 3.9 |
| 0827 | 0.6 | 0754 | 0.9 |
| SU 1514 | 3.7 | M 1438 | 3.6 |
| 2036 | 1.1 | 2005 | 1.1 |
| **9** 0325 | 3.9 | **24** 0245 | 3.8 |
| 0926 | 0.7 | 0840 | 0.9 |
| M 1613 | 3.5 | TU 1523 | 3.5 |
| 2134 | 1.3 | 2053 | 1.2 |
| **10** 0428 | 3.8 | **25** 0332 | 3.8 |
| 1025 | 0.8 | 0930 | 0.9 |
| TU 1715 | 3.4 | W 1613 | 3.5 |
| ◗ 2234 | 1.4 | 2144 | 1.2 |
| **11** 0533 | 3.7 | **26** 0423 | 3.7 |
| 1126 | 1.0 | 1023 | 0.9 |
| W 1817 | 3.4 | TH 1706 | 3.5 |
| 2338 | 1.5 | ◑ 2240 | 1.2 |
| **12** 0637 | 3.6 | **27** 0518 | 3.7 |
| 1227 | 1.1 | 1121 | 1.0 |
| TH 1917 | 3.4 | F 1804 | 3.5 |
| | | 2341 | 1.3 |
| **13** 0043 | 1.5 | **28** 0620 | 3.7 |
| 0738 | 3.6 | 1223 | 1.0 |
| F 1328 | 1.2 | SA 1907 | 3.5 |
| 2012 | 3.4 | | |
| **14** 0149 | 1.4 | **29** 0045 | 1.2 |
| 0836 | 3.6 | 0725 | 3.7 |
| SA 1424 | 1.2 | SU 1327 | 1.0 |
| 2102 | 3.5 | 2009 | 3.6 |
| **15** 0247 | 1.4 | **30** 0151 | 1.1 |
| 0928 | 3.6 | 0833 | 3.8 |
| SU 1512 | 1.2 | M 1429 | 0.9 |
| 2145 | 3.6 | 2108 | 3.8 |

### JULY

| Time | m | Time | m |
|---|---|---|---|
| **1** 0253 | 1.0 | **16** 0404 | 1.3 |
| 0936 | 3.9 | 1031 | 3.5 |
| TU 1526 | 0.9 | W 1611 | 1.3 |
| 2202 | 3.9 | 2236 | 3.8 |
| **2** 0352 | 0.8 | **17** 0441 | 1.2 |
| 1034 | 4.0 | 1110 | 3.6 |
| W 1618 | 0.8 | TH 1645 | 1.1 |
| 2253 | 4.1 | 2311 | 3.8 |
| **3** 0445 | 0.6 | **18** 0513 | 1.0 |
| 1128 | 4.0 | 1144 | 3.6 |
| TH 1705 | 0.7 | F 1716 | 1.1 |
| ● 2341 | 4.2 | ○ 2343 | 3.9 |
| **4** 0536 | 0.4 | **19** 0542 | 0.9 |
| 1218 | 4.0 | 1216 | 3.7 |
| F 1750 | 0.7 | SA 1746 | 1.0 |
| **5** 0027 | 4.2 | **20** 0016 | 4.0 |
| 0625 | 0.4 | 0611 | 0.8 |
| SA 1308 | 3.9 | SU 1250 | 3.7 |
| 1834 | 0.8 | 1818 | 0.9 |
| **6** 0115 | 4.2 | **21** 0052 | 4.0 |
| 0714 | 0.4 | 0644 | 0.8 |
| SU 1356 | 3.8 | M 1326 | 3.7 |
| 1920 | 0.9 | 1854 | 0.9 |
| **7** 0204 | 4.1 | **22** 0132 | 4.0 |
| 0805 | 0.5 | 0723 | 0.7 |
| M 1445 | 3.7 | TU 1406 | 3.7 |
| 2008 | 1.0 | 1934 | 0.9 |
| **8** 0254 | 4.0 | **23** 0215 | 4.0 |
| 0856 | 0.7 | 0807 | 0.7 |
| TU 1535 | 3.6 | W 1450 | 3.7 |
| 2059 | 1.1 | 2019 | 0.9 |
| **9** 0348 | 3.9 | **24** 0300 | 4.0 |
| 0948 | 0.8 | 0854 | 0.8 |
| W 1627 | 3.4 | TH 1536 | 3.7 |
| 2153 | 1.3 | 2108 | 1.0 |
| **10** 0445 | 3.7 | **25** 0349 | 3.9 |
| 1040 | 1.1 | 0945 | 0.9 |
| TH 1723 | 3.3 | F 1627 | 3.6 |
| ◗ 2251 | 1.4 | ◗ 2202 | 1.1 |
| **11** 0548 | 3.5 | **26** 0444 | 3.8 |
| 1136 | 1.3 | 1043 | 1.0 |
| F 1823 | 3.3 | SA 1726 | 3.5 |
| 2353 | 1.5 | 2305 | 1.3 |
| **12** 0652 | 3.4 | **27** 0548 | 3.6 |
| 1236 | 1.4 | 1149 | 1.2 |
| SA 1923 | 3.3 | SU 1836 | 3.5 |
| **13** 0103 | 1.6 | **28** 0019 | 1.3 |
| 0755 | 3.4 | 0705 | 3.6 |
| SU 1342 | 1.5 | M 1305 | 1.3 |
| 2019 | 3.4 | 1950 | 3.5 |
| **14** 0217 | 1.5 | **29** 0138 | 1.3 |
| 0854 | 3.4 | 0825 | 3.6 |
| M 1443 | 1.5 | TU 1419 | 1.2 |
| 2111 | 3.5 | 2057 | 3.7 |
| **15** 0318 | 1.4 | **30** 0251 | 1.1 |
| 0947 | 3.4 | 0934 | 3.7 |
| TU 1532 | 1.4 | W 1522 | 1.1 |
| 2157 | 3.6 | 2156 | 3.9 |
| | | **31** 0352 | 0.8 |
| | | 1033 | 3.9 |
| | | TH 1613 | 0.9 |
| | | 2246 | 4.1 |

### AUGUST

| Time | m | Time | m |
|---|---|---|---|
| **1** 0443 | 0.6 | **16** 0447 | 0.9 |
| 1123 | 3.9 | 1121 | 3.7 |
| F 1657 | 0.8 | SA 1651 | 0.9 |
| ● 2331 | 4.2 | ○ 2319 | 4.0 |
| **2** 0528 | 0.4 | **17** 0513 | 0.7 |
| 1207 | 3.9 | 1150 | 3.8 |
| SA 1737 | 0.7 | SU 1720 | 0.8 |
| | | 2349 | 4.1 |
| **3** 0012 | 4.3 | **18** 0542 | 0.6 |
| 0610 | 0.3 | 1221 | 3.9 |
| SU 1248 | 3.9 | M 1751 | 0.7 |
| 1814 | 0.7 | | |
| **4** 0052 | 4.2 | **19** 0023 | 4.2 |
| 0652 | 0.4 | 0614 | 0.5 |
| M 1327 | 3.8 | TU 1255 | 3.9 |
| 1853 | 0.8 | 1825 | 0.6 |
| **5** 0133 | 4.2 | **20** 0102 | 4.2 |
| 0734 | 0.5 | 0652 | 0.5 |
| TU 1406 | 3.7 | W 1334 | 3.9 |
| 1935 | 0.9 | 1904 | 0.7 |
| **6** 0216 | 4.0 | **21** 0143 | 4.2 |
| 0818 | 0.7 | 0734 | 0.6 |
| W 1447 | 3.6 | TH 1416 | 3.9 |
| 2020 | 1.0 | 1948 | 0.7 |
| **7** 0301 | 3.8 | **22** 0229 | 4.1 |
| 0904 | 0.9 | 0820 | 0.7 |
| TH 1532 | 3.5 | F 1503 | 3.8 |
| 2109 | 1.1 | 2038 | 0.9 |
| **8** 0351 | 3.6 | **23** 0320 | 3.9 |
| 0952 | 1.2 | 0913 | 0.9 |
| F 1621 | 3.4 | SA 1554 | 3.6 |
| ◗ 2205 | 1.4 | ◗ 2136 | 1.1 |
| **9** 0450 | 3.4 | **24** 0417 | 3.7 |
| 1045 | 1.4 | 1014 | 1.2 |
| SA 1722 | 3.3 | SU 1656 | 3.5 |
| 2308 | 1.6 | 2245 | 1.3 |
| **10** 0604 | 3.2 | **25** 0530 | 3.5 |
| 1145 | 1.6 | 1128 | 1.4 |
| SU 1834 | 3.2 | M 1816 | 3.4 |
| **11** 0019 | 1.7 | **26** 0010 | 1.6 |
| 0719 | 3.2 | 0703 | 3.4 |
| M 1256 | 1.7 | TU 1256 | 1.5 |
| 1942 | 3.3 | 1940 | 3.5 |
| **12** 0149 | 1.6 | **27** 0139 | 1.3 |
| 0827 | 3.3 | 0828 | 3.5 |
| TU 1414 | 1.6 | W 1417 | 1.4 |
| 2042 | 3.4 | 2052 | 3.7 |
| **13** 0301 | 1.5 | **28** 0253 | 1.0 |
| 0925 | 3.3 | 0937 | 3.7 |
| W 1511 | 1.5 | TH 1517 | 1.2 |
| 2132 | 3.6 | 2151 | 3.9 |
| **14** 0346 | 1.3 | **29** 0348 | 0.7 |
| 1011 | 3.5 | 1031 | 3.8 |
| TH 1550 | 1.3 | F 1604 | 1.0 |
| 2214 | 3.8 | 2239 | 4.1 |
| **15** 0419 | 1.1 | **30** 0433 | 0.5 |
| 1049 | 3.6 | 1115 | 3.9 |
| F 1622 | 1.1 | SA 1643 | 0.8 |
| 2248 | 3.9 | ● 2320 | 4.2 |
| | | **31** 0512 | 0.4 |
| | | 1153 | 3.9 |
| | | SU 1719 | 0.7 |
| | | 2355 | 4.2 |

Chart Datum: 0·20 metres above Ordnance Datum (Dublin). HAT is 4·5 metres above Chart Datum.

**TIME ZONE (UT)**
For Summer Time add ONE hour in **non-shaded areas**

## DUBLIN (NORTH WALL)  LAT 53°21′N  LONG 6°13′W
### TIMES AND HEIGHTS OF HIGH AND LOW WATERS

Dates in red are SPRINGS
Dates in blue are NEAPS

YEAR **2008**

S Ireland

### SEPTEMBER

| Time m | Time m |
|---|---|
| **1** M 0549 0.4 / 1224 3.9 / 1753 0.7 | **16** TU 0512 0.4 / 1150 4.0 / 1723 0.5 / 2355 4.3 |
| **2** TU 0028 4.2 / 0625 0.4 / 1255 3.8 / 1827 0.7 | **17** W 0545 0.3 / 1224 4.0 / 1759 0.5 |
| **3** W 0103 4.1 / 0701 0.6 / 1328 3.8 / 1904 0.8 | **18** TH 0033 4.3 / 0623 0.4 / 1304 4.0 / 1839 0.5 |
| **4** TH 0141 4.0 / 0739 0.8 / 1405 3.7 / 1945 0.9 | **19** F 0117 4.2 / 0705 0.6 / 1348 4.0 / 1925 0.7 |
| **5** F 0222 3.8 / 0820 1.0 / 1445 3.6 / 2030 1.1 | **20** SA 0206 4.1 / 0753 0.8 / 1436 3.9 / 2019 0.9 |
| **6** SA 0308 3.6 / 0905 1.2 / 1529 3.5 / 2123 1.3 | **21** SU 0301 3.8 / 0849 1.1 / 1532 3.7 / 2123 1.1 |
| **7** SU 0401 3.3 / 0959 1.5 / 1623 3.4 / ◐ 2228 1.6 | **22** M 0405 3.6 / 0957 1.4 / 1639 3.6 / ◑ 2240 1.3 |
| **8** M 0516 3.1 / 1103 1.7 / 1741 3.2 / 2343 1.7 | **23** TU 0531 3.4 / 1118 1.6 / 1806 3.5 |
| **9** TU 0645 3.1 / 1217 1.8 / 1905 3.2 | **24** W 0008 1.3 / 0706 3.4 / 1249 1.6 / 1931 3.6 |
| **10** W 0113 1.7 / 0800 3.1 / 1341 1.7 / 2011 3.4 | **25** TH 0136 1.2 / 0826 3.5 / 1405 1.4 / 2042 3.8 |
| **11** TH 0232 1.4 / 0901 3.3 / 1442 1.5 / 2105 3.6 | **26** F 0242 0.9 / 0929 3.7 / 1501 1.2 / 2139 4.0 |
| **12** F 0315 1.2 / 0947 3.5 / 1522 1.3 / 2146 3.8 | **27** SA 0332 0.7 / 1019 3.8 / 1546 1.0 / 2226 4.1 |
| **13** SA 0347 0.9 / 1023 3.7 / 1553 1.0 / 2220 3.9 | **28** SU 0414 0.5 / 1100 3.9 / 1624 0.8 / 2305 4.2 |
| **14** SU 0415 0.7 / 1053 3.8 / 1622 0.8 / 2250 4.1 | **29** M 0451 0.5 / 1133 3.9 / 1700 0.7 / ● 2337 4.2 |
| **15** M 0442 0.5 / 1121 3.9 / 1651 0.6 / ○ 2321 4.2 | **30** TU 0526 0.5 / 1200 3.9 / 1733 0.7 |

### OCTOBER

| Time m | Time m |
|---|---|
| **1** W 0006 4.1 / 0558 0.6 / 1226 3.8 / 1806 0.7 | **16** TH 0520 0.3 / 1158 4.2 / 1738 0.4 |
| **2** TH 0039 4.0 / 0631 0.7 / 1257 3.8 / 1841 0.8 | **17** F 0013 4.3 / 0559 0.4 / 1241 4.1 / 1822 0.5 |
| **3** F 0115 3.9 / 0705 0.9 / 1333 3.8 / 1919 0.9 | **18** SA 0101 4.2 / 0644 0.6 / 1328 4.1 / 1913 0.6 |
| **4** SA 0155 3.7 / 0742 1.1 / 1412 3.7 / 2001 1.1 | **19** SU 0154 4.0 / 0735 0.9 / 1420 4.0 / 2011 0.8 |
| **5** SU 0238 3.5 / 0825 1.3 / 1455 3.6 / 2051 1.3 | **20** M 0255 3.8 / 0836 1.2 / 1520 3.8 / 2119 1.0 |
| **6** M 0329 3.3 / 0917 1.5 / 1545 3.4 / 2154 1.5 | **21** TU 0407 3.6 / 0946 1.5 / 1632 3.7 / ◐ 2235 1.2 |
| **7** TU 0437 3.1 / 1025 1.7 / 1650 3.3 / ◐ 2308 1.6 | **22** W 0531 3.4 / 1105 1.6 / 1754 3.7 / 2356 1.2 |
| **8** W 0607 3.0 / 1141 1.8 / 1818 3.2 | **23** TH 0654 3.5 / 1227 1.6 / 1911 3.7 |
| **9** TH 0027 1.6 / 0725 3.1 / 1256 1.8 / 1930 3.3 | **24** F 0113 1.1 / 0807 3.6 / 1339 1.5 / 2019 3.9 |
| **10** F 0140 1.4 / 0825 3.3 / 1358 1.6 / 2026 3.6 | **25** SA 0217 0.9 / 0907 3.7 / 1435 1.3 / 2116 4.0 |
| **11** SA 0230 1.2 / 0912 3.5 / 1442 1.3 / 2109 3.7 | **26** SU 0307 0.8 / 0956 3.8 / 1522 1.1 / 2205 4.0 |
| **12** SU 0306 0.9 / 0948 3.7 / 1517 1.0 / 2145 3.9 | **27** M 0350 0.7 / 1036 3.9 / 1603 1.0 / 2246 4.1 |
| **13** M 0338 0.6 / 1020 3.9 / 1550 0.8 / 2218 4.1 | **28** TU 0428 0.7 / 1110 3.9 / 1641 0.9 / ● 2319 4.0 |
| **14** TU 0410 0.4 / 1053 4.0 / 1623 0.6 / ○ 2253 4.2 | **29** W 0503 0.7 / 1137 3.9 / 1716 0.9 / 2349 4.0 |
| **15** W 0443 0.3 / 1122 4.1 / 1659 0.5 / 2331 4.3 | **30** TH 0535 0.8 / 1203 3.9 / 1750 0.9 |
|  | **31** F 0021 3.9 / 0606 0.9 / 1234 3.9 / 1825 0.9 |

### NOVEMBER

| Time m | Time m |
|---|---|
| **1** SA 0057 3.8 / 0639 1.0 / 1309 3.9 / 1902 1.0 | **16** SU 0055 4.1 / 0631 0.8 / 1317 4.2 / 1907 0.6 |
| **2** SU 0135 3.7 / 0714 1.2 / 1348 3.8 / 1942 1.1 | **17** M 0151 4.0 / 0724 1.0 / 1412 4.1 / 2006 0.7 |
| **3** M 0218 3.5 / 0755 1.3 / 1431 3.7 / 2028 1.3 | **18** TU 0253 3.8 / 0824 1.2 / 1513 4.0 / 2110 0.8 |
| **4** TU 0307 3.4 / 0844 1.5 / 1519 3.6 / 2122 1.4 | **19** W 0402 3.7 / 0929 1.4 / 1620 3.9 / ◐ 2218 1.0 |
| **5** W 0405 3.2 / 0946 1.7 / 1614 3.5 / 2227 1.5 | **20** TH 0514 3.5 / 1039 1.5 / 1730 3.8 / 2328 1.1 |
| **6** TH 0517 3.2 / 1057 1.8 / 1719 3.4 / ◐ 2335 1.5 | **21** F 0626 3.5 / 1152 1.6 / 1840 3.8 |
| **7** F 0632 3.2 / 1205 1.7 / 1828 3.4 | **22** SA 0038 1.1 / 0733 3.6 / 1302 1.5 / 1945 3.8 |
| **8** SA 0039 1.4 / 0734 3.3 / 1305 1.6 / 1929 3.5 | **23** SU 0143 1.1 / 0832 3.7 / 1404 1.4 / 2045 3.9 |
| **9** SU 0135 1.2 / 0824 3.5 / 1354 1.4 / 2019 3.7 | **24** M 0238 1.0 / 0923 3.7 / 1457 1.3 / 2138 3.9 |
| **10** M 0220 0.9 / 0905 3.7 / 1437 1.1 / 2104 3.9 | **25** TU 0324 1.0 / 1007 3.8 / 1543 1.2 / 2223 3.9 |
| **11** TU 0301 0.7 / 0942 3.9 / 1518 0.9 / 2147 4.1 | **26** W 0405 1.0 / 1043 3.9 / 1624 1.1 / 2301 3.8 |
| **12** W 0340 0.6 / 1020 4.1 / 1558 0.7 / 2231 4.2 | **27** TH 0442 1.0 / 1115 3.9 / 1702 1.1 / ● 2334 3.8 |
| **13** TH 0420 0.5 / 1059 4.2 / 1640 0.5 / ○ 2316 4.3 | **28** F 0516 1.0 / 1145 3.9 / 1739 1.0 |
| **14** F 0501 0.5 / 1141 4.2 / 1725 0.5 | **29** SA 0007 3.8 / 0547 1.1 / 1217 3.9 / 1813 1.0 |
| **15** SA 0003 4.2 / 0544 0.6 / 1227 4.2 / 1814 0.5 | **30** SU 0042 3.7 / 0619 1.1 / 1251 3.9 / 1848 1.1 |

### DECEMBER

| Time m | Time m |
|---|---|
| **1** M 0119 3.7 / 0653 1.2 / 1328 3.9 / 1924 1.1 | **16** TU 0144 4.0 / 0712 0.9 / 1400 4.3 / 1954 0.5 |
| **2** TU 0159 3.6 / 0731 1.3 / 1409 3.8 / 2004 1.2 | **17** W 0241 3.9 / 0805 1.1 / 1456 4.2 / 2051 0.7 |
| **3** W 0243 3.5 / 0814 1.4 / 1453 3.8 / 2048 1.2 | **18** TH 0340 3.7 / 0903 1.2 / 1555 4.0 / 2149 0.8 |
| **4** TH 0332 3.4 / 0903 1.5 / 1541 3.7 / 2138 1.3 | **19** F 0441 3.6 / 1004 1.4 / 1657 3.9 / ◐ 2249 1.0 |
| **5** F 0426 3.4 / 0959 1.6 / 1633 3.6 / ◐ 2234 1.3 | **20** SA 0545 3.5 / 1108 1.5 / 1801 3.8 / 2353 1.2 |
| **6** SA 0525 3.3 / 1101 1.6 / 1729 3.6 / 2335 1.3 | **21** SU 0648 3.5 / 1217 1.6 / 1906 3.7 |
| **7** SU 0627 3.4 / 1204 1.6 / 1829 3.6 | **22** M 0059 1.3 / 0748 3.5 / 1327 1.6 / 2008 3.6 |
| **8** M 0036 1.2 / 0726 3.5 / 1303 1.4 / 1928 3.7 | **23** TU 0204 1.3 / 0844 3.6 / 1431 1.5 / 2108 3.6 |
| **9** TU 0134 1.1 / 0819 3.7 / 1358 1.3 / 2027 3.8 | **24** W 0259 1.3 / 0934 3.7 / 1526 1.4 / 2200 3.6 |
| **10** W 0226 0.9 / 0909 3.8 / 1449 1.0 / 2123 4.0 | **25** TH 0346 1.3 / 1016 3.8 / 1612 1.3 / 2243 3.6 |
| **11** TH 0316 0.7 / 0957 4.0 / 1540 0.8 / 2216 4.1 | **26** F 0425 1.2 / 1054 3.9 / 1651 1.2 / 2320 3.7 |
| **12** F 0403 0.7 / 1024 4.2 / 1629 0.6 / ○ 2308 4.2 | **27** SA 0459 1.2 / 1128 3.9 / 1727 1.1 / ● 2353 3.7 |
| **13** SA 0449 0.7 / 1130 4.3 / 1718 0.5 / 2358 4.2 | **28** SU 0531 1.1 / 1200 4.0 / 1800 1.0 |
| **14** SU 0535 0.7 / 1217 4.3 / 1808 0.4 | **29** M 0026 3.7 / 0601 1.1 / 1232 4.0 / 1830 1.0 |
| **15** M 0050 4.1 / 0622 0.8 / 1307 4.3 / 1900 0.4 | **30** TU 0059 3.7 / 0632 1.1 / 1307 4.0 / 1900 1.0 |
|  | **31** W 0135 3.7 / 0705 1.1 / 1344 4.0 / 1934 1.0 |

Chart Datum: 0·20 metres above Ordnance Datum (Dublin). HAT is 4·5 metres above Chart Datum.

## 5.10  WICKLOW

Wicklow **52°58'·98N 06°02'·70W** ✿✿✿🌊🌊🌸🌸

**CHARTS** AC 1468, 633, 5621; Imray C61; Irish OS 56

**TIDES** –0010 Dover; ML 1·7; Duration 0640

**Standard Port DUBLIN (NORTH WALL)** (⟵)

| Times | | | | Height (metres) | | | |
|---|---|---|---|---|---|---|---|
| High Water | | Low Water | | MHWS | MHWN | MLWN | MLWS |
| 0000 | 0700 | 0000 | 0500 | 4·1 | 3·4 | 1·5 | 0·7 |
| 1200 | 1900 | 1200 | 1700 | | | | |
| Differences **WICKLOW** | | | | | | | |
| –0019 | –0019 | –0024 | –0026 | –1·4 | –1·1 | –0·4 | 0·0 |

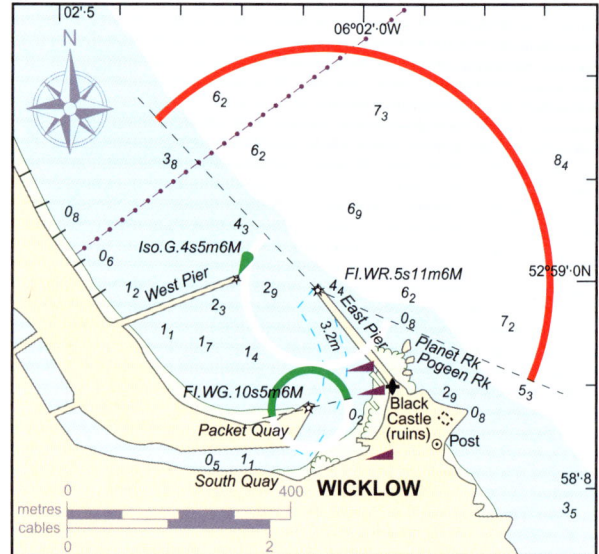

**SHELTER** Very safe, and access H24. Outer hbr is open to NE winds which cause a swell. Moorings in NW of hbr belong to SC and may not be used without permission. 4 berths on E Pier (2·5m) are convenient except in strong winds NW to NE, with fender boards/ladders provided. W pier is not recommended. ⚓ in hbr is restricted by ships' turning circle. Inner hbr (river) gives excellent shelter in 2·5m on N and S Quays, which are used by FVs. Packet Quay is for ships (2·5m), but may be used if none due; fender board needed. Yachts should berth on N or S quays as directed and/or space available.

**NAVIGATION** WPT 52°59'·20N 06°01'·80W, 220°/0·27M to ent. Appr presents no difficulty; keep in the R sector of the E pier lt to avoid Planet Rk and Pogeen Rk.

**LIGHTS AND MARKS** No ldg marks/lts; lts are as on the chartlet. W pier head lt, Iso G 4s, is shown H24. ☆ Fl WG 10s on Packet Quay hd is vis 076°-G-256°-W-076°.

**R/T** VHF Ch 12, **14**, 16. Wicklow SC Ch M 16 (occas).

**TELEPHONE** (Code 0404) HM ☎/📠 67455; MRCC (01) 6620922; Coast/Cliff Rescue Service 69962; ⊖ 67222; Police 67107; Dr 67381.

**FACILITIES East Pier, S and N Quays**, L, FW, AB €14.00/craft, reductions for longer stay, P & D (cans; bulk: see HM); **Wicklow SC** ☎ 67526, Slip (except LWS), M, L, FW, Bar; **Services**: ME, El, C, Kos, Gaz. **Town** CH, 🛒, R, Bar, ✉, Ⓑ, ⇄, ✈ (Dublin).

## 5.11  ARKLOW

Wicklow **52°47'·60N 06°08'·20W** ✿✿✿🌊🌊🌸🌸

**CHARTS** AC 1468, 633, 5621; Imray C61; Irish OS 62

**TIDES** –0150 Dover; ML 1·0; Duration 0640

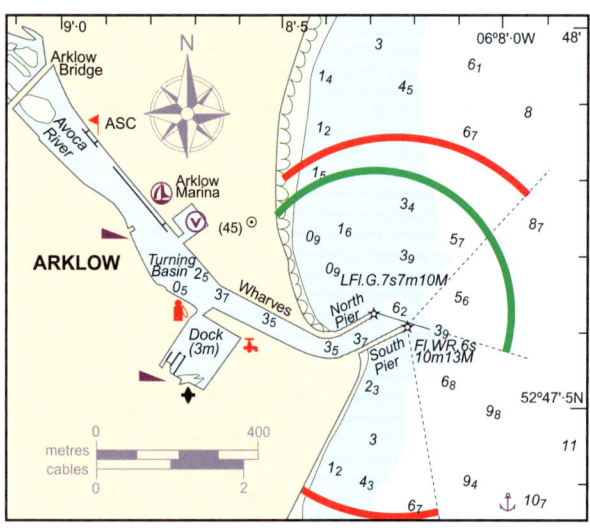

**Standard Port DUBLIN (NORTH WALL)** (⟵)

| Times | | | | Height (metres) | | | |
|---|---|---|---|---|---|---|---|
| High Water | | Low Water | | MHWS | MHWN | MLWN | MLWS |
| 0000 | 0700 | 0000 | 0500 | 4·1 | 3·4 | 1·5 | 0·7 |
| 1200 | 1900 | 1200 | 1700 | | | | |
| Differences **ARKLOW** (Note small Range) | | | | | | | |
| –0315 | –0201 | –0140 | –0134 | –2·7 | –2·2 | –0·6 | –0·1 |
| **COURTOWN** | | | | | | | |
| –0328 | –0242 | –0158 | –0138 | –2·8 | –2·4 | –0·5 | 0·0 |

**SHELTER** Good, access H24.

• Entrance unsafe in strong or prolonged NE to SE winds, when seas break across the bar.

A 60 berth marina lies on NE side of river. Good ⚓ in bay; avoid whelk pots. One AB for ❤ (1.4m) at ASC quay. AB on SE wall of Dock (ent is 13·5m wide; 3m depth) in perfect shelter, but amidst FVs. **Arklow Roadstone Hbr**, 1M S of Arklow, is not for yachts.

**NAVIGATION** WPT 52°47'·60N 06°07'·50W, 270°/0·40M to ent. No navigational dangers, but beware ebb setting SE across hbr ent; give S pierhd a wide berth. Ent is difficult without power, due to blanking by piers. 3kn speed limit. Night entry, see below. Caution: Up-river of Dock ent keep to NE side of river.

**LIGHTS AND MARKS** No ldg lts/marks, see 5.3 and chartlet Conspic factory chy 2·5ca NW of piers.

• Beware the Pier Hd lts are very difficult to see due to powerful orange flood lts near the root of both piers shining E/ENE onto them (to assist pilotage of departing shipping).
• Best advice to visitors is to approach from the NE with R sector just showing, or enter by day.

**R/T** Marina Ch 16 12 (HJ); Arklow SC Ch 10.

**TELEPHONE** (Code 0402) HM 32466, 📠 31068; MRCC (01) 6620922/3; Coast/Cliff Rescue Service 32430; RNLI 32901; ⊖ 32553; Police 32304/5; Dr 32421.

**FACILITIES** (from seaward) **Dock** €15.00/craft (2nd day free), use showers and toilets in LB Hse, D (Dock ent, HO); **Marina** (60 inc ❤ €3·35), ☎ 39901/32610. **Arklow SC** (NE bank, 500m up-river from Dock), showers, pontoon €15.00, 1 ⚓. **Services:** FW, P & D (cans ½M), ME, El, ✖, C (20 ton mobile), Kos. **Town** limited CH for yachts, 🛒, R, P & D (cans), Bar, ✉, Ⓑ, Wi-fi, @, ⇄, ✈ (Dublin).

### MINOR HARBOURS S OF ARKLOW

**COURTOWN**, Wexford, **52°38'·55N 06°13'·50W**. AC 1787. 10M S of Arklow is feasible in settled weather and offshore winds. Caution: 10m wide ent; only 1m (maintained by local YC) at MLWS due to silting. AB on E wall or pick up vacant mooring.

**MINOR HARBOURS S OF ARKLOW** *continued*

**POLDUFF PIER**, Wexford, **52°34'·15N 06°11'·97W**. AC 1787. 14M S of Arklow. Pier, 100m long, extends in NE direction from shore. NW side of pier has slipway from shore and 1m depth alongside. Local moorings W of pier. Good shelter for small boats in S to W winds. Swell in winds E of S. Appr in daylight only. Appr is clear from NE to E. Rks extend from shore E'ward 200m N of pier but steering along line of pier will clear them. Pub near pier. Village (Ballygarrett) 1·25M W.

## 5.12  WEXFORD

Wexford **52°20'·10N 06°27'·00W** ⚓🔱🏴🏵️🏵️

**CHARTS**  AC 1787, 1772, 5621; Imray C61; Irish OS 77

**TIDES**  –0450 Dover; ML 1·3; Duration 0630

**Standard Port COBH (⟶)**

| Times | | | | Height (metres) | | | |
|---|---|---|---|---|---|---|---|
| High Water | | Low Water | | MHWS | MHWN | MLWN | MLWS |
| 0500 | 1100 | 0500 | 1100 | 4·1 | 3·2 | 1·3 | 0·4 |
| 1700 | 2300 | 1700 | 2300 | | | | |
| Differences WEXFORD | | | | | | | |
| +0126 | +0126 | +0118 | +0108 | –2·1 | –1·7 | –0·3 | +0·1 |

**SHELTER**  250m of AB available just below bridge. Sheltered ⚓ off town quays in 2·3m, but streams are strong. Some 🛟s are provided by WHBC, close N of Ballast Bank. There are no commercial users, other than FVs. Work continues on new waterfront on W side of river.

**NAVIGATION**  For regularly updated local information visit www.whbtc.com/harbour.htm or ☎ 053 9122039.
- Entry is hazardous in strong winds between SE and NE when the sea breaks on the bar. Entry is also difficult at any time for vessels with a draft >1.3m.
- For strangers best entry is HW±2.
- From N steer 225° from North Long Buoy for approx 2·4M keeping outside 5m contour to avoid Slaney Wreck and Dogger Bank; from S steer 358° for approx 4M from West Holdens Buoy. PHM Bar Buoy (52°19'·58N 06°19·57W (2007 position)) on 10m contour marks entrance to the channel.
- New narrow chan into Wexford was laid in 2006. Keep close to all PHM buoys. Beware the S training wall (covers) and pass well S of Black Man SHM Bn at end of N training wall.
- Proceed either to the quays or by arrangement (☎ 053 9122039 or Ch 16/69) to club visitor's mooring.

**LIGHTS AND MARKS**  The marks and tracks on chartlet should be treated with great caution. The white marks on the embankment along the N side of hbr have only limited relevance to the shifting chan. There are no ldg lts. The 2 church spires at Wexford give useful general orientation.

**R/T**  Wexford Hbr BC VHF Ch 16 (best time to try 1000–1200 hrs).

**TELEPHONE** (Code 053) Wexford Hbr BC 9122039; MRCC (01) 6620922/3; ⊜ 9133116; Police 9122333; Dr 9131154; ⊕ 9142233.

**FACILITIES Wexford Quays**, AB (free), Slip, P, D, FW, ME, El, 🛒, CH; **Wexford Hbr Boat Club**, Slip, C (5 ton), Bar; **Town** ✉, Ⓑ, 🚆, ✈ (Waterford).

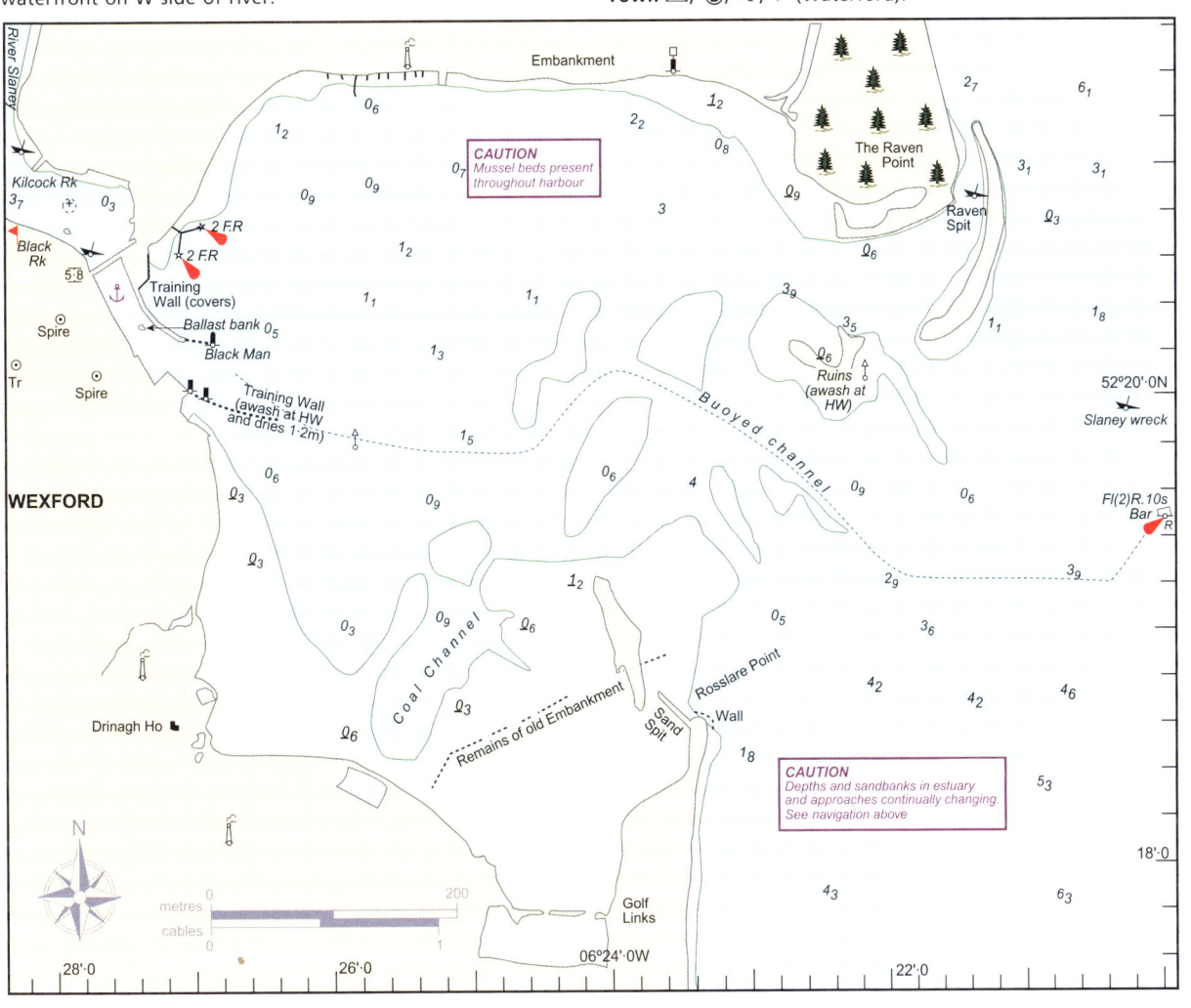

## 5.13   ROSSLARE EUROPORT

Dublin **52°15'·30N 06°20'·90W** ✿✿✿✿✿✿

**CHARTS** AC 1787, 1772, 5621; Imray C61, C57; Irish OS 77

**TIDES** –0510 Dover; ML 1·1; Duration 0640

**Standard Port COBH** (→)

| Times | | | | Height (metres) | | | |
|---|---|---|---|---|---|---|---|
| High Water | | Low Water | | MHWS | MHWN | MLWN | MLWS |
| 0500 | 1100 | 0500 | 1100 | 4·1 | 3·2 | 1·3 | 0·4 |
| 1700 | 2300 | 1700 | 2300 | | | | |
| Differences ROSSLARE EUROPORT | | | | | | | |
| +0045 | +0035 | +0015 | –0005 | –2·2 | –1·8 | –0·5 | –0·1 |

**SHELTER** Useful passage shelter from SW'lies, but few facilities for yachts which may berth on E wall of marshalling area (⚓ on the chartlet, 3·7m), or ⚓ about 0·5M W of hbr. *Small craft harbour (5ca W) is not recommended. In winds from WNW-NNE it is often uncomfortable and, if these winds freshen, dangerous; leave at once, via S Shear.* Rosslare has 160 ferry/high-speed catamaran (41kn) movements per week.

**NAVIGATION** WPT 52°14'·82N 06°15·60W (abeam S Long SCM buoy, VQ (6)+L Fl 10s), 285°/2·92M to bkwtr lt. Main appr from E, S and W is via S Shear, buoyed/lit chan to S of Holden's Bed, a shoal of varying depth; the tide sets across the chan. From S, beware rks off Greenore Pt, and overfalls here and over The Baillies. From the N, appr via N Shear. Tuskar TSS is approx 8M ESE of hbr. Yachts, bound N/S, will usually navigate to the W of Tuskar Rk where the 3·5M wide chan lies to seaward of The Bailies. A passage inshore of The Bailies requires local knowledge and should not be attempted at night. In heavy weather or poor vis, passage E of Tuskar Rk is advised.

**LIGHTS AND MARKS** Tuskar Rk, Q (2) 7·5s 33m 28M, is 5·8M SE of hbr. Water tr (R lt, 35m) is conspic 0·8M SSE of hbr ent. Bkwtr lt, Oc WRG 5s 15m 13/10M, see 5.3. Its two W sectors (188°-208° and 283°-286°) cover N and S Shear respectively. Note: Powerful floodlights in the hbr make identification of navigational lights difficult.

**R/T** VHF Ch **12** (H24) before entering hbr.

**TELEPHONE** (Code 053) HM 9157921, mobile 087 2320251, ▨ 9133206; MRCC (01) 6620922/3; LB Lookout Stn 9133205; ⊜ 9133116; Police 053 65200/33149; Dr 9131154; ⊕ 9142233.

**FACILITIES** **Hbr Ops** ☎ 9157929, No dues, P&D (cans), L, FW (by hose on Berths 2 and 3), ME, C, Divers, Kos, El. **Village**; 🍴, R, Bar, ✉, Ⓑ, ≈, ✈ (Dublin). Ferries to Fishguard, Pembroke Dock, Cherbourg and Roscoff.

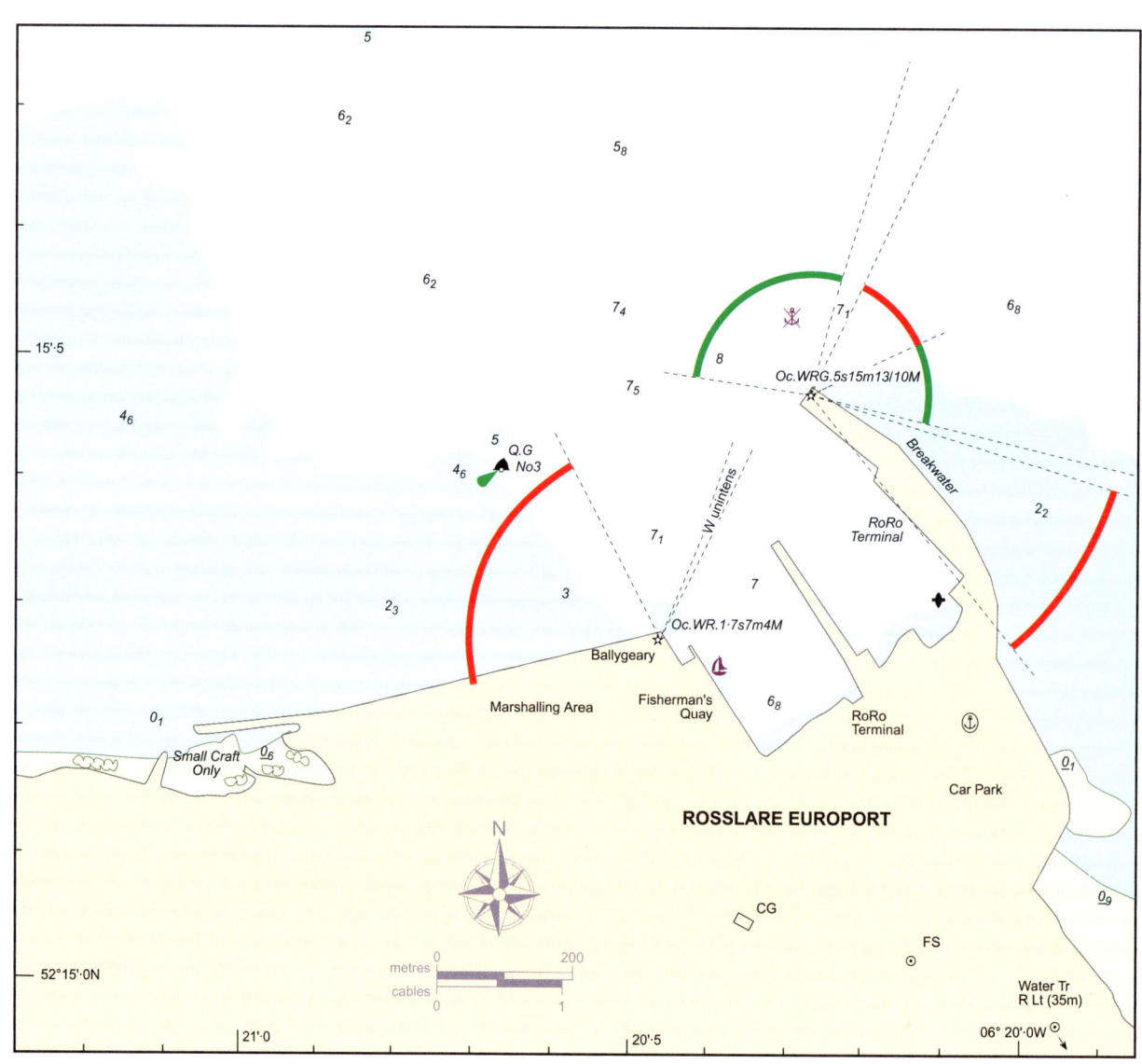

## 5.14 KILMORE QUAY

Wexford **52°10'·25N 06°35'·15W** ✿✿✿🌊🌊 ✿✿✿

**CHARTS** AC *2049*, 2740, 5621; Imray C61, C57; Irish OS 77

**TIDES** −0535 Dover; ML No data; Duration 0605

**Standard Port COBH (→)**

| Times | | | | Height (metres) | | | |
|---|---|---|---|---|---|---|---|
| High Water | | Low Water | | MHWS | MHWN | MLWN | MLWS |
| 0500 | 1100 | 0500 | 1100 | 4·1 | 3·2 | 1·3 | 0·4 |
| 1700 | 2300 | 1700 | 2300 | | | | |
| **Differences BAGINBUN HEAD** (5M NE of Hook Hd) | | | | | | | |
| +0003 | +0003 | −0008 | −0008 | −0·2 | −0·1 | +0·2 | +0·2 |
| **GREAT SALTEE** | | | | | | | |
| +0019 | +0009 | −0004 | +0006 | −0·3 | −0·4 | No data | |
| **CARNSORE POINT** | | | | | | | |
| +0029 | +0019 | −0002 | +0008 | −1·1 | −1·0 | No data | |

**SHELTER** Excellent in marina (3·0m depth), but hbr ent is exposed to SE'lies. FVs berth on W and E piers, close S of marina.

**NAVIGATION** WPT 52°09'·22N 06°35'·32W, SWM buoy (Apr-Sep), 007°/1·0M to pier hd lt, on ldg line. Great (57m) and Little (35m) Saltee Islands lie 3M and 1·7M to SSW and S, respectively, of hbr, separated by Saltee Sound. From the E, safest appr initially is via Saltee Sound, then N to WPT. Caution: In bad weather seas break on the Bohurs and The Bore, rks 2M E of

Saltee Islands. Beware Goose Rk (2·6m) close W of Little Saltee and Murroch's Rk (2·1m) 6ca NW of Little Saltee. St Patrick's Bridge, 650m E of the WPT, is a 300m wide E/W chan used by FVs and yachts, but carrying only 2·4m; care needed in strong onshore winds. It is marked by a PHM buoy, Fl R 6s, and a SHM buoy, Fl G 6s, (laid Apr to mid-Sep); general direction of buoyage is E. From the W, appr is clear but keep at least 5ca off Forlorn Pt to avoid Forlorn Rk (1·5m).

**LIGHTS AND MARKS** See 5.3 and chartlet. Ldg lts/marks lead 008° to the hbr.

- From W, ldg lts are obsc'd by piers until S of hbr ent. Turn 90° port into hbr ent, just past ✫ QRG at W Quay Hd; do not overshoot into shoal water ahead. The R sectors of this ✫ QRG warn of Forlorn Rock and The Lings to W of the ldg line and shingle banks drying 0·6m close E of the ldg line.

A white-gabled church is conspic from afar, as are two 20m high flood lt pylons on the E quay. A disused lt ship at the inner end of W quay is a museum of no navigational significance.

**R/T** VHF Ch 09 (occas).

**TELEPHONE** (Code 053) HM ☎/📠 9129955; 🖥 9133741; MRCC (01) 6620922/3; Emergency/Dr/Police 999.

**FACILITIES** **Marina** Ch 09 16 (35+20 Ⓥ) ☎/📠 9129955, €2.20, Slip, ⚓, D & P, El, ME, LB; **Village** Showers at Stella Maris (10 mins walk), Gaz, CH, ME, El, D & P (cans) is 3M away, R, Bar, 🍴, ✉, Ⓗ (Wexford 15M).

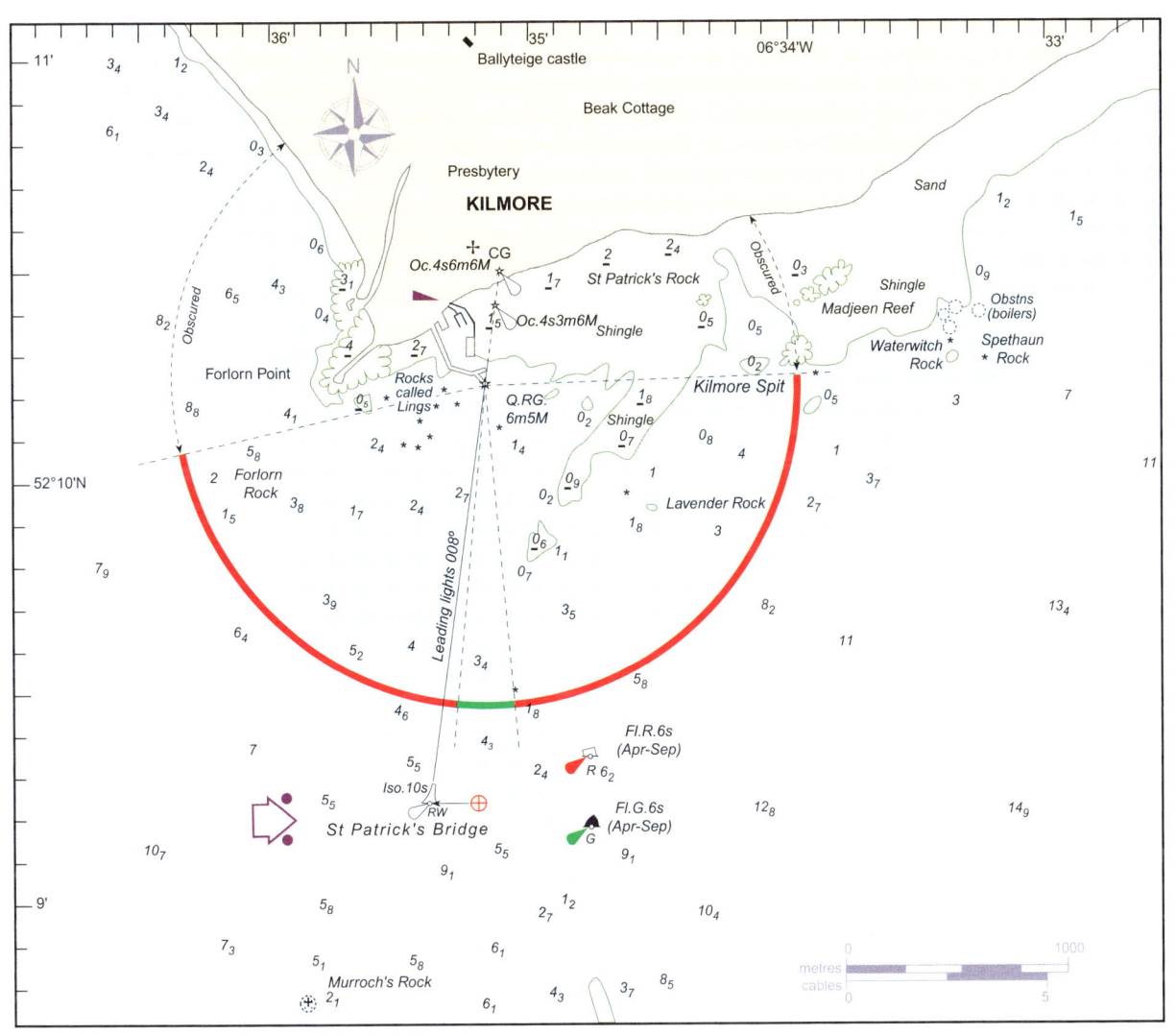

## 5.15   WATERFORD

**Waterford 52°15'·50N 07°06'·00W** ✿✿✿✿⚓⚓✿✿

**CHARTS** AC *2049, 2046*, 5621, 5622; Imray C57; Irish OS 76

**TIDES** −0520 Dover; ML 2·4; Duration 0605

**Standard Port COBH** (→)

| Times | | | | Height (metres) | | | |
|---|---|---|---|---|---|---|---|
| High Water | | Low Water | | MHWS | MHWN | MLWN | MLWS |
| 0500 | 1100 | 0500 | 1100 | 4·1 | 3·2 | 1·3 | 0·4 |
| 1700 | 2300 | 1700 | 2300 | | | | |
| **Differences WATERFORD** | | | | | | | |
| +0057 | +0057 | +0046 | +0046 | +0·4 | +0·3 | −0·1 | +0·1 |
| **CHEEKPOINT** | | | | | | | |
| +0022 | +0020 | +0020 | +0020 | +0·3 | +0·2 | +0·2 | +0·1 |
| **KILMOKEA POINT** | | | | | | | |
| +0026 | +0022 | +0020 | +0020 | +0·2 | +0·1 | +0·1 | +0·1 |
| **NEW ROSS** | | | | | | | |
| +0100 | +0030 | +0055 | +0130 | +0·3 | +0·4 | +0·3 | +0·4 |

**SHELTER** Very good on 4 long marina pontoons after Nanny pontoon(first one/private) on S bank, abeam cathedral spire. Beware strong tidal stream. Up the estuary are many excellent ⚓s: off S side of R Suir in King's Chan (only to be entered W of Little Is); and up the R Barrow near Marsh Pt (about 2M S of New Ross) and 0·5M S of New Ross fixed bridge.

**NAVIGATION** WPT 52°06'·50N 06°58'·50W, 002°/6·7M to Dir lt at Duncannon. From the E, keep clear of Brecaun reef (2M NE of Hook Hd). Keep about 1·5M S of Hook Hd to clear Tower Race and overfalls, especially HW Dover ±2. From the W beware Falskirt Rk (3m), 2ca off Swine Head and 2M WSW of Dunmore East (5.16). Marine Farms off Creadan Hd and Broomhill Pt; cruise liners and large container ships go up to Waterford; beware ferry between Passage East and Ballyhack.

**LIGHTS AND MARKS** The estuary and R Suir are very well buoyed/lit all the way to Waterford. The estuary ent is between Dunmore East and Hook Hd. Duncannon dir lt, F WRG, leads 002° into the river. R Barrow is also well lit/marked up to New Ross. The railway swing bridge at the river ent opens at its W end. Call bridge-keeper VHF Ch 14.

**R/T** Waterford and New Ross VHF Ch **14** 16.

**TELEPHONE** (Code 051) Marina 873501, mobile 087 2384944; HMs Waterford 301400, 🖷 301409, New Ross 421303; Waterford SC 383389 MRCC (01) 6620922; ⊜ 862100; Police 305300; Dr 855411; Ⓗ 848000.

**FACILITIES** Yacht pontoons, FW, ⏚, AB €2.00 2m all tides both sides; showers at Tower Hotel Leisure Centre (approx 300m). **Services:** ME, El, ⚒, C, BY (Ballyhack). **City** P, D (by arrangement with marina), Gaz, all facilities, Bus and ⇌ to Rosslare for UK ferries, ✈ (Cork) for UK/Continent, ✈ (Waterford) for Manchester and Luton and summer seasonal to Lorient.

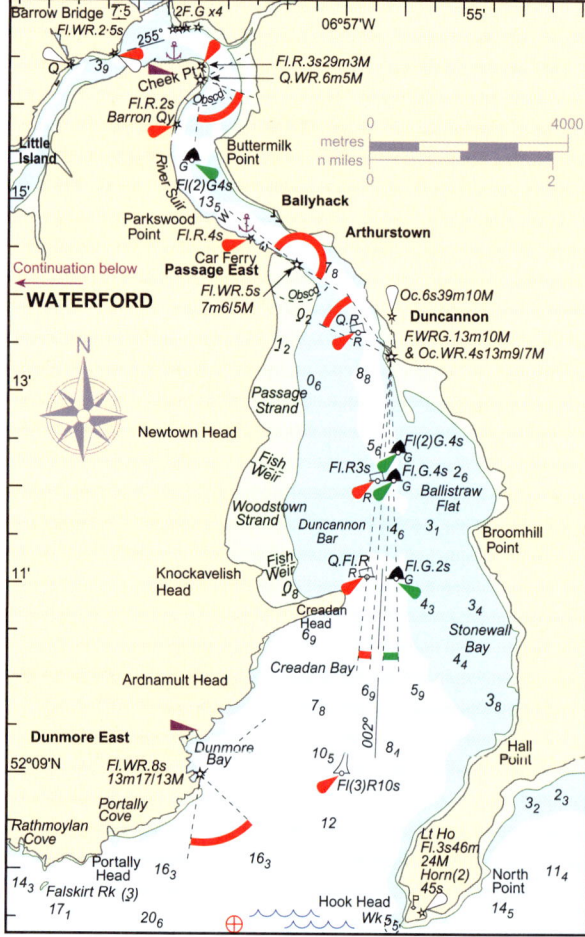

Continuation below

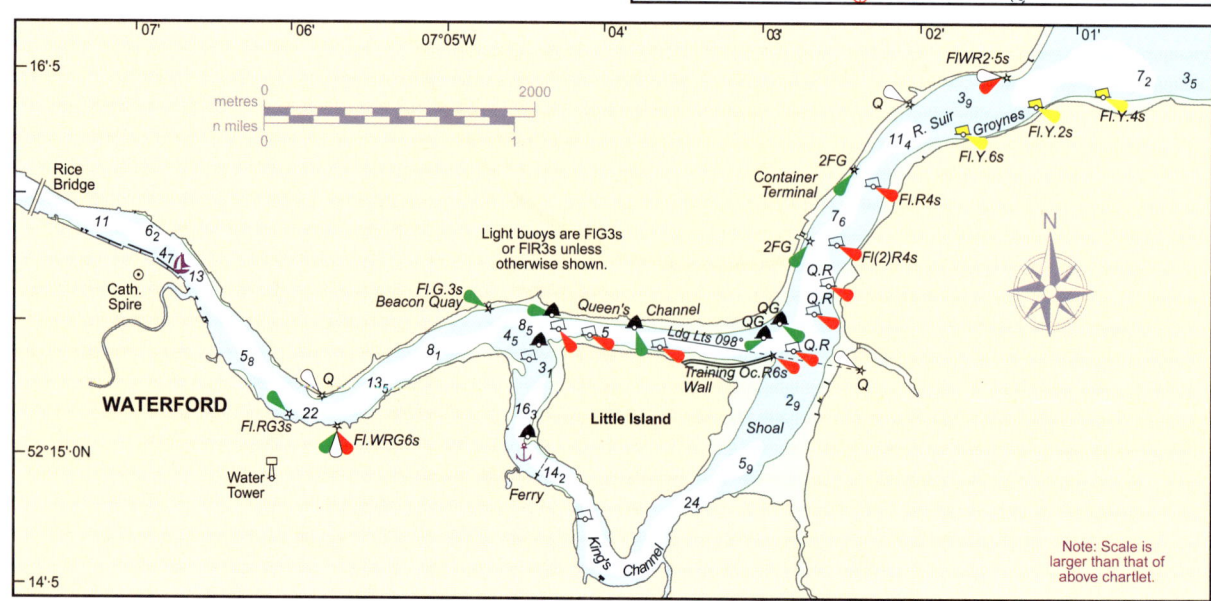

## 5.16   DUNMORE EAST

Waterford 52°08'·95N 06°59'·37W ✿✿✿🌸🌸 ✿

**CHARTS** AC *2049, 2046*, 5621, 5622; Imray C57, C61; Irish OS 76

**TIDES** –0535 Dover; ML 2·4; Duration 0605

**Standard Port COBH (→)**

| Times | | | | Height (metres) | | | |
|---|---|---|---|---|---|---|---|
| High Water | | Low Water | | MHWS | MHWN | MLWN | MLWS |
| 0500 | 1100 | 0500 | 1100 | 4·1 | 3·2 | 1·3 | 0·4 |
| 1700 | 2300 | 1700 | 2300 | | | | |
| Differences DUNMORE EAST | | | | | | | |
| +0008 | +0003 | 0000 | 0000 | +0·1 | 0·0 | +0·1 | +0·2 |
| DUNGARVAN HARBOUR | | | | | | | |
| +0004 | +0012 | +0007 | –0001 | 0·0 | +0·1 | –0·2 | 0·0 |

**SHELTER** Very good in hbr, but moorings exposed in E-ESE'lies >F6. ⚓ N of the hbr. Visitors welcome, moorings administered by Waterford SC (☎ 051 383389). A useful passage port/refuge. Primarily a busy FV hbr and large cruise liners ⚓ off. In bad weather berth on FVs at W Wharf, clear of ice plant, in at least 2m or go up R Suir to Waterford (5.15).

**NAVIGATION** WPT (see also 5.15) 52°08'·00N, 06°58'·00W, 317°/1·2M to bkwtr lt. Enter under power. From E, stay 1·5M off Hook Hd to clear Tower Race; then steer for hbr in R sector of E pier lt ho. In calm weather Hook Hd can be rounded 1ca off. From W, beware Falskirt Rk (off Swines Hd, 2M WSW) dries 3·0m. By night track E for Hook Hd until in R sector of E pier lt, then alter to N.

**LIGHTS AND MARKS** Lts as chartlet and see 5.3.

**R/T** VHF Ch 14 16 (Pilot Station).

**TELEPHONE** (Code 051) HM 383166, 🖷 383607, mobile 087 7931705; Hbr Foreman 383688; Fuel 087 2503510; Police 383112; ⊖ 875391; MRCC (01) 6620922/3; Duty Coastguard Mob 0868 501764; Health Centre 383347.

**FACILITIES Hbr** ☎ 383166, D, FW (E pier), Slip, scrubbing grid, Kos, CH, BH (230 ton); **Waterford Hbr SC** ☎ 383389, R, Bar, showers; **Village** P (cans), Bar, R, 🛒, Ⓑ, ✉, ✈ (Waterford).

## 5.17   YOUGHAL

Cork 51°56'·54N 07°50'·20W ✿✿🌸🌸🌸 ✿✿

**CHARTS** AC *2049*, 2071, 5622; Imray C57; Irish OS 81, 82

**TIDES** –0556 Dover; ML 2·1; Duration 0555

**Standard Port COBH (→)**

| Times | | | | Height (metres) | | | |
|---|---|---|---|---|---|---|---|
| High Water | | Low Water | | MHWS | MHWN | MLWN | MLWS |
| 0500 | 1100 | 0500 | 1100 | 4·1 | 3·2 | 1·3 | 0·4 |
| 1700 | 2300 | 1700 | 2300 | | | | |
| Differences YOUGHAL | | | | | | | |
| 0000 | +0010 | +0010 | 0000 | –0·2 | –0·1 | –0·1 | –0·1 |

**SHELTER** Good, but strong S'lies cause swell inside the hbr. Possible AB 1.3m with drying patches just off quay. ⚓ as chartlet; no dues. Strong tides run throughout anchorages.

**NAVIGATION** WPT, East Bar, 51°55'·62N 07°48'·00W, 302°/1·8M to Fl WR 2·5s lt. Beware Blackball Ledge (ECM lt buoy) and Bar Rks (SCM lt buoy), both outside hbr ent in R sector of lt ho. From W, appr via West Bar (1·7m) is shorter route and E Bar has 2·0m.

- Both Bars in E to SSW'lies >F6 are likely to have dangerous seas.
- Beware salmon nets set during June-July, Mon-Thurs 0400-2100.
- Red Bank is continually changing, obtain local knowledge.

**LIGHTS AND MARKS** See 5.3. and chartlet. Water tr is conspic from seaward; clock tr and ✠ tr within hbr. Up-river, 175° transit of convent belfry tr/town hall clears W of Red Bank.

**R/T** VHF Ch 14 16 0900-1700 and when ships expected.

**TELEPHONE** (Code 024) HM Mobile 0872511143 MRCC (066) 9476109; Coast Guard 93252 or mob 0868 501769; ⊖ (021) 4325000; Police 92200; Dr 92702. Youghal Shipping 92577 (for poss AB).

**FACILITIES Services:** L, FW, Slip, AB (☎Youghal Shipping). **Town** P & D (cans), 🛒, R, Bar, ✉, Ⓑ, Bus (Cork/W'ford), ✈(Cork).

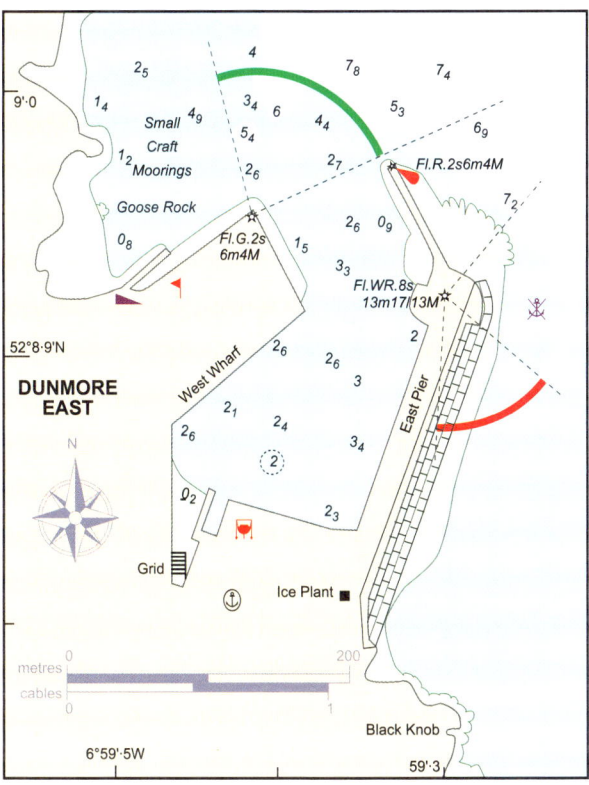

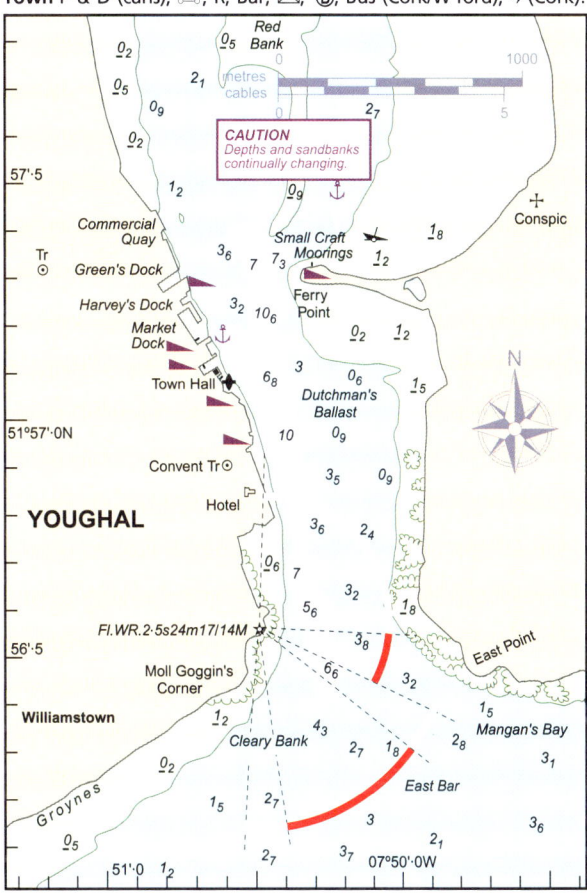

**TIME ZONE (UT)**
For Summer Time add ONE hour in **non-shaded areas**

## COBH   LAT 51°51'N   LONG 8°18'W
### TIMES AND HEIGHTS OF HIGH AND LOW WATERS

Dates in red are **SPRINGS**
Dates in blue are **NEAPS**

**YEAR 2008**

### JANUARY

| Date | Time m | Time m | Time m | Time m |
|---|---|---|---|---|
| **1** TU | 0533 1.2 | 1126 3.4 | 1805 1.3 | 2345 3.3 |
| **16** W | 0452 1.1 | 1051 3.7 | 1717 1.2 | 2313 3.6 |
| **2** W | 0631 1.3 | 1225 3.3 | 1904 1.4 | |
| **17** TH | 0555 1.2 | 1154 3.6 | 1825 1.3 | |
| **3** TH | 0050 3.3 | 0730 1.4 | 1329 3.3 | 2003 1.4 |
| **18** F | 0022 3.5 | 0709 1.3 | 1306 3.5 | 1943 1.3 |
| **4** F | 0156 3.4 | 0829 1.3 | 1430 3.4 | 2100 1.3 |
| **19** SA | 0139 3.5 | 0829 1.2 | 1423 3.5 | 2102 1.1 |
| **5** SA | 0257 3.5 | 0926 1.2 | 1525 3.5 | 2154 1.2 |
| **20** SU | 0259 3.6 | 0945 1.0 | 1535 3.7 | 2211 0.9 |
| **6** SU | 0351 3.7 | 1017 1.1 | 1615 3.7 | 2240 1.0 |
| **21** M | 0409 3.8 | 1048 0.8 | 1636 3.8 | 2308 0.7 |
| **7** M | 0438 3.8 | 1101 1.0 | 1658 3.8 | 2320 0.9 |
| **22** TU | 0505 4.0 | 1140 0.6 | 1727 4.0 | ○2356 0.5 |
| **8** TU | 0520 3.9 | 1140 0.9 | 1737 3.9 | ●2357 0.8 |
| **23** W | 0553 4.2 | 1225 0.4 | 1811 4.1 | |
| **9** W | 0558 4.0 | 1217 0.8 | 1812 3.9 | |
| **24** TH | 0039 0.4 | 0634 4.2 | 1306 0.4 | 1851 4.1 |
| **10** TH | 0032 0.7 | 0634 4.1 | 1253 0.8 | 1846 3.9 |
| **25** F | 0120 0.4 | 0714 4.2 | 1345 0.5 | 1929 4.0 |
| **11** F | 0108 0.7 | 0710 4.1 | 1330 0.8 | 1921 3.9 |
| **26** SA | 0158 0.5 | 0752 4.1 | 1422 0.6 | 2005 3.9 |
| **12** SA | 0147 0.7 | 0748 4.0 | 1409 0.8 | 1959 3.9 |
| **27** SU | 0235 0.6 | 0828 3.9 | 1459 0.8 | 2040 3.8 |
| **13** SU | 0227 0.8 | 0828 4.0 | 1450 0.9 | 2041 3.9 |
| **28** M | 0312 0.8 | 0905 3.8 | 1534 1.0 | 2116 3.7 |
| **14** M | 0311 0.8 | 0911 3.9 | 1533 1.0 | 2126 3.8 |
| **29** TU | 0350 1.0 | 0942 3.6 | 1612 1.1 | 2156 3.5 |
| **15** TU | 0358 0.9 | 0958 3.8 | 1621 1.1 | ☽2216 3.7 |
| **30** W | 0431 1.2 | 1023 3.5 | 1657 1.3 | ☽2242 3.4 |
| **31** TH | 0523 1.3 | 1113 3.3 | 1755 1.5 | 2341 3.2 |

### FEBRUARY

| Date | Time m | Time m | Time m | Time m |
|---|---|---|---|---|
| **1** F | 0628 1.5 | 1218 3.2 | 1907 1.5 | |
| **16** SA | 0642 1.3 | 1243 3.2 | 1920 1.4 | |
| **2** SA | 0059 3.2 | 0740 1.5 | 1344 3.2 | 2019 1.5 |
| **17** SU | 0125 3.3 | 0818 1.3 | 1416 3.2 | 2055 1.2 |
| **3** SU | 0223 3.3 | 0851 1.4 | 1500 3.3 | 2126 1.4 |
| **18** M | 0259 3.5 | 0943 1.0 | 1533 3.5 | 2208 0.9 |
| **4** M | 0329 3.5 | 0954 1.2 | 1557 3.5 | 2221 1.0 |
| **19** TU | 0406 3.7 | 1043 0.7 | 1630 3.8 | 2302 0.6 |
| **5** TU | 0420 3.7 | 1045 1.0 | 1643 3.7 | 2304 0.8 |
| **20** W | 0456 4.0 | 1130 0.5 | 1715 4.0 | 2345 0.4 |
| **6** W | 0503 3.9 | 1124 0.7 | 1722 3.9 | 2340 0.6 |
| **21** TH | 0538 4.2 | 1210 0.3 | 1755 4.1 | ○ |
| **7** TH | 0540 4.0 | 1200 0.6 | 1757 4.0 | ● |
| **22** F | 0023 0.3 | 0615 4.2 | 1246 0.3 | 1830 4.1 |
| **8** F | 0014 0.5 | 0615 4.1 | 1236 0.5 | 1829 4.0 |
| **23** SA | 0057 0.3 | 0649 4.2 | 1319 0.4 | 1903 4.1 |
| **9** SA | 0049 0.5 | 0650 4.1 | 1310 0.5 | 1903 4.0 |
| **24** SU | 0129 0.4 | 0722 4.1 | 1350 0.5 | 1934 4.0 |
| **10** SU | 0126 0.5 | 0714 4.2 | 1347 0.5 | 1939 4.0 |
| **25** M | 0200 0.5 | 0753 3.9 | 1420 0.7 | 2004 3.9 |
| **11** M | 0204 0.5 | 0804 4.1 | 1425 0.6 | 2017 4.0 |
| **26** TU | 0231 0.7 | 0824 3.8 | 1450 0.8 | 2037 3.8 |
| **12** TU | 0246 0.6 | 0844 4.0 | 1505 0.7 | 2058 3.9 |
| **27** W | 0304 0.9 | 0857 3.7 | 1522 1.0 | 2112 3.6 |
| **13** W | 0330 0.7 | 0928 3.8 | 1550 0.9 | 2144 3.7 |
| **28** TH | 0341 1.1 | 0933 3.5 | 1600 1.2 | 2154 3.4 |
| **14** TH | 0420 1.0 | 1018 3.6 | 1642 1.1 | ☽2240 3.5 |
| **29** F | 0428 1.3 | 1018 3.3 | 1653 1.4 | ☽2248 3.2 |
| **15** F | 0523 1.2 | 1121 3.4 | 1751 1.3 | 2352 3.3 |

### MARCH

| Date | Time m | Time m | Time m | Time m |
|---|---|---|---|---|
| **1** SA | 0535 1.5 | 1118 3.0 | 1813 1.6 | |
| **16** SU | 0631 1.3 | 1235 3.0 | 1911 1.3 | |
| **2** SU | 0003 3.0 | 0656 1.6 | 1249 2.9 | 1938 1.5 |
| **17** M | 0126 3.2 | 0815 1.2 | 1411 3.1 | 2051 1.1 |
| **3** M | 0147 3.1 | 0815 1.4 | 1431 3.1 | 2053 1.3 |
| **18** TU | 0253 3.4 | 0933 0.9 | 1522 3.4 | 2158 0.8 |
| **4** TU | 0302 3.3 | 0923 1.1 | 1533 3.4 | 2151 1.0 |
| **19** W | 0351 3.7 | 1027 0.6 | 1613 3.7 | 2246 0.5 |
| **5** W | 0353 3.6 | 1016 0.9 | 1618 3.6 | 2236 0.7 |
| **20** TH | 0437 3.9 | 1110 0.4 | 1656 3.9 | 2326 0.3 |
| **6** TH | 0435 3.9 | 1058 0.6 | 1656 3.8 | 2314 0.5 |
| **21** F | 0516 4.1 | 1147 0.3 | 1733 4.0 | ○ |
| **7** F | 0513 4.0 | 1135 0.4 | 1731 4.0 | ●2349 0.3 |
| **22** SA | 0000 0.2 | 0550 4.1 | 1220 0.3 | 1806 4.0 |
| **8** SA | 0549 4.1 | 1210 0.3 | 1805 4.0 | |
| **23** SU | 0031 0.3 | 0622 4.1 | 1250 0.4 | 1835 4.0 |
| **9** SU | 0025 0.3 | 0624 4.2 | 1246 0.3 | 1839 4.1 |
| **24** M | 0059 0.4 | 0651 4.0 | 1317 0.5 | 1903 3.9 |
| **10** M | 0102 0.2 | 0701 4.2 | 1323 0.3 | 1916 4.1 |
| **25** TU | 0126 0.6 | 0719 3.9 | 1345 0.7 | 1932 3.9 |
| **11** TU | 0142 0.3 | 0739 4.1 | 1402 0.4 | 1954 4.1 |
| **26** W | 0155 0.7 | 0748 3.8 | 1412 0.8 | 2003 3.8 |
| **12** W | 0224 0.4 | 0821 4.0 | 1443 0.6 | 2036 3.9 |
| **27** TH | 0227 0.9 | 0819 3.6 | 1443 1.0 | 2039 3.6 |
| **13** TH | 0310 0.6 | 0905 3.7 | 1530 0.8 | 2124 3.7 |
| **28** F | 0303 1.1 | 0855 3.5 | 1521 1.2 | 2119 3.4 |
| **14** F | 0403 0.9 | 0957 3.5 | 1624 1.0 | ☽2221 3.4 |
| **29** SA | 0350 1.3 | 0940 3.3 | 1612 1.4 | ☽2211 3.2 |
| **15** SA | 0507 1.1 | 1104 3.2 | 1736 1.3 | 2339 3.2 |
| **30** SU | 0455 1.4 | 1038 3.0 | 1728 1.5 | 2321 3.0 |
| **31** M | 0616 1.5 | 1158 2.9 | 1855 1.5 | |

### APRIL

| Date | Time m | Time m | Time m | Time m |
|---|---|---|---|---|
| **1** TU | 0054 3.1 | 0734 1.4 | 1340 3.0 | 2009 1.3 |
| **16** W | 0228 3.4 | 0906 0.8 | 1455 3.4 | 2130 0.7 |
| **2** W | 0217 3.3 | 0841 1.1 | 1450 3.3 | 2109 1.0 |
| **17** TH | 0322 3.6 | 0957 0.6 | 1545 3.7 | 2218 0.5 |
| **3** TH | 0312 3.6 | 0935 0.8 | 1538 3.6 | 2157 0.7 |
| **18** F | 0407 3.8 | 1041 0.5 | 1628 3.8 | 2258 0.4 |
| **4** F | 0357 3.8 | 1021 0.5 | 1620 3.8 | 2240 0.4 |
| **19** SA | 0447 3.9 | 1118 0.4 | 1705 3.9 | 2332 0.4 |
| **5** SA | 0438 4.0 | 1103 0.3 | 1659 4.0 | 2320 0.3 |
| **20** SU | 0522 3.9 | 1151 0.5 | 1739 3.9 | ○ |
| **6** SU | 0518 4.1 | 1143 0.2 | 1737 4.1 | ● |
| **21** M | 0002 0.5 | 0553 3.9 | 1220 0.5 | 1808 3.9 |
| **7** M | 0001 0.2 | 0557 4.2 | 1223 0.2 | 1816 4.2 |
| **22** TU | 0029 0.6 | 0622 3.8 | 1248 0.6 | 1836 3.9 |
| **8** TU | 0042 0.2 | 0638 4.2 | 1304 0.2 | 1856 4.2 |
| **23** W | 0056 0.7 | 0650 3.8 | 1315 0.7 | 1906 3.8 |
| **9** W | 0126 0.2 | 0721 4.1 | 1346 0.3 | 1938 4.1 |
| **24** TH | 0126 0.8 | 0719 3.7 | 1345 0.8 | 1939 3.7 |
| **10** TH | 0211 0.4 | 0806 3.9 | 1432 0.5 | 2024 3.9 |
| **25** F | 0200 0.9 | 0752 3.6 | 1419 1.0 | 2015 3.6 |
| **11** F | 0301 0.6 | 0854 3.7 | 1522 0.7 | 2115 3.6 |
| **26** SA | 0240 1.0 | 0831 3.5 | 1459 1.1 | 2057 3.5 |
| **12** SA | 0357 0.8 | 0950 3.4 | 1621 0.9 | ☾2217 3.4 |
| **27** SU | 0327 1.2 | 0916 3.3 | 1551 1.3 | 2148 3.3 |
| **13** SU | 0503 1.0 | 1059 3.1 | 1734 1.1 | 2339 3.2 |
| **28** M | 0427 1.3 | 1013 3.2 | 1657 1.3 | ☾2251 3.2 |
| **14** M | 0627 1.1 | 1227 3.0 | 1905 1.1 | |
| **29** TU | 0539 1.3 | 1122 3.1 | 1813 1.3 | |
| **15** TU | 0114 3.2 | 0758 1.0 | 1351 3.2 | 2030 0.9 |
| **30** W | 0006 3.2 | 0651 1.2 | 1242 3.1 | 1923 1.2 |

Chart Datum: 0·13 metres above Ordnance Datum (Dublin). HAT is 4·5 metres above Chart Datum.

**FREE** monthly updates from
www.reedsalmanac.co.uk

**TIME ZONE (UT)**
For Summer Time add ONE
hour in **non-shaded areas**

## COBH  LAT 51°51′N  LONG 8°18′W
TIMES AND HEIGHTS OF HIGH AND LOW WATERS

Dates in red are SPRINGS
Dates in blue are NEAPS

YEAR **2008**

### MAY

| | Time m | | Time m |
|---|---|---|---|
| **1** TH | 0121 3.4 / 0756 1.0 / 1352 3.4 / 2023 0.9 | **16** F | 0242 3.5 / 0916 0.8 / 1506 3.5 / 2139 0.7 |
| **2** F | 0222 3.6 / 0852 0.8 / 1449 3.6 / 2116 0.7 | **17** SA | 0329 3.6 / 1002 0.7 / 1551 3.7 / 2222 0.7 |
| **3** SA | 0314 3.8 / 0943 0.6 / 1538 3.8 / 2206 0.5 | **18** SU | 0412 3.7 / 1043 0.7 / 1632 3.7 / 2300 0.7 |
| **4** SU | 0402 4.0 / 1032 0.4 / 1626 4.0 / 2254 0.3 | **19** M | 0450 3.7 / 1119 0.7 / 1709 3.8 / 2332 0.7 |
| **5** M ● | 0449 4.1 / 1119 0.3 / 1712 4.1 / 2341 0.2 | **20** TU ○ | 0525 3.8 / 1152 0.7 / 1743 3.8 |
| **6** TU | 0536 4.1 / 1205 0.2 / 1757 4.2 | **21** W | 0002 0.7 / 0557 3.7 / 1223 0.7 / 1815 3.8 |
| **7** W | 0028 0.2 / 0622 4.1 / 1251 0.2 / 1843 4.1 | **22** TH | 0033 0.8 / 0628 3.7 / 1254 0.8 / 1847 3.8 |
| **8** TH | 0116 0.2 / 0709 4.0 / 1339 0.3 / 1930 4.0 | **23** F | 0106 0.8 / 0700 3.7 / 1327 0.8 / 1922 3.7 |
| **9** F | 0205 0.4 / 0758 3.8 / 1428 0.4 / 2020 3.9 | **24** SA | 0143 0.9 / 0736 3.6 / 1404 0.9 / 2000 3.7 |
| **10** SA | 0258 0.5 / 0850 3.6 / 1521 0.6 / 2114 3.7 | **25** SU | 0225 1.0 / 0816 3.5 / 1447 1.0 / 2043 3.6 |
| **11** SU | 0355 0.7 / 0946 3.4 / 1620 0.8 / 2215 3.5 | **26** M | 0311 1.1 / 0901 3.5 / 1535 1.1 / 2131 3.5 |
| **12** M ◐ | 0458 0.9 / 1049 3.3 / 1727 0.9 / 2326 3.3 | **27** TU | 0403 1.1 / 0953 3.4 / 1631 1.1 / 2226 3.5 |
| **13** TU | 0610 1.0 / 1201 3.2 / 1842 1.0 | **28** W | 0503 1.2 / 1052 3.4 / 1733 1.1 / 2327 3.5 |
| **14** W | 0041 3.3 / 0722 0.9 / 1313 3.2 / 1952 0.9 | **29** TH | 0607 1.1 / 1156 3.4 / 1838 1.1 |
| **15** TH | 0148 3.4 / 0824 0.9 / 1414 3.4 / 2050 0.8 | **30** F | 0032 3.5 / 0710 1.0 / 1302 3.5 / 1940 0.9 |
| | | **31** SA | 0135 3.6 / 0810 0.9 / 1403 3.6 / 2039 0.8 |

### JUNE

| | Time m | | Time m |
|---|---|---|---|
| **1** SU | 0234 3.7 / 0908 0.7 / 1501 3.8 / 2137 0.6 | **16** M | 0335 3.5 / 1007 0.9 / 1559 3.6 / 2226 0.9 |
| **2** M | 0331 3.9 / 1005 0.6 / 1557 3.9 / 2234 0.5 | **17** TU | 0420 3.6 / 1050 0.9 / 1643 3.7 / 2305 0.9 |
| **3** TU ● | 0426 4.0 / 1100 0.4 / 1652 4.0 / 2327 0.3 | **18** W ○ | 0502 3.7 / 1129 0.8 / 1723 3.8 / 2341 0.8 |
| **4** W | 0520 4.0 / 1152 0.3 / 1744 4.1 | **19** TH | 0540 3.7 / 1204 0.8 / 1800 3.8 |
| **5** TH | 0019 0.3 / 0610 4.0 / 1243 0.3 / 1834 4.1 | **20** F | 0015 0.8 / 0614 3.7 / 1237 0.8 / 1834 3.8 |
| **6** F | 0109 0.3 / 0700 4.0 / 1332 0.3 / 1924 4.1 | **21** SA | 0051 0.8 / 0648 3.7 / 1312 0.8 / 1910 3.8 |
| **7** SA | 0159 0.4 / 0750 3.9 / 1422 0.4 / 2014 3.9 | **22** SU | 0129 0.8 / 0724 3.7 / 1350 0.8 / 1947 3.8 |
| **8** SU | 0251 0.5 / 0840 3.7 / 1514 0.5 / 2105 3.8 | **23** M | 0209 0.9 / 0802 3.7 / 1430 0.9 / 2027 3.8 |
| **9** M | 0343 0.6 / 0931 3.6 / 1607 0.6 / 2158 3.6 | **24** TU | 0251 0.9 / 0844 3.6 / 1514 0.9 / 2111 3.7 |
| **10** TU ◐ | 0438 0.8 / 1024 3.4 / 1702 0.8 / 2254 3.5 | **25** W | 0337 1.0 / 0930 3.6 / 1601 0.9 / 2158 3.7 |
| **11** W | 0536 0.9 / 1121 3.3 / 1802 0.9 / 2354 3.4 | **26** TH ◑ | 0426 1.0 / 1021 3.6 / 1654 1.0 / 2251 3.6 |
| **12** TH | 0635 1.0 / 1221 3.3 / 1902 1.0 | **27** F | 0521 1.0 / 1117 3.6 / 1753 1.0 / 2350 3.6 |
| **13** F | 0055 3.3 / 0733 1.0 / 1322 3.3 / 1959 1.0 | **28** SA | 0624 1.1 / 1219 3.5 / 1859 1.0 |
| **14** SA | 0153 3.4 / 0827 1.0 / 1418 3.4 / 2052 1.0 | **29** SU | 0055 3.6 / 0731 1.0 / 1325 3.6 / 2007 0.9 |
| **15** SU | 0246 3.4 / 0919 1.0 / 1511 3.5 / 2141 0.9 | **30** M | 0202 3.6 / 0839 0.9 / 1432 3.7 / 2115 0.8 |

### JULY

| | Time m | | Time m |
|---|---|---|---|
| **1** TU | 0308 3.7 / 0946 0.8 / 1539 3.8 / 2220 0.6 | **16** W | 0356 3.5 / 1026 1.0 / 1622 3.6 / 2244 0.9 |
| **2** W | 0411 3.8 / 1047 0.6 / 1641 3.9 / 2318 0.5 | **17** TH | 0443 3.6 / 1110 0.8 / 1706 3.8 / 2323 0.8 |
| **3** TH ● | 0509 3.9 / 1142 0.4 / 1736 4.1 | **18** F ○ | 0524 3.7 / 1146 0.7 / 1744 3.9 / 2359 0.7 |
| **4** F | 0010 0.3 / 0600 4.0 / 1233 0.3 / 1825 4.1 | **19** SA | 0600 3.8 / 1220 0.7 / 1819 3.9 |
| **5** SA | 0059 0.3 / 0649 4.0 / 1321 0.3 / 1912 4.1 | **20** SU | 0033 0.7 / 0634 3.8 / 1253 0.6 / 1853 3.9 |
| **6** SU | 0146 0.3 / 0735 3.9 / 1407 0.3 / 1958 4.0 | **21** M | 0109 0.7 / 0707 3.8 / 1329 0.6 / 1927 3.9 |
| **7** M | 0232 0.4 / 0820 3.8 / 1453 0.4 / 2042 3.9 | **22** TU | 0146 0.7 / 0742 3.8 / 1407 0.7 / 2004 3.9 |
| **8** TU | 0318 0.6 / 0904 3.7 / 1538 0.6 / 2126 3.7 | **23** W | 0225 0.7 / 0820 3.8 / 1447 0.7 / 2044 3.9 |
| **9** W | 0403 0.7 / 0948 3.6 / 1623 0.7 / 2211 3.6 | **24** TH | 0306 0.7 / 0902 3.8 / 1530 0.8 / 2127 3.8 |
| **10** TH ◐ | 0450 0.9 / 1033 3.5 / 1710 0.9 / 2259 3.4 | **25** F | 0350 0.9 / 0947 3.7 / 1617 0.9 / 2216 3.7 |
| **11** F | 0540 1.1 / 1123 3.3 / 1803 1.1 / 2354 3.3 | **26** SA | 0440 1.0 / 1040 3.6 / 1714 1.0 / 2313 3.6 |
| **12** SA | 0635 1.2 / 1222 3.2 / 1901 1.2 | **27** SU | 0542 1.1 / 1143 3.5 / 1823 1.1 |
| **13** SU | 0056 3.2 / 0735 1.2 / 1329 3.2 / 2001 1.2 | **28** M | 0022 3.4 / 0658 1.2 / 1257 3.4 / 1942 1.1 |
| **14** M | 0202 3.2 / 0835 1.2 / 1433 3.3 / 2101 1.2 | **29** TU | 0140 3.4 / 0819 1.1 / 1418 3.5 / 2102 1.0 |
| **15** TU | 0303 3.3 / 0934 1.1 / 1532 3.5 / 2157 1.1 | **30** W | 0256 3.5 / 0935 0.9 / 1533 3.7 / 2213 0.7 |
| | | **31** TH | 0404 3.7 / 1039 0.6 / 1635 3.9 / 2310 0.5 |

### AUGUST

| | Time m | | Time m |
|---|---|---|---|
| **1** F ● | 0500 3.9 / 1132 0.4 / 1727 4.1 / 2359 0.3 | **16** SA ○ | 0503 3.8 / 1124 0.6 / 1722 3.9 / 2337 0.6 |
| **2** SA | 0548 4.0 / 1219 0.2 / 1812 4.2 | **17** SU | 0539 3.8 / 1156 0.5 / 1756 4.0 |
| **3** SU | 0042 0.3 / 0631 4.1 / 1302 0.2 / 1853 4.2 | **18** M | 0010 0.5 / 0610 3.9 / 1228 0.5 / 1828 4.0 |
| **4** M | 0124 0.3 / 0712 4.0 / 1342 0.3 / 1932 4.1 | **19** TU | 0044 0.5 / 0642 3.9 / 1302 0.5 / 1901 4.0 |
| **5** TU | 0204 0.4 / 0751 3.9 / 1421 0.4 / 2010 4.0 | **20** W | 0120 0.5 / 0716 3.9 / 1339 0.5 / 1936 4.0 |
| **6** W | 0242 0.5 / 0828 3.8 / 1459 0.6 / 2047 3.8 | **21** TH | 0157 0.6 / 0752 3.9 / 1419 0.6 / 2015 4.0 |
| **7** TH | 0320 0.7 / 0905 3.7 / 1537 0.8 / 2125 3.6 | **22** F | 0237 0.7 / 0832 3.8 / 1502 0.7 / 2057 3.8 |
| **8** F | 0359 0.9 / 0944 3.5 / 1616 1.0 / 2205 3.4 | **23** SA ◑ | 0321 0.8 / 0917 3.7 / 1549 0.9 / 2145 3.7 |
| **9** SA | 0442 1.1 / 1028 3.4 / 1703 1.2 / 2251 3.3 | **24** SU | 0411 1.0 / 1011 3.6 / 1646 1.1 / 2244 3.4 |
| **10** SU | 0536 1.3 / 1123 3.2 / 1803 1.4 / 2353 3.1 | **25** M | 0515 1.2 / 1118 3.4 / 1800 1.3 |
| **11** M | 0644 1.4 / 1238 3.1 / 1914 1.4 | **26** TU | 0001 3.2 / 0638 1.3 / 1245 3.3 / 1930 1.3 |
| **12** TU | 0118 3.1 / 0757 1.4 / 1404 3.2 / 2025 1.4 | **27** W | 0132 3.2 / 0812 1.2 / 1420 3.4 / 2100 1.0 |
| **13** W | 0237 3.2 / 0906 1.2 / 1510 3.4 / 2131 1.2 | **28** TH | 0255 3.4 / 0931 0.9 / 1532 3.7 / 2208 0.7 |
| **14** TH | 0336 3.4 / 1004 1.0 / 1602 3.6 / 2222 0.9 | **29** F | 0357 3.7 / 1031 0.6 / 1627 4.0 / 2259 0.5 |
| **15** F | 0423 3.6 / 1048 0.8 / 1645 3.8 / 2302 0.8 | **30** SA ● | 0447 3.9 / 1119 0.3 / 1712 4.1 / 2342 0.3 |
| | | **31** SU | 0530 4.1 / 1200 0.2 / 1752 4.2 |

Chart Datum: 0·13 metres above Ordnance Datum (Dublin). HAT is 4·5 metres above Chart Datum.

**TIME ZONE (UT)**

For Summer Time add ONE hour in **non-shaded areas**

## COBH  LAT 51°51'N  LONG 8°18'W
### TIMES AND HEIGHTS OF HIGH AND LOW WATERS

Dates in red are SPRINGS
Dates in blue are NEAPS

**YEAR 2008**

| SEPTEMBER | | OCTOBER | | NOVEMBER | | DECEMBER | |
|---|---|---|---|---|---|---|---|
| Time m | Time m | Time m | Time m | Time m | Time m | Time m | Time m |

### SEPTEMBER

**1** 0021 0.3 / 0609 4.1 / M 1238 0.2 / 1828 4.2
**16** 0541 4.0 / 1200 0.4 / TU 1759 4.1

**2** 0057 0.3 / 0645 4.1 / TU 1312 0.3 / 1902 4.1
**17** 0017 0.4 / 0614 4.1 / W 1236 0.4 / 1833 4.2

**3** 0130 0.4 / 0718 4.0 / W 1345 0.5 / 1934 4.0
**18** 0054 0.4 / 0650 4.1 / TH 1315 0.4 / 1911 4.1

**4** 0203 0.6 / 0751 3.9 / TH 1418 0.6 / 2007 3.8
**19** 0133 0.5 / 0728 4.0 / F 1356 0.5 / 1951 4.0

**5** 0236 0.8 / 0824 3.7 / F 1451 0.8 / 2040 3.7
**20** 0215 0.6 / 0810 3.9 / SA 1442 0.7 / 2035 3.8

**6** 0310 1.0 / 0900 3.6 / SA 1527 1.1 / 2116 3.5
**21** 0302 0.8 / 0858 3.7 / SU 1533 0.9 / 2126 3.6

**7** 0348 1.2 / 0942 3.4 / SU 1611 1.3 / ☽ 2159 3.3
**22** 0357 1.0 / 0956 3.5 / M 1634 1.1 / ☽ 2230 3.3

**8** 0440 1.4 / 1034 3.2 / M 1713 1.5 / 2256 3.1
**23** 0506 1.2 / 1109 3.3 / TU 1752 1.3 / 2354 3.1

**9** 0556 1.5 / 1148 3.0 / TU 1831 1.6
**24** 0635 1.3 / 1249 3.2 / W 1930 1.3

**10** 0025 3.0 / 0719 1.5 / W 1334 3.1 / 1950 1.5
**25** 0131 3.2 / 0811 1.1 / TH 1419 3.5 / 2055 1.0

**11** 0210 3.1 / 0834 1.3 / TH 1445 3.3 / 2059 1.2
**26** 0247 3.5 / 0923 0.8 / F 1521 3.7 / 2153 0.7

**12** 0310 3.4 / 0932 1.0 / F 1535 3.6 / 2151 1.0
**27** 0342 3.8 / 1016 0.5 / SA 1609 4.0 / 2240 0.5

**13** 0355 3.6 / 1016 0.8 / SA 1616 3.8 / 2232 0.7
**28** 0428 4.0 / 1100 0.3 / SU 1651 4.1 / 2320 0.4

**14** 0434 3.8 / 1053 0.6 / SU 1652 4.0 / 2308 0.6
**29** 0508 4.1 / 1137 0.3 / M 1728 4.2 / ● 2355 0.4

**15** 0508 3.9 / 1126 0.5 / M 1725 4.1 / ○ 2342 0.5
**30** 0544 4.1 / 1211 0.3 / TU 1801 4.1

### OCTOBER

**1** 0027 0.4 / 0617 4.1 / W 1242 0.5 / 1831 4.1
**16** 0550 4.2 / 1216 0.4 / TH 1811 4.2

**2** 0058 0.6 / 0647 4.0 / TH 1311 0.6 / 1901 3.9
**17** 0034 0.4 / 0630 4.2 / F 1259 0.4 / 1852 4.1

**3** 0127 0.7 / 0717 3.9 / F 1340 0.8 / 1930 3.8
**18** 0117 0.5 / 0713 4.1 / SA 1344 0.5 / 1937 4.0

**4** 0156 0.9 / 0749 3.8 / SA 1412 1.0 / 2002 3.7
**19** 0203 0.6 / 0800 3.9 / SU 1433 0.7 / 2025 3.8

**5** 0228 1.1 / 0825 3.6 / SU 1448 1.2 / 2038 3.5
**20** 0255 0.8 / 0852 3.7 / M 1528 0.9 / 2120 3.6

**6** 0306 1.2 / 0907 3.4 / M 1532 1.4 / 2121 3.3
**21** 0354 1.0 / 0954 3.5 / TU 1632 1.1 / ☽ 2226 3.3

**7** 0358 1.4 / 0958 3.2 / TU 1633 1.5 / ☽ 2216 3.1
**22** 0505 1.2 / 1110 3.4 / W 1751 1.2 / 2348 3.2

**8** 0512 1.6 / 1106 3.1 / W 1751 1.6 / 2333 3.0
**23** 0631 1.2 / 1241 3.4 / TH 1921 1.2

**9** 0637 1.6 / 1241 3.1 / TH 1910 1.5
**24** 0114 3.3 / 0756 1.0 / F 1358 3.5 / 2033 1.0

**10** 0116 3.1 / 0750 1.3 / F 1401 3.4 / 2017 1.3
**25** 0223 3.5 / 0900 0.8 / SA 1455 3.8 / 2127 0.8

**11** 0227 3.4 / 0849 1.1 / SA 1454 3.6 / 2110 1.0
**26** 0317 3.8 / 0951 0.6 / SU 1543 3.9 / 2213 0.6

**12** 0315 3.6 / 0936 0.8 / SU 1536 3.8 / 2155 0.7
**27** 0402 3.9 / 1034 0.5 / M 1624 4.0 / 2253 0.6

**13** 0355 3.8 / 1017 0.6 / M 1615 4.0 / 2236 0.6
**28** 0442 4.0 / 1112 0.5 / TU 1701 4.1 / ● 2328 0.5

**14** 0434 4.0 / 1056 0.5 / TU 1653 4.2 / ○ 2315 0.4
**29** 0518 4.1 / 1145 0.6 / W 1734 4.0 / 2359 0.6

**15** 0512 4.1 / 1135 0.4 / W 1732 4.2 / 2354 0.4
**30** 0551 4.0 / 1214 0.7 / TH 1804 4.0

**31** 0028 0.7 / 0621 4.0 / F 1243 0.8 / 1833 3.9

### NOVEMBER

**1** 0057 0.8 / 0651 3.9 / SA 1312 0.9 / 1902 3.8
**16** 0110 0.5 / 0706 4.2 / SU 1340 0.5 / 1930 4.0

**2** 0126 1.0 / 0724 3.8 / SU 1344 1.1 / 1934 3.7
**17** 0200 0.6 / 0757 4.0 / M 1431 0.7 / 2021 3.8

**3** 0159 1.1 / 0801 3.7 / M 1422 1.2 / 2011 3.6
**18** 0253 0.7 / 0851 3.9 / TU 1526 0.9 / 2116 3.6

**4** 0239 1.2 / 0843 3.6 / TU 1507 1.4 / 2055 3.5
**19** 0351 0.9 / 0951 3.7 / W 1627 1.0 / ◑ 2217 3.5

**5** 0331 1.4 / 0933 3.4 / W 1603 1.5 / 2148 3.3
**20** 0456 1.0 / 1057 3.5 / TH 1736 1.1 / 2325 3.4

**6** 0435 1.5 / 1033 3.3 / TH 1711 1.5 / ◑ 2254 3.2
**21** 0609 1.1 / 1209 3.5 / F 1850 1.1

**7** 0549 1.5 / 1144 3.3 / F 1825 1.5
**22** 0038 3.4 / 0721 1.0 / SA 1319 3.5 / 1955 1.1

**8** 0011 3.3 / 0700 1.4 / SA 1258 3.4 / 1930 1.3
**23** 0144 3.5 / 0824 0.9 / SU 1417 3.6 / 2051 1.0

**9** 0125 3.4 / 0801 1.2 / SU 1359 3.6 / 2027 1.1
**24** 0240 3.6 / 0917 0.9 / M 1507 3.8 / 2140 0.9

**10** 0223 3.6 / 0854 0.9 / M 1450 3.8 / 2118 0.9
**25** 0329 3.8 / 1003 0.8 / TU 1552 3.8 / 2223 0.8

**11** 0313 3.9 / 0943 0.7 / TU 1538 4.0 / 2206 0.7
**26** 0413 3.9 / 1045 0.8 / W 1633 3.9 / 2301 0.8

**12** 0400 4.0 / 1031 0.6 / W 1624 4.1 / 2252 0.5
**27** 0453 3.9 / 1710 3.9 / TH 1710 3.9 / ● 2336 0.8

**13** 0446 4.2 / 1117 0.5 / TH 1710 4.2 / ○ 2337 0.5
**28** 0530 4.0 / 1152 0.9 / F 1743 3.9

**14** 0532 4.2 / 1204 0.4 / F 1756 4.2
**29** 0007 0.8 / 0603 4.0 / SA 1222 0.9 / 1814 3.9

**15** 0023 0.4 / 0618 4.2 / SA 1251 0.4 / 1842 4.1
**30** 0037 0.9 / 0636 4.0 / SU 1254 1.0 / 1845 3.9

### DECEMBER

**1** 0108 1.0 / 0710 3.9 / M 1328 1.1 / 1918 3.8
**16** 0154 0.5 / 0751 4.2 / TU 1425 0.6 / 2012 4.0

**2** 0143 1.0 / 0746 3.8 / TU 1406 1.2 / 1955 3.7
**17** 0244 0.6 / 0842 4.0 / W 1515 0.7 / 2102 3.8

**3** 0223 1.1 / 0827 3.7 / W 1449 1.2 / 2037 3.6
**18** 0336 0.7 / 0933 3.9 / TH 1607 0.9 / 2153 3.7

**4** 0310 1.2 / 0912 3.7 / TH 1538 1.3 / 2125 3.5
**19** 0430 0.9 / 1026 3.7 / F 1703 1.0 / ◑ 2247 3.5

**5** 0403 1.3 / 1003 3.6 / F 1632 1.4 / ◑ 2220 3.5
**20** 0528 1.0 / 1123 3.6 / SA 1802 1.1 / 2346 3.4

**6** 0502 1.4 / 1100 3.6 / SA 1734 1.4 / 2322 3.5
**21** 0631 1.1 / 1224 3.5 / SU 1904 1.2

**7** 0607 1.3 / 1202 3.6 / SU 1840 1.3
**22** 0050 3.4 / 0733 1.2 / M 1327 3.5 / 2004 1.2

**8** 0028 3.5 / 0712 1.2 / M 1306 3.6 / 1943 1.2
**23** 0154 3.4 / 0833 1.2 / TU 1426 3.5 / 2101 1.2

**9** 0133 3.6 / 0814 1.1 / TU 1406 3.8 / 2043 1.1
**24** 0253 3.5 / 0929 1.1 / W 1519 3.6 / 2153 1.1

**10** 0234 3.8 / 0914 0.9 / W 1505 3.9 / 2140 0.9
**25** 0345 3.7 / 1018 1.1 / TH 1608 3.7 / 2239 1.0

**11** 0332 4.0 / 1011 0.8 / TH 1601 4.0 / 2235 0.7
**26** 0432 3.8 / 1101 1.0 / F 1651 3.8 / 2318 0.9

**12** 0428 4.1 / 1106 0.6 / F 1655 4.1 / ○ 2327 0.5
**27** 0514 3.9 / 1136 1.0 / SA 1729 3.9 / ● 2352 0.9

**13** 0522 4.2 / 1157 0.5 / SA 1746 4.2
**28** 0551 4.0 / 1208 0.9 / SU 1803 3.9

**14** 0016 0.4 / 0612 4.3 / SU 1247 0.4 / 1835 4.2
**29** 0023 0.8 / 0625 4.0 / M 1241 0.9 / 1835 3.9

**15** 0105 0.4 / 0702 4.3 / M 1335 0.5 / 1923 4.1
**30** 0055 0.8 / 0658 4.0 / TU 1314 0.9 / 1907 3.9

**31** 0129 0.9 / 0732 4.0 / W 1351 1.0 / 1941 3.8

Chart Datum: 0·13 metres above Ordnance Datum (Dublin). HAT is 4·5 metres above Chart Datum.

》》 FREE monthly updates from 《《
www.reedsalmanac.co.uk

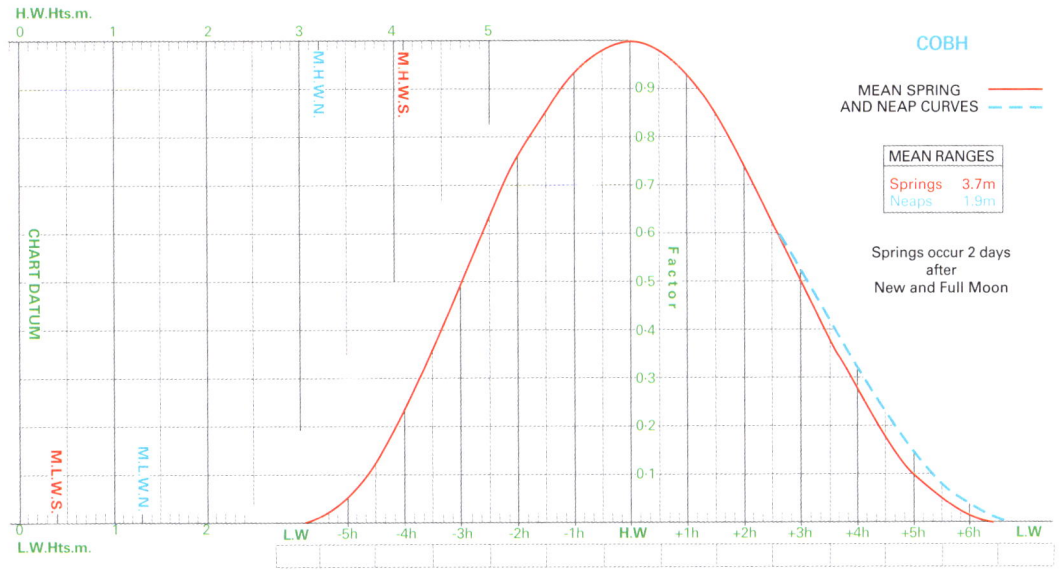

**COBH**

MEAN SPRING AND NEAP CURVES

| MEAN RANGES | |
|---|---|
| Springs | 3.7m |
| Neaps | 1.9m |

Springs occur 2 days after New and Full Moon

## 5.18   CORK HARBOUR

Cork **51°47'·50N 08°15'·54W** ✻✻✻✿✿✿⚓✿✿✿

**CHARTS** AC 1765, *1777*, 1773, 5622; Imray C57, C56; Irish OS 81, 87

**TIDES** –0523 Dover; ML 2·3; Duration 0555

**Standard Port COBH** (←)

| Times | | | | Height (metres) | | | |
|---|---|---|---|---|---|---|---|
| High Water | | Low Water | | MHWS | MHWN | MLWN | MLWS |
| 0500 | 1100 | 0500 | 1100 | 4·1 | 3·2 | 1·3 | 0·4 |
| 1700 | 2300 | 1700 | 2300 | | | | |
| **Differences BALLYCOTTON** (15M ENE of Roche's Point) | | | | | | | |
| –0011 | +0001 | +0003 | –0009 | 0·0 | 0·0 | –0·1 | 0·0 |
| **RINGASKIDDY** | | | | | | | |
| +0005 | +0020 | +0007 | +0013 | +0·1 | +0·1 | +0·1 | +0·1 |
| **MARINO POINT** | | | | | | | |
| 0000 | 0000 | 0000 | +0010 | +0·1 | +0·1 | 0·0 | 0·0 |
| **CORK CITY** | | | | | | | |
| +0005 | +0010 | +0020 | +0010 | +0·4 | +0·4 | +0·3 | +0·2 |
| **ROBERTS COVE** (approx 4M SW of Roche's Point) | | | | | | | |
| –0005 | –0005 | –0005 | –0005 | –0·1 | 0·0 | 0·0 | +0·1 |

**SHELTER** Very good in all conditions, esp in Crosshaven and East Passage. There are 3 main marinas at Crosshaven (see Facilities), plus a small private marina and several ⚓s up the Owenboy River, in particular at Drake's Pool. There is a marina at E Ferry at the E end of Great Island. Cobh, Ringaskiddy and Cork City are commercial and ferry ports; contact Port Ops for advice on yacht berths.

**NAVIGATION** WPT 51°46'·57N, 08°15'·39W, 005°/1M to Roche's Pt lt; also on 354°ldg line. Safe hbr with no dangers for yachts; ent is deep and well marked. Sp rate is about 1½kn in ent. Main chan up to Cork and the chan to E Ferry are marked, but shoal outside navigable chan. Ent to Crosshaven/Owenboy River carries at least 3m at LWS, and the chan is buoyed.

**LIGHTS AND MARKS** See 5.3. The 24·5m high hammerhead water tr S of Crosshaven and the R/W power stn chy NE of Corkbeg Is are conspic from seaward. Two set Ldg lts/marks lead through The Sound, either side of Hbr Rk (5·2m), not a hazard for yachts; but do not impede merchant ships. The chan to Crosshaven is marked by C1 SHM lt buoy, C1A SHM lt buoy; C2A PHM lt buoy, C2 PHM lt buoy; and C4 PHM lt buoy.

**R/T** Call: *Cork Hbr Radio* (Port Ops) VHF Ch 12 14 16 (H24); *Crosshaven BY* Ch **M** (Mon–Fri: 0830–1730LT). *Royal Cork YC*

Marina Ch **M** (0900–2359LT) and RCYC water taxi, *Salve Marine and East Ferry Marina* both Ch **M** 0830-1730.

**TELEPHONE** (Code 021) HM 4273125, ▣ 4276284, info@portofcork.ie; Port Ops 4811380; MRSC (066) 9476109; IMES 4831448; ⊖ 4311024; Police 4831222; Dr 4831716; Ⓗ 4546400.

**FACILITIES** Crosshaven BY Marina (100 + 20Ⓥ) ☎ 4831161, ▣ 4831603, cby@eircom.net, €2.50, BH (40 ton), C (1.5 tons), M, Ⓔ, CH, D, P (cans), El, Gaz, Kos, SM, ME, ⚒.
**Salve Marine** (45 + 12 Ⓥ) ☎ 4831145, ▣ 4831747, AB €2.50, M, BY, El, ME, C, CH, R, D, P (cans), Slip.
**Royal Cork YC Marina** (170 + 30Ⓥ) ☎ 4831023, ▣ 4831586, www.royalcork.com, €3.00, P , Bar, R, Slip, ♿.
**Crosshaven Pier/Pontoon** AB €21.00 any size.
**East Ferry Marina** (85 + 15Ⓥ) ☎ 4811342, €2.50, D, Bar, R, Slip; access all tides, max draft 5·5m.
**Crosshaven Village** FV pier in 3·5m at Town quay, L, Slip HW±4(for RIBs & small power craft), Grid, SM, Bar, Dr, ✉, R, 🛒 + ATM, ▣.
**Cork City** All facilities. Ferries (to UK and France), ⇒, ✈.

### MINOR HARBOUR 16M ENE of YOUGHAL
**DUNGARVAN BAY**, Waterford, **52°05'·15N 07°36'·70W**.✻✻⚓✿✿✿. AC 2017, 5622. HW –0540 on Dover; Duration 0600. See 5.15. A large bay, drying to the W, entered between Helvick Hd to the S and to the N Ballynacourty Pt, Fl (2) WRG 10s; see 5.3. Appr in W sector (274°-302°) of this lt, to clear Carricknamoan islet to the N, and Carrickapane Rk and Helvick Rk (ECM buoy Q (3) 10s) to the S. 5ca W of this buoy are The Gainers, a large unmarked rky patch (dries 0·8m). Beware salmon nets. Off Helvick hbr are 8 Y ⚓s or ⚓ in approx 4m. Dungarvan town hbr is accessible HW+3, via buoyed (FlG/FlR) chan which shifts, the buoys being moved to suit; there are now no ldg lts. Appr is difficult in SE'lies >F6. ⚓ in the pool below the town or AB on pontoon (dries to soft mud), S bank below bridge; craft can stay overnight beyond double Y lines. Facilities: D & P (cans), Bar, Ⓑ, ✉, ▣, R, 🛒, Kos.

### MINOR HARBOUR 15M ENE of ROCHE'S POINT
**BALLYCOTTON**, Cork, **51°49'·70N 08°00·19W**. AC 2424, 5622. HW –0555 on Dover; Duration 0550. See above. Small, NE-facing hbr at W end of bay suffers from scend in strong SE winds; 3m in ent and about 1·5m against piers. Many FVs alongside piers, on which yachts should berth, rather than ⚓ in hbr, which is foul with old ground tackle. 6 Y ⚓s are outside hbr, or good ⚓ in offshore winds in 6m NE of pier, protected by Ballycotton Is. Lt ho Fl WR 10s 59m 21/17M, B tr in W walls; 238°-W-048°-R-238°; Horn (4) 90s. Facilities: FW on pier. **Village** Hotel, R, ✉, 🛒, LB, Kos.

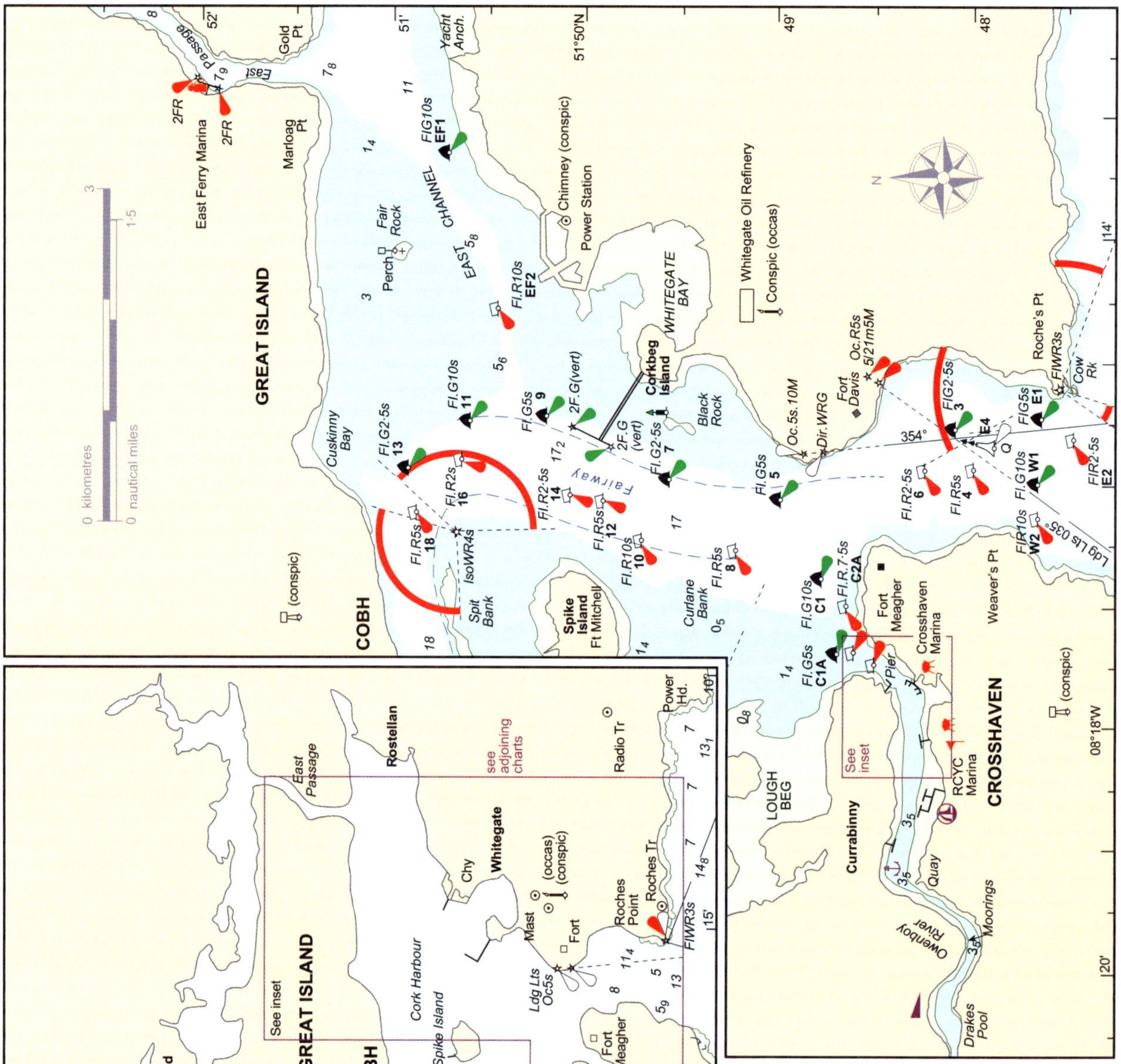
GREAT ISLAND
East Ferry Marina
2FR
Marloag Pt
Gold Pt
East Passage
Yacht Anch.
Fair Rock
Perch
EAST CHANNEL
Fl G10s EF1
Fl.R10s EF2
Chimney (conspic)
Power Station
WHITEGATE BAY
Whitegate Oil Refinery
Conspic (occas)
Corkbeg Island
Black Rock
2F.G(vert)
Fairway
Cuskinny Bay
Fl.G2·5s 13
Fl.R2s 16
Fl.R5s 18
IsoWR4s
Spit Bank
COBH
(conspic)
Spike Island
Ft Mitchell
Fl.G10s 11
Fl.G5s 9
Fl.G2·5s 7
Fl.G5s 5
Fl.R2·5s 14
Fl.R5s 12
Fl.R10s 10
Fl.R5s 8
Curlane Bank
Oc.5s.10M
Dir.WRG
Fort Davis
Oc.R5s 5/21m5M
Fl G2·5s 3
E4
354°
Fl.G5s E1
Fl.G10s W1
Fl.R2·5s 6
Fl.R5s 4
Fl.R2·5s E2
FlWR3s
Roche's Pt
Cow Rk
Fl.R10s W2
Ldg Lts 035°
Fl.G10s C1
Fl.G5s C1A
Fl.R.7·5s C2A
Fort Meagher
Crosshaven Marina
Weaver's Pt
Pier
LOUGH BEG
Currabinny
See inset
RCYC Marina
CROSSHAVEN
Quay
Moorings
Owenboy River
Drakes Pool
(conspic)
0 kilometres 3
0 nautical miles 1·5
51°50'N
08°18'W

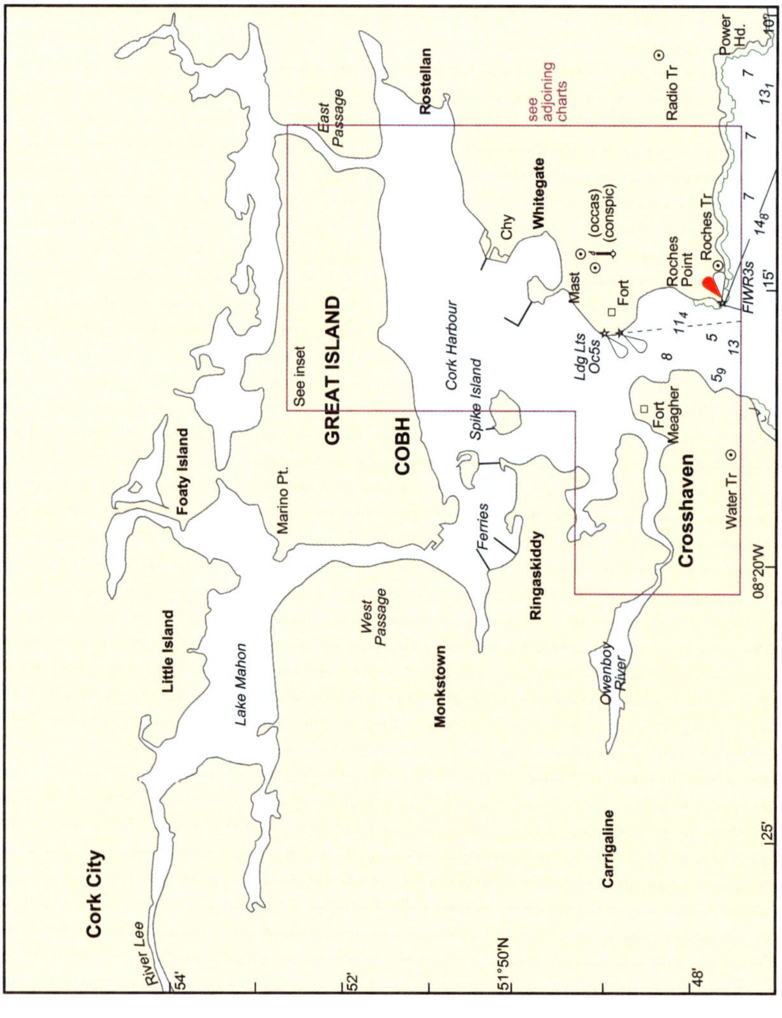
Cork City
River Lee
Little Island
Lake Mahon
Foaty Island
Marino Pt.
GREAT ISLAND
COBH
See inset
East Passage
Rostellan
see adjoining charts
Whitegate
Chy
(occas) (conspic)
Mast
Fort
Ldg Lts Oc5s
Cork Harbour
Spike Island
Ferries
Ringaskiddy
West Passage
Monkstown
Carrigaline
Owenboy River
Crosshaven
Fort Meagher
Roches Point
Roches Tr
FlWR3s
Radio Tr
Power Hd.
Water Tr
51°50'N
08°20'W

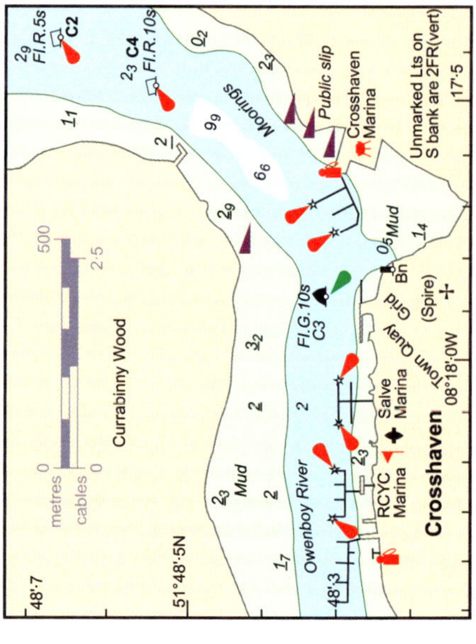
Fl.R.5s C2
Fl.R.10s C4
Currabinny Wood
Moorings
Public slip
Crosshaven Marina
Unmarked Lts on S bank are 2FR(vert)
Mud
Bn
Fl.G.10s C3
Grid
(Spire)
Town Quay
Salve Marina
RCYC Marina
Owenboy River
Crosshaven
0 metres 500
0 cables 2·5
51°48'·5N
08°18'·0W

## 5.19 KINSALE

Cork **51°40'·80N 08°30'·00W** ✳✳✳⚓⚓⚓❀❀❀

**CHARTS** AC 1765, 2053, 5622, 5623; Imray C56; Irish OS 87

**TIDES** –0600 Dover; ML 2·2; Duration 0600

**Standard Port COBH** (←)

| Times | | | | Height (metres) | | | |
|---|---|---|---|---|---|---|---|
| High Water | | Low Water | | MHWS | MHWN | MLWN | MLWS |
| 0500 | 1100 | 0500 | 1100 | 4·1 | 3·2 | 1·3 | 0·4 |
| 1700 | 2300 | 1700 | 2300 | | | | |
| Differences KINSALE | | | | | | | |
| –0019 | –0005 | –0009 | –0023 | –0·2 | 0·0 | +0·1 | +0·2 |

**SHELTER** Excellent, except in very strong SE winds. Access H24 in all weathers/tides. Marinas at Kinsale YC and Castlepark; ❿'s berth on outside of pontoons in 10m in both cases; NNW of latter is FV pontoon and no ⚓ area. Hbr speed limit 6kn. Possible AB (Sun-Thurs) at Trident Hotel. No ⚓ allowed in main channel or within 700m of Town Pier. Contact HM prior to ⚓. All craft have to pay harbour dues as well as berthing/launching fees.

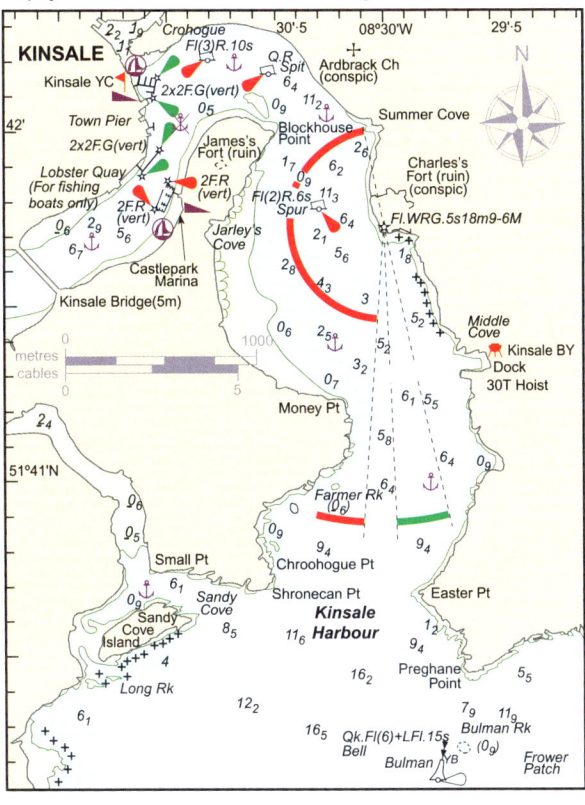

**NAVIGATION** WPT 51°40'·00N 08°30'·00W, 001°/1·7M to Charles's Fort lt. Beware: Bulman Rk (0·9m; SCM lt buoy) 4ca S of Preghane Pt; and Farmer Rk (0·6m) ¾ca off W bank.

**LIGHTS AND MARKS** See 5.3 and chartlet. Chan is marked by PHM lt buoys. Marina lts are 2 FG or FR.

**R/T** KYC VHF Ch M 16. Castlepark marina 06 16 M. HM **14** 16.

**TELEPHONE** (Code 021) HM 4772503 (HO), 4773047 (OT), 🖷 4774695; MRCC (066) 9476109; Coast/Cliff Rescue Service 4772346; ⊜ 4311044/4315422; Police 4772302; Dr 4772253; Ⓗ 4546400.

**FACILITIES** Kinsale BY, ☎ 4774774, 🖷 4775405. D, ❿, FW, ME, ✂, EI, BH (30 ton). **Kinsale YC Marina** (170 + 50❿), €2·70, ☎ 4772196, mobile 087 6787377, 🖷 4774455, Slip, D, R, Bar, ⌖; **Trident Hotel**, D, FW, AB, Sun-Thur try Sail Ireland ☎ 4772927, 🖷 4774170, Mobile 0877 502737. **Castlepark Marina** (150 inc 20 ❿), €5·00, ☎ 4774959, mob 0877 502737, D (fuel pontoon), Slip, R, Bar, EI, ☐; ferry (3 mins) to town. **Services:** ME, EI, Ⓔ, Divers, C (30 ton), D, SM, Gas, Gaz. **Town** @ & Wi-fi, P (cans), 🖷, R, Bar, ✉, Ⓑ, (bus to Cork), ⇌, ✈.

### ANCHORAGE 2M EAST OF KINSALE

**OYSTERHAVEN**, Cork, **51°41'·20N 08°26'·90W**. ✳✳🔹❀❀❀. AC 1765, 2053, 5622. HW –0600 on Dover; ML 2·2m; Duration 0600. Use 5.18. Good shelter but ⚓'s subject to swell in S winds. Enter 0·5M N of Big Sovereign, a steep islet divided into two. Keep to S of Little Sovereign on E side of ent. There is foul ground off Ballymacus Pt on W side, and off Kinure Pt on E side. Pass W of Hbr Rk (0·9m) off Ferry Pt, the only danger within hbr. ⚓ NNW of Ferry Pt in 4·6m on soft mud/weed. NW arm shoals suddenly about 5ca NW of Ferry Pt. Also ⚓ up N arm of hbr in 3m off the W shore. Weed in higher reaches may foul ⚓. No lts, marks or VHF radio. Coast/Cliff Rescue Service ☎ (021) 4770711.

Oysterhaven Yacht Harbour (strictly private) 51°42'·10N 08°26'·58W, ☎ (021) 4770878.

## 5.20 COURTMACSHERRY

Cork **51°38'·22N 08°40'·90W** ✳✳⚓⚓❀❀❀

**CHARTS** AC 2092, 2081, 5622, 5623; Imray C56; Irish OS 87

**TIDES** HW –0610 on Dover; Duration 0545

**Standard Port COBH** (←)

| Times | | | | Height (metres) | | | |
|---|---|---|---|---|---|---|---|
| High Water | | Low Water | | MHWS | MHWN | MLWN | MLWS |
| 0500 | 1100 | 0500 | 1100 | 4·1 | 3·2 | 1·3 | 0·4 |
| 1700 | 2300 | 1700 | 2300 | | | | |
| Differences COURTMACSHERRY | | | | | | | |
| –0025 | –0008 | –0008 | –0015 | –0·1 | –0·1 | 0·0 | +0·1 |

**SHELTER** Good shelter up-river, but in strong S/SE winds seas break on the bar (2·3m), when ent must not be attempted. Dry out in small inner hbr or AB afloat on jetty (FVs) or on yacht pontoon (18·5m). ⚓ NE of Ferry Pt in about 2·5m or N of pontoon. Weed may foul ⚓; best to moor using two ⚓s.

**NAVIGATION** WPT, 51°37'·50N 08°40'·17W, 324°/0·8M to Wood Pt. Appr in the W sector of Wood Pt lt, between Black Tom and Horse Rk (dries 3·6m); the latter is 3-4½ca E of Barry Pt on the W shore. Black Tom (2·3m), with SHM buoy Fl.G.5s 5ca SSE, is close NE of the appr. Further to NE, in centre of bay, Barrel Rk (dries 2·6m), has unlit SCM perch (no topmark). To NNW and E of it are Inner Barrels (0·5m) and Blueboy Rk. Hbr ent is between Wood Pt and SHM buoy 2ca NE, Fl G 3s. Chan (2m but 1·4m reported close inside ent) is marked by 3 unlit SHM spar buoys after these; keep close N of moorings on S side of harbour.

**LIGHTS AND MARKS** Wood Pt, Fl (2) WR 5s 15m 5M.

**R/T** None.

**TELEPHONE** (023) HM/RNLI(Boathouse) 46170/46600; Dr 46186; HN 1850 335999; Police 46122; Coast Rescue Service 40110.

**FACILITIES** Quay AB (min €15/craft). ⟁, 🚾, FW, ⌖, D (Pier 0930-1800 on request), Slip, LB, R. **Village**, Bar, R, 🖷, (bus to Cork), ⇌, ✈.

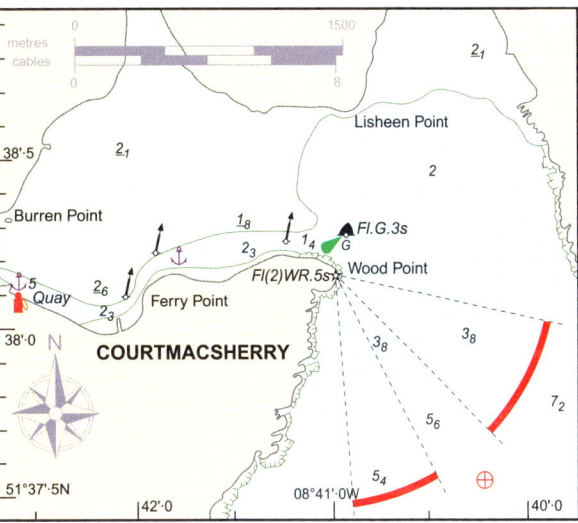

## 5.21 GLANDORE

Cork, **51°33'·70N 09°07'·20W** ✿⚓⚓🏔🏵🏵🏵

**CHARTS** AC *2092*, 5622, 5623; Imray C56; Irish OS 89

**TIDES** Approx as for 5.21 Castletownshend

**SHELTER** Excellent. 12 Y ⚓s or ⚓ 1½ca SW of Glandore Pier in 2m or 1ca NE of the New pier at Unionhall in 3m.

**NAVIGATION** WPT 51°32'·35N 09°05'·10W, 129°/1·2M to Outer Dangers. Approach between Adam Is and Goat's Hd, thence keep E of Eve Is and W of the chain of rocks: Outer, Middle and Inner Dangers and Sunk Rk. Before altering W for Unionhall, stand on to clear mudbank 1ca off S shore. Speed limit 3kn.

**LIGHTS AND MARKS** See 5.3. Galley Hd, Fl (5) 20s, is 5M E of ent. Outer Dangers are marked by GRG lt buoy, and PHM bn; Middle and Inner Dangers by 2 SHM bns; and Sunk Rk by a NCM lt buoy.

**R/T** HM Ch 06.

**TELEPHONE** (Code 028) HM Glandore/Unionhall 34737, mob 0866081944; Police (023) 23088; Dr 23456; Coast Rescue 33115.

**FACILITIES Glandore** GHYC, ⚓s €14.00/craft (contact Glandore Inn ☎ 33468/33518), FW, ✉, R, Bar, Kos. **Unionhall** AB(outside of FVs/drying AB Old Quay) €15.00/craft, FW, D(occ quayside) or D & P (by cans from Leap 2M), ME, Gas, showers, 🚻, ✉, R, Bar, 🛒.

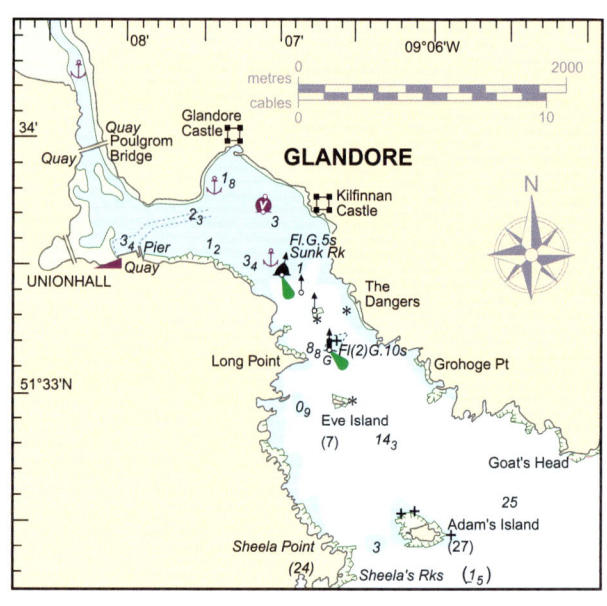

## 5.22 CASTLE HAVEN

Cork **51°30'·90N 09°10'·70W** ✿⚓⚓🏔🏵🏵🏵

**CHARTS** AC *2092, 2129*, 5623; Imray C56; Irish OS 88, 89

**TIDES** +0605 Dover; ML 2·2; Duration 0605

**Standard Port COBH (⟵)**

| Times | | | | Height (metres) | | | |
|---|---|---|---|---|---|---|---|
| High Water | | Low Water | | MHWS | MHWN | MLWN | MLWS |
| 0500 | 1100 | 0500 | 1100 | 4·1 | 3·2 | 1·3 | 0·4 |
| 1700 | 2300 | 1700 | 2300 | | | | |
| **Differences CASTLETOWNSHEND** | | | | | | | |
| −0020 | −0030 | −0020 | −0050 | −0·4 | −0·2 | +0·1 | +0·3 |
| **CLONAKILTY BAY** (5M NE of Galley Head) | | | | | | | |
| −0033 | −0011 | −0019 | −0041 | −0·3 | −0·2 | No data | |

**SHELTER** Excellent ⚓ in midstream SE of Castletownshend slip, protected from all weathers and available at all tides; but the outer part of hbr is subject to swell in S winds. Or ⚓ N of Cat Island, or upstream as depth permits. Caution: An underwater cable runs E/W across the hbr from the slip close N of Reen Pier to the slip at Castletownshend.

**NAVIGATION** WPT 51°30'·28N, 09°10'·26W, 351°/7ca to Reen Pt lt. Enter between Horse Is (35m) and Skiddy Is (9m) both of which have foul ground all round. Black Rk lies off the SE side of Horse Is and is steep-to along its S side. Flea Sound is a narrow boat chan, obstructed by rks. Colonel's Rk (0·5m) lies close to the E shore, 2ca N of Reen Pt. Beware salmon nets.

**LIGHTS AND MARKS** Reen Pt, Fl WRG 10s; a small slender W bn; vis shore-G-338°-W-001°-R-shore. A ruined tr is on Horse Is.

**R/T** None.

**TELEPHONE** (Code 028) MRCC (066) 9746109; Coast/Cliff Rescue Service 21039; ⊖ Bantry (027) 50061; Police 36144; Dr 23456; 🅷 21677.

**FACILITIES Reen Pier** L, FW; **Sailing Club** ☎ 36100; **Castletownsend Village** Slip, Bar, R, 🛒, FW, ✉, Ⓑ (Skibbereen), ⇌, ✈ (Cork).

**BARLOGE CREEK**, Cork, **51°29'·57N 09°17'·58W**. AC 2129. Tides approx as Castletownshend. A narrow creek, well sheltered except from S/SE winds. Appr with Gokane Pt brg 120°. Enter W of Bullock Is, keeping to the W side to clear rks S of the island. ⚓ W of the Is in 3m but weedy. No facilities.

## 5.23 BALTIMORE

Cork **51°28'·30N 09°23'·40W** ✿✿✿⚓⚓✿✿✿

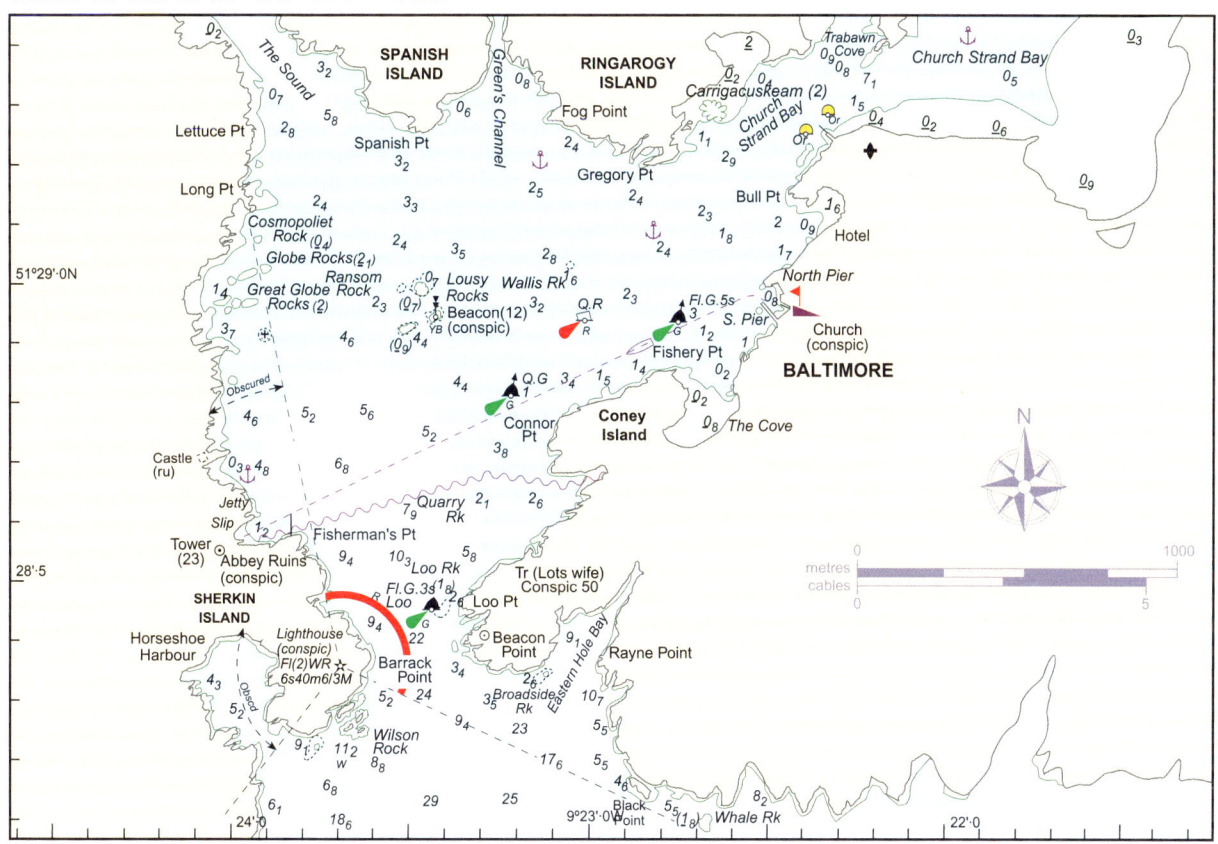

**CHARTS** AC 2129, 3725, 5623; Imray C56; Irish OS 88

**TIDES** –0605 Dover; ML 2·1; Duration 0610

**Standard Port COBH (⟵)**

| Times | | | | Height (metres) | | | |
|---|---|---|---|---|---|---|---|
| High Water | | Low Water | | MHWS | MHWN | MLWN | MLWS |
| 0500 | 1100 | 0500 | 1100 | 4·1 | 3·2 | 1·3 | 0·4 |
| 1700 | 2300 | 1700 | 2300 | | | | |
| Differences BALTIMORE | | | | | | | |
| –0025 | –0005 | –0010 | –0050 | –0·6 | –0·3 | +0·1 | +0·2 |

**SHELTER** Excellent. Access H24 from the S. At Baltimore, pontoon (Apr-Sep) on S Pier, AB for up to 20 yachts in 1·5m depth. Inner Hbr, partly drying between N and S piers, mostly used by ferries, local boats and FVs; the latter also berth on N pier. ⚓ about 200m W of S pier, or about 200m N of N Pier avoiding extensive moorings. In strong NW'lies ⚓ in Church Strand Bay. Its are required. Do not ⚓ in dredged chan between Wallis Rk buoy and N Pier, or in chan to Church Strand Bay. In strong W winds ⚓ in lee of Sherkin Is off Castle ruins or berth on pontoon.

**NAVIGATION** WPT 51°27'·93N 09°23'·46W, 000°/5ca to Loo Rk SHM lt buoy. No passage between buoy and mainland. Beware Lousy Rks (SCM bn) and Wallis Rk (PHM lt buoy) in middle of bay. From/to the N The Sound needs careful pilotage; AC 3725 and ICC SDs essential. R Ilen is navigable on the flood for at least 4M above The Sound. Speed limit 6kn within river and hbr.

**LIGHTS AND MARKS** See 5.3 and chartlet. Ent easily identified by Barrack Pt lt ho and conspic W tr (Lot's Wife) on Beacon Pt.

**R/T** VHF (HM) Ch 09, 16.

**TELEPHONE** (Code 028) HM 087 2351485; MRCC and Coast/Cliff Rescue Service (066) 9476109; ⊖ (027) 53210; Police 20102; Dr 23456/after hrs 1850 335999, Ⓗ 21677.

**FACILITIES** Berthing: May-Sept from €20/craft, ☎ 22145, 0872 351485 or www.atlanticboat.ie; slip, AB, D (☎ 20106), FW on pontoon; **Baltimore SC,** ☎ 20426, visitors welcome, bar, showers; **Glenans Irish Sailing School** ☎ (01) 6611481; Hotel ☎ 20361. **Services:** D (hose), BY (on R Ilen at Old Court), ME, EI, CH, 🛒, Gas, Gaz, Kos, ACA; **Village:** Bar, ✉, bus to Cork for ⇌, ✈.

**ADJACENT ANCHORAGES**

**HORSESHOE HARBOUR, 51°28'·20N 09°23'·86W.** Small unlit hbr on Sherkin Is, 3ca WSW of ent to Baltimore. Keep to the W at narrow ent. ⚓ in about 5m in centre of cove.

**CLEAR ISLAND, N HARBOUR, 51°26'·60N 09°30'·20W.** AC 2129, 5623. Tides approx as Schull, 5.23. A tiny, partly drying inlet on N coast of Clear Is, exposed to N'ly swell. Rks either side of outer appr 196°. Inside the narrow (30m), rky ent keep to the E. Lie to 2⚓s on E side in about 1·5m or drying berth in Inner Hbr clear of ferry bad weather berth. **Facilities** D & P (cans), FW, 🛒, ✉,email, R, Bar.

**ROARINGWATER BAY,** Long Island Bay AC 2129, 5623. Entered between Cape Clear and Mizen Hd and extends NE into Roaringwater Bay, beware extensive marine farms with narrow chans between them. Fastnet Rk/Lt Ho, is 4M to seaward. Safest appr, S of Schull, is via Carthy's Sound (51°30'N 09°30'W). From the SE appr via Gascanane Sound, but beware Toorane Rks, Anima Rk and outlying rks off many of the islands. Shelter in various winds at ⚓s clockwise from Horse Island: 3ca E and 7ca NE of E tip of Horse Is; in Ballydehob B 2m; Poulgorm B 2m; 5ca ENE of Mannin Is in 4m; 2ca SE of Carrigvalish Rks in 6m. Rincolisky Cas (ru) is conspic on S side of bay. The narrow chan E of Hare Is and N of Sherkin Is has two ⚓s; also leads via The Sound into Baltimore hbr. Local advice useful. Temp'y fair weather ⚓s in Carthy's Islands. Rossbrin Cove safe ⚓ 2·5M E of Schull, but many local moorings; no access from E of Horse Is due to drying Horse Ridge. Ballydehob has a good quay for tenders and most facilities.

## 5.24 SCHULL

Cork **51°30'·80N 09°32'·00W** ✲✲✲⚓⚓⚓✿✿

**CHARTS** AC 2184, 2129, 5623; Imray C56; Irish OS 88

**TIDES** +0610 Dover; ML 1·8; Duration 0610

**Standard Port COBH (←—)**

| Times | | | | Height (metres) | | | |
|---|---|---|---|---|---|---|---|
| High Water | | Low Water | | MHWS | MHWN | MLWN | MLWS |
| 0500 | 1100 | 0500 | 1100 | 4·1 | 3·2 | 1·3 | 0·4 |
| 1700 | 2300 | 1700 | 2300 | | | | |
| Differences SCHULL | | | | | | | |
| −0040 | −0015 | −0015 | −0110 | −0·9 | −0·6 | −0·2 | 0·0 |

**SHELTER** Good, except in strong S/SE winds when best shelter is N of Long Island. Schull Hbr access H24. 12 Y ⚓s in NE part of hbr or ⚓ in 3m 1ca SE of pier, usually lit by street lts all night; keep clear of fairway marked by 8 unlit lateral buoys (summer time only).

**NAVIGATION** WPT 51°29'·60N 09°31'·60W, 346°/2·1M to front ldg lt. In hbr ent, Bull Rk (dries 1·8m), R iron perch, can be passed either side.

**LIGHTS AND MARKS** See 5.3 and chartlet. Ldg lts, lead 346° between Long Is Pt, W conical tr, and Amelia Rk SHM lt buoy; thence E of Bull Rk and toward head of bay. By day in good vis 2 W radomes conspic on Mt Gabriel (2M N of Schull) lead 355° with Long Is Pt lt ho in transit.

**R/T** None.

**TELEPHONE** (Code 028) Water Sports Centre 28554; HM 086-1039105; MRCC (066) 9476109; Coast/Cliff Rescue Service 35318; ⊜ (027) 51562; Police 28111; Dr 28311; Ⓗ (027) 50133.

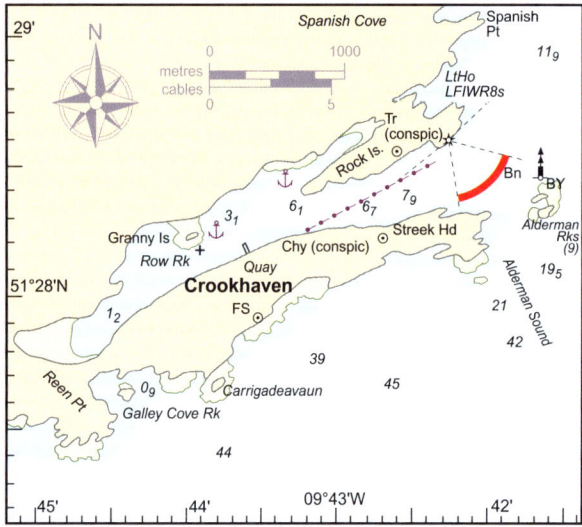

**FACILITIES** **Schull Pier/Hbr** Slip (H24 except LWS) FV pier/pontoon for tenders (v.crowded at times), AB tempy, ⚓s €6.35, M, D (large quantities by arrangement), FW, SM; **Sailing Club** ☎ 37352; **Services:** Kos, BY, ✕, CH. **Village** P & D (cans from Ballydehob 5M), ME, El, ⊞, @/Wi-fi, Charts, R, Bar, ▣, ✉, Ⓑ, bus to Cork for: ⇌, ✈, car ferry.

## 5.25 CROOKHAVEN

Cork **51°28'·50N 09°42'·00W** ✲✲⚓⚓✿✿✿

**CHARTS** AC 2184, 5623; Imray C56; Irish OS 88

**TIDES** +0550 Dover; ML 1·8; Duration 0610

**Standard Port COBH (←—)**

| Times | | | | Height (metres) | | | |
|---|---|---|---|---|---|---|---|
| High Water | | Low Water | | MHWS | MHWN | MLWN | MLWS |
| 0500 | 1100 | 0500 | 1100 | 4·1 | 3·2 | 1·3 | 0·4 |
| 1700 | 2300 | 1700 | 2300 | | | | |
| Differences CROOKHAVEN | | | | | | | |
| −0057 | −0033 | −0048 | −0112 | −0·8 | −0·6 | −0·4 | −0·1 |
| DUNMANUS HARBOUR | | | | | | | |
| −0107 | −0031 | −0044 | −0120 | −0·7 | −0·6 | −0·2 | 0·0 |
| DUNBEACON HARBOUR | | | | | | | |
| −0057 | −0025 | −0032 | −0104 | −0·8 | −0·7 | −0·3 | −0·1 |

**SHELTER** Excellent. There are 8 Y ⚓s and 10 dayglow R ⚓s. Short stay pontoon for up to 4 boats (FW/stores/passengers). ⚓s in middle of bay in 3m; off W tip of Rock Is; and E of Granny Is; last two are far from the village. Holding is patchy, especially in strong SW'lies; beware weed, shellfish beds around shoreline and submarine pipeline from Rock Is to Crookhaven.

**NAVIGATION** WPT 51°28'·50N 09°40'·50W, 274°/1M to Rock Is lt ho. Ent between this lt and NCM bn on Black Horse Rks (3½ca ESE). From S, keep 1ca E of Alderman Rks and ½ca off Black Horse Rks bn. Passage between Streek Hd and Alderman Rks is not advised for strangers. Inside the bay the shores are steep to.

**LIGHTS AND MARKS** Lt ho on Rock Is (conspic W tr) L Fl WR 8s 20m 13/11M; vis outside hbr: W over Long Is Bay-281°-R-340°; vis inside hbr: 281°-R-348°-W-shore(N).

**R/T** None.

**TELEPHONE** (Code 028) HM (O'Sullivan's Bar) 35319; MRCC (066) 9476109; Coast/Cliff Rescue at Goleen 35318; ⊜ (027) 50061; Dr 35148; ✉ 35200.

**FACILITIES Village** ⚓s €8.00, Bar, R, FW, ⊞, ✉, D (cans), ME, Ⓑ (Schull), taxi to Goleen then bus to Cork, ✈, ⇌.

### ADJACENT HARBOURS

**GOLEEN** (Kireal-coegea), Cork, **51°29'·65N 09°42'·21W**. AC 2184, 5623. Tides as Crookhaven. A narrow inlet 6ca N of Spanish Pt; good shelter in fair weather, except from SE. 2 churches are easily seen, but ent not visible until close. Keep to S side of ent and ⚓ fore-and-aft just below quay, where AB also possible. Facilities: P, ⊞, Bar.

**DUNMANUS BAY**, Cork. AC 2552, 5623. Tides see 5.24. Appr between Three Castle Hd and Sheep's Hd, Fl (3) WR 15s 83m 18/15M; no other lts. Ent to **Dunmanus Hbr**, 51°32'·70N 09°39'·86W, is 1ca wide; breakers both sides. ⚓ in 4m centre of B. **Kitchen Cove**, 51°35'·50N 09°38'·05W, best of the 3 hbrs; enter W of Owens Is and ⚓ 1ca NNW of it or 2ca further N in 3m. Exposed to S, but good holding. Quay at Ahakista village: AB (drying) FW, ⊞, R, Bar. **Dunbeacon Hbr**, 51°36'·35N 09°33'·60W, is shallow and rock-girt. Quay possible AB in 2m (used by FVs), Slip; ⚓'ge E or SE of Mannion Is. Durrus (¾M): Fuel (cans), R, Bar.

**WGS84 DATUM**

## 5.26 BANTRY BAY

Cork 51°34'N 09°57'W ✿✿✿≋≋✿✿✿

**CHARTS** AC *2552*, 1840, 1838, 5623; Imray C56; Irish OS 84, 85, 88

**TIDES** +0600 Dover; ML 1·8; Duration 0610

**Standard Port COBH** (←)

| Times | | | | Height (metres) | | | |
|---|---|---|---|---|---|---|---|
| High Water | | Low Water | | MHWS | MHWN | MLWN | MLWS |
| 0500 | 1100 | 0500 | 1100 | 4·1 | 3·2 | 1·3 | 0·4 |
| 1700 | 2300 | 1700 | 2300 | | | | |
| **Differences BANTRY** | | | | | | | |
| −0045 | −0025 | −0040 | −0105 | −0·7 | −0·6 | −0·2 | +0·1 |
| **CASTLETOWN** (Bearhaven) | | | | | | | |
| −0048 | −0012 | −0025 | −0101 | −0·9 | −0·6 | −0·1 | 0·0 |
| **BLACK BALL HARBOUR** (51°36N 10°02W) | | | | | | | |
| −0115 | −0035 | −0047 | −0127 | −0·7 | −0·6 | −0·1 | +0·1 |

**SHELTER/NAVIGATION** Bantry Bay extends 20M ENE from Sheep's Hd, Fl (3) WR 15s 83m 18/15M. Access is easy, but the Bay is exposed to W'lies. The shore is clear everywhere except off Bear Is and Whiddy Is. Some of the many well sheltered ⚓s on the N shore are detailed on this page. The S shore has few ⚓s.

**CASTLETOWNBERE, 51°38'·80N 09°54'·45W.** AC 1840, 5623. Sheltered ⚓ in 2·4m NW of Dinish Is, to E of 010° ldg line, but never far from FVs; also ⚓ at **Dunboy Bay,** W of Piper Sound (open to E). 4 Y ⚓s are laid Apr-Sep 3ca E of Dinish Is. Lts: At W ent, Ardnakinna Pt, Fl (2) WR 10s 62m 17/14M, H24. At E ent to Bearhaven: Roancarrigmore, Fl WR 3s 18m 18/14M. Appr W of Bear Is on 024° Dir lt, Oc WRG 5s 4m 14/11M (024°-W-024·5°); then inner ldg lts 010°, both Oc 3s 4/7m 1M, vis 005°-015°, via ent chan which narrows to 50m abeam Perch Rk lt bn. Beware Walter Scott Rk (2·7m), SCM lt buoy, and Carrigaglos (0·6m high) S of Dinish Is. VHF Ch 14 16. HM ☎ (027) 70220, ⌕ 70329. Facilities: FW & D on quay; BH on Dinish Is. **Town** El, ME, ✖, P (cans), Bar, Ⓑ, ✉, ⛟, R, Kos.

**LAWRENCE COVE MARINA, 51°38'·28N 09°49'·28W**; AC 1840, 5623. *See inset on chartlet below.* Good shelter on N side of Bear Island. Marina on S side of cove has NE/SW pontoon 90m long (40 AB in 3-3·5m). From E keep clear of Palmer Rk and a shoal patch, both 1·8m. ☎/⌕ 027 75044; VHF Ch 16 M. AB (€1.52), FW, ⟐, D, BH, ▣. Friendly welcome at the only marina between Kinsale and Dingle. There are 4 Y ⚓s in 3m close S of Ardagh Pt, or ⚓ in 4m to W of Turk Is. At Rerrin village: BY, Slip, Gaz, ⛟, R, Bar, ✉, storage facilities. Bus to Cork and all storage facilities.

**LONEHORT HARBOUR, 51°38'·12N 09°47'·80W.** AC 1840, 5623. At E tip of Bear Is, good shelter but keep S at ent to clear unmarked rks; then turn ENE to ⚓ in 2·7m at E end of cove.

**ADRIGOLE, 51°40'·51N 09°43'·22W.** AC 1840, 5623. Good shelter, but squally in W/N gales. Beware Doucallia Rk, dries 1·2m, 1M SSW of ent. Beyond the 2ca wide ent, keep E of Orthons Is (rks on W side). 7 Y ⚓s NE of Orthons Is. ⚓s to suit wind direction: off pier on E shore 4m; N or NW of Orthons Is. Drumlave (½M E): Slip, FW, showers (sailing school), D (cans), Gaz, ⛟, ✉.

**Trafrask Bay,** 2M to the E, has 1 Y ⚓ at 51°40'·8N 09°40'·1W; ⛟, Bar/R.

**GLENGARRIFF, 51°44'·20N 09°31'·90W.** AC 1838, 5623. Tides as Bantry. Beautiful ⚓ S of Bark Is in 7-10m; or to NE in 3m, where there are 6 Y ⚓s. Better for yachts than Bantry hbr. Ent between Big Pt and Gun Pt. No lts/marks. Keep 1ca E of rks off Garinish Island (Illnaculien) and Ship Is; beware marine farms. Rky chan W of Garinish, with HT cable 15m clearance, should not be attempted. Facilities: Eccles hotel, showers. **Village** FW (ferry berth 1800-1900), Bar, D & P (cans), ✉, R, ⛟, Kos.

**BANTRY, 51°40'·85N 09°27'·85W.** AC 1838, 5623. Beware Gerane Rks ½M W of Whiddy Is. Appr via the buoyed/lit N chan to E of Horse and Chapel Is; keep 2ca off all islands to clear unlit marine farms. The S chan, fair weather only. Appr Relane Pt hdg 063° with HW mark S.Beach (seaward edge of airfield) ∅ Reenbeg Cliff (distant rounded hill) to clear Cracker Rk, then leave Blue Hill and S Beach to stbd. ⚓'s call Bantry Hbr Ch 14 or ☎ 027 51253; VHF Ch 14 11 16 (H24). HM (027) 53277; ⌕ 50061; Police 50045; Dr 50405; ⊞ 50133. MRCC (066) 9476109. Facilities: **Pier** AB(drying), L, FW, Gaz; **Bantry Bay SC** ☎ 50081 ⚓'s(free),Slip, L, FW, Showers; **Town** @ (Vickery's Inn), P & D (cans), Kos, ME, CH, ⛟, R, Bar, ✉, Ⓑ, bus to Cork.

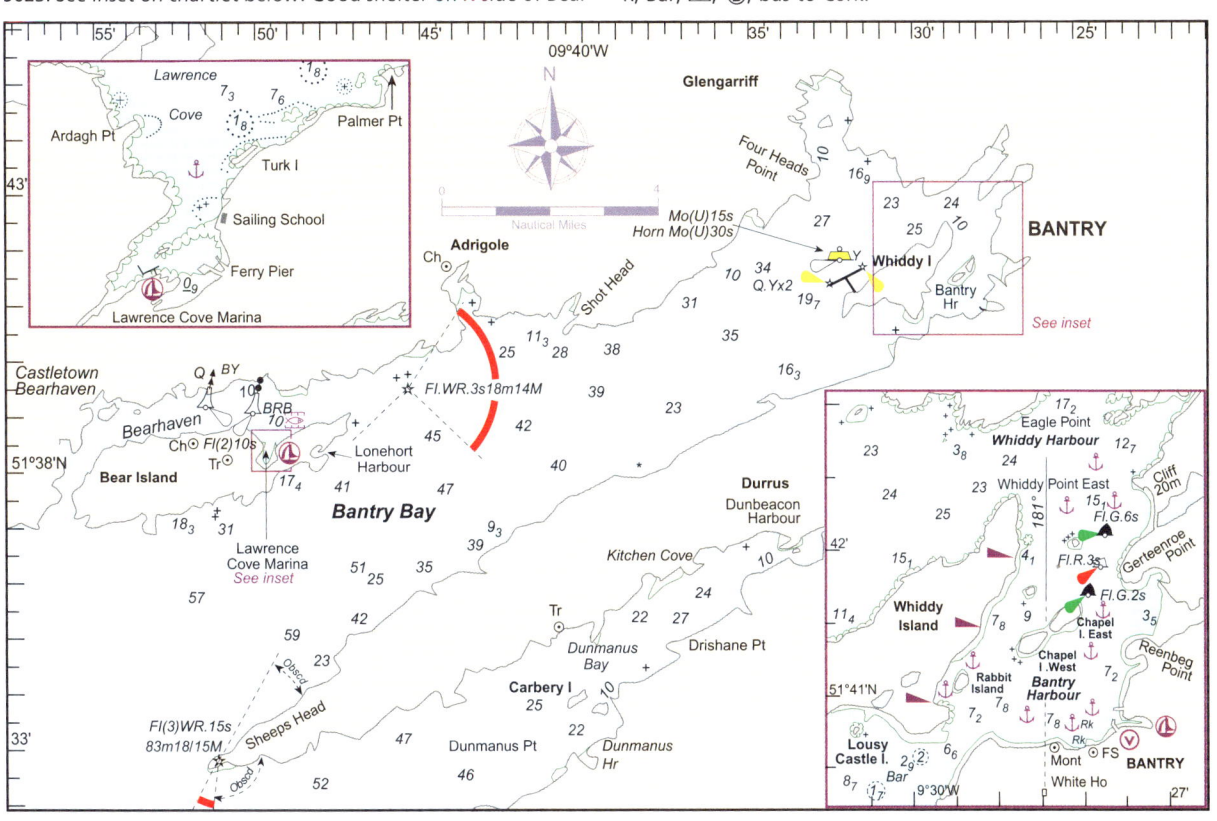

## 5.27 KENMARE RIVER

Kerry 51°45'·00N 10°00'·00W ✲✲✲❀❀

**CHARTS** AC *2495*; Imray C56; Irish OS 84

**TIDES** +0515 Dover; Duration Dunkerron 0620

**Standard Port COBH (◄──)**

| Times | | | | Height (metres) | | | |
|---|---|---|---|---|---|---|---|
| High Water | | Low Water | | MHWS | MHWN | MLWN | MLWS |
| 0500 | 1100 | 0500 | 1100 | 4·1 | 3·2 | 1·3 | 0·4 |
| 1700 | 2300 | 1700 | 2300 | | | | |
| Differences BALLYCROVANE HARBOUR (Coulagh Bay) | | | | | | | |
| −0116 | −0036 | −0053 | −0133 | −0·6 | −0·5 | −0·1 | 0·0 |
| DUNKERRON HARBOUR | | | | | | | |
| −0117 | −0027 | −0050 | −0140 | −0·2 | −0·3 | +0·1 | 0·0 |
| WEST COVE (51°46'N 10°03'W) | | | | | | | |
| −0113 | −0033 | −0049 | −0129 | −0·6 | −0·5 | −0·1 | 0·0 |
| BALLINSKELLIGS BAY | | | | | | | |
| −0119 | −0039 | −0054 | −0134 | −0·5 | −0·5 | −0·1 | 0·0 |

**SHELTER** Garnish Bay (S of Long I): is only good in settled weather and W'ly winds. ⚓ either W or 1ca S of the Carrigduff concrete bn.

**Ballycrovane:** in NE of Coulagh B is a good ✗, but open to W'ly swell which breaks on submerged rks in SE. N and E shores are foul 5ca NE of Bird Is.

**Cleanderry:** ent NE of Illaunbweeheen (Yellow Is) is only 7m wide and rky. ⚓ ENE of inner hbr. Beware marine farms.

**Ardgroom:** excellent shelter, but intricate ent over rky bar. Appr with B bn brg 135°; then 2 W bns (front on Black Rk, rear ashore) lead 099° through bar. Alter 206° as two bns astern come in transit. When clear, steer WNW to ⚓ 0·5 ca E of Reenavade pier; power needed. Beware marine farms off Ardgroom & Kilmakilloge.

**Kilmakilloge:** is a safe ⚓ in all winds. Beware mussel beds and rky shoals. On appr keep S side of ent, steer W of Spanish Is, but pass N of it. Bunaw Hbr ldg lts 041°, front Oc R 3s, rear Iso R 2s, (access only near HW; AB for shoal draft). Keep S side of ent; ⚓ 2ca W of Carrigwee bn; S of Eskadawer Pt; or Collorus Hbr W side only.

**Ormond's Hbr:** good shelter except in SW or W winds, but beware rk 2½ca ENE of Hog Is. ⚓ in S half of bay.

**Kenmare:** good shelter. Access only near HW via narrow ch marked by poles on S side. Poss AB (☎ (064) 83171) rafted at end of pier (FW available) at N side of river, just below town. ⚓ in pool (2.5m) just downstream of concrete suspension bridge. Beware very strong ebbs at springs and after heavy rains.

**Dunkerron Hbr:** ent between Cod Rks and The Boar to ⚓ 1ca NW of Fox Is in 3·2m; land at Templenoe pier. 4ca E of Reen Pt behind pier FW available.

**Sneem:** enter between Sherky Is and Rossdohan Is. Hotel conspic NE of hbr. 3 Y ⚓s and ⚓ NE of Garinish Is, but uncomfortable if swell enters either side of Sherky Is. Beware of marine farms.

**Darrynane:** 1¾M NW of Lamb's Hd, is appr'd from the S between Deenish and Moylaun Islands, but not with high SW swell. Enter with care on the ldg marks/lts 034°, 2 W bns, both Oc 3s 10/16m 4M. 3 Y ⚓s (beware unmkd drying rk close N) and safe ⚓ (3m) NE of Lamb's Hd. Also ⚓s in Lehid Hbr, R Blackwater, Coongar Hbr & W Cove.

**NAVIGATION** WPT 51°40'·00N 10°17'·20W, 065°/15·6M to 0.5M S of Sherky Island. From SW, keep NW of The Bull and Dursey Is. From SE, Dursey Sound is possible in fair weather but narrow (beware Flag Rk 0·3m) and with cable car, 21m clearance. To clear dangerous rks off Coulagh Bay, keep twr on Dursey Is well open of Cod's Head 220°. From NW, there are 3 deep chans off Lamb's Head: between Scarriff Is and Deenish Is which is clear; between Deenish and Moylaun Is which has rky shoals; and between Moylaun and Two Headed Is which is clear and 4½ca wide. A night appr into the river is possible, but close appr to hbrs or ⚓s is not advised. Up-river from Sneem Hbr, keep N of Maiden Rk, dries 0·5m, and Church Rks; also Lackeen Rks and Carrignarona beg. Beware marine farms, also salmon nets Jun-Sep. See 5.4.

**LIGHTS AND MARKS** On Dursey Is: Old Watch Twr (conspic) 250m. Eagle Hill (Cod's Hd) 216m. Lights are as on chartlet.

**R/T** None.

**TELEPHONE** (Code 064) MRCC (066) 9476109; Coast/Cliff Rescue Service (Waterville) (066) 74320; ⊖ Bantry (027) 50061; Ⓗ 4108; Police 41177.

**FACILITIES**

**ARDGROOM Pallas Hbr:** D & P (cans), ▦, R, Bar, Kos, ✉ at Ardgroom village (2M SSW of Reenavade pier).

**KILMAKILLOGE: Bunaw Pier,** AB, ▦, Bar/R; 2M to D(cans), Kos, ✉.

**KENMARE:** AB. **Town** D & P (cans), Kos, Gaz, R, ▦, Bar, Ⓗ, ✉ inc @, Ⓑ, ⊕ (bus to Killarney), ✈ (Cork or Killarney).

**SNEEM:** L at Hotel Parknasilla and Oysterbed Ho pier (FW).

**Town** (2M from hbr), P & D (cans), R, Bar, ✉, ▭, Gaz, Kos.

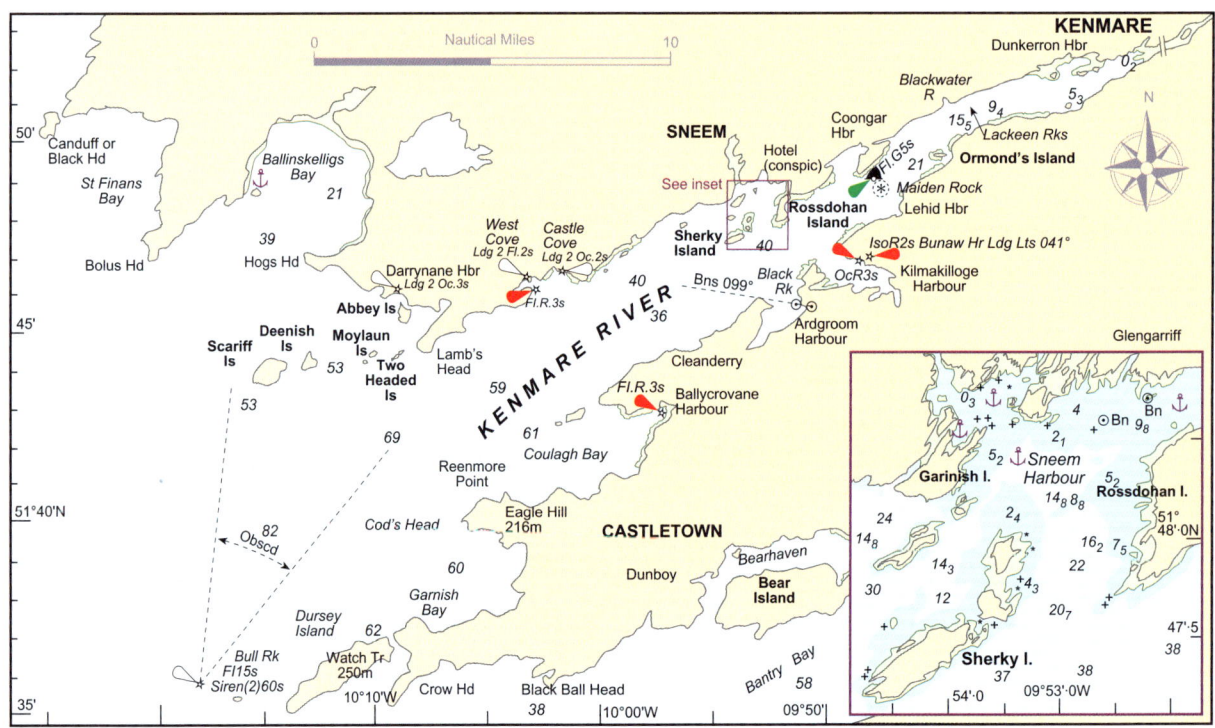

## 5.28   DINGLE BAY

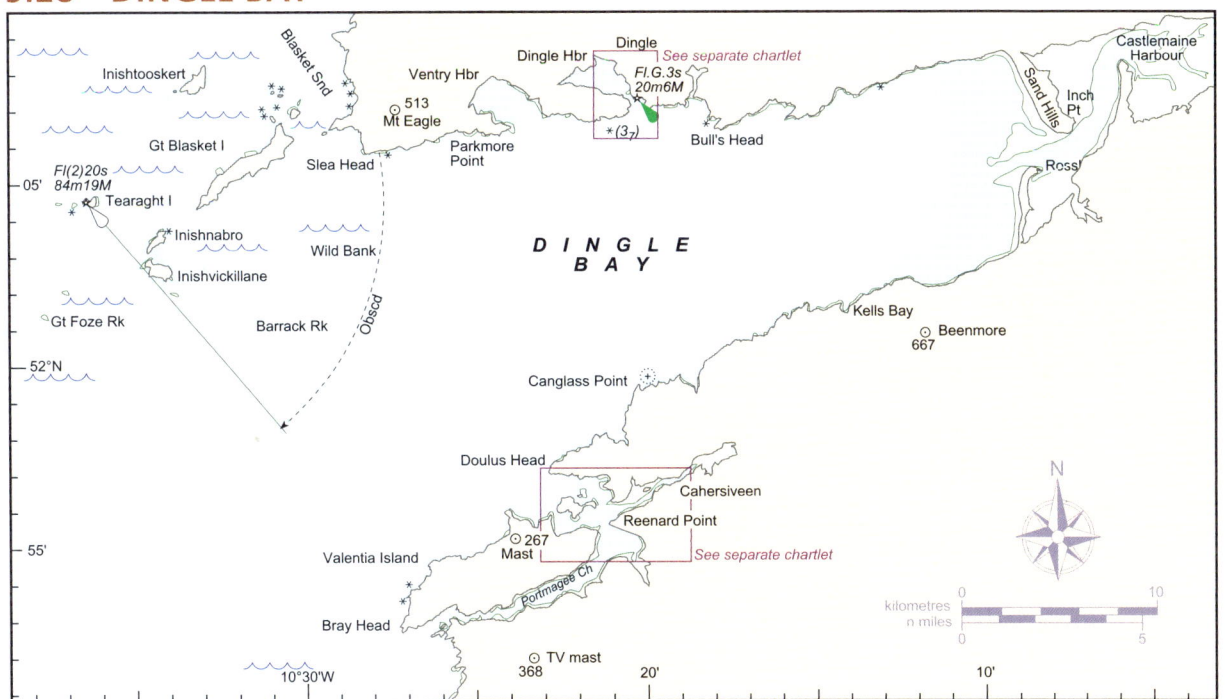

## 5.29   VALENTIA HARBOUR

**Kerry** 51°55'·7N 10°17'·1W ✳✳✳✳

**CHARTS** AC 2125; Imray C56; Irish OS 84

**TIDES** +0515 Dover

**Standard Port COBH** (←)

| Times | | | | Height (metres) | | | |
|---|---|---|---|---|---|---|---|
| High Water | | Low Water | | MHWS | MHWN | MLWN | MLWS |
| 0500 | 1100 | 0500 | 1100 | 4·1 | 3·2 | 1·3 | 0·4 |
| 1700 | 2300 | 1700 | 2300 | | | | |
| **Differences VALENTIA HARBOUR** (Knight's Town) | | | | | | | |
| −0118 | −0038 | −0056 | −0136 | −0·6 | −0·4 | −0·1 | 0·0 |

**SHELTER** Good ⚓s at: Glanleam B, 6ca S of Fort Pt in 4m; 1ca NW of LB slip in 2·5m, with 6 Y ⚓s (beware The Foot, spit drying 1·2m,

marked by ECM lt buoy; SE of Ferry Pier at Knight's Town (E end of the island) in 4m; in bay on the S side of Beginish Is in 3m.

**NAVIGATION** Wpt 51°56'·84N 10°20'·15W 147°/1M to Fort Pt lt. Appr the NE end of Valentia Is, either via;

- Doulus Bay, N of Beginish Is (avoid if swell is running). Clear Black Rks by ½ca then head for E end of Beginish Is immediately Reenard Pt opens to port of it. When Lamb Is and the N point of Beginish are about to open astern, alter course to keep them so till Reenard Point opens to the E of Church Is. Then steer to pass 50m E of Church Is to avoid Passage Rk (1₅) 1ca E of Is.
- Better ent, between Fort Pt and Beginish Is (easy access except in strong NW'lies). Beware Hbr Rk, 2·6m, 3ca SE of Fort Pt and 100m SW of ldg line and marked by ECM lt Bn.

For **Cahersiveen Marina** from Valentia Is start as early on the tide possible to cross the Caher Bar (buoyed WC, EC ,SH & PHMs), using the ldg lts/lines 019-199°, 100°-280°, 076°-256°, 053°-233°, 035°-215° and then keep to the middle of the river.

For appr S of Island via Portmagee chan see **Portmagee** overleaf for info on availability of the swing bridge across the chan.

**LIGHTS AND MARKS** See 5.3 and chartlet.

**R/T** Cahersiveen Marina VHF Ch 80.

**TELEPHONE** Knightstown HM (066) 9476124, 🖷 9476309; CG 9476109; ⊖ 7128540; Dr 9472121; Police 9472111; Ⓗ 9472100; Cahersiveen Marina ☎ 947 2777, 🖷 9472993, www.cahersiveenmarina.ie.

**FACILITIES** **Knight's Town**: 6 Y ⚓s; BY, ✗, ME, Kos, 🗑, R, Bar, ▢. Ferry/bus to Cahersiveen (2½M) for usual shops; EC Thurs. Bus to 🚃 (Tralee and Killarney), ✈ (Kerry, Shannon, Cork). **Cahersiveen Marina** (2M upriver): (min depth 2.5m in basin, 93 incl Ⓥ) €2, BH(14T), ME, El, Ch, Ⓔ, ✗, P & D, ▢, 🗑, Ⓑ, ✉, R, Bar.

## 5.30 DINGLE

Kerry 52°07'·14N 10°15'·48W ✿✿✿✿♒♒♒✿✿✿

**CHARTS** AC 2789, 2790; Imray C55, C56; Irish OS 70

**TIDES** +0540 Dover; ML 2·1m; Duration 0605

**Standard Port COBH (←)**

| Times | | | | Height (metres) | | | |
|---|---|---|---|---|---|---|---|
| High Water | | Low Water | | MHWS | MHWN | MLWN | MLWS |
| 0500 | 1100 | 0500 | 1100 | 4·1 | 3·2 | 1·3 | 0·4 |
| 1700 | 2300 | 1700 | 2300 | | | | |
| **Differences DINGLE** | | | | | | | |
| –0111 | –0041 | –0049 | –0119 | –0·1 | 0·0 | +0·3 | +0·4 |
| **SMERWICK HARBOUR** | | | | | | | |
| –0107 | –0027 | –0041 | –0121 | –0·3 | –0·4 | No data | |
| **FENIT PIER** (Tralee Bay) | | | | | | | |
| –0057 | –0017 | –0029 | –0109 | +0·5 | +0·2 | +0·3 | +0·1 |

**SHELTER** Excellent at marina (5m depth) in landlocked hbr. *See RMWG*. A busy fishing port. There are 4 Y ⚓s at **Kells Bay** (52°01'·6N 10°06'·3W), 8M SE of Dingle ent.

**NAVIGATION** WPT 52°06'·20N 10° 15'·48W, 360°/1·06M to lt Fl G 3s. Easy ent H24. Beware Crow Rk (dries 3·7m), 0·8M SW off Reenbeg Pt and rky ledge SW of Black Pt.

• **Castlemaine Hbr**, approx 15M E at the head of Dingle Bay, largely dries and should not be attempted without local knowledge or inspection at LW.

**LIGHTS AND MARKS** Eask Twr (195m, with fingerpost pointing E) is conspic 0·85M WSW of ent. Lt tr, Fl G 3s 20m 6M, on NE side of ent. Ent chan, dredged 2·6m, is marked by 5 SHM lt buoys and 3 PHM lt buoys, as chartlet. Ldg lts, both Oc 3s, (W ◇s on B poles) lead from astern 182° to hbr bkwtrs. Sectored lt Oc RWG 4s on W side of Main Pier.

**R/T** Ch **14** 16, but no calls required. Valentia Radio (Ch 24 28) will relay urgent messages to Dingle HM.

**TELEPHONE** (Code 066) HM 9151629; Coastguard (066) 9476109; ⊕ 7121480; Dr 9152225; Ⓗ 9151455; Police 9151522. All emergencies: 999 or 112.

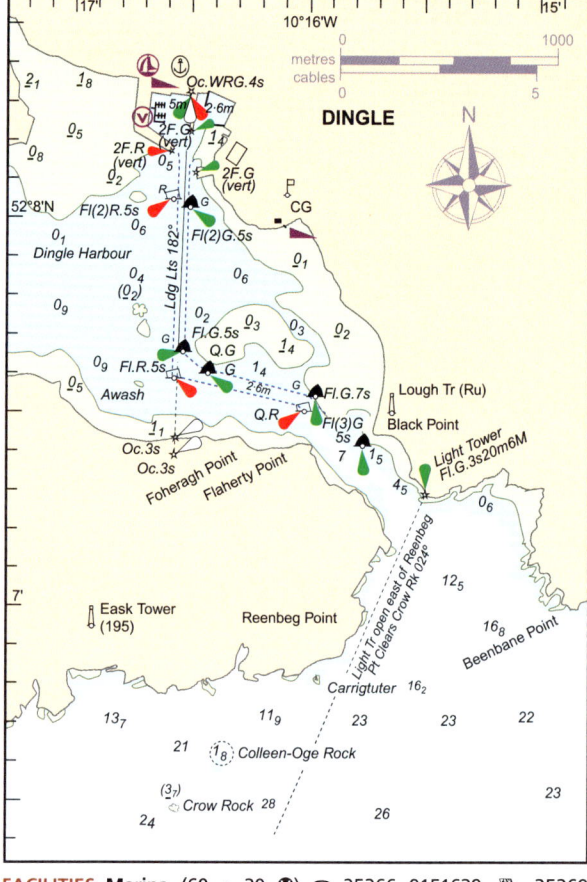

**FACILITIES Marina** (60 + 20 Ⓥ) ☎ 35366 9151629, 🖷 35369 9152542, www.dinglemarina.com, €1.80, D, Slip (launching €2.00), 🖻, ♿, C (hire). **Town** P (cans), Kos, ME, Ⓔ, Gas, Gaz, SM, ✉, R, Bar, 🛒, Ⓑ, ⇌ Tralee (by bus), ✈ (Kerry 30M).

### ANCHORAGE SW VALENTIA ISLAND

**PORTMAGEE**, Kerry, **51°53'·20N 10°22'·29W**. AC 2125. HW +0550 on Dover; ML 2·0m; Duration 0610; See 5.28. A safe ⚓ 2·5M E of Bray Head in Portmagee Sound between the mainland and Valentia Is. The ent to the Sound often has bad seas, but dangers are visible. Care required E of Reencaheragh Pt (S side) due rks either side. Deepest water is N of mid-chan. 6 Y ⚓s at 51°53'·3N 10°22'·5W (N side), or ⚓ off the pier (S side) in 5m, opposite Skelling Heritage Centre (well worth a visit). AB on pier is not recommended due to strong tides. Facilities: FW, 🛒, showers (at hotel), R, Bar, Kos. It is currently uncertain as to whether Swing road bridge 1ca E of pier can be opened for yachts; check with HM at Knight's Town (5.28) for present arrangement, if any.

### ANCHORAGE CLOSE W OF DINGLE BAY

**VENTRY** Kerry, **52°06·70N 10°20'·30W**. AC 2789, 2790. HW +0540 on Dover; ML 2·1m; Duration 0605; Use 5.29. Ent is 2M W of conspic Eask Tr. A pleasant hbr with easy ent 1M wide and good holding on hard sand; sheltered from SW to N winds, but open to swell from the SE, and in fresh W'lies prone to sharp squalls. Beware Reenvare Rks 1ca SE of Parkmore Pt; also a rky ridge 2·9m, on which seas break, extends 2·5ca SSE of Ballymore Pt. No lts. ⚓s in about 4m off Ventry Strand (✠ brg W, the village NE); or in 3m SW side of bay, 1ca N of pier; also 3 Y ⚓s. On N side 3 Y ⚓s off pier at Ventry village. Both piers access HW±3 for landing. Facilities: P, Slip, 🛒, Kos, Bar, R, ✉.

### ANCHORAGES BETWEEN THE BLASKETS AND KERRY HD

**SMERWICK HARBOUR**, Kerry, **52°13'·00N 10°24'·00W**. AC 2789. Tides 5.29. Adequate shelter in 1M wide bay, except from NW'ly when considerable swell runs in. Ent between The Three Sisters (150m hill) and Dunacapple Is to the NE. Beacon Fl.R.3s at pier end at Ballnagall Pt. ⚓s at: the W side close N or S of the Boat Hr in 3-10m; to the S, off Carrigveen Pt in 2·5m; or in N'lies at the bay in NE corner inside 10m line. Facilities at Ballynagall village on SE side: 4 Y ⚓s, pier (0·5m), limited 🛒, Bar, Bus.

**BRANDON BAY**, Kerry, **52°16'·10N 10°09'·92**W. AC 2739. Tides as Fenit 5.29. A 4M wide bay, very exposed to the N, but in moderate SW-W winds there is safe ⚓ in 6m close E of drying Brandon Pier, 2FG (vert). Cloghane Inlet in SW of Bay is not advised. Facilities at Brandon: limited 🛒, P (1M), ✉, R, Bar, bus.

**TRALEE BAY**, Kerry, **52°18'·00N 09°56'·00W**. AC 2739. HW –0612 on Dover; ML 2·6m; Duration 0605. See 5.29. Enter the bay passing 3M N of Magharee Islands. Pick up the W sector (W140°–152°) of Little Samphire Is lt, Fl WRG 5s 17m 16/13M; see 5.3 for sectors. Approach between Magharee Is and Mucklaghmore (30m high).

# 5.31  FENIT HARBOUR

Kerry **52°16'·20N 09°51'·61W** ✳✳✳🏊🏊🏊❀❀❀

**CHARTS** AC 2254, 2739; Imray C55; Irish OS 70

**TIDES** -0612 Dover; ML 2·6m; Duration 0605

**Standard Port COBH** (⟵)

| Times | | | | Height (metres) | | | |
|---|---|---|---|---|---|---|---|
| High Water | | Low Water | | MHWS | MHWN | MLWN | MLWS |
| 0500 | 1100 | 0500 | 1100 | 4·1 | 3·2 | 1·3 | 0·4 |
| 1700 | 2300 | 1700 | 2300 | | | | |
| Differences FENIT PIER (Tralee Bay) | | | | | | | |
| -0057 | -0017 | -0029 | -0109 | +0·5 | +0·2 | +0·3 | +0·1 |

**SHELTER** Good shelter in marina (2.7m depth), but a few berths exposed to SE'ly conditions.

**NAVIGATION**  Appr on 146° to WPT 52°16'·00N 09° 53'·00W, Little Samphire Is, conspic lt ho, Fl WRG 5s 17m 16/13M, thence 7ca E to Samphire Is; lt QR 15m 3M vis 242°–097°. Fenit Pier Hd 2 FR (vert) 12m 3M, vis 148°–058°. Easy ent H24.

**LIGHTS AND MARKS** See 5.3 and chartlet.

**R/T** Neptune (Tralee SC) VHF Ch 14 16. Port Manager: VHF Ch 16 **14 M** (0900-2100UT).

**TELEPHONE** (Code 066) Port Manager ☎ 7136231, 📠 7136473; ⊖ ☎ 7121480.

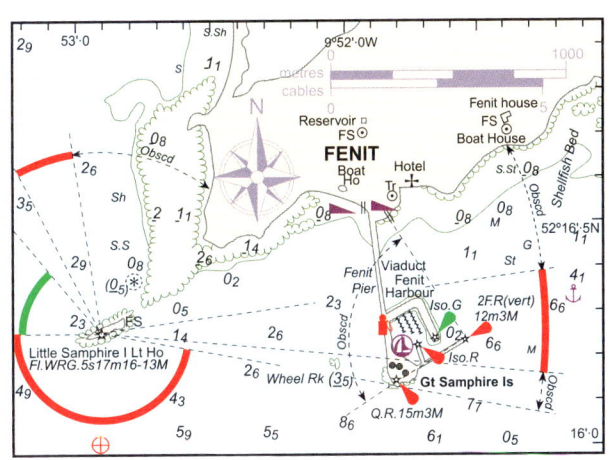

**FACILITIES Marina** (130 inc 15 Ⓥ; max LOA 25m, €1.60 min €16.00/craft), FW, ⛽, D, ▢, &; For ⚓s call Neptune (Tralee SC); **Village** Slip, C, P (cans), ME, 🍴, Bar, R, ✉, Ⓑ, ⇌ Tralee (by bus), ✈ (Kerry 30M).

# 5.32  SHANNON ESTUARY

Clare (N); Kerry and Limerick (S) **52°35'·00N 09°40'·00W**

**CHARTS** AC 1819, 1547, 1548, 1549, 1540; L. Derg 5080; L. Ree 5078. Imray C55. OS 63, 64. The ICC's Sailing Directions for S & W Ireland and/or Admiralty Irish Coast Pilot are essential.

**TIDES**

| HW at | HW Galway | HW Dover |
|---|---|---|
| Kilbaha & Carrigaholt | –0015 | +0605 |
| Tarbert Island | +0035 | –0530 |
| Foynes | +0050 | –0515 |
| Limerick | +0130 | –0435 |

At Limerick strong S-W winds increase the height and delay the times of HW; strong N-E winds do the opposite.

**SHELTER** The Shannon Estuary is 50M long (Loop Hd to Limerick). For boats on passage N/S the nearest ⚓ is Kilbaha Bay, 3M inside Loop Hd; it has ⚓s sheltered in winds from W to NE, but is exposed to swell and holding is poor. 6M further E, Carrigaholt Bay has ⚓s and good shelter from W'lies; ⚓ just N of the new quay, out of the tide. Kilrush Marina (5.33) with all facilities is 7M further E. From Kilcredaun Head in the W to the R Fergus ent (about 25M) there are ⚓s or ⚓s, protected from all but E winds, at Tarbert Is, Glin, Labasheeda, Killadysert (pontoon) and among the islands in the Fergus mouth. There is a pontoon off the YC S of Foynes Is and drying quays at Ballylongford Creek (Saleen), Knock and Clarecastle (S of Ennis, off chartlet). Yachts may enter Limerick Dock, but this is a commercial port with usual problems; major improvements planned.

**NAVIGATION** WPT 52°32'·50N 09°46'·90W, Ballybunnion NCM By VQ, 064°/4·2M to Tail of Beal Bar buoy WCM, Q (9) 15s. For notes on ent and tidal streams see 5.4. The ebb can reach 4kn. Ldg lts, Oc. 5s, 046·4° on Corlis Pt. The lower estuary between Kerry and Loop Heads is 9M wide, narrowing to 2M off Kilcredaun Pt.

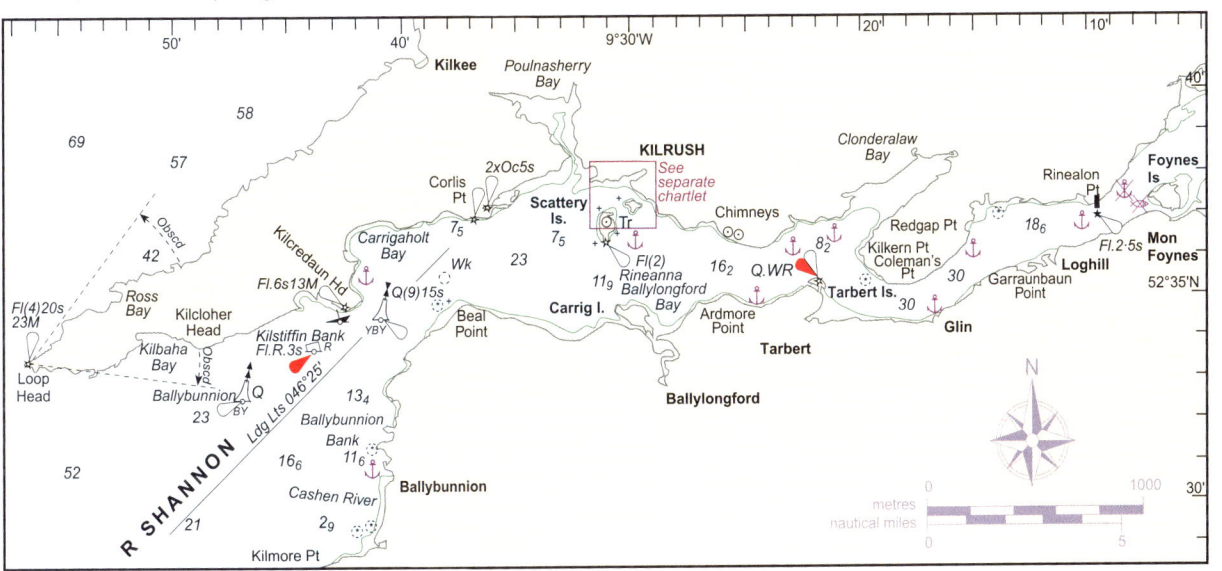

**SHANNON ESTUARY** *continued*

Here the chan is well buoyed in mid-stream and then follows the Kerry shore, S of Scattery Is. From Tarbert Is to Foynes Is the river narrows to less than 1M in places, before widening where the R Fergus joins from the N, abeam Shannon airport. Above this point the buoyed chan narrows and becomes shallower although there is a minimum of 2m at LWS. AC 1540 is essential for the final 15M stretch to Limerick.

**RIVER SHANNON** The Shannon, the longest navigable river in the UK or Ireland, is managed by Limerick Hbr Commissioners up to Limerick. Up-stream it effectively becomes an inland water-way; progress is restricted by locks and bridges. Info on navigation and facilities can be obtained from the Waterways Service, Dept of Art, Culture & the Gaeltacht, 51 St Stephen's Green, Dublin 2, ☎ 01-6613111; or from the Inland Waterways Association of Ireland, Kingston House, Ballinteer, Dublin 4, ☎ 01-983392; also from Tourist Offices and inland marinas.

**LIGHTS AND MARKS** See 5.3. There are QW (vert) aero hazard lts on tall chimneys at Money Pt power station 3M ESE of Kilrush. 2 chys at Tarbert Is are conspic (R lts).

**R/T** Foynes Ch 12 13 16 (occas). *Shannon Estuary Radio* Ch 12 13 16 (HO).

**FACILITIES** Marine facilities are available at several communities on the Shannon; M, P & D (cans), FW, ⛟, can be found at many villages. ⚓s are being laid at Labasheeda, Glin Pier (pontoon) and Foynes. E of Aughanish Is on S shore, R Deal is navigable 3M to Askeaton. Ent, marked by RW bn, is 8ca SE of Beeves Rk with 1m in buoyed chan. BY at Massey's Pier ☎ 069 73100, ☒ 392344, ⚓s, FW, C, CH, ⟶, D, Slip. Facilities at Foynes and Limerick include: **Foynes** Slip, L, AB, P & D (cans), FW, ☒, Ⓑ, Dr, ⛟, R, Bar; **Foynes YC** ☎ (069) 65261, AB (pontoon), Bar, R. **Limerick:** Hbr Commission ☎ (061) 315377; ⊖ ☎ 415366. **City** Slip, AB, L, FW, P & D (cans), Kos, Gas, Gaz, ME, El, Dr, Ⓗ, ☒, all usual city amenities, ⇌, ✈ (Shannon).

## 5.33 KILRUSH

Clare **52°37'·90N 09°29'·70W** ✸✸✸✿≋≋≋❀❀❀

**CHARTS** AC 1819, 1547; Imray C55; Irish OS 63

**TIDES** −0555 Dover; ML 2·6; Duration 0610

**Standard Port GALWAY (⟶)**

| Times | | | | Height (metres) | | | |
|---|---|---|---|---|---|---|---|
| High Water | | Low Water | | MHWS | MHWN | MLWN | MLWS |
| 1000 | 0500 | 0000 | 0600 | 5·1 | 3·9 | 2·0 | 0·6 |
| 2200 | 1700 | 1200 | 1800 | | | | |
| Differences KILRUSH | | | | | | | |
| −0006 | +0027 | +0057 | −0016 | −0·1 | −0·2 | −0·3 | −0·1 |

**SHELTER** Excellent in Kilrush Marina (2·7m), access via lock H24. Day ⚓ in lee of Scattery Is.

**NAVIGATION** WPT 52°37'·18N 09°31'·64W, 063°/1M to SWM buoy. From seaward usual appr is N of Scattery Is (conspic Round Twr, 26m); beware Baurnahard Spit and Carrigillaun to the N. Coming down-river between Hog Is and mainland, beware Wolf Rk.

**LIGHTS AND MARKS** SWM By L Fl 10s marks ent to buoyed chan (dredged 2·5m), with ldg lts 355°, both Oc 3s, to lock. Fl G 3s 2M, S side of lock.

**R/T** Marina Ch 80. Kilrush Ch 16, 12.

**TELEPHONE** (Code 06590) Marina 52072 Mobile 086 2313870; Lock 52155; MRCC (066) 9476109; Coast/Cliff Rescue Service 51004; ⊖ (061) 415366; Weather (061) 62677; Police 51017; Dr (065) 51581 also 51470.

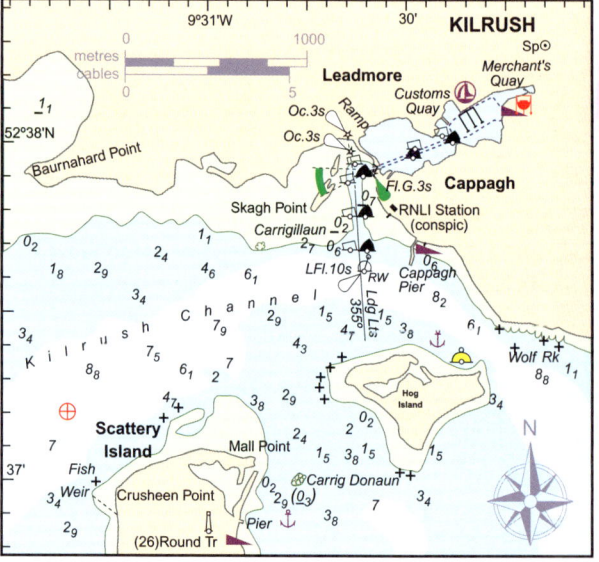

**FACILITIES** **Marina** (120+50) ☎ 52072, ☒ 51692, Lock 52155, €1.90, (minimum €16.00/craft), D, P (cans), Slip, BY, CH, Gas, Gaz, Kos, BH (45 ton), C (26 ton), ME, El, ▣, ⛟; **Town** El, CH, ⛟, R, Bar, Dr, ☒, Ⓑ, ⇌ (bus to Limerick), ✈ (Shannon).

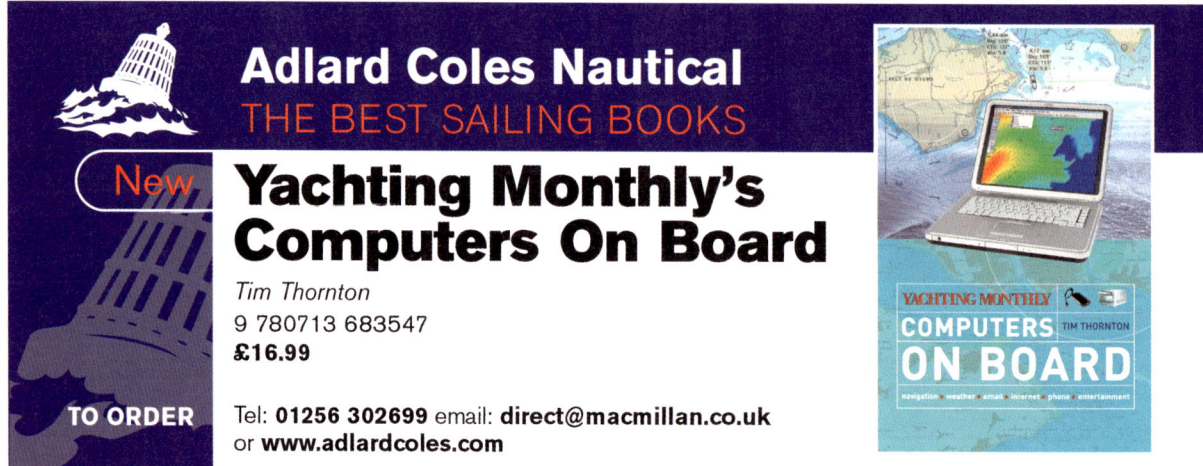

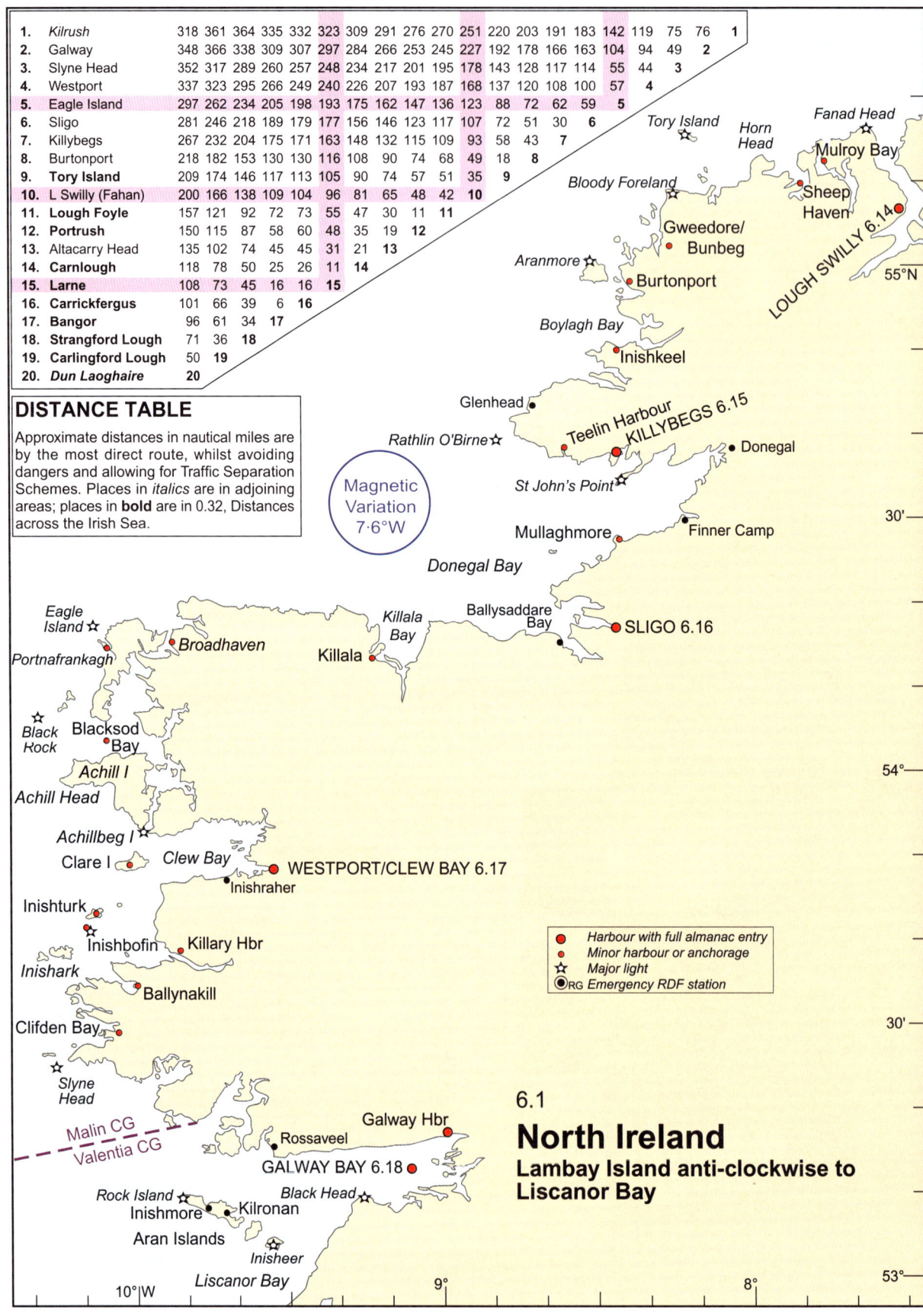

| | | | | | | | | | | | | | | | | | | | | |
|---|---|---|---|---|---|---|---|---|---|---|---|---|---|---|---|---|---|---|---|---|
| **1.** | *Kilrush* | 318 | 361 | 364 | 335 | 332 | 323 | 309 | 291 | 276 | 270 | 251 | 220 | 203 | 191 | 183 | 142 | 119 | 75 | 76 | **1** |
| **2.** | Galway | 348 | 366 | 338 | 309 | 307 | 297 | 284 | 266 | 253 | 245 | 227 | 192 | 178 | 166 | 163 | 104 | 94 | 49 | **2** | |
| **3.** | Slyne Head | 352 | 317 | 289 | 260 | 257 | 248 | 234 | 217 | 201 | 195 | 178 | 143 | 129 | 117 | 114 | 55 | 44 | **3** | | |
| **4.** | Westport | 337 | 323 | 295 | 266 | 249 | 240 | 226 | 207 | 193 | 187 | 168 | 137 | 120 | 108 | 100 | 57 | **4** | | | |
| **5.** | Eagle Island | 297 | 262 | 234 | 205 | 198 | 193 | 175 | 162 | 147 | 136 | 123 | 88 | 72 | 62 | 59 | **5** | | | | |
| **6.** | Sligo | 281 | 246 | 218 | 189 | 179 | 177 | 156 | 146 | 123 | 117 | 107 | 72 | 51 | 30 | **6** | | | | | |
| **7.** | Killybegs | 267 | 232 | 204 | 175 | 171 | 163 | 148 | 132 | 115 | 109 | 93 | 58 | 43 | **7** | | | | | | |
| **8.** | Burtonport | 218 | 182 | 153 | 130 | 130 | 116 | 108 | 90 | 74 | 68 | 49 | 18 | **8** | | | | | | | |
| **9.** | **Tory Island** | 209 | 174 | 146 | 117 | 113 | 105 | 90 | 74 | 57 | 51 | 35 | **9** | | | | | | | | |
| **10.** | L Swilly (Fahan) | 200 | 166 | 138 | 109 | 104 | 96 | 81 | 65 | 48 | 42 | **10** | | | | | | | | | |
| **11.** | **Lough Foyle** | 157 | 121 | 92 | 72 | 73 | 55 | 47 | 30 | 11 | **11** | | | | | | | | | | |
| **12.** | **Portrush** | 150 | 115 | 87 | 58 | 60 | 48 | 35 | 19 | **12** | | | | | | | | | | | |
| **13.** | Altacarry Head | 135 | 102 | 74 | 45 | 45 | 31 | 21 | **13** | | | | | | | | | | | | |
| **14.** | **Carnlough** | 118 | 78 | 50 | 25 | 26 | 11 | **14** | | | | | | | | | | | | | |
| **15.** | **Larne** | 108 | 73 | 45 | 16 | 16 | **15** | | | | | | | | | | | | | | |
| **16.** | **Carrickfergus** | 101 | 66 | 39 | 6 | **16** | | | | | | | | | | | | | | | |
| **17.** | **Bangor** | 96 | 61 | 34 | **17** | | | | | | | | | | | | | | | | |
| **18.** | **Strangford Lough** | 71 | 36 | **18** | | | | | | | | | | | | | | | | | |
| **19.** | **Carlingford Lough** | 50 | **19** | | | | | | | | | | | | | | | | | | |
| **20.** | *Dun Laoghaire* | **20** | | | | | | | | | | | | | | | | | | | |

## DISTANCE TABLE

Approximate distances in nautical miles are by the most direct route, whilst avoiding dangers and allowing for Traffic Separation Schemes. Places in *italics* are in adjoining areas; places in **bold** are in 0.32, Distances across the Irish Sea.

Magnetic Variation 7·6°W

Tory Island

Horn Head

Fanad Head

Mulroy Bay

Bloody Foreland

Sheep Haven

LOUGH SWILLY 6.14

Gweedore/ Bunbeg

55°N

Aranmore

Burtonport

Boylagh Bay

Inishkeel

Glenhead

Rathlin O'Birne

Teelin Harbour

KILLYBEGS 6.15

Donegal

St John's Point

30'

Mullaghmore

Finner Camp

Donegal Bay

Ballysaddare Bay

Killala Bay

Eagle Island

Broadhaven

Killala

SLIGO 6.16

Portnafrankagh

Black Rock

Blacksod Bay

Achill I

Achill Head

54°

Achillbeg I

Clare I

Clew Bay

WESTPORT/CLEW BAY 6.17

Inishraher

Inishturk

Inishbofin

Killary Hbr

Inishshark

Ballynakill

Clifden Bay

30'

Slyne Head

| | |
|---|---|
| ● | Harbour with full almanac entry |
| • | Minor harbour or anchorage |
| ☆ | Major light |
| ◉RG | Emergency RDF station |

Malin CG

Valentia CG

Galway Hbr

Rossaveel

## 6.1

# North Ireland

**Lambay Island anti-clockwise to Liscanor Bay**

GALWAY BAY 6.18

Rock Island

Inishmore

Kilronan

Black Head

Aran Islands

Inisheer

Liscanor Bay

10°|W

9°

8°

53°

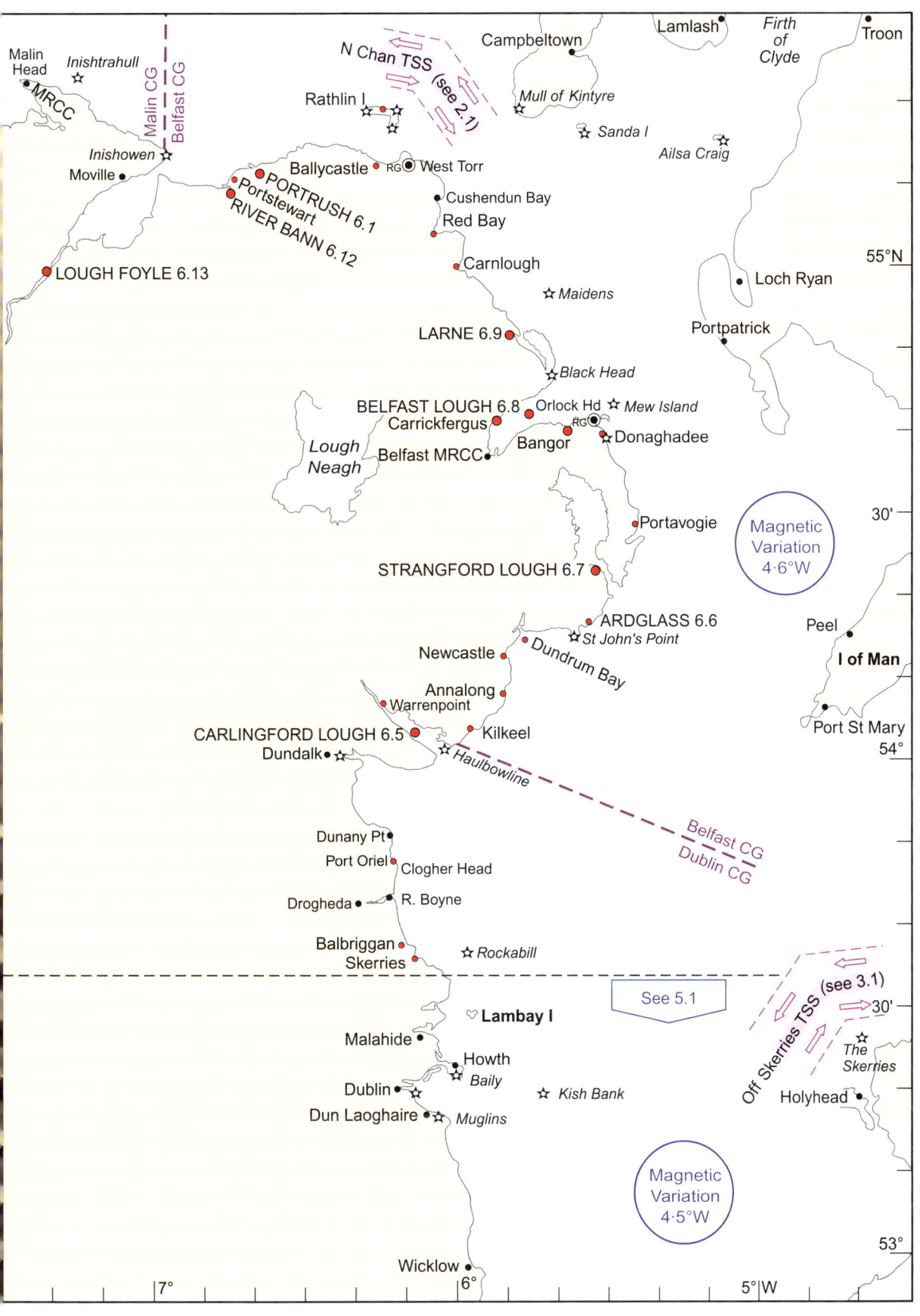

Malin Head
Inishtrahull
MRCC

N Chan TSS (see 2.1)

Campbeltown
Lamlash
Firth of Clyde
Troon

Mull of Kintyre

Malin CG
Belfast CG

Rathlin I

Sanda I

Ailsa Craig

Moville
Inishowen

Ballycastle
RG West Torr
PORTRUSH 6.1
Portstewart
RIVER BANN 6.12

Cushendun Bay
Red Bay

Carnlough

Loch Ryan

55°N

LOUGH FOYLE 6.13

Maidens

LARNE 6.9

Portpatrick

Black Head

BELFAST LOUGH 6.8
Carrickfergus
Lough Neagh
Belfast MRCC
Bangor

Orlock Hd
RG
Mew Island
Donaghadee

Portavogie

Magnetic Variation 4·6°W

30'

STRANGFORD LOUGH 6.7

ARDGLASS 6.6
St John's Point

Peel

I of Man

Newcastle
Dundrum Bay

Annalong
Warrenpoint

CARLINGFORD LOUGH 6.5
Dundalk

Kilkeel
Haulbowline

Port St Mary

54°

Belfast CG
Dublin CG

Dunany Pt
Port Oriel
Clogher Head
Drogheda
R. Boyne

Balbriggan
Skerries

Rockabill

See 5.1

Off Skerries TSS (see 3.1)

30'

Lambay I

Malahide

Howth
Baily

Dublin
Dun Laoghaire
Muglins

Kish Bank

The Skerries

Holyhead

Magnetic Variation 4·5°W

53°

Wicklow

7°

6°

5° W

## 6.2 NORTH IRELAND TIDAL STREAMS

The tidal arrows (with no rates shown) off the S and W coasts of Ireland are printed by kind permission of the Irish Cruising Club, to whom the Editor is indebted. They have been found accurate, but should be used with caution.

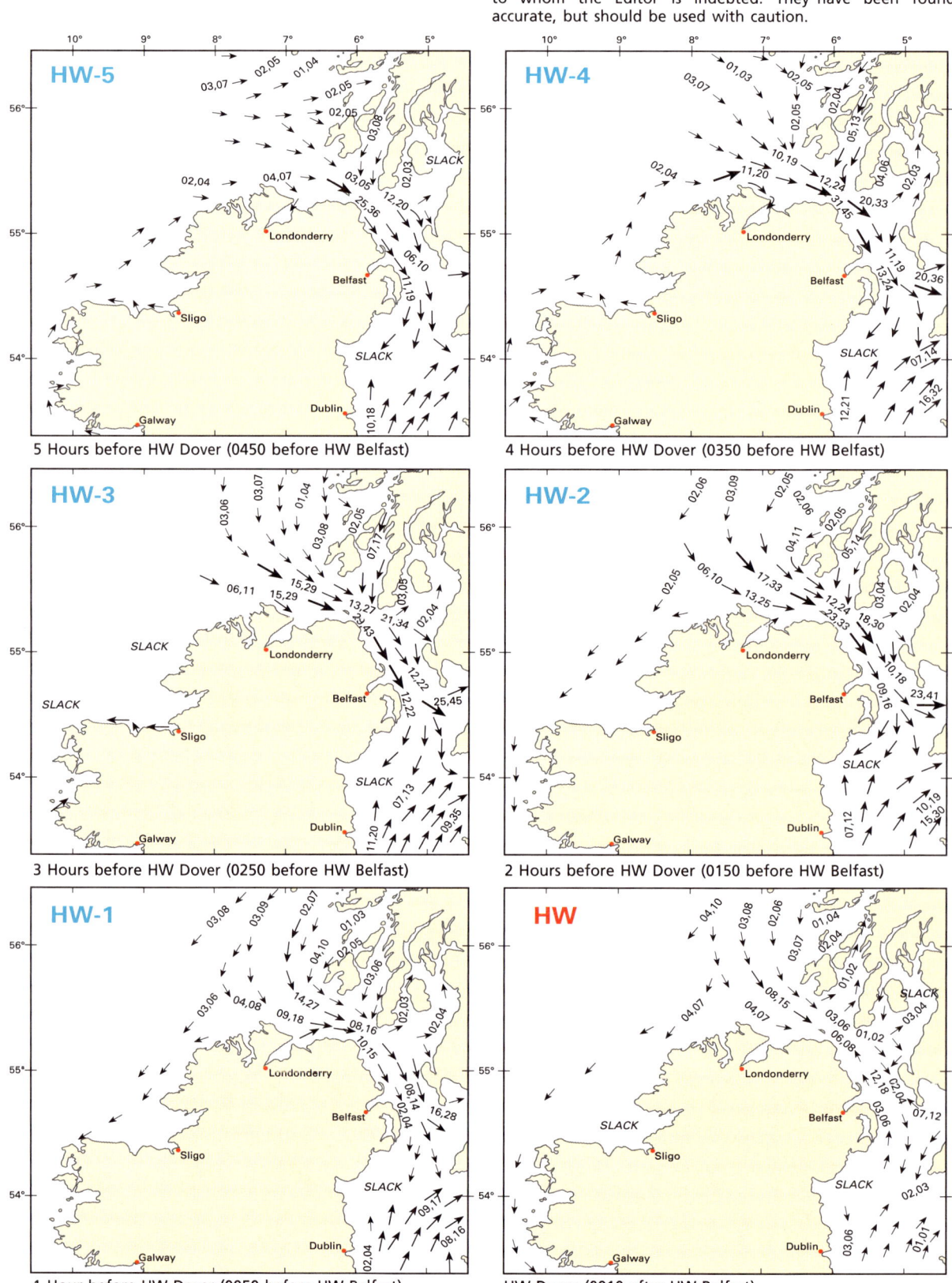

5 Hours before HW Dover (0450 before HW Belfast)

4 Hours before HW Dover (0350 before HW Belfast)

3 Hours before HW Dover (0250 before HW Belfast)

2 Hours before HW Dover (0150 before HW Belfast)

1 Hour before HW Dover (0050 before HW Belfast)

HW Dover (0010 after HW Belfast)

Rathlin Island 6.10     SW Scotland 2.2
Mull of Kintyre 2.10    South Ireland 5.2
North Irish Sea 3.2

The tidal arrows (with no rates shown) off the S and W coasts of Ireland are printed by kind permission of the Irish Cruising Club, to whom the Editor is indebted. They have been found accurate, but should be used with caution.

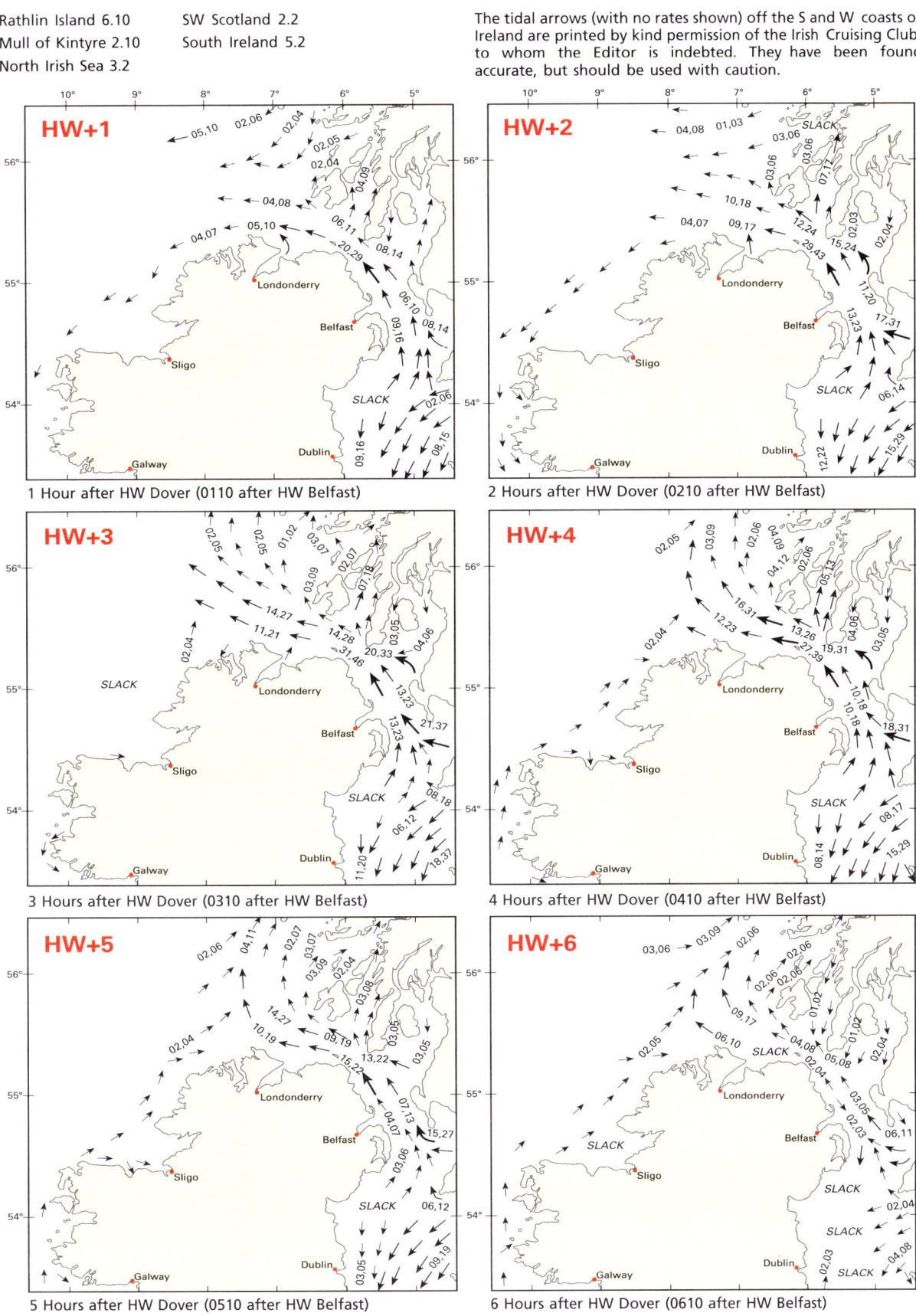

1 Hour after HW Dover (0110 after HW Belfast)

2 Hours after HW Dover (0210 after HW Belfast)

3 Hours after HW Dover (0310 after HW Belfast)

4 Hours after HW Dover (0410 after HW Belfast)

5 Hours after HW Dover (0510 after HW Belfast)

6 Hours after HW Dover (0610 after HW Belfast)

N Ireland

## 6.3 LIGHTS, BUOYS AND WAYPOINTS

**Bold** print = light with a nominal range of 15M or more. CAPITALS = place or feature. *CAPITAL ITALICS* = light-vessel, light float or Lanby. *Italics* = Fog signal. ***Bold italics*** = Racon. See 0.2 for Abbreviations.

### LAMBAY ISLAND TO DONAGHADEE

**Rockabill** ☆ 53°35'·82N 06°00'·25W Fl WR 12s 45m **W22M, R18M;** W twr, B band; vis: 178°-W-329°-R-178°.
Cross Rock ⌐ Fl R 10s; 53°35'·30N 06°06'·55W.

### DROGHEDA and DUNDALK

**Drogheda, Port Approach** Dir lt 53°43'·30N 06°14'·73W WRG 10m **W19M, R15M,** G15M; vis: 268°-FG- 269°-Al WG-269·5°-FW-270·5°-Al WR-271°-FR-272°; H24.
Dunany ⌐ Fl R 3s; 53°53'·56N 06°09'·47W.
Imogene ⌐ Fl (2) R 10s; 53°57'·41N 06°07'·02W.
**Dundalk, Pile Light** ☆ 53°58'·56N 06°17'·70W Fl WR 15s 10m **W21M, R18M;** W Ho; vis: 124°-W-151°-R-284°-W-313°-R-124°. Fog Det lt VQ 7m, vis: when brg 358°; *Horn (3) 60s*.

### CARLINGFORD LOUGH and NEWRY RIVER

Carlingford ⌐ L Fl 10s; 53°58'·76N 06°01'·06W.
Hellyhunter ⌐ Q (6) + L Fl 15s; *Racon;* 54°00'·35N 06°02'·10W
No. 1 ⌐ Fl (3) G 6s; 54°00'·73N 06°03'·41W.
No. 4 ⌐ Fl R 4s; 54°01'·08N 06°04'·07W.
No. 6 ⌐ Fl R 2s; 54°01'·24N 06°04'·39W.
No. 5 ⌐ Fl R 2s; 54°01'·38N 06°04'·50W.
**Haulbowline** ☆ 54°01'·19N 06°04'·74W Fl (3) 10s 32m **17M;** Gy twr; reserve lt 15M; Fog Det lt VQ 26m; vis: 330°. Turning lt ⌐ FR 21m 9M; same twr; vis: 196°-208°; *Horn 30s*.
Carlingford Marina Ent. ⌐ Q R 5m 1M; 54°03'·11N 06°11'·38W.
Warren Pt Bkwtr Hd ⌐ Fl G 3s 6m 3M; 54°05'·79N 06°15'·26W.

### KILKEEL and ANNALONG

Kilkeel Pier Hd ⌐ Fl WR 2s 8m 8M; vis: R296°-W313°-017°; 54°03'·46N 05°59'·30W.
Annalong E Bkwtr Hd ⌐ Oc WRG 5s 8m 9M; twr; vis: 204°-G-249°-W-309°-R-024°; 54°06'·51N 05°53'·73W.

### DUNDRUM BAY and ARDGLASS

**St John's Point** ☆ 54°13'·61N 05°39'·30W Q (2) 7·5s 37m **25M;** B twr, Y bands; H24 when horn is operating. **Auxiliary Light** ☆ Fl WR 3s 14m **W15M,** R11M; same twr, vis: 064°-W-078°-R-shore; Fog Det lt VQ 14m vis: 270°; *Horn (2) 60s*.
Ardglass S Pier Hd ⌐ Fl R 3s 10m 5M; 54°15'·67N 05°36'·16W.

### STRANGFORD LOUGH

Strangford ⌐ L Fl 10s; 54°18'·61N 05°28'·67W.
Bar Pladdy ⌐ Q (6) + L Fl 15s; 54°19'·34N 05°30'·51W.
Angus Rock ⌐ Fl R 5s 15m 6M; 54°19'·84N 05°31'·56W.

### S ROCK, PORTAVOGIE, BALLYWATER and DONAGHADEE

Butter Pladdy ⌐ Q (3) 10s; 54°22'·45N 05°25'·74W.
*SOUTH ROCK* ⌐ 54°24'·49N 05°22'·02W Fl (3) R 30s 12m **20M**. R hull and lt twr, W Mast, *Horn (3) 45s, Racon (T) 13M*.
Plough Rock ⌐ 54°27'·40N 05°25'·12W Fl R 3s.
Skulmartin ⌐ L Fl 10s; *Whis;* 54°31'·82N 05°24'·80W.
**Donaghadee** ☆, S Pier Hd 54°38'·70N 05°31'·86W Iso WR 4s 17m **W18M,** R14M; W twr; vis: shore-W-326°-R-shore; *Siren 12s*.

### DONAGHADEE TO RATHLIN ISLAND

Governor Rocks ⌐ Fl R 3s; 54°39'·36N 05°31'·99W.
Deputy Reefs ⌐ Fl G 2s; 54°39'·51N 05°31'·94W.
Foreland Spit ⌐ Fl R 6s; 54°39'·63N 05°32'·31W.

### BELFAST LOUGH, BANGOR and CARRICKFERGUS

**Mew I** ☆ NE end 54°41'·91N 05°30'·79W Fl (4) 30s 37m; B twr, W band; *Racon (O) 14M*.

Briggs ⌐ 54°41'·19N 05°35'·72W Fl (2) R 10s.
Bangor N Pier Hd ⌐ Iso R 12s 9m14M; 54°40'·03N 05°40'·34W.
Belfast Fairway ⌐ LFl10s; *Horn (1) 16s; Racon(G);* 54°41'·71N 05°46'·24W.
Carrickfergus E Pier Hd ⌐ Fl G 7·5s 5m 4M; G col; 54°42'·63N 05°48'·37W.
Marina E Bkwtr Hd ⌐ QG 8m 3M; 54°42'·58N 05°48'·69W.
**Black Hd** ☆ 54°45'·99N 05°41'·33W Fl 3s 45m **27M;** W 8-sided twr.
N Hunter Rock ⌐ Q; 54°53'·04N 05°45'·13W.
S Hunter Rock ⌐ VQ (6) + L Fl 10s; 54°52'·69N 05°45'·22W.

### LARNE, CARNLOUGH and RED BAY

Larne No. 1 ⌐ QG; 54°51'·68N 05°47'·67W.
Larne No. 3 ⌐ Fl (2) G 6s; 54°51'·27N 05°47'·64W.
**Chaine Twr** ☆ Iso WR 5s 23m **16M;** Gy twr; vis: 230°-W-240°-240°-R-shore; 54°51'·27N 05°47'·90W.
Larne No. 2 ⌐ Fl R 3s; 54°51'·07N 05°47'·55W.
**East Maiden** ⌐ Fl (3) 20s 29m **24M;** W twr, B band; *Racon (M) 11-21M*. Auxiliary lt Fl R 5s 15m 8M; 54°55'·74N 05°43'·65W; same twr; vis:142°-182° over Russel and Highland Rks.
Carnlough Hbr N Pier ⌐ Fl G 3s 4m 5M; 54°59'·59N 05°59'·29W.
Red Bay Pier ⌐ Fl 3s 10m 5M; 55°03'·93N 06°03'·21W.

### RATHLIN ISLAND TO INISHTRAHULL
#### RATHLIN ISLAND

Rue Pt ⌐ Fl (2) 5s 16m 14M; W 8-sided twr, B bands; 55°15'·53N 06°11'·47W.
Drake Wreck ⌐ 55°17'·00N 06°12'·48W Q (6) + L Fl 15s.
**Altacarry Head Rathlin East** ☆ 55°18'·06N 06°10'·30W Fl (4) 20s 74m **26M;** W twr, B band; vis: 110°-006° and 036°-058°; *Racon (G) 15-27M*.
**Rathlin W** 0·5M NE of Bull Pt ⌐ 55°18'·05N 06°16'·82W Fl R 5s 62m **22M;** W twr, lantern at base; vis: 015°-225°; H24.

### PORTRUSH, RIVER BANN and COLERAINE

N Pier Hd ⌐ Fl R 3s 6m 3M; vis: 220°-160°; 55°12'·34N 06°39'·58W.
Portstewart Point ⌐ Oc R 10s 21m 5M; R □ hut; vis: 040°-220°; 55°11'·33N 06°43'·26W.
River Bann W Mole ⌐ Fl G 5s 4m 2M; Gy mast; vis: 170°-000°; 56°10'·25N 06°46'·45W.

### LOUGH FOYLE APPROACHES

Foyle ⌐ L Fl 10s; 55°15'·32N 06°52'·60W.
Tuns ⌐ Fl R 3s; 55°14'·00N 06°53'·46W.
**Inishowen Dunagree Pt** ☆ 55°13'·56N 06°55'·75W Fl (2) WRG 10s 28m **W18M,** R14M, G14M; W twr, 2 B bands; vis: 197°-G-211°-W-249°-R-000°. Fog Det lt VQ 16m vis: 270°.
**Inishtrahull** ☆ 55°25'·86N 07°14'·62W Fl (3) 15s 59m **19M;** W twr; obscd 256°-261° within 3M; *Racon (T) 24M 060°-310°*.

### INISHTRAHULL TO BLOODY FORELAND
#### LOUGH SWILLY

**Fanad Head** ☆ 55°16'·57N 07°37'·91W Fl (5) WR 20s 39m **W18M,** R14M; W twr; vis 100°-R-110°-W-313°-R-345°-W-100°.
Swilly More ⌐ Fl G 3s; 55°15'·12N 07°35'·79W.
Dunree ⌐ Fl (2) WR 5s 46m W12M, R9M; vis: 320°-R-328°-W-183°-R-196°; 55°11'·88N 07°33'·25W.
Colpagh ⌐ Fl R 6s; 55°10'·42N 07°31'·55W.
White Strand Rocks ⌐ Fl R 10s; 55°09'·06N 07°29'·95W.

### MULROY BAY, SHEEPHAVEN and TORY SOUND

Limeburner ⌐ Q Fl; 55°18'·54N 07°48'·40W.
Ravedy Is ⌐ Fl 3s 9m 3M; twr; vis: 177°-357°; 55°15'·14N 07°46'·90W.
Downies Bay Pier Hd ⌐ Fl R 3s 5m 2M; vis: 283° through N till obsc by Downies Pt; 55°11'·35N 07°50'·51W.
**Tory Island** ☆ 55°16'·36N 08°14'·97W Fl (4) 30s 40m **27M;** B twr, W band; vis: 302°-277°; *Racon (M) 12-23M;* H24.
Bloody Foreland ⌐ Fl WG 7·5s 14m W6M, G4M; vis: 062°-W-232°-G-062°; 55°09'·51N 08°17'·03W.

## WGS84 DATUM
*Plot waypoints on chart before use*

### BLOODY FORELAND TO RATHLIN O'BIRNE

#### GOLA and OWEY SOUND

Glassagh. Ldg lts 137·4°. Front, Oc 8s 12m 3M; 55°06'·83N 08°18'·97W. Rear, 46m from front, Oc 8s 17m 3M; synch.

Inishsirrer, NW end ⚲ Fl 3·7s 20m 4M; W ☐ twr vis: 083°-263°; 55°07'·40N 08°20'·93W.

Gola I s Ldg lts 171·2°. Front, Oc 3s 9m 2M; W Bn, B band; 55°05'·11N 08°21'·07W. Rear, 86m from front, Oc 3s 13m 2M; B Bn, W band; synch with front.

Gola Spit ⚲ Fl R 3s; 55°04'·50N 08°21'·02W.

Middle Rock ⚲ Fl (2) R 6s; 55°04'·91N 08°20'·39W.

Rinnalea Point ⚲ 55°02'·59N 08°23'·72W Fl 7·5s 19m 9M; ☐ twr; vis: 132°-167°.

**Aranmore, Rinrawros Pt** ☆ 55°00'·90N 08°33'·66W Fl (2) 20s 71m **27M**; W twr; obsc by land about 234°-007° and about 013°. Auxiliary lt Fl R 3s 61m 13M, same twr; vis: 203°-234°.

#### S SOUND OF ARAN and RUTLAND S CHANNEL

Illancrone I ⚲ Fl 5s 7m 6M; W☐ twr; 54°56'·27N 08°28'·57W.

Wyon Point ⚲ Fl (2) WRG 10s 8m W6M, R3M; W☐ twr; vis: shore-G-021°-W-042°-R-121°-W-150°-R-shore; 54°56'·51N 08°27'·54W.

Turk Rocks ⚲ 54°57'·30N 08°28'·18W Fl G 5s 6m 2M; G ☐ twr.

**Rathlin O'Birne, W side** ☆ 54°39'·80N 08°49'·94W Fl WR 15s 35m **W18M**, R14M; W twr; vis: 195°-R-307°-W-195°; *Racon (O) 13M, vis 284°-203°*.

### RATHLIN O'BIRNE TO EAGLE ISLAND

#### DONEGAL BAY and KILLYBEGS

Bullockmore ⚲ Qk Fl (9) 15s; 54°33'·98N 08°30'·14W.

**Rotten I** ☆ 54°36'·97N 08°26'·41W Fl WR 4s 20m **W15M**, R11M; W twr; vis: W255°- R008°- W039°-208°.

Killybegs Outer ⚲ VQ (6) + L Fl 10s; 54°37'·92N 08°29'·15W.

#### SLIGO

Wheat Rock ⚲ Q (6) + LFl 15s; 54°18'·84N 08°39'·10W.

Black Rock ⚲ Fl WR 5s 24m 10/8M; vis: 130°-W-107°-R-130° (R sector covers Wheat and Seal rks); W twr, B band; 54°18'·45N 08°37'·06W.

Lower Rosses, ( N of Cullaun Bwee) ⚲ Fl (2) WRG 10s 8m 13 -10M; W hut on piles; vis: G over Bungar bank-066°-W-070°-R over Drumcliff bar; shown H24; 54°19'·72N 08°34'·41W.

Bungar Bank ⚲ Q; 54°19'·09N 08°36'·76W.

#### BROAD HAVEN BAY

Gubacashel Point ⚲ Iso WR 4s 27m W17M, R12M; 110°-R-133°-W-355°-021° W twr; 54°16'·06N 09°53'·33W.

### EAGLE ISLAND TO SLYNE HEAD

**Eagle Is, W end** ☆ 54°17'·02N 10°05'·56W Fl (3) 15s 67m **19M**; W twr.

**Black Rock** ☆ 54°04'·03N 10°19'·25W Fl WR 12s 86m **W20M, R16M**; W twr; vis: 276°-W-212°-R-276°.

### BLACKSOD BAY, ACHILL SOUND and ACHILL ISLAND

Carrigeenmore ⚲ Q(3) 10s 3M; 54°06'·56N 10°03'·4W.

Blacksod ⚲ Q (3) 10s; 54°05'·89N 10°03'·01W.

Achill I Ridge Point ⚲ Fl 5s 21m 5M; 54°01'·78N 09°58'·50W.

Achill Sound ⚲ QR; R Bn; 53°56'·05N 09°55'·30W.

Achillbeg E lt Bn ⚲ Fl R 2s 5m; R ☐ twr; 53°52'·11N 09°56'·60W.

### CLEW BAY and WESTPORT

**Achillbeg I S Point** ☆ 53°51'·51N 09°56'·85W Fl WR 5s 56m **W18M, R18M, R15M**; W☐ twr on ☐ building; vis: 262°-R-281°-W-342°-R-060°-W- 092°-R(intens)-099°-W-118°.

Cloughcormick ⚲ Q (9) 15s; 53°50'·56N 09°43'·20W.

Dorinish ▲ Fl G 3s; 53°49'·48N 09°40'·50W.

Inishgort S Point ⚲ L Fl 10s 11m 10M; W twr. Shown H24; 53°49'·61N 09°40'·25W.

Westport Appr ⚲ Fl 3s; 53°47'·98N 09°34'·33W.

### INISHBOFIN and CLIFDEN BAY

Inishlyon Lyon Head ⚲ Fl WR 7·5s 13m W7M, R4M; W post; vis: 036°-W-058°-R-184°-W-325°-R-036°; 53°36'·74N 10°09'·56W.

**Slyne Head,** North twr, Illaunamid ☆ 53°23'·99N 10°14'·06W Fl (2) 15s 35m **19M**; B twr.

### SLYNE HEAD TO BLACK HEAD

Inishnee ⚲ Fl (2) WRG 10s 9m W5M, R3M, G3M; W col on W☐base; vis: 314°-G-017°-W-030°-R-080°-W-194°; 53°22'·75N 09°54'·53W.

Croaghnakeela Is ⚲ Fl 3·7s 7m 5M; W col; vis: 034°-045°, 218°-286°, 311°-325°; 53°19'·40N 09°58'·21W.

### GALWAY BAY and INISHMORE

**Eeragh, Rock Is** ☆ 53°08'·90N 09°51'·40W; Fl 15s 35m **18M**; W twr, two B bands; vis: 297°-262°.

Killeany ▲ Fl G 3s; 53°07'·26N 09°38'·24W.

**Straw Is** ☆ 53°07'·06N 09°37'·85W Fl (2) 5s 11m **15M**; W twr.

### CASHLA BAY, SPIDDLE and GALWAY

Cannon Rock ▲ Fl G 5s; 53°14'·09N 09°34'·35W.

Lion Pt Dir lt Iso WRG 5s 6m (H24), G6M, W8M, R6M,(night), G2M, W3M, R2M(day); vis: 005°-G- 008·5°-W-011·5°-R-015°; 53°15'·84N 09°33'·95W.

Spiddle Pier Hd ⚲ Fl WRG 3·5s 11m W6M, R4M, G4M; Y col; vis: 102°-G-282°-W-024°-R-066°; 53°14'·42N 09°18'·55W.

Margaretta Shoal ▲ Fl G 3s; *Whis*; 53°13'·68N 09°05'·99W.

Black Rock ⚲ Fl R 3s; 53°14'·00N 09°06'·55W.

Tawin Shoals ▲ Fl (3) G 10s; 53°14'·30N 09°04'·26W.

Mutton Is ⚲ Fl (2)R 6s; 53°15'·07N 09°02'·93W.

Peter Rock ⚲ 53°15'·17N 09°01'·09W.

Black Hd ⚲ Fl WR 5s 20m W11M, R8M, W ☐ twr; vis: 045°- R268°-276°; 53°09'·26N 09°15'·83W.

Finnis Rock ⚲ Q (3) 10s; 53°02'·82N 09°29'·14W.

**Inisheer** ☆ 53°02'·78N 09°31'·58W Iso WR 12s 34m **W20M, R16M**; vis: 225°-W(partially vis >7M)-231°, 231°-W-245°-R-269°-W-115°; *Racon (K) 13M*.

---

## 6.4 PASSAGE INFORMATION

For all Irish waters the Sailing Directions published by the Irish Cruising Club are strongly recommended, and particularly on the N and W coasts, where other information is scarce. They are published in 2 volumes: *E and N coasts of Ireland* which runs anti-clockwise from Carnsore Pt to Bloody Foreland, and *S and W coasts of Ireland* which goes clockwise.

### CROSSING THE IRISH SEA

(AC 1123, 1121, 1411) Passages across the Irish Sea can range from the fairly long haul from Land's End to Cork (140M), to the relatively short hop from Mull of Kintyre to Torr Pt (11M). Such distances are deceptive, because the average cruising yacht needs to depart from and arrive at a reasonably secure hbr. ▶ *In the North Chan strong tidal streams can cause heavy overfalls.* ◀ Thus each passage needs to be treated on its merits. See 0.29 for distances across the Irish Sea.

Many yachts use the Land's End/Cork route on their way to (and from) the delightful cruising ground along the S coast of Ireland, see 5.4. Penzance Bay, or one of the Scilly Is ⚓s, make a convenient place from which to leave, with good lights to assist departure.

▶ *Although the Celtic Sea is exposed to the Atlantic, there are no dangers on passage and the tidal streams are weak.* ◀ A landfall between Ballycotton and Old Hd of Kinsale (both have good lights) presents no offlying dangers, and in poor vis decreasing soundings indicate approach to land. There is a likelihood, outward bound under sail, that the boat will be on the wind – a possible benefit on the return passage. If however the wind serves, and if it is intended to cruise along the southern coast, a landfall at the Fastnet with arrival at (say) Baltimore will place the yacht more to windward, for little extra distance.

From Land's End the other likely destination is Dun Laoghaire. A stop at (say) Milford Haven enables the skipper to select the best time for passing the Smalls or Bishops (see 3.23) and roughly divides the total passage into two equal parts. From S Bishop onwards there are the options of making the short crossing to Tuskar Rk and going N inside the banks (theoretically a good idea in strong W winds), or of keeping to seaward. ▶ *But in bad weather the area off Tuskar is best avoided; apart from the Traffic Separation Scheme, the tide is strong at sp and the sea can be very rough.* ◀

The ferry route Holyhead/Dun Laoghaire is another typical crossing, and is relatively straightforward with easy landfalls either end. ▶ *The tide runs hard round Anglesey at sp, so departure just before slack water minimises the set N or S.* ◀ Beware also the TSS off The Skerries.

The Isle of Man is a good centre for cruising in the Irish Sea, and its hbrs provide convenient staging points whether bound N/S or E/W.

## CROSSING TO SCOTLAND

(AC 2198, 2199, 2724) Between Scotland and Northern Ireland there are several possible routes, but much depends on weather and tide. ▶ *Time of departure must take full advantage of the stream, and avoid tide races and overfalls (see 2.26). Conditions can change quickly, so a flexible plan is needed.* ◀

▶ *From Belfast Lough ent, the passage distance to Mull of Kintyre is about 35M and, with a departure at HW Dover (also local HW) providing at least 6 hrs of N-going tides, fair winds make it possible to get past the Mull or Sanda Is on one tide. But to be more confident of reaching Port Ellen or Gigha Island a departure from Carnlough or Red Bay at HW makes a shorter passage with better stream advantage. The inshore side of the TSS coincides with the outer limit of the race S and SW off the Mull of Kintyre; this occurs between HW Dover +0430 and +0610 when a local S-going stream opposes the main N-going stream.* ◀

For information on submarine exercises/activity see Subfacts.

## LAMBAY ISLAND TO FAIR HEAD

(AC 44, 2093, 2198/9) The coast is fairly steep-to except in larger bays, particularly Dundalk. ▶ *Streams offshore run up to 2·5kn as far as Rockabill, but are weaker further N until approaching Belfast Lough.* ◀ Lambay Island is private, and steep-to except on W side, where there can be overfalls. Skerries Islands (Colt, Shenick's and St Patrick's) are 1M E and SE of Red Island, to E of Skerries hbr. Shenick's Island is connected to shore at LW. Pass between Colt and St Patrick's Islands, but the latter has offliers 3ca to S. Rockabill, two steep-to rks with lt ho, is 2·5M E of St Patrick's Island.

NE'wds from Carlingford Lough, after rounding Hellyhunter SCM, there are no offshore dangers until Strangford Lough where ▶ *the tidal cycle is approx 3 hours later than in the N Channel. Flood runs for 6 hrs from HW Dover –0345 (HW Belfast –0330), with a maximum rate of 7.5kn at Rue Point.* The strong flow flattens the sea in onshore winds and entrance can be made in strong winds. *Ebb runs for 6 hours from HW Dover +0215 (HW Belfast +0230), max rate 7.5kn, E of Angus Rk. If entering against ebb use West Channel with care. Smoothest water near Bar Paddy Buoy when leaving.* ◀

There is a marina at Ardglass. N of Strangford keep 5ca off Ballyquintin Pt. 3M to NE are Butter Pladdy Rks; keep to E of these. 2M further N is South Rk, with disused lt ho, part of group

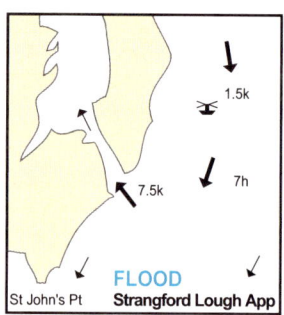 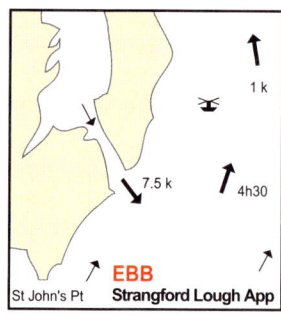

FLOOD  Strangford Lough App    EBB  Strangford Lough App

of rks to be avoided in poor vis or bad weather by closing South Rk lt float. In good vis pass inshore of South Rk, between it and North Rks (AC 2156), rounding South Ridge PHM buoy.

Three routes lead into Belfast Lough: **a.** E of Mew Is, but beware Ram Race (to the N on the ebb, and the S on the flood). **b.** Copeland Sound, between Mew Is and Copeland Is, is passable but not recommended; **c.** Donaghadee Sound is buoyed and a good short cut for yachts. ▶ *Here the stream runs SSE from HW Belfast +0530 and NW from HW Belfast –0030, 4.5kn max. An eddy extends S to Ballyferris Pt, and about 1M offshore.* ◀ For Donaghadee, see AC 3709.

N from Belfast L, Black Hd is clean. Pass E of Muck Is, which is steep-to. Hunter Rk (0·8m), 2·5M NE of Larne, is marked by N & S cardinals. 2M further N are the Maidens, two dangerous groups of rks extending 2·5M N/S; E Maiden is lit.

Glenarm Marina provides good shelter for yachts and is useful for yachts on passage to the W.coasts of Scotland or Ireland . Other anchs in offshore winds are at Red Bay 5M further N, and in Cushendun B, 5M NNW of Garron Pt. All provide useful anch on passage to/from the Clyde or Western Is. Fair Hd is a bold 190m headland, steep-to all round, but with extensive overfalls in Rathlin Sound.

## FAIR HEAD TO BLOODY FORELAND

(AC 2723) This is a good cruising area, under the lee of land in SW'lies, but very exposed to NW or N. Beware fishing boats and nets in many places and the North Channel TSS.

▶ *A fair tide is essential through Rathlin Sound, as sp rates reach 6kn, with dangerous overfalls. The main stream sets W from HW Dover + 0030 for 5 hrs, and E from HW Dover –0530 for 5 hrs. The worst overfalls are S of Rue Pt (Slough-na-more) from HW Dover +0130 to +0230, and it is best to enter W-bound at the end of this period, on the last of fair tide. E-bound enter the Sound at HW Dover –0500. Close inshore between Fair Hd and Carrick-mannanon Rk a counter eddy runs W from HW Dover –0030, and an E-going eddy runs from HW Dover +0200 to +0300.* ◀ Pass outside Carrickmannanon Rk (0·3m) and Sheep Is. There are small hbrs in Church Bay (Rathlin Is) and at Ballycastle.

Proceeding to Portrush, use Skerries Sound in good weather. ▶ *Enter Lough Foyle by either the North Chan W of The Tuns, or S chan passing 2ca N of Magilligan Pt and allowing for set towards The Tuns on the ebb (up to 3·5kn).* ◀

Tor Rks, Inishtrahull and Garvan Is lie NE and E of Malin Hd. In bad weather it is best to pass at least 3M N of Tor Rks. Inishtrahull is lit and about 1M long; rks extend N about 3ca into Tor Sound. ▶ *Inishtrahull Sound, between Inishtrahull and Garvan Is, is exposed; tidal streams up to 4kn sp can raise a dangerous sea with no warning. Stream also sets hard through Garvan Isles, S of which Garvan Sound can be passed safely in daylight avoiding two sunken rks, one 1½ca NE of Rossnabarton, and the other 5ca NW. The main stream runs W for only 3hrs, from HW Galway –0500 to –0200. W of Malin Hd a W-going eddy starts at HW Galway +0400, and an E-going one at HW Galway –0300.* ◀

**W of Malin Hd the direction of buoyage changes to E.** From Malin Hd SW to Dunaff Hd, at ent to Lough Swilly, keep 5ca offshore. Trawbreaga Lough (AC 2697) gives shelter, but is shallow, and sea can break on bar; only approach when no swell, and at half flood. Ent to L Swilly is clear except for Swilly Rks off the W shore, SSE of Fanad Hd.

W from Lough Swilly the coast is very foul. Beware Limeburner Rk (2m), 6·8M WNW of Fanad Hd. Mulroy Bay has good anchs but needs accurate pilotage, as in *ICC SDs*.

Between Mulroy B and Sheephaven there is an inshore passage S of Frenchman's Rk, and between Guill Rks & Carnabollion, safe in good weather; otherwise keep 1M offshore. Sheep Haven B is easy to enter between Rinnafaghla Pt and Horn Hd, and has good anchs except in strong NW or N winds. Beware Wherryman Rks, dry 1·5m, 1ca off E shore.

Between Horn Hd and Bloody Foreland (AC 2752) are three low-lying islands: Inishbeg, Inishdooey and Inishbofin. The latter is almost part of the mainland; it has a temp anch on S side and a more sheltered anch on NE side in Toberglassan B. 6M offshore is Tory Is (lt, fog sig, RC) with rks for 5ca off SW side. Temp anch in good weather in Camusmore B. ▶ *In Tory Sound the stream runs W from HW Galway +0230, and E from HW Galway –0530, sp rates 2kn.* ◀

### BLOODY FORELAND TO EAGLE ISLAND

(AC 2725) Off low-lying Bloody Foreland (lt) there is often heavy swell. The coast and islands 15M SW to Aran Is give good cruising (AC 1883). An inshore passage avoids offlying dangers: Buniver and Brinlack shoals, which can break; Bullogconnell 1M NW of Gola Is; and Stag Rks 2M NNW of Owey Is. Anchs include Bunbeg and Gweedore Hbr, and Cruit B which has easier access. Behind Aran Is are several good anchs. Use N ent, since S one is shallow (AC 2792). Rutland N Chan is main appr to Burtonport.

Boylagh B has shoals and rks N of Roaninish Is. Connell Rk (0·3m) is 1M N of Church Pool, a good anch, best approached from Dawros Hd 4·5M to W. On S side of Glen B a temp anch (but not in W or NW winds) is just E of Rinmeasa Pt. Rathlin O'Birne Is has steps E side; anch SE of them 100m offshore. Sound is 5ca wide; hold Is side to clear rks off Malin Beg Hd.

In Donegal B (AC 2702) beware uncharted rks W of Teelin, a good natural hbr but exposed to S/SW swell. Killybegs has better shelter and is always accessible. Good shelter with fair access in Donegal Hbr (AC 2715). Good anch or ⚓ via YC at Mullaghmore in fair weather; sea state is calm with winds from SE through S to NW. Inishmurray is worth a visit in good weather, anch off S side. There are shoals close E and NE of the Is, and Bomore Rks 1·5M to N. Keep well clear of coast S to Sligo in onshore winds, and watch for lobster pots.

Killala B has temp anch 1M S of Kilcummin Hd, on W side. Proceeding to Killala beware St Patrick's Rks. Ent has ldg lts and marks, but bar is dangerous in strong NE winds.

The coast W to Broadhaven is inhospitable. Only Belderg and Portacloy give a little shelter. Stag Rks are steep-to and high. Broadhaven (AC 2703) is good anch and refuge, but in N/NW gales sea can break in ent. In approaches beware Slugga Rk on E side with offlier, and Monastery Rk (0·3m) on S side.

### EAGLE ISLAND TO SLYNE HEAD

(AC 2420) This coast has many inlets, some sheltered. ▶ *Streams are weak offshore.* ◀ There are few lights. Keep 5ca off Erris Hd, and further in bad weather. Unless calm, keep seaward of Eagle Is (lt) where there is race to N. Frenchport (AC 2703) is good temp anch except in strong W winds. Inishkea Is (AC 2704) can be visited in good weather; anch N or S of Rusheen Is. On passage keep 5ca W of Inishkea to avoid bad seas if wind over tide. The sound off Mullett Peninsula is clear, but for Pluddany Rk 6ca E of Inishkea N.

Blacksod B (AC 2704) has easy ent (possible at night) and good shelter. In the approaches Black Rk (lt) has rks up to 1·25M SW. From N, in good weather, there is chan between Duvillaun Beg and Gaghta Is, but in W gales beware breakers 1M SE of Duvillaun More.

Rough water is likely off impressive Achill Hd. Achill Sound (AC 2667) is restricted by cables 11m high at swing bridge. ▶ *Anchs each end of Sound, but the stream runs strongly.* ◀

Clare Is has Two Fathom Rk (3·4m) 5ca off NW coast, and Calliaghcrom Rk 5ca to the N; anch on NE side. In Clew Bay Newport and Westport (AC 2667, 2057) need detailed pilotage directions. S of Clare Is beware Meemore Shoal 1·5M W of Roonagh Hd. 2M further W is the isolated rk Mweelaun. The islands of Caher, Ballybeg, Inishturk (with anch on E side) and Inishdalla have few hidden dangers, but the coast to the E must be given a berth of 1·5M even in calm weather; in strong winds seas break much further offshore.

Killary B (AC 2706) and Little Killary both have good anchs in magnificent scenery. Consult sailing directions, and only approach in reasonable weather and good vis.

Ballynakill Hbr (AC 2706), easily entered either side of Freaghillaun South, has excellent shelter; Tully mountain is conspic to N. Beware Mullaghadrina and Ship Rk in N chan. Anch in Fahy, Derryinver or Barnaderg B. There is anch on S side of Inishbofin (lt), but difficult access/exit in strong SW wind or swell. Rks and breakers exist E of Inishbofin and S of Inishshark; see AC 2707 for clearing lines. Lecky Rks lie 1M SSE of Davillaun. Carrickmahoy is a very dangerous rk (1·9m) between Inishbofin and Cleggan Pt.

Cleggan B is moderate anch, open to NW but easy access. High Is Sound is usual coasting route, not Friar Is Sound or Aughrus Passage. Clifden B (AC 2708) has offlying dangers with breakers; enter 3ca S of Carrickrana Bn and anch off Drinagh Pt, in Clifden Hbr or Ardbear B.

Slyne Hd Lt Ho marks SW end of the rocks and islets stretching 2M WSW from coast. ▶ *Here the stream turns N at HW Galway –0320, and S at HW Galway +0300. It runs 3kn at sp, and in bad weather causes a dangerous race; keep 2M offshore.* ◀ Seas break on Barret Shoals, 3M NW of Slyne Hd.

### SLYNE HEAD TO LISCANNOR BAY

(AC 2173) In good visibility the Connemara coast (AC 2709, 2096) and Aran Islands (AC 3339) give excellent cruising. But there are many rks, and few navigational marks. Between Slyne Hd and Roundstone B are many offlying dangers. If coasting, keep well seaward of Skerd Rks. A conspic twr (24m) on Golan Head is a key feature. Going E the better hbrs are Roundstone B, Cashel B, Killeany B, Greatman B and Cashla B. Kilronan (Killeany B) on Inishmore is only reasonable hbr in Aran Islands, but is exposed in E winds. Disused lt ho on centre of island is conspic.

Normal approach to Galway B is through N Sound or S Sound. N Sound is 4M wide from Eagle Rk and other dangers off Lettermullan shore, to banks on S side which break in strong winds. S Sound is 3M wide, with no dangers except Finnis Rk (0·4m) 5ca SE of Inisheer. The other channels are Gregory Sound, 1M wide between Inishmore and Inishmaan, and Foul Sound between Inishmaan and Inisheer. The latter has one danger, Pipe Rk and the reef inshore of it, extending 3ca NW of Inisheer.

The N side of Galway Bay is exposed, with no shelter. Galway is a commercial port, with possible marina plans. 3M SE, New Hbr (AC 1984) is a more pleasant anch with moorings off Galway Bay SC. Westward to Black Hd there are many bays and inlets, often poorly marked, but providing shelter and exploration. The coast SW to Liscannor Bay is devoid of shelter. O'Brien's Twr is conspic just N of the 199m high Cliffs of Moher.

## Special notes for Ireland: See 5.5.

### MINOR HARBOURS AND ANCHORAGES TO THE NORTH WEST OF LAMBAY ISLAND

**SKERRIES**, Dublin, **53°35'·09N 06°06'·49W**. AC 633. Tides as Balbriggan, 6.5. E & SE of Red Island (a peninsula) lie Colt, Shenick's and St Patrick's Is, the latter foul to S and SW. Inshore passage between Colt and St Patrick's Is uses transit/brg as on chart to clear dangers. Good shelter and holding in 3m at Skerries Bay, W of Red Is. Appr from E or NE outside PHM buoy, Fl R 10s, off Red Is. ⌇ WNW of pier, Oc R 6s 7m 7M, vis 103°-154°; clear of moorings. Most facilities; Skerries SC ☎ 1-849 1233, Slip (HW±3). Rockabill Lt, Fl WR 12s 45m 22/18M, is conspic 2·4M ExN of St Patrick's Is.

**BALBRIGGAN**, Dublin, **53°36'·76N 06°10'·84W**. AC 44, 1468. Tides see 6.5. Good shelter in small hbr, dries about 0̲·9m, access approx HW ±2. Hbr unattractive, mainly FV's. Appr on SW, to open the outer hbr which is entered on SE; thence to inner hbr and AB on SE quay. Beware shoaling on both sides of outer hbr. Lt, Fl (3) WRG 20s 12m 13/10M, conspic W tr on E bkwtr head, vis 159°-G193°-W-288°-R-305°. Facilities: FW, D (by tanker from Skerries), Gas, Slip (HW±2), R, Bar, ▒.

**PORT ORIEL**, Louth, **53°47'·94N 06°13'·37W**. AC 44. Tides see 6.5 (Dunany Pt). Good shelter, except in strong NW'lies, in small new fishing harbour. Appr from NE on ldg marks 180°; Pier Hd Lt FR 5s. AB on pier in 4m or dry out in inner hbr. HM ☎ 087 2628777. D by tanker, ▒ in Clogher Hd village (1·2M).

## 6.5 CARLINGFORD LOUGH

Louth/Down **54°01'·25N 06°04'·30W** ✿✿♒♒♒ ✿✿✿

**CHARTS** AC 44, 2800, 5621; Imray C62; Irish OS 29, 36

**TIDES** Cranfield Pt +0025 and Warrenpoint +0035 Dover; ML 2·9; Duration Cranfield Pt 0615, Warrenpoint 0540

**Standard Port DUBLIN (NORTH WALL) (←)**

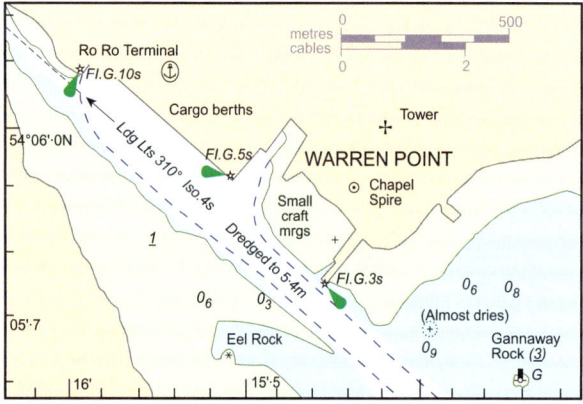

| Times | | | | Height (metres) | | | |
|---|---|---|---|---|---|---|---|
| High Water | | Low Water | | MHWS | MHWN | MLWN | MLWS |
| 0000 | 0700 | 0000 | 0500 | 4·1 | 3·4 | 1·5 | 0·7 |
| 1200 | 1900 | 1200 | 1700 | | | | |
| **Differences CRANFIELD POINT** | | | | | | | |
| −0027 | −0011 | +0005 | −0010 | +0·7 | +0·9 | +0·3 | +0·2 |
| **WARRENPOINT** | | | | | | | |
| −0020 | −0010 | +0025 | +0035 | +1·0 | +0·7 | +0·2 | 0·0 |
| **NEWRY (VICTORIA LOCK)** | | | | | | | |
| −0005 | −0015 | +0045 | Dries | +1·2 | +0·9 | +0·1 | Dries |
| **DUNDALK (SOLDIERS POINT)** | | | | | | | |
| −0010 | −0010 | 0000 | +0045 | +1·0 | +0·8 | +0·1 | −0·1 |
| **DUNANY POINT** | | | | | | | |
| −0028 | −0018 | −0008 | −0006 | +0·7 | +0·9 | No data | |
| **RIVER BOYNE BAR** | | | | | | | |
| −0005 | 0000 | +0020 | +0030 | +0·4 | +0·3 | −0·1 | −0·2 |
| **BALBRIGGAN** | | | | | | | |
| −0021 | −0015 | +0010 | +0002 | +0·3 | +0·2 | No data | |

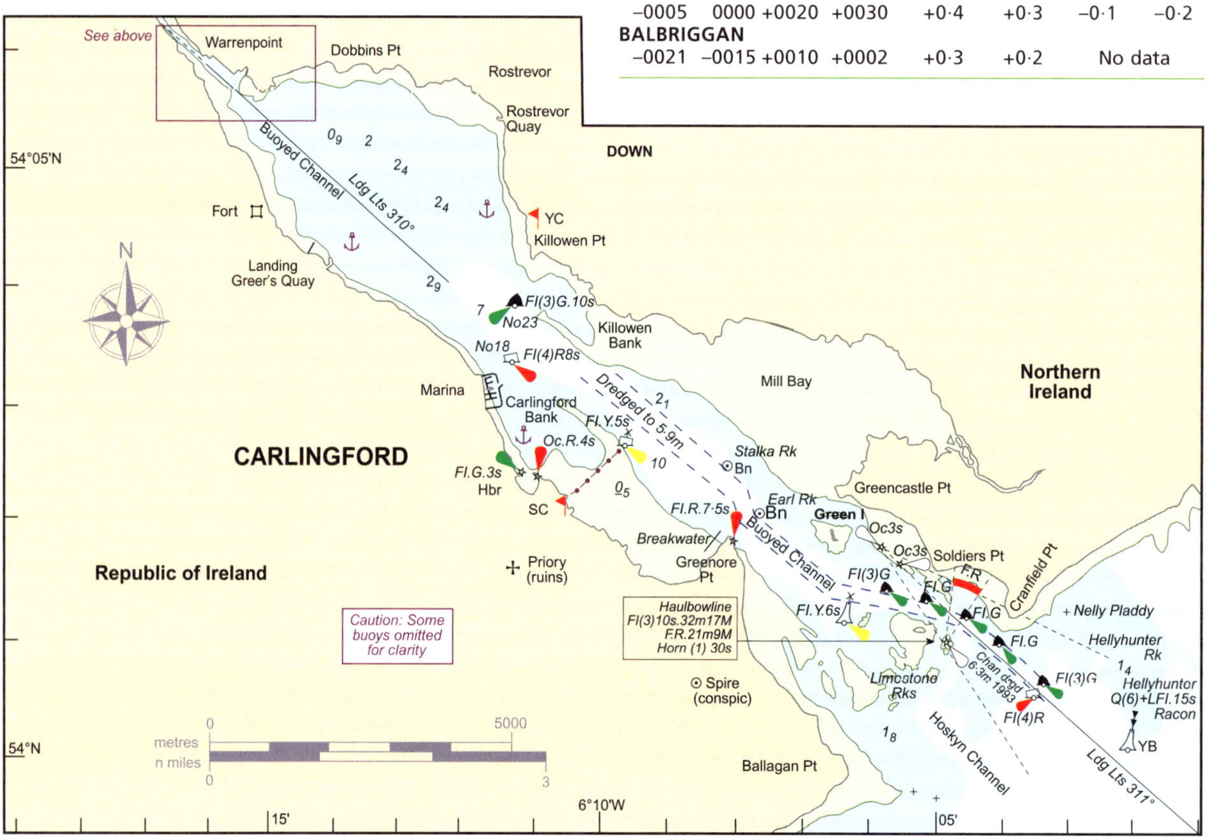

**N Ireland**

**SHELTER Carlingford Marina** protected on S side by sunken barge; depths 1·4m–3·5m. Visitors should check depth of berth offered by marina against depth drawn. Appr from N with Nos 18 and 23 buoys in transit astern 012°, to clear the tail of Carlingford Bank (dries) and beware of marine farms in vicinity.

**Carlingford Hbr** (dries 2·2m), AB at piers.

**Warrenpoint** has pontoons on NW side of bkwtr (Fl G 3s); access dredged 1·1m. ⚓s clockwise from ent include: at Greenore Pt, between SW end of quay and bkwtr, in 3m clear of commercial tfc; off Greer's Quay in 2m; off Rostrevor Quay, Killowen Pt (YC) and off derelict pier at Greencastle Pt (beware rks). Limited space may be available for short-stay visiting craft in the mussel fishing complex (approx £15/night). Call at least 24 hours before arrival.

**NAVIGATION** WPT 54°00'·09N 06°02'·00W, (2½ ca S of Hellyhunter SCM lt buoy) 311°/1M to first chan buoys.

- The main chan is Carlingford Cut (6·3m), about 3ca SW of Cranfield Pt, and passing 2ca NE of Haulbowline lt ho. Drying rks and shoals obstruct most of the ent.
- Small craft should at all times keep clear of commercial shipping in the narrow dredged channel.
- The NE bank is **Northern Ireland**, SW bank is **Republic of Ireland**. Craft may be stopped by Naval vessels.
- The lough becomes choppy in S'ly winds: due to the funnelling effect of the mountains NW winds cause a worse sea state within the lough than outside it.
- The ent is impassable in strong on-shore winds.
- Tides run up to 5kn off Greenore Pt and entry is impracticable against the ebb.
- Beware sudden squalls and waterspouts.
- Extensive shellfish beds along the NE side of the lough and the head is shallow.

**LIGHTS AND MARKS** Haulbowline Fl (3) 10s 32m 17M; granite tr; also turning lt FR 21m 9M, vis 196°-208°, horn 30s. Ldg lts 310°26': both Oc 3s 7/12m 11M, vis 295°-325°; R △ front, ▽ rear, on framework trs. Greenore Pier Fl R 7·5s 10m 5M. Newry R: Ldg lts 310°, both Iso 4s 5/15m 2M, stone columns. Channel from Green ls to Warren Pt marked by lit lateral buoys.

**R/T** Greenore (*Ferry Greenore*) Ch 12 16 (HJ). Carlingford marina Ch M 16. Warrenpoint Ch 12 16 (H24); call Ch 12 at By No. 23 to enter dredged chan. Dundalk Ch 14 16 (HW±3).

**TELEPHONE** (Code Greenore/Carlingford 042; Warrenpoint 028). MRCC (01) 6620922/3 or (02891) 463933; Irish ⊖: Dundalk (042) 34114; Marinecall 09068 969655; Dr (042) 73110; Ⓗ Newry (028) 3026 5511, Dundalk (042) 34701; Police (042) 9373102, (028) 4172 2222.

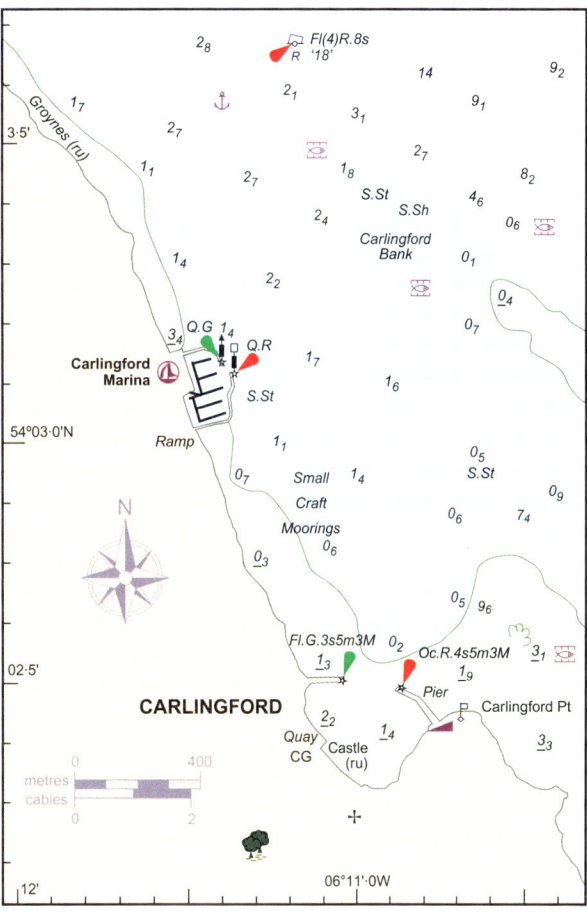

**FACILITIES**
**Carlingford Marina** ☎ 937 3073, mob 0872 321567, ▣ 937 3075. 290 inc ⓥ Wi-fi + @, €2.60 (min€17/craft), short stay <5hrs€12.50/craft, D (0900-2100), C, CH, BH (50T), ME ☎ 0872 301319, Rigger ☎ (048)44 828882, Divers, Slip, ▣, Bar, R. **Carlingford YC** ☎ (041) 685 1951, Slip, Bar, M, FW.
**Village** P (cans), ▤, R, Bar, Ⓑ, ✉. **Hbr** AB, Slip, ME, El, ✗, Kos, Gas.
**Warrenpoint** HM ☎ (02841) 752878, ▣ (02841) 773962; AB, M (but no access at LW), FW, P, D, ✉ also at Rostrevor, Ⓑ also Dundalk, ⇌ (Dundalk, Newry), ✈ (Dublin).

---

**MINOR HARBOURS BETWEEN CARLINGFORD LOUGH AND ST JOHN'S POINT**

**KILKEEL**, Down, **54°03'·47N 05°59'·26W**. AC 44, 2800. HW +0015 on Dover; ML 2·9m; Duration 0620. See 6.6. Inner basin is completely sheltered, but gets crowded by FVs; depth off quays approx 1m. Secure in inner basin and see HM. There are drying banks both sides of ent chan and SW gales cause a sandbank right across ent. This is dredged or slowly eroded in E winds. S bkwtr lt Fl WR 2s 8m 8M, 296°-R-313°-W-017°, storm sigs. Meeney's pier (N bkwtr) Fl G 3s 6m 2M. VHF Ch **12** 14 16 (Mon-Fri: 0900-2000). HM ☎ (028 417) 62287; Facilities: FW on quay, BY (between fish market and dock), El, ME, ✗, Slip. **Town** (⅜M) Bar, ✉, R, ▤, Gas, ▣.

**ANNALONG HBR**, Down, **54°06'·50N 05°53'·65W**. AC 44, 5621. Tides as Kilkeel, see 6.6. Slight silting rep't 2006. Entry HW ±2. Excellent shelter in small drying hbr, dredged to 1·5m 80m beyond pier with 30m pontoon (£10/craft), FW. Appr in W sector of S bkwtr lt, Oc WRG 5s 8m 9M, vis 204°-G-249°-W-309°-R-024°. Hug N side of the bkwtr to avoid rky shore to stbd. Surge gate at hbr ent may be closed in SE winds (3R lts vert shown). IPTS shown at ent. HM ☎ mob 07739 527036 Facilities: ▤, Bar, ✉.

**DUNDRUM BAY**, Down. AC 44. Tides see 6.6. This 8M wide bay to the W of St John's Pt is shoal to 5ca offshore and unsafe in onshore winds. The small drying hbr at **Newcastle** (54°11'·8N 05°53'·0W) is for occas use in fair weather. HM ☎ (02843) 722804, mob 07803 832515. **Dundrum Hbr (54°14'·2N 05°49'·4W)** No longer used by commercial tfc, provides ⚓ in 2m for shoal draft; the bar carries about 0·3m. A steep sea can run at the bar in onshore winds. HW Dundrum is approx that of HW Liverpool; see also 6.6 Newcastle. *The Irish Cruising Club's Sailing Directions* are essential for the 1M long, buoyed appr chan. 3 unlit DZ buoys offshore are part of the Ballykinler firing range, 2M E of hbr; R flag/lts indicate range active.

## 6.6 ARDGLASS

Down **54°15′·63N 05°35′·96W** ✿✿✿⚓⚓✿✿

**CHARTS** AC 2093, 633; Imray C62; Irish OS 21

**TIDES** HW +0025 Dover; ML 3·0; Duration 0620

**Standard Port BELFAST (⟶)**

| Times | | | | Height (metres) | | | |
|---|---|---|---|---|---|---|---|
| High Water | | Low Water | | MHWS | MHWN | MLWN | MLWS |
| 0100 | 0700 | 0000 | 0600 | 3·5 | 3·0 | 1·1 | 0·4 |
| 1300 | 1900 | 1200 | 1800 | | | | |
| **Differences KILKEEL** | | | | | | | |
| +0040 | +0030 | +0010 | +0010 | +1·2 | +1·1 | +0·4 | +0·4 |
| **NEWCASTLE** | | | | | | | |
| +0025 | +0035 | +0020 | +0040 | +1·6 | +1·1 | +0·4 | +0·1 |
| **KILLOUGH HARBOUR** | | | | | | | |
| 0000 | +0020 | No data | | +1·8 | +1·6 | No data | |
| **ARDGLASS** | | | | | | | |
| +0010 | +0015 | +0005 | +0010 | +1·7 | +1·2 | +0·6 | +0·3 |

**SHELTER** Good, except in strong winds from E to S. It is the only all-weather, all-tide shelter between Howth and Bangor. Phennick Cove marina is on W side of hbr, with depths 1·0m to 2·8m. Visitors should check depth of berth offered by marina against depth drawn. The busy fishing port is in South Hbr, with quays (2·1m) on inside of extended S pier. At NW end of hbr, old drying N Dock is also used by FVs.

**NAVIGATION** WPT 54°15′·30N 05°35′·32W, 131°/5ca to hbr ent. Appr 311° in W sector of WRG Dir lt. Depth in chan 2·4m. The inner bkwtr is marked by an ECM buoy, VQ (3) 4s. Thence chan 232° into the marina is marked by Nos 2 and 4 PHM buoys, QR and Fl R 4s; and by Nos 3 and 5 SHM buoys, QG and Fl G 4s. (These buoys are not shown on chartlet due to small scale.) Do not cross the drying SW portion of inner bkwtr, marked by two unlit SCM perches.

**LIGHTS AND MARKS** Dir lt, 311°, conspic W tr at inner hbr, Iso WRG 4s 10m 8/7/5M, 308°-W-314°; reported hard to see against shore lts. S bkwtr Fl R 3s 10m 5M. W roof of shed on S bkwtr is conspic. If entering S Hbr, avoid Churn Rk, unlit SCM bn. Entrance to marina is buoyed. Castle, spire and water tr (off plan) are conspic to W.

**R/T** Hbr VHF Ch 12 14 16. Marina Ch M, 80.

**TELEPHONE** (Code 028) HM 4484 1291, mob 07790 648274; MRCC 9046 3933; Marinecall 09068 969655; Police 4461 5011; Dr 9084 1242.

**FACILITIES Phennick Cove Marina** (55 inc 30✓ £1.60), ☎/📠 44842332, www.ardglassmarina.co.uk, ardglassmarina@tiscali.co.uk; Slip(£3.00), D, P (cans), 🗑, ♿. **Town** P (cans), Bar, ✉, R, 🛒, Gas.

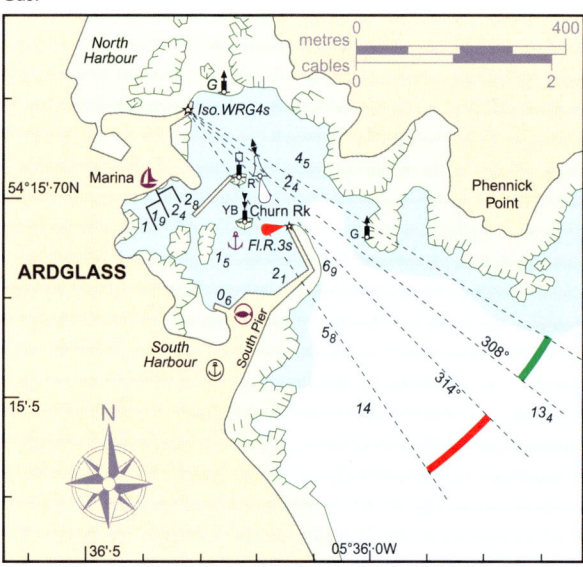

## 6.7 STRANGFORD LOUGH

Down **54°19′·33N 05°30′·85W** (Narrows) ✿✿⚓⚓✿✿✿

**CHARTS** AC 2156, 2159; Imray C62; Irish OS 21

**TIDES** Killard Pt 0000, Strangford Quay +0200 Dover; ML 2·0; Duration 0610

**Standard Port BELFAST (⟶)**

| Times | | | | Height (metres) | | | |
|---|---|---|---|---|---|---|---|
| High Water | | Low Water | | MHWS | MHWN | MLWN | MLWS |
| 0100 | 0700 | 0000 | 0600 | 3·5 | 3·0 | 1·1 | 0·4 |
| 1300 | 1900 | 1200 | 1800 | | | | |
| **Differences STRANGFORD (The Narrows)** | | | | | | | |
| +0147 | +0157 | +0148 | +0208 | +0·1 | +0·1 | −0·2 | 0·0 |
| **KILLARD POINT (Entr)** | | | | | | | |
| +0011 | +0021 | +0005 | +0025 | +1·0 | +0·8 | +0·1 | +0·1 |
| **QUOILE BARRIER** | | | | | | | |
| +0150 | +0200 | +0150 | +0300 | +0·2 | +0·2 | −0·3 | −0·1 |
| **KILLYLEAGH** | | | | | | | |
| +0157 | +0207 | +0211 | +0231 | +0·3 | +0·3 | No data | |
| **SOUTH ROCK** | | | | | | | |
| +0023 | +0023 | +0025 | +0025 | +1·0 | +0·8 | +0·1 | +0·1 |
| **PORTAVOGIE** | | | | | | | |
| +0010 | +0020 | +0010 | +0020 | +1·2 | +0·9 | +0·3 | +0·2 |

**SHELTER** Excellent; largest inlet on E coast. Good ⚓s in the Narrows at Cross Roads; in Strangford Creek (NW of Swan Island, which is marked by 3 lt bns to S, E and N); in Audley Rds and Ballyhenry Bay. 3 ⚓s at Strangford. Portaferry has a small marina with a few visitors' berths. Many good ⚓s and some ⚓s up the lough, by villages and YCs; dues, if applicable, are seldom collected.

**NAVIGATION** WPT Strangford SWM buoy, L Fl 10s, 54°18′·63N 05°28′·62W, 306°/2·05M to Angus Rk lt tr.

Strangers should use the E Chan. Beware St Patricks Rk, Bar Pladdy and Pladdy Lug; also overfalls in the SE apprs and at the bar, which can be dangerous when ebb is against strong onshore winds.

During flood the bar presents no special problem, preferable to enter on the young flood or at slack wayer. Strong (up to 7kn at sp) tidal streams flow through the Narrows. The flood starts in the Narrows at HW Belfast −3½ and runs for about 6 hrs; the ebb starts at HW Belfast +2½. Beware car ferry plying from Strangford, S and E of Swan Is, to Portaferry.

Swan Island, seen as a grassy mound at HW, is edged with rks and a reef extends 32m E ending at W bn, Fl (2) WR 6s. Further up the lough, AC 2156 is essential. Pladdies are drying patches, often un-marked.

**LIGHTS AND MARKS** See chartlet. Ent identified by Strangford SWM buoy, W tr with R top on Angus Rk, Pladdy Lug bn (W), Bar Pladdy SCM lt buoy and St Patrick's Rock perch. See chartlet for clearance lines.

**R/T** HM at Strangford Ferry Terminal Ch 12 14 16 M (Mon-Fri 0900-1700LT). Some YCs Ch **80** M.

**TELEPHONE** (Code 028) Strangford HM 4488 1637; MRCC 9146 3933; Marinecall 09068 969655; Police 4461 5011; Medical Clinic 4461 3016; Casualty 4461 3311.

**FACILITIES**
**STRANGFORD** 3 ⚓s SE of Swan Is. **Islander Marine** ☎ 4488 1449: FW, Slip, El, Ⓔ, ⚒, D (cans). Village: 🛒, R, Bar, ✉.
**PORTAFERRY: Marina,** ☎ 42729598, mobile 07703 209780,📠 42729784; barholm.portaferry@virgin.net. AB(limited) £1.50, Gas, Gaz, P & D (cans), 🛒, R, Bar, ✉, Ⓑ, aquarium. **Cook St Pier** (2ca S), limited AB, FW.
**QUOILE RIVER: Quoile YC** ☎ 4461 2266. AB, M, Slip, FW.
**KILLYLEAGH:** M, P & D (cans), L, CH, SM (Irish Spars & Rigging ☎ 4482 8882), 🛒, Gas, Gaz, Kos, R, Ⓑ, Bar, ✉; **Killyleagh YC** ☎ 4482 8250; N of village, **East Down YC** ☎ 4482 8375, AB (about 1M NE of town).
**RINGHADDY QUAY:** CC, M, AB drying, FW, Slip.
**SKETRICK ISLAND:** In White Rk B, **Strangford Lough YC,** ☎ 9754 1883, L, AB, FW, BY, CH, R, Bar. To the NW in the Dorn, **Down CC,** (Old Lightship) FW, D, Bar.
**KIRCUBBIN** (tidal): Gas, P & D (cans), Ⓑ, R, Bar, 🛒, ✉.

**STRANGFORD LOUGH** *continued*

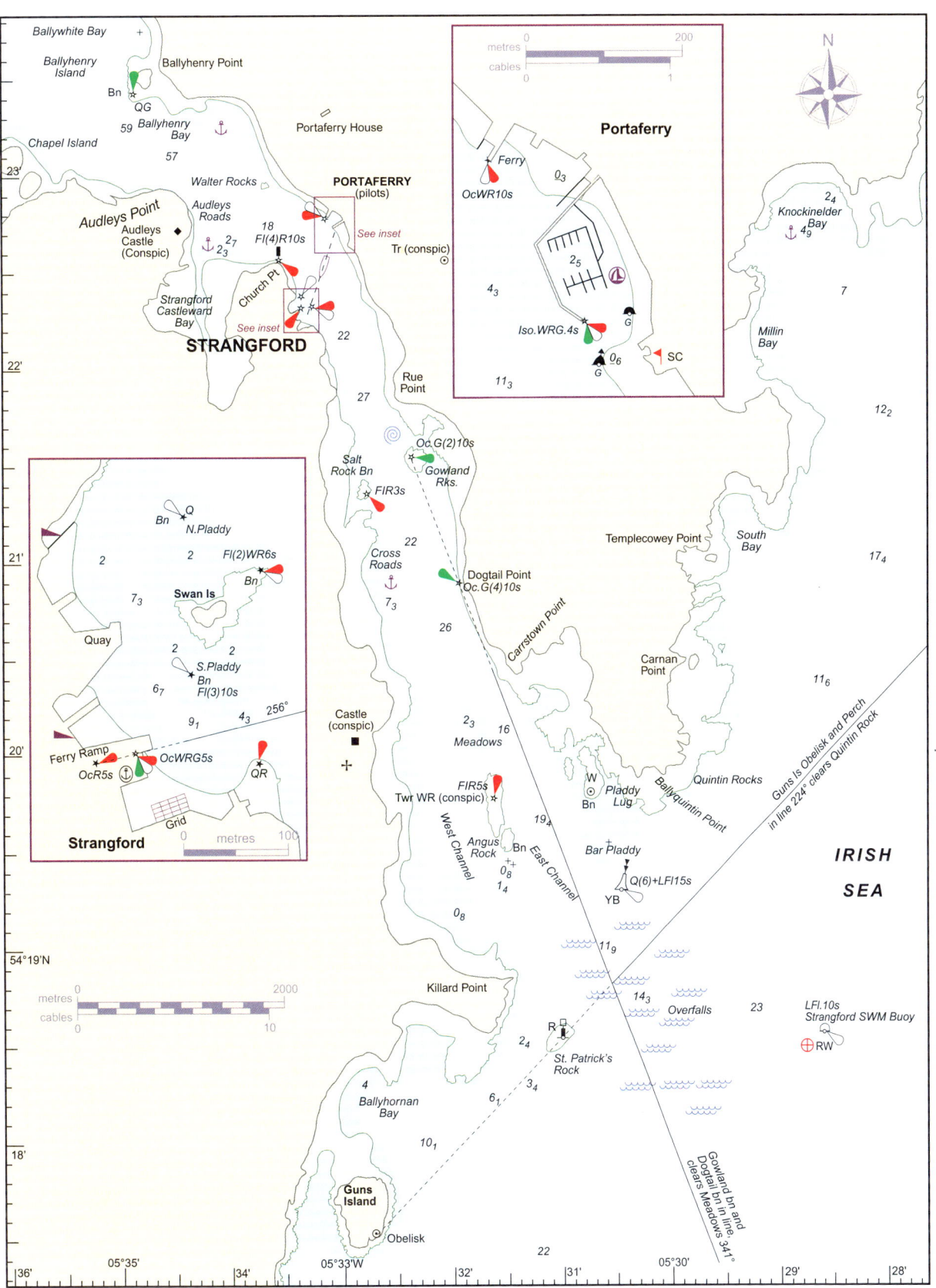

N Ireland

# 6.8 BELFAST LOUGH

County Down and County Antrim **54°42'N 05°45'W**
Bangor ✿✿✿△△△✿✿; Carrickfergus ✿✿✿△△✿✿

CHARTS AC 2198, 1753; Imray C62, C64; Irish OS 15

TIDES +0007 Dover; ML Belfast 2·0, Carrickfergus 1·8; Duration 0620

**Standard Port BELFAST (→)**

| Times | | | | Height (metres) | | | |
|---|---|---|---|---|---|---|---|
| High Water | | Low Water | | MHWS | MHWN | MLWN | MLWS |
| 0100 | 0700 | 0000 | 0600 | 3·5 | 3·0 | 1·1 | 0·4 |
| 1300 | 1900 | 1200 | 1800 | | | | |
| Differences CARRICKFERGUS | | | | | | | |
| +0005 | +0005 | +0005 | +0005 | −0·3 | −0·3 | −0·2 | −0·1 |
| DONAGHADEE | | | | | | | |
| +0020 | +0020 | +0023 | +0023 | +0·5 | +0·4 | 0·0 | +0·1 |

SHELTER Main sailing centres, clockwise around Belfast Lough, are at Bangor, Cultra and Carrickfergus.
**Donaghadee:** small marina at SE ent to the Lough.
**Ballyholme Bay:** good ⚓ in offshore winds.
**Bangor:** exposed to N winds, but well sheltered in marina (depths 2·9m to 2·2m). Speed limits: 4kn in marina, 8kn between Luke's Pt and Wilson's Pt.
**Cultra:** in offshore winds good ⚓ & moorings off RNoIYC.
**Belfast Harbour** is a major commercial port, but there are pontoons on the NW bank at Donegal Quay (54°36'·16N 05°55'·20W) between Lagan Bridge, 8m clearance, and Lagan Weir. To enter call *Belfast Port Control* VHF Ch **12**.
**Carrickfergus:** very good in marina, depths 1·8m to 2·3m. The former commercial hbr has 10 yacht berths on the W quay. A stub bkwtr, marked by 2 PHM bns, extends NNE into the hbr from the W pier. The ent and SW part of the hbr are dredged 2·3m; the NE part of the hbr dries 0·7m. Good ⚓ SSE of Carrickfergus Pier, except in E winds.

NAVIGATION WPT Bangor 54°41'·00N 05°40'·00W, 190°/1M to bkwtr lt. Rounding Orlock Pt beware Briggs Rocks extending ¾M

offshore. The Lough is well marked. WPT Carrickfergus 54°41'·71N 05°46'·16W, Fairway SWM buoy marks start of the chan to Belfast Hbr. It also bears 121°/301° from/to Carrickfergus Marina, 1.7M. Carrickfergus Bank liable to shift. Deep draft yachts should not enter/leave at LW±2. High speed ferries operate in the area.

LIGHTS AND MARKS Bangor Dir Oc WRG 10s lt; W sector 105° leads into ent. Chan to Belfast Hbr is well marked/lit by buoys and bns. Beyond No 12 PHM bn it is dangerous to leave the chan. Carrickfergus is easily recognised by conspic castle to E of Marina. On Marina Bkwtr, 30m W of the ☆ QR 7m 3M, is a Dir lt 320°, Oc WRG 3s 5m 3M, (H24).

R/T Bangor Marina Ch **80** M (H24); Bangor HM Ch **11** (H24). Royal N of Ireland YC (at Cultra) Ch **16**; **11** (H24) 80. *Belfast Port Control* (at Milewater Basin) Ch **12** 16 (H24); VTS provides info on request to vessels in port area. The greater part of Belfast Lough is under radar surveillance. Carrickfergus Marina Ch M, 80, M2.

TELEPHONE (Codes: Belfast 028) HM Bangor 91453297, ☒ 9145 3450; HM Belfast 90553012, ☒ 90553017; Belfast VTS 9055 3504; MRCC 91463933; Weather (08494) 22339; Marinecall 09068 969655; Police 90558411, 93362021, 91454444; Dr 91468521.

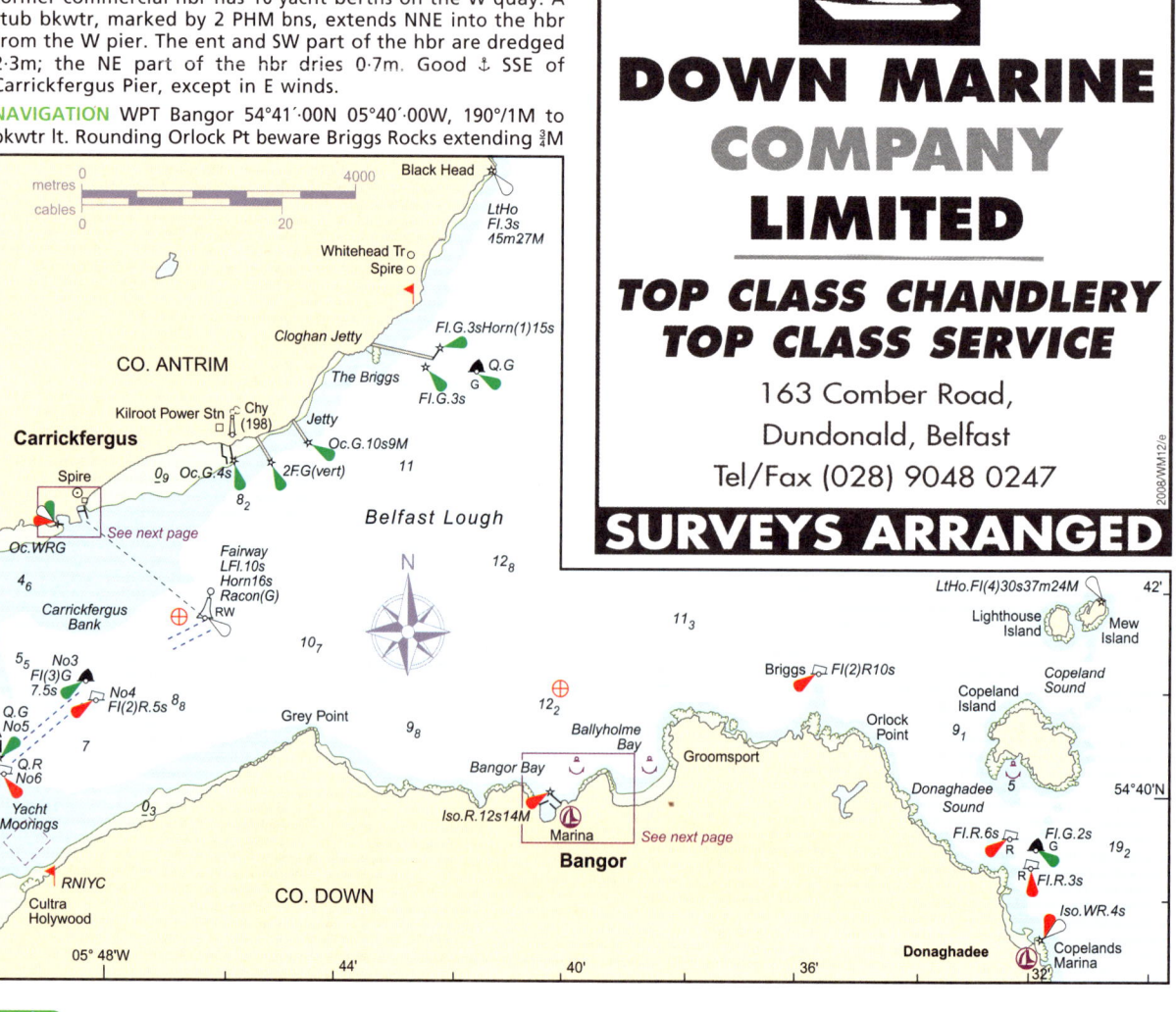

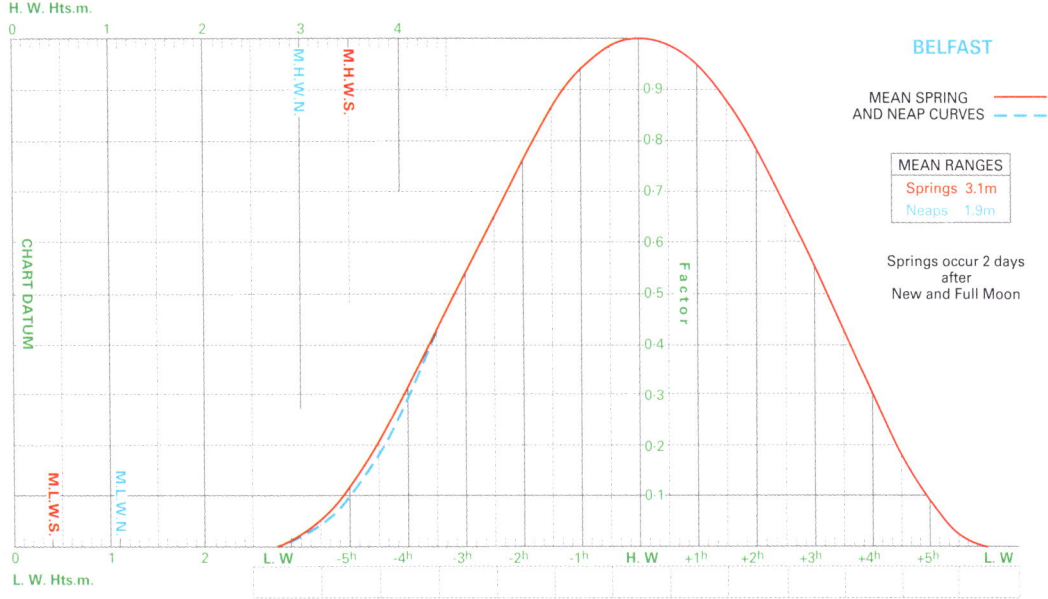

**H. W. Hts.m.**

**BELFAST**

MEAN SPRING
AND NEAP CURVES

MEAN RANGES
Springs 3·1m
Neaps 1·9m

Springs occur 2 days
after
New and Full Moon

CHART DATUM

M.H.W.N.
M.H.W.S.

M.L.W.S.
M.L.W.N.

Factor

L. W   -5h  -4h  -3h  -2h  -1h  H. W  +1h  +2h  +3h  +4h  +5h  L. W

**L. W. Hts.m.**

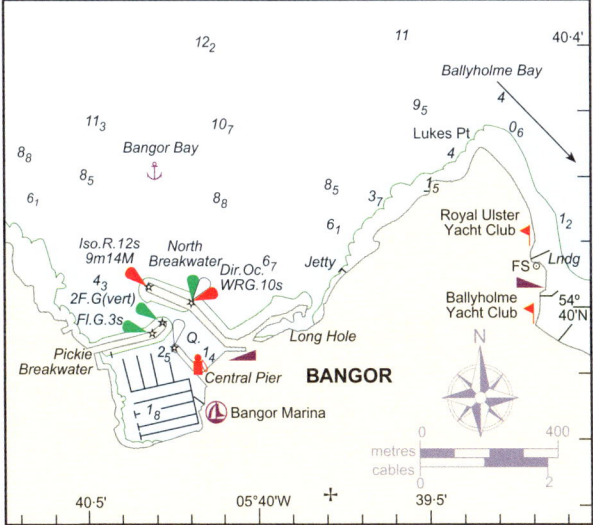

Ballyholme Bay

Lukes Pt

Bangor Bay

Royal Ulster
Yacht Club

FS

Lndg

Iso.R.12s
9m14M

North
Breakwater

Dir.Oc.
WRG.10s

Jetty

Ballyholme
Yacht Club

2F.G(vert)

Fl.G.3s

Pickie
Breakwater

Long Hole

Central Pier   **BANGOR**

Bangor Marina

metres
cables

0   400
0   2

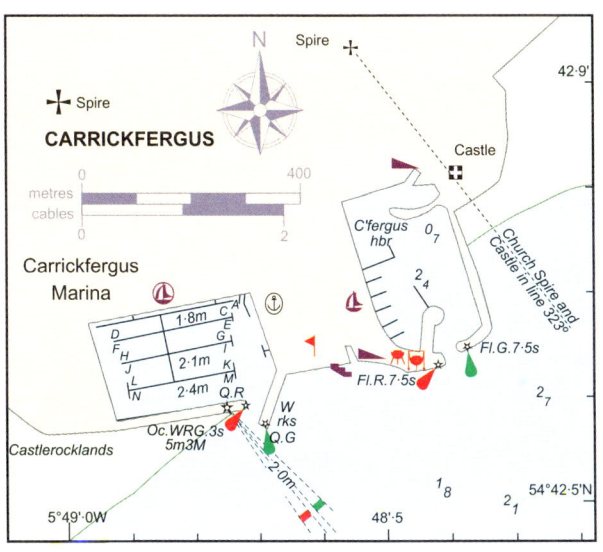

Spire

Spire

**CARRICKFERGUS**

Castle

C'fergus
hbr

Church Spire and
Castle in line 323°

Carrickfergus
Marina

metres
cables

0   400
0   2

Fl.G.7·5s

Fl.R.7·5s

Q.R

W
rks
Q.G

Oc.WRG.3s
5m3M

Castlerocklands

**FACILITIES** Clockwise around the Lough:
**GROOMSPORT BAY** HM ☎ 91278040, M, Slip, FW; **Cockle Island Boat Club**, Slip, M, FW, L, R.
**BALLYHOLME BAY** Ballyholme YC ☎ 9127 1467, two ⚓s, R, Bar; **Royal Ulster YC** ☎ 91270568, M, R, Bar.
**BANGOR** Bangor Marina (560 + 40♥) inc ♿ £1·80) ☎ 91453297, 🖷 91453450, ajaggers@quaymarinas.com, www.quaymarinas.com, Wi-fi, P, D, C, CH, BH (40 ton), ME, El, Ⓔ, ⚒, Gas, Gaz, Slip, SM, 🛒, 🖥; **Todd Chart Agency** ☎ 91466640, 🖷 9147 1070 ACA, CH. **Services:** BY, Diving, Gas, ME, El, ⚒. **Town** 🛒, R, Bar, ✉, Ⓑ, ⛟, ✈ (Belfast).
**CULTRA Royal North of Ireland YC,** ☎ 90428041, M, L, AB, FW, Slip, P (½M), D, R, Bar. **Services:** ME, El, ⚒; **Town** P, CH, 🛒, R, Bar, ✉, Ⓑ, ⛟, ✈.
**BELFAST** River Manager ☎ 90328507, AB, P, D, FW, ME, El, ⚒, CH, C (200 ton), SM, Gas. **City** EC Wed; all facilities, ⛟, ✈.
**CARRICKFERGUS Marina** (280 inc ♥) ☎ 93366666, 🖷 93350505, bwithers.marina@carrickfergus.org; £2, Wi-fi, El, ⚒, Rigging, ME, Ⓔ. **Carrick SC** ☎ 351402, M, L, FW, C, AB
**Hbr:** 10 AB, D, BH (45 ton).
**Town:** 🛒, R, Ⓑ, ✉, ⛟, ✈ (Belfast).

**MINOR HARBOURS BETWEEN STRANGFORD AND BELFAST LOUGHS**
**PORTAVOGIE,** Down, 54°27′·45N 05°26′·08W. 🌼🌼⚓⚓🌸. AC 2156. HW +0016 on Dover; ML 2·6m; Duration 0620. See 6.7. Good shelter, but hbr so full of FVs as to risk damage; best only for overnight or emergency. Entrance dangerous in strong onshore winds. Beware Plough Rks to SE marked by PHM buoy, Fl (2) R 10s, and McCammon Rks to NE of ent. Keep in W sector of outer bkwtr lt, Iso WRG 5s 9m 9M, shore-G-258°-W-275°-R-348°. Inner bkwtr 2 FG (vert) 6m 4M. VHF Ch 12 14 16 (Mon-Fri: 0900-1700LT). HM ☎ (028) 4277 1470. Facilities: Slip, FW (on central quay) ⚒, ME, El. **Town** CH, D & P (cans), ✉, R, Gas, 🛒. No 🛢.

**DONAGHADEE,** Down, 54°38′·71N 05°31′·85W. 🌼🌼⚓⚓🌸🌸🌸. AC 1753, 3709. HW +0025 on Dover; see 6.8; ML no data; Duration 0615. Excellent shelter and basic facilities in tiny marina, access HW±4 over sill; covers approx 1.1m at half tide. Appr on about 275° on ldg marks, orange △s to tricky ent with sharp 90° port turn into marina (pilots available). Appr in strong winds or at night not advised. 3ca to the N, the Old Hbr is small and very full; scend often sets in. Beware rocky reef with less than 2m extends 1·5ca ENE from S pier hd. Max depth in hbr is approx 2·5m, dries at SW end; best berth alongside SE quay. S pier lt, Iso WR 4s 17m 18/14M, W shore–326°, R326°–shore. HM ☎/🖷 (028) 9188 2377. Police 9188 2526. Facilities: **Copelands Marina** ☎ 9188 2184, mobile 07802 363382; VHF Ch **16** 11 80; AB for 6 ♥, D, C (20 ton). **Old Hbr** AB £4. **Town** Bar, D, P, Gas, ✉, R, 🛒, Ⓑ, ⛟ (Bangor), ✈ (Belfast).

**TIME ZONE (UT)**
For Summer Time add ONE hour in **non-shaded areas**

## BELFAST   LAT 54°36'N   LONG 5°55'W
### TIMES AND HEIGHTS OF HIGH AND LOW WATERS

Dates in red are SPRINGS
Dates in blue are NEAPS

YEAR 2008

### JANUARY

| Day | Time | m | Day | Time | m |
|---|---|---|---|---|---|
| 1 TU | 0511 / 1115 / 1720 / 2345 | 2.9 / 1.2 / 3.2 / 1.0 | 16 W | 0422 / 1018 / 1638 / 2306 | 3.1 / 0.9 / 3.3 / 0.8 |
| 2 W | 0606 / 1217 / 1819 | 2.9 / 1.3 / 3.1 | 17 TH | 0524 / 1123 / 1747 | 3.0 / 1.0 / 3.2 |
| 3 TH | 0044 / 0706 / 1321 / 1924 | 1.1 / 2.9 / 1.3 / 3.0 | 18 F | 0020 / 0632 / 1243 / 1905 | 0.9 / 3.0 / 1.1 / 3.1 |
| 4 F | 0141 / 0812 / 1421 / 2031 | 1.2 / 3.0 / 1.2 / 3.1 | 19 SA | 0135 / 0745 / 1404 / 2024 | 0.9 / 3.1 / 1.0 / 3.1 |
| 5 SA | 0233 / 0908 / 1514 / 2127 | 1.1 / 3.1 / 1.1 / 3.1 | 20 SU | 0240 / 0854 / 1511 / 2131 | 0.9 / 3.2 / 0.8 / 3.2 |
| 6 SU | 0319 / 0955 / 1558 / 2213 | 1.1 / 3.3 / 1.0 / 3.2 | 21 M | 0337 / 0952 / 1607 / 2227 | 0.8 / 3.4 / 0.6 / 3.3 |
| 7 M | 0401 / 1036 / 1637 / 2253 | 1.0 / 3.4 / 0.9 / 3.2 | 22 TU ○ | 0428 / 1043 / 1657 / 2316 | 0.7 / 3.6 / 0.5 / 3.3 |
| 8 TU ● | 0439 / 1112 / 1713 / 2329 | 0.9 / 3.5 / 0.8 / 3.3 | 23 W | 0515 / 1129 / 1742 | 0.7 / 3.7 / 0.4 |
| 9 W | 0517 / 1144 / 1749 | 0.9 / 3.5 / 0.7 | 24 TH | 0003 / 0558 / 1214 / 1824 | 3.2 / 0.7 / 3.7 / 0.4 |
| 10 TH | 0000 / 0554 / 1211 / 1824 | 3.3 / 0.8 / 3.5 / 0.6 | 25 F | 0048 / 0640 / 1257 / 1904 | 3.2 / 0.7 / 3.7 / 0.4 |
| 11 F | 0030 / 0631 / 1241 / 1902 | 3.2 / 0.8 / 3.6 / 0.6 | 26 SA | 0131 / 0720 / 1339 / 1942 | 3.1 / 0.7 / 3.7 / 0.5 |
| 12 SA | 0106 / 0710 / 1319 / 1941 | 3.2 / 0.8 / 3.6 / 0.5 | 27 SU | 0212 / 0759 / 1421 / 2020 | 3.1 / 0.8 / 3.6 / 0.6 |
| 13 SU | 0149 / 0750 / 1402 / 2023 | 3.2 / 0.8 / 3.6 / 0.6 | 28 M | 0252 / 0838 / 1504 / 2059 | 3.0 / 0.8 / 3.5 / 0.7 |
| 14 M | 0235 / 0834 / 1449 / 2110 | 3.2 / 0.8 / 3.5 / 0.6 | 29 TU | 0333 / 0920 / 1547 / 2142 | 3.0 / 0.9 / 3.3 / 0.9 |
| 15 TU ◑ | 0327 / 0923 / 1540 / 2204 | 3.1 / 0.9 / 3.5 / 0.7 | 30 W ◑ | 0416 / 1009 / 1635 / 2233 | 2.9 / 1.1 / 3.1 / 1.0 |
| | | | 31 TH | 0505 / 1114 / 1728 / 2342 | 2.9 / 1.2 / 3.0 / 1.2 |

### FEBRUARY

| Day | Time | m | Day | Time | m |
|---|---|---|---|---|---|
| 1 F | 0602 / 1236 / 1832 | 2.8 / 1.3 / 2.8 | 16 SA | 0002 / 0607 / 1238 / 1858 | 1.1 / 2.9 / 1.0 / 2.9 |
| 2 SA | 0059 / 0714 / 1347 / 1955 | 1.3 / 2.8 / 1.2 / 2.9 | 17 SU | 0129 / 0734 / 1404 / 2027 | 1.1 / 3.0 / 0.9 / 2.9 |
| 3 SU | 0204 / 0844 / 1447 / 2110 | 1.2 / 2.9 / 1.1 / 2.9 | 18 M | 0237 / 0848 / 1511 / 2131 | 0.9 / 3.1 / 0.7 / 3.0 |
| 4 M | 0257 / 0938 / 1536 / 2157 | 1.1 / 3.1 / 0.9 / 3.0 | 19 TU | 0333 / 0944 / 1604 / 2221 | 0.8 / 3.3 / 0.5 / 3.1 |
| 5 TU | 0342 / 1018 / 1616 / 2236 | 0.9 / 3.2 / 0.7 / 3.1 | 20 W | 0421 / 1031 / 1649 / 2305 | 0.6 / 3.5 / 0.3 / 3.1 |
| 6 W | 0422 / 1052 / 1653 / 2309 | 0.8 / 3.3 / 0.5 / 3.2 | 21 TH ○ | 0504 / 1114 / 1728 / 2346 | 0.6 / 3.6 / 0.3 / 3.1 |
| 7 TH ● | 0459 / 1119 / 1729 / 2336 | 0.7 / 3.4 / 0.4 / 3.2 | 22 F | 0542 / 1155 / 1804 | 0.5 / 3.6 / 0.3 |
| 8 F | 0535 / 1143 / 1804 | 0.6 / 3.5 / 0.4 | 23 SA | 0025 / 0617 / 1234 / 1835 | 3.1 / 0.6 / 3.6 / 0.4 |
| 9 SA | 0004 / 0622 / 1216 / 1839 | 3.2 / 0.6 / 3.6 / 0.3 | 24 SU | 0101 / 0650 / 1313 / 1907 | 3.0 / 0.6 / 3.5 / 0.5 |
| 10 SU | 0040 / 0646 / 1256 / 1916 | 3.2 / 0.5 / 3.6 / 0.3 | 25 M | 0136 / 0723 / 1351 / 1939 | 3.0 / 0.6 / 3.5 / 0.6 |
| 11 M | 0121 / 0725 / 1339 / 1956 | 3.2 / 0.5 / 3.6 / 0.4 | 26 TU | 0211 / 0758 / 1429 / 2014 | 3.1 / 0.7 / 3.4 / 0.7 |
| 12 TU | 0206 / 0807 / 1425 / 2040 | 3.2 / 0.5 / 3.6 / 0.5 | 27 W | 0248 / 0836 / 1510 / 2053 | 3.0 / 0.8 / 3.2 / 0.9 |
| 13 W | 0255 / 0854 / 1516 / 2131 | 3.2 / 0.6 / 3.4 / 0.7 | 28 TH | 0329 / 0920 / 1555 / 2138 | 3.0 / 0.9 / 3.0 / 1.0 |
| 14 TH ◑ | 0349 / 0948 / 1614 / 2234 | 3.1 / 0.8 / 3.2 / 0.9 | 29 F ◑ | 0417 / 1016 / 1648 / 2237 | 2.9 / 1.1 / 2.8 / 1.2 |
| 15 F | 0452 / 1056 / 1728 | 3.0 / 1.0 / 3.0 | | | |

### MARCH

| Day | Time | m | Day | Time | m |
|---|---|---|---|---|---|
| 1 SA | 0513 / 1154 / 1750 | 2.8 / 1.2 / 2.7 | 16 SU | 0553 / 1239 / 1906 | 2.9 / 0.9 / 2.7 |
| 2 SU | 0018 / 0620 / 1316 / 1906 | 1.3 / 2.7 / 1.2 / 2.6 | 17 M | 0120 / 0725 / 1400 / 2024 | 1.1 / 2.9 / 0.7 / 2.8 |
| 3 M | 0135 / 0751 / 1417 / 2043 | 1.2 / 2.7 / 1.0 / 2.7 | 18 TU | 0228 / 0834 / 1503 / 2119 | 0.9 / 3.1 / 0.5 / 2.9 |
| 4 TU | 0232 / 0905 / 1507 / 2131 | 1.1 / 2.9 / 0.7 / 2.9 | 19 W | 0323 / 0927 / 1553 / 2205 | 0.8 / 3.3 / 0.3 / 3.0 |
| 5 W | 0318 / 0944 / 1549 / 2206 | 0.9 / 3.1 / 0.5 / 3.0 | 20 TH | 0408 / 1012 / 1633 / 2245 | 0.6 / 3.4 / 0.3 / 3.1 |
| 6 TH | 0359 / 1014 / 1627 / 2235 | 0.7 / 3.2 / 0.4 / 3.1 | 21 F ○ | 0447 / 1053 / 1707 / 2322 | 0.6 / 3.5 / 0.3 / 3.1 |
| 7 F ● | 0436 / 1041 / 1702 / 2303 | 0.6 / 3.4 / 0.3 / 3.2 | 22 SA | 0522 / 1131 / 1736 / 2357 | 0.5 / 3.5 / 0.4 / 3.1 |
| 8 SA | 0510 / 1113 / 1737 / 2336 | 0.5 / 3.5 / 0.2 / 3.3 | 23 SU | 0553 / 1207 / 1804 | 0.5 / 3.4 / 0.5 |
| 9 SU | 0545 / 1151 / 1812 | 0.4 / 3.6 / 0.2 | 24 M | 0028 / 0622 / 1243 / 1832 | 3.1 / 0.6 / 3.4 / 0.6 |
| 10 M | 0015 / 0621 / 1234 / 1849 | 3.3 / 0.3 / 3.6 / 0.2 | 25 TU | 0059 / 0652 / 1318 / 1903 | 3.1 / 0.6 / 3.3 / 0.6 |
| 11 TU | 0058 / 0701 / 1319 / 1931 | 3.3 / 0.3 / 3.6 / 0.3 | 26 W | 0133 / 0725 / 1355 / 1937 | 3.1 / 0.6 / 3.2 / 0.7 |
| 12 W | 0143 / 0744 / 1408 / 2016 | 3.3 / 0.4 / 3.5 / 0.5 | 27 TH | 0209 / 0803 / 1435 / 2016 | 3.1 / 0.7 / 3.1 / 0.8 |
| 13 TH | 0232 / 0833 / 1502 / 2108 | 3.3 / 0.5 / 3.3 / 0.8 | 28 F | 0247 / 0846 / 1520 / 2100 | 3.1 / 0.9 / 2.9 / 1.0 |
| 14 F ◑ | 0327 / 0930 / 1606 / 2214 | 3.1 / 0.7 / 3.1 / 1.0 | 29 SA ◑ | 0332 / 0939 / 1614 / 2156 | 3.0 / 1.0 / 2.8 / 1.2 |
| 15 SA | 0432 / 1048 / 1726 / 2354 | 3.0 / 0.9 / 2.8 / 1.2 | 30 SU | 0429 / 1105 / 1718 / 2319 | 2.8 / 1.1 / 2.6 / 1.3 |
| | | | 31 M | 0537 / 1241 / 1827 | 2.7 / 1.1 / 2.6 |

### APRIL

| Day | Time | m | Day | Time | m |
|---|---|---|---|---|---|
| 1 TU | 0058 / 0647 / 1343 / 1941 | 1.3 / 2.7 / 0.9 / 2.7 | 16 W | 0206 / 0809 / 1441 / 2055 | 1.0 / 3.3 / 0.5 / 2.9 |
| 2 W | 0158 / 0755 / 1433 / 2038 | 1.1 / 2.9 / 0.6 / 2.9 | 17 TH | 0301 / 0901 / 1528 / 2139 | 0.8 / 3.3 / 0.4 / 3.0 |
| 3 TH | 0246 / 0847 / 1516 / 2119 | 0.9 / 3.1 / 0.4 / 3.1 | 18 F | 0346 / 0946 / 1606 / 2218 | 0.7 / 3.4 / 0.4 / 3.1 |
| 4 F | 0328 / 0927 / 1554 / 2155 | 0.7 / 3.2 / 0.3 / 3.2 | 19 SA | 0425 / 1027 / 1638 / 2254 | 0.6 / 3.4 / 0.5 / 3.1 |
| 5 SA | 0405 / 1005 / 1630 / 2232 | 0.6 / 3.4 / 0.2 / 3.3 | 20 SU ○ | 0459 / 1105 / 1706 / 2327 | 0.6 / 3.3 / 0.6 / 3.1 |
| 6 SU ● | 0441 / 1046 / 1707 / 2312 | 0.4 / 3.5 / 0.2 / 3.4 | 21 M | 0530 / 1139 / 1734 / 2357 | 0.6 / 3.3 / 0.6 / 3.2 |
| 7 M | 0519 / 1130 / 1745 / 2355 | 0.3 / 3.6 / 0.2 / 3.4 | 22 TU | 0559 / 1213 / 1803 | 0.6 / 3.3 / 0.6 |
| 8 TU | 0559 / 1217 / 1826 | 0.3 / 3.6 / 0.3 | 23 W | 0028 / 0628 / 1248 / 1834 | 3.2 / 0.7 / 3.2 / 0.8 |
| 9 W | 0041 / 0642 / 1307 / 1911 | 3.5 / 0.3 / 3.5 / 0.4 | 24 TH | 0102 / 0701 / 1325 / 1909 | 3.3 / 0.7 / 3.2 / 0.8 |
| 10 TH | 0129 / 0729 / 1401 / 2000 | 3.5 / 0.3 / 3.4 / 0.6 | 25 F | 0138 / 0739 / 1406 / 1950 | 3.3 / 0.7 / 3.1 / 0.9 |
| 11 F | 0220 / 0822 / 1459 / 2057 | 3.4 / 0.5 / 3.2 / 0.9 | 26 SA | 0215 / 0822 / 1452 / 2036 | 3.2 / 0.8 / 2.9 / 1.0 |
| 12 SA | 0315 / 0925 / 1607 / 2209 | 3.2 / 0.6 / 3.0 / 1.1 | 27 SU | 0257 / 0914 / 1547 / 2130 | 3.1 / 0.9 / 2.8 / 1.1 |
| 13 SU ◑ | 0421 / 1053 / 1730 / 2340 | 3.1 / 0.8 / 2.8 / 1.2 | 28 M ◑ | 0350 / 1021 / 1649 / 2236 | 2.9 / 1.0 / 2.7 / 1.2 |
| 14 M | 0541 / 1227 / 1858 | 3.0 / 0.8 / 2.7 | 29 TU | 0455 / 1151 / 1753 / 2356 | 2.9 / 0.9 / 2.7 / 1.2 |
| 15 TU | 0059 / 0704 / 1342 / 2004 | 1.1 / 3.0 / 0.6 / 2.8 | 30 W | 0603 / 1257 / 1855 | 2.9 / 0.8 / 2.8 |

Chart Datum: 2·01 metres below Ordnance Datum (Belfast). HAT is 3·8 metres above Chart Datum.

>> **FREE** monthly updates from
www.reedsalmanac.co.uk <<

**TIME ZONE (UT)**
For Summer Time add ONE hour in **non-shaded areas**

## BELFAST  LAT 54°36′N  LONG 5°55′W
TIMES AND HEIGHTS OF HIGH AND LOW WATERS

Dates in red are SPRINGS
Dates in blue are NEAPS

YEAR **2008**

N Ireland

### MAY

| Day | Time m | Time m | Time m | Time m |
|---|---|---|---|---|
| 1 TH | 0106 1.1 | 0705 3.0 | 1350 0.6 | 1949 3.0 |
| 2 F | 0201 0.9 | 0800 3.1 | 1435 0.5 | 2036 3.1 |
| 3 SA | 0248 0.8 | 0850 3.3 | 1517 0.3 | 2121 3.3 |
| 4 SU | 0331 0.6 | 0937 3.5 | 1557 0.3 | 2205 3.4 |
| 5 M ● | 0413 0.5 | 1025 3.5 | 1639 0.3 | 2251 3.5 |
| 6 TU | 0457 0.4 | 1115 3.6 | 1722 0.4 | 2339 3.6 |
| 7 W | 0543 0.3 | 1206 3.6 | 1809 0.5 | |
| 8 TH | 0028 3.6 | 0630 0.3 | 1300 3.5 | 1858 0.6 |
| 9 F | 0119 3.6 | 0722 0.3 | 1356 3.3 | 1952 0.8 |
| 10 SA | 0211 3.5 | 0818 0.4 | 1456 3.1 | 2052 0.9 |
| 11 SU | 0306 3.4 | 0924 0.6 | 1603 3.0 | 2201 1.0 |
| 12 M ◐ | 0407 3.3 | 1042 0.6 | 1719 2.8 | 2314 1.1 |
| 13 TU | 0518 3.2 | 1159 0.7 | 1830 2.8 | |
| 14 W | 0023 1.1 | 0631 3.1 | 1307 0.6 | 1930 2.9 |
| 15 TH | 0128 1.0 | 0735 3.2 | 1404 0.6 | 2021 2.9 |
| 16 F | 0226 0.9 | 0829 3.2 | 1452 0.6 | 2106 3.0 |
| 17 SA | 0315 0.8 | 0917 3.3 | 1531 0.6 | 2147 3.1 |
| 18 SU | 0358 0.8 | 1000 3.3 | 1605 0.7 | 2225 3.1 |
| 19 M | 0436 0.8 | 1039 3.3 | 1636 0.8 | 2259 3.2 |
| 20 TU ○ | 0510 0.8 | 1114 3.2 | 1707 0.8 | 2331 3.3 |
| 21 W | 0541 0.7 | 1149 3.2 | 1739 0.8 | |
| 22 TH | 0005 3.3 | 0612 0.7 | 1224 3.2 | 1813 0.9 |
| 23 F | 0040 3.4 | 0645 0.7 | 1301 3.1 | 1850 0.9 |
| 24 SA | 0114 3.4 | 0723 0.7 | 1341 3.1 | 1932 0.9 |
| 25 SU | 0150 3.3 | 0805 0.8 | 1426 3.0 | 2017 1.0 |
| 26 M | 0231 3.2 | 0852 0.8 | 1519 2.9 | 2108 1.0 |
| 27 TU | 0318 3.1 | 0947 0.8 | 1617 2.9 | 2203 1.1 |
| 28 W ◑ | 0414 3.1 | 1050 0.8 | 1717 2.9 | 2302 1.1 |
| 29 TH | 0516 3.1 | 1156 0.7 | 1814 2.9 | |
| 30 F | 0004 1.0 | 0620 3.1 | 1258 0.6 | 1908 3.0 |
| 31 SA | 0107 1.0 | 0721 3.2 | 1352 0.5 | 2000 3.2 |

### JUNE

| Day | Time m | Time m | Time m | Time m |
|---|---|---|---|---|
| 1 SU | 0206 0.8 | 0820 3.3 | 1442 0.5 | 2052 3.3 |
| 2 M | 0301 0.7 | 0916 3.4 | 1531 0.5 | 2143 3.4 |
| 3 TU ● | 0353 0.6 | 1010 3.5 | 1619 0.5 | 2234 3.5 |
| 4 W | 0444 0.4 | 1103 3.5 | 1708 0.5 | 2326 3.6 |
| 5 TH | 0534 0.4 | 1157 3.5 | 1758 0.6 | |
| 6 F | 0016 3.7 | 0625 0.3 | 1251 3.4 | 1850 0.7 |
| 7 SA | 0107 3.7 | 0717 0.3 | 1347 3.3 | 1944 0.8 |
| 8 SU | 0159 3.6 | 0812 0.4 | 1446 3.1 | 2040 0.9 |
| 9 M | 0251 3.6 | 0910 0.5 | 1546 3.0 | 2139 0.9 |
| 10 TU ◐ | 0346 3.4 | 1014 0.6 | 1648 2.9 | 2239 1.0 |
| 11 W | 0444 3.3 | 1118 0.7 | 1748 2.9 | 2340 1.0 |
| 12 TH | 0546 3.2 | 1218 0.7 | 1845 2.9 | |
| 13 F | 0040 1.1 | 0650 3.1 | 1315 0.8 | 1938 2.9 |
| 14 SA | 0141 1.0 | 0751 3.1 | 1407 0.8 | 2029 3.0 |
| 15 SU | 0238 1.0 | 0846 3.1 | 1453 0.9 | 2115 3.1 |
| 16 M | 0329 0.9 | 0934 3.1 | 1533 0.9 | 2158 3.2 |
| 17 TU | 0413 0.9 | 1017 3.1 | 1610 0.9 | 2236 3.3 |
| 18 W ○ | 0451 0.8 | 1055 3.2 | 1646 0.9 | 2313 3.3 |
| 19 TH | 0524 0.8 | 1131 3.2 | 1721 0.9 | 2347 3.4 |
| 20 F | 0557 0.7 | 1205 3.1 | 1757 0.9 | |
| 21 SA | 0020 3.4 | 0630 0.7 | 1240 3.1 | 1834 0.8 |
| 22 SU | 0051 3.4 | 0706 0.7 | 1315 3.1 | 1914 0.8 |
| 23 M | 0125 3.4 | 0745 0.6 | 1357 3.0 | 1956 0.8 |
| 24 TU | 0204 3.4 | 0827 0.6 | 1444 3.0 | 2041 0.9 |
| 25 W | 0249 3.3 | 0914 0.6 | 1536 3.0 | 2129 0.9 |
| 26 TH ◑ | 0338 3.3 | 1006 0.7 | 1632 3.0 | 2221 0.9 |
| 27 F | 0434 3.2 | 1105 0.7 | 1730 3.0 | 2319 1.0 |
| 28 SA | 0537 3.2 | 1211 0.7 | 1828 3.0 | |
| 29 SU | 0025 1.0 | 0646 3.2 | 1318 0.7 | 1928 3.1 |
| 30 M | 0137 0.9 | 0756 3.2 | 1420 0.7 | 2028 3.2 |

### JULY

| Day | Time m | Time m | Time m | Time m |
|---|---|---|---|---|
| 1 TU | 0245 0.8 | 0901 3.3 | 1516 0.6 | 2126 3.4 |
| 2 W | 0346 0.6 | 1001 3.3 | 1609 0.6 | 2221 3.5 |
| 3 TH ● | 0440 0.4 | 1055 3.4 | 1700 0.6 | 2312 3.6 |
| 4 F | 0530 0.3 | 1147 3.3 | 1749 0.6 | |
| 5 SA | 0002 3.7 | 0618 0.3 | 1239 3.3 | 1838 0.7 |
| 6 SU | 0052 3.7 | 0706 0.3 | 1331 3.2 | 1927 0.7 |
| 7 M | 0140 3.7 | 0753 0.3 | 1423 3.1 | 2016 0.8 |
| 8 TU | 0228 3.6 | 0841 0.4 | 1514 3.0 | 2106 0.8 |
| 9 W | 0316 3.5 | 0931 0.6 | 1603 3.0 | 2157 0.9 |
| 10 TH ◐ | 0405 3.4 | 1024 0.7 | 1651 2.9 | 2251 1.0 |
| 11 F | 0456 3.2 | 1122 0.9 | 1741 2.9 | 2352 1.1 |
| 12 SA | 0552 3.0 | 1222 1.0 | 1837 2.9 | |
| 13 SU | 0056 1.1 | 0659 2.9 | 1322 1.1 | 1942 2.9 |
| 14 M | 0201 1.1 | 0813 2.9 | 1417 1.1 | 2044 3.0 |
| 15 TU | 0301 1.0 | 0913 3.0 | 1505 1.0 | 2135 3.1 |
| 16 W | 0350 0.9 | 1000 3.0 | 1548 1.0 | 2218 3.3 |
| 17 TH | 0430 0.7 | 1040 3.1 | 1626 0.9 | 2255 3.3 |
| 18 F ○ | 0504 0.7 | 1115 3.1 | 1702 0.8 | 2328 3.4 |
| 19 SA | 0537 0.6 | 1146 3.1 | 1738 0.8 | 2354 3.4 |
| 20 SU | 0610 0.6 | 1213 3.1 | 1814 0.7 | |
| 21 M | 0020 3.4 | 0644 0.5 | 1245 3.1 | 1851 0.7 |
| 22 TU | 0055 3.4 | 0720 0.5 | 1323 3.1 | 1929 0.7 |
| 23 W | 0136 3.5 | 0757 0.5 | 1408 3.1 | 2010 0.7 |
| 24 TH | 0219 3.5 | 0839 0.5 | 1456 3.1 | 2055 0.7 |
| 25 F ◑ | 0307 3.4 | 0928 0.6 | 1550 3.1 | 2145 0.8 |
| 26 SA | 0400 3.3 | 1024 0.7 | 1648 3.0 | 2243 0.9 |
| 27 SU | 0504 3.1 | 1132 0.9 | 1754 3.0 | 2355 1.0 |
| 28 M | 0622 3.0 | 1258 0.9 | 1903 3.0 | |
| 29 TU | 0127 1.0 | 0744 3.0 | 1411 0.9 | 2012 3.2 |
| 30 W | 0243 0.8 | 0858 3.1 | 1511 0.8 | 2116 3.3 |
| 31 TH | 0343 0.6 | 0958 3.2 | 1603 0.7 | 2210 3.5 |

### AUGUST

| Day | Time m | Time m | Time m | Time m |
|---|---|---|---|---|
| 1 F ● | 0435 0.4 | 1049 3.2 | 1651 0.6 | 2259 3.6 |
| 2 SA | 0522 0.3 | 1136 3.2 | 1736 0.6 | 2345 3.7 |
| 3 SU | 0605 0.2 | 1222 3.2 | 1819 0.6 | |
| 4 M | 0031 3.7 | 0645 0.3 | 1307 3.1 | 1901 0.7 |
| 5 TU | 0116 3.6 | 0728 0.4 | 1351 3.1 | 1942 0.7 |
| 6 W | 0200 3.6 | 0801 0.5 | 1433 3.0 | 2023 0.8 |
| 7 TH | 0243 3.5 | 0840 0.6 | 1514 3.0 | 2105 0.9 |
| 8 F ◐ | 0326 3.3 | 0921 0.8 | 1557 3.0 | 2153 1.0 |
| 9 SA | 0412 3.1 | 1009 1.0 | 1644 2.9 | 2255 1.1 |
| 10 SU | 0504 2.9 | 1115 1.2 | 1738 2.9 | 2344 1.1 |
| 11 M | 0014 1.2 | 0606 2.8 | 1238 1.3 | 1843 2.8 |
| 12 TU | 0127 1.2 | 0736 2.7 | 1344 1.2 | 2014 2.9 |
| 13 W | 0231 1.1 | 0856 2.8 | 1439 1.1 | 2113 3.1 |
| 14 TH | 0322 0.9 | 0943 3.0 | 1524 1.0 | 2156 3.2 |
| 15 F | 0403 0.7 | 1021 3.1 | 1604 0.8 | 2230 3.3 |
| 16 SA ○ | 0438 0.6 | 1053 3.1 | 1640 0.7 | 2257 3.4 |
| 17 SU | 0511 0.5 | 1118 3.2 | 1714 0.7 | 2318 3.4 |
| 18 M | 0544 0.4 | 1141 3.2 | 1748 0.6 | 2348 3.5 |
| 19 TU | 0617 0.4 | 1213 3.2 | 1823 0.6 | |
| 20 W | 0025 3.5 | 0650 0.4 | 1252 3.2 | 1859 0.6 |
| 21 TH | 0108 3.6 | 0727 0.4 | 1336 3.3 | 1939 0.6 |
| 22 F | 0152 3.5 | 0808 0.5 | 1423 3.2 | 2025 0.7 |
| 23 SA ◑ | 0241 3.4 | 0856 0.7 | 1516 3.2 | 2116 0.8 |
| 24 SU | 0336 3.2 | 0951 0.9 | 1617 3.1 | 2217 1.0 |
| 25 M | 0445 3.0 | 1105 1.1 | 1730 3.0 | 2344 1.1 |
| 26 TU | 0613 2.8 | 1252 1.1 | 1849 3.0 | |
| 27 W | 0130 1.3 | 0748 2.9 | 1406 1.0 | 2006 3.1 |
| 28 TH | 0241 0.7 | 0901 3.0 | 1505 0.9 | 2108 3.3 |
| 29 F | 0338 0.5 | 0953 3.1 | 1554 0.7 | 2158 3.5 |
| 30 SA ● | 0425 0.3 | 1037 3.2 | 1638 0.6 | 2243 3.6 |
| 31 SU | 0506 0.3 | 1119 3.2 | 1718 0.6 | 2326 3.6 |

Chart Datum: 2·01 metres below Ordnance Datum (Belfast). HAT is 3·8 metres above Chart Datum.

## BELFAST LAT 54°36'N LONG 5°55'W
### TIMES AND HEIGHTS OF HIGH AND LOW WATERS

TIME ZONE (UT)
For Summer Time add ONE hour in **non-shaded areas**

Dates in red are SPRINGS
Dates in blue are NEAPS

YEAR 2008

### SEPTEMBER

| Time | m | | Time | m |
|---|---|---|---|---|
| **1** M | 0543 0.3 / 1158 3.2 / 1755 0.6 | **16** TU | 0514 0.4 / 1111 3.3 / 1719 0.6 / 2320 3.6 |
| **2** TU | 0007 3.6 / 0615 0.4 / 1237 3.1 / 1830 0.7 | **17** W | 0546 0.4 / 1146 3.4 / 1754 0.5 |
| **3** W | 0048 3.6 / 0647 0.5 / 1314 3.1 / 1905 0.7 | **18** TH | 0000 3.6 / 0621 0.4 / 1227 3.4 / 1832 0.5 |
| **4** TH | 0128 3.5 / 0720 0.6 / 1351 3.1 / 1941 0.8 | **19** F | 0045 3.6 / 0700 0.5 / 1311 3.4 / 1915 0.6 |
| **5** F | 0207 3.4 / 0754 0.7 / 1429 3.1 / 2020 0.9 | **20** SA | 0132 3.5 / 0744 0.6 / 1359 3.4 / 2003 0.7 |
| **6** SA | 0248 3.2 / 0832 0.9 / 1511 3.1 / 2105 1.0 | **21** SU | 0224 3.4 / 0833 0.8 / 1454 3.3 / 2058 0.8 |
| **7** SU | 0333 3.1 / 0916 1.1 / 1558 3.0 / ☽ 2200 1.2 | **22** M | 0326 3.1 / 0932 1.1 / 1558 3.1 / ☽ 2206 1.0 |
| **8** M | 0425 2.9 / 1011 1.3 / 1653 2.9 / 2333 1.3 | **23** TU | 0443 2.9 / 1058 1.3 / 1716 3.0 / 2353 1.1 |
| **9** TU | 0526 2.7 / 1147 1.4 / 1756 2.8 | **24** W | 0619 2.8 / 1244 1.3 / 1841 3.1 |
| **10** W | 0053 1.2 / 0642 2.6 / 1311 1.4 / 1914 2.9 | **25** TH | 0125 0.9 / 0749 2.9 / 1356 1.1 / 1956 3.2 |
| **11** TH | 0157 1.1 / 0828 2.8 / 1409 1.2 / 2036 3.0 | **26** F | 0232 0.7 / 0850 3.0 / 1453 0.9 / 2053 3.4 |
| **12** F | 0248 0.9 / 0914 2.9 / 1456 1.0 / 2119 3.2 | **27** SA | 0324 0.5 / 0937 3.1 / 1540 0.8 / 2140 3.5 |
| **13** SA | 0331 0.7 / 0949 3.1 / 1536 0.9 / 2150 3.3 | **28** SU | 0408 0.4 / 1018 3.2 / 1620 0.7 / 2223 3.6 |
| **14** SU | 0407 0.5 / 1018 3.2 / 1612 0.7 / 2216 3.4 | **29** M | 0444 0.4 / 1056 3.2 / ● 1657 0.7 / ● 2304 3.6 |
| **15** M | 0441 0.4 / 1043 3.3 / 1646 0.7 / ○ 2245 3.5 | **30** TU | 0515 0.5 / 1132 3.2 / 1730 0.7 / 2342 3.6 |

### OCTOBER

| Time | m | | Time | m |
|---|---|---|---|---|
| **1** W | 0544 0.6 / 1206 3.2 / 1801 0.7 | **16** TH | 0517 0.5 / 1127 3.6 / 1730 0.5 / 2344 3.7 |
| **2** TH | 0019 3.5 / 0612 0.7 / 1239 3.3 / 1833 0.8 | **17** F | 0557 0.5 / 1210 3.6 / 1813 0.5 |
| **3** F | 0056 3.4 / 0643 0.8 / 1312 3.3 / 1908 0.8 | **18** SA | 0033 3.7 / 0640 0.6 / 1257 3.6 / 1900 0.6 |
| **4** SA | 0134 3.3 / 0717 0.9 / 1350 3.3 / 1946 0.9 | **19** SU | 0125 3.5 / 0728 0.8 / 1348 3.6 / 1951 0.7 |
| **5** SU | 0215 3.2 / 0755 1.0 / 1431 3.3 / 2030 1.0 | **20** M | 0223 3.3 / 0822 1.0 / 1444 3.4 / 2051 0.8 |
| **6** M | 0300 3.1 / 0839 1.1 / 1517 3.2 / 2123 1.1 | **21** TU | 0329 3.1 / 0927 1.2 / 1548 3.3 / ☽ 2206 0.9 |
| **7** TU | 0353 2.9 / 0933 1.3 / 1613 3.0 / ☽ 2241 1.3 | **22** W | 0447 2.9 / 1054 1.3 / 1704 3.2 / 2344 1.0 |
| **8** W | 0454 2.7 / 1047 1.4 / 1717 2.9 | **23** TH | 0616 2.9 / 1223 1.3 / 1825 3.2 |
| **9** TH | 0014 1.2 / 0603 2.7 / 1228 1.4 / 1824 2.9 | **24** F | 0104 0.9 / 0729 2.9 / 1332 1.2 / 1934 3.3 |
| **10** F | 0118 1.1 / 0718 2.8 / 1331 1.3 / 1930 3.0 | **25** SA | 0208 0.7 / 0825 3.1 / 1430 1.0 / 2030 3.4 |
| **11** SA | 0209 0.9 / 0820 3.0 / 1420 1.1 / 2023 3.2 | **26** SU | 0259 0.6 / 0912 3.2 / 1517 0.9 / 2118 3.5 |
| **12** SU | 0253 0.7 / 0901 3.1 / 1502 0.9 / 2104 3.4 | **27** M | 0341 0.6 / 0953 3.3 / 1559 0.8 / 2201 3.6 |
| **13** M | 0331 0.6 / 0937 3.3 / 1539 0.8 / 2141 3.5 | **28** TU | 0415 0.7 / 1031 3.3 / ● 1635 0.8 / ● 2241 3.5 |
| **14** TU | 0406 0.5 / 1011 3.4 / 1614 0.7 / ○ 2219 3.6 | **29** W | 0445 0.7 / 1107 3.4 / 1708 0.8 / 2318 3.5 |
| **15** W | 0441 0.4 / 1047 3.5 / 1651 0.6 / 2300 3.7 | **30** TH | 0514 0.8 / 1139 3.4 / 1740 0.8 / 2353 3.4 |
| | | **31** F | 0544 0.9 / 1210 3.4 / 1811 0.9 |

### NOVEMBER

| Time | m | | Time | m |
|---|---|---|---|---|
| **1** SA | 0029 3.4 / 0615 0.9 / 1245 3.5 / 1845 0.9 | **16** SU | 0029 3.6 / 0629 0.8 / 1250 3.8 / 1852 0.5 |
| **2** SU | 0107 3.3 / 0650 1.0 / 1322 3.5 / 1923 0.9 | **17** M | 0125 3.5 / 0720 0.9 / 1342 3.7 / 1947 0.6 |
| **3** M | 0148 3.2 / 0730 1.1 / 1401 3.4 / 2006 1.0 | **18** TU | 0223 3.3 / 0817 1.1 / 1436 3.6 / 2047 0.7 |
| **4** TU | 0233 3.1 / 0815 1.2 / 1444 3.3 / 2056 1.1 | **19** W | 0328 3.2 / 0921 1.2 / 1537 3.5 / ☽ 2158 0.8 |
| **5** W | 0325 3.0 / 0908 1.3 / 1535 3.2 / 2157 1.2 | **20** TH | 0439 3.0 / 1034 1.3 / 1644 3.4 / 2316 0.8 |
| **6** TH | 0425 2.9 / 1010 1.4 / 1635 3.1 / ☽ 2313 1.2 | **21** F | 0551 3.0 / 1147 1.3 / 1755 3.4 |
| **7** F | 0528 2.9 / 1122 1.4 / 1740 3.0 | **22** SA | 0027 0.8 / 0655 3.0 / 1254 1.2 / 1901 3.4 |
| **8** SA | 0024 1.1 / 0630 2.9 / 1234 1.3 / 1841 3.1 | **23** SU | 0129 0.8 / 0751 3.1 / 1354 1.1 / 2000 3.4 |
| **9** SU | 0120 0.9 / 0727 3.1 / 1331 1.2 / 1937 3.2 | **24** M | 0222 0.8 / 0841 3.2 / 1447 1.0 / 2052 3.4 |
| **10** M | 0208 0.8 / 0816 3.2 / 1419 1.0 / 2026 3.4 | **25** TU | 0306 0.9 / 0926 3.3 / 1534 1.0 / 2139 3.4 |
| **11** TU | 0250 0.7 / 0901 3.4 / 1504 0.9 / 2113 3.5 | **26** W | 0345 0.9 / 1008 3.4 / 1615 0.9 / 2221 3.4 |
| **12** W | 0331 0.6 / 0944 3.5 / 1546 0.8 / 2159 3.6 | **27** TH | 0419 0.9 / 1045 3.4 / 1651 0.9 / ● 2300 3.4 |
| **13** TH | 0413 0.6 / 1028 3.6 / 1630 0.6 / ○ 2247 3.7 | **28** F | 0452 1.0 / 1119 3.5 / 1725 0.9 / 2335 3.4 |
| **14** F | 0456 0.6 / 1113 3.7 / 1715 0.6 / 2337 3.7 | **29** SA | 0524 1.0 / 1152 3.5 / 1758 0.9 |
| **15** SA | 0541 0.7 / 1201 3.8 / 1802 0.5 | **30** SU | 0010 3.3 / 0557 1.0 / 1227 3.6 / 1831 0.9 |

### DECEMBER

| Time | m | | Time | m |
|---|---|---|---|---|
| **1** M | 0047 3.3 / 0634 1.0 / 1302 3.6 / 1907 0.9 | **16** TU | 0119 3.4 / 0713 0.8 / 1332 3.8 / 1940 0.5 |
| **2** TU | 0126 3.2 / 0713 1.0 / 1338 3.5 / 1947 0.9 | **17** W | 0215 3.3 / 0806 0.9 / 1424 3.8 / 2035 0.5 |
| **3** W | 0208 3.1 / 0757 1.1 / 1416 3.4 / 2032 0.9 | **18** TH | 0313 3.2 / 0903 1.0 / 1518 3.7 / 2134 0.6 |
| **4** TH | 0255 3.1 / 0844 1.1 / 1459 3.3 / 2122 1.0 | **19** F | 0412 3.1 / 1002 1.1 / 1615 3.5 / ☽ 2237 0.7 |
| **5** F | 0349 3.0 / 0936 1.2 / 1549 3.3 / ☽ 2218 1.0 | **20** SA | 0512 3.0 / 1105 1.1 / 1715 3.4 / 2340 0.9 |
| **6** SA | 0447 3.0 / 1032 1.2 / 1647 3.2 / 2319 1.0 | **21** SU | 0612 3.0 / 1208 1.2 / 1819 3.3 |
| **7** SU | 0544 3.0 / 1133 1.3 / 1750 3.2 | **22** M | 0041 1.0 / 0710 3.0 / 1312 1.2 / 1923 3.2 |
| **8** M | 0021 0.9 / 0640 3.1 / 1236 1.2 / 1852 3.2 | **23** TU | 0139 1.0 / 0808 3.1 / 1413 1.1 / 2024 3.2 |
| **9** TU | 0121 0.9 / 0735 3.2 / 1338 1.1 / 1952 3.3 | **24** W | 0231 1.1 / 0901 3.2 / 1510 1.1 / 2118 3.2 |
| **10** W | 0215 0.8 / 0829 3.3 / 1435 1.0 / 2050 3.4 | **25** TH | 0318 1.1 / 0948 3.3 / 1558 1.0 / 2205 3.3 |
| **11** TH | 0306 0.7 / 0921 3.5 / 1528 0.8 / 2145 3.5 | **26** F | 0358 1.0 / 1029 3.4 / 1638 0.9 / 2246 3.3 |
| **12** F | 0355 0.7 / 1012 3.6 / 1619 0.7 / ○ 2239 3.6 | **27** SA | 0435 1.0 / 1107 3.5 / 1712 0.9 / ● 2323 3.3 |
| **13** SA | 0443 0.7 / 1102 3.7 / 1708 0.5 / 2331 3.6 | **28** SU | 0509 1.0 / 1141 3.5 / 1744 0.8 / 2358 3.2 |
| **14** SU | 0532 0.7 / 1151 3.8 / 1758 0.5 | **29** M | 0544 0.9 / 1214 3.6 / 1817 0.8 |
| **15** M | 0024 3.5 / 0622 0.8 / 1241 3.9 / 1848 0.4 | **30** TU | 0031 3.2 / 0619 0.9 / 1244 3.5 / 1851 0.8 |
| | | **31** W | 0104 3.2 / 0656 0.9 / 1313 3.5 / 1927 0.8 |

Chart Datum: 2·01 metres below Ordnance Datum (Belfast). HAT is 3·8 metres above Chart Datum.

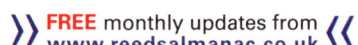

## 6.9 LARNE

Antrim 54°51'·20N 05°47'·50W ✿✿✿⚓⚓❀❀

**CHARTS** AC 2198, 1237; Imray C62, C64; Irish OS 9

**TIDES** +0005 Dover; ML 1·6; Duration 0620

**Standard Port BELFAST (←)**

| Times | | | | Height (metres) | | | |
|---|---|---|---|---|---|---|---|
| High Water | | Low Water | | MHWS | MHWN | MLWN | MLWS |
| 0100 | 0700 | 0000 | 0600 | 3·5 | 3·0 | 1·1 | 0·4 |
| 1300 | 1900 | 1200 | 1800 | | | | |
| **Differences LARNE** | | | | | | | |
| +0005 | 0000 | +0010 | −0005 | −0·7 | −0·5 | −0·3 | 0·0 |
| **RED BAY** | | | | | | | |
| +0022 | −0010 | +0007 | −0017 | −1·9 | −1·5 | −0·8 | −0·2 |
| **CUSHENDUN BAY** | | | | | | | |
| +0010 | −0030 | 0000 | −0025 | −1·7 | −1·5 | −0·6 | −0·2 |

**SHELTER** Secure shelter in Larne Lough or ⚓ overnight outside hbr in Brown's Bay (E of Barr Pt) in 2-4m. Hbr can be entered H24 in any conditions. Larne is a busy commercial and ferry port; W side is commercial until Curran Pt where there are two YCs with congested moorings. ⚓ S of Ballylumford Power Stn. No AB

available for visitors. Yachts should not berth on any commercial quays, inc Castle Quay, without HM's permission. Boat Hbr (0·6m) 2ca S of Ferris Pt only for shoal draft craft.

**NAVIGATION** WPT 54°51'·70N 05°47'·47W, 184°/2·1M to front ldg lt. Beware Hunter Rk 2M NE of hbr ent. Magnetic anomalies exist near Hunter Rk and between it and the mainland. Inside the narrow ent, the recommended chan is close to the E shore. Tide in the ent runs at up to 3½kn.

**LIGHTS AND MARKS** No1 SHM Q G 1½ca off chartlet N edge; Ldg lts 184°, Oc 4s 6/14m 12M, synch and vis 179°-189°; W ◇ with R stripes. Chaine Tr and fairway lts as chartlet. Note: Many shore lts on W side of ent may be mistaken for nav lts.

**R/T** VHF Ch **14** 11 16 *Larne Port Control*. Traffic, weather and tidal info available on Ch 14.

**TELEPHONE** (Code 02828) HM 872100 🖷 872209; MRCC 9146 3933; Pilot 273785; Marinecall 09068 969655; Dr 275331; Police 272266.

**FACILITIES Pier** ☎ 27 9221, M, L, FW, C (32 ton); **E Antrim Boat Club** ☎ 277204, Visitors should pre-contact Sec'y for advice on moorings; Slip, L, 🛠, FW, Bar; **Services:** D, Gas, ⚒, El. **Town** P & D (delivered, tidal), CH, 🛠, R, Bar, ✉, Ⓑ, ⇌, Ferry to Cairnryan and Stranraer, ✈ (Belfast City and Belfast/Aldergrove).

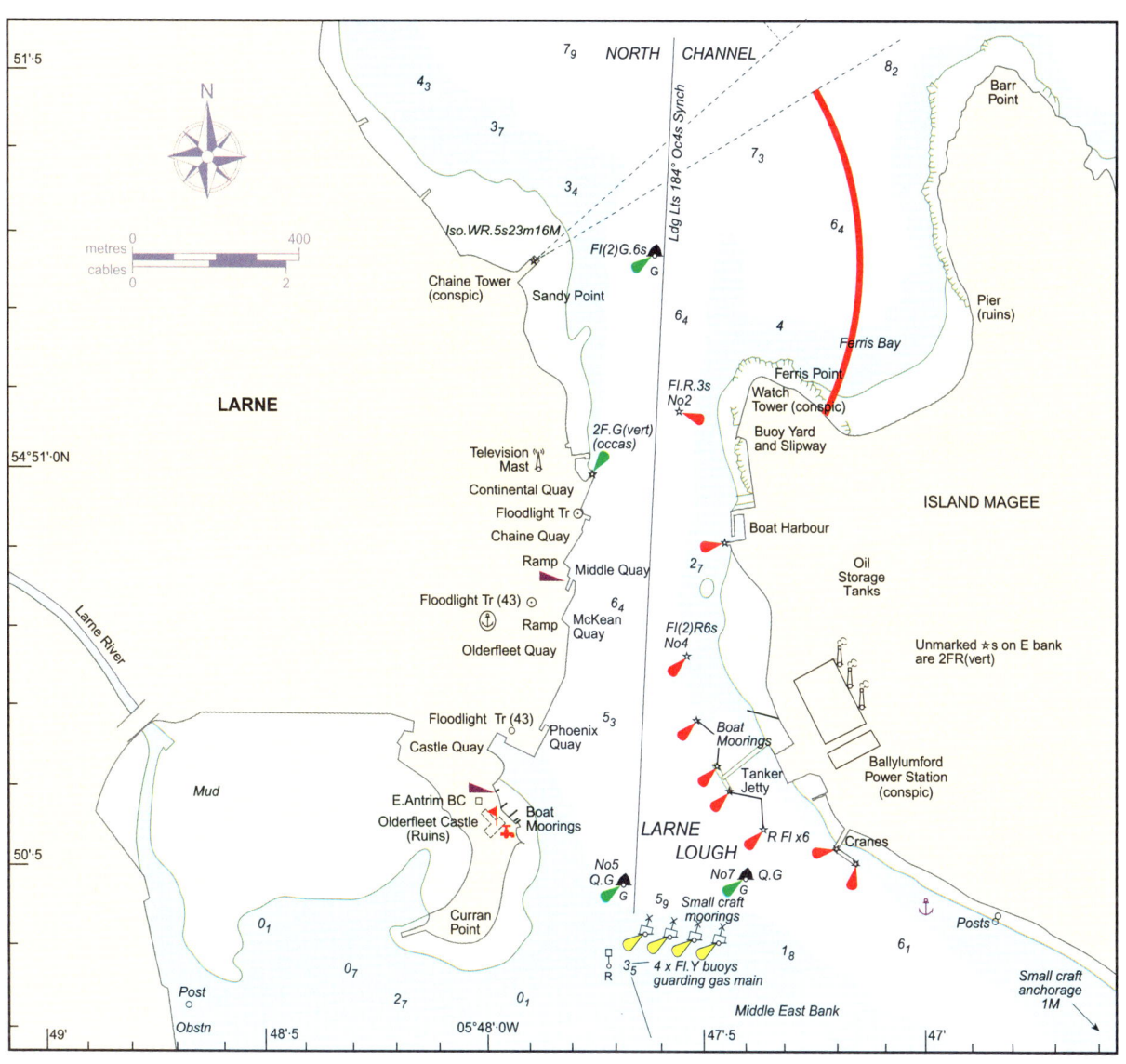

## HARBOURS AND ANCHORAGES BETWEEN LARNE AND PORTRUSH

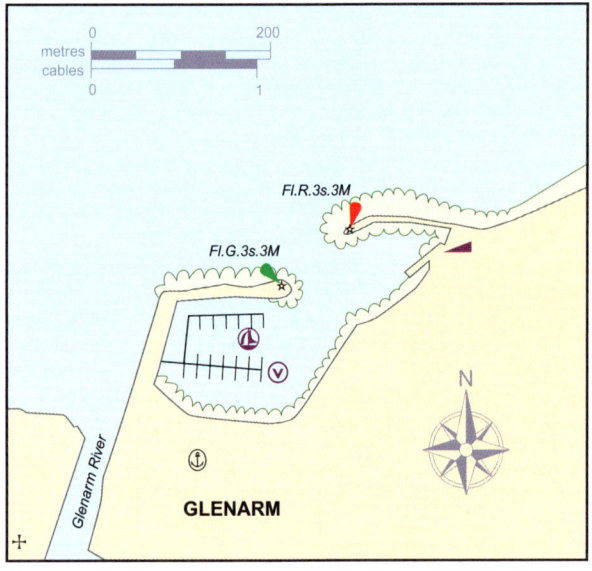

**GLENARM**, Antrim, **54°58′N 05°57′W**. AC 2198, *2199*. HW +0006 on Dover, +0005 on Belfast; HW −1·6m on Belfast; ML no data; Duration 0625. Good shelter in marina. Hbr ent lts Q.G.3s3M and Q.R.3s3M. HM and Marina ☎ 028 2884 1285, Mob 07703 606763. **Marina** 40 AB inc ⓥ in 4-6m, £1.00, FW, D, ⛽. **Village** 🍴, P (cans).

**CARNLOUGH HARBOUR**, Antrim, **54°59′·87N 05°59′·20W**. AC 2198. HW +0006 on Dover, +0005 on Belfast; HW −1·6m on Belfast; ML no data; Duration 0625. Good shelter, except in SE gales; do not enter in fresh/strong onshore winds. Entrance shoaling due to build up of kelp, minimum depth 1m (2004). Ldg marks 310°, Y ▽s on B/W posts. N pier lt, Fl G 3s 4m 5M; S pier Fl R 3s 6m 5M, both lts on B/W columns. Beware fish farms in the bay marked by lt buoys (unreliable); and rks which cover at HW on either side of ent. Small harbour used by yachts and small FVs; visitors welcome. HM ☎ (Mobile) 07703 606763. Facilities: **Quay** AB £1, AC (see HM), D (by arrangement), FW, Slip. **Town** P (cans), Gas, Gaz, ✉, R, 🍴, Bar, ♿.

**RED BAY**, Antrim, **55°03′·91N 06°03′·13W**. AC 2199. HW +0010 on Dover; ML 1·1m; Duration 0625. See 6.9. Good holding, but open to E winds. Beware rks, 2 ruined piers W of Garron Pt and fish farms, marked by lt buoys, on S side of bay, approx ⅓M from shore. Glenariff pier has lt Fl 3s 10m 5M. In S and E winds ⚓ 2ca off W stone arch near hd of bay in approx 3·5m; in N or W winds ⚓ S of small pier in 2–5m, ½M NE of Waterfoot village. **Facilities:** **Cushendall** (1M N of pier) Bar, D & P (cans), ✉, R, 🍴, Gas. **Services:** CH, El, Slip. **Waterfoot** Bar, R, ✉.

---

**BALLYCASTLE**, Antrim, **55°12′·47N 06°14′·27W**. AC 2798, 2494. Tides as for Rathlin Is; ML 0·8m; −0320 on Dover. Ferries to Campbeltown (Mull of Kintyre) and Rathlin Island berth inside the N breakwater. The marina is in the S part of the harbour with 2·3m. Outside the harbour is a fair weather anchorage clear of strong tidal streams, but liable to sudden swell and exposed to onshore winds. Lights: see chartlet and 6.3. HM ☎ (028) 20768525, mobile 07803 505084; CG ☎ 20762226; Ⓗ 20762666. **Marina** 74 AB , £2·00 <9·14m. El, Slip, D, P (cans), Gas. **Town** R, Bar, 🍴, ✉, Ⓑ, ♿.

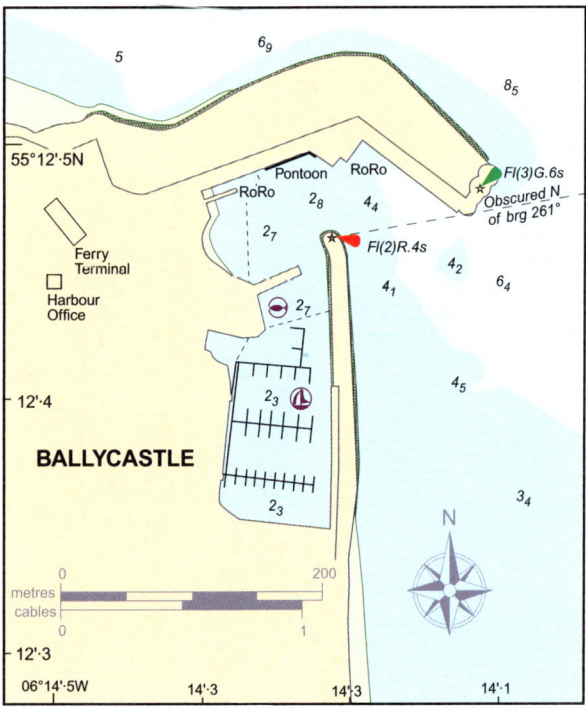

**RATHLIN ISLAND**, Antrim, **55°17′·47N 06°11′·78W**. AC 2798, 2494. HW sp −0445, nps −0200 on Dover. Small harbour in NE corner of Church Bay, sheltered from winds NW through E to SSE. Ferries run from the the Inner Harbour to Ballycastle. Beware sp streams up to 6kn in Rathlin Sound (6.10) and the North Channel TSS, just 2M NE of the island. Pass N or E of a wreck 6ca SW of hbr, marked on its SE side by a SCM lt buoy. When clear, appr on NNE to the W and S piers which form an outer hbr. The white sector of Manor House lt, Oc WRG 4s, leads 024·5° to Inner Harbour (2m) ent via channel dredged to 3·5m. AB on yacht pontoons just S of Inner Harbour. ⚓ in outer hbr on NW side in about 1.2m clear of ferry ramp; or outside hbr, close to W pier in about 5m. **Facilities:** Church Bay R, Bar, 🍴, ✉, ferry to Ballycastle.

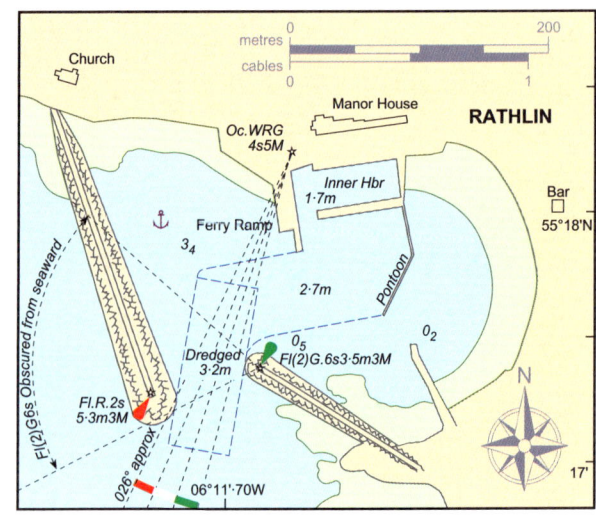

# 6.10  TIDAL STREAMS AROUND RATHLIN ISLAND

North Ireland 6.2
North Irish Sea 3.2

Off Mull of Kintyre 2.10
SW Scotland 2.2

South Ireland 5.2

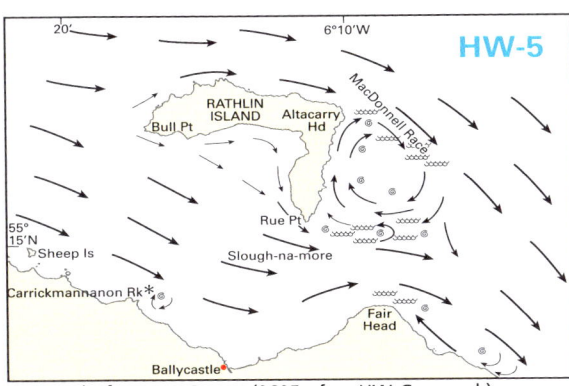

5 Hours before HW Dover (0605 after HW Greenock)

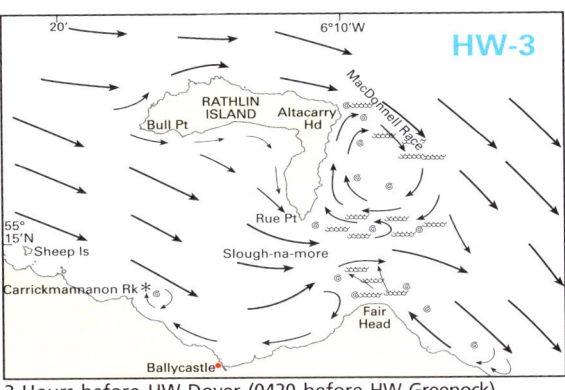

3 Hours before HW Dover (0420 before HW Greenock)

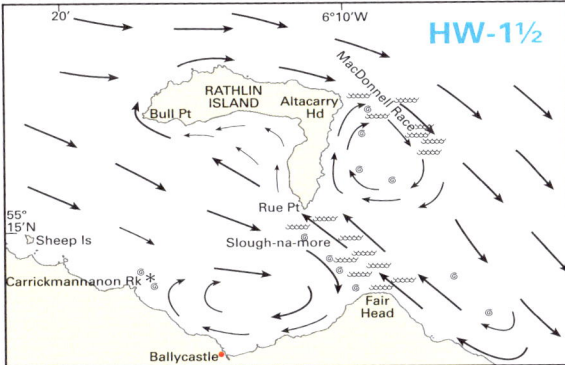

1½ Hours before HW Dover (0250 before HW Greenock)

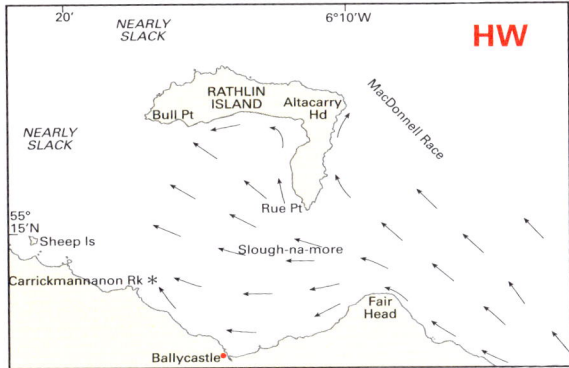

HW Dover (0120 before HW Greenock)

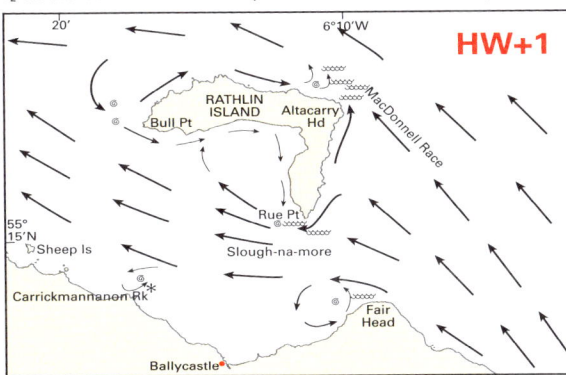

1 Hour after HW Dover (0020 before HW Greenock)

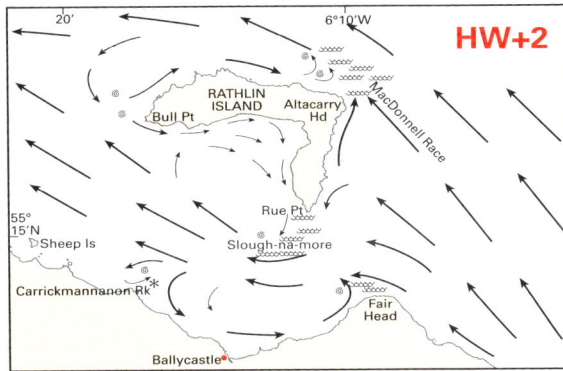

2 Hours after HW Dover (0040 after HW Greenock)

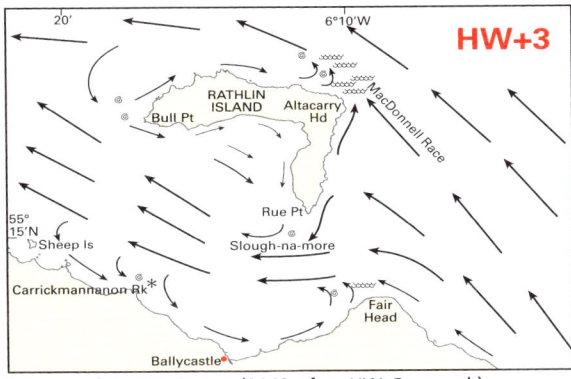

3 Hours after HW Dover (0140 after HW Greenock)

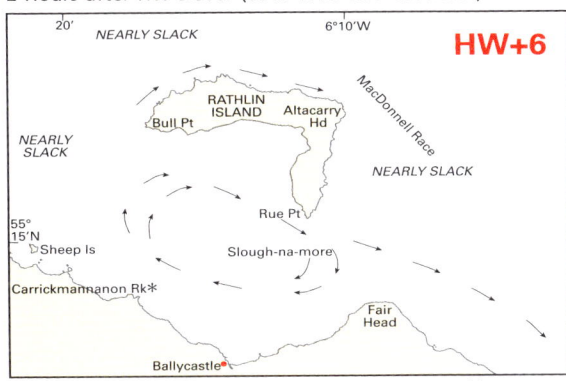

6 Hours after HW Dover (0440 after HW Greenock)

## 6.11 PORTRUSH

**Antrim 55°12'·34N 06°39'·49W** ⚙⚙🔱🔱🔱✿✿✿

**CHARTS** AC 2798, 2499, 49; Imray C53, C64; Irish OS 4

**TIDES** –0400 Dover; ML 1·1; Duration 0610

**Standard Port BELFAST (⟶)**

| Times | | | | Height (metres) | | | |
|---|---|---|---|---|---|---|---|
| High Water | | Low Water | | MHWS | MHWN | MLWN | MLWS |
| 0100 | 0700 | 0000 | 0600 | 3·5 | 3·0 | 1·1 | 0·4 |
| 1300 | 1900 | 1200 | 1800 | | | | |
| Differences PORTRUSH | | | | | | | |
| –0433 | | –0433 | | –1·6 | –1·6 | –0·3 | 0·0 |

**SHELTER** Good in hbr, except in strong NW/N winds. Berth on N pier or on pontoon at NE end of it and see HM. A ⚓ may be available, but very congested in season. ⚓ on E side of Ramore Hd in Skerries Roads 1ca S of Large Skerrie gives good shelter in most conditions, but open to NW sea/swell.

**NAVIGATION** WPT 55°13'·00N 06°41'·00W, 128° to N pier lt, 1·1M.

Ent with onshore winds >F 4 is difficult. Beware submerged bkwtr projecting 20m SW from N pier. Depth is 2·8m in hbr entrance.

**LIGHTS AND MARKS** Ldg lts 028° (occas, for LB use) both FR 6/8m 1M; R △ on metal bn and metal mast. N pier Fl R 3s 6m 3M; vis 220°-160°. S pier Fl G 3s 6m 3M; vis 220°-100°.

**R/T** VHF Ch 12 16 (0900-1700LT, Mon-Fri; extended evening hrs June-Sept; Sat-Sun: 0900–1700, June-Sept only).

**TELEPHONE** (Code 028) HM 7082 2307; MRCC 9146 3933; Marinecall 09068 969655; Police 7034 4122; Dr 7082 3767; ⊞ 7034 4177.

**FACILITIES** Hbr AB £14, D(0900-1800), FW, M, Slip (launching £3), Gas, El, Ⓔ, ♿; Portrush YC ☎ 7082 3932, Bar; **Town** @ Library, 🛒, R, Bar, ▣, D & P (cans), ✉, Ⓑ, ⇌, ✈ (Belfast). Giant's Causeway is 10M ENE.

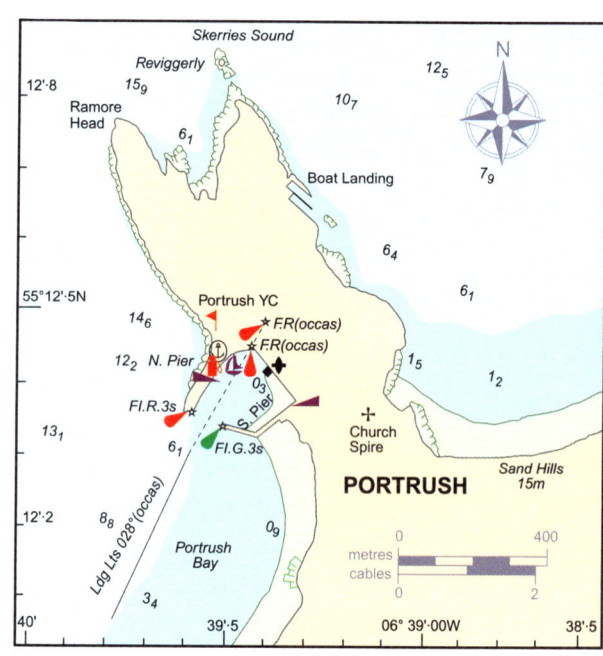

**PORTRUSH**

**Portstewart**, Antrim, **55°11'·21N 06°43'·21W**. AC 49. Tides as for Portrush. A tiny hbr 1·1ca S of Portstewart Pt lt, Oc R 10s 21m 5M, vis 040°–220°, obscd in final appr. A temp, fair weather berth (£10) at S end of inner basin in 0·8–1·7m; the very narrow ent is open to SW wind and swell. Visitors should obtain fuel at Portrush before proceeding to Portstewart. Beware rocks close to S bkwtr.

**Facilities**: @ Library, FW, Gas, Slip, Bar, 🛒, R.

## 6.12 RIVER BANN and COLERAINE

**Londonderry/Antrim 55°10'·32N 06°46'·35W** ⚙⚙🔱🔱🔱✿✿

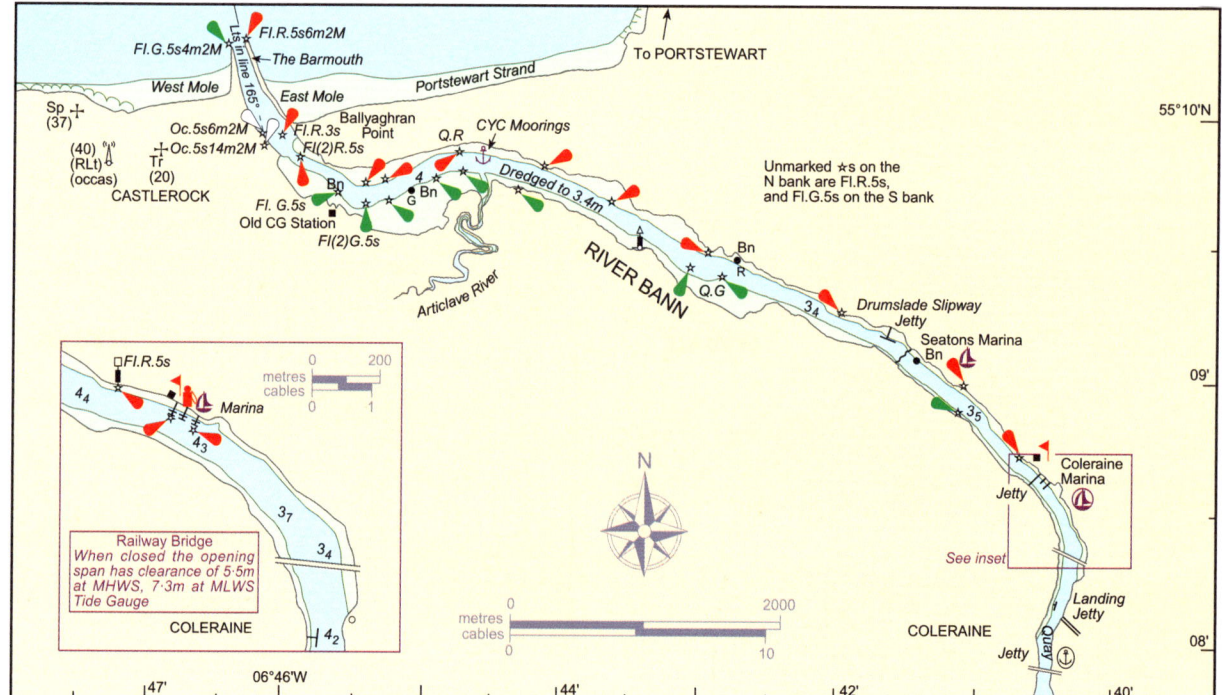

**RIVER BANN** *continued*

**CHARTS** AC 2723, 2798, 2494; Imray C64; Irish OS 4

**TIDES** –0345 Dover (Coleraine); ML 1·1; Duration 0540

**Standard Port BELFAST (←)**

| Times | | | | Height (metres) | | | |
|---|---|---|---|---|---|---|---|
| High Water | | Low Water | | MHWS | MHWN | MLWN | MLWS |
| 0100 | 0700 | 0000 | 0600 | 3·5 | 3·0 | 1·1 | 0·4 |
| 1300 | 1900 | 1200 | 1800 | | | | |
| Differences COLERAINE | | | | | | | |
| –0403 | | –0403 | | –1·3 | –1·2 | –0·2 | 0·0 |

**SHELTER** Good, once inside the river ent (The Barmouth) between 2 training walls, extending 2ca N from the beaches. Do not try to enter in strong on-shore winds or when swell breaks on the pierheads. If in doubt call Coleraine Hbr Radio or ring HM. ⚓ upstream of old CG stn, or berth at Seaton's or Coleraine marinas, 3½M & 4½M from ent, on NE bank.

## 6.13 LOUGH FOYLE

Londonderry (to SE)/Donegal (to NW) **55°14'N 06°54W**

**CHARTS** AC 2723, 2798, 2499; Imray C53, C64; Irish OS 3, 4, 7

**TIDES**
Warren Point: –0430 Dover
Moville: –0350 Dover; –0055 Londonderry; –0400 Belfast
Culmore Point: –0025 Londonderry
Londonderry: –0255 Dover
ML 1·6; Duration 0615

**Standard Port GALWAY (←)**

| Times | | | | Height (metres) | | | |
|---|---|---|---|---|---|---|---|
| High Water | | Low Water | | MHWS | MHWN | MLWN | MLWS |
| 0200 | 0900 | 0200 | 0800 | 5·1 | 3·9 | 2·0 | 0·6 |
| 1400 | 2100 | 1400 | 2000 | | | | |
| Differences LONDONDERRY | | | | | | | |
| +0254 | +0319 | +0322 | +0321 | –2·4 | –1·8 | –0·8 | –0·1 |
| INISHTRAHULL | | | | | | | |
| +0100 | +0100 | +0115 | +0200 | –1·8 | –1·4 | –0·4 | –0·2 |
| PORTMORE | | | | | | | |
| +0120 | +0120 | +0135 | +0135 | –1·3 | –1·1 | –0·4 | –0·1 |
| TRAWBREAGA BAY | | | | | | | |
| +0115 | +0059 | +0109 | +0125 | –1·1 | –0·8 | | No data |

**SHELTER** The SE side of the Lough is low lying and shallow. The NW rises steeply and has several village hbrs between the ent and Londonderry (often referred to as Derry).

**White Bay**: close N of Dunagree Point is a good ⚓ on passage.

**Greencastle**: a busy fishing hbr, open to swell in winds SW to E. Only advised for yachts in emergency.

**Moville**: the pier, with 1·5m at the end, is near the village (shops closed all day Wed), but is much used by FVs. ⚓ outside hbr is exposed; inside hbr for shoal draft only. 8 Y ⚓s are about 600m up-stream.

**Carrickarory**: pier/quay is used entirely by FVs. ⚓ in bay is sheltered in winds from SW to NNW.

**Culmore Bay**: complete shelter. ⚓ 1½ca W of Culmore Pt in pleasant cove, 4M from Londonderry.

**Londonderry, Foyle Pontoon**: AB adjacent to the centre of historic city or ⚓ close below Craigavon Bridge clearance 1·7m. Commercial operations are now at Lisahally (55°02'·6N 07°15'·6W).

**NAVIGATION** WPT Tuns PHM buoy, Fl R 3s, 55°14'·00N 06°53'·49W, 235°/2·5M to Warren Pt lt, 2·5M. The Tuns bank lies 3M NE of Magilligan Pt and may dry. The main or N Chan, ¾M wide, runs NW of The Tuns; a lesser chan, min depth 4m, runs 3ca off shore around NE side of Magilligan Pt. Beware commercial traffic. Foyle Bridge at Rosses Pt has 32m clearance. In June and July the chan

is at times obstructed by salmon nets at night. N Chan tides reach 3½kn, and up-river the ebb runs up to 6kn.

**LIGHTS AND MARKS** Inishowen Fl (2) WRG 10s 28m 18/14M; W tr, 2 B bands; vis G197°–211°, W211°–249°, R249°–000°. Warren Pt Fl 1·5s 9m 10M; W tr, G abutment; vis 232°–061°. Magilligan Pt QR 7m 4M; R structure. The main chan up to Londonderry is very well lit. Foyle Bridge centre FW each side; VQ G on W pier; VQ R on E.

**R/T** VHF Ch 14 12 16 (H24). Traffic and nav info Ch 14.

**TELEPHONE** (Code 028) HM (at Lisahally) 7186 0555, ☎ 7186 1168; MRCC 9146 3933; ⊖ 7126 1937 or 9035 8250; Marinecall 09068 969655; Police 7776 6797; Dr 7126 4868; Ⓗ 7034 5171.

**FACILITIES** **Londonderry** ☎ 7186 0313 or Ch 14 for Foyle Pontoon, £1·40, M, FW; **Prehen Boat Club** ☎ 7034 3405. **City** P & D (cans), ME, El, 🛒, R, Bar, ✉, Ⓑ, ⇌, ✈. **Culdaff Bay** (10M W of Foyle SWM buoy) 6 Y ⚓s at 55°18'N 07°09'·1W, off Bunnagee Port.

---

Above the R Bann entry, right column:

**NAVIGATION** WPT 55°11'·00N, 06°46'·65W, 165°/0·72M to ent. Appr from E of N to bring ldg lts into line at bkwtr ends. The sand bar is constantly moving but ent is dredged to approx 3·5m. Beware commercial traffic.

**LIGHTS AND MARKS** Ldg lts 165°, both Oc 5s 6/14m 2M, front on W pyramidal metal tr; rear W ☐ tr. Portstewart Pt, Oc R 10s, is 2M ENE.

**R/T** Coleraine Hbr Radio Ch 12 (Mon-Fri: HO and when vessel due). Coleraine Marina Ch M.

**TELEPHONE** (Code 028) HM 70342012, ☎ 70352000; MRCC 91463933; Marinecall 09068 969655; Rly Bridge 7032540; Police 70344122; Ⓗ 70344177; Dr 70344831.

**FACILITIES** **Seatons Marina** ☎ 70832086, mobile 07733100915, BH (14 ton), Slip (£3). **Coleraine Hbr** ☎ 7034 2012, BH (35 ton); **Coleraine Marina** (90+5Ⓥ), ☎ 70344768, £20, ME, ⚓ (by arrangement), ⚒, 🛒, Slip, D(H24), R, BH (12.5 ton); **Coleraine YC** ☎ 70344503, Bar, M; **Services**: Gas, Kos, El, Ⓔ. **Town** P & D (cans), 🛒, R, ✉, Ⓑ, ⇌, ✈ (Belfast).

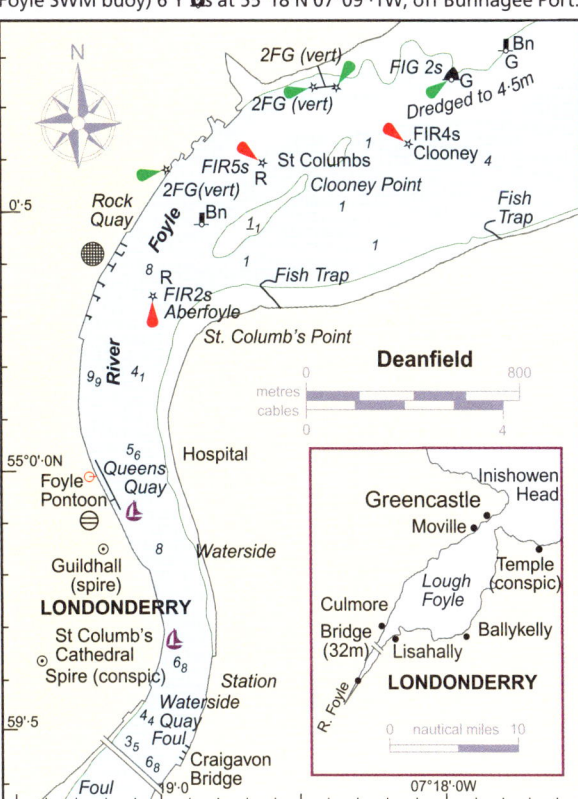

## 6.14 LOUGH SWILLY

Donegal 55°17'N 07°34'W

**CHARTS** AC 2697; Irish OS 2, 3, 6; Imray C53

**TIDES** –0500 Dover; ML 2·3; Duration 0605

**Standard Port GALWAY (→)**

| Times | | | | Height (metres) | | | |
|---|---|---|---|---|---|---|---|
| High Water | | Low Water | | MHWS | MHWN | MLWN | MLWS |
| 0200 | 0900 | 0200 | 0800 | 5·1 | 3·9 | 2·0 | 0·6 |
| 1400 | 2100 | 1400 | 2000 | | | | |
| **Differences FANAD HEAD** | | | | | | | |
| +0115 | +0040 | +0125 | +0120 | –1·1 | –0·9 | –0·5 | –0·1 |
| **RATHMULLAN** | | | | | | | |
| +0125 | +0050 | +0126 | +0118 | –0·8 | –0·7 | –0·1 | –0·1 |
| **MULROY BAY** (BAR) | | | | | | | |
| +0108 | +0052 | +0102 | +0118 | –1·2 | –1·0 | No data | |
| **SHEEP HAVEN (DOWNIES BAY)** | | | | | | | |
| +0057 | +0043 | +0053 | +0107 | –1·1 | –0·9 | No data | |

**SHELTER** Good, but beware downdrafts on E side. ⚓s N of 55°05'N may suffer from swell. ⚓s from seaward: Ballymastocher Bay, also 8 Y ⚓s, but exposed to E'lies; inside Macamish Pt, sheltered from SE to N; Rathmullan Roads N of pier, where yacht pontoon lies N/S in 3·6m MLWS; Fahan Creek and marina ent at HW–1.

**NAVIGATION** WPT 55°17'·50N 07°34'·50W, 172°/5·7M to

Dunree Hd lt. Ent is easy and main chan is well lit/buoyed. Beware: off W shore, Swilly More Rks, Kinnegar Spit and Strand; off E shore, Colpagh Rks and Inch Flats. These dangers are buoyed, as is Fahan Creek. There are many marine farms and shellfish beds S from Scraggy Bay (☎ 074 50172/59071 for permission to use pier).

**LIGHTS AND MARKS** Fanad Hd lt, Fl (5) WR 20s 39m 18/14M, touching Dunree Hd lt, Fl (2) WR 5s 46m 12/9M, leads 151° into the Lough. Thence Ballygreen Pt and Hawk's Nest in line at 202°.

**R/T** None.

**TELEPHONE** (Codes: both sides of lough 074) Rathmullan Pontoon 9158131, 9158315 (eves); MRCC 9370243; Police 9153114 (Milford) and 9361555 (Buncrana); Dr 9158416 (Rathmullan), 1850 400911(out of hours), and 9363611 (Buncrana).

**FACILITIES** **Rathmullan** Pontoon (Easter–October) ☎ 087 2480132 €10/craft/day, €20/craft/overnight, FW, slip, ▯, R, Hotel, Bar, D & P (cans), Kos, 🛒, ✉. **Ramelton** AB (drying), BY ☎ 9151082, Bar, R, D & P (cans), FW, Kos, 🛒, ✉. **Fahan Marina** ☎ 086 1082111, 4 ▼, €2/m. **Fahan**, Slip, FW, Bar, R, ✉, **Lough Swilly YC** www.loughswillyyc.com. Services (1M SE): 🛒, D & P (cans), ⛽, ✈ (Londonderry 10M bus/taxi). **Buncrana** AB (congested), Hotel, R, Bar, Ⓑ, ✉, 🛒, ▯, D & P (cans), Kos.

## OTHER HARBOURS AND ANCHORAGES IN DONEGAL

**MULROY BAY**, Donegal, **55°15´·30N 07°46´·30W**. AC 2699; HW (bar) –0455 on Dover. See 6.14. Beware Limeburner Rk, (NCM buoy, Q) 3M N of ent & the bar which is dangerous in swell or onshore winds. Obtain local advice as the depths on the bar change considerably. Ent at half flood (not HW); chan lies between Bar Rks and Sessiagh Rks, it is rep'd to run along the alignment of the charted drying spit thence through First, Second and Third Narrows (with strong tides) to Broad Water. HW at the head of the lough is 2¼ hrs later than at the bar. ‡s: Close SW of Ravedy Is (Fl 3s 9m 3M); Fanny's Bay (2m), excellent; Rosnakill Bay (3·5m) in SE side; Cranford Bay; Milford Port (3 to 4m). Beware power cable 6m, over Moross chan, barring North Water to masted boats. Facilities: **Milford Port** AB, FW, ☷; **Fanny's Bay** ✉, Shop at Downings village (1M), hotel at Rosepenna (⅜M).

**SHEEP HAVEN**, Donegal, **55°11´·00N 07°51´·00W**. AC 2699. HW –0515 on Dover. See 6.14. Bay is 2M wide with many ‡s, easily accessible in daylight, but exposed to N winds. Beware rks off Rinnafaghla Pt, and further S: Black Rk (6m) and Wherryman Rks, which dry, 1ca off E shore. ‡ or 8 Y ⚓s in Downies Bay to SE of pier; in Pollcormick inlet close W in 3m; in Ards Bay for excellent shelter, but beware the bar in strong winds. Lts: Portnablahy ldg lts 125°, both Oc 6s 7/12m 2M, B col, W bands; Downies pier hd, Fl R 3s 5m 2M, R post. Facilities: (Downies) EC Wed; ☷, FW, P (cans 300m), R, Bar; (Portnablahy Bay) ☷, P (cans), R, Bar.

**GWEEDORE HBR/BUNBEG**, Donegal, **55°03´·75N 08°18´·87W**. AC 1883. Tides see 6.15. Gweedore hbr, the estuary of the R Gweedore, has sheltered ‡s or temp AB at Bunbeg Quay, usually full of FVs. Apprs via Gola N or S Sounds are not simple especially in poor visibility. N Sound is easier with ldg lts 171°, both Oc 3s 9/13m 2M, B/W bns, on the SE tip of Gola Is. (There are also ‡s on the S and E sides of Gola Is.) E of Bo Is the bar 0·4m has a Fl G 3s and the chan, lying E of Inishinny Is and W of Inishcoole, is marked by a QG and 3 QR. A QG marks ent to Bunbeg. Night ent not advised. Facilities: FW, D at quay; ☷, ✉, Ⓑ, Bar at village ⅛M.

**BURTONPORT**, Donegal, **54°58´·93N 08°26´·60W**. AC 1879, 2792. HW –0525 on Dover; ML 2·0m; Duration 0605. See 6.15. Only appr via N Chan. Ent safe in all weathers except NW gales. Hbr very full, no space to ‡; berth on local boat at pier or go to Rutland Hbr or Aran Roads: 6 Y ⚓s 250m NE of Black Rks, Fl R 3s. Ldg marks/lts: N Chan ldg lts on Inishcoo 119·3°, both Iso 6s 6/11m 1M; front W bn, B band; rear B bn, Y band. Rutland Is ldg lts 138°, both Oc 6s 8/14m 1M; front W bn, B band; rear B bn, Y band. Burtonport ldg lts 068°, both FG 17/23m 1M; front Gy bn, W band; rear Gy bn, Y band. HM ☎ (075) 42155 (43170 home), 🖷 (074) 41205; VHF Ch 06, 12, **14**, 16. Facilities: D (just inside pier), FW (root of pier), P (⅛M inland). **Village** Bar, ✉, R, ☷, Kos.

**INISHKEEL**, Donegal, **54°50´·82N 08°26´·50W**. AC 2792. 6 Y ⚓s in Church Pool, 3ca E of Inishkeel. Open to N/NE'lies.

**TEELIN HARBOUR**, Donegal, **54°37´·50N 08°37´·87W**. AC 2792. Tides as 6.15. A possible passage ‡, mid-way between Rathlin O'Birne and Killybegs. But Hbr is open to S'ly swell and prone to squalls in NW winds. Ent, 1ca wide, is close E of Teelin Pt lt, Fl R 10s, which is hard to see by day. 4 Y ⚓s and ‡ on E side in 3m to N of pier, or ‡ on E side near pier. Many moorings and, in the NE, mussel rafts. Facilities: possible FW, D, ☷ at Carrick, 3M inland.

## 6.15 KILLYBEGS

**Donegal 54°36´·90N 08°26´·80W** ✹✹✹⚓❀

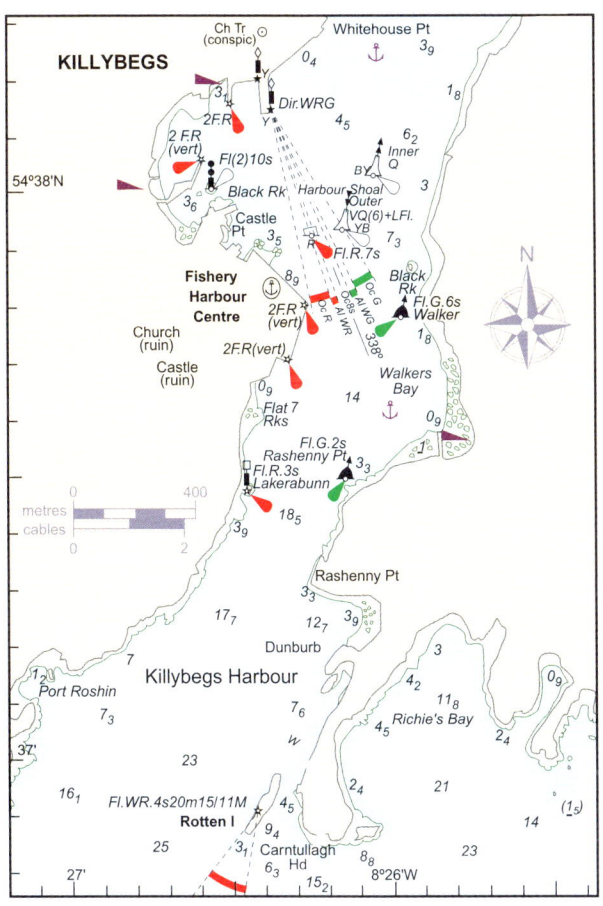

**CHARTS** AC 2702, 2792; Irish OS 10; Imray C53

**TIDES** –0520 Dover; ML 2·2; Duration 0620

**Standard Port GALWAY (⟶)**

| Times | | | | Height (metres) | | | |
|---|---|---|---|---|---|---|---|
| High Water | | Low Water | | MHWS | MHWN | MLWN | MLWS |
| 0600 | 1100 | 0000 | 0700 | 5·1 | 3·9 | 2·0 | 0·6 |
| 1800 | 2300 | 1200 | 1900 | | | | |
| **Differences KILLYBEGS** | | | | | | | |
| +0040 | +0050 | +0055 | +0035 | −1·0 | −0·9 | −0·5 | 0·0 |
| **GWEEDORE HARBOUR** | | | | | | | |
| +0048 | +0100 | +0055 | +0107 | −1·3 | −1·0 | −0·5 | −0·1 |
| **BURTONPORT** | | | | | | | |
| +0042 | +0055 | +0115 | +0055 | −1·2 | −1·0 | −0·6 | −0·1 |
| **DONEGAL HARBOUR (SALTHILL QUAY)** | | | | | | | |
| +0038 | +0050 | +0052 | +0104 | −1·2 | −0·9 | No data | |

**SHELTER** Secure natural hbr, but some swell in SSW winds. A busy major FV port, H24 access. ‡ about 2½ca NE of the Pier, off blue shed (Gallagher Bros) in 3m, clear of FV wash. Or contact HM and berth at pier. **Bruckless Hbr**, about 2M E at the head of McSwyne's Bay, is a pleasant ‡ in 1·8m but is severely restricted due to fish cages(2005), sheltered from all except SW winds. Ent on 038° between rks; ICC SDs are essential.

**NAVIGATION** WPT 54°36´·00N 08°27´·00W, 022°/0·94M to Rotten Is lt. From W, beware Manister Rk (covers at HW; dries at LW) off Fintragh B. Keep mid chan until off new Killybegs Fishery Centre, then follow the Dir lt or Y ◊ ldg marks 338° into hbr.

**LIGHTS AND MARKS** Rotten Is lt, Fl WR 4s 20m 15/11M, W tr, vis W255°-008°, R008°-039°, W039°-208°. Dir lt 338°, Oc WRG 6s 17m; W sector 336°-340° (see 6.3). Harbour Shoal (2·3m) is marked by a SCM and NCM lt buoy.

**R/T** HM Ch **14**; essential to request a berth.

**TELEPHONE** (Code 07497) HM 31032, 🖷 31840; MRCC (01) 6620922/3; Bundoran Inshore Rescue ☎ (072) 41713; ⊜ 31070; Police 31002; Dr 31148 (Surgery).

**FACILITIES Town Pier** ☎ 31032, AB (free), M, D & P (cans), FW, ME, El, CH ⚒, C (12 ton), Kos, Ⓔ, Slip, ☷, R, Bar. **Black Rock Pier** AB, M, Slip, D. **Town** ✉, Ⓑ, ⇌ (bus to Sligo), ✈ (Strandhill).

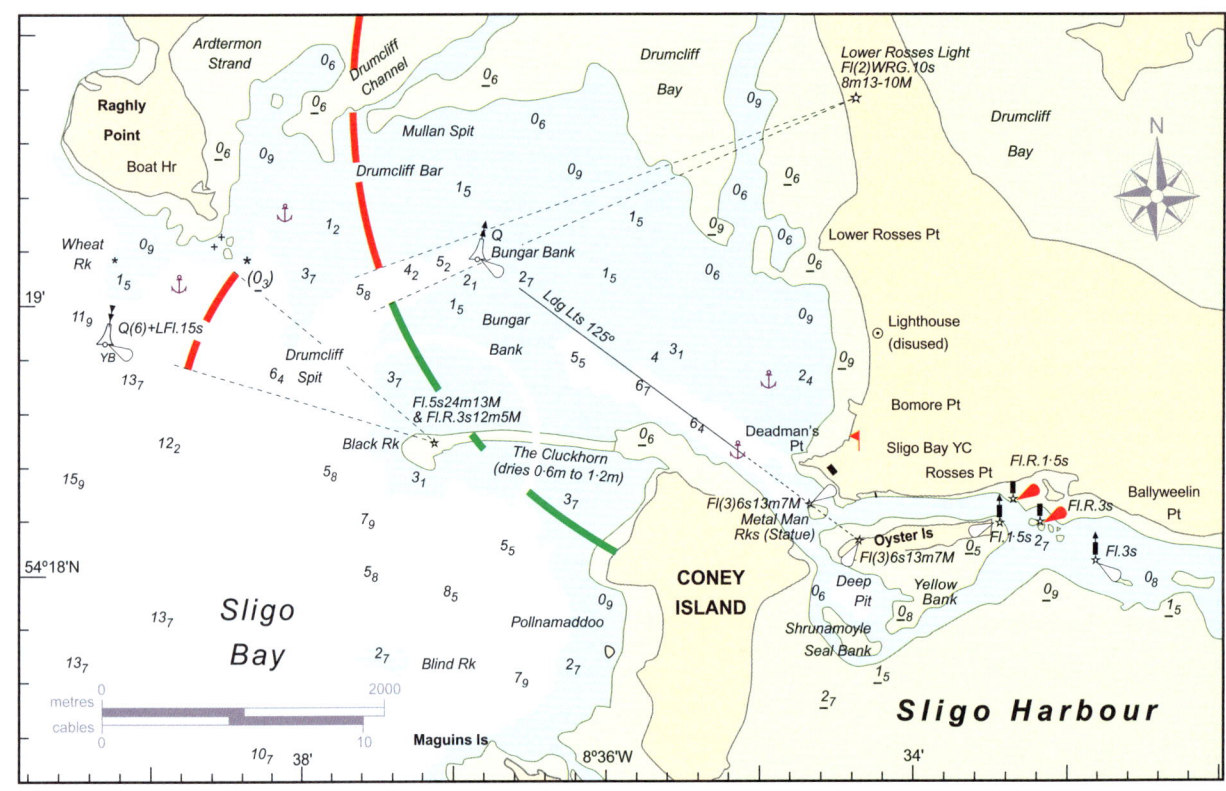

# 6.16 SLIGO

Sligo 54°18'·30N 08°34'·70W ✿✿✿✿✿✿✿✿

**CHARTS** AC 2767, 2852; Imray C54; Irish OS 16, 25

**TIDES** –0511 Dover; ML 2·3; Duration 0620

**Standard Port GALWAY** (→)

| Times | | | | Height (metres) | | | |
|---|---|---|---|---|---|---|---|
| High Water | | Low Water | | MHWS | MHWN | MLWN | MLWS |
| 0600 | 1100 | 0000 | 0700 | 5·1 | 3·9 | 2·0 | 0·6 |
| 1800 | 2300 | 1200 | 1900 | | | | |
| **Differences SLIGO HARBOUR (Oyster Is)** | | | | | | | |
| +0043 | +0055 | +0042 | +0054 | −1·0 | −0·9 | −0·5 | −0·1 |
| **MULLAGHMORE** | | | | | | | |
| +0036 | +0048 | +0047 | +0059 | −1·4 | −1·0 | −0·4 | −0·2 |
| **BALLYSADARE BAY (Culleenamore)** | | | | | | | |
| +0059 | +0111 | +0111 | +0123 | −1·2 | −0·9 | No data | |
| **KILLALA BAY (Inishcrone)** | | | | | | | |
| +0035 | +0055 | +0030 | +0050 | −1·3 | −1·2 | −0·7 | −0·2 |

**SHELTER** The lower hbr is fairly exposed; ⚓ along N side of Oyster Island, or proceed 4M (not at night) up to the shelter of Sligo town; 2nd berth below bridge for yachts.

**NAVIGATION** WPT 54°19'·15N 08°36'·77W, 125°/1·6M to front ldg lt.

- The passage between Oyster Island and Coney Island is marked 'Dangerous'.
- Pass N of Oyster Is leaving Blennick Rks to port. Passage up to Sligo town between training walls. Appr quays at HW-3 or higher.
- Some perches are in bad repair. Pilots at Raghly Pt and Rosses Pt. *Tide Tables* (based on Inishraher/Inishgort, published by Westport Hbr Comm.) available locally.

**LIGHTS AND MARKS** See 6.3 and chartlet. Channel to Sligo Deepwater Quay is well marked by lit bcns.

**R/T** Pilots VHF Ch 12 16. HM Ch 16.

**TELEPHONE** (Code 071) Hbr Office ☎/🖷 9161197, mob 086 8526233; MRCC (01) 6620922/3; ⊖ 9161064; Police 9157000; Dr 9142886; ℍ 9171111.

**FACILITIES No 3 berth** (next to bridge) AB 20-30ft €19.00, P & D (in cans), FW, ME, El, ✕, CH, C (15 ton); **Sligo YC** ☎ 9177168, 🛥s, FW, Bar, Slip. **Services:** Slip, D, ME, El, ✕, SM, Gas; **Town** 🛒, R, Bar, ✉, Ⓑ, ⇌ Irish Rail ☎ 9169888, Bus ☎ 9160066, ✈ (Strandhill) ☎ 9168280.

**MINOR HARBOUR ON S SIDE OF DONEGAL BAY**

**MULLAGHMORE 54°27'·90N 08°26'·80W**. AC 2702. Tides see 6.16. Pierhead lit Fl G 3s 5m 3M. Fair weather ⚓ in 2-3m off hbr ent, sheltered by Mullaghmore Head, except from N/NE winds. For 🛥s near hbr ent, call Liam Carey at BY, ☎/🖷 071 66106, mobile ☎ 087 2574497. Keep close to N pier to avoid shingle bank drying 1m, ⅜ of the way across the ent toward the S pier. Take the ground or dry out against the piers inside hbr berth on pontoon on bkwtr (min 1m at MLWS). Access approx HW±2 when least depth is 2m. VHF Ch 16, 8, 6. Facilities: FW at S Pier and on bkwtr, BY, ✕, D (cans), 🛒, R, Bar.

**MINOR HARBOUR/ANCHORAGE TO THE WEST**

**KILLALA BAY**, Sligo/Mayo, **54°13'·02N 09°12'·80W**. AC 2715. Tides, see 6.16. The bay, open to the N-NE, is entered between Lenadoon Pt and Kilcummin Hd, 6M to the W. 1·1M W of Kilcummin Hd are 8 Y 🛥s off Rathlackan pier, well sheltered from W'lies. Carrickpatrick ECM lt buoy, in mid-bay marks St Patrick's Rks to the W. Thence, if bound for Killala hbr, make good Killala SHM lt buoy, 7½ca to the SSW. The Round Tr and cathedral spire at Killala are conspic. Four sets of ldg bns/lts lead via a narrow chan between sand dunes and over the bar (0·3m) as follows:

- 230°, Rinnaun Pt lts Oc 10s 7/12m 5M, □ concrete trs.
- 215°, Inch Is, □ concrete trs; the rear has Dir lt Fl WRG 2s.
- 196°, Kilroe lts Oc 4s 5/10m 2M, W □ trs, which lead to ⚓ in Bartragh Pool, 6ca NE of Killala hbr; thence
- 236°, Pier lts Iso 2s 5/7m 2M, W ◇ daymarks, lead via narrow, dredged chan to pier where AB is possible in about 1·5m.

**Facilities:** FW, P & D (cans), 🛒 in town ½M.
Other hbrs in the bay: R Moy leading to Ballina should not be attempted without pilot/local knowledge. Inishcrone in the SE has a pier and lt; see 6.3.

# 6.17 WESTPORT (CLEW BAY)

Mayo 53°47'·85N 09°35'·40W

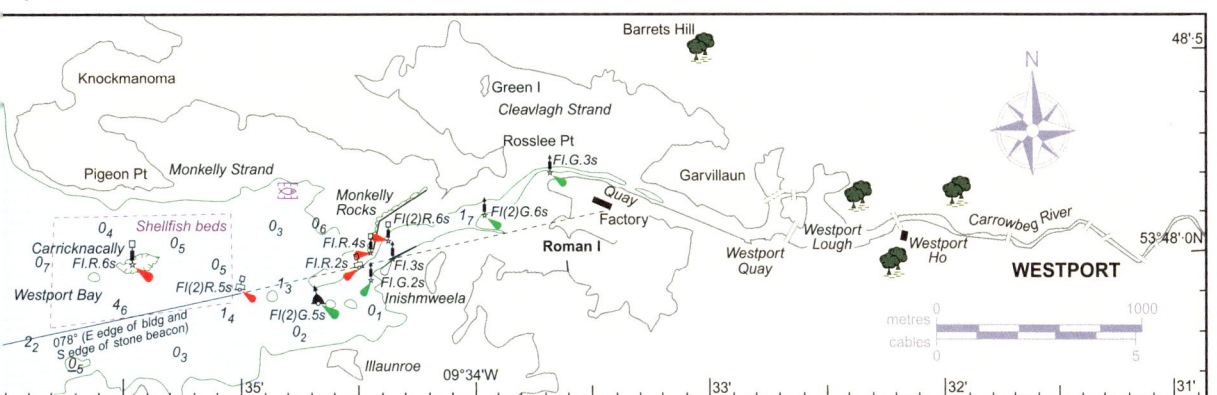

CHARTS AC 2667, 2057; Imray C54; Irish OS 30, 31

TIDES –0545 Dover; ML 2·5; Duration 0610

Standard Port GALWAY (→)

| Times | | | | Height (metres) | | | |
|---|---|---|---|---|---|---|---|
| High Water | | Low Water | | MHWS | MHWN | MLWN | MLWS |
| 0600 | 1100 | 0000 | 0700 | 5·1 | 3·9 | 2·0 | 0·6 |
| 1800 | 2300 | 1200 | 1900 | | | | |
| **BROADHAVEN** | | | | | | | |
| +0040 | +0050 | +0040 | +0050 | –1·4 | –1·1 | –0·4 | –0·1 |
| **BLACKSOD QUAY** | | | | | | | |
| +0025 | +0035 | +0040 | +0040 | –1·2 | –1·0 | –0·6 | –0·2 |
| **CLARE ISLAND** | | | | | | | |
| +0015 | +0021 | +0039 | +0027 | –0·6 | –0·4 | –0·1 | +0·2 |
| **INISHGORT/CLEW BAY** | | | | | | | |
| +0035 | +0045 | +0115 | +0100 | –0·7 | –0·5 | –0·2 | +0·2 |
| **KILLARY HARBOUR** | | | | | | | |
| +0021 | +0015 | +0035 | +0029 | –1·0 | –0·8 | –0·4 | –0·1 |
| **INISHBOFIN HARBOUR** | | | | | | | |
| +0013 | +0009 | +0021 | +0017 | –1·0 | –0·8 | –0·4 | –0·1 |
| **CLIFDEN BAY** | | | | | | | |
| +0005 | +0005 | +0016 | +0016 | –0·7 | –0·5 | No data | |
| **SLYNE HEAD** | | | | | | | |
| +0002 | +0002 | +0010 | +0010 | –0·7 | –0·5 | No data | |

SHELTER Secure ⚓s amongst the islands at all times, as follows: E of Inishlyre in 2m; 2ca NE of Dorinish More, good holding in lee of Dorinish Bar (dries); 6 ⚓s in Rosmoney Hbr 53°49'·75N 09°37'·34W; Westport Quay HW±1½, to dry out on S side; Newport Hbr (dries) can be reached above mid-flood with careful pilotage (AC 2667); dry out against N quay or ⚓ at E end of Rabbit Is.

NAVIGATION WPT 53°49'·20N 09°42'·10W, 071°/1·2M to Inishgort lt ho. Contact Tom Gibbons (Inishlyre Is) ☎ (098) 26381 for pilotage advice. Approaches to Westport Channel between Monkellys Rks and Inishmweela are well marked by lit PHMs and SHMs. Beware fish farms E of Clare I and in Newport Bay. Do not anchor or ground in the Carricknacally Shellfish Bed Area.

LIGHTS AND MARKS Westport Bay entered via Inishgort lt, L Fl 10s 11m 10M (H24), and a series of ldg lines, but not advised at night. Final appr line 080° towards lt bn, Fl 3s. but beware of drying patches on this lead inwards from Pigeon PHM. Chan from Westport Bay to Westport Quay, 1½M approx, is marked by bns.

R/T None.

TELEPHONE (Code 098) MRCC (01) 6620922/3; ⊖ (094) 9021131; Police 9025555; Ⓗ (094) 9021733.

FACILITIES Westport Quays M, AB free, Slip, ⬚, R, Bar; Services: Kos, El, Ⓔ; Town P & D (cans), ✉, Ⓑ, ⇶, ✈ (Galway/Knock). Mayo SC Rosmoney ☎ 9026160, Slip, Bar; Glénans Irish SC ☎ 9026046 on Collanmore Is;

OTHER ANCHORAGES FROM EAGLE IS TO SLYNE HEAD

BROAD HAVEN, Mayo, 54°16'·00N 09°53'·20W. AC 2703. A safe refuge except in N'lies. Easy appr across Broad Haven Bay to the ent between Brandy Pt and Gubacashel Pt, Iso WR 4s27m 12/9M, W tr. 7ca S of this lt is Ballyglas Fl G 3s on W side. ⚓ close N or S of Ballyglas which has pier (2m) and 8 Y ⚓s. In E'lies ⚓ 3ca S of Inver Pt out of the tide. Further S off Barrett Pt, the inlet narrows and turns W to Belmullet. Facilities: ⬚, ✉.

PORTNAFRANKAGH Mayo, 54°14'·95N 10°06'·00W. AC 2703. Tides approx as Broad Haven. A safe passage ⚓, close to the coastal route, but swell enters in all winds. Appr toward Port Pt, thence keep to the N side for better water; middle and S side break in onshore winds. ⚓ in 4–5m on S side, close inshore. L and slip at new pier. Unlit, but Eagle Is lt, Fl (3) 10s 67m 26M H24, W tr, is 2M N. No facilities; Belmullet 4M, ⬚.

BLACKSOD BAY, Mayo, 54°05'·00N 10°02'·00W. AC 2704. HW – 0525 on Dover; ML 2·2m; Duration 0610. See 6.17. Easy appr, accessible by night. Safe ⚓s depending on wind: NW of Blacksod Pt 6 Y ⚓s in 3m; at Elly B in 1·8m; Elly Hbr 6 Y ⚓s; Saleen Bay (ldg lts 319°, both Oc 4s, lead to pier); N of Claggan Pt. Beware drying rk 3·5ca SSE of Ardmore Pt. Lts: Blacksod Pt, Fl (2) WR 7·5s 13m 9M, see 6.3. ECM buoy Q (3) 10s. Ldg lts 181°, Oc W 5s, lead to Blacksod pier hd. Few facilities; nearest town is Belmullet.

CLARE ISLAND, Mayo, 53°48'·1N 09°56'·7W. 6 ⚓s on SE side untenable in E winds. Hotel, Bar, some ⬚.

INISHTURK, Mayo, 53°42'·3N 10°05'·2W. 8 Y ⚓s Garranty Hbr. sheltered SW to NNW winds. Slip, quay, Bar, R, ✉, 6 ⚓s on E side.

KILLARY HARBOUR, Mayo/Galway, 53°37'·83N 09°54'·00W, 4ca W of Doonee Is. AC 2706. Tides 6.17. A spectacular 7M long inlet, narrow and deep. Caution fish farms, some with Fl Y lts. Appr in good vis to identify Doonee Is and Inishbarna bns ldg 099° to ent. ⚓s off Dernasliggaun, Bundorragha and, at head of inlet, Leenaun with 8 Y ⚓s. (Village: L, ⬚, Bar, hotel). Enter **Little Killary Bay** 4ca S of Doonee Is; drying rks at ent. Good ⚓ in 3m at head of bay.

BALLYNAKILL, Galway, 53°34'·95N 10°03'·00W. AC 2706. Tides as Inishbofin/Killary. Easy appr between Cleggan Pt, Fl (3) WRG 15s and Rinvyle Pt. Then pass N of Freaghillaun South Is, E of which is good passage ⚓ in 7m. Further E, Carrigeen and Ardagh Rks lie in mid-chan. Keep N for ⚓ in Derryinver B. S chan leads to ⚓s: off Ross Pt; S of Roeillaun; in Fahy Bay with 8 Y ⚓s sheltered by bar dries 0·2m. No facilities.

INISHBOFIN, Mayo, 53°36'·60N 10°13'·20W. AC 1820, 2707. HW – 0555 on Dover; ML 1·9m. See 6.17. Very safe hbr once inside narrow ent. 2 conspic W trs lead 032°. ⚓ between new pier and Port Is. Old pier to the E dries. Gun Rock, Fl (2) 6s 8m 4M, vis 296°-253°. Facilities: FW, R, Bar, ⬚, Hotel ☎ (095) 45803.

CLIFDEN BAY, Galway, 53°29'·40N 10°05'·90W. AC 1820, 2708. HW –0600 on Dover; Duration 0610. Tides at 6.17. Before entering identify the conspic W bn on Carrickrana Rks. To the E keep clear of Coghan's Rks and Doolick Rks. Ldg marks: W bn at Fishing Pt on 080° with Clifden Castle (ruin); caution bar 0·4m off Fishing Pt. 8 Y ⚓s are 3ca S of Castle ruins, or ⚓ NE of Drinagh Pt. In the drying creek to Clifden beware ruined trng wall; dry out against the quay. Or enter Ardbear Bay to ⚓ SE of Yellow Slate Rks in 3·4m. Keep clear of fish farms. Facilities: **Town** Bar, Ⓑ, CH, D, P, ✉, R, ⬚, Kos, FW, ⬚, R, Dr, Ⓗ. Bus to Galway.

## 6.18  GALWAY BAY

Galway **53°12'N 09°08'W**

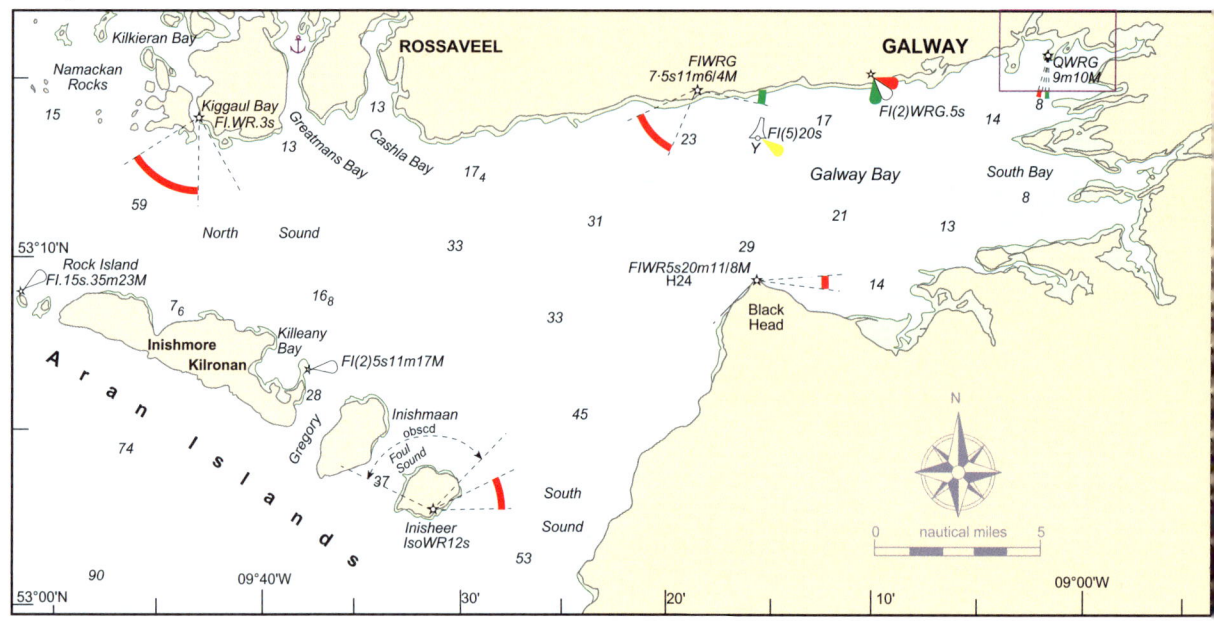

**CHARTS** AC 2173, 3339, 1984,1904; Imray C55; Irish OS 45, 46, 51

**TIDES** –0555 Dover; ML 2·9; Duration 0620

**Standard Port GALWAY (→)**

| Times | | | | Height (metres) | | | |
|---|---|---|---|---|---|---|---|
| High Water | | Low Water | | MHWS | MHWN | MLWN | MLWS |
| 0600 | 1100 | 0000 | 0700 | 5·1 | 3·9 | 2·0 | 0·6 |
| 1800 | 2300 | 1200 | 1900 | | | | |
| **Differences KILKIERAN COVE** | | | | | | | |
| +0005 | +0005 | +0016 | +0016 | –0·3 | –0·2 | –0·1 | 0·0 |
| **ROUNDSTONE BAY** | | | | | | | |
| +0003 | +0003 | +0008 | +0008 | –0·7 | –0·5 | –0·3 | –0·1 |
| **KILLEANY BAY** (Aran Islands) | | | | | | | |
| –0008 | –0008 | +0003 | +0003 | –0·4 | –0·3 | –0·2 | –0·1 |
| **LISCANNOR** | | | | | | | |
| –0003 | –0007 | +0006 | +0002 | –0·4 | –0·3 | No data | |

**SHELTER** Galway Bay is sheltered from large swells by Aran Is, but seas get up in the 20M from Aran Is to Galway. Beware salmon drift nets in the apps to many bays. The better ⚓s from Slyne Head and clockwise around Galway Bay are:

**Bunowen Bay**: (53°24'·6N 10°06'·9W). Sheltered in W-NE winds; unsafe in S'ly. Easy appr with Bunowen House brg 000°, leaving Mullauncarrickscoltia Rk (1·1m) to port. ⚓ in 3-4m below conspic Doon Hill.

**Roundstone Bay**: AC2709 (Off chartlet at 53°23'N 09°54'·5W). Safe shelter/access, except in SE'ly. 4 Y ⚓s are 5ca SSE of Roundstone, or ⚓ in 2m off N quay. There are other ⚓s E'ward in Bertraghboy and Cashel Bays.

**Kilkieran Bay**: Easy ent abm Golam Tr (conspic). 12 Y ⚓s off Kilkieran. Many ⚓s in 14M long, sheltered bay.

**Kiggaul Bay**: Easy ent, H24; ⚓ close W/NW of lt Fl WR 3s 5/3M. Depth 3 to 4m; exposed to S/SE winds.

**Greatman Bay**: Beware English Rk (dries 1·2m), Keeraun Shoal (breaks in heavy weather), Arkeena Rk, Trabaan Rk, Rin Rks and Chapel Rks. ⚓ off Natawny Quay (E side), or on 4 Y ⚓s off Maumeen Quay (dries), AB possible.

**Cashla Bay**: Easiest hbr on this coast; ent in all weather. ⚓ and 8 Y ⚓s off Sruthan Quay. Rossaveel, on E side, is a busy fishing and ferry hbr.

**Note**: There is no safe hbr from Cashla to Galway (20M).
**Bays** between Black Hd and Galway have rocks and shoals,

but give excellent shelter. Kinvarra B, Aughinish B, South B and Ballyvaghan B are the main ones. Enter Kinvarra B with caution on the flood; beware rks. Berth in small drying hbr. Beware fish farm in South B. Ballvaghan B, entered either side of Illaunloo Rk, leads to two piers (both dry) or ⚓ close NE in pool (3m). Best access HW±2.

**NAVIGATION** Enter the Bay by one of four Sounds:
- North Sound between Inishmore and Golam Tr (conspic), 4½M wide, is easiest but beware Brocklinmore Bank in heavy weather.
- Gregory Sound between Inishmore and Inishmaan, is free of dangers, but give Straw Island a berth of 2-3ca.
- Foul Sound between Inishmaan and Inisheer; only danger is Pipe Rock (dries) at end of reef extending 3ca NW of Inisheer.
- South Sound between Inisheer and mainland. Only danger Finnis Rock (dries 0·4m) 4½ca SE of E point of Inisheer (marked by ECM buoy Q (3) 10s). From S, beware Kilstiffin Rocks off Liscanor Bay.

**LIGHTS AND MARKS** Roundstone Bay: Croaghnakeela Is Fl 3·7s 7m 5M. Inishnee lt Fl (2) WRG 10s 9m 5/3M, W sector 017°-030°. Kiggaul Bay: Fl WR 3s 5m 5/3M, 329°-W-359°-R-059°.
Cashla Bay: Killeen Pt Fl (3) WR 10s 6/3M; Lion Pt Dir lt 010°, Iso WRG 4s 8/6M, 008·5°-W-011·5°. Rossaveel ldg lts 116°, Oc 3s. Black Head lt Fl WR 5s 20m 11/8M H24, vis 045°-W-268°-R (covers Illanloo Rk)-276°.

**FACILITIES**
**Bunowen Bay**: No facilities.
**Roundstone Bay**: ⚒, FW, Bar, ✉, Bus to Galway.
**Kilkieran Bay**: Bar, ☎, P, ⚒, Bus to Galway.
**Kiggaul Bay**: Bar (no ☎), shop at Lettermullen (1M).
**Greatman Bay**: Maumeen ⚒, P (1M), Bar.
**Cashla Bay: Carraroe** (1M SW) ⚒, Hotel, ☎; **Rossaveel** HM ☎ 091 572108, FW, D, ME; **Costelloe** (1½M E), Hotel, ✉, Gge.

**ARAN ISLANDS** Beware marine farm activity, only reasonable shelter is off Inishmore in Killeany Bay, but exposed to E/NE winds and crowded with FVs. HM ☎ 099 61150; 8 Y ⚓s available; or ⚓ S of Kilronan pier; or ⚓ E of Killeany Pt; or in good weather ⚓ at Portmurvy. Kilronan, facilities: 8⚓s, ⚒, D, FW, ✉; Ferry to Galway, ✈ to Galway from airstrip on beach. **Lights and marks**: Inishmore: Eeragh Island (Rk Is) Fl 15s 35m 23M, W tr, B bands. Killeany Bay: Straw Is, Fl (2) 5s 11m 17M. Kilronan pier Fl WG 1·5s. Ldg lts 192° both Oc 5s for Killeany hbr. Inishmaan unlit. Inisheer: Iso WR 12s 34m 20/16M, Racon, vis 225°-W-245° (partially obscd 225°-231° beyond 7M), R sector covers Finnis Rk.

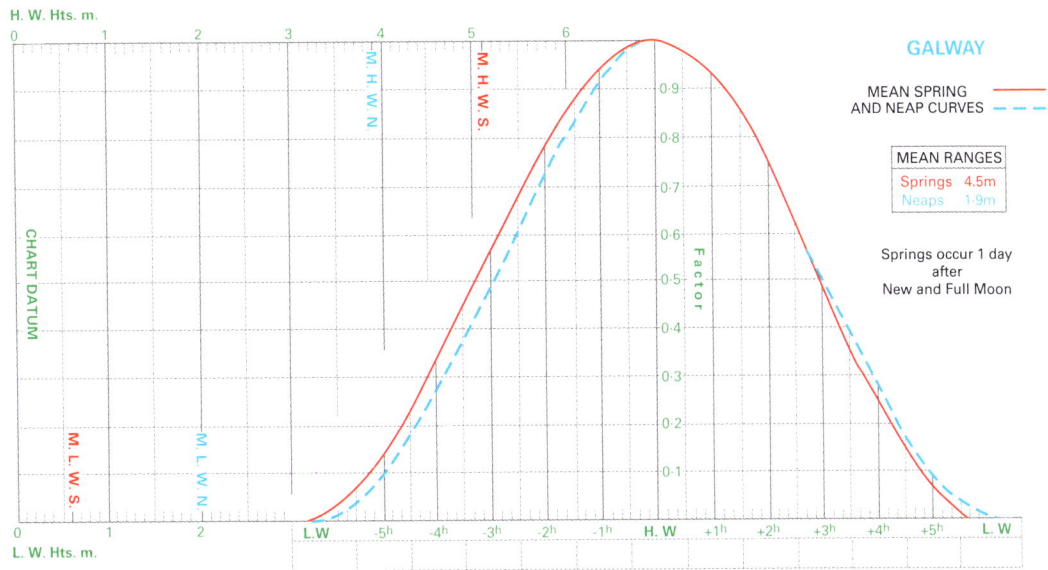

**GALWAY**

MEAN SPRING ——— AND NEAP CURVES - - - -

MEAN RANGES
Springs 4.5m
Neaps 1·9m

Springs occur 1 day
after
New and Full Moon

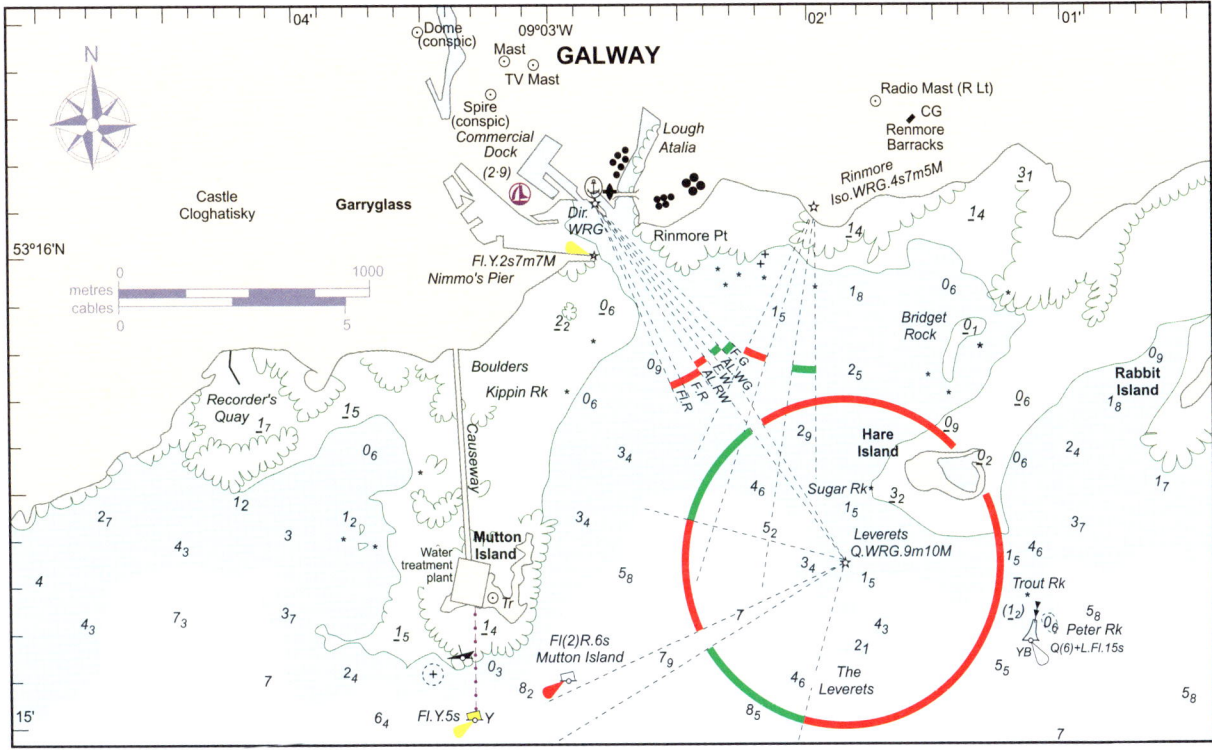

**GALWAY HARBOUR** **53°16'·07N** **09°02'·74W**

**SHELTER** Very good in Galway hbr, protected from SW'lies by Mutton Island. Dock gates open HW–2 to HW, when min depth is 6m. Enter Galway Dock and secure in SW corner of basin, or ask HM for waiting berth on lead-in pier. It is dangerous to lie in the 'Layby' (a dredged cut NE of New pier) when wind is SE or S; if strong from these points, seas sweep round the pierhead. New Harbour (2·5M ESE and home of Galway Bay SC) is nearest safe ⚓ to Galway.

**NAVIGATION** Galway WPT 53°14'·80N 09°03'·40W, 061°/1·1M to Leverets lt. Tidal information see www.gsmtides.com. Shipping information see www.aislive.com.

**LIGHTS AND MARKS** See 6.3 and chartlet. Leverets Q WRG 9m 10M; B tr, W bands; Rinmore Iso WRG 4s 7m 5M; W ☐ tr. Appr chan 325° is defined by a Dir lt WRG 7m 3M on New Pier.

**R/T** Call *Galway Harbour Radio* VHF Ch **12** 16 (HW–2½ to HW+1). Call Galway Pilots on VHF Ch **12** in case ship movements are imminent or under way and follow their instructions on berthing.

**TELEPHONE** (Code 091) HM 561874, 🖷 563738; MRCC (066) 9476109; Coast/Cliff Rescue Service (099) 61107; Police 538000; Dr 562453.

**FACILITIES Dock** AB €15 if space available, FW, D (by r/tanker not small quantities), El, ME, ⚒, C (35 ton), CH, LB, PV, SM, 🛒, R, Bar; **Galway YC** M, Slip, FW, C, CH, Bar; **Galway Bay SC** ☎ 794527, M, CH, Bar; **Town** P, D, ACA, Gas, Gaz, Kos, 🛒, R, Bar, ✉, Ⓑ, ⛽, ✈ Carnmore (6M to the E of Galway City direct flights to UK see www.aerann.com). The nearest D by pump is Rossaveal.

**TIME ZONE (UT)**
For Summer Time add ONE hour in **non-shaded areas**

## GALWAY  LAT 53°16′N  LONG 9°03′W
TIMES AND HEIGHTS OF HIGH AND LOW WATERS

Dates in red are **SPRINGS**
Dates in blue are **NEAPS**

YEAR **2008**

| JANUARY | | FEBRUARY | | MARCH | | APRIL | |
|---|---|---|---|---|---|---|---|
| Time  m | Time  m | Time  m | Time  m | Time  m | Time  m | Time  m | Time  m |
| **1** 0450 2.1 1117 3.9 TU 1719 1.9 | **16** 0412 1.7 1041 4.3 W 1636 1.6 2326 4.1 | **1** 0617 2.2 1213 3.4 F 1857 2.2 | **16** 0014 3.8 0630 1.9 SA 1257 3.9 1910 2.0 | **1** 0537 2.2 1124 3.3 SA 1826 2.4 | **16** 0007 3.7 0628 1.8 SU 1255 3.8 1910 2.0 | **1** 0120 3.6 0735 1.8 TU 1431 3.6 2005 1.9 | **16** 0218 4.3 0829 1.2 W 1447 4.4 2041 1.4 |
| **2** 0002 3.9 0557 2.1 W 1219 3.8 1830 2.0 | **17** 0521 1.8 1148 4.2 TH 1745 1.7 | **2** 0118 3.6 0738 2.1 SA 1415 3.5 2016 2.1 | **17** 0148 4.0 0807 1.6 SU 1424 4.0 2031 1.7 | **2** 0011 3.4 0709 2.2 SU 1409 3.3 1950 2.2 | **17** 0140 3.9 0801 1.5 M 1418 4.0 2023 1.7 | **2** 0233 3.9 0826 1.4 W 1510 4.0 2049 1.4 | **17** 0306 4.5 0909 1.0 TH 1529 4.6 2120 1.1 |
| **3** 0104 3.9 0705 2.1 TH 1331 3.7 1942 2.0 | **18** 0036 4.1 0645 1.8 F 1305 4.2 1914 1.7 | **3** 0241 3.8 0843 1.9 SU 1522 3.7 2107 1.8 | **18** 0256 4.3 0908 1.3 M 1525 4.3 2122 1.3 | **3** 0225 3.6 0816 1.9 M 1510 3.6 2043 1.8 | **18** 0243 4.3 0857 1.2 TU 1511 4.3 2107 1.3 | **3** 0315 4.2 0908 1.0 TH 1543 4.4 2128 1.0 | **18** 0348 4.7 0945 0.9 F 1607 4.8 2156 0.9 |
| **4** 0205 4.0 0807 2.0 F 1437 3.8 2037 1.9 | **19** 0152 4.3 0805 1.6 SA 1423 4.3 2030 1.6 | **4** 0331 4.0 0929 1.5 M 1604 4.0 2147 1.5 | **19** 0347 4.6 0954 0.9 TU 1612 4.6 2203 1.0 | **4** 0314 3.9 0903 1.5 TU 1545 4.0 2123 1.4 | **19** 0331 4.6 0937 0.9 W 1554 4.6 2145 1.0 | **4** 0352 4.6 0947 0.6 F 1616 4.7 2206 0.6 | **19** 0427 4.8 1020 0.8 SA 1643 4.9 2233 0.8 |
| **5** 0257 4.1 0858 1.8 SA 1528 4.0 2120 1.7 | **20** 0257 4.5 0907 1.3 SU 1526 4.5 2125 1.3 | **5** 0411 4.3 1009 1.2 TU 1640 4.3 2224 1.2 | **20** 0432 4.9 1034 0.6 W 1655 4.8 2243 0.8 | **5** 0351 4.2 0943 1.0 W 1618 4.3 2200 1.0 | **20** 0413 4.8 1012 0.6 TH 1634 4.8 2221 0.7 | **5** 0429 4.9 1023 0.4 SA 1650 5.0 2243 0.4 | **20** 0505 4.8 1053 0.8 SU 1718 4.9 ○ 2308 0.8 |
| **6** 0341 4.3 0943 1.6 SU 1611 4.1 2159 1.6 | **21** 0351 4.7 0959 1.0 M 1619 4.7 2212 1.1 | **6** 0448 4.5 1046 0.8 W 1715 4.5 2300 0.9 | **21** 0514 5.0 1112 0.4 TH 1736 4.9 ○ 2321 0.6 | **6** 0426 4.5 1019 0.7 TH 1651 4.6 2236 0.7 | **21** 0453 5.0 1047 0.5 F 1712 4.9 ○ 2258 0.6 | **6** 0507 5.1 1059 0.2 SU 1725 5.2 ● 2320 0.2 | **21** 0542 4.8 1124 0.9 M 1753 4.9 2341 0.8 |
| **7** 0421 4.5 1023 1.3 M 1650 4.3 2237 1.4 | **22** 0441 5.0 1046 0.7 TU 1708 4.9 ○ 2257 0.9 | **7** 0525 4.8 1121 0.6 TH 1750 4.7 ● 2336 0.7 | **22** 0555 5.1 1148 0.3 F 1815 5.0 2358 0.5 | **7** 0502 4.8 1055 0.3 F 1724 4.9 ● 2311 0.4 | **22** 0532 5.0 1121 0.5 SA 1748 5.0 2333 0.5 | **7** 0547 5.3 1136 0.1 M 1802 5.2 2359 0.2 | **22** 0617 4.7 1153 1.0 TU 1827 4.8 |
| **8** 0500 4.6 1102 1.1 TU 1728 4.5 ● 2315 1.2 | **23** 0528 5.1 1129 0.5 W 1753 4.9 2339 0.8 | **8** 0602 4.9 1156 0.4 F 1825 4.8 | **23** 0633 5.1 1222 0.4 SA 1852 4.9 | **8** 0538 5.1 1129 0.1 SA 1757 5.0 2346 0.3 | **23** 0608 5.0 1153 0.5 SU 1823 4.9 | **8** 0627 5.2 1214 0.2 TU 1840 5.2 | **23** 0014 1.0 0651 4.5 W 1223 1.2 1901 4.5 |
| **9** 0539 4.7 1139 0.9 W 1806 4.6 2351 1.1 | **24** 0612 5.2 1209 0.4 TH 1836 4.9 | **9** 0010 0.6 0637 5.1 SA 1230 0.3 1858 4.9 | **24** 0033 0.6 0709 5.0 SU 1254 0.5 1927 4.8 | **9** 0614 5.2 1203 0.1 SU 1831 5.1 | **24** 0007 0.6 0643 4.9 M 1224 0.7 1856 4.8 | **9** 0040 0.3 0708 5.1 W 1254 0.5 1919 5.0 | **24** 0048 1.1 0725 4.3 TH 1255 1.4 1936 4.4 |
| **10** 0618 4.8 1214 0.8 TH 1844 4.6 | **25** 0020 0.7 0653 5.1 F 1248 0.4 1917 4.9 | **10** 0046 0.6 0713 5.1 SU 1304 0.3 1932 4.8 | **25** 0108 0.7 0744 4.8 M 1326 0.8 2001 4.6 | **10** 0022 0.2 0649 5.2 M 1235 0.2 1904 5.0 | **25** 0040 0.8 0716 4.7 TU 1253 0.9 1929 4.6 | **10** 0123 0.5 0753 4.8 TH 1337 0.9 2004 4.6 | **25** 0123 1.4 0802 4.1 F 1329 1.6 2015 4.2 |
| **11** 0027 1.1 0656 4.9 F 1250 0.7 1920 4.6 | **26** 0059 0.8 0734 5.0 SA 1324 0.6 1957 4.7 | **11** 0122 0.6 0748 5.0 M 1341 0.5 2007 4.7 | **26** 0142 1.0 0817 4.5 TU 1358 1.1 2036 4.3 | **11** 0100 0.3 0726 5.1 TU 1316 0.4 1939 4.8 | **26** 0112 1.0 0748 4.4 W 1323 1.2 2002 4.4 | **11** 0212 0.9 0844 4.4 F 1426 1.4 2059 4.3 | **26** 0202 1.6 0843 3.9 SA 1407 1.9 2101 4.0 |
| **12** 0104 1.1 0733 4.9 SA 1326 0.7 1958 4.6 | **27** 0137 1.0 0812 4.8 SU 1400 0.8 2037 4.5 | **12** 0202 0.9 0826 4.8 TU 1421 0.9 2046 4.4 | **27** 0217 1.3 0850 4.2 W 1431 1.5 2115 4.0 | **12** 0140 0.6 0806 4.8 W 1356 0.8 2019 4.5 | **27** 0146 1.3 0822 4.1 TH 1354 1.5 2039 4.1 | **12** 0310 1.3 0950 4.0 SA 1528 1.8 ◐ 2218 3.9 | **27** 0248 1.8 0933 3.7 SU 1455 2.2 2156 3.8 |
| **13** 0143 1.2 0811 4.8 SU 1405 0.8 2038 4.5 | **28** 0216 1.2 0851 4.5 M 1438 1.2 2120 4.2 | **13** 0247 1.2 0911 4.5 W 1507 1.2 2139 4.2 | **28** 0256 1.7 0929 3.8 TH 1507 1.8 2201 3.8 | **13** 0225 1.0 0853 4.4 TH 1442 1.3 2110 4.2 | **28** 0222 1.6 0902 3.8 F 1429 1.9 2125 3.8 | **13** 0432 1.6 1112 3.8 SU 1705 2.1 2355 3.9 | **28** 0353 2.0 1032 3.6 M 1611 2.3 ◑ 2256 3.7 |
| **14** 0226 1.3 0852 4.7 M 1449 1.0 2126 4.3 | **29** 0258 1.5 0930 4.2 TU 1518 1.5 2205 4.0 | **14** 0341 1.5 1012 4.2 TH 1603 1.6 ◑ 2249 3.9 | **29** 0344 2.0 1020 3.5 F 1554 2.2 ◑ 2258 3.5 | **14** 0320 1.4 0956 4.1 F 1539 1.7 ◑ 2225 3.9 | **29** 0306 1.9 0953 3.6 SA 1514 2.2 ◑ 2223 3.6 | **14** 0613 1.6 1240 3.8 M 1847 2.0 | **29** 0543 1.9 1138 3.6 TU 1824 2.2 |
| **15** 0314 1.5 0942 4.5 TU 1538 1.3 ◑ 2222 4.2 | **30** 0346 1.9 1014 3.9 W 1606 1.9 ◑ 2256 3.8 | **15** 0451 1.8 1127 3.9 F 1717 1.9 | | **15** 0437 1.8 1119 3.8 SA 1707 2.1 | **30** 0438 2.2 1056 3.4 SU 1755 2.4 2328 3.5 | **15** 0116 4.0 0733 1.5 TU 1354 4.1 1956 1.7 | **30** 0001 3.8 0647 1.7 W 1301 3.8 1921 1.9 |
| | **31** 0452 2.1 1104 3.6 TH 1714 2.2 2356 3.6 | | | | **31** 0633 2.1 1224 3.3 M 1911 2.2 | | |

Chart Datum: 0·20 metres above Ordnance Datum (Dublin). HAT is 5·6 metres above Chart Datum.

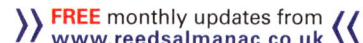
>> **FREE** monthly updates from <<
www.reedsalmanac.co.uk

**TIME ZONE (UT)**
For Summer Time add ONE hour in **non-shaded areas**

## GALWAY   LAT 53°16′N   LONG 9°03′W
TIMES AND HEIGHTS OF HIGH AND LOW WATERS

Dates in red are SPRINGS
Dates in blue are NEAPS

YEAR **2008**

N Ireland

### MAY

| Time m | Time m |
|---|---|
| **1** 0116 4.0 / 0741 1.5 / TH 1412 4.1 / 2010 1.5 | **16** 0234 4.3 / 0836 1.3 / F 1458 4.4 / 2051 1.3 |
| **2** 0221 4.3 / 0829 1.1 / F 1456 4.4 / 2053 1.1 | **17** 0319 4.4 / 0915 1.2 / SA 1537 4.6 / 2130 1.2 |
| **3** 0309 4.6 / 0911 0.8 / SA 1535 4.8 / 2134 0.9 | **18** 0400 4.5 / 0952 1.2 / SU 1614 4.6 / 2208 1.1 |
| **4** 0353 4.9 / 0951 0.6 / SU 1614 5.0 / 2214 0.5 | **19** 0439 4.5 / 1026 1.2 / M 1649 4.7 / 2244 1.1 |
| **5** 0437 5.1 / 1031 0.4 / M 1654 5.2 / ● 2256 0.3 | **20** 0516 4.5 / 1058 1.2 / TU 1724 4.7 / ○ 2320 1.1 |
| **6** 0523 5.2 / 1111 0.4 / TU 1737 5.3 / 2340 0.3 | **21** 0553 4.4 / 1129 1.3 / W 1801 4.7 / 2356 1.1 |
| **7** 0609 5.2 / 1154 0.5 / W 1821 5.2 | **22** 0630 4.4 / 1202 1.4 / TH 1838 4.6 |
| **8** 0025 0.3 / 0655 5.1 / TH 1239 0.7 / 1907 5.0 | **23** 0032 1.2 / 0707 4.3 / F 1237 1.5 / 1916 4.5 |
| **9** 0113 0.5 / 0744 4.8 / F 1325 1.0 / 1956 4.7 | **24** 0110 1.3 / 0746 4.2 / SA 1314 1.6 / 1956 4.3 |
| **10** 0204 0.8 / 0837 4.5 / SA 1417 1.4 / 2054 4.4 | **25** 0150 1.4 / 0827 4.1 / SU 1355 1.8 / 2040 4.2 |
| **11** 0303 1.2 / 0940 4.2 / SU 1519 1.7 / 2208 4.2 | **26** 0234 1.5 / 0913 4.0 / M 1443 1.9 / 2130 4.1 |
| **12** 0416 1.4 / 1053 4.0 / M 1642 1.9 / ◑ 2328 4.0 | **27** 0326 1.6 / 1005 3.9 / TU 1542 2.0 / 2225 4.0 |
| **13** 0538 1.5 / 1206 4.0 / TU 1807 1.9 | **28** 0427 1.7 / 1101 3.9 / W 1702 2.0 / ◑ 2322 4.1 |
| **14** 0039 4.1 / 0649 1.5 / W 1316 4.1 / 1914 1.8 | **29** 0536 1.6 / 1200 4.0 / TH 1823 1.9 |
| **15** 0142 4.2 / 0749 1.4 / TH 1412 4.3 / 2008 1.5 | **30** 0023 4.2 / 0643 1.5 / F 1304 4.2 / 1925 1.6 |
| | **31** 0128 4.3 / 0743 1.3 / SA 1406 4.4 / 2017 1.3 |

### JUNE

| Time m | Time m |
|---|---|
| **1** 0229 4.5 / 0835 1.1 / SU 1458 4.7 / 2105 1.0 | **16** 0335 4.1 / 0925 1.5 / M 1547 4.4 / 2147 1.4 |
| **2** 0323 4.8 / 0922 0.9 / M 1545 5.0 / 2151 0.7 | **17** 0417 4.2 / 1003 1.5 / TU 1624 4.5 / 2227 1.2 |
| **3** 0414 4.9 / 1008 0.7 / TU 1632 5.1 / ● 2238 0.5 | **18** 0457 4.2 / 1040 1.4 / W 1702 4.5 / ○ 2306 1.1 |
| **4** 0505 5.0 / 1054 0.6 / W 1720 5.2 / 2327 0.4 | **19** 0536 4.3 / 1116 1.3 / TH 1741 4.6 / 2344 1.1 |
| **5** 0556 5.1 / 1140 0.7 / TH 1809 5.2 | **20** 0615 4.3 / 1151 1.3 / F 1820 4.6 |
| **6** 0015 0.4 / 0645 5.0 / F 1228 0.8 / 1858 5.1 | **21** 0021 1.0 / 0652 4.4 / SA 1227 1.3 / 1858 4.6 |
| **7** 0104 0.5 / 0734 4.8 / SA 1315 1.0 / 1948 4.9 | **22** 0058 1.0 / 0730 4.3 / SU 1304 1.3 / 1937 4.5 |
| **8** 0153 0.7 / 0825 4.6 / SU 1404 1.2 / 2042 4.6 | **23** 0135 1.0 / 0808 4.3 / M 1342 1.4 / 2017 4.5 |
| **9** 0245 0.9 / 0920 4.3 / M 1458 1.5 / 2144 4.3 | **24** 0214 1.1 / 0848 4.2 / TU 1424 1.5 / 2101 4.4 |
| **10** 0343 1.2 / 1020 4.1 / TU 1602 1.7 / ◑ 2249 4.1 | **25** 0257 1.2 / 0932 4.2 / W 1513 1.6 / 2151 4.3 |
| **11** 0449 1.4 / 1122 4.0 / W 1715 1.9 / 2353 4.0 | **26** 0346 1.3 / 1023 4.1 / TH 1610 1.7 / ◑ 2247 4.2 |
| **12** 0555 1.6 / 1224 4.0 / TH 1825 1.9 | **27** 0442 1.4 / 1118 4.1 / F 1718 1.8 / 2346 4.2 |
| **13** 0055 4.0 / 0659 1.7 / F 1326 4.0 / 1928 1.8 | **28** 0544 1.5 / 1219 4.2 / SA 1834 1.7 |
| **14** 0156 4.0 / 0756 1.7 / SA 1421 4.1 / 2021 1.6 | **29** 0051 4.2 / 0654 1.5 / SU 1327 4.3 / 1946 1.5 |
| **15** 0249 4.0 / 0844 1.6 / SU 1507 4.2 / 2106 1.5 | **30** 0201 4.3 / 0804 1.4 / M 1432 4.5 / 2046 1.2 |

### JULY

| Time m | Time m |
|---|---|
| **1** 0305 4.5 / 0902 1.2 / TU 1528 4.8 / 2139 0.9 | **16** 0404 4.0 / 0946 1.6 / W 1610 4.3 / 2212 1.2 |
| **2** 0401 4.7 / 0954 1.0 / W 1619 5.0 / 2229 0.6 | **17** 0444 4.1 / 1025 1.4 / TH 1649 4.4 / 2251 1.0 |
| **3** 0454 4.9 / 1043 0.8 / TH 1710 5.1 / ● 2318 0.4 | **18** 0523 4.3 / 1102 1.2 / F 1726 4.6 / ○ 2328 0.8 |
| **4** 0545 4.9 / 1130 0.7 / F 1800 5.1 | **19** 0559 4.4 / 1138 1.0 / SA 1804 4.7 |
| **5** 0005 0.3 / 0633 5.0 / SA 1216 0.7 / 1847 5.1 | **20** 0003 0.7 / 0635 4.5 / SU 1213 1.0 / 1840 4.7 |
| **6** 0050 0.3 / 0719 4.9 / SU 1300 0.8 / 1934 5.0 | **21** 0038 0.6 / 0710 4.6 / M 1247 0.9 / 1916 4.7 |
| **7** 0134 0.5 / 0804 4.7 / M 1343 0.9 / 2021 4.7 | **22** 0112 0.6 / 0744 4.5 / TU 1321 1.0 / 1951 4.7 |
| **8** 0217 0.7 / 0851 4.5 / TU 1428 1.2 / 2110 4.5 | **23** 0148 0.7 / 0818 4.5 / W 1400 1.1 / 2028 4.6 |
| **9** 0303 1.0 / 0940 4.3 / W 1517 1.5 / 2204 4.2 | **24** 0227 0.9 / 0854 4.4 / TH 1443 1.3 / 2113 4.4 |
| **10** 0354 1.4 / 1032 4.0 / TH 1616 1.8 / ◑ 2300 3.9 | **25** 0312 1.2 / 0939 4.2 / F 1534 1.5 / ◑ 2211 4.2 |
| **11** 0453 1.7 / 1127 3.9 / F 1727 1.9 | **26** 0404 1.4 / 1036 4.1 / SA 1637 1.7 / 2316 4.1 |
| **12** 0000 3.7 / 0559 1.9 / SA 1229 3.8 / 1842 2.0 | **27** 0506 1.6 / 1143 4.0 / SU 1757 1.8 |
| **13** 0109 3.6 / 0711 2.0 / SU 1339 3.8 / 1951 1.9 | **28** 0028 4.0 / 0622 1.7 / M 1301 4.1 / 1933 1.6 |
| **14** 0221 3.7 / 0814 1.9 / M 1442 3.9 / 2047 1.7 | **29** 0148 4.1 / 0751 1.6 / TU 1422 4.3 / 2042 1.3 |
| **15** 0318 3.8 / 0904 1.8 / TU 1530 4.1 / 2132 1.5 | **30** 0258 4.3 / 0855 1.4 / W 1523 4.6 / 2135 0.9 |
| | **31** 0355 4.6 / 0946 1.1 / TH 1614 4.9 / 2222 0.6 |

### AUGUST

| Time m | Time m |
|---|---|
| **1** 0445 4.8 / 1032 0.8 / F 1702 5.1 / ● 2307 0.3 | **16** 0503 4.4 / 1041 1.0 / SA 1708 4.7 / ○ 2303 0.6 |
| **2** 0532 4.9 / 1116 0.6 / SA 1747 5.2 / 2348 0.2 | **17** 0537 4.6 / 1142 0.8 / SU 1742 4.8 / 2337 0.4 |
| **3** 0616 5.0 / 1157 0.5 / SU 1831 5.2 | **18** 0611 4.7 / 1149 0.6 / M 1816 4.9 |
| **4** 0028 0.2 / 0658 5.0 / M 1237 0.6 / 1912 5.0 | **19** 0010 0.4 / 0643 4.8 / TU 1222 0.6 / 1849 5.0 |
| **5** 0107 0.4 / 0738 4.8 / TU 1316 0.7 / 1952 4.8 | **20** 0044 0.4 / 0714 4.8 / W 1257 0.7 / 1922 4.9 |
| **6** 0144 0.6 / 0818 4.6 / W 1354 1.0 / 2033 4.5 | **21** 0119 0.6 / 0745 4.7 / TH 1333 0.8 / 1957 4.7 |
| **7** 0223 1.0 / 0858 4.4 / TH 1434 1.3 / 2116 4.2 | **22** 0157 0.8 / 0818 4.5 / F 1415 1.1 / 2040 4.5 |
| **8** 0304 1.4 / 0941 4.1 / F 1521 1.7 / ◑ 2204 3.8 | **23** 0241 1.2 / 0900 4.3 / SA 1504 1.4 / ◑ 2140 4.2 |
| **9** 0354 1.8 / 1028 3.8 / SA 1626 2.0 / 2301 3.6 | **24** 0333 1.6 / 0959 4.1 / SU 1607 1.8 / 2256 3.9 |
| **10** 0504 2.1 / 1124 3.6 / SU 1801 2.1 | **25** 0440 1.9 / 1117 3.9 / M 1741 1.9 |
| **11** 0017 3.4 / 0633 2.2 / M 1247 3.6 / 1926 2.0 | **26** 0019 3.8 / 0616 2.0 / TU 1255 3.9 / 1938 1.7 |
| **12** 0206 3.4 / 0748 2.1 / TU 1428 3.7 / 2030 1.8 | **27** 0148 4.0 / 0750 1.8 / W 1422 4.2 / 2042 1.3 |
| **13** 0310 3.7 / 0843 1.9 / W 1520 4.0 / 2114 1.5 | **28** 0255 4.3 / 0848 1.4 / TH 1518 4.6 / 2128 0.9 |
| **14** 0352 3.9 / 0926 1.6 / TH 1558 4.2 / 2151 1.1 | **29** 0345 4.6 / 0934 1.1 / F 1604 4.9 / 2208 0.6 |
| **15** 0428 4.2 / 1004 1.3 / F 1633 4.5 / 2227 0.8 | **30** 0430 4.8 / 1016 0.6 / SA 1647 5.1 / ● 2247 0.3 |
| | **31** 0512 5.0 / 1055 0.6 / SU 1728 5.2 / 2324 0.2 |

Chart Datum: 0·20 metres above Ordnance Datum (Dublin). HAT is 5·6 metres above Chart Datum.

# Galway Tides

**TIME ZONE (UT)**
For Summer Time add ONE hour in **non-shaded areas**

## GALWAY   LAT 53°16′N   LONG 9°03′W
### TIMES AND HEIGHTS OF HIGH AND LOW WATERS

Dates in red are **SPRINGS**
Dates in blue are **NEAPS**

YEAR **2008**

### SEPTEMBER

| Day | Time m | Time m | Time m | Time m |
|---|---|---|---|---|
| 1 M | 0553 5.1 | 1134 0.5 | 1808 5.2 | |
| 16 TU | 0538 4.9 | 1121 0.5 | 1747 5.1 | 2339 0.3 |
| 2 TU | 0001 0.3 | 0631 5.0 | 1211 0.5 | 1846 5.1 |
| 17 W | 0610 5.0 | 1155 0.4 | 1821 5.2 | |
| 3 W | 0036 0.5 | 0708 4.9 | 1246 0.7 | 1922 4.9 |
| 18 TH | 0014 0.4 | 0642 5.0 | 1231 0.5 | 1856 5.1 |
| 4 TH | 0110 0.8 | 0743 4.7 | 1321 1.0 | 1958 4.6 |
| 19 F | 0051 0.6 | 0715 4.9 | 1310 0.7 | 1935 4.9 |
| 5 F | 0144 1.1 | 0819 4.5 | 1356 1.3 | 2035 4.2 |
| 20 SA | 0131 0.9 | 0752 4.7 | 1353 1.0 | 2022 4.5 |
| 6 SA | 0219 1.5 | 0856 4.2 | 1435 1.7 | 2118 3.9 |
| 21 SU | 0216 1.3 | 0837 4.4 | 1443 1.4 | 2125 4.2 |
| 7 SU | 0259 1.9 | 0940 3.9 | 1524 2.1 | ◗ 2214 3.5 |
| 22 M | 0311 1.8 | 0939 4.1 | 1550 1.8 | ◗ 2247 3.9 |
| 8 M | 0403 2.3 | 1034 3.7 | 1727 2.3 | 2326 3.3 |
| 23 TU | 0428 2.1 | 1108 3.9 | 1749 1.9 | |
| 9 TU | 0609 2.4 | 1142 3.5 | 1857 2.2 | |
| 24 W | 0017 3.9 | 0624 2.1 | 1254 4.0 | 1932 1.6 |
| 10 W | 0155 3.4 | 0720 2.2 | 1408 3.7 | 2001 1.9 |
| 25 TH | 0142 4.1 | 0739 1.8 | 1410 4.3 | 2028 1.3 |
| 11 TH | 0252 3.7 | 0815 1.9 | 1458 4.0 | 2045 1.5 |
| 26 F | 0241 4.4 | 0832 1.5 | 1502 4.7 | 2109 0.9 |
| 12 F | 0328 4.0 | 0858 1.6 | 1534 4.3 | 2122 1.1 |
| 27 SA | 0327 4.7 | 0914 1.1 | 1545 5.0 | 2146 0.7 |
| 13 SA | 0401 4.3 | 0937 1.2 | 1607 4.6 | 2157 0.8 |
| 28 SU | 0408 5.0 | 0954 0.9 | 1626 5.2 | 2222 0.5 |
| 14 SU | 0434 4.6 | 1013 0.9 | 1640 4.8 | 2232 0.5 |
| 29 M | 0447 5.1 | 1032 0.7 | 1705 5.2 | ● 2258 0.5 |
| 15 M | 0506 4.8 | 1048 0.6 | 1713 5.0 | ○ 2306 0.3 |
| 30 TU | 0525 5.1 | 1109 0.6 | 1742 5.2 | 2332 0.6 |

### OCTOBER

| Day | Time m | Time m | Time m | Time m |
|---|---|---|---|---|
| 1 W | 0601 5.1 | 1144 0.7 | 1819 5.0 | |
| 16 TH | 0537 5.2 | 1131 0.4 | 1756 5.3 | 2347 0.5 |
| 2 TH | 0004 0.8 | 0636 5.0 | 1218 0.9 | 1853 4.8 |
| 17 F | 0615 5.2 | 1210 0.5 | 1838 5.2 | |
| 3 F | 0036 1.1 | 0711 4.8 | 1251 1.1 | 1928 4.5 |
| 18 SA | 0028 0.7 | 0655 5.1 | 1253 0.7 | 1923 5.0 |
| 4 SA | 0108 1.4 | 0746 4.6 | 1326 1.4 | 2005 4.2 |
| 19 SU | 0112 1.0 | 0738 4.9 | 1339 1.0 | 2014 4.6 |
| 5 SU | 0142 1.7 | 0824 4.3 | 1402 1.7 | 2048 3.9 |
| 20 M | 0200 1.5 | 0828 4.6 | 1432 1.4 | 2119 4.3 |
| 6 M | 0220 2.1 | 0908 4.0 | 1446 2.1 | 2143 3.6 |
| 21 TU | 0300 1.9 | 0934 4.2 | 1542 1.7 | ◗ 2239 4.0 |
| 7 TU | 0311 2.4 | 1001 3.8 | 1633 2.3 | ◗ 2251 3.5 |
| 22 W | 0426 2.1 | 1103 4.1 | 1736 1.8 | |
| 8 W | 0540 2.5 | 1103 3.7 | 1816 2.2 | |
| 23 TH | 0003 4.1 | 0607 2.1 | 1233 4.2 | 1906 1.6 |
| 9 TH | 0058 3.5 | 0645 2.3 | 1230 3.7 | 1916 2.0 |
| 24 F | 0119 4.3 | 0715 1.9 | 1344 4.4 | 2002 1.4 |
| 10 F | 0211 3.8 | 0738 2.0 | 1413 4.0 | 2005 1.6 |
| 25 SA | 0216 4.5 | 0808 1.6 | 1437 4.7 | 2045 1.1 |
| 11 SA | 0249 4.1 | 0824 1.7 | 1454 4.3 | 2046 1.2 |
| 26 SU | 0302 4.8 | 0851 1.3 | 1522 4.9 | 2122 1.0 |
| 12 SU | 0323 4.4 | 0931 1.3 | 1530 4.6 | 2123 0.9 |
| 27 M | 0342 4.9 | 0931 1.1 | 1602 5.0 | 2157 0.9 |
| 13 M | 0355 4.7 | 0942 1.0 | 1604 4.9 | 2159 0.6 |
| 28 TU | 0420 5.0 | 1008 1.0 | 1640 5.0 | ● 2231 0.9 |
| 14 TU | 0427 5.0 | 1018 0.7 | 1639 5.1 | ○ 2234 0.5 |
| 29 W | 0456 5.1 | 1045 0.9 | 1717 5.0 | 2304 1.0 |
| 15 W | 0501 5.1 | 1053 0.5 | 1716 5.3 | 2309 0.4 |
| 30 TH | 0532 5.0 | 1120 1.0 | 1753 4.9 | 2335 1.2 |
| 31 F | 0608 4.9 | 1154 1.1 | 1829 4.7 | |

### NOVEMBER

| Day | Time m | Time m | Time m | Time m |
|---|---|---|---|---|
| 1 SA | 0007 1.4 | 0644 4.8 | 1229 1.3 | 1905 4.5 |
| 16 SU | 0013 0.8 | 0643 5.2 | 1244 0.6 | 1915 5.0 |
| 2 SU | 0041 1.6 | 0721 4.6 | 1305 1.5 | 1944 4.3 |
| 17 M | 0101 1.1 | 0731 5.0 | 1332 0.9 | 2008 4.7 |
| 3 M | 0118 1.9 | 0800 4.4 | 1344 1.7 | 2027 4.0 |
| 18 TU | 0152 1.4 | 0823 4.8 | 1425 1.2 | 2109 4.4 |
| 4 TU | 0158 2.1 | 0843 4.2 | 1428 1.9 | 2118 3.8 |
| 19 W | 0250 1.7 | 0927 4.5 | 1529 1.5 | ◗ 2220 4.2 |
| 5 W | 0248 2.4 | 0933 4.0 | 1526 2.1 | 2219 3.7 |
| 20 TH | 0405 2.0 | 1041 4.3 | 1653 1.7 | 2332 4.2 |
| 6 TH | 0436 2.5 | 1029 3.9 | 1711 2.2 | ◗ 2325 3.7 |
| 21 F | 0529 2.0 | 1156 4.3 | 1821 1.7 | |
| 7 F | 0558 2.4 | 1128 3.9 | 1822 2.0 | |
| 22 SA | 0041 4.3 | 0639 1.9 | 1305 4.3 | 1926 1.6 |
| 8 SA | 0041 3.9 | 0654 2.2 | 1235 4.1 | 1917 1.7 |
| 23 SU | 0142 4.4 | 0737 1.8 | 1405 4.4 | 2016 1.5 |
| 9 SU | 0147 4.1 | 0744 1.9 | 1346 4.3 | 2004 1.4 |
| 24 M | 0232 4.6 | 0825 1.6 | 1455 4.6 | 2056 1.4 |
| 10 M | 0232 4.5 | 0828 1.5 | 1440 4.6 | 2046 1.1 |
| 25 TU | 0315 4.7 | 0908 1.4 | 1538 4.6 | 2133 1.3 |
| 11 TU | 0311 4.8 | 0909 1.2 | 1525 4.9 | 2126 0.9 |
| 26 W | 0354 4.8 | 0948 1.3 | 1618 4.7 | 2209 1.3 |
| 12 W | 0349 5.0 | 0949 0.9 | 1608 5.1 | 2204 0.7 |
| 27 TH | 0430 4.8 | 1026 1.3 | 1655 4.7 | ● 2242 1.4 |
| 13 TH | 0429 5.2 | 1030 0.6 | 1653 5.3 | ○ 2245 0.6 |
| 28 F | 0507 4.8 | 1103 1.2 | 1733 4.6 | 2316 1.4 |
| 14 F | 0512 5.3 | 1112 0.5 | 1739 5.3 | 2328 0.7 |
| 29 SA | 0545 4.8 | 1140 1.3 | 1811 4.6 | 2350 1.5 |
| 15 SA | 0557 5.3 | 1157 0.5 | 1826 5.2 | |
| 30 SU | 0624 4.8 | 1216 1.3 | 1849 4.5 | |

### DECEMBER

| Day | Time m | Time m | Time m | Time m |
|---|---|---|---|---|
| 1 M | 0026 1.6 | 0702 4.7 | 1253 1.4 | 1928 4.4 |
| 16 TU | 0053 0.9 | 0724 5.2 | 1324 0.6 | 1957 4.9 |
| 2 TU | 0105 1.7 | 0741 4.6 | 1331 1.5 | 2009 4.2 |
| 17 W | 0141 1.1 | 0814 5.0 | 1411 0.8 | 2050 4.6 |
| 3 W | 0145 1.9 | 0821 4.4 | 1412 1.6 | 2054 4.1 |
| 18 TH | 0232 1.4 | 0908 4.7 | 1503 1.2 | 2149 4.4 |
| 4 TH | 0230 2.0 | 0905 4.3 | 1457 1.7 | 2145 4.0 |
| 19 F | 0330 1.7 | 1009 4.4 | 1603 1.5 | ◗ 2252 4.2 |
| 5 F | 0323 2.2 | 0954 4.2 | 1550 1.8 | ◗ 2240 4.0 |
| 20 SA | 0437 1.9 | 1112 4.2 | 1715 1.7 | 2355 4.1 |
| 6 SA | 0431 2.2 | 1047 4.2 | 1653 1.8 | 2336 4.0 |
| 21 SU | 0549 2.0 | 1217 4.1 | 1833 1.8 | |
| 7 SU | 0546 2.2 | 1143 4.2 | 1803 1.8 | |
| 22 M | 0057 4.1 | 0656 2.0 | 1324 4.0 | 1940 1.8 |
| 8 M | 0035 4.2 | 0652 2.0 | 1246 4.3 | 1911 1.6 |
| 23 TU | 0158 4.2 | 0757 1.9 | 1427 4.1 | 2032 1.8 |
| 9 TU | 0137 4.4 | 0749 1.7 | 1353 4.5 | 2007 1.4 |
| 24 W | 0250 4.3 | 0848 1.7 | 1518 4.2 | 2114 1.7 |
| 10 W | 0232 4.7 | 0840 1.4 | 1453 4.7 | 2057 1.2 |
| 25 TH | 0334 4.5 | 0932 1.6 | 1602 4.3 | 2153 1.6 |
| 11 TH | 0321 4.9 | 0928 1.1 | 1546 4.9 | 2143 1.0 |
| 26 F | 0414 4.6 | 1013 1.4 | 1642 4.4 | 2229 1.5 |
| 12 F | 0408 5.1 | 1014 0.8 | 1637 5.1 | ○ 2229 0.8 |
| 27 SA | 0453 4.6 | 1053 1.3 | 1721 4.4 | ● 2306 1.4 |
| 13 SA | 0457 5.3 | 1102 0.6 | 1728 5.2 | 2317 0.8 |
| 28 SU | 0531 4.7 | 1130 1.2 | 1759 4.5 | 2342 1.3 |
| 14 SU | 0546 5.3 | 1149 0.5 | 1818 5.2 | |
| 29 M | 0610 4.8 | 1206 1.1 | 1836 4.5 | |
| 15 M | 0004 0.8 | 0635 5.3 | 1237 0.5 | 1907 5.1 |
| 30 TU | 0017 1.3 | 0647 4.8 | 1241 1.0 | 1912 4.5 |
| 31 W | 0053 1.4 | 0724 4.7 | 1315 1.0 | 1949 4.4 |

Chart Datum: 0·20 metres above Ordnance Datum (Dublin). HAT is 5·6 metres above Chart Datum.

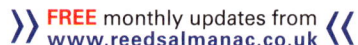

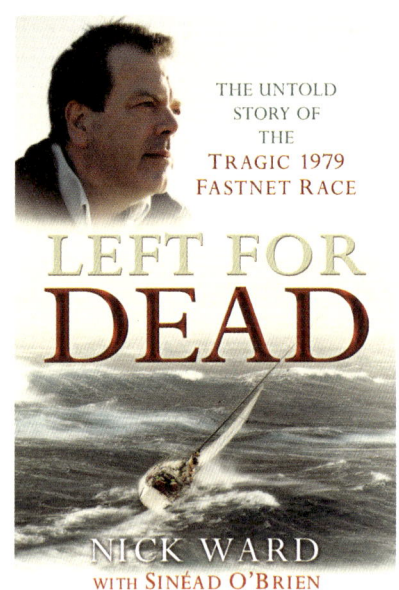